Church of England Record Society

Volume 8

TUDOR CHURCH REFORM

THE HENRICIAN CANONS OF 1535
AND THE
REFORMATIO LEGUM ECCLESIASTICARUM

The English Reformation began as a dispute over questions of canon law, and reforming the existing system was one of the state's earliest objectives. A draft proposal for this, known as the Henrician canons, has survived, revealing the state of English canon law at the time of the break with Rome, and providing a basis for Cranmer's subsequent, and much better known, attempt to revise the canon law, which was published by John Foxe under the title 'Reformatio legum ecclesiasticarum' in 1571. Although it never became law, it was highly esteemed by later canon lawyers and enjoyed an unofficial authority in ecclesiastical courts. The Henrician canons and the 'Reformatio legum ecclesiasticarum' are thus crucial for an understanding of Reformation church discipline, revealing the problems and opportunities facing those who wanted to reform the Church of England's institutional structure in the mid-Tudor period, an age which was to determine the course of the church for centuries to come.

This volume makes available for the first time full scholarly editions and translations of the whole text, taking all the available evidence into consideration, and setting the 'Reformatio' firmly in both its historical and contemporary context.

GERALD BRAY is Anglican Professor of Divinity at Beeson Divinity School, Samford University.

TUDOR CHURCH REFORM

THE HENRICIAN CANONS OF 1535 AND THE *REFORMATIO LEGUM ECCLESIASTICARUM*

EDITED BY

Gerald Bray

THE BOYDELL PRESS

CHURCH OF ENGLAND RECORD SOCIETY

First published 2000

A Church of England Record Society publication
Published by The Boydell Press
an imprint of Boydell & Brewer Ltd
PO Box 9, Woodbridge, Suffolk IP12 3DF, UK
and of Boydell & Brewer Inc.
PO Box 41026, Rochester, NY 14604–4126, USA
website: http://www.boydell.co.uk

ISBN 0 85115 809 9

ISSN 1351–3087

Series information is printed at the back of this volume

A catalogue record for this book is available
from the British Library

This publication is printed on acid-free paper

Printed in Great Britain by
St Edmundsbury Press Ltd, Bury St Edmunds, Suffolk

CONTENTS

ACKNOWLEDGMENTS

The publication of *The Anglican canons 1529-1947* by Boydell and Brewer Press, under the auspices of the Church of England Record Society closed an important gap in the study of Anglican canon law, but as always in such cases, it also revealed other gaps which needed to be filled. Ideally, both of the documents contained in this volume should have been tucked in between the canons of the convocation of 1529 and the legatine constitutions of Cardinal Pole (1556), but they were far too long to be able to fit comfortably in an already lengthy collection. They are also quite distinct in their nature from other Anglican canons, since both were attempts to edit (and even to some extent rewrite) the entire canon law and neither was ever an official document. Furthermore, the Henrician canons of 1535 were effectively lost from 1571 until 1974, and the many different problems posed by the existence of a draft manuscript of the *Reformatio legum ecclesiasticarum* alongside John Foxe's printed edition of 1571, as well as of a hitherto neglected fragment of a sixteenth-century English translation, have never been adequately addressed. A separate edition was therefore required, though one which would demonstrate the close links which there are between both of these documents and other canonical materials.

In preparing these texts for publication, I am once again deeply indebted to the Church of England Record Society, which has very kindly made me an honorary life member, and in particular to its secretary, Dr Stephen Taylor of the University of Reading, who has patiently edited the typescript, has been a constant source of enlightenment in both technical and scholarly matters. I am also grateful to Dr Diarmaid MacCulloch of the University of Oxford, who took the time to read through a draft of the introduction and made a number of valuable suggestions and corrections, and to Mrs Alsion Fincham, who read every word of both the Latin and the English, picking up several errors in the process and making a number of other useful improvements.

In the United States, it has been a great pleasure to have been able to draw on the vast fund of knowledge possessed by Professor Richard Helmholz of the University of Chicago Law School, who has put his time and expertise at my disposal in reading through the introduction and the translation of the Henrician canons with the eye of a legal expert. Even more, I cannot begin to thank adequately Emeritus Professor Donald Logan of Emmanuel College, Boston, without whose rediscovery of the Henrician canons in the British Library in 1974 this book would have been literally impossible, and whose meticulous

scholarship has improved it beyond measure. Professor Logan has been most generous in sharing with me his knowledge of the sources, and my debt to him is incalculable.

Part of the introduction has already appeared in a collection of essays offered to Bishop Eric Kemp of Chichester, entitled *English canon law* and published by the University of Wales Press (1998). I am indebted to two of that volume's editors, Mark Hill and Norman Doe, both of whom are leading exponents of Anglican ecclesiastical law, for their invitation to me to contribute a chapter on the later history of the *Reformatio*, which obliged me to investigate the remarkable way in which that text has been used (and abused) in English legal history, and to bring the story of that document down to the threshold of modern times.

Preparation of the manuscripts for publication would not have been possible without the use of the facilities of the British Library's Manuscript Students' Room (including, for a brief period in the final stages, the new Manuscripts Room at St Pancras), and of the library of the Inner Temple, where the texts are held. In particular, I must thank John Jackson of Worcester College, Oxford, who spent many hours with me in the British Museum going over the manuscripts and checking their readings, against transcriptions which I had made from microfilms and from the printed editions of the *Reformatio*. I am also very grateful to the staff of the House of Lords Record Office who were kind enough to respond promptly and efficiently to my inquiries by e-mail. At different times I have consulted material in the Public Record Office, the Squire Law Library in Cambridge, and in Lambeth Palace Library, and have made full use of the excellent facilities of the University Library at Cambridge. I must thank the staff of the Rare Books Room, the Manuscripts Room, the Official Publications Room and (of course) the Tea Room of that library for their patience and consistent co-operation over an extended period.

In the United States I have used the Samford University Library in Birmingham, Alabama, with its excellent inter-library loan facilities, the Cumberland Law Library at Samford, the Gorgas Library at the University of Alabama in Tuscaloosa, and particularly that university's Bounds Law Library, which has a remarkable collection of canon law materials, as well as the Pitts Theological Library, the Woodruff Library and the McMullen Law Library of Emory University in Atlanta. At two particularly crucial junctures I was also able to use the library system of McGill University, Montreal, where much of the introduction was written.

As before, I am also very grateful to the dean of the Beeson Divinity School, Dr Timothy George, and my colleagues, who have supported me throughout my work on this project. The friendly and co-operative atmosphere of the Divinity School has greatly expedited the completion of the text for publication.

ABBREVIATIONS

A.C.	*The Anglican canons 1529-1947*, ed. G. L. Bray (Church of England Record Society, VI, Woodbridge, 1998).
B.C.P.	Book of common prayer (1662)
c.	canon or chapter (*caput*)
c.	circa
C.	Causa (*Corpus iuris canonici*)
C.J.	*Journals of the house of commons*
Clem.	*Extravagantes Clementinae*
C.O.D.	*Decrees of the ecumenical councils (Conciliorum oecumenicorum decreta)*, ed. N. Tanner (London and Washington, 1990).
Cod. Iust.	*Codex Iustiniani (Corpus iuris civilis)*
Comm.	*Extravagantes communes (Corpus iuris canonici)*
D	*Distinctio (Decretum Gratiani, Corpus iuris canonici)*
de cons.	*De consecratione (Decretum Gratiani, Corpus iuris canonici)*
D.E.R.	*Documents of the English reformation*, ed. G. L. Bray (Cambridge, 1994).
Dig.	*Digest(a) (Corpus iuris civilis)*
DP	Distinctio de paenitentia (part of C. 33 in the *Corpus iuris canonici*).
Ep.	epistle
E.R.	*English reports*
Extrav. Ioh.	*Extravagantes Iohannis XXII (Corpus iuris canonici)*
fl.	floruit (flourished)
fo.	folio
F	The first printed edition of the *Reformatio legum ecclesiasticarum* (1571)
Fr	*Corpus iuris canonici*, ed. E. L. Richter and E. Friedberg (2 vols., Leipzig, 1879-81).
G	E. Gibson, *Codex iuris ecclesiastici Anglicani* (2 vols., London, 1713).
H.C.	The Henrician canons (in this volume).
HS	*Councils and ecclesiastical documents relating to Great Britain and Ireland to 871*, ed. A.W. Haddan and W. Stubbs (3 vols., Oxford, 1869-73).
Inst.	*Institutes (Corpus iuris civilis)*
L	W. Lyndwood, *Constitutiones provinciales, seu provinciale* (Oxford, 1679).
L.J.	*Journals of the house of lords*

MS   manuscript
n.   note
no.   number
Nov.   *Novellae* (*Corpus iuris civilis*)
PC   *Councils and synods, with other documents relating to the
                        English church 1205-1313*, ed. F. M. Powicke and C. R.
                        Cheney (2 vols., Oxford, 1964-81).
q.   quaestio
R   The *Reformatio legum ecclesiasticarum* (in this volume)
Reg.   register
R.S.T.C.   *A short-title catalogue of books printed in England,
                        Scotland, Ireland and Wales, and of English works printed
                        in other countries, 1475-1640*, ed. A. W. Pollard and G.
                        R. Redgrave; revised 2nd edn. ed. W. A. Jackson, F. S.
                        Ferguson and K. F. Pantzer (3 vols., London, 1976-91).
R.S.T.C. (Wing)   *A short-title catalogue of books printed in England, Scotland,
                        Ireland, Wales and British America, and of English works
                        printed in other countries, 1641-1700*, ed. D. G. Wing,
                        revised 2nd edn., ed. J. J. Morrison, C. W. Nelson and M.
                        Seccombe (4 vols., New York, 1972-98).
S   The second printed edition of the *Reformatio legum
                        ecclesiasticarum* (1640)
s.   section or (rarely) statute
S. P.   State papers (in the Public Record Office, London).
S.R.   *Statutes of the realm* (12 vols., London, 1810-28).
ST   supplementary text(s)
VI   *Liber sextus* (*Corpus iuris canonici*)
vol.   volume
W   *Concilia Magnae Britanniae et Hiberniae a synodo
                        Verulamensi A.D. 446 ad Londiniensem A.D. 1717*, ed. D.
                        Wilkins (4 vols., London, 1737).
WBB   *Councils and synods, with other documents relating to the
                        English church 871-1204*, ed. D. Whitelock, M. Brett and
                        C.N.L. Brooke (2 vols., Oxford, 1981).
X   *Liber extra* (*Corpus iuris canonici*)

1237   Legatine constitutions of Otho (PC)[1]
1268   Legatine constitutions of Othobon (PC)[2]
1529   Canons of the convocation of 1529 (*A.C.*)
1536   First Henrician injunctions (*D.E R.*)

---

[1]The text of both this and the following can be found in PC, and references to it are
given in the main text. For the gloss, however, it is necessary to refer to L, where it is
printed in full.
[2]See previous note.

1538	Second Henrician injunctions (*D.E.R.*)
1547	Edwardian injunctions (*D.E.R.*)
1556	Legatine constitutions of Cardinal Pole (*A.C.*)
1559	Elizabethan injunctions (*D.E.R.*)
1566	Advertisements (*A.C.*)
1571	Canons of 1571 (*A.C.*)
1575	Canons of 1575 (1576) (*A.C.*)
1583	Archbishop Whitgift's articles (*A.C.*)
1584	Canons of 1584 (1585) (*A.C.*)
1587	Archbishop Whitgift's statutes for the ecclesiastical courts (*A.C.*)
1597	Canons of 1597 (1598) (*A.C.*)
1603	Canons of 1603 (1604) (*A.C.*)
1640	Canons of 1640 (*A.C.*)
1969	*The canons of the Church of England* (London, 1969-).

Books of the Bible are abbreviated as follows:

Gn	Genesis
Ex	Exodus
Lv	Leviticus
Nm	Numbers
Dt	Deuteronomy
Jo	Joshua
Jd	Judges
Rt	Ruth
Sa	Samuel (I and II)
Ki	Kings (I and II)
Ch	Chronicles (I and II)
Ez	Ezra
Ne	Nehemiah
Es	Esther
Jb	Job
Ps	Psalms
Pr	Proverbs
Ec	Ecclesiastes
So	Song of Songs (Solomon)
Is	Isaiah
Je	Jeremiah
La	Lamentations
Ek	Ezekiel
Da	Daniel
Ho	Hosea
Jl	Joel
Am	Amos

Ob	Obadiah
Jh	Jonah
Mi	Micah
Na	Nahum
Hb	Habakkuk
Zp	Zephaniah
Ha	Haggai
Ze	Zechariah
Ma	Malachi
Si	Sirach (Ecclesiasticus)
Wi	Wisdom of Solomon
Mt	Matthew
Mk	Mark
Lk	Luke
Jn	John (also I, II and III John)
Ac	Acts
Ro	Romans
Co	Corinthians (I and II)
Ga	Galatians
Ep	Ephesians
Ph	Philippians
Cl	Colossians
Th	Thessalonians (I and II)
Ti	Timothy (I and II)
Tt	Titus
Pl	Philemon
He	Hebrews
Ja	James
Pe	Peter (I and II)
Ju	Jude
Re	Revelation (Apocalypse)

INTRODUCTION

The origins of canon law reform

The reform of English canon law may be said to have begun on 10 May 1532, when Edward Fox, the royal almoner, presented the convocation of Canterbury with three articles for their acceptance. The articles were the end result of several months of debate over the legislative and judicial powers of the clergy, which had already produced a protest from the house of commons on 18 March,[1] followed by a point by point refutation from the bishops on 12 April.[2] They came from King Henry VIII, or rather from Thomas Cromwell, a protégé of Cardinal Wolsey who had managed to survive his benefactor's downfall, and who was already exercising considerable influence in ecclesiastical affairs.[3] The articles were debated for a few days, but although many of the clergy were unhappy with them and the exchanges were heated, they were assented to without alteration on 15 May.[4] They read as follows:

> First, [we] do offer and promise, *in verbo sacerdotii*,[5] here unto your highness, submitting ourselves most humbly to the same, that we will never from henceforth enact, put in ure, promulge, or execute any new canons or constitutions provincial, or any other new ordinance, provincial or synodal, in our convocation or synod in time coming, which convocation is, always has been, and must be assembled only by your highness's commandment or writ, unless your highness by your royal assent shall license us to assemble our convocation and to make, promulge and execute such constitutions and ordinances as shall be made in the same; and thereto give your royal assent and authority.
>
> Secondly, that whereas divers of the constitutions, ordinances and canons provincial or synodal, which have been heretofore enacted, be

---

[1] 'The supplication of the commons', *D.E.R.*, pp. 51-6.
[2] *Ibid.*, pp. 57-70.
[3] He would later become the king's vicar-general in spirituals, though this title did not emerge until 21 January 1535, and then only with respect to the visitation which he undertook that year. The title was not conferred on him in the full sense until 18 July 1536. See F. D. Logan, 'Thomas Cromwell and the vicegerency in spirituals: a revisitation', *English Historical Review*, CIII (1988), 658-67. On Cromwell's career generally, see G. R. Elton, *Reform and renewal. Thomas Cromwell and the common weal* (Cambridge, 1973).
[4] This was also the day on which Sir Thomas More resigned as lord chancellor.
[5] 'On the word of the priesthood', or 'priest's honour' as we might say today.

thought to be not only much prejudicial to your prerogative royal, but also overmuch onerous to your highness's subjects, your clergy aforesaid is contented, if it may stand so with your highness's pleasure, that it be committed to the examination and judgment of your grace, and of thirty-two persons, whereof sixteen to be of the upper and nether house of the temporalty, and other sixteen of the clergy, all to be chosen and appointed by your most noble grace.

So that finally, whichsoever of the said constitutions, ordinances or canons, provincial or synodal, shall be thought and determined by your grace and by the most part of the said thirty-two persons not to stand with God's laws and the laws of your realm, the same to be abrogated and taken away by your grace and the clergy; and such of them as shall be seen by your grace, and by the most part of the said thirty-two persons, to stand with God's laws and the laws of your realm, to stand in full strength and power, your grace's most royal assent and authority once impetrate and fully given to the same.[6]

The following day, Archbishop William Warham took the convocation's assent to the king and made his personal submission to Henry's authority at the same time.[7] The way was now clear for the government to act as it wished, though as yet there was no concrete proposal for serious reform of the existing canon law. Elaborating such a proposal would clearly have taken some time, but a framework for change had been established, which would endure (in slightly different guises) into the next reign and eventually bear fruit in the *Reformatio legum ecclesiasticarum*. Archbishop Warham died on 22 August 1532, and following the custom of the time, the appointment of Peter Ligham as his official principal (dean of the arches)[8] lapsed as well. Cromwell seized the opportunity and on 18 September he appointed Richard Gwent as Ligham's successor, even

---

[6]Text in *D.E.R.*, 71.

[7]See M. Kelly, 'The submission of the clergy', *Transactions of the Royal Historical Society*, 5th series, XV (1965), 97-119. Kelly's conclusions were largely adopted by S. E. Lehmberg, *The reformation parliament 1529-1536* (Cambridge, 1970), pp. 142-3. Warham also brought Henry the seventeen canons which had been agreed by convocation earlier in the year. The king ratified them and they were subsequently included in the official act book. See *A.C.*, xxxiv-xl, 2-67.

[8]The ancient distinction between these offices effectively disappeared after 1504, when Humphrey Hawarden was appointed to them both jointly, a practice which has been followed ever since, though it did not become law until 37-8 Victoria, c. 85 (7 August 1874). The arches court originally handled the legal affairs of the thirteen London parishes which belonged to the peculiar jurisdiction of the archbishop of Canterbury, though it soon became the court of appeal for the whole province, which it still remains. Its name derived from the fact that from *c.* 1280 until the great fire of 1666 it sat in the crypt of St Mary-le-Bow ('St Mary of the arches') church. Why the official principal came to be known by the lesser of the two titles is unknown, but the habit persists to this day and is adopted here as a matter of convenience.

before Thomas Cranmer could be installed as the new archbishop.[9] This procedure was irregular, because the dean of the arches was the archbishop's personal appointee, but it seems that Cromwell was unwilling to wait any longer than necessary. Probably he wanted to make the point that the crown was now the dominant force in ecclesiastical affairs, and it can be said with some certainty that Cranmer was not able to appoint his own man until after Gwent's death in 1543.[10] Gwent was one of the king's chaplains and seems to have been a reformer of sorts, though not in the sense which that term would soon acquire.[11]

What happened next is obscure, but it is known that the legislation authorizing the appointment of the commission of thirty-two was piloted through both houses of parliament during the course of March 1534, and received the royal assent at the closing session on 30 March, the day before the convocation of Canterbury voted to abjure the papal supremacy.[12] The relevant portions of this act read as follows:

> 1. Where the king's humble and obedient subjects, the clergy of this realm of England, have not only acknowledged according to the truth, that the convocation of the same clergy is, always has been, and ought to be assembled only by the king's writ, but also submitting themselves to the king's majesty, have promised *in verbo sacerdotii* that they will never from henceforth presume to attempt, allege, claim or put in ure, or enact, promulge or execute any new canons, constitutions, ordinances provincial or other, or by whatsoever other name they shall be called in the convocation, unless the king's most royal assent and licence may to them be had, to make, promulge and execute the same; and that his majesty do give his most royal assent and authority in that behalf:

---

[9]Cranmer, who was abroad at the time, was approached to become archbishop after Warham's death, but he delayed for a while and did not return to England until January 1533. See D. MacCulloch, *Thomas Cranmer* (New Haven and London, 1996), pp. 41-78.
[10]In a letter to Cromwell dated 2 November 1535, Cranmer tried to have Sir William Petre appointed as dean of the arches, but without success. See *Letters and papers, foreign and domestic, of the reign of Henry VIII* (21 vols., London, 1861-1910), IX, 252-3, no. 741 (S.P. 1/98, pp. 192-3).
[11]On Gwent, see G. Williams, 'Two neglected London-Welsh clerics, B. Richard Gwent', in *Transactions of the Honourable Society of Cymmrodorion* (1961), 33-43. He was admitted to doctors' commons on 20 April 1526 (G. D. Squibb, *Doctors' commons. A history of the college of advocates and doctors of law* (Oxford, 1977), p. 143). For further details of his career and appointments, see A. B. Emden, *A biographical register of the university of Oxford, A. D. 1501 to 1540* (Oxford, 1974), p. 252.
[12]*D.E.R.*, pp. 109-10. This action was followed by the university of Cambridge (2 May), the convocation of York (2 June) and finally the university of Oxford (27 June), by which time the king had already acknowledged it (9 June). It became law on 4 November by the act of supremacy, 26 Henry VIII, c. 1, 1534 (*S.R.*, III, 492).

And where divers constitutions, ordinances and canons, provincial or synodal, which heretofore have been enacted, and be thought not only to be much prejudicial to the king's prerogative royal, and repugnant to the laws and statutes of this realm, but also overmuch onerous to his highness and his subjects; the said clergy have most humbly besought the king's highness that the said constitutions and canons may be committed to the examination and judgment of his highness and of two-and-thirty persons of the king's subjects, whereof sixteen to be of the upper and nether house of the parliament of the temporalty, and the other sixteen to be of the clergy of this realm; and all the said two-and-thirty persons to be chosen and appointed by the king's majesty, and that such of the said constitutions and canons as shall be thought and determined by the said two-and-thirty persons, or the more part of them, worthy to be abrogated and annulled, shall be abolished and made of no value accordingly; and such other of the same constitutions and canons as by the said two-and-thirty or the more part of them, shall be approved to stand with the laws of God and consonant to the laws of this realm, shall stand in their full strength and power, the king's most royal assent first had and obtained to the same:

Be it therefore now enacted by authority of this present parliament, according to the said submission and petition of the said clergy, that they, nor any of them, from henceforth shall presume to attempt, allege, claim or put in ure any constitutions or ordinances, provincial or synodal, or any other canons, nor shall enact, promulge or execute any such canons, constitutions or ordinances provincial, by whatsoever name or names they may be called, in their convocations in time coming (which alway shall be assembled by authority of the king's writ), unless the same clergy may have the king's most royal assent and licence to make, promulge and execute such canons, constitutions and ordinances, provincial or synodal, upon pain of every one of the said clergy doing contrary to this act, and being therefore convict, to suffer imprisonment and make fine at the king's will.

2. And forasmuch as such canons, constitutions and ordinances as heretofore have been made by the clergy of this realm cannot now at the session of the present parliament, by reason of shortness of time, be viewed, examined and determined by the king's highness, and thirty-two persons to be chosen and appointed according to the petition of the said clergy in form above rehearsed: be it therefore enacted by authority aforesaid that the king's highness shall have power and authority to nominate and assign at his pleasure the said two-and-thirty persons of his subjects, whereof sixteen to be of the clergy, and sixteen to be of the temporalty of the upper and nether house of the parliament, and if any of the said two-and-thirty persons so chosen shall happen to die before their full determination, then his highness to nominate other from time to time of the said two houses of parliament, to supply the number of the said two-and-thirty; and that the same two-and-thirty, by his

highness so to be named, shall have power and authority to view, search and examine the said canons, constitutions and ordinances, provincial and synodal, heretofore made, and such of them as the king's highness and the said two-and-thirty, or the more part of them, shall deem and adjudge worthy to be continued, kept and obeyed, shall be from thenceforth kept, obeyed and executed within this realm, so that the king's most royal assent under his great seal be first had to the same; and the residue of the said canons, constitutions, or ordinance provincial, which the king's highness and the said two-and-thirty persons or the more part of them shall not approve, or deem and judge worthy to be abolished, abrogate and made frustrate, shall from thenceforth be void and of none effect, and never be put in execution within this realm.

3. Provided alway that no canons, constitutions or ordinances shall be made or put in execution within this realm by authority of the convocation of the clergy, which shall be contrariant or repugnant to the king's prerogative royal or the customs, laws or statutes of this realm; anything contained in this act to the contrary hereof notwithstanding.

7. Provided also that such canons, constitutions, ordinances and synodals provincial being already made, which be not contrariant or repugnant to the laws, statutes and customs of this realm, nor to the damage or hurt of the king's prerogative royal, shall more still be used and executed as they were afore the making of this act, till such time as they be viewed, searched or otherwise ordered and determined by the said two-and-thirty persons, or the more part of them, according to the tenor, form and effect of this present act.[13]

This act forbade convocation to legislate independently of the king, though whether this meant that it required the assent of parliament as well was less clear and was later disputed by parliament, which naturally assumed that its approval was also needed.[14] What the act envisaged was a new and streamlined version of the existing canon law which would replace all previous legislation, though as section 7 indicates, provision was made for the existing law to remain in force

---

[13]25 Henry VIII, c. 19, 1534 (*S.R.*, III, 460-1). Sections 1 and 3 are still on the statute book today. Sections 2 and 7 were both repealed by the statute law (repeals) act, 1969, c. 52 (22 October 1969).

[14]In 1604 James I ratified the canons of that year even though parliament refused to accept them, and he got away with it. His son Charles I tried something similar in 1640 (though with the added complication that he allowed convocation to continue sitting after the dissolution of parliament, something which was regarded as unconstitutional) but was unsuccessful. However, the legal position was never clarified and remained ambiguous until 1919, when a representative national assembly with limited legislative powers was established for the Church of England. Even then, the exact status of the 1640 canons was still in doubt; they were not finally (and unambiguously) disposed of until 7 May 1969, when the current revised canons were promulgated.

until the royal assent was given to a new set of canons, as long as it did not contradict any of the laws, statutes or customs of the realm or go against the royal prerogative.[15] By the time the act was passed, determining what the canon law of England actually was had become a matter of urgency, because the simultaneous abjuration of papal supremacy made further appeal to Rome impossible,[16] and there is evidence that a preparatory committee (at least) was set to work more or less immediately. This evidence comes from a letter written by Dr Thomas Thirlby,[17] one of the king's chaplains, to Cromwell. It is dated 25 July 1534 and reads as follows:

> By the king's command we have met sundry times at the Blackfriars, London, to debate such matters as you proposed to us but cannot set them forth without the help of men learned in the laws of God and of the realm. We have required several times the assistance of Master Saint German,[18] but he has excused himself. We therefore await for your further pleasure.[19]

[15]The pre-reformation canon law still retains a residual authority in the Church of England, at least to the extent that it has not been repealed by statute. For the history and the current position, see Lynne Leeder, *Ecclesiastical law handbook* (London, 1997), pp. 5-9, who concludes, p. 9: 'All pre-reformation canon law, so far as this is not repugnant nor contrary to the laws of England, forms part of the ecclesiastical law of England.'

[16]It may be recorded that a parallel development occurred later on in Pennsylvania, where on 12 October 1776 the house of delegates asked for a similar clarification of the law after having broken with the British crown. Interestingly, in that case too, achievement of the aim proved to be just as elusive. See P. Miller, *The life of the mind in America from the revolution to the civil war* (New York, 1965), pp. 239-65.

[17](c.1506-70). He was a king's chaplain by 1533 and archdeacon of Ely by 1534, since he sat in the convocation (16 January-30 March) under that title. Note, however, that he was not a member of doctors' commons until 7 February 1536. (See Squibb, *Doctors' commons*, p. 147.) Thirlby was to have a long and chequered career as bishop of Westminster (1540-50), Norwich (1550-4) and Ely (1554-9), eventually becoming one of Mary I's most loyal servants and even a (reluctant) participant in Archbishop Cranmer's degradation on 14 February 1556. He was deprived in 1559 and went into retirement until his death. See J. Venn and J. A. Venn, *Alumni Cantabrigienses. Part I (to 1751)* (4 vols., Cambridge, 1922-7), IV, 220.

[18]Christopher Saint German (c.1460-1540) was a leading legal theorist, who had recently engaged Thomas More in a pamphlet debate over church-state relations. Saint German sided with the king, on the whole, and blamed the clergy for their own misfortunes. For an account of the debate from More's point of view, see P. Ackroyd, *The life of Thomas More* (London, 1998), pp. 309-43.

[19]*Letters and papers*, VII, 384, no. 1008 (S.P. 1/85, pp. 86-7), dated at London, 25 July 1534.

This letter was signed by Thirlby and four members of doctors' commons - John Oliver, dean of King Henry VIII's College, Oxford, from 1533 to 1545,[20] Edward Carne, recently returned from Rome, where he had tried to pilot the king's annulment suit through the papal curia,[21] William Bretten (Breyten or Brytten)[22] and John Hewys (Hughes).[23] As three of these were among the four who eventually produced the Henrician canons, we may assume that this letter represents the failure of a first attempt at them.

But how did a relatively unknown person like Thirlby come to be put in charge of such an important task? Is there any way that we can close the gap between the first mention of a commission of thirty-two in May 1532 and the activities of the draft committee in mid-1534? A letter from Thomas Cranmer to Nicholas Hawkins, archdeacon of Ely, dated 16 June 1533 lists Drs Hewys, Oliver and Bretten as among those who had been appointed to try Katharine of Aragon on 8 May 1533, so there is evidence that the three men were working together at that time.[24] They obviously all supported the king in his annulment proceedings, which was probably a key factor in their appointment to redraft the canons. If that is the case, we may find a further lead in a list which is appended to a memorandum in Cromwell's hand, which has been preserved among the state papers.[25] The list is in another hand and contains twenty-four names, fourteen of which have been pricked through. There is no indication what this list might have been for, nor why the names were pricked, but, in so far as the people

---

[20](d.1552). Admitted to doctors' commons on 12 November 1522. (See Squibb, *Doctors' commons*, p. 139.) He was forced to resign the deanship when the college was reorganized as Christ Church (10 May 1545), and returned to doctors' commons in London where he remained active in the church's legal affairs until his death. See Emden, *Biographical register 1501-40*, p. 425.

[21](c.1496-1561). Admitted to doctors' commons on 13 November 1525. See Squibb, *Doctors' commons*, p. 142. He was to be the English ambassador to the holy see again under Mary I (1553-8) and died in exile as a recusant, though he avoided declaring this, so as not to have his property in England confiscated. See Emden, *Biographical register 1501-40*, pp. 103-4.

[22](d.1552). Admitted to doctors' commons on 25 April 1518 (Squibb, *Doctors' commons*, p. 136). See also Venn, *Alumni Cantabrigienses*, I, 212.

[23](d. c.1543). Admitted to doctors' commons on 9 December 1532 (Squibb, *Doctors' commons*, p. 146). According to J. Foster, *Alumni Oxonienses* (4 vols., Oxford, 1891), II, 761, he took his M.A. at Merton College, Oxford in 1506 and was proctor of that university from 10 April 1510. In 1528 he was refused admission to the doctorate of civil laws at Oxford. Emden, *Biographical register 1501-40*, p. 286, records two people by the name of John Hewys, the second of whom is probably the same as this one, but the details of his career given there are very different.

[24]*Letters and papers*, VI, 299-300, no. 661 (MS Harleian 6, 148, fo. 25).

[25]*Ibid.*, VI, 68-9, no. 150 (S.P. 1/74, pp. 169-70). The memorandum is not dated but has been calendared between 11 and 12 February 1533, which may be regarded as the *terminus ante quem*. Lehmberg, *Reformation parliament*, pp. 167-8, concludes, on the basis of a report from the imperial ambassador Chapuys, that the meeting to which the memorandum refers took place on 5 February.

on it can be identified, it seems that they were all supporters of the king in his battle for an annulment.[26] Furthermore, it is obvious that the list is not a random one. It contains the names of nine lords spiritual, drawn up in order of seniority, followed by a number of others, most (though not all) of whom appear to have been both members of the lower house of the convocation of Canterbury and doctors of civil or canon law. The names given are as follows (an asterisk indicates the ones which are pricked):

1. *The archbishop of Canterbury [Thomas Cranmer][27]
2. The archbishop of York [Edward Lee][28]
3. *The bishop of London [John Stokesley][29]
4. *The bishop of Winchester [Stephen Gardiner][30]
5. *The bishop of Lincoln [John Longland][31]
6. *The bishop of St Asaph [Henry Standish][32]
7. *The abbot of Hyde [John Capon, *alias* Salcot][33]
8. *The abbot of St Benet [Dr William Rugge, or Repps][34]
9. *The abbot of Burton [Dr William Boston][35]

[26]MacCulloch, *Thomas Cranmer*, pp. 84-5 believes that the list was drawn up in order to form a committee to discuss the legitimacy of the king's annulment proceedings. See also G. Elton, *Studies in Tudor and Stuart politics and government* (4 vols., Cambridge, 1974-92), II, 99-101, where it is suggested that this committee was convened primarily in order to amend the draft of 24 Henry VIII, c. 12, 1533 (*S.R.*., III, 427-9) which ended appeals to Rome. Elton's view is followed by Lehmberg, *Reformation parliament*, pp. 167-8 and may well be correct. If so, it complements the suggestion put forward here. What we are dealing with is a committee of canon-law experts summoned to advise Cromwell and the king, and this body would doubtless have formed the nucleus of any group subsequently appointed to undertake the full-scale revision of that law.

[27](1489-1556). Consecrated 21 February 1533. Noted in Venn, *Alumni Cantabrigienses*, I, 413.

[28](*c*.1482-1544). Appointed 20 October 1531. Noted in *ibid.*, III, 61.

[29](*c*.1475-1539). Appointed 28 March 1530. Noted in A. B. Emden, *A biographical register of the university of Oxford to A. D. 1500* (3 vols., Oxford, 1957-9), III, 61.

[30](*c*.1483-1555). Appointed 20 October 1531. Noted in Venn, *Alumni Cantabrigienses*, II, 193 and also in Emden, *Biographical register 1501-40*, p. 227.

[31](1473-1547). Appointed 20 March 1521. Noted in Emden, *Biographical register to 1500*, II, 1160-2.

[32](d.1535). Appointed 11 July 1518. Noted in Venn, *Alumni Cantabrigienses*, IV, 145.

[33](d.1557). Appointed bishop of Bangor sometime between November 1533 and January 1534; consecrated 19 April 1534. In 1539 he was translated to Salisbury. Noted in *ibid.*, I, 290.

[34](d.1550). Elected bishop of Norwich on 31 May 1536. Noted in *ibid.*, III, 497.

[35](*c*.1500-49). *Alias* William Benson, of Boston, Lincs., he took his Cambridge D.D. in 1528 and was appointed abbot of Burton-on-Trent on 27 May 1531. He was translated to Westminster Abbey on 12 May 1533, the first monk from outside the chapter to become its abbot. He was a faithful supporter of Cromwell's policies and on 16 January 1540 he surrendered the abbey to the crown, but he survived Cromwell's fall and on 17 December 1540 he became the dean of the new cathedral foundation. Noted in *ibid.*, I, 136.

10. The dean of the king's chapel [Richard Sampson][36]
11. *The king's almoner [Edward Fox][37]
12. *Dr [John] Oliver[38]
13. *Dr [John] Tregonwell[39]
14. *Dr Lee[40]
15. *Dr [Richard] Gwent[41]
16. Dr [Robert] Aldridge[42]
17. Dr [Thomas] Goodrich[43]
18. Dr [Thomas] Thirlby[44]
19. Dr [Richard] Curwen[45]
20. Nicholas [del Burgo][46]
21. *The Carmelite friar[47]
22. Dr [William] Tresham[48]

[36](d.1554). Entered doctors' commons on 20 March 1514 (Squibb, *Doctors' commons*, p. 132); elected bishop of Chichester 3 June 1536. Noted in Venn, *Alumni Cantabrigienses*, IV, 12.

[37](c.1496-1538). Appointed bishop of Hereford 20 August 1535. Noted in *ibid.*, II, 169.

[38]See above, n. 20.

[39](d.1565). Entered doctors' commons on 9 December 1522 (Squibb, *Doctors' commons*, p. 140); made a judge of the court of admiralty by 1535 and was active in dissolving the monasteries from then until 1539. Noted in Emden, *Biographical register 1501-40*, pp. 575-6.

[40]Probably Rowland Lee (d.1543), who entered doctors' commons on 8 October 1520 (Squibb, *Doctors' commons*, p. 138) and became bishop of Coventry and Lichfield on 10 January 1534, but possibly his cousin Thomas Legh (d.1545), who entered doctors' commons on 7 October 1531 (*ibid.*, p. 146) and played a large part in the visitations of the universities in 1535. Both men are noted in Venn, *Alumni Cantabrigienses*, III, 65.

[41]See above, n. 11.

[42](d.1556). Appointed bishop of Carlisle on 18 July 1537. Noted in *ibid.*, I, 14 and in Emden, *Biographical register 1501-40*, pp. 4-5.

[43](d.1554). Appointed bishop of Ely on 6 March 1534. He later became a member of the 1551 canon law commission. From 22 December 1551 he was keeper of the privy seal and served as chancellor from 19 January 1552. Both appointments lapsed on the death of King Edward VI (6 July 1553). Noted in Venn, *Alumni Cantabrigienses*, II, 237.

[44]See above, n. 17.

[45](d.1543). Canon of Salisbury from 1533; archdeacon of Oxford, 1535. Noted in Emden, *Biographical register 1501-40*, pp. 138-9.

[46](Dates unknown). An Italian who had studied in Paris, and was incorporated at Oxford in 1523. He lectured in theology at Cardinal College, Oxford from 1525 to 1535, when he returned to Italy. Noted in *ibid.*, pp. 85-6.

[47]Giacomo Calco (d.1533), an Italian Carmelite who came to England in 1529 and was a strong supporter of the king's bid for an annulment of his marriage. But for his death, he would have become bishop of Salisbury. I am grateful to Dr James Carley of York University (Toronto) for allowing me to use some as yet unpublished research of his.

[48](1495-1569). Commissary (vice-chancellor) of Oxford university from 1532 to 1547, and again in 1556 and 1558. In 1559 he was deprived of all his benefices, except for Towcester. Noted in Emden, *Biographical register 1501-40*, pp. 576-7.

23. Mr [Thomas] Bedyll[49]
24. Mr [Edward] Leighton[50]

The above list was clearly intended for a purpose, but what was it? The decision to appoint a commission of thirty-two to review the canon law had envisaged that sixteen would be clergy, and it is probable that the intention was that eight should be drawn from the upper house of convocation and eight from the lower.[51] If we look at the names on this list which are pricked, we find that exactly eight (including the abbots) are lords spiritual. The omission of the archbishop of York may be explained by the fact that as the metropolitan of another province he was not a member of the convocation of Canterbury.[52] When we look at the lower clergy, we immediately spot Drs Oliver and Gwent, who are known to have been involved at a later stage. Dr Thirlby is also on the list, though his name is not pricked. Can it be that we are dealing here with a list of possible candidates for the eight clergy seats on the proposed commission?

The omission of the dean of the king's chapel is surprising, especially as it appears that he must have been deliberately passed over, but the answer may be that he was put in charge of the whole operation, and may even have done the pricking himself. Once again there is a cryptic letter in the state papers, this time from Dr Sampson to Cromwell, which suggests that this may have been the case. The letter reads:

The lords of the council have committed the matter you know to Mr Almoner [Edward Fox], Tregonwell, Oliver, Carne and me, and charged us to be diligent about it, to the exclusion of all other things.[53]

---

[49](1486-1537). Clerk of the king's council. He was a canon of Chichester and prebendary of Hampstead (1528) and archdeacon of London from 3 or 5 August 1533 to 30 December 1534, when he was instituted as rector of All Hallows the Great, London. On 2 March 1535 he was appointed archdeacon of Cornwall. He died shortly before 5 September 1537. Noted in Emden, *Biographical register to 1500*, I, 148-9.

[50](d.1549). King's chaplain by 1533, canon and prebendary of King Henry VIII's College, Oxford (1532-45). Noted in Emden, *Biographical register 1501-40*, p. 349.

[51]This was not explicitly stated in the legislation, but the sixteen lay members were to be equally divided between the upper and lower houses of parliament, and it seems reasonable to assume that the same principle would have been applied to the clergy. It was certainly followed in 1551, when eight bishops and eight doctors of theology were appointed.

[52]It might be thought that both convocations would be represented on a commission purporting to draw up national legislation, but this was not the case at any time until 1868. At the most, York was asked to ratify what Canterbury had already decided, but even that formality was occasionally omitted (as with the canons of 1597, for example).

[53]*Letters and papers*, VI, 603, no. 1490 (S.P. 1/80, p. 104). The letter is undated, but calendared as of 2 December 1533.

It is known that Drs Oliver and Carne[54] were at work on the revision not long after this, and, if our hunch is correct, we can add Edward Fox and Dr Tregonwell to the list of those involved with the canons at an early stage. It seems entirely natural to suppose that Cromwell would have assigned the task to people like Sampson and Fox, who were prominent members of the court, and not gone over their heads to appoint Thirlby or Gwent. But equally, if Sampson and Fox were too busy to get involved with the details of the work (as they surely must have been) it is entirely plausible that Sampson, as the main person in charge, should have delegated the responsibility to one of his assistants, which Dr Thirlby then was.

A reconstruction of events based on these conjectures would suggest that moves were afoot at the beginning of 1533 to appoint a commission of thirty-two, but that in practice the work was entrusted to a pool of clerical lawyers initially headed by Dr Sampson but then delegated to Dr Thirlby. Dr Tregonwell must have dropped out on being appointed a judge of the admiralty court (which probably occurred in 1534), and so did Dr Bretten, though the reason for his departure is not known. At some point after 25 July 1534 Cromwell appointed Dr Gwent to take Thirlby's place, since we know that he was in charge of the operation in October 1535.

As far as we can tell, Gwent's relations with the new archbishop were fairly good. In the summer of 1533 the two men both took part in the heresy trial of Elizabeth Barton, the 'nun of Kent', who was outspokenly opposed to the king's annulment proceedings. In September of the following year, Gwent went as Cranmer's commissary to Merton College, Oxford, and substantially revamped its statutes. After that Gwent was elected prolocutor of the lower house of convocation in 1536, and again in 1540 and 1541.[55] He survived the fall of Thomas Cromwell, possibly with Cranmer's assistance, and was one of the judges who ruled on the annulment of the king's marriage to Anne of Cleves. He was also a commissioner in London for the implementation of the act of six articles.[56] One of his last acts was to undertake a series of heresy trials in Kent, evidently with Cranmer's blessing.[57] Both Gwent and Cranmer were loyal to Henry VIII through all the ups and downs of the late 1530s and early 1540s, and their co-operation is best understood in that light. At a deeper level the two men came from different worlds and had Gwent lived into the next reign it is possible that their fundamental incompatibility would have revealed itself. With Gwent in charge of the revision of the canon law there was no chance of a real reformation; the most that could be hoped for was an updating of the existing law

---

[54]Carne's absence from the earlier list may have been due to the fact that he had not yet returned from his embassy to Rome.

[55]As prolocutor, it was Gwent who on 19 June 1536 presented a list of heresies condemned by the lower house to the upper house which includes many 'protestant' beliefs to which the archbishop was at least sympathetic. See W, III, 804-7.

[56]31 Henry VIII, c. 14 (*S. R.*, III, 739-43).

[57]*Letters and papers*, XVIII, 2, 291-378, no. 546 (Corpus Christi College Cambridge MS 128). Gwent is mentioned on pp. 332, 359 (fos. 164, 267).

carried out from within a deeply conservative guild of lawyers. On the other hand, when Cranmer finally had a relatively free hand in the matter, Gwent's efforts were treated with respect and even used to some extent, though it was clear to all involved at that time that they were totally inadequate to meet the needs of a church which was at last embarking on real change.

To summarize our findings, although the evidence is not strong enough to allow us to reconstruct the history of the drafting committee with any certainty, it does at least suggest that we are dealing with one fairly small circle of canon lawyers, all of whom supported the king in his annulment proceedings and most of whom would have associated with each other both socially and professionally in the nascent doctors' commons.[58] It is with Dr Thirlby's chairmanship of the committee that plausibility becomes probability and with Dr Gwent that we enter the realm of certainty.

1. The Henrician canons

Origin

The commission envisaged in 1534 was never formally appointed, but we may conclude from the above that plans for it were under way.[59] Richard Gwent was a worthy successor to Thirlby as chairman of the drafting committee, though it should not be assumed that he was the natural choice merely because of his position.[60] He was joined by John Oliver, Edward Carne and John Hewys, who had already been involved in the business, and they formed the group which was to produce the Henrician canons as we now have them. When this new team first got together is unknown, though it may have been at any point after 25 July 1534. What is certain is that they had already been at work for some time when Gwent wrote to Cromwell on 6 October 1535 as follows:

> This St Faith's Day, Dr Oliver, Mr Carne, Mr Hewys and I came from Uxbridge, where we have tarried a good while on account of the sickness at London. If it be your pleasure we will come and report to you how far forward we are in these new laws; but we dare not until we

---

[58]On the character of this body in its formative years, see F. D. Logan, 'Doctors' commons in the early sixteenth century: a society of many talents', *Historical Research*, LXI (1988), 151-65.

[59]John Foxe's opinion to the contrary may reflect his awareness that there were plans to appoint a full committee, or even just the fact that he knew that the Henrician canons were the work of more than one person. That there were only four (as far as we know) would not have disturbed him, since about the same number worked on the later *Reformatio legum ecclesiasticarum*, even though both a full commission of thirty-two and a drafting committee of eight had clearly been appointed.

[60]When the commission was eventually established in 1551, the then dean of the arches, Griffith (or Griffin) Leyson, was not a member of it.

hear from you. I beg that you will dispense with me, that I may keep the court of arches this day, and I shall sue further for your licence under the great seal. Many have come from far countries for expedition of their causes, but I dare determine none without your licence, considering that your general visitation doth now depend. Let me know by bearer your pleasure for this one court. This *crastino Fidis* is the first court done in the arches and the prerogative the morrow after.

Doctors' Commons.
St Faith's Day.[61]

They were evidently in Uxbridge because of the threat of plague in London, though when they went there is unknown. Most probably it was after the closure of the ecclesiastical courts for the summer recess (31 July), which would have given them two months of relative seclusion in which to complete the main body of the work as we now have it. They were forced to return to London for the re-opening of the courts, but they had not completed their task, as a further letter from Gwent to Cromwell, dated 27 October, makes plain:

Mr Oliver, Mr Carne and myself have remained here at London, occupied as you know, and are now very desirous to see the king at this holy time of All Saints, if we may do so after the late proclamation against Londoners going near where he is.[62]

It appears that Gwent got a favourable reception to his first letter, but what happened after the second one is unknown. Whether he was able to see the king or not, no more is heard of this group of four. Writing almost a generation later (in 1571), John Foxe noted the rather mysterious interruption of their activities, but did not know whether this was because of the distemper of the times or the sluggishness of those involved. In favour of the former possibility is the fact that it was during the time that the men were at Uxbridge that the faculty of canon law at Oxford was dissolved.[63] This was part of a wider process of creating a

---

[61]*Letters and papers*, IX, 181-2, no. 549 (S.P. 1/97, p. 127). For the dates of the law terms as used in the court of arches, see C. R. Cheney, *A handbook of dates for students of British history* (3rd edn., Cambridge, 1997), pp. 73-4.

[62]*Letters and papers*, IX, 232, no. 690 (SP 1/98, p. 80).

[63]This probably happened on 6 September 1535, when the visitation injunctions were delivered to Oxford, and was certainly complete by 12 September. It is recorded in a letter of that date from Dr Richard Layton, who administered the dissolution, to Thomas Cromwell, in *Letters relating to the suppression of monasteries*, ed. T. Wright (London, 1843), pp. 70-1. The Cambridge faculty was dissolved on 22 October 1535, when Dr Thomas Legh, acting as Thomas Cromwell's surrogate, published the king's injunctions in that university. See *Collection of statutes for the university and colleges of Cambridge* (London, 1811), pp. 196-201. The suppression of the canon law faculty is mentioned on p. 200. See also J. E. Mullinger, *The university of Cambridge from the earliest times to*

single legal culture, and reinforcing the canon law, in whatever form, would have been a barrier to that.[64] But in favour of Foxe's second suggestion is the fact that, shortly after Gwent announced that the draft canons were nearly ready, a bill was prepared and enacted in parliament which once again authorized the king to appoint a commission of thirty-two (on the ground that that had not been done in 1534), but this time set a limit of three years for the commission to complete its work.[65] The time limit was probably intended as a spur to get the process moving, but nothing happened and Gwent was soon busily involved in helping to oversee the dissolution of the monasteries. By the time he was finished with that, the three years had run out and nothing more was heard of the canons.

That the manuscript which we now have must have been composed in late 1535 or early 1536 has been cogently argued by F. D. Logan (b. 1930), who rediscovered them in 1974 in a manuscript in the British Library.[66] On the basis of internal evidence, Dr Logan concluded that the document was produced before the dissolution of the monasteries began, because provision is made for them, but after the break with Rome, since Henry VIII's prefatory declaration refers to him as supreme head of the Church of England.[67] Confirmation that they were indeed in their present form by about 27 October 1535 comes from the fact that the text takes careful note of all the statutes relating to ecclesiastical matters which were passed by the reformation parliament during its first seven sessions (covering the period from 3 November 1529 to 18 December 1534) but betrays no knowledge of those passed during the eighth and final session (4 February to 14 April 1536) or later. We must therefore conclude that by the time legislation for the renewal of the commission of thirty-two was introduced on 16 February

the royal injunctions of 1535 (Cambridge, 1873), p. 630. On the visitations themselves, see F. D. Logan, 'The first royal visitation of the English universities, 1535', English Historical Review, CVI (1991), 861-88.

[64] Another indication of this process at work is that an English translation of Lyndwood and of the legatine constitutions of Otho and Othobon was commissioned at the same time. The translator is unknown, but he may well have been Sir William Petre, whom Cranmer hoped to make dean of the arches in place of Gwent. Petre was passed over by Cromwell, perhaps because he saw no reason to lose Gwent at such a crucial moment, but on 13 January 1536 Cromwell made him his deputy for the probate of testaments and the administration of (intestate) estates, and he survived to become a member of the commission appointed in 1551-2 (see below).

[65] 27 Henry VIII, c. 15, 1536 (S.R., III, 548-9). The three-year period was to be counted from 14 April 1536, the last day of the parliamentary session.

[66] F. D. Logan, 'The Henrician canons', Bulletin of the Institute of Historical Research, XLVII (1974), 99-103. Dr Logan taught at Emmanuel College, Boston, until his retirement in 1995. I am indebted to him for much of what follows, and must pay tribute to a truly great scholar who has most generously put his time and knowledge at my disposal.

[67] The title was granted to the king by the act of supremacy (4 November 1534) but he does not seem to have used it before 15 January 1535.

1536[68] the Henrician canons as we now have them were already in existence. Furthermore, as Dr Logan noted, the quality of the copying is such that the extant text may well have been the one prepared for the king himself.

Did Henry VIII ever set eyes on it? In the present state of our knowledge this question cannot be answered one way or the other, although it is certain that if he did, it made no lasting impression on him. Quite possibly the text was shelved by Cromwell himself, on the ground that it did not fit in with his plans for church reform. Things were moving so fast by 1536 that any attempt to codify the existing situation would have been out of date almost before it was written, and it was not in Cromwell's interest to tie himself to a code which would have been much too conservative for his taste. However one looks at it, the years 1536-40 were not a time for reaching the sort of long-term conclusions which an official revision of the canon law would have entailed. We may therefore conclude that, although there were doubtless many factors involved, the decisive one was that, in the eyes of those in power, the Henrician canons were both unwanted and inappropriate, and that their disappearance was the natural consequence of that fact.

Content

The Henrician canons consist of thirty-six separate titles, which may be subdivided into about 360 distinct canons.[69] They are mostly taken from already existing legislation, and a large portion of the text is copied verbatim from the sources. These can be identified as follows:

1. The canonical collections known to us as the *Corpus iuris canonici*. The compilers used Gratian's *Decretum*, the *Decretals* (*Liber extra*) of Pope Gregory IX (5 September 1234), the *Liber sextus* (*Sext*) of Pope Boniface VIII (3 March 1298) and the *Clementines* of Pope Clement V, issued by his successor Pope John XXII (25 October 1317). However, there is no sign of the *Extravagantes* of Pope John XXII (compiled between 1325 and 1327) or the so-called *Extravagantes communes*, both of which were added by Jean Chappuis in his edition of 1500.[70]

---

[68]The date is known from the despatch of Eustace Chapuys, imperial ambassador in London from 1529 to 1545. See *Letters and papers*, X, 308, translated from Chapuys MS, 1536, fo. 42-3. This MS is in the Haus-, Hof- und Staatsarchiv, Vienna, catalogued in the Statenabteilung England, Karton 4.

[69]The exact number depends on how the text is divided. Generally speaking, the compilers respect the divisions indicated by their sources, but not always. The divisions adopted in this edition combine those of the manuscript with those of the original sources. References to them are abbreviated as H.C., followed by the title and canon numbers, e.g. H.C., 1.1.

[70]Chappuis subsequently added four further canons to the *Extravagantes communes* in his second edition (1503).

2. The Roman law collections known to us as the *Corpus iuris civilis*. There are citations from Justinian's *Digest* and from the *Codex Iustinianus*. It is possible that the compilers also used the *Institutions of Justinian* but there is no evidence that any use was made of the *Novellae*.

3. English church legislation, much (but not all) of which is contained in William Lyndwood's *Provinciale*, composed in 1430 and published in 1433. The compilers also used the legatine constitutions of Otho (1237) and Othobon (1268), which were normally printed together with Lyndwood's *Provinciale*.

In addition to these, Gwent and his companions made full use of the statutes of the realm as they stood at the end of 1534, and it appears that they had independent access to the canons of the fourth Lateran council (1215), since H.C., 14.11 is an adaptation of one of them (c. 49) which is not in the *Corpus iuris canonici*.

That the compilers would have used these sources is hardly surprising, but the way in which they selected from them calls for some comment. In some cases it seems that they did little more than run down the pages of the editions which they had and extracted those elements which they believed were still in force.[71] But questions arise in two areas. First, there is the curious order in which the canons are presented, which is quite unlike that of the sources they were using. What (if anything) can explain that? Second, there is the fact that quite often the compilers have modified their sources in different ways. Omissions from a text may be accidental as well as deliberate, and alterations may sometimes be the result of variant textual sources or of careless copying. But additions are almost invariably deliberate, and in some cases may result in a change to the existing law, even if that was not intended.

The shape of the collection

To deal first with the order in which the canons are presented, it is immediately clear that the overall shape of the collection bears no resemblance to the established canonical tradition, nor does it seem to possess any inner coherence of its own. From the appearance of the *Compilatio prima* in 1191, it had become the custom to divide canonical legislation into five categories, which were usually represented by separate books in the different collections. These categories were abbreviated as follows:

---

[71]This should be understood to mean *theoretically* in force; not necessarily in practice. What actually transpired in the courts is very hard to determine, and we must await Professor R. H. Helmholz's forthcoming history of English canon law, based (as it largely is) on surviving court records, before we can gauge this at all accurately.

1. Iudex	Judge (i.e. ecclesiastical officials)
2. Iudicium	Judgment (i.e. court procedures)
3. Clerus	Clergy (their duties and status)
4. Connubium	Marriage (including divorce)
5. Crimen	Crime (mainly matters of church discipline)

This order was so ingrained that it was used without question by everyone from Gregory IX in 1234 to Jean Chappuis in 1500, including William Lyndwood. The only other model which the compilers of 1535 knew about was Gratian's *Decretum*, but nobody had ever imitated that. It would therefore have been expected that the Henrician canons would at least try to follow the customary order, if only to make it easier for people to find their way around, but this was not the case. Furthermore, although the compilers often did little more than extract whole pages from the *Corpus iuris canonici* (and - though much less frequently - from the *Corpus iuris civilis* as well), so that blocks of material are readily identifiable, there is relatively little orderly progression from one title to the next. Even when we can identify a series of canons as coming, let us say, from Book 1 of the *Decretals* (X), this does not mean that the block in question starts at the beginning of that book and works its way through. Furthermore, even when title headings are identical, or virtually so, this does not guarantee that the content has been drawn from the earlier material contained under that title, and not from somewhere else.

This is particularly evident in the first title ('On the Trinity and the catholic faith'), which is the standard introduction to all the classical collections. The Henrician canons take over the heading but not the content, which comes from elsewhere, including parts of Book 5. In other cases the Henrician canons have altered the original heading but retained the content, as for example in H.C., 8 ('On blasphemy') which comes from X, 5.26 ('De maledicis'), whereas in still other cases both the title and the content are so altered that any relationship between the classical canons and the Henrician compilation becomes highly questionable. Taking the titles of the *Decretals* as our model, what we find is the following:

Decretals		*Henrician canons*	
1.1	The Trinity and the catholic faith	1.	The Trinity and the catholic faith
1.6	Election	15.	Elections
1.9	Renunciation (Resignation)	16.	Renunciation (Resignation)
1.10	Correcting negligence	17.	Correcting negligence
1.11	The times of ordinations	18.	The time of ordinations
1.27	The office of the guardian	34.	Churchwardens' accounts
1.38	Procurators	29.	Procurators
2.17	Sequestration	33.	Sequestrations
2.28	Appeals	36.	Appeals

3.4	Non-resident clerics	19. Non-resident clerics
3.7	Institutions	20. Institutions
3.19	Exchanges	21. Exchanges
3.26	Last wills and testaments	31. Testaments
3.29	Parish clergy and strangers	32. Parish boundaries
3.30	Tithes	24. Tithes
3.39	Payments, etc.	28. Stipends
3.48	Building and repairing churches	30. Dilapidation
4.1	Betrothals and marriage	22. Betrothal and marriage
4.19	Divorce	23. Divorce
5.1	Accusations	11. Accusations
5.2	Calumniators	9. Defamation and abuse
5.3	Simony	3. Simony
5.16	Adultery and fornication	4. Adultery and fornication
5.20	Crime of forgery	5. Crime of forgery
5.21	Fortune telling	7. Fortune telling
5.26	Cursing	8. Blasphemy
5.31	Excesses of prelates and subordinates	10. Excesses in general
5.34	Canonical purgation	12. Purgation
5.35	Popular purgation	12. Purgation
5.37	Penalties	13. Penalties and ecclesiastical penalties
5.39	Sentence of excommunication	14. Sentence of excommunication

The mid-sections of Books 1 and 5 present the most coherent sequences, and Book 5 has been treated more thoroughly than the others, but one is still struck by the large number of gaps. It is true that several matters are dealt with under other headings, so that the above is not a complete picture - for example, there is an extensive treatment of heresy (X, 5.7) in H.C., 1. This means that we cannot use the list of titles as a reliable index of sources without a certain amount of distortion, although a complete listing of them would only confirm our impressions as far as the overall relationship of the Henrician canons to the *Decretals* is concerned. No doubt some of the original titles would have had little relevance in the sixteenth century, especially in a reformed church, but that still does not account for the all but total absence of Book 2, for example. A glance at the later *Reformatio legum ecclesiasticarum* will show immediately that there is a much more extensive use made there of that book, as there is of Book 1 as well. The conclusion must be that the collection as we have it is incomplete, a judgment which is supported by the fact that the last canon breaks off in mid-sentence.

In addition to the above, there are six titles in the Henrician canons which at first sight do not have any obvious textual antecedents in the classical canonical tradition. These are:

2. The office of preaching
6. Perjury and breach of faith
25. London tithes
26. Lepers
27. Mortuaries
35. Procedure [in the ecclesiastical courts]

A closer look at these reveals that the sources are as follows:

2. From the canons of the (anti-Lollard) council of Oxford, 1407.
6. Vaguely linked to X, 2.24 ('Oaths') but mainly from Gratian's *Decretum* (C. 22).
25. A local ordinance of March-April 1534.
26. X, 3.48.2, but may be taken directly from Lateran III, c. 23, 1179.
27. A reference to 21 Henry VIII, c. 6 (1529).
35. Drawn from different sources, including X, 2.27 and English statutes.

It thus appears that four (H.C., 2, 25, 27 and part of 35) are drawn from local English legislation, whilst three (H.C., 6, 26 and part of 35) have Roman canonical antecedents. The insertion of H.C., 2, 6, 25 and 26 in the main body of the text appears to be dependent on their connexion, real or imagined, with the title immediately preceding them, and it is possible that H.C., 35 was meant to head up a new section on judicial procedure which was never finished. The position of H.C., 27 is doubtless due to the fact that it deals with a source of clerical income as the titles before (H.C., 24-6) and after (H.C., 28) it do, but why it should come before 'Stipends' and not after it is impossible to say. Once again, we appear to be dealing with a series of vaguely connected titles which have been thrown together without much thought being given to the overall logic of the presentation.

Yet perhaps a closer examination of the canons as they are, rather than against the background of what we assume they should have been, will present a less bleak picture. We can only conjecture what may have been in the mind of the compiler(s) who placed them in their present order, and any reconstruction must be pure guesswork, but it may be that some sense can be made of it as follows:

A. The clergy and clerical discipline (1-14)
a. Clerical crimes and misdemeanours (1-10)
b. The procedure for dealing with clerical crimes and abuses (11-14)

B. The clergy and their ministry (15-31)
  a. Clerical status (15-21)
  b. Clerical duties (22-31)
C. Parochial administration (32-4)
D. The ecclesiastical courts (35-6; unfinished)

If such a reconstruction is plausible, then it is clear that the revisers intended to break with the mindset of the past while retaining what to them were the sounder elements of its substance. In this connexion it may be noticed that the order of the titles bears some resemblance, not only to the *Reformatio legum ecclesiasticarum* (which would be expected) but also to the canons of 1603 (1604), which became the classical expression of Anglican canon law.[72] Is it therefore possible to say that the Henrician canons are the harbinger of a new and 'Anglican' approach to canon law, preserving much of its medieval inheritance whilst at the same time moulding it into a fundamentally different shape? That is probably going too far, since such an idea would not have occurred to Richard Gwent and his companions, but perhaps there is some method behind their apparently chaotic approach which bears a resemblance (however slight) to what has happened in the Church of England since that time.

Use of the source materials

Turning next to the way in which the source materials were used, we can examine this most conveniently in terms of omissions, modifications of existing material and additions. Given that a large number of the canons were copied verbatim from earlier sources, this is a relatively easy task, though it is not always clear why a particular alteration was made. Omissions, by their very nature, are the hardest to classify - were they deliberate, accidental or merely the result of a variant source? Often we can only guess, and where the meaning is basically unaffected there is little point in trying to reach a conclusion one way or the other. But there are cases where omissions do affect the meaning, and here it is of some interest and importance to try to determine why they were made. Sometimes it is possible to say that the omission was deliberate, because the source text reflects a situation which no longer obtained after the break with Rome. A good example of this occurs with the canon 'Suffraganeis',[73] which was originally a pronouncement of Pope Alexander III (1159-81). The compilers of 1535 reproduced it verbatim (H.C., 15.11) but without the clause 'etiamsi pallium non receperit' ('even if he has not received the pallium') immediately

---

[72]Promulgated on 6 September 1604, they remained in force until 7 May 1969, when they were replaced by the current 'revised' canons. The content is now rather different from what it was, but the structure of the older compilation has been retained more or less intact.
[73]X, 1.6.11 (Fr, II, 53).

after 'confirmationem electionis suae'. The reason for the omission is obvious, because the pallium was the vestment which Rome traditionally sent as its confirmation of the election, and it can hardly be regarded as accidental. But indications as clear as this one are rare, and it would be unwise to make assumptions about most of the omissions without supporting evidence.

There is however at least one clear case of substantial omission which cannot be accidental or explained by the break with Rome. It occurs in the very first canon, which is a long list of heresies, taken ultimately from the writings of Isidore of Seville (c. 560-636) but more immediately from Gratian's *Decretum*.[74] In the text as it is printed in the *Decretum* there are sixty-eight distinct heresies named (plus eleven other unnamed ones), but only sixteen of them are taken up by the Henrician canons. They are listed in the original order,[75] but with a number of impressive gaps which cannot all be readily explained, and the names given to them by Isidore and Gratian are left out. The result is a list of heretical teachings which the compilers presumably felt were still relevant in their own day, but their criteria of selection remain opaque. For example, why did they include the ancient Judaizing insistence on the need for circumcision, which could not have been a major problem in 1535, whilst leaving out the major Christological and Trinitarian heresies of the fourth and fifth centuries, some of which were reappearing in their own time?

It hardly seems plausible that Gwent and his colleagues could have contented themselves with a random selection of false doctrines, since only the year before parliament had passed a statute against heresy which had failed to define what it was, and the need to do so was pressing.[76] As the prescribed penalty for heresy was burning at the stake, the legal system had a genuine interest in determining what constituted guilt, and randomness would not have provided a satisfactory criterion. The trouble is that an examination of the items selected for inclusion in the list found in H.C., 1.1 fails to reveal any obvious principle at work, although it is true that the compilers prefaced their list with a general statement which Isidore (and Gratian) put at the end. This states that anything which goes against the teaching of Scripture is to be regarded as a heresy, and that must be regarded as the overarching legal principle which governed the rest. The following selection would then be just a sample of the sorts of things which would come under the definition of heresy, without attempting to relate specific items to heresies which actually existed in 1535. However we look at it, H.C., 1.1 is an incomplete and inadequate definition of what was unacceptable even in the post-reformation church. When we consider

---

[74]C. 24, q. 3 c. 39 (Fr, I, 1001-6); from Isidore of Seville, *Etymologiae*, VIII, 5.
[75]They are nos. 1, 3, 6-7, 10-11, 23, 25-8, 32-3, 45, 58 and 63.
[76]25 Henry VIII, c. 14, 1534 (*S.R.*, III, 454-5). For the problems of definition surrounding this act, and contemporary awareness of them, see Lehmberg, *Reformation parliament*, pp. 186-7.

that much of what was needed could have been supplied by making greater use of the source actually quoted this inadequacy becomes all the more difficult to explain.

Modifications made to existing material present a different range of problems. In some cases they are probably no more than stylistic variations adopted for no reason other than personal preference. An example can be found in H.C., 26.1, where the second sentence, which originally began 'caveant tamen ut', has been joined to the first, so that it now reads 'ita tamen ut'. The meaning is not altered significantly, but the change is more than just a copyist's error. Who made it and why? It is impossible to say, other than to remark that exact reproduction of a source was not as important in the middle ages as it is today. It may well have been a variant reading found in the text which the compilers were using, but even if they were responsible for it, they may not have given the matter much thought. Other changes clearly are due to careless copying, as for example in H.C., 25.1 where 'vino' has been written as 'omni' and 'caponibus' as 'panonibus', though these too may go back to a faulty source and not be attributable to a scribal error by one of the collaborators on the 1535 project.

More serious are the cases where a modification has made a real difference in the meaning, the most extreme example being H.C., 11.18. Even allowing for the fact that the canon is a paraphrase of the original,[77] and not a direct copy of it, it is still the case that where the source talks about 'publice concubinarios ... in eos fuit excommunicationis sententia lata' ('clergy who keep concubines publicly ... a sentence of excommunication has been laid against them') the text of H.C., 11.18 has been altered to read 'publicas concubinas ... excommunicatas' ('public concubines ... [who have been] excommunicated'). This change may reflect a belief on the compilers' part that the canonical text was corrupt, since they probably knew that in earlier times the concubine was more likely to suffer the penalty in question than the clergyman who kept her. As celibate clergymen themselves, it is also possible that they thought that such a rectification was in their own interests. But the change may well have been made at an earlier stage, probably for essentially the same reason, and thus found its way into the manuscript which the compilers were using. Whatever the explanation for it is, it provides a good example of how a textual modification, which must have been deliberate, has inverted the meaning of the original completely and would have changed the law quite drastically if it had been sanctioned.

Additions to the source texts are numerous, and very often substantial. On the whole, they represent clarifications of the originals, rather than conscious attempts to alter their meaning, though where one ends and the other begins may not always be easy to decide. In particular, the compilers were fond of writing in the specific terms which by custom and tradition attached to particular provisions. For example, if it were decreed that a clergyman should be suspended

---

[77] X, 5.1.20 (Fr, II, 741), originally a decretal of Pope Innocent III (1198-1216).

for some offence, the compilers would characteristically add a phrase like 'per triennium' to indicate how long the suspension would normally have lasted, even if that had not previously been specified in the law itself.

The most interesting clarification of this kind is in H.C., 19.2 where it is decreed that a non-resident incumbent shall contribute one fortieth of his annual income to poor relief in the parish. The principle that a non-resident should make such a contribution had been stated for the first time in the legatine constitutions of Othobon,[78] and it was subsequently repeated by Archbishop John Stratford in the fourth of his canons of 1342,[79] but no rate had ever been specified. Whether two and a half per cent had become customary at this time or not is uncertain, but it obviously seemed reasonable, and the 1535 compilers inserted it into their collection. It is of interest to us now because it also appears in the royal injunctions of 1536,[80] where the context and the tone both suggest that it was a new thing. Was there perhaps some input from the Henrician canons (or from one of their compilers) into the injunctions? Or are we dealing with a general rule of thumb which most people had come to accept and which Cromwell, like the compilers of 1535, thought ought to be standardized?

Another addition which reflects a similar desire to tie down things which had previously been left hanging is found in H.C., 22.28, where it is declared that marriage in the direct line of consanguinity is henceforth to be forbidden. This had always been accepted in the case of parents and children, of grandparents and grandchildren and even of great-grandparents and great-grandchildren, but there had never been a blanket prohibition of the kind proposed here. No doubt the compilers believed that they were merely tidying up a loose end, and it seems that the matter was frequently debated among canonists in the later middle ages. But this kind of prohibition was not the law then, nor is it the law in England now. However odd it may seem, it is perfectly legal for great-great-grandparents to marry their great-great-grandchildren! Roman canonists took the matter sufficiently seriously that in 1917 they introduced a blanket prohibition of consanguineous marriages in the direct line of descent into the new *Codex iuris canonici* (*c*.1076) which has carried over into the 1983 revision (*c*.1091), but, although it was proposed in 1535, the Church of England has never done the same.

Another matter affecting marriage is the question of where the wedding should take place if the parties were from different parishes (H.C., 22.17). It was apparently the custom then, as it is now, for such weddings to take place in the church of the bride, though there was (and is) no law on the subject. The 1535 compilers wanted to make this custom official, and so they wrote it into the canon regardless of the inconvenience which it would certainly have caused in

---

[78] 1268/9 (PC, 757-8).
[79] L, 3.4.4 (W, II, 697).
[80] 1536/8 (*D.E.R.*, p. 178).

any number of cases. They also managed to simplify the law regarding betrothals (cf. H.C., 22.19), by giving expression to what had apparently already become general practice, though it had never received canonical confirmation.

In sum, it can be said that although the Henrician canons are generally no more than a statement of what the law was (or was thought to be) at the time they were compiled, there are instances where real changes were introduced. Even if many of them were thought of as corrections or clarifications of the existing law, and not as innovations, innovations are what they actually were. Whether they would have survived the sort of scrutiny which would have been required if they were ever to be enacted into law is uncertain, but their appearance in this compilation is a reminder to us of how difficult it is for anyone to undertake a comprehensive codification of the law without changing it in the process.

Transmission of the manuscript

After the winter of 1535-6 the Henrician canons ceased to play any active part in the development of the reformation, although they did not disappear from view immediately. It is probable that the text which we now have is the only one to have survived, although it is obviously a fair copy made from one or more rough drafts. It is written on eighty-nine folio pages in a single, neat court hand, which suggests that it was prepared for presentation to the king. The corrections are all scribal and most of them were made in the course of copying. The only exceptions are found in H.C., 25.1, where the scribe altered 'cives tamen et inhabitantes' to read 'cives tamen occupantes sive inhabitantes'; in H.C., 25. 8, where he added 'decem annis ultra praeteritis'; and in H.C., 25.11, where he added 'et panni chrismales in purificationibus mulierum', using a different pen after the main text had been completed. Since H.C., 25 is probably a direct transcription of the London tithe agreement reached at the end of March 1534 (of which no other example appears to have survived), it may be assumed that these changes are no more than the corrections needed in order to make the canon correspond exactly to the original text.

At the same time, it is hard to believe that the compilers had got no further than the point where the manuscript breaks off, since it ends in mid-sentence; more likely, the scribe paused at that point and before he could resume his task the need for it was gone. Whatever rough drafts were lying about at that stage were probably thrown out at some point, but the fair copy was kept, perhaps for future use if the occasion should arise. That was a real possibility at the time, especially after legislation was passed authorizing the reappointment of a canon law commission for a three-year period from 14 April 1536. Had that commission ever been constituted, it is quite likely that the Henrician canons would have been an important starting point for its deliberations. That did not

happen, and whatever Gwent did with the manuscript, no more is heard of it until after his death in July 1543, when Cranmer was finally able to appoint his own man to succeed him.[81]

Shortly after this, parliament returned to the subject of canon law and enacted a new statute for its revision, giving the still theoretical commission of thirty-two the power to propose new laws (provided that they were not repugnant to the common law of the realm or to the king's prerogative), in addition to its earlier right to revise the old ones, with the result that the work of Gwent and his companions, which was no more than a revision of the existing law, was effectively superseded.[82] But the abandoned manuscript had not been forgotten. Thomas Cranmer was well aware of its existence and apparently knew where to find it when the need arose. When Henry VIII asked him to produce a list of those who had worked on the earlier compilation, as well as a copy of the work itself, Cranmer replied to the king as follows:

> I sent for the bishop of Worcester[83] incontinently, and declared unto him your majesty's pleasure, in such things as your majesty willed to be done. And first, where your majesty's pleasure was to have the names of such persons as your highness in times past appointed to make laws ecclesiastical for your grace's realm, the bishop of Worcester promised me with all speed, to enquire out their names, and the book which they made, and to bring the names and also the book unto your majesty; which I trust he hath done before this time.[84]

What happened next is unknown, but it is at least clear that the commission which prepared the *Reformatio legum ecclesiasticarum* was neither ignorant of the Henrician canons nor deprived of access to them. On the contrary, in a small number of cases it is virtually certain that they made use of the earlier document, and more extensive borrowings from it cannot be excluded, although they are

---

[81]This was John Cockes, the first layman to hold the office of dean of the arches. It is interesting to speculate whether Gwent's death had anything to do with the subsequent revival of the canon law legislation. Had he been obstructing progress in some way? Or did the need to appoint a successor to him simply jog Cranmer's memory and persuade him that it was time to try to revive the moribund project?

[82]35 Henry VIII, c. 16, 1544 (*S.R.*, III, 976). See below.

[83]This was Nicholas Heath who was bishop of Rochester from 4 April 1540 until his translation to Worcester on 20 February 1544. He was deprived on 10 October 1551 for his opposition to the reformation, but was restored to the see by Mary I on 15 March 1555. On 21 June in the same year he became archbishop of York until he was deprived a second time on 5 July 1559. He died in 1579. Evidently he and Cranmer were still on good terms in 1546. Noted in Emden, *Biographical register 1501-40*, pp. 278-9 and in Venn, *Alumni Cantabrigienses*, II, 347.

[84]*Letters and papers*, XXI, 1, 48-9, no. 109 (SP 1/213, p. 144). The letter is dated 23 January 1546.

impossible to prove.[85] At some point the manuscript seems to have come into the possession of John Foxe (1517-87), most probably through the good offices of Archbishop Matthew Parker, who also gave Foxe his copy of the *Reformatio*.[86] Foxe printed its preface on the assumption that the Edwardian commission which produced the *Reformatio* was just a continuation of the one supposedly appointed by Henry, but although he noted that the contents of the earlier document were very different from those of the later one, he did not venture to print it.[87] Nevertheless, we know that it was from our manuscript that Foxe got his information, because on fo. 13r the following words are written: 'Ecclesiastical lawes devesed in King Henry the VIIIth *his* dayes', followed immediately by 'of Master John Foxe' in a different hand.[88] Foxe seems to have owned the manuscript and not merely had the use of it, because it never went back to the archbishop or to an ecclesiastical archive. From him it passed to Robert Beale (1541-1601), who was clerk to the council of Queen Elizabeth I.[89] On his death, it went to his daughter Margaret, who was the wife of Sir Henry Yelverton (1566-1629), and it remained in the Yelverton family until 1795. In that year it was given, along with the rest of the collection, to a cousin of the family, Sir Henry Gough-Calthorpe (1749-98), on the understanding that he would look after it properly. In 1953 it was sold to the British Museum by one of his descendants, Brigadier R. H. Anstruther-Gough-Calthorpe (1908-85). From there it passed to the British Library when that was created on 1 July 1973, although it continued to be housed in the museum until the autumn of 1998 when it was moved, along with the rest of the manuscript collection, to the library's new site at St Pancras.

[85]See the next section for the details.

[86]Foxe is best known for his classic *Acts and monuments of these latter and perillous days, touching matters of the church* (London, 1563), which was published in a second and definitive edition in 1570. A year later the bishops made it the official history of the English reformation, and every clergyman was ordered to obtain a copy for his personal edification (1571/1.9).

[87]He made a number of alterations in the preface, three of which must be retained for the text to make grammatical sense. The others are probably just misreadings of the original. Foxe's version has been reproduced on several occasions, e.g. by J. Strype, *Memorials of Thomas Cranmer* (3 vols., Oxford, 1840), II, 778-80; W, III, 779-80; G, 989; and E. Cardwell, *The reformation of the ecclesiastical laws of England* (Oxford, 1850).

[88]The first hand is probably that of a scribe, who subsequently crossed out 'his'. The second hand is probably that of Robert Beale, who gained possession of the MS after Foxe. There is also a third hand, in which is written: 'Speciatim. E. Jhon.'

[89]Dr T. S. Freeman has suggested to me that Foxe got the MS from Sir William Cecil but returned it to him after he had finished with it, and that Cecil later passed it on to Beale. It should be noted that Beale was a learned canonist in his own right.

The manuscript was noted by E. Bernard in his catalogue of 1697,[90] by which time it had been bound with other ecclesiastical material of the same period. Bernard apparently failed to appreciate what it was and it remained unnoticed until Dr Logan identified it in 1974. Formerly it was catalogued as MS Yelverton 45, but it is now British Library Additional MS 48040, ff. 14r-103r. Although it has been referred to quite often in recent scholarship,[91] only now is it being edited, translated and published for the first time.

2. The *Reformatio legum ecclesiasticarum*

The royal commission

The 1536 legislation authorizing a new canon law commission was repeated in 1544, but this time it was allowed to continue for the duration of the king's life and could also introduce new canonical legislation, not merely revamp the old.[92] Yet once again no commission came into being, and when Henry died on 28 January 1547 the act automatically lapsed. It would therefore take a third act of parliament to get the job of canon law revision under way, but that had to wait until the third session of Edward VI's first parliament, which did not open until 4 November 1549. In that session there was a two-pronged attempt to reform the ecclesiastical jurisdiction. In the house of lords on 14 November the bishops present complained that episcopal authority was being ignored and undermined by royal proclamations, and that this was a serious cause of popular disorder. This was almost certainly a reference to the way in which the duke of Somerset had used proclamations to deal with religious matters, and Somerset's fall on 10 October made it possible for them to complain openly for the first time, but it may also have been a way to reopen the whole canon law question.[93] The lords listened sympathetically and directed the bishops to prepare a draft statute dealing with the matter, which could then be debated by parliament and enacted

---

[90]*Catalogi librorum manuscriptorum Angliae et Hiberniae in unum collecti* (Oxford, 1697), II, i. 139-40. Bernard notes only the words of Foxe on fo. 13r, and lists a few of the titles. His description served as the model for the subsequent report of the Historical Manuscripts Commission (II, 39-46).
[91]Most recently MacCulloch, *Thomas Cranmer*, p. 121. There is a good notice of it in *The British Library catalogue of additions to the manuscripts. The Yelverton manuscripts*, ed. M. A. F. Borrie (2 vols., London, 1994), pp. 141-3. The introduction to the volume gives a complete history of the Yelverton collection (*ibid.*, pp. ix-xviii).
[92]35 Henry VIII, c. 16, 1544, (*S.R.*, III, 976).
[93]This ulterior motive was assumed, for example, in W. Cobbett, *The parliamentary history of England from the Norman conquest in 1066 to the year 1803* (36 vols., London, 1806-20), I, cols. 591-2.

into legislation.[94] The bishops who made the complaint were the fourteen diocesans who were present for the parliamentary session, out of the twenty-four or five who could have been there.[95] Listed by seniority, the fourteen were the following (an asterisk denotes those who were later to be on the 1551-2 canon law commission):

1. *Canterbury [Thomas Cranmer][96]
2. Durham [Cuthbert Tunstall][97]
3. *Ely [Thomas Goodrich][98]
4. Coventry and Lichfield [Richard Sampson][99]
5. *Bath and Wells [William Barlow][100]

[94]*L.J.*, I, 359 reads: 'Hodie quaesti sunt episcopi, contemni se a plebe; audere autem nihil pro potestate sua administrare, eo quod per publicas quasdam denuntiationes, quas proclamationes vocant, sublata esset penitus sua iurisdictio, adeo ut neminem iudicio sistere, nullum scelus punire, neminem ad aedem sacram cogere, neque cetera id genus munia ad eos pertinentia exequi audent. Haec querela ab omnibus proceribus non sine merore audita est, et, ut quam citissime huic malo subveniretur, iniunctum est episcopis ut formulam aliquam statuti hac de re scriptam traderent, quae, si consilio postea praelecta omnibus ordinibus proberetur, pro lege omnibus sententiis sanciri posset.' ('Today the bishops complained that they are being scorned by the [common] people and that they dare not exercise any of their powers, claiming that their jurisdiction has been completely removed by certain public announcements which are called proclamations, as a result of which they dare not summon anyone to judgment, punish any crime, compel anyone to come to church or execute any of the other functions of this type which belong to them. This complaint was heard by all the peers with sympathy, and in order that this evil should be alleviated as soon as possible, the bishops were enjoined to submit a written draft of a statute dealing with the matter which, if after being read, were to be approved by all the orders, might be sanctioned as law by a vote of the whole.')

[95]There were then twenty-seven dioceses in all, but London and Gloucester were both vacant at this time, and Norwich was nearly so. Of the remainder, Bangor (Arthur Bulkeley), Chester (John Bird), Exeter (John Veysey), Llandaff (Anthony Kitchin), Oxford (Robert King) and Peterborough (John Chamber or Chambers) were represented by proxies, whereas Bristol (Paul Bush), Salisbury (John Salcot *alias* Capon), Winchester (Stephen Gardiner) and York (Robert Holgate) simply failed to appear.

[96]See above, n. 27.

[97](1474-1559). Bishop of London (1522-30) and Durham (1530-59). He resigned his see shortly before his death. He was one of the earliest members of doctors' commons, having been admitted to the college of advocates c.1506 (see Squibb, *Doctors' commons*, p. 125). Noted in Emden, *Biographical register to 1500*, III, 1913-15; Venn, *Alumni Cantabrigienses*, IV, 271.

[98]See above, n. 43.

[99]See above, n. 36.

[100](d.1568). Bishop of St Asaph (1535), St David's (1536), Bath and Wells (1548-53) and Chichester (1559). He spent the Marian years in exile but was not highly regarded by his peers and had little influence on events. Noted in Emden, *Biographical register 1501-40*, p. 27.

6. St Asaph [Robert Warton *alias* Parfew][101]
7. Carlisle [Robert Aldridge][102]
8. Hereford [John Skip][103]
9. Worcester [Nicholas Heath][104]
10. Westminster [Thomas Thirlby][105]
11. Chichester [George Day][106]
12. Lincoln [Henry Holbeach *alias* Rands][107]
13. *Rochester [Nicholas Ridley][108]
14. St David's [Robert Ferrar][109]

On the same day, a bill was introduced into the commons which would have restricted the administration of ecclesiastical justice to university graduates with at least four years of training in the civil law.[110] The bill was engrossed on 18 November and passed on 3 December, when it was sent up to the lords.[111] There it was read for the first time on 5 December and for the second on 10 December, after which no more was heard of it.[112]

Meanwhile the bishops had drawn up legislation and presented to the upper house, also on 18 November. Their draft was rejected because it appeared to give too much power to the episcopate, but a committee was formed to make amendments to it and to bring it back.[113] There were twelve members of this

---

[101](d.1557). Bishop of St Asaph (1536-54) and then Hereford (1554-7). Noted in Venn, *Alumni Cantabrigienses*, III, 304.

[102]See above, n. 42.

[103](d.1552). Bishop of Hereford (1539-52). Noted in Venn, *Alumni Cantabrigienses*, IV, 86.

[104]See above, n. 83.

[105]See above, n. 17.

[106](*c.*1501-56). Bishop of Chichester (1543-51); deprived 10 October 1551. Noted in Venn, *Alumni Cantabrigienses*, II, 22.

[107](d.1551). Bishop of Rochester (1544-7) and Lincoln (1547-51). Noted in *ibid.*, III, 419.

[108](*c.*1500-55). Bishop of Rochester (1547) and London (1550), he was a close friend of Cranmer's and one of the most prominent martyrs under Mary I (16 October 1555). Noted in *ibid.*, III, 458.

[109](d.1555). Bishop of St David's (1548-53); deprived sometime after 19 July 1553. Noted in *ibid.*, II, 134.

[110]*C.J.,*, I, 11.

[111]*Ibid.*, I, 12.

[112]*L.J.*, I, 366-7.

[113]*Ibid.*, I, 360 says: 'Hodie lecta est billa pro iurisdictione episcoporum et aliorum ecclesiasticorum quae cum proceribus, eo quod episcopi nimis sibi arrogare viderentur, non placeret, visum est deligere prudentes aliquot viros utriusque ordinis, qui habita matura tantae rei inter se deliberatione, referrent toti consilio quid pro ratione temporis et rei necessitate, in hac causa expediret.' ('Today a bill for the jurisdiction of bishops and other ecclesiastics was read which, since it displeased the peers because the bishops seemed to be claiming too much power for themselves, it was decided to choose some wise men of each order who, after mature deliberation among themselves, might report

committee all told, of whom four were bishops.[114] The revised draft of the bishops' bill took three weeks to emerge, although it eventually passed in the house of lords.[115] The bill was then sent to the commons where it was read on 24 December and again on 8 January 1550, but it failed in the third reading on 22 January.[116] By then however, a third bill for ecclesiastical jurisdiction had been submitted to the commons. It received its first two readings and was engrossed on 21 January, only to fail at the third reading on 31 January.[117] In addition to that, on 21 January 1550 the commons initiated another bill which revived the Henrician legislation for a canon law commission, though with only sixteen members instead of thirty-two. That bill was read again and passed on the following day, after which it was sent to the house of lords.[118]

In the interval, the lords were debating yet another bill, this one intended to give formal approval to the ordinal. They had already given it a first reading on 8 January, and were to give it a second reading on 23 January and a third on 25 January. On its final reading the bill was passed, against the opposition of five of the bishops, and sent to the commons.[119] The lords then received the canon law commission bill and gave it its first two readings on the same day.[120] During the following week they proceeded to restore the original number of thirty-two commissioners, and passed the amended bill on the afternoon of Friday 31 January, at the same time as they passed the ordinal bill which had just returned from the commons. The five bishops who had originally voted against the ordinal maintained their opposition, but when it came to the canon law commission ten of the eleven bishops present voted against it; only William Barlow of Bath and Wells being recorded as in support.[121] It then returned to the house of commons

back to the whole council what the most expedient course of action might be, given the constraints of time and the urgency of the matter.')

[114]Canterbury, Durham, Ely and Coventry and Lichfield. There were also four lay peers, the marquess of Dorset (Henry Grey, later duke of Suffolk), Lord Wharton, Lord Stafford and Lord Montague. The remaining four were royal officials, *viz.* the chief justice of the common pleas (Sir Edward Montague), the chief baron of the exchequer court (Sir Roger Cholmley), the attorney-general (Henry Bradshaw) and the solicitor-general (Edward Griffin or Griffith).

[115]*L.J.,*, I, 367-71. It was read for the first time on 11 December and for the second on 17 December, at which point it was committed to the king's attorney for revision. It was brought back to the lords and engrossed on 23 December and was read for the third time on 24 December, when it was passed.

[116]*C.J.*, I, 13-15.

[117]*Ibid.*, I, 15-16.

[118]*Ibid.*

[119]*L.J.*, I, 377, 383-4. The dissenting bishops were Durham, Carlisle, Worcester, Chichester and Westminster.

[120]*L.J.*, I, 384.

[121]*L.J.*, I, 387. The only bishop recorded as having been present and not voting against was William Barlow of Bath and Wells, which is something of a mystery. Barlow had no reason to break rank with his fellow bishops, and was sufficiently in tune with Cranmer to be appointed to the eventual commission. It may be that his name was overlooked,

for final approval, which was granted in a first reading on the same day and the two further readings on 1 February 1550, the last day of the session.[122] As in the 1536 statute, an obligation was laid on the commission to have its work completed and ready for enactment within three years from that date.

Why did the bishops vote against the re-establishment of the canon law commission? The late J. C. Spalding claimed that the fact that ten bishops voted against the bill means that they opposed lay interference in church affairs.[123] This is possible, especially in the case of the five who voted against the ordinal, but it may be that their opposition had as much to do with the doubling of the number of members as anything else, since four of them were subsequently appointed to the commission and it was completely dominated by the clerical interest.

The format of thirty-two members had by this time become traditional (even though the commission had still never met), providing for equal representation from the clergy and the laity, though there were some differences of detail from what had obtained previously. According to the 1550 statute, the clergy had to include at least four bishops, but the lay representatives were no longer required to be members of the two houses of parliament. Instead, at least four had to be common lawyers.[124] Nothing more was done until 6 October 1551, when the privy council finally approved a provisional list of thirty-two names.[125] With one or two slight alterations, this list reappears in the journal of King Edward VI for 10 February 1552,[126] and the actual commission, containing the final list of approved names, is in the patent rolls, dated 12 February 1552.[127] The privy council also provided for the appointment of a drafting committee of eight, drawn equally from each of the four groups which made up the commission,

either in the list of dissenters or in the list of those present at the session. Coventry and Lichfield, Hereford and St Asaph had absented themselves for the afternoon, though it is possible that they were attending convocation instead, as was the bishops' habit on a Friday. The same three had been absent on Friday 17 January, along with Rochester, and convocation seems to have been the most likely reason. Perhaps Barlow went to convocation in Ridley's place on 31 January and the *Lords Journal* simply fails to record his absence (an infrequent but by no means unprecedented lapse).

[122]*C.J.*, I, 16. It became law as 3-4 Edward VI, c. 11, 1549-50 (*S.R.*, IV, 111-12).

[123]J. C. Spalding, 'The *Reformatio legum ecclesiasticarum* of 1552 and the furthering of discipline in England', *Church History*, XXXIX (1970), 162-71.

[124]The number four is an anachronistic survival from the earlier draft, when a commission of only sixteen had been suggested. This is clear from that fact that when the thirty-two were appointed, the bishops and the common lawyers each numbered eight. It will be remembered that earlier legislation had not specified how the clerical representation was to be apportioned.

[125]*Acts of the privy council*, III (1550-2), 382.

[126]*Literary remains of King Edward the Sixth*, ed. J. G. Nichols (London, 1857), p. 397.

[127]*Calendar of the patent rolls preserved in the Public Record Office. Edward VI* (4 vols., London, 1926), IV (1550-3), 354. Permission for action to be taken, but no list of names, is found in the *Acts of the privy council*, III, 471-2, dated 2 February 1552.

which was constituted by royal proclamation on 11 November 1551.[128] It was envisaged that this committee would do the work of preparing and editing the proposed canons, which it would then submit to the full commission for ratification. What happened next is not entirely clear, but there is no reason to doubt that the *Reformatio* as we now have it is essentially the work of this drafting committee (or part of it). Whether the full commission of thirty-two ever met to ratify their work is unknown and probably unlikely, but if it did, that meeting can only have taken place shortly before Archbishop Cranmer presented the finished work to the house of lords at the beginning of March 1553, and could hardly have done any more than rubber stamp the finished text. The names of the commissioners, with those of the drafting committee in bold type, were:

Bishops	*Divines*
Thomas Cranmer (Canterbury)[129]	John Taylor[130]
Thomas Goodrich (Ely)[131]	**Richard Cox**[132]
Nicholas Ridley (London)[133]	Matthew Parker[134]

[128]The proclamation is printed at the beginning of the *Reformatio*, immediately after Foxe's preface. Approval for it to be issued was given by the privy council on 9 November. See *Acts of the privy council*, III, 410.

[129]See above, n. 27.

[130](*c*.1503-54). A canon of Lincoln who became bishop of that diocese in 1552. He was a member of the committee which produced the first Edwardian book of common prayer (1549). Noted in Venn, *Alumni Cantabrigienses*, IV, 205.

[131]See above, n. 43. He was about to become keeper of the privy seal (22 December 1551) and chancellor (19 January 1552).

[132](1500-81). Tutor and almoner to Edward VI, chancellor of Oxford University and dean of Christ Church. He later became a leader of the Marian exiles at Frankfurt and was consecrated bishop of Ely in 1559. Noted in Emden, *Biographical register 1501-40*, pp. 146-7.

[133]See above, n. 108.

[134](1504-75). Vice-chancellor of Cambridge University and dean of Lincoln (1552). He was consecrated archbishop of Canterbury in 1559 and became a great collector of manuscripts, most of which he deposited at Corpus Christi College, Cambridge. The definitive copy of the *Reformatio* was in his possession in 1570, but what happened to it after that is unknown. Noted in Venn, *Alumni Cantabrigienses*, III, 307.

John Ponet (Winchester)[135] Hugh Latimer[136]/Nicholas Wotton[137]
Miles Coverdale (Exeter)[138] Sir Anthony Cooke[139]
William Barlow (Bath and Wells)[140] **Peter Martyr Vermigli**[141]

[135](c. 1514-56). Bishop of Rochester (1550) and Winchester (1551). He fled England in 1553 and eventually joined Peter Martyr Vermigli at Strasbourg, where he died. Noted in *ibid.*, III, 390.

[136](c. 1485-1555). Noted preacher and bishop of Worcester (1535-9), he resigned his see after the passage of the act of six articles. He inclined towards a puritan viewpoint, and was martyred with Nicholas Ridley on 16 October 1555. His name did not appear on either list in February 1552. Noted in *ibid.*, III, 49.

[137](c. 1497-1567). Dean of both Canterbury and York, he was a member of Edward VI's privy council and secretary of state in 1549-50. He was a traditionalist in doctrinal matters, and was admitted to doctors' commons on 29 October 1530 (Squibb, *Doctors' commons*, p. 145). Noted in Emden, *Biographical register 1501-40*, pp. 639-40.

[138](1488-1569). Famous for completing William Tyndale's translation of the Old Testament and publishing the first English-language Bible (1535), he became bishop of Exeter in 1551. He was in exile from 1540-8 and again under Mary I (1553-8). He refused to resume his bishopric in 1559 because of his puritan sympathies. Noted in Venn, *Alumni Cantabrigienses*, III, 406.

[139](c. 1505-76). Privately educated himself, he became a tutor to Edward VI and a member of parliament for Lewes (1547-53). His daughter married Sir William Cecil, and he went into exile at Strasbourg (with Peter Martyr Vermigli) under Mary I. Later he represented Essex in the parliaments of 1559 and 1563. Noted in S. T. Bindoff, *The house of commons 1509-58* (3 vols., London, 1982), I, 689-91.

[140]See above, n. 100.

[141](1500-62). An Italian protestant, he fled to Zürich in 1542 and went straight to Strasbourg, where he became a professor of theology. In 1547 Thomas Cranmer invited him to England, and he became regius professor of divinity at Oxford. When Mary I came to the throne he returned to Strasbourg, but in 1557 he went back to Zürich as professor of Hebrew, in order to escape the Lutheran-Reformed controversy which had broken out in the former city. On his career in England, see P. McNair, 'Peter Martyr in England', *Peter Martyr Vermigli and Italian reform*, ed. J. C. McLelland (Waterloo, ON, 1980), pp. 85-105.

John Hooper (Gloucester)[142]   Sir John Cheke[143]
John Scory (Rochester)[144]   John a Lasco (Łaski)[145]

Civil lawyers   *Common lawyers*

Sir William Petre[146]   Sir James Hales[147]
Sir William Cecil[148]   Sir Thomas Bromley[149]

[142](d.1555). Bishop of Gloucester (1550), he caused controversy by refusing to be consecrated with the traditional ceremonies. After being put in prison for his contumacy, he was finally consecrated in 1551 and spent his short episcopate introducing Zwinglian church order into his diocese. He was martyred under Mary I. Noted in Emden, *Biographical register*, pp. 296-7.

[143](1514-57). Tutor to Edward VI and member of parliament for Bletchingley (1547-53), he became secretary of state for a brief period in 1553. He fled to Belgium under Mary I but was captured and sent back to England, where he recanted under pressure. This recantation was insincere, and he was troubled by it until his death. Noted in *ibid.*, pp. 114-15 and in Bindoff, *House of commons*, I, 626-30, who overstates his *rôle* in the composition of the *Reformatio*.

[144](d.1585). Bishop of Rochester (1551) and Chichester (1552). He recanted under Mary I but later fled to the continent. In 1559 he was consecrated bishop of Hereford. Noted in Venn, *Alumni Cantabrigienses*, IV, 30.

[145](1499-1560). Polish nobleman and archdeacon of Warsaw, he was the superintendent of the Stranger Church in London under Edward VI. He was a strict protestant and organized this Stranger Church along Zwinglian lines. In 1553 he returned to Poland, where he died.

[146](c.1505-72). Principal secretary from 1544-57, a privy council member and member of parliament for Downton (1536) and Essex (1547-63). He presided over convocation as Cromwell's deputy on 16 June 1536, became keeper of the great seal for ecclesiastical affairs in 1547, and managed to adapt himself to both Mary I and Elizabeth I. He was admitted to doctors' commons on 8 March 1533 (Squibb, *Doctors' commons*, p. 145). Noted in Emden, *Biographical register 1501-40*, pp. 445-6 and Bindoff, *House of commons*, III, 92-6.

[147](c.1469-1554). King's sergeant in 1544 and prominent on ecclesiastical commissions under Edward VI. He was imprisoned under Mary I and committed suicide after having been forced to recant his protestant beliefs. Noted in A. W. B. Simpson, *Biographical dictionary of the common law* (London, 1984), p. 222.

[148](1520-98). Secretary of state (1550-3) and again from 1558-72, he was a member of parliament for an unknown constituency in 1542, for Stamford in 1547-52 and for Lincolnshire (Oct. 1553-9), as well as for Northamptonshire in 1563. He became one of Elizabeth I's chief advisers and was created Lord Burghley in 1571. However he was not a civil lawyer, having been to Gray's Inn where he was trained in the common law instead, and why he should have been included among them is unknown. Noted in Venn, *Alumni Cantabrigienses*, I, 313 and in Bindoff, *House of commons*, I, 603-6.

[149](c.1505-55). Member of the privy council, he became king's sergeant in 1540 and a judge in the court of common pleas in 1544. His nephew, also called Thomas Bromley, was lord chancellor from 1579-87. Bromley was a member of parliament for an unknown constituency (1529-36). Noted in Bindoff, *House of commons*, I, 508-10.

Rowland Taylor[150]   John Gosnold[151]
William May[152]   William Stamford[153]
Bartholomew Traheron[154]   John Caryll[155]
Sir Thomas Smith[156]/William Cooke[157]   John Lucas[158]

[150](d.1555). Chancellor of the diocese of London, he was one of Cranmer's chaplains and was martyred under Mary I. He was admitted to doctors' commons sometime during 1539 (Squibb, *Doctors' commons*, p. 148). On King Edward VI's list, he appears among the divines. Noted in Venn, *Alumni Cantabrigienses*, IV, 209.

[151](*c.*1507-54). Member of parliament for Ipswich (1547-52; Oct. 1553), he seems to have opposed the attempt to make Lady Jane Grey queen, and may also have expressed himself in parliament against the restoration of Catholicism under Mary I. He was also a solicitor in the court of augmentations and solicitor general (1552-3). Noted in Bindoff, *House of commons*, II, 237-8.

[152](d.1560). Dean of St Paul's from 1546 and a master of requests under Edward VI. He was nominated archbishop of York in 1559 but died before being consecrated. Noted in Venn, *Alumni Cantabrigienses*, III, 167.

[153](1509-58). Also called Stanford, Staunford. Member of parliament for Stafford (1542-5) and Newcastle-under-Lyme (1547-52), he served on a number of ecclesiastical commissions under Edward VI. Under Mary I he became a judge. Noted in Simpson, *Biographical dictionary*, p. 484 and in Bindoff, *House of commons*, III, 366-8.

[154](*c.*1510- *c.*1558). Member of parliament for Barnstaple (1547-52). Although a layman, he was made dean of Chichester in 1552. He spent the Marian years first in Frankfurt, where he was one of Richard Cox's ablest assistants, and later in Wesel, where he is thought to have died. Noted in Emden, *Biographical register 1501-40*, pp. 573-4 and in Bindoff, *House of commons*, III, 473-4.

[155](*c.*1505-66). Eldest son of another John Caryll (d.1523), who was the first modern-style English law reporter. This Caryll was a member of the Inner Temple and became sergeant at law in 1552. He was a member of parliament for an unknown constituency in 1542, for Taunton (1547-52), Lancaster (March 1553) and Sussex (October 1553-9). Noted in Bindoff, *House of commons*, I, 590-1.

[156](1513-77). Privy councillor under Edward VI and secretary of state (1548-9; 1572-6), he was a member of parliament for Marlborough (1547-52), Grampound (October 1553), Liverpool (1559) and Essex (1571-2). He was not on either of the February 1552 lists, and was not admitted to doctors' commons until 29 May 1574 (Squibb, *Doctors' commons*, p. 160), but he was appointed to the reconstituted commission on 6 April 1571. Noted in Venn, *Alumni Cantabrigienses*, IV, 110 and in Bindoff, *House of commons*, III, 338-40.

[157](*c.*1507-58). King's sergeant in 1550 and judge in the court of common pleas (1552), he was a member of parliament for New Woodstock (October 1553) and Portsmouth (April 1554). He was admitted to doctors' commons on 15 October 1537 (Squibb, *Doctors' commons*, p. 147). His name replaced that of Sir Thomas Smith on the two February 1552 lists. Noted in Bindoff, *House of commons*, I, 692-3.

[158](*c.*1512-56). He was a member of parliament for Colchester (1545-53) and served as one of Edward VI's masters of requests. Noted in Bindoff, *House of commons*, II, 553-5.

Richard Lyell[159]   Robert Brooke[160]/(Thomas Gaudy)[161]
Ralph Skinner[162]/Richard Rede[163] **Richard Goodrich**[164]

A sociological analysis of the final list reveals the following (membership of the drafting committee being indicated in brackets):

	Number		*Percentage*	
Lords spiritual (bishops)	8	(2)	25	(25)
Lords temporal	0	(0)	0	(0)
Lower clergy	6	(3)	18.75	(37.5)
Foreign divines	2	(1)	6.25	(12.5)
Members of parliament	12	(2)	37.5	(25)
Other laymen[165]	4	(0)	18.75	(0)
Total	32	(8)	100	(100)

[159](d. *c.*1563). He may have been a member of parliament under Edward VI, but is not recorded as such in Bindoff, *House of commons*. He was admitted to doctors' commons on 7 March 1538 (Squibb, *Doctors' commons*, p. 147), and his name does not appear on King Edward VI's list. Noted in Emden, *Biographical register 1501-40*, p. 368.

[160](*c.*1507-58). Also spelled Broke. Recorder of London (1545-52) and then a serjeant. He was also a member of parliament for London from 1545 and the speaker of the house of commons (1554). Noted in Simpson, *Biographical dictionary*, pp. 78-9 and in Bindoff, *House of commons*, I, 504-6.

[161](*c.*1509-56). Also spelled Gawdy. On King Edward VI's list instead of Brooke, whose name was restored on the patent roll. He was a member of parliament for Salisbury (1545), Lynn (1547-52) and Norwich (October 1553). Noted in Bindoff, *House of commons*, II, 199-201.

[162](*c.*1513-63). A correspondent of Heinrich Bullinger, Zwingli's successor at Zürich. His name appeared on King Edward VI's list of 10 February 1552, but was not on the final patent roll. He was a member of parliament for Leicester (1547-52), Penryn (Oct. 1553-4), Bossiney (1555) and Westbury (1559). In January 1560 he was ordained and made dean of Durham later in the year. He was also commissioner for ecclesiastical causes in the province of York from 1561 until his death. Noted in Emden, *Biographical register 1501-40*, p. 518 and in Bindoff, *House of commons*, III, 324-5.

[163](1511-79). He participated in the dissolution of the monasteries and later helped to remove the conservative bishops in Edward VI's reign, when he may also have been a master of requests. He was admitted to doctors' commons on 21 July 1540 (Squibb, *Doctors' commons*, p. 148) and replaced Skinner on the patent roll list, 12 February 1552. Noted in Emden, *Biographical register 1501-40*, IV, 481.

[164](*c.*1508-62). Nephew of Thomas Goodrich, he was the member of parliament for Grimsby from 1545-52. Noted in Venn, *Alumni Cantabrigienses*, II, 237 and in Bindoff, *House of commons*, II, 231-3.

[165]These include one former member of parliament (Sir Thomas Bromley) and Richard Lyell, who may have been an M. P. at this time.

The distribution which this table reveals is interesting from several points of view. On the clergy side, the number of sixteen has been respected in the right proportions, though only the episcopal list can really be regarded as straightforward.[166] The eight members of the lower clergy contain two foreign divines, and the distribution is uneven, since two other clergymen are classed with the civil lawyers. This was confusing even at the time, as we can see from King Edward VI's list, where Rowland Taylor is placed among the divines by mistake. The reason for this shift however is apparent, since it is the clerical members of the civil law list who served on the drafting committee, giving the clergy an overall majority of six to two![167]

The lay representation shows a disproportionately high number of members of parliament (fifty percent more than they would have had in 1534) but this is deceptive, as they were proportionately represented on the drafting committee, where they both appear among the common lawyers. That too conceals more than it reveals, because Richard Goodrich was the bishop of Ely's nephew, and therefore hardly an independent lay voice, and John Lucas was actually a civilian who appears to have changed places with Sir William Cecil, a common lawyer who for some reason has been placed on the civil law list![168] It is hard not to avoid the conclusion that what we are witnessing here is a sleight of hand by which a drafting committee totally subservient to clerical interests was created, whilst preserving the appearance of equal representation from clergy and laity alike.

Even more striking however, is the complete absence of lay peers from the list. There is no doubt that those who were appointed to serve on the commission were all qualified to do so, and that it would have been difficult to find eight lords temporal of similar calibre. But although a meritocratic approach may have exercised some influence on the appointments, it is hard to believe that the complete exclusion of the lay peers was due to that cause alone. A much more probable reason is the fact that the aristocracy were generally more conservative in their religious views, and it would have been very difficult to find enough noble candidates who would sympathize with the aims of the canon law commission. By contrast, the over-represented commoners were almost all convinced protestants, and many of them were to show their mettle during the Marian persecution. Putting all the evidence together, the conclusion must surely

[166]The only point of interest is the omission of Thomas Thirlby, then bishop of Norwich, who might have been included given his earlier experience of canon law reform (see above). But perhaps he was no longer interested in the matter, or unsympathetic to the kind of reforms being proposed in 1551-2.

[167]It should be said that there is an earlier list of eight, dated 4 November 1551, which has the names of Nicholas Ridley (instead of Thomas Goodrich), Bartholomew Traheron (instead of William May) and John Gosnold (instead of Richard Goodrich). For the two lists, see *Calendar of the patent rolls, Edward VI*, IV, 114.

[168]Lucas was a close associate of Edward Carne, who like him was a master in the court of requests at this time. Why Carne was not asked to join the commission, given his earlier experience, is unknown, but perhaps he was unsympathetic to so wide-ranging a reform.

be that the *Reformatio* was intended to be a document drawn up by reforming clerics, which would then receive the approval of protestant-leaning (but eminently qualified) laymen. The hope must have been that this would create a consensus among the learned so impressive that the lay lords would not dare to oppose it.

Things did not work out that way, of course, and the failure of the final text to gain lay support in the March 1553 session of the house of lords was to show just how politically unwise the omission of the lords temporal was. Yet it is hard to believe that the privy council, which was largely responsible for the commission's composition, would have approved either the full commission or the drafting committee which it did, if it thought that there was no chance that the lay lords would be persuaded to go along with the final result. At the very least, it seems that the two swords of government were working harmoniously together in the autumn of 1551 in a way which would not be true only eighteen months later, when their divergent interests and understanding of what the relationship between church and state in a reformed polity should be had become only too apparent. From hindsight that clash appears to have been inevitable (or at least highly understandable) but it was not so clear to those responsible for shaping policy in the autumn of 1551, and there is no reason to think that the lay peers who knew about it (including the all-important John Dudley, then still only earl of Warwick but soon to become the duke of Northumberland) disagreed with the strategy adopted.

The drafting committee began its work on 12 December 1551[169] and was in full swing by early March 1552.[170] But not everyone was pleased by this progress, and there is some evidence that Nicholas Ridley and Thomas Goodrich were doing their best to hinder its work because they feared what the consequences of too radical a reform would be.[171] Anxiety over the approaching deadline soon set in and became sufficiently serious that a bill for a new commission was read twice in the house of lords and engrossed on 1 April 1552.[172] It got no further, but on 14 April the house of commons voted to extend

---

[169]The date is given in a letter from a German student at Oxford, known as John ab Ulmis, to Heinrich Bullinger (1504-75), dated 10 January 1552. See *Original letters relative to the English reformation, written during the reigns of King Henry VIII, King Edward VI, and Queen Mary, chiefly from the archives of Zürich*, ed. H. Robinson (2 vols., Cambridge, 1846-7), II, 444.

[170]As indicated in a letter from Peter Martyr Vermigli to Bullinger, 8 March 1552. See *ibid.*, p. 503. There is also a letter from Ralph Skinner to Bullinger, dated 5 January, but no year is given. Robinson thought it was 1550, but 1552 seems much more likely. See *ibid.*, I, 313-14.

[171]At least this is what Martin Micronius (1523-59), Dutch chaplain in London from 1549-53, claimed in a letter to Bullinger, 9 March 1552. See *ibid.*, p. 504.

[172]*L.J.*, I, 419. There were thirteen bishops present: Canterbury, York, London, Winchester, Bath and Wells, St Asaph, Carlisle, Chichester, Norwich, Bristol, St David's, Gloucester and Exeter. Six of them (Canterbury, London, Winchester, Bath and Wells, Exeter and Gloucester) were on the existing commission.

the three-year time limit for completing the work, and sent the bill to the lords. There it was read twice but failed to pass, as parliament was adjourned the following day and there was no time to get it through.[173]

The need to respect the 1 February 1553 deadline seems to have concentrated minds wonderfully, especially when we consider that many of the same people were concurrently engaged on a new prayer book and on what were to become the forty-two articles of religion. In a letter to Heinrich Bullinger dated 5 October 1552, Richard Cox mentioned that the revised prayer book had been approved[174] and the articles of religion were calendared among the state papers on 20 October.[175] The same letter makes a veiled allusion to difficulties being encountered in the production of the *Reformatio*, and two letters dated the previous day also mention it.[176] Then on Saturday 8 October the privy council asked Cranmer to delay his departure from London until the following Tuesday, because they wanted to discuss 'certain matters' with him.[177] Among those matters may have been canon law reform, which according to a note penned by King Edward VI (on 13 October) figured on the council's agenda at that time. But if Cranmer was present for the discussion, it must have occurred on 11 October, since he retired to Canterbury the following day.[178] It seems quite possible, even probable, that this meeting provided the occasion for which the manuscript which we now identify as MS Harleian 426 was compiled. It is clearly in an unpolished state, which may be explained by the need for haste at

[173]*C.J.*, I, 23; *L.J.*, I, 428.
[174]It was authorized in the act of uniformity passed on 15 April 1552 (5-6 Edward VI, c. 1 - *S.R.*, IV, 130-1) and came into use on 1 November 1552. The letter is in *Original letters*, ed. Robinson, I, 123-4.
[175]*Calendar of state papers, domestic series, of the reign of Edward VI*, ed. C. S. Knighton (London, 1992), p. 268, no. 739 (SP 10/15, no. 28). They had been in preparation for about a year, and a rough draft was circulated to the bishops on 2 May 1552. After further changes, Archbishop Cranmer sent the final text to Sir William Cecil and Sir John Cheke on 19 September 1552 and about a fortnight later (on their recommendation) to the king. The articles then went to a committee of six divines (John Harley, William Bill, Robert Horne, Andrew Perne, Edmund Grindal and John Knox) which approved them and sent them back on 20 October. At that time there were forty-five articles, but it seems that when they were returned to Archbishop Cranmer for revision (on 20 November), he combined articles 29-32 into a single article on the Lord's supper, whilst leaving the text itself unchanged. The resulting forty-two articles were not approved by convocation, though they were mandated by the king on 19 June 1553 (W, IV, 79). See *D.E.R.*, pp. 284-311 for the complete text and its relationship to the thirty-nine articles of 1563 (1571).
[176]One is from Cranmer to Calvin, printed in *Corpus Reformatorum* XLII (*Calvini opera* XIV), col. 370. The other is from Peter Martyr Vermigli to Heinrich Bullinger, printed in *Gleanings of a few scattered ears, during the period of the reformation in England*, ed. G. C. Gorham (London, 1857), p. 286.
[177]*Acts of the privy council*, IV, 138.
[178]Nichols, *Literary remains*, p. 547. According to the privy council records, Cranmer did not attend any of its meetings from 12 October 1552 until 21 February 1553.

this juncture. It may be that Archbishop Cranmer put together the titles which he already had, re-ordering them along the way, in anticipation of his discussion with the privy council. Drafting was still going on and at the last minute four extra titles were included, though this happened too late for them to be edited or even added to the table of contents. It may even be that the one or two changes which are in an unidentified hand were made at this meeting by someone who was particularly sensitive to the claims of the royal supremacy.[179] In any event, it seems that the privy council must have encouraged the work to go forward towards completion in time to meet the deadline, since that is what actually happened.

MS Harleian 426 (British Library)

MS Harleian 426 may thus reasonably be dated to mid-October 1552, and it is the only direct evidence we have of the drafting committee's work. As it now stands, it contains all but eight of the fifty-five titles which make up the final text. Fortunately for us, it was the working copy used by Archbishop Cranmer, with the result that we can trace the changes which he and others made at different stages of the editorial process. Three, or perhaps four of these stages are still clearly discernible, and may be categorized as follows:

A. This is the state of the different portions of the MS as they were submitted to Cranmer by the scribes who wrote up the deliberations of the committee. There must have been earlier drafts of the text, but they are no longer extant, and A represents the earliest version which we can now recover. It must of course be remembered that A is not a single, coherent document, but represents the work of three scribes who submitted their material to Cranmer in apparently piecemeal fashion.

B[1]. This was Cranmer's first attempt at ordering the material. It can be detected by the folio page numbers and running heads which he introduced, as well as by the table of contents which he drew up and placed at the beginning of the MS.

B[2]. This is the MS as it was after Cranmer reordered it and corresponds to fos. 1-269 as we now have them.[180]

B[3]. This is an extension of B[2], rather than as a separate stage of the redactional process. It comprises B[2] plus additional titles which were added after Cranmer had completed his table of contents. There are four of these (now R, 15-17, 27) and they make up fos. 270-88.

[179]This is particularly true of the changes in R, 20.23. The one in R, 21.1 (in the same unknown hand) is just a simple clarification of the meaning.
[180]Unless otherwise indicated, the folio page numbers are those devised by Cranmer, not the ones introduced by a curator of the British Museum in December 1875. The two systems are correlated on p. 733.

The initial scribal drafts (A)

A is not a single document, but a collection of independent compositions written in at least three different hands. Two of these (referred to here as hands I and II) produced the theological and doctrinal titles, whilst the third (hand III) was responsible for the ones on ecclesiastical court procedure.

It seems fairly clear that the drafting committee was subdivided into two separate groups, *viz.* the bishops and divines on the one hand, and the lawyers on the other. Whether there were further subdivisions is very difficult to say and depends entirely on how we interpret the editorial corrections. For example, the fact that R, 2-3 (originally joined as one) was extensively edited by Archbishop Cranmer makes it somewhat unlikely that he was one of its original composers, but we cannot be certain about this. It is equally possible that he had second thoughts about it after putting the collection together, and that he made his (largely editorial) changes at that stage. Some of the doctrinal issues raised in the title, like the anti-Lutheran statements on the eucharist and the attacks on the anabaptists, seem to reflect the views of Peter Martyr Vermigli, but we cannot say that they are so distinctively his that they cannot be attributed to the other members of the committee (who obviously approved them). In addition, the title contains one or two emendations by Vermigli which may reflect second thoughts on his part also.

What is certain is that fos. 1-69 are in a single scribal hand (I) and that at some point they constituted a distinct document, since they all have running heads put there by Cranmer himself, a feature which is not found elsewhere in the MS. Analysis of the handwriting and general presentation of the material suggests that the thirteen titles concerned can be subdivided into four separate batches, though we have no way of knowing when or how each of these was put together. The result looks like this, with the numbers in brackets indicating where they are now to be found:

Batch 1:	1. The Trinity and the catholic faith	(1)
	2. Heresies and judgments against heresies	(2; 3)
	3. Blasphemy	(4)
Batch 2:	4. Oaths and perjury	(39)
	5. Forgery	(44)
	6. Preachers	(7)
Batch 3:	7. Matrimony	(8)
	8. Prohibited degrees	(9)
	9. Adultery and divorce	(10)
Batch 4:	10. Violence against clerics	(48)
	11. Admission to ecclesiastical benefices	(11)
	12. Defamation	(50)
	13. Conferring benefices without loss	(18)

The remaining six titles written in hand I cannot be so easily tied together, and there is no indication in the MS that they were ever part of a single document. Perhaps the first four originally formed a sequence, but if so, two other titles have now been interpolated to divide the sequence in half, and the last two titles look as if they have been inserted among the ones dealing with ecclesiastical court procedure. A note in Archbishop Cranmer's hand indicates that the title on tithes was reviewed by Dr Walter Haddon,[181] who also edited R, 21-2, but whether there was any other connexion between them is doubtful. The overall picture is as follows:

14.	Form for reconciling excommunicates	(33)
15.	Church and its ministers	(20)
16.	Schools in cathedral churches	(23)
17.	Universities	(24)
18.	Tithes	(25.1-18)
19.	Pensions and visitations	(25.19; 26)

To these must be added the three titles which are in hand II. They occupy fos. 70-81, and thus come immediately after the first thirteen titles in hand I and before the form for reconciling excommunicates. They are:

1.	Celebration of the divine offices	(19)
2.	Sacraments	(5)
3.	Idolatry, etc.	(6)

These titles survived intact and in order in the MS, but the first of them was detached from the others in the final version of the text, when the other two were placed immediately after the title on blasphemy. The only curious feature about them is that the title on sacraments contains a running head in the scribe's own hand, though the other two do not. Perhaps this is an indication that the others were written first, but that the scribe then discovered what Cranmer wanted and placed his own running heads on the third title. Why the other two were not subsequently emended is impossible to say; perhaps both the scribe and Cranmer

---

[181](c.1516-71). Educated at Eton and King's College, Cambridge, he was noted for his elegant Latin, and was employed by Archbishop Cranmer to improve the style of the *Reformatio*. He was admitted as a doctor of civil law at Cambridge in 1549 and was appointed master of Trinity Hall in February 1552. On 10 October 1552 the crown made him president of Magdalen College, Oxford, though this was in flagrant violation of the college's statutes, and he retired (before being ejected) on Mary I's accession. He made his peace with the Marian regime and was admitted to doctors' commons on 5 May 1555 (Squibb, *Doctors' commons*, p. 152), but his protestant sympathies were sufficiently clear that he was able to play a major *rôle* in establishing the Elizabethan settlement in 1559. He was a member of parliament for Reigate (1555), Thetford (1558), Poole (1559) and Warwick (1563). Noted in Venn, *Alumni Cantabrigienses*, II, 280 and in Bindoff, *House of commons*, II, 272-3.

felt that there was no room for running heads in the other titles, or that they would spoil the appearance of them! In any case, it is safe to say that they came from the same general source as the titles in hand I, *viz.* the subcommittee of bishops and divines.

As far as the titles dealing with ecclesiastical court procedure are concerned, it is clear from the editing that Cranmer and Vermigli worked on them, probably in succession to one another. We know this because in R, 52 the first four canons have been sectioned off and headed by Cranmer whilst the remainder were done by Vermigli. The most natural explanation for this is that Cranmer began the work and then turned it over to Vermigli for completion. If that was the case, we have to ask ourselves whether the current MS order of these titles is the original one, since the titles edited by Vermigli do not form a block which follows naturally on those edited by Cranmer. The nature of the problem can best be observed by looking at the titles composed by hand III in tabular form, with the breaks indicating possible 'batches' of material, submitted at different times. The name on the right indicates the editor of the particular 'batch' in question.

1.	Churchwardens	(21)	Haddon
2.	Parish boundaries	(22)	
3.	Witnesses	(45)	Cranmer
4.	Presumptions	(49)	Cranmer
5.	Trials	(41)	
6.	Possession	(42)	
7.	Custom	(46)	Vermigli
8.	Joinder of issue	(38)	Cranmer
9.	Oath of calumny	(40)	
10.	Delays	(51)	
11.	Judgments	(34-6)	
12.	Credibility of documents	(43)	
13.	Exceptions	(52)	Vermigli[182]
14.	Prescriptions	(47)	
15.	Appeals	(54)	
16.	Office and jurisdiction of all judges	(37)	Cranmer

---

[182]Cranmer began to edit this title and turned it over to Vermigli.

| 17. | Sentence and matter judged | (53) | Vermigli |
| 18. | Rules of law | (55) | Cranmer |

Title 3 (R, 45) on witnesses stands alone because each of its canons has a heading of its own, put there by the scribe, and there are only one or two minor alterations in Cranmer's hand. Title 4 (R, 49) may have been connected with the next two (as indicated here) or may have been handed in separately; in any case, it is divided from the others in the MS by the titles on tithes and visitations (in hand I) which have been interpolated between them. What we cannot now decide is whether Cranmer edited a group of titles in a different order and turned the whole lot over to Vermigli for completion, or whether he edited them as they came in and gave the ones which he did not have time to deal with himself.

The fact that these titles later underwent a substantial reordering suggests that the second of these possibilities is the more probable one, although lack of further evidence makes it impossible to be dogmatic on this point. Nevertheless, the fact that what are now titles R, 2 and R, 3 were divided and edited by Cranmer before he put them in the present collection[183] suggests that much, if not most, of the editing took place before the MS order of the titles was decided.

The re-ordering of the MS (B)

The second stage, which has three discernible subdivisions, is the re-ordering of the scribal drafts which took place as they were put together to form the MS which we now have. We do not know whether Cranmer started re-ordering the material as soon as he received it or not, but we can tell from the MS that he put together fos. 1-69 and then edited them, dividing the second title (on heresies) into two as he did so. After fo. 69, the interleaving of material in hand I with titles in hands II and III suggests that some rearrangement took place, though it may also be the order in which Cranmer received the drafts. The fact that the running heads which he put on fos. 1-69 do not continue beyond that point suggests that they all came in later - including the titles written in hand I. What we know for certain is that in the process of drawing up a table of contents, Cranmer moved three of the titles to new positions, though he did not renumber the folios to take account of this. As a result, it appears as if a number of folios are missing when in fact they have merely been relocated within the MS and renumbered accordingly. For our present purposes, the original table of contents has been designated B^1 and the revised version B^2, but apart from this reordering there is no difference between them.

Most (if not all) of the editorial corrections appear to have been made at the B^1 stage. It seems that Cranmer got the material from the scribes (A) and edited

---

[183]We know this because they were reckoned separately in Cranmer's table of contents; see below, p. 736.

it without any substantial re-ordering of the titles. When he began that task is unknown, though it is clear that the B^2 stage was simultaneous with the composition of the table of contents. If our supposition about the MS is correct, the titles which are not part of Cranmer's table were added in haste, in order to get all the then existing material ready for the privy council meeting on 11 October 1552. This process may be regarded either as an extension of B^2 or as a distinct B^3, since it appears that the extra titles were not added by Cranmer himself.

As distinct from B^2, B^3 consists of four titles, three of which are written in scribal hand III and one in a different hand (hand IV), which appears to be that of a private individual.[184] None of these titles has been edited, and it is possible that Archbishop Cranmer did not even read them before they were included in the MS as we now have it. The titles in question can be set out as follows, with those in hand III given first:

1.	Dilapidation	(15)
2.	Alienation of church property	(16)
3.	Election(s)	(17)
4.	Testaments	(27)

The final text

MS Harleian 426 makes a fairly detailed reconstruction of the composition of the *Reformatio* possible up to mid-October 1552, but there the story comes to an abrupt end. The next textual evidence we have does not appear until the first printed edition (F) which was published by John Foxe shortly before 6 April 1571. Foxe was using a different and substantially revised manuscript as his main source (though he also used MS Harleian 426) which at that time was in the possession of Archbishop Parker. In his 1850 edition, Edward Cardwell suggested that Parker had taken the 1552 text (either MS Harleian 426 or a fair copy made from it) and revised it early in Elizabeth's reign, rather in the way that both the prayer book and the articles of religion were revised at the same time. We must therefore try to reconstruct the intermediate stages between MS Harleian 426 and F, and work out, if we can, which text Foxe based his edition on. To do this properly, we must first consider what the main differences between F and B^{2-3} are. These can be set out as follows:

1. F has eight more titles than B^{2-3} and the ones they have in common are in a substantially different order. Furthermore, the eight additional

---

[184]It does not respect the normal scribal conventions regarding margins, paragraphs, etc. and has a generally unpolished look.

ones are split into two blocks which are interpolated into the text (R, 12-14; 28-32); they are not added to the end in the way that B^3 is added to B^2, for example.

2. At least ninety-nine percent of the shared text is identical, but compared with B^{2-3}, F has some additions, alterations and especially deletions in addition to those accounted for by the editorial corrections made by Archbishop Cranmer, Dr Walter Haddon and Peter Martyr Vermigli.

Archbishop Matthew Parker had been one of the thirty-two commissioners appointed in 1551 and however he came into possession of the manuscript he gave to Foxe, he would certainly have known where it came from and what it represented. Is there any evidence that he himself had made the revisions which differentiate his manuscript from MS Harleian 426, or did he merely give Foxe the fair copy (which we shall call C) which Cranmer offered to the house of lords, already revised, in March 1553? Parker's MS is no longer extant, but we know something about it from two independent sources. The first of these consists of a series of notes and jottings which Foxe made on the pages of MS Harleian 426 (presumably sometime in 1570-1, when he was preparing his printed edition). The second is a fragment of an English translation of the text, covering R, 44.3-45.19, which is preserved among the Petyt manuscripts in the library of the Inner Temple, London.[185]

Foxe's jottings were evidently designed to help the reader of MS Harleian 426 compare that text with Parker's MS, which Foxe knew was the superior copy, though he may not have understood that MS Harleian 426 was no more than a preparatory draft.[186] At the very beginning of the MS, immediately after Cranmer's table of contents, Foxe penned the corresponding list in Parker's MS, from which we learn that it was the same as that found in his printed edition. A further note of his at the end of Cranmer's list gives the eight missing titles and indicates on what folio page in Parker's MS they could be found.[187] There is also a partial list on fo. 23r which tells us that the Parker MS placed the title on preachers between the one on idolatry and the one on matrimony, though whoever wrote that list initially made the mistake of thinking that the title on preachers was not in MS Harleian 426 at all, and had to correct his error later on.[188]

Most of the differences between F and B^{2-3} are clearly errors made by the typesetter, or by an editor who misread the original MS, and can therefore be

---

[185]MS Petyt 538/38, fos. 231r-46r.

[186]For example, Foxe wrote the text of R, 25.18 into MS Harleian 426, apparently on the ground that it had been 'omitted' by mistake. In fact, it appeared as R, 46.5, and had been marked by Peter Martyr Vermigli for transfer to R, 25.

[187]See below, pp. 736-9.

[188]See below, pp. 740-1.

discounted. Deliberate changes occur in only a few canons, and almost all of them are just odd words here and there. They may be set out in tabular form as follows. In F, odd words have been:

Added	Altered	Deleted
1.9		
	2.7	
	2.17	
2.19		
	2.20	
	2.22	
		8.11
		9.2
		9.5
		15.2
	20.1	
	20.2	
27.11	27.11	
		27.13
27.22	27.22	
33.1	33.1	33.1
	36.3	
38.14		
		51.1
54.40		

In addition to these, there are more substantial deletions in R, 2.7 and 53.5, as well as the curious case of R, 7.(5-7) where three canons which Cranmer marked for transfer elsewhere in MS Harleian 426 appear to have been deleted by accident. There are also cases where material marked in that MS for eventual inclusion (cf. R, 3.4, 10) or deletion (cf. R, 3.2) in C was not taken into account in the printed edition. The most reasonable explanation for this is that this material never found its way into C in the first place, since Parker would hardly have omitted it (and changed nothing else) in a revision of his own. Why Cranmer's proposed alterations never got into C is unknown. The copyist would hardly have chosen to ignore them, and it is unlikely that he had already completed his work before these particular alterations were made. The most plausible explanation is that the drafting committee which met to consider Cranmer's suggestions decided to reject them and that they were not included in the final version. That must have been the case with R, 7.(5-7), and there is no reason to doubt that the same was true of the other missing alterations as well. The remaining differences between MS Harleian 426 and F are few, and even if one or two of them are significant, they do not amount to a revision of the text as a whole. They might easily have been made by Cranmer or another member of the drafting committee shortly after 11 October 1552, been approved by that

committee and included in C when it was copied. In one place (R, 53.6), it appears that C had an error which Foxe or his typesetters decided to retain because it was in the MS, but which they corrected in a marginal note.[189] But there are no other examples of variant readings in F, and if Parker or one of his associates made any changes to C before giving it to Foxe, they can only have been very minor ones. It must therefore be concluded that Parker's MS, on which F was based, was C itself, with few if any subsequent alterations.[190]

The other evidence for C comes from MS Petyt 538/38. This is a translation which is clearly based on the order of both C and F, and it is difficult to say which of those two it was translated from. What swings the evidence in favour of C as the source rather than F is a curious error which the translator made in R, 45.50. Again, setting this out in tabular form is the easiest way to appreciate what happened:

MS Harleian 426 has:	*ne tueantur*
F has:	*ne teneantur*
The translator read:	*ne timeant(ur)*

F conveys basically the same meaning as the MS, and may be regarded as a typesetter's mistake. But the translator has produced a different (and much less probable) reading altogether. He did not misread MS Harleian 426, which he was not using, and he would hardly have made such a mistake on the basis of F. The conclusion must therefore be that he was using another manuscript in which the word 'tueantur' may have been poorly copied. That would account both for his mistake and for Foxe's attempt to make sense of the text. The conclusion must therefore be that, like Foxe, the translator was using C, to which he may have had access once Foxe was finished with it.[191] What happened to C after that is

---

[189]F has 'exegentiam' instead of the correct 'exegeticam', but a marginal note reads 'alias exegeticam', showing that Foxe and/or his printers were aware of the correct reading.

[190]This conclusion agrees with L. Sachs, 'Thomas Cranmer's *Reformatio legum ecclesiasticarum* of 1553 in the context of English church law from the later middle ages to the canons of 1603', unpublished J. C. D. dissertation, Catholic University of America (Washington, D. C.), 1982, pp. 79-82. Sachs refutes Edward Cardwell's contention (*Reformation*, p. x) that Archbishop Parker was responsible for a substantial revision of C.

[191]We do not know when the translator began his work, but it seems clear that he broke off at R, 51.19, because his text ends in the middle of the page and has a final flourish underneath, indicating the end. Perhaps he broke off there because by then it was clear that the *Reformatio* would not become law and that a translation would not be needed. Edward Cardwell (*Reformation*, p. xii) drew attention to some evidence in a tract written by the separatist John Penry (1563-93), *A treatise wherein is manifestlie proved, that reformation and those that favor the same, are unjustly charged to be enemies, unto hir majestie* (Edinburgh, 1590). In a note to the reader between the preface and the main text, Penry wrote: 'Mr Dr Haddon delivered in parliament a Latin book concerning church discipline, written in the days of King Edward VI by Mr Cranmer and Sir John Cheke, knight, etc. this book was committed by the house to be translated unto the said Mr

unknown, but probably it was stored at St Paul's cathedral in London, together with the records of the convocation of Canterbury. If that was the case, it was burnt along with them in the great fire of 2-6 September 1666.[192]

MS Harleian 426 seems to have remained in Foxe's possession after 1571 and eventually it became the property of John Strype (1643-1737), though how this happened is unclear. The most widely accepted theory is that the manuscript remained in the Foxe family until it was given to Strype by Sir Richard Willis (1614-90), who was one of Foxe's descendants. Another story is that it passed into the hands of Sir Michael Hicks (1543-1612), who was Lord Burghley's secretary for many years, and remained in that family for about a century, until Sir William Hicks (1629-1703), Michael's great-grandson, gave it to Richard Chiswell the elder (1639-1711), apparently on the understanding that it would be edited and published by Strype, who was then in Chiswell's employ. But in 1699 Hicks was declared to be insane, and both Chiswell and his son, Richard Chiswell the younger (1673-1751), claimed that Hicks had sold it to them. In the ensuing confusion, Strype would simply have hung on to the MS. Either way, there is no doubt that Strype sold it to Robert Harley (1661-1724) in 1711, the year in which Harley was elevated to the peerage as the earl of Oxford. It then passed to his son Edward Harley (1689-1741), the second earl, and remained in his widow's possession until 1753, when she sold the entire Harley collection to the state for £10,000. It was deposited in the newly-founded British Museum, and remained in its possession until the creation of the British Library (1 July 1973).[193] It has never been published as a separate document, but oddly enough, a translation of it appeared in 1992 (see below).

F remained the only printed text of the *Reformatio* until 1640, when an anonymous person or group decided that it should be reprinted. A number of obvious typographical errors were corrected, but it is clear that whoever did this had not consulted either manuscript source. Some of the corrections are right, a few are wrong, and a number of F's mistakes are not corrected at all, because

Haddon, Mr George [*sic*] Bromley, Mr Norton, etc. if thou canst good reader help me, or any other that labour in the cause unto the said book, I hope (though I never saw it), that in so doing thou shalt do good service unto the Lord and his church.' Much of Penry's history is clearly wrong - Haddon was dead, for example - but although we have no independent confirmation that the house of commons ordered an English translation to be made, the text that Penry was trying to find does in fact exist, so his account, however wrong in its details, may nevertheless contain a kernel of truth.

[192]If the fragmentary English translation was salvaged from the ruins of St Paul's by William Petyt (which is quite possible), this theory would be strengthened. C may also have been stored at St Mary-le-Bow, with the records of the court of the arches, though that is less likely. They too were burnt in 1666. It was not used in the preparation of the second printed edition (S) in 1640, which endeavoured to correct the errors of F. Perhaps it had already disappeared by that stage, but more probably the editors of S either did not know of its existence or did not think of consulting it.

[193]Along with British Library Additional MS 48040 (the Henrician canons) it stayed in the British Museum until the autumn of 1998, when it was moved to the new library building at St Pancras.

they make sense as they stand.[194] This edition was then reprinted, with a few further corrections, in the following year.[195] In the eighteenth century, Bishop Edmund Gibson seems to have used the 1571 edition, but in the early nineteenth century, the majority of citations were taken from one of the two later printings. All three texts were effectively superseded in 1850, when Edward Cardwell (1787-1861)[196] published his edition which inaugurated the modern critical study of the text. Cardwell's text was republished in a facsimile edition as recently as 1968, and is only now being replaced by a truly critical edition and translation.[197]

The sources of the *Reformatio*

It is immediately obvious to anyone who compares the *Reformatio* with the Henrician canons of 1535 that they are very different kinds of document. Whereas the Henrician canons are little more than a compilation of existing sources, occasionally reworded, contracted or even slightly expanded, the *Reformatio* is an independent work in its own right. Only very occasionally can it be shown to have quoted directly from an earlier source,[198] and in many cases what we are really looking for are *precedents,* rather than sources in the strict sense of the term. But although this is true, it would be a great mistake to go to the opposite extreme and claim that the *Reformatio* was a serious attempt to suppress medieval canon law and replace it with something which reflects the protestant reformation, the ideas of certain reformed theologians, or a humanist desire to recover the 'purity' of ancient Roman law. Once we understand that the drafting committee of 1551-2 was at least as concerned with producing a text in what to them was an elegant Latin style as it was in changing the law, we shall see that behind the rhetorical flourishes and reclassicized grammar there is a very substantial continuity with the medieval tradition. This is particularly true in the titles which deal with purely legal matters,[199] where the medieval inheritance accounts for at least ninety-five percent of the material, and virtually all of the remainder can be ascribed to the work of fifteenth and sixteenth century canonists working in that tradition. Protestantism is largely confined to the doctrinal titles,[200] though reformed ideas can also be found in the titles which

---

[194]*Reformatio legum ecclesiasticarum*, printed by Thomas Harper and Richard Hodgkinson (London, 1640).
[195]*Ibid.*, printed by the Stationers' Company (London, 1641). The corrections are mainly to the punctuation, though in a few cases indicative verbs have been put into the subjunctive, *e.g.* 'creavit' may become 'creaverit', etc.
[196]Principal of St Alban's Hall, Oxford, 1831-61, a personal friend of W. E. Gladstone and uncle of Edward, Viscount Cardwell (1813-86).
[197]Cardwell's edition and modern studies are treated in a separate section below.
[198]R, 46.1, for example, comes from D, 1 c. 5 (Fr, I, 2).
[199]R, 11-18, 25-32, 34-55.
[200]R, 1-7.

deal with worship and church order.[201] The titles dealing with matrimony and divorce are something of a grey area, in that they touch on both doctrine and ecclesiastical law, which may explain why most of the disputes about legal 'innovations' in the *Reformatio* have focussed on them.[202]

The first and most obvious place to look for sources is in the Henrician canons of 1535, which the *Reformatio* was originally intended to take over and complete. There are a large number of thematic correspondences between the two documents, though it is difficult to be sure how much use the drafting committee made of the earlier text, since it also had access to the original sources and may have got its material directly from them instead. Nevertheless, there are certain titles where the correspondence is so great, not merely in the content but (more importantly) in the order in which it is reproduced, that direct dependence on the Henrician canons is virtually certain. Furthermore, these titles are all among those which do not appear in MS Harleian 426. Consider the following (canons which are not in the same order in both documents are asterisked):

Subject	R	HC
Resignation	12.2	16.1-2
	12.4	16.3
	12.5	16.6
Exchange of benefices	13.1	21.1
	13.4	21.3
Purgation	14.1	12.1
	14.6	12.8*
	14.8	12.2
	14.9	12.3
	14.10	12.4
	14.13	12.6
	14.14	12.5*
Penalties	28.1	13.1
	28.2	13.2
	28.3	13.3
	28.4	13.5
	28.5	13.6
	28.6	13.9
	28.7	13.11

[201]R, 19-24, 33.
[202]R, 8-10.

	28.8	13.17
	28.9	13.15*
Sequestration	30.1	33.1, 3*
	30.2	33.2
	30.3	33.4
	30.4	33.6
Excommunication	32.4-5	14.12*
	32.10	14.2*
	32.11	14.1
	32.12	14.7
	32.13	14.20

It is true that two of the later titles are missing from this list,[203] but as neither of them is treated separately in the Henrician canons (or anywhere else, for that matter) not much can be made of this. On the other hand, there is nothing in the titles which are in MS Harleian 426 to indicate any similarly high level of borrowing, and if the Henrician canons were used in composing them, it was with considerably greater circumspection.[204] It is difficult to avoid the conclusion that in the final stages of putting C together, the drafting committee speeded up the process by taking over as many of the Henrician canons as they could, adding further items as they occurred. This is less true of the title on excommunication, but as that was a particularly contentious issue at the time, we should probably expect to find a more thorough reworking of it. We may therefore conclude that the Henrician canons came to the rescue of the drafting committee when it was running out of time, but until that point was reached, relatively little use was made of them.

When we look back behind the Henrician canons to the medieval tradition of canon law, we discover that the compilers of the *Reformatio* were familiar with it and made extensive use of the *Corpus iuris canonici*, though once again without adopting the order of the *Decretals*.[205] There is a good deal of rewriting of the original material, but relatively little in the way of addition. Omissions (and deletions) are more frequent, but although the abolition of papal supremacy over the Church of England was certainly a factor in this, obsolescence and general inapplicability also played an important *rôle*. Cases where the old canon law was deliberately altered because of a changed theological perspective

---

[203]R, 29 on suspension and R, 31 on deprivation.
[204]In R, 27 (testaments) and in R, 54 (appeals) there is a good deal of material which is also found in H.C., 31 and in H.C., 36 respectively, but the order is quite different and direct borrowing is unlikely.
[205]See below, pp. 742-7 for the details.

resulting from the reformation are extremely rare, and even in the doctrinal titles there are often canonical precedents for what appear at first sight to be 'protestant' ideas.[206]

The 'protestantism' of the *Reformatio* is most evident in matters of controversy which were living issues in 1552, rather than in historical disputes involving the *Corpus iuris canonici*. Thus, for example, the definition of which biblical books are canonical Scripture was formulated with respect to the then recent decision of the council of Trent, since the subject was not mentioned in the old canon law at all.[207] There are even cases, such as the determination of the number of ecumenical (general) church councils, where the conservative drafters of the *Reformatio* appealed to the canonical tradition for support *against* what was then coming to be accepted at Rome.[208]

There can be no doubt that the drafting committee regarded the *Corpus iuris canonici* as their legal inheritance, just as much as it was of any other church in western Christendom, and that they felt free to use it as such.[209] The same is true of the work of the classical canonists, which they consulted much more extensively than the compilers of the Henrician canons had. There is no doubt that they made considerable use of Panormitanus, not least because his work was already easily available in more than one printed edition.[210] They also made great use of the *Speculum iudiciale* of William Durand (known as the 'Speculator'), which had just appeared in print.[211] The drafting committee may also have possessed a copy of the *Tractatus universi iuris*,[212] an eighteen-volume

---

[206]For example, the belief that the Hebrew and Greek originals of the texts of Holy Scripture should be regarded as the authentic ones for legal purposes (R, 1.12) seemed to most people in the sixteenth century to be a 'protestant' idea, but it appears in Gratian's *Decretum* (D, 9 c. 6 – Fr, I, 17), a fact which must have been known to at least some of the members of the drafting committee.

[207]R, 1.6-8. Cf. The decision taken at the fourth session of the council of Trent, 8 April 1546 (*C.O.D.*, 663-4).

[208]R, 1.14. Cf. D, 15 cc. 1-2 (Fr, I, 34-6). The ecumenical status of the council of Trent was an obvious bone of contention between Rome and the protestants (not to mention the Eastern Orthodox churches), and gradually the custom of accepting it, along with fourteen medieval councils, as 'ecumenical' in addition to the first four was accepted in Roman Catholic theology. But this has never been defined by the magisterium, as the editors of the *Conciliorum oecumenicorum decreta* (Bologna, 1973) were careful to point out in their preface.

[209]On this subject, see R. H. Helmholz, *Roman canon law in medieval England* (Cambridge, 1990).

[210]Nicholas de Tudeschis (1386-1445) was bishop of Palermo (Panormus) and wrote a major commentary on the *Liber extra* which was published in nine volumes (Venice, 1475) and later in six (Lyon, 1524). Either edition could easily have been used by the drafting committee.

[211](1231-96). Bishop of Mende (France). Durand completed his *Speculum* about 1271 and revised it about 1287. Additions were later made by Baldus de Ubaldis (*c.*1327-1400), which were included in the first printed edition (Lyon, 1547).

[212]Published at Lyon, 1549.

encyclopedia of canon law which was then brand new, and it is quite likely that they also consulted Hostiensis, who had long been popular in England, though his works were still available only in manuscript.[213] Beyond that it is hard to say, since the canonists readily copied each other and it is always possible that the drafting committee picked up ideas from lesser known works. All we can do is trace the ideas expressed in the canons of the *Reformatio* to a plausible source in the canonists, which is enough to demonstrate the former's lack of originality or innovation. What actually transpired in the committee, however, is now impossible to determine.

Another obvious source of legal material is the collection which we now call the *Corpus iuris civilis*, the great compendium of Roman law which had been enjoying a considerable revival since the mid-fifteenth century. Those who promoted this revival were well aware of the links between canon and civil law, but they tended to regard the former as inferior to the latter in its understanding and application of Roman jurisprudence. This point of view was certainly familiar to the drafting committee and was probably shared by them, at least in a general way.[214] Certainly they did not hesitate to adopt large portions of the Roman civil law, though they were careful to recognize that it was subordinate to English custom and parliamentary statute.[215] This raises the question of the ongoing relationship between Roman law and English custom, which we have grown used to understanding as the progressive defeat of the former by the latter, even if it is generally recognized that modern English common law has absorbed a number of Roman elements into its system.

History is usually written by the victors, and there is no doubt that the common view is broadly correct if the longer-term historical perspective is taken into account. But we must not forget that matters were much less clear in the sixteenth century, when the English legal situation was not all that different from what obtained elsewhere. Most European countries had operated systems of

---

[213]Henricus de Segusio, bishop of Ostia (*c.*1190/1200-71), wrote a famous compendium of canon law called the *Summa aurea* (1250-1) and a commentary on the *Liber extra* (1271). The former was first printed at Lyon (1587) and the latter at Venice (1581), but both had been widely quoted by John of Athon (*c.*1340) and William Lyndwood (1430) and thus were well known and highly respected in England. Moreover, he had been in England from 1236-44 as part of the household of Queen Eleanor and had therefore witnessed the legation of Otho (1237-41) and perhaps also the initial implementation of Gregory IX's *Decretals* in England. For the impact of his years in England on his subsequent writings, see Noel Didier, 'Henri de Suse en Angleterre (1236?-1244)', *Studi in onore di Vincenzo Arangio-Ruiz nel XLV anno del suo insegnamento* (4 vols., Naples, 1953), II, 333-51.

[214]We should not forget that when the canon law faculties were suppressed in the universities (1535) they were replaced by chairs in civil law.

[215]Cf. R, 27.43.

customary law throughout the middle ages, and, if England was exceptional, it was only in the degree of organization which the existence of a centralized and relatively efficient monarchy permitted.[216]

What is less well known (at least in England) is that from about 1450 these same countries were faced with the challenge of 'receiving' Roman law into their systems, a process which continued for several centuries and eventually resulted in the almost complete victory of the Roman tradition over local custom. This victory was facilitated by the relative absence of strong central governments with an entrenched legal establishment which could resist change. As other European countries began to develop centralized state structures, local customs were a barrier to unity, and so Roman principles tended to prevail over them. This did not happen in England because it was not necessary – national unification had already occurred under the common law. But this does not mean that the reception of Roman law was never seriously entertained in England. On the contrary, English travellers to the continent were well aware that their country was falling behind in the process of legal modernization, and at least one of them, Thomas Starkey (d.1538), wrote a lengthy treatise advocating the wholesale reception of Roman law in England.[217] This may have been a utopian ideal, but it should not be dismissed merely for that reason.[218] Debates of that kind evidently took place for much of the sixteenth century, and a decision to adopt Roman law wholesale might have proved no more difficult (or unpopular) than the adoption of the metric system of weights and measures has proved in our time. Certainly almost everyone agrees that the victory of the common law over the Roman system was not finally assured until 1640, after which the ecclesiastical law was increasingly subjected to its influence.[219]

In the sixteenth-century context, adoption of the *Reformatio* could have been regarded by 'progressive' secularizers as part of a movement towards the adoption of Roman civil law in general, and this possibility must be borne in mind when we consider its widespread adoption of Roman principles and

---

[216]See R. C. Van Caenegem, *The birth of the English common law* (2nd edn., Cambridge, 1988).

[217]*England in the reign of King Henry the eighth. A dialogue between Cardinal Pole and Thomas Lupset, by Thomas Starkey*, ed. J. M. Cowper (Early English Texts Society, extra series, XII, 2, London, 1871). See Van Caenegem, *Birth*, pp. 105-6.

[218]As is done, for example, by A. Borkowski, *Textbook on Roman law* (2nd edn., London, 1997), p. 383. Perhaps it is worth recalling that utopia was invented by one of Henry VIII's most prominent statesmen!

[219]Not without resistance, however, as a number of eighteenth-century treatises and Edmund Gibson's *Codex* attest. See J. H. Baker, *Monuments of endelesse labours* (London, 1998) for the details. Even as recently as 1963, when the ecclesiastical courts were overhauled and the appellate jurisdiction of the judicial committee of the privy council over them was restricted, it was explicitly stated that nothing decided during the period of that committee's jurisdiction (1 February 1833 - 1 March 1965) would constitute a precedent for the future. See the ecclesiastical jurisdiction measure, 1963/no. 1, s. 45 (3).

ideas.[220] Certainly whatever reasons may be put forward to explain the *Reformatio*'s failure to get through the house of lords in 1553, it cannot be said that its bias towards Roman legal norms was one of them.

The relationship of the *Reformatio* to the work of the protestant reformers is a more complex question. On the one hand, there can be no doubt that the document was intended to form the third great pillar of the reformation, standing for church discipline alongside reformed doctrine (the articles of religion) and worship (the book of common prayer), and so one might expect to find changes of a similar degree of magnitude in a revised canon law. On the other hand, the text itself is inherently conservative (as was the legal establishment) and in the purely administrative and procedural titles most of its 'changes' can be reduced to attempts to improve the speed, fairness and cost of the administration of justice – universal sources of complaint which scarcely needed a religious reformation to make themselves heard.

The connexion between the *Reformatio* and the main constitutional documents of the English reformation is not difficult to establish. The early titles have a clear link to the forty-two articles of 1553, covering most of the same themes in somewhat greater detail.[221] Similarly, there are occasional references to the 1552 prayer book as the only recognized form of worship.[222] John Foxe expressed objections to this in his preface, as well as in a marginal note next to R, 19.1, but it seems that he was mainly bothered by those 'remnants of popery' which the prayer book still contained and did not object to set prayers as such.[223] In any case, it is perfectly clear that the *Reformatio* merely supplemented the various acts of uniformity on this point, and would not have required alteration as long as the principle of having a set form of worship was maintained. The *Ordinal* (1550) which is attached to the prayer book but is not a part of it, is not mentioned in the *Reformatio* at all, though the threefold pattern of holy orders and the requirements placed on them are clearly assumed by it. Its main effect seems to have been to make a title dealing with ordination unnecessary, and there is nothing specifically geared to that subject in the text. The *Homilies* (1547)[224] are not mentioned either, although it was clearly assumed that a homily would

---

[220]The notion that there may have been a tacit alliance between protestant reformers and a reactionary nativist tradition in legal affairs, which has sometimes been advanced with regard to Luther's revolt in Germany, cannot be sustained as far as England is concerned. See M. Bellomo, *The common legal past of Europe, 1000-1800* (Washington, D. C., 1995), p. 220.

[221]See below, p. 808 for the details.

[222]R, 5.10; 19.16.

[223]Of course, Foxe was referring primarily to the 1559 book, which retreated somewhat from the protestantism of the 1552 book (which was the one referred to in the canon). The extent of his 'puritan' leanings is unclear, and it is known that he did not fully support 'puritanism' as it developed after 1571.

[224]Only the first book of homilies was available when the *Reformatio* was written; the second book did not appear until 1563, and the last homily in it was not added until 1571.

be read when a sermon was not preached.[225] It is obviously inconceivable that the drafting committee would have produced a text which did not coincide with the other foundational documents of the Edwardian church; the only surprise is that so little is said about them. In fact all the classic formularies of the Church of England, apart from the articles of religion, could have been altered or abandoned without necessitating any corresponding change in the *Reformatio*.[226]

Of course, the heart of the matter does not lie in these things, but in the influence, real or imaginary, which was exercised by those protestant theologians who openly challenged traditional social values, and in particular, the long-standing bans on clerical marriage and on divorce *a vinculo*.[227] Generally speaking, the reformers wanted to introduce the former and recognize the latter, at least in certain circumstances. On the subject of clerical marriage, the *Reformatio* obviously followed this pattern, which in any case had already been legislated as a parliamentary statute.[228] Furthermore, it was not simply a matter of granting permission for clerical marriage; denying its validity was regarded as a heresy, and that was clearly a concession to protestant sentiment.

The question of divorce *a vinculo* is rather different. The scriptural basis for allowing this is not as clear as it is in the case of clerical matrimony, and is restricted to cases of adultery.[229] Traditional canon law had not made this connexion however, probably because it was foreign to Roman law. The Romans regarded adultery as a crime which could be punished like any other felony, whereas divorce was just the dissolution of a marriage and was more about the restitution of the dowry than about punishment in the usual sense. The old canon law had respected this distinction, treating adultery in Book 5 of the *Decretals* and divorce (however that was understood) in Book 4. The Henrician canons followed suit, in spite of their general re-ordering of the traditional shape of the canons. Here the *Reformatio* clearly innovated along scriptural lines, not only by putting adultery and divorce together in a single title for the first time, but also by allowing for the latter principally in the case of the former.

Little more would have to be said about this were it not for the suggestion, apparently first made by John Keble (1792-1866) in 1857,[230] but since repeated and developed by a number of different authorities,[231] to the effect that the

---

[225]Cf. R, 7.(7).

[226]This is a reminder to us of the importance of the articles within the overall settlement; the popular modern view that the essence of Anglicanism is to be found in the prayer book and ordinal, rather than in the articles, cannot be sustained from the evidence. Where the *Reformatio* is concerned, at least, it was the other way round.

[227]This is what we now understand by divorce, i.e. the dissolution of a legally valid marriage. See the next section for a detailed discussion.

[228]R, 2.20. Cf. 2-3 Edward VI, c. 21, 1549-50 (*S.R.*, IV, 67).

[229]Mt. xix. 9.

[230]J. Keble, *Sequel to the argument against unduly repealing the laws which treat the nuptial bond as indissoluble* (Oxford, 1857), pp. 201-4.

[231]See below. Sachs, 'Thomas Cranmer's *Reformatio*', pp. 105-16, has the fullest discussion of the subject.

doctrine of the *Reformatio* on divorce is dependent on the influence of continental reformers, and more especially on Martin Bucer (1491-1551), who is known to have written extensively on the subject after his arrival in England in April 1549. Furthermore, it is well known that Bucer's remarks, which take up a considerable portion of his *De regno Christi*, a treatise on the Christian reformation of the state addressed to King Edward VI and actually presented to him (*via* Sir John Cheke) on 21 October 1550, were excerpted and translated by John Milton in the seventeenth century, as part of Milton's campaign in favour of lax divorce laws.[232] This circumstance led Keble and others like him to suppose that Milton's 'liberal' views on the subject went back to the first generation of reformers and found their way into the *Reformatio* because of Bucer's close connexions with men like Archbishop Thomas Cranmer, Peter Martyr Vermigli, Walter Haddon and Sir John Cheke. What evidence is there to support such a view?

Bucer died on 28 February 1551, about eight months before the canon law commission was appointed, but probably he would have been asked to join it had he been alive and well enough to take part.[233] Sir John Cheke had a copy of *De regno Christi* which would presumably have been available for the commission's use, though it was not printed until 1557.[234] There is no doubt that Bucer's views would have been known to most, if not all, of the members of the drafting committee, who may well have shared them to some extent. But if there is a certain degree of affinity between Bucer's thought and that of the *Reformatio*, consanguinity is another matter altogether. The big difference between the *De regno Christi* and the *Reformatio* lies in the fact that the former advocates complete state control of both marriage and divorce, which the latter does not. Bucer followed the precepts of Roman civil law, many of which were already current in New Testament times, a fact which is often reflected in the works of the church fathers, as he pointed out. But none of the drafters of the *Reformatio* had any thought of relinquishing ecclesiastical jurisdiction over these matters, nor did they show much interest in adopting Roman civil law as their basis for deciding them.[235] In their eyes, matrimony was still 'holy' even if it was no longer technically a sacrament, and they intended to keep it that way.[236] The point was not lost on John Milton, who praised Bucer to the skies because he supported civil marriage and divorce, but who made no mention of the *Reformatio* (even though it had been reprinted twice only a few years before he

---

[232]M. Bucer, *De regno Christi*, ed. F. Wendel (Paris, 1955). Translated (except for the titles on divorce) by W. Pauck, *Melanchthon and Bucer* (Philadelphia, 1969). Milton's translation of most (but not all) of the titles on divorce, originally published on 15 July 1644, can be found in *Complete prose works of John Milton* (8 vols., New Haven, 1953-82), II, 416-79.

[233]He was ill for much of his short stay in England, and was only able to lecture at Cambridge (where he was regius professor of divinity) for a few months in 1550.

[234]At Basel.

[235]In sharp contrast, for example, to what they had to say about testaments. Cf. R, 27.43.

[236]Cf. article 26 of 1553 (25 of 1571), *D.E.R.*, pp. 298-300.

wrote his tract and he must have known about it), probably because it was much less favourable to his cause. The conclusion therefore must be that the similarities between Bucer and the *Reformatio* are not strong enough to indicate direct dependence of the latter on the former, and that in its basic structure and intention, the *De regno Christi* is a different kind of work from the one which the drafting committee was trying to produce.

The possibility that Jan Łaski may have made a similar contribution with respect to church discipline was put forward by the late Basil Hall, who based his belief on the fact that the privy council granted Łaski a sum of money on 19 November 1551.[237] Unfortunately, the acts of the privy council do not say what the money was for, and Hall's assertion that it was a payment for services rendered in the composition of the *Reformatio* is made impossible by the date, which is too early for that.[238] Perhaps Łaski did have some say in the final text, since he was a member of the commission of thirty-two, but what that might have been is unknown and is unlikely to have been very significant.

The political failure of the *Reformatio legum ecclesiasticarum*

When Archbishop Cranmer presented the final text of the *Reformatio* to the house of lords it was criticized and rejected by John Dudley (1502-53), duke of Northumberland and effective head of the government.[239] Cranmer and Northumberland were never close, and the latter seems to have objected in principle to the kind of church discipline which adoption of the document would have imposed – on the laity as well as on the clergy. But John Foxe believed that the king would have approved it if he had lived to attain his majority, and that its failure to pass in 1553 was due to a political accident rather than to any deep difference of policy between the spiritual and the temporal authorities.[240] Our

---

[237]*Acts of the privy council*, III (1550-2), p. 420.

[238]B. Hall, 'John a Lasco, the humanist turned protestant, 1499-1560', *Humanists and protestants* (Edinburgh, 1990), pp. 171-207. See especially p. 201. This article was originally published as a separate pamphlet (London, 1971).

[239]Dudley was made earl of Warwick on 16 February 1547, less than three weeks after Edward VI became king. He effectively replaced the duke of Somerset in a kind of *coup d'état* on 10 October 1549, though he did not assume Somerset's title of lord protector. On 11 October 1551 he had himself created duke of Northumberland, but after the failure of his attempt to place Lady Jane Grey on the throne (6-19 July 1553), he forfeited his titles and was executed (22 August 1553). David Loades describes him in *The reign of Mary Tudor. Politics, government and religion in England, 1553-1558* (2nd edn., London, 1991), p. 98: 'Having been hailed as "an intrepid soldier of Christ" after his break with the conservative Wriothesly in 1550, he had become by 1553 the outstanding example of a "carnal gospeller" – one who paid lip-service to the faith but whose actions belied his words.'

[240]What is certain is that if it had passed in March 1553 it would have been repealed later in the year by Mary I, who dismantled all Edward VI's ecclesiastical legislation as soon as she could. See 1 Mary I, c. 2, 1553 (*S. R.*, IV, 202).

knowledge of what happened in the parliament of March 1553 comes from two main sources. The first is the *Journal of the house of lords* which records the various religious bills which were debated but says nothing about the canon law project. The other source is a diplomatic despatch sent by the imperial ambassador Jehan Scheyfve to Charles V on 10 April 1553.[241] Scheyfve was not a particularly good diplomat and he did not speak English, which made him reliant on the reports of others when it came to proceedings in parliament. He was also hostile to the protestant regime and presented it in an unfavourable light whenever he could. Furthermore, his despatch is a highly condensed version of events which summarizes the results of the March 1553 parliament but does not give us a blow-by-blow account of what actually transpired. Nevertheless, he seems to have captured the prevailing atmosphere of distrust between the bishops and the lords temporal, which is known from other contemporary sources, and to that extent the broad outline of his report may be regarded as accurate. Scheyfve moreover puts the canon law discussion at the top of his paragraph dealing with religious affairs, demonstrating that he regarded it as the most important ecclesiastical issue to have come before the parliament, although it tells us nothing about the chronological sequence of events. Scheyfve wrote his despatch in French cipher, which has been translated and published as follows:

Nothing new was done in matters of religion, and although the bishops had a volume of canon law ready, it was not accepted. The bishop [*sic*] of Canterbury presented it to parliament but the duke of Northumberland said openly and before all to him that it should come to nothing, and warned him and his brother bishops to take good care what they were about, as parliament had entrusted a charge to them, but could not stand judge [of their fidelity to the trust]. He added that if they did not teach the true doctrine and word of Christ, they should be punished; and he went on to say that certain agitators had dwelt recently on the incorporation of church property and lands and on the dividing up of bishoprics contemplated by the king, proclaiming that those who sought to diminish and restrict the rightful perquisites of the church were heretics, breaking God's law. This, he declared, was scandalous behaviour, tending to foster disorders and sedition. Let the bishops henceforth take care that the like should not occur again, and let them forbear calling into question in their sermons the acts of the prince and his ministers, else they should suffer with the evil preachers. The said [archbishop of] Canterbury excused himself, saying that he had heard nothing of it; and if something had been said, it was aimed at correcting and showing up vices and abuses. The duke of Northumberland replied

---

[241]*Calendar of letters, despatches and state papers relating to the negotiations between England and Spain, preserved in the archives at Vienna, Simancas, Besançon and Brussels* (13 vols., London, 1862-1954), XI, 32-4. Scheyfve was ambassador from 19 May 1550 until 17 October 1553.

that there were vices enough to denounce, that the fruits of their lives seemed meagre enough, that therefore some were saying that men would easily fall back into the old religion, others that bills regarding religion and other matters were being held back and postponed to another season for certain respects and considerations, and especially those touching the authority and absolute power with which the king was to have been invested. This last point, however, is supposed by some to have been put forward intentionally by the said duke, who is said to have previously circulated the rumour in order to ascertain the opinion of the public and what inferences and conclusions might be drawn therefrom.[242]

Scheyfve may have overdrawn this account somewhat but its basic assertions appear to be correct. His claim that Cranmer presented the finished text to the house of lords and that Northumberland scotched it in public debate may be true, though it is odd that the official record says nothing about it. Perhaps what really happened was that Cranmer presented it to a meeting of the privy council in the week before parliament opened, and Northumberland warned him there that his project was a non-starter.[243] If not, their exchange of views is most likely to have taken place at the first working session of the parliament on Monday 6 March, when the bill for regulating leases made by incumbents was given its first reading, though we have no way of knowing this.[244] Whatever the case, there is no reason to doubt that the main reason for this was, as Scheyfve stated, that there were preachers in London who had been attacking the rapacious seizure of church lands and property by the aristocracy, and that the bishops had done nothing to silence them. It is hard to believe that Cranmer was as unaware of this as he apparently claimed, and quite likely that he sympathized with their complaint, as Scheyfve implied. It is also probable that Northumberland reacted against the canon law proposal because of the immediate political situation (in which he saw a potential threat to his power coming from clerical rabble rousers)

---

[242]*Ibid.*, p. 33. The translation is by R. Tyler, the editor of volume XI. The original document is in the imperial archives at Vienna, catalogued as E. 20.

[243]Cranmer was present at council meetings on 21, 25, 27 and 28 February 1553, and it is hard to believe that Northumberland and the rest of the council would by then still have been unaware that the canon law revision was complete. However, the privy council records say nothing about it and so we must accept Scheyfve's account, in spite of its oddity at this point.

[244]See *L.J.*, I, 431-45. Cranmer was present at all twenty-five sessions, of which that on 6 March was the third, but Northumberland was there for only seventeen of them. We can therefore exclude the sessions on 7, 14, 16, 22, 25, 28 and 30 March (both morning and afternoon on the last of these days) when Northumberland was absent, but we know no more than that. The bill concerning leases was read a second time on 8 March and then sent to a committee, which returned it on 14 March, when Northumberland was absent. The third and final reading was on 20 March, when it passed with Northumberland's consent. The closing session of the parliament was on the afternoon of Friday 31 March.

and not from any serious consideration of the text itself. It is true that the *Reformatio* has a title dealing with the alienation of church property (R, 16), but that was a longstanding grievance going back several centuries and there is no indication that R, 16 was drawn up primarily with the post-reformation situation in view. The canons which it contains are either medieval in origin, which means that they were technically part of the existing law and not innovations at all, or else derived from the *Novellae* of Justinian. Furthermore, as Dr Diarmaid MacCulloch has pointed out, if Northumberland had read Cranmer's text, he would have found any number of other things in it to object to in addition to this one, but there is no indication that he did so.[245]

On the other hand, it is quite possible that Northumberland realized that there was a danger inherent in giving the church control of its own affairs. In constitutional terms, it was not clear whether passage of the *Reformatio* would have been an abdication of parliamentary responsibility for the church or a confirmation of it – or a curious combination of both. The likelihood is that it would have resulted in a form of legislative autonomy similar in some ways to that which the Church of England has enjoyed since 1919, in which parliament would have claimed supremacy over the church in theory but left most of the day-to-day running of affairs to the bishops and clergy. However, that could easily have led to a situation in which the bishops would pursue policies highly displeasing to parliament, of which the attempt to recover lost property was a prime example, but which would have been awkward for parliament to deal with without calling the whole idea of autonomy into question.[246] It certainly looks as if Northumberland saw such a situation developing and decided not to take any risks. Whether Edward VI would have pursued a different policy after attaining his majority, as John Foxe claimed, is impossible to say, though no doubt he would have had to put Northumberland in his place if he were to rule effectively at all. Perhaps that would have led to the enactment of the *Reformatio* a few years later, but the problems inherent in granting ecclesiastical legislative autonomy would not have gone away. We can only speculate of course, but the probability is that even if the *Reformatio* had become law it would sooner or later have been abrogated, or allowed to become a dead letter, and real control would have reverted to the crown, if only because the church was too large and powerful an institution to be left to its own devices.

The parliament of 1571

As it was, Edward VI died on 6 July 1553 and both Cranmer and Northumberland were removed from power as soon as Mary I gained control.

---

[245]MacCulloch, *Thomas Cranmer*, pp. 533-4.
[246]It is enough to recall the crisis over prayer book revision in 1927-8, when changes approved by the church assembly were defeated in parliament, to see how easily – and quickly – something analogous could have happened in the 1550s.

The reformed canon law disappeared, although it was resurrected under Elizabeth I. On 27 February 1559 a bill to revive the canon law commission was given its first reading in the house of commons. The second reading followed on 1 March, when the bill was engrossed, and the third reading came on 17 March, when the bill was passed. It was then sent to the lords on 20 March, where it was rejected after its first reading on 22 March.[247] But the idea resurfaced in the run-up to the parliament of 1563 and may have been mentioned in the convocation of Canterbury at that time.[248] What happened after that is obscure, but there is no evidence that the question of the *Reformatio* was raised in either house of parliament in 1563 or 1566.[249]

What is certain however is that six bills for church reforms of various kinds, now known as 'alphabetical' because they were lettered A-F, were brought to the 1566 parliament. Bill A would have given statutory confirmation to the thirty-nine articles of religion which had been passed in the convocation of Canterbury on 19 February 1563. It was given its first reading in the commons on 5 December, engrossed on 10 December, passed on 13 December and sent to the lords the following day.[250] It was read in the lords on 14 December but was taken no further.[251] Bills B-F were brought to the commons on 6 December 1566 but they were not debated, presumably because of lack of time.[252] But all six were held in reserve and reintroduced in 1571, at which point their history became entangled with that of the *Reformatio*. On 2 April 1571 Sir Nicholas Bacon, lord keeper of the privy seal,[253] addressed the opening of parliament as follows:

---

[247]*C.J.*, I, 55-8; *L.J.*, I, 566-8. The bishops present for the first reading of the bill were: York (Nicholas Heath), London (Edmund Bonner), Winchester (John White), Worcester (Richard Pates), Llandaff (Anthony Kitchin), Coventry and Lichfield (Ralph Baynes), Chester (Cuthbert Scott), Carlisle (Owen Oglethorpe) and the abbot of Westminster (John de Feckenham). All of them except Llandaff were Marian creations or supporters, and were gone by the end of the year.

[248]See *General note of matters to be moved by the clergy*, 1563, 3.1 (*A.C.*, p. 730). This anonymous source also recommended the immediate adoption of R, 33 (ibid., 3.46 in *A.C.*, p. 736). J. Strype, *Annals of the reformation* (4th edn., 4 vols., Oxford, 1824), I, 500 says that Bishop Edwin Sandys of Worcester proposed in convocation that the commission of thirty-two should be revived.

[249]For a review of this question, see N. L. Jones, 'An Elizabethan bill for the reformation of the ecclesiastical law', *Parliamentary History*, IV (1985), 171-87. However there was a bill presented to the lords on 30 March 1563 which picked up some of the failed legislation of 1549-50 and would have ensured that chancellors, commissaries and officials in the ecclesiastical courts would all be university graduates. It failed after a second reading on 31 March. See *L.J.*, I, 611. The matter was eventually covered by 1571/4.1 (*A.C.*, pp. 184-5), which was later incorporated into 1603/127 (*A.C.*, pp. 426-9).

[250]*C.J.*, I, 79-80.

[251]*L.J.*, I, 658.

[252]*C.J.*, I, 79.

[253](1509-79). He was a close friend and brother-in-law of Sir William Cecil (Lord Burghley) and a strong supporter of the protestant reformation. He became lord keeper on 22 December 1558 and remained in that office until his death on 20 February 1579. His

And because in all counsels and conferences first and chiefly there should be sought the advancement of God's honour and glory as the sure and infallible foundation whereupon the policy of every good public weal is to be erected and built, and as the straight line whereby it is principally to be directed and governed, and as the chief pillar and buttress wherewith it is continually to be sustained and maintained, therefore, for the well performing of the former, touching laws you are to consider first, whether the ecclesiastical laws concerning the discipline of the church be sufficient or no, and if any want shall be found, to supply the same; and thereof the greatest care ought to depend on my lords the bishops, to whom the execution thereof especially pertains, and to whom the imperfections of the same be best known, this is the time *gladius gladium iuvaret*.[254]

Following this, one of the members of the house of commons, William Strickland,[255] stood up on 6 April 1571 and made a speech in which he mentioned the existence of a text on which 'great and learned men of this realm had travailed, as Peter Martyr, Paulus Fagius[256] and other[s] whose works hereupon were extant'.[257] According to an anonymous diarist who was present and recorded the speech, Strickland went on to say:

...before this time thereof an offer was made in parliament that it might be approved,[258] but either the slackness or somewhat else of some men in that time was the let thereof – or what else (he said) he would not say. The book, he said, rested in the custody of Mr Norton as he guessed, a man neither ill-disposed to religion or a negligent keeper of such matters of charge, and thereupon requested Mr Norton might be required to produce the same. He added also that after so many years as now by God's providence we have been learning the purity of God's truth, that we should not permit for any cause of policy or other

speeches at the opening and closing of the parliaments are models of their kind and have become justly famous. Noted in Venn, *Alumni Cantabrigienses*, I, 65.

[254]The text is in *Proceedings of the parliaments of Elizabeth I*, ed. T. E. Hartley (3 vols., Leicester, 1981-95), I, 183 (spelling modernized here). The Latin means 'sword should help sword', a reference to the two swords, or branches of government (spiritual and temporal).

[255](d.1598). He represented Scarborough in the 1571 parliament, and was responsible for getting Thomas Norton to present the *Reformatio* to the house. Noted in P. W. Hasler, *The house of commons 1558-1603* (3 vols., London, 1981), III, 457-8.

[256](1504-49). He was a Hebrew scholar and colleague of Martin Bucer at Strasbourg. The two men came to England in the spring of 1549 and both went to Cambridge, where Fagius fell ill and died in mid-November. He could therefore not have taken part in the preparation of the *Reformatio*, which did not begin until late in 1551.

[257]Hartley, *Proceedings*, I, 200.

[258]A reference to the bill presented on 27 February 1559.

pretence any errors in matters of doctrine to continue among us. And therefore, said he, the book of common prayer, although (God be praised) it is drawn very near to the sincerity of the truth, yet there are some things inserted more superstitious or erroneous than in so high matters be tolerable, as namely, in the ministration of the sacrament of baptism, the sign of the cross to be made with some ceremonies, and the ministration of the sacrament by women in time of extremity, and some such other errors, all which, he said, might well be without note of chopping or changing of our religion changed, or whereby the enemies might slander us, being a reformation not consonant but directly personant to our profession, that is to have all things brought to the purity of the primitive church and institution of Christ.[259]

This speech may fairly be regarded as the earliest expression of 'puritanism' in parliament, but Strickland's linking of the passage of the canons to a further revision of the prayer book was unwise, to say the least. His speech evidently took Thomas Norton[260] by surprise. Norton was the late Archbishop Cranmer's son-in-law, the owner of MS Harleian 426 and the political agent of Sir William Cecil, the secretary of state, who had been created Lord Burghley on 25 February 1571.[261] The anonymous journalist describes the scene as follows:

Mr Norton, a man wise, bold and eloquent, standing up, said he was not ignorant (but had long time since learned) what it was to speak on a sudden, or first before the rest of men in parliament; yet being occasioned by Mr Strickland, he was to say that truth it is he had a book tending to that effect, but (quoth he) the book was not drawn by those learned men whom he named, but by virtue of the act of 32 [Henry VIII, c. 26][262] at the assignation or by the devise of seven [sic] bishops, eight deans, eight civilians and eight temporal lawyers, who having in charge to make ecclesiastical constitutions, took in hand the same, which was drawn by that learned man Mr Doctor Haddon, and penned by that excellent learned man Mr Cheke, whereupon he said that consideration had been, and some travail bestowed by Mr Foxe of late, and that there was a book newly imprinted to be offered to that house, which he did then and there presently show forth... It was concluded by

---

[259]Hartley, *Proceedings*, I, 200 (spelling modernized).
[260](*c.*1532-84). He represented London in the 1571 parliament. Noted in Hasler, *House of commons*, III, 145-9 and in Venn, *Alumni Cantabrigienses*, III, 269. On his career generally, see M. A. R. Graves, *Thomas Norton, the parliament man* (Oxford, 1994). On matters dealing with the *Reformatio*, Graves follows the views of Jones, 'An Elizabethan bill'.
[261]*C.J.*, I, 83.
[262]1540 (*S.R.*, III, 783-4).

the house that twenty-one [*sic*] should be especially assigned to have care of that book, and to have conference with the bishops therein.[263]

What, if anything, lay behind these manoeuvres at the opening of the 1571 parliament? It was suggested by Sir John Neale (1890-1975) that behind the scenes there was a campaign being launched by a group of 'proto-puritans', including Norton and Strickland, to initiate a more far-reaching reform of the church.[264] This view was disputed by Michael Graves (b. 1933), who suggested instead that the whole project was the work of the bishops and some privy councillors who were using Norton and Strickland as their agents,[265] a position which he has maintained in his recent biography of Norton.[266] However, this scenario has recently (and rightly) been challenged by Dr T. S. Freeman (b. 1959).[267] In both the Neale and Graves interpretations of events Strickland's speech was a set piece, deliberately structured so as to invite Norton's reply. Norton, who just 'happened' to have a copy of the *Reformatio* in his pocket, was then given the perfect opportunity to elaborate on the overall scheme.

Unfortunately, as Dr Freeman points out, this interpretation can only be sustained by distorting some of the key facts - notably Norton's apparent surprise when Strickland mentioned the text, and Strickland's equally apparent ignorance of its recent publication. One would have thought that a coordinated plan would have been better organized than that. Dr Freeman's own solution is to suggest that Norton was in league not with Strickland but with John Foxe, who saw the *Reformatio* as the key to church reform. He points out that Foxe had a long-standing interest in church discipline, and that he may even have written a contribution for the attention of the 1551-2 commissioners.[268] He further reminds us that Foxe was active in the anti-vestiarian movement of the mid 1560s, and suggests that he may have had a hand in shaping the 'alphabetical' bills of 1566,

[263]Hartley, *Proceedings*, I, 201 (spelling modernized). The numbers have been corrupted in transmission. 'Seven' bishops should read 'eight', as indeed MS Cotton Titus F 1, one of the sources used by Hartley, actually does. Similarly, 'twenty-one' should be 'twenty'. The same event was recorded much more briefly by John Hooker, *alias* Vowell (c.1527-1601), who was a member for Exeter in 1571 and whose diary, rediscovered in the nineteenth century, has been published in ibid., cf. I, 245. Hooker is noticed in Hasler, *House of commons*, II, 333-5 and in Foster, *Alumni Oxonienses*, I, 741.

[264]J. E. Neale, *Elizabeth I and her parliaments* (2 vols., London, 1953-7), I, 193-5.

[265]M. A. R. Graves, 'The management of the Elizabethan house of commons. The council's men of business', *Parliamentary History*, II (1983), 11-38.

[266]Graves, *Thomas Norton*, pp. 292-4.

[267]T. S. Freeman, 'Thomas Norton, John Foxe and the parliament of 1571', *Parliamentary History*, XVI (1997), 131-47.

[268]See C. Davies and J. Facey, 'A reformation dilemma. John Foxe and the problem of discipline', *Journal of Ecclesiastical History*, XXXIV (1988), 37-65, where it is argued that Foxe's book on the subject, *De censura*, may have been written with this intention.

which Neale regarded as a major part of the 'proto-puritan' campaign for reform.[269] Did Foxe therefore decide to print the *Reformatio* as the next stage in this wider scheme and enrol Norton's support for it?

According to Dr Freeman, Foxe was in London on 28 March 1571, where he was staying with John Day, the man who printed his edition of the *Reformatio*. Presumably he was there to see the manuscript through the press, and the first print run came out in the following week, just as parliament was meeting. Norton obviously acquired one of the earliest available copies, and (as those who covet newly-published works know) it is not at all surprising that he should have had it in his pocket for several days so that he could take a good look at it in his spare moments. That Strickland should have mentioned it by coincidence at that very moment obviously unsettled Norton, who had not yet had time to digest it properly and probably did not know quite what to say in reply. His hesitant reaction is typical of a person who has been caught off guard, but he recovered his composure and produced the text as requested, correcting Strickland's misconceptions as he did so.

Norton may well have been involved in a scheme hatched by Foxe, but if so, it appears that Strickland's untimely (and unexpected) intervention threw him off course. Instead of seizing the opportunity to advocate the adoption of the *Reformatio*, Norton moved off in a rather different direction. He continued with a speech in which he supported Strickland's demands for legislation against simony, but in the course of it he distanced himself from Strickland's somewhat impetuous radicalism, especially over the vexed question of further prayer book reform.[270] Nevertheless, he and Strickland were fundamentally on the same side, as can be seen from the fact that Norton was induced to support the revival of the 'alphabetical' bills which were to form a major part of the parliament's business in the 1571 session. But of the *Reformatio* we hear nothing. Norton would hardly have been against it, but the evidence which we have does not support the idea that he was part of a plot to get it adopted. On balance, it is probably best to drop the notion of a 'plot' altogether, even if we accept that Foxe rushed his edition into print in time for the parliamentary session.

Parliament responded to this unexpected rediscovery of a half-forgotten text by appointing a committee to consider both the *Reformatio* and the revived bill A, though it is possible that some members would have preferred to appoint a new commission of thirty-two to continue and complete the work of the earlier one.[271] In its initial form, this committee consisted of twenty members of the house of commons, including all five members of the privy council who sat in

---

[269]Freeman, 'Thomas Norton', pp. 134-7.

[270]Foxe, of course, was in favour of that, as his preface to the *Reformatio* makes clear, but like Norton, he probably wanted to move cautiously – certainly much more cautiously than Strickland.

[271]This at least is the argument of Jones, 'An Elizabethan bill', which is based on his discovery of a draft bill to that effect found among the Hastings papers at the Huntington Library in California, which he dates to the 1571 parliament.

that house. A request was then sent to the house of lords, which appointed another twenty-one members, ten lords spiritual and eleven lords temporal. When word of this was brought back to the commons on 10 April,[272] a further twelve committee members were appointed by that house, bringing the total number of commoners to thirty-two. This suggests that the house of commons was aware that the original provision had been for thirty-two members, but mistakenly assumed that each house of parliament would be expected to provide that number, which would have made an overall total of sixty-four! The list of those appointed makes it clear that both houses took the matter seriously, since it included many of the most prominent people in the 1571 parliament. The members of the committee were the following:

Appointed by the house of commons on 6 April 1571:[273]

1. Sir Francis Knollys[274]
2. Sir James Croft[275]
3. Sir Ralph Sadler[276]
4. Sir Walter Mildmay[277]
5. Sir Thomas Smith[278]
6. Sir Henry Neville[279]
7. Sir John Thynne[280]

---

[272]The messengers were Sir Richard Rede (1511-79) who had been a member of the 1552 commission (see above), and Dr Thomas Yale (*c*.1526-77), who entered doctors' commons on 10 November 1557 (Squibb, *Doctors' commons*, p. 153). Neither man was a member of either house at the time. According to *C.J.*, I, 84, there were supposed to be only twenty members of the upper house; the eleventh lay peer seems to have gone unnoticed.

[273]*C.J.*, I, 83.

[274](*c*.1512-96). He became a member of the privy council on 14 January 1559 and represented Oxfordshire in the 1571 parliament. Noted in Hasler, *House of commons*, II, 409-14 and in Venn, *Alumni Cantabrigienses*, III, 31.

[275](*c*.1518-90). He became a member of the privy council on 24 May 1570 and represented Herefordshire in the 1571 parliament. Noted in Hasler, *House of commons*, I, 672-5.

[276](1507-87). He became a member of the privy council on 20 November 1558 and represented Hertfordshire in the 1571 parliament. Noted in *ibid.*, III, 318-21.

[277](*c*.1523-89). He became a member of the privy council sometime in July or August 1566, and represented Northamptonshire in the 1571 parliament. Noted in *ibid.*, III, 53-6 and in Venn, *Alumni Cantabrigienses*, III, 188.

[278](1513-77). He became a member of the privy council in March 1571, and represented Essex in the 1571 parliament. His name had been suggested for the 1551 commission but did not figure in the final list. Noted in Hasler, *House of commons*, III, 400-1 and in Venn, *Alumni Cantabrigienses*, IV, 110.

[279](d.1593). He represented Berkshire in the 1571 parliament. Noted in Hasler, *House of commons*, III, 124-5.

[280](*c*.1513/15-80). He represented Wiltshire in the 1571 parliament. Noted in *ibid.*, III, 506-7.

8. Sir Thomas Lucy[281]
9. Sir Henry Gates[282]
10. The master of the requests[283]
11. Thomas Heneage[284]
12. Mr Recorder [Thomas Wilbraham][285]
13. Robert Bell[286]
14. Henry Knollys, Senior[287]
15. Robert Monson[288]
16. Thomas Norton[289]
17. William Strickland[290]
18. Henry Goodere[291]
19. William More[292]
20. Dr Henry Berkeley (Barclay)[293]

[281](*c.*1532-1600). He represented Warwickshire in the 1571 parliament. Noted in *ibid.*, II, 496-7.

[282](*c.*1515-89). He represented Yorkshire in the 1571 parliament. Noted in *ibid.*, II, 173-5.

[283]Probably Thomas Seckford (1515/16-87), who became a master of the requests on 9 December 1558 and represented Suffolk in the 1571 parliament. Noted in *ibid.*, III, 362-4. But it may also have been Thomas Wilson (1523-81), who became a master of the requests about the same time as he entered doctors' commons on 3 March 1561 (Squibb, *Doctors' commons*, p. 154). He represented Lincoln in the 1571 parliament. Noted in Hasler, *House of commons*, III, 629-31 and in Venn, *Alumni Cantabrigienses*, IV, 432.

[284](*c.*1532-95). A close friend of Dr Walter Haddon, he represented Lincolnshire in the 1571 parliament. Noted in Hasler, *House of commons*, II, 290-3 and in Venn, *Alumni Cantabrigienses*, II, 354.

[285](1531-73). He served briefly as recorder of London from March 1569 until about 23 April 1571, when he was made a judge in the court of wards. The recorder of London was traditionally elected to the commons as one of the city's four representatives. Noted in Hasler, *House of commons*, III, 617 and in Venn, *Alumni Cantabrigienses*, IV, 405.

[286](d.1577). He represented King's Lynn in the 1571 parliament and was speaker of the house from 1572-6. Noted in Hasler, *House of commons*, I, 421-4 and in Venn, *Alumni Cantabrigienses*, I, 128.

[287](*c.*1521-83). He represented Guildford in the 1571 parliament. Noted in Hasler, *House of commons*, II, 414-15.

[288](d.1583). He represented Lincoln in the 1571 parliament. Noted in *ibid.*, III, 66-7.

[289]See above, n. 260.

[290]See above, n. 255.

[291](1534-95). He represented Coventry in the 1571 parliament. Noted in Hasler, *House of commons*, II, 202-4.

[292](1520-1600). He represented Surrey in the 1571 parliament. Noted in *ibid.*, III, 86-9.

[293](*c.*1536-87). He became a member of doctors' commons on 29 October 1567 (Squibb, *Doctors' commons*, p. 157) and represented East Grinstead in the 1571 parliament. Noted in Hasler, *House of commons*, I, 430 and in Foster, *Alumni Oxonienses*, I, 113.

Appointed by the house of commons on 10 April 1571:[294]

    21. The master of the rolls [Sir William Cordell][295]
    22. Sir Henry Norris[296]
    23. Sir William Butts[297]
    24. John Astley[298]
    25. Roger Manwood[299]
    26. Adrian Stokes[300]
    27. William Fleetwood[301]
    28. George Carleton[302]
    29. Edward Aglionby[303]
    30. Christopher Yelverton[304]
    31. James Dalton[305]
    32. Robert Snagge[306]

[294]*C.J.*, I, 84.

[295](*c.*1522-81). He represented Westminster in the 1571 parliament. Noted in Hasler, *House of commons*, I, 657-8 and in Venn, *Alumni Cantabrigienses*, I, 397.

[296](*c.*1525-1601). He represented Oxfordshire in the 1571 parliament. Noted in Hasler, *House of commons*, III, 136-7.

[297](1513-83). He represented Norfolk in the 1571 parliament. Noted in *ibid.*, I, 522-3 and in Venn, *Alumni Cantabrigienses*, I, 276.

[298](*c.*1507-96). He represented Lyme Regis in the 1571 parliament. Noted in Hasler, *House of commons*, I, 359-60 and in Venn, *Alumni Cantabrigienses*, I, 50.

[299](*c.*1532-92). He represented Sandwich in the 1571 parliament. Noted in Hasler, *House of commons*, III, 15-17.

[300](*c.*1533-85). He represented Leicestershire in the 1571 parliament. Noted in *ibid.*, III, 449-50.

[301](*c.*1525-94). He represented St Mawes in the 1571 parliament. He became recorder of London about 23 April 1571 and remained in that office until 1592. Noted in *ibid.*, II, 133-8 and in Foster, *Alumni Oxonienses*, I, 506.

[302](1529-90). He represented Poole in the 1571 parliament. Noted in Hasler, *House of commons*, I, 552-4.

[303](1520-*c.*1591). He represented Warwick in the 1571 parliament. Noted in *ibid.*, I, 329-30 and in Venn, *Alumni Cantabrigienses*, I, 9.

[304](*c.*1537-1612). He represented Northampton in the 1571 parliament. His son Henry later acquired what is now British Library Additional MS 48040, containing the Henrician canons (see above). Noted in Hasler, *House of commons*, III, 679-81 and in Venn, *Alumni Cantabrigienses*, IV, 489.

[305](d.1601). He represented Saltash in the 1571 parliament. Noted in Hasler, *House of commons*, II, 8-9 and in Foster, *Alumni Oxonienses*, I, 368.

[306](d.1605). He represented Lostwithiel in the 1571 parliament. Noted in Hasler, *House of commons*, III, 408-9.

Appointed by the house of lords on 10 April 1571:[307]

Lords spiritual:

1. Canterbury [Matthew Parker][308]
2. London [Edwin Sandys][309]
3. Hereford [John Scory][310]
4. Ely [Richard Cox][311]
5. Salisbury [John Jewel][312]
6. St David's [Richard Davies][313]
7. Rochester [Edmund Gest (Guest)][314]
8. Carlisle [Richard Barnes][315]
9. Chichester [Richard Curtis (Curteys)][316]
10. Lincoln [Thomas Cooper][317]

Lords temporal:

1. Marquis of Northampton [William Parr][318]
2. Earl of Oxford [Edward de Vere][319]

[307] As given in *L.J.*, I, 672, the list is in strict order of precedence, with the archbishop of Canterbury coming first, followed by the marquis of Northampton, the six earls, the two viscounts, the nine bishops and the two barons.

[308] A member of the 1552 commission. See above, n. 134.

[309] (*c.*1516-88). Bishop of Worcester (1559-70), London (1570-7) and archbishop of York (1577-88). Noted in Venn, *Alumni Cantabrigienses*, IV, 19.

[310] A member of the 1552 commission. See above, n. 144.

[311] The lone survivor from the drafting committee of 1552. See above, n. 99.

[312] (1522-71). Bishop of Salisbury from 1560-71 and a leading apologist for the Elizabethan settlement. Noted in Emden, *Biographical register 1500-40*, pp. 317-18.

[313] (*c.*1501/9-81). Bishop of St David's from 1561-81. Noted in *ibid.*, pp. 162-3.

[314] (1518-77). Bishop of Rochester from 1560-71 and then of Salisbury from 1571-7. Noted in Venn, *Alumni Cantabrigienses*, II, 272.

[315] (1532-87). Bishop of Carlisle from 1570-7 and of Durham (1577-87). Noted in Foster, *Alumni Oxonienses*, I, 75 and in Venn, *Alumni Cantabrigienses*, I, 93. His appointment, as a bishop from the northern province, was unprecedented.

[316] (*c.*1532-82). Bishop of Chichester from 1570-82. Noted in *ibid.*, I, 434.

[317] (*c.*1511-94). Bishop of Lincoln from 1571-84 and of Winchester from 1584-94. Noted in Emden, *Biographical register, 1500-40*, pp. 135-6 and in Venn, *Alumni Cantabrigienses*, I, 392.

[318] (1513-71), made famous by his suit for divorce (1547-52) which was finally resolved by a special act of parliament. He became the seventeenth earl of Essex in 1543 and was created marquis of Northampton in 1547. He lost the second title under Mary I (1553) but it was restored to him in 1559. He was a favourite of Queen Elizabeth I, who paid for his funeral.

[319] (1550-1604). He succeeded to the title in 1562.

3.   Earl of Arundel [Henry Fitzalan][320]
4.   Earl of Worcester [William Somerset][321]
5.   Earl of Sussex [Thomas Radcliffe][322]
6.   Earl of Huntingdon [Henry Hastings][323]
7.   Earl of Bedford [Francis Russell][324]
8.   Viscount Hereford [Walter Devereux][325]
9.   Viscount Montagu [Anthony Browne][326]
10. Lord Cobham [William Brooke][327]
11. Lord Grey of Wilton [Arthur Grey][328]

Did this committee ever meet to discuss the *Reformatio*? It has sometimes been claimed that it did, and that its failure to reach a consensus between moderates and 'puritans' forced the bishops to act on their own, but this suggestion is mere conjecture and on balance it seems unlikely that it did so.[329] Fifty-three would have been an unwieldy number at the best of times, and it is hard to see how so large a body could have met for such wide-ranging business during a parliamentary session, when many of its members were taken up with other things. Only a smaller working party could have accomplished the necessary work, and there is some evidence to suggest that an attempt was actually made to do this. On 7 April the commons delegated Edward Grimston[330] and William Strickland to confer with the bishops about matters of religion and Strickland at least would probably have included the *Reformatio* in the discussion.[331]

---

[320](1512-80). He succeeded to the title in 1544. Noted in Foster, *Alumni Oxonienses*, I, 502.
[321](c.1527-89). He succeeded to the title in 1549.
[322](c.1525-93). He succeeded to the title in 1557. Noted in Venn, *Alumni Cantabrigienses*, III, 414.
[323](1536-95). He succeeded to the title in 1560. Noted in *ibid.*, II, 328.
[324](1527-85). He succeeded to the title in 1555. Noted in *ibid.*, III, 499.
[325](1539-76). Granted the title in 1558, he became earl of Essex in 1572 and was the father of Robert (1566-1601), the queen's celebrated favourite.
[326](c.1528-92). He succeeded to the title in 1554. Noted in Foster, *Alumni Oxonienses*, I, 192.
[327](1527-97). He succeeded to the title in 1558 and was the brother-in-law of William Parr, marquis of Northampton.
[328](1536-93). He succeeded to the title in 1562.
[329]See *e.g.*, Neale, *Elizabeth I and her parliaments*, I, 196-7. In his closing speech on 29 May 1571 Sir Nicholas Bacon relayed the queen's rebuke to those members of the lower house who had shown themselves to be 'audacious, arrogant and presumptuous' in their desire to involve themselves in matters beyond their competence, but there is no reference to the *Reformatio* as such. See Hartley, *Proceedings*, I, 188.
[330](c.1508-1600), member for Ipswich in the 1571 parliament. Noted in Hasler, *House of commons*, II, 229-30.
[331]*C.J.*, I, 83.

Whether anything ever came of that is doubtful, because on 14 April Strickland made a fiery speech in the commons demanding prayer book reform, as a result of which the queen ordered him to be suspended and arraigned before the privy council.[332] Pleas from the commons restored him to that house on 21 April and he does not appear to have suffered any further handicap as a result of his indiscretion.[333] The next we hear is that on 25 April the commons sent a delegation of six members to confer with Archbishop Parker, only three of whom (John Astley, Sir Henry Gates and Henry Knollys, Senior) had been appointed to the committee of fifty-three.[334] The others were Sir Robert Lane,[335] Miles Sandys[336] and Peter Wentworth,[337] who by all accounts was no more diplomatic than Strickland.

Evidence that this group of seven (including Parker) may have made a serious attempt to revise the *Reformatio* comes from the copy of Foxe's edition which is located in the Parker Library at Corpus Christi College, Cambridge and which almost certainly belonged to the archbishop himself. That copy contains marginal markings next to R, 8.4 (beginning with the words 'praecipimus, ut'), and R, 10.3, 5 and 19. In addition, a section of R, 19.16 (which Foxe singled out in his preface as a canon which needed revision) is underlined, beginning with 'ne quicquam' and ending with 'esse iussimus'. Were these jottings made by Parker in anticipation (or even as the result) of this consultation? Quite possibly they were, but it has to be emphasized that even if this conjecture is correct, matters never proceeded any further than that. Three days later the commons appointed a new committee of only four members - Henry Knollys, Senior, Robert Monson, William Strickland and Christopher Yelverton, all of whom were on the larger committee of fifty-three - and entrusted the management of the religious bills to them.[338] Presumably they could have pursued the question of the *Reformatio* further had they been so inclined, but no more is heard of it. Instead the bishops drafted new canons, some of which incorporated material from the *Reformatio*, a fact which suggests that they had given up on the full text, at least for the time being.[339] It appears that these canons were ready by the close of the

---

[332]*Ibid.*

[333]*Ibid.*, I, 85.

[334]*Ibid.*, I, 86.

[335](1527- *c.*1588), member for Northamptonshire in the 1571 parliament. Noted in Hasler, *House of commons*, II, 436.

[336](d.1601), member for Lancaster in the 1571 parliament. Noted in *ibid.*, III, 341-3.

[337](1524-97), member for Barnstaple in the 1571 parliament and later to be one of the most prominent advocates of radical church reform. Noted in *ibid.*, III, 597-601.

[338]*C.J.*, I, 86.

[339]R, 20 in particular was widely used in the 1571 canons. See *A.C.*, p. 952 for the details. It should be noted that the bishops who signed these canons were not the ten appointed to the commission. Carlisle did not sign them, but Winchester, Worcester, Chester, Bath and Wells, Coventry and Lichfield, Norwich, Bangor and Exeter all did. In addition, Canterbury signed for York, Winchester signed for Durham, Worcester signed for Peterborough and Bangor signed for both St Asaph and Llandaff.

parliamentary session on 29 May, and they were probably approved by convocation before it dissolved on the following day. Certainly they were presented to the queen on 4 June and she approved them verbally, though she never signed them.[340]

Whatever went on behind the scenes, it is certain that no version of the *Reformatio* ever resurfaced in the form of parliamentary legislation. Its demise is as obscure as that of the Henrician canons in 1535-6, which tempts us to ask whether Foxe's alternative explanations for that have any applicability to this situation. Can we suppose that the *Reformatio* disappeared because of the distemper of the times, or that there was ill-will in high places which prevented it from being taken seriously? The second of these possibilities is the easier one to evaluate, and it can be dealt with first. There is little doubt that ill-will on the part of the duke of Northumberland had been largely responsible for the *Reformatio*'s failure in 1553, but there is no record of any lingering animosity towards the *Reformatio* in the house of lords or anywhere else.[341] The people most directly concerned with it were the members of the 1551-2 commission, and an examination of the careers of those who survived into Elizabeth's reign shows that they would have been well-placed to counter whatever opposition there may have been. The effective survival rate of the commission's members[342] may be tabulated as follows:

Category	1563	1571
Bishops	Barlow Scory	Scory
Divines	Cox Parker Wotton Cooke	Cox Parker
Civil lawyers	Petre Cecil	Cecil

Of the divines of 1552, Cox (the only one to have been on the drafting committee) was the bishop of Ely ten years later and Parker was archbishop of Canterbury. Cooke, a layman, was a member of parliament. Of the civil lawyers, both were members of parliament in 1563, and Cecil (Burghley), as secretary of

---

[340]See *A.C.*, pp. 172-209. They may have been revised by the queen and her advisers before being printed and distributed sometime in July or August 1571.

[341]The presence on the 1571 commission of men such as the marquis of Northampton and his brother-in-law Lord Cobham would surely argue the opposite, since they (at least) must have been in favour of the controversial divorce provisions, for example.

[342]*I.e.*, those who were not only alive but still occupying positions of power and influence.

state, was the queen's chief adviser. So although their numbers were few and thinning, their influence was great and growing in the period up to 1571. There seems to be little reason to doubt that Parker, Cox and Burghley could have pursued the matter and carried the day if they had been determined to do so. Certainly it is hard to imagine that there could have been any opposition strong enough to stand up to them, unless it came from the queen herself. This view was put forward by Edward Cardwell in his edition of 1850, and it has proved to be remarkably popular.[343] Unfortunately, there is no evidence to suggest that the queen was opposed to the *Reformatio* as such, and so other explanations for its failure have also been canvassed. The most popular one is the theory that it never got anywhere because of William Strickland's foolish outbursts against the prayer book on 14 April, when he even went to the point of introducing a bill proposing a revision of it.[344] Much has been made of this incident and the fact that Foxe had mentioned the desirability of further liturgical reform in the preface to his edition of the *Reformatio* may have brought it under suspicion as well. The Strickland affair cannot have helped the cause of reform, but we have to look both at the fate of the ecclesiastical bills which were debated in the 1571 parliament and at Strickland's role in them before trying to decide what its real impact on the course of events was.

To take the 'alphabetical' bills first, four of them were in fact debated (and two of them became law) in the course of this parliamentary session. As it has been assumed by supporters of the 'proto-puritan' campaign theory that the subject matter of these bills was closely connected to the *Reformatio*, and that if the latter had been passed they would have been made redundant, it is necessary to take a brief look at what they were. They are listed here in order, with the ones which eventually passed indicated in bold type. Corresponding canons in the 1535 draft (H.C.) and in Foxe's edition of the *Reformatio* (R) are also noted, with vague or uncertain resemblances indicated in parentheses:

---

[343]Cardwell, *Reformation*, pp. x-xi. See, e.g., Neale, *Elizabeth I and her parliaments*, I, 197; W. P. Haugaard, *Elizabeth and the English reformation* (Cambridge, 1968), pp. 333-41; C. Cross, *The royal supremacy in the Elizabethan church* (London, 1969), pp. 68-95; and W. T. MacCaffrey, *Queen Elizabeth and the making of policy, 1572-1588* (Princeton, NJ, 1981), pp. 59-60.

[344]*C.J.*, I, 84. For this view, see Graves, 'The management of the Elizabethan house of commons', pp. 11-38 and G. R. Elton, *The parliament of England 1559-1581* (Cambridge, 1986), p. 209.

		H.C.	R
A.	Confirmation of the articles of religion.[345]	-	-
B.	**The qualifications for ordination.**[346]	18	(11.7-11)
C.	The residence of beneficed clergy.	19.1-3	(11.12-15)
D.	Corrupt presentations.[347]	3.1-2	(11.24)
E.	**Fraudulent leases.**[348]	-	-
F.	Pensions paid out of benefices.[349]	28	-
G.	Against the commutation of penance.[350]	10.11	28.11

Unfortunately we know very little about the content of these bills, but it is fair to say that the agenda (if it can be called that) of B-F resembles the Henrician canons of 1535 more readily than it does the *Reformatio*, which does not deal with E or F at all and which treats the others in a somewhat cursory and indirect fashion. Indeed, it could almost be argued that the 'alphabetical' bills were meant to plug gaps in the *Reformatio,* or at least to deal directly and specifically with pressing problems which that text mentions only in a cursory and inadequate way.

The progress of the alphabetical bills through the houses of parliament appears to have been quite regular, and although it may have been postponed by the Strickland affair (14-21 April), there is no sign that it was seriously impeded by it. The readings in the two houses can be tabulated as follows:

[345]Dr N. L. Jones ('An Elizabethan bill') has argued that this bill, which the queen had blocked in 1566 (see Elton, *The parliament of England*, pp. 205-7), was replaced in 1571 by what amounted to another bill A, which would have given statutory force to the *Reformatio*. Whatever the case, no more was heard of it.

[346]This included clerical subscription to the articles of religion. It passed into law as 13 Elizabeth I, c. 12, 1571 (*S.R.*, IV, 546-7).

[347]This bill is frequently confused with E in the literature, but in fact there was no legislation against simony until 31 Elizabeth I, c. 6, 1589 (*S.R.*, IV, 802-4). This was reinforced by 1603/40 (*A.C.*, 324-7) and by much later legislation. See *A.C.*, 324, n, 183 for the details.

[348]This bill was described as 'concerning simony' before it was passed into law as 13 Elizabeth I, c. 20, 1571 (*S.R.*, IV, 556), a fact which has led to its being confused with D in much of the secondary literature. See also 1571/1.7 (*A.C.*, 176).

[349]In 1571 this bill disappeared, probably because it was thought to have been covered by E.

[350]Introduced in the 1571 parliament and added to the others. It vanished in a committee of the house of lords, but something of its intention was enacted by convocation in 1576. See 1575/12 (13) in *A.C.*, 214.

House of commons[351]

	First reading	Second reading	Third reading
A.[352]	-	-	-
B.	28 April	30 April	3 May
C.	12 May	14 May	16 May
D.[353]	11 April	9 May	11 May[354]
E.	13 April	2 May	7 May
F.[355]	-	-	-
G.	10 May	15 May	17 May

House of lords[356]

	First reading	Second reading	Third reading
B.	7 May	11 May	21 May
C.	17 May	-	-
D.	12 May	15 May	17 May
E.	7 May	16 May	17 May
G.	17 May	-	-

Passage of these bills in the house of lords was somewhat complicated by the fact that on 7 May the lords read a bill designed to prevent fraudulent gifts to evade responsibility for dilapidations.[357] After being reviewed by a committee, the bill came back for a second reading on 16 May; it was then engrossed and passed after the third reading on the following day.[358] Meanwhile on 11 May a separate simony bill was introduced in the upper chamber.[359] It received its second reading on 15 May, at which point it was coupled with bill D and referred to a committee of four bishops and six lay peers.[360] Both bills were brought back to the house on 17 May and were passed.[361] After that bills B, D and E, as well

---

[351]*C.J.*, I, 83-90.

[352]Sent to a committee on 7 April; see *ibid.*, I, 83.

[353]We are told that there was much argument and debate when this bill was presented. See *ibid.*, I, 84.

[354]*C.J.* does not record when this bill was passed but the date is known from John Hooker's journal. See Hartley, *Proceedings*, I, 251.

[355]Apparently combined with E.

[356]*L.J.*, I, 682-9.

[357]*Ibid.*, I, 682.

[358]*Ibid.*, I, 688.

[359]*Ibid.*, I, 684.

[360]*Ibid.*, I, 686. The bishops were Winchester (Robert Horne), Ely (Richard Cox), Salisbury (John Jewel) and Lincoln (Thomas Cooper). The lay peers were the earls of Huntingdon (Henry Hastings) and Bedford (Francis Russell), and Lords Burghley, Chandos, Hastings and Hunsdon.

[361]*Ibid.*, I, 689.

as the lords' bills on fraudulent gifts and simony were returned to the commons where they were read, approved and returned to the lords, who passed bills B and E, as well as their own bill on fraudulent gifts. They do not appear to have done anything with their bill on simony, but the bill on corrupt presentations was read three times before it finally failed to pass.[362] What happened can best be presented in tabular form as follows:

	Lords to commons	Commons to lords	Final result
B.	21 May	23 May	Passed (23 May)[363]
D.	19 May	26 May	Failed (28 May)
E.	19 May	23 May	Passed (24 May)[364]
Fraud	19 May	23 May[365]	Passed (24 May)[366]
Simony	19 May	22 May	Ignored

That bill D was in trouble can be seen from the fact that on 25 May the commons appointed a committee to confer with the lords about it. We do not know whether they ever met with representatives of the upper house, but the names of the thirteen members of the commons who were on the committee are recorded and nearly half of them were also on the committee of fifty-three, as can be seen from the following list in which they are designated by an asterisk:

1. *Sir Thomas Smith[367]
2. Sir William Paulet[368]
3. Sir Francis Hastings[369]
4. *Thomas Heneage[370]
5. *William Fleetwood[371]
6. *Adrian Stokes[372]
7. Thomas Browne[373]

[362]C.J., I, 91-2; L.J., I, 692-9.

[363]13 Elizabeth I, c. 12, 1571 (S.R., IV, 546-7).

[364]13 Elizabeth I, c. 10, 1571 (S.R., IV, 544-5).

[365]The commons read it on successive days (21-3 May) and made amendments which the lords accepted.

[366]13 Elizabeth I, c. 20, 1571 (S.R., IV, 556).

[367]See above, n. 278.

[368](c.1532-98), member for Dorset in the 1571 parliament. He inherited the title of marquess of Winchester from his father on 4 November 1576. Noted in Hasler, House of commons, III, 189-90.

[369](c.1545-1610), member for Leicestershire in the 1571 parliament. Noted in ibid., II, 270-2.

[370]See above, n. 284.

[371]See above, n. 301.

[372]See above, n. 300.

[373](d.1597), member for Arundel in the 1571 parliament. Noted in ibid., II, 505-6.

8. Mr Hussey[374]
9. John Hastings[375]
10. Thomas Snagge[376]
11. *Robert Snagge[377]
12. *William Strickland[378]
13. Nicholas St. John[379]

Another ecclesiastical bill of great importance in the 1571 parliament was the one designated 'for coming to church and receiving holy communion' which was designed to flush out recusants by making both of those things compulsory. It was actually introduced in the house of commons and given its first reading on 4 April, two days before Strickland's famous speech in which he brought up the *Reformatio*.[380] The second reading followed on 6 April, the same day as Strickland's speech, when a number of amendments were made and a committee of nine members was appointed to discuss them.[381] They were (with members of the committee of fifty-three asterisked):

1. *Sir Thomas Smith[382]
2. Sir Owen Hopton[383]
3. Sir Thomas Scott[384]
4. *Thomas Seckford[385]
5. Thomas Wilson[386]
6. *Roger Manwood[387]
7. John Jeffrey[388]

[374]Either Thomas (*c*.1520 - *c*.1576), member for Weymouth in the 1571 parliament (noted in *ibid*., II, 357-8) or John, member for Horsham (noted in *ibid*., II, 356-7). The former is thought to have been more likely however, given his other ecclesiastical interests.
[375](*c*.1525 - *c*.1585), member for Reading in the 1571 parliament. Noted in *ibid*., II, 274-5.
[376](1536-93), brother of Robert and member for Bedfordshire in the 1571 parliament. Noted in *ibid*., III, 410.
[377]See above, n. 306.
[378]See above, n. 255.
[379](*c*.1526-89), member for Great Bedwyn in the 1571 parliament. Noted in *ibid*., III, 322-3.
[380]*C.J.*, I, 82.
[381]*Ibid*., I, 83.
[382]See above, n. 278.
[383](*c*.1519-95), member for Suffolk in the 1571 parliament. Noted in Hasler, *House of commons*, II, 336-7.
[384](*c*.1535-94), member for Kent in the 1571 parliament. Noted in *ibid*., III, 356-8.
[385]See above, n. 283.
[386]See above, n. 283.
[387]See above, n. 299.
[388](*c*.1524-78), member for East Grinstead in the 1571 parliament. Noted in *ibid*., II, 374-5.

8. *William Fleetwood[389]
9. Miles Sandys[390]

The committee reported back to the house on 9 April when the revised bill was given its first reading, although according to the *Journal of the house of commons* there was a lot of argument about it and a number of further amendments were proposed.[391] The second reading was delayed until 20 April, possibly because of the Strickland affair but probably also because of the controversy which the bill itself had engendered.[392] On the following day, when Strickland returned to the house, an addition to the bill was proposed and given its first reading.[393] A further proviso was also added, and read twice.[394] At this point yet another committee was formed, consisting of thirteen members as follows (those on the committee of fifty-three are once again asterisked):

1. *Treasurer [Sir Francis Knollys][395]
2. *Chancellor of the duchy of Lancaster [Sir Ralph Sadler][396]
3. *Sir Thomas Smith[397]
4. *William More[398]
5. *Henry Knollys, Senior[399]
6. Thomas St. Poll or Sampole[400]
7. *Robert Monson[401]
8. *Robert Bell[402]
9. *Christopher Yelverton[403]
10. John Agmondesham[404]
11. Thomas Bowyer[405]

---

[389]See above, n. 301.
[390](d.1601), member for Lancaster in the 1571 parliament. Noted in *ibid.*, III, 341-3.
[391]*C.J.*, I, 83.
[392]*Ibid.*, I, 85.
[393]*Ibid.*
[394]*Ibid.*
[395]See above, n. 274.
[396]See above, n. 276.
[397]See above, n. 278.
[398]See above, n. 292.
[399]See above, n. 287.
[400](c.1539-82), member for Great Grimsby in the 1571 parliament. Noted in Hasler, *House of commons*, III, 332-3.
[401]See above, n. 288.
[402]See above, n. 286.
[403]See above, n. 304.
[404](c.1511-73), member for Reigate in the 1571 parliament. Noted in *ibid.*, I, 330-1.
[405](1537-95), member for Midhurst in the 1571 parliament. Noted in *ibid.*, I, 473-4.

12. Thomas Snagge[406]
13. *William Strickland[407]

It will be noted that William Strickland lost no time in returning to the fray and that he was immediately involved in a matter of the utmost sensitivity. The committee actually met on 22 April and again on 28 April, before bringing the revised bill back for its second reading on 30 April, when it was engrossed.[408] The third reading followed on 4 May when the bill was finally passed and sent to the lords.[409] The lords received it on 5 May and gave it its first reading on 7 May.[410] The second reading followed on 9 May, when a committee of thirteen was appointed to study it further.[411] That committee consisted of four bishops, eight lay peers and a serjeant-at-law, as follows (those on the committee of fifty-three being asterisked, and those who had served on the 1551-2 commission in bold type):

1. Winchester [Robert Horne][412]
2. **Hereford** [John Scory][413]
3. *Salisbury [John Jewel][414]
4. *Lincoln [Thomas Cooper][415]
5. *Earl of Sussex [Thomas Radcliffe][416]
6. *Earl of Huntingdon [Henry Hastings][417]
7. *Earl of Bedford [Francis Russell][418]
8. *Viscount Montagu [Anthony Browne][419]
9. **Lord Burghley** [William Cecil][420]
10 *Lord Cobham [William Brooke][421]
11. Lord [John] Lumley[422]

[406]See above, n. 376.

[407]See above, n. 255.

[408]*C.J.*, I, 85-6. The record calls this the third reading, which was technically true in the case of the proviso.

[409]*Ibid.*, I, 87.

[410]*L.J.*, I, 681-2.

[411]*Ibid.*, I, 683.

[412](*c.*1519-80), bishop of Winchester from 1561. Noted in Venn, *Alumni Cantabrigienses*, II, 408.

[413]See above, n. 144.

[414]See above, n. 312.

[415]See above, n. 317.

[416]See above, n. 322.

[417]See above, n. 323.

[418]See above, n. 324.

[419]See above, n. 326.

[420]See above, n. 148.

[421]See above, n. 327.

[422](*c.*1534-1609). He inherited the title from his grandfather in 1544, but had to be restored to it (in 1547) because of his father's attainder. Noted in *ibid.*, III, 117.

12. Lord [Edward] Hastings of Loughborough[423]
13. Serjeant [Nicholas] Barham[424]

The bill passed on its third reading on 17 May and was returned to the commons.[425] On 20 May the commons appointed a committee of twenty members to study it, including the five privy councillors who then sat in the house (listed first).[426] As can be seen from the list, three-quarters of them were also on the committee of fifty-three which was supposed to look at the *Reformatio* (names asterisked):

1. *Sir Francis Knollys[427]
2. *Sir James Croft[428]
3. *Sir Ralph Sadler[429]
4. *Sir Walter Mildmay[430]
5. *Sir Thomas Smith[431]
6. Lord president [Sir Christopher Wray][432]
7. Sir Nicholas Arnold[433]
8. Sir Owen Hopton[434]
9. *Adrian Stokes[435]
10. *Robert Monson[436]
11. *Robert Bell[437]
12. *Christopher Yelverton[438]
13. Sir Francis Hastings[439]
14. *Henry Knollys, Senior[440]

---

[423](c.1519-72). Raised to the peerage on 19 January 1558. Noted in Bindoff, *House of commons*, II, 315-17.

[424](d.1577). He became a serjeant-at-law on 17 February 1567. See J. H. Baker, *The order of serjeants at law. A chronicle of creations, with related texts and a historical introduction* (London, 1984), pp. 171-2, 498.

[425]*L.J.*, I, 688.

[426]*C.J.*, I, 91.

[427]See above, n. 274.

[428]See above, n. 275.

[429]See above, n. 276.

[430]See above, n. 277.

[431]See above, n. 278.

[432](c.1522-92), member for Ludgershall in the 1571 parliament. Noted in Hasler, *House of commons*, III, 653-4.

[433](c.1509-80), member for Cricklade in the 1571 parliament. Noted in *ibid.*, I, 349-51.

[434](c.1519-95), member for Suffolk in the 1571 parliament. Noted in *ibid.*, II, 336-7.

[435]See above, n. 300.

[436]See above, n. 288.

[437]See above, n. 286.

[438]See above, n. 304.

[439]See above, n. 369.

[440]See above, n. 287.

15. Edward Hastings[441]
16. *William Strickland[442]
17. *George Carleton[443]
18. *William More[444]
19. *Thomas Norton[445]
20. *James Dalton[446]

Apparently all was well because the bill was returned to the lords on 23 May.[447] The lords looked at it on the morning of 24 May, and made further amendments before sending it back to the commons, evidently with a request for a conference to discuss the matter further.[448] Whether that conference ever took place is unknown, but the bill was back in the lords by the following day, where it failed to pass.[449]

The history of the ecclesiastical bills in the 1571 parliament demonstrates quite clearly that the Strickland affair, unsettling though it was at the time, did not seriously interrupt the business at hand, nor did it remove Strickland himself from a position of influence. Furthermore, the evidence shows that people responsible for the *Reformatio* were prominently represented on the committees formed to discuss other important legislation, and we must assume that had they been determined to bring it before parliament there is no way that they could or would have been prevented from doing so.

Foxe's alternative explanation for the failure of the Henrician canons, *viz.* that the distemper of the times made it unadvisable to proceed any farther at that time, is on balance more plausible, though in the nature of the case it cannot be pinned down to specific people or events. We know that the queen had been excommunicated by Pope Pius V (1566-72) on 18 February 1570, and that the 1571 parliament had to consider what response to make to that. In particular, the pope had ordered his loyal followers to try to overthrow Elizabeth, and in the charged atmosphere of the time, who could say whether or not some fanatic might manage to assassinate her and open the succession to the catholic Mary, queen of Scots? The moment demanded a re-affirmation of protestantism, which happened when papal bulls were declared to be invalid[450] and also when the thirty-nine articles were finally ratified and enjoined on the clergy for

---

[441](d. *c.*1603, member for Tregonwy in the 1571 parliament. Noted in *ibid.*, II, 269-70.
[442]See above, n. 255.
[443]See above, n. 302.
[444]See above, n. 292.
[445]See above, n. 260.
[446]See above, n. 305.
[447]*C.J.*, I, 92.
[448]*Ibid.*; *L.J.*, I, 695.
[449]*Ibid.*, I, 697.
[450]13 Elizabeth I, c. 2, 1571 (*S.R.*, IV, 528-31).

subscription,[451] but there was not the same need to accept a document which had proved controversial even in the highly protestant atmosphere of Edward VI's last days.

The debates over the 'alphabetical' bills demonstrate that other issues were higher on the agenda, and the *Reformatio* may have appeared to many as something of a red herring which could only divert attention from more immediately pressing matters. It would certainly have required extensive revision,[452] but that would have taken a long time and would have had to be very carefully considered; it could not have been rushed through in the charged atmosphere of 1571. Another important point, suggested by Dr Freeman, is that enactment of the *Reformatio* would have greatly increased the power of the clerical establishment in the church at a time when popular sentiment was moving the other way. It is perfectly possible that an independent convocation would have been spurred on by the more radical members of the lower house to make the kinds of changes which the 'proto-puritans' in the house of commons wanted to see - in this respect, opinions on church reform cut across traditional clergy-lay divisions. It is even possible that, left to themselves, the clergy would have enacted most, if not all, of the measures proposed in the 'alphabetical' bills, as they did with bill G in the convocation of 1576 (see below).

But however true this may be, the fact remains that the lay members of parliament had grown accustomed to having their say in church affairs, which many of them took just as seriously as any clergyman. They would not easily have given this up, and probably only a concerted drive by the queen and the bishops, acting together, could have deprived them of their voice. But would the queen have allied herself with the bishops on such a key issue against the lay majority in both houses of parliament? When a later king and archbishop of Canterbury tried just that, they were deprived of their heads by a laity which would not be excluded from church government and it is most unlikely that the ever-cautious Elizabeth would ever have painted herself into such a corner.[453] The queen certainly regarded herself as supreme over both church and state, but this meant that just as she did not tolerate parliamentary interference in church affairs if it went against her settlement of religion, so she also treated her bishops

---

[451] 13 Elizabeth I, c. 12, 1571 (*S.R.*, IV, 546-7). The articles had been approved in convocation on 19 February 1563, but article 29 was suspended for fear of offending the Lutherans. Eight years later this objection was overruled, and all thirty-nine of them were once more approved by convocation (3 April 1571) and ratified in the form which they still have today.

[452] Quite apart from legal matters, the entire first title would have had to be rewritten in order to make it conform more closely to the changes which had been made to the articles of religion in 1563.

[453] Archbishop Laud's went first (10 January 1645) to be followed four years later by that of King Charles I (30 January 1649).

as servants, not as equals.[454] She may have been amenable to most of what the *Reformatio* proposed in terms of law and doctrine, especially since much of it was already in force by other means, but she saw no reason (and had no need) to favour the clergy in a way which would have alienated the lay lords and commons. There is no doubt that many of the latter would have smelled 'popery' if the ecclesiastical establishment had been given wide-ranging powers of discipline over the laity, and Elizabeth, who was threatened enough by genuine popery not to need a bogeyman masquerading under the same name, knew when and where to stop. All things considered, therefore, the weight of probability suggests that if there was a single, main reason why the *Reformatio* never got any further, it was the distemper of the times, not the ill-will of the queen or some other highly-placed persons, which was the main culprit.

The aftermath

The 1571 parliament should probably be regarded as a qualified success in terms of ecclesiastical reform, but those who desired change most deeply could only think of the unfinished business which it had left behind. Among this business was the *Reformatio,* but what chance (if any) did it have of being resurrected at this stage? When a new parliament was summoned on 8 May 1572 it was not long before one of the reforming measures which had failed in 1571 reappeared. On 22 May the old bill D was brought back to the lords and it reached a second reading (31 May) before it was finally abandoned.[455] In the commons the potential for trouble over prayer book reform was such that the queen had to order the suspension of all religious bills (also on 22 May) and tell the members not to introduce any which had not previously been approved by the clergy.[456] Apparently some members thought that this was the beginning of a royal retreat from protestantism, and the following day Elizabeth had to reassure them that the reformed faith was safe in her hands.[457] Not everyone was convinced, and in the charged atmosphere of the time two clergymen, John Field (d.1588) and Thomas Wilcox (c.1549-1608), sat down to pen their famous *Admonition to the parliament* which was already circulating when the session ended on 30 June,

---

[454]In this respect the Anglican settlement was (and is) quite different from the Roman imperial model on which it was supposedly based. In the Christian Roman empire the emperor was *isapostolos* ('equal to the apostles') but not superior to them or to their successors. Relations between emperors and popes or patriarchs were by no means always harmonious and the lay authorities often tried to silence the clergy, but this was unconstitutional and on several occasions led to the emperor's ultimate defeat. See G. Dagron, *Empereur et prêtre. Etude sur le 'césaropapisme' byzantin* (Paris, 1995).
[455]*L.J.*, I, 711-15.
[456]*C.J.*, I, 97.
[457]*Ibid.*

leaving the reformers with nothing to show for it.[458] This was followed by a number of tracts, including a *Second admonition* which was written by Thomas Cartwright (1535-1603) in October 1572. This provoked a number of replies from those in authority, most notably from John Whitgift (*c*.1530-1604), who was then master of Trinity College, Cambridge. Finally, on 11 June 1573, the queen stepped in and issued a proclamation ordering the tracts to be destroyed.[459] Parliament was not summoned again until 8 February 1576, but the desire for further church reform had not abated. The bill on coming to church and receiving holy communion returned to the lords on 13 February and was read a second time two days later.[460] It did not get any further, but later on in the session the requirement of attendance at holy communion was dropped and the bill was brought in again, only to fail after its first reading on 3 March.[461] Meanwhile the commons wanted to make additions to 13 Elizabeth I, c. 10, 1571 (the old bill E), and introduced a bill to that effect on 21 February.[462] It was read a second time on 8 March and passed two days later.[463] The lords received it on the same day and read it twice, passing it on 13 March.[464] Meanwhile on 29 February the lower house had addressed a petition to the queen asking her to do more to further the reformation of church discipline.[465] It was signed by the following twenty-two members (those who had been on the committee of fifty-three in the 1571 parliament are asterisked):

1.   *Sir James Croft[466]
2.   *Sir Francis Knollys[467]
3.   *Sir Walter Mildmay[468]
4.   *Sir Ralph Sadler[469]
5.   *Sir Thomas Smith[470]
6.   Francis Walsingham[471]

---

[458]Thomas Cooper, the bishop of London, preached against it at Paul's cross on 27 June. See M. MacLure, *Register of sermons preached at Paul's cross 1534-1642* (rev. edn., Ottawa, 1989), pp. 52-3. The text of the admonition and its sequel is in *Puritan manifestoes*, ed. W. H. Frere and C. E. Douglas (London, 1907).

[459]*Tudor royal proclamations*, ed. P. L. Hughes and J. F. Larkin (3 vols., New Haven, 1964-9), III, 375-6 (no. 597).

[460]*L.J.*, I, 731-2.

[461]*Ibid.*, I, 740.

[462]*C.J.*, I, 108.

[463]*Ibid.*, I, 112-13.

[464]*L.J.*, I, 745-6. It became law as 18 Elizabeth I, c. 11, 1576 (*S.R.*, IV, 622-3).

[465]*C.J.*, I, 109.

[466]See above, n. 275.

[467]See above, n. 274.

[468]See above, n. 277.

[469]See above, n. 276.

[470]See above, n. 278.

[471](*c*.1532-90), member for Surrey in the 1572-81 parliament. Noted in Hasler, *House of commons*, III, 571-4.

7. John Russell[472]
8. *The master of requests [Thomas Seckford][473]
9. Sir Thomas Scott[474]
10. *Sir Henry Gates[475]
11. Sir Henry Wallop[476]
12. The lieutenant of the tower [Sir Owen Hopton][477]
13. *William More[478]
14. Mr Popham[479]
15. *Christopher Yelverton[480]
16. Edward Lewknor[481]
17. *Henry Knollys, Senior[482]
18. John Croke[483]
19. Tristram Pistor[484]
20. *William Fleetwood[485]
21. *Robert Snagge[486]
22. John Audley[487]

Even after five years, the number of signatories who had had some connexion with the *Reformatio* is striking, and they still formed a bare majority of twelve out of the twenty-two. They agreed to confer with the lords and present the petition to the privy council by way of those signatories who were members of that body (the first six on the list). The consultation duly took place and when the petition was presented to the queen on 2 March it bore the names of four peers

---

[472](d.1584), member for Bridport in the 1572-81 parliament and elevated to the lords in 1581. Noted in *ibid.*, III, 308.

[473]See above, n. 283.

[474]See above, n. 384.

[475]See above, n. 282.

[476](c.1531-99), member for Southampton in the 1572-81 parliament. Noted in *ibid.*, III, 567-8.

[477]See above, n. 434.

[478]See above, n. 292.

[479]Either Edward (c.1530-86), member for Bridgwater in the 1572-81 parliament (noted in *ibid.*, III, 233-4) or more likely his brother John (c.1532-1607), member for Bristol in the same parliament (noted in *ibid.*, III, 234-6).

[480]See above, n. 304.

[481](1542-1605), member for New Shoreham in the 1572-81 parliament. Noted in *ibid.*, II, 472-3.

[482]See above, n. 287.

[483](1530-1608), member for Buckinghamshire in the 1572-81 parliament. Noted in *ibid.*, I, 676-7.

[484](c.1520 - c.1582), member for Stockbridge in the 1572-81 parliament. Noted in *ibid.*, III, 224-5.

[485]See above, n. 301.

[486]See above, n. 306.

[487](d.1588), member for West Looe in the 1572-81 parliament. Noted in *ibid.*, I, 365-6.

and three members of the lower house, all of them privy councillors. Their eminence speaks for itself, and five of them (names asterisked) had either been on the committee of fifty-three in 1571 or (as in the case of Lord Burghley) had been closely linked with the *Reformatio* at an earlier stage:

1.   *The lord treasurer [Sir William Cecil, Lord Burghley][488]
2.   The lord steward [Edward Clinton or Fiennes, earl of Lincoln][489]
3.   *The lord chamberlain [Thomas Ratcliffe, earl of Sussex][490]
4.   The earl of Leicester [Robert Dudley][491]
5.   *Mr Treasurer [Sir Francis Knollys][492]
6.   *Mr Comptroller [Sir James Croft][493]
7.   *Mr Chancellor of the exchequer [Sir Walter Mildmay][494]

No more powerful combination of statesmen could have been imagined, and it is remarkable that the representatives of the lower house were able to secure the support of the lords closest to the queen, including even the experienced and normally cautious Burghley. As presented to the queen on 2 March, the petition reads as follows:

To the queen's most excellent majesty, our most sovereign lady:

In most humble wise beseeching your highness, your majesty's most loving, faithful and obedient subjects the commons in this present parliament assembled, that whereas by the lack of the true discipline of the church amongst other abuses a great number of men are admitted to occupy the place of ministers in the Church of England, who are not only altogether unfurnished of such gifts as are by the Word of God necessarily and inseparably required to be incident to their calling, but also are infamous in their lives and conversations. And also many of the ministry whom God has endued with ability to teach are by mean[s] of non-residence, pluralities, and such like dispensations so withdrawn from their flocks that their gifts are almost altogether become unprofitable, whereby an infinite number of your majesty's subjects for want of the preaching of the Word – the only ordinary means of salvation of souls and the only good means to teach your majesty's subjects to know their true obedience to your majesty and to the

---

[488]See above, n. 148.
[489](1512-85).
[490]See above, n. 322.
[491](1532/3-88). The queen's favourite at this time.
[492]See above, n. 274.
[493]See above, n. 275.
[494]See above, n. 277.

magistrates under you, and without the which the Lord God hath pronounced that the people must needs perish[495] – have already run headlong into destruction, and many thousand of the residue yet remain in great peril (if speedy remedy be not provided) daily to fall into the ditch and to die in their sins, to the great danger and charge of those to whom the Lord God hath committed the care of provision for them in this behalf. And by means whereof the common blaspheming of the Lord's name, the most licentiousness of lief, the abuse of excommunication, the great number of atheists, schismatics and heretics daily springing up. And to conclude, the hindrance and increase of obstinate papists, which ever since your majesty's sworn enemy the pope did by his bulls pronounce definitive sentence against your highness' person and proceedings, have given evident testimony of their corrupt affection to him and of their wilful disobedience to your majesty in that they forbear to participate with your majesty's faithful subjects in prayer and administration of sacraments, wherein they most manifestly declare that they carry very unsound and undutiful hearts unto your majesty.

In consideration therefore of the premisses, having regard first and principally to the advancement of the glory of God, next to the long and most blessed continuance of your majesty's reign and safety (which we most instantly beseech Almighty God long to preserve), then to the discharge of our most bounden obedience, which in all duty and reverence we bear unto your majesty, besides being moved to pitiful consideration of the most lamentable estate of so many thousands of your majesty's subjects daily in danger to be lost for want of the food of the Word and true discipline, and lastly respecting the peace of our consciences and the salvation of our souls, being at this present assembled by your majesty's authority to open the griefs and to seek the salving of the sores of our country; and this before remembered, beyond measure exceeding in greatness all the residue which can be disclosed in your majesty's commonwealth: we are most humbly to beseech your highness, seeing the same is of so great importance, if the parliament at this present may not be so long continued as that, by good and godly laws established in the same, provision may be made for supply and reformation of these great wants and grievous abuses, that yet by such other good means as to your majesty's most godly wisdom shall seem best, a perfect redress may be had of the same; which doing you shall do such acceptable service to the Lord God which cannot but procure at his hands the sure establishment of your seat and sceptre, and the number of your majesty's most faithful subjects (the bond of conscience being of all other most straightest) by mean of preaching and discipline be so multiplied and the great swarms of malefactors,

[495] Am. viii. 11.

schismatics, atheists, anabaptists and papists, your most dangerous enemies, so weakened and diminished, that by the help and assistance of Almighty God, if all popish treasons and traitorous practices should conspire together in one against your majesty, they should not be able to shake the state. And we your majesty's most loving and obedient subjects together with the remembrance of those inestimable and innumerable benefits by which your majesty's means the Lord God hath already blessed us withal, far beyond any other of our neighbours round about us, shall not only be more and more stirred up to dutiful thankfulness unto your majesty and continual and earnest prayer unto Almighty God (which we will nevertheless) for the long and prosperous continuance of your majesty's reign, but also both we are the residue of your majesty's most faithful subjects and our posterities shall be most bounden to continue in that obedient duty which we owe to your most royal majesty. And to conclude, your majesty shall be recommended to all posterities for such a pattern to be followed, that nothing may seem to be added to the perfection of your renown.[496]

Some of the reforms proposed in this petition may have been inspired by titles in the *Reformatio* (e.g. R, 7 on preachers), but there was no suggestion that the text should be adopted as it stood. The petitioners received a reply from Elizabeth on 9 March. As the *Journal of the house of commons* records it:

Mr Chancellor of the exchequer [Sir Walter Mildmay], touching the petition for reformation of discipline in the church, doth bring word from the lords, that their lordships having moved the queen's majesty touching the said petition, her highness answered their lordships, that her majesty, before the parliament, had a care to provide, in that case, of her own disposition, and at the beginning of this session her highness had conference therein with some of the bishops, and gave them in charge to see due reformation thereof, wherein, as her majesty thinketh, they will have good consideration, according unto her pleasure, and express commandment, in that behalf, so did her highness most graciously and honourably declare further, that, if the said bishops should neglect or omit their duties therein, then her majesty, by her supreme power and authority over the Church of England, would speedily see such good redress therein, as might satisfy the expectation of her loving subjects, to their good contentation, which message and report was most thankfully and joyfully received by the whole house with one accord.[497]

---

[496]British Library Additional MS 33271, fos. 13v-14 (spelling modernized). The text in the original spelling is printed in Hartley, *Proceedings*, I, 445-7.
[497]*C.J.*, I, 113. For an alternative version of this speech, see Hartley, *Proceedings*, I, 447.

Thus it was up to the convocation of Canterbury to enact the desired reforms, and it did so by passing fifteen canons, most of them dealing with clerical discipline, and one with the commutation of penance – in effect an implementation of the old bill G of 1571.[498] However, two of the canons, one on private baptism and the other on times allowed for marriage, went beyond the demands of the petition and were struck out by the queen, perhaps for that reason. It was a meagre harvest after so much labour and fell a long way short of what the passage of the *Reformatio* might have accomplished. But it seems to be what the potential supporters of that text believed was politically possible in 1576 and if so, it shows that any serious attempt to turn Cranmer's book of discipline into law had come to an end. One day there would be other (and much more radical) attempts at reform, but by then the *Reformatio* would be little more than a historical curiosity to those few who were aware of its existence and irrelevant to the needs and desires of a later age.

But if it is true that Foxe's text disappeared after 1571, it was not entirely forgotten.[499] As we have already mentioned, it was republished in 1640 when the canon law was once more a matter of dispute, and the appearance of a third edition in 1641[500] suggests that it was in some demand. At that time, the *Reformatio* might reasonably have been taken to represent 'puritan conformity', i.e. a strict church discipline within the traditional establishment, and in the early 1640s adoption of it must have seemed to some to offer a reasonable solution to the political and religious crisis of the time.

This did not happen of course, and the *Reformatio* disappeared again, this time for good. The restored church of 1660 was in no mood to consider it as a possible way forward, nor did it resurface in the more accommodating atmosphere of 1689, when a serious attempt was made to modify the restoration settlement in a way which would comprehend as many nonconformists as possible. Given that the *Reformatio* had little of the latitudinarian spirit which dominated those attempts at reconciliation, we should not be surprised at this –

---

[498] 1575/12(13). See *A.C.*, pp. 211-15 for these canons. They are remarkable in being the first canons to have been drafted in English. Those of 1571 had been translated from Latin almost immediately, but there is no Latin version of the 1575 (1576) canons extant. English was also used in the drafting of the 1584 and 1603 (1604) canons, though the Latin translations were the official texts. Since 1604 English has been used exclusively, except for the period 1921-48, when Latin translations were once again provided. In the convocations it seems that English was the language of debate from at least 1558, though it did not become the language of record until 25 March 1733.

[499] There are occasional references to it, as for example in the convocation of 1580, where it was stated that the *Reformatio* preferred 'imprisonment and mulct pecuniary' to excommunication. See E. Cardwell, *Synodalia. A collection of articles of religion, canons and proceedings of convocations in the province of Canterbury, from the year 1547 to the year 1717* (2 vols., Oxford, 1842), II, 550-1.

[500] The corrections made in 1641 mainly concern punctuation, which was improved, though a number of verbs were put in the subjunctive as well. They are not noted in this edition, since they were purely stylistic embellishments which make no difference to the meaning of the text.

its strict discipline could never have been adapted to the needs of religious comprehension as this was understood in the late seventeenth century. Its subsequent influence on English ecclesiastical law, which was to be considerable, owed much to the efforts of someone who was of quite a different theological stamp, and it is to that extraordinary history that we must now turn.

Gibson's *Codex*

The man who did more than anyone else to rescue the *Reformatio* from oblivion was Edmund Gibson (1669-1748), bishop of Lincoln from 1716 and of London from 1723, and author of the famous *Codex iuris ecclesiastici Anglicani* (1713), which rapidly established itself as the *vademecum* of ecclesiastical lawyers.[501] While he was vicar of Lambeth (1704-10), Gibson collected all the material which made up the ecclesiastical law of England (including historical statutes and canons which had been superseded), and arranged it in a systematic order. He then added his own commentary, which became the standard interpretation of the texts, in which he drew on the *Corpus iuris canonici*, the *Corpus iuris civilis*, the *Provinciale* of William Lyndwood and the *Reformatio legum ecclesiasticarum*. His motive for including the last of these is stated quite explicitly in the preface:

> The citations of ancient and modern councils and synods which have been held at home and abroad (as they are annexed here by way of commentary to our present laws) are designed to show, on one hand, that though many of the laws are modern, the constitution is ancient; and on the other hand to facilitate the improvement of this constitution by suggesting such useful rules of order and discipline as have been established abroad or attempted at home. With which last view it is that many of the passages out of the body of ecclesiastical laws entitled *Reformatio legum etc.* are grafted into this commentary as candidates for a place in our constitution in case the convocation shall think them deserving, or at least as not unworthy the consideration of that learned and venerable assembly.[502]

Gibson's hope was not to be realized, because only four years after his *Codex* appeared, business transactions in convocation were suspended, not to be resumed on a regular basis until 1852. But that was not to make much difference, because Gibson quoted from the *Reformatio* in such a way as to grant it surrogate authority, regardless of what any legislative body might have said about it.

---

[501]For a recent assessment of Gibson, see J. H. Baker, 'Famous English canon lawyers VIII: Edmund Gibson and David Wilkins', *Ecclesiastical Law Journal*, III (1995), 371-8; idem., *Monuments*, pp. 95-107.
[502]G, xiv.

Gibson was well aware of the history of the text, and included a full account of it in the *Codex*. But although he knew that the *Reformatio* had no official status, the way in which he handled it tells a rather different story. For instance, he not infrequently quoted it as a handy summary of earlier, more complex legislation, thereby granting it practical authority as a work of reference without pronouncing on its legal status. A good example of this technique can be found in what he had to say about the royal supremacy, where he quoted R, 37.2 as a useful statement of how that was viewed in the time of King Edward VI.[503] He did the same with many other matters, including the absolution of those who have laid violent hands on a clergyman,[504] the alienation of ecclesiastical property,[505] simony,[506] the office of rural deans,[507] the procedure for appeals,[508] the commutation of penance[509] and excommunication.[510] In each of these instances Gibson claimed no more than that *the Reformatio* was summarizing and repeating earlier legislation, but the fact that he preferred to quote it rather than the legally correct sources shows that he accepted it as an authoritative summary of those canons and statutes.

Once the *Reformatio*'s usefulness in this respect was established, it was but a short step to regarding it as proof of sixteenth-century practice, whether there was any other evidence to support that claim or not. Gibson was not averse to doing this, particularly when its rules looked eminently desirable. A good example of his method can be found in what he had to say about the resignation of a clergyman from his benefice. Traditionally, this could be done by proxy, but Gibson did not think that that was a good idea, and neither did the *Reformatio,* which insisted than a man should resign his benefice in person. So Gibson simply overrode Lyndwood's testimony, as well as the evidence of traditional writs (both of which he mentioned), and stated categorically that resignation must be made in person, citing the *Reformatio* as his only source for this.[511] He dealt in a similar way with the penalties to be inflicted on those who ignored orders of suspension, even going so far as to pronounce that lay people could be excommunicated, once again solely on the basis of the *Reformatio*'s testimony.[512] He did the same again when he claimed that the church had the right to proceed in a spiritual way against criminals, after they had been sentenced in the temporal courts,[513] and also when he rejected leniency in the commutation of penance.[514]

---

[503]G, II, 3 (p. 63).
[504]G, I, 4 (pp. 10-11), quoting R, 48.1-2.
[505]G, XXX, 1 (p. 688), quoting R, 16.1.
[506]G, XXXIV, 4 (pp. 840-1), quoting R, 11.24.
[507]G, XLII, 8 (pp. 1011-12), quoting R, 20.5.
[508]G, XLV, 6 (p. 1080), quoting R, 28.11.
[509]G, XLVI, 3 (p. 1092), quoting R, 28.11.
[510]G, XLVI, 4 (p. 1095), quoting R, 32.3-4.
[511]G, XXXIV, 11 (p. 869), quoting R, 12.5.
[512]G, XLVI, 3 (p. 1093), alluding to R, 29.5.
[513]G, XLV, 5 (p. 1078), quoting R, 32.16.
[514]G, XLVI, 4 (p. 1095), quoting R, 32.4.

The fact that these matters, particularly the ones involving the laity, were extremely sensitive at that time makes his audacity all the more remarkable.

On the other hand, it is true that Gibson recognized that the *Reformatio* has a prescriptive side which was never realized in practice, and he occasionally mentioned this, as when he suggested that coadjutors should be appointed to assist incapacitated bishops,[515] that bishops should attend the examination of future incumbents in person,[516] that parental consent for underage marriages should be compulsory[517] and that Sunday schools should be formed for instructing the young.[518] On these matters it was impossible to pretend that things had once been different, nor could Gibson simply lay down the law.[519] But there is one instance in which Gibson mentioned an actual court case in which he believed that the decision had been made on the basis of rules laid down in the *Reformatio*. It concerned the question of whether illegitimate relations counted in the table of kindred and affinity, and Gibson commented that there are two rules in the *Reformatio* which help us to understand what these are. He then went on to quote a case where a man was charged for marrying his sister's bastard daughter, in which he claimed that the principles of the *Reformatio* were actually applied.[520]

The *Reformatio rediviva*

Of course, Gibson's attempt to rescue the *Reformatio legum* from oblivion did not change the law, and the practice of the ecclesiastical courts carried on as it always had. The titles dealing with matrimonial causes would have been of particular interest to a generation which was having to deal with the scandalous increase in clandestine marriages, but Gibson was good enough a historian to recognize that the line taken by the *Reformatio,* on divorce in particular, had never been the law and could not simply be introduced by what amounted to stealth. It needed an issue where the existing law was unclear, but where the *Reformatio* offered an answer, to test whether it could be applied and thus acquire some kind of authority. Such a case arose in 1792, when the Rev. John

---

[515]G, V, 3 (p. 158), quoting R, 20.16.
[516]G, XXXIV, 5 (p. 850), quoting R, 11.7.
[517]G, XXII, 3 (p. 507), quoting R, 8.4.
[518]G, XIX, 1 (p. 453), quoting R, 19.9.
[519]For example, he mentions that parliament had tried unsuccessfully to make parental consent for the marriage of minors obligatory, once in 1541 and again in 1689. See G, XXII, 3 (p. 507).
[520]G, XXII, 1 (p. 499), quoting R, 9.6. The case is *Haynes v. Jescott, Modern Reports*, V, 168-70. It was heard in January 1696. Unfortunately the published report does not confirm Gibson's citation of it. The case certainly made use of the Levitical laws, which are found in the *Reformatio*, but there is no indication that the *Reformatio* was the source appealed to. On the other hand, Gibson may have had personal knowledge of details of the case which have not been recorded elsewhere.

Hutchins, vicar of St Botolph, Aldersgate, brought charges against one of his churchwardens because the latter had tried to prevent the use of chanting in the church, which he had authorized. In giving his judgment in the London consistory court, Sir William Scott (1745-1836)[521] had to say:

If then, chanting was unlawful anywhere but in cathedrals and colleges these canons[522] are strangely worded and are of disputable meaning. But in order to show that they are not liable to such imputation, I shall justify my interpretation of them by a quotation from the *Reformatio legum* - a work of great authority in determining the practice of those times, whatever may be its correctness in matters of law. With respect to parish churches in cities, it is there observed: '*eadem parochiarum in urbibus constitutarum erit omnis ratio, festis et dominicis diebus, quae prius collegiis et cathedalibus ecclesiis (ut vocant) attributa fuit*'.[523]

What stands out in the above remark is Scott's estimation of the *Reformatio* as 'a work of great authority in determining the practice of those times'. He did not form that impression solely from Gibson, who, although he probably believed it, was far too careful to say so. More probably, Scott was dependent on another legal authority, William Salkeld (1671-1715), who had been a serjeant in the court of king's bench from 1689 to 1711. In his well-known and widely used case notes, Salkeld claimed the following:

Divorce for adultery was anciently *a vinculo matrimonii* and therefore in the beginning of the reign of Queen Elizabeth, the opinion of the Church of England was that after a divorce for adultery the parties might marry again. But in Fuljambe's case, *anno* 44 Elizabeth, in the star chamber, that opinion was changed. And Archbishop [*sic*] Bancroft, upon the advice of divines, held that adultery was only a cause of divorce *a mensa et thoro*.[524]

---

[521]He was a judge in the consistory court of London from 1788-1821, when he was created the first Baron Stowell and resigned his appointment. On Scott in general, see H. J. Bourguignon, *Sir William Scott, Lord Stowell. Judge of the high court of admiralty* (Cambridge, 1987).

[522]Scott means the injunctions of 1559, of which the forty-ninth is in dispute here. For the text, see *D.E.R.*, pp. 344-5.

[523]*Hutchins* v. *Denziloe*, 1 Haggard Consistory 179 (*English Reports*, CLXI, 518), quoting R, 19.6, which says: 'The same pattern will apply in urban parishes, on feasts and Sundays, which formerly applied to colleges and cathedral churches (as they are called).' The date was 9 February 1792.

[524]3 Salkeld 138 (*English Reports*, XCI, 738). For a discussion of the case *Rye* v. *Fuljambe* and Salkeld's error concerning it, see the memorandum of Sir Lewis Dibdin presented to the royal commission on divorce and matrimonial causes on 1 November 1910 and contained in its report, vol. III, 53-4 (see below for further details). Bancroft was

Salkeld did not mention the *Reformatio* by name, but it is hard to see what other source he could have had in mind, and later generations assumed that he was referring to it. But if Scott was prepared to use the *Reformatio* in that way, he was more careful than Salkeld not to trespass into areas where such statements might be challenged. In the landmark case of *Dalrymple* v. *Dalrymple*, for example, Scott pointed out that after the reformation matrimony was no longer regarded as a sacrament by the protestant churches, but despite the golden opportunity which this provided for quoting the *Reformatio*, or even just Salkeld's judgment, he did not do so.[525]

This point must be borne in mind because of what happened next. In the first edition of his *Ecclesiastical law*, Richard Burn quoted Gibson to the effect that parliament had occasionally allowed divorces *a vinculo* in accordance with the famous 'Matthaean exception' of Jesus, as prescribed by the *Reformatio*.[526] But in the ninth edition of the same work, thoroughly revised and updated by Sir Robert Phillimore,[527] this information was supplemented by an extensive quotation from the *History of England* which had been published in 1830 by Sir James Mackintosh (1765-1832). There Mackintosh stated:

> The articles on marriage (in the *Reformatio*) relate to questions ... [which] affect the civil rights of all men, as well as the highest of all the moral interests of society. The book, not having received the royal confirmation, is not indeed law, but it is of great authority, and conveys the opinions of our first reformers on problems which the law of England has not yet solved.[528]

That Mackintosh's view was not an isolated one can be confirmed by the testimony given to a select committee of the house of lords on 18 March 1844 by Sir John Stoddart (1773-1856), who made the following remarks about the indissolubility of late Tudor marriages:

> The *Reformatio legum* had expressly broken in upon the principle, and would have been, in all probability, if King Edward VI had lived, the law of England. But although it was not the law of the land, it was the recognized opinion and sentiment of the English church, as I apprehend, at that time, because the *Reformatio legum* was drawn up by a subcommittee of eight persons out of the thirty-two nominated

---

still bishop of London in 1602.

[525]2 Haggard Consistory 67-8 (*English Reports*, CXLI, 670), 16 July 1811.

[526]The Matthaean exception is in Mt. xix. 9. R. Burn, *Ecclesiastical law* (2 vols., London, 1763), II, 40-1, referring to G, XXII, 17 (p. 536) and R, 10.5, 17. Gibson's chief evidence was the famous 'Parr case', in which the marquess of Northampton, Lord Parr, remarried after divorcing his first wife for adultery. The marriage was declared lawful by a private act of parliament in 5-6 Edward VI (1552).

[527]4 vols., London, 1842.

[528]As quoted in *ibid.*, II, 503a.

according to the directions of the act of parliament, and at the head of those was Archbishop Cranmer; and therefore I apprehend that the *Reformatio legum*, having been published as a work of authority, although not of absolute legislative authority, it must have been, and in all probability was, followed, and that for that reason in the spiritual courts there were dissolutions of marriage, because I believe that from about the year 1550 to the year 1602 marriage was not held by the church, and therefore not held by the law, to be indissoluble. But in 1602 Archbishop [*sic*] Bancroft summoned together an assembly of divines, who were of opinion that marriage was indissoluble, though not upon the ground of its being a sacrament, but of its having, as Lord Stowell once described it, something sacramental in its nature. They held upon what I suppose to be sufficient authority of Scripture, that it was indissoluble, and then I apprehend that, in the same manner as Archbishop Cranmer's doctrine was followed down to 1602, the opinion of Archbishop [*sic*] Bancroft and the divines of that time has been followed to the present day in the spiritual courts.

Stoddart's historical reconstruction was demonstrably inaccurate, since it must have been clear to everyone that divorces *a vinculo* would not have been granted under Mary I (1553-8). He also repeated Salkeld's error regarding Archbishop Bancroft, who in 1602 was still bishop of London and lacked the authority which Stoddart attributed to him. But in spite of these obvious blemishes, nobody called Stoddart's opinion into question, and it was quoted as an authority both in the report of the divorce commission of 1853[529] and in the report of the royal commission on divorce and matrimonial causes in 1912.[530] In fairness, neither Salkeld nor Stoddart claimed that divorce *a vinculo* was a written law in the sixteenth century. Their point was that it was then the generally held opinion of most leading divines, and that the church courts followed their theology, which meant that divorce *a vinculo* was valid even without being formally legislated. They were wrong to suppose this, but their authority carried all before it and issued in the matrimonial causes act which received the royal assent on 25 August 1857.[531] It was the *Reformatio*'s greatest triumph, because thanks to it, the reformers of 1857 could maintain that in providing (once more,

---

[529] *First report of the commissioners appointed by her majesty to enquire into the law of divorce, and more particularly into the mode of obtaining divorces* a vinculo matrimonii (London, 1853), p. 5. The commission was appointed on 10 December 1850, but in its report it incorporated material from the house of lords' hearings in 1844.
[530] *Report of the royal commission on divorce and matrimonial causes* (London, 1912), appendix I, p. 18. The commission was appointed on 10 November 1909 and again (following the death of King Edward VII) on 21 June 1910. It submitted its report on 2 November 1912.
[531] 20-1 Victoria, c. 75.

in their view) for divorce *a vinculo,* they were merely fulfilling the wishes of the great reformers of the Church of England, which had unfortunately been frustrated by Richard Bancroft in 1602.

The second death of the *Reformatio*

But as often happens, it was at the moment of victory that the seeds of doubt and eventual destruction were sown. When Edward Cardwell's edition appeared in 1850, the *Reformatio* became readily available for the first time in over two hundred years. Cardwell wrote a preface to the work, making it quite clear that it had never received the royal assent, and claiming that Queen Elizabeth I was quite antipathetic to it. Cardwell's interpretation was somewhat exaggerated and inaccurate in places, but on the main point it was correct and was noted as such by John Keble in his pamphlet objecting to the law of 1857.[532] Keble quoted extracts from the *Reformatio* and claimed that they tallied with what Martin Bucer had written in *De regno Christi.* This was subsequently picked up by Oscar Watkins (1848-1926), whose book on the subject was referred to by the divorce commission in 1912. Watkins wrote:

> The important collection of proposed canons known as the *Reformatio legum ecclesiasticarum,* by which it was intended to replace the ancient canon law of England, was exceedingly lax on the subject of divorce. Not only adultery, but desertion, continued absence, murderous enmity in the case of either party and also cruelty in the case of the husband, was held to justify divorce *a* vinculo, and to leave the parties free to marry again. Happily for England, the *Reformatio* never became law and is therefore only a historical curiosity.[533]

No one, not even Keble, had been quite as rude about the *Reformatio* before, but although Watkins' views were often distorted by his anti-protestant theological bias, he was correct to say that the *Reformatio* had never become law. When the issue surfaced again in the divorce commission of 1910-12, the church's big guns were ready for the attack. Sir Lewis Dibdin (1852-1938), dean of the arches from 1903 to 1934 and a leading evangelical, prepared a

---

[532]Keble, *Sequel,* pp. 201-4. Keble quotes R, 10.5, 8-11.
[533]O. D. Watkins, *Holy matrimony. A treatise on the divine laws of marriage* (London, 1895), p. 426. He reproduces Keble's quotes from the *Reformatio* on p. 401.

memorandum which he read out before the commission at its hearing on 1 November 1910 and which he subsequently expanded for publication.[534] In this he stated:

> The conclusion seems to me to be inevitable that the *Reformatio legum* as we have it, so far as the section on divorce is concerned, is merely a literary relic representing the views derived from continental sources of certain individual churchmen of great eminence and influence. These views were no doubt also adopted by the rank and file of a section of extreme protestants in this country, but except during a few years of Edward VI's reign, were never dominant in the Church of England. On the other hand, the opinion that adultery was on biblical grounds a valid reason for the complete dissolution of marriage seems to have been widely, I should even say generally, held by English divines in the latter half of the sixteenth century.[535]

Sir Lewis backed up his opinion with a wealth of evidence never seen before (or since) on the matter, and it was impossible for the commission to ignore it, despite a feeble attempt to retain Stoddart's view as a viable alternative. But although Sir Lewis Dibdin could and did uphold the indissolubility of late Tudor marriage and discredit the *Reformatio* as evidence to the contrary, he could not ensure that a recognizably Christian doctrine of marriage would continue to be the law of the land. As the understanding of marriage and the grounds for divorce relied less and less on religious principles, the *Reformatio* ceased to be of any practical relevance. It had served a purpose in the run-up to 1857, because then it had allowed divorce reformers to remain within the umbrella of Christian teaching, even if that teaching had not previously been adopted by the ecclesiastical courts. But by 1910 those courts had long ceased to have any say in the matter. Divorce on many grounds was on the way, regardless of what any divines, living or dead, might think about it. Within a generation it would be widespread, not only among the laity but among the clergy as well. The unofficial canons of 1553 had served their purpose, and when both church and society moved on to a new and unprecedented departure from traditional Christian standards of morality and behaviour, they were no longer needed. As 'law', the *Reformatio* was dead, and had at last become what Oscar Watkins insisted it had been all along – just a historical curiosity.

---

[534]The memorandum is in the minutes of evidence of the commission's *Report*, III, 42-58 and the resulting book is L. Dibdin, *English church law and divorce. Part I: Notes on the Reformatio legum ecclesiasticarum* (London, 1912). On Dibdin's career generally, see E. S. S. Sunderland, *Dibdin and the English establishment* (Bishop Auckland, 1995).
[535]Divorce commission *Report*, appendix I, p. 18, taken from the minutes of evidence, III, p. 52.

Modern critical study of the *Reformatio*

As we have already observed, modern critical study of the *Reformatio* began with Edward Cardwell's edition in 1850. Cardwell took F as his principal text (being the one closest to the missing C), and used both the two seventeenth-century reprints and MS Harleian 426 only when these helped him to correct apparent errors in it. His instinct was basically sound, but it is clear that he did not fully understand the relationship between the MS and F. He believed that there had been a much longer and more extensive period of revision than was in fact the case, and thought that C was as much the work of Archbishop Parker in the 1560s as it was of Archbishop Cranmer in the 1550s. Cardwell made no attempt to trace the sources of the *Reformatio,* nor did he translate the text. He knew nothing of the Henrician canons of course, nor was he aware of the English-language fragment in the Inner Temple. Furthermore, his introduction barely discusses the relationship between the *Reformatio* and the church of the reformation, and cannot be regarded as making a serious contribution to our knowledge of that subject. Because he focussed on F, and believed that C was a product of the 1560s, he gave more attention to the early Elizabethan period, which is irrelevant to the contents of the *Reformatio*, than he did to the late Edwardian years, which is where the document really belongs. For all these reasons therefore, Cardwell's text, though worthy enough in itself, is inadequate for the needs of modern study.

The next person to embark on a detailed study of the *Reformatio* was Leslie Raymond Sachs (b. 1955), who wrote a doctoral dissertation on it which he defended in 1982.[536] Sachs used Cardwell's text as his only source, and did not consult any manuscripts, even though he was aware of the existence of both MS Harleian 426 and the Henrician canons of 1535.[537] In his dissertation he included a lot of background material, situating the *Reformatio* within the wider context of canon law reform from 1535 to 1603 (1604). His was the first (and to date remains the only) attempt to analyse the contents of the text, and to give some indication of what its sources were. In the course of his study Sachs also translated some of the canons, which had never been done before. Generally speaking, his work is stronger on contemporary reformed texts like the articles of religion and Martin Bucer's De *regno Christi,* than it is on the medieval background, which he did not study systematically. His dissertation is more of a survey of the *Reformatio* than an in-depth study of the legal and theological problems which it raises, but in what he covers Sachs is generally accurate, and his judgment is sound. In particular, he did a good job of refuting Cardwell's

---

[536]He was then a member of the Reformed Church in America, although he submitted his dissertation to the canon law faculty of the Catholic University of America in Washington, D. C. (See n. 190 above.) Since 1984 he has been a freelance writer and in 1997 he set up Pussycat Press in Richmond, VA. His books include *How to buy your new car for a rock-bottom price* (New York, 1987) and *The Virginia ghost murders* (Richmond, VA, 1998).
[537]However, it does not seem that he knew about the fragmentary English translation.

views of the *rôle* played by Archbishop Parker, and of situating the *Reformatio* where it belongs – in 1553. Sachs' greatest weakness is his relative ignorance of the Church of England, which allowed him to regard the *Reformatio* as a blueprint for 'the church that never was',[538] when in fact much of it is descriptive of conditions as they actually were (and in some cases still are).

The third person who has made a sizeable contribution to the modern study of the *Reformatio* is James C. Spalding (1921-96),[539] who published a translation of MS Harleian 426 in 1992.[540] Spalding's work challenged that of both Cardwell and Sachs. Unlike Cardwell, he regarded the MS as the most important text, and treated F as a later and less authentic form of it. In Spalding's opinion, it was MS Harleian 426 which Cranmer presented to the house of lords in 1553, and virtually all subsequent modifications can be attributed to Archbishop Parker's supposed revision. He was therefore deeply opposed to the view of Sachs, which he criticized at some length in his introduction.

Spalding's thesis has the merit of focussing our attention on the draft MS, which has not received the attention it deserves. But his interpretation of what happened between the compilation of that draft and the publication of F is wrong to the point of perversity, and this unfortunately diminishes the value of his insights regarding the MS itself. Another difficulty is that Spalding used a microfilm version of the MS, with the result that he misread a number of words in it and produced wrong translations.[541] Considering that not only could he have consulted the MS without difficulty, but that most of the MS readings can be found in an appendix to Cardwell's edition, this is inexcusable. Even when he had the correct text though, his translations are often faulty because of his unfamiliarity with the subject matter, a defect which is particularly apparent in the titles dealing with ecclesiastical court procedure.[542] He also betrays no knowledge of the Henrician canons of 1535, in spite of the fact that they had been known for eighteen years and had been mentioned by Sachs, whose work he used extensively.[543] This unfortunately makes large sections of his introduction worthless, because the evidence for the 1535 canons (of which he *was* aware) has inevitably been misinterpreted. Finally, by producing a translation without the original text, and then attempting to indicate where the

---

[538]The title of his chapter four; see Sachs, 'Thomas Cranmer's *Reformatio*', pp. 136-77.
[539]He taught at the University of Iowa until his retirement in 1992.
[540]*The reformation of the ecclesiastical laws of England, 1552*, ed. J. C. Spalding (Sixteenth Century Essays and Studies, XIX, Kirksville, MO, 1992).
[541]For example, in R, 33.1 he read 'cena' ('coena') instead of 'ceno' ('caeno'), with the result that he has sinners wallowing in the *banquet* of their sins, instead of the more usual *mire*.
[542]For example, in R, 49.13, his failure to understand the context allows him to interpret 'presumption from habit (*habitus*)' as: 'Anyone is presumed to be of such a kind as he is habitually found to be', rather than the correct: 'A man is presumed to be of the rank (order) indicated by his clothing.'
[543]Spalding also appears to have had no knowledge of the fragmentary English translation, which is a great pity, considering what he was trying to do.

folio page divisions are located, as well as what words were added, deleted, or modified by Cranmer or Vermigli – both things which can only be done properly by referring to the Latin – he leaves his readers wondering what the original actually says.[544] In sum, although Spalding raised some interesting and important questions, he almost invariably gave the wrong answers, and produced a translation which is too inaccurate and misleading to be of any real value.

The sad fact is that the *Reformatio* has not been well served by modern scholarship, and it is one of the chief aims of this edition to make it available to scholars in a form which is both accurate and informative. MS Harleian 426 and F are given equal importance, with all variants being recorded in their proper place. The evidence of the 1640 reprint, though secondary, is also provided in order to show how far it was possible to correct Foxe's typographical errors merely by guesswork. In addition, connexions with other canonical material are explored with the aim of pointing out what sources may have been consulted in the composition of the text. In many cases this does not amount to proof that these were indeed the sources used, but at least we can say with complete assurance that the canons in question were not invented by protestant reformers in an attempt to replace corrupt medieval laws. On the contrary, the more we look at the *Reformatio*, the more we realize how deeply traditional it is, particularly in its more legal sections. It cannot be regarded without qualification as a reliable statement of sixteenth-century ecclesiastical law, but neither is it an oddity which is of no real value for understanding what that law was. As so often in such matters, the truth lies somewhere in the middle, and one of the main purposes of this edition is to make it easier for scholars to find it.

3. The church order of the *Reformatio*

Introduction

The *Reformatio legum ecclesiasticarum* in its final form (C or F) can be analyzed into different thematic sections, along the following lines:

I. The doctrine, organization and discipline of the church (1-33)

A. The doctrine of God **(1-4)**
    - affirmative   (1)
    - negative   (2-4)

---

[544]On top of everything else, he generally attributes Haddon's alterations to Cranmer, presumably because he could not distinguish the two men's handwriting in the microfilm copy.

B. The sacraments   **(5-10)**
- affirmative   (5)
- negative   (6)
- ministry   (7)
- matrimony   (8-10)

C. Benefices   **(11-13; 15-18)**
D. Worship   **(19)**
E. Ministry   **(20-7)**
- in the parish   (20-2)
- in education   (23-4)
- legal aspects of   (25-7)

F. Discipline   **(14; 28-33)**
- general   (28)
- of the innocent   (14)
- of the guilty   (29-33)

II. Ecclesiastical courts and their procedure (34-55)

G. Courts and their procedure   **(34-47; 49; 51-4)**
- preliminary definitions   (34-6)
- judges   (37)
- trials and evidence   (38-45)
- points of procedure   (46-7; 49)
- delays and exceptions   (51-2)
- sentences and appeals   (53-4)

H. Crimes   **(48; 50)**
J. The rules of law   **(55)**

R, 14, which deals with purgation, is clearly out of place among the titles dealing with benefices, and ought to have been put after R, 28 with the section on discipline. It was probably composed by the same people who put the disciplinary titles together, and at the same time, but the compiler separated them and put R, 14 in the wrong place. R, 48, which deals with violence against clergy, was moved to its present position by Archbishop Cranmer, having originally come between what are now R, 10 (adultery and divorce) and R, 11 (on admission to benefices). Cranmer probably did this because the title deals with a crime, but it sits awkwardly between prescriptions and presumptions. In the old canon law the subject was dealt with in the title on excommunication,[545] but it might have been politically difficult to have put it there in the mid-sixteenth century, when feelings ran high both about excommunication and the nature of

[545]X, 5.39.

clerical privilege.[546] Finally, R, 50 on defamations was originally added to MS Harleian 426 after the MS had been put together, and it seems to have been thrown in here more or less arbitrarily by whoever created C. But as long as we allow for a few loose ends like these, it can be said that on the whole, the *Reformatio* presents a coherent and systematic picture of the church and its disciplinary structure. In this section, we shall look briefly at each of the above categories in turn.

A. The doctrine of God (1-4)

The opening titles of the *Reformatio* were put there deliberately, as we can see from R, 1.1, which argues that it is necessary to understand the Christian doctrine of God before going on to other matters, since all of them ultimately derive from that. The doctrine expressed in these titles is based on the following sources:

> 1. Holy Scripture
> 2. The three creeds
> 3. The first four ecumenical councils
> 4. Other church councils
> 5. The teaching of the church fathers

This scheme is hierarchical. Scripture is the sole ultimate authority for Christian doctrine, and anything which goes against its teaching must be rejected, even if it has been approved by church authorities in the past. But the *Reformatio* does not insist that Scripture's authority is exclusive, in the way that the puritans were later to do. Practices which are consonant with biblical teaching may be retained in the church, even if they are not specifically sanctioned by any particular text.[547] The three creeds are regarded as reliable interpretations of Scripture, and are to be accepted as such, so that to deny one of their articles is to deny the authority of the Bible itself. Similarly, the acts and decrees of the first four ecumenical councils are also deemed to be in accordance with the teaching of Scripture, and must be accepted on the same basis as the three creeds. Beyond that, other church councils and the witness of the church fathers are acceptable in so far as they are in accordance with the three chief authorities. This allowed the reformed Church of England to claim the essence of the medieval doctrinal heritage of the western church, while at the same time making it possible for it to reject unwelcome accretions, like compulsory clerical celibacy and transubstantiation. The trouble is that it also opened up a grey area in which

---

[546]It is hard to see where it really belongs, though perhaps it could be placed immediately after R, 37.

[547]This view was perhaps most cogently expressed in the preface to the 1549 book of common prayer, which is reprinted in the 1662 version under the heading 'Of ceremonies'.

deciding what is and what is not consonant with the teaching of Scripture became a matter of interpretation within the church. It would not be too much to say that a great deal of the dissension which has subsequently divided the Church of England into competing theological parties owes its origin to this vagueness in the formulations of the reformers.[548]

The titles on heresy present the negative side of Christian doctrine, and they are of particular interest because they reveal what the main theological concerns of the drafting committee were. Their importance in the overall scheme of things can be measured by the fact that R, 2-3 (originally a single title) were revised much more thoroughly by Cranmer than any of the other titles; in fact, between them they probably contain about half of the total number of revisions to the MS. We are not surprised to find condemnations of the classical Christian heresies, though it is important to notice that the theological sophistication shown here is much greater than that found in H.C., 1.1, which also purports to condemn them. Nor is it surprising to find a clear repudiation of those things which protestants generally regarded as Roman inventions (i.e. deviations from the truth), since after Henry VIII's death the protestant character of the Church of England's reformation could (and did) express itself much more freely than had been possible before, and in ways which would have been inconceivable in 1535.

What stands out is the prominence given in R, 2 to attacks on other forms of protestantism. These include a blanket condemnation of anabaptism, which in mid-sixteenth century England was a minor nuisance at best, and the clear repudiation of the Lutheran doctrine of the ubiquity of Christ's resurrection body. The former reflects a mental atmosphere more than a social reality, and may be compared to the anti-communist scares which swept through various western countries in the mid-twentieth century. Anabaptists were seen as revolutionaries who preached strange doctrines, even if it was not always clear what those doctrines were. Although a rejection of infant baptism united all anabaptist groups, the word covered different strands of belief, only a few of which were truly heretical or immoral. Unfortunately, they had acquired notoriety after one of the more extreme groups had seized the city of Münster on 9 February 1534 and introduced revolutionary changes there, which they immediately tried to export to the Netherlands. The Münster experiment was crushed on 25 June 1535 after a bloody campaign led by the city's expelled bishop, but by then all Europe had been aroused to the danger. Fear of similar happenings elsewhere dictated official policies towards anyone calling himself an anabaptist, and these policies of repression were common to most European countries. The English scene reflects the general European panic with the added complication that all real and supposed anabaptists were foreigners, a

---

[548]To be fair, the reformers themselves were much clearer about the meaning of their statements than appears from nineteenth-century debates, for example. There can be little doubt that most of them would have seen matters more or less in the light of something like Calvin's *Institutes*, and that the attempts of the tractarians (1833-41) to prove otherwise would have scandalized them.

circumstance which made them doubly suspect.[549] Anabaptists were condemned by name in the 1553 articles of religion, but the references to them were deleted in the 1563 (1571) revision, probably because the danger they presented was recognized as being more theoretical than real.[550]

The anti-Lutheran statements were more purely theological in origin, and reflect the evolving situation in England itself at that time. Whether Cranmer ever subscribed to the Lutheran doctrine of the ubiquity of Christ's body and blood is unclear and depends on what his early allegiance to Lutheranism is understood to have included. In the thirteen articles of 1538 Cranmer had accepted the Lutheran doctrine of the real presence of Christ in the eucharist, though the question of ubiquity is not specifically addressed there.[551] Whatever the case may be, there is no doubt that Cranmer moved away from the Lutheran position in the course of 1547-8, and adopted the more radical views of Martin Bucer and Johannes Oecolampadius (1482-1531), whose work *De genuina verborum Christi* (Basel, 1525) was to be especially influential on his intellectual development. In the parliamentary debate which took place in the house of lords from 14-19 December 1548, Cranmer expounded this view in detail, and later wrote it up as a treatise.[552] The mixed reception given to the first English prayer book after it was issued on 9 June 1549 was also an important factor motivating Cranmer to clarify matters as much as possible. The conservative bishops were prepared to use the new communion service precisely because they thought they could read the traditional doctrine of Christ's real presence into it, and Cranmer was determined to do everything in his power to disabuse them of that notion. To him and to those around him (like Bucer) the Lutheran doctrine of the ubiquity of Christ's ascended body was a form of the real presence doctrine which had

[549]England never produced an indigenous form of anabaptism, at least not at this stage. The first English baptists were converted to that view of baptism when they were in exile in the Netherlands, in the opening years of the seventeenth century, but they absorbed other aspects of anabaptism (e.g. pacifism and communism) only very imperfectly, if at all. They were perceived as radicals when they returned to England, but within a generation or two they had become a respectable nonconformist group, distinguished from the others mainly by their rejection of infant baptism. See J. F. McGregor, 'The baptists, fount of all heresy', in *Radical religion in the English revolution*, ed. J. F. McGregor and B. Reay (Oxford, 1984), pp. 23-63.
[550]Cf. article 8 of 1553 (9 of 1571), in *D.E.R.*, pp. 289-90, and possibly article 41 of 1553 in *D.E.R.*, p. 310.
[551]See article 7 (*D.E.R.*, p. 192) based on article 10 of the Augsburg confession of 1530 (*D.E.R.*, p. 610), which does not mention ubiquity either.
[552]*A defence of the true and catholick doctrine of the sacrament* (London, 1550). R.S.T.C. 6000-1. See MacCulloch, *Thomas Cranmer*, pp. 379-409 for a full discussion of these events.

survived in one part of the reformed church. It was therefore necessary to disavow it, although it is noteworthy that this disavowal did not appear in the forty-two articles of 1553 and was not fully accepted even ten years later.[553]

R, 3 was originally joined to R, 2 but was separated out by Cranmer to form a title on heresy trials. At first sight it might seem more appropriate to put R, 3 much later in the text, along with the other titles dealing with courts and trial procedure (R, 34-6), but this was not the way it appeared in the sixteenth century. Heresy trials were in a category all their own, and had been for at least 300 years in some parts of Europe, though not in England, where a separate judicial régime for dealing with them was not introduced until 1401.[554] Theoretically, the system functioned in the same way as other ecclesiastical courts, but the clear preference for trials by judicial inquest (*inquisitio*) gave it the name by which it is most commonly known today. A peculiar feature of the inquisition was that it empowered ecclesiastical judges to pronounce sentences of capital punishment which were normally the preserve of the secular courts. The terror which it provoked was largely due to the technical nature of so much heresy, which made it relatively easy for an ecclesiastical court to condemn innocent but theologically ignorant people, who were unaware of the subtleties of Christian doctrine. Abuse was rife, but the system persisted in one form or another as long as most people were convinced that false beliefs should not only be punished but also extirpated from the body politic. In England that was the case at least until 1640, and something of the principle survived as late as 1688-9, when a limited toleration was finally enacted.[555]

The main fact which has to be borne in mind here is that the system did not follow the traditional model envisaged by Cranmer, unless one excepts the inquisitorial proceedings under Mary I (1553-8) which caught the archbishop and his fellow reformers in their net. What eventually emerged was a court system known as 'high commission' which is generally reckoned to have been established by Elizabeth I on 19 July 1559[556] and which lasted until 1 August 1641.[557] Tribunals functioned at both provincial and diocesan levels, and dealt

---

[553]It appeared as article 29 in 1563 and was approved by convocation, but at the last minute it was suspended, for fear of giving offence to the Lutherans. It was finally included in 1571.

[554]The original impetus for special measures to deal with heresy went back to c. 3 of Lateran IV, 1215 (*C.O.D.*, 233-4), later included in the *Decretals* as X, 5.7.13 (Fr, II, 787-9), but it took some time to get the machinery for dealing with it up and running. England was one of the last countries in Europe to co-operate, and that was only in the wake of the perceived threat of Lollardy. The statute authorizing trials and punishments for heresy was 2 Henry IV, c. 15, 1401 (*S.R.*, II, 125-8). It was replaced by 25 Henry VIII, c. 14, 1534 (*S.R.*, III, 454-5), but that was repealed and the earlier statute restored by 1-2 Philip and Mary I, c. 6, 1554 (*S.R.*, IV, 244). It then remained on the statute book until it was finally repealed by 29 Charles II, c. 9, 1677 (*S.R.*, V, 850).

[555]1 William III and Mary II, c. 18, 1689 (*S.R.*, VI, 74-6).

[556]1 Elizabeth I, c. 1, s. 8, 1559 (*S.R.*, IV, 350-5).

[557]16 Charles I, c. 11, 1641 (*S.R.*, V, 112-13).

with a wide range of offences using the inquisitorial procedure. They also functioned as appellate courts. The high commission was still in its infancy when the *Reformatio* was reintroduced in the 1571 parliament, and the question of how it would relate to the *Reformatio* if that document ever became law was not raised. On the other hand, it seems quite likely that the reprints of Foxe's edition in 1640 and 1641 were somehow related to the crisis and demise of the high commission system at that time. Perhaps those who wanted to promote the *Reformatio* thought that it offered a viable pattern of ecclesiastical courts, including courts for trying heresy cases, which more faithfully reflected the original intentions of the reformers than the high commission did. But whether it would have avoided the criticisms levelled at the latter if it had been implemented is doubtful, since the underlying principle was basically the same. Sooner or later there would have been a clash between those who wanted to enforce anti-heresy laws and those who wanted toleration of heterodox views, and it is hard to believe that R, 3 would have resisted the eventual onslaught against traditional attitudes and behaviour in that sphere.

The late medieval punishments for heresy were also to be retained in the reformed church, and as R, 4 indicates, they were even to be extended to cases of 'blasphemy', which meant swearing as much as anything else.[558] One is tempted to think that had it been rigorously applied, the majority of the male population (at least) would have been burnt at the stake, but the absurdity of such an extreme application should not blind us to the fact that there was a real aversion to swearing at that time and that people are known to have been punished for it. The *Reformatio* should therefore not be regarded as extremist or utopian on this point, even if the punishments actually inflicted were much less draconian than the ones which it envisaged.[559]

B. The sacraments (5-10)

The titles on the sacraments are interesting because they implicitly retain the traditional medieval view that there were seven of them, even though the articles of religion had officially limited their number to the two sacraments of the gospel. R, 5 contains canons dealing specifically with ordination, matrimony, confirmation and the visitation of the sick (a thinly veiled reference to extreme unction). The only one omitted is penance, which may perhaps be explained by the shift in emphasis away from external acts of contrition towards heartfelt and spiritual repentance which is so characteristic of protestantism, and which Cranmer is known to have emphasized.[560]

---

[558]See R, 4.1.
[559]See Helmholz, *Roman canon law*, p. 110.
[560]See J. A. Null, 'Thomas Cranmer's doctrine of repentance', unpublished Ph.D. dissertation, University of Cambridge, 1994. Originally the reformers had retained penance as the third 'gospel' sacrament. See the ten articles of 1536, no. 3 *(D. E. R.,* pp.

R, 6 deals with idolatry and witchcraft, which were the negative image of the sacramental principle because they represented the use of material objects by evil, rather than by good spiritual powers.[561] Idolatry in the strict sense must have been rare in the mid-sixteenth century, though of course the protestant reformers were quick to apply the concept to the traditional veneration of images and the like.[562] Witchcraft on the other hand was very much a going concern and did not fade out of judicial consciousness (largely because educated people ceased to believe in it) until the seventeenth century or even later.[563] There had been a statute against it in 1542,[564] although it was repealed in 1547 as part of a general abolition of all felonies which had appeared for the first time in the reign of Henry VIII.[565] Thus it happened that when the *Reformatio* was composed there was no statutory legislation on witchcraft, though that situation did not last long. Another statute was enacted in 1563[566] which was replaced in 1604.[567] That survived until 1736 when witchcraft was finally taken out of the jurisdiction of the courts altogether.[568]

R, 7 deals with 'preachers', who are put in the place where one would expect a title on holy orders, although it was not strictly necessary for a preacher to be ordained.[569] This title is the most obviously protestant one in the *Reformatio*, because the beliefs that preaching was the chief means of grace and that the ministry of the Word should replace the ministry of the sacrament as the chief focus of worship were among the most important distinguishing characteristics of the reformed church. The canons faithfully reflect the difficulties which a doctrinal change of that kind entailed, and their content is programmatic rather than descriptive of any existing norm. No one was to be allowed to exercise the office of a preacher without a licence to do so, a provision which had first appeared in the wake of Lollardy and which still remains in force today, at least

---

166-9).

[561]Later canons have simply omitted these subjects altogether.

[562]There is a draft article among Cranmer's papers, usually attached to the thirteen articles though not one of them, which is devoted to this subject. See *D.E.R.*, pp. 219-21.

[563]The last burning for witchcraft in England occurred in 1612, but there were burnings in Massachusetts as late as 1692 and in Scotland in 1696. See K. Thomas, *Religion and the decline of magic* (London, 1971) for a full discussion of the subject.

[564]33 Henry VIII, c. 8, 1541-2 (*S.R.*, III, 837).

[565]1 Edward VI, c. 12, 1547 (*S.R.*, IV, 18-22).

[566]5 Elizabeth I, c. 16, 1563 (*S.R.*, IV, 446-7).

[567]1 James I, c. 12, 1604 (*S.R.*, IV, 1028-9).

[568]9 George II, c. 5, 1736.

[569]In the Henrician canons of 1535 the title on preachers comes immediately after the one on heresies, which reflects the medieval perception of the danger associated with them. R, 7.4 mentions only ordained clergy as persons to whom the task of preaching properly belongs, but if this was the ideal, it was a long time before it was realized. Lay preaching was abolished at an early date (1575/9), but despite attempts to upgrade the standard of clerical education (cf. *e.g.* 1575/3), non-preaching ministers were still to be found as late as 1603 (1604). See 1603/46 for provisions regarding them.

within the Church of England.[570] Such a licence would only be granted to those who were both sound in doctrine and upright in moral character, but although it was clearly specified what was to be required in these respects, there was no provision for any examination or other mechanism to ensure that the standard would be maintained.[571] One point which concerned Cranmer was the need to maintain public harmony among preachers and to avoid using the pulpit for theological controversy. This seems to have gone unnoticed at the time but the idea was picked up and greatly expanded in the 1603 (1604) canons, no doubt because the rise of puritanism had made it a real matter of concern by then.[572]

Detailed instructions were also given as to how a preacher should go about disciplining his flock, and the tone is often closer to that of a pastoral homily than to a legal document. It was further envisaged that there would be a clear plan for regular preaching not only in cathedrals and universities, but also in towns and villages. Three of the canons dealing with this subject were marked by Cranmer in MS Harleian 426 for transfer to different places in the text, but unfortunately they seem to have got lost in transit, with the result that they do not appear in any of the printed editions. Preachers were also to meet regularly at diocesan conventions for what we would today call in-service training, and that provision was subsequently incorporated in the 1571 canons.[573] There were also canons making attendance at Sunday sermons compulsory[574] and providing for sanctions against those who interrupted them or caused any distraction in church.[575]

R, 7 is one of the titles whose provisions were not realized in practice, much to the chagrin of the hotter sort of protestants within the church. If what is recommended here were being carried out in 1553, the title (much of which has a transitional character) would soon have had to be revised, but at least things would have been moving in the right direction. As it was, failure in this area was to cost the church dear, as the demand for good preaching outstripped the ability to provide it, and preachers began to emerge from unofficial (and deeply suspect) sources. The 1571 canons picked up some of these recommendations,[576] but they were a pale shadow of R, 7 and soon had to be supplemented with more adequate provisions.[577]

---

[570]2 Henry IV, c. 15, 1400-1 (S.R., II, 125-8).
[571]However there was to be a thorough examination for those admitted to benefices. See R, 11.2, 7-11.
[572]1603/53 (A.C., 340-1).
[573]1571/1.3 (A.C., 172-5).
[574]This was concurrently provided for by 5-6 Edward VI, c. 1, 1552 (S.R., IV, 130-1).
[575]This was in essence a revival of 1 Richard II, c. 15, 1377 (S.R., II, 5).
[576]1571/6 (A.C., 196-9).
[577]1575/1-11 (A.C., 211-14).

Matrimony and divorce (8-10)

Moving on to the next three titles, which are devoted to matrimony and divorce, it would be no exaggeration to say that more attention has been paid to them than to the rest of the *Reformatio* put together, though not all of this comment has been properly informed.[578] R, 8, the title on contracting marriage, is largely traditional. One novelty however is a provision requiring parental consent for minors (R, 8.4), which was eventually incorporated in the canons of 1584 and 1603 (1604),[579] perhaps because it accorded with the general sentiment among protestant divines.[580] The reading of the banns was maintained, as was the traditional age of fourteen for boys and twelve for girls. There were sanctions against people who might unlawfully try to prevent a marriage and a clear statement of what were, and were not to be regarded as impediments to it. Marriage was to be open to all including clergy, as had recently been permitted by statute;[581] polygamy was to be avoided, disputes and quarrels were insufficient grounds for separation, and a marriage could be annulled if it had been contracted by force or fear. All of these except clerical marriage had clear medieval precedents, but the last canon (R, 8. 13/*14*) is an oddity. It states that mothers are to breast-feed their children rather than give them to a wet nurse. The reformers felt strongly about this because they believed that it was a mother's God-given duty to care for her children in this way, but it has to be said that such a provision is unique in the history of canon law! It never resurfaced in later legislation, in spite of the controversy which it seems to have engendered in sixteenth-century England.[582]

R, 9 deals with prohibited degrees of consanguinity and affinity but although it is new from the standpoint of the canonical tradition, it is really little more than a return to the principles laid down in the Old Testament. The medieval church had got itself into difficulty by insisting on a broad definition of kinship which originally extended to the seventh degree, and it had already been forced to restrict this to four.[583] Even then there were difficulties, and the reformers not unnaturally thought that the biblical solution was the right one. A table of kindred and affinity in line with what is stated in this title was drawn up by

[578]See E. J. Carlson, *Marriage and the English reformation* (Oxford, 1994) for the most recent discussion of the subject.
[579]1584/3.2 (*A.C.*, 224-5); 1603/100 (*A.C.*, 400-1).
[580]The case for it was argued at length by Marin Bucer, *De regno Christi*, II, 18, and it is possible that his views inspired the drafting committee at this point (see above).
[581]2-3 Edward VI, c. 21, 1549 (*S.R.*, IV, 67).
[582]See D. Cressy, *Birth, marriage and death. Ritual, religion and the life-cycle in Tudor and Stuart England* (Oxford, 1997), pp. 87-94.
[583]The seven-degree rule came into vogue in the eighth century and was maintained until the fourth Lateran council in 1215, when it was relaxed by c. 50 (*C.O.D.*, 257-8). This was subsequently included in the canon law as X, 4.14.8 (Fr, II, 703-4). See J. A. Brundage, *Law, sex and Christian society in medieval Europe* (Chicago, 1987) for a full discussion of the issue.

Archbishop Matthew Parker and passed in the convocation of 1563.[584] As in the case of witchcraft, something which was not the law when the *Reformatio* was composed had become so by the time the final text came up for reconsideration in 1571, and the fact that Foxe's edition does not reflect this development merely confirms our opinion, established on solid textual grounds, that the 1553 text was not seriously revised for publication at that time.

The greatest interest (and controversy) has surrounded R, 10, which deals with adultery and divorce. As we have already mentioned, the combination of these two things was new, and this must be attributed once again to the reformers' biblical emphasis. Adultery had always been a crime, and the medieval church had gone to great lengths to stamp out clerical concubinage, so there is nothing new about the canons which deal with those subjects. Similarly, there had long been canonical provision for divorce in cases of desertion, danger to one of the spouses (almost invariably the wife) and maltreatment. On the other hand, it had also been understood that arguments between spouses were not enough to provoke divorce, nor was illness or impotence, unless these had been concealed from the other spouse before the marriage. Other matters, such as incitement to commit adultery or false accusations, had also long been the object of canonical censure and the traditional position is upheld in the *Reformatio*. The innovations which R, 10 contains amount in the end to only two:

> 10.5:   The innocent party may (lawfully) contract a fresh
>   marriage.
> 10.19: Separation 'from bed and board' shall be abolished.

These two things belong together and require some explanation. 'Divorce' in the general usage of this period could have one of three different meanings:

> 1. The dissolution of a legitimate marriage, which permitted the wife to recover her dowry and both parties to remarry. This was divorce *a vinculo*, which existed in Roman law but was not recognized by the Christian church and therefore did not exist for practical purposes at this time.[585]

---

[584]It remained the law of England *in toto* until 1907, when it was slightly modified, but it was not revised by the church until 1946. See *A.C.*, 890-1.

[585]Until 11 January 1858 the only way to obtain a divorce *a vinculo* in England was by private parliamentary statute. There were a good many of these, especially in the eighteenth and early nineteenth centuries, but they obviously fell far short of the potential demand and never represented more than a minuscule proportion of marriages contracted. The Church of England has never recognized it, and still does not sanction the remarriage of divorced persons within the lifetime of a former spouse. On 25 January 2000 the Church published an official report entitled *Marriage in church after divorce*, which would alter this rule in specific cases. The report is due to be debated within the Church and the results will come before the general synod, probably in 2002. But even if the report is adopted, the Church will still be less generous to divorced persons than it would

2. Divorce *a thoro et mensa* ('from bed and board'), which is what we would now call legal separation. The couple was permitted (and sometimes compelled) to live apart, but could not remarry. The husband retained the dowry. This is what the ecclesiastical law normally meant by the term 'divorce'.

3. Annulment. This dissolved the marriage by declaring that it had never existed. The wife's dowry was returned, both parties were free to marry (technically for the first time), but children born of the earlier union were illegitimate. This affected Henry VIII, who was forced to pass legislation legitimizing both of his daughters after his marriages to their mothers were annulled.[586]

What the *Reformatio* envisaged was a fourth option, according to which 'divorce' would be *a vinculo,* but only the 'innocent' party would have the right to remarry, and a guilty wife could not recover her dowry. This option presupposed that such a divorce would normally be granted only in cases of adultery, as Jesus had allowed, though it could also be extended to cover such matters as desertion, where the principle had long been applied in practice. If both parties were guilty of adultery, there could be no divorce, and they would be condemned to live together as their punishment – exactly the same solution as the medieval canon law had recommended.

For all the ink spilled and the invective directed against it in the late nineteenth and early twentieth centuries, it is hard to see how the proposal put forward in the *Reformatio* can be regarded as a radical departure from traditional Christian morality. The reformers knew (as their latter-day critics must also have known) that in a society where there is no provision for divorce, or where it is very hard to obtain, what happens in practice is that couples split up and cohabit with other partners, often producing illegitimate children. In many cases such arrangements can go on for years, but when one of the original parties dies, the 'concubine' and her illegitimate children find themselves disinherited, even though very often the 'husband' or 'wife' has long disappeared and may well be in a similar 'union' with someone else.[587] Although marital breakdown entails a host of problems, if there is no divorce to deal with it the latter state can easily be worse than the first. The reformers opted for the lesser of two evils, but it would be a great mistake to think of this as laxity on their part. The restrictions which they continued to insist on demonstrate that they were still a very long way from the 'no fault divorce' situation which is increasingly prevalent today. The suggestions made in the *Reformatio* were never adopted, and in that respect the divorce commission of 1850 was wrong, but whether we should rejoice at this

have been if it had adopted the *Reformatio* in the sixteenth century.

[586]25 Henry VIII, c. 22, 1533-4 (*S.R.*, III, 471-4); 28 Henry VIII, c. 7, 1536 (*S.R.*, III, 655-62).

[587]This is a very common situation in the Republic of Ireland, which did not introduce divorce until 1995-6 and which continues to make it difficult to obtain.

in the way that Oscar Watkins did is another matter. It is at least possible that the adoption of the *Reformatio* in the sixteenth century might have led to a sane approach to the whole question which would have avoided both the hypocrisies and the overreactions of later times.

C. Benefices (11-13; 15-18)

The seven titles which deal with benefices and their incumbents reveal the solid structure of the parochial system of the Church of England which has remained remarkably unchanged over the centuries. Many of their provisions are still familiar to a modern reader who is likely to notice only a few, relatively minor modifications in matters of detail. R, 11 deals with the admission of ministers to benefices and contains several canons concerning the examination of appointees (R, 11.2, 7-11, 18-24). These all have medieval precedents and the only novelty is that here they are applied to candidates for admission to benefices, as distinct from holy orders.[588]

The basic responsibility for carrying out the examination belonged to the bishop but was normally delegated to the archdeacon, who was expected to draw on expert advice and assistance. All candidates had to swear an oath beforehand and diligent inquiry was to be made into their family background and education. Illegitimate children were normally to be excluded, and Old Testament precedent was cited for this, though the main reason for it seems to have been that lay patrons were in the habit of providing for their illegitimate sons in this way.[589] An attempt was made to make it possible for the physically handicapped to be admitted if they were otherwise suitable candidates, though this was not to be done if the handicap was such that the person concerned could not fulfil his duties properly.

In principle, the model for ministry which was to be followed was that set down by the Apostle Paul in his letters to Timothy and Titus. More specifically, candidates were to be asked to explain their views on the catholic faith of the creeds (especially the doctrine of the Trinity), the authority of the Holy

---

[588]The *Reformatio* does not cover admission to holy orders, presumably because that had already been dealt with in the ordinal (1550), but it may be doubted whether Cranmer really intended there to be two parallel sets of examinations. He probably assumed that one examination ought to suffice for both ordination and institution to a benefice, though since there were still many clergy in 1553 who had been ordained without such an examination and who could not have passed one, the provisions of R, 11 must have seemed like a necessary safeguard.

[589]Before the reformation, of course, it was the (officially celibate) clergy who provided for their illegitimate sons in this way. The old law against it was simply dusted off and reused in new circumstances. It was never applied, though in 1947 the revisers of the canon law tried to reintroduce the provision for reasons which are obscure (cf. 1947/55.5 – A.C., 652 and accompanying note). The current canons state explicitly that illegitimacy is not a bar to ordination; cf. 1969/ C 2.4, 4.4.

Scriptures and current controversies. They were also to be asked to expound the catechism point by point. The object of this exercise was to determine their orthodoxy, which was the *sine qua non* for any appointment. It was further specified that a bishop must be at least thirty years old, a priest at least twenty-five, and a deacon at least twenty-one, the assumption being that the last of these would be ordained before undertaking his theological training. It is not altogether clear from the Latin text of the *Reformatio* how these ages were to be calculated, and the preface to the ordinal of 1550 has to be consulted for greater precision. There it appears that the ages for bishops and deacons were to be reckoned as thirty or twenty-one completed years, but that the age for a priest was to be twenty-four (*i.e.* his twenty-fifth year). The ages prescribed for bishops and priests had ancient precedents, but deacons were originally supposed to be twenty-five at least.[590] In fact, twenty-one came to be regarded as too young, and in 1662 the age limit was raised to twenty-three, which it still is.[591]

Of great interest and importance are the canons dealing with patronage (R, 11.3-6), the first two of which were new and sufficiently important to have been adopted in a slightly modified form by the 1571 canons.[592] Between 1535 and 1553 a revolution in patronage had occurred in the Church of England, largely because of the dissolution of the monasteries. Their patronage had covered a very large proportion of parishes and had been redistributed among a wide range of lay people. Colleges in the universities had acquired a share, and the crown retained a good many, but individual laymen were often able to buy the right of presentation ('advowson') to a particular church or churches and abuse was rife. The crown often failed to appoint incumbents, preferring to cream off the tithe revenue itself, and private patrons might do almost anything. Some had alienated church property, including valuable farmland; others had stripped buildings of lead and other valuable materials; still others had made highly unsuitable appointments, including of their own illegitimate children, as we have already seen. These abuses had reached scandalous proportions by 1553 and the need to do something about them had become urgent, though it was here that the reformers met with their most determined opposition. Those who had profited from the dissolution of the monasteries were not going to surrender their dubiously gotten gains, and even Mary I was unable to restore catholicism until she obtained an assurance from the pope that the restitution of monastic lands would not be demanded. In such circumstances canons of this kind could hardly be much more than pious wishes. Serious reform of the patronage system did not begin until the nineteenth century, and it is still going on.[593] Perfection will never

---

[590]See D, 77 cc. 5-7 (Fr, I, 273-4 (Fr I, 273-4).
[591]See *D.E.R.*, pp. 277-8.
[592]Cf. 1571/10.1 (*A.C.*, 202-3).
[593]Beginning with the ecclesiastical commissioners act, 3-4 Victoria, c. 115, 11 August 1840. For the details, see the interesting and informative account by R. E. Rodes, *Law and modernization in the Church of England. Charles II to the welfare state* (Notre Dame, 1991), pp. 183-95.

be attained, but it is safe to say that the conduct of both private patrons and the crown has improved beyond recognition since the sixteenth century, and that the intentions of the *Reformatio* are more nearly fulfilled today than they have ever been in the past.

R, 11.5-6 attempt to deal with the problem of vacant livings. Quite apart from the pastoral damage which long vacancies cause, many patrons (and especially the crown) were not averse to seizing the tithe and other revenues during such vacancies which they then had little incentive to terminate. To deal with this problem the medieval practice of withdrawing patronage rights after six months was continued by the *Reformatio*. A patron's rights were to devolve to the bishop and from him to the archbishop, and thence to the crown, but with the ingenious addition that if the crown failed to act, the patronage would return to its owner for a further six months and the cycle would be repeated! That innovation excepted, these canons remained an accurate statement of the law until very recently and their basic outline is still recognizable today.[594] R, 11.12-15 contains the traditional stipulations enforcing residence and outlawing pluralism, whose history parallels that of patronage. Real progress on these fronts had to wait until the nineteenth century when a reasonably satisfactory system of clerical discipline in these matters was gradually established and enforced.[595] The result is that here too, we can say that the *Reformatio*'s intentions are being realized today far better than they have ever been in the past.

R, 11.25 was added by Cranmer after the rest of the title had been put together, but it was essentially taken from the *Decretals*.[596] Its purpose was to prevent the illegal seizure of benefices by barring those who were guilty of doing so from ever holding another ecclesiastical office. Presumably this is still the law today, though instances of its happening are so rare that it is almost never applied. No doubt it was a more common offence in the sixteenth century, but it cannot have been too widespread since none of the post-reformation canons makes any mention of it.

R, 12 basically repeats already existing legislation on the resignation of benefices and requires little comment except for R, 12.5, which altered the wording of a medieval canon in order to forbid the surrender of benefices by proxy. The failure of the *Reformatio* ensured that the law was not changed on this point, but as we have already seen, Edmund Gibson felt that such an amendment was so desirable that he wrote it in himself.[597] His authority seems

---

[594]No lapse from the crown has ever been recognized in English law. By the provisions of s. 16 of the patronage (benefices) measure of 18 July 1986 (1986/no. 3), which came into force on 1 January 1989, the six month period was extended to nine months and the benefice lapses only once – to the archbishop, who may act without constraint of time. The measure does not apply to crown benefices.

[595]Beginning with the pluralities act, 1-2 Victoria, c. 106, 14 August 1838. See Rodes, *Law and modernization*, pp. 195-207.

[596]Cf. X, 1.7.3 (Fr, II, 98-9).

[597]Gibson, *Codex*, XXXIV, 11 (p. 869). See above.

to have been sufficient to put an end to proxy resignations which (as far as anyone can tell) have been regarded as invalid ever since and would certainly not be accepted nowadays.

R, 13 is basically an appendix to R, 11 and R, 12 and deals very briefly with the exchange of benefices, the history of which is intimately linked with the matters dealt with in the two preceding titles. All the canons are of medieval origin and there is nothing new in any of them. As always, the real problem was one of enforcement, which was not finally brought under control until the nineteenth century.

R, 15 on dilapidations is drawn almost entirely from earlier English legislation and all the evidence suggests that the problem was both serious and getting worse in the mid-sixteenth century.[598] The royal injunctions of 1536, 1547 and 1559 all ordered incumbents to set aside a fifth of their annual income for repairs as needed, and it is therefore somewhat surprising to see this figure reduced to one seventh in R, 15.2. Once again, enforcement was the real problem, especially since lay patrons were often unwilling to spend the funds needed to repair their churches and many clergymen and parishes were too poor to do so. The problem has never really been solved, and even today it is not unusual to find church buildings in poor repair because of lack of funds.

R, 16 is another short title, dealing this time with the alienation or letting of church property. Most of it is taken from Justinian's *Novellae*, which is a somewhat unusual source, but nothing in the title can really be regarded as new. Alienation of church property was another longstanding problem which the rapid growth of lay patronage had only exacerbated, and as usual the main difficulty was enforcing the legislation which already existed. As with the other titles in this section, real improvement had to wait until the nineteenth century when the matter was brought under some kind of control. Even so, there are still cases today in which an incumbent or a church council disposes of church property without the proper authorization, so it is premature to suggest that the problem has finally been solved.

R, 17 on elections is drastically reduced and somewhat forlorn when compared with H.C., 15 on the same subject, but the dissolution of the monasteries in the interval, as well as the realization that royal control over the election of bishops had come to stay,[599] made detailed provisions unnecessary. It is, however, noteworthy that this title does say that traditional customs were to be maintained as far as possible, so in fact, no reform was contemplated beyond what had already occurred.

R, 18 deals with the trade in ecclesiastical offices and describes the various forms which that might take. As with the other titles dealing with irregularities in the conferral of benefices there is nothing new in the provisions made, but enforcement was as always the major difficulty. It is very doubtful whether

---

[598] See R. Houlbrooke, *Church courts and the people during the English reformation, 1520-1570* (Oxford, 1979), pp. 151-62.
[599] It was originally established by 25 Henry VIII, c. 20, 1534 (*S.R.*, III, 462-4).

passing the *Reformatio* would have made any difference, since the practices condemned were widespread and deeply rooted. Only in recent times, when the whole financial structure of the church has been overhauled, has it been possible to resolve this issue by making it financially pointless, as well as legally impossible, to engage in the fraudulent activities mentioned in this title.[600]

D. Worship (19)

The form of worship has always been a sensitive subject in the Church of England, and regulations concerning it have a special importance. At the time the *Reformatio* was composed, the matter had already been regulated by one parliamentary statute which was about to be replaced by another, and legislation governing worship has remained typical of the reformed church.[601] The drafting committee had to work within a new but already existing framework, which accounts for most of the innovations, many of which were picked up by subsequent canons.[602] In that light what is surprising is how much of R, 19 is rooted in medieval canons which had already regulated such matters as the times at which divine service should be celebrated, the frequency of the administration of holy communion, the attendance of the clergy at and their duties in public worship. Even the way in which the lessons should be read and the psalms chanted was taken over virtually unchanged. Some matters, like the prohibition against private masses, may have appeared to be new at the time, but in fact reflected existing (if somewhat ancient) provisions in Justinian's *Novellae* and in Gratian's *Decretum*.

The new canons deal mostly with the pattern of worship to be observed in parish churches, both urban and rural, and the emphasis is placed squarely on regular preaching. Celebration of the eucharist, on the other hand, appears to be discouraged, but this is only relative to what had become common in the later middle ages, when priests frequently said mass daily whether there was a congregation or not. This practice was ruled out, and in R, 19.7 it was decreed that communion was to be celebrated only on Sundays and feast days, and then only in the presence of a congregation.[603]

---

[600]Reform began with the benefices act, 61-2 Victoria, c. 48, 12 August 1898 and has continued ever since. See Rodes, *Law and modernization*, pp. 187-95.

[601]The first act of uniformity was 2-3 Edward VI, c. 1, 1549 (*S.R.*, IV, 37-9) and the second was 5-6 Edward VI, c. 1, 1552 (*S.R.*, IV, 130-1). By the time the *Reformatio* was printed, there was a third act, 1 Elizabeth I, c. 2, 1559 (*S.R.*, IV, 355-8) and the church's worship is currently regulated by a fourth act, 14 Charles II, c. 4, 1662 (*S.R.*, V, 364-70) and its many subsequent amendments. The full text of all four of these acts is printed in *D.E.R.*

[602]R, 19.7 was adapted to become 1603/113; R, 19.9 became 1571/4.8 and then 1603/59; R, 19.11 became 1571/4.3 and R, 19.14 (not really an innovation) became 1571/4.6.

[603]This was later picked up by 1603/113 and remains the general rule in the Church of England today, though there are many exceptions at local parish level.

R, 19.11, which states how decrees of excommunication were to be published during services seems somewhat out of place and might have been better in R, 32 which deals specifically with the subject, but its presence here is a reminder that excommunications were meant to be a regular feature of worship which would serve to teach congregations the importance of spiritual discipline. Excommunications were never as frequent as the church authorities would have liked, but they did remain a feature of parish life until the procedure was abolished in 1813.[604]

The most notorious canon in this title is R, 19.16, which was singled out by John Foxe in his preface as one which in his opinion needed revision. The main problem is that it enjoined worship according to the prayer book and imposed penalties on anyone who refused to comply. It is enough to remember that there had been no fewer than three different prayer books in use in the *Reformatio*'s short lifetime for us to realize the importance of this provision and the potential problems which might arise from trying to enforce it strictly.[605] On the one hand, conservative tendencies could still be found in many places and would not be fully eradicated until the pre-reformation generation of priests had passed from the scene.[606] But on the other hand there was a rising generation of future 'puritans' who wanted more sweeping reforms and who might have been happy, even at this early stage, to do without a book altogether. At the very least they wanted much greater freedom in interpreting the rubrics of the 1559 prayer book than R, 19.16 would have allowed, and the fact that Foxe singled out this canon for special mention shows just how significant it was felt to be.

As it turned out there were periodic bouts of tension in the Elizabethan church whenever enforcement of the rules was attempted, and it was probably only Archbishop John Whitgift's undoubted commitment to Calvinism which made it possible for him to persuade the 'puritans' to moderate their demands. Discipline slackened for a while under the fairly tolerant James I (1603-25) but it returned with a vengeance in the reign of Charles I (1625-49) when it was to become one of the major causes of the disaffection which eventually led to civil war and revolution. The restored Church of England once again imposed conformity, but at the price of losing much of its 'puritan' element. From then until the mid-nineteenth century prayer book discipline was maintained reasonably well, but it broke down with the revival of ritualism. There were many attempts to enforce the law against the ritualists, but public opinion found it hard to accept that a man should be imprisoned for matters of that kind. After 1892 prosecution for ritualist offences became much more difficult than it had

---

[604]By 53 George III, c. 127, 12 July 1813.

[605]The first was in force from 9 June 1549 and the second from 1 November 1552. It was withdrawn from 20 December 1553 but continued in use among the Marian exiles at Frankfurt, in spite of calls from John Knox and others for further reform. The third book (basically the second with elements of the first integrated into it) was authorized from 24 June 1559.

[606]See E. Duffy, *The stripping of the altars. Traditional religion in England, 1400-1580* (New Haven and London, 1992) for a detailed assessment of this.

been before,[607] and a *de facto* anarchy in matters of worship prevailed which continues to the present time. Indeed, it would be no exaggeration to say that in spite of the much greater freedom which is now legally available, the variety of unapproved worship styles which can be found is larger than ever. Worship is still theoretically regulated by law in the Church of England but nowhere are the canons flouted more openly than in this respect, and at the present time it looks extremely doubtful that anything like R, 19.16 will ever be enforceable in the church again.

E. Ministry (20-7)

The titles on ministry can be subdivided into R, 20-2, which deal with ministers (both clerical and lay) in the church and parish; R, 23-4, which concentrate on educational establishments;[608] and R, 25-7, which cover different legal aspects of a clergyman's duties.

Ministry in the parish (20-2)

In R, 20 the different ministries of the church are catalogued in reverse order, which is surprising but may not be very significant, since it is quite clear that the traditional hierarchical structure has been maintained. Also noticeable is the fact that the distinction between laymen and clergy is played down, though it obviously continued to exist. The officers mentioned and defined are the following:

1.	Parish clerks	(laymen)
2.	Churchwardens	(laymen)
3.	Deacons	
4.	Presbyters	
5.	Archpresbyters	(Rural deans)
6.	Archdeacons	
7.	Deans of cathedrals	
8.	Prebendaries of cathedrals[609]	
9.	Bishops	
10.	Archbishops	

---

[607]The clergy discipline act, 55-6 Victoria, c. 32, 27 June 1892 effectively suspended the writ *De contumace capiendo* which had been used to prosecute ritualists.

[608]The link between the parish and the school was closer then than it is now, and we sometimes have to make a conscious effort to remind ourselves that in 1553, and for three hundred years after that, many schools and the two universities were effectively seminaries training young men for the ministry, even if they did allow other students in as well.

[609]Here the ascending hierarchical order is (exceptionally) reversed.

There is nothing odd or unusual about the duties assigned to the last eight of these, all of which correspond to standard medieval practice, though there are certain modern touches, like the requirement for presbyters to own copies of the Bible.[610] Our real focus of attention must be on the first two, who now appear for the first time in canonical legislation, though their offices were not new.

The parish clerk is a somewhat mysterious figure. The duties ascribed to him combine those of the *primicerius*[611] and the *sacrista* or sexton,[612] and so in a sense the office may be said to go back to medieval times. The canons of 1603 (1604) translated the term 'parish clerk' as *(h)ostiarius*, thereby assimilating it to a minor order which had disappeared in the upheavals of the reformation, if not before.[613] This error was picked up by Edmund Gibson, and from there it has entered the common understanding of the church.[614] In the *Reformatio* the parish clerk is called the *aedituus*, which is also confusing, because this word is just a Latin translation of the Greek *oeconomus*, which is used in the very next canon as the equivalent of *gardianus* ('churchwarden').[615] This sort of confusion probably indicates that a new office was envisaged, which would combine different functions thitherto performed by a wide range of officials. Certainly it is true that parish clerks never established themselves in the way that churchwardens did, and for a long time now their existence has been residual at best.[616]

Churchwardens are more definable and have proved to be much more resilient in the life of the church. An extraordinarily large amount of space is given to them and to their functions in the *Reformatio*, something which is unprecedented in earlier canons. The office of churchwarden had existed at least since the thirteenth century, since we first hear of it in 1287.[617] As we have already seen, nomenclature was a problem. In theory, the churchwarden corresponded to the *custos* of the old canon law,[618] but although this word is

---

[610]According to the ordinal of 1550, they would have been given a copy at their ordination, a practice which still continues. Perhaps this is why the canon stresses that presbyters should possess a copy of the Scriptures in Latin *as well*, since they would presumably have had to buy that themselves.

[611]Cf. X, 1.25.1 (Fr, II, 155).

[612]Cf. X, 1.26.1 (Fr, II, 155).

[613]1603/91 (*A.C.*, 386-9). On the *(h)ostiarius*, see D, 23 c. 19 (Fr, I, 85).

[614]Gibson, *Codex*, IX, 14 (p. 214). The belief that parish clerks were once in orders is perpetuated, for example, by the Worshipful Company of Parish Clerks, which distributes an information leaflet claiming this. The leaflet and other materials relating to parish clerks can be obtained by writing to: The Clerk, Parish Clerks Company, c/o 1 Dean Trench Street, London, SW1P 3HB.

[615]The confusion is compounded by 1571/5, which uses *aedituus* for 'churchwarden'.

[616]It may be significant, for example, that there is no mention of them in the 1571 canons, which otherwise drew extensively on this title.

[617]See the statutes of Exeter II, 12 (PC, 1005-8). For further evidence from this period see C. Drew, *Early parochial organisation in England. The origins of the office of churchwarden* (York, 1954).

[618]X, 1.27.1 (Fr, I, 155).

sometimes found, the usual designation for him was *gardianus,* a Latinization of the French word *gardien.*[619] This was not good humanist Latin, and so other terms were looked for which sounded better. In the *Reformatio* it seems as if the divines preferred to use *oeconomus* (originally a steward, or controller of the episcopal or monastic household), whereas the lawyers opted for *syndicus,* which had a wide range of possible meanings.[620] However, it is clear that in this case the confusion is merely one of humanist 'elegance' and has nothing to do with the office itself, since *gardianus* almost invariably appears alongside it in order to explain what is meant. The *Reformatio* gives the first detailed account of this office, which is all the more valuable in that it comes from different sources which have not been harmonized in the text.

R, 20 closes with a number of canons (18-23) which deal with synods, which were normally meant to be called by the archbishop at the provincial or by the bishop at the diocesan level. But it is here that we come across the royal supremacy for the first time, because thanks to a textual emendation made by an unknown hand, unsatisfactory deliberations in a diocesan synod were to be referred to the king for judgment.[621] There is no reason to doubt that these provisions corresponded to the true situation on the ground, though the royal supremacy was much more powerful than is suggested here.[622]

R, 21 is a separate title dealing with churchwardens, though this probably an accident. Most likely it comes from a different source which for some reason has not been integrated into R, 20 to make a unified whole.[623]

R, 22 deals with parish boundaries and needs little comment. The beating of the parish bounds which it mentions was an old custom which still takes place in some areas. Otherwise the union of small benefices goes on much as it always has done, though it now takes many different forms (e.g. team and group ministries) which were not available until recently. The *Reformatio* captures this process at a particular moment in history, but it neither adds to nor alters anything in it.

---

[619]*Gardien* is in turn an adaptation of a Germanic word beginning with 'w', which is represented in English by 'warden'. Compare the doublets 'war/*guerre*', 'William/*Guillaume*', 'warranty/*garanti* (guarantee)', etc.

[620]In R, 27.2 there was a space left blank in the manuscript, in order to let somebody else insert the correct word, which turned out to be *syndicus.*

[621]R, 20.23.

[622]After the reformation, diocesan synods met only rarely and hardly ever deliberated independently. The convocations were more active, but they always met in tandem with parliament and were strictly controlled until they were effectively suppressed in 1717. The revived convocations of Canterbury (1852) and York (1861) had more independence, but they could not legislate on their own. The national assembly of the Church of England, established in 1919, acquired semi-legislative powers which have been inherited in an expanded version by the general synod (established in 1970), but the latter is still not entirely free from state control. Furthermore, it was not until 24 February 1966 that the convocations were given permission to meet outside parliamentary sessions (1966, c. 2).

[623]Probably R, 20 was composed by the clergy and R, 21 by the lawyers. See above.

Ministry in education (23-4)

R, 23 deals with schools and those in charge of them, drawing heavily on secular legislation, and including a number of regulations which appear to be new, though whether they represent an existing situation or an ideal one is hard to say. Probably they are a combination of both; the drafters may well have been guided by the practice of some schools and thought that it would be a good idea to set standards for everyone. The ancient connexion of schools to cathedrals is retained, as is the responsibility of the bishop to oversee them. The programme of study is heavily weighted in favour of religious subjects, and pupils were expected to know the English version of the catechism by heart before being admitted. They were also expected to bring an English New Testament with them and move on to Latin after a year. Particularly revealing is R, 23.4 which tells us that a schoolmaster would be allowed to decide his teaching method for himself. Those who teach in academic institutions know that such things, obvious though they may seem, can never be taken for granted! Church and cathedral schools still exist of course, as do a number of other foundations from this period, and although the curriculum has changed somewhat over the years the basic aim of giving the pupils a Christian education is still maintained today.

R, 24 applies the same principles to the universities, which are treated as theological colleges first and foremost. For example, if a shortage of funds should make it necessary to cut down on the number of students, the theological faculty was to be maintained at full strength and the cuts were all to be made elsewhere. Poor scholars were to receive bursaries, something which was already provided for in the royal injunctions of 1536 and 1547. Most importantly, graduates were not to stay at the university any longer than was strictly necessary, but were to go to their parishes and minister there as soon as possible. This too had already been provided for by statute, and so was not new. The system described in R, 24 remained recognizably the same until the university reforms in the mid-nineteenth century, but only a few remnants can be detected now, even if the residual presence of the Church of England at Oxford and Cambridge can still impress onlookers today.

Legal aspects of ministry (25-7)

R, 25, the title on tithes, is derived almost entirely from already existing sources, as was to be expected. Between 1535 and 1553 there were three important parliamentary statutes passed which governed the details of tithe payments and tried to reinforce the ability of the church authorities to collect them.[624] Collection was always difficult, and often became a major source of conflict between the rector of the parish and his parishioners, who did their best to evade

---

[624] 27 Henry VIII, c. 20, 1536 (*S.R.*, III, 551-2); 32 Henry VIII, c. 7, 1540 (*S.R.*, III, 751-2); 2-3 Edward VI, c. 13, 1549 (*S.R.*, IV, 55-8). See Houlbrooke, *Church courts*, pp. 117-50.

them. There was a further complication in that provision also had to be made for vicars who stood in for absentee rectors, since the latter were often remiss in their duty to give their substitutes adequate financial support.

Tithes were either 'personal' or 'predial'. The former were paid on income from wages and salaries after expenses were deducted, and to that extent they may be compared to modern income tax. Predial tithes were levies on agricultural products (e.g. wheat) and there was no provision for deducting expenses beforehand. There was also a third category of 'mixed' tithes, which covered animal products like wool, cheese and milk, as well as calves, lambs, piglets and so on. Here too, there was no provision for the prior deduction of expenses. But as in any tax system, there were many special regulations which also had to be taken into account. A number of items were not tithable at all, and there were longstanding disputes over things like minerals, fishponds, mills and timberwood. The royal courts, and the common lawyers attached to them, did their best to limit the range of ecclesiastical tithes and the threat they posed was felt more acutely in the post-reformation church than it had been before. There were also problems arising from uncertainties about parish boundaries, local customs granting special exemptions and shared tithes – on common pasture land, for example, or on flocks of sheep which grazed in one parish but were shorn in another. The *Reformatio* attempted to deal with these by defining parish boundaries more clearly (R, 22), by invalidating special exemptions (R, 25.18) and by detailing as precisely as possible how shared tithes were to be assessed, but in none of these areas can it be said that it made an original contribution to the development of the law. Its only value is that it gives some idea of the state of affairs obtaining in 1553, though there are many gaps which have to be filled in from other sources. The most noticeable omission, especially when compared with H.C., 25, is the almost total absence of any reference to London tithes, which were in a category all their own.

R, 25.19 on pensions was originally a separate title but it was so short that Foxe included it under tithes.[625] It sought to abolish the custom whereby some rectors would live in idle luxury off the revenue of their benefice(s), paying a pittance to a vicar who would be expected to shoulder his parochial duties. It is interesting mainly because, if it had succeeded, the word 'pension' would have been restricted to its modern meaning – a payment made to the old and infirm. Tithe continued to be a major feature of English life until the early nineteenth century, when changing economic conditions and the toleration of religious dissent combined to alter and then abolish the system completely, so that the church no longer receives any income from this source.[626] Clergy pensions, on

[625]It was still present in C, as Foxe's handwritten list of that manuscript's titles makes clear. See below, pp. 738-9.
[626]The first major change came in the tithe commutation act, 6-7 William IV, c. 71, 13 August 1836. Other acts followed until tithe was finally abolished by the tithe act, 26 George V and 1 Edward VIII, c. 43, 31 July 1936. According to its provisions, the last payments were made on 1 October 1996. See Rodes, *Law and modernization*, pp. 97-103.

the other hand, are now well established, and given that incumbents must now retire at age seventy, their importance has increased. So to some extent at least, it can be said that the intentions of R, 25.19 have been fulfilled in modern times.

R, 26 on visitations is thoroughly traditional and best regarded as simply a statement of existing fact apart from R, 26.7, which goes against the old canon law granting privileges to exempt places. But even if this canon is new it may not have been understood as such at the time, since the royal stranglehold on the church after 1534 would have made the old canon law inoperative (and inoperable) in any case. An increase in the frequency and quality of visitations does however seem to have been one of the major accomplishments of the reformation in the sphere of church administration and we are well informed about them thanks to the publication of visitation articles and injunctions for the period up to 1640.[627] After the restoration they seem to have become more of a formality and were eventually abandoned altogether, being replaced by questionnaires sent to incumbents and churchwardens. Today they have ceased entirely, though supervision of local parish affairs is still carried out by various diocesan and national church bodies appointed for the purpose.

R, 27 on testaments was certainly composed by a single individual and was published with almost no editorial emendations. It was probably submitted by a specialist in the field, though to what extent it can be regarded as a statement of actual practice is unclear. For example, although the last canon states explicitly that the general framework for resolving testamentary questions was the *Corpus iuris civilis*, it also says that this could not overrule English statute or custom. However, in R, 27.11-13 there is a clear case in which ancient Roman practice is affirmed against the prevailing English one. This concerns the 'lawful portion', or *legitim,* which the next of kin could claim from the deceased's estate, whether it was specifically willed to them or not.

Apparently this Roman law was applied in England in the thirteenth century, but the practice gradually died out and was all but extinct by the time the *Reformatio* was written.[628] But in that case, why was it included and (just as important) left standing in subsequent editions of the title? Did whoever wrote these canons think they were (or ought to be) the law, and include them for that reason, perhaps believing that Roman law would soon supersede English custom in any case? Was the issue still not clearly decided one way or the other, in spite of the fact that English custom did not support the notion of a *legitim*? Or was the Roman principle actually being applied at the time without anyone raising

---

[627] *Visitation articles and injunctions of the period of the reformation*, ed. W. H. Frere and W. P. M. Kennedy (3 vols., London, 1910); *Visitation articles and injunctions of the early Stuart church*, ed. K. Fincham (2 vols., Woodbridge, 1993-7).

[628] See R. H. Helmholz, 'Legitim in English legal history', *University of Illinois Law Review* (1984), 659-74; reprinted in *idem.*, *Canon law and the law of England* (London, 1987), pp. 247-62. English statute law did not recognize the principle of *legitim* (in a modified form) until 1-2 George VI, c. 45, which received the royal assent on 13 July 1938, no more than 1978 years after the Romans felt a need for something of the kind and passed the *Lex Falcidia* in 40 B. C.

objections to it? The most likely answer is that the *Reformatio* was prescriptive as well as descriptive, and that its statements about the *legitim* are a clear example of the former.[629]

Testamentary jurisdiction remained in the hands of the church courts until 11 January 1858 and accounted for a very large proportion of their business. As a result there were a number of treatises written which deal with testamentary matters in detail, of which Henry Swinburne's classic, *A brief treatise of testamenta and last wills*[630] was the archetype. Swinburne greatly expanded the *Reformatio*'s treatment of the subject, but said nothing of the *legitim*, for example, which must make us doubt whether that had any currency in the sixteenth century. We probably ought to conclude from this that when R, 27 and Swinburne agree we are dealing in the former with matters of actual practice, but that where they differ (or where there is no specific agreement) Swinburne is to be preferred as the more reliable historical source.

F. Discipline (14; 28-33)

The section on discipline contains seven titles, of which one (R, 14) is misplaced, and one (R, 33) is not a legal text at all. Furthermore, as we have already seen, this group of titles was put together later than the others, and with the notable exception of R, 33 is more heavily dependent on the Henrician canons than any other part of the *Reformatio*. Among other things, that means that this section is largely traditional in content and is one of those least influenced by the theology and special concerns of the protestant reformation.

R, 14 defines and defends the concept of purgation, which has no equivalent in the common law and which could not be used with respect to a proceeding in any common law court. Its main purpose was to counteract rumour and gossip prejudicial to the defendant, and it involved producing a number of compurgators, *i.e.* people who would swear on oath that the former was innocent of the crime of which he was accused. The precise number of compurgators required varied from three to as many as ten, according to the gravity of the offence, though usually there were no more than six at the most. The practice was widespread in the mid-sixteenth century and Ralph Houlbrooke (b. 1944) has evaluated its significance as follows:

Between two-thirds and three-quarters of those known to have attempted purgation succeeded in clearing their names. When men failed in purgation they usually did so because they were unable to produce a sufficient number of compurgators, or because those they did bring refused to take the oath, not because of objections by interested

---

[629]The best study of testamentary administration for the mid-sixteenth century remains Houlbrooke, *Church courts*, pp. 89-116.
[630]London, 1590-1.

parties, which were rare. Purgation was a primitive and unreliable means of discovering the truth, but a useful means of avoiding conflict and maintaining social harmony. It allowed the putative offender to produce those of his neighbours who were willing to speak in his favour under an external supervision which gave the proceedings solemnity and reduced the likelihood that gross fraud or injustice would be perpetrated.[631]

Purgation was effectively abolished in 1661,[632] although there was some argument about this among legal scholars like Edmund Gibson.[633] In any case it disappeared in the late seventeenth century and has never been revived.

R, 2 8 is a statement of general principles, of which the only ones of particular interest are R, 28.3, which maintains the right of the clergy to trial in their own courts, a principle which was being gradually whittled away in the sixteenth century and disappeared completely in the early nineteenth, and R, 28.11, which allows monetary commutation of penance in certain circumstances. This was not a popular idea with the church's disciplinarians, who did their best to stamp it out, though without much success.[634] An interesting detail is that here, as elsewhere in the *Reformatio*, financial penalties were to be paid into the poor box of the parish, a new institution designed to replace medieval almsgiving.[635] Poor relief was a major protestant concern, and the application of such fines to this purpose was a result of that influence.[636]

R, 29 deals with suspension, which had never been treated before under that heading, but which on inspection turns out to be nothing other than what was generally known as the lesser excommunication. This barred a person from receiving or administering the sacraments (unless he was dying, in which case he could receive them) without cutting him off from society in general. Anyone who was suspended would be given a year to do the penance required of him, after which he would be subjected to the greater excommunication, which theoretically removed him from all social intercourse. Suspension of this kind was practised with reasonable frequency until 1640, but after the restoration it was difficult to enforce, even though it was not formally abolished until 1813.[637] Disciplinary action against clergymen is still possible of course, and it

---

[631]Houlbrooke, *Church courts*, pp. 45-6.

[632]13 Charles II, s. 1, c. 12, s. 4, 1661 (*S.R.*, V, 315-16).

[633]See Rodes, *Law and modernization*, pp. 23-4.

[634]It was forbidden by 1575/12(13), but this was relaxed by 1584/2 which was repeated and extended by 1597/9. Nothing was said about the matter in the canons of 1603 (1604), but it seems that 1597/9 retained its authority. See *A.C.*, pp. 246-8.

[635]The poor box was set up following the royal injunctions of Edward VI (1547/29). See *D.E.R.*, pp. 255-6. In the 1549 prayer book opportunity was given to the parishioners to contribute to it before receiving holy communion.

[636]For example, it was the 'sixth law' of Martin Bucer's ideal Christian commonwealth. See *De regno Christi*, II, 14.

[637]53 George III, c. 127, 12 July 1813.

occasionally happens that a priest's licence will be withdrawn for some reason, but the legal procedure by which this is done is now different from that which obtained at the time the *Reformatio* was written.

R, 30 deals with the process of sequestration, by which funds could be seized for a variety of different reasons. Sequestration occurred when it was necessary to provide for the repair of dilapidated church property, when possession of a benefice was contested, or when an incumbent vacated the living. The last of these still occurs, but the others have been made redundant by changes in church administration. A peculiar instance of sequestration is mentioned in R, 30.3, where it is stated that a woman involved in a matrimonial suit may be sequestered for her own protection until the issue is resolved. This has nothing to do with the other forms of sequestration mentioned in this title, and probably should have been put in R, 10, but it is a good example of how the form of words used in a canon could be more important than its content and determine where it would be placed in a code of law.

R, 31 is a short title on deprivation, which has no exact precedent in medieval canon law, although most of the content is found there in different places. The main point of interest is that provision is made for the deprivation of bishops (R, 31.2) where a new procedure was required. Before the reformation, a bishop could only be deprived by the pope, but in the *Reformatio* this is entrusted to the archbishop and two other bishops, acting together. Deprivation was an extreme measure, but it remains possible and modern ecclesiastical law makes provision for it in ways which are fundamentally similar to the ones described in this title.

R, 32 deals with (the greater) excommunication, laying down the rules for it in considerable detail. Of special interest are the canons which state that no one is to be excommunicated without being given advance warning (R, 32.4), and that only individuals, not the universities or colleges to which they might belong, can be excommunicated (R, 32.5). The utmost care was to be taken in pronouncing sentence, which had to be delivered in writing, and there were severe penalties for a judge who abused this power. Once a person was excommunicated, notice of this was to be given in his own parish church, as well as in the neighbouring ones, and failure to repent after forty days would lead to imprisonment under the writ of *significavit*. None of this was new, and excommunication was a commonly used weapon in the ecclesiastical courts, even though it was frequently defied by those affected. It was finally abolished in 1813 (see R, 30 above).

R, 33 is a liturgical piece composed independently (and probably before) R, 32, to which it was later connected.[638] It is hard for us to imagine any occasion on which this form of service would have been used, but there was a demand for it to be introduced in 1563, whether as part of the *Reformatio* or not.[639] The 'puritan' elements among the reformers believed strongly in the salutary

---

[638]We know this because R, 33 is in MS Harleian 426, whereas R, 32 is not.
[639]In the *General note of matters to be moved by the clergy*, 3.46. See *A.C.*, p. 736.

properties of public shaming, which would become a prominent feature of law enforcement wherever they were in a position to determine its nature.[640] They would have welcomed a public demonstration of the reconciliation of a penitent, if only to reinforce the message that it was best to avoid being caught in a position where such penitence would be necessary. But no service of this type has ever entered the public worship of the Church of England, even though there has been a service of commination, or 'denouncing of God's anger and judgments against sinners' in every prayer book since 1549.

G. Courts and their procedure (34-47; 49; 51-4)

These titles outline the pattern of ecclesiastical justice, and they are thoroughly traditional, the only real innovation being the (inevitable) substitution of royal for papal supremacy. Otherwise these titles are little more than a summary of the standard practice which had long been in place. It would not be necessary to say very much about them, except that the procedure of the church courts is little known or understood nowadays, and so some explanation of how they functioned has to be given if the content of these titles is to be understood.[641]

The *Reformatio* does not list the actual courts themselves, no doubt because they were so familiar to contemporaries, but incidental remarks make it clear that knowledge of them was assumed. A wide range of ecclesiastical officials had courts in which they dispensed justice, and there were even some secular courts which had the right to administer certain aspects of the ecclesiastical law. The system can best be explained by using the following tabular form:

1. *The high court of delegates.* This was a crown court set up in 1534 to hear appeals which had previously gone to the Roman curia. It did not sit permanently, but was constituted on an *ad hoc* basis, and in its early years it was dominated by the higher clergy.[642] The court survived until 1 February 1833, when it was replaced by the then newly-formed judicial committee of the privy council.

---

[640]It was particularly prominent in New England for most of the seventeenth century.

[641]For this, see R. E. Rodes, *Ecclesiastical administration in medieval England* (Notre Dame, 1977); *idem.*, *Lay authority and reformation in the English church* (Notre Dame, 1982); Houlbrooke, *Church courts*. For a more popular account with a number of helpful illustrations, see A. Tarver, *Church court records. An introduction for family and local historians* (Chichester, 1995).

[642]This changed later on, and after 1750 no bishop is known to have sat in this court. It was dissolved on 1 February 1833, when its powers were transferred to the judicial committee of the privy council. Some of them still remain there, but since 1 March 1965 most have been transferred to a new court, that of ecclesiastical causes reserved, which operates under the rules of canon law, unlike the judicial committee which follows common law procedures.

2. *The archbishops' courts.* There were audience courts, in which the archbishops were supposed to preside in person (though they usually delegated this to others), provincial appeal courts, and various peculiar courts. In the province of Canterbury there was also a prerogative court for the probate of testaments.[643] The provincial appeal courts still exist, but the prerogative and peculiar courts were abolished on 11 January 1858 and the audience courts disappeared on 1 March 1965, although they had become moribund long before.[644]

3. *The bishops' courts.* These paralleled those of the archbishops, with both audience and diocesan courts. The latter were normally known as consistory courts, except that in the diocese of Canterbury the term 'commissary court' was used instead.[645] It has to be said that audience courts were fading out at the time the *Reformatio* was composed and that the few attempts which were made to reinvigorate them were unsuccessful. The consistory courts still exist today, but as in the case of the archbishops' courts, the audience courts were formally abolished on 1 March 1965 after having been moribund since the seventeenth century.

4. *The archdeacons' courts.* These were the normal courts of first instance, especially for matters concerning parish furnishings and so on. They were abolished and their business was taken over by the diocesan consistory courts on 1 March 1965.[646]

5. *Other courts.* These were provided for peculiar jurisdictions. There were also manorial courts, in which secular judges sometimes handled matters such as the probate of testaments.[647] They were abolished at different times, the last ones on 11 January 1858.[648]

The jurisdiction of the ecclesiastical courts had been defined by the *Articuli cleri* of 1316, which were regarded as a statute of the realm.[649] The *Reformatio*

---

[643]The prerogative court ceased to function on 11 January 1858, when testamentary jurisdiction was secularized. The provincial appeal courts still exist, though since 1874 they have been combined to the extent that their presidents must always be the same person for both courts. Since 1 March 1965 they are no longer courts of first instance.

[644]The Canterbury court of audience does not appear to have met at all after 1640, though its York equivalent seems to have struggled on until early in the eighteenth century.

[645]This distinction is still preserved.

[646]Curiously enough, there are now (2000) proposals to revamp the consistory courts which, if adopted, will leave *only* the former archdeaconry courts' business in their hands.

[647]Most of these were abolished by orders-in-council after 1836, and any which survived ceased to function on 11 January 1858, when their jurisdiction was secularized. For the details, see *A.C.*, pp. 909-10.

[648]See *ibid.* for the details.

[649]9 Edward II, c. 1, 1316 (*S.R.*, I, 171-4). The statute was gradually whittled away until it was finally repealed *in toto* by the ecclesiastical jurisdiction measure (1963/no. 1), which received the royal assent on 31 July 1963 and became law on 1 March 1965.

lists the areas of their competence, and by comparing these with the topics which it treats in some detail, we can discover which of them really functioned in practice and which were moribund. The list is as follows, with the relevant title(s) given in brackets:

1.	Benefices	(11)
2.	Matrimony and divorce	(8-10)
3.	Testamentary causes	(27)
4.	Tithes and offerings	(25)
5.	Usury[650]	
6.	Heresy	(2-3)
7.	Sexual sins	(10)
8.	Sacrilege	(6)
9.	Perjury	(39)
10.	Blasphemy	(4)
11.	Breach of faith	(39)
12.	Defamation	(50)
13.	Violence against the clergy	(48)
14.	Disturbing divine worship	(19)
15.	Correction of morals[651]	
16.	Church accounts	(21)
17.	Dilapidation and other debts	(15)

Preliminary definitions (34-6)

These titles were originally one, but were divided by Archbishop Cranmer at the drafting stage, and this division was preserved in the printed editions. R, 34 begins by defining what a judgment is, and explaining that it may take one of two forms, which are called 'ordinary' and 'extraordinary' (or more usually 'summary') judgments. In the first of these the order of procedure was followed in all respects, whereas in the second it was shortened or even avoided altogether by what we would now call an 'out-of-court' settlement. Every effort was made to do this if possible, because of the strong desire to limit both the time and the expense of litigation in the courts, but it was made quite clear that the summary procedure could not be used if doing so would cause prejudice to the interests of either party involved. Indeed, it would not be too much to say that the determination to avoid unnecessary time and expense dominated most of what

---

[650]Ecclesiastical jurisdiction over usury was first challenged by 37 Henry VIII, c. 9, 1545 (*S.R.*, III, 996-7) and by 13 Elizabeth I, c. 8, 1571 (*S.R.*, IV, 542-3). See Helmholz, *Roman canon law*, p. 116, who says that even though both statutes recognized the jurisdiction of the church courts in this area, in fact ecclesiastical causes related to usury 'all but ceased'.

[651]There is no title devoted to this subject, but it could be argued that elements related to it are scattered through several others.

the *Reformatio* had to say about judicial procedure in the ecclesiastical courts, and virtually all of its 'innovations' are connected with this.[652]

R, 35 is a short title which defines what a crime is and how proceedings may be initiated. Crimes were divided into two kinds – those which were 'notorious' and those which were not. A 'notorious' crime was defined as one which was so obvious that no judicial proceedings were required. All that was necessary in such cases was for sentence to be pronounced, though if the guilty party wished to defend his action he was allowed to do so, provided that his defence was within the provisions of the law. That judgments of this kind were summary would seem to go without saying, but it should be noted that the *Reformatio* was careful to state as much explicitly (R, 3 5.2). Crimes which were not 'notorious', *i.e.* where there was some doubt about who may have committed them, had to be tried in court. However, it was provided that summary procedure would normally be used in so-called 'instance' cases. These dealt with disputes brought by the parties themselves and concerned such things as benefices, matrimony, testaments, tithes and usury. Other matters would normally be handled by a judge acting *ex officio* according to the ordinary procedure, unless the parties agreed to waive it or some order from a higher authority intervened to impose the summary procedure instead.

There were four ways in which an *ex officio,* or 'office' cause might be initiated. These are listed in R, 35.1 as follows:[653]

1. Accusation
2. ('Evangelical') denunciation
3. Inquisition (inquest)
4. Exception

The first type (also known as ex *officio promoto*), was initiated by a plaintiff, who had to present his accusation(s) in a document known as a *libellus* ('libel').[654] He also had to agree that if his case failed, he would be subject to the penalty which the other party would have received if he had been convicted, unless he appealed the case to a higher court. That was a powerful deterrent, and generally ensured that accusation was a little-used form of procedure. The second type was initiated by an ecclesiastical superior against one of the clergy or officials under his jurisdiction in cases where the latter had refused to comply with disciplinary measures instituted by that superior. It was well known to the post-reformation courts in the form of 'presentments' which were regularly made

---

[652]For example, it was decreed that no ecclesiastical cause should last more than one year (R, 36.19), a stipulation which had medieval precedents of a kind but which must be regarded as new in this context.

[653]The list occurs in two other places, *viz.* R, 3.2 and R, 44.2.

[654]The word means 'booklet', but in modern English usage, 'libel' has so changed in meaning that its use in this context must now be regarded as highly technical and specialized.

by churchwardens and parish clergy against recalcitrant parishioners, a procedure which endured as long as the church courts exercised jurisdiction over the laity in matters of tithe, probate and matrimony. Today presentments are made only against errant clergy, though some legal opinion holds that lay people who work for the church might also be subject to them in certain circumstances.[655]

Inquisition, the third type, is familiar to us from the system of heresy trials described under R, 3 above, but that specialized usage makes it preferable for us to use the word 'inquest' when describing the standard procedure, as was in fact done in contemporary English usage. An inquest was a cause initiated by the judge *ex officio mero*, which meant that it did not require a plaintiff. The fourth type resulted from objections raised by the accused in an attempt to discredit the plaintiff by showing that the latter's accusation(s) were inadmissible, either because they were not properly made or because the plaintiff was guilty of the same crimes he was accusing the defendant of. In crimes of exception the plaintiff had the right of reply (or counter-exception), to which the defendant could in turn answer ('triplication'). This pattern would continue until one of the parties either ran out of objections or one of his objections was rejected by the judge, at which point he would be declared the loser.[656] Sometimes one cause would lead to another which emerged in the course of proceedings, in which case the presiding judge had the authority to hear the emergent cause as well as long as he did not confuse it with the main cause.[657]

R, 36.1-5 lays down the rules for deciding who could be regarded as a competent judge in any given case. A litigant could choose a judge outside his own jurisdiction, provided that all parties in the suit agreed, but if he did so, he was bound to accept the result. Jurisdiction passed automatically from a judge to his successor, and there were rules to determine who was ineligible for such a post (R, 36.3). Furthermore, if there was evidence that a judge might be prejudiced in favour of one of the parties, his jurisdiction could be rejected. Trials were divided into three distinct parts, which are defined in R, 36.6 as follows:

1. From the beginning up to the joinder of issue.
2. From the joinder of issue to the conclusion of the cause.
3. The process of sentencing.

The initial stage dealt with preliminaries, which are spelled out in the remainder of this title. Once a judge initiated or accepted a cause, he would issue a citation to the person accused, ordering him to appear in court on a fixed day.

---

[655] See *Halsbury's laws of England* (4th edn., London, 1975-), XIV, paragraphs 1350-1.
[656] A whole title is given over to exceptions (R, 52), explaining when and how they could be made. The procedure still operates today in faculty causes. See T. Briden and B. Hanson, *Moore's introduction to English canon law* (3rd edn., London, 1992), pp. 117-18.
[657] R, 36.18.

Theoretically citations were issued three times if necessary, but this process was short-circuited in practice by issuing one peremptory citation.[658] In instance causes the citation might also include the plaintiff's libel, so that the accused person could prepare his reply in advance and thereby cut down the amount of time spent in court. In fact it seems that in many cases issue of such a citation was enough to prompt the other party to seek an out-of-court settlement, which made it a particularly useful legal device.[659] Persons cited were expected to appear, but in most circumstances they could be represented by 'proctors', a word which in this context means 'advocates'.[660] Normally, the hearing was held in the court of the jurisdiction in which the accused person dwelt, but it could also be held where the crime had been committed, as long as it took place in a recognized courtroom (R, 36.13-15). Hearings could be terminated by a higher judge and were automatically suspended if the judge in the case was promoted to higher office within the same jurisdiction. But suspension did not occur when one of the litigants died. In that case the judge would proceed against his proctor, if he had one, though any judgment would be borne by the deceased litigant's heir or executor (R, 36.17). All cases were supposed to be wound up within a year, and could not be prolonged by the judge acting on his own initiative (R, 36.19-20). At the end of the case the judge was compelled to pronounce sentence one way or the other, but if it could be proved that this sentence was malicious or fraudulent he could be severely punished for it (R, 36.21). There were further provisions stating that a defendant who refused to appear for sentencing forfeited his right to appeal (R, 36.22) and that minors could not be litigants in their own right (R, 36.23).

Judges (37)

In post-reformation England the ultimate source of all legal jurisdiction, both civil and ecclesiastical, was (and still is) the crown (R, 37.2). But beneath the crown the pre-reformation hierarchy was preserved intact and continued to function as it had done previously. Theoretically, the judges who presided in the ecclesiastical courts were the church dignitaries to whom the courts belonged, but in practice only the archdeacons sat at all regularly in them.[661] This made it essential to define the rôle and the rights of their substitutes, who were of two different types. First of all there were judges with the right to preside, and then there were those who were merely delegated for a particular purpose or duration of time. In the former category were the chancellors, or vicars general, who were

---

[658]R, 36.7. the matter is covered at greater length in R, 51.20-3.
[659]Houlbrooke, *Church courts*, p. 40.
[660]One of the astonishing things about the *Reformatio* is that it says virtually nothing about the personnel who administered the ecclesiastical court system. Advocates are referred to from time to time as proctors for the litigants, but the officials known to us as 'proctors' are never mentioned. Nor is anything said about the registrars who issued the citations (and could therefore often control their use) or about the apparitors who delivered them.
[661]There were no juries.

appointed by the bishop of the diocese but who were not directly dependent on him.[662] In the latter category was anyone else who was given a personal commission to act as a judge. Both kinds of judge had full access to all the resources of the law required to fulfill their functions. The essential difference between them was that an official who was a judge in his own right could subdelegate his functions to someone else, but one who was already a delegated judge could not subdelegate his authority any further. This did not apply to ecclesiastical judges who were delegates of the king (i.e. who sat in the high court of delegates), any more than it had previously applied to those who had been delegates of the pope.[663] All judges lost their posts when the person who appointed them died or was translated to another see, because the basis of government in both church and state remained personal.[664]

It should be pointed out that the *Reformatio* paid close attention to misdemeanours on the part of judges, and made provision for punishing them if necessary. It was also possible for one or both of the parties to reject a judge if there was a good reason to suspect his impartiality, but not just because he was from another diocese, although judges were not to take causes from outside their jurisdiction.[665] The final canons of R, 37 specify further instances in which the competence of a particular judge was recognized or restricted, as the case may be.

Trials and evidence (38-42)

R, 38 deals with the joinder of issue, which marked the beginning of the trial. This was the second but most important stage of the judgment, because it was then that the arguments on either side were debated and a case was made out for the judge to decide. If the accused person confessed his guilt, there would be no need to proceed any further, and the trial would move straight to the sentence. But if the accused decided to defend himself, he would be subjected to a detailed interrogation by the judge, based on the contents of the plaintiff's libel, although the plaintiff himself was not obliged to be present. The accused could block

---

[662]The position is well expressed in Briden and Hanson, *Moore's introduction*, p. 115: 'He [the chancellor] is appointed by the bishop; but thereupon he becomes an independent judge in one of the queen's courts, deriving his authority not from the bishop, but from the law, and charged, like all judges, with hearing and determining impartially causes in which the bishop or the crown may have an interest.'

[663]This is a good example of how the royal supremacy replaced the papal one without altering the fundamental structure of the church.

[664]However, such a judge could terminate any cause which was then in progress, unless he was named to succeed the man who had originally appointed him. Normally judges were reappointed by the bishop's successor, but this was not automatic, and strong-willed prelates could ignore it. Archbishop Laud, for example, wasted no time in replacing his predecessor's official principal with a man more to his own liking as soon as he got to Canterbury.

[665]Cf. R, 36.21; 37.18-21.

proceedings by raising objections ('exceptions') which were of two types. Dilatory exceptions served to postpone the joinder of issue, and peremptory exceptions, if admitted, would end the cause altogether. These were dealt with in greater detail in two separate titles (R, 51-2).

Proceedings in the joinder of issue opened with the swearing of the oaths (R, 39), something which was taken with the utmost seriousness in the sixteenth century when a man's word was his bond even more than it is today. Rash swearing (*i.e.* using religious language disrespectfully) was strongly disliked (cf. R, 4.1-2) and punished with a fine, but oaths were not regarded as unlawful in principle and they were demanded of all litigants as a form of insurance against perjury. Perjury was regarded as one of the most serious crimes and was severely punished, with the result that it became important to distinguish it from things like lapses of memory or ignorance which could lead to inadvertent lying, but which were not punishable offences. The most important of the oaths were the ones against calumny and malice (R, 40), which all parties to a suit had to take, including the judge.[666]

Once the oaths were sworn, the judge would proceed to an examination of the evidence (R, 41). Different types of evidence were admissible, but documentary proof was preferred. The plaintiff was expected to support his accusations with such evidence and if he could not do so the case would be quashed, and he would have to reimburse the accused party for any expenses incurred as a result of the accusation. The best form of evidence consisted of public records which bore the seal of the appropriate authority, though in certain circumstances private documents were also admissible. Such documents were not entirely above suspicion however, and the *Reformatio* goes to great lengths in describing how their authenticity was to be determined (R, 43). These directions are of some interest to us, because they are a reminder that, even after a century of printing, handwritten documents were still the preferred norm, as they were to remain for several centuries. Forgery was regarded as a crime equal to perjury, and was likewise severely punished (R, 44).

The burden of proof normally lay with the plaintiff, though there were subtle variations on this according to circumstances. For example, if a creditor sued his debtor for payment and the latter claimed to have paid, it was up to the accused to produce evidence to support his claim (R, 41.11). It was also possible for the person accused to assume the burden of proof, though he was not compelled to do so (R, 41.17). The ancient maxim that 'possession is nine-tenths of the law' is borne out by R, 42, a very short title which was originally part of R, 41 and which affirms that in property disputes the burden of proof lay not with the possessor but with the plaintiff. If both claimed possession, the one with the older title would prevail.

---

[666] Judges were allowed to take it only once, when entering upon their offices (R, 40.2). The difference between the oath against calumny and the oath against malice is explained in R, 40.5.

R, 41.14 makes brief mention of the *testes synodales*, but the casual reader would have no idea from what it says how important the *rôle* of these men was. 'Synodal witnesses' originated in the middle ages when it was the custom to decide parish disputes at diocesan and other synods. In an attempt to discover the truth, a number of respected parishioners would be formally sworn and asked to give testimony at these gatherings. As time went on, 'sworn men' came to be regarded as local officials who had a duty to keep an eye on things in their parish and report misdemeanours to the authorities. In normal circumstances their testimony was used to support that of the churchwardens and/or the incumbent in their presentations. They were frequently referred to as 'questmen' (*quaestores*) or as 'synodsmen', though the latter term was soon corrupted to 'sidesmen' which it remains to this day, though modern sidesmen might be surprised to discover what their predecessors' duties were.[667]

Oral witnesses (or written depositions submitted by them) were also common, and the *Reformatio* gives detailed instructions for determining their admissibility (R, 45). Normally witnesses could not be accepted before the joinder of issue, but this rule was waived in cases where it was feared that the witness might die before the hearing or be otherwise unavailable for it, and any witnesses brought in to support a dilatory or peremptory exception would have to be heard beforehand, since the joinder of issue hung on the outcome of their testimony.[668] The same rules of oath-taking and perjury applied to witnesses as applied to the principal parties in the suit, and consideration was given to determining what kind of people (and how many) should be admitted in any given instance. Witnesses could be summoned from any part of the country, but certain people did not have to appear, *e.g.* royal officials and soldiers on active duty. Their expenses were to be paid by the party which called them to testify (R, 45.32) and there were clear guidelines as to how their statements were to be interpreted. Virtually all of this material was culled from the medieval canon law and its commentators, and here the *Reformatio* is merely describing established practice.

Points of procedure (46-7, 49)

The remaining titles dealing with procedure cover a number of miscellaneous matters which are not treated elsewhere but about which it was necessary to say something. For example, there is a short title on custom (R, 46), which defines what it is and when it can be accepted as valid, and a longer one dealing with prescriptions (R, 47), many of which were rooted in customary practices. As the title indicates, prescriptions in the ecclesiastical law of the sixteenth century were mainly to do with tithe revenue and other income, and the chief concern seems to have been that parishes would claim to be exempt from having to pay certain tithes, or from having to contribute to the expenses of an episcopal visitation.

---

[667] The form 'sidemen' is also found in sixteenth- and seventeenth-century documents.
[668] These provisions are also found in R, 38.10-12.

There is also an interesting title on presumptions (R, 49), which was obviously pieced together from many different sources. As is common with such lists it is hard to say what principles, if any, guided the selection of material.[669] There does not appear to be any inner logic in the selection, though no doubt each individual item had its place in contemporary thinking. It is quite possible, perhaps even probable, that whoever composed the title put things down more or less as they occurred to him, without giving much thought to the overall effect.

Delays and exceptions (51-2)

The long title on delays (R, 51) shows how much importance was given to this subject, which was a major source of public dissatisfaction with the ecclesiastical courts. However, it has to be said that the title was more concerned to explain the rules for granting delays and to establish what business could and could not be transacted on particular holidays than it was to shorten proceedings overall. As a result, its contents are thoroughly traditional and do not merit the designation 'reform' in any meaningful sense. The following title on exceptions (R, 52) is somewhat more reforming in intention, but it too says virtually nothing which does not derive from some medieval source.

Sentences and appeals (53-4)

The last two titles in the procedural section deal with the third part of the judgment: the passing of sentence and the right of appeal resulting from it (R, 53-4). As there was no jury, responsibility for the final decision rested on the shoulders of the judge, and it was therefore essential to make sure that he was being guided by the law and not by his own intuition ('conscience'). It was also important to define what constituted a sentence, since in the course of the joinder of issue the judge might be called upon to make any number of pronouncements which might sound like a sentence without being one. This difficulty was dealt with by distinguishing two types of sentence, of which the first and less important was the 'interlocutory' one. This might be given at any time during the course of the hearing and its main purpose was to clear the way for the main issue to be dealt with. It could also be revoked by the judge at any time during the proceedings. The second type of sentence was the final ('definitive') one, which required much greater care to be taken in framing and pronouncing it. Once it was pronounced it could not be revoked, and if the condemned party wished to object to it, he had no alternative but to appeal to a higher judge. The issue then became a *res iudicata* ('judgment rendered'), and was consigned for execution, after a short delay to allow for a possible appeal.[670]

---

[669]Cf. R, 55 for a similar situation.

[670]This was normally ten days, but in R, 51.4 it was given first as twelve and then as fifteen. Perhaps this was an intended reform of the existing practice, but it may have been no more than a confusion arising from a well-established habit of extending the deadline.

R, 54 is taken up with the many provisions which existed for appeals, none of which can be regarded as innovatory in any way. As with the other procedural matters, the title must be seen as a handy guide to existing practice, which could be confusing for those who were not familiar with it, and not as a blueprint for reform. Whether appeals were very common may be doubted, since it was always possible to bypass the lower courts and take a matter straight to the provincial ones, which many people did in order to save unnecessary time and expense, but as long as a hierarchy of courts existed an appeals procedure had to be spelled out.[671]

The titles on procedure can be summed up by saying that they look more like self-contained set pieces on a given topic than like parts of an integrated whole. In some cases they read very much like student essays which contain everything that the writer knows about the matter, whether it is directly relevant to the subject or not, but do not necessarily cover everything they should. One result of this is that there is a good deal of overlap, and anyone who wants to know the law on citations, exceptions or appeals, for example, has to look in more than one title. Probably this would not have bothered the civilians, who were used to doing that with much larger volumes, and who generally knew what to do in any case, but the uninitiated (who might well include the principal parties in any given suit) could easily have found themselves confused or inadequately informed. A careful edit and rearrangement (of the kind found in R, 2-3) was what was required, but probably Archbishop Cranmer was not enough of a lawyer to be able to do it, and may not have been particularly interested in trying.[672]

Anyone who wonders whether these titles could ever have served as a practical guide for those who practised in the ecclesiastical courts has only to look at the manual prepared towards the end of the sixteenth century by an otherwise unknown proctor, Francis Clarke (*fl. c.*1596).[673] Not only is Clarke's presentation of the material infinitely more systematic than what we find in the *Reformatio*, it is also much longer and more complete, taking no fewer than 339 titles to cover what the *Reformatio* condenses into twenty or so. Clarke's work was complemented by his contemporary Henry Swinburne (*c.*1575-1624), whose two treatises on marriage and testaments likewise went into much greater detail

---

[671]Since 1 March 1965 it is no longer possible to bypass the diocesan consistory courts, which may have the effect of making appeals more common than they once were.

[672]This may explain why he turned the 'editing' over to Peter Martyr Vermigli, who did not do much either. Both men seem to have been content to supply the canons with individual headings, many of which merely abbreviate their contents.

[673]Written in 1596, Clarke's work circulated in manuscript for seventy years, being finally printed by Thomas Bladen as *Praxis Francisci Clarke, tam ius dicentibus quam aliis omnibus qui in foro ecclesiastico versantur apprime utilis* (Dublin, 1666). Unfortunately, the printed edition is corrupt and often unreliable. An English version was prepared by Henry Consett and entitled *The practice of the spiritual or ecclesiastical courts* (London, 1685). It was reprinted in 1700 and again in 1708. See Baker, *Monuments*, pp. 71-6.

than the *Reformatio* did on those particular subjects.[674] By the mid-eighteenth century there were manuals by John Godolphin (1617-78),[675] John Ayliffe (1676-1732)[676] and Thomas Oughton (d. *c.*1740),[677] the first of whom was a practising advocate and the other two proctors in the ecclesiastical courts, and all of these were much more comprehensive than anything found in the *Reformatio*. We may therefore say without any hesitation that as a practical tool for determining proper procedure the *Reformatio* would have been superseded very quickly indeed if it had been authorized either in 1553 or in 1571.

H. Crimes (48; 50)

Interpolated among the titles on procedure are two short ones dealing with miscellaneous crimes. The first one, on violence against clergy (R, 48), was put there deliberately by Archbishop Cranmer, who knew that it did not belong with the titles on benefices but seems to have been at a loss as to where it ought to go. Special treatment for the clergy was greatly resented, as R, 48.2 demonstrates, and from 1576 clergy accused of secular offences had to be tried in the secular courts along with everyone else.[678] Even so, remnants of clergy privilege, known as 'benefit of clergy', survived for a long time in English law and were not finally abolished until 1827.[679]

The second title, on defamation (R, 50), was added to MS Harleian 426 after Cranmer's re-ordering, and it does not really fit anywhere in particular either. It deals very briefly with a matter which was gradually coming to be regarded as the province of the secular courts, though the church courts were kept busy with defamation suits involving sexual offences for some time after the reformation.[680] Defamation cases in the church courts became less common in the seventeenth century and eventually almost disappeared, though the ecclesiastical jurisdiction over them was not abolished until 1855.[681]

---

[674]*A briefe treatise of testaments and last willes, very profitable to be understoode of all the subjects of this realme of England* (London, 1590-1); *Of spousals* (London, 1686). The latter was unfinished and not published until long after Swinburne's death. See Baker, *Monuments*, pp. 57-70.

[675]*The orphan's legacy, or a testamentary abridgement* (London, 1674); *Repertorium canonicum* (London, 1678). See Baker, *Monuments*, pp. 77-86.

[676]*Parergon iuris canonici Anglicani, or a commentary, by way of supplement to the canons and constitutions of the Church of England* (London, 1726). See Baker, *Monuments*, pp. 87-8.

[677]*Ordo iudiciorum, sive methodus procedendi in negotiis et litibus in foro ecclesiastico-civili britannico et hibernico* (2 vols., London, 1728). See Baker, *Monuments*, pp. 89-94.

[678]18 Elizabeth I, c. 7, 1576 (*S.R.*, IV, 617-18).

[679]7-8 George IV, c. 28, 21 June 1827.

[680]The canons are taken from the *Corpus iuris civilis*, but the medieval canon law had sanctioned this. Cf. X, 5.36.9 (Fr, II, 880) and so had the commentators. Helmholz, *Roman canon law*, pp. 58-60 discusses post-reformation developments in this area.

[681]18-19 Victoria, c. 41, 26 June 1855.

Both titles are remnants of Book 5 of the *Decretals*, which the drafting committee had dismembered and rearranged, leaving only these loose ends which had nowhere else to go.

J. The rules of law (55)

These are all derived from earlier sources, mainly in the *Corpus iuris civilis* or the *Corpus iuris canonici*. Not infrequently they are found in both, since the canonical list was compiled by Pope Boniface VIII (1294-1303) from ancient Roman sources. There is little internal order in them, except that occasionally rules on a given subject (*e.g.* testaments) may be found together. Some of the subjects are dealt with in other titles, but on the whole the rules are just a checklist of general principles which had to be applied and interpreted in particular cases if they were to have any meaning at all. Archbishop Cranmer went to the trouble of indicating the sources in the left margin of the manuscript, and these were repeated without elaboration in both Foxe's and Cardwell's editions. Since the notation system which Cranmer used is hard for a non-specialist to follow, as well as being incomplete and occasionally inaccurate, it has been replaced in this edition with a complete apparatus which respects modern critical norms. The sources of the eighty-two rules listed may be broken down as follows:

Decretals (X):	1
Sext (VI) only:	37
Digest only:	30
Digest/Sext:	12
Digest/other:	1
Other:	1

From this it can be seen that the compiler did not look very far, and it may be added that the rules which he selected represent only a fraction of the total, particularly where the *Digest* is concerned. We can only assume that these are the ones which he found relevant to the sixteenth-century situation, though as with other lists of this kind it is virtually impossible to detect any rational principle of selection behind it.

4. Conclusion

The spirit of the *Reformatio*

In conclusion, it can be said that the *Reformatio* was not only conceived within the framework of the Cranmerian reformation (of which it was intended to be the disciplinary pillar alongside the doctrinal and liturgical ones), but that it also reflects the kind of conservative reform which the church establishment desired.

It conformed to the many changes which the articles of religion and the book of common prayer introduced and fully supported them, but when dealing with purely legal matters it was little more than a restatement of existing (and largely medieval) canons and customs. There were only the most minimal moves towards 'reform', and many of these may have been the result of accident or misunderstanding as much as of deliberate policy. The reformers clearly saw no need to tamper with the well-established system of ecclesiastical justice, and they contented themselves with trying to explain its inner workings in a way which makes the second half of the *Reformatio* read more like a handy reference work than anything else.

But although this is true, it cannot be the final word on the *Reformatio* as a text bearing witness to the nature of the sixteenth-century upheaval in the Church of England. The committee which drafted it, and the people who preserved and published it, lived in an age when God walked among men in a way which made even the greatest among them willing to sacrifice all they had, if only they might somehow 'build Jerusalem in England's green and pleasant land'. They not only believed that such a goal was achievable – they also thought that God had called them to achieve it. We ought not to forget that John Foxe published the *Reformatio* only a few weeks after putting the finishing touches on the second edition of his *Acts and monuments*; it was his very next project, and one which he must have thought would honour the reformation martyrs just as much as his more famous work did.

A secular age such as our own finds it hard to understand this, but we should not hasten to dismiss the *Reformatio* on that account. It is quite possible, and in the longer perspective of history almost certain, that the present secularism will one day give way to a new age of religious conviction, and when that happens people who pick up the *Reformatio* may appreciate it more deeply than we can today. It is worth remembering that as long as the ecclesiastical courts survived in their traditional form the *Reformatio* found its admirers, and that criticism of it did not become dominant until the circumstances in which it could have been applied had ceased to exist. In the event of revived interest in the *Reformatio* at some future date it will be those changed circumstances, rather than any defects in the document itself, which will seal its fate. For even if a generation arises which understands its spiritual purpose and wants to put it into effect, the social and legal situation with which it will have to deal will be so different that the *Reformatio* will be unable to contribute any more than its spirit to such an enterprise. Perhaps that is just as well, since anachronistic attempts to revive a long dead past are always unworkable and often disastrous. If the *Reformatio* survives as something more than a historical curiosity it will only be as a spiritual inspiration to future generations, not as a practical programme for action. In that sense its time has passed and it is the historians, not the practitioners of either theology or law, who now lay claim to its legacy.

Characteristics of this edition

The Henrician canons

This edition basically reproduces the MS, including the corrections and deletions found in it, but with a few minor alterations. First, it has been necessary to modify the punctuation to some extent because that of the original does not always make sense to a modern reader and is sometimes defective. Similarly, the paragraph divisions of the MS have been retained when they occur within particular canons, but when they indicate a new source, a new canon has been created to reflect this. In no case does this affect the sense of the original in any way. Other alterations concern the spelling, which has been standardized according to the modern dictionary norm. This involves the following changes:

1. 'Ae' and 'oe' in place of 'e'. *E.g.* 'poenae' is now distinguished from 'paene', whereas in the MS both are written 'pene'.
2. 'Dif-' sometimes becomes 'de-'. *E.g.* 'defamatio' replaces 'diffamatio'.
3. 'C' and 't' are distinguished along etymological lines. *E.g.* 'officium' instead of 'offitium'; 'ratio' instead of 'racio', etc.

Such a policy will displease some scholars, but they will have no trouble restoring the MS spelling and normalization means that others will be able to find the words in a dictionary without any difficulty. All abbreviated words have also been written out in full.[682] Other modifications to the MS are noted in the text as they occur.

The Reformatio legum ecclesiasticarum

In general, the same principles as those outlined above apply, especially where questions of spelling and punctuation are concerned. The existence of three printed editions, as well as of a MS with many alterations, makes it almost impossible to use one of them as a standard in such matters, or to give every variant. However, care has been taken to indicate those places where Archbishop Cranmer deliberately altered the punctuation in MS Harleian 426.

All textual variants have been placed in the main body of the Latin text, whether they are significant or not, on the assumption that those able to consult it will also be able to decide for themselves which reading is to be preferred, or whether either is possible. The variants have been transcribed in such a way as to indicate their nature, so that when the difference is one of a few letters in a word which has probably been misread, this is shown in such a way as to

---

[682]Case endings are frequently dropped in the MS, for example. Such practices were deplored by Archbishop John Whitgift in his statutes for the ecclesiastical courts of 1587 (7.2 – see *A.C.*, p. 799), but that came too late to affect this particular document.

highlight that fact. Beyond that, the basic rule is that deletions are shown in *italic,* and additions in **bold type;** once that principle has been mastered, the rest should follow logically. However, a detailed explanation of all signs and variations used is given at the beginning of the text. As far as the English translation goes, textual variants in the Latin are only reproduced when they are (at least possibly) deliberate and materially affect the meaning. This means that there are far fewer of them, though occasionally a very minor alteration to the Latin requires a whole new clause in English translation in order to bring out the difference in meaning.

A problem with the Latin text is that it is written in an artificially elevated style which in Greek would be called *katharevousa*,[683] and which often cannot be rendered literally into English without sounding ridiculous. In these circumstances, a certain amount of simplification and clarification is essential. As far as possible, modern terms have been used, particularly when describing matters relating to the church and its administration, since to do otherwise would only invite confusion. But there are a number of words and phrases which have no ready modern equivalent, and the sixteenth century terms have to be retained, however misleading they may now be.[684]

As far as possible, technical terms have been translated in only one way, though complete consistency has not been achieved. For example, *lis* has normally been translated as 'lawsuit', but in the phrase *litis contestatio* it is 'issue', since this phrase is normally rendered in English as 'the joinder of issue'. Occasionally, recourse has been had to a 'neutral' word when the Latin is capable of meaning different things. For example, since *reus* in Latin may mean 'defendant' or 'guilty', the ambiguous word 'accused' has generally been preferred in this translation. Similarly, *iudicium* can have a wide range of meanings, but as far as possible, 'judgment' has been used to translate it, even in cases where this sounds somewhat odd to an English ear.

A further difficulty is that English common law often uses the same vocabulary as Roman civil/canon law does, but in a different way. In this translation, the Roman context of the original has been respected as far as possible, and the English reader is asked to make the necessary adjustment. However, there are times when some concessions have been made, e.g. *inquisitio* has been translated as 'inquest' rather than as 'inquisition', because of the rather narrow and negative sense which the latter term has acquired in English. But when the thing itself no longer exists or cannot be expressed in contemporary language without causing confusion, the original term has been retained, e.g. *evangelica denuntiatio* is simply anglicized to 'evangelical denunciation', even

---

[683] 'Puristic'. This is the name given to a form of modern Greek which seeks to archaize the grammar and style as much as possible. It delights in odd phrases and expressions, and in its concern to avoid modernisms, is often rather vague in meaning.

[684] The word 'libel', meaning a 'little book' containing the plaintiff's accusation(s) against the defendant, is an obvious example of this.

though this is incomprehensible (or highly misleading) to most modern readers. In such cases, the notes and/or the introduction provide guidance in making the correct interpretation.

In the commentary and appendixes every effort has been made to achieve maximum clarity and usefulness, with 'chapter and verse' references to the canons being preferred to page numbers which are less specific. Citations of source materials are given in their standard forms, and can be interpreted with the assistance of the guide to abbreviations at the beginning and the bibliography at the end of the work. Lastly, the subject index has been designed to make it as easy as possible to find a particular theme and trace it through the canons, and it is hoped that it is comprehensive enough to meet the needs of most users of the present volume.

Excursus: the educational background of the canon law reformers

There were in all 117 men who at different times were engaged, or might have been engaged, on the reform of the canon law. This number has to be divided into a 'pool', covering all 117 (of whom six are counted twice because they were engaged in more than one of the attempts at reform),[685] and a 'core', consisting only of those who are known to have taken an active part in the work. Looking at their educational backgrounds, we find the following:

A. The 'pool'

	1535	1551-2	1571
Oxford	13	11	8
Cambridge	16	14	21
Both	1	1	3
Neither	1	11	23
Total	31	37	55

Doctors' commons members

	1535	1551-2	1571
Oxonians	5	3	1
Cantabrigians	4	2	2
Both	0	1	0
Neither	0	1	0
Total	9	7	3

[685]Two served in both 1535 and 1551-2 and four served in both 1551-2 and 1571.

B. The 'core'

For 1535, this consists of four men, all of whom were Oxonians and members of doctors' commons.

For 1551-2 it is harder to determine who should be included in this category, but a generous assessment might yield nine – the eight members of the drafting committee and Dr Walter Haddon. This produces only two Oxonians, but five Cantabrigians, one (Dr Haddon) from both and one (John Lucas) from neither. There are only two members of doctors' commons, Rowland Taylor (of Cambridge) and Walter Haddon, though Haddon was not admitted until 1555.

For 1571 there is no core, because no drafting committee was ever constituted.

An analysis of these data shows that even in 1535 the pool of Cambridge men available was considerable, even if that had no immediate impact and the actual work was done exclusively by Oxonians. As the reformation progressed, however, the university which more clearly supported it gained in influence, so that by 1571 nearly half those appointed to the commission were Cantabrigians. Equally remarkable is the large number of laymen, unconnected with either university, who were involved in 1551-2 and the even higher percentage in 1571 – a clear indication that secularization was making inroads even into the field of ecclesiastical law. A further sign of this is that although members of doctors' commons were well represented in 1535, when that body was still in its infancy and had not acquired anything like a monopoly of civil lawyers, its members were fewer in 1551-2 and barely in evidence in 1571, despite the fact that by then it had acquired much greater prestige and a growing monopoly of civil lawyers practising in the ecclesiastical courts. In other words, any reform which might have been undertaken in 1571 would have been carried out without the benefit of experts in the field, even though such men clearly existed – a recipe for failure from the very beginning.

THE HENRICIAN CANONS

Signs used in the text

Roman	Present in MS.
Italic	Deleted in MS.
Bold	MS text virtually identical to source.
/Roman/	Added to MS text as a scribal correction.
[Roman]	Emended by John Foxe in 1571.

An asterisk (*) before the number of a canon means that the canon in question is not separated off from the one(s) before it in the MS, although it comes from a different source.

Prohoemium

Henricus octavus, Dei gratia Angliae et Franciae rex, fidei defensor et dominus
Hiberniae, ac in terris Ecclesiae Anglicanae, sub Deo caput supremum, omnibus
archiepiscopis, episcopis, abbatibus, clericis, ducibus, marchionibus, comitibus,
baronibus, militibus, generosis, ac aliis cuiuscunque generis hominibus, subditis
et legeis nostris, per regnum nostrum et dominia nostra ubilibet commorantibus,
salutem et evangelicae veritatis incrementum.

Cum vos optimi cives mei, mihique carissimi, me nunc unum atque solum
huius regni principem, in terris secundum Deum huius Ecclesiae Anglicanae
coryphaeum unicum, supremumque caput, quemadmodum divini atque humani
iuris ratio postulat, potestatemque tam ecclesiasticae quam mundanae politiae
mihi maioribusque meis ipso iure divino concessam[1] (verum multis saeculis unius
Romani episcopi malitia, fraude, dolis atque astutia ereptam) ad me et
successores meos pertinere, viva voce uno omnium assensu agnoscitis, non
possum indies magis magisque muneris atque officii mei rationem non habere,
deque illustranda Dei gloria, de Christianae pietatis vera doctrina propaganda, de
imperii huius incolumnitate et quiete tuenda, summa animi cura atque cogitatione,
[14v] non esse sollicitus. Occurrunt enim subinde animo meo verba illa quae
Sapientiae capite sexto habentur ad hunc modum:

> Audite reges et intelligite quoniam data est a Domino potestas vobis et
> virtus ab Altissimo, qui interrogabit opera vestra et scrutabitur
> cogitationes. Ad vos ergo reges sunt hi sermones mei, ut discatis
> sapientiam et ut [non] excidatis; qui enim custodiunt iustitiam iuste
> iudicabuntur et qui didicerunt iusta invenient quid respondeant.[2]

Hinc facile perspici potest exactissime a regibus potestatis suae reddendam esse
rationem, illosque gravissimas manere poenas, si non ut oportuit in republica
administranda sese gesserint.

Quod si tanta cura ac sollicitudine, quibuscunque regibus opus est, quam
anxios igitur ac sollicitos Christianos reges esse debere censendum est, quibus
non politica modo ac civilis vel ecclesiastica etiam potestas data est. Hos enim
non ea tantum quae ad humanam societatem pertinent, sed etiam quae divinae
Christianaeque religionis maxime consentanea sunt, curare necesse est,

---

[1] The MS and F both have 'concessis'.
[2] Wi. vi. 2,4,10-11. The MS omitted 'non' by mistake, and F corrected it by replacing 'ut'
with 'ne'. The effect is the same.

Preface

Henry the eighth, by the grace of God king of England and France, defender of the faith and lord of Ireland, and on earth supreme head under God of the Church of England, to all archbishops, bishops, abbots, clergy, dukes, marquises, earls, barons, knights, gentlemen and other men of whatever sort, our subjects and liege men, wherever they may dwell throughout our kingdom and our dominions, greeting and increase of Gospel truth.

Seeing that you, most excellent citizens of mine and most dear to me, now audibly and with one common accord acknowledge me to be the one and only prince of this realm, on earth the sole summit after God of this Church of England, and its supreme head, in so far as the nature of divine and human right allows, and that the power over the ecclesiastical as well as the earthly commonwealth granted[1] to me and to my predecessors by that same divine right, (but which for many centuries has been seized by the wickedness, fraud, deceits and cleverness of the sole bishop of Rome), belongs to me and to my successors, I cannot but be concerned, with the utmost care and thought of my mind, to take more and more account every day of my duty and office, which is to glorify God, to proclaim the true doctrine of the Christian religion and to preserve the peace and quiet of this state. In which respect, those words which are written in the sixth chapter of Wisdom come to my mind as follows:

> Hear, O kings, and understand that power is given to you from the Lord and strength from the most high, who will try your works and examine your thoughts. Wherefore to you, O kings, are these my words, that you might learn wisdom and [not] depart from it, for those who maintain justice will be justly judged, and those who have learned justice will find what to answer.[2]

From this it may easily be seen that the most exact account of their power will be required from kings, and that they will receive the most severe punishment if they have not conducted themselves as they ought to in the government of the commonwealth.

Wherefore if such great care and concern is required of all kings whatsoever, how much must it be judged that Christian kings, to whom not only secular and civil, but also ecclesiastical power has been given, should be anxious and concerned. For they must take care not only of those things which pertain to human society, but also of those things which are most agreeable to the divine Christian religion. It is the duty of Christian princes so to order the present

5

praesentem huius saeculi felicitatem principes [15r] Christianos metiri convenit, ut hac potestate sua ad Dei cultum dilatandum utantur, ut in hoc incumbant, ut recta doctrina propagetur orneturque Dei gloria.

Cum igitur a Christianis regibus, iustitia[m] in imperio, pacis tuendae cura[m], pieta[s/tem],[3] studium iuvandae et ornandae religionis Christianae exigi animadverterem, nihil mihi potius esse debere iudicabam, quam ut omnes inirem rationes quo minus in hoc meo regno haec a me desiderentur, et quoad possem, muneri imposito satisfacerem. Hoc ut facilius expeditiusque facere valeam, non ignoratis vos, quantam curam adhibuerim in illis rebus promovendis tuendisque quae huic negotio maxime conducere atque adiumento esse videbantur; quae contra impedire atque obesse visa sunt, quanto studio tollere ac delere conatus sum, assidueque conor. Abunde enim vobis declaratum hactenus fuit, [15v] quam in hac nostra Britannia multis retro saeculis episcopi Romani vis iniusta ac non ferenda sacrosancto divino nomini inimica fuit; quantopere religionis Christianae verae doctrinae propagandae adversata est; quantum huius reipublicae pacem ac tranquillitatem saepissime inturbavit, potestatemque regiam divinitus constitutam labefactando, civium omnium oboedientiam a vero ac iusto principis sui imperio, contra omne ius divinum et humanum, ad se transferre ausus est. Huius potestatem huic cum divino munere sublatam manifestum est. Ne quid superesset, quo non plane fractam illius vim esse constaret, leges omnes, decreta atque instituta quae ab auctore episcopo Romano profecta sunt, prorsus abroganda esse censimus. Quorum loco, ut felicius in posterum Dei optimi maximi gloria illustretur et vera philosophia Christiana, regnumque Christi vigere possit, et quo omnia decenter et ordine [16r] in Christi hac ecclesia gerantur; en vobis auctoritate nostra editas leges damus, quas a vobis omnibus suscipi, coli et observari volumus, et sub nostrae indignationis poena mandamus, ut vestra in Deum pietas, amor erga patriam, principemque vestrum oboedientia, non sine immensa divini nominis gloria omnibus conspicua sit, ac vos ipsos non minus de vestris rationibus sollicitos ostendatis, quam ego vestra causa de officio fuerim meo, stricte praecipientes ut his nostris constitutionibus vos omnes et singuli tam in iudiciis quam in gymnasiis utamini, severe prohibentes ne quisquam vestrum alias praeter has et regni nostri leges admittere praesumat.

Valete

Sequitur de summa Trinitate et fide Catholica.

---

[3]These emendations were made by John Foxe in his edition of 1571.

happiness of this world that they may use this power of theirs to further the worship of God, and to continue in this, so that true doctrine might be spread and God's glory advanced.

Therefore, when I realized that justice in the state, keeping the peace, godliness[3] and a desire to assist and advance the Christian religion, are demanded of Christian kings, I decided that nothing was more required of me than that I should look into all the ways in which these things might be expected of me in this my realm, and that I should fulfil the task required to the best of my ability. You are not unaware how much care I have devoted, in order to achieve this more easily and expediently, to promoting and preserving those things which seem to be helpful and most conducive to this matter, nor with what dedication I have tried and continue to try to remove and destroy those things which seem to go against this aim and to hinder it. For this reason it has already been declared to you how, in this our Britain, for many centuries the unjust and intolerable power of the bishop of Rome was hostile to the most holy name of God, how far it was opposed to the preaching of the true doctrine of the Christian religion, how frequently it disturbed the peace and tranquillity of this commonwealth, and how, by undermining divinely established royal power, he dared to transfer from the true and just rule of its prince to himself the due obedience of all citizens, contrary to all divine and human right. It is clear that the power of this man has now been taken away with divine sanction. In order that nothing might remain by which it might be said that his power has not been completely broken, we have determined that all decrees and statutes which originated with the bishop of Rome shall from henceforth be abrogated. In their place, so that the glory of the most high God may in future be more happily magnified, that the kingdom of Christ might flourish by true Christian learning, and that everything in Christ's church might be done decently and in order, behold - we are giving you laws published by our authority, which we desire to be received, studied and observed by you all; and under pain of our displeasure we order that your faithfulness to God, your love towards your country, and your obedience to your prince may be clear to all men, to the great glory of the divine name, and that you may show yourselves no less concerned for your responsibilities than I have been for mine on your behalf, strictly decreeing that each and every one of you shall employ these our constitutions both in the courts and in the schools, and severely prohibiting any of you to presume to accept laws other than these and those of the realm.

Farewell.

Here follows the section on the highest Trinity and the Catholic faith.

[16v] 1. De summa Trinitate et fide Catholica

1.[4] Qui falsas ac novas opiniones contra fidem catholicam vel gignunt vel sequuntur, **aut aliter Sacram Scripturam intelligunt, quam sensus Spiritus Sancti flagitat**, quales sunt hi:

qui dicunt creaturam non a Deo sed a virtute quadam superna creatam,[5]

qui passum Iesum abnegant,[6]

qui dicunt Christum hominem fuisse tantum, et de utroque sexu progenitum,[7]

qui circumcisionem observant,[8]

qui Christum de virgine nihil corpus assumpsisse asserunt,[9]

qui dicunt Christum non in veritate Deum sed hominem in phantasia apparuisse,[10]

qui resurrectionem non credunt ac Vetus Testamentum non recipiunt,[11]

qui Deum Verbum non credunt,[12]

qui adventum Spiritus Sancti in apostolos negant,[13]

qui denegant paenitentibus veniam peccatorum, qui damnant nuptias viduarum,[14]

qui dicunt non semper fuisse Christum sed a Maria sumpsisse initium,[15]

qui coniugia omnia prohibent, qui damnant baptisma parvulorum,[16]

qui rebaptizant baptizatos,[17]

[17r] qui asserunt Mariam post Christum natum viro suo fuisse commixtam,[18]

qui dicunt animam cum corpore mori,[19]

---

[4]C 24 q. 3, c. 39, s. 70 (Fr, I, 1006). The canon comes from Isidore of Seville, *Etymologiae*, VIII, 5.

[5]*Ibid.*, s. 1. The heresy was attributed by Isidore to Simon Magus (cf. Ac. viii. 9-24) and his followers.

[6]*Ibid.*, s. 3. Attributed to the gnostic heretic Basilides and his followers.

[7]*Ibid.*, s. 6. Attributed to the gnostic heretic Carpocrates and his followers.

[8]*Ibid.*, s. 7. Attributed to the gnostic heretic Cerinthus and his followers.

[9]*Ibid.*, s. 10. Attributed to the gnostic heretic Valentinus and his followers.

[10]*Ibid.*, s. 11. Attributed to the gnostic heretic Apelles and his followers.

[11]*Ibid.*, s. 23. Attributed to an unknown gnostic heretic, Severus, and his followers.

[12]*Ibid.*, s. 25. Attributed to the so-called 'Alogoi' of Asia Minor, who denied the apostolic origin of the Apocalypse.

[13]*Ibid.*, s. 26. Attributed (falsely) to the so-called 'Cataphrygians', or Montanists.

[14]*Ibid.*, s. 27. Attributed to the Cathars, descendants of the ancient Manichaeans.

[15]*Ibid.*, s. 28. Attributed to the so-called 'adoptionists', followers of Paul of Samosata, who was condemned at Antioch in 268.

[16]*Ibid.*, s. 32. Attributed to the gnostic heretic Heraclites and his followers.

[17]*Ibid.*, s. 33. Attributed to the third-century Roman schismatic Novatian and his followers.

[18]*Ibid.*, s. 45. Attributed to the so-called 'Antidicomaritans', who are otherwise unknown.

[19]*Ibid.*, s. 58. Attributed to the 'Arabici', so called from their supposed land of origin, but otherwise unknown.

1. Of the highest Trinity and the Catholic faith.

1.[4] Those who invent or follow false and new opinions against the catholic faith, **or understand Holy Scripture in a way different from what the Holy Spirit requires,** like those:

who say that creation was made not by God but by some supernatural power,[5]

who deny that Jesus suffered,[6]

who say that Christ was just a man and engendered by both sexes,[7]

who practise circumcision,[8]

who claim that Christ did not receive a body from a virgin,[9]

who say that Christ did not appear as God in reality but as a man in fantasy,[10]

who do not believe in the resurrection or accept the Old Testament,[11]

who do not believe that the Word is God,[12]

who deny the coming of the Holy Spirit on the apostles,[13]

who refuse forgiveness of sins to those who repent, who condemn the marriage of widows,[14]

who say that Christ did not always exist, but took his beginning from Mary,[15]

who forbid all marriages, who condemn the baptism of infants,[16]

who rebaptize those already baptized,[17]

who claim that Mary had intercourse with her husband after the birth of Christ,[18]

who say that the soul dies with the body,[19]

qui dicunt virginem Mariam, non Dei sed hominis tantummodo matrem,[20]

qui dicunt non prodesse homini ieiunare aut orare,[21]

qui de sacramentis ecclesiae aliter sentire vel docere praesumant, quam Sacra Scriptura et Ecclesia nostra Anglicana docet et affirmat.[22]

Hi enim et generaliter alii quicunque qui falsas et erroneas opiniones contra Sacram Scripturam tenent, docent aut praedicant, nisi ab erroribus suis edocti discesserint, haeretici sunt censendi, ac a communione fidelium et participatione sacramentorum sint prorsus alieni.[23] Eosdem tamen, si **sententiam suam, quamvis falsam atque perversam, nulla *t...* pertinaci animositate defendant, sed quaerunt cauta solicitudine veritatem,** ac ab erroribus suis edocti discedere **parati sunt, nequaquam haereticos esse** iudicamus.[24] Volumus quod archiepiscopi [17v] et episcopi in dioecesibus suis, in locis tam exemptis quam non exemptis, et sede vacante hi ad quos de consuetudine iurisdictio ecclesiastica illic spectaverit, ac ab eis specialiter deputati in negotiis haereticae pravitatis, iudices sint competentes.

2.[25] Iudices autem adversus praesentatos, detectos sive accusatos de haeresi iuxta statuta nostra procedentes eosdem per litteras aut nuntium iuratum

---

[20]*Ibid.*, s. 63. Attributed to Nestorius (*c.* 381-*c.* 451), patriarch of Constantinople from 428-31, who challenged the popular view that Mary was *Theotokos* ('God-bearer'). Nestorius wanted to say that she was *Christotokos*, because he believed that the person of Christ was the result of the conjunction of two natures, divine and human, each of which possessed its own individual identity (*hypostasis*) both before and after the incarnation.

[21]This is a curious inclusion, since it was actually stated by Pope Pius I (*c.* 140-55), *Ep.*, 1, and is found in the canon law under D, 3 *de cons.*, c. 23 (Fr, I, 1417-18). No doubt it was thought to apply to Martin Luther (1483-1546) because of his denial of the efficacy of works for salvation.

[22]Apparently adapted from C. 24 q. 1, c. 15 (Fr, I, 970), with the specific reference to the sacraments taken from C. 24 q. 1 c. 22 (Fr, I, 974) and other similar canons in the same section of the *Decretum*. It was probably aimed at the followers of John Wycliffe (*c.* 1330-84), Jan Hus (*c.* 1372-1415), Martin Luther (1483-1546), against whom Henry VIII had written his *Assertio septem sacramentorum* in 1521, and Huldrych Zwingli (1484-1531), as well as the Anabaptists, who were already known in England, though to a very limited extent. But the substitution of 'Anglicana' for 'Romana' was clearly a blow to the teaching authority claimed by Rome, and allowed the Church of England to establish its own sacramental teaching. The ratification of the ten articles in June 1536 was a first step in that direction, but any tendency towards a departure from the traditional teaching was countered by the act of six articles (31 Henry VIII, c. 14, 1539 – *S.R.*, III, 739-43). Real divergence from the Roman position did not become law in England until the passing of the sacrament act in 1547 (1 Edward VI, c. 1 – *S.R.*, IV, 2-3).

[23]C. 24, q. 3, c. 31 (Fr, I, 998), originally Augustine, *De civitate Dei*, XVIII, 51. For the addition of excommunication, see C. 24, q. 3, c. 37 (Fr, I, 1000), taken from a letter of Pope Urban II (1088-99).

[24]C. 24, q. 3, c. 29 (Fr, I, 998), originally from Augustine, *Ep.*, 162.

[25]The procedure here is laid down in 23 Henry VIII, c. 9, 1531-2 (*S.R.*, III, 377-8), but it is not applied specifically to heresy trials. Cf. also 1237/26 (PC, 256-7).

who say that the Virgin Mary was not the Mother of God but only of a man,[20]

who say that it does not profit a man to fast or pray,[21]

who presume to think or teach differently about the sacraments of the church from what Holy Scripture and our Church of England teach and affirm.[22]

For these and generally all others who hold, teach or preach false and erroneous opinions, contrary to Holy Scripture, are to be regarded as heretics unless they are educated out of their errors and abandon them, and they are to be cut off from henceforth from the communion of the faithful and from participation in the sacraments.[23] Nevertheless, those who **defend their position, however false and perverse it may be, without any obstinate animosity, but who seek the truth with careful concern**, and who, once they are educated out of their errors, **are ready** to abandon them, we **by no means** judge **to be heretics**.[24] We will that archbishops and bishops in their dioceses, in places both exempt and non-exempt, and during an interregnum, those to whom by custom ecclesiastical jurisdiction in that place would belong, and those specially delegated by them to handle matters of heretical depravity, shall be competent judges.

2.[25] Judges proceeding against those who have been presented, caught in or accused of heresy according to our statutes, shall cite them personally by letters

personaliter si appraehendi potuerint citent. Sin autem per publicae citationis edictum, ac recepto certificatorio legitimo de citatione huiusmodi, eosdem si contumaciter abfuerunt, sententiam excommunicationis feriant. In qua si per quadraginta dies post publicationem dictae sententiae perstiterint in sua contumacia perdurantes, procedant ad testium receptionem et alias probationes legitimas, habitaque deinde informatione legitima omni dilatione semota, sententient, declarent, faciantque quod est iustum, ipsorum contumacium absentiis [18r] in aliquo non obstantibus. Taliter vero de haeresi condemnatos, per officiarios nostros, ad mandatum condemnantis depraehendi volumus et eidem cum celeritate accommoda praesentari; qui exposito eis errore de quo condemnati sunt, nisi infra triduum haeresim abiuraverint, et paenitentiam eis provide iniungendam subire voluerint, curiae tradantur saeculari.

3.[26] Praesentes quidem per iudices competentes de dicto crimine condemnati, nisi infra triduum a die latae sententiae, haeresi abiurata, ab erroribus suis resipiscant, et paenitentiam condignam ad arbitrium ordinarii sui subire se obtulerint sine spe veniae, curiae tradantur saeculari.[27] Porro qui abiurare velint, omnem haeresim abiurare teneantur.

4.[28] **Post abiuratam haeresim si quis relapsus inveniatur, sine ulla penitus audientia curiae tradatur saeculari.** Relapsum vero eum declaramus, qui post abiuratam [18v] haeresim vel in eandem aut aliam quamcunque inciderit.

Traditis vero curiae saeculari si postmodum paeniteant et paenitentiae signa in eis apparuerint, nequaquam sunt paenitentiae sacramenta et eucharistiae deneganda.

5.[29] Abiurati de crimine haeresis si paenitentiam eis iniunctam (legitima cessante causa) non adimpleverint et inde legitime convicti fuerint, pro haereticis condemnentur, et perpetuis tradentur carceribus.

6.[30] In causa haeresis appellandi adimimus facultatem nisi post condemnationem ad nos contigerit appellari. Sic vero appellantem a carceribus dimitti nolumus nisi datis fideiussoribus aut aliis cautionibus ad arbitrium iudicis a quo fuerit appellatum.

7.[31] **Inventi autem solummodo de haeresi notabiliter suspecti**, aut publice de ea infamati, ad arbitrium ordinarii sui [19r] innocentiam suam purgent, aut paenitentiam ab eodem iniunctam subeant, alioquin **anathematis gladio feriantur, et usque ad satisfactionem condignam ab omnibus evitentur, ita quod si per sex menses in excommunicatione huiusmodi perstiterint, extunc velut haeretici condemnentur.** Notabiliter autem suspecti eos esse declaramus, apud quos libri postquam sint condemnati haeretica pravitate, aut penes quos

---

[26]25 Henry VIII, c. 14, s. 6, 1533-4 (S.R., III, 454-5).

[27]For this detail, see X, 5.7.13 (Fr, II, 787-9), originally a decretal of Pope Innocent III, published as canon 3 of Lateran IV, 1215 (C.O.D., 233).

[28]VI, 5.2.4 (Fr, II, 1071-2), originally a decretal of Pope Alexander IV (1254-61).

[29]25 Henry VIII, c. 14, s. 6, 1533-4 (S.R., III, 454-5).

[30]Ibid., s. 8.

[31]X, 5.7.13 (Fr, II, 787-9), c. 3 of Lateran IV, 1215 (C.O.D., 233-5); 2 Henry IV, c. 15, 1400-1 (S.R., II, 125-8).

or by a sworn messenger, if they can be found. But if, after a public citation has been issued and a lawful confirmation of the said citation has been received, those cited are contumaciously absent, the judges shall impose a sentence of excommunication. In which, if they continue after forty days from the publication of the said sentence persisting in their contumacy, the judges shall proceed to the reception of witnesses and other lawful investigations, and then, when lawful information is obtained, they shall express, declare and do what is just, without any delay, the absence of these contumacious people notwithstanding. We will that those so condemned for heresy shall be arrested by our officers on the order of the one convicting them, and that they shall be presented to him with all convenient speed. And if, when the error for which they have been convicted is explained to them, they do not abjure their heresy within three days and voluntarily submit to the penance which shall rightly be imposed on them, they shall be handed over to the secular court.

3.[26] Those present and condemned for the said crime by competent judges shall be handed over to the secular court with no hope of pardon, unless they abjure their heresy and repent of their errors within three days from the day that sentence is given, and offer themselves for appropriate penance at the discretion of their ordinary.[27] Moreover, those who want to abjure shall be required to abjure all heresy.

4.[28] **If anyone is found to have relapsed after abjuring heresy, he shall be handed over to the secular court without any further hearing.** By 'relapsed' we mean someone who, after abjuring a heresy, falls back into the same one or into any other one whatsoever.

But if those who have been handed over to the secular court shall later repent, and the signs of repentance appear in them, then the sacraments of penance and the eucharist shall on no account be denied to them.

5.[29] If those who have abjured their heresy do not do the penance imposed on them, (barring lawful impediment), and have been lawfully convicted of the same, they shall be condemned as heretics and consigned to perpetual imprisonment.

6.[30] In a cause of heresy we do not allow any right of appeal unless, after the condemnation, it seems appropriate that the cause should be appealed to us. But we do not wish such an appellant to be set free from prison unless he has given sureties or other guarantees at the discretion of the judge from whom the appeal has been made.

7.[31] **Those however, who have been found no more than seriously suspect of heresy**, or who have been publicly defamed for it, may purge their innocence at the discretion of their ordinary, or else undergo the penance imposed by him; otherwise they **shall be punished with the sword of anathema and cut off from everyone until they make appropriate satisfaction, and if they continue in this excommunication for six months, then they shall be condemned as heretics.** By 'seriously suspect' we mean those in whose possession are found books, which have been condemned for

scienter inquisiti reperiuntur haeretici, aut qui secretas haereticorum lectiones, aut illorum conventicula frequentant, et alii qui haereticos defendere et auctorizare praesumunt. Publice vero defamatos *ill...* illos reputamus qui apud *apud* vicinos suos, eorum conversationis et vitae notitiam habentes ad numerum decem infamantur.

8.[32] Cum haereticus non est censendus, qui edoctus de sententia sua quamvis falsa et perversa discedere paratus sit, [19v] tamen ut pertinacibus omnis occasio eludendi iudicia nostra auferatur, volumus quod laici, nisi haeresim docere aut defendere praesumant, de haeresi iuxta statuta nostra delati, accusati, indictati, sive detecti, si cum primum ad iudicem venerint errorem suum confiteantur, ac edocti ab ea discedere parati sunt, absque omni abiuratione ab omni iudicio dimittantur, iniuncta prius illis discreta paenitentia per quam satisfiet omnibus, quatenus possibile est, qui per ipsam haeresim laesi aut scandalizati fuerint, et qui illam paenitentiam non adimpleverit aut in eandem haeresim inciderit, abiuretur, et si abiurare noluerit, ut haereticus iudicetur, verum si postquam confessi sunt haeresim suam in ea perstiterint donec feratur sententia aut si nolunt errorem suum confiteri donec convincantur legitimis probationibus in his casibus ut haeretici iudicentur.

[20r] 9.[33] **Praecipiatur his** qui pro paenitentia haeresi paenitentiam sunt acturi ut ubi inde infamati extiterint, vel haeresim praedicaverint, docuerint aut asseruerint, **ibi ac aliis locis circumvicinis profiteantur et praedicent fidem catholicam, ac confundant et protestantur omnem haereticam pravitatem** et illam praecipue in specie quam tenuerunt, aut de qua notabiliter suspecti vel infamati sunt, **sic deinceps vitam suam bonis adornantes operibus ut infamia convertatur in bonam famam et omne scandalum ac suspicio de catholicorum mentibus deleatur.**

10.[34] Archiepiscopis, episcopis et aliis iudicibus in causis haeresis deputatis, registrum, acta et processus alterius cuiuscunque iudicis contra haereticos sibi per censuras ecclesiasticas sibi exhiberi faciendi necnon inclusorum propter haeresim in carcere vel muro poenam mitigandi vel mutandi, [20v] cum viderint expedire plenam concedimus facultatem.

11.[35] **In examinatione testium** qui super crimine haeresis producuntur **adhibeantur duae honestae ac discretae personae in quarum praesentia et notarii publici (si commode haberi possit) aut eius loco in praesentia duorum aliorum virorum idoneorum dicti testes per iudicem fideliter** examinentur ac **depositiones eorundem conscribantur.**

---

[32]Adapted from X, 5.7.9 (Fr, II, 780-2), a decretal of Pope Lucius III (1181-5).

[33]X, 5.34.10 (Fr, II, 872-4), a decretal of Pope Innocent III, dated 7 May 1199; L, 5.5.2, c. 4 of the council of Oxford, 1407.

[34]Cf. X, 5.7.13 (Fr, II, 787-9), c. 3 of Lateran IV, 1215 (*C.O.D.*, 233-5); VI, 5.2.20 (Fr, II, 1078), a decretal of Pope Boniface VIII (1294-1303).

[35]VI, 5.2.11 (Fr, II, 1073-4), a decretal of Pope Clement IV (1265-8).

heresy, or in whose houses are found persons known to be wanted for heresy, or who attend secret lectures given by heretics or their meetings, as well as others who presume to defend and support heretics. By 'publicly defamed' we mean those who have been denounced by at least ten of their neighbours, who have noticed their lifestyle and behaviour.

8.[32] When a person who has been educated out of his opinion, however false or perverse it may be, is ready to abandon it, he is not to be regarded as a heretic. Nevertheless, in order that any chance of escaping our judgments shall be removed from the obstinate, it is our will that if lay people who have been denounced, accused, indicted or detected for heresy , as long as they do not presume to teach or defend heresy, come and confess their error, according to our statutes, before a judge at the first available opportunity, and having been educated out of it, are prepared to abandon it, they shall be dismissed without any abjuration or judgment, as soon as a specific penance is imposed on them, which as far as possible shall give satisfaction to everyone who has been offended or scandalized by that heresy. And whoever does not do that penance or who falls into the same heresy shall abjure it, and if he does not want to abjure it, then he shall be condemned as a heretic. But if those who have confessed their heresy persist in it afterwards until the sentence is given, or if they do not want to confess their error until they are convicted of it by lawful examination, then in these cases they shall be judged as heretics.

9.[33] **Let it be enjoined on those** who are about to do penance for heresy, **that they shall profess and preach the catholic faith, and confute and deny all heretical error**, particularly the one which they have held, or of which they have been seriously suspected or accused, **in the place** where they were so accused, or preached, taught or asserted heresy, **and in other neighbouring localities, so adorning their life from henceforth with good works, that the evil rumour about them may be turned into a good report, and all scandal and suspicion be removed from the minds of Catholics.**

10.[34] We grant full power to archbishops, bishops and other judges deputed to handle heretical causes, to have the acts of the registrars and the proceedings of any other judge against heretics, to be shown to him on pain of ecclesiastical censure, as well as to mitigate or modify the punishment of those imprisoned or cloistered on account of heresy, as they may see fit.

11.[35] **In the examination of witnesses** produced in a crime of heresy **two honest and discreet persons shall be summoned, in whose presence and that of a notary public (if one is readily available), or instead of him, in the presence of two other suitable men, the said witnesses shall be faithfully** examined **by the judge and their depositions shall be recorded.**

12.[36] **Notarii** et alii personae in causa haeresis notoriae **coram iudicibus causarum** huiusumodi **iuramentum praestabunt** corporale **quod eorum officia** in causis supradictis **fideliter** in omnibus **exercebunt**.

Sequitur de officio contionandi.

[21r] **2. De officio contionandi.**

1.[37] Nullus praesumet publice vel privatim praedicatoris officium exercere, nisi aut metropolitani infra provinciam suam aut episcopi infra dioecesim suam etiam in locis exemptis licentia prius obtenta et sub sigillo concedentis curato paroechiae ubi contionari intendit primitus ostensa.

Rectoribus tamen et vicariis ac aliis quibus cura imminet animarum in ecclesiis et locis sibi commissis, liberam concedimus praedicandi facultatem.

2.[38] Prohibemus praeterea ne quis libellum aut tractatum aliquem noviter compositum vel post hac componendum priusquam fuerit approbatus publice vel privatim docere praesumat, quia nimis est grave, ad exterminationem haereticae pravitatis non agere quod ipsius contagiosa enormitas agendum requirit, grave est quoque et damnatione dignissimum malitiose insontibus eandem imponere [21v] pravitatem. Archiepiscopis igitur et episcopis ac aliis haereticae pravitatis iudicibus quibuscunque *iud...* praecipimus ut sic aeque et iuste contra eos qui de haeretica pravitate iuxta formam dicti statuti nostri fuerint accusati sive delati procedant, quod neque odii gratia vel amoris aut lucri sive commodi temporalis obtentu contra iustitiam et conscientiam suam omittant contra quemcumque procedere ubi fuerit procedendum super huiusmodi pravitate.

3. De simonia.

1.[39] Ordines ab episcopis gratis conferantur. Si episcopus ordines pro pecunia aut alicuius muneris gratia contulerit, ipso facto ab executione officii sui sit suspensus donec absolutionis beneficium ab archiepiscopo suo meruit obtinere. Ordinatum vero a sic suspenso ab executione suae ordinationis per triennium [22r] suspensum esse volumus.

---

[36]*Clem.*, 5.3.1 (Fr, II, 1181-2), a decretal of Pope Clement V, published at the council of Vienne, 1311-12.
[37]2 Henry IV, c. 15, 1400-1 (*S.R.*, II, 125-8); also L, 5.5.1, originally cc. 1-2 of the council of Oxford, 1407, in response to a claim of John Wycliffe which was condemned at the council of Constance on 4 May 1415 (*C.O.D.*, 412).
[38]L, 5.4.2, c. 6 of the council of Oxford, 1407.
[39]X, 5.3.1 (Fr, II, 749), originally a decretal of Pope Gregory I (590-604); X, 5.3.45 (Fr, II, 767), originally a decretal of Pope Gregory IX (1227-34). See also X, 5.3.4 (Fr, II, 750), originally a decretal of either Pope Adeodatus I (615-18) or Adeodatus II (672-6).

12.[36] **Notaries** and other such persons in a cause of notorious heresy, **shall swear a** corporal **oath before the judges of causes of this kind, that they will faithfully execute their duties** in the aforesaid causes in every respect.

Here follows the section on the office of preaching.

2. Of the office of preaching.

1.[37] No one shall presume to exercise the office of preaching, publicly or privately, unless a licence which he has previously obtained either from the metropolitan within his province or from the bishop within his diocese, even in exempt places, and under the seal of the one granting it, has first been shown to the curate of the parish where he intends to preach.

However, we grant complete freedom to rectors, vicars and others to whom the cure of souls belongs, to preach in the churches and places committed to them.

2.[38] Furthermore, we forbid anyone to presume to teach, publicly or privately, any book or tract which has recently been written, or which shall hereafter be written, before it has been approved, for if it is a serious thing not to act for the extermination of heretical depravity to the degree which that contagious evil requires, it is also serious and most worthy of damnation to impose the same error maliciously on the innocent. Therefore we enjoin archbishops, bishops, and other judges of heretical error whatsoever that they proceed in so fair and just a way against those who have been accused or denounced for heretical depravity according to the form of our said statute, and that they shall not neglect to proceed against whoever ought to be proceeded against for error of this kind, either for the sake of hatred or love, or for financial reward or the acquisition of temporal gain, contrary to justice and their conscience.

3. Of simony.

1.[39] Orders shall be conferred by bishops free of charge. If a bishop grants orders for money, or in return for any reward, he shall automatically be suspended from the exercise of his office until he has shown himself worthy to obtain the benefit of absolution from the archbishop. And we will that anyone ordained by someone so suspended shall himself be suspended from the exercise of his ordination for a three year period.

2.[40] Pro litteris ordinum aut quocumque alio circa ordinandos ministerio, nihil detur registrario, ianitori sive alicui alii in ea parte ministro. Quod si contra factum fuerit, dans ab executione ordinis sic suscepti et a receptione aliorum per annum, recipiens vero ab officio suo et a sacramentorum perceptione usque ad condignam satisfactionem sit suspensus. Ut igitur huic malo via praecludatur, volumus et sub nostrae indignationis poena mandamus, quod episcopi omnia et singula onera in ea parte necessaria suis sumptibus supportent.

3.[41] Quoties ad consecrandum vel reconciliandas ecclesias episcopi invitentur non quasi ex debito munus aliquod requirant; polluentes tamen ecclesiam seminis vel violenta sanguinis effusione ad fabricam eiusdem ecclesiae summam quinque librarum solvere coga{n}tur, et qui solvendo non sit, [22v] publicam ad arbitrium ordinarii sui agat paenitentam.

*4.[42] Polluto coemeterio ecclesia non censeatur esse polluta, sed polluta ecclesia coemeterium contiguum sit ipso facto pollutum.

5.[43] Prohibemus ne abbas aut prior vel quisquam alius praesidens alicuius monasterii, prioratus seu cuiuscunque alterius loci religiosi, ab aliquo illius loci religionem ingredi volente pecuniam vel aliquod aliud munus exigat vel recipiat, sub poena privationis ab officio suo. Pactiones quibus ut beneficia ecclesiastica pro munere vel {*poena* pecunia} resignentur conventum est, item transactiones, etiam iuramento firmat{*ae*/as} super beneficiis ecclesiasticis in litigium deductas, vel super ecclesiastica subiectione habitas et factas, dummodo in eis superioris auctoritas non intercesserit, speciem decernimus /continere/ simoniae quam amissione eius, quod sic est acquisitum puniri volumus.

[23r] 6.[44] Prohibemus ne quis ad ecclesiam paroechialem, dignitatem, praebendam, liberam capellam aut aliud beneficium ecclesiasticum, quocunque censeatur nomine, eligatur, praesentetur, aut per donationem, collationem sive alium quemcunque modum admittetur interventu pecuniae aut alicuius muneris gratia. Contrarium vero facientes simoniacos esse iudicamus, iuste enim uterque corripiendus est, et qui pro ecclesiae ambitu munera largitur, et qui, ut aliter ecclesiam adeat, quicquam praesumat accipere, ille quippe ecclesia quam emere cupit privetur. Hic autem ius suum quod vendere voluit, pro illa vice amittat et collatio illius ad ordinarium pro illa vice spectabit.

(De adulteriis et stupris)

---

[40]L, 3.22.3, c. 19 of Archbishop John Stratford, 1342. Cf., C. 1, q. 2, c. 4, a letter of Pope Gregory I (590-604); X, 5.3.1 (Fr, II, 749), a decretal of Pope Gregory I; X, 5.3.18 (Fr, II, 754-5), a decretal of Pope Alexander III (1159-81).
[41]Cf. X, 5.3.10 (Fr, II, 751), originally a decretal of Pope Alexander III. See also 1268/3 (PC, 750-1) and 1268/12 (PC, 762-4).
[42]VI, 3.21.1 (Fr, II, 1059), a decretal of Pope Boniface VIII (1294-1303).
[43]Cf. X, 5.3.19 (Fr, II, 755-6), originally a decretal of Pope Alexander III, and X, 5.3.30 (Fr, II, 759-60), originally a letter from Pope Innocent III (1198-1216) to Archbishop Hubert Walter of Canterbury (1193-1205), dated 1201.
[44]1268/34 (PC, 780-1).

2.[40] For letters of orders or for any other service connected with ordinands, nothing shall be given in payment to the registrar, doorkeeper or to anyone else who serves in that respect. If anything shall be done contrary to this, the giver shall be suspended from the exercise of the order so obtained and from the reception of others for a year, and the recipient shall be suspended from his office and from receiving the sacraments until he has made appropriate satisfaction. Therefore, in order for the way into such evil to be closed, we will, and under pain of our displeasure we command, that bishops shall defray all and every expense necessary for this purpose out of their own funds.

3.[41] Whenever bishops are invited to consecrate or reconsecrate churches, they shall not demand any payment, as if it were due to them. But those who desecrated a church by violently spilling sperm or blood shall be compelled to pay the sum of five pounds towards the fabric of that church, and whoever does not pay shall do penance at the discretion of his ordinary.

*4.[42] If the churchyard is desecrated the church shall not be deemed to have been desecrated, but if the church is desecrated, the adjoining churchyard shall be considered desecrated as a matter of course.

5.[43] We forbid an abbot, prior or other head of any monastery, priory or other religious house, to receive money from anyone wanting to enter the order of that house, or to demand or receive any other reward, under pain of being deprived of his office. We consider that arrangements by which it is agreed that ecclesiastical benefices may be resigned for reward or payment, and likewise transactions involving ecclesiastical benefices, even those affirmed by oath, which have been brought to court, or which have been had and made concerning ecclesiastical jurisdiction, without the authority of their superior, involve a form of simony, and we will that this be punished by the loss of whatever has been so acquired.

6.[44] We forbid anyone to be elected, presented or admitted by donation, collation or any other means, to a parish church, dignity, free prebend, chapel or any other ecclesiastical benefice, whatever it may be called, on the payment of money or for the sake of any reward. Those who do otherwise we judge to be simoniacs, and both parties are to be justly punished, the one who pays out money in order to obtain a church and the one who presumes to take something, in order for another to enter into possession of a church. The first of these shall therefore be deprived of the church which he wants to buy, while the other, who was prepared to sell his right, shall lose it for that turn, and the collation of the benefice shall revert for that turn to the ordinary.

(On adultery and dishonour)

7.[45] Volumus ut quibusvis excommunicatis aut suspensis, in forma ecclesiae se absolvi petentibus, absolutionis beneficium gratis (salvis tamen expensis ratione suae contumaciae factis) impendatur.

[23v] **4. De adulteriis et stupro.**

1.[46] Adulterium, incestum, stuprum et fornicationem infra regnum et dominia nostra severe puniri mandamus iuxta tamen arbitrium et moderationem episcoporum et aliorum qui de praedictis criminibus cognoscendi ac iudicandi habent potestatem super quo eorum consciencias oneramus.

2.[47] **Aliud est fornicatio, aliud stuprum, aliud adulterium, aliud incestus.**

Fornicatio autem, licet videatur esse genus cuiuslibet illiciti coitus, qui fit extra uxorem legitimam, tamen specialiter intelligitur in usu viduarum vel meretricum vel concubinarum.

Stuprum autem proprie est virginum illicita defloratio, quando videlicet non praecedente coniugali pactione utriusque voluntate virgo corrumpitur.

Adulterium vero est alieni thori violatio. Unde adulterium dicitur, quasi ad alterius thorum accessus.

Incestus est consanguineorum vel affinium abusus in gradibus prohibitis.

[24r] 3.[48] Deflorans virginem illam ducat in uxorem, quam si nolit aut non possit in uxorem ducere, illam ad arbitrium ordinarii per censuras ecclesiasticas dotare cogatur.

4.[49] **Clerici in sacris ordinibus constituti qui publice tenent concubinas, licet ad eas abiurandas compelli non debent, ne in eandem fornicationem redeuntes periurii reatum incurrant; ipsos tamen per condignam paenitentiam volumus arctius compelli ut mulieres ipsas a se ita removeant quod de illis postmodum sinistra non habeatur suspicio. Et si qui ipsorum clericorum ad illas redire vel alias mulieres suspectas accipere praesumant,** volumus eos severius per ordinarium castigari.

5.[50] Si clericus notorius fuerit fornicator, ut quia de hoc in iudicio confessus convictus vel legitime condemnatus est, ipso facto a celebratione divinorum sit suspensus, donec iniunctam sibi paententiam adimpleverit.

[24v] 6.[51] Praecipimus ut episcopi et alii iudices ecclesiastici contra adulteros, incestuosos et concubinarios in suis visitationibus inquisitionem faciant

---

[45]VI, 5.11.7, a decretal of Pope Innocent IV (1243-54).
[46]Cf. 13 Edward I, c. 1, s. 34, 1285 (*S.R.*, 87).
[47]C. 36, q. 1, c. 2 (Fr, I, 1288-9).
[48]X, 5.16.1 (Fr, II, 805-6), a quote from Ex. xxii. 16.
[49]X, 3.2.3 (Fr, II, 454), originally a decretal of Pope Alexander III (1159-81).
[50]Cf. X, 3.2.10 (Fr, II, 457), a decretal of Pope Gregory IX (1227-41), published before 1234.
[51]The general principle is stated in X, 5.1.25 (Fr, II, 747), c. 6 of Lateran IV, 1215 (*C.O.D.*, 236-7). Cf. 4.2 above.

7.[45] We will that the benefit of absolution shall be dispensed free of charge (apart from the expenses incurred by reason of their contumacy) to all who are excommunicated or suspended and who seek to be absolved in the manner laid down by the church.

4. Of adultery and dishonour.

1.[46] We order that adultery, incest, dishonour and fornication within our kingdom and dominions shall be severely punished, but according to the discretion and moderation of the bishops and others who have the power to investigate and judge the aforesaid crimes, about which we burden their consciences.

2.[47] **Fornication, dishonour, adultery and incest must be distinguished from each other.**

Fornication, although it is any kind of illicit intercourse which takes place with someone other than a man's lawful wife, is nevertheless particularly understood as making use of widows, harlots or concubines.

Dishonour, properly speaking, is the unlawful deflowering of virgins, when a virgin is corrupted by the will of either party without any prior marriage contract.

Adultery is the violation of someone else's marriage bed. It is called adultery because it is access 'to someone else's' marriage bed.

Incest is the abuse of those within the prohibited degrees of kindred or affinity.

3.[48] A man who deflowers a virgin shall take her to wife, and if he does not want, or is unable to do so, he shall be obliged by means of ecclesiastical censures to provide her with a dowry at the discretion of the ordinary.

4.[49] **Although clergy ordained in holy orders, who publicly maintain concubines, must not be forced to abjure them, lest they incur the accusation of perjury by falling back into the same fornication, yet we will that they shall be so strictly compelled by appropriate penance that they will send these women away from them, so that there may be no more sinister suspicion about them. And if any of these clergy presume to go back to them or to take on any other suspect women,** it is our will that they shall to be punished all the more severely by the ordinary.

5.[50] If a clergyman has been a notorious fornicator, to the point where he has confessed it in court, been convicted and lawfully condemned, he shall be suspended from the celebration of divine service as a matter of course, until he has done the penance imposed on him.

6.[51] We order that bishops and other ecclesiastical judges shall make diligent inquiry against adulterers, incestuous persons and concubines in their visitations,

diligentem, et constitutiones nostras in ea parte exquisite studeant observare, ac in eos, quos culpabiles invenerint, debitum officii sui exequantur; quorum conscientias in hac parte oneramus.

5. De crimine falsi.

1.[52] Cunctis iudicibus ecclesiasticis potestatem damus, pro qualitate delicti, animadvertendi in eos, qui in eorum iudiciis falsas producunt litteras vel instrumenta aut falsum dicunt testimonium, quive illis scienter usi sunt, aut testes, ut falsum proferant testimonium, corrumpere praesumant, aut ordinariorum sigilla corrumpunt adulterantve.

Iudex qui scripta aliqua aut eorum sigilla vel signa viderit de falsitate probabiliter suspecta vel redarguenda, nullam eis fidem prius adhibeat, quam de ipsorum [25r] veritate plene constiterit.

2.[53] Decernimus ut non solum ante sententiam verum etiam post, obiici potest exceptio falsitatis huiusmodi. Ideo cum falsorum instrumentorum praetextu lata fuerit sententia, comperta postmodum veritate quandocunque poterit rectractari. Qui absentium nomina tanquam praesentium scienter et dolo malo inscribunt vel inscribi faciunt in munimentis vel instrumentis aliquibus, arbitrio iudicantium punientur ac talia munimenta vel instrumenta non valebunt.

3.[54] Statuimus praeterea quod sigillum capitulare vel conventuale alicuius ecclesiae, collegii vel hospitalis ecclesiastici nulli instrumento apponatur, nisi in praesentia et cum consensu praesidentis et maioris partis praesentium de capitulo. Quod si aliter factum fuerit, qui fecerit aut fieri procuraverit, ad arbitrium ordinarii puniaturi et tale instrumentum ut falsum reiiciatur, cuiusque [25v] tamen loci statutis et fundatione semper salvis.

4.[55] **Qui testamentum, ultimam voluntatem aut codicillum dolo malo mutaverit, aut ut verum non appareat, celaverit, deleverit, interleverit, quive testamentum, ultimam voluntatem aut codicillum falsum scripserit, signaverit, recitaverit, vel dolo malo id fieri procuraverit,** per iudicem qui de valore ipsius testamenti, ultimae voluntatis aut codicilli, aut de contentis in eodem iudicabit ut falsarius punietur et omni commodo quod habiturus esset ex illo privetur.

5.[56] Qui sibi ipsi contrarius in testimonio suo reperitur **quive contra signum suum falsum reddit testimonium, falsi testis poena punietur.**

6.[57] Qui citationes, inhibitiones, decreta aut alia scripta vel edicta iudicum ecclesiasticorum auctoritate proposita malitiose violant aut corrumpunt, quive

---

[52] 1237/27 (PC, 257).
[53] X, 2.25.6 (Fr, II, 377-8), a decretal of Pope Innocent III, 3 August 1206; *Dig.* 44.1.11, originally Modestinus, *Responsa*, 13.
[54] Cf. 1237/26 (PC, 256-7).
[55] *Dig.*, 48.10.2, originally Paulus, *Ad Sabinum*, 3.
[56] *Dig.*, 48.10.27, originally Modestinus, *Regularum*, 8.
[57] 1237/26 (PC, 256-7); 1268/25 (PC, 772-3).

and that they shall take particular care to observe our constitutions which deal with the subject, and in this respect we burden their consciences to carry out their duty towards those whom they find guilty.

5. Of the crime of forgery.

1.[52] To all ecclesiastical judges we grant the power to punish, in proportion to the crime, those who produce false letters or instruments in their courts, or who give false testimony, or who knowingly make use of them, or who presume to bribe witnesses to offer false testimony, or who counterfeit or forge the seals of the ordinaries.

A judge who sees any documents, or their seals and signatures which are suspected of probably being false, or which are disputable, shall attribute no validity to them until their authenticity is fully proved.

2.[53] We decree that not only before the sentence, but also afterwards, an objection of forgery of this kind may be made. Therefore, if a sentence is pronounced on the basis of false documents and the truth is later discovered, it may be cancelled at any time. Whoever knowingly, and with evil intent, writes down the names of absentees as if they were present or causes them to be written down in any pieces of evidence or documents, shall be punished at the discretion of the judges, and such pieces of evidence and documents shall not be valid.

3.[54] Furthermore we ordain that the capitular or conventual seal of any church, college or ecclesiastical boarding school shall not be affixed to any document, except in the presence and with the consent of the president and the majority of those present from the chapter. If anything other than this is done, the one who has done it or who has caused it to be done shall be punished at the discretion of the ordinary and such a document shall be rejected as false, provided that this accords with the statutes and foundation of the place.

4.[55] **Whoever alters a testament, last will or codicil in bad faith, or else conceals, deletes or adds to it so that its true meaning does not appear, or whoever writes, signs or reads out any false testament, last will or codicil, or else causes this to be done in bad faith,** shall be punished as a forger and deprived of any benefit which he may have obtained thereby, by the judge who shall rule on the value of the testament, last will or codicil, or on what is contained therein.

5.[56] Whoever is discovered to contradict his own testimony, or **whoever gives false testimony against his own seal, shall be punished as a false witness.**

6.[57] Whoever maliciously violates or alters citations, inhibitions, decrees or other documents or edicts issued by the authority of the ecclesiastical judges, or

eorum nomine falsas litteras exequuntur vel edictum falsum proponunt, arbitrio [26r] illius iudicis in ea parte contempto, pro huiusmodi contemptu paenitentiam subeant.

7.⁵⁸ Qui deceptus ab alio falso utitur instrumento, si innocentiam suam probaverit, se a poena liberabit, nec exemplum originalis instrumenti aliter per errorem scriptum, quam ibi veritas postularet, originali patimur praeiudicare, cum non nisi dolo malo falsum commitentes crimini subiungentur.

6. De periurio et fidei laesione.

1.⁵⁹ Quicunque in re quavis, cuius examinatio ad iudicem spectat ecclesiasticum, periurii crimine incurrunt, aut fidem interpositam non observant ipsius iudicis arbitrio debita coerceantur poena.

2.⁶⁰ Cum **iuramenti causa est ut omnis qui iurat ad hoc iurat ut quod verum est loquatur**, periurus aestimandus est qui autem in dolo iurat aut qui aliter facturus est quam promittit, vel qui nequiter decipit credentem.

*3.⁶¹ Ille [26v] autem qui sub iuramento aut interposita fide promittit se aliquid facturum, quod postea non praestat, si in ea re iuste excusare se possit, periurus aut fidei violator non est aestimandus. Qui enim facit quod possit ut impleat quod iuratum est, non est periurus licet non fit quod iuramento promissus est.

4.⁶² Qui iuratus fideliter et veraciter respondere contraria respondet est periurus.

5.⁶³ Si quis verborum arte iurat eius iuramentum ita accipiendum est, sicut ille cui iuratur, secundum communem sensum intelligit.

6.⁶⁴ Cum alter alterius mandato sciens peierat, uterque periurus est, et mandans et iurans.

7.⁶⁵ **Contra bonos mores praestitum iuramentum non est servandum.** Qui tamen temere iuravit poenam suae temeritatis debitam luat.

8.⁶⁶ **Episcopi et alii praelati qui suum transgrediuntur iuramentum sunt tanto gravius puniendi, quanto maiori praeemi**[27r]**nent dignitate, ne eorum exemplo facilius ad talia ceteri provocentur.**

---

⁵⁸Cf. *Dig.*, 48.10.3, originally Ulpian, *Disputationes*, 4.
⁵⁹Cf. X, 2.24.27 (Fr, II, 371), a decretal of Pope Innocent III (1198-1216).
⁶⁰C. 22, q. 5, c. 12 (Fr, I, 886), attributed to John Chrysostom (d. 407).
⁶¹C. 22, q. 4, cc. 1-23 (Fr, I, 875-82); X, 2.24.3 (Fr, II, 360), a decretal of Pope Gregory III (731-41); VI, 2.11.1 (Fr, II, 1003-4), a decretal of Pope Nicholas III (1277-80).
⁶²C. 22, q. 5, c. 10 (Fr, I, 885), from Augustine (354-430), *Hom. de verbis Apostoli*, 30.
⁶³C. 22, q. 5, c. 9 (Fr, I, 885), Isidore, *Sententiarum*, II, 31.
⁶⁴C. 22, q. 5, c. 1 (Fr, I, 883), attributed to Pope Pius I (*c.* 142-55).
⁶⁵VI, 5.13.58 (Fr, II, 1123), one of the rules of Pope Boniface VIII (1294-1303).
⁶⁶X, 2.24.12 (Fr, II, 363), originally a decretal of Pope Urban III (1185-7).

whoever draws up false letters in their name or issues a false decree in contempt of the judge's discretion in that respect, shall undergo penance for the said contempt.

7.[58] Whoever is deceived by another into making use of a false document, will free himself from punishment if he proves his innocence, nor do we allow that a copy of the original document shall compromise the original because by some mistake it has been written differently from what the truth there requires, since those making the mistake are not guilty of a crime, unless they have done it in bad faith.

6. Of perjury and breach of faith.

1.[59] Those who incur the crime of perjury in any matter, the examination of which pertains to an ecclesiastical judge, or who do not act according to their deposited bond, shall be punished with due punishment, at the discretion of the judge himself.

2.[60] Since **the reason for swearing an oath is that everyone who swears it is swearing that he will tell the truth**, anyone who swears with evil intent or who does otherwise than he promises, or who wickedly deceives someone who trusts him, is to be regarded as a perjurer.

*3.[61] But if someone who promises under oath or by pledging faith that he will do something, which later on he does not do, can justly excuse himself in that matter, he shall not be considered to be a perjurer or breaker of trust. Whoever does what he can to fulfil what has been sworn is not a perjurer, even if what he has promised on oath is not done.

4.[62] Whoever is sworn to respond faithfully and truly but who responds in the opposite way is a perjurer.

5.[63] If someone swears in an ambiguous form of words, his oath is to be accepted in the way that the person to whom it is sworn understands it, according to the ordinary meaning.

6.[64] When one person knowingly perjures himself on the order of another, both the one who orders and the one who swears are perjurers.

7.[65] **An immoral oath is not to be kept.** Whoever has recklessly so sworn shall pay the due penalty for his recklessness.

8.[66] **Bishops and other prelates who go against their oath are to be punished all the more severely, as befits their higher station, lest others be more easily encouraged by their example to do the same thing.**

*9.[67] Clerici qui iuramenta auctoritate ordinaria praestita scienter violare comprobantur, si beneficiati sunt, eorum beneficiis priventur. Si vero beneficia non habuerint, ad beneficia sint inhabiles et ab executione ordinum suorum suspendantur.

*10.[68] Qui generaliter iurant statuta et consuetudines ecclesiarum vel fundationes aliorum locorum quorumcumque servare, non tenentur praetextu talis iuramenti aliqua illicita vel impossibilia aliquatenus facere vel adimplere, nec eorum intentio ad talia debebit referri.

7. De sortilegiis.

1.[69] Prohibemus ne quis infra regnum aut dominia nostra, sortilegio, idolatria, incantatione, superstitioneve uti praesumat. Qui contra fecerit anathema sit, et pro suo commisso publicam agat paenitentiam arbitrio ordinarii sui imponendam. **Sortilegi habendi sunt, qui sub [27v] nomine fictae religionis per quasdam sortes divinationis scientiam profitentur aut quarumcunque scripturarum inspectione futura promittunt,**[70] vel occulta inquirunt. **Divinos autem eos accipimus, qui coniectura mentis suae incerta futurorum quasi vera pronuntiant absque divinorum auctoritate verborum.**[71]

*2.[72] **Superstitiosum iudicandum est, quicquid institutum est ab hominibus ad facienda idola et colenda, vel ad colendum sicut deum creaturam, vel ad consultationes et pacta cum daemonibus pertinens, quibus utuntur magi, hauruspices et auguri.**

Ad hoc etiam genus pertinent omnes ligaturae atque remedia quae medicorum quoque disciplina condemnat sive in praecantationibus, sive in quibusdam notis quas characteres vocant, sive in quibuscumque rebus suspendendis atque ligandis.

His adiunguntur milia inanissimarum observationum si [28r] membrum aliquod salierit, si iniunctim ambulantibus amicis canis aut lepus vulpesve medius intervenerit, aut si vestis a soriscibus roditur.

Omnes igitur artes huiusmodi vel nugatoriae vel noxiae superstitionis ex quadam pestifera societate hominum et daemonum, quasi pacta infidelis et dolosae amicitiae constituta penitus sunt repudiandae et fugiendae Christiano.

---

[67]X, 2.24.10 (Fr, II, 362, originally a letter of Pope Alexander III (1159-81) to the bishops of London (or perhaps Lincoln) and Worcester concerning a suit filed by one 'R', a canon of Lincoln.

[68]VI, 2.11.1 (Fr, II, 1003-4), originally a decretal of Pope Nicholas III (1277-80), dated 18 March 1280. Cf. also X, 2.24.35 (Fr, II, 373).

[69]Cf. X, 5.21.1 (Fr, II, 822), from the penitential of Theodore.

[70]C. 26, q. 1, c. 1 (Fr, I, 1020), from Isidore, *Etymologiae*, 8.9.

[71]D, 37, c. 4 (Fr, I, 136).

[72]C. 26, q. 2, c. 6 (Fr, I, 1021-2), from Augustine, *De doct. Chr.*, II, 19-21.

*9.[67] Clergymen who are proved to have knowingly violated oaths sworn on the authority of their ordinary, shall be deprived of their benefices if they are beneficed. But if they are unbeneficed, they shall be rendered ineligible for any benefice and suspended from the exercise of their orders.

10.[68] Those who swear in general terms to obey the statutes and customs of churches, or the foundations of any other places whatsoever, are not obliged, on the pretext of such an oath, to do or to fulfil anything which might be unlawful or impossible, nor shall their promise be held to apply to such things.

7. Of fortune telling.

1.[69] We forbid anyone within our kingdom or dominions to presume to make use of fortune telling, idolatry, incantation or superstition. Anyone who does otherwise shall be anathema and for his transgression shall do public penance, to be imposed at the discretion of his ordinary. **Fortune tellers are** to be defined as **those who, in the name of a fictitious religion, claim a knowledge of divination gained by means of random selection, or who prophesy future events by examining certain writings,**[70] or who seek after the occult. **Diviners are those who proclaim the uncertain conjectures of their own minds regarding the future as if they were true, without the authority of the Word of God.**[71]

*2.[72] **To the category of the superstitious belongs anything which is established by men for making and worshipping idols, or for worshipping the creature as a god, or which pertains to consultations or pacts with demons, which magicians, soothsayers and augurs make use of.**

Also to this category belong all bandages and remedies which even the medical profession also condemns, whether in incantations, or in certain marks which are called characters, or in certain things which are hung up and tied.

To these may be added thousands of the most absurd observations - if some part of the body suddenly jumps, if a dog, a hare or a fox should come between friends when they are walking together, or if clothing is gnawed by mice.

Therefore all arts of this kind, whether of empty or of harmful superstition, coming out of some pestilential union of men and demons, are to be totally repudiated and avoided by the Christian, as if they were agreements based on a disloyal and treacherous friendship.

3.[73] **Si quis ariolos, hauruspices vel incantatores** aut artem magicam exercentes consuluerit vel **observaverit aut philacteriis eorum usus fuerit** publicam subeat paenitentiam.

4.[74] **Si quis paganorum consuetudinem sequens divinatores aut sortilegos in domum suam introduxerit quasi ut malum foras mittant, aut maleficia inveniant** parem **agant paenitentiam.**

5.[75] **Admoneant fideles sacerdotes populum** quater ad minus [28v] in anno inter divinorum solemnia diebus dominicis vel festiviis **magicas artes incantationesque nihil remedii quibuslibet infirmitatibus hominum posse conferre, non animalibus languentibus claudicantibusve, seu etiam moribundis quicquam mederi, sed haec esse laqueos et insidias antiqui hostis, quibus ille perfidus genus humanum decipere nititur.** Eorum est scientia punienda et severissimis merito legibus iudicandi, qui magicis accincti artibus aut contra salutem hominum moliri aut pudicos animos ad libidinem deflectere deteguntur.

6.[76] Omnes sortilegos, divinos, magos, incantatores et idolatrias pronuntiamus irregulares et propterea neque ad ordines provehi, neque in susceptis debent ordinibus ministrare.

7.[77] Astrologis tamen non prohibemus ea praedicere ad quae corpora caelestia se inclinant, nec medicis [29r] aut rusticis stellarum aut planetarum cursum observare, modo non credant aliquam inesse necessitatem.

8. De blasphemia.

1.[78] **Si quis contra Deum aut aliquem sanctorum suorum linguam in blasphemiam publice laxare praesumpserit, per ordinarium poenae subdatur** condignae.

9. De defamatione et convitio.

1.[79] Prohibemus ne quis aliquod crimen alicui malitiose imponat aut scripturam in alicuius infamiam publice fingat, aut ab alio fictam dolose manifestat vel manifestari faciat, verbave contumeliosa, defamatoria vel convitiosa contra

---

[73]C. 26, q. 5, c. 1 (Fr, I, 1027), c. 12 of a council of Rome, 721.

[74]C. 26, q. 5, c. 3 (Fr, I, 1027-8), c. 72 of the *Capitula* of Martin of Braga.

[75]C. 26, q. 7, c. 15 (Fr, I, 1045), attributed to Augustine; c. 42 of the third council of Tours, 813.

[76]C. 26, q. 5, c. 6 (Fr, I, 1028), c. 38 of the council of Agde, 506; C. 26, q. 5, c. 9 (Fr, I, 1029), c. 32 of the first council of Orléans, 511; C. 26, q. 5, c. 13 (Fr, I, 1031-2), c. 7 of the thirteenth council of Toledo, 683.

[77]Cf. C. 26, q. 2, c. 6 (Fr, I, 1021-2), from Augustine, *De doct. Chr.*, II, 19-21.

[78]X, 5.26.2 (Fr, II, 826-7), a decretal of Pope Gregory IX (1227-41), published in 1234.

[79]*Cod. Iust.*, 9.36.1, a letter of the emperors Valentinian I and Valens, 16 February 363.

3.[73] **If anyone has** consulted or **observed fortune tellers, soothsayers, enchanters** or people who practise magical arts, **or has made use of their devices**, he shall undergo public penance.

4.[74] **If anyone, following the custom of pagans, has invited diviners or fortune tellers into his house, either to exorcise it, or to uncover evil, they shall do like penance.**

5.[75] **Faithful priests shall warn the people** at least four times a year, during the celebration of divine service on Sundays and holy days, **that magical arts and incantations cannot provide any kind of cure to human infirmities, nor can they heal animals who are suffering, lame or dying, but these things are traps and tricks of the old enemy, by which that perfidious one tries to deceive the human race.** Knowledge of these things is to be punished, and those who are in bondage to magical arts and attempt to destroy the salvation of men, or turn chaste minds to sin, are to be rightly judged by the most severe laws.

6.[76] We declare that all fortune tellers, diviners, magicians, enchanters and idolaters are outlaws, and for this reason they may neither be ordained, nor minister if they have already received holy orders.

7.[77] Nevertheless, we do not forbid astrologers to predict which way the heavenly bodies are heading, nor do we forbid doctors or farmers to observe the course of the stars or planets, as long as they do not believe that there is any particular fate bound up in them.

8. Of blasphemy.

1.[78] **If anyone shall presume to loose his tongue publicly in blasphemy against God, or against any one of his saints, he shall be subjected to** appropriate **punishment by the ordinary.**

9. Of defamation and abuse.

1.[79] We forbid anyone to impute any crime to someone else maliciously, or to publish any document which slanders someone else, or to exhibit with evil intent, or cause to be exhibited, a document written by someone else, or maliciously to

aliquem malitiose proferat. Qui contra hanc prohibitionem nostram alicui crimen imposuerit, imponive fecerit, aut quemquam defamaverit, excommunicatus sit. Qui vero convitium fecerit, ab ingressu ecclesiae et sacramentorum [29v] perceptione suspensus existat, donec pro arbitrio iudicantis parti laesae satisfecerit, et condignam paenitentiam subiverit. Qui non convitii consilio aut infamandi animo aliquid dixisse probare poterit, fides veri a calumnia eum defendit.

2.[80] **Sane quidam sunt, qui defamare aut convitium facere non possunt utputa furiosus et impubes, qui doli mali capax non est, hi namque talia pati facere non solent, quoniam huiusmodi ex affectu facientis consistunt.**

3.[81] Is qui plura convitia ab eodem passus est, si de eis agere velit, tenetur ipsa quae simul sustinuit coniungere.

4.[82] **Si plures simul aliquem** infamaverint, **aut convitium cuiquam fecerint, singulorum proprium est maleficium, et tanto maior est excessus, quanto a pluribus admissus est. Immo tot iniuriae sunt quot et personae facientium.**

10. De excessibus in genere.

1.[83] Si aliquis licitis ordinarii sui mandatis parere [30r] contempserit, per eundem donec paruerit excommunicetur. Si clericus fuerit ioculator,[84] scurra,[85] aleator aut crapulae vel ebrietati deserviens,[86] nisi ab ordinario suo monitus resipuerit, ab officio suo per annum suspendatur.

2.[87] Apostatae qui non possunt induci, ut abiectum habitum *reaffirment* /reassument/, licite possunt incarcerari et alias acriter affligi donec professae religionis habitum duxerint reassumendum.

Apostata vero reputatur qui absque legitima dispensatione vel abiecto suae religionis habitu vel sine sui superioris assensu extra coepta monasterii sui vagatur.[88]

3.[89] Qui sacrum ordinem ut apostata recipit, quantumlibet fuerit reconciliatus suo praeposito decernimus non posse in suscepto per eum ordine, absque legitima dispensatione ministrare.

---

[80]*Dig.*, 47.10.3.1, originally Ulpian, *Ad edictum*, 56.
[81]*Dig.*, 47.10.7.5, originally Ulpian, *Ad edictum*, 57.
[82]*Dig.*, 47.10.34, originally Gaius, *Ad edict. Prov.*, 13.
[83]X, 3.1.9 (Fr, II, 450-1), a decretal of Pope Gregory VII (1073-85).
[84]VI, 3.1.1 (Fr, II, 1019), a decretal of Pope Boniface VIII (1294-1303).
[85]D 46, c. 6 (Fr, I, 168).
[86]X, 3.1.14 (Fr, II, 452-3), c. 15 of Lateran IV, 1215 (*C.O.D.*, 242-3).
[87]X, 5.9.5 (Fr, II, 791-2), a decretal of Pope Honorius III (1216-27), dated 6 May 1218.
[88]For the definition, see L, 5.6.1, gloss on *apostasiae*.
[89]X, 5.9.6 (Fr, II, 792), a decretal of Pope Honorius III, dated 10(11) August 1225.

express injurious, defamatory or abusive words against anyone else. Anyone who attributes a crime to someone else against this our prohibition, or who causes it to be attributed, or who defames someone, shall be excommunicated. And anyone who abuses another shall be suspended from entering the church and from receiving the sacraments, until he has made satisfaction to the offended party at the discretion of the judge, and undergone appropriate punishment. If anyone can prove that he did not speak with the intention of abusing or of attacking someone else, the reliability of the truth defends him from calumny.

2.[80] **Of course there are some who cannot defame or abuse anyone, for example a madman or a child who is incapable of evil intent, such people usually suffer such things but do not do them, since they arise out of the attitude of the culprit.**

3.[81] If someone has suffered several injuries from the same person and wants to do something about it, he must combine everything he has endured on any one occasion into a single complaint.

4.[82] **If many people** have slandered **someone at the same time, or cast abuse on someone, the wrongdoing is common to all of them, and the transgression is all the greater when it is confessed by many. Indeed, there are as many injuries done as there are people who have done them.**

10. Of excesses in general.

1.[83] If anyone disdains to obey the lawful commands of his ordinary, he shall be excommunicated by the latter until he obeys them. If a cleric is a gamer,[84] playboy,[85] gambler, or addicted to drunkenness or inebriation,[86] and does not repent after having been warned by his ordinary, he shall be suspended from his office for a year.

2.[87] Apostate monks who cannot be persuaded to go back to the habit they have rejected, may be lawfully imprisoned and severely punished in other ways until they are prepared to return to the habit of the order in which they were professed.

An apostate may be defined as one who has thrown off the habit of his order without lawful dispensation or who has wandered outside the confines of his monastery without the agreement of his superior.[88]

3.[89] We decree that anyone ordained as an apostate cannot minister in the order which he has received as long as he is not reconciled to his superior, unless he is lawfully dispensed.

4.[90] **De infantibus qui mortui reperiuntur cum patre et matre et non apparet, utrum a patre vel a matre oppressi** [30v] **sunt vel suffocati vel propria morte defuncti, non debent inde securi esse parentes nec etiam sine poena. Sed tamen consideratio debet esse pietatis ubi non voluntas, sed eventus mortis causa fuerit**, et ideo statuimus quod parentes ipsi arbitrio ordinarii sui debitam subeant paenitentiam.

5.[91] **Si quis, causa implendae libidinis vel odii meditatione, sibi aut cuivis alteri homini aut mulieri aliquid fecerit vel ad potandum dederit, ut non possit generare aut concipere, vel ut soboles nasci nequeat,** per annum sub arcta custodia, ad peragendam paenitentiam in carceribus teneatur.

6.[92] Si quis aliquod ecclesiasticum sacramentum praeter baptismatis in casu necessitatis ministraverit, cum ad id non sit legitime ordinatus, propter suam temeritatem de ecclesia abiiciatur nunquam postea ordinandus.

7.[93] Prohibemus ne quis ad aliquos promoveatur ordines ecclesiasticas nisi secundum ritum et observationem Ecclesiae nostrae [31r] Anglicanae; qui vero aliter promotus fuerit ab executione ordinum sic susceptorum sit suspensus et ad alios non admittatur.

8.[94] Uniones ecclesiarum perpetuas fieri prohibemus, nisi ex evidenti necessitate aut ecclesiarum utilitate per locorum ordinarios id fiat.

9.[95] **Cum grave sit crimen in Christianis qui malefecerint inde gloriari, contingitque interdum qui nonnulli ex eis non erubescunt in publico confiteri se mulieres carnaliter cognovisse, quo fit vel possit fieri quod viri uxores abiiciunt, quibus fuerant matrimonialiter copulati, stricte prohibemus ne talia decetero committantur, et si quisquam clericorum contrarium attemptaverit ab officio et beneficio suspendatur, laici vero condigna paenitentia puniantur. Viri autem qui suas uxores ex illa occasione non probato crimine dimiserint, eas statim recipiant,** [31v] **atque eis, sicut iustum fuerit, officium exhibeant maritale.**

10.[96] Statuimus ut nullus sacerdos peccatorem sibi in foro paenitentiae de suis peccatis confessum, vel etiam peccata sibi taliter confessa, **verbo aut signo, aut alio quovismodo revelet, et si contrarium fecerit, non solum a sacerdotali officio** *depon...* **deponetur, verum etiam ad agendum perpetuam paenitentiam in arctum monasterium detrudetur.**

---

[90]X, 5.10.3 (Fr, II, 793), a decretal of Pope Lucius III (1181-5).

[91]X, 5.12.5 (Fr, II, 794), of uncertain origin. Cf. *Dig.*, 48.19.38.5, originally Paulus, *Sententiarum*, 5.

[92]X, 5.28.1 (Fr, II, 833), a decretal of Pope Hormisdas (514-23), which however, forbade baptizing as well. Lay baptism in case of necessity was authorized by L, 3.24.1, originally c. 22 of Richard Poore's statutes for the diocese of Salisbury, *c.* 1217-19 (PC, 68-9).

[93]L, 1.9.1, originally c. 46 of an unknown English diocese, *c.* 1225 (PC, 147).

[94]1268/22 (PC, 770-1); X, 5.31.8 (Fr, II, 837), a decretal of Pope Celestine III (1191-8); cf. C. 16, q. 1, cc. 48-9 (Fr, I, 776), two letters of Pope Gregory I (590-604).

[95]X, 5.31.9 (Fr, II, 837), a decretal of Pope Innocent III (1198-1216), dated 4 May 1198.

[96]X, 5.38.12 (Fr, II, 887-8), c. 21 of Lateran IV, 1215 (*C.O.D.*, 245).

4.[90] **As for children who are found dead in bed with their father and mother, and it is not clear whether they have been crushed by the father or mother, been smothered, or simply died, the parents must not on that account be excused or go without punishment. But when the cause of death is accidental and not deliberate, the main concern should be for godliness,** and therefore we ordain that the parents themselves shall undergo due penance at the discretion of their ordinary.

5.[91] **If anyone shall make some kind of drug and either take it himself or give it to someone else, whether male or female, to drink for the purpose of fulfilling his lust or from thoughts of hatred, so that the recipient is not able to generate or conceive, or bear offspring,** then he shall be kept in prison for a year under strict custody, in order to do penance.

6.[92] If anyone administers any sacrament of the church, apart from baptism in case of necessity, when he is not lawfully ordained to do so, he shall be expelled from the church for his temerity and shall never afterwards be ordained.

7.[93] We forbid anyone to be ordained to any ecclesiastical orders except according to the rite and observance of our Church of England. If anyone is promoted in any other way, he shall be suspended from the exercise of the orders so assumed, and shall not be admitted to any others.

8.[94] We forbid churches to be united in perpetuity, unless this is done by the local ordinaries either from obvious necessity or to the advantage of the churches.

9.[95] **Since it is a serious crime for Christians to glory in their wrongdoing, and it happens from time to time that some of them are not ashamed to confess in public that they have known women carnally, with the result that it happens or may happen that men leave the wives to whom they have been joined in matrimony, we strictly forbid that such things shall be done in future. And if a clergyman tries to go against this, he shall be suspended from his office and benefice, and lay people shall be punished with appropriate penance. And husbands who have sent their wives away for this reason, without any crime having been proved, shall take them back again and perform their marital duty as it is right to do.**

10.[96] We decree that no priest **shall reveal** the identity of a sinner who has confessed to him in the context of penance, or any sins so confessed to him, **by word or sign or in any other way, and if he does otherwise, he shall not only be deposed from his priestly office but shall also be confined in a closed monastery in order to do perpetual penance.**

11.[97] Prohibemus insuper ne archiepiscopi, episcopi, archidiaconi vel alii iudices ecclesiastici, **pro corrigendis excessibus aut criminibus, a clericis vel laicis poenam pecuniariam** contra statuta regni[98] **exigant,** sub poena suspensionis ab officio suo per annum.

12.[99] Cum excommunicati ecclesiastica carere debeant sepultura, exemptis et non exemptis stricta interdictione praecipimus ne aliquos in excommunicatione defunctos, aut mortem sibi ipsis [32r] inferentes **in suis ecclesiis vel earum coemeteriis sepelire** praesumant, et, si de facto tales sepelierint, e{i/o}s **extra** ecclesias vel **coemeteria** ad mandatum ordinariorum suorum **eiiciant. Quod si facere noluerint,** ordinarii ipsi eorum suppleant defectum, ipsos nihilominus pro suae praesumptionis excessu debita animadversione nostra auctoritate compescendo. Per invocationem privilegii nemini intelligimus ius novum acquiri, sed vetus si quod fuerat, illibatum conservari.

13.[100] Quaecunque divinum perturbaverint officium aut oculos divinae maiesta{rum/tis} offendant sint ab ecclesiis prorsus aliena, ne ubi peccatorum est postulanda venia ibi peccandi detur occasio, aut depraehendantur peccata committi.

14.[101] Praelati, rectores, vicarii et alii clerici qui divinis in ecclesia deputantur officiis, si in illis negligentes fuerint, [32v] et a superioribus suis legitime moniti non emendaverint, debite castigentur.

11. De accusationibus.

1.[102] **Eorum qui accusantur causas discutere non licet priusquam legitime vocati ad iudicium veniant, et praesens per praesentem agnoscat veritatem et intelligat quae ei obiciuntur.**

2.[103] **Si quem paenituerit accusasse de eo quod non potuerit probare, si cum accusato innocenti convenerit, invicem se absolvant. Si vero iudex eum qui accusatus est criminosum esse, et inter re***r***um et accusatorem per collusionem conventum esse cognoverit, collusores pro arbitrio suo puniat.**

---

[97]X, 5.37.3 (Fr, II, 880-1), a letter of Pope Alexander III (1159-81) to the archbishop of Canterbury; 23 Henry VIII, c. 9, s. 4, 1531-2 (*S.R.*, III, 377-8).
[98]9 Edward II, s. 1, c. 2, 1315-16 (*S.R.*, I, 171).
[99]X, 5.33.5 (Fr, II, 850-1), a letter of Pope Alexander III to the archbishop of Canterbury, dated 23 March 1175; cf. X, 3.28.12 (Fr, II, 553), a decretal of Pope Innocent III (1198-1216).
[100]Cf. 1 Richard II, c. 15, 1377 (*S.R.*, II, 5).
[101]X, 1.9.10 (Fr, II, 107-12), a decretal of Pope Innocent III, 1 March 1206; X, 1.31.13 (Fr, II, 191), c. 7 of Lateran IV, 1215 (*C.O.D.*, 237); *Clem.*, 1.9.1 (Fr, II, 1140-1), a decretal of Pope Clement V (1305-14), published at the council of Vienne, 1311-12.
[102]C. 11, q. 3, c. 76 (Fr, I, 664), *Ep.* 6 of Pope Damasus I (366-84).
[103]C. 2, q. 3, c. 8 (Fr, I, 453-4), a letter of Pope Gregory I (590-604).

11.[97] In addition, we forbid archbishops, bishops, archdeacons and other ecclesiastical judges **to demand a financial penalty** which is against the statutes of the realm,[98] **from clergy or lay people for correcting excesses or crimes,** under pain of suspension from their office for a year.

12.[99] Since excommunicated persons ought to go without a church burial, we decree by strict prohibition that neither exempt nor non-exempt clergy shall presume to bury anyone who has died excommunicate, or who has committed suicide, in their churches or churchyards, and that if they have in fact buried such people, they shall throw their remains out of the church or churchyard at the command of their ordinaries. If they refuse to do this, their ordinaries themselves shall step in and do it, and shall also punish them, by our authority and with due consideration, for their excess of presumption. By invoking this privilege we do not understand that a new right is being given to anyone, but rather that an old right which may have lapsed, is being preserved.

13.[100] Whatever has interrupted divine service or offended the eyes of the divine majesty shall from henceforth be expelled from the church, lest opportunity should be given for committing sins, or it should be discovered that sins are being committed in the very place where one is expected to ask for sins to be forgiven.

14.[101] If prelates, rectors, vicars and other clergy appointed to divine offices in the church, neglect their duties, and after being lawfully warned by their superiors, do not mend their ways, they shall be duly punished.

11. Of accusations.

1.[102] **It is not permissible to discuss the cases of those who have been accused before they have been lawfully called to come to the court and the accused, being present, confesses the truth in person and understands what it is he is being accused of.**

2.[103] **If someone wishes to withdraw an accusation because he has not been able to prove it, if it turns out that the accused person is innocent, both parties shall absolve each other. But if the judge finds the person accused guilty, and discovers that there has been collusion between the guilty party and his accuser, then he shall punish both of them at his discretion.**

3.[104] Qui aliquem de crimine ad forum ecclesiasticum pertinenti accusaverit quod probare non possit, eandem paenitentiam sustinebit quam passus esset accusatus, si de crimine illo legitime fuisset convictus, nisi se a calumnia legitimis [33r] excusaverit argumentis.

4.[105] **Neganda est accusatis nisi suas suorumque iniurias prosequantur licentia** communicandi **in pari vel minore crimine, priusquam se crimine quo praemunitur eximunt.**

5.[106] **Non est credendum contra alios eorum confessioni, qui criminibus implicantur, nisi se prius probaverint innocentes, quia periculosa res est et admitti non debet, rei adversus quemcunque professio.**

6.[107] **Si legitimus non fuerit accusator non fatigetur accusatus.**

*7.[108] **Valde grave est ut vir de quo gravia crimina nuntiantur, cum ante requiri et discuti debeat, honoretur.**

8.[109] **Nulli episcoporum ab accusatione sua liceat repellere quos, antequam se ab eis impetendum cognosceret, a sua communi familiaritate neglexerit separare.**

9.[110] **De his criminibus, de quibus absolutus est accusatus,** [33v] **non potest accusatio replicari,** nisi praevaricatum fuisse doceatur.

10.[111] **Repellantur ab accusatione** inimici aut **cohabitantes inimicis quia infestationes blasphemiae affectio solet amicitiae** vel inimicitiae **incitare.**

11.[112] **Evidentia patrati sceleris non indiget clamore accusatoris.**

12.[113] **Monachi, nisi alia rationabilis /causa/ impediat, non sunt ab accusatione sui praelati repellendi, eo quod eius obedientia esse dinoscuntur, quamvis alios accusare minime possunt; quibus siquidem monachis, cum proprium non habent, de rebus monasterii debeant expensae necessariae, donec causa finem debitum accipiat, ministrari.**

13.[114] Statuendo ordinamus quod licet ad prosequendum accusationem, criminaliter intentatam admitti non debeat procurator, nihilominus tamen licebit, tam accusa[34r]tori quam accusato causas absentiae et alias excusationes sive exceptiones crimen propositum non tangentes in causa criminali per procuratorem

---

[104]C. 2, q. 3, cc. 1-6 (Fr, I, 451-2). Cf. also *Cod. Iust.*, 9.1.3, originally a judgment of Alexander Severus sent to Rufus on 3 February 222. See also 11.28 below.

[105]C. 3, q. 11, c. 2 (Fr, I, 535); *Cod. Iust.*, 9.1.19, originally a judgment given by Valentinian, Valens and Gratian to Laodicius, governor of Sardinia, 12 August 374.

[106]C. 3, q. 11, c. 3 (Fr, I, 535), a decretal of Pope Hadrian I (772-95).

[107]X, 5.1.1 (Fr, II, 733), a decretal wrongly attributed to Pope Felix II (355-65); true origin unknown.

[108]X, 5.1.4 (Fr, II, 733), attributed to Pope Gregory I (590-604).

[109]X, 5.1.5 (Fr, II, 734), a decretal of Pope Paschal II (1099-1118).

[110]X, 5.1.6 (Fr, II, 734), from the Council of Mainz, 813.

[111]X, 5.1.7 (Fr, II, 734), wrongly attributed to Pope Stephen I (254-7); true origin unknown.

[112]X, 5.1.9 (Fr, II, 734), from Augustine of Hippo, *Comm. in Gen. ad litt.*, 4.

[113]X, 5.1.11 (Fr, II, 735), a decretal of Pope Alexander III (1159-81).

[114]Rubric to X, 5.1.15 (Fr, II, 737), a decretal of Pope Innocent III (1198-1216).

3.[104] Whoever has accused someone of a crime pertaining to the ecclesiastical courts which he cannot prove shall undergo the same penance that the accused would have suffered if he had been lawfully convicted of the crime, unless he can excuse himself from calumny by legitimate explanations.

4.[105] **Accused parties shall not be permitted to** give evidence regarding **a similar or lesser crime, unless they are pursuing harm done to them or to their families, until they have been cleared of the crime of which they have been accused.**

5.[106] **Testimony against others from those who are involved in crimes is not to be believed until they have proved themselves to be innocent, because the statement of an accused person made against someone else is a dangerous thing and ought not to be accepted.**

6.[107] **If the accuser is not legitimate the accused shall not be troubled.**

*7.[108] **It is a very serious matter that a man concerning whom grave crimes are alleged should be honoured when he ought rather to be summoned and examined.**

8.[109] **No bishop shall be allowed to reject accusations from those with whom he neglected to break off relations before realizing that he was going to be accused by them.**

9.[110] **Concerning those crimes of which the accused has been absolved, the accusation cannot be repeated,** unless it appears that he was lying.

10.[111] **Enemies or those who dwell with enemies are to have their accusations dismissed, because a feeling of friendship** or enmity **has a way of stirring up slanderous attacks.**

11.[112] **Evidence of a crime committed is not strengthened by the shouts of the accuser.**

12.[113] **Unless some other reasonable cause prevents them, monks are not to be refused permission to make an accusation against their superior on the ground that they are considered to be under obedience to him, although they are unable to accuse others. As they have nothing themselves, necessary expenses must be paid to such monks out of monastic funds until the cause reaches its due conclusion.**

13.[114] We ordain by statute that it is not lawful for any proctor to be admitted to prosecute an accusation which was made with criminal intent; yet nevertheless it shall be lawful both for the accuser and for the accused to propound or submit the causes of his absence as well as other excuses and exceptions which do not have any bearing on the crime itself in a criminal case by a proctor, and through

proponere, seu allegare ac per ipsum in causa huiusmodi quoad praemissa iudicialiter experiri. Id excommunicationis tamen poenam agere et defendere per procuratorem permittimus.

14.[115] **Cum varie de criminibus procedi possit, per accusationem, videlicet denuntiationem, inquisitionem et exceptionem, volumus ut accusationem praecedat legitima inscriptio, denuntiationem caritativa monitio, inquisitionem vero clamosa insinuatio.**

Cum autem excipiendo crimen fuerit obiectum, distinguetur quare oppositum sit et quando; si enim obiciatur ut ab accusatione et testificatione quis repellatur, non est necesse inscribi. Sed cum opponatur ut quis a promotione excludatur, siquidem ante [34v] confirmationem obiectum sit, non cogitur quisquam inscribere, quia crimen eo modo probatum impedit promovendum, sed non eiicit iam promotum. Post confirmationem vero, cum scilicet ordinandus fuerit aliquis vel consecrandus, quia tunc etiam ab obtinendo repellit et deiicit ab obtento, ad extraordinariam poenam iuxta arbitrium discreti iudicis citra vinculum inscriptionis est excipiens astringendus. Si defecerit in probando pro eo quod crimine sic probato perdit quod per electionem et confirmationem ei fuerat acquisitum.

Sed ob hoc prius habitum non amittit, licet enim agatur tunc de crimine, non est tamen huiusmodi quaestio criminalis, unde per procuratorem recte poterit agitari.

15.[116] **Formam iurisiurandi** quod inquisitores ab inquisitis, cum de criminibus generaliter inquiratur, recipiant, [35r] **talem esse volumus, ut videlicet iurent** inquisiti huiusmodi **quod super his quae sciunt vel credunt esse inter se reformanda, tam in capite quam in membris (exceptibus occultis criminibus) meram et plenam dicant, ipsis inquisitoribus veritatem.**

16.[117] Non licebit de veritate criminum contra quoscunque inquirere, nisi prius de infamia legitimis constiterit probationibus, postquam tamen quis crimina fuerit in iudicio confessus, frustra confessionem suam (quominus puniatur ex ea pro ut iustitia suadeat) eo praetextu impugnare contendit, quod super eisdem criminibus non fuerat antea defamatus vel quod per eundem inquisitorem capitula super quibus contra ipsum inquireret, sibi tradita non fuerunt. Atque is qui negat obiecta, de fama non probata obiicere [35v] non potest. Ceterum ad petitionem eorum qui schedulas vel libellos infamationis porrigunt contra aliquos in occulto nolumus super contentis in eis criminibus ad inquisitionem contra quoscunque procedi, nec etiam stari dictis eorum contra aliquos qui post iuramentum vel ante tacite vel expresse inimicos se asserunt eorundem, nisi forsan ante iuramentum in fraudem id facere praesumantur. Sane propter famam et deponentium credulitatem dumtaxat, non erit contra aliquem ad depositionis sententiam

---

[115]X, 5.1.16 (Fr, II, 737-8), a decretal of Pope Innocent III (1198-1216), dated 11 February 1203; X, 5.1.24 (Fr, II, 745-7), c. 8 of Lateran IV, 1215 (*C.O.D.*, 237-9).
[116]X, 5.1.17 (Fr, II, 738-9), a decretal of Pope Innocent III, dated 29 January 1206.
[117]X, 5.1.19 (Fr, II, 740-1), a decretal of Pope Innocent III, dated 1 September 1206.

him to test the matter judicially, as far as it permitted in a cause of this kind. Nevertheless we allow anything involving the penalty of excommunication to be handled and defended by a proctor.

14.[115] **Since there are different ways of proceeding in criminal cases, namely, by accusation, by denunciation, by inquest and by exception, we desire that lawful registration shall precede an accusation, that a charitable admonition shall come before a denunciation and that a private investigation shall precede a formal inquest.**

When a ruling has been objected to by the process of exception, it must be discovered why it was objected to and when. For if it is objected that someone has been prevented from making an accusation and deposition, it need not be recorded. But when it is objected that someone has been prevented from taking up an appointment, if the objection is made before the appointment is confirmed, no one is obliged to register it, for a crime proved like that will block an appointment, but it does not remove someone who has already been appointed. But after an appointment has been confirmed, and the person in question is about to be ordained or consecrated, the person making the objection is subject to an exceptional penalty, within the prescribed limits, at the discretion of the judge, because then the objection prevents him from obtaining the appointment, or removes him if he has already obtained it. If [the accused] fails under examination, because the crime is thereby proved, he shall lose whatever he may have gained by his election and confirmation.

But he shall not on that account lose what he previously had, for although a crime is involved, the criminal matter is nevertheless not such that it cannot properly be handled by a proctor.

15.[116] **It is our will that the form of oath**, which inquisitors take from those being investigated whenever they inquire about crimes, **shall be such that** those being investigated **shall swear that they are telling the inquisitors the simple and complete truth about what they know or believe must be corrected among themselves, both in the head and in the members (hidden crimes excepted).**

16.[117] It shall not be lawful to inquire concerning the truth of crimes against whoever, unless the crime is first substantiated by lawful proofs, but after someone has confessed his crimes in court, it is pointless for him to try to withdraw his confession (so as not to be punished for it, as far as justice demands) on the ground that he has not previously been defamed for these crimes, or because the matters about which an inquest is being made against him have not been conveyed to him by the same inquisitor. And the man who denies the charges cannot object that they are based on lack of proof of [public] defamation against him. But with respect to the petition of those who present lists or libels of accusation against others in secret matters, we do not want an investigation to be launched against any such people concerning the crimes contained in them, nor to be based on the reports of those who, after [taking the] oath or before, have silently or openly indicated that they are enemies of the accused, unless perchance they have presumed to do this fraudulently, before

procedendum, sed infamatio legitima poterit indici purgatio{ne}, secundum arbitrium iudicantis qui propter dicta paucorum eum non debebit reputare infamatum cuius apud bonos et graves laesa non existit opinio. Et cum ad inquisitionem contra aliquos merito fuerit procedendum, non inimici seu periuri, [36r] vel alias inidonei; sed viri honesti habiles et idonei ad prosequendum inquisitionis causam et testimonium perhibendum in eadem debebunt admitti.

17.[118] **Debet esse praesens is contra quem facienda est inquisitio, nisi se per contumaciam absentaverit, et exponenda sunt ei illa capitula de quibus fuerit inquirendum, ut facultatem habeat defendendi se ipsum. Et non solum dicta sed etiam nomina ipsa testium sunt ei ut quid et a quo sit dictum appareat, publicanda, necnon exceptiones et replicationes legitime admittendae, ne per suppressionem nominum infamandi, per exceptionum vero exclusionem deponendi, falsa audacia praebeatur.**

18.[119] Public{a/o}s concubina{rio}s excommunicat{a/o}s et conspirantes ac etiam eos qui caritative secundum praescriptum evangelii non praemonuerunt, a denuntiatione volumus esse alienos.

[36v] 19.[120] Cum cui beneficium ecclesiasticum constiterit fore legitime collatum, nolumus propter obiecta sibi ab aliquo crimina, ab adipiscenda possessione beneficii huiusmodi impediri, nisi de criminibus ipsis **publice fuerit infamatus. Deinde si legitimus accusator in tali casu apparuerit, audiantur quae fuerint huic inde proposita, et si praedicta crimina vel eorum aliquod (quod nihil obstet) legitime fuerit probatum, tunc ipsi qui pro beneficio instat silentium imponatur super eodem. Si vero contra ipsum legitimus accusator non apparuerit, et ipse super praedictis criminibus infamatur, purgatio ei indicetur legitima, in qua si defecerit imponatur ei silentium, ea vero praestita purgatione, contradictores ab eius debent molestia compesci et in expensis legitimis condemnari.**

20.[121] Quoties contra ecclesiarum praelatos de consumptione bonorum suorum ecclesiarum *absque* /aliisque/ excessibus legitime denun[37r]tiatos fuerit de veritate criminum huiusmodi procedendum seu inquirendum, eisdem denuntiatis vendendi, dandi, infeodandi in pignus vel hypothecam concedendi seu alias quomodolibet alienandi bona ecclesiarum suarum huiusmodi potestatem interim volumus interdici.

21.[122] **Non ideo minus crimine tenetur is qui iuste accusatus est, quoniam dicit alium se huiusmodi facti mandatorem habuisse, namque hoc casu praeter principalem reum mandatorem, quoque ex sua persona conveniri posse ignotum non est.**

---

[118]X, 5.1.24 (Fr, II, 745-7), c. 8 of Lateran IV, 1215 (*C.O.D.*, 237-9).

[119]X, 5.1.20 (Fr, II, 741), a decretal of Pope Innocent III (1198-1216). The text may have been deliberately altered by the compilers to 'correct' a supposed corruption of the original.

[120]X, 5.1.23 (Fr, II, 744-5), a decretal of Pope Innocent III.

[121]X, 5.1.27 (Fr, II, 748), a decretal of Pope Gregory IX, 27 April 1227.

[122]*Cod. Iust.*, 9.2.5, originally a judgment given by Gordian to Paulinus, 11 September 241.

taking the oath. Indeed, there shall be no attempt to proceed against anyone to the sentence of deposition on the basis of defamation, or of the credulity of those making the accusation, but the slander may be countered by lawful purgation, at the discretion of the judge, who shall not consider someone to be defamed because of the words of a few people when his reputation is not harmed among those who are good and serious. And when it is right to launch an inquest against some people, it is not enemies or perjurers, or other unsuitable people who ought to be admitted, but honest men who are capable and suitable to pursue the cause of inquest and give testimony in it.

17.[118] **Unless he absents himself by his contumacy, the man against whom the inquest is to be made must be present and have the matters about which he will be asked explained to him, so that he may be able to defend himself. And not only the statements, but also the names of the witnesses are to be revealed to him, so that it may be clear what has been said and by whom, and exceptions and replies are to be lawfully allowed, lest (by the suppression of the names) the slanderer, or (by exception or exclusion) the accuser should be emboldened to lie.**

18.[119] We will that {those who keep} public concubines, {those} who have been excommunicated, conspirators, and all those who do not practise love according to the Gospel ordinance, shall be ineligible to make a denunciation.

19.[120] When someone has been lawfully collated to an ecclesiastical benefice, we do not want him to be prevented from entering into the benefice simply on account of crimes objected against him by someone, unless **he has been publicly defamed** for these crimes. **Then if a legitimate accuser appears in such a case, the matters he has been accused of shall be heard, and if any of them (provided there is no legal impediment) is lawfully proved, then silence on the matter shall be imposed on the one seeking the benefice. But if no legitimate accuser appears against him, and he is defamed for the aforesaid crimes, lawful purgation shall be imposed upon him. If he fails in this, then silence shall be imposed on him, but if he succeeds in his purgation, his accusers shall be forced to stop bothering him and shall be condemned to pay legitimate expenses.**

20.[121] Whenever it is necessary to proceed or make inquest about the truth of allegations made against prelates of churches, who have been lawfully accused of consuming the goods of their churches and of other excesses, we will that during the proceedings, those so accused shall be forbidden to sell, give, lease, mortgage or otherwise alienate the goods of their churches.

21.[122] **Someone who is justly accused shall not be considered to have committed a lesser crime because he claims that he acted on the mandate of someone else, for in this case, in addition to the one giving the orders, who is chiefly guilty, it is not unknown for the one who actually did the deed to be in agreement with it.**

22.[123] **Ne reformatio monasteriorum** et aliorum locorum quorum abbates vel praesidentes fuerint denuntiati ulla **valeat** occasione **retardari** vel impediri, statuimus ut eidem abbates vel praesidentes [37v] post inceptum inquisitionis negotium in eorum monachos seu subditos denuntiantes vel adhaerentes eisdem nihil quicquam faciant aut attemptent, quod ipsum negotium aut dictos denuntiantes quoad prosecutionem eiusdem quovismodo impedire aut turbare possit, irritum decernentes, quicquid contra hanc constitutionem nostram actum fuerit, ipsosque contemptores debita poena plectendos; volumus tamen ut denuntiantes huiusmodi debitam suis abbatibus et praesidentibus in reliquis, pendente etiam dicto negotio, exhibeant oboedientiam.

23.[124] **Qui de crimine in accusatione deductus est ab alio super eodem crimine apud eundem vel alium iudicem, deferri non potest. Si tamen ex eodem facto plura crimina nascuntur, et de uno crimine in accusationem fuerit deductus, de altero non prohibetur apud** [38r] **eundem iudicem etiam ab alio deferri. Iudex autem super utroque crimine audientiam accommodabit, licebitque**[125] **ei separatim de uno crimine sententiam proferre priusquam plenissima** examinatio **super altero quoque crimine fiat.** Neminem ad iudicium vocari volumus nisi quem iudex per suas litteras aut nuntium iuratum specialiter vocari prius mandaverit; contra praesentem tamen procedere non prohibemus. Si plures de eodem crimine accusati fuerint, uno mortuo, adversus reliquos non est abolita accusatio.

24.[126] **Accusationem a qua discedere te** publice in iudicio **professus es repetere non debes.**

25.[127] **Si is qui crimen intendit cognitionem moratur, certa perferendae accusationis tempora iudex competens praestet intra quae, si agere supersederit, renuntiasse causam intelligitur.**

26.[128] **Si accusator decesserit aliave iusta causa eum impedierit, quominus accusare possit, reus a iudicio si petierit absolvetur, alii tamen licebit ex integro cum infra triginta dies post absolutionem huiusmodi accusare.**

[38v] 27.[129] Qui accusare volunt crimen personamque specialiter designent ac mensem et locum commissi criminis profiteri etiam debent in instituta accusatione perseveraturi, usque ad sententiam, et obiectum crimen debite probaturi, alioquin sponte subituri eandem paenitentiam quam rei, si legitime essent convicti, agerent.

---

[123]X, 5.1.26 (Fr, II, 747), a decretal of Pope Gregory IX issued sometime between 1227 and 1234.

[124]*Cod. Iust.*, 9.2.9, originally a judgment of Diocetian and Maximian, 19 August 289.

[125]The original source reads 'nec enim licebit' ('nor shall it be lawful') which gives the opposite sense to what is found here.

[126]*Cod. Iust.*, 9.1.6, a judgment of Alexander Severus given to Probus, 3 May 224.

[127]*Cod. Iust.*, 9.1.7, a judgment of Alexander Severus given to Felix, 18 August 230.

[128]*Dig.* 48.2.4, originally Paulus, *De adulteriis*, III.

[129]*Cod. Iust.*, 9.2.17, a judgment of Honorius and Theodosius II, 423.

22.[123] In order that there should be **no** occasion given for **delaying or hindering the reformation of monasteries** and of other places whose abbots or presidents have been accused, we ordain that once the business of inquest has begun, the same abbots or presidents shall not do or attempt anything against their monks or subjects who have accused them, or against their supporters, which might in any way hinder or disturb the business itself, or the said accusers in their prosecution of the same, declaring that whatever is done against this our constitution shall be invalid, and that those who ignore it shall pay the required penalty; nevertheless we desire that the said accusers shall show due obedience to their abbots and presidents in other matters, as long as the said business is in progress.

23.[124] **Whoever is accused a second time for the same crime cannot be brought before the same or another judge for it. But if several crimes arise from the same deed, and he has been formally accused of only one crime, it shall not be forbidden for him to be accused of a second one, and be indicted either before the same judge or before another one. Moreover, the judge shall provide a hearing for both crimes, and**[125] **it will be lawful for him to pronounce sentence separately for the one crime, before a full examination is made into the other crime also.** We do not want anyone to be summoned to court unless the judge has previously ordered him to be specially summoned, either by his letters or by a sworn messenger; but we do not forbid proceedings to be launched against anyone who is present. If many people have been accused of the same crime and one of them has died, the accusation against the others is not thereby cancelled.

24.[126] **You must not repeat an accusation from which you have already dissociated yourself** publicly in court.

25.[127] **If the person who intends to prosecute the crime delays his submission, a competent judge shall set a certain time limit for presenting the accusation, within which, if he fails to act, he is to be understood as having abandoned the cause.**

26.[128] **If the accuser dies or if some other just cause hinders him from making his accusation, the accused may be absolved by the court if he so desires, but someone else will be allowed to accuse him, without prejudice, within thirty days after an absolution of this kind.**

27.[129] Those who want to accuse someone must declare the crime, the person, the month and the place where the crimes were committed, and must persevere with the accusation, once it is made, until the sentence, and must duly prove the crime charged. Otherwise they shall automatically undergo the same penance as the accused parties would have undergone had they been convicted.

28.[130] Qui ad accusandum ex adiecta causa vel qualitate admitti petit, non prius audietur quam causam seu qualitatem probaverit.

*29.[131] Feminae,[132] impuberes,[133] periuri, item calumnia aut infamia notati, quive praevaricati sunt, vel ob accusandum pecuniam acceperunt,[134] ab accusatione repellendi sunt, nisi suam suorumve iniuriam prosequantur.

30.[135] **Si plures existunt qui eundem de publicis criminibus simul accusare volunt, iudex eligere debet eum qui accuset, causa scilicet cognita, aestimatis accusatorum personis, vel de dignitate vel ex eo quod interest, vel aetate vel moribus vel alia iusta de causa.**

[39r] **12. De purgatione.**

1.[136] Cum quis de crimine aliquo, cuius examinatio ad forum nostrum ecclesiasticum pertinet, publice apud bonos et graves infamatus sit, quod tamen legitime probari non possit, ad arbitrium iudicis de huiusmodi crimine purgare se debet, in qua purgatione si defecerit, (legitimo cessante impedimento) pro convicto de eodem habeatur.

*2.[137] **Porro purgationis tenor erit huiusmodi.** Infamatus primum iurabit ad sancta Dei evangelia quod obiectum crimen non commisit, **purgatores deinde iurabunt, quod ipsi credunt eum verum iurasse.**

*3.[138] **Purgatores omnes illius honestatis et opinionis esse volumus, quod verisimile sit eos nolle amore vel odio seu obtentu pecuniae, aliave quavis de causa deierare; ut autem idonei appareant, necesse est ut eius quem purgare debent vitam et conversationem cognoscant.**

4.[139] Defamatos purgationis faciendae causa a loco habitationis suae ultra duodecim milia invitos vocari prohibemus,[140] et in [39v] iudicenda purgatione non super quinque purgatores pro fornicatione et similibus, septem vero pro adulterio vel maioribus criminibus quisque iudicum nostrorum ecclesiasticorum assignet sub poena suspensionis ab officio suo, quam contra facientem incurrere volumus ipso facto.

---

[130]Cf. *Dig.*, 48.2.7.2, originally Ulpian, *De officio consulis*, 7.

[131]*Dig.*, 48.2.8, originally Macer, *De publicis iudiciis*, 2; *Dig.*, 48.2.9, originally Paulus, *Sententiarum*, 5; *Dig.*, 48.2.11, originally Macer, *De publicis iudiciis*, 2.

[132]*Dig.*, 48.2.1, originally Pomponius, *Ad Sabinum*, 1; *Dig.*, 48.2.2, originally Papinian, *De adulteriis*, 1; *Cod. Iust.*, 9.1.12, a judgment of Diocletian and Maximian, 3 May 293.; VI, 2.1.2 (Fr, II, 995), a decretal of Pope Boniface VIII (1294-1303).

[133]VI, 2.1.3 (Fr, II, 996), a decretal of Pope Boniface VIII.

[134]*Dig.*, 48.2.4, originally Ulpian, *De adulteriis*, 2.

[135]*Dig.*, 48.2.16, originally Ulpian, *De officio consulis*, 2.

[136]L, 5.14.1, c. 32 of the council of Oxford, 1222 (PC, 116).

[137]X, 5.34.5 (Fr, II, 870-1), a decretal of Pope Innocent III (1198-1216).

[138]X, 5.34.7 (Fr, II, 871), a decretal of Pope Alexander III (1159-81).

[139]Cf. X, 5.34.10 (Fr, II, 872-4), a decretal of Pope Innocent III, dated 7 May 1199.

[140]According to 23 Henry VIII, c. 9, 1531-2 (*S.R.*, III, 377-8) no-one could be summoned outside his diocese.

28.[130] Whoever seeks to be allowed to make an accusation for some additional cause or consideration, shall not be heard before he has justified this cause or consideration.

*29.[131] Women,[132] children,[133] perjurers noted for calumny or slander, or those who have lied or have taken money from the accused,[134] shall be forbidden to make any accusation unless they are prosecuting an injury done to them or their family.

30.[135] **If there are many people who want to accuse the same man of public crimes simultaneously, the judge must select the one who will make the accusation, from his knowledge of the cause and his judgment of the characters of the accusers, based on their social standing, their interest in the case, their age, their manners or some other just cause.**

12. Of purgation.

1.[136] When someone has been publicly defamed among good and serious people of some crime, the examination of which belongs to our ecclesiastical court, which crime however cannot be lawfully proved, he must purge himself of the said crime at the discretion of the judge, and if he fails in this purgation (barring lawful impediment) he shall be regarded as convicted of the crime.

*2.[137] **Moreover, the purgation shall take the following form.** First, the accused shall swear on the Holy Gospels of God that he has not committed the crime of which he has been accused, and **then the purgators will swear that they believe that he has sworn truly.**

*3.[138] **We will that all the purgators shall be of such honesty and reputation that it is probable that they would not wish to swear falsely out of love, or hate, or because of bribery, or for any other reason. For them to be considered suitable, it is essential that they should be familiar with the life and behaviour of the person whom they have to purge.**

4.[139] We forbid those who have been defamed to be summoned, against their will, more than twelve miles from the place of their dwelling,[140] for the purpose of making purgation, and in ordering purgation there shall not be more than five purgators for fornication and the like; but each of our ecclesiastical judges shall assign seven for adultery and major crimes, under pain of suspension from his office, which we desire shall automatically befall anyone who does anything contrary to this.

5.[141] Postquam infamatus de crimine, inde se legitime purgaverit, deinceps boni testimonii per decretum iudicis annuntietur et compescantur qui eum ulterius de eodem infamare praesumpserint. Et ut maledicentium ora veritatis testimonio obturentur, volumus ut iudex apud quem facta est huiusmodi purgatio, litteras suas authentice sigillatas praedicto testificanti, ipsi infamato se ut supra purganti, cum commode illud petierit, scribi et dari ac publicari faciet.

6.[142] **Clerici pro suis criminibus detenti a saeculari potestate, et tandem pro convictis suis rest{it}u{t}i ordinariis non faciliter liberentur, nec perfunctione ad purgationem admittantur,** [40r] **sed cum debita iuris solemnitate et tam provida circumspectione, ut oculos maiestatis nostrae vel aliorum quos studium aequitatis exagitat purgatio eorum non praesumatur offendere.** In qua etiam purgatione non minor numerus quam duodecim purgatorum admittatur.[143]   *7.[144] Purgationes vulgares quae videlicet per duellum, ignem ardentem, ferrum vel aliam materiam candentem, aquamve ferventem, seu alia peregrina iudicia solent (eo quod per eas nocens plerumque absolvitur et innocens condemnatur, divinaque ex eis temptatur omnipotentia) decetero interdicimus, et qui tales deinceps purgationes subire non formidaverint arbitrio iudicantium extraordinarie puniantur et nihilominus legitimas super excessibus unde infamati sunt facere tenentur purgationes.

8.[145] Cum purgatio sit facienda, volumus ut in ecclesia paroechiali eius qui se purgare debet, aut si ecclesiam paroechialem certam non habuerit, tunc in ecclesia cathedrali illius loci ubi purgatio [40v] est facienda publice inter divinorum officia cum maior adfuerit populi multitudo, moneantur omnes et singuli qui dictae purgationi contradicere aut eam ullo modo impedire volunt, quod certis die et loco ad hoc competenter assignatis compareant dicturi et proposituri quod ipsam purgationem quovis ne impedire possit.

---

[141]This was well-attested practice; cf. e.g. L, 5.5.1, originally cc. 1-2 of the council of Oxford, 1407.

[142]This corresponds to L, 5.14.3, an undatable canon of Archbishop John Peckham (1279-92). The original text is in PC, 1122. See also C. R. Cheney, 'The punishment of felonious clerks', *English Historical Review*, LI (1936), 215-36, especially 232-4. See also 23 Henry VIII, c. 1, 1531-2 (*S.R.*, III, 362-3) and 25 Henry VIII, c. 11, 1531-2 (*S.R.*, III, 379).

[143]The number twelve was prescribed by X, 5.24.1 (Fr, II, 869-70).

[144]X, 5.35.1-3 (Fr, II, 877-8), decretals of Pope Celestine III (1191-8), Pope Innocent III (1198-1216), dated 22 March 1203, and Pope Honorius III (1216-27).

[145]X, 5.34.10 (Fr, II, 872-4), a decretal of Pope Innocent III, 7 May 1199, provides the canonical basis for this. Objections to purgation were common in late medieval England, and it was probably felt that this was the best way to regulate them.

5.[141] After the person defamed of the crime has lawfully purged himself of it, he shall be declared to be of good report by decree of the judge, and those who presume to slander him any further shall be restrained. And in order that the mouths of those who curse may be stopped by the witness of the truth, we desire that the judge before whom a purgation of this kind has been made shall cause his letters, authentically sealed by the aforesaid witness, to be recorded, published and given to the person defamed, if he purges himself as aforesaid, as soon as he requests them.

6.[142] **Clerics arrested for their crimes by the secular power and returned to their ordinaries as convicted, shall not be set free easily, nor shall they be admitted to purgation as a matter of course, but with the due solemnity of law and with such careful circumspection, that their purgation shall not presume to offend the eyes of our majesty or of others who are deeply concerned for justice.** In which purgation there shall be admitted no less than the number of twelve purgators.[143]

*7.[144] Popular forms of purgation, for example, by duel, burning fire, iron or other hot metal, boiling water or other extraordinary judgments, we from henceforth forbid (because through them the guilty party is often absolved and the innocent condemned, and God's omnipotence is tried by them). From henceforth those who do not scruple to undergo purgations of this kind shall be specially punished at the discretion of the judges, and in addition shall be obliged to make lawful purgations for the excesses of which they have been defamed.

8.[145] When purgation is to be made, we desire that in the parish church of the person who must purge himself, or if he does not have a particular parish church, then in the cathedral church of the place where the purgation is to be made, publicly during the time of divine service when the greater number of the people shall be present, all and singular who want to object to the said purgation or impede it in any way, shall be advised to appear on a particular day, and in a particular place specially reserved for this, in order to state and declare whatever might prevent the said purgation.

13. De publicis paenitentiis et aliis poenis ecclesiasticis.

1.[146] Cum pro modo et gravitate criminum poenae moderari debent, volumus ut iudices ecclesiastici in excessibus corrigendis causam, personas, locum, tempus, qualitatem, quantitatem ac eventum considerent, et pro iustitiae aeqitatisque ratione, aut iustam poenam imponant aut temperamentum admittant.

2.[147] Prohibemus ne aliquis praelatorum aut aliorum iudicum nostrorum ecclesiasticorum, eum quem semel iuxta constitutiones nostras punierit, iterum cum est functus officio suo alia pro eodem crimine afficiat paenitentia.

3.[148] **Clericos de criminibus suis** in iure **confessos vel** legitime **convictos, eorum excessibus et personis ceterisque circumstantiis provida consideratione pensatis, ad tempus vel** [41r] **in perpetuum** iuxta moderamen iudicantis **ad peragendam paenitentiam carceribus** per suos iudices **mancipari** posse concedimus.

4.[149] Clerici qui per suam temeritatem absque auctoritate legitima ecclesias paroechiales seu quaecunque beneficia ecclesiastica occupant et in eisdem intruduntur, servata iuris forma excommunicari debent necnon beneficiis illis perpetuo carere. Et si post latam in eos excommunicationis sententiam, in intensione huiusmodi per duos menses omnino pertinaci remanserint per locorum dioecesanos ubi alia habent beneficia, ad denuntiationem illorum in quorum dioecesibus se intruserunt seu intrudi procurarunt, quorumque excommunicationem contempserunt, proventus illorum beneficiorum quousque congrue satisfecerint eis subtrahantur, et si per annum eidem intrusi in huiusmodi excommunicationis sententia perseveraverint, extunc ad alia beneficia ecclesiastica minime admittantur.

5.[150] **Impunitas delicti propter aetatem non datur si in ea quis sit aetate, in qua crimen quod intenditur cadere poterit.**

[41v] 6.[151] **Sancimus ibi esse poenam ubi et noxa est, peccataque volumus suos tenere auctores, nec ulterius progrediatur metus quam inveniatur delictum.**

7.[152] Eum accipiemus condemnatum qui sententia sui iudicis condemnatus legitime non appellaverit, neque de nullitate conquestus est, ceterum si appellaverit aut de nullitate conquestus sit pendente appellatione aut nullitatis querela, non reputabitur condemnatus.

---

[146]X, 5.38.3 (Fr, II, 884-5), a decretal of Pope Alexander III (1159-81); X, 5.38.8 (Fr, II, 886), a decretal of Pope Innocent III (1198-1216), 19 April 1201.
[147]L, 5.16.12, gloss on *canonicas sanctiones*.
[148]VI, 5.9.3 (Fr, II, 1091), a decretal of Boniface VIII (1294-1303).
[149]Cf. 1268/10, (PC, 759-61).
[150]*Cod. Iust.*, 9.47.7, a judgment of Alexander Severus (222-35) to Isidore (undated).
[151]*Cod. Iust.*, 9.47.22, a judgment of Arcadius and Honorius to Eutychianus, 25 July 399.
[152]Based on X, 3.28.5 (Fr, II, 411), a letter of Pope Alexander III to the archbishop of Reims.

13. Of public penances and other ecclesiastical penalties.

1.[146] Since punishments ought to be gauged according to the type and seriousness of the crimes, we will that when correcting excesses, ecclesiastical judges shall consider the cause, persons, place, time, quality, quantity and result, and for the sake of justice and equity, either impose a just penalty or allow mitigation.

2.[147] We forbid any of the prelates or other of our ecclesiastical judges to impose penance a second time, for the same crime, on someone else, after the one whom he has already punished once according to our constitutions has done what was demanded of him.

3.[148] We allow that clerics who have confessed their crimes in court and who have been lawfully convicted, once their excesses have been weighed with due consideration being given to the persons and other circumstances, may be bound in prison by their judges, to do penance either for a time or in perpetuity, according to the decision of the one pronouncing judgment.

4.[149] Clerics who by their own temerity, and without lawful authority, occupy parish churches or any ecclesiastical benefices whatsoever, and are intruded into them, must be excommunicated according to the due form of the law, and surrender those benefices in perpetuity. And if, after the sentence of excommunication has been given against them, they remain in stubborn determination for a full two months, the fruits of those benefices shall be taken away from them, to the extent deemed appropriate, by the diocesan bishops of the places where they have other benefices, after having been informed by those into whose dioceses they have been intruded and whose excommunication they have ignored. And if these intruders persist in the said sentence of excommunication for a year, they shall not be admitted to any other ecclesiastical benefices from that point onward.

5.[150] **Immunity from punishment on grounds of age is not granted if the person concerned is old enough to have committed the crime intended.**

6.[151] **We decree that wherever there is injury there shall be punishment, and we desire that sins shall render their authors liable, so that there shall be no fear [of a punishment] which is out of proportion to the gravity of the crime.**

7.[152] We accept that a man stands condemned if, having been condemned by the sentence of his judge, he does not make a lawful appeal or sue for a decree of nullity. But if he appeals or sues for a decree of nullity, he shall not be regarded as condemned as long as the appeal or the suit for nullity is still pending.

8.[153] **Ea quae frequenti praevaricatione iterantur frequenti sententia condemnentur.** Contumacia enim cumulat poenam.

9.[154] **Ne iudicialis evanescat auctoritas, adversus iudices verbis vel factis contumeliose se gerens iuxta dicti iudicis arbitrium digna poterit animadversione puniri.**

10.[155] Archiepiscopis eorum provincias tempore congruo visitantibus manifest{a/o}s et notori{a/o}s offensus tunc eis vel suis quomodolibet illat{a/o}s, etiam si eorum iurisdictionem ex hoc non contingat impediri de speciali concessione nostra puniendi [42r] libera sit facultas.

11.[156] **Praegnantis mulieris paenitentiam differri** volumus **quoad pariat,** quinimmo nec ad iudicium cum periculo uteri sui eam vocari permittimus.

12.[157] Respiciendum **est iudicanti ne quid aut durius aut remissius constituatur quam causa depositi, nec enim aut severitatis aut clementiae gloria affectanda est, sed perpenso iudicio prout quaeque res expostulat, statuendum est. Plane in lenioribus causis proniores ad lenitatem iudices esse debent; in gravioribus autem severitatem legum cum aliquo temperamento** iustitiae **sequantur.**

13.[158] **Cogitationis poenam nemo patitur.**

14.[159] **Sanctio legum quae novissime certam poenam generaliter irrogat, ei{s} qui legis praeceptis non obtemperaverit, ad eas species pertinere non videtur, quibus ipsa lege poena specialiter addita est, nec ambigitur** [42v] **speciem generi derogari nec sane verisimile est delictum unum eadem lege variis aestimationibus coerceri.**

15.[160] **Interpretatione legum poenae moliendae sunt potius quam exasperandae.**

(De publica poena et aliis poenis ecclesiasticis.)

16.[161] Ultimo damnatis supplicio, nolumus paenitentiae sacramentum denegari contrariam consuetudinem reprobantes.

17.[162] Transgressores constitutionum nostrarum, in quos statutae poenae non sunt, ad arbitrium iudicis puniri volumus.

---

[153]X, 5.37.1 (Fr, II, 880); origin unknown.
[154]X, 5.37.11 (Fr, II, 882-3), a decretal of Pope Innocent III (1198-1216), dated 5 January 1211.
[155]VI, 5.9.1 (Fr, II, 1090), a decretal of Pope Innocent IV (1243-54).
[156]*Dig.*, 48.19.3, originally Ulpian, *Ad Sabinum*, 14.
[157]*Dig.*, 48.19.11, originally Marcian, *De publicis iudiciis*, 2.
[158]DP (C. 33, q. 3) 1, c. 14 (Fr, I, 1161); *Dig.*, 48.19.18, originally Ulpian, *Ad edictum*, 3.
[159]*Dig.*, 48.19.41, originally Papinian, *Definitiones*, 2.
[160]VI, 5.13.49 (Fr, II, 1123), one of the rules of Pope Boniface VIII (1294-1303), taken from *Dig.*, 48.19.42, originally Hermogenianus, *Epitomae*, 1.
[161]*Clem.*, 5.9.1 (Fr, II, 1190), a decretal of Pope Clement V(1305-14), published at the council of Vienne, 1311-12.
[162]Cf. *Dig.*, 48.19.41, originally Papinian, *Definitiones*, 2.

8.[153] **The more often a person prevaricates about something, the more often must he be sentenced for it**, for contumacy makes the punishment greater.

9.[154] **In order that judicial authority may not disappear, anyone who behaves abusively, in words or deeds, towards judges may be punished with an appropriate punishment, at the discretion of the said judge.**

10.[155] By special permission on our part, full authority shall be given to archbishops, during the time of their regular visitations of their provinces, even if their jurisdiction does not appear to be hindered in this matter, to punish open and notorious offences which are brought to them or to their servants at that time, by whatever means.

11.[156] We will that **the penance of a pregnant woman shall be deferred until after she has given birth.** On no account do we permit her to be called into court when there may be danger to her womb.

12.[157] **It must be** respected **by the person judging that nothing shall be done which is either harsher or more lenient than the cause of the matter laid before them, nor is anyone to boast of his severity or of his clemency. Rather, it is decreed that judgment is to be weighed according to what each case requires. Clearly, in lighter causes the judges must be more inclined to show leniency, whereas in weightier causes they must follow the severity of the laws, with some mitigation** of justice.

13.[158] **No one shall be punished for his thoughts.**

14.[159] **The sanction of the laws, which nowadays generally requires a fixed punishment for those who do not comply with a law's provisions, does not seem to apply to those cases in which a punishment is specifically added by the law itself; nor is there any doubt that a specific case gives way to a general principle, for it is hardly likely that one crime should be punished by different assessments of the same law.**

15.[160] **In applying the laws, punishments are to be moderated rather than made harsher.**

(On public punishment and other ecclesiastical punishments.)

16.[161] We do not desire that the sacrament of penance shall be denied to those who are condemned to death, and we denounce any custom to the contrary.

17.[162] We desire that transgressors of our constitutions, against whom there are no fixed punishments, shall be punished at the discretion of the judge.

14. De sententia excommunicationis.

1.[163] Qui cum excommunicato priusquam a suo iudice absolvatur scienter communicat, ab ingressu ecclesiae ipso facto sit suspensus.

2.[164] Excipimus tamen uxorem, filios suos, necnon eos qui ad obsequia familiaria praestandi de iure obligantur,[165] divine eorum concilio scelera non perpetrantur. Ac eos etiam qui ignoranter excommunicatis communicant, aut qui excommunicatis in sustentatione non superbiae sed humanitatis causa dare [43r] aliquid voluerint, aut ut citius resipiscantur concilium dederunt.

3.[166] Qui in criminibus damnatis cum excommunicato participant, vel in praesentia excommunicati scienter celebrant, maioris excommunicationis sententiam ipso facto incurrant. In reliquis autem, participantes non prius maioris excommunicationis sententia percellantur, quam legitime moniti a participatione huiusmodi non desistant. Legitima autem monitio tunc aestimanda est, si hi qui monendi fuerint nominatim et in specie exprimantur ac competentia dierum intervalla in huiusmodi monitione assignata fuerint. Excommunicati et sic denuntiati, nisi de eorum absolutione per litteras absolventium, vel alias legitime possunt docere, ut excommunicati semper debebunt evitari.

4.[167] Si excommunicatus ab eodem iudice diversis sententiis ob diversas causas ab una ipsarum fuerit beneficium absolutionis assecutus, non erit propter hoc communioni fidelium restituendus, quantum aliis sententiis adhuc remanet [43v] alligatus. Absolutione vero ab una (tacitis aliis sententiis) obtenta, tanquam surreptitiam volumus impetranti suffragari et ideo in eius commodum non debebit efficiaciter denuntiari.

5.[168] Excommunicatus a nullo absolvatur praeterquam a suo excommunicatore aut eius vicem gerente, nisi causa ad superiorem per viam appellationis sive querelae de nullitate deducta fuerit, in quibus casibus, sive iniustam esse huiusmodi sententiam sive nullam, aut absolutionem debite petitam iniuste sibi denegatam, conquestus fuerit excommunicatus, vocata adversa parte, eundem statim absolvat superior, nisi ex adversa obiiciatur et infra quindecim dies probetur ob manifestos offensus ipsam excommunicationis sententiam fuisse latam, in quo casu ad excommunicatorem remittatur, et non {absolvatur}

---

[163]X, 5.39.15 (Fr, II, 894-5) and X, 5.39.18 (Fr, II, 895-6), both decretals of Pope Clement III (1187-91). See also C. 11, q. 3, c. 38 (Fr, I, 654).

[164]C. 11, q. 3, c. 103 (Fr, I, 672-3), a decretal of Pope Gregory VII (1073-85) at a Roman council, 1078.

[165]This clause was added by X, 5.39.31 (Fr, II, 901-2), a decretal of Pope Innocent III (1198-1216).

[166]X, 5.39.55 (Fr, II, 912), a decretal of Pope Gregory IX (1227-41), promulgated before 1234; VI, 5.10.3 (Fr, II, 1094), c. 1, 21 of Lyon I, 1245 (C.O.D., 292).

[167]X, 5.39.17 (Fr, II, 898-9), a decretal of Pope Innocent III, 1198. Cf. X, 1.38.6 (Fr, II, 214-15), which is a fuller version of the same decretal.

[168]X, 5.39.40 (Fr, II, 906-7), a decretal of Pope Innocent III, 17 February 1203; VI, 5.11.7 (Fr, II, 1096-1101), a decretal of Pope Innocent IV, published as c. 1,20 at Lyon I, 1245 (C.O.D., 291-2). See also VI, 5.11.7a (Fr, II, 1096-1100), supposedly a decretal of Pope Alexander IV, 11 July 1254.

14. Of the sentence of excommunication.

1.[163] Whoever knowingly communicates with an excommunicated person before he has been absolved by his judge shall automatically be suspended from entering the church.

2.[164] Nevertheless we make an exception for his wife, his children, and those who by law are obliged to be present at household funerals,[165] in whose company crimes are unlikely to be committed, along with those who unknowingly have dealings with the excommunicated, or who wish to give something to excommunicated people, not in order to bolster their pride but for humanitarian reasons, or who consort with them in order that they might repent more quickly.

3.[166] Those who participate with an excommunicated person in crimes which have been condemned, or who knowingly celebrate [mass] in the presence of an excommunicate, shall automatically incur the sentence of greater excommunication, but otherwise the participants shall not be punished with the sentence of greater excommunication before they have been lawfully warned and then have not ceased from the said participation. By 'lawful warning' we mean that those to be warned have been named individually and particularly, and that a reasonable period of time has been allowed for the said warning. Those who have been excommunicated and who have been proclaimed as such must always be avoided as excommunicates, unless they can show that they have been absolved by letters from those absolving them, or by some other lawful means.

4.[167] If a person who has been excommunicated by the same judge under different sentences and for different reasons receives the benefit of absolution for one of them, he is not on that account to be restored to the society of the faithful as long as he remains bound by the other sentences. But if absolution is obtained from one of them (with nothing being said about the other sentences), it is our will that it shall be regarded as a kind of secret advantage to the recipient, and therefore, for his benefit, it must not be publicly proclaimed.

5.[168] An excommunicate shall not be absolved by anyone other than the person who excommunicated him or his deputy, unless the cause has been taken to a superior by way of appeal or suit for nullity, in which cases, if the excommunicate has complained that the sentence of this kind is unjust, or invalid, or that he has been unjustly denied absolution after having duly requested it, the other party shall be called and the superior shall absolve him immediately, unless the other party objects and it is proved within fifteen days that the said sentence of excommunication had been imposed for open offences, in which case he shall be sent back to the one who excommunicated him, and shall not [be absolved] until he has sworn a guarantee towards the payment of the

priusquam praes{ti}terit cautionem de solvendis expensis, et super eo pro quo fuerit excommunicatus satisfaciendo. Concedimus tamen facultatem superiori ad quem appellatum vel querelatum fuerit huiusmodi excommunicatum ad diem cum videbitur [44r] expedire, interim dum vocetur adversa pars absolvere.

Sed si compertum fuerit male fuisse appellatum et bene iudicatum, vel appellationem ipsam seu querelam esse desertam, super eo pro quo fuerat excommunicatus aut infra viginti dies a die sententiae latae, vel appellationis seu querelae desertae, satisfaciat, vel in pristinam sententiam reincidat.

6.[169] **Manifesta autem offensio illa intelligenda est, quae vel per confessionem vel probationem legitimam {m/n}ota fuerit, aut evidentia rei quae nulla possit tergiversatione celari.**

7.[170] Qui excommunicatus fuerit, non prius absolvetur quam iuramentum praestiterit, quod stabit iudicis legitimis in ea parte mandatis.

*8.[171] Hac generali prohibemus constitutione, **ne quis in aliquem excommunicationis sententiam promulgare praesumat, nisi competente admonitione praemissa, ex manifesta et rationabili causa** *ad* **ad huiusmodi excommunicationem procedat**, et sententiam suam huiusmodi in scriptis proferat, ac causam excommunicationis [44v] expresse conscribat, propterquam sententiam ipsam duxerit proferendam, exemplum quoque scripturae huiusmodi, si congrue petatur, tradat excommunicato infra quattuor dies ab illa petitione continue numerandos; qui vero contra fecerit ingressum ecclesiae per mensem unum sibi noverit interdictum.[172]

9.[173] **Superior vero ad quem pro hoc recurritur sententiam contra** dict{a/u}m ordinem latam, absque difficultate relaxans excommunicatorem **in expensis et interesse condemnet excommunicato, eumque alias suo arbitrio puniat, ut docente poena discant iudices, quam grave sit contra instituta nostra excommunicare. Haec vero quae in excommunicationis statuimus in suspensionis et interdicti sententiis volumus observari.**

*10.[174] **Porro si iudex qui excommunicationis sententiam tulit suum recognoscens errorem, paratus sit, talem (quam iniuste tulit) sententiam revocare, priusquam excommunicatus superiorem iudicem appellandi vel querelandi adiverit, et is, pro quo lata fuerat, ne absque satisfactione [45r] revocetur appellet, appellationi huiusmodi nequaquam deferat, nisi talis sit error, de quo merito debeat dubitari et tunc sufficienti cautione recepta, quod coram eo ad quem appellatum extiterit, vel delegato ab ipso,** iudicis **parebit** mandatis, **excommunicatum absolvat, sicque poenae praescriptae**

---

[169]X, 5.40. 24 (Fr, II, 921), a decretal of Pope Innocent III (1198-1216), 25 May 1207.
[170]X, 5.39.51 (Fr, II, 910), a decretal of Pope Honorius III (1216-27).
[171]Most of what follows comes from X, 5.39.48 (Fr, II, 909-10), a decretal of Pope Innocent III, published as c. 47, Lateran IV, 1215 (*C.O.D.*, 255-6).
[172]Cf. VI, 5.11.1 (Fr, II, 1093-4), c. 1, 19 of Lyon I, 1245 (*C.O.D.*, 291).
[173]*Ibid.*
[174]X, 5.39.48 (Fr, II, 909-10), a decretal of Pope Innocent III, published as c. 47, Lateran IV, 1215 (*C.O.D.*, 255-6).

expenses [incurred], and made satisfaction with respect to the matter for which he was excommunicated. We then grant power to the superior to whom the matter has been appealed or sued, to absolve the excommunicate on a day when it seems convenient, and that meanwhile the other party shall be summoned to perform the absolution.

But if it appears that the appeal was groundless and that the person had been rightly excommunicated, or if either the appeal or the suit is dropped, he shall either make satisfaction for the matter about which he had been excommunicated within twenty days, from the imposition of the sentence or from the abandonment of the appeal or suit, or else go back to serve the sentence as it was first given.

6.[169] **By 'manifest offence' we mean one which has been uncovered by confession or by lawful investigation, or evidence of guilt which cannot be hidden by turning one's back on it.**

7.[170] No one who has been excommunicated shall be absolved before he has sworn an oath, that he will comply with the lawful commands of the judge in that respect.

*8.[171] By this general constitution, we forbid **anyone to presume to pronounce a sentence of excommunication against someone without adequate warning in advance or a clear and reasonable cause, whereupon a judge shall proceed to the said excommunication** and issue his sentence in writing, and he shall specifically record the reason for the excommunication, on account of which he has pronounced the sentence, and if asked, he shall give the excommunicated person a copy of the said document within four days immediately following his request; and anyone who does not do this shall find himself barred from entering the church for one month.[172]

9.[173] **But the superior to whom a sentence imposed against the said order is appealed shall without difficulty condemn the excommunicator to pay the excommunicated person's expenses with interest, and punish him in other ways at his discretion, so that by the instruction of punishment judges may learn how serious a matter it is to excommunicate someone against our laws. And we desire that what we are decreeing in sentences of excommunication shall also be observed in sentences of suspension and interdict.**

*10.[174] **Moreover, if the judge who pronounced the sentence of excommunication recognizes his mistake and is prepared to withdraw the sentence (which he unjustly imposed) before the excommunicated person can lodge an appeal or suit with a superior judge, and the man on whose behalf the sentence was granted appeals that it should not be removed until satisfaction has been made, the judge shall in no case defer to an appeal of this kind, unless the mistake is such that there may be genuine doubt about it, and then, on receipt of adequate security, he shall comply with the** orders of the judge **and shall absolve the person he has excommunicated, in the presence of the one to whom the appeal has been made, or his deputy. That way he shall escape the prescribed punishment, taking care that he shall**

minime subiacebit. **Cavens omnino, ne voluntate perversa in alterius praeiudicium mentiatur errorem si debitam voluerit effugare ultionem.**

11.[175] Excommunicato iniuste expensas intuitu gravaminis factas, restitui volumus licet excommunicans revocando errorem illum sponte velit absolvere.

12.[176] **Excommunicationum sententiae nec in specie nec in genere pro culpis praeteritis vel praesentibus absque competenti monitione praemissa fulminentur, et si contra praesumptum fuerit** irritae sunt sententiae et inanes, eisque similes fiant **excommunicationum sententiae, quae sive generaliter sive specialiter, in aliquos pro futuris culpis, ita videlicet si tale quid fecerint vel etiam pro iam commissis sub hac videlicet forma: 'Si de illis infra tale tempus non satisfecerint' proferantur,** [45v] **nisi mora culpa vel offensus aut alia rationalis causa subesse dinoscatur, quam etiam in ipsis sententiis exprimi volumus seu recitari. Praeterea in universitatem vel collegium** excommunicationis sententiam proferri interdicimus, quia nonnunquam ex hoc contingeret innoxios sententia huiusmodi irriteri, quapropter in illos tamen de collegio vel universitate, quos culpabiles esse constiterit, et non in alios promulgatur.

13.[177] **Decernimus ut iudices saeculares post publicam denuntiationem** excommunicationis contra aliquem latae et eisdem cognitae excommunicatum repellant ab actibus ei de iure interdictis.

14.[178] **Si presbyter aut alius clericus fuerit ab officio pro suis criminibus suspensus vel interdicti sententia innodatus, et ipse per contemptum et superbiam aliquid de ministerio sibi interdicto agere praesumpserit,** *et* **eo ipso sit excommunicatus, et quicunque cum eo scienter communicaverit, similiter se sciat excommunicatus.**

15.[179] **Si vero post excommunicationem ante absolutionem divina officia celebraverint, perpetuae depositionis sententiam, pro ausu** [46r] **tantae temeritatis incurrant.**

*16.[180] **De his autem clericis qui tempore suspensionis aut interdicti vel excommunicationis huiusmodi ignari celebrant divina, ordinamus quod si eorum circa hoc probabilis fuerit ignorantia, ipsos reddere debebit excusatos.**

17.[181] Nominatim excommunicatis et publice denuntiatis beneficia ecclesiastica conferri non possunt, qui vero talibus scienter beneficia contulerint, eorum collatione pro ea vice sint privati.

[175]C. 49, Lateran IV, 1215 (*C.O.D.*, 257).

[176]VI, 5.11.5 (Fr, II, 1095), a decretal of Pope Innocent IV (1243-54).

[177]VI, 5.11.8 (Fr, II, 1101), originally a decretal of Pope Alexander IV (1254-61).

[178]X, 5.27.2 (Fr, II, 827), c. 29 of the council of Antioch, *c.* 341.

[179]X. 5.27.3 (Fr, II, 827), a letter of Pope Alexander III (1159-81) to Bishop Gilbert Foliot of London (1163-87).

[180]X, 5.27.9 (Fr, II, 832), a decretal of Pope Gregory IX, 22 April 1227.

[181]X, 5.27.7 (Fr, II, 830-1), a decretal of Pope Innocent III, 15 May 1207.

not, out of ill will and to the prejudice of another person, lie about the mistake in order to escape due punishment.

11.[175] It is our will that expenses unjustly incurred by reason of the action shall be reimbursed to the person excommunicated, even if the excommunicating judge has voluntarily absolved him by correcting his mistake.

12.[176] **Sentences of excommunication are not to be pronounced either in particular or in general, for earlier or for present faults, without adequate forewarning, and if anything is done to the contrary,** the sentences will be null and void, as likewise will be **those sentences of excommunication which are pronounced against some people either generally or specifically for future sins, on the assumption that they may do something of the kind, and also for sins already committed, with the formula: 'If they do not make satisfaction concerning these matters within such a time', unless there is some delay, fault, offence or other reasonable cause, which it is our will shall be expressed or recited in the same sentences. Moreover, we forbid a sentence of excommunication to be pronounced against a university or college, because when this is done it sometimes happens that innocent people are ensnared by a sentence of this kind, which is why the sentence should be pronounced against those in the college or university who are guilty, and not against the others.**

13.[177] **We decree that secular judges, after a public announcement of excommunication has been given against someone and has been made known to them, shall bar the excommunicated person from those acts which are forbidden to him.**

14.[178] **If a presbyter or other cleric has been suspended from office for his crimes or has been bound by the sentence of interdict, and has presumed through his contempt and pride to perform some of the ministerial duties forbidden to him, he shall be automatically excommunicated, and anyone who knowingly enters into communion with him will know that he has also been excommunicated.**

15.[179] **And if they celebrate the divine offices after excommunication but before absolution, they shall incur a sentence of perpetual deposition for having dared to do such an outrageous thing.**

*16.[180] **But concerning those clerics who, during the time of their said suspension or interdiction or excommunication, do ignorantly celebrate the divine offices, we ordain that if their ignorance concerning this matter seems probable, it must suffice to excuse them.**

17.[181] Ecclesiastical benefices cannot be conferred upon persons who have been excommunicated by name and publicly denounced, and those who have knowingly conferred benefices on such people shall be deprived of their [right of] collation to them for that turn.

Qui scienter in ecclesiis aut aliis locis, per ordinarium loci ecclesiasticis suppositis interdictis, divina officia celebrare aut alios ad celebrandum cogere praesumpserint quive[182] **excommunicatos publice vel interdictos, de *a* ecclesiis dum in ipsis missarum aguntur solemnia a celebrantibus moniti ut exeant, exire prohibent vel impediunt,** excommunicationis sententiam ipso facto incurrant, a qua non absolvantur donec peracta ab eis paenitentia, absolutionis beneficium mereantur obtinere.

Ipsi vero excommunicati vel interdicti, si sic moniti, ab ecclesiis [46v] non exeant, si clerici sint et beneficia habuerint, a suorum beneficiorum fructibus; si autem beneficia non habuerint, ab executione officii etiam post obtentam ab ipsa excommunicatione absolutionem, sint per annum suspensi. Laici autem qui taliter deliquerint arbitrio ordinariorum acriter puniantur.

18.[183] Eos qui ab excommunicatione iuris vel hominis propter mortis periculum vel aliud impedimentum legitimum, ab eo qui eos alias absolvere non poterit fuerint absoluti, nisi cessante periculo vel impedimento huiusmodi se illis a quibus alias absolvi debeant quam cito commode poterint duxerint praesentandos, ipsorum super his pro quibus fuerint excommunicati mandatum recepturi et secundum iustitiam satisfacturi in eandem excommunicationem decernimus reincidere. Idem quoque statuimus de his quibus (cum absolvantur) iniungitur ut aliorum conspectui se praesentent, et iniuriam passis satisfactionem exhibeant, si hoc cum primum commode poterint non duxerint adimplendi.

19.[184] Nullus excommunicationis, suspensionis vel interdicti sententiam publicare [47r] aut denuntiare praesumat, nisi prius iudicis qui sententiam tulit, aut eius superioris mandatum super hoc per litteras authentice sigillatas prius receperit.

20.[185] Quoties aliquem obstinate in excommunicatione post publicam denuntiationem eiusdem per quadraginta dies et ultra stare constiterit, tunc enim episcopus cuius dioecesis vel iurisdictionis fuerit ille excommunicatus, id in scriptis sub suo sigillo nobis aut alteri regalia in loco domicilii eiusdem excommunicati tenenti significabit ut nos aut regalia tenens huiusmodi pro eius corporis captione iuxta consuetudinem regni nostri Angliae scribere valeamus.

---

[182]From here to the end of the paragraph is from *Clem.*, 5.10.2 (Fr, II, 1191-2), a decretal of Pope Clement V (1305-14).

[183]VI, 5.11.22 (Fr, II, 1105), a decretal of Pope Boniface VIII (1294-1303).

[184]L, 5.17.4, c. 27 of the council of Lambeth, 8-13 May 1261. Cf. also VI, 5.11.1, a decretal of Pope Innocent IV (1243-54). This canon must also have been designed to meet the objections of the House of Commons, which had complained of abuses in its supplication to the king, 18 March 1532 (*D.E.R.*, 51-6). In their reply, the ordinaries implicitly accepted the justice of the accusation (*ibid.*, 57-70; cf. esp. s. 8, pp. 61-2).

[185]This refers to the peculiarly English custom of issuing a royal writ, *De excommunicato capiendo*, following a request (known as a *Significavit*) from a bishop or other authorized person. It was established following the separation of the ecclesiastical from the secular courts by King William I in 1072, and continued to be the practice until 1813, when a new writ, *De contumace capiendo* replaced it. Following the clergy discipline act of 1892 the whole procedure fell into abeyance, but it was not finally abolished until the ecclesiastical jurisdiction measure, 1963, which came into force on 1 March 1965.

Whoever knowingly presumes to celebrate the divine offices or to encourage others to celebrate them in churches or in other places which are under an ecclesiastical interdict imposed by the ordinary of the place, and **whoever**[182] **prevents or hinders those who are publicly excommunicated or banned from leaving the church during the celebration of mass, when they are warned by the celebrants to do so,** shall automatically incur the sentence of excommunication, from which they shall not be absolved until they have done penance and have earned the right to obtain the benefit of absolution.

But those who are excommunicated or banned, if they have been so warned and do not leave the church, shall be suspended from the revenues of their benefices if they are beneficed clergy, and if they are unbeneficed, from the execution of their office for a year, even after obtaining absolution from their excommunication. Lay people who sin in this way shall be severely punished at the discretion of their ordinaries.

18.[183] We decree that those who have been absolved from the excommunication of the law or of man because of the danger of death or for any other lawful impediment, by a judge who could not otherwise have absolved them, shall return to their excommunicated state when the said danger or impediment has ceased, unless they hasten to present themselves as soon as they conveniently can to those from whom they ought to be seeking absolution, in order to receive their order concerning the things for which they had been excommunicated and to render satisfaction according to justice. We decree exactly the same thing for those who are bound (when they are absolved) to present themselves to the sight of others and render satisfaction to those who have suffered wrong, if they do not hasten to fulfil this [requirement] as soon as they conveniently can.

19.[184] No one shall presume to publish or announce a sentence of excommunication, suspension or interdict unless he has first received the order of the judge who issued the sentence or of his superior concerning this, by letters bearing an authentic seal.

20.[185] Whenever someone obstinately remains excommunicate for forty days and more after the public announcement of his excommunication, the bishop in whose diocese or jurisdiction he was excommunicated, shall signify it in writing under his seal to us or to someone else who exercises the king's authority in the place of residence of this excommunicate person, so that we, or someone holding the said royal authority, may be able to issue an order for his arrest, according to the custom of our kingdom of England.

21.[186] Cum vero quisquam excommunicatus depraehensus ea de causa fuerit, incarceretur donec excommunicans nobis aut huiusmodi regalia tenenti denuo scribat de excommunicato deliberando.

22.[187] In loco ecclesiastico supposito interdicto, aut sanguinis vel seminis effusione polluto, sacramenta baptismatis, confirmationis, paenitentiae et eucharistiae, quoties opus fuerit, celebrari, [47v] consecrationem chrismatis **in coena Domini et missae semel in hebdomada ianuis clausis celebrationem, pro conficienda eucharistia fieri permittimus**. In festis quoque Natalis Domini, Paschae, Pentecostes et Assumptionis Mariae Virginis,[188] solemniter (**excommunicatis et his qui interdicto causam de**b/d/**erunt solum exclusis**) divina celebrari concedimus.

15. De electionibus.

1.[189] Statuimus ut ecclesia regularis vel alia post pontificalem dignitatem ecclesiastica administratio quaecunque ad quam quis per electionem assumi debeat, ultra tres menses non vacet, infra quos, iusto impedimento cessante, si electio non fuerit celebrata, qui eligere debuerant, eligendi potestatem careant ea vice, et cum electio fuerit celebranda, vocatis ad locum capitularem ecclesiae vacantis electoribus omnibus qui sunt intra eandem provinciam, ac praesentibus illis si volunt et possunt commode interesse per praesidentem capituli cum consensu maioris partis eiusdem assumantur tres scrutatores de collegio fide digni et notarius ac duo testes, qui quidem notarius [48r] in praesentia testium huiusmodi, vota ipsorum scrutatorum secrete et sigillatim primum exquirat, et in scriptis redigat moxque ipsi scrutatores praesente notario et testibus praedictis, vota ceterorum eligentium simili modo exquirant, et in scriptis redactis statim publicent in capitulo, ac eis pro electo habeatur in quem omnes vel maior pars capituli consentit vel saltem eligendi potestas aliquibus viris idoneis ab omnibus electoribus committatur, qui vice omni ecclesiae pastoris regimine destitutae provideant de pastore. Aliter electio facta non valeat, nisi forte communiter esset ab omnibus quasi per inspirationem absque vitio celebrata. Porro cum per scrutinium facta fuerit electio, si omnes electores, seu saltem maiorem partem capituli in aliquam certam personam, vota sua nequaquam direxisse (facta publicatione) appareat, statim continuato capitulo, omissa omni iuris solemnitate denuo ad novam procedant electionem secundum formam praescriptam, idque de die in diem durante tempore eiusdem ad eligendum [48v] assignato faciant, donec omnes aut maior pars capituli in unam et certam personam consenserint. Qui vero

---

[186]This was consequent on the preceding paragraph. Cf. L, 3.28.5, c. 13 of Archbishop John Stratford, 1342.
[187]X, 5.39.57 (Fr, II, 912), a decretal of Pope Gregory IX (1227-34).
[188]15 August.
[189]Cf. X, 1.6.41 (Fr, II, 88), a decretal of Pope Innocent III (1198-1216), published as c. 23 of Lateran IV, 1215 (*C.O.D.*, 246); also, X, 1.6.42 (Fr, II, 88-9), a decretal of Pope Innocent III published as c. 24 of the same council (*C.O.D.*, 246-7).

21.[186] And when an excommunicated person is arrested for that reason, he shall be imprisoned until the one excommunicating him writes to us or to whoever exercises such royal authority again, to free the excommunicated person.

22.[187] Whenever it is necessary to celebrate the sacraments of baptism, confirmation, penance or holy communion in a place which has been placed under ecclesiastical interdict, or which has been polluted by the spilling of blood or sperm, **we permit** consecration of the chrism **during the Lord's Supper** [i.e. on Maundy Thursday], **and the celebration of mass once a week behind closed doors, in order for the eucharist to be made.** We also allow divine service to be solemnly celebrated on the feasts of the Birth of the Lord, Easter, Pentecost and the Assumption of the Virgin Mary[188] **(excluding only those who are excommunicate or who have been the reason for the interdict)**.

15. Of elections.

1.[189] We decree that a monastic [i.e. cathedral] church, or any other ecclesiastical administration whatsoever, below the episcopal dignity, to which someone ought to be appointed by election, shall not remain vacant beyond the space of three months, during which, barring lawful impediment, if no election has been held, those who ought to have elected shall lose their power of election for that turn, and when the election is held, all the electors who are within the same province shall be summoned to the chapter house of the vacant church, and in their presence, if they will and can conveniently attend, three trustworthy invigilators shall be appointed from among the college by the president of the chapter, with the consent of the majority of it, plus a notary and two witnesses, which notary, in the presence of the said witnesses, shall first ask for the votes of the invigilators themselves in secret and under seal, and shall record them in writing, and then the same invigilators, in the presence of the notary and the aforesaid witnesses shall ask for the votes of the other electors following the same procedure, and as soon as they have recorded them in writing, they shall publish them in the chapter, and those shall be deemed elected on whom all or the greater part of the chapter agrees; or failing this, the power of election shall be entrusted to certain suitable men chosen from among the electors, who shall provide a pastor for a church each time it is deprived of pastoral oversight. An election held in any other way will not be valid, unless it happens to have been commonly agreed by everyone, without fraud, as if by inspiration. Furthermore, when an election is held by ballot, if it appears (when the results are published) that all the electors, or at least the greater part of the chapter, have been unable to agree on a particular candidate, the chapter shall continue to sit, and laying aside all the formalities of the law, shall immediately proceed to a new election according to the form prescribed, and they shall do this from day to day during the time appointed for the election of the same, until all or the greater part of the chapter

secundum aliquam praescriptarum formarum electionem infra tempus illis datum ad eligendum non celebraverint, eligendi potestate ea vice sint privati, ac in praedictis privationis casibus, ipsa eligendi potestas ad eum qui proximum praeesse dinoscitur devolvatur, qui deinde prae oculis habens non differat ultra triginta dies vacantem ecclesiam de persona idonea providere. Quod si superior ille facere infra praedictum tempus neglexerit, tunc ad eius proximum superiorem simili modo deferatur.

2.[190] Sane cum a maiori parte capituli (minori contempta) celebrata fuerit electio, **licet pars illa minor in uno solo consistit, cassari debet talis electio, si contemptus prosequatur, cum plus contemptus unius obesse consueverit quam multorum contradictio**, nisi propter bonum pacis hi qui contempti fuerint ei postmodum curaverint consentire.

*3.[191] Prohibemus ne quis ad regimen monasterii aut ecclesiae cuiuscunque regularis eligatur, nisi qui tricesimum [49r] aetatis suae annum attigerit ac prius eiusdem loci regulas didicit et professus fuerit.

4.[192] Minoris viginti quinque annis et qui expresse professi non sunt, ad praestandum in electione suffragium nullatenus admittantur. Frustra igitur tales ex eo quod ad electiones una cum aliis admissi non fuerint de contemptu conquaeruntur, aut electiones easdem ea occasione moliuntur impugnare. Variare nequeunt electores postquam scrutinium fuerit publicatum nisi cum ob deficitum consensus maioris partis capituli ad novam electionem procedatur, in quo casu liberum sit cuiquam in quemcunque voluerit votum suum dirigere.

5.[193] **Nulli licere decernimus postquam in scrutinio nominaverit aliquem vel postquam praestiterit electioni de ipso ab aliis celebratis consensum illum super electione ipsa (nisi ex causis postea emergentibus) impugnare, vel nisi ei morum ipsius antea celata de novo pandatur improbitas, seu alterius latentis vitii vel defectus quae verisimiliter ignorare [49v] potuerit veritas reveletur, opponens autem de ignorantia huiusmodi fidem faciat proprio iuramento.**

6.[194] **Vota conditionalia, alternativa, vel incerta, ab electoribus volumus esse aliena, statuentes ut talibus votis pro non adiectis habitis ex puris consensibus celebrentur electiones. Voces enim illorum qui non pure consenserint vicibus illis penes pure consentientes resideant.**

7.[195] **Cupientes indemnitatibus ecclesiarum vacantium opportune providere, hoc ordinamus decreto ut si quando fuerit electio in aliqua ecclesia celebrata, electores ipsam, quanto citius commode potuerit, electo praesentare, ac petere consensum infra mensem a tempore praesentationis**

---

[190]X, 1.6.36 (Fr, II, 82-3), a decretal of Pope Innocent III (1198-1216).

[191]X, 1.6.27 (Fr, II, 71), a decretal of Pope Innocent III, dated 24 June 1203; also, X, 1.6.49 (Fr, II, 91), a decretal of Pope Honorius III (1216-27).

[192]VI, 1.6.14 (Fr, II, 953-4), a decretal of Pope Innocent IV (1243-54).

[193]VI, 1.6.8 (Fr, II, 950-1), a decretal of Pope Innocent IV.

[194]VI, 1.6.2 (Fr, II, 946), a decretal of Pope Innocent IV, published as c. 1, 5 of Lyon I, 1245 (C.O.D., 285).

[195]VI, 1.6.6 (Fr, II, 950), a decretal of Pope Innocent IV.

agree on one particular person. But those who have not held an election according to one of the prescribed forms within the time appointed for them to elect, shall be deprived of the power of electing for that turn, and in the aforesaid cases of deprivation, the power to elect shall revert to the one who is recognized as being immediately superior, who shall then keep the matter before his eyes, and not delay more than thirty days in providing the vacant church with a suitable person. But if the superior neglects to do this within the aforesaid time, then the matter shall be transferred in like manner to his immediate superior.

2.[190] But when an election is held by the majority of the chapter and a minority has been ignored, **even if that minority consists of only one person, such an election must be annulled if contempt is alleged, for it is better to avoid the contempt of one person than the opposition of many,** unless for the sake of peace those who have been ignored decide to agree to the election afterwards.

*3.[191] We forbid the election of anyone to the headship of a monastery or of any monastic [i.e. cathedral] church who has not attained the thirtieth year of his age and has already mastered the rules of that place and been professed.

4.[192] Those under twenty-five years of age, and those who have not been explicitly professed shall on no account be allowed to cast a vote in an election. Therefore it is pointless for such people to complain that they have not been allowed to take part in the elections along with the others because of some contempt shown to them, or to try to contest the elections themselves for that reason. The electors cannot change their minds once the result has been published, except when, for want of a consensus among the majority of the chapter, a new election is called for, in which case everyone is free to vote for whomever he likes.

5.[193] **We decree that no one is allowed, after he has voted for someone or after he has sworn his consent to the election of the same person carried out by others, to object to his election (unless there are reasons which emerge later), or unless the previously hidden worthlessness of his character is subsequently revealed, or the truth of some other latent vice or defect which had almost certainly been unknown is revealed, but whoever stands up against such ignorance [of a defect] shall swear on oath that he is telling the truth.**

6.[194] **We do not want the electors to cast any conditional, alternative or unclear votes, and decree that such votes are to be regarded as invalid, and that the elections are to be held on the basis of simple consent. Let the voices of those who do not give their simple consent be given to those who do, for those turns.**

7.[195] **Desiring to make appropriate provision for the expenses of vacant churches, we ordain by the present decree that whenever an election is held in any church, the electors are bound to present the church to the person**

huiusmodi teneatur, quod si electus ipse praestare ultra distulerit, iure si quod ei ex ea electione fuerat acquisitum, extunc se noverit eo ipso privatum, nisi forsan ea sit electae personae conditio, ut electioni de se factae absque superioris sui licentia consentire non possit, quo casu idem electus seu eius electores, licentiam consentiendi ab eius superiore [50r] cum celeritate accommoda petere studeant et obtinere. Alioquin si lapso tempore pro huiusmodi petenda licentia, ea contingat non habere, electores extunc aliam celebrandi electionem habeant facultatem. Ceterum quivis electus infra tres menses, postquam electioni de se factae consenserit, eius confirmationem petere studeat. Quod si iusto impedimento cessante infra tempus huiusmodi omiserit, electio eadem viribus vacuetur eo ipso.

8.[196] Si electio ex eo non sortiatur effectum, quoniam electus consentire recusat, vel post consensum *viri* iuri suo renuntiat aut forte diem clausit extremum, seu propter occulta eius vitia irritatur, electores qui iam fecerint quod spectabat ad ipsos infra iuris terminum, eligendi habebunt a dissensu, renuntiatione, morte vel irritatione huiusmodi, ac si vacatio nova esset, tempus integrum ad *in* electionem aliam celebrandam, divine nil fraudulenter egerint in praemissis.

9.[197] Priore electione quae modo electionis et non vitio electi [50v] corruit promotionem eius in eadem vel alia ecclesia ad quam postea canonice eligatur nolumus impediri. Nominatim excommunicatus aut suspensus et sic denuntiatus, nec eligere nec eligi possit, donec absolutionis beneficium obtinuerit.

10.[198] Statuimus cum quis ad episcopatum electus fuerit, confirmationem ac consecrationem suam infra tres menses a tempore electionis huiusmodi, legitimo cessante impedimento, ab illis qui per statuta nostra ad hoc designantur petat, quo decurso tempore, is ad quem spectant beneficia quae habebat de illis disponere licite possit. Inferiora autem beneficia sive ministeria curam habentia nemo suscipiat nisi qui vicesimum quintum suae aetatis annum attigerit scientiaque et moribus existat commendatus. Cum autem assumptus fuerit, si archidiaconus in diaconum, et decanus et reliqui in presbyteros, infra annum a tempore possessionis beneficii huiusmodi adepto ordinati non fuerint, ab isto removeantur officio, et beneficia sive ministeria illa aliis conferantur qui velint et possint illud officium convenienter implere. [51r] Illos tamen decanos, quibus cura animarum non est commissa hac nostra constitutione nolumus ligari.

11.[199] Suffraganeis alicuius metropolitani ad mandatum ipsius post confirmationem electionis, licitum erit electum, qui ad eius iurisdictionem pertinet consecrare.

---

[196]VI, 1.6.26 (Fr, II, 962), a decretal of Pope Boniface VIII (1294-1303).

[197]Cf. X, 1.6.39 (Fr, II, 84), a decretal of Pope Innocent III (1198-1216), dated 8 February 1207.

[198]X, 1.6.54 (Fr, II, 93-4), a decretal of Pope Honorius III (1216-27).

[199]X, 1.6.11 (Fr, II, 53), a decretal of Pope Alexander III (1159-81).

elected as soon as may be convenient, and to seek his agreement within a month of the time of the said presentation. But if the person elected defers his consent beyond that time, then by law he shall find himself deprived from then on of anything which he may have acquired by that election, unless there happens to have been a condition placed on the person elected, to the effect that he cannot agree to the election result without the permission of his superior, in which case either the man elected or those who elected him shall do their utmost, with all deliberate speed, to seek and obtain permission from his superior for him to accept. Otherwise, if the time for seeking permission of this kind runs out and it has not arrived, the electors will be empowered to hold another election. But whoever is elected shall do his utmost to seek confirmation of the election within three months after he agrees to accept its result. But if he does not do this within the time appointed, barring lawful impediment, the election will be automatically declared null and void.

8.[196] If the election has no effect because the man elected refuses to agree to it, or after agreeing to it renounces his right, or perhaps has breathed his last, or is disqualified on account of his secret faults, the electors who have already done their duty within the time limit, shall have the full election period from the moment of such refusal, renunciation, death or disqualification, as if there were a new vacancy, in order to hold another election, provided that nothing in the aforesaid has been done fraudulently.

9.[197] If a previous election fails because of the method of election and not because of the fault of the man elected, we do not want the latter's chances of promotion in that or in any other church to which he may later be canonically elected to be compromised. Anyone who has been excommunicated by name or suspended and proclaimed as such can neither elect nor be elected until he has obtained the benefit of absolution.

10.[198] We decree that when someone has been elected to a bishopric, he shall seek his confirmation and consecration from those who by our statutes are appointed for this purpose, within three months from the time of the said election, barring lawful impediment, after which time the proprietor of the benefices which he had may lawfully dispose of them. But no one shall accept lesser benefices or ministries with cure of souls, unless he has attained the twenty-fifth year of his age, and is well thought of for his learning and morals. And once he is appointed, if an archdeacon has not been ordained a deacon, nor a dean and the rest been ordained priests within a year after taking possession of such a benefice, they shall be removed from their office and the benefices or ministries shall be conferred on those who are willing and able to fulfil that office properly. But we do not want those deans to whom the cure of souls is not committed to be bound by this our constitution.

11.[199] It will be lawful for the suffragans of any metropolitan, after confirmation of the latter's election, to consecrate the man elected, who belongs to that jurisdiction.

12.[200] Episcopi vero rite electi et legitime confirmati licet adhuc munus consecrationis non susceperint ea possunt, quae sunt iurisdictionis, sed non quae sunt ordinis pontificalis exercere; ea tamen quae sunt ordinis sive iurisdictionis personis idoneis committere possint.

13.[201] Frivole nititur unius monasterii monachus postquam alterius abbas fuerit effectus, vocem in capitulo prioris monasterii vendicare, etiam si tale ius ab abbate et monachis illius monasterii prioris sibi reservatum fuerit.

14.[202] **Si religiosus cuius arbitrium non ex sua (cum velle non habeat neque nolle), sed ex ipsius quem supra caput** [51v] **suum posuit et cuius potestati se subiecit voluntate dependet electioni, de se ad prolationem aliquam extra suum monasterium, vel suam ecclesiam sui superioris. Qui** scitus et concensus, **dare ipsa valeat, non petita licentia et obtenta praesumpserit consentire, sic praestitus non teneat consensus, et in poenam praesumptionis illius electio eadem viribus vacuetur ipso facto.** Abbas quidem monacho electo de se factae electioni consentiendi licentiam negans, per superiorem ad id compellatur, nisi legitimam negandi causam coram illo probaverit.

15.[203] **Cum licentia religioso ab eius superiore prius concessa ut electioni vel provisioni, si quam de ipso in futurum fieri contigerit, suum dare possit assensum ambitio{nis} vitio viam parat,** nullius eam volumus existere firmitatis.

16.[204] Cum eligentes vota sua in duo reperiantur dimissa, electus a maiori parte capituli debebit consummari dummodo tempore electionis suae eum constiterit fuisse [52r] idoneum, alioquin si vel in aetate, vel in ordinibus, vel in scientia ipsum constiterit, tunc passum fuisse defectum, atque ab eligentibus scienter electum is qui a minore parte electus est (si dignus reperiatur) confirmari debebit.

17.[205] Illud prae omnibus sit curandum ne in electionibus datio quibuscunque modis interveniat praemiorum, neve talis eligatur persona, quae illicitis eligentium affectibus velit deservire.

18.[206] **Confirmationem petentium desideria, si nihil est quod impediat electum, impleantur. Electi tamen vitia et actus quanto melius possunt, ubi est conversatus agnosci inquiratur ibidem.**

---

[200]X, 1.6.9 (Fr, II, 52-3), a decretal of Pope Alexander III (1159-81), which is also c. 3, Lateran III, 1179 (*C.O.D.*, 212).

[201]X, 1.6.47 (Fr, II, 90-1), a decretal of Pope Honorius III (1216-27).

[202]VI, 1.6.27 (Fr, II, 962), a decretal of Pope Boniface VIII (1294-1303).

[203]*Clem.*, 1.3.8 (Fr, II, 1138), a decretal of Pope Clement V (1305-14), published at the council of Vienne, 1311-12.

[204]X, 1.6.22 (Fr, II, 64-6), a decretal of Pope Innocent III (1198-1216), dated 13 April 1203.

[205]X, 1.6.2 (Fr, II, 48-9), c. 2 of the council of Serdica, 343.

[206]X, 1.6.3 (Fr, II, 49), a decretal of Pope Gregory I (590-604), found in his register (10.19).

12.[200] And bishops who have been duly elected and lawfully confirmed, although they have not yet received the gift of consecration, can exercise those powers which belong to their jurisdiction, but not those of their episcopal order. Once they are consecrated they can delegate the powers of their order or jurisdiction to suitable persons.

13.[201] A monk from one monastery, once he has been made abbot of another, is foolish to try to exercise his right to speak in the chapter of his former monastery, even if that right had been reserved to him by the abbot and the monks of that former monastery.

14.[202] **If a monk, whose will is not his own (because he cannot choose one way or the other) but that of him whom he has placed over his head and to whose power he has subjected himself, is a candidate for election to some preferment outside his monastery or outside the church of his own superior, who if he is informed and is agreeable has the power to grant such things, if he presumes to consent without having asked for and obtained permission, the consent so sworn shall not be valid and the election itself shall automatically be deprived of all validity under pain of presumption.** Moreover, an abbot who refuses to give permission to a monk who has been independently elected shall be compelled to do so by his superior, unless he can prove to him that he has a legitimate reason for refusing it.

15.[203] **Since prior permission granted to a monk by his superior to give his assent, if the occasion arises, to his future election or appointment, opens the way to the sin of ambition**, it is our will that such permission shall have no force whatever.

16.[204] When the electors are known to have split their votes, the man elected by the majority of the chapter must be appointed, provided that at the time of his election he appears to have been suitable, but if it appears that he was then suffering from some defect in age, or in orders, or in knowledge, but was knowingly chosen by the electors, then the man who was elected by the minority (if he is worthy) shall be confirmed.

17.[205] Above all else, every effort must be made to ensure that in elections no giving of bribes should intervene in any way whatsoever, nor should any person be elected who wishes to pander to the unlawful desires of the electors.

18.[206] **The desires of those who seek confirmation shall be fulfilled, if there is nothing which stands in the way of the one elected. At that point the faults and deeds of the one elected, and also what company he has kept, shall be investigated as thoroughly as possible.**

19.[207] Concedendi dignitates, officia, beneficia vel praebendas aut alias disponendi de rebus ecclesiae electo, ante suam confirmationem adimimus potestatem, in universum prohibentes, ne quisquam ad regimen ecclesiasticum electus administrationem dignitatis aut officii ad quod electus fuerit *priu...* priusquam electio de ipso facto confirmetur sub oeconomatus [52v] vel procurationis nomine aut alio quaesito colore in spiritualibus vel temporalibus per se vel per alium seu alios pro parte vel in totum gerere vel recipere aut illis se quomodolibet immiscere praesumat, decernentes illum qui contra fecerit, iure, si quod ei ex electione huiusmodi acquisitum fuerit privatum esse ipso facto.

20.[208] Cum rationi non congruit, ut homines disparis professionis vel habitus, simul in eodem monasterio, cohabitent, prohibemus ne religiosus aliquis in abbatem vel praelatum alterius religionis vel habitus, decetero eligatur, quod si secus actum exstiterit irritum habeatur eo ipso. Per hoc tamen quantum religiosus in episcopatum saecularis vel regularis ecclesiae possit eligi non intendimus prohibere.

21.[209] Si quis iusto impedimento detentus in electionis negotio commode nequeat interesse, potest non solum uni, sed et pluribus eiusdem capituli vires suas committere, dum tamen eorum cuilibet insolutam *det* det potestatem. Eritque tunc melior conditio occupantis, verum si ambo simul concurrant et postulent se admitti, eos audire non [53r] expedit. Quoniam possunt vota sua in diverso *corn...* dirigendo, exitum rei impedire, et quod ab eis sic fieret non valeret. Sed is admittatur dumtaxat quem capitulum vel pars maior duxerit eligendi, vel si concordare nequeunt, is qui primo in instrumento, vel litteris procurationis extiterit nominatus. Si autem nullus ipsorum fuerit insolide nominatus, tunc eadem ratione non debebit quisquam ipsorum admitti, imputetque sibi ipsi, qui eos sic constiterit indiscrete.

Porro cum unus fuerit procurator simpliciter constitutus et is unum suo et alium domini sui nomine in scrutinio elegerit nihil agit nisi certa persona eligenda, dominus sibi dederit mandatum speciale, tunc enim in illam eius et in aliam suo nomine, licite possit consentire personam.

Sancimus ut in confirmationibus electionum vocentur nominatim ubi est coelectus vel certus apparet contradictor alias generaliter in ecclesia in qua electio facta est contradicere volentes, assignato peremptorio termino [53v] competente, infra quem si qui sunt, qui se velint opponere compareant, quae etiam si electio fuerit concorditer celebrata volumus observari.

22.[210] Is qui plene non probaverit, quod in formam electionis opponit, ad expensas quas propter hoc altera pars fecerit condemnetur. Qui vero

---

[207]VI, 1.6.5 (Fr, II, 949-50), a decretal of Pope Innocent IV (1243-54).
[208]*Clem.*, 1.3.1 (Fr, II, 1135), a decretal of Pope Clement V (1305-14), published at the council of Vienne, 1311-12.
[209]VI, 1.6.46 (Fr, II, 970), a decretal of Pope Boniface VIII (1294-1303), deliberately inended to modify X, 1.6.42 (Fr, II, 88-9), c. 24 of Lateran IV, 1215 (*C.O.D.*, 246-7).
[210]VI, 1.6.1 (Fr, II, 945-6), a decretal of Pope Innocent IV (1243-54).

19.[207] We withhold the power of granting positions, offices, benefits and prebends, or of otherwise disposing of the possessions of the church from the man elected before his confirmation, totally forbidding anyone who has been elected to ecclesiastical government **to control or receive in spirituals or in temporals, by himself or through another person or persons, in part or in whole,** the administration of the position or office to which he has been elected, **in the name of guardianship or deputation or, or to presume to involve himself in them in any way before the election result has been confirmed, and decree that anyone who does otherwise, if he has gained anything as a result of the said election, shall be automatically deprived [of such gains] by law.**

20.[208] **Since it does not accord with reason that men of different profession and habit should dwell together in the same monastery, we forbid any monk to be elected from henceforth as the abbot or prelate of another order or habit, and if anything is done to the contrary it shall automatically be declared invalid. But we do not mean by this to prevent a monk from being elected to the government of a secular or monastic church.**

21.[209] **If someone is prevented by lawful impediment from conveniently taking part in the business of an election, he may delegate his powers not only to one but also to many of the same chapter, as long as he gives complete power to every one of them. The position of the occupier will then be better, but if both appear together and seek admission, it is not expedient to hear them, because they might hinder the outcome of the matter by voting in different ways, and what would thus be done by them would have no validity. But if that happens, the one whom the chapter or the majority of it decides to elect shall be admitted, and if they cannot agree, the one who is named first in the document or letters of deputation shall prevail. But if none of them is clearly named, then by the same reasoning one of them should not be admitted and claim for himself the rights which belong to them all without distinction.**

Furthermore, when only one man has been appointed proxy, and in the ballot he casts one vote in his own name and another in the name of his master, he is only doing what his master gave him special permission to do, by electing a certain person, for then he may lawfully choose one person in his own name and another in the name of his master.

We decree that in the confirmations of elections, when there is a tie or when a particular objector appears, or when there are a number of people in the church in which the election was made who wish to object to it, they shall be summoned by name and present their complaints within a period assigned for that purpose, during which time any who wish to oppose the election may appear, and if the election was held harmoniously, it is our will that the result shall be observed.

22.[210] **He who does not fully prove what he objects to in the electoral procedure shall be compelled to pay the expenses which the other party has incurred on this account. And whoever fails to prove what he objects to in**

defecerit in probatione eius quod obiicit in personam electi a beneficiis et administrationibus spiritualibus triennio sit suspensus, ad quae si infra illud temere se iniecerit, eis ipso iure perpetuo sit privatus absque spe regressus ad eadem, nisi manifestissimis ostenderit documentis causam probabilem se a vitio calumniae excusasse.

23.[211] Potestatem compromissariis datam ad eligendum praelatum (re desinente esse integra) nequeunt eligentes revocare. Rem quam definimus non esse integram postquam compromissarii inceperint de electione tractare.

24.[212] Frustra renituntur compromittentes electum recipere a [54r] compromissariis, nisi sit indignus vel contra formam compromissi electus.

25.[213] Electus per tres ex septem compromissariis si unus ex ipsis fuerit et consentiat electioni de se factae, ac idoneus reperiatur, confirmari debebit.

26.[214] Si compromissarius in quem transfertur eligendi potestas negligenter praetermittat eligere infra tempus statutum a iure ad superiorem devolvitur potestas providendi, sibique compromittentes imputent, qui in talem transtulerunt huiusmodi potestatem. Si vero eligat, sed indignum, tunc sive scienter id fecerit (cum dolus ipsius eis qui non sunt in culpa nequeat imputari) sive etiam ignoranter, cum suo sit functus officio, eligendi potestas nisi et ipsi scienter electionem talem ratam habuerint libere revertitur ad eosdem.

Idem sit cum eligit idoneum, sed electus renuit consentire. Porro eo casu, cum scilicet indignus eligitur [54v] a compromissario, compromittentes quos illius odio non convenit praegravari, nequaquam (nisi sicut praemittitur ratum habuerint) puniuntur, sed ipse ut poena suum teneat auctorem poena debita punietur.

27.[215] Expensas quas eligentes pro electione praelati necessarie erogant de bonis praelaturae volumus resarciri.

28.[216] Ea quae de electionibus et earum formis superius statuimus ad electiones quae in collegiis et aliis locis ecclesiasticis, ex statuto, fundatione, privilegio vel consuetudine, alias fieri debeant nolumus pertinere, sed secundum statuta, fundationes, privilegia et consuetudines eorundem locorum eas volumus celebrari.

16. De renuntiatione.

1.[217] Si praelatus aut quisquam alius, qui ecclesiasticum beneficium obtinet, suae praelaturae aut beneficio propter infirmitatem aut aliam quamcunque legitimam

[211]X, 1.6.30 (Fr, II, 74-6), a decretal of Pope Innocent III (1198-1216).
[212]X, 1.6.32 (Fr, II, 77-9), a decretal of Pope Innocent III, dated 5 April 1208.
[213]X, 1.6.33 (Fr, II, 79), a decretal of Pope Innocent III, dated 22 November 1208.
[214]VI, 1.6.37 (Fr, II, 966), a decretal of Pope Boniface VIII (1294-1303).
[215]X, 1.6.45 (Fr, II, 90), a decretal of Pope Honorius III (1216-27).
[216]VI, 1.6.22 (Fr, II, 961), a decretal of Pope Boniface VIII.
[217]X, 1.9.1 (Fr, II, 102-3), a decretal of Pope Alexander III (1159-81).

the person of the man elected shall be suspended from his benefices and spiritual administrations for the space of three years, and if he dares to involve himself in them during that period, he shall by the same law be deprived of them in perpetuity, with no hope of returning to them, unless he demonstrates by the clearest possible evidence that there is a plausible reason why he should not be charged with the sin of calumny.

23.[211] Electors cannot withdraw the power given to their deputies to elect a prelate (once the process has begun). We define a process as having begun once the delegates have started to take part in the election.

24.[212] Those who delegate authority to elect are wasting their time if they try to overrule the choice made by their deputies, unless the man so elected is unworthy or has been elected in contravention of the provisions of the deputation.

25.[213] A man elected by three out of seven deputies, if he was himself one of them and he agrees with the election result, and he is found to be suitable, ought to be confirmed.

26.[214] **If a deputy to whom the power of electing has been transferred neglects to elect within the time appointed by law, the power of appointment shall devolve to his superior, and those who deputed him shall bear the responsibility for this. But if he elects and the man he chooses is unworthy, then whether he did this knowingly (since his wrongdoing cannot be attributed to those who are not at fault) or whether he did it in ignorance, when he has discharged his duty, the power of electing shall revert unconditionally to those who deputed him, unless they knowingly assent to the election result.**

The same thing shall happen when he elects a suitable person, but the man elected refuses to accept. Furthermore, in a case where, for example, someone unworthy is elected by a deputy, as it is not right for those who deputed him to be weighed down by his hatred, they are in no way punished (unless, as is presumed, they have gone along with him), but he himself will be punished with the appropriate penalty, so that the penalty may affect the one who deserves it.

27.[215] It is our will that the expenses which the electors have necessarily incurred because of the election shall be reimbursed from the revenues of the bishopric.

28.[216] We do not want the things which we have decreed above, concerning elections and their procedures, to apply to elections in colleges and other ecclesiastical places which by statute, foundation, privilege or custom ought to be held in some other way; rather it is our will that they should take place according to the statutes, foundations, privileges and customs of those places.

16. Of resignation.

1.[217] If a bishop, or anyone else who obtains an ecclesiastical benefice, wishes to give up his bishopric or benefice on account of infirmity or for some other

causam cedere vult eius superior, cum huiusmodi cedendi causam utilem et [55r] honestam esse prospexerit, ipsius desiderium in hoc admittere debet. Sic tamen ut quamdiu in hoc saeculo vitam tenuerit huiusmodi redens, cum illum ab officio suo non crimen sed necessitas, infirmitas, aliave iusta et probabilis causa *ad...* abducit, sumptus ei debitos et necessarios de eadem ecclesia ministrari faciet aliumque idoneum ad regimen huiusmodi praelaturae seu beneficii cedentis loco substituat, substituive faciat secundum ordinationem constitutionum nostrarum, dignitates enim et beneficia ecclesiastica sicut non possunt absque superioris assensu obtineri, sic nec eo inconsulto dimitti.

2.[218] Cum personae ecclesiasticae, ecclesiis aut beneficiis suis nisi ex superioris licentia redere non possunt, volumus ut omnis renuntiatio huiusmodi beneficiorum non prius rata habeatur quam ad eius notitiam deducta per eundem admittatur.

3.[219] Qui beneficii sui sponte resignationem fecerit et eandem [55v] efficaciter admitti procuraverit, illud postea repetere ex priore titulo non potest. Ceterum si denuo eligatur, praesentetur aut alias assumetur ad idem, illud tametsi iuravit, non repetere absque metu periurii canonice possit obtinere.

4.[220] Qui se gratia adversarii sui submisit, quive litteras beneficiales quarum vigore adeptus est beneficium, suo superiori reddidit et eius misericordiae se subiecit non videtur pro hoc iuri suo in aliquo renuntiasse.

5.[221] Renuntiationem enim nisi de voluntate redentis clare constata admitti nolumus.

6.[222] **Cum collusio et variatio in personis ecclesiasticis maxime sint vitandae, praesente constitutione sancimus ut si quis ad** *rea...* **renuntiandum alicui dignitati vel beneficio procuratorem libere et sponte constituerit, et ipsum ignoranter postmodum duxerit quomodolibet revocandum, teneri debeat cessio per eum facta, antequam ad ipsius procuratoris vel illius, in cuius manibus cessio fuerat [56r] facienda, notitiam revocatio huiusmodi sit deducta nisi forte per ipsos aut alios factum fuerit, quominus ad eos vel eorum alterum ante cessionem potuerit revocatio pervenisse.**

17. De supplenda negligentia.

1.[223] Patroni ecclesiarum nisi ad ecclesias seu alia quaecunque beneficia sui patronatus vacantia, infra sex menses a tempore notitiae vacationis huiusmodi computandos personas idoneas locorum ordinariis praesentaverint, ius

---

[218]X, 1.9.4 (Fr, II, 104), a decretal of Pope Alexander III (1159-81).

[219]1268/33 (PC, 780); also X, 1.9.2 (Fr, II, 103) and X, 1.9.3 (Fr, II, 103), both decretals of Pope Alexander III (1159-81).

[220]X, 1.9.13 (Fr, II, 113-14), a decretal of Pope Honorius III (1216-27).

[221]Cf. L, 2.5.1, gloss on *renuntians*.

[222]*Clem.*, 1.4.1 (Fr, II, 1138), a decretal of Pope Clement V (1305-14), published at the council of Vienne, 1311-12.

[223]Cf. X, 1.10.3-5 (Fr, II, 116-17), decretals of Pope Innocent III (1198-1216).

lawful reason, his superior, when he has ascertained that the reason for this resignation is appropriate and honourable, must accept his desire in this matter. But [he must do so] in such a way that for as long as the person resigning continues to live in this world, he shall make sure that he receives his due and necessary income from the same church, since it is not crime but necessity, illness or some other just and plausible cause which has taken him away from his office, and in place of the man resigning he shall substitute, or cause to be substituted, another suitable person for the government of that bishopric or benefice, according to the order of our constitutions, for just as it is impossible for appointments and ecclesiastical benefices to be obtained without the consent of one's superior, so it is also impossible for them to be resigned without consulting him.

2.[218] Since ecclesiastical persons cannot resign their churches or benefices without the permission of their superior, it is our will that no such resignation of benefices shall be deemed valid until the matter has been brought to the superior's notice by the person [intending to resign].

3.[219] Whoever voluntarily resigns his benefice and succeeds in having his resignation accepted, cannot subsequently reclaim it on the basis of his former title. But if he is re-elected, re-presented or otherwise reappointed to it, even if he has sworn not to reclaim it, he may obtain it canonically, without fear of perjuring himself.

4.[220] A man who has withdrawn for the sake of his opponent, or who has returned the letters of appointment to the benefice, on the strength of which he had taken the benefice on, and has gone back to his superior and cast himself on his mercy, is not thereby regarded as having renounced his rights in any way.

5.[221] We do not want any resignation to be accepted unless it is clearly the will of the person resigning.

6.[222] **Since collusion and untrustworthiness in ecclesiastical persons are to be avoided, we decree by the present constitution that if someone has freely and voluntarily appointed a proctor for the purpose of resigning some position or benefice and after the proctor has acted, dismisses him for some reason, in ignorance [of what the proctor has done], the resignation accomplished by the proctor must stand if it was done before the dismissal was made known to the same proctor or to him in whose hands the resignation had been placed, unless it has been done by them or by others in such a way that it was impossible for the dismissal to have reached them, or one of them, before the resignation took place.**

17. Of correcting negligence.

1.[223] If patrons of churches do not present to the local ordinaries persons suitable for the churches or any other vacant benefices in their patronage, within six months to be reckoned from the time of the notification of the said vacancy, they

praesentandi pro illa vice amittant ac ordinarii ipsi eisdem ecclesiis de personis idoneis infra triginta dies a tempore notitiae post lapsum dictorum sex mensium numerandos provideant, pro illa vice dumtaxat.

Et si ordinarii huiusmodi hoc facere neglexerint, tunc eorum proximus superior a tempore lapsus dictorum triginta dierum infra alios triginta dies, simile ne provideat. Is quoque ad quem collatio alicuius beneficii ecclesiastici pertinere dinoscitur, infra sex menses a tempore vacationis [56v] eiusdem personae idoneae illud contulerit, pro ea vice ius conferendi illud amittat. Ac eius immediate superior, ea vice illud conferendi ius habeat, infra triginta dies a tempore notorie post lapsum dictorum sex mensium computandos. Cum omnes vero ad quos ut supra ecclesiasticorum beneficiorum collatio divolvitur, infra tempora illis assignata, non contulerint, tunc ipsis beneficiis per nos pro illa vice provideatur. Per hanc tamen constitutionem iuri aut praerogativae nostris, sive speciali fundatione cuicunque nolumus in aliquo derogari. Licet collatio beneficii facta ab eo, ad quem spectat post lapsum temporis a iure statuti viribus non subsistit, is *t...* tamen cui talis collatio facta sit potest ex illa collatum sibi beneficium (mediante toleratione superioris) retinere.

2.[224] Patronus ecclesiasticus qui scienter indignum praesentat, vel indigno scienter beneficium confert, pro ea vice ius praesentandi et conferendi amittat, quod ipso iure ad ordinarium loci vel proximum superiorem devolvetur.

[57r] **18. De tempore ordinationum.**

1.[225] Minores ordines diebus dominicis et aliis festis; sacros autem in quattuor ieiuniorum temporibus, aut sabbato sancto vel sabbato ante dominicam de passione aut (si viderint illud expedire) quibuscunque diebus festis, episcopis nostris conferre suis dioecesanis liberum sit.

2.[226] Nullus nisi vicesimum quartum suae aetatis annum compleverit aut per ordinatorem examinatus, idoneus moribus et scientia iudicetur ad sacros promoveatur ordines. Si vero ante dictam aetatem aliquem ordinatum esse constiterit, ordinator a collatione ordinum per annum, ordinatus autem ab executione ordinum sic receptorum, donec pervenerit ad legitimam aetatem ipso facto sit suspensus.

---

[224]X, 1.6.44 (Fr, II, 89-90), c. 26 of Lateran IV, 1215 (*C.O.D.*, 247-8).

[225]X, 1.11.3 (Fr, II, 118), a decretal of Pope Alexander III (1159-81).

[226]The age limit was twenty-five according to D, 77 c. 5 (Fr, I, 273) which is canon 4 of the third council of Carthage, 397: *ibid.*, c. 6 (Fr, I, 273-4), canons 16-17 of the council of Agde, 506; and *ibid.*, c. 7 (Fr, I, 274), canon 20 of the fourth council of Toledo, 633. This was repeated in VI, 1.6.14 (Fr, II, 953-4), which is c. 13 of Lyon II, 1274 (*C.O.D.*, 321-2). The suspension of the ordaining bishop is VI, 1.6.15 (Fr, II, 954), c. 15 of Lyon II, 1274 (*C.O.D.*, 322).

shall lose the right of presentation for that turn and the ordinaries themselves shall provide suitable persons for the said churches, for that turn only, within thirty days, to be counted from the time of notification after the expiry of the said six months.

And if the said ordinaries fail to do this, then their immediate superior shall likewise provide within another thirty days after the expiry of the first thirty days. Also, if the person who is recognized as having the collation to any benefice has not arranged to collate some suitable person to the benefice within six months from the time the vacancy occurs, he shall also lose the right of collating to it for that turn. And his immediate superior shall have the right to collate to it for that turn, within thirty days to be reckoned from the time appointed after the expiry of the said six months. But if none of those who have the above-mentioned right of collation to ecclesiastical benefices has collated to it within the time allotted to them, then for that turn the benefice shall be provided by us, but we do not want any right or prerogative of ours, or special privilege, to be diminished in any way merely on the basis of this constitution. Although a collation to a benefice which is made by the person responsible for it after the expiry of the time limit imposed by law is without any force, nevertheless the man to whom such a collation has been granted may retain the benefice he has been collated to (as long as his superior is agreeable).

2.[224] An ecclesiastical patron who knowingly presents someone unworthy, or who knowingly confers a benefice on someone who is unworthy, shall lose the right of presentation and conferment for that turn, which by the same right shall devolve upon the ordinary of the place or to his immediate superior.

18. Of the time of ordinations.

1.[225] Our bishops are free to confer minor orders on men from their dioceses on Sundays and other holy feast days, and holy [orders] on ember days, on Holy Saturday or on the Saturday before Passion Sunday, or (if it seems expedient) on any feast days whatsoever.

2.[226] No one shall be ordained unless he has completed the twenty-fourth year of his age and is judged to be suitable in morals and learning. But if someone is ordained before the said age, the ordainer shall automatically be suspended from the granting of orders for a year and the ordained person will automatically be suspended from the exercise of the orders so received until he reaches the lawful age.

3.[227] Prohibemus ne quis episcoporum duos sacros ordines eodem uno die conferat, et si secus factum fuerit, tam episcopus a collatione quam clericus ab executione ordinum huiusmodi [57v] per sex menses maneant suspensi.

4.[228] **Qui scienter** vel per affectatam ignorantiam, seu alio quocunque figmento **clericum vel paroechianum alterius episcopi, sine ipsius licentia speciali ordinaverit,** per annum **a collatione ordinum ipso facto sit suspensus;** qui vero taliter ordinatus est, ab executione sic susceptorum ordinum et a receptione aliorum maneat suspensus, **donec a suo episcopo relaxationis gratiam obtinuerit.** Illi tamen quorum episcopi a collatione ordinum sunt suspensi, etiam absque eorum licentia, cum eorum suspensio manifesta fuerit, interim ordines recipiendi si tamen alias idonei inventi sint, a vicinis episcopis liberam habeant facultatem.

5.[229] Proprius **episcopus is** *t...* **intelligendus est, de cuius dioecesi qui promoveri desiderat, oriundus est, sive in eadem beneficium obtinet ecclesiasticum, vel ibidem, licet alibi natus fuerit, domicilium habet** per triennium.

[58r] **Episcopo in remoto agente, ipsius in spiritualibus vicarius generalis vel (sede episcopali vacante) capitulum seu is ad quem tunc administratio spiritualium pertineat dare possunt licentiam ordinandi.** Alii vero, nisi sit eis specialiter indultum, ut aut ab episcopo speciali commissione vel compositione concessum, hoc facere nullatenus *potest* possunt.

6.[230] **Nullus deinceps abbas vel prior monachos vel canonicos suos ab alio quam loci dioecesano faciat ordinari, nisi cum litteris dimissoriis sui proprii episcopi seu eius, qui ius eas concedendi habet,** vel nisi hoc habent ex speciali privilegio.

7.[231] Sancimus ne deinceps promovendus ad sacros ordines sine certo titulo unde convenienter sustentari possunt, per eorum ordinatores vel suos successores tam diu provideatur, donec ecclesiastica consequantur beneficia nisi talis ordinatus sufficiens patrimonium habeat unde competenter vivere possit.

[58v] 8.[232] Quando episcopus ordinationem facere disponit, omnes qui ad sacrum ministerium accedere voluerint, pridie ante ipsam ordinationem vocandi sunt ad locum ordinationis et tunc episcopus a latere suo eligere debet sacerdotes et alios prudentes viros grav{o/e}s dominicae legis, excitatos in ecclesiasticis sanctionibus, qui ordinandorum vitam, genus, patriam, aetatem, institutionem,

---

[227]X, 1.11.15 (Fr, II, 122-3), a decretal of Pope Honorius III (1216-27).
[228]This is taken from L, 1.4.3, originally canon 5 of Archbishop Richard of Dover (1174-84), which is itself a collage of four decretals: one of Pope Urban II (1088-99) (D, 70 c. 2 – Fr, I, 257); one of Pope Innocent I (401-17) (D, 71 c. 2 – Fr, I, 258); canon 6 of the council of Chalcedon, 451 (D, 70 c. 1 – Fr, I, 257 – *C.O.D.*, 90) and canon 21 of the third council of Carthage, 397 (D, 72 c. 2 – Fr, I, 259-60).
[229]VI, 1.9.3 (Fr, II, 975-6), a decretal of Pope Boniface VIII (1294-1303).
[230]L, 1.4.4, originally canon 50 of the canons for an unknown English diocese, *c.* 1225.
[231]X, 1.11.13 (Fr, II, 130), a decretal of Pope Alexander III (1159-81), which is also c. 5, Lateran III, 1179 (*C.O.D.*, 214).
[232]Cf. Lateran V, s. 11, 19 December 1516 (*C.O.D.*, 636).

3.[227] We forbid any bishop to confer two holy orders on a single day, and if he does otherwise, both shall remain suspended for six months - the bishop from ordaining and the cleric from the exercise of such orders.

4.[228] **Whoever knowingly** or by feigned ignorance or by any other device **ordains a cleric or a parishioner of another bishop without his special permission, shall automatically be suspended** for a year **from the granting of orders**, and whoever is thus ordained shall remain suspended from the exercise of the orders so received and from the reception of any others **until he has received a dispensation from his own bishop.** But those whose bishops have been suspended from the granting of orders, once their suspension has been made known, shall for the duration have full permission to receive orders from neighbouring bishops, as long as they are found to be otherwise suitable, even without the permission of their own.

5.[229] **By 'one's own bishop' is to be understood the man from whose diocese the person seeking orders comes, or in which he is receiving an ecclesiastical benefice or where he has had his residence** for the space of three years, **even though he was born elsewhere.**

If the bishop is away on business his vicar general in spirituals or (if the episcopal see is vacant) the chapter, or the person to whom the administration of spirituals then belongs, may grant a licence for ordination. But others may on no account do this, unless they have received special permission, granted to them either by special commission from the bishop, or by composition.

6.[230] **From henceforth no abbot or prior shall allow his monks or canons to be ordained by any but the local diocesan, except with letters dimissory from his own bishop or from whoever has the right to grant them,** or unless they have this right by special privilege.

7.[231] We ordain that from henceforth anyone who is to be ordained to holy orders without a definite title on which they can be adequately maintained shall be provided for by those ordaining him, or their successors, until they find ecclesiastical benefices, unless the said ordinand has sufficient income to be able to live adequately.

8.[232] When a bishop decides to hold an ordination, all those who may want to enter the sacred ministry shall be summoned to the place of ordination on the day before the said ordination takes place, and then the bishop, on his side, shall choose priests and other men learned in the law of God and well-versed in the rules of the church, who shall examine the life, family, background, age, and

locum ubi educati sunt, si bene sunt litterati, si instructi in lege Dei et ante omnia diligenter investigent, si fidem catholicam firmiter teneant, et verbis simplicibus asserere sciant. Episcopi autem quibus cura talis committitur cavere debent ne aut favoris gratia aut cuiuscunque muneris cupiditate, indignum et minus idoneum ad sacros ordines admittant. Quod si aliter fecerint, et ille qui indigne accesserit ab altari removebitur, et ill{e/i} qui donum Spiritus Sancti vendere conati sunt ecclesiastica dignitate [59r] carebunt. Nam procul dubio Deus offenditur, si ad sacros ordines quisquam non ex merito sed ex favore (quod absit) aut venalitate provehitur.

9.[233] Cum periculosum sit indignos, idiotas, illitteratos et extraneos, aut sine vero et certo titulo aliquos ordinare, statuimus ut ante collationem ordinum per episcopum de his omnibus inquisitio ac indagatio diligens habeatur et ne in excommunicatione reprobati clanculo immiscere se approbatis valeant numerus scribatur et nomina probatorum, et postmodum in ordinationis limine *l...* perlecta scriptura discretione solita requirantur probati, ipsaque scriptura in registro conservetur.[234]

10.[235] **Clerici qui ab episcopo excommunicat**{i/o} **vel suspens**{i/o} **igno**[59v]**ranter ordines recipiunt**, cum eorum ignorantia sit probabilis, licite possunt in susceptis ordinibus ministrare.

11.[236] Illud servari mandamus ut omnes ad ecclesiasticos ordines gradatim accedant, primo ut sit ostiarius, deinde lector, postea exorcista inde sacretur acolythus, deinde vero subdiaconus, deinde diaconus et postea presbyter. Exinde si meretur, episcopus consecretur.

12.[237] Inhibemus ne personae quae in ecclesiis ad animarum curam fuerint ordinandae, instituantur in ipsis, nisi scientia, moribus et aetate ad id inveniantur idoneae et tales praeterea sint, quae in minoribus constitutae infra tempus legitimum, in presbyteros possunt ordinari. Mandantes praeterea ne dignitates vel personatus [60r] quibus etiam animarum cura non imminet. Item paroechiae quae vicarios habent perpetuos, minoribus viginti annis aut illis qui discretione vel morum honestate idonei non sint, nec minoribus ordinibus constituti, ac habitum clericalem non deferentes concedantur, aut a quoquam conferantur, irritum decernentes quicquid, contra hanc ordinationem nostram factum fuerit, eiusque transgressores debite et severiter castigandos.

13.[238] **De servorum ordine statuimus ut nullus episcoporum eos ad sacros ordines scienter promoveat, nisi prius a dominis suis libertatem fuerint**

[233]Cf. VI, 1.6.11 (Fr, II, 952), c. 10 of Lyon II, 1274 (*C.O.D.*, 321).

[234]The latter part of this section appears to have been taken from 1237/6 (PC, 248).

[235]X, 1.13.2 (Fr, II, 125), a decretal of Pope Gregory IX, 1234.

[236]Cf. D 25, c. 1 (Fr, I, 89-91).

[237]The first sentence is from X, 1.14.4 (Fr, II, 126-7), a decretal of Pope Alexander III (1159-81). The second sentence (from 'mandantes') is taken from VI, 1.10.1 (Fr, II, 976), a decretal of Pope Boniface VIII (1294-1303).

[238]X, 1.18.2 (Fr, II, 141-2), of unknown origin.

upbringing of the ordinands, the place where they have been educated, whether they are well taught, whether they are instructed in the law of God, and above all else, whether they have a firm grasp of the Catholic faith and know how to explain it in simple terms. And the bishops to whom this responsibility is entrusted must be careful not to admit any unworthy or less suitable person to holy orders, either out of favouritism or in the hope of some financial reward. If they do otherwise, both the man who has unworthily been ordained shall be removed from the altar, and those who have tried to sell the gift of the Holy Spirit shall be stripped of their ecclesiastical position. For without doubt, God is offended if someone is elevated to holy orders not on his merit but by favouritism (which should never be) or venality.

9.[233] Because it is dangerous to ordain those who are unworthy, stupid, illiterate and outsiders, or who lack a true and certain title, we decree that before the granting of orders by the bishop there should be a diligent inquiry and investigation into all these matters, and in order that no one under the ban of excommunication might secretly mix in with those who have been approved, the number and names of those approved shall be recorded, and afterwards, at the point of ordination, the document shall be read out and those approved shall be tested with the usual discretion, and the said document shall be kept in the [bishop's] register.[234]

10.[235] Clerics who have unwittingly received ordination from an excommunicated or suspended bishop, if their ignorance was probably genuine, may lawfully minister in the orders received.

11.[236] We order the principle to be maintained, that everyone should enter ecclesiastical orders by stages, that first one should be a parish clerk, then a reader, then an exorcist, then be ordained an acolyte, then a subdeacon, then a deacon and afterwards a presbyter. Finally, if he is worthy, he may be consecrated a bishop.

12.[237] We forbid those persons who are to be ordained to the cure of souls in churches to be instituted in them, unless they are found to be suitable in learning, morals and age, and moreover those who are ordained in minor orders shall be such as are able to become presbyters within the lawful time. Moreover, we command that the same be applied also to positions and parsonages which do not contain a cure of souls; likewise, parishes which have perpetual vicars shall not be granted to, or conferred by anyone on men who are less than twenty years old, nor to those who are unsuitable because they lack judgment or are of dubious moral character, who are not ordained in minor orders, and who do not wear clerical dress. We decree that anything done contrary to this our order shall be invalid, and those who transgress it are to be duly and severely punished.

13.[238] **Concerning the ordination of serfs, we decree that no bishop shall knowingly promote them to holy orders unless they have first obtained**

consecuti, et si servus fugiens dominum suum qualibet calliditate, aut fraude ad ordines pervenerit ecclesiasticos, ab eorum executione tam diu stet suspensus, donec fuerit legitime manumissus.

[60v] 14.[239] Qui corpore adeo enormiter vitiati sunt, ut sine scandalo non possunt solemniter celebrare, aut commissum illis officium congrue perficere, ad sacros ordines non provehantur, quod si post susceptos ordines taliter vitiati sunt, ab administratione sacramentorum quae sine scandalo aut congrue ministrari non possunt suspendantur.[240]

15.[241] Clerici peregrini qui ad alienas dioeceses, ubi non cognoscuntur, sine litteris testimonialibus ordinariorum suorum de susceptis ordinibus, ac sine litteris commendatitiis vel dimissoriis ordinariorum suorum in quorum dioecesi interim per longum tempus conversati sunt, se conferunt, priusquam eorum conversatio fuerit approbata, deque eorum legitima ordinatione vitae munditia pariter et litteraturae constiterit, nec in susceptis ordinibus ministrare, nec ad maiores debent promoveri aut ad divinorum [61r] celebrationem infra regna et dominia nostra, ecclesiis deserviendo admitti.

19. De clericis non residentibus.

1.[242] Clerici qui in ecclesiis, dignitatibus, personatibus, praebendis seu aliis suis beneficiis ecclesiasticis quibuscunque iuxta tenorem et effectum statutorum nostrorum non resideant,[243] nisi admoniti per ordinarios suos ad illa infra sex menses redierint, divine non sunt iusto impedimento detenti iuste eisdem privari possunt. Qui vero ita sunt absentes, ut nesciatur ubi sint, vel ad illos ordinariorum admonitio commode venire non possit, publicae citationis edicto in ecclesiis aut beneficiis suis huiusmodi citentur ad competentem terminum, post quem si ultra sex menses, legitimo cessante impedimento, [61v] redditum suum distulerint, huiusmodi beneficiis priventur, et eis de personis idoneis iuxta vim et ordinationem constitutionum nostrarum provideatur.

2.[244] Statuimus ut rectores et vicarii perpetui in ecclesiis suis non residentes, per firmarios vel deputatos suos quadragesimam partem valoris beneficiorum suorum singulis annis inter pauperes paroechianos ibidem distribuant. Item religiosi ac alii qui beneficia ecclesiastica sibi appropriata obtinent, quadragesimam partem valoris beneficiorum huiusmodi annis singulis pauperibus

---

[239]Based on X, 1.20 (Fr, II, 144-6), but not identical to it.
[240]The last clause, from 'quod si' is taken from X, 3.6.4 (Fr, II, 482), a decretal of Pope Clement III (1187-91).
[241]Based on X, 1.22 (Fr, II, 148-9), but not identical.
[242]X, 3.4.11 (Fr, II, 462-3), a decretal of Pope Innocent III, 20 April 1207.
[243]21 Henry VIII, c. 13, 1529 (S.R., III, 292-6).
[244]1536/8 (D.E.R., 178); cf. 1268/9 (PC, 757-8) and L, 3.4.4, c. 21 of Archbishop John Stratford, 1342.

permission from their masters, and if a serf who is trying to escape from his master by trickery or fraud should manage to get ordained, he shall be suspended from the exercise of those orders until he is legally emancipated.

14.[239] Those who are so seriously handicapped physically that they cannot celebrate properly without causing scandal, or fulfil the office entrusted to them as they should, shall not be admitted to holy orders, and if after receiving orders they should become so handicapped, then they shall be suspended from the administration of the sacraments which they cannot administer appropriately or without scandal.[240]

15.[241] Itinerant clerics who move to other dioceses where they are not known without letters testimonial from their ordinaries concerning the orders they have received, and without letters commendatory or dimissory from the ordinaries in whose dioceses they have lived for a long period since that time, must neither minister in the orders they have received, nor be promoted to higher ones, nor be admitted to serve the church in the celebration of divine services within our kingdoms and dominions, until their behaviour has been approved of and the legitimacy of their ordination, as well as the soundness of both their life and learning, has been demonstrated.

19. Of non-resident clerics.

1.[242] Clerics who do not reside in their churches, dignities, parsonages, prebends or other ecclesiastical benefices, whatever [they may be], according to the intention and purpose of our statutes,[243] may rightly be deprived of them if, after being warned by their ordinaries, they do not return to them within six months, provided that they have not been hindered by some lawful impediment. But those who are so absent that nobody knows where they are, or else the warning of the ordinaries cannot easily reach them, shall be officially summoned, by the issue of a public citation, to appear in their churches or benefices within a reasonable time, after which they shall be deprived of the said benefices, if they put off their return beyond six months, barring lawful impediment, and suitable persons shall be provided in their stead, according to the force and direction of our constitutions.

2.[244] We decree that rectors and perpetual vicars who are not resident in their churches shall, through their lessees or deputies, distribute the fortieth part of the value of their benefices each year among the poor parishioners there. Likewise monks and others who obtain ecclesiastical benefices appropriated to them, shall be obliged by the local ordinaries to distribute the fortieth part of the value of the

paroechianis ibidem per locorum ordinarios distribuere compellantur, per poenam sequestrationis et sub{s}tractionis fructuum et proventuum beneficiorum huiusmodi, donec in praemissis paruerint competenter.

3.[245] Quotidianas distributiones quae tantum residentibus [62r] in ecclesiis, et his qui intersunt horis canonicis, ab antiquo debentur et distribui solent, absentibus etiam ex legitima causa nullo modo tribui volumus, nisi specialis ecclesiae ordinatio aliud voluerit.

4.[246] Qui unum beneficium cum cura animarum obtinet, si secundum simile contra statut{i/a} parliamenti nostri[247] in ea parte edita acceperit, primo beneficio sit privatus ipso facto. Qui vero duo beneficia curata legitime possidet, si tertium simile contra statuta praedicta accipere praesumpserit, secundo suo beneficio quod ante tertium habuit ipso iure privetur, et si quartum simili modo acceperit privetur tertio, et sic deinceps, nec ullo modo plura beneficia curata, quam statuta nostra permittunt, quisquam retinere pariatur; decernentes praeterea ut in una eademque ecclesia nullus plures dignitates aut [62v] personatus seu praebendas habere praesumat, cum singula officia in ecclesiis assiduitatem exigant personarum.

5.[248] Praecipimus ne una ecclesia pluribus rectoribus aut vicariis regenda committatur, exceptis illis ecclesiis, quae ab antiquo divisae fuerint et sic hactenus regi solebant.

6.[249] Clericus aegrotus de ecclesia sua omnia percipiat, quae si sanus esset percipere deberet, verum si perpetua sit eius aegritudo et talis ut administrationi seu curae sibi commissis superesse non possit, cum non crimen sed infirmitas illum ab officio suo abducit, necessaria illi quamdiu vixerit ministrari debet, et dandus est ei per ordinarium loci coadiutor,[250] vir providus et honestus, qui curam animarum habeat et possit eius [63r] curam omnem agere, ac locum illius in regimine ecclesiae conservare quicquid ad huiusmodi regimen, et ad aegroti defectum supplendum, per omnia sit idoneus; qui quidem coadiutor de facultatibus ecclesiae ad sustentationem suam congruam portionem iuxta assignationem ordinarii recipiet. Cum coadiutorum episcoporum et superiorum praelatorum datio intelligenda sit de causis maioribus, et ideo ad nostram referenda maiestatem, ac a nobis tantummodo postulanda.

*7.[251] Volumus tamen ut episcopus se senio aut valetudine corporali gravatus, vel etiam alias adeo impeditus perpetuo ut officium suum nequeat exercere, possit de sui et assensu capituli vel maioris partis ipsius, unum vel duos auctoritate nostra coadiutores nominare ac nobis praesentare, ut per nos si idonei recepti [63v] fuerint, ad dictum officium exequendum admitterentur.

---

[245]VI, 1.3.1 (Fr, II, 1019-20), a decretal of Pope Boniface VIII (1294-1303).

[246]This is based on L, 3.5.2, originally canon 4 of the council of Reading, 1279.

[247]21 Henry VIII, c. 13, 1529 (S.R., III, 292-6).

[248]1237/12 (PC, 250-1); 1268/11 (PC, 761-2).

[249]X, 1.6.1 (Fr, II, 481), a letter of Pope Gregory I (590-604) to Bishop Candidus of Civitavecchia, taken from Gregory's register (II, 8).

[250]X, 3.6.3 (Fr, II, 482), a decretal of Pope Lucius III (1181-5).

[251]X, 3.6.5 (Fr, II, 482), a decretal of Pope Innocent III, dated 2 December 1204.

said benefices each year to the poor parishioners, under pain of sequestration and subtraction of the fruits and revenues of the said benefices, until they appear to be fulfilling the above adequately.

3.[245] We do not wish the daily disbursements which by ancient custom are owed and usually distributed only to those who are resident in churches and to those who are present at the canonical hours, to be in any way given to those who are absent, even if it is for a legitimate reason, unless there is a special regulation of the church which decrees otherwise.

4.[246] Whoever obtains one benefice with cure of souls and who then accepts a second similar benefice, contrary to the statutes of our parliament issued in that respect,[247] shall automatically be deprived of the first benefice. And if anyone who lawfully possesses two benefices with cure presumes to accept a third in violation of the aforesaid statutes, he shall automatically be deprived of the second benefice which he held before the third one, and likewise if he accepts a fourth he shall be deprived of the third, and so on, nor shall anyone in any way be allowed retain more benefices with cure than our statutes permit. Moreover we decree that no one shall presume to hold several positions, parsonages or prebends in the same church, since every single office in the churches demands the full attention of its holder.

5.[248] We decree that no one church shall be entrusted to the government of more than one rector or vicar, except for those churches which were so divided of old and which have ever since then been customarily so governed.

6.[249] An infirm cleric shall receive from his church everything that he should have received had he been well, but if the illness is permanent and such that he cannot stay on top of the administration or cure entrusted to him, since it is not a crime but illness which is taking him away from his duty, he must be provided with the necessities as long as he lives, and an assistant is to be given to him by the ordinary,[250] a prudent and honest man, who shall have the cure of souls and may do everything pertaining to the cure, and take the other man's place in the government of the church, and who shall in every way be suitable to take on the government of the church and make up for the inadequacy of the infirm man, which assistant shall receive an appropriate portion of the revenues of the church for his own maintenance, according to the assignment of the ordinary. Since the granting of assistants to bishops and senior prelates is to be understood to be for major reasons only, it must therefore be referred to our majesty and be proposed only by us.

*7.[251] Nevertheless we wish that a bishop who is weighed down by old age or bodily illness, or who is otherwise disabled to the point where he will never again be able to exercise his office, may with his own agreement and that of the chapter, or the majority of it, nominate one or two assistants on our authority and present them to us, so that if they are accepted by us as suitable, they may be admitted to perform the said duty.

8.[252] Si vero episcopus demens fuerit, et quid velit, aut nolit exprimere nesciat, sive vero senio, aut incurabili morbo, gravatus, vel perpetuo impedimento detentus, et ea occasione ad sui executionem officii inutilis, coadiutorem tamen assumere vel habere noluerit, tunc nihil per capitulum innovetur, sed idem capitulum episcopi et ecclesiae suae conditionem et statum ac facti circumstantias universas, quam cito poterit fideliter et explicite referat ad notitiam nostram, recepturum humiliter et efficaciter impleturum quod super hoc per nos contigerit ordinari. Quod de episcopis praemittitur ad superiores etiam praelatos referri volumus.

Statuimus quod coadiutores abstineant ab [64r] alienatione qualibet bonorum mobilium aut immobilium ipsorum praelatorum vel ecclesiarum ipsarum, nisi sunt talia, quae servari commode non possunt, in collationibus sive praesentationibus beneficiorum, coadiutores nihil agant, absque consensu illorum, quibus dantur coadiutores, nisi illi sic mente alienati sunt, quod consentire non possunt.

20. De institutionibus.

1.[253] Cum ad officium episcoporum vel officialium suorum in ecclesiasticis beneficiis instituere pertineat, statuimus ut quicunque beneficia ecclesiastica absque dioecesanorum institutione occupata detinent, ab eisdem beneficiis removeantur, nisi ab illis instituti fuerint, qui speciali privilegio, concessione aut consuetudine instituendi ius habeant.

2.[254] Is ad quem spectat collatio beneficiorum seipsum [64v] instituere non potest, cum inter dantem et accipientem debet esse distinctio personalis.

3.[255] Si is ad quem rectoris praesentatio in aliqua paroechiali ecclesia noscitur pertinere, quempiam non constitutum in sacris praesentet ad eam, ipsum, dummodo alias sit idoneus et infra tempus a iure statutum ad ordines quos ipsius ecclesiae cura requirit, valeat promoveri, decernimus admittendum.

4.[256] Cum quis ad ecclesiam aliquam, nullo contradicente legitime praesentetur, si episcopus aut alius cui instituendi ius est praesentatum huiusmodi, ultra duos menses admittere, nisi ad mandatum archiepiscopi id fecerit, aut quare non facit *in...* causam rationabilem non allegaverit, tunc ius instituendi ad illud pro ea vice ad archiepiscopum [65r] provinciae devolvatur.

5.[257] Si vero per archidiaconum, vel quemvis alium ad quem ius inducendi pertinet, steterit quominus institutus infra quindecim dies post mandatum

---

[252]VI, 3.5.1 (Fr, II, 1034), a decretal of Pope Boniface VIII (1294-1303).
[253]The first clause is from X, 3.7.3 (Fr, II, 483-4), a decretal of Pope Alexander III (1159-81).
[254]X, 3.7.7 (Fr, II, 487), a decretal of Pope Innocent III, dated 20 June 1207.
[255]Cf. 1237/11 (PC, 249-50).
[256]1268/30 (PC, 777-9).
[257]Based on X, 3.7.6 (Fr, II, 485-6), a letter of Pope Innocent III (1198-1216) to the bishop of Ely, who must have been Eustace (1197-1215), and the archdeacon of Norwich (or possibly Northampton).

8.[252] But if the bishop is mentally ill and unable to state what his wishes are, or if he is weighed down by old age or some incurable disease, or hindered by some permanent impediment, and at that time is unable to exercise his duty, but nevertheless does not want to employ or have a coadjutor, then nothing shall be initiated by the chapter, but the same chapter shall refer the condition of the bishop and his church and the situation and all the circumstances of the situation faithfully and in detail to our attention as quickly as possible, and shall humbly accept and fully implement whatever we decide to order in this case. And what applies to bishops we wish to apply to the higher prelates as well.

We decree that coadjutors shall refrain from alienating any of the goods, moveable or immoveable, of those prelates or of those churches, unless they are such as cannot be conveniently preserved. In appointments or presentations to benefices coadjutors shall do nothing without the consent of those to whom the coadjutors have been given, unless the latter are so mentally deficient that they cannot give their consent.

20. Of institutions.

1.[253] As far as the duty of bishops or their officials to institute in ecclesiastical benefices is concerned, we ordain that whoever holds ecclesiastical benefices which they have occupied without the institution of the diocesans shall be removed from those benefices unless they have been instituted by those who have the right to institute by special privilege, concession or custom.

2.[254] The one to whom the granting of benefices pertains may not institute himself, since there must be a distinction of persons between the giver and the receiver.

3.[255] If the one who is recognized as having the right to present the rector in any parish church should present someone who is not ordained, we decree that he may be admitted, provided that he is otherwise suitable and is qualified to be promoted to the orders which the cure of that church requires within the time specified by law.

4.[256] When someone is presented to a church and there is no one who lawfully objects, if the bishop or whoever has the said right of institution fails to admit the man so presented for more than two months, unless this is by order of the archbishop, or gives no reasonable cause why he has not done so, then the right of institution to that benefice shall devolve for that turn upon the archbishop of the province.

5.[257] And if it transpires that the man instituted has not been inducted by the archdeacon or by someone else who has the right of induction, into real

instituentis sibi exhibitum in realem possessionem fuerit inductus, nec causam rationabilem quare id non fecerit coram instituente allegaverit, tunc ius inducendi ad instituentem pro illa vice devolvatur, prohibentes ne quisquam archidiaconus pro litteris inductionis ultra id quod solvi consueverat aliquid recipere praesumat.

6.[258] **Episcopus clerico quem ad ecclesiam admittit litteras patentes super sua admissione concedat, inter alia continentes [65v] in quo consistat ordine, etiam quo titulo ad huiusmodi beneficium admittatur**, pro quibus praeter id quod consuetum est nihil recipiet.[259]

7.[260] **Nulla ecclesiastica ministeria seu beneficia vel ecclesiae tribuantur alicui seu promittantur antequam vacent, ne desiderare quis mortem proximi videatur in cuius locum et beneficium se crediderit successurum.**

*8.[261] **Qui vero contra hanc ordinationem in vivorum loco scienter poni se passi sunt, ab ecclesiastica communione pellantur** et sic receptis beneficiis priventur,[262] et de huiusmodi beneficiis cum vacaverint non obstantibus promissionibus quibuscunque ante vacationem factis libere et idonee provideatur.

*9.[263] Cum donatio praebendarum sive ecclesiasticorum beneficiorum quorumcunque ad capitulum et praelatum simul pertineat, si infra tempus legitimum de illis ordinare [66r] neglexerint, sicut nec a praelato ad capitulum, ita nec a capitulo ad praelatum devolvitur potestas conferendi, sed ad superiorem transit donatio, nisi forte praelatus, non ut praelatus sed ut canonicus cum capitulo ius habeat conferendi, in quo casu nisi dolose impedierit collationem, a capitulo ad illum ius conferendi devolvitur.

*10.[264] Mandamus ut clericus paroechialis, ab his qui eum consuetudine aut compositione eligere debent, nominatus non prius in officio suo ministret quam per vic... rectores aut vicarios seu alios qui curam ibi habent animarum, aut illis hoc indebitum recusantibus, per ordinarium ad huiusmodi officium idoneus esse fuerit approbatus, sub poena perpetuae privationis ab huiusmodi officio.

*11.[265] Decernentes insuper ut paroechiani ad solvendum huiusmodi clerico [66v] debita et consueta stipendia per censuras ecclesiasticas, si opus fuerit, per ordinarios suos compellantur.

12.[266] Si quis ad beneficium ab alio per institutionem et inductionem aut aliter possessum de facto institui aut admitti et induci se faciat, huiusmodi institutio seu admissio et inductio omni iuris affectu careant, nisi prius huiusmodi possessor sufficiente auctoritate finaliter ab ipso beneficio fuerit amotus, quod si

---

[258]L. 3.6.3, c. 24 of the council of Lambeth, 1281.

[259]L, 3.6.4, c. 20 of the statutes of Archbishop John Stratford, 1343.

[260]X, 3.8.2 (Fr, II, 488), canon 8 of Lateran III, 1179 (*C.O.D.*, 215).

[261]X, 3.8.1 (Fr, II, 488), a decretal of Pope Gelasius I (492-6).

[262]X, 3.8.3 (Fr, II, 488), a letter of Pope Alexander III (1159-81) to the archbishop of York.

[263]X, 3.8.15 (Fr, II, 499-500), a decretal of Pope Innocent III (1198-1216), dated 10 January 1212.

[264]X, 1.12.1 (Fr, II, 124-5), a decretal of Pope Innocent III, 15 March 1206.

[265]X, 1.14.13 (Fr, II, 130), a decretal of Pope Innocent III.

[266]1237/11 (PC, 249-50); 1268/10 (PC, 759-61).

possession within fifteen days after the order of the person instituting has been shown to him, and the latter gives the instituting bishop no reasonable explanation why he has not done it, then the right of induction shall revert to the instituting bishop for that turn. We forbid any archdeacon to presume to accept anything beyond what he is usually paid for letters of induction.

6.[258] **A bishop shall give any cleric whom he admits to a church letters patent concerning his admission, which among other things shall state in what order and also by what title he has been admitted to the said benefice,** for which the bishop shall receive nothing beyond the usual fee.[259]

7.[260] **No ecclesiastical ministries or benefices or churches shall be granted to anyone or promised before they are vacant, lest it appear that someone is looking forward to the death of his neighbour, whose place and benefice he thinks he will inherit.**

*8.[261] **Those who, in violation of this ordinance, have knowingly allowed themselves to be placed in the post of the living, shall be expelled from the communion of the church** and deprived of the benefices thus received,[262] and when the benefices fall vacant, they shall be freely and suitably filled, regardless of any promises which were made before the vacancy occurred.

*9.[263] When the gift of prebends or any ecclesiastical benefices belongs to the chapter and the bishop together, if they fail to appoint to them within the lawful time, the power of conferment does not revert from the bishop to the chapter, any more than from the chapter to the bishop, but the gift goes to the archbishop, unless it happens that the bishop, not in his capacity as bishop but as a canon has the right of conferment as a member of the chapter, in which case the right of conferment shall devolve upon him from the chapter, unless he has fraudulently hindered the conferment.

*10.[264] We order that a parish clergyman who has been nominated by those who must elect him by custom or composition, shall not minister in his office before he has been approved as suitable for the said office by the rectors or vicars or others who have the cure of souls in that place, or if they refuse to do this duty, by the ordinary, under pain of permanent deprivation from the said office.

*11.[265] Moreover, we decree that the parishioners shall be compelled, if necessary by ecclesiastical censures, by their ordinaries to pay the said curate the stipends customarily due [to him].

12.[266] If someone has himself instituted or admitted and inducted to a benefice *de facto*, which is already possessed by someone else by virtue of institution and induction or otherwise, such institution or admission and induction shall lack any legal validity, unless the said possessor has first been definitively removed from the benefice by adequate authority, and if something

contra hoc factum fuerit, sic scienter instituens vel admittens aut inducens iure proprio vel delegato ab officio et beneficio tam diu sit suspensus donec huiusmodi possessori resarciatur ut convenit omne damnum. Qui vero scienter sic institutus aut admissus fuerit censeatur intrusus, et prior possessor ante omnia restituatur et deinde de titulo discutiatur.

[67r] *13.[267] Cum ecclesia vacante nihil debeat innovari quicquid in damnum eius interim factum fuerit non valebit, sed in pristino statu sit et habeatur.

*14.[268] **Si ad episcopum et capitulum communiter pertineat collatio beneficiorum seu praebendarum, episcopo a beneficiorum collatione suspenso, poterit capitulum vacantes conferre praebendas seu ecclesias etiam si episcopus interesse habeat in collatione huiusmodi ut praelatus. Idem poterit episcopus si capitulum ab ipsa collatione suspendi contingat vel singulariter omnes de capitulo maioris excommunicationis vinculo innodari. Cum vero ad solum episcopum praebendarum seu beneficiorum spectat collatio, cum con{c/s}ilio sui capituli, suspenso episcopo (nisi episcopus in petenda relaxatione suspensionis huiusmodi sit in mora), capitulum se non potest intromittere de eisdem. Ubi vero de speciali alicuius ecclesiae consuetudine vel statuto beneficiorum** [67v] **collatio ad aliquem cum consilio episcopi noscitur pertinere, sublato episcopo de medio (cum consilium nequeat tunc peti ab eo) non erit propter hoc vacantis beneficii collatio differenda, nec etiam si egerit in remotis ita quod non possit ipsius praesentia in brevi haberi, quoniam in petendo vel expectando eius consilio posset vacanti beneficio periculum imminere.**

15.[269] Cum ius praesentandi ad collegia aliqua saecularia vel regularia pertineat, eorum praesidentes, magistri seu gubernatores, quocunque nomine vocentur, sine consensu conventus sive capituli vel maioris partis eiusdem praesentare non possunt, **nisi ex antiqua et approbata consuetudine vel concessa libertate** vel **probaverint commissi sibi collegii non debere in ecclesiarum seu beneficiorum collationibus requiri consensum.**

[68r] 16.[270] Episcopus ecclesias paroechiales vel obventiones ipsarum etiam de consensu patroni et aliorum quorum interest, nisi de licentia nostra et accedente consensu capituli sui, aut maioris partis eiusdem cuicunque collegio sive loco religioso dare, appropriare sive in perpetuos usus concedere non potest.

17.[271] In ordinationibus ecclesiasticis praevaleat semper et suum consequatur effectum quod a praesidente et maiore parte capituli fuerit constitutum, donec a paucioribus aliquid rationabiliter obiectum fuerit et probatum, non obstante contraria consuetudine quacunque nec contradictio minoris numeri aut eius cuius non interest maioris partis capituli ordinationem quovismodo impedire debet.

---

[267]X, 3.9.1 (Fr, II, 500-1), a decretal of Pope Innocent III, 14 March 1206.
[268]VI, 3.8.1 (Fr, II, 1041-2), a decretal of Pope Boniface VIII (1294-1303).
[269]X, 3.10.6 (Fr, II, 503-4), a decretal of Pope Celestine III (1191-8).
[270]X, 3.10.9 (Fr, II, 505), a letter of Pope Innocent III to Eustace, bishop of Ely (1197-1215), dated 10 January 1204.
[271]X, 3.11.1 (Fr, II, 506), canon 25 of Lateran III, 1179 (*C.O.D.*, 223).

is done contrary to this, the person who knowingly institutes and admits or inducts, on his own or on delegated authority, shall be suspended from his office and benefice until all damages are reimbursed to the possessor, as is right. And whoever has knowingly been instituted or admitted in this way shall be considered an intruder, and the former possessor shall first of all be restored and then his entitlement [to the benefice] may be discussed.

*13.[267] Since no changes should be made while a church is vacant, whatever is done to its damage during the vacancy shall have no validity, but the church shall remain and be kept in its original state.

*14.[268] **If the collation to benefices or prebends belongs to the bishop and the chapter together and the bishop has been suspended from appointing to benefices, the chapter may confer vacant prebends or churches even if the bishop or prelate has to be personally involved in such a collation [in his capacity] as prelate. The bishop may do likewise if it happens that the chapter has been suspended from making the collation, or all the members of the chapter individually have been bound by the chain of greater excommunication. But when the collation to benefices or prebends belongs to the bishop alone, with the agreement of his chapter, and the bishop has been suspended (unless the bishop has been dilatory in requesting the lifting of his suspension), the chapter cannot interfere with them. But where by a special custom of a particular church or by a statute, the collation to the benefices is recognized as belonging to someone on the advice of the bishop, and the bishop is out of the picture (so that no advice may then be sought from him), the collation to the vacant benefice shall not on that account be deferred, nor if he is so far away that his presence cannot be had by letter, because some danger might befall the vacant benefice in the time needed for seeking and awaiting the bishop's advice.**

15.[269] When the right of presentation belongs to any secular or monastic colleges, their presidents, masters or governors, whatever they may be called, cannot present without the agreement of the council or the chapter or the majority of it, **unless they can prove on the basis of an ancient and approved custom or liberty granted, that the agreement of the college committed to their charge is not required in collations made to churches or benefices.**

16.[270] A bishop cannot give, appropriate or grant on perpetual lease, parish churches or their revenues, to any college or religious house whatsoever, even with the agreement of the patron and other interested parties, without our permission and the accompanying agreement of his chapter, or the majority of it.

17.[271] In ecclesiastical ordinations whatever has been decided by the president and the majority of the chapter shall prevail and take effect, until something is reasonably objected and proved by the minority, any custom to the contrary notwithstanding, and any objection made by a minority or by someone who is absent, must not impede the decision of the majority of the chapter in any way.

18.[272] Quod per praelatum et maiorem partem capituli communiter statutum est de reditibus canonicorum residentium pro reparatione fabricae ecclesiae et aliis similibus praevalebit.

[68v] 19.[273] Cum beneficia ecclesiastica sine diminutione debent conferri, prohibemus ne quis cum conferat ecclesiasticum beneficium, aliquam partem proventium ipsius, ex pacto aut quovis alio colore sibi retinere praesumat.

20.[274] **Si una ecclesia alteri ecclesiae seu dignitati alicui vel praebendae per episcopum, suo consentiente capitulo, uniatur, aut religioso loco donetur, ex eo quod rector ipsius ad hoc vocatus, vel si vacabat, defensor ei super hoc datus non extitit, nequaquam id poterit impugnari.**

21.[275] Licet donationesve concessiones ecclesiarum, si quae fiant privatis personis, viventibus illis qui ipsas ecclesias possident, nullius sint momenti.

*22.[276] Aliis tamen ecclesiis, dignitatibus, aut praebendis, seu religiosis locis, ab episcopo vel eius auctoritate huiusmodi ecclesiarum appropriationes sive uniones rite factae ratae sunt habendae, ita quod personae quae iam dictas [69r] ecclesias possident, sine ipsorum assensu eis in vita sua non debeant spoliari.

*23.[277] Omnino decernentes quod singulis ecclesiis paroechialibus, monasteriis aut collegiis unitis *a* et appropriatis ubi iam non sunt perpetui vicarii, auctoritate ordinarii perpetuus ordinetur vicarius, cui per ordinarium debita fructuum assignetur portio.

21. De permutatione.

1.[278] Praebendas, dignitates et alia beneficia ecclesiastica absque ordinariorum et patronorum consensu permutare prohibemus. **Si autem episcopus causam inspexerit necessariam licite poterit de uno loco ad alium, accedente patroni consensu, transferre personas, ut quae uno loco primis sunt utiles, alibi se valeant utilius exercere.**

2.[279] Cum spiritualia pro temporalibus dari sit illicitum, [69v] permutationem etiam spiritualium cum temporalibus illicitam esse decernimus.

---

[272]X, 3.11.4 (Fr, II, 509), a decretal of Pope Innocent III, dated 9 June 1198.

[273]X, 3.12.1 (Fr, II, 509-12), a letter of Pope Innocent III to the archbishop of Milan, dated 24 September 1198.

[274]*Clem.*, 3.4.2 (Fr, II, 1160), a decretal of Pope Clement V (1305-14), published at the council of Vienne, 1311-12.

[275]1268/33 (PC, 780).

[276]1237/12 (PC, 250-1); 1268/11 (PC, 761-2).

[277]X, 3.5.30 (Fr, II, 478-9), c. 32 of Lateran IV, 1215 (*C.O.D.*, 249-50); 1237/12 (PC, 250-1).

[278]X, 3.19.5 (Fr, II, 522-3), a decretal of Pope Urban III (1185-7).

[279]X, 3.19.9 (Fr, II, 524-5), a decretal of Gregory IX (1227-41), published before 1234.

18.[272] Whatever has been jointly determined by the bishop and the majority of the chapter concerning the contributions of the residentiary canons towards the repair of the fabric of the church and other similar matters shall prevail.

19.[273] Since ecclesiastical benefices must be conferred without diminution, we forbid anyone, when conferring an ecclesiastical benefice, to presume to retain for himself any part of the revenues of that church, by agreement or on any other pretext.

20.[274] **If one church is united to another church or to any dignity or prebend by the bishop, with the consent of his chapter, or is given to a religious house, this act can in no way be contested on the ground that its rector who has been summoned for this purpose, if it is vacant, the defender who has been given to it for this reason, has not appeared [in order to contest it].**

21.[275] If grants and awards of churches are made by private persons during the lifetime of those who possess the church, such grants shall have no force.

*22.[276] Nevertheless, in other churches, appointments, prebends or religious houses, appropriations or unions of such churches, properly made by the bishop or on his authority, are to be approved, as long as the persons who already possess the said churches are not deprived during their lifetime without their consent.

*23.[277] As a general rule we decree that in individual parish churches, monasteries or colleges united and appropriated, where there are as yet no perpetual vicars, a perpetual vicar shall be appointed on the authority of the ordinary, and a portion of the fruits shall be assigned to him by the ordinary.

21. Of exchanges.

1.[278] We do not allow anyone to exchange prebends, positions and other ecclesiastical benefices without the agreement of the ordinaries and patrons. **But if the bishop discerns some necessary cause, he may lawfully transfer clergy from one place to another, with the consent of the patron, so that those who were first useful in one place may prove themselves to be even more useful elsewhere.**

2.[279] Since it is illegal for spiritual things to be given [in exchange] for temporal ones, we decree that the exchange of spirituals for temporals is illegal.

3.[280] **Si aliqua beneficia ex causa permutationis ab aliquibus resignata, aliis quam ipsis permutare volentibus conferantur nullius firmitatis huiusmodi sit collatio,** sed omnia in eo statu permaneant in quo fuerint ante permutationem.

22. De sponsa et matrimoniis.

1.[281] Coniugia omnia ac etiam sponsalia clandestine fieri prorsus inhibemus, statuentes ut priusquam matrimonium contrahatur, banna matrimonialia tribus diebus dominicis aut festivis inter se distantibus in ecclesiis paroechialibus volentium contrahere, inter divinorum solemnia iuxta morem Ecclesiae nostrae Anglicanae publice edantur in quibus per sacerdotes perquiratur de libertate et immunitate eorum qui volunt contrahere, et si nihil apparuerit aut obiectum fuerit, quod huiusmodi matrimonium impediat, tunc solemnizetur ex more inter eos matrimonium, secundum ritum et [70r] consuetudinem ecclesiae nostrae praedictae.

*2.[282] Matutina vero sponsalia inter aliquas personas contracta de quarum consensu per duos aut tres testes idoneos non constiterit clandestina esse censemus.

*3.[283] Sane si alter sponsorum a legitime contractis sponsalibus, altero invito recedere absque legitima causa voluerit, poenam etiam pecuniariam arbitrio ordinarii moderandam personae repudiatae solvere per censuras ecclesiasticas compelletur.

*4.[284] Mulieres quae post matrimonium contractum, viros suos quantocunque tempore absentes expectaverint, non prius cum aliis nuptias contrahere auctoritate ecclesiae permittendae sunt, quam certum iudicium recipiant de morte virorum.

*5.[285] Si vero post contracta tantum sponsalia, viri (sponsis suis incognitis) terram dimittat, ad alias partes se transferentes, liberum erit mulieribus ipsis in hoc [70v] casu ad alia se vota transferre.

6.[286] Contracto semel matrimonio, vir et uxor cogendi sunt, ut illud solemnizari facient, et se invicem maritali affectione tractent.

---

[280]*Clem.*, 3.5.1 (Fr, II, 1161), a decree of Pope Clement V, published at the council of Vienne (1311-12).

[281]Based on X, 4.3.3 (Fr, II, 679-80), c. 51 of Lateran IV, 1215 (*C.O.D.*, 258).

[282]This is most clearly stated in c. 24 of the statutes of Chichester (II), 6 October 1289 (PC, 1086), which appears to be an adaptation of c. 25 of the statutes of York (I), *c.* 1241-55 (PC, 490). See also c. 83 of Richard Poore's statutes for the diocese of Salisbury (I), *c.* 1217-19 (PC, 87) and c. 43 of the statutes of London (II), *c.* 1245-59 (PC, 643)

[283]Cf. *Dig.*, 23.1.10, originally Ulpian, *Disputationes*, 3.

[284]X, 4.1.19 (Fr, II, 668), a decretal of Pope Clement III (1187-91); also X, 4.21.2 (Fr, II, 730-1), a decretal of Pope Lucius III (1181-5).

[285]X, 4.1.15 (Fr, II, 662), a decretal of Pope Alexander III (1159-81).

[286]C. 30, q. 5, cc. 1-5 (Fr, I, 1104-6).

3.[280] **If any benefices are resigned by anyone in view of an exchange and are then conferred on people other than those desiring to make the exchange, the said collation shall be of no validity**, but everything will remain in the state it was in before the exchange.

22. Of betrothal and marriages.

1.[281] From now on we forbid all marriages as well as betrothals to take place clandestinely, decreeing that before a marriage is contracted, the banns of matrimony shall be read publicly, according to the custom of our Church of England, during divine service, on three separate Sundays or feast days in the parish churches of those wishing to contract matrimony, at which [times] inquiry will be made by the priests concerning the liberty and eligibility of those who wish to marry, and if nothing appears or is objected, which would prevent the said marriage, then the marriage between them shall be solemnized in the usual way, according to the rite and custom of our aforesaid church.

*2.[282] But we decree that early morning betrothals, contracted between certain persons whose consent is not witnessed by two or three suitable people, are clandestine.

*3.[283] And if one of the betrothed parties in a lawfully contracted betrothal wishes to break it off without a legitimate reason, against the will of the other party, he shall be compelled by the censures of the church to pay a financial penalty to the person rejected, [the amount] to be determined at the discretion of the judge.

*4.[284] Women who, after contracting marriage, wait for their absent husbands for however long a time, shall not be permitted to contract marriage with other men by the authority of the church, until they have received a definite ruling confirming the death of their husbands.

*5.[285] But if, when only betrothal has occurred, men (unknown to their fiancées) leave the country and go somewhere else, the women in that case will be free to make other vows.

6.[286] Once marriage has been contracted, the man and his wife shall be obliged to have it solemnized and to treat each other with marital affection.

*7.[287] Monendi praeterea sunt omnes, qui aliorum uxores a viris suis, aut viros ab uxoribus detinerint, ut debitam faciant restitutionem et si moniti non acquieverint per censuras compellantur.

8.[288] Matrimonium per vim aut metum, qui liberum consensum impedit, contractum ipso iure nullum esse definimus, nisi invicem postea sponte cohabitent, taliter contrahent, aut aliter tacite vel expresse de novo libere consenserint. Si vero per sex menses sponte et absque reclamatione cohabitaverint, probatio de violentia non est audienda, cum mora tanti temporis huiusmodi probationem excludit.

[71r] 9.[289] Si quis mulierem quam desponsaverit post fidem praestitam cognoverit, cum ea matrimonium solemnizare secundum formam praedictam cogendus est.

*10.[290] Mutus et surdus et quicunque specialiter non prohibentur, matrimonium contrahere possunt, quorum autem consensus verbis declarari non valeat, illis signa quomodocunque consensum exprimentia sufficient.

11.[291] Furiosus et qui consentire non *potest* possunt, nec matrimonium contrahere possunt. Sed furor post matrimonium superveniens non dirimit contractum.

12.[292] Districtius inhibemus ne masculus qui sextum decimum, mulier vero quae quartum decimum suae aetatis annum non compleverit, matrimonium seu sponsalia contrahat, et quod contra factum fuerit, nullum esse decernimus, nisi urgentissima aliqua necessitas interveniat, utpote pro bono pacis sponsalia tamen inter minores tolerantur.

*13.[293] **Sponsalia sunt repromissio** [71v] **futurarum nuptiarum.**

*14.[294] Cum ad impedienda illicita coniugia matrimonium ante bannorum editionem solemnizare prohibitum sit, statuimus etiam ut **si** inter bannorum editionem **probabilis apparuerit coniectura**, aut aliquid obiectum fuerit quod huiusmodi matrimonium impedire possit, **contractus interdicatur expresse, donec quid fieri debeat super eo manifestis constiterit documentis.**

---

[287]X, 4.1.11 (Fr, II, 664-5), a letter of Pope Alexander III sent to the archbishops and bishops of the Church of England.

[288]X, 4.1.21 (Fr, II, 668-9), a decretal of Pope Clement III.

[289]X, 4.1.30 (Fr, II, 672), a decretal of Pope Gregory IX (1227-41), published before 1234.

[290]X, 4.1.23 (Fr, II, 669-70), a decretal of Pope Innocent III, dated 13 July 1198.

[291]The first sentence is from X, 4.1.24 (Fr, II, 670), a decretal of Pope Innocent III, dated 28 December 1204.

[292]Based on X, 4.2.1-14 (Fr, II, 672-9); VI, 4.2.1 (Fr, II, 1066-7), but not identical with either of them.

[293]*Dig.*, 23.1.1; C. 30, q. 5, c. 3 (Fr, I, 1105), a letter of Pope Nicholas I (858-67) to the Bulgarians. The phrase also occurs in c. 7 of the statutes of the diocese of Exeter (II), 16 April 1287 (PC, 996-9).

[294]X, 4.3.3 (Fr, II, 679-80), canon 51 of Lateran IV, 1215 (*C.O.D.*, 258).

*7.[287] Moreover, all those who hold the wives of other men back from their husbands, or men from their wives, shall be warned to make due restitution, and if, after being warned, they do not do so, they shall be compelled by censures.

8.[288] We declare that a marriage which has been contracted by force or fear, which prevents free consent, shall be automatically null and void, unless those so contracting voluntarily live together afterwards or otherwise freely give their consent again, either silently or verbally. And if they dwell together for six months voluntarily and without complaint, evidence of violence is not to be entertained, since so long a period of time rules out proof of that kind.

9.[289] If a man sleeps with a woman to whom he is betrothed after plighting his troth, he shall be obliged to solemnize matrimony with her according to the aforesaid form.

*10.[290] The dumb and the deaf and whoever is not specifically prohibited from marrying may contract matrimony, but as they are unable to give their consent in words, signs expressing consent will suffice in their case.

11.[291] The insane and those who cannot give their consent cannot contract matrimony either. But madness appearing after marriage does not break the contract.

12.[292] We strictly forbid any male who has not attained the age of sixteen years, and any female who has not attained the age of fourteen years to contract matrimony or betrothal, and anything done to the contrary we declare to be null and void, unless some very urgent necessity intervenes, for betrothals between minors can be tolerated only for the sake of keeping the peace.

*13.[293] **Betrothals are a promise of future marriage.**

*14.[294] Since it is forbidden to solemnize matrimony before the reading of the banns in order to prevent illegal marriages, we decree that if, during the reading of the banns, **a plausible suspicion should appear**, or something is objected which may hinder the said marriage, **the contract will be expressly forbidden until a clear written indication is received of what should be done about it.**

Si quis contra hoc statutum nostrum contrahere, aut clandestinum matrimonium, ullo pacto inire de facto praesumpserit, excommunicationis sententia percellatur, non prius absolvendus quam ad arbitrium ordinarii sufficientem propter hoc fecerit emendam.

Sane paroechialis sacerdos qui tales coniunctiones prohibere contempserit, aut illas de facto solemnizare praesumpserit, quive clandestina matrimonia quovismodo solemnizare an suum consensum adhibere ausus fuerit **per triennium** [72r] **ab officio suo suspendatur.**

*15.[295] Ut igitur haec /constitutio/ *constitutio* nostra melius observetur, volumus ut paroechiales sacerdotes quater ad minus in anno eam publice paroechianis suis in vulgari exponant diligenter eos admonentes ne quid contra ipsam attemptent.

*16.[296] Sacerdos sive saecularis sive regularis, exemptus sive non exemptus, qui solemnizationem interdum vel clandestini matrimonii facere sive etiam *libitum* licitum et permissum matrimonium inter alios quam suos paroechianos scienter absque dioecesanorum vel curatorum ipsorum contrahentium licentia solemnizare aut huiusmodi solemnizationi conscius praemissorum interesse praesumpserit, maioris excommunicationis sententiam ipso facto incurrat a qua non absolvetur donec ab episcopo loci legitima satisfactione praemissa absolutionem obtinere meruerit.

17.[297] Solemnizationem matrimonii in ecclesia paroechiali contrahentium si eiusdem fuerint paroechiae, alioquin in ecclesia paroechiali mulieris fieri [72v] volumus, nisi de consensu ordinarii aut curati dictae paroechiae aliter fieri permittatur.

Paroechiam propriam illam esse decernimus, in qua quis per integrum annum animo perpetuo manendi habitaverit, et qui matrimonium solemnizare velit, in aliqua paroechia, antequam illic per annum manserit, non permittatur, nisi litteras testimoniales presbyteri et gardianorum paroechiae ubi alias per annum habitaverit super sua immunitate ostenderit.

18.[298] Qui post matrimonium legitime contractum secundam (vivente praevia) ducit uxorem, relicta secunda, adhaerere primae, et pro arbitrio iudicis condignam de hoc paenitentiam agere per ecclesiasticas censuras compelletur.

---

[295]Cf. L, 4.3.1, c. 8 of Archbishop Simon Mepham, 1329.
[296]*Ibid.* See also L, 4.3.2, c. 11 of Archbishop John Stratford, 1342.
[297]This is most clearly stated in c. 24 of the statutes for the diocese of York, *c.* 1241-55 (PC, 490), repeated as c. 23 of the statutes for the diocese of Chichester (II), 6 October 1289 (PC, 1086); c. 12 of the statutes for the diocese of Wells, *c.* 1258 (PC, 598), repeated as c. 28 of the statutes for the diocese of Winchester (III), *c.* 1262-5 (PC, 707) and in c. 7 of the statutes for the diocese of Exeter (II), 16 April 1287 (PC, 996-9); c. 47 of the statutes for the diocese of London (II), *c.* 1245-59 (PC, 644). However, none of these specifies that the marriage is to take place in the bride's parish church if the parties come from different parishes.
[298]C. 34, qq.1-2, c. 1 (Fr, I, 1256-7), a letter of Pope Leo I, 458; X, 4.21.2 (Fr, II, 730), a decretal of Pope Lucius III (1181-5).

If anyone shall presume to contract or in fact enter a secret marriage under some agreement contrary to this our statute, he shall be punished with the sentence of excommunication and shall not be absolved until he has made sufficient amends, at the discretion of the ordinary.

But a parish priest who refuses to prohibit such relations or who presumes to solemnize them *de facto*, or who has dared to solemnize secret marriages in some way or to permit them without consent being given, **shall be suspended from his office for the space of three years.**

*15.[295] Therefore, in order that this our constitution may be better observed, it is our will that parish priests shall publicly expound it to their parishioners at least four times a year, in the vulgar tongue, warning them not to try anything contrary to it.

*16.[296] Any priest, whether secular or regular, exempt or non-exempt, who meanwhile presumes to perform the solemnization of a secret marriage, or knowingly to solemnize a lawful and permitted marriage between persons other than his parishioners without the permission of the diocesans or of the curates of the contracting parties, or who, being aware of the above, takes part in a solemnization of this kind, shall automatically incur the sentence of greater excommunication, and shall not be absolved from it until he has earned absolution from the bishop of the place, after making lawful satisfaction as aforesaid.

17.[297] It is our will the solemnization of the marriage to take place in the parish church of the contracting parties, if they are of the same parish; otherwise, in the parish church of the woman, unless with the agreement of the ordinary or the curate of the said parish some other arrangement is allowed.

We define one's own parish to be that in which one has resided for a full year with every intention of remaining there. And if one wishes to solemnize the marriage in some parish where one was living before that year, this will not be permitted, unless one can show letters testimonial, concerning one's freedom to marry, from the priest and wardens of the other parish where one had dwelt for a year.

18.[298] Whoever takes a second wife after contracting lawful matrimony (while the former wife is still living), shall be forced to abandon the second wife and return to the first one, and to do appropriate penance for this by the censures of the church, at the discretion of the judge.

19.[299] Sponsalia autem per matrimonium postea contractum prorsus dissolvi volumus.

*20.[300] Si de matrimonio quaestio habeatur interim dum lis pendeat, iudex qui de causa cognoscit prohibere debet, ne [73r] litigantes cum aliis contrahant, donec cum per sententiam finiatur. Qui contra huiusmodi prohibitionem iudicis contraxerunt excommunicentur et ab invicem separentur donec causa terminetur.

21.[301] Qui sub honesta conditione matrimonium aut sponsalia cum aliqua contrahit, non prius cogendus est praestitam fidem implere, quam conditio impleatur, nisi postea eam per carnalem copulam cognoverit, aut alias tacite vel expresse a conditione recesserit.

22.[302] Contracto matrimonio inter aliquas personas sub conditione, si pendente conditione, alter contrahentium pure cum tertia contraxerit, secundum purum et non primum conditionale matrimonium valere volumus.

23.[303] **Si autem conditiones contra substantiam coniugii inserantur puta si alter dicat alteri: 'Contraho tecum si generationem prolis evites', vel 'donec inveniam h... aliam honore vel [73v] facultatibus digniorem', aut 'si pro quaestu adulterandam te tradas', matrimonialis contractus quantumcunque sit favorabilis caret effectu, licet aliae conditiones appositae in matrimonio (si turpes aut impossibiles fuerint), debeant propter favorem eius pro non adiectis haberi.**

24.[304] Si post contracta sponsalia alter contrahentium leprae morbum incurrat, alter ab huiusmodi sponsalibus impune recedere potest.

25.[305] Si liber homo cum ancilla, aut libera cum servo ignoranter matrimonium contraxerit, nec postquam intellexit conditionem ipsius facto aut verbo huiusmodi nuptiis consenserit, soluto propter hoc per iudicium ecclesiae huiusmodi matrimonio liberam cum aliis contrahendi habeat facultatem.

26.[306] Cum affinitas non tantum ex licito verum etiam ex illicito coitu pervenit, statuimus ut si post contracta sponsalia [74r] quovismodo superveniat, matrimonium consanguinea cognite contrahi non permittatur, sed sponsalia prorsus dissolvatur, et matrimonium si quod post huiusmodi affinitatem de facto sequatur nullum esse pronuntiamus, verum si post legitime contractum matrimonium sequatur affinitas matrimonii nihilominus ratum manebit.

---

[299]This is a simplification of the old canon law, which allowed for future betrothals to be broken by marriage, but not for present ones. If a person married someone else when he or she was already officially betrothed, the marriage was declared null and void. See X, 4.1.31 (Fr, II, 672), a decretal of Pope Gregory IX, 1234 and X, 4.1.22 (Fr, II, 669), a decretal of Pope Innocent III, 25 February 1198.

[300]X, 4.4.4 (Fr, II, 681), a decretal of Pope Alexander III (1159-81).

[301]X, 4.5.6 (Fr, II, 683-4), a decretal of Pope Innocent III, dated 12 July 1203.

[302]VI, 4.1.1 (Fr, II, 1065-6), a decretal of Pope Boniface VIII (1294-1303).

[303]X, 4.5.7 (Fr, II, 684), a decretal of Pope Gregory IX (1227-41), published before 1234.

[304]X, 4.8.3 (Fr, II, 691), a decretal of Pope Urban III (1185-7).

[305]X, 4.9.4 (Fr, II, 692-3), a decretal of Pope Innocent III (1198-1216).

[306]X, 4.13.2 (Fr, II, 696-7), a decretal of Pope Alexander III (1159-81).

19.[299] It is our will that betrothals shall be utterly without force once matrimony has been contracted.

*20.[300] If there is some question about the marriage, while the suit is pending, the judge handling the cause must forbid the litigants to make a contract with anyone else, until the cause is terminated by sentencing. Those who make a contract in violation of this prohibition by the judge shall be excommunicated and separated from each other until the cause is brought to an end.

21.[301] Whoever has placed an acceptable condition on the matrimony or betrothal which he has contracted with someone, shall not be obliged to fulfil his plighted troth before the condition is met, unless he has already slept with her or otherwise tacitly or expressly backed away from the condition.

22.[302] If a marriage has been contracted between particular persons subject to some condition, and before the condition is met, one of the contracting parties contracts an unconditional marriage with a third party, it is our will that the second straightforward marriage, and not the first conditional one, shall be valid.

23.[303] **However, if conditions are inserted which go against the very nature of marriage, for instance, if one party says to the other: 'I contract with you as long as you avoid bearing children', or 'until I find someone else who is of a higher class or social standing', or 'if you are prepared to commit adultery for financial gain', the contract of matrimony, however favourable it may be, shall have no effect, although any other conditions placed on the marriage (if they are wicked or impossible) must for its sake be regarded as not having been made.**

24.[304] If, after making a betrothal, one of the parties contracts the disease of leprosy, the other may break the betrothal off without penalty.

25.[305] If a free man unwittingly contracts marriage with a maidservant, or a free woman with a manservant, and after finding out what the position of the other is, refuses by word or deed to consent to such a marriage, the marriage shall be dissolved by a judgment of the church on that ground, and the person in question shall be perfectly free to enter into a contract with someone else.

26.[306] Since affinity arises not only from lawful but also from unlawful intercourse, we decree that if something like that happens after a betrothal has been made, the marriage cannot be permitted because of the blood tie, but rather the betrothal shall be broken off, and any marriage which may follow the discovery of this affinity we declare to be null and void, but if the affinity comes about after the marriage has been contracted, it shall remain valid notwithstanding.

27.[307] Cum ad dissolvendum matrimonium vir uxoris suae consanguineam carnaliter se cognovisse fateatur et mulier illa id etiam affirmat, atque aliqua pars vicinii hoc acclamare dicatur, tum **propter eorum confessionem tantum, vel rumorem vicinii separari non dentur, ne colludendi contra matrimonium occasio coniugalis detur, quia sic ad confessionem incestus facile prosilirent, si suo iudicio crederent per iudicium ecclesiae succurrendum. Rumor autem viciniae, non adeo est iudicandus validus, quod nisi rationabiles ac fide dignae** [74v] **probationes accedant, possit bene contractum matrimonium irritar**{e/i} nec ad dictum unius asserentis affinitatem inter coniuges praecessisse matrimonium rite contractum, separari debet.[308]

28.[309] Matrimonium inter ascendentes et descendentes in *lu*... linea recta quoniam parentum et liberorum loco sunt, usque in infinitum contrahi prohibemus.

29.[310] Sed nec quis uxorem patris seu patrui vel avunculi sui aut uxorem fratris sui, vel amitam aut materteram suam seu matrem aut sororem, vel filiam uxoris suae, vel filiam filii aut filiae uxoris suae, aut sororem suam ex patre sive ex matre matrimonio sibi coniungat, et si tales personae de facto matrimonium contraxerint, quia naturali et dominico iure huiusmodi personae coire prohibentur, nefarias atque incestas nuptias ac ipso iure nullas contraxisse pronuntiamus.

*30.[311] Eorum praeterea coniunctionem, qui secundo consanguinitatis vel affinitatis gradu aequali se invicem attingunt, [75r] fieri prorsus inhibemus, decernentes matrimonium quod contra hanc prohibitionem contractum fuerit ipso iure esse nullum, ac eos qui scienter in gradibus consanguinitatis vel affinitatis *gradu aequali se invicem attingunt, fieri prorsus inhibemus, decernentes matrimonium* huiusmodi contraxerint quive inter eos matrimonium scienter celebrare praesumpserint, excommunicationis sententiae ipso facto subiacere, a qua non prius absolventur, quam suum humiliter recognoscentes errorem ad arbitrium ordinarii condignam paenitentiam peregerint.

*31.[312] Si post contractum matrimonium probetur alterum coniugum, naturali aut quovis alio perpetuo impedimento, quod ante matrimonium extitit, eoque nulla medicorum arte reparabili impotentem esse ad debitum coniugale per iudicium ecclesiae huiusmodi matrimonium separari possit, et qui habilis est, cum alio si voluerit, matrimonium contrahere possit. Si vero de impedimento [75v] huiusmodi constare liquido non possit, tunc tam diu cohabitent huiusmodi

---

[307]X, 4.13.5 (Fr, II, 697-8), a decretal of Pope Celestine III (1191-8).

[308]X, 4.13.3 (Fr, II, 697), a decretal of Pope Alexander III.

[309]Cf. *Dig.* 23.2.68, originally Paulus, *Ad senatusconsultum Turpillianum*, 1. It was not in the old canon law, and much debated, though it could be implied, e.g. from C. 35, qq. 2-3, c. 18 (Fr, I, 1268), originally c. 32 of the synod of Worms, 868. Rome finally adopted it in 1917 (1917/1076.1; cf. 1983/1091.1) but it has never been part of English law.

[310]25 Henry VIII, c. 22, s. 2, 1533-4 (*S.R.*, III, 471-4).

[311]*Clem.*, 4.1.1 (Fr, II, 1177-8), a decretal of Pope Clement V (1305-14) published at the council of Vienne, 1311-12.

[312]X, 4.15.3 (Fr, II, 705), a decretal of Pope Alexander III (1159-81).

27.[307] If, in order to dissolve a marriage, a man says that he has slept with a blood relative of his wife and the woman affirms that this is true, and a certain part of the neighbourhood is said to agree with this, **they shall not be allowed to separate merely on the ground of their confession and the rumour of the neighbourhood, in order not to give occasion for some joint collusion against the marriage, for such people will easily leap to a confession of incest if, in their judgment, they think that it will be accepted by a church court. Furthermore, the rumour of the neighbourhood is not to be considered valid, because a properly contracted marriage cannot be invalidated without reasonable and trustworthy proofs**, nor ought the couple to be separated on the word of one person who asserts that there was some affinity between them before the marriage was duly contracted.[308]

28.[309] We forbid marriage to be contracted between ascendants and descendants in the direct line of parents and children, as far as that line may extend.

29.[310] Nor shall anyone join to himself in marriage the wife of his father or his father's brother or his mother's brother or the wife of his brother, or his father's sister or his mother's sister or his mother or his sister, or the daughter of his wife, or the daughter of his wife's son or daughter, or his half-sister on either side, and if such persons have in fact contracted matrimony, because such persons are prevented by natural and divine law from having intercourse, we decree that they have contracted a marriage which is evil and incestuous, and therefore invalid.

*30.[311] Moreover, we utterly forbid the joining together of those who are related to each other in the second degree of consanguinity or affinity, decreeing that any marriage which has been contracted in violation of this prohibition shall for that reason be null and void, and that those who have knowingly contracted matrimony within the degrees of consanguinity and affinity, or who have presumed to celebrate matrimony between such persons, shall automatically incur the sentence of excommunication, from which they shall not be absolved until they humbly acknowledge their error and do appropriate penance at the discretion of the ordinary.

*31.[312] If after the marriage has been contracted it is proved that one of the partners, because of some natural or other impediment which existed before the marriage, and which no medical technique can put right, is unable to fulfil the marital obligation, the said marriage may be dissolved by a judgment of the church, and the party which is able to, may contract matrimony with someone else if he or she so desires. But if the existence of this impediment cannot be clearly proved, then the said couple shall live together until the impediment is

coniuges, donec per iustum iudicium impedimentum hoc probetur et si post matrimonium ex hac causa solutum, constiterit *ecclesiasticum* ecclesiam fuisse deceptam, reintegrabitur huiusmodi matrimonium.

32.[313] Qui scienter cum impotente ad debitum coniugale contraxerit ab ea non sep{e/a}retur, sed quam ut uxorem habere non possit, habeat ut sororem.

33.[314] Cum aliquem ex viro et uxore post legitime contractum matrimonium natum esse per legitimas probationes constiterit, licet vir et mulier non in matrimonio sed in concubinatu se suscepisse dictam prolem affirmaverint, idque opinio maioris partis viciniae comprobaverit, dubitandum non est, in hoc casu, eundem pro legitimo filio habendum esse.

34.[315] Cum quaeritur an quis de legitimo matrimonio natus sit, coram iudice ecclesiastico hanc causam agitari et definiri volumus. [76r] Incongruum esse iudicamus ut eius matrimonium, quod dum viveret reputabatur validum, ipso iam mortuo impetatur, nisi ad effectum successionis discutiendae.

35.[316] Contracto matrimonio si vir aut mulier absens fuerit, et legitimi accusatores aut testes appareant, qui huiusmodi matrimonium illicitum esse probare possunt, absens cum omni diligentia requiratur, et si nequiunt inveniri, testes recipi et causam huiusmodi fine debito terminari possit.

36.[317] Parentes et consanguinei, quia suam genealogiam melius scire putantur, ac cum matrimonium contrahitur plurimum eorum interest adesse in causa matrimoniali super affinitate, consanguinitate ac etiam contractu, testimonium (si disparitas aut aliud non impediat) legitime dare possunt.

37.[318] Qui ut quaestum faciat, matrimonium accusat, ab accusatione repellatur.

[76v] 38.[319] **Si is qui cum banna secundum consuetudinem in ecclesiis edebantur extra dioecesim fuit, vel alias inscius de bannorum editione, aut si tunc propter nimiam infirmitatem aut furorem vel minorem aetatem, seu propter aliam legitimam causam contradicere huiusmodi nuptiis non valebat, post contractum matrimonium illud accusare voluerit, non est propter hoc repellendus. Is vero qui prius in ipsa dioecesi (cum banna edebantur) fuit eademque minime ignoravit et tunc contradicere potuit, tanquam suspectus repellatur, si postea voluerit accusare, nisi proprio firmaverit iuramento, quod postea didicerit ea quae obiecerit, et ad hoc ex malitia non procedat, quia tunc etiamsi didicisset ab illis qui denuntiationis tempore siluerint claudi non debet eidem aditus accusandi, quoniam etsi ab impetitione huiusmodi culpa de silentio tali contracta illos excluderet, iste tamen amoveri nequit, cum culpabilis non existit.**

---

[313]X, 4.15.4 (Fr, II, 705), a decretal of Pope Lucius III (1181-5).
[314]X, 4.17.12 (Fr, II, 713-14), a decretal of Pope Innocent III, dated 5 August 1198.
[315]X, 4.17.5 (Fr, II, 711), a decretal of Pope Alexander III (1159-81).
[316]X, 4.18.1 (Fr, II, 717-18), a decretal of Pope Alexander III.
[317]X, 4.18.3 (Fr, II, 718-19), a decretal of Pope Clement III (1187-91).
[318]X, 4.18.5 (Fr, II, 719), a decretal of Pope Innocent III, dated 15 June 1204.
[319]X, 4.18.6 (Fr, II, 719-20), a decretal of Pope Innocent III, dated 29 October 1212.

proved by fair judgment, and if, after a marriage has been dissolved for that reason, it turns out that the church has been deceived, the said marriage will be reconstituted.

32.[313] Anyone who has knowingly entered into marriage with someone who is impotent shall not be separated from her, but as he cannot treat her as a wife he shall treat her as a sister.

33.[314] When it is determined by lawful proofs that someone has been born to a man and his wife after a lawfully contracted marriage, even if the man and woman state that they conceived the said child not in matrimony but out of wedlock, and the opinion of the majority of the neighbourhood agrees with this, there can be no doubt that in this case the child is to be considered legitimate.

34.[315] When a question is raised as to whether someone was born legitimate or not, it is our will that the cause shall be debated and decided before an ecclesiastical judge. We think that it is inappropriate that a person's marriage, which was regarded as valid during his lifetime, should be called into question once he is dead, unless it involves a matter of succession which must be decided.

35.[316] If a marriage has been contracted, [and] in the absence of the man or woman, legitimate accusers or witnesses appear who can prove that the said matrimony was illegal, the absent party shall be sought out with all diligence, and if they cannot be found, the witnesses may be accepted and the cause brought to a proper conclusion.

36.[317] Parents and relatives, because they are thought to know their genealogy better, and when a marriage is contracted most of them have an interest in being present in a matrimonial cause, may lawfully give testimony (if disagreement or something else does not stand in the way) concerning affinity, consanguinity and the contract as well.

37.[318] Anyone who calls a marriage into question in the hope of some financial gain shall be barred from pursuing his case.

38.[319] **If a man was outside the diocese when the banns were read in the churches according to custom, or he was otherwise unaware of the reading of the banns, or if at that time he was unable to object to the marriage because he was too ill, or mad, or under age, or for some other lawful reason, and after the marriage has taken place he wants to object to it, he is not to be barred from doing so on that account. But a man who was in the diocese (when the banns were being read) and was perfectly aware of the fact, and who could have objected at that time, shall be barred as being suspect, if later on he wants to object, unless he swears on oath that he only discovered the things he is objecting to afterwards, and that he is not taking action out of malice, for if he has discovered things which were not mentioned by the parties concerned at the time the banns were read, he must not be barred from making his accusation, and if as a result of the said petition the parties concerned are found guilty of having kept quiet, at least he himself will not be removed, because he will not be guilty.**

[77r] **23. De divortiis.**

1.[320] Si vir ab uxore, vel uxor a viro sua auctoritate absque iudicio ecclesiae diverit, spoliatus ante omnia est restituendus, nisi petenti restitutionem opponatur impedimentum consanguinitatis vel affinitatis in gradibus lege divina prohibitis, et probationes de eo offeruntur, incontinenter paratae recepto prius iuramento quod talis obiectio malitiose non fiat, in quo casu donec auditis probationibus et discussis causa terminetur, restitutio est differenda.

2.[321] Si propter metum mortis aut saevitiam coniugis alter coniugum ab altero sua auctoritate absque iudicio ecclesiae divertat, sufficiente (si fieri potest) securitate promissa, ante omnia spoliato restitutio est facienda, verum **si trepidanti non possit sufficiens securitas provideri, non solum non debet fieri restitutio, sed qui in periculo aut metu est ab altero potius a mutua cohabitatione amoveri** per [77v] iudicium ecclesiae debet.

3.[322] Pendente lite inter virum et uxorem in causa restitutionis ad obsequia coniugalia sive divortii, quo ad vinculum vel quo ad thorum et mensam[323] sumptus litis et alimoniae ad mandatum iudicis per maritum mulieri volumus ministrari.

4.[324] Si episcopus seu alius quicunque qui de matrimonio cognoscere et iudicare possit aliquos per legitimas probationes, noverit in gradibus prohibitis aut alias illicite coniunctos esse, licet non appareant accusationes, tamen ex officio suo matrimonium illud quod illicite contractum est dissolvere possit.

5.[325] Cum de restitutione eius qui recessit a coniuge sua agatur, **si notorium est mulierem adulterium commisisse, ad eam recipiendam vir cogi non debet, nisi constat ipsum quoque cum alia quoque adulterium commisisse.**

[78r] 6.[326] Si vir sciens uxorem suam deliquisse, quae non egerit paenitentiam, sed **eo consentiente**{*m*} permanet in fornicatione, et vixerit cum illa, pro arbitrio iudicis legitimam subeat paenitentiam; quod si mulier dimissa egerit paenitentiam et voluerit ad virum suum reverti, **potest vir eam recipere, sed propter adulterium quod praecessit matrimonium, vir uxorem suam deserere non potest.**

---

[320]Based on X, 4.19.3 (Fr, II, 720-1), a decretal of Pope Alexander III.

[321]X, 2.13.13 (Fr, II, 286-8), a decretal of Pope Innocent III (1198-1216).

[322]1237/23, gloss on *matrimoniales causae*. John de Athon takes his authority from X, 5.1.11 (Fr, II, 735), which says that monks should be supported while their suits are pending because they have no resources of their own, and from *Cod. Iust.*, 7.19.7, a rescript of Emperor Constantine I (306-37), dated to *c.* 317-19, which says the same thing about slaves.

[323]Divorce *a vinculo* was known from Roman law but not granted by the church courts. Divorce *a thoro et mensa* was a legal separation which did not permit remarriage of either party or require the return of the dowry. See L. Dibdin, *English church law and divorce* (London, 1912).

[324]X, 4.19.3 (Fr, II, 720-1), a decretal of Pope Alexander III (1159-81).

[325]X, 4.19.4 (Fr, II, 721), a decretal of Pope Alexander III.

[326]X, 5.16.3 (Fr, II, 806), supposed to have come from a council of Arles.

23. Of divorces.

1.[320] If a man leaves his wife, or a wife leaves her husband, on their own authority, without the sanction of the church, the abandoned party is to have the other restored to him or her, unless an impediment of consanguinity or affinity within the degrees prohibited by the law of God is offered as an objection to the party seeking the restoration, and immediate proof of this is presented, an oath having been sworn beforehand that the said objection is not being made maliciously, in which case the restoration is to be postponed until the proofs have been heard and discussed, and the cause is closed.

2.[321] If because of fear of death, or the cruelty of a spouse, one of the spouses leaves the other on his or her own authority, without the sanction of the church, above all else, restoration is to be made to the one abandoned and (if possible) adequate security is to be promised, but **if adequate security cannot be provided for the fearful party, not only must the restoration not take place, but the party who is in danger or fear of the other** must **rather be removed from mutual cohabitation** by the judgment of the church.

3.[322] While a suit is pending between a man and his wife in a cause of restoration of conjugal rights or divorce, either of the marriage bond or of bed and board,[323] it is our will that the costs of the suit and of alimony should be paid by the husband at the order of the judge.

4.[324] If a bishop or whoever else who can hear and decide matrimonial causes, discovers by lawful proofs that particular people are joined within the prohibited degrees or in some other unlawful way, even if there are no accusations against them, he may on his own authority dissolve that marriage which has been unlawfully contracted.

5.[325] When it is a matter of restoring a man who has left his wife, **if it is notorious that the woman has committed adultery, the man must not be obliged to take her back unless it appears that he has also committed adultery with someone else.**

6.[326] If a man knows that his wife has offended and has not done penance, but remains in fornication **with his consent**, and he has lived with her, he shall undergo lawful penance at the discretion of the judge. But if the wife is sent away, does penance and wants to go back to her husband, **the man may take her back, but a man may not leave his wife on account of adultery which has taken place before marriage.**

7.[327] Vir ab uxore adultera separari non debet, si et ipsum quoque adulterum esse constiterit, **quoniam matrimonii ius in utroque laesum consistat et paria delicta mutua compensatione tollantur**, quare indicta illis pro adulterio paenitentia ad invicem permanere, et maritali affectione se tractare cogantur.

8.[328] Qui iuravit aliquam ducere in uxorem, propter fornicationem quam tunc ignoravit eam impune relinquere [78v] potest, nec ullo modo eam ducere cogitur.

9.[329] Si mulier absente viro suo post legitime contractum matrimonium (nondum habita absentis coniugis certitudine), cum alio de facto, propria auctoritate, matrimonium contraxerit, et post hoc de prioris coniugis vita constiterit, relictis adulterinis amplexibus, ad priorem coniugem revertere cogatur.

10.[330] Si alter coniugum adulterium se commisisse fuerit confessus aut per testes idoneos legitime inde convictus, divortium quoad thorum et mensam, dumtaxat per iudicem in ea parte competentem, ad petitionem alterius coniugis donec se reconciliaverint fieri permittimus.

11.[331] Matrimonium sane efficitur per consensum de praesente declaratum, puta: 'Accipio te, volo habere te, nolo habere *te* aliam nisi te' ac aliis verbis expressum consensum de praesente exprimentibus.

[79r] **24. De decimis.**

1.[332] De **frugibus, pascuis, herbis, piscatoris umariis, et stagnis, columbariis, proventibus boscorum, pannagiis silvarum et ceterarum** *hi....* **arborum, et de fructibus omnium arborum**, ac silvis caeduis,[333] **pecoribus, seminibus, cuniculis et aliis bestiis guerrenarum, curtilagiis, lino,** {*omni* **vino**}, **grano, de turvis quoque in locis in quibus fodiuntur, de cygnis,** {*panonibus* **caponibus**}, **aucis, et anatibus, ovis, ac de pullis gallinaris, porcellis teneris agrorum, de apibus quoque, ac melle et cera, de molendinis,** fodinis et lapiditiis, ac de omni denique fructu terrae illi ecclesiae, infra cuius paroechiam praedictam contingunt, proveniunt, seu crescunt, decimam partem integre ac statim collectis fructibus omnes subditos nostros persolvere, atque de *subst...* subtractis et retentis dignam satisfactionem exhibere mandamus, nisi tales sunt, ut inde decimas statuta regni

---

[327]X, 5.16.7 (Fr, II, 807), a decretal of Pope Innocent III, dated 13 June 1208.

[328]X, 2.24.25 (Fr, II, 368-9), a decretal of Pope Innocent III, dated 1 September 1207.

[329]X, 4.21.2 (Fr, II, 730), a decretal of Pope Lucius III (1181-5).

[330]C. 32, q. 7, c. 3 (Fr, I, 1140-1), a quotation from Augustine of Hippo (354-430), and ibid., c. 5 (Fr, I, 1141), c. 17 of the second council of Milevis, 402.

[331]Based on X, 4.1.9 (Fr, II, 663-4), a decretal of Pope Alexander III (1159-81).

[332]Much of this is based on L, 3.16.5, which may have been a canon of Archbishop Boniface (1249-69), though its origin is uncertain, and on L, 3.16.7, which is of unknown origin. Both were attributed by Lyndwood to Archbishop Robert Winchelsea (1293-1313) and dated to 1305.

[333]This is the subject of L, 3.16.3, originally a statute of Archbishop John Stratford (1333-48), probably the fifth canon of a council held in 1342.

7.[327] A man may not be separated from his adulterous wife if it transpires that he is also an adulterer, **because then the right of matrimony has been offended on both sides and the sins cancel one another out**; wherefore the penance towards one another, imposed on them for adultery, is to be maintained, and they must be obliged to treat each other with marital affection.

8.[328] Whoever has sworn to marry a woman may abandon her without penalty on account of [some previous] fornication of which he was unaware at the time, and there is no way that he can be forced to marry her.

9.[329] If after a lawful marriage and in the absence of her husband (assuming that [the death of] the absent spouse is not yet confirmed) a woman contracts a marriage with another man on her own authority, and afterwards it is discovered that her first husband is still alive, she shall be obliged to abandon her adulterous relationship and return to her former spouse.

10.[330] If one of the spouses confesses to having committed adultery or is lawfully convicted of the same by suitable witnesses, we allow there to be a separation from bed and board at the request of the other spouse, as long as it is decreed by a judge who is competent in this respect, until they are reconciled.

11.[331] Matrimony is effected by a declaration of present consent, for example: 'I take you, I want to have you, I do not want to have anyone else but you' or present consent expressed in other words.

24. Of tithes.

1.[332] We command all our subjects to pay a full tenth part as soon as the fruits are collected, and to provide adequate satisfaction for whatever things have been subtracted and held back, unless they are such that the statutes of our realm expressly forbid tithes to be paid or demanded for them, on **the crops, pastures, grasslands, fish hatcheries and ponds, dovecotes, products of the woods, roots of the forests and of other trees, and of the fruits of all trees**, and of timber woods,[333] **cattle, seeds, rabbits and other beasts for fowling, courtyards, flax, wine, grain, of turfs also in the places in which they are dug, swans, capons, geese and ducks, eggs, hens' chickens, tender piglets of the fields, bees also, and honey and wax, mills**, digs and quarries, and of all the fruit of the earth, to that church within whose aforesaid parish they belong,

nostri solvi seu exigi expresse prohibent, [79v] de modo autem solvendi huiusmodi decimam, cuiusque loci consuetudinem observari volumus. Decimas vero personales, videlicet quae ex piscatione in fluminibus publicis, sive in mare, sive ex negotiatione aut artificio, vel quovis alio iusto labore proveniunt, nisi pro illis aliter ex consuetudine seu compositione satisfactum fuerit, illi ecclesiae deductis prius necessariis expensis solvi volumus, cuius paroechiani sunt huiusmodi piscatores, artifices seu negotiatores, in tempore Paschae quando videlicet sacramenta ecclesiastica recipere et decimas huiusmodi solvere consueverunt. De foetu autem et fructu animalium decima solvatur, ita videlicet de agnis quod si pauciores sunt quam septem agni, pro quolibet agno obolus detur pro decima, si septem sunt agni in numero, agnus septimus detur pro decima rectori. Ita tamen quod rector ecclesiae qui septimum agnum recipit, tres obolos in recompensationem solvat paroechiano a quo decimam illam recipit. [80r] Qui octavum recipit det denarium, qui vero {unum nonum} det obolo paroechiano, et ita intelligendum est de decima lanae, sed si oves alibi in hieme, alibi in aestate nutriantur, dividenda {m} est decima. Similiter si quis medio tempore emerit oves et certum sit a qua paroechia illae oves veniunt, dividenda est earundem decima, sicut de re quae sequitur duo domicilia; si autem incertum fuerit, habeat illa ecclesia totam decimam infra cuius limites tempore tonsionis inveniuntur. De lacte vero volumus quod *den*... decima solvatur dum durat, videlicet de caseo tempore suo et de lacte in auctumno et hieme, nisi paroechiani velint pro talibus facere competentem redemptionem.

2.[334] **Statuimus** etiam **quod ad ecclesias in quarum paroechiis oves a tempore tonsionis usque ad festum Sancti Martini**[335] **in hieme continue pascuntur et cubant, decima lanae, lactis** [80v] **et casei eiusdem temporis licet postea amotae fuerint ab illa paroechia et alibi tondeantur, integre persolvatur, et ne fraus fiat in casu praemissorum, praecipimus quod antequam oves amoveantur a pasturis vel etiam distrahantur ecclesiarum rectoribus** *sol*... **sufficienter de solvenda decima caveatur.**

Quod si infra praedictum tempus ad diversarum paroechiarum pasturam transferantur quaelibet ecclesia pro rata temporis portione decimam percipiet eorundem, minori triginta dierum spatio in rata temporis minime computando. Si vero per totum tempus praedictum cubant in una paroechia et pascuntur continue in alia, inter ipsas ecclesias decima dividatur.

Quoties oves in una paroechia per mensem pasci aut ultra, atque postea in aliam agi paroechiam contingat, toties decimas lanae et agnorum pro rata temporis dividat, [81r] minori triginta dierum spatio minime computando. Decima vero lactis et casei de vaccis et capris proveniens ubi cubant et pascuntur ibi solvatur, alioquin si cubant in una paroechia et pascuntur in

---

[334]This is based on L, 3.16.6, originally canon 77 of Bishop William of Bitton I, made for the diocese of Bath and Wells about 1258.
[335]11 November.

come or grow. As for the method of paying the tithe, it is our will that the custom of each place shall be observed. But as for personal tithes, like those which arise from fishing in public rivers or in the sea, or from business or crafts or some other honest labour, unless satisfaction is made for them in some other way, by custom or composition, we wish them to be paid to that church whose parishioners the fishermen, craftsmen or traders are, after necessary expenses have been deducted, at the time of Easter, which is when they are accustomed to receive the sacraments of the church and to pay the said tithes. A tithe shall also be paid on the seed and offspring of animals; so that in the case of lambs, for example, if there are fewer than seven lambs, a halfpenny shall be given as tithe for each one, if there are seven lambs in number, the seventh lamb shall be given to the rector as a tithe. And so the rector of the church who receives the seventh lamb must pay three halfpence in compensation to the parishioner from whom he has received that tithe. Whoever receives an eighth lamb shall pay a penny, and whoever receives a ninth shall give a halfpenny to the parishioner, and the same is to be understood of the tithe on wool, but if the sheep graze in one place in winter and in another in summer, the tithe is to be divided. Likewise, if someone buys sheep during the course of the year, and it is clear what parish those sheep have come from, the tithe on them is to be divided, just as on anything which has two domiciles. But if it is uncertain where they have come from, that church, within whose limits the sheep are found at the time of shearing, shall receive the whole tithe. As for milk, it is our will that a tithe shall be paid as long as it lasts, namely on cheese in its season and on milk in the autumn and winter, unless the parishioners wish to make a block payment in lieu of them.

2.[334] **Furthermore, we decree that the tithes of wool, milk and cheese in its season shall be paid in full to the churches in whose parishes the sheep graze and sleep right through from shearing time until the feast of St Martin[335] in the winter, even if afterwards they are taken away from that parish and sheared elsewhere, and in order to prevent fraud in the case of the foregoing, we decree that before the sheep are removed from the pastures and even sold, there must be a guarantee to pay the tithe to the rectors of the churches.**

But if within the aforesaid time they are transferred to pasture in different parishes, each church shall receive a tithe in proportion to the time [spent in them], not counting any period which is less than the space of thirty days. But if during the whole of the aforesaid time they sleep in one parish and normally graze in another, the tithe shall be divided between those churches.

Whenever it happens that sheep are grazed in one parish for a month and afterwards are moved to another parish, the tithes of wool and of lambs shall be divided in proportion to the time, not counting a period which is less than thirty days in length. A tithe which comes from cow's or goat's milk shall be paid in the place where they sleep and graze, but if they sleep

alia paroechia decima inter rectores dividatur omnino. Vituli vero, pulli equini, et alii foetus decimales ubi oriuntur, *saula* salva semper laudabili cuiuslibet loci consuetudine, decimentur.

Quid vero pro decima debeatur, ubi lac propter paucitatem vaccarum vel ovium ad caseum faciendum non sufficit, et quid pro agnis, vitulis, pullis equinis, velleribus, aucis aut aliis huiusmodi de quibus eorum paucitatem decima certa dari non *possunt* potest, consuetudini locorum duximus relinquendam. Item praecipimus quod si quis post festum Sancti Martini [81v] oves occiderit, aut si oves quovis casu fortuito moriantur, decimam legitimam iuxta laudabilem loci consuetudinem paroechiali ecclesiae solvere non postponant. Et si oves extraneae in alicuius paroechia tondeantur, decima ibidem tradetur rectori ecclesiae, nisi sufficienter doceri posset, quod pro decima sit alibi satisfactum, ut solutionem ibidem faciendam modo legitimo valeat impedire. Speciali tamen locorum consuetudine legitime praescripta, seu compositioni vel privilegio, nolumus per hanc constitutionem nostram quovismodo derogari.

3.[336] Decimam fructuum terrae quae alicuius certae paroechiae non sit aut illius fuerit paroechiae, cuius ecclesia casu vel vetustate esse desit, ad arbitrium episcopi in cuius dioecesi terra illa sita sit alicui alteri ecclesiae assignari volumus, nisi homines illius paroechiae cuius ecclesia esse desit, in aliqua certa ecclesia per longum tempus, [82r] videlicet per decem annos divina audire et sacramenta ac sacramentalia recipere consueverunt, in quo casu ibidem decimas huiusmodi solvere teneantur. Religiosi et alii qui habent privilegia de non solvendis decimis, de terris quas ab aliis conducunt, decimas solvere teneantur.

4.[337] Ubi per concessiones decimarum quae per privilegia seu aliter locis religiosis aut aliis quibuscunque fiunt, ecclesiae paroechiales adeo gravantur, quod earum rectores seu vicarii de ipsarum redditibus congrue sustentari et debita iura commode exhiberi non possunt, provideatur per locorum ordinarios, et taliter ordinetur, quod eisdem rectoribus aut vicariis tamen de illarum relinquantur proventibus quod exinde competentem sustentationem habere et debita onera supportare valeant.

5.[338] Religiosi omnes tam exempti quam non exempti de terris [82v] et possessionibus acquisitis hactenus et amodo acquirendis decimas integre solvant illis ecclesiis quibus de iure, consuetudine, praescriptione aut compositione eaedem possessiones et terrae sunt decimales ac per locorum dioecesanos ad illud compellantur, nisi super speciali iure aut privilegio sint muniti.[339]

---

[336]X, 3.30.13 (Fr, II, 560-1), a decretal of Pope Alexander III (1159-81).

[337]X, 3.30.34 (Fr, II, 568-9), c. 55 of Lateran IV, 1215 (*C.O.D.*, 260).

[338]X, 3.30.4 (Fr, II, 557), a letter of Pope Hadrian IV (1154-9) to 'Thomas, Archbishop of Canterbury'. But Thomas Becket did not become archbishop until 1162; the archbishop during Hadrian's pontificate was Theobald of Bec (1138-61).

[339]VI, 3.13.2 (Fr, II, 1048-50), a decretal of Pope Alexander IV (1254-61).

in one parish and graze in another the tithe shall simply be divided between the rectors. Calves, goats and other tithable offspring shall be tithed where they are born, approved local custom always excepted.

Something shall be owed for tithe where there is not enough milk for making cheese because of the lack of cows or sheep, and when a fixed tithe cannot be given for lambs, calves, goats, fleeces, geese or other similar things because of their small number, we have decided that the tithe shall be left to the custom of those places. Likewise we decree that if someone kills sheep after the feast of St Martin, or if sheep happen to die in some way or other, they shall not delay in paying the lawful tithe to the parish church, according to the honourable custom of the place. And if sheep from outside the parish are sheared within it, the tithe shall be given to the rector of the church there, unless it can be adequately demonstrated that the tithe has been paid elsewhere, so that it is lawful not to pay it in that place. But it is not our wish to derogate, by this our constitution, from any special custom of particular places which is lawfully prescribed, or from any composition or privilege.

3.[336] We will that the tithe of the fruits of the earth which do not belong to any particular parish, or which belonged to a parish whose church has disappeared by accident or old age, shall be assigned to some other church, at the discretion of the bishop in whose diocese that land is situated, unless the men of the parish whose church has vanished have been accustomed to attend divine service and to receive the sacraments and sacramentals in a particular church for a long time, that is, for ten years, in which case they shall be bound to pay such tithes there. Monks and others who have the privilege of not paying tithes, shall be bound to pay tithes on lands which they lease from others.

4.[337] Where parish churches are particularly burdened by concessions on tithes which by privileges or otherwise have been granted to religious houses or to someone else, because their rectors or vicars cannot be suitably maintained on their revenues and their due rights cannot easily be claimed, it shall be provided by the local ordinaries, and so ordained, that there shall be reserved for these rectors or vicars enough of the revenues of those parishes that they may have a reasonable maintenance and carry out their due obligations.

5.[338] All religious, both exempt and non-exempt, shall pay full tithes on lands and possessions already acquired or hereinafter to be acquired, to those churches to which by law, custom, prescription or composition the same possessions and lands are tithable, and they shall be compelled to do this by the local diocesans, unless they possess some special right or privilege.

6.[340] Compositio super decimis legitime facta per privilegium quod postea concessum fuerit, tolli non potest, nisi de illa nominatim in privilegio caveatur.

7.[341] Cum ad paroechiales ecclesias decima omnium rerum quae infra limites eiusdem proveniunt, de iure pertineat, statuimus quod si quis in aliena paroechia certum locum decimalem aut decimas certas legitime praescripserit, alium locum seu alias decimas quem sive quas non praescripsit ea ratione sibi vendicare non possit.

[83r] 8.[342] Qui vitulos vendit aut ad suum proprium usum occidit, decimam partem pretii, rectori pro dictis vitulis solvet. Qui vero vitulos nutrit, si septem habuerit, unum pro decimis solvet, et tres denarios a rectore recipiet, qui octo habet, unum solvet, et duos denarios recipiet, qui novem habet unum solvet et denarium recipiet, qui decem habet unum pro decima solvet, qui pauciores quam septem habet, pro quolibet unum denarium nomine decimarum solvet rectori, nisi rector donec habuerit decem velit expectare.

Sancimus praeterea quod quicunque decimas, oblationes, sive alia iura ecclesiastica, iuxta et secundum exigentia harum constitutionum nostrarum solvere recusant, per locorum ordinarios per censuras ecclesiasticas ad id compellantur, [83v] aut ad requisitionem ordinariorum per constabularios, ballivos, maiores, vicecomites et iustitiarios nostros ad id sine mora cogantur.

Quicunque malitiose impediunt, impedireve faciunt vel procurant, viros ecclesiasticos ad quos spectat perceptio decimarum vel eorum servitores quominus liberum ingressum et egressum in praedia et a praediis de quibus huiusmodi decimae proveniunt, habere possint, pro ipsis decimis colligendis, custodiendis, vel quo voluerint abducendis, quive ipsas decimas scienter tollerant a suis aut aliorum animalibus conteri et consinui, ipsarum collectionem et abductionem debito et conveniente tempore fieri prohibentes excommunicantur, et pro excommunicatis auctoritate ordinarii loci denuntientur, nec prius absolventur quam in ea parte condignam satisfactionem fecerint.

[84r] 9.[343] Si sacellum aut oratorium in aliqua paroechia sit, decimae, oblationes et cetera iura ecclesiastica, non oratorio aut sacello, sed paroechiali ecclesiae solum debent, nisi specialiter aliud legitime permissum fuerit. De oblationibus et aliis obventionibus ecclesiasticis, statuimus quod cuiusque loci consuetudo hactenus observata inconcusse teneatur et ad earum solutionem paroechiani ac alii qui eas solvere debeant per ordinarium loci debitis censuris cogantur.

---

[340]X, 3.30.3 (Fr, II, 556-7), a letter from Pope Hadrian IV to Gilbert Foliot, bishop of Hereford (1148-63) and the bishop of Worcester, who was probably John of Pagham (1151-7) but may have been Alfred (1158-60).
[341]X, 3.30.29 (Fr, II, 566), a decretal of Pope Innocent III, 17 May 1210.
[342]An order of Archbishop William Courtenay, 3 July 1389 (W: III, 205-7).
[343]1268/16 (PC, 766).

6.[339] A composition for tithes lawfully made cannot be taken away by a privilege granted later on, unless provision for it is expressly made in the privilege.[340]

7.[341] Since the tithe of everything which originates within the boundaries of the parish belongs to the parish church by law, we decree that if anyone has lawfully prescribed a certain place as tithable or certain tithes in another parish, he cannot on that basis claim for himself another place or other tithes which he has not prescribed.

8.[342] Whoever sells calves or kills them for his own use shall pay a tenth part of the price of the said calves to the rector. But whoever raises calves, if he has seven, shall pay one for his tithes, and shall receive three pence from the rector; whoever has eight, shall pay one and receive two pence; whoever has nine shall pay one and receive a penny, whoever has ten shall pay one for his tithe. Whoever has less than seven shall pay one penny for each of them to the rector as his tithe, unless the rector is willing to wait until he has ten.

Moreover, we order that whoever refuses to pay tithes, offerings or other ecclesiastical dues according to and in accordance with the demands of these our constitutions, shall be compelled to do so by ecclesiastical censures imposed by the local ordinaries, or at the request of the ordinaries, shall be compelled to it without delay by our constables, bailiffs, mayors, sheriffs and justices.

Whoever maliciously hinders, or causes or procures someone else to hinder the ecclesiastical agents to whom the collection of tithes pertains, or their servants, so that they do not have free entry and exit into and from the fields from which the tithes come, in order to collect, keep or divert the tithes wherever they want, or whoever knowingly allows the same tithes from their own animals or those of others to be miscalculated or falsified, prohibiting their collection and removal at the due and convenient time, shall be excommunicated and shall be denounced as excommunicate by the authority of the local ordinary, nor shall they be absolved until they have made appropriate satisfaction in that respect.

9.[343] If there is a chapel or oratory in any parish, the tithes, offerings and other ecclesiastical dues must be paid only to the parish church and not to the oratory or chapel, unless there is some other special arrangement which is lawful. As for offerings and other ecclesiastical revenues, we decree that the custom of each place which has been observed hitherto shall be maintained intact and that the parishioners and others who ought to pay them shall be forced to do so by the local ordinary, by means of the appropriate censures.

25. De decimis Londiniensibus.[344]

1. Ad cives tamen *et* /occupantes sive/ inhabitantes civitatem nostram London aut suburbia et libertates eiusdem has nostras constitutiones de solvendis decimis editas, extendi nolumus ullo pacto, eo quod apud illos solvendi decimas mos est, non pro quantitate personalis aut praedialis lucri sed iuxta et secundum quantitatem redditus quae [84v] infra eandem civitatem aut suburbia et libertates eiusdem solvunt. Idcirco statuimus et decernimus quod cives *et* /occupantes sive/ inhabitantes ipsi posthac nomine decimarum et pro decimis annuatim ad quattuor anni terminos, Paschae, Sancti Iohannis Baptistae,[345] Michaelis[346] et Natalis dum solvent modo et forma sequentibus; videlicet, quilibet civis *et* /occupans sive/ inhabitans huiusmodi solvens redditum decem solidorum, solvet rectori sive vicario infra cuius paroechiam praedium sive aedificium pro quo redditus ille solvitur situm est, pro decimis et nomine decimarum sedecim denarios et obolum unum; et qui solvit redditum viginti solidorum solvit pro decimis duos solidos et novem denarios, atque sic ascendendo pro singulis decem solidis pro redditu solutis solventur pro decimis sedecim denarii et obolus unus, volentes quod inhabitantes /sive per se vel alios occupantes/ propria aedificia sive praedia solvent pro decimis, iuxta ratum redditum pro quo aedificium sive praedium illud locari consuevit et possit, puta sedecim [85r] denarios et obolum unum pro singulis decem solidis huiusmodi redditus. Cives tamen et inhabitantes praedicti, talium paroechiarum et locorum dictae civitatis sive suburbium eiusdem, infra quadraginta annos ultra praeteritos, ultra octo denarios nomine decimarum pro singulis sex solidis et octo denariis pro redditu solutis solvere non solebant, ad aliquam maiorem summam pro decimis solvendam per has nostras constitutiones non teneri declaramus.

2. Nolumus insuper quod domini sive proprietarii praediorum sive aedificiorum infra dictam civitatem sive libertatem eiusdem vacantium quidcunque pro decimis solvant durante tempore vacationis eorundem.

3. Quoties vero contingit redditum alicuius aedificii sive praedii infra dictam civitatem aut libertatem, ratione structurae sive novae aedificationis augeri, toties volumus decimas [85v] secundum rationem augeri.

---

[344]This chapter contains the text of an agreement made by Archbishop Thomas Cranmer, Lord Chancellor Sir Thomas Audley, Bishop Stephen Gardiner of Winchester, Thomas Cromwell and the two chief justices, Sir John FitzJames and Sir Robert Norwich, early in 1534 and confimed by royal proclamation on 2 April in that year. See Hughes and Larkin, *Tudor royal proclamations*, I, 215-16, no. 145. It was confirmed by a second proclamation in February 1535 (*ibid.*, I, 224-5, no. 153) and reinforced by 27 Henry VIII, c. 21, 1535 (*S.R.* III, 552). The arrangement was enforced from Easter (28 March) 1535 and was subsequently modified by 37 Henry VIII, c. 12, 1546 (*S.R.* III, 998-9), which is followed by a decree of Archbishop Thomas Cranmer, dated 24 February 1546 (*S.R.* III, 999-1000). See J. A. F. Thomson, 'Tithe disputes in later medieval London', *English historical review*, LXXVIII (1963), 1-17.

[345]24 June.

[346]29 September.

25. Of London tithes.[344]

1. Nevertheless, we do not want these our constitutions, published concerning the payment of tithes, to apply in any way to the citizens, occupiers or inhabitants of our city of London, its suburbs or the liberties thereof, because among them the customary method of paying tithes does not depend on the amount of their personal or agricultural wealth, but goes according to the rents they pay within the said city, its suburbs and the liberties thereof. Therefore we decree and determine that those citizens, occupiers or inhabitants shall pay in the name of tithes and as tithes, annually at the four terms of the year, viz. Easter, St John the Baptist,[345] Michaelmas[346] and Christmas, according to the form following, that is: Any such citizen, occupier or inhabitant who pays a rent of ten shillings, shall pay to the rector or vicar within whose parish the field or building for which the rent is paid is situated, sixteen and a half pence as tithes and in the name of tithes, and whoever pays twenty shillings in rent shall pay two shillings and nine pence in tithes, and so on, so that for every ten shillings paid in rent there shall be sixteen and a half pence in tithes. We will that the inhabitants, either by themselves or through others who occupy their buildings or fields, shall pay in tithes according to the rent for which the building or field can be and usually is let, the sum of sixteen and a half pence for every ten shillings paid in rent. But we declare that those aforesaid citizens and inhabitants of the said parishes and places of the said city or the suburbs thereof, who for the past forty years have not been accustomed to paying more than eight pence in the name of tithes for every six shillings and eight pence paid in rent, shall not be obliged by these our constitutions to pay any higher sum in tithes.

2. Furthermore we do not want owners or proprietors of fields or buildings within the said city or the liberties thereof, which are vacant, to pay anything for them in tithes during the time of the vacancy thereof.

3. Whenever it happens that the rent of some building or field within the said city or liberty is increased because of improvements or new construction, it is our will that the tithes shall be increased proportionately.

4. Qui conducit aedificium sive praedium infra dictam civitatem sive libertatem pro certo redditu, et illud inter duos aut plures subtenentes dividens ab illis plus redditus recipit quam solvit, decimas solvere teneatur iuxta redditum quem recipit, nisi subtenentes illum velint exonerare, et electioni rectoris relinquimus, utrum a primo conducente aut subtenente decimas exigere velit.

5. Intuitu vero paupertatis decernimus, nihil esse debitum pro decimis aut nomine decimarum ab his, qui infra dictam civitatem suburbiave aut libertates eiusdem minus quam decem solidos pro redditu solvunt.

6. Ne tamen fraudi locum dare videamur, statuimus quod conducens aedificium sive praedium aliquod redditus decem solidos et ultra, si illud subtenentibus locans, inter subtenentes [86r] sic dividit quod eorum quidam aut nullus, decem solidos pro redditu solvit, decimas solvere teneatur, tantas quantas ante divisionem solvere consueverat. Pari modo statuentes quod conducens sive occupans plura aedificia pro quorum singulis minus quam decem solidi solvi consueverat pro redditu pro quibus ille iunctim decem solidos aut ultra nomine redditus solvit, decimas solvet, /ac/ *aut* si unicum esset beneficium.

7. Tenens sive occupans aedificium, cuius redditus decem solidos excedere consueverat, cuius partem alteri locat, pro qua minus quam decem solidos recipit, quo fiat etiam quod ille forsitan residuum solvit nomine redditus minus quam decem solidos, decimas integre solvere teneatur, ut ante divisionem solvi solebat. Si vero antiquum redditum aedificiorum ruina, infrequentia loci, aliove casu minui contingat decimas similiter minui aequum est.

[86v] 8. Ne fraus noceat ecclesiae aut alicui commodum ferat, statuimus quod domini aedificiorum sive praediorum partem redditus dolo remittentes, ut minus quam decem solidi pro redditu solvatur, quo fiet quod nihil possit pro decimis exigi, in eo casu integram solvent inhabitantes decimam, iuxta ratum redditum qui /decem annis ultra praeteritis/ solvi consueverat, eadem lege plectentes illos, qui pecuniam paratam recipiunt prae manibus ut minor solvatur redditus.

9. Statuimus insuper patrem familias, qui secundum formam praescriptam infra dictam civitatem vel suburbia et libertates eiusdem decimas solvit, ad aliquas alias decimas vel oblationes solvendas cogi non deberi. Matres vero familias, libros servientes et apprentitios omnes qui in festo Paschatis in specie panis corpus recipiunt Dominicum, ad solvendum duos denarios nomine oblationum tempore communionis astringimus.

[87r] 10. Pater quoque familias qui nihil solvit nomine decimarum eorum minus quam decem solidos solvit nomine redditus, duos denarios nomine oblationum tempore communionis solvere teneatur.

11.[347] Et quoniam laudabiles et honestas ecclesiarum consuetudines violari nolumus, idcirco statuendo decernimus quod candelae *sereae* /cereae/ in die

---

[347]C. 21 of the statutes for the diocese of Worcester (II), 1229 (PC, 174).

4. Whoever lets a building or a field within the said city or liberty for a certain rent, and after dividing it between two or more subtenants, receives more in rent than he pays, shall be obliged to pay tithes according to the rent which he receives, unless the subtenants agree to pay it for him, and we leave it to the choice of the rector, whether he wishes to demand tithes from the primary lessee or a subtenant.

5. But in cases of poverty we decree that nothing is owed in tithes or in the name of tithes by those who, within the said city, the suburbs or liberties thereof, pay less than ten shillings in rent.

6. Nevertheless, in order not to appear to be giving opportunity for fraud, we decree that the one who leases any building or field of which the rent is ten shillings or more, if he lets it to subtenants, and divides it among the subtenants in such a way that some of them, or even none of them, pays as much as ten shillings in rent, then he shall be required to pay tithes in the amount that he would ordinarily have paid before the property was divided. Likewise we decree that the lessee or occupier of several buildings, for each of which less than ten shillings has ordinarily been paid in rent, but for which, taken together, he pays ten shillings or more in rent, shall pay tithes as if they were all one property.

7. The tenant or occupier of a building whose rent normally exceeds ten shillings, who lets a part of it to someone else, for which he receives less than ten shillings, with the result that he perhaps pays the remainder as a rent of less than ten shillings, shall be obliged to pay tithes in full, as he used to do before the division of the property. But if it happens that the former rent of the buildings has decreased because of ruin, abandonment or some other cause, it is fair for the tithes to be reduced accordingly.

8. In order that fraud may not harm the church or bring benefit to anyone, we decree that the owners of buildings or fields who cheat by remitting a part of the rent, so that less than ten shillings is paid in rent, with the result that nothing can be charged for tithes, in that case the inhabitants shall pay the whole tithe in proportion to the rent which has normally been paid for the preceding ten years, punishing by the same law those who take cash in hand so that a lower rent may be paid.

9. In addition we decree that the father of a household, who pays his tithes according to the prescribed form within the said city or suburbs and the liberties thereof, must not be forced to pay any other tithes or offerings. But we constrain mothers of families, free servants and all apprentices who receive the Lord's body in the form of bread on the feast of Easter, to pay two pence in the name of offerings at the time of communion.

10. Also, the father of a household who pays nothing in tithes, because he pays less than ten shillings in rent, shall be obliged to pay two pence in the name of offerings at the time of communion.

11.[347] And because it is not our wish that the laudable and honourable customs of churches should be violated, we therefore decree by statute that wax

purificationis Virginis deiparae³⁴⁸ /et panni chrismales in purificationibus mulierum/ iuxta et secundum antiquam consuetudinem in dicta civitate hactenus usitatam offerantur, et ad commodum et usum rectoris convertantur.

12. Oblationes quoque in exequiis mortuorum, solemnizationeve matrimoniorum aut purificationibus mulierum aut aliis de causis sponte factas, ad rectorem ecclesiae in qua fiunt pertinere volumus, nisi eas consensu aliter fieri conventum sit. Pro officio mortuorum ultra sex denarios pro solemnizatione matrimonii ultra sex denarios ad usum rectoris vel curati exigi prohibemus.

13. Duos tamen ramos cereos cum funere ad summum altare [87v] offerri consuetos, ad rectorem ecclesiae in qua offeruntur pertinere declaramus.

14. Praeter et ultra superius narrato nomine decimarum aut oblationum, cives et inhabitantes dictam civitatem London suburbiave et libertates eiusdem nihil solvere compellantur, ad quae omnia et singula superius nominata et secundum modum et formam praedictam solvenda, cives et inhabitantes huiusmodi per iudices ecclesiasticos in ea parte competentes per censuras ecclesiasticas cogentur et compellantur, atque ad id per iudices ecclesiasticos requisiti. Maior, vicecomites et aldermanni dictae civitatis pro tempore existentes, eosdem cives et inhabitantes ad huiusmodi decimas et oblationes modo et forma praenarratis solvendas cogere et compellere teneantur.

[88r] **26. De leprosis.**

1.³⁴⁹ **Cum tot leprosi simul sub communi vita fuerint congregati, quod ecclesiam cum coemeterio sibi constituere et proprio gaudere valeant presbytero, sine contradictione aliqua haec habere permittantur, ita tamen ut iniuriosi paroechialibus ecclesiis in iure paroechiali nequaquam existant. Quod enim eis pietate conceditur, ad aliorum iniuriam nolumus redundare. Statuimus etiam ut de hortis, et nutrimentis animalium suorum quae in communi possident decimas tribuere non cogantur.**

27. De mortuariis.

1.³⁵⁰ Mortuaria secundum ordinationem, vim et effectum statuti in parliamento nostro editi solvantur, et qui ea cum debeant solvere iniuste recusant, ordinarii auctoritate debite compellantur.

---

³⁴⁸2 February. Popularly known as Candlemas.
³⁴⁹X, 3.48.2 (Fr, II, 652), c. 23 of Lateran III, 1179 (*C.O.D.*, 222-3). Freedom from tithe was granted to lepers by a bull of Pope Nicholas IV (1288-92), dated 20 March 1291 (W, II, 180-3).
³⁵⁰21 Henry VIII, c. 6, 1529 (*S.R.*, III, 288-9).

candles on the day of the purification of the Virgin Mother of God[348] and the chrism cloths used hitherto in the purification of women according to and following ancient custom in the said city, shall be turned over for the benefit and use of the rector.

12. Also it is our will that offerings voluntarily made at funerals of the dead, or at the solemnization of marriages, or at the purifications of women, or for other reasons, shall belong to the rector of the church in which they are made, unless it is agreed that something else should be done with them. We forbid more than six pence to be charged, for the use of the rector or curate, for a funeral service or more than six pence to be charged for the solemnization of matrimony.

13. We declare that the two wax branches which are customarily offered on the high altar at a funeral shall belong to the rector of the church in which they are offered.

14. Above and beyond the above named tithes and offerings, the citizens and inhabitants of the said city of London, its suburbs and the liberties thereof, shall not be obliged to pay anything. But the said citizens and inhabitants shall be forced and compelled by ecclesiastical judges competent in this matter, to pay all and singular the tithes mentioned above according to the prescribed method and form, subject to the censures of the church, and they shall be required to do this by the ecclesiastical judges. The mayor, sheriffs, and aldermen of the said city for the time being, shall be obliged to force and compel those citizens and inhabitants to pay such tithes and offerings in the manner and form spelled out above.

26. Of lepers.

1.[349] **When enough lepers are gathered together in community that they can form their own church with a cemetery and enjoy their own priest, they shall be permitted to have these things without any objection, as long as they are in no way detrimental to parish churches in matters of parish law. For we do not want what is granted to them out of kindness to redound to the hurt of others. Furthermore we decree that they shall not be forced to pay tithes on the grasses and animal feeds which they possess in common.**

27. Of mortuaries.

1.[350] Mortuaries are to be paid according to the regulation, force and effect of the statute passed in our parliament, and those who wrongly refuse to pay them shall be duly compelled to do so by the authority of the ordinary.

[88v] **28. De pensionibus.**

1.[351] Quicunque pensionem aut portionem ecclesiasticam de consuetudine, compositione aut alias debitam, *an...* ac solvi consuetam ei cui debet iniuste solvere recusaverit per locorum ordinarios aut alios iudices ecclesiasticos in ea parte competentes eandem solvere compellantur, huiusmodi vero pensione sive portione de novo constitui aut antiquitus constituta nomine augeri aut tolli sine auctoritate ordinaria ac consensu patroni et incumbentis prohibemus.

2.[352] Quoties pensionem personalem alicui beneficio suo cedenti per ordinarium loci iuxta formam statuti in parliamento nostro editi[353] ex causis eum moventibus de consensu patroni et incumbentis, ad terminum vitae cedentis assignari contigerit, eam de fructibus ecclesiae resignatae iuxta formam decreti per ordinarium in ea parte interpositi quicunque huiusmodi beneficium possidet solvere compellatur.

*3.[354] Si vero sine consensu [89r] patroni huiusmodi pensio per ordinarium ex consensu incumbentis assignata fuerit, mortuo aut cedente vel privato ipso incumbente, liberam ecclesiam esse a solutione huiusmodi pensionis volumus.

*4.[355] Huiusmodi tamen pensiones personales quacunque auctoritate hactenus constitutas, aut imposterum constituendas, eo anno quo primi fructus iuxta statuta nostra solvuntur, incumbens solvere minime teneatur.

5.[356] Si personae cum ad ecclesiarum regimen vocantur ad solvendum vel augendum censum, qui de iure solvi aut augeri non debet iuramentum praestiterint ab huiusmodi iuramento, imposita illis prius congrua paenitentia absolvantur, ac ab illicita praestatione omnino liberentur.

6.[357] Qui ecclesias quas tenent ea ratione constituunt censuales, ut post decessum eorum eaedem ecclesiae ad [89v] amicos vel consanguineos suos transferantur, propter hoc ab eisdem ecclesiis removeantur.

29. De procurat{*ori*}/ion/ibus.

1.[358] Procurationes et synodaticae cathedraticae, archiepiscopis, episcopis, archidiaconis aut aliis quibus de iure, consuetudine seu compositione, ratione

---

[351]L, 3.23.10, c. 1 of Archbishop Simon Islip, 1329; L, 3.23.11, c. 1 of Archbishop Simon Sudbury, 1378.
[352]L, 3.7.1, gloss on *de consensu*.
[353]26 Henry VIII, c. 3, s. 19, 1534 (*S.R.*, III, 493-9).
[354]L, 3.7.1, gloss on *beneficii*.
[355]This canon covers a loophole left (unintentionally ?) by 26 Henry VIII, c. 3, 1534 (*S.R.*, III, 493-9). The matter was rectified by 27 Henry VIII, c. 8, 1536 (*S.R.*, III, 537-8).
[356]X, 3.39.15 (Fr, II, 626), a decretal of Pope Clement III (1187-91).
[357]X, 3.39.11 (Fr, II, 624), a letter of Pope Alexander III (1159-81) to the archbishop of Canterbury and his suffragans.
[358]X, 3.39.23 (Fr, II, 632), c. 33 of Lateran IV, 1215 (*C.O.D.*, 250); also VI, 3.20.3 (Fr, II, 1057-8), a decretal of Pope Boniface VIII (1294-1303).

28. Of pensions.

1.[351] Anyone who wrongly refuses to pay an ecclesiastical pension or portion due by custom or composition or otherwise due and normally paid to the person to whom he owes it, shall be obliged to pay the same by the local ordinaries or other ecclesiastical judges competent in that respect, and we forbid any like pension or portion to be newly created, or if it already exists, to be augmented or reduced, without the ordinary's authority and the agreement of the patron and the incumbent.

2.[352] Whenever it happens that a personal pension is assigned to someone for life, on the surrender of his benefice, by the local ordinary, according to the form of the statute passed in our parliament,[353] for reasons moving him, with the agreement of the patron and incumbent, whoever possesses the said benefice shall be compelled to pay it out of the fruits of the church resigned, according to the form of the decree laid down in this respect by the ordinary.

*3.[354] But if the said pension is appointed by the ordinary with the agreement of the incumbent, but without the agreement of the patron, when that incumbent has died, resigned or been deprived, it is our will that the church shall be freed from having to pay the said pension.

*4.[355] The incumbent shall not be obliged to pay personal pensions of this kind, by whatever authority they are appointed or shall hereinafter be appointed, in the same year in which the first fruits are paid, according to our statutes.

5.[356] If parsons, when they are called to govern a church, swear an oath that they will pay or increase a rate which by law ought not to be paid or increased, they shall first be absolved and an appropriate penance imposed on them, and shall in no way be liable to keep that oath or make that unlawful payment.

6.[357] Whoever makes the churches which they hold rateable in such a way that, after their death, the same churches may be transferred to their friends or relatives, shall on that account be removed from the same churches.

29. Of procurations.

1.[358] It is our will and command that procurations and diocesan quotas, which by right, custom or composition, are normally paid in cash to archbishops, bishops,

visitationis, aut alia quarumque legitima de causa in pecunia solvi consuetae, deinceps sub censuris ecclesiasticis dari, solvi, praestari temporibus debitis volumus et mandamus.

2.[359] Cum visitationis officium exercentes non quae sua sunt, sed quae Iesu Christi quaerere debeant, statuimus ut cum archiepiscopus provinciam suam aut episcopus dioecesim suam, archidiaconusque in suis generalibus capitulis seu alii qui de iure, consuetudine, compositione aur privilegio loca suae iurisdictioni subiecta visitant, praedicationi Verbi Dei exhortationi, [90r] correctioni et reformationi diligenter vacent, /et/ de peccatis a clero aut populo illic commissis diligenter secundum ordinem constitutionum nostrarum inquirent, et comperta severiter pro auctoritate sua vindicare studeant.

Inquirant praeterea vistatores praedicti, utrum presbyteri et alii viri ecclesiastici ac eorum ministri in praedicatione Verbi Dei, administratione sacramentorum ac aliis quibuscunque quae ad eorum q... officia pertineant diligentes fuerint, et si aliquos in ea parte culpabiles invenerint, debite ac indilate eos corrigant. De reparatione praeterea fabricae ecclesiarum et cancellarum, de libris, de vestimentis, calicibus, et ornamentis, ac rebus aliis quae ad divina officia de iure aut consuetudine requiruntur, diligentem adhibeant considerationem et si aliquos [90v] invenerint defectus circa huiusmodi, certum praefigant terminum, infra quem emendentur vel suppleantur, indicta e... poena etiam pecuniaria pro arbitrio iudicis ad pios usus amplicanda, in eos qui eorum in hoc mandatis non paruerint.

3.[360] Provincias, dioeceses, archidiaconatus et loca alia visitari solita, per archiepiscopos, episcopos, archidiaconos et alios, ad quos visitandi ius pertinet, visitari volumus et mandamus, temporibus illis quibus visitationes ipsae fieri consueverant, iuxta et secundum consuetudines laudabiles hactenus in ea parte con/ob/servatas.

4.[361] Contra visitationes ordinariorum quorumcunque procurationesve inde debitas, nullam cuiuiscunque generis praescriptionem admitti volumus, statuentes insuper quod archiepiscopus sive episcopus ultra duos dies et tres [91r] noctes in uno monasterio, unius vistitationis iure non permaneat et, ne tunc monasterio onerosus existat, praecipimus ut archiepiscopus non ultra viginti, episcopus vero non ultra duodecim sumptibus monasterii comitatus existat nec procurationes nisi consuetas etiam sponte oblatas per se aut suos recipiat, nec quicquam inter ministros suos distribui permittat.

---

[359]VI, 3.20.3 (Fr, II, 1057-8), a decretal of Pope Boniface VIII.
[360]Cf. *e.g.* X, 1.23.6 (Fr, II, 151), a decretal of Pope Alexander III (1159-81) to the bishop of Coventry and the abbot of Chester; X, 1.31.15 (Fr, II, 192), c. 10 of Lateran IV, 1215 (*C.O.D.*, 239-40); X, 3.39.23 (Fr, II, 632), c. 33 of Lateran IV, 1215 (*C.O.D.*, 250).
[361]1268/18 (PC, 767-8); cf. c. 7 of Lateran IV, 1215 (*C.O.D.*, 237).

archdeacons or others, by reason of visitation or for some other lawful cause shall from henceforth be given, paid and pledged at the proper time, subject to the censures of the church.

2.[359] Since those who exercise the office of visitation ought to seek not their own, but the things of Jesus Christ, we decree that when an archbishop visits his province or a bishop his diocese, or an archdeacon in his general chapters, or others who by right, custom, composition or privilege visit places subject to their jurisdiction, they shall diligently make time for the preaching of the Word of God, for correction, exhortation and reformation, and shall make diligent inquiry concerning the sins of the clergy or the people committed to them, according to the order of our constitutions, and shall do all in their power to put right what they have discovered.

Moreover the aforesaid visitors shall make inquiry as to whether the priests and other ecclesiastical men and their servants are diligent in the preaching of the Word of God, in the administration of the sacraments and in the other things which pertain to their offices, and if they find that any of them are guilty in this respect, they shall duly and without delay correct them. Moreover they shall give diligent consideration to the repair of the fabric of the churches and chancels, to the books, the vestments, the chalices, the ornaments and the other things which, by law or custom, are required for the divine offices, and if they find any defects in this respect they shall set a certain date by which these defects must be corrected and put right, with a stated penalty which shall also be financial and applied to pious uses at the discretion of the judge, for those who do not obey them in these commands.

3.[360] We will and command that the provinces, dioceses, archdeaconries and other places habitually visited by archbishops, bishops, archdeacons and others to whom the right of visitation belongs, shall be visited at the times when those visitations customarily take place, according to and following the laudable customs hitherto observed in that respect.

4.[361] We will that no prescription of any kind shall be allowed against the visitations of any ordinaries or the procurations which they are owed, and we furthermore decree that an archbishop or bishop shall not stay more that two days and three nights in any one monastery by right of a single visitation; and in order that he may not be burdensome to the monastery on that occasion, we decree that an archbishop shall not maintain a retinue of more than twenty, or a bishop of more than twelve, at the expense of the monastery, nor shall he receive for himself or for his retinue any procurations other than the usual ones, or ones voluntarily offered, nor shall he allow anything to be distributed among his servants.

30. De dilapidatione.

1.[362] Statuimus atque praecipimus ut universi clerici suorum beneficiorum domos et cetera aedificia prout indiguerint reficere studebant conde/ce/nter ad quod per suos episcopos vel archidiaconos sollicite moneantur. Si quis post episcopi aut archidiaconi sui monitionem infra legitimum tempus arbitrio eorum moderando id facere cessaveri{n}t, extunc episcopus aut archidiaconus, *p...* ipsius clerici sumptibus id fieri faciat diligenter, de fructibus ipsius ecclesiae vel beneficii quos ad effectum praedictum sequestrari valeant [91v] praesentis auctoritate statuti tantum accipi faciens quantum ad refectionem huiusmodi peragendam cum necessariis expensis facto intuitu ipsius sequestrationis. Cancellas etiam ecclesiae per eos qui ad hoc tenentur refici faciant prout superius est expressum. Archiepiscopos vero episcopos ac alios inferiores praelatos domos ac aedificia sua et in statu suo conservare ac tenere sub indignatione nostra praecipimus, et episcopi ea reficiant, quae refectionem noverint indigere. Ad aedificationem et reparationem unius ecclesiae, ad clausuram coemeterii, ad inveniendum et reparandum libros, calices, vestimenta et cetera ornamenta ecclesiastica aut res alias quascunque quae in administratione sacramentorum aut celebratione divinorum necessarie decentes vel convenientes sunt et usitatas, patroni singularum ecclesiarum regni et dominiorum nostrorum teneantur, et per ordinarios locorum ad praedicta debitis censuris compellantur, nisi de consuetudine aut compositione praedicta onera ad alios pertinere docere possunt. Aedificatio autem et reparatio cancelli [92r] tam interius quam exterius ad rectores ecclesiarum pertineat, nisi rector probare potest consuetudine aut compositione huiusmodi onus ad alios spectare, ut sic semper hi ad quos pertinet reparationem facere in omnibus praedictis suis sumptibus per locorum ordinarios ad id debite compellantur.

2.[363] Si rector vel vicarius alicuius ecclesiae, aut alia quaecunque ecclesiastica persona, quae praebendam, liberam capellam, hospitale, collegium, aut aliud quodcunque beneficium ecclesiasticum possidet, decedens aut aliter a beneficio suo huiusmodi recedens seu amotus, cancellum, domos, aut aedificia quaecunque ad beneficium suum huiusmodi pertinentia ad quae aedificanda et reparanda dum vixerit tenebatur, diruta relinquerit vel ruinosa, tunc viri fide digni arbitrio ordinarii munerandi et eligendi in forma iuris iurati (ipso cuius interest personaliter si appraehendi poterit; alioquin per publicae citationis edictum in illa ecclesia de cuius aedificiorum ruina tractatur, [92v] ad hoc primitus vocato), integram et veram aestimationem defectuum et ruinae, in domibus et aliis ad beneficia huiusmodi spectantibus diligenter investigent ac iudici in ea parte procedenti fideliter repraesentent, ipseque iudex tamen de bonis dicti decedentis aut aliter tradentis vel amoti per censuras ecclesiasticas solvi faciat, quantum

---

[362] 1268/17 (PC, 766-7).
[363] L, 3.27.1, c. 68 of the statutes of Richard Poore for the diocese of Salisbury, *c.* 1217-19 (PC, 82).

30. Of dilapidation.

1.[362] We decree and order that all clergy shall take appropriate care to repair their houses and other buildings in so far as they require it, and that they shall be carefully warned of this by their bishops and archdeacons. If after being warned by his bishop or archdeacon, someone fails to do this within the lawful time appointed by them, then the bishop or archdeacon shall take care to have it done at the expense of that clergyman, out of the fruits of that church or benefice which may be sequestered for the aforesaid purpose, using the authority of the present statute to have as much taken as is required for carrying out the repairs, with all necessary expenses included in the reckoning made of the said sequestration. They shall also have the chancels of the church repaired by those who are obliged to do that, as is stated above. And we order archbishops and bishops and other inferior prelates to keep and maintain their houses and buildings in their proper state, subject to our displeasure, and the bishops shall rebuild what they know requires rebuilding. And the patrons of each church in our kingdom and dominions shall be responsible for the construction and repair of their own church, for fencing the churchyard, for finding and repairing books, chalices, vestments and other ecclesiastical ornaments, or anything else which is of necessity proper, convenient and customary in the administration of the sacraments or in the celebration of divine service, and shall be compelled by the local ordinaries to accomplish the aforesaid by due censures, unless by custom or composition, they can show that the aforesaid burdens belong to others. But the construction and repair of the chancel, both inside and outside, shall belong to the rectors of the churches, unless the rector can prove that that burden belongs to others by custom or composition, so that those whose responsibility it is to do repairs in all the aforesaid shall be duly compelled by the local ordinaries to do them at their own expense.

2.[363] If the rector or vicar of any church, or any other ecclesiastical person, who possesses a prebend, free chapel, hospital, college or any other ecclesiastical benefice, shall die or otherwise depart or be removed from his benefice, and shall leave the chancel, houses or other buildings belonging to the said benefice, for whose construction and repair he was responsible during his lifetime, destroyed or in ruins, then trustworthy men shall be appointed and chosen at the discretion of the ordinary and sworn in the form of the law (after first summoning the man who is directly interested in the matter, if he can be found; otherwise by the issuing of a public citation in that church, the ruin of whose buildings is being dealt with), who shall diligently assess the full and true estimate of the defects and ruin in the houses and other things belonging to the said benefices, and proceeding diligently, they shall report to the judge in charge of the matter, and the judge himself shall order it to be paid, subject to ecclesiastical censures, out of the goods of the said [clergyman] deceased, or otherwise departed or removed,

sufficiat ad reparandum et supplendum ipsos defectus ac in reparationem ipsorum defectuum converti faciat infra terminum competentem ipsius arbitrio moderando.

31. De testamentis.

1.[364] Insinuationes ac approbationes testamentorum et bonorum decedentium ab intestato administrationis commissionem quorumcunque ad ordinarium loci pertinere volumus, nisi ad alios per compositionem, privilegium, aut legitime praescriptam consuetudinem, pertinere dinoscitur, salva semper praerogativa archiepiscoporum hactenus usitata, cui per praemissa nolumus in aliquo derogari.

2.[365] Testamenta quae coram presbytero et tribus vel duabus aliis personis idoneis, aut absente presbytero, coram tribus ad minus fide dignis [93r] fide dignis [*sic*] facta sunt firma decernimus permanere sub excommunicationis poena prohibentes ne quisquam audeat huiusmodi testamenta sic probata (si alias sunt legitima) rescindere, aut ne debite exequantur quovismodo impedire.

3.[366] Minoribus tamen quattuordecim annis, furiosis et dementibus testandi adimimus potestatem;[367] testamentum etiam propria manu decedentis scriptum vel subscriptum et suo sigillo sigillatum, postquam illud propria manu defuncti scriptum vel subscriptum esse, cum depositionibus testium qui illud testamentum saltem clausum, viderint et sigillaverint vel subscripserint[368] probatum sit, nolumus impugnari.

4.[369] Quae specialiter ex decedentis testamentis sunt legata, vel ut in pios usus convertantur quovismodo relicta, per locorum ordinarios executores testamentorum huiusmodi, secundum defuncti voluntatem, eadem solvere et expendere /cogi/ volumus. Ac omnes denique executores [93v] post susceptum onus executionis per dioecesanum cogi debent testatoris explere ultimam voluntatem.

5.[370] Bona eorum qui intestati moriuntur quia aut nullum testamentum fecerint, aut nullum executorem nominaverint, aut qui nominatus est executionis onus in se assumere recusat, aut quod factum est testamentum ex defectu probationum aut aliis legitimis causis per ordinarios locorum approbatum non fuerit, secundum dispositionem statutorum in parliamento nostro editorum[371]

---

[364]Cc. 19-22 of the provincial council held by Archbishop Boniface at Lambeth, 13 May 1261 (PC, 681-2). Their provisions were restated by Archbishop John Stratford in c. 7 of 1342 (L, 3.13.5).

[365]X, 3.26.10 (Fr, II, 541), a decretal of Pope Alexander III (1159-81).

[366]Justinian, *Inst.*, 2.12; *Dig.*, 28.1.5, originally Ulpian, *Ad Sabinum*, 6.

[367]*Dig.*, 28.1.17, originally Paulus, *Sententiae*, 3.

[368]*Dig.*, 28.1.22, originally Ulpian, *Ad edictum*, 39.

[369]X, 3.26.17 (Fr, II, 545), a decretal of Pope Gregory IX, 1234.

[370]21 Henry VIII, c. 5, s. 2, 1529 (*S.R.*, III, 285-8).

[371]21 Henry VIII, c. 4 (*S.R.*, III, 285) and ibid., c. 5 (*S.R.*, 285-8).

as much as is necessary for repairing and making up the defects, and he shall order the said funds to be applied to the repair of those defects within a reasonable time, at the discretion of the judge himself.

31. Of testaments.

1.[364] It is our will that the validations and probations of testaments, and the commission of administration of the goods of whoever dies intestate, shall belong to the local ordinary, unless it is recognized that they belong to others by composition, privilege or lawfully prescribed custom, saving always the prerogative of the archbishops which has been customary hitherto, which we do not want to see restricted in any way by the foregoing.

2.[365] Testaments which have been made in front of a priest and three or two other suitable persons, or in the absence of a priest, in front of at least three trustworthy persons, we decree shall stand firm, forbidding under pain of excommunication that anyone should dare to withdraw such testaments so proved (if they are otherwise lawful) or in some way hinder them from being duly executed.

3.[366] We withhold the power of making a testament from minors under the age of fourteen years,[367] from the mad and from the insane, but we do not want a testament which has been written in the very hand of the deceased or signed and sealed with his seal, to be contested after it has been written in the very hand of the deceased or signed, and proved by the depositions of witnesses who have seen, sealed and signed the testament once it was closed.[368]

4.[369] What has been specially bequeathed in the testaments of the deceased, or left in order that it might be turned over to pious uses, it is our will that the executors of such testaments shall be obliged by the local ordinaries to pay and disburse these things according to the will of the deceased. And all executors, after assuming the burden of execution, must be obliged by the diocesan to carry out the last will of the testator.

5.[370] The goods of those who die intestate either because they have not made a testament, or because they have not named an executor, or because the person nominated refuses to take on the burden of execution, or because the testament which has been made has not been proved by the local ordinaries because of some defect of proof or for other lawful reasons, shall be administered according to the provision of the statutes passed in our parliament,[371] at the discretion of the

arbitrio ordinarii administrentur, recepta prius ab illis quibus committitur huiusmodi administratio sufficiente securitate quod fideliter huiusmodi bona administrabunt ac ordinarium adversus omnes indemnem conservabunt.

6.[372] Si executores testamentorum voluntates infra annum post legitimam monitionem ab ordinario illis factam, quam tempore probati testamenti fieri volumus implere neglexerint, ordinarius eosdem ad debitas implendas ipsas defunctorum voluntates per ecclesiasticas censuras cogat, eosque legato aut alio quocunque emolumento [94r] a testatore eisdem hoc nomine relicto propter eorum circa executionem negligentiam privet.

7.[373] Religiosus executor aut bonorum administrator sive distributor ab aliquo in sua voluntate ultima deputatus, non potest (cum velle aut nolle non habeat) huiusmodi officium suscipere vel exequi **nisi[374] a superiore sua petita super hoc licentia et obtenta, in quo casu etiam eius superior cavere debet pro suo religioso quod sufficienter exequetur administrabit** sive distribuet bona huiusmodi, **et fideliter ac integre reddat rationem de residuis, si quae fuerint et quod de damnis quae per ipsum emerserint, absque difficultate qualibet loci ordinario rendebit.**

8.[375] **Sane pluribus a testatore simpliciter executoribus** *deputis* **deputatis, uno eorum mortuo vel in remoto agente, aut onus executionis in se assumere forte nolens, ne voluntatem testatoris impedire vel nimium deferri contingat, poterit alius, (nisi testator aliud expresserit) officium executionis suscipere** [94v] **et illud libere adimplere.**

9.[376] Statuimus quod executores omnes testamentorum, ac administratores bonorum ab intestato decendente, licet tales sint, qui quocunque privilegio aut ordinatione a iurisdictione ordinarii loci, coram quo approbata fuerint huiusmodi testamenta, sive per quem commissa fuerit administratio bonorum, exempti sunt, ipsi tamen huiusmodi ordinario debitam de executione seu administratione sua reddere rationem, ac de ea eidem reddere teneantur, non obstante ullo suo privilegio, cui remunerare illos, quo ad hunc effectum volumus ante susceptam executionem seu administrationem huiusmodi.

10.[377] Cum in testamento executor nominatus non fuerit aut testamentum legitime factum devenerit ad causam intestati ex eo quod executores in eo nominati onus executionis eiusdem in se assumere nolunt, volumus ut ordinarius in commissione administrationis bonorum faciat ut huiusmodi testamentum pro facultatibus defuncti per [95r] administratores impleatur.

[372]X, 3.26.3 (Fr, II, 539), a decretal of Pope Gregory I (590-604), *Reg.*, 4.8; X, 3.26.6 (Fr, II, 540), perhaps from an unidentified council of Mainz.
[373]VI, 3.11.2 (Fr, II, 1045), a decretal of Pope Boniface VIII (1294-1303).
[374]L, 3.13.3, originally canon 21 of the council of Lambeth, 1281.
[375]VI, 3.11.2 (Fr, II, 1045), a decretal of Pope Boniface VIII.
[376]*Clem.*, 3.6.1 (Fr, II, 1161), a decretal of Pope Clement V (1305-14) published at the council of Vienne, 1311-12.
[377]21 Henry VIII, c. 5, s. 2, 1529 (*S.R.*, III, 285-8).

ordinary, sufficient surety having first been received from those to whom such administration is entrusted, that they will faithfully administer such goods and ensure that the ordinary is not made liable to anyone.

6.[372] If the executors of the testaments fail to fulfil the wishes [of the deceased] within a year after they have been lawfully directed [to do so] by the ordinary, which we desire shall be done at the time when the testament is proved, the ordinary shall oblige them to fulfil the said wishes of the deceased as they are bound to, and shall deprive them of whatever remuneration has been left to them by the testator for the said purpose, on account of their negligence in executing the testament.

7.[373] If the executor or administrator or distributor of goods appointed by someone in his last will is a monk, he cannot undertake this duty or execute the will (since it is not in his power to decide one way or the other) **unless**[374] **he asks for and obtains the permission of his superior to do this, in which case his superior must ensure that his monk will adequately execute, administer** or distribute the said goods, **and faithfully and fully render account of the remainder, if there is any, and he shall report whatever costs he has incurred, without any hesitation, to the local ordinary.**

8.[375] **And if there are several executors clearly appointed by the testator, and one of them has died or is far away, or is unwilling to take on the burden of execution, in order not to hinder the will of the testator or delay it too long, someone else (unless the testator has indicated otherwise) may undertake the duty of execution and fulfil it with complete freedom.**

9.[376] We decree that all executors of testaments and administrators of the goods of someone dying intestate, even if they are such as are exempted, by some privilege or provision, from the jurisdiction of the local ordinary before whom the said testaments have been proved, or by whom the administration of the goods was assigned, shall nevertheless be obliged to give due account of their execution or administration to the said ordinary, and to give it to him, notwithstanding any privilege he may have rewarded them with, and it is our will that the ordinary shall inform them of this before they undertake such execution or administration.

10.[377] When no executor has been named, or a lawfully made testament turns into a case of intestacy because the executors named in it do not want to take on the burden of execution, it is our will that the ordinary shall so act, in entrusting the administration of the goods to others, that the said will may be fulfilled by the administrators according to the means of the deceased.

11.[378] Si vero bonorum administratio, ex eo quod defunctus nullum testamentum condidit alicui commissa fuerit, volumus quod solutis debitis funeralibus et aliis ordinariis oneribus, quicquid bonorum dicti defuncti reliquum fuerit, iuxta et secundum arbitrium ac discretionem ordinarii, inter uxorem et liberos ac propinquiores consanguineos dicti defuncti qui maxime egent, si qui extant, alioqui{n} in pios usus distribuatur. Volumus praeterea quod executores testamentorum et administratores bonorum defuncti si inventarium iuxta formam ac ordinationem statutorum nostrorum inde editorum[379] fecerint, ultra vires huiusmodi inventarii minime onerentur.

12.[380] Executores in testamento nominati, nisi vocati et moniti per ordinarium, testamenti executionem infra tempus per eum assignatum, aut cum non fuerint vocati et moniti infra annum a die obitus testatoris (legitimo cessante impedimento) in se [95v] assumpserint, tunc ab executione ac omni commodo huiusmodi testamenti per ipsum ordinarium excludantur, ac bona defuncti quae ad eos pervenerint restituere compellantur, et bonorum administratio iuxta statuta nostra per eundem iudicem committatur.

13.[381] Cum plures fuerint unius testamenti executores, volumus quod illi omnes coram iudice qu{ae/i} dictum testamentum approbavit pro legatis et aliis oneribus eis ratione dicti testamenti incumbentibus, licet in diversis dioecesibus sive iurisdictionibus resideant conveniri valeant, et per eundem iudicem ad faciendum quod /causa/ exigat et iustitia suadet coartari.

14.[382] Executores vero et administratores sicut aequaliter onerantur, sic volumus inter eos defunctorum bona aequaliter distribuere et ad id per ordinarium cogi et compelli, nisi aliter inter eos convenerit, aut aliter intuitu liberorum aut relicta dicti defuncti fieri videatur ordinatio.

[96r] 15.[383] Ordinarii locorum et alii ad quos testamentorum insinuatio et approbatio aut bonorum ab intestato defuncto administrationis commissio pertinere dinoscitur, executores et administratores quoscunque, lapso anno a tempore approbati testamenti aut commissae administrationis, ad computum administrationis suae reddendum vocare et cogere valeant et possunt, quo quidem computo plene et fideliter reddito executores et administratores huiusmodi ab ulteriore computi redditione liberentur et exonerentur (ceterum si super visum computi huiusmodi compertum fuerit, aliquid de bonis defuncti, debite non esse administratum, id iuxta dicti defuncti voluntatem, ubi de eo constiterit, alioquin ad mandatum et moderamen iudicis in ea parte, per eundem executorem sive administratorem in pios usus distribuatur).

---

[378]*Ibid.*
[379]L, 3.13.5, originally c. 7 Archbishop John Stratford, 1342.
[380]X, 3.26.3 (Fr, II, 539), a decretal of Pope Gregory I (590-604), *Reg.*, 4.8.
[381]L, 3.13.5, gloss on *laicis*; 1268/15, gloss on *fidem.*
[382]L, 3.13.5, gloss on *propriis suis bonis*; 1268/15, gloss on *libertatem.*
[383]Cf. 13 Edward I, c.1, s. 23, 1285 (*S.R.*, I, 83); 4 Henry IV, c. 8, 1402 (*S.R.*, II, 195-6); the constitution of Archbishop Henry Chichele, 1 July 1416 (W, III, 377).

11.[378] But if the administration of goods is entrusted to someone because the deceased has left no testament, it is our will that, once the debts, funeral and other normal expenses have been paid, whatever is left of the goods of the said deceased shall be distributed, according to and following the decision and discretion of the ordinary, among the wife and children and nearest relatives of the said deceased who are in greatest need, and otherwise be given to pious uses. Moreover, it is our will that the executors of testaments and administrators of the goods of the deceased, if they have made an inventory according to the form and order of our statutes passed in that behalf,[379] shall not be burdened beyond the limits of the said inventory.

12.[380] If the executors who are named in a testament, after being summoned and directed by the ordinary, have not taken on themselves the execution of the testament within the time appointed by him, or when they have not been summoned and directed, have not done so within a year from the day of the testator's death (barring lawful impediment), then they shall be excluded from the administration and all benefit of the said testament by the same ordinary, and shall be compelled to return the goods of the deceased which have come to them, and the administration of the goods will be assigned by the same judge according to our statutes.

13.[381] When there are several executors of one testament, it is our will that all of them who are to prove the said testament shall come together in the presence of the judge who has proved the said testament with respect to the legacies and other responsibilities incumbent upon them by reason of the said testament, even though they may reside in different dioceses and jurisdictions, and they shall be obliged by the said judge to do what the cause demands and what justice indicates.

14.[382] And just as executors and administrators are equally responsible, so it is our will that the goods of the deceased shall be distributed equally among them, and that they shall be forced and compelled by the ordinary to do this, unless they have agreed to do otherwise, or unless it appears that some other provision has been made for the sake of the children or by the widow of the said deceased.

15.[383] Local ordinaries and others to whom the validation and probation of testaments, or the commission of administration of the goods of someone dying intestate, is recognized as belonging, are empowered and may summon and oblige any executors and administrators, once a year has elapsed from the time the testament has been proved or the administration has been commissioned, to render an account of their administration, and as soon as this account is fully and faithfully rendered, the said executors and administrators shall be dispensed and exonerated from making any further report (but if, on seeing the said report, it is discovered that a portion of the goods of the deceased has not been properly administered, it shall be distributed by the same executor or administrator, in accordance with the will of the said deceased, if there is some indication of that, or else given to pious uses by the order and at the discretion of the judge in that respect).

16.[384] Cum de viribus testamenti non dicti probati in foro ecclesiastico [96v] contendatur, vel cum dubitatur quibus personis bonorum administratio committi debeat, iuxta bona defuncti, ne dilapidarentur donec causa terminetur, vel de praemissis constiterit, possit sequestrari, ac sequestri custodiam personis idoneis committere.

17.[385] Executor si de onere executionis testamenti acceptando vel recusando ex causa legitima duxerit deliberando ad colligendum bona defuncti, sub computo inde reddendo iuxta distinctionem iudicis possit, (dummodo non ultra sex menses) admitti, idem quoque statuimus de{c...} eo cui administratio bonorum ab intestato decedente committi debeat, cum id duxerit ex simili causa postulandam.

18.[386] Prohibemus ne quisquam bona defunctorum sine auctoritate iudicis in ea parte competentis administrare praesumat, exceptis his quae circa funeralia necessarie expendenda sunt aut quae commode servari non possunt.

[97r] 19.[387] Statuimus praeterea quod nullus executor vel bonorum administrator aliquid de bonis defuncti sibi applicet nisi quod fuerit illi a testatore donatum, aut quod pro ipsius executoris vel administratoris labore ordinarii arbitrio fuerit assignatum, aut pro moderatis expensis suae administrationis.

20.[388] Si mulier in viduitate sua testamenti executionem aut bonorum administrationem ab intestato decedente susceperit, ac postea nubat, maritus eius illa vivente seu mortua secundum facultates defuncti legata solvere, ac alia testamenti onera per iudicem qui administrationem seu executionem huiusmodi commisit cogatur.

21.[389] Executor vel bonorum administrator, qui moritur antequam plene administravit, onus complendae administrationis suo executori aut bonorum administratori arbitrio ordinarii commit[97v]tendum *relinquunt* relinquit.

Ita quod ipse executor executoris, vel bonorum administrator succedens bonorum administratori, ad omnia teneatur ad quae executor ille vel bonorum administrator cui succedit tenebatur, iuxta vires bonorum primi vel secundi defuncti, quae ad eius manus pervenerint.

22.[390] Verum quia circa testamenta ac ultimas voluntates necnon bonorum ab intestato decedente administrationes, legataque, computus et cetera inde

---

[384]The constitution of Archbishop Henry Chichele, 1 July 1416 (W, III, 377).

[385]L, 3.13.4, gloss on *commissionem administrationis*.

[386]L, 3.13.5, gloss on *prius*.

[387]The constitution of Archbishop Henry Chichele, 1 July 1416 (W, III, 377).

[388]Cf. 1268/15, gloss on *libertatem*; L, 3.13.5, gloss on *propriarum uxorum*, for the view that a widow could execute her husband's testament. The assumption that she lost this right on remarriage comes from the common law, cf. H. de Bracton, *De legibus et consuetudinibus Angliae libri quinque*, ed. T. Twiss (6 vols., London, 1878) and G. E. Woodbine (4 vols., New Haven, 1915-41), fo. 32 a: 'Omnia quae uxoris sunt, sunt ipsius viri, nec habeat uxor potestatem sui, sed vir.' ('Everything which belongs to the wife belongs to her husband, and a wife has no power of her own, but rather her husband.')

[389]25 Edward III, s. 5, c. 5, 1351 (*S.R.*, II, 319-24).

[390]Cf. 25 Henry VIII, c. 19, s. 5, 1534 (*S.R.*, III, 460-1).

16.[384] When the validity of a testament which has not been declared proved is being debated in an ecclesiastical court, or when there is some doubt as to which persons the administration of the goods should be entrusted, the goods of the deceased may be sequestered, so that they will not be diminished until the cause is terminated and agreement is reached concerning the above, and custody of the sequestered property may be entrusted to suitable people.

17.[385] If for some legitimate reason an executor continues to debate whether he should accept or refuse the responsibility of executing a testament, he may be allowed to collect the goods of the deceased subject to rendering account, according to the decision of the judge (provided that this does not continue beyond six months). We decree the same also concerning him to whom the administration of the goods of a person dying intestate ought to be entrusted, if he takes the matter on for some similar reason.

18.[386] We forbid anyone to presume to administer the goods of the deceased without the authority of the judge who is competent in that respect, except for those things which must necessarily be spent on the funeral service or which cannot easily be preserved.

19.[387] Moreover we decree that no executor or administrator of goods shall take anything from those goods for himself, unless it is something which has been donated to him by the testator, or which has been assigned to him at the discretion of the ordinary, specifically for his work as an executor or administrator, or for the reasonable expenses of his administration.

20.[388] If a woman in her widowhood undertakes the execution of a testament or the administration of the goods of a person dying intestate, and then remarries, her husband shall be obliged by the judge who entrusted the said administration or execution to pay the things bequeathed and other requirements of the testament, according to the abilities of the deceased, whether the woman is alive or dead.

21.[389] An executor or administrator of goods who dies before he has completed the administration, leaves the responsibility of completing the administration to his executor or to the administrator of his goods, at the discretion of the ordinary, so that the executor's executor, or the administrator of goods who succeeds the administrator of goods shall be obliged to do all the things that the executor or administrator whom he is succeeding was obliged to do, in accordance with the resources of the first or second deceased, which have come into his hands.

22.[390] And because in reality there are more things concerning testaments and last wills, not to mention the administrations of the goods of those dying intestate, and legacies, accounts and other things depending on them, than our

dependentia plura de facto contingere possunt quam constitutiones nostrae praemissae complectuntur, sancimus ut alia omnia et singula praemissa concernentia, de quibus in his constitutionibus nostris certa determinatio non habetur, secundum leges civiles quatenus iur{a/ibus}[391] regni nostri seu constitutionibus nostris, praedictis non adversantur, aut repugnant, examinari, discuti et [98r] definiri volumus.

32. De limitibus paroechiarum.

1.[392] Cum in causis ecclesiasticis in foro ecclesiae pendentibus inciderit quaestio de limitibus paroechiarum sine quarum cognitione causae ipsae dependentes terminari nequeant, statuimus, ut super illis limitibus testes ac aliae probationes in foro ecclesiastico recipi valeant, et causae pendentes fine debito terminari.

33. De sequestrationibus.

1.[393] Beneficiati omnes, sive resideant sive non resideant in suis beneficiis, ad deserviendum eis vel deserviri faciendum congrue et ad alia onera illis ratione beneficiorum suorum incumbentia debita perimplenda, per sequestrationem fructuum beneficiorum suorum ac alias poenas ecclesiasticas ab ordinariis locorum seu aliis iudicibus competentibus compellantur.

[98v] 2.[394] Si de titulo beneficii antequam ad eius possessionem aliquis per ordinarium fuerit admissus contendatur, lite pendente fructus beneficii per ordinarium sequestrari, ac finita lite, deductis omnibus ecclesiae interim incumbentibus, ei qui beneficium obtinuerit restitui volumus.

*3. Si[395] vero aliquo possidente beneficium ecclesiasticum sententia contra possessorem proferatur, a qua provocatum existit, fructus beneficii huiusmodi, probabili suspicione, de dilapidatione laborante, appellatione etiam pendente rationaliter possunt sequestrari, ita quod interim ecclesia debitis non fraudetur obsequiis.

---

[391]See 35.3 below.
[392]Cf. X, 3.29.4 (Fr, II, 555) a decretal of Pope Urban III (1185-7); X, 2.19.13 (Fr, II, 314), a decretal of Pope Honorius III (1216-27).
[393]X, 3.4.16 (Fr, II, 464), a decretal of Pope Gregory IX (1227-41), issued before 1234.
[394]*Clem.*, 2.6.1 (Fr, II, 1146), a decretal of Pope Clement V promulgated at the council of Vienne, 1311-12.
[395]X, 2.16.3 (Fr, II, 305), a decretal of Pope Gregory IX, published before 1234.

aforesaid constitutions include, it is our command and will that all and singular additional matters concerning the aforesaid, about which there is no definite instruction in these our constitutions, shall be examined, discussed and defined according to the civil laws, in so far as they are not opposed to the laws[391] of our kingdom or repugnant to our aforesaid constitutions.

32. Of parish boundaries.

1.[392] When a question concerning parish boundaries occurs in causes which are pending in a church court, without determination of which matters depending upon that cause cannot be terminated, we decree that witnesses and other proofs concerning these boundaries may be accepted in the ecclesiastical court and the causes pending brought to their due conclusion.

33. Of sequestrations.

1.[393] All beneficed men, whether they reside on their benefices or not, shall be compelled by the local ordinaries or other competent judges, through sequestration of the fruits of their benefices and other ecclesiastical penalties, to serve the benefice, or have it served in an appropriate manner, and to fulfil the other duties which are duly incumbent on them by reason of their benefices.

2.[394] If someone who has been admitted by the ordinary has the title to his benefice contested before he enters into possession of it, it is our will that, while the suit is pending, the revenues of the benefice shall be sequestered by the ordinary, and that, when the suit is finished, after everything needed for the church during the time [of the sequestration] has been deducted, they shall be restored to the man who obtained the benefice.

3.[395] But if someone is in possession of an ecclesiastical benefice and sentence is given against the possessor, from which an appeal has been made, the revenues of the said benefice may reasonably be sequestered, even while the appeal is pending, if there is a credible suspicion that they will be dissipated, so that in the meantime the church will not be deprived of its due services.

4.[396] Cum de iniurio quaestio habeatur, et de violentia inferenda mulieri, cuius animus est indagandus, aut de eius corruptione timeatur, in eam domum in qua nihil timere oporteat, ipsam donec causa terminetur et sententia executioni demandari valeat, sequestrari volumus.

*5.[397] In reliquis autem [99r] causis omnibus, nominatim in constitutionibus nostris non expressis sequestrationem fieri prohibemus, nisi evidens et legitima causa id fieri postulaverit.

6.[398] **Si quis sequestrationem ex causis veris et iustis in casibus a iure permissis interpositam et debite publicatam violaverit maioris excommunicationis sententiam ipso facto incurrat. Si tamen a sequestro fuerit appellatum et appellatio legitime prosecuta, ea pendente, possessor** {e} **sua possessione libere et impune utatur.**

34. De computo gardianorum.

1.[399] Volumus ac mandamus ut gardiani et ecclesiarum oeconomi ad computum iuxta morem et consuetudinem suarum paroechiarum fideliter reddendum, ceterique paroechiani, tam ad contributionem pro reparatione ecclesiarum, et aliorum onerum eis de iure, consuetudine seu compositione incumbentium, quam ad restitutionem bonorum ad ecclesiam pertinentium in eorum [99v] manibus existentium, per episcopum, archidiaconum aut alium iudicem in ea parte competentem cogantur et compellantur.

35. De modo procedendi in causis ecclesiasticis.

1.[400] Statuimus quod in omnibus causis ecclesiasticis, absque aliqua solemnitate, sola facti veritate inspecta, ad sententiam definitivam procedatur, videlicet

---

[396]This is based on X, 2.19.14 (Fr, II, 314-15), a decretal of Pope Honorius III (1216-27). The connection with sequestration is made clear by Speculum, 4.2, *De sequestratione possessionum et fructuum*, 1.7.

[397]1268/15 (PC, 765-6).

[398]L, 2.4.1, originally c. 15 of Archbishop John Stratford, 1342.

[399]The office of the 'oeconomus' was established by the cc. 25-6 of the council of Chalcedon in 451 (*C.O.D.*, 98-9) but it was reserved to members of the ordained clergy. These canons were taken up into the medieval canon law (D 75, c. 2 – Fr, I, 265-6 and C. 16, q. 7, c. 21 – Fr, I, 806 respectively), and the clerical nature of the office was stressed (C. 16, q. 7, c. 21 – Fr, I, 806-7) but it seems that by the early fourteenth century the office was being exercised by laymen, at least in England. Regular accounts are common from about 1350, though provision was made for them in the statutes of Exeter II, c. 12, 1287 (PC, 1005-8).

[400]Cf. X, 2.27.2 (Fr, II, 393), a statement of Pope Gregory I (590-604), *Reg.* 3.8; *Clem.*, 2.1.2 (Fr, II, 1143), a decretal of Pope Clement V (1305-14), published at the council of Vienne, 1311-12. On submissions in writing, cf. X, 2.3.1 (Fr, II, 255-6), c. 7 of the third council of Soissons, 852.

4.[396] When there is a question of harm and of violence done to a woman whose mind is deranged, or there are fears for her corruption in the house where nothing ought to be feared, it is our will that the house be sequestered until the cause is terminated and the sentence is ready to be pronounced for execution.

5.[397] But we forbid sequestration to be made in all other causes not expressly named in our constitutions, unless some clear and lawful cause suggests that it should be made.

6.[398] If someone violates a sequestration which has been imposed and duly published for true and just reasons in cases permitted by law, he shall automatically incur the sentence of greater excommunication. But if the sequestration has been appealed and the appeal is being lawfully pursued, the possessor may have full and unrestricted use of his possession while it is pending.

34. Of churchwardens' accounts.

1.[399] It is our will and command that wardens and treasurers of churches shall be obliged and compelled by the bishop, archdeacon or other judge competent in that respect, to render faithful account, according to the habit and custom of their parishes, and that the other parishioners shall be obliged and compelled both to contribute to the repair of the churches and the other expenses incumbent on them by law, custom or composition, and to the restoration of those goods, belonging to the church, which happen to be in their hands.

35. Of procedure in ecclesiastical causes.

1.[400] We decree that in all ecclesiastical causes the final sentence shall be proceeded to without any formality, once the simple truth of the matter has been

libellus non exigatur, sed simpliciter et pure factum ipsum rei veritatem continens quomodocunque in scriptis proponatur, litis contestatio non postuletur, dilationum materia amputetur, et iudex quantum poterit litem faciat breviorem, exceptiones et appellationes dilatorias et frustratorias repellendo, pertinentium advocatorum et procuratorum contentiones, et testium superfluam multitudinem refrenando.

2.[401] Nolumus tamen probationes necessarias aut defen[100r]siones legitimas citationesve aut iuramenta de calumnia, malitia sive veritate dicenda ne veritas occultetur ullo pacto, per praemissa excludi.

3.[402] Ad clariorem expeditionem litium, plenioremque causarum definitionem, in causis omnibus ad examen fori ecclesiastici ex concessione nostra pertinentibus, leges civiles quatenus statutis et legibus regni nostri aut hisce nostris constitutionibus expresse non repugnant, observari permittimus ac concedimus.

4.[403] Cum semper bonas litteras in summo pretio habuimus, idcirco (ad iura civilia, ceterasque bonas artes studendas, iuvenes allicere cupientes) statuimus et ordinamus, quod quilibet in academiis nostris Oxoniensi et Cantabrigensi legum baccalareus, aut in artibus magister admissus possit, medi[100v]ante dispensatione legitima, duo etiam curata beneficia quaecunque recipere et retinere, aliquo statuto in parliamento nostro edito, non obstante.

36. De appellationibus et nullitatum querelis.

1.[404] Appellationes et nullitatum querelas infra quindecim dies a tempore notitiae latae sententiae aut gravaminis a quo per constitutiones nostras appellare sive querelare liceat, in scriptis coram iudice a quo, aut si plures sint iudices, coram maiore parte ipsorum etiam separatim, si eius aut eorum copiam commode haberi possit; alias in praesentia honestorum virorum, contestatione super hoc proposita, fieri volumus. Alioquin rebus prius iudicatis standum esse decernimus.

*2.[405] Permittimus tamen ut a sententia definitiva statim apud acta iudice pro tribunali sedente, viva voce appellare sive querelare cuique liceat.

[101r] 3.[406] Prohibemus ne iudex ad quem appellari sive querelari contigerit, iudici a quo prius inhibeat, quam appellatum sive querelatum fuisse legitime sibi constiterit, nisi a definitiva statim, iudice pro tribunali sedente viva voce apud

---

[401]Cf. VI, 2.3.2 (Fr, II, 998), a decretal of Pope Boniface VIII (1294-1303).

[402]Cf. 25 Henry VIII, c. 19, s.5, 1534 (*S.R.*, III, 460-1).

[403]This refers to 21 Henry VIII, c. 13, 1529 (*S.R.*, III, 292-6).

[404]X, 2.28.4 (Fr, II, 410-11); X, 2.28.5 (Fr, II, 411); X, 2.28.33 (Fr, II, 420-1), all decretals of Pope Alexander III (1159-81); X, 2.28.47 (Fr, II, 435-7), a decretal of Pope Innocent III, 9 July 1209.

[405]*Dig.*, 49.1.2, originally Macer, *De appellationibus*, 1; *Dig.*, 49.1.5.4, originally Marcian, *De appellationibus*, 1.

[406]VI, 2.15.7 (Fr, II, 1017), a decretal of Pope Boniface VIII (1294-1303); cf. also X, 2.28.38 (Fr, II, 422-3), a decretal of Pope Clement III (1187-91).

investigated; in particular, a formal libel shall not be required, but the fact itself, containing the truth of the matter, shall be put down simply and clearly in some form of writing, joinder of issue shall not be required, reasons for delay shall be removed, and the judge shall make the suit as brief as possible by excluding exceptions and appeals designed to delay and frustrate the proceedings, and also by refraining both the arguments of the relevant advocates and proctors and an excessive number of witnesses.

2.[401] But we do not want necessary examinations, or lawful exceptions, or citations, or the oaths of calumny, malice or telling the truth to be excluded by the above, lest the truth be hidden by some conspiracy.

3.[402] In order to expedite suits more efficiently and render a fuller judgment of the causes, we allow and permit, that in all the causes pertaining by our permission to the examination of an ecclesiastical court, the civil laws may be observed, in so far as they are not expressly repugnant to the statutes and laws of our kingdom or of these our constitutions.

4.[403] Since we have always prized sound learning highly, therefore (desiring to encourage young men to study civil law and other noble arts), we decree and ordain that whoever may be admitted as a bachelor of laws or master of arts in our universities of Oxford and Cambridge, subject to lawful dispensation, may receive and retain any two benefices with cure, any statute passed in our parliament notwithstanding.

36. Of appeals and suits of nullity.

1.[404] It is our will that appeals and suits of nullity shall be made within fifteen days from the time of notice of the sentence given, or of the grievance from which it is permissible, according to our constitutions, to appeal or sue, and that this should be in writing before the judge from whom [the appeal is lodged], or if there are many judges, before the majority of them individually, if a copy of it or them may readily be had; or else the suit shall be lodged in the presence of honest men. Otherwise we decree that the matters previously adjudicated shall be allowed to stand.

*2.[405] But we allow that anyone may appeal or bring a suit of nullity orally against the final sentence, while the proceedings are still going on and the judge is sitting in court.

3.[406] We forbid the judge to whom an appeal or suit has been made to restrain the judge from whom it has been made, before the matter has been lawfully appealed or sued to him, unless it has been immediately appealed or sued from the final sentence orally, while the judge was sitting in court, during

acta fuerit appellata sive querelata, in quo casu ad effectum praedictum sufficiet iudici ad quem de hoc per appellantis aut eius procuratoris sufficiens ad hoc mandatum habentis, iuramento constare, addentes insuper ut ubi a gravamine appellatur sive querelatur, probablilis ac legitima causa in appellatione sive querela exprimatur.

4.[407] In causis ecclesiasticis ante sententiam definitivam appellare sive de nullitate querelare prohibemus, ne a sententia censurarum aut correctionis ubi modus exceditur, aut ubicunque damnum aut gravamen [101v] illatum per appellationem a definitiva non est reparabile, in quibus casibus appellare aut etiam querelare, ante sententiam definitivam licebit.

5.[408] Cum a sententia definitiva appellatum fuerit vel de nullitate querelatum gravamen quodcunque quod per interlocutoriam illatum sit, licite per appellationis iudicem emendari possit.

6.[409] Cum appellaverit vel de nullitate conquestus fuerit, nisi infra duos menses a tempore appellationis sive querelae interpositae eandem prosecutus fuerit, et iudici a quo de prosecutione huiusmodi per citationem aut nihilitionem superioris certiorem fecerit, ac infra sex menses a fine ipsorum duorum mensium numerandos, ipsam appellationem sive querelam, legitimo cessante impedimento, finiri obtinuerit, sententiae contra eum prius latae stare compelletur. Si eorum possessio qui appellant turbata fuerit, iudici a quo extitit appellatum eam reformare licet, [102r] eo de quo appellatio est interposita praetermisso. Appellans vero si appellatione pendente appellatum turbaverit in possessione, quia appellationi deferri neglexit, se reddit appellationis beneficio indignum.

7.[410] **Sententia censurarum sub conditione lata**, veluti nisi quis infra viginti dies satisfecerit excommunicatus sit, **suspenditur si ante conditionis eventum fuerit appellatum.**

8.[411] Qui post appellationem ad superiorem factam, coram iudice inferiore super concernentibus ipsam appellationem comparuerit, appellationi suae

---

[407]This follows the procedure of civil law, to which the ancient canons were opposed. Cf. X, 2.28.12 (Fr, II, 413), a decretal of Pope Alexander III (1159-81). However, it is clear that the thirteenth-century canonists preferred the civil procedure, cf. *e.g.* X, 2.28.59 (Fr, II, 437), c. 35 of Lateran IV, 1215 (*C.O.D.*, 251).

[408]Cf. *Dig.*, 49.5.2, originally Scaevola, *Regularum*, 4. Speculum, 2.3, *De sententia*, 2.1 says: '...dixit Iohannes de Deo interlocutoriam non obtinere vim rei iudicatae...quia potest revocari...' ('John of God said that an interlocutory [sentence] does not acquire the force of a matter adjudged...since it can be revoked...'). A footnote quotes the source as follows: 'Interlocutoriam revocare posse; si tamen non suspendatur per appellationem intra decem dies, transit in rem iudicatam...' ('It is possible to revoke an interlocutory [sentence]; but if it is not suspended by an appeal within ten days, then it becomes a matter adjudged...').

[409]Based on X, 2.28.4 (Fr, II, 410-11), a letter of Pope Alexander III (1159-81) to Bishop William Turbe of Norwich (1147-74).

[410]X, 2,28.40 (Fr, II, 423), a decretal of Pope Celestine III (1191-8), 1193. Cf. also X, 1.31.8 (Fr, II, 189), a decretal of Pope Innocent III, 1 June 1198; X, 2.28.16 (Fr, II, 414-15), a decretal of Pope Alexander III; X, 2.28.26 (Fr, II, 418-19), c. 6 of Lateran III, 1179 (*C.O.D.*, 214); X, 2.28.55 (Fr, II, 433-5), a decretal of Pope Innocent III, 2 January 1207.

[411]X, 2.28.54 (Fr, II, 432-3), a decretal of Pope Innocent III, 12 December 1207.

the proceedings, in which case it shall suffice for the aforesaid effect, that the judge to whom the appeal has been made shall confirm it by the oath of the appellant or of his proctor, having sufficient authority to do this, adding moreover that when an appeal or suit is made on the basis of a ruling, that a plausible and lawful reason [for it] shall be stated in the appeal or suit.

4.[407] In ecclesiastical causes we forbid any appeals or suits of nullity before the final sentence, except from a sentence of censures or correction where the procedure has been violated, or wherever the injury or grievance cannot be remedied on appeal from the final sentence, in which cases it shall be lawful to appeal or sue even before the final sentence.

5.[408] When an appeal or complaint for a suit of nullity has been made, any interlocutory ruling may lawfully be emended by the appeal judge.

6.[409] When someone has made an appeal or suit for nullity, unless he has pursued it within two months from the time of the deposition of the appeal or suit of nullity, and notice of such prosecution has been given to the judge from whom the appeal has been made, either by citation or by annulment from his superior, and [unless] within six months, counting from the end of those two months, he has managed, barring lawful impediment, to bring the appeal or suit to an end, he shall be forced to abide by the sentence previously passed against him. If the possession of those appealing has been disturbed, it is lawful for the judge from whom the cause has been appealed to restore it, without reference to the one from whom the appeal has been made. But if, while the appeal is pending, an appellant interferes with the possession of the person being appealed against, he shall be held unworthy of the benefit of appeal since he has not bothered to defer to the appeal.

7.[410] **A sentence of censures given subject to a condition**, such as that whoever has not given satisfaction within twenty days shall be excommunicated, **shall be suspended if an appeal has been made before the fulfilment of the condition.**

8.[411] Whoever appears before an inferior judge on matters to do with his appeal, after the appeal has been made to a superior, will appear to have

renuntiare videtur, nisi protestetur quod propter hoc non intendit renuntiare huiusmodi appellationi, in quo casu, tanquam contraria allegans, coram inferiori non est audiendus.

Per appellationem legitime interpositam, et causa principalis ex qua extitit appellatum, et eius accessoria, et ab [102v] ea dependentia, ad ipsius iudicis referri debent examen ad quem est appellatum.

9.[412] **Si plures qui communi iure iuventur, idemque negotium et eandem defensionis causam habent, una sententia condemnati...**

---

[412]X, 2.28.72 (Fr, II, 443), a decretal of Pope Gregory IX (1227-41) before 1234. The main clause is missing here; it reads: 'Si unus solus ad appellationis beneficium convolaverit, illius victoria iure communi ceteris suffragatur.' ('If only one should avail himself of the benefit of appeal, his victory shall, by common law, be valid for the others.') Cf. R, 54.12a, 15.

renounced that appeal, unless it is objected that he did not mean to renounce the appeal on that account, in which case, although he claims the opposite, he shall not be heard before the inferior judge.

In an appeal lawfully made, both the main reason for which the appeal exists, as well as the secondary cause and the things dependent on it, must be referred to the examination of that judge to whom the appeal has been made.

9.[412] **If there are many people who are supported by the same law, who have the same business and the same ground of defence, who have been condemned by the same sentence...**

THE *REFORMATIO LEGUM ECCLESIASTICARUM*

Signs used in the text

Manuscript readings:

Roman	Present in MS, F and S.
Italic	Deleted in MS and absent from F and S.
*Italic**	Deleted in MS but present in F and S.
Bold	Added to MS and present in F and S.
Bold*	Added to MS but absent from F and S.
Bold italic	Added to MS and deleted from it.
<u>Underline</u>	Underlined in MS (probably intended for deletion).
>Roman<	Transferred from this place in the MS.
<Roman>	Transferred to this place in the MS.
/---------/	Addition to MS text (often a scribal correction).

1571 Foxe edition (F):

[*Italic*]	Present in MS but not in F or S.
[**Bold**]	Absent from MS but present in F and S.
[*Italic*/**Bold**]	Former deleted from MS by F and S and latter added.
[Roman/**Bold**] in	Former deleted from MS in F but restored in S; latter F only.
[[**Bold**]]	Present in F, but not in MS or S.
[[*Italic*]]	Absent from F, but present in MS and S.
[>Roman<]	Transferred in F and S from this place in the MS.
[<Roman>]	Transferred to this place in F and S.

NB: When secondary changes have been made to a text which is already in *italic* or **bold**, then the *italic* or the **bold** becomes the default type. In these cases, deletions to an *italic* text and additions to a **bold** text are both in roman type. Conversely, additions to an *italic* text and/or deletions from a **bold** text are both in ***bold italic***.

1640/1641 editions (S):

Romanly additions in **bold** to F are also present in S, because S is based on F and not on the MS. But S has variations on F (including a number of attempted corrections to it), and these are indicated as follows:

{*Italic*}	S has replaced this reading, which is in both MS and F.
{**Bold**}	S has added this reading, which is in neither MS nor F.
{Roman}	S has omitted something common to MS and F.

{*Italic*} and {Roman} are distinguished because the former is used only when accompanied by an addition in **bold**, and may therefore be regarded as a deliberate alteration. Roman type indicates a simple omission, which is most probably a printing error.

The text of MS Petyt 538/38, fos. 231r-246r (Inner Temple)

This sixteenth-century translation of a part of the *Reformatio* (44.3-51.19) is printed on pp. 583-651 as it stands in the MS. Basically it follows the Foxe edition of 1571, though not entirely. In order to account for the alterations which were made within MS Harleian 426 and between that MS and the Foxe edition, the deletions have been supplied in *italic* type (for MS Harleian 426) and in [*italic*] for the Foxe edition, as has been done in the rest of the translation.

However, where the translator deleted words from his own text, angular brackets have been used to indicate this: e.g. <*italic*>. Conversely, where the translator has **not** followed changes made in the Foxe edition (which are marked in [**bold**]), that has been indicated by using inverted angular brackets, e.g. [>**bold**<]. In those cases, the MS Petyt fragment follows the reading in italic or in Roman type.

REFORMATIO LEGUM ECCLESIASTICARUM

Ex auctoritate primum Regis Henrici VIII incohata, deinde per Regem Edovardum VI provecta adauctaque in hunc modum, atque nunc ad pleniorem ipsarum reformationem in lucem edita.

Ad doctum et candidum lectorem praefatio (I. F.)[1]

Cum nihil sit, quod vel ad communem omnium naturam, vel ad privatam cuiusque salutem propius pertineat, quam ut in quaque reipublicae societate recta religionis doctrina retineatur, tum ad hanc ipsam optimae religionis institutionem non parum retulerit, optimarum pariter legum accedere disciplinam; quarum altera nos ad pietatem informet, altera externam, hominum inter ipsos vitam moresque componat. Quae duae res simul coniunctae ut plurimum in omni republica recte administranda valent, seseque mutuo iuvant, ita si divellantur, perinde ac si navem seces mediam, haud ita multum video, quid aut haec sine illa, aut utraque pars sine altera, his praesertim temporibus contulerit. Nam ut nulla quantumvis morata civitas aut regnum commode haberi possit, si absit aut aberret religionis regula, sic neque religio rursus quantumlibet exculta praestiterit ad absolvendam felicitatis perfectionem, ubi nec morum cura habetur, nec iudiciorum servatur severitas. Unde non inscite ab Augustino dictum est, qui de Dei scribens civitate, posse rempublicam felicem esse negat, ubi stantibus quidem moenibus, mores ruinam patiuntur.[2] Ideoque non abs re a sapientissimis maioribus prospectum arbitror, qui praemia pariter cum poenis temperantes, simulque cum religione legum colligantes instituta, omni reipublicae parti consulendum putaverunt, quo videlicet nec bonis deesset, quo ad virtutes sincerumque Dei cultum incitari possent, nec malis suppliciorum abesset metus, quo revocentur a flagitio; simulque iniuriarum controversiae, (si quae emergerent) tolli eodem pacto et finiri possent.

Ceterum diligens hic cum primis, et multiplex adhibenda cautio est. Quemadmodum enim non omnis admittenda est in coetus politicos religio, nisi quae ad expressam divinae voluntatis normam quam simplicissime respondeat; ita et in condendis legibus prudenti cum primis delectu utendum censeo, ut

---

[1] The initials are those of John Foxe.
[2] The actual quotation is from Augustine, *De civitate Dei*, I, 33: 'Neque enim censebat ille felicem esse rempublicam stantibus moenibus, ruentibus moribus.' ('He (Scipio) did not think that the state could be happy if the walls were standing but morals were collapsing').

THE REFORMATION OF THE ECCLESIASTICAL LAWS

First begun by the authority of King Henry VIII, then continued and extended by King Edward VI, and now published for their further reformation.

A preface to the learned and candid reader (J. F.)[1]

As there is nothing more relevant to the common nature of all men, or to the particular salvation of any one individual, than that the correct teaching about religion should be maintained in every community within the state, the discipline of the best laws must be accepted in order for the best religion to be established. For the latter instructs us in godliness and the former regulates the outward life and behaviour of people towards one another. When these two things are joined together, they help each other to promote the best government in any state, but if they are separated it is as if you were to cut a ship in two - I cannot see how this part can function without that one, or how either can operate without the other, especially at the present time. For just as no city or kingdom, however well-behaved it may be, can be governed well if the rule of religion is absent or defective, so also religion, however widely it is practised, cannot deliver the perfection of happiness where there is no attention paid to behaviour and the strict rule of law is not maintained. For this reason it was wisely said by Augustine in writing his *City of God*, when he denied that it was possible for a state to be happy when 'its walls are standing but its morals are being destroyed'.[2] Likewise, I think that it was correctly foreseen by the wisest of our ancestors, who thought it advisable to provide for every part of the state by balancing rewards equally with punishments and by linking the institutions of law together with religion, so that good people would not be without something by which they might be encouraged to virtue and the true worship of God, and wicked people would not go without fear of punishment, by which they might be pulled back from their error, and at the same time disputes over wrongdoing (if any should arise) might be removed and brought to an end by the same means.

But in this matter above all, a careful and many-faceted caution must be exercised. For just as not all religion is to be accepted in public life, if it does not correspond in the clearest possible way to the stated norm of the divine will, so in making the laws, I believe that above all a prudent choice should be exercised,

reipublicae accommodentur, non quae temere cuiusvis effundit temeritas, aut tyrannis obtrudit, sed quae ad archetypum aequi et honesti atque ad perfectae rationis regulam accedant quam proxime. Prospiciendum deinde, ne aut fisci lucrum oleant, aut privatam sapiant utilitatem, cuiusmodi Epitadae fuisse feruntur, qui cum legem tulisset, ut liberum esset cuique sua, cui vellet, relinquere, nihil interim agebat, nisi ut ipse filium quem odisset, posset exhaeredare.[3] Porro ne crudelitatem spirent, quales erant Draconis[4] et Phalaridis[5] Agrigentinorum tyranni, quibus et episcopi Romani addas licebit. Profuerit et illud insuper cavere, ne leges immodica superfluitate ac multitudine scitorum onerent magis quam ornent rempublicam.

Quamquam vero longe id praestantissimum fuerat, votisque omnibus optandum, eiusmodi omnium esse Christianorum mores, ut non paucis aut moderatis modo, sed nullis potius omnino opus esset legibus; tantumque posse religionis vigorem apud omnes, ut de nobis vere affirmari posset Paulinum illud: 'Lex iusto posita non est, etc.'[6] Verum quando hoc in tanta vitae infirmitate obtinere non datur, nescio etiam an sperare liceat, in invisibili hac ecclesia, ubi promiscue cum bonis ita permisti mali sunt, ut amplior plerumque pars vincat meliorem; idcirco legum necessario comparata sunt praesidia, ut quos ducere religio nequeat, disciplinae saltem legumque retineat coercio. Sine quibus nullam posse humanae societatis gubernationem constare, non modo recentiorem temporum exempla, sed vetustissimae etiam antiquitatis, ubique comprobant historiae; sive Atticam primum, sive Spartanam spectemus rempublicam. Quarum utraque post varias civilium conflictationum agitationes, tandem acceptis altera a Solone,[7] altera a Lycurgo[8] legibus, multo dehinc pacatior auctiorque est reddita. Sic enim de Athenis constat, quod cum sine certo aliquo iure tres simul per id tempus factiones inter se contenderent, eaque dissensio, gliscentibus magis odiis, universis exitium minaretur, Soloni respublica mandata est. Is leges tulit, quibus libertatem et otium per quingentos postea annos ei restituit reipublicae.

---

[3] According to Plutarch, *Lives, Agis*, 4, Epitadeus was a Spartan ephor who introduced this law about 400 BC. Spartan inheritance laws were different from those of other Greek states in that they gave equal rights to women, a feature which left about two-thirds of the arable land in female hands by the late third century BC and provoked a crisis in the time of Kings Agis IV and Cleomenes III, about which Plutarch was writing. However, any connexion between these laws and Epitadeus is certainly fictitious.

[4] Lawgiver of Athens, *c.* 621 BC, who was known for his severity. His law code was replaced by that of Solon about 575 BC.

[5] Tyrant of Acragas (Agrigento) in Sicily who died about 554 BC. His laws were known for their harshness, but in ancient times Phalaris himself was often highly regarded for his humanity.

[6] I Ti. i. 9.

[7] Solon (*c.*630-*c.*560 BC) was archon of Athens about 594 and composed his law code some twenty years after that. He was renowned for his sense of justice and widely contrasted with his severe predecessor, Draco.

[8] Lawgiver of Sparta who may have lived in the second half of the seventh century BC. He has traditionally been credited with having established the military-like discipline under which the Spartans of antiquity lived.

so that it will not be whatever the boldness of any one person should dare to pour out, nor what a tyrant might insist on, which will be enjoined on the state, but rather those things which correspond most closely to the model of fairness and decency, and to the rule of perfect reason. Furthermore, care must be taken to ensure that the laws do not oil the greed of the treasury or serve the ends of private persons, as is reported of Epitades, who made a law to the effect that everyone was free to leave his goods to whomever he wished, the only purpose of which was to make it possible for him to disinherit his son, whom he detested.[3] Furthermore, laws should not breathe cruelty, as did those of Draco[4] and Phalaris,[5] tyrants of Agrigentum, to which you might add those of the bishop of Rome. It would also be helpful to ensure that the laws do not burden the state by an immoderate excess and number of provisions, instead of adorning it.

For although it would be by far the most preferable thing, and to be desired by everyone's prayers, that the behaviour of all Christians should be such that there should not only be no need for a few or for moderate laws, but rather than there should be no need for any laws at all, and that the strength of religion should be so great among everyone that Paul's statement might truly be said of us: 'There is no law for the righteous, etc.',[6] yet attaining this is not granted in the great weakness of this life, nor do I think that we can dare to hope for it in this invisible church, where the wicked are so thoroughly mixed together with the good that the larger and more numerous part can overcome the better one. For this reason the defences of the laws have had to be made ready, so that the force of discipline and the laws may restrain those whom religion cannot control. Without them the government of human society is impossible, as not only the examples of recent times but also those of the most ancient antiquity demonstrate, and histories everywhere prove, whether we look first at the Athenian or at the Spartan city-states. For after separate outbreaks of civil unrest each of them in turn accepted laws, the first from Solon[7] and the second from Lycurgus,[8] and after that they were both much more peaceful and prosperous. In the case of Athens, it appears that when there was no fixed law of any kind there and three factions were fighting with each other at the same time, and as hatreds grew ever greater, this quarrelling threatened everybody with death, so the state was turned over to Solon. He gave laws by which he restored freedom and rest

Porro ut non puduit Atticos ea tempestate Aegyptias leges quasdam usucapere, atque in suam transferre rempublicam, (ut testis est Herodotus),[9] idem et Romanis postea usu venit, quos cum publica cogeret necessitas leges in civitate sua conscribere, missi sunt in Graeciam decemviri,[10] qui ex Atticis legibus Solonis, Zaleuci[11] apud Locros, Charondae[12] apud Thurinos, Lycurgi apud Lacedaemonios, Phoronei[13] apud Argivos, certas legum formulas colligerent, et de republica instituenda summos in Graecia homines consulerent.

Atque ex eis demum leges duodecim tabularum conflatae sunt, quibus tantum tribuit M. Cicero,[14] ut alicubi de optimo civitatis statu disputans a natura discedere praedicat, qui a Romanis legibus dissident. Breviter, nulla gens, nulla civitas aut patria tam immanis unquam aut barbara fuit, quae non leges, etsi non ubique consimiles, non aliquas tamen habuerit, quibus si non omnia propellerentur vitia, at aliquam saltem morum honestatem retineret. Sic neque Angliae nostrae iam olim sua defuerunt legum decreta sapienter a prudentissimis maioribus constituta. Declarant id Bracthonis[15] nomothetica, Inae[16] regis, Eduardi

---

[9]Herodotus, *Historiae*, II, 177. Solon borrowed a law from the Egyptians and imposed it at Athens.

[10]Pomponius, quoted in *Digest*, I, 2, 2, 3-4 mentions this. According to legend, the Romans appointed a committee of ten men in 451 BC, following a plebeian revolt, to draw up laws for the city. These 'decemviri', as they are known, drew up ten laws and were reappointed in 450 BC, when they added two more. When they failed to resign in 449, they were overthrown, but the Twelve Tables became the foundation of Roman public law. If the decemviri existed, they may have gone to Magna Graecia (Southern Italy), but there would not have been time to go further afield. In any case, resemblances between the Twelve Tables and Greek law codes are few, and most probably accidental.

[11]Zaleucus wrote the earliest known law code in the Greek world for the south Italian colony of Locri, sometime around 660 BC.

[12]Misspelt as 'Chacondas' in F. Charondas (*fl. c.*600 BC), was a Greek from Sicily who gave laws to several cities there and in southern Italy, including Thurii, which is mentioned here.

[13]Phoroneus was a mythical king of Argos. His 'laws' are of unknown prehistoric origin.

[14]Marcus Tullius Cicero (106-43 BC) defended traditional Roman republicanism against Julius Caesar and his great-nephew Octavian, later the emperor Augustus. At the height of this struggle, he wrote at length on the Roman constitution in *De re publica*, of which only fragments survive. There is nothing which directly parallels Foxe's allusion, but it is consonant with what he says in II, 1-3 and in a surviving fragment of III.

[15]Henry de Bracton (d.1268), wrote *De legibus et consuetudinibus Angliae*, one of the earliest treatises on the English common law and long regarded as a classic exposition of it.

[16]F has 'Ivae', an error which was corrected in 1640. Ine (or Ini) was king of Wessex from 688-726 and wrote the earliest known Anglo-Saxon law code. It was later appended to the laws of King Alfred the Great.

to the city for the next fifty years. Furthermore, just as the Athenians of that time were not ashamed to make use of Egyptian laws and adapt them to their own state (as Herodotus testifies),[9] so likewise it later came about that when public necessity obliged the Romans to write down laws for their state, ten men[10] were sent to Greece, who gathered together certain forms of laws taken from the Athenian laws of Solon, the laws of Zaleucus[11] for Locri, those of Charondas[12] for Thurii, of Lycurgus for Sparta and of Phoroneus[13] for Argos, and consulted with the greatest men of Greece as to how to govern a state.

And so out of this material were eventually put together the laws of the twelve tables, of which Cicero[14] said, when arguing in one of his works about the best form of state, that those who reject the Roman laws are turning their backs on nature itself. In conclusion, there has been no race, no state and no country, however wild or barbarous it may have been, which has not had laws of some kind, even if they have not been everywhere alike, by which, if not all vices have been excluded, at least some moral decency has been preserved. Thus even here in England decrees of laws, wisely composed by the ablest of our ancestors, were not lacking, even in ancient times. Bracton's[15] legal treatise and the laws given

senioris,[17] Aethelstani,[18] Eadmundi,[19] Edgari,[20] Aluredi,[21] Ethelredi,[22] Canuti,[23] ceterorumque principum auspiciis institutae sanctiones. Quae leges quam diu suam tueri auctoritatem potuerunt, viguit aliqua saltem in hoc regno morum disciplina. Tandem non multo post haec descendit in orchestram scenicus plane artifex suam saltaturus fabulam, urbis Romae pontifex; qui ceteris paulatim explosis actoribus, solus ipse scenam occupare, omnesque omnium actiones sustinere voluit.[24] Primumque profanis magistratibus ea tantum relinquens, quae profana videbantur, reliquam partem illam de moribus universam ad se populumque suum transtulit ecclesiasticum, callidissimo nimirum commento, dum se fingit Christi in terris vicarium et apostolicae cathedrae haereditarium successorem. Quod simul atque semel principibus esse persuasum sensisset, hinc illico maiora conandi materiam accipit. Neque porro defuit occasioni audacia. Pergens itaque in coepta fabula mirus hic histrio, postquam exordium sibi tam pulchre videt procedere, ad reliquas similiter actionis partes se parat, quas nihilo etiam segnius tractat. Ac primum ad reges ipsos summosque monarchas affectat viam, eorum auctoritatem paulatim vellicare, mox et aequare, tum superare etiam, superatamque sub iugum mittere pertentat. Hoc ubi etiam succedere intelligit, maiore sumpta fiducia, ulterius adhuc progreditur sese dilatare, ac pennas nido maiores distendere, nihil iam humile aut plebeium de se cogitans. Qui prius humili socco incedebat, nunc alto cothurno ingreditur, ex pontifice rex factus plane tragicus. Quin nec amplius subditi iam nomen agnoscit, qui iubetur a Christo, ne dominetur suis.

Denique eousque intumescit magnitudinis hic ecclesiarcha, ut qui leges prius ab aliis accipere, atque in ordine teneri sit solitus, nunc inversa rerum scena, leges ipse imponit aliis, ac iura praescribit universis, quod ius nunc canonicum appellamus. In quo ipso iure neque ullum tamen modum tenet illius impudentia,

---

[17]Edward the Elder was a son of Alfred the Great and succeeded him as king of Wessex (899-924).

[18]Son of Edward the Elder who ruled Wessex from 924-40. As a result of his conquests, he was the first Anglo-Saxon king to rule over almost the whole of England.

[19]Edmund I was king of Wessex from 939-46.

[20]King of Wessex from 959 and of England from 973 to 975.

[21]This is presumably Alfred the Great, king of Wessex (871-99), though for some reason he is out of chronological order.

[22]Ethelred II 'the Unready', king of England from 978 to 1013 and again from 1014-16.

[23]Canute (Cnut or Knut) the Dane was king of England from 1013-35.

[24]Here Foxe is referring to the papal revival of the mid-eleventh century, when claims to universal jurisdiction were pressed against the kings of western Europe. The most notorious exponent of this position was Hildebrand, who reigned as Pope Gregory VII (1073-85). But his predecessor, Pope Alexander II (1961-73) had already demanded the 'reform' of the English Church as his price for supporting William I's invasion in 1066. Alexander got want he wanted when William established an independent ecclesiastical jurisdiction in England, probably in 1072.

under the auspices of King Ine,[16] Edward the Elder,[17] Athelstan,[18] Edmund,[19] Edgar,[20] Alfred,[21] Ethelred,[22] Canute[23] and other rulers demonstrate this. As long as these laws were able to retain their authority, at least some moral discipline existed in this kingdom. Yet not long after this a *deus ex machina* appeared on the stage and set about creating his own plot - the pope of the city of Rome. Before long he had chased the other actors offstage and occupied it all by himself, wanting to control everybody and everything they did.[24] First of all, he left to the secular magistrates only those matters which appeared to be secular, and then by the cleverest of lies he transferred all remaining moral matters to himself and his church people, while he made himself into the vicar of Christ on earth and the hereditary successor of the apostolic see. As soon as he sensed that the secular rulers were persuaded of this, he had the wherewithal to attempt even greater enormities. Nor indeed was his boldness unequal to the opportunity. For once the play had started and he saw how the introduction had turned out so beautifully for him, this amazing actor went on and prepared himself to play the other parts too, which he did no less skilfully. First of all he made his way to the kings and supreme monarchs themselves, and bit by bit whittled away at their authority. Soon he was their equal and then he even surpassed them, and did his best to put their vanquished authority under his yoke. When he realized that he was succeeding he became even more confident, and lost no time in going still further, spreading his wings far beyond the nest, and showing no sign of lowliness or humility in himself. The man who had previously walked in humble slippers, now strutted about in high books, turning himself from a pontiff into the real king of the drama. The man who was ordered by Christ not to lord it over his flock no longer acknowledged the designation of 'subject'.

Finally, so great did this hierarch become that he who had previously accepted laws from others and had been accustomed to be kept in order, now, in a complete reversal of rôles, himself gave laws to others and prescribed ordinances for everyone, which we now call canon law. In this law his insolence

quin leges²⁵ legibus, decreta²⁶ decretis, ac eis insuper decretalia²⁷ aliis alia atque item alia accumulet, nec ullum paene statuit cumulandi finem, donec tandem suis Clementinis,²⁸ Sextinis,²⁹ intra et extravagantibus,³⁰ constitutionibus provincialibus et synodalibus,³¹ paleis, glossulis, sententiis, capitulis, summariis, rescriptis, breviculis, casibus longis et brevibus, ac infinitis rhapsodiis adeo orbem consarcinavit, ut Atlas mons, quo sustineri coelum dicitur, huic (si imponeretur) oneri vix ferendo sufficeret. Atque hunc quidem in modum habuit pontificiae huius fabulae epitasis satis quidem turbulenta et prodigiosa. In qua mirum quas ille turbas dedit, quos mundo ludos fecit, et quos errores involvit, foris nonnullam quidem religionis faciem obtendens, sed ita ut propius intuenti haud difficile esset videre longe aliud mysterium in animo eum instituisse, nempe ut ecclesiasticum imperium aliquod in hoc mundo eminentiae singularis attolleret. Tum nec his contentus ius fori sui haud prius destitit hactenus dilatare, quoad totum etiam civilem gladium cum plena potestate in suam traduxisset possessionem; non huc spectans interim, ut morum disciplinam in melius proveheret (quod fortassis numquam illi serio curae fuit) sed partim ut sedis dignitatem omnibus munitam modis constabiliret, partim ut opes undecunque quam maximas ad explendam ipsius avaritiam converteret, haud multum dissimili exemplo, quale de Dionysio Syracusano commemorat Plutarchus,³² qui cum insidioso consilio quam plurimas tulisset leges, alias super alias ingerens, tum easdem pari rursus astutia a populo negligi patiebatur, quo cunctos hac ratione sibi obnoxios redderet. Nec aliud in consilio fuisse huic pontifici videtur in tot

---

²⁵The medieval popes claimed the right to make laws, based on an agreement with the Emperor Justin I in 519, which healed the so-called 'Acacian schism' between Rome and Constantinople and gave the Roman pontiff 'jurisdiction' in the former western Roman empire, as well as on the forged *Donation of Constantine*. It was a 'right' which was sharply contested by almost every secular ruler who was powerful enough to do so. The papacy never renounced it, but by 1571 it had become a dead letter almost everywhere in western Europe.

²⁶A reference to Gratian's *Concordantia discordantium canonum*, or *Decretum*, issued about 1140. It eventually supplanted earlier collections.

²⁷Decretals were issued by the popes, and were collected from about 1190 onwards. Five of these collections, now known as the *Quinque compilationes antiquae*, were in use when Pope Gregory IX replaced them with his *Liber extra*, issued on 5 September 1234.

²⁸The series of decretals issued by Pope Clement V on 21 March 1314 after the close of the Council of Vienne (1311-12), where they were supposedly promulgated.

²⁹The *Liber Sexta*, issued by Pope Boniface VIII on 3 March 1298.

³⁰There are no 'intravagantes', but there are two collections of *Extravagantes*, one issued by Pope John XXII on 13 November 1334 and named after him; the other, known as the *Extravagantes communes*, compiled in the fifteenth century and gradually accepted as authoritative.

³¹This refers to William Lyndwood's *Provinciale*, which was finished in 1430 and published in 1433.

³²This is Dionysius II of Syracuse (367-57), whose incompetence weakened the state and led to his overthrow. Plutarch mentions him in his life of Timoleon, who prevented Dionysius from regaining control of the city in 343 BC.

knew no limit, but piled laws[25] upon laws, decrees[26] upon decrees, and decretals[27] on top of them, and so on, one thing on top of another. Nor did he declare any end to it, until he had burdened the world with his Clementines,[28] the Sext,[29] *intra-* and *extravagantes*,[30] provincial and synodal constitutions,[31] *palea*, glosses, sentences, chapters, summaries, rescripts, writs, cases long and short, and endless rhapsodies, so that even Mount Atlas, by which heaven is said to be held up, would hardly be enough to bear the burden (if it were to be imposed upon it). And indeed, a rather disorderly and bizarre cult of this pontifical comedy pushed him on even further in the same direction. In all this it was astonishing what crowds he attracted, what games he invented for the world, and what errors he devised, presenting to the outside world a certain appearance of religion, but in such a way that it was hardly very difficult for anyone who took a closer look to see that in his heart he had formed a very different conception, which quite clearly was to raise up some ecclesiastical empire of unique eminence in this world. But not content with all this, he did not stop trying to extend the law of his court until he had brought the entire civil sword, with its full power, into his own possession, not considering in the meantime whether he might be helping to improve moral discipline (which perhaps he never took seriously) but partly in order to establish the dignity of his see by strengthening it by every means, and partly to acquire as much wealth as possible from wherever he could, in order to satisfy his greed. Plutarch records a similar example in the case of Dionysius of Syracuse,[32] who passed so many laws with insidious intent, laying one upon another and then with equal cleverness allowing them to be disregarded by the people, so that in this way he made them all answerable to him. It seems that the pope had much the same idea in making up such a complex pattern of laws that he could hold almost everyone guilty of having broken his canonical precepts, with the result that his income from dispensations and condemnations grew even greater. And just think - this was the dénouement of this farce. For just as old comedies usually end in a wedding, so almost all the pope's efforts ended in

congerendis legum centonibus, quam ut plurimos canonicis suis articulis irretitos
teneret, quo uberior quaestus ei ex dispensationibus et condemnationibus
accresceret. Atque hanc puta catastrophen esse huius choragii. Nam ut veteres
olim comoediae exibant fere in nuptias, ita pontificis omnes fere molitiones
desinebant in pecunias. Breviter sub hoc pontifice ita gubernata est res
ecclesiastica, ut in peiori loco nec alias fuerit unquam, nec tum esse potuerit,
quando nihil in religione fere rectum, in moribus nihil sanum, nihil in
conscientiis liberum, nec in cultu sincerum relinquebatur, nec in legibus
quicquam nisi quod ad inutiles quasdam ceremonias vel absurda dogmata, vel ad
ordinis magnificentiam tuendam pertinebat. Et si in consistoriis ostendebatur
nonnulla forsan iustitiae umbra et morum inspectio, sic tamen res gerebatur, ut
pretio nulli non venalis foret impunitas. Cui et hoc porro accedebat incommodi,
quod cum ab eis iudiciis procul omnis politica potestas arceretur, interim tota fori
tractatio nescio quibus canonistis et officialibus patebat, quorum magna pars ex
litibus victitans suum magis spectabat compendium, quam virtutis ac morum
rectitudinem. Ut multa hic supprimam modestiae causa, fortassis non
praetereunda, si non pudori magis consulere quam calamo indulgere hoc loco
libuisset.

Postulabat sane haec tanta rerum dissipatio necessariam emendationem.
Neque fefellit ecclesiam suam divina providentia, cuius singulari beneficio coepit
tandem utcunque scintillare, velut e crassa nebula, promicans sincerioris
religionis aura, regnante auspicatissimae memoriae Rege Henrico octavo; qui
regum omnium in hoc regno primus, magno reipublicae bono, pontificis huius
nomen cum superbissimis fascibus prorsus e regni finibus excusserat. Quin nec
eo contentus cordatus rex, ut nomen nudosque solum titulos a se suisque
depelleret, nisi et iura decretaque omnia, quibus adhuc obstringebatur ecclesia,
perfringeret; huc quoque animum adiecit, ut universam secum rempublicam in
plenam assereret libertatem. Quocirca cum ex ipsius,[33] tum ex publico senatus[34]
decreto delecti sunt viri aliquot, usu et doctrina praestantes, numero triginta duo,
qui penitus abolendo pontificio iuri (quod canonicum vocamus), cum omni illa
decretorum et decretalium facultate, novas ipsi leges, quae controversiarum et
morum iudicia regerent, regis nomine et auctoritate surrogarent. Id quod ex ipsius
regis epistula, quam huic praefiximus libro,[35] constare poterit, quae et serium
ipsius in hac re studium et piam voluntatem aperiat. Laudandum profecto regis
propositum, nec illaudandi fortassis eorum conatus, qui leges tum illas, licet his
longe dissimiles, conscripserant. Sed nescio quo modo quaque occasione res
successu caruit, sive temporum iniquitate, sive nimia eorum cessatione, quibus
tunc negotium committebatur. Sequitur post haec regis tandem Henrici mors,
aequo pulsans pede pauperum tabernas regumque turres. Post quem subiit in

---

[33]Presumably the three articles sent to the convocation of Canterbury on 10 May 1532 and
approved by that body five days later.

[34]25 Henry VIII, c. 19, 1534 (*S. R.*, III, 460-1).

[35]In the 1571 edition, this letter came before Edward VI's proclamation. It is reproduced
here in its original setting, at the beginning of the Henrician Canons.

money. In a word, under the pope church business was so managed that things could hardly have been in a worse condition, nor could it have been otherwise when almost nothing in religion was right, nothing in morals was healthy, and nothing in conscience was free, nor was there any sincerity left in worship, or anything in the laws, except what led to certain pointless ceremonies and absurd doctrines, or what helped preserve the worldly splendour of the hierarchy. And if perhaps in the consistories there was some shadow of justice and supervision of morals shown, yet the matter was handled in such a way that there was no price at which acquittal would not be sold. Furthermore, there was the additional inconvenience, in that since all civil power was far removed from these tribunals, all court business was actually handled by goodness knows what canonists and officials, a large number of whom lived off the litigation and paid more attention to their own profit than to any standard of virtue and morality. For modesty's sake, I am here leaving out many things which perhaps ought not to be passed over, except that it is better to beware of scandal than to let my pen run riot at this point.

Obviously, degradation on this scale demanded the necessary correction. Nor did the providence of God betray his church. Rather it began, by his exceptional blessing, to shine like a ray of pure religion breaking forth out of a dark cloud in the reign of King Henry VIII, of most auspicious memory, who was the first of all the kings in this realm who threw the name of the pope, with his haughty paraphernalia, right out of the bounds of the kingdom, to the great good of the state. But not content merely to drive away the name and the empty titles from himself and his people, without also destroying the laws and all the decrees by which the church had been bound up to that time, that wise king also turned his mind towards obtaining full liberty both for himself and for the whole state. Therefore, both by a royal decree[33] and by a statute of parliament,[34] some men of outstanding experience and learning were appointed, thirty-two in number, who set about abolishing papal law (which we call canon law), with all its apparatus of decrees and decretals, and in its place proposed new laws, in the name and by the authority of the king, to govern judgments in matters of controversy and morals. It is also clear from the king's letter, which we have prefixed to this book,[35] that his intentions in this matter were serious and his desire godly. The king's intention must be praised, and perhaps also the attempts of those who compiled those laws, even though they are very different from the present ones. But I do not know how or why their attempt failed, whether it was due to the evil of the times or to too great a lack of perseverance on the part of those to whom the task had been entrusted. Following on these events came King Henry's death, something which strikes both the cottages of the poor and the castles of kings with equal force. After him, the reins of power passed to his

regni habenas relictus a patre filius nunquam satis laudati nominis Edovardus sextus.[36] Qui in emendanda primum religione, quam adhuc incohatam reliquit pater, maiores impetus ac vires addidit, nec omnino profecit infeliciter. Quo factum, ut religionis fontes multo quam antea purgatiores nativo quodammodo nitori sint restituti. Sed iniquissimi illorum temporum mores, longe a professione dissidentes et religioni labem, et bonis omnibus dolorem non mediocrem asperserunt. In causa creditur, quod cum doctrina reformata non item adhibita essent legum idonea repagula, quae effrenem multitudinis impunitatem cohiberent. Durabant enim adhuc haec ipsa, quae et hodie regnant in curiis, et consistoriis pontificii iuris instituta et constitutiones provinciales, quae praeter verbosam ceremoniarum congeriem nihil fere habebant, quod corrigendae Christianorum vitae magnopere conduceret. Neque interim hoc nesciebat pro divina sua indole Edovardus noster. Itaque, coacto mox senatu, indictoque frequentissimis comitiis parlamento, non solum in animo habuit, sed diligenter etiam curavit, paternum secutus exemplum, ut quod ille factum prius voluisset in reformandis pontificiorum canonum decretis, id ipse absolutiori expeditione perfectum redderet.

Quid multis? Ex communi ordinum omnium[37] suffragio datum id negotii est viris, si non eisdem, quibus superius, at pari tamen numero, nec impari excellentia praeditis, triginta videlicet duobus (quod idem etiam ab Henrico prius octavo instituebatur) partim ex episcopis, partim ex theologia, partim ex utriusque iuris prudentia,[38] partim ex communis quoque iuris professione, ad octenos in quattuor classes ad hoc ipsum designatis, ut ipsorum arbitrio certa quaedam sanctionum capita in legum formulas redacta figerentur, quae in locum suffecta Romanarum constitutionum, reipublicae et moribus in melius formandis quam maxime salutares proponerentur. Nec longum erat quin regis voluntati satisfactum sit. Res enim, tanquam pensum, in varias distributa operas felicitate non minori quam celeritate confecta est, hoc observato ordine; ut duo hi et triginta (quos diximus) in quattuor classes aequa proportione ita dividerentur, ut in singulis octonariis duo episcopi, duo item theologi, rursusque duo iuris utriusque similiter et communis iuris consulti totidem continerentur. Inter quos sic denique conventum est, ut quod in singulis classibus conclusum et definitum esset, id per reliquas classes considerandum atque inspiciendum transmitteretur. Quamquam vero ex hoc ipso omni numero octo potissimum selecta fuerunt capita, quibus prima operis praeformatio quasique materiae praeparatio commitebatur, quorum nomina regis in Edovardi epistula compraehensa videre liceat. Atque hoc modo confectae hae quidem leges sunt, sive eas ecclesiasticas sive politicas appellare libeat. Quarum materia ab optimis undique legibus petita videtur, non solum ecclesiasticis sed civilibus etiam, veterumque Romanarum

---

[36]Though only a minor, Edward VI knew about (and presumably approved of) the compilation of the *Reformatio*. For a critical analysis of the Edwardian committee and its work, see the Introduction.

[37]There were three estates – the clergy, the lords and the commons.

[38]*I.e.*, Roman civil and canon law.

surviving son, Edward VI, whose name has never been sufficiently praised.[36] He brought greater force and strength to the correction of religion, which his father had only begun, and he was quite successful. As a result, the founts of religion became much purer than they had previously been and were restored to something like their natural beauty. But people's practice in those days was extremely wicked, and far removed from what they preached, which brought decay to religion and great grief to all good people. The fact of the matter is that although doctrine had been reformed there had not been a comparable refashioning of the laws which would restrain the unbridled impudence of the masses. For the very same statutes of papal law and provincial constitutions, which apart from a long-winded series of rituals contain almost nothing which is of any use in correcting the lives of Christians, still remained in force in the courts and consistories, as they do to this day. Nor was our Edward unaware of this, thanks to his divine genius. Therefore, convocation was soon convened and parliament was charged with frequent committee meetings, because he not only intended but following his father's example, actually saw to it that what Henry had previously wanted to do by way of reforming the decrees of the papal canons, he would himself bring to completion with more determined resolution.

Why say a great deal about this? By the unanimous vote of all the estates[37] the task was given to men who, though not the same as those mentioned above, were nevertheless equal in number to them and endowed with comparable excellence, that is to thirty-two (which was the number previously decided upon by Henry VIII), drawn partly from the bishops, partly from the theologians, partly from each branch of jurisprudence[38] and partly from the common law profession and divided into four groups of eight for this purpose, that at their discretion, certain chapters of sanctions should be edited into forms of law, which would take the place of the Roman constitutions and be put forward as the most wholesome laws possible for the state and for the better advancement of morals. It was not long before the king's desire was satisfied. For the matter was divided up into different tasks as planned, and it was completed both successfully and speedily. The following order was adopted: the thirty-two (as we have already said) were divided into four equal groups in such a way that each group of eight had two bishops, two theologians, and likewise two experts in Roman law and two in common law. Finally, it was agreed among them that what was decided and defined in each individual group should then be sent to the other groups for their consideration and inspection. But out of the total number eight men in particular were singled out, to whom the first preliminaries and the virtual preparation of the work were entrusted. Their names may be seen included in King Edward's letter. This is how these laws were put together, whether one prefers to call them ecclesiastical or civil. It is clear that their substance has been taken from the best laws, wherever they may be found, not only ecclesiastical ones but civil ones as well, deriving from the most extreme antiquity of the ancient Romans. Thomas Cranmer, archbishop of Canterbury, was in charge of the whole business. Walter Haddon, a gifted man and not

praecipua antiquitate. Summae negotii praefuit Thomas Cranmerus, archiepiscopus Cantuariensis. Orationis lumen et splendorem addidit Gualterus Haddonus, vir disertus, et in hac ipsa iuris facultate non imperitus. Quin nec satis scio an Iohannis Checi, viri singularis, eidem negotio adiutrix adfuerit manus. Quo factum est, ut cultiori stylo concinnatae sint istae leges, quam pro communi ceterarum legum more. Atque equidem lubens optarim, si quid votis meis proficerem, ut consimili exemplo, nec dissimili etiam oratione ac stylo, prosiliat nunc aliquis, qui in vernaculis nostris legibus perpoliendis idem efficiat, quod in ecclesiasticis istis praestitit clarissimae memoriae hic Haddonus. Sed haec aliorum relinquens perpensioni, ad eccelsiasticas nostras redeo, quae quemadmodum elaboratae fuerint, quibusque auctoribus conscriptae, iam aperuimus. Restabat nunc de illarum dignitate et aestimatione aliquid porro mihi disserendum. Sed quia nolim meo iudicio ceteris praecurrere, liberam suam cuique censuram relinquo. Nobis sat erit, quoniam iampridem in superioribus monumentis nostris promissa sunt, studiosis lectoribus haec proposuisse, non ut vim illico legum auctoritatemque induant, sed ut specimen dumtaxat rei, velut ad gustum ista lectitare volentibus, exhiberemus, quae ubi perlecta fuerint, pro suo quisque captu, quid de eis statuendum putet, libere secum pensitet. Ut nihil est, nec unquam fuit, tam feliciter humano elucubratum ingenio, cui non aliquid inhaesit naevi, ita neque hic fortasse defutura sunt, quae δευτέρας φροντίδας et acriorem lectoris discussionem flagitare nonnullis videbuntur. In quo genere praeter alia quae brevitatis causa transilire cogor, hoc unum minime vel praetereundum mihi vel doctis iudiciis admittendum videtur, quod lex ista vetat in titulo *De divinis officiis* capite 16[39] ne quicquam omnino praeter praescripta peragatur, et formulas illius libri nostra communi lingua scripti, quem proprium et perfectum omnis divini cultus magistrum esse statuit, etc. Nos vero perfectum omnis divini cultus magistrum solum Dei Verbum agnoscimus, cum interim in hoc libro non esse nulla constat, quae per omnia minus quadrare ad amussim ecclesiasticae reformationis videantur, multoque rectius fortasse mutarentur. Sed haec ab aliis rectius perspici{*entur*}, quam a me admoneri poterint. Interim, illustrissimi principis Edovardi nostri tam piam vereque Christianam sollicitudinem nunquam satis laudare queo, nec minus praeclare eorum etiam doctorum hominum navatam diligentiam arbitror, qui congerendis his legibus praefuerunt, quas summa approbatione et applausu illorum tum temporum fuisse receptas constat. Nec dubium quin parlamentari etiam auctoritate eaedem sanctiones istae constabilitae atque in publicum usum consecratae fuissent, si vita regi paulo longior suppetisset. Quod ut valde tum dolendum est non contigisse, ita nunc vicissim optandum, quod per praematuram mortem regis illius negatum est ecclesiae felicitati, per feliciora tempora serenissimae reginae nostrae Elizabethae suppleatur, accedente publica huius nunc parlamenti auctoritate, simulque faventibus doctorum hominum suffragiis. Quos ut nostram hanc in edendo audaciam boni consulant, impense rogamus.

---

[39]R, 19.16. This probably correlates with Foxe's marginal annotation in Harleian MS 426, placed opposite R, 19.1.

unskilled in the field of the law, contributed the light and splendour of his style. I am not entirely sure whether John Cheke, a most notable man, lent a helping hand to the work or not. It is for this reason that these laws were written in a more educated style than is the normal custom for other laws. And if I might pray for something, I would willingly choose that someone else should now undertake to do the same thing for the revision of our vernacular laws as Haddon, of most noble memory, did for these ecclesiastical ones, following his example and imitating his diction and style. But leaving this to the consideration of others, I return to our ecclesiastical laws. We have already explained how they were devised and by whom they were written. There remains now the need for me to discourse somewhat further on their appropriateness and their value. But because I do not want my judgment to outpace that of others, I leave each one free to form his own opinion. It will be enough for us to lay these matters before our eager readers, since we have long since promised to do so in our earlier writings, not so that they should assume the authority and force of the laws, but merely to give a sample demonstration of the matter to suit the taste of those who enjoy reading such things. Once they have been read through, each person may feel free, on the strength of his own investigation, to decide what he thinks ought to be done about them. For just as there is nothing, and never has been anything, which has been so successfully worked out in the human mind which has not got something wrong with it, so here too there will probably be things which will seem to some people to require 'second thoughts' and more careful discussion on the reader's part. Of these, apart from other things which I am forced to skip over because of lack of space, there is at least one matter which I cannot overlook or leave to the learned judgments of others, which is that this law forbids (in the title *De divinis officiis*, section 16)[39] anything at all to be done [in worship] apart from those things which are prescribed in the rubrics of that book, written in our common language, which has been declared to be the proper and perfect guide to all divine worship, etc. But we recognize only the Word of God to be the perfect guide to all divine worship, whereas it appears that there are some things in that book which appear not to square exactly with the need of ecclesiastical reformation, and which probably ought rather to be changed. But these things can be considered by others better than they can be pointed out by me. Meanwhile, I am as always quite unable to give enough praise to the godly and truly Christian concern of our most illustrious Prince Edward, nor do I consider the zealous diligence of those learned men, who presided over the compiling of these laws, which it is agreed were received in their time with the greatest approval and applause, to be any less outstanding. Nor is there any doubt that these same laws would have been ratified and authorized for public use by the authority of parliament, if only the king had lived a little longer. So just as we must regret that this did not happen, so now we must hope that what was denied to the happiness of the church because of the premature death of the king may now be put right in the happier times of our most serene Queen Elizabeth, accompanied by the public authority of this present parliament, along with the supporting votes of learned men, whom we earnestly beg to look favourably on our boldness in publishing these laws.

REX EDOVARDUS SEXTUS

Edovardus sextus, Dei gratia Angliae, Franciae et Hiberniae rex, fidei defensor, et in terra Ecclesiae Anglicanae et Hibernicae supremum caput, reverendissimo in Christo patri, Thomae eadem gratia Cantuariensi archiepiscopo, totius Angliae primati et metropolitano, reverendoque in Christo patri, Thomae Eliensi episcopo, ac dilectis nobis in Christo, Richardo Cox eleemosynario nostro, Petro Martyr, sacrae theologiae professoribus, Wilhelmo Maye, Rolando Taylor de Hadley, legum doctoribus, nec non dilectis et fidelibus nostris, Iohanni Lucas et Richardo Goodrich, armigeris, salutem.

Cum vos triginta duos viros ad leges nostras ecclesiasticas perlegendas et componendas iuxta vim, formam et effectum cuiusdam acti parlamenti, in tertio regni nostri anno apud Westmonasterium facti,[1] brevi assignare et deputare proponimus, et ubi numerus praedictus ad tractatum legum praedictarum describendarum et componendarum nimius videtur, tametsi id tum propter consultationem et iudicium super eo habendum, tum etiam propter perfectionem et complementum earundem longe expediens existit, nobis, moventibus consiliariis nostris a secretis, consentaneum magis videtur, huius rei initium introitum primam formam et lineaturam numero octavo, qui doctorum triginta erit portio, committere; nempe quasi praeparationem quandam grandiori numero futuram.

Quapropter de prudentia, scientia et diligentia vestris plurimum confidentes, de sententia concilii nominavimus et deputavimus vos commissarios nostros, et vobis auctoritatem per praesentes impartimus, ut loco et tempore congruis et opportunis, celeritate conveniente qua poteritis maxima, insimul conveniatis, cursumque legum ecclesiasticarum, infra regnum nostrum in usu existentium, aut antehac uti solitarum, diligenter perlegatis, consideretis et ponderetis, eoque facto, illarum loco et vice, collectionem, compilationem et ordinem talium legum ecclesiasticarum inveniatis faciatis et in scripta redigi faciatis, quales in usu esse practicari et in quibuscunque curiis et iurisdictionibus nostris ecclesiasticis infra istud regnum nostrum et alia nostra dominia proponi et publicari, de scientia, sapientia et iudicio vestris maxime expediens fore putaveritis; habentes considerationem et respectum debitum ad tenorem statuti praedicti, pro praeservatione legum nostrarum communium in suo vigore remanentium, et pro omnibus aliis articulis et ramis dicti statuti. Et quamprimum leges praedictae per vos adinventae formatae descriptae et compilatae fiunt, easdem statim nobis exhiberi et in scriptis tradi volumus, ut eas de concilii nostri sententia, de residuo triginta duorum, una vobiscum, pro ulteriore legum praedictarum

---

[1] 2-3 Edward VI, c. 13, 1548-9 (*S.R.*, IV, 55-8).

KING EDWARD THE SIXTH

Edward VI, by the grace of God, king of England, France and Ireland, defender of the faith, and in earth supreme head of the Church of England and Ireland, to the most reverend father in Christ, Thomas, by the same grace archbishop of Canterbury, primate of all England and metropolitan, to Thomas bishop of Ely, and to our beloved in Christ, Richard Cox our almoner [and] Peter Martyr, professors of sacred theology, William May, Roland Taylor of Hadley, doctors of law, and also to our beloved and faithful John Lucas and Richard Goodrich, esquires, greeting.

As we propose shortly to appoint and designate you thirty-two men to review and compile our ecclesiastical laws according to the force, form and effect of a certain act of parliament, made at Westminster in the third year of our reign,[1] and as the aforesaid number seems to be too great for the business of defining and compiling the aforesaid laws, even though it ought to be held for the purpose of consultation and decision concerning this matter, as well as being highly expedient for the perfecting and completing of those laws, it seems better to us, with the agreement of our privy council, to entrust the initial stages of the work, including the format and framework, to eight men who are a part of the thirty [*sic*] doctors. Obviously, they will serve as a preparatory group for the subsequent gathering of the entire number.

Thus, with the greatest confidence in your wisdom, knowledge and diligence, on the advice of the council we have nominated and appointed you as our commissioners, and by these presents grant you the authority to come together at an appropriate and convenient time and place, with as much suitable speed as you possibly can, and carefully review, consider and ponder the corpus of ecclesiastical laws actually in use in this kingdom, or customarily used in the past, and having done that, in their place and stead to compose, make and cause to be recorded in writing, a collection, compilation and catalogue of such ecclesiastical laws as you think, on the basis of your knowledge, wisdom and judgment, ought most expediently to be in force and in which of our ecclesiastical courts and jurisdictions within this our kingdom and our other dominions they ought to be propounded and published, having consideration and due regard for the tenor of the aforesaid statute, for the preservation of our common laws remaining in force, and for all the other articles and branches of the said statute. And as soon as the aforesaid laws have been made, formed, defined and compiled by you, we want them to be shown and sent to us in

ecclesiasticarum ratificatione et perfectione, tanquam commissariorum nostrorum, iuxta formam statuti praedicti, coniunctim nominandorum transmittamus.

Et quamvis vos ea modestia et sapientia praeditos esse scimus, quod onus istud humeris vestris commissum et impositum haud parvi esse momenti et ponderis aestimabitis; considerantes tamen, quod propositum nostrum non est aliud quam praeparationis cuiusdam gratia istud a vobis effectum reddi; ita quod maior numerus ad consultationem et perfectionem eiusdem magis certo et ordinate procedere valeat, certiores vos esse volumus, quod actiones et studia vestra in hac parte cum erunt nobis gratissima, tum autem benignissima et maxime favorabili interpretatione accepta.

Et praeterea volumus quod statim post receptionem praesentium una conveniatis, et hac in re celeritate et expeditione ea utamini, quam causa exposcit; mandantes et stricta praecipientes omnibus et singulis personis, quarum consilio sententia et ope in hac parte vos opus habebitis, quod illi per vos requisiti opem praestent consulant et iuvent, quemadmodum nobis placere cupiunt. In cuius rei testimonium has litteras nostras fieri fecimus patentes. Teste me ipso apud Westmonasterium XI die Novembris anno regni regis quinto [11 November 1551].

Marton.

Per ipsum Regem, et de data praedicta auctoritate parlamenti.

writing immediately, so that we may pass them on for the opinion of our council, and of the rest of the thirty-two who have been appointed, along with you, according to the form of the aforesaid statute, as our commissioners for the further ratification and perfecting of the aforesaid ecclesiastical laws.

And although we know that you are blessed with such modesty and wisdom that you will consider this burden committed to your shoulders to be of great moment and weight, nevertheless, considering that our proposal is only that this matter should be launched by some preparation on your part, so that a larger number may then be enabled to proceed to the revising and perfecting of the same with greater confidence and sense of direction, we want you to be all the more certain that your actions and efforts in this respect will not only be most pleasing to us, but will also be received with the kindest and most favourable understanding.

And moreover it is our will that you shall meet together immediately after receiving these presents, and employ such speed and efficiency in this matter as the case requires, commanding and strictly enjoining all and singular persons, of whose counsel, advice and help you will be in need in this respect, that they, upon being requested by you, shall offer help, advice and assistance, in so far as they desire to please us. In witness of which matter we have caused these our letters patent to be made. Witnessed by me at Westminster, on the eleventh day of November in the fifth year of the king's reign [11 November 1551].

Marton.

By the king himself, and with the aforesaid authority of parliament given.

[1r; 1a]   **1. DE SUMMA TRINITATE ET FIDE CATHOLICA**

1. De fide Christiana ab omnibus amplectenda et profitenda.[1]

Quoniam regni potestas et legum administrandarum ius ad nos ex Deo pervenit, principium nobis ab eodem Deo capiendum erit. De cuius natura cum recte fuerit et ordine constitutum, facilior erit reliquarum legum provisio, quas ad confirmandum in regno nostro verum Dei cultum, et ad [*pi*/**ips**]um ecclesiae statutum conservandum, adhiberi curavimus. Quapropter omnes homines ad quos imperium nostrum ulla ratione pertinet, Christianam religionem suscipere et profiteri volumus et iubemus. Contra quam qui cogitationes aut actiones ullas suscipiunt, impietate sua Deum a se abalienant; nos autem qui divinae maiestatis administri sumus, et facultates universas et ipsam denique vitam illis abiudicandam esse statuimus, quicunque tam immani se scelere impietatis obligaverint. Et hoc in omnibus *nos* valeat nostris subditis, quocunque nomine, loco vel conditione censeantur.

2. De natura Dei et beata Trinitate, quid sit credendum.[2]

Omnes filii Dei per Iesum Christum renati, ex [1v] corde puro, conscientia bona et fide non ficta credant et confi[1b]teantur unum esse vivum et verum Deum, aeternum et incorporeum, impassibilem, immensae potentiae, sapientiae et bonitatis, creatorem et conservatorem omnium rerum tum visibilium tum invisibilium; et in unitate eius divinae naturae tres esse personas, eiusdem essentiae ac aeternitatis, Patrem, Filium et Spiritum Sanctum; Patrem vero a seipso esse, nec ab alio quoquam vel generari vel procedere; et Filium quidem a Patre generari; Spiritum Sanctum vero et a Patre et a Filio procedere;[3] nec

---

[1]26 Henry VIII, c. 1, 1534 (*S.R.*, III, 492). Cf. Also the preface to H.C.

[2]X, 1.1.1 (Fr, II, 5-6), originally c. 1 of Lateran IV, 1215 (*C. O. D.*, 230-1); X, 1.1.2 (Fr, II, 6-7), originally c. 2 of Lateran IV, 1215 (*C. O. D.*, 231-2), the Athanasian creed (*Quicunque vult*) and Article 1 of 1553 and 1571.

[3]The double procession of the Holy Spirit, often referred to as the *Filioque* controversy, because of the addition of this word to the Latin version of the Nicene Creed, was (and is) the classic dogmatic controversy between the Eastern and Western churches, but the classical Western position was not challenged by the protestant reformers. For the canon law on the subject, see D, 5 *de cons.*, c. 39 (Fr, I, 1423) and D, 5 *de cons.*, c. 40 (Fr, I, 1424).

1. OF THE HIGHEST TRINITY AND THE CATHOLIC FAITH

1. Of the Christian faith, to be embraced and professed by all.[1]

Since the power to rule and the right to administer laws has come to us from God, we ought to learn about him first. For once his nature is rightly and properly understood, the meaning of the other laws which we have taken care to be applied to the confirmation of the true worship of God in our kingdom, and to preserving the [*godly* **same**] state of the church, will be easier. For this reason, it is our will and command that all people to whom our rule in any way extends, shall accept and profess the Christian religion. Those who engage in any thoughts or deeds contrary to it turn God away from them by their ungodliness; moreover, we who are servants of the divine majesty decree that all goods, and finally even life itself shall be confiscated from those who have involved themselves in that enormous crime of ungodliness. And this shall apply to all our subjects, of whatever name, rank or condition they may be.

2. What is to be believed about the nature of God and the blessed Trinity.[2]

All children of God who are born again by Jesus Christ, shall believe with a pure heart, a good conscience and an unfeigned faith, and they shall confess that there is one living and true God, eternal and incorporeal, impassible, of unlimited power, wisdom and goodness, the creator and preserver of all things, both visible and invisible, and that in the unity of that divine nature there are three persons, of the same essence and eternity, the Father, the Son and the Holy Spirit, and that the Father is of himself, neither begotten of anyone else nor proceeding, and that the Son is begotten of the Father, and that the Holy Spirit proceeds from the Father and the Son,[3] and that no diversity or inequality is to be understood in this

ullam naturae diversitatem aut inaequalitatem in ista personarum distinctione poni, sed quoad substantiam, vel (ut dicunt), essentiam divinam, omnia inter eos paria et aequalia esse.

3. De Christo et mysteriis nostrae redemptionis.[4]

Credatur etiam, cum venisset plenitudo temporis, Filium qui est Verbum Patris, in utero beatae virginis Mariae, ex ipsius carnis substantia, naturam humanam assumpsisse, ita ut duae naturae, divina et humana, integre atque perfecte in unitate personae, fuerint inseparabiliter coniunctae; ex quibus unus est Christus, verus Deus et verus homo; qui vere passus est, crucifixus, mortuus et sepultus, descendit ad inferos ac tertia die resurrexit, nobisque per suum sanguinem reconciliavit Patrem, sese hostiam offerens illi, non solum pro culpa originis, verum etiam pro omnibus peccatis quae homines propria voluntate adiecerunt.

[2r] 4. De duabus Christi naturis post resurrectionem.[5]

Credatur item Dominus noster Iesus Christus, etiam post resurrectionem, duplici natura constare; divina quidem, immensa, incircumscripta et infinita, quae ubique sit et [2a] omnia impleat; humana vero, finita et descripta humani corporis terminis ac finibus, qua, postquam peccata nostra perpurgavisset, in caelos ascendit, ibique ita sedet ad dexteram Patris, ut non ubique sit,[6] quippe quem oportet in caelo remanere, usque ad tempus restitutionis omnium, cum ad iudicandum vivos et mortuos veniet, ut reddat cuique iuxta opera sua.

5. De tribus symbolis.[7]

Et quoniam omnia ferme, quae ad fidem spectant catholicam, (tum quoad beatissimam trinitatem, tum quoad mysteria nostrae redemptionis), tribus

---

[4]X, 1.1.1 (Fr, II, 5-6), c. 1 of Lateran IV, 1215 (*C.O.D.*, 230-1). Articles 2-4 of 1553 and 1571.

[5]Article 4 of 1553 and 1571.

[6]The 'ubiquity' of Christ's ascended body was a Lutheran doctrine which was rejected by most of the Swiss reformers because it denied that the ascended Christ retained the natural properties (including finitude) of a human body. It was important in eucharistic controversies, because the Lutherans claimed that Christ's 'ubiquitious' body could be present 'in, with and under' the species of bread and wine, but in a 'heavenly and spiritual manner' (i.e., not by transubstantiation). The Swiss, including Calvin, rejected this and claimed that the presence of Christ in the sacrament was spiritual only. See R, 2.5 below. On Lutheran doctrine, see W. Maurer, *Historical commentary on the Augsburg Confession* (Philadelphia, 1986), pp. 258-61, 408-9.

[7]Article 7 of 1553 (8 of 1571).

distinction of persons, but that according to the divine substance, or (as they say) essence, they share everything alike and equally.

3. Of Christ and the mysteries of our redemption.[4]

Furthermore, it is to be believed that when the fulness of time was come, the Son, who is the Word of the Father, took on a human nature in the womb of the blessed virgin Mary, of the substance of her flesh, so that the two natures, divine and human, have been inseparably conjoined, fully and perfectly, in unity of person. Out of them there is one Christ, true God and true man, who truly suffered, was crucified, died and was buried, he descended into hell and on the third day he rose again, and by his blood he has reconciled the Father to us, offering himself to him as a sacrifice, not only for original guilt, but also for all the sins which people have added to that by their own will.

4. Of the two natures of Christ after the resurrection.[5]

Likewise it is to be believed that our Lord Jesus Christ, even after the resurrection, had a double nature; one divine, incomprehensible, unlimited and infinite, which is everywhere and fills all things, and one human, finite and defined by the limits and bounds of the human body, in which, after he had purged our sins, he ascended into heaven, and there he sits at the right hand of God in such a way as not to be everywhere,[6] since it is necessary for him to remain in heaven until the time of the restoration of all things, when he shall come to judge the living and the dead, in order to reward each one according to his works.

5. Of the three creeds.[7]

And since virtually all things which pertain to the catholic faith (both as regards the most blessed Trinity and as regards the mysteries of our redemption) are

symbolis, hoc est, Apostolico,[8] Nicaeno[9] et Athanasii[10] breviter continentur; idcirco ista tria symbola, ut fidei nostrae compendia quaedam, recipimus et amplectimur, quod firmissimis divinarum et canonicarum Scripturarum testimoniis facile probari poss[u/i]nt.

6. Quae sint canonicae Scripturae, quoad Vetus Testamentum.[11]

Ut autem quae s[u/i]nt Scripturae illae canonicae ex quibus solis religionis et fidei dogmata constare [2v] et confirmari debent, non ambigant fideles, illarum catalogum hic ascribendum duximus, secuti in Veteri Testamento illum quo Hebraei utuntur ordinem,[12] qui sic habet:

Libri Moysis quinque.

Iosuae.
Iudicum.
Samuelis 2.
Regum 2.
Isaias.
Ieremias.
Ezechiel.

---

[8]Based on the old Roman creed which can be traced back to the second century, though the earliest example of it in its present form goes back only to 724. See J. N. D. Kelly, *Early Christian creeds*, 3rd edn. (London, 1972), pp. 368-434.

[9]Not the creed adopted at the first council of Nicaea in 325. It is rather a creed which was composed at or shortly after the first council of Constantinople in 381, and which was canonized as 'Nicene' at the council of Chalcedon in 451. See Kelly, *Creeds*, pp. 296-331.

[10]Ascribed to Athanasius, archbishop of Alexandria (*c.* 296-373), because of his reputation as a defender of orthodoxy, though it was originally composed in Latin, probably in Gaul during the first half of the sixth century, and possibly by Caesarius, who was bishop of Arles from 502 to 542. See J. N. D. Kelly, *The Athanasian creed* (London, 1964).

[11]This is the Hebrew canon, preferred by Jerome (340-420) and by all protestants, but rejected by Augustine (354-430) and by the council of Trent, fourth session, 8 April 1546 (*C.O.D.*, 663-4). See Article 5 of 1553 (6 of 1571), which lists the books in the Septuagint order, which is the one normally followed in Christian Bibles today.

[12]The Hebrew canon is divided into three main parts, known as the law (Torah), the prophets and the 'writings'. The division given here reflects this, but the details are more complicated. The order of the books of the law was always fixed, but that of the prophets could vary. The order given here is the one retained by Jerome, though there were at least eight other possibilities. As for the writings, at least seventy different orders are found, of which the standard one today dates from a thirteenth-century German manuscript (De Rossi) which happened to be the one most widely printed in the sixteenth century. However, the order given here is a different one, and is not found anywhere among the seventy which are known. See R. T. Beckwith, *The Old Testament canon of the New Testament church* (London, 1985), pp. 450-64.

briefly contained in the three creeds, that is, the Apostles',[8] the Nicene[9] and the Athanasian,[10] therefore we receive and embrace these three creeds as summaries of our faith, for they can easily be proved by the most certain testimonies of the divine and canonical Scriptures.

6. What Scriptures are canonical in the Old Testament.[11]

And in order that believers shall not be in any doubt as to what those canonical Scriptures are, by which alone the doctrines of religion and faith must stand and be confirmed, we have drawn up a list of them, following in the Old Testament the order which the Jews use,[12] as follows:

The five books of Moses.

Joshua.
Judges.
Samuel (2).
Kings (2).
Isaiah.
Jeremiah.
Ezekiel.

Prophetae minores 12.
Psalterium.
Iob.
Proverbia.
Daniel, sepositis apocryphis.
Paralipomenon 2.
Canticum Canticorum.
Ruth.
Threni.
Ecclesiastes.
Esther.
Esdras et Nehemias.

Libri

[2b] Omnes isti libri, quos recensuimus, certo sunt canonici.

7. Libri sacri, non tamen canonici.[13]

Liber vero qui Sapientia Salomonis inscribitur, Ecclesiasticus, item Iudith, Tobias, Baruch, tertius et quartus Esdrae, libri Machabaeorum, cum apocryphis Esther et Danielis, leguntur quidem a fidelibus et in ecclesia recitantur, quod ad aedificationem plebis plurima in illis valeant, quibus tamen non tantum auctoritatis tribuitur, ut fidei nostrae dogmata ex [*h*/**ips**]is solis et separatim citra alios indubitatae Scripturae locos constitui, constabilirique, vel possint vel debeant. [3r] Sunt ergo et cum iudicio et sobrie isti tum audiendi tum legendi.

8. De libris canonicis Novi Testamenti.[14]

In Novo autem Testamento, pro canonicis libris agnoscit et admittit ecclesia hos qui sequuntur.

Quattuor Evangelia, videlicet: Matthaei, Marci, Lucae, Iohannis.
Acta Apostolica.

---

[13]Article 5 of 1553 (6 of 1571). These are the so-called 'apocryphal' or 'deuterocanonical' books. See Beckwith, *OT canon*, pp. 338-433.

[14]Article 5 of 1553 (6 of 1571), which however, does not list them as is done here. They are listed for the first time in this order by Athanasius, *Ep. Fest.* 39, 367, and also by the fourth session of the council of Trent, 8 April 1546 (*C.O.D.*, 663-4). See B. Metzger, *The canon of the New Testament. Its origin, development and significance* (Oxford, 1987) for the full history.

The twelve minor prophets.
The psalter.
Job.
Proverbs.
Daniel, apart from the apocryphal sections.
Chronicles (2).
The Song of Songs.
Ruth.
Lamentations.
Ecclesiastes.
Esther.
Ezra and Nehemiah.

Books

All these books which we have listed are certainly canonical.

7. Books which are sacred, but not canonical.[13]

But the book which is entitled the Wisdom of Solomon, Ecclesiasticus, likewise Judith, Tobit, Baruch, Third and Fourth Esdras, the books of the Maccabees, with the apocryphal sections of Esther and Daniel, are read by believers and recited in church, because many things in them are valuable for the edification of the people, yet there is not such great authority attributed to them that the doctrines of our faith either can or ought to be formed and established on the basis of them alone, apart from other passages of undoubted Scripture. They are therefore to be listened to and read with judgment and discretion.

8. Of the canonical books of the New Testament.[14]

And in the New Testament, the church recognizes and admits the following books as canonical:

The four Gospels, namely: Matthew, Mark, Luke and John.
The Acts of the Apostles.

Epistulas Pauli ad:
  Romanos
  Corinthios 2.
  Galatas.
  Ephesios.
  Philippenses.
  Colossenses.
  Thessalonicenses 2.
  Timotheum 2.
  Titum.
  Philemonem.
  Hebraeos.
[3a] Epistulas canonicas:[15]
  Iacobi 1.
  Petri 2.
  Iohannis 3.
  Iudae 1.
Apocalypsim.

9. Omnia credenda ex canonicis haberi Scripturis.[16]

Haec igitur generatim est Sancta Scriptura, qua omnia creditu [**ad salutem**] necessaria, plene et perfecte contineri credimus, usque adeo ut quicquid in ea non legitur, nec reperitur, nec denique ex eadem aut consequitur, aut convincitur, a nemine sit exigendum ut tamquam articulus fidei credatur.

[3v] 10. Suprema est in ecclesia Scripturae Divinae auctoritas.[17]

Divinae Scripturae tanta credatur auctoritas, ut nulla creaturae cuiusvis excellentia ipsi vel anteponenda sit vel aequanda.

[15]This title was added by Archbishop Cranmer in the MS. In Latin 'canonicas' was commonly used alongside 'catholicas', though in English only the second title is at all common.
[16]Article 5 of 1553 (6 of 1571).
[17]D, 9 c. 10 (Fr, I, 18).

The Epistles of Paul to:
> the Romans.
> the Corinthians (2).
> the Galatians.
> the Ephesians.
> the Philippians.
> the Colossians.
> the Thessalonians (2).
> Timothy (2).
> Titus.
> Philemon.
> the Hebrews.

The Catholic Epistles:[15]
> James (1).
> Peter (2).
> John (3).
> Jude (1).

Revelation.

9. Every required belief must come from the canonical Scriptures.[16]

This is the sum of Holy Scripture, in which we believe that all things which must be believed [**for salvation**] are fully and perfectly contained, so that if something is not read or contained in it, neither does it follow nor is it deduced from it, cannot be demanded of anyone that it should be believed as an article of faith.

10. The authority of the divine Scripture is supreme in the church.[17]

The authority of divine Scripture is to be believed to be so great, that no excellence of any creature may be set above it or equated with it.

11. Ecclesia contra Scripturas nil potest constituere, nilque praeter easdem obtrudere debet necessario credendum.[18]

Quamobrem non licet ecclesiae quicquam constituere, quod Verbo Dei scripto adversetur, neque potest sic unum locum exponere, ut alteri contradicat. Quamquam ergo divinorum librorum testis sit et custos et conservatrix ecclesia, haec tamen praerogativa ei minime concedi debet, ut contra hos libros vel quicquam decernat, vel absque horum librorum testimonio ullos fidei articulos condat, eosque populo Christiano credendos obtrudat.

[3b] 12. Ad codices Hebraicos in Veteri Testamento recurrendum, a[*t*/c] in Novo ad Graecos.[19]

Ceterum in lectione Divinarum Scripturarum si qua occurrerint ambigua vel obscura in Veteri Testamento, eorum interpretatio ex fonte Hebraicae veritatis petatur, in Novo autem Graeci codices consulantur.

13. Symbola fidei utilia sunt ad interpretandam Scripturam.[20]

Summa praeterea fidei capita (quae articulos appellamus) e Sacris Scripturis clarissimis desumpta, [4r] et in Symbolis breviter *desumpta* compraehensa, in exponendo sacras litteras ob oculos perpetuo habeantur, ne quid contra ea aliquando interpret[e/**a**]mur aut definiamus.[21]

14. De conciliis quid sentiendum.[22]

Iam vero conciliis, potissimum generalibus, tametsi ingentem honorem libenter deferimus, ea tamen longe omnia infra Scripturarum canonicarum dignitatem ponenda iudicamus, sed et inter ipsa concilia magnum discrimen ponimus. Nam quaedam illorum, qualia sunt praecipua illa quattuor, Nicaenum,[23]

---

[18]D, 9 c. 8 (Fr, I, 17-18).
[19]D, 9 c. 6 (Fr, I, 17).
[20]Article 1 of the Wittenberg Articles of 1536 (*D. E. R.*, 119-20) and article 1 of the Ten Articles of 1536 (*D. E. R.*, 164-5). This may also have been conceived as a response to the second decree of the fourth session of the council of Trent, 8 April 1546 (*C.O.D.*, 664-5).
[21]In the MS this form of the word is written in Foxe's hand above the reading 'diffiniamus'.
[22]D, 15 c. 1 (Fr, I, 34-5); D, 15 c. 2 (Fr, I, 35-6), originally from Pope Gregory I, *Reg.* 1, 24.
[23]The first council of Nicaea, which met there on 19 June 325.

11. The church may determine nothing against the Scriptures, and must not impose anything apart from them as necessarily to be believed.[18]

For this reason the church may not determine anything which is contrary to the Word of God written, nor may it so interpret one passage as to contradict another. Therefore, although the church is the witness, guardian and keeper of the divine books, yet this prerogative must never be granted to it, that it should either decree anything contrary to these books or that it should make any articles of faith without the witness of these books, and impose them on Christian people as requirements of faith.

12. Reference is to be made to the Hebrew manuscripts in the Old Testament and to the Greek in the New Testament.[19]

But if, in the reading of the divine Scriptures, things come up in the Old Testament which are ambiguous or obscure, their interpretation is to be sought from the original Hebrew, and in the New the Greek manuscripts are to be consulted.

13. The creeds are useful for interpreting Scripture.[20]

Moreover, in expounding Holy Writ, the main points of the faith (which we call articles), derived from the clearest passages of Holy Scripture and briefly *derived* summarized in the creeds, are to be kept continually in view, so that we shall not interpret or define anything which is contrary to them.[21]

14. What is to be thought about councils.[22]

Although we freely grant great honour to the councils, and especially to the ecumenical ones, yet we judge that all of them must be placed far below the dignity of the canonical Scriptures, and even among the councils themselves we make a huge distinction. For some of them, such as the special four, Nicaea,[23] the

Constantinopolitanum primum,[24] Ephesinum[25] et Chalcedonense,[26] magna cum reverentia amplectimur et suscipimus. Quod quidem iudicium de multis aliis quae postea celebrata sunt ferimus, in quibus videmus et confitemur sanctissimos patres de beata et summa Trinitate, de Iesu Christo Domino et Servatore nostro, et humana redemptione per eum procurata, iuxta Scripturas Divinas multa gravissime et perquam sancte constituisse. Quibus tamen **non** aliter fidem nostram obligandam esse censemus, nisi quatenus ex Scripturis Sanctis confirmari possint. Nam concilia nonnulla interdum errasse, et contraria inter sese defini[4a]visse, partim in actionibus [*nost*/ **iu**]ris, partim etiam in fide, manifestum est *liquidissime constat.*[27] Itaque legantur concilia quidem cum honore atque Christiana reverentia, sed interim ad Scripturarum piam certam rectamque regulam examinentur.

[4v] 15. Quae sanctorum patrum auctoritas.[28]

Postremo, orthodoxorum patrum etiam auctoritatem minime censemus esse contemnendam; (sunt enim permulta ab illis praeclare et <u>utiliter</u> dicta). Ut tamen ex eorum sententia de sacris litteris iudicetur, non admittimus. Debent enim Sacrae Litterae nobis omnis Christianae doctrinae et regulae esse et iudices. Quin et ipsi patres tantum honoris sibi deferri recusarunt, saepius admonentes lectorem ut tantisper suas admittat sententias et interpretationes, quoad cum sacris litteris consentire eas animadverterit. Maneat ergo illis sua auctoritas et reverentia, sed quae sacrorum librorum sententiae, veritati atque auctoritati cedat et subiiciatur.

16. Epilogus.

Ceterum quoniam perlongum esset, et plane opus valde laboriosum, omnia nunc distincte scribere quae catholica fide sunt credenda, sufficere iudicamus quae breviter de summa trinitate, de Iesu Christo Domino nostro, et de salute per eum humano generi parta diximus.

---

[24]The first council of Constantinople, which concluded its business on 9 July 381.
[25]The first council of Ephesus, which met there from 7 June to 22 July 431.
[26]The council of Chalcedon met from 1 September to 22 October 451.
[27]This is more cautiously stated in Article 22 of 1553 (21 of 1571).
[28]D, 9 c. 10 (Fr, I, 18); D, 12 c. 5 (Fr, I, 28).

first of Constantinople,[24] Ephesus[25] and Chalcedon,[26] we embrace and accept with great reverence. And we make the same judgment with regard to many others which were held later on, in which we see and confess that the most holy fathers determined many things, in a most serious and holy manner, concerning the blessed and highest Trinity, our Lord and Saviour Jesus Christ, and the redemption of mankind procured by him. But we do **not** regard them as binding on our faith except in so far as they can be proved out of the Holy Scriptures. For it is *most obvious* clear that some councils have occasionally erred, and defined things which are contrary to each other, partly in [*our* **legal**] actions and partly even in faith.[27] Therefore the councils are to be studied with honour and Christian reverence, but at the same time they are to be tested against the godly, certain and right rule of the Scriptures.

15. What authority the holy fathers have.[28]

Finally, we consider that the authority of the orthodox fathers is also not at all to be despised, for a great many things are said by them in a most clear and helpful way. Yet we do not allow that the meaning of Holy Writ can be determined by their opinion. For Holy Writ must be our rule and judge for all Christian teaching. Moreover, the fathers themselves refused to accept so great an honour, often warning their readers to accept their opinions and interpretations only so far as they found them to be agreeable to Holy Writ. Therefore their authority and reverence shall remain to them, but it shall give way and be subject to the teaching, truth and authority of the holy books.

16. Conclusion.

But since it would take far too long, and clearly be a laborious task, to write down here all the details of what must be believed as part of the catholic faith, we judge that what we have briefly stated concerning the highest Trinity, our Lord Jesus Christ, and the salvation imparted through him to the human race is sufficient.

17. Pereunt qui catholicae fidei adversantur vel ab ea deficiunt.[29]

Hoc ipsum tamen silentio praeterire non possumus, eos omnes misere perire qui orthodoxam catholicamque fidem amplecti nolunt, et longe gravius eos esse damnandos, qui ab ea semel agnita et suscepta defecer[i/u]nt.

---

[29]These are the opening (and closing) words of the Athanasian creed: 'Whosoever will be saved must above all things hold the catholic faith, which, except a man do believe wholly and undefiled, he shall perish everlastingly.'

17. Those who oppose the catholic faith or who reject it shall perish.[29]

Nevertheless we cannot pass over this in silence, that all those who are unwilling to embrace the catholic faith shall perish miserably, and that those who have rejected it, having once known and accepted it, shall be punished far more severely.

[6r; 4b]   **2. DE HAERESIBUS**

1. Qui sint haeretici et qui non sint.[1]

Haereticos statuimus omnes quicunque communis nostrae fidei decretum aliquod secus accipiunt, quam Sacra Scriptura determinatum est, et in errore sic habitant, ut omnino se non sinant ab illo removeri. Nec illud in hoc genere spectandum est, utrum aliquis ipse sibi erroris fuerit auctor, an illum aliunde acceptum ipse sequatur et defendat. Qui vero non commorantur in haeresi, n[ec/**on**] ill[a/**u**]m defendunt, sed inquirunt [*in*] veritatem et cum a legitimis iudicibus plene fuerint instructi, suam ipsi culpam agnoscunt, et in eo se corrigi facile patiuntur, in haereticorum numero poni non debent.

2. Schismatici, et haeretici quomodo differant.[2]

Schismaticos plerique cum haereticis confuderunt. Sed tamen magna inter illos est differentia. Nec enim schismatici fidem aliam habent quam ceteri, sed a communi illa, quae inter [6v] Christianos esse debe*a**t, societate se dis[t]i[*u*]ngu[**u**]nt. Itaque nonnunquam usu venit, /ut/ cum longe a piis aliorum institutis et officiis peregrinati sunt, tandem ad aliquam haeresim dilabantur, ut se vehementius a recepta bonorum communitate segregent.

3. Ex haeresibus quae prima sit.
***4*. 3. De** [*e*/h]**is qui Sacrarum Scripturarum auctoritatem reiiciunt.**[3]

Capitalis Christiani nominis hostis Satan, ad salutare Divinarum Scripturarum semen in Dei ecclesia sparsum, tam pestilentem haeres[*u*/i]m [*vim*], (quasi loliorum et zizaniorum), [5a] infu[**n**]dit, ut universae vix enumerari possint hae faces, quibus ecclesia conflagravit, et adhuc miserabiliter ardet, diabolo maiorem quotidie falsarum opinionum materiam accu[mu/-]lante,. *n*/**Nos**[4] igitur his constitutionibus nostris breviter per illas haereses praetervehemur, quarum praesens pestis [in/-] perniciem religionis nostrorum temporum adhuc incubat. In quo genere teterrimi illi sunt, (itaque a nobis primum nominabuntur), qui

---

[1]C. 24, q. 3, c. 28 (Fr, I, 998); C. 24, q. 3, c. 29 (Fr, I, 998).
[2]C. 24, q. 3, c. 26 (Fr, I, 997); L, 5.4.1, gloss on *schismaticum*.
[3]C. 24, q. 3, c. 27 (Fr, I, 997-8); C. 24, q. 3, c. 39, s. 70 (Fr, I, 1006).
[4]Cranmer began a new sentence here.

2. OF HERESIES

1. Who are heretics and who are not.[1]

We decree that heretics are all those who receive any doctrine of our common faith in a way which is contrary to what has been determined by Holy Scripture, and who so dwell in error that they make no attempt whatsoever to be delivered from it. Nor is any distinction to be made in this matter between someone who has been the author of his own error and someone who follows and defends an error which he has received from elsewhere. But those who are not confirmed heretics [*and*] do not defend it, but seek [*after*] the truth, and when they have been fully instructed by lawful judges, themselves acknowledge their guilt and are easily open to correction in this matter, ought not to be counted as heretics.

2. How schismatics differ from heretics.[2]

Many people have confused schismatics with heretics. But there is a great difference between them. For schismatics do not have a faith which is any different from others, but [*separate* **distance**] themselves from that common fellowship which ought to exist among Christians. Therefore it sometimes happens, /that/ when they have wandered far away from the godly doctrines and worship of others, that they end up in some heresy, which then cuts them off even more from the recognized fellowship of the good.

3. *What the first of the heresies is.*
***4.* 3. Of those who reject the authority of the Holy Scriptures.**[3]

Satan, who is the chief enemy of the Christian name, infuse[*d*/**s**] such pestilential [*force of*] heresy (like weeds and tares) into the saving seed of the divine Scriptures, which is scattered about in the church of God, that the total number of these fireballs by which the church is inflamed and continues to burn miserably can hardly be counted, as the devil daily piles up even more firewood in the shape of false opinions. Therefore[4] in these constitutions of ours we shall briefly go over those heresies, the present plague of which still incubates [to/-] the harm of religion in our times. Of this type the most frightening (who shall

Sacras Scripturas ad infirm*i*orum **tantum** hominum debilitatem ablegant et detrudunt, sibi sic ipsi interim prae[*f*/s]identes ut *ad* earum auctoritate*m nullum omnino respectum habeant; et hi* **se teneri non putent, sed** peculiarem quendam *sibi* spiritum *arrogant* **iactant**, a quo **sibi omnia** suppeditari *scientiam rerum affirmant* **aiunt, quaecunque docent et faciunt.**

[7r] **4.** *Quae secunda, tertia, quarta.* **De** [*e*/h]**is qui Vetus Testamentum aut totum reiiciunt, aut totum exigunt.**[5]

Deinde quomodo priscis temporibus Marcionitarum[6] sordes, Valentinianorum[7] et Manichaeorum[8] fluxerunt, et aliae similes earum multae faeces, (a quibus Vetus Testamentum ut absurdum **malum[que]**, et cum Novo dissidens, repudiabatur); sic multi nostris temporibus inveniuntur, (inter quos Anabaptistae praecipue sunt collocandi),[9] ad quos si quis Vetus Testamentum alleget, illud pro *nihilo* **abrogat[o/a] iam et obsoleto penitus** habent, omnia quae in illo posita sunt ad prisca maiorum nostrorum tempora referentes. Itaque nihil eorum ad nos statuunt pervenire debere. Aliorum autem contrarius est, sed eiusdem impietatis error, qui usque adeo Vetus ad Testamentum adhaerescunt, ut ad circumcisionem et a Moyse quondam institutas caeremonias necessario nos revocent.

*Subsequitur etiam tertius illorum error qui morte*m *Christi talem nobis licentiam concessam et impunitatem omnium rerum ita permissam arbitrantur, ut ne morum quidem illis solemnibus* **decalogi** *praeceptis teneamur, nec ullis denique reliquis vitae sanctis institutis, quibus Sacrae Scripturae perspersae sunt.*

5. *Quinta* de **duabus** naturis Christi.[10]

Circa duplicem Christi naturam perniciosus est et varius error, ex quibus alii sunt ex Arianorum [7v] secta,[11] [5b] Christum ita ponentes hominem ut Deum negent.

---

[5]C. 24, q. 3, c. 39, ss. 7-8 (Fr, I, 1001); *ibid.*, s. 23 (Fr, I, 1002); Article 6 of 1553 (7 of 1571).
[6]Marcion was a second-century heretic who rejected the Old Testament.
[7]Valentinus was a second-century gnostic, who believed that matter was evil.
[8]Mani (third century) preached a dualism derived from the Zoroastrianism of Persia.
[9]On 4 June 1535 fourteen Dutch Anabaptists were burnt in London, and the remainder were expelled from England on 16 November 1538. See *Tudor royal proclamations*, ed. P. L. Hughes and J. F. Larkin (3 vols., New Haven, 1964), I, 270-6, no. 186. However, they were pardoned on 26 February 1539; see *ibid.*, I, 278-80, no. 188. The extent of the denunciation in this title is without parallel in other English sources, and may reflect the concerns of Peter Martyr Vermigli, who had experienced them first-hand on the continent.
[10]X, 5.7.7 (Fr, II, 779), originally a decretal of Pope Alexander III (1159-81).
[11]C. 24, q. 3, c. 39, s. 42 (Fr, I, 1004). Arius (*c.* 256-336) was condemned at the first council of Nicaea, 325.

therefore be named first by us) are those who misread and distort the Holy Scriptures to the hurt of weak men **only**, thus all the while *confirming that they have no respect for their authority, and they arrogate to themselves some special spirit by which they claim that they are supplied with the knowledge of things* **demonstrating that they do not think themselves bound by their authority, but boast of some special spirit by which they say that everything which they teach and do is revealed to them.**

4. *What the second, third and fourth ones are.* **Of those who either reject the Old Testament completely or who insist that it be kept to the letter.**[5]

Likewise, just as in early times the rubbish of the Marcionites,[6] the Valentinians[7] and the Manichees,[8] and a lot of other dirt much like it, poured out, according to which the Old Testament was held to be absurd, **wicked [and]** discordant with the New, so many people can be found in our time, (among whom the Anabaptists in particular are to be grouped),[9] to whom if someone refers to the Old Testament, they immediately claim that it is *worthless* **now abrogated and obsolete**, limiting everything which is contained in it to the primitive times of our ancestors. Therefore they ordain that none of it ought to apply to us. But there is another opposite error, of equal ungodliness, which is that of those who cling so firmly to the Old Testament that they call us back to a need for circumcision and the other ceremonies instituted by Moses.

 Following on from this there is a third error of those who those who think that by *the death of Christ such great licence has been given to us and liberty to do anything and everything has been so permitted, that we are not even bound by those solemn moral precepts* **of the Ten Commandments** *nor by any of the other holy ordinances of life, with which the Holy Scriptures are saturated.*

5. *The fifth*, of the **two** natures of Christ.[10]

Concerning the double nature of Christ there is a pernicious error which takes different forms. Some are of the sect of the Arians,[11] holding that Christ is man in such a way as to deny that he is God. Others consider that he is God in such

Alii eum sic Deum iudicant ut hominem non agnoscant, et de corpore nugantur de caelo divinitus **assumpto, et in virginis uterum**[12] lapso, quod tanquam in transitu per Mariam quasi per canalem aut fistulam praeterfluxerit. **Quidam Verbum etc.***[13] [>Quidam corpus ipsum saepe dicunt, et subinde factum esse. *Quae tria* **qui errores omnes** Sacrarum Scripturarum auctoritate sic corrigendi sunt, ut Christus meliore natura Deus **sempiternus** accipiatur, (et quidem aequalis sit Dei Patris); humana vero corpus habeat **ex tempore factum, neque saepius quam semel, neque ex alia materia quam** ex Mariae virginis **vera et** sola substantia, *factum et expressum; quod sane corpus ut tantum semel est effectum, ita semel et unico tempore in crucem pro communi salute nostra vere sublatum, et ibi Deo Patri oblatum est* **ac quemadmodum reliqua humana corpora suis loci finibus circumscriptum.**<]

Sexta de corpore Christi et septima de Spiritu Sancto.

Quidam *Eutychetis*[14] *somnium de corpore Christi resuscitant, quod* **Verbum in carnis naturam conversum asserunt, quae,** quamprimum **a morte** in caelum fuit recept*um*/**a**, *statim* **rursus** volunt *integrum* in naturam divinam *con*/reversu/am et absorpt*u*/am esse.[15] Quorum illi delirium imitantur, qui corpori Christi tam latos fines dant, ut illo credant **vel aut** omne*m*/s loc*um*/os **simul, aut** *plurima* [*in*] **numeros** obsideri,. q/**Q**uod[16] si confiteremur, humanam e Christo naturam eximeremus. [8r] Quemadmodum enim Dei natura sibi hoc assumit, ut per omnia permeet, sic humanae semper illud attributum est, ut certis locorum finibus circumscript*um*/**a** sit. [<Quidam corpus ipsum saepe dicunt, et subinde factum esse. Qui errores omnes Sacrarum Scripturarum auctoritate sic corrigendi sunt, ut Christus meliore natura Deus sempiternus accipiatur, et quidem aequalis sit Dei Patris; humana vero corpus habeat ex tempore factum, neque saepius quam semel, neque ex alia materia quam ex Mariae virginis vera et sola substantia, ac quemadmodum reliqua humana corpora suis loci finibus circumscriptum.>]

---

[12]Cranmer put 'Valentinus' in the margin here. Cf. C. 24, q. 3, c. 39, s. 10 (Fr, I, 1002).
[13]These words were inserted by Cranmer to indicate that this paragraph, originally in the following section, should follow immediately here. The next passage, in brackets, was marked for transfer to the bottom of the section, but this was not actually done in the MS.
[14]A fifth-century Alexandrian condemned by the council of Chalcedon, 451.
[15]The heresy of the Theodosians, cf. C. 24, q. 3, c. 39, s. 66 (Fr, I, 1005).
[16]Cranmer started a new sentence here.

a way that they do not recognize him as a man, and concerning his body, they pretend that he *fell in* **assumed** one of a divine nature from heaven, **and fell into a virgin's womb**,[12] rather as if he were in transit through Mary and flowed through her as through a canal or a tube. **Some... the Word, etc.*** [>Some say that the body itself was often reincarnated here on earth. *Which three* **All of which errors** are to be corrected by the authority of Holy Scripture in such a way that Christ is to be accepted as **the eternal** God in his higher nature, and therefore as the equal of God the Father, but that in his human nature he has a body, made *and manifested* **in time, not more than once, nor** of **any matter other than** the **true and** sole substance of the virgin Mary, *which body indeed, just as it was made only once, so also it was* <u>*lifted up on the cross*</u> *for our* <u>*common*</u> *salvation only one single time,* <u>*and there*</u> *offered to God the Father,* **and was circumscribed by the limits of finitude just as other human bodies are.**<]

The sixth, of the body of Christ, and the seventh, of the Holy Spirit.

Some *resuscitate the delusion of Eutyches*[14] *concerning the body of Christ* **assert that the Word was changed into the nature of flesh, which** they claim was *immediately* **once more** turned **back** and absorbed into the divine nature as soon as it was taken up into heaven **from the dead**.[15] Others imitate their madness by giving the body of Christ such broad limits that they believe that it occupies *every place* **either all places at the same time, or [in/-]numerable ones**. But[16] if we believe this, then we are depriving Christ of any human nature. For just as the nature of God takes upon itself the ability to permeate everything, so it has always been a property of human nature that it should be circumscribed by certain spatial limits. [<Some say that the body itself was often reincarnated here on earth. All of these errors are to be corrected by the authority of Holy Scripture so that Christ is accepted as the eternal God in his higher nature, and therefore as the equal of God the Father, but that in his human nature he has a body, made in time, not more than once, nor of any matter other than the true and sole substance of the virgin Mary, and was circumscribed by the limits of finitude just as other human bodies are.>]

6. De Spiritu Sancto.

Quomodo vero haec putida membra sunt ab ecclesiae corpore segreganda, quae de Christo capite tam perverse sentiunt, sic illorum etiam est execrabilis impudentia, qui cum Macedonio[17] contra Spiritum Sanctum conspiraverunt, illum pro Deo non agnoscentes.[18]

7. *Octava haeresis,* de peccato originis, libero arbitrio, **et** iustificatione.[19]

In labe peccati ex ortu nostro contracta, quam vitium originis appellamus, primum quidem Pelagianorum,[20] dein[6a]de etiam Anabaptistarum nobis vitandus et submovendus est error, quorum in eo consensus contra *auctoritatem* **veritatem** Sacrarum Scripturarum est, quod peccatum originis **in Adamo solo haer**/serit *dicunt*, **et non ad posteros transi*sse*/erit, nec *n*ullam afferat naturae nostrae perversitatem, nisi quod ex Adami delicto propositum sit peccandi noxium exemplum, quod homines ad eandem pravitatem invitat imitandam et usurpandam. /Et/ similiter nobis contra illos progrediendum est, qui tantum in libero arbitrio roboris et nervorum ponunt, ut eo solo sine **alia speciali** Christi gratia recte *et perfecte* [8v] ab hominibus vivi posse constituant. Deinde nec illi sunt audiendi, quorum impietas salutarem /et/ in Sacris Scripturis fundatam iustificationis nostrae doctrinam oppugna[n]t, in qua tenendum est non operum momentis, iustitiam hominum [**collocari** *ponderari, sed existere illam ex sola fide, quam habemus in Iesu Christo defixam. Id tamen semper in omnibus sequi debet, ut cum fide iusti sunt facti bonis in operibus se collocent, quae Sacra Scriptura flagitat, quasi fructus necessarios ex vera et sincera fide profectos.*]

8. *Nona,* de *innocentia* **perfectione** iustificatorum,[21] et *decima,* de operibus supererogationis.[22]

Illorum etiam superbia legibus nostris est frangenda, qui tantam vitae perfectionem hominibus iustificatis attribuunt, quantam nec imbecillitas nostrae naturae fert, nec quisquam sibi praeter Christum sumere potest; nimirum ut omnis peccati sint expertes, si mentem ad recte pieque vivendum instituerint,. e/**Et**[23] hanc volunt absolutam morum perfectionem in hanc praesentem vitam

---

[17]A fourth-century heretic condemned at the first council of Constantinople, 381.
[18]C. 24, q. 3, c. 39, s. 43 (Fr, I, 1004).
[19]Article 5 of the Ten Articles, 1536 (*D. E. R.*, 170-1); Article 8 of 1553 (9 of 1571).
[20]C. 24, q. 3, c. 39, s. 62 (Fr, I, 1005). Pelagius taught at Rome *c.*418 and was severely condemned by Augustine for his views on free will.
[21]C. 24, q. 3, c. 39, s. 27 (Fr, II, 1002); Article 14 of 1553 (15 of 1571).
[22]Article 13 of 1553 (14 of 1571).
[23]Cranmer began a new sentence here.

6. Of the Holy Spirit.

And just as these gangrenous members, who have such perverse notions of Christ its head, are to be cut out of the body of the church, so also is the execrable impudence of those who, with Macedonius,[17] have conspired against the Holy Spirit, not recognizing him as God.[18]

7. *The eighth heresy*, of original sin, free will and justification.[19]

In the inheritance of sin which is contracted at our birth, which we call original sin, we must first of all avoid the error of the Pelagians[20] and also of the Anabaptists, whose agreement on this point goes against the *authority* **truth** of the Holy Scriptures, because they say that original sin **belonged only to Adam and did not extend to his descendants, nor** did *not* it contribute any perversity to our nature, except in so far as Adam's sin set forth a bad example of sinning which invites people to imitate and take over the same depravity. /And/ likewise we must take steps against those who put such confidence in the free will of our strength and nerves, that they contend that people can live rightly *and perfectly* by that alone, without any **other special** grace of Christ. Finally, we must not listen to those whose ungodliness attacks the saving doctrine of our justification, which is /also/ grounded in the Holy Scriptures, according to which it is to be held that the righteousness of men is not to be [*weighed* **placed**] in particular works, [*but that it exists on the basis of faith alone, which we have fixed in Jesus Christ. Yet it must always follow in all cases, that when people have been made righteous by their faith they will concentrate on good works, which Holy Scripture commands, as the necessary fruits stemming from a true and sincere faith.*]

8. *The ninth*, of the *innocence* **perfection** of the justified,[21]
and *the tenth*, of works of supererogation.[22]

Moreover, the pride of those who attribute to people a perfection of life so great that the weakness of our nature cannot bear it and no one apart from Christ can achieve it, must be broken by our laws, as well as the belief that people are set free from every sin if they devote their lives to right and godly living. And[23] they want this absolute moral perfection to occur in this present life, even though it

cadere, cum debilis ipsa si*nt* et fragilis, et ad omnes virtutis et officii ruinas praeceps. Tum et illorum arrogantia comprimenda est, et auctoritate legum domanda, qui supererogationis opera quaedam importaverunt, quibus existimant [9r] non solum cumulate Dei *et* legibus, et explete satisfieri, sed aliquid etiam in illis amplius superesse quam Dei mandata postulent, **unde et sibi mereri, et aliis merita applicari possint.**

[6b] **9.** *Undecima*, de *statu* **casu** iustificatorum et *duodecima, de mortali peccato* **peccato in Spiritum Sanctum.**[24]

Etiam illi de iustificatis perverse sentiunt, qui credunt illos, postquam iusti semel facti si/**unt** *Licet in hoc saeculo versentur tamen*, in peccatum non posse incidere, aut si forte quicquam eorum faciunt, quae Dei legibus prohibentur, ea Deum pro peccatis non accipere,. *q*/**Quibus**[25] opinione contrarii, sed impietate pares sunt, qui quodcumque peccatum mortale, quod post baptismum a nobis susceptum voluntate nostra committitur, illud omne contra Spiritum Sanctum affirmant gestum esse, **et remitti non posse.**[26]

10. *13.* De missis et purgatorio.[27]

Quorundam *enim est* nimis **est** curiosa *e...* perversitas, qui veniam quidem peccatorum expectant, sed hanc, morte Christi per solam fidem ad [n/v]os accommodata[**m**], **plene** non credunt et omnibus partibus impleri,. *q*/**Quapropter**[28] alia conquirunt sacrificia, quibus perpurgari possint, et ad hanc rem [9v] missas [*ad*/**ex**]hibent. *In quibus, etc. fo. 14* [<in quibus sacrificium Deo Patri credunt oblatum esse, nimirum corpus et sanguinem Domini nostri Iesu Christi vere, quomodoque illi dicunt realiter, ad veniam peccatorum impetrandam, et salutem tam mortuorum quam vivorum procurandam; *quibus etiam* reg[n/*i*]*um tam* [licentiosum *latum*] *dant ut illis aliquando minui, nonnunquam omnino tolli purgatorii tormenta statuant.** Qua in re sacrificium illud unicum (quod Christus Dei Filius in cruce Deo Patri repraesentavit et plenissime exhibuit) largiter imminuunt, et sacerdotium quod unius Christi proprium est, ad miserabilem hominum conditionem devolvunt.>][29] *v*/**Verum**[30]

---

[24]Articles 14-15 of 1553 (15-16 of 1571).
[25]Cranmer began a new sentence here.
[26]The unforgivable sin of blasphemy against the Holy Spirit is found in Mt. xii. 31; Mk. iii. 29; Lk. xii. 10.
[27]Article 10 of the Ten Articles, 1536 (*D. E. R.*, 173-4); Article 23 of 1553 (22 of 1571).
[28]Cranmer began a new sentence here.
[29]A marginal note in Foxe's hand reads: 'Hoc caput in codice Domini Matthaei Cantuariensis habetur pro 10; in codice isto refertur ad appendicem capitis 19, folio 14.' ('In the codex of Matthew, Archbishop of Canterbury, this section is no. 10; in this codex it is placed at the end of section 19 on folio 14'). A note in Cranmer's hand ('In quibus,

is weak and fragile, and prone to destroy every form of virtue and duty. Therefore the arrogance of those who have introduced certain works of supererogation, by which they think that not only have they fully and completely satisfied the laws of God, but that they have also done something more than what the commands of God require, **on which basis they can obtain merit for themselves and apply their merits to others**, must be restrained and bridled by the authority of the laws.

9. *The eleventh*, of the *state* **case** of the justified, and *the twelfth,* of *mortal* sin **against the Holy Spirit.**[24]

Those who believe that the justified can no longer fall into sin *even though they are still living in this world*, or that if they happen to do something which is forbidden by the laws of God, God will not count that as sin, also have a perverse conception of justification. Opposed[25] to this opinion, but equally ungodly, are those who believe that any sin which may be committed by our will after we have received baptism is mortal, and who say that all such sin has been done against the Holy Spirit **and cannot be forgiven.**[26]

10. *13.* Of masses and purgatory.[27]

Moreover the perversity of those who continue to wait for the forgiveness of their sins and who do not believe that this has already been [**fully**] granted to [us **you**] by Christ's death through faith alone and completed in every respect, is extremely odd. Because[28] of this, they look for other sacrifices by which they may be completely cleansed, and for this purpose they [*offer* **present**] masses [<in which they believe that a sacrifice has been offered to God the Father, even the body and blood of our Lord Jesus Christ truly, or as they put it, really, to obtain the forgiveness of sins and procure the salvation of both the dead and the living, *to which they grant such licentious power that they maintain that their torments in purgatory are sometimes lessened and occasionally taken away altogether.**** In which matter they greatly diminish that one unique sacrifice (which Christ the Son of God offered and fully presented to God the Father on the cross), and bring the priesthood, which is the property of Christ alone, down to the miserable level of men.>][29] But[30] the Holy Scriptures reserve the death of

Sacrae Scripturae solam Christi mortem nobis [*ad* **et**] delictorum purgationem reservant, nec ullum ponunt aliud sacrificium quod ad hanc rem valere possit, imo de purgatorio sane ipsorum ne una quidem syllaba Sacris in Scripturis invenitur.

[7a] **11.** *14.* De *naturali lumine* **incredulorum et impiorum damnatione.**
15. De poenis temporariis damnatorum.[31]

Horribilis est et i[*mm*/**n**]anis illorum audacia, qui contendunt in omni religione vel secta, quam homines professi fuerint, salutem illis esse sperandam, si tantum ad innocentiam et integritatem vitae pro viribus [*an*/**e**]nitantur iuxta lumen, quod illis praelucet a natura infusum, auctoritate vero Sacrarum Litterarum confixae sunt huiusmodi pestes,. *s*/Solum[32] enim et unicum ibi Iesu Christi nomen nobis commendatum est, ut omnis ex eo salus ad nos perveniat. Nec minor est illorum *illorum* amentia, qui periculosam Origenis[33] haeresim in hac aetate nostra rursus excitant; nimirum omnes homines (quantumcunque sceleribus se contaminaverint) salutem ad extremum consecuturos cum *ex praescripto divinae providentiae magnitudine poenarum propter peccata sibi* [10r] *impositarum Dei iustitiae satisfecerint* **definito tempore a iustitia divina, poenas de admissis flagitiis luerint.** Sed Sacra Scriptura damnatos saepe pronuntiat, *impios et sceleros* [in **im**]perpetui/**o**s cruciatus et aeternas flammas praecipitari.

12. *16.* De animarum interitu vel somno **et**
17. De* resurrectione *animarum.*[34]

Quidam impie philosophantur animas hominum ex hac vita migrantium, quando semel ex corporibus excesserunt, usque ad supremum ultimi iudicii tempus vel somno involvi, vel prorsus ad nihilum recidere; tum autem cum [*pos*/**ex**]tremi iudicii dies erit, illas rursus vel a somno excitari, vel cum propriis corporibus ab interitu resurgere. Affinis est eis error de resurrectione quam multi (cum Hym[-/**a**]en[*ae*]o consentientes et Phileto)[35] perfectam /iam/ esse dicunt et conclusam; quia solum debet ad animum referri quem *iam vero* Christus *animum* (affusa nobis beneficio suae mortis gratia) prorsus ex morte peccatorum excitavit. Sed

---

etc. fo. 14') indicates that it was moved on his instructions.
[30]Cranmer began a new sentence here.
[31]X, 5.7.3 (Fr, II, 778), from Fulgentius, *De fide ad Petrum diaconum*, but traditionally attributed to Augustine.
[32]Cranmer began a new sentence here.
[33]Origen (*c.*186-*c.*254) was not condemned until long after his death (traditionally at the second council of Constantinople, 553).
[34]Articles 39-40 of 1553 (omitted in 1563 and 1571).
[35]Mentioned in II Ti. ii. 17.

Christ alone [*for* **and**] the cleansing of our sins, and allow no other sacrifice which can achieve this, and not even a single syllable is found in the Holy Scriptures concerning that purgatory of theirs.

11. *14.Of the light of nature* **the damnation of unbelievers and the ungodly.**
15. Of the temporary punishments of the damned.[31]

Horrible and insane is the daring of those who maintain that salvation may be hoped for in every religion or sect which men have professed, as long as they strive as hard as they can for innocence and integrity of life according to the light which has been put in them by nature, for plagues of this kind are condemned by the authority of Holy Writ. For[32] there the one and only name of Jesus Christ is commended to us, that all salvation may come to us from him. Nor is the madness any less of those who are stirring up the dangerous heresy of Origen[33] once again in our time, to wit that all people (however many sins they may have committed) will be saved in the end when *by the decree of divine providence, they shall have satisfied the justice of God by the magnitude of the penalties imposed on them for their sins* **over a particular period of time they have paid the penalties of divine justice for the sins they have confessed.** But Holy Scripture frequently declares that *the ungodly and wicked* are condemned to be cast into perpetual torment and eternal flames.

12. *16.* Of the annihilation or sleep of souls **and**
17. Of the resurrection *of souls.*[34]

Some people wrongly imagine that the souls of men departing this life, when once they have left the body, are either wrapped in sleep until the time of the last judgment, or else return to nothing, but then when the day of the last judgment comes, they are either wakened again from sleep or rise again from destruction with their own bodies. Related to these is the error concerning the resurrection which many (agreeing with Hymenaeus and Philetus)[35] say is /already/ perfect and completed, because it ought to refer only to the mind, which *mind* Christ (by the grace poured out on us by the blessing of his death) has *already* raised from

haec illorum abrupta est et curta doctrina. Quemadmodum enim ipse Iesus Christus a morte [7b] ad vitam *et* corpore integro, vero et perfecto revocatus est, **nec eius interim animus /aut/ interiit aut dormivit**; ita nos qui membra [*Christi*] sumus [**Christi**] **post mortem quidem animo vivimus**, caput **vero** nostrum [10v] secuti, cum animis et corporibus ad extremum illud iudicium consurgemus.

13. *18.* De magistratibus *tollendis*.

Qu[in/**m**] et Anabaptistarum profligandus est agrestis stupor, qui negant licere Christianis magistratum gerere, quasi propterea Christus in terras descenderit, ut rerum publicarum administratione[*m*/**s**] aboleret. Imo vero Spiritus Sanctus statuit principes et magistratus esse Dei ministros ut benefactis favorem suum impartiant, et maleficia suppliciis constringant, quae duo si rebus humanis abessent, maxima sequeretur omnium rerum confusio. *Igitur in nostra republica legitimi magistratus omnis generis permanebunt et cum humanas tum imprimis divinas leges firme et inviolate servari curabunt.*

14. *19.* De communitate bonorum **et**
20. *De communitate* uxorum.

Excludatur etiam ab eisdem Anabaptistis inducta bonorum et possessionum communitas, quam *tam corpore* **tantopere** urgent, ut nemini quicquam relinquant proprium et suum. In quo mirabiliter loquuntur, [11r] cum furta prohiberi *lege Dei* **divina Scriptura** cernant, et eleemosynas in utroque Testamento laudari videant, quas ex propriis facultatibus nostris elargimur; quorum sane neutrum consistere posset, nisi Christianis proprietas bonorum et possessionum suarum relinqueretur. Emergunt etiam ex Anabaptistarum lacunis quidam Nicolaitae,[36] *in* inquinatissimi sane homines qui feminarum, **imo et uxorum** disputant usum per omnes promiscue pervagari debere.[37] Quae foeda illorum et conscelerata libido, primum pietati contraria est et Sacris Litteris, deinde cum universa civili honestate et naturali illa incorruptaque in men[8a]tibus nostris accensa luce vehementer pugnat.

---

[36] An obscure sect mentioned in Re. ii. 6, 15.
[37] C. 24, q. 3, c. 39, s. 4 (Fr, I, 1001).

the death of sin. But this teaching of theirs is partial and inadequate. For just as Jesus Christ himself was called back to life from death with a complete, real and perfect body, **but in the interval his mind did not /either/ perish or sleep**, so we who are members of Christ **continue to live in our mind after death, but**, following our head, we shall rise with our souls and bodies at that last judgment.

13. *18.* Of *removing* magistrates.

Furthermore the boorish foolishness of the Anabaptists must be reprimanded, who deny that Christians should rule the state, as if Christ had come to earth in order to abolish all governments. But in fact the Holy Spirit has ordained that princes and magistrates are God's servants in order to show his favour on good deeds and to restrain evil deeds by punishment, and if these two things were absent from human affairs the greatest confusion of all things would follow. *Therefore in our state lawful magistrates of all kinds will remain and ensure that both human and, above all, divine laws will be kept firm and inviolate.*

14. *19.* Of the sharing of goods **and**
20. Of the sharing of wives.

It is also proclaimed by the same Anabaptists that there shall be a forced sharing of goods and possessions, which they insist on *even physically* **so strongly**, that they leave nobody with anything of his own. In this they speak strangely, since they can discover that theft is prohibited *by the law of God* **by divine Scripture**, and they can see that almsgiving, which we offer out of our own resources, is praised in both Testaments, neither of which would be possible unless the ownership of their goods and possessions were left to Christians. There even emerge from the recesses of the Anabaptists some Nicolaitans,[36] truly the most wicked of men, who argue that the use of women **and even of wives** should be promiscuously spread around by everybody.[37] First of all, this evil and criminal desire of theirs is contrary to godliness and Holy Writ, and second, it contends violently against universal civility and that uncorrupted light of nature which has been lit in our minds.

15. *21.* De iuramentis et *communione sacramentorum* **participatione Dominicae coenae.**
22. De communicatione.

Praeterea nec iuramentorum Anabaptistae legitimum relinquunt usum, in quo contra Scripturarum sententiam e*x*/**t** Veteris Testamenti patrum exempla, Pauli etiam Apostoli, imo Christi, imo Dei Patris procedunt; quorum iuramenta saepe sunt in Sacris Litteris repetita. [11v] Deinde ab ecclesiae corpore se ips[*i*/**os**] segregant, et ad sacrosanctam Domini mensam cum aliis recusant accedere, seque dicunt d[*is*/**e**]tineri vel ministrorum improbitate, vel aliorum fratrum, quasi prius excommunicatio possit in quoquam intelligi, quam ecclesia sententiam excommunicationis contra ill**um**/*os* direxerit, in qua pronuntiatur ill*os*/**um** non secus vitandu*s*/**m**, quam ethnicu*s*/**m** et publicanu*s*/**m**.

16. *23.* De ministris et ordinibus.
24. De baptismo infantium.

Similis est illorum amentia, qui institutionem ministrorum ab ecclesia[*m*] disiungunt, negantes in certis locis certos doctores, pastores atque ministros collocari debere; nec admittunt legitimas vocationes, nec solemnem manuum impositionem, sed per omnes publice docendi potestatem divulgant, qui sacris litteris ut[c/r]unque sunt aspersi, **et Spiritum sibi vendicant**; nec illos solum adhibent ad docendum, sed etiam ad moderandam ecclesiam et distribuenda sacramenta; quae sane universa cum scriptis apostolorum manifeste pugnant.

[>18. De baptismo.[38]

Deinde crudelis illorum impietas in baptismum irruit, quem infantibus impartiri nolunt, sed omnino nulla ratione,. *n*/Nec[39] enim minus ad Deum [12r] et ecclesiam pertinent Christianorum infantes quam liberi quondam Hebraeorum pertinebant, quibus in infantia cum circumcisio adhiberetur, nostris etiam infantibus debet baptismus admoveri, quoniam eiusdem promissionis et foederis divini participes sunt, et a Christo sunt etiam summa cum humanitate suscepti.

---

[38] Added by Cranmer and given this number, with the intention that it should be moved. A 'b' in the margin collates with another 'b' at the end of s. 17, to confirm this. On the doctrine, see Article 28 of 1553 (27 of 1571).
[39] Cranmer began a new sentence here.

15. *21.* Of oaths and *the communion of the sacraments* **participation in the Lord's supper.**
22. Of communion.

Furthermore, the Anabaptists even give up the lawful use of oaths, in this matter going against the teaching of the Scriptures **and** the examples of the fathers of the Old Testament, as well as of the Apostle Paul, and even of Christ, even of God the Father, whose oaths are often recorded in Holy Writ. Finally, they separate themselves from the body of the church and refuse to come to the most holy table of the Lord along with everyone else, saying that they are held back either by the unworthiness of the ministers, or of the other brethren, as if excommunication can be understood of someone before the church has pronounced a sentence of excommunication against *them* **him**, in which it is stated that it is not wrong to avoid *them* **him** as a pagan and a publican.

16. *23.* Of ministers and orders.
24. Of infant baptism.

Similar to this is the madness of those who divorce the institution of ministers from the church, denying that certain teachers, pastors and ministers ought to be appointed to particular places, neither do they accept lawful callings nor the solemn laying on of hands, but they grant the power of teaching publicly to everyone who has even a smattering of sacred learning, **and claims the Spirit for himself**, nor do they allow them only to teach, but also to govern the church and distribute the sacraments, which things are all clearly repugnant to the writings of the apostles.

[> **18. Of baptism.**[38]

Furthermore, their cruel ungodliness extends to baptism, which they do not want to be administered to infants, though for no reason whatsoever. For[39] the children of Christians do not belong any less to God and the church than the children of the Hebrews once did, and since circumcision was given to them in infancy so also baptism ought to be imparted to our children, since they are participants in the same divine promise and covenant, and have been accepted by Christ with the greatest human kindness.

25. De baptismi externa ceremonia.
26. De baptismi necessitate.

Plures item ab aliis cumulantur errores in baptismo, quem aliqui sic attoniti spectant, ut ab ipso illo externo credant elemento Spiritum Sanctum emergere, vimque eius omnem et virtutem ex qua recreamur, et gratiam et reliqua ex eo proficiscentia dona in ipsis baptismi fonticulis innatare. In summa totam regenerationem nostram illi sacro puteo deberi volunt, qui in sensus nostros incurrit. Verum salus animarum, instauratio Spiritus, et beneficium adoptionis, (quo nos Deus pro filiis agnoscit), a misericordia divina per Christum ad nos dimanante, tum etiam ex promissione Sacris in Scripturis apparente proveniunt. Illorum etiam impia [12v] videri deben*t* scrupulosa superstitio, qui Dei gratiam et Spiritum Sanctum tantopere cum sacramentorum elementis colligant, ut plane affirment nullum Christianorum infantem aeternam salutem esse consecuturum, qui prius a morte fuerit occupatus, quam ad baptismum adduci potuerit; quod longe secus **habere iudicamus** *est*. Salus enim illis solum adimi*t*atur, qui sacrum hunc baptismi fontem contemnunt, aut superbia quadam ab eo, vel contumacia resiliunt; quae importunitas cum in puerorum aetatem non cadat, nihil contra salutem illorum auctoritate Scripturarum decerni potest, immo contra cum illos communis promissio pueros in se compraehendat, optima nobis spes de illorum salute concipienda est.<]

17.[40] *18. 27.* De sacramentorum natura.[41]

Contraria **Magna quoque** temeritas illorum est, qui sacramenta sic extenuant ut ea pro nudis *tantum* signis et externis **tantum** indiciis capi velint, quibus tanquam notis hominum Chri[8b]stianorum religio possit a ceteris internosci, nec animadvertunt quantum sit scelus, haec sancta [*Dei*] instituta *exhaurire et obterere* **inania et vacua** cred*d*ere. Quae cum inter nos dispertiuntur, vi Divini Spiritus fides confirmatur, [13r] erigitur conscientia, promissio etiam veniae peccatorum per Christum [*exhibitae*]. *Deinde Dei gratia et Spiritus Sanctus in Christianorum mentibus disseminatus* [**facta intrinsecus exhibetur, extrinsecus vero**] istis sacramentis *tamquam communi quadam* v... *nota* **quasi sigillo quodam** consignatur. Praeterea verbo Dei quod intercedit, et symbolorum adhibitorum naturis erudiuntur fideles *in* **de** pretio nostrae redemptionis per Christum comparatae, **Spiritus Sanctus et gratia in mentibus fidelium** u[*b*/lt]**erius instillatur**, tum etiam foede*u*s quod per Christum inter Deum et nos ictum est, corroboratur, ut nobis ille proprius sit Deus, nos illi peculiaris populus, et astringimus nos ipsos ad peccatorum abolitionem, et integritatem vitae

---

[40]There is an 'a' in the margin in Cranmer's hand to indicate that this section should precede the one on baptism.
[41]Article 26 of 1553 (25 of 1571).

25. Of the external rite of baptism.
26. Of the necessity of baptism.

Likewise there are many errors which are piled up by others in baptism, which some are so impressed by that they think the Holy Spirit emerges from the mere external element itself, as well as all the force and power by which we are re-created, and that grace and the other gifts which come from it swim in the very fonts of baptism. In sum, they want our entire regeneration to be owed to that sacred well, which flows into our senses. But the salvation of souls, the indwelling of the Spirit, and the blessing of adoption (by which God recognizes us as his children), come from the divine mercy flowing to us through Christ, as well as from the promise which appears in the Holy Scriptures. For the scrupulous superstition of those who combine the grace of God and the Holy Spirit with the elements of the sacraments so closely as to affirm plainly that no child of Christian parents shall receive eternal salvation if he has been seized by death before he has been able to be brought to baptism, must be regarded as ungodly, because *it is* **we judge it to be** quite wrong. For salvation is denied only to those who despise this sacred font of baptism, or who turn away from it because of a certain pride or contumacy, but since this misfortune does not occur at the age of children, nothing can be determined against their salvation by the authority of the Scriptures, but rather the opposite, for since the common promise includes those children in it, the best hope for their salvation ought to be conceived by us.<]

17.[40] *18. 27.* Of the nature of sacraments.[41]

The opposite **Another great** boldness belongs to those who so dilute the sacraments that they want them to be understood as *mere* bare signs and **mere** external symbols, by which signs however, the religion of Christian people may be recognized by others, and they do not notice what a great crime it is *to believe that this exhausts and destroys* **renders** these holy institutions **null and void.** For when they are distributed among us, faith is confirmed by the power of the Holy Spirit, the conscience is awakened, and the promise of forgiveness of sins through Christ [*is revealed. Furthermore, by the grace of God, the Holy Spirit, who is also implanted in Christian minds* **is revealed as made internally, while externally it**] is symbolized by those sacraments *as though by some common sign* **as if by some seal.** Moreover by the Word of God which intervenes, and by the nature of the symbols presented, believers are instructed *in* **about** the price of our salvation bought by Christ, **the Holy Spirit and grace are instilled more** [*richly* **deeply**] **in the minds of believers**, for then the covenant which has been made by Christ between God and us is reaffirmed, that God is nearer to us, that we are his peculiar people, and that we are dedicating ourselves to the abolition

suscipiendam. Quae si recte ponderentur, necesse est ut obmutescat illorum calumnia, qui sacramentorum inopem volunt, et nudam naturam relinquere.[42]

[<**18**. De baptismo.

Deinde crudelis illorum impietas in baptismum irruit, quem infantibus impartiri nolunt, sed omnino nulla ratione. Nec enim minus ad Deum et ecclesiam pertinent Christianorum infantes quam liberi quondam Hebraeorum pertinebant, quibus in infantia cum circumcisio adhiberetur, nostris etiam infantibus debet baptismus admoveri, quoniam eiusdem promissionis et foederis divini participes sunt, et a Christo sunt etiam summa cum humanitate suscepti.

Plures item ab aliis cumulantur errores in baptismo, quem aliqui sic attoniti spectant, ut ab ipso illo externo credant elemento Spiritum Sanctum emergere, vimque eius [*omnem* **nomen**] et virtutem ex qua recreamur, et gratiam et reliqua ex eo proficiscentia dona in ipsis baptismi fonticulis innatare. In [9a] summa totam regenerationem nostram illi sacro puteo deberi volunt, qui in sensus nostros incurrit. Verum salus animarum, instauratio Spiritus, et beneficium adoptionis quo nos Deus pro filiis agnoscit, a misericordia divina per Christum ad nos dimanante, tum etiam ex promissione Sacris in Scripturis apparente proveniunt. Illorum etiam impia videri debet scrupulosa superstitio, qui Dei gratiam et Spiritum Sanctum tantopere cum sacramentorum elementis colligant, ut plane affirment nullum Christianorum infantem aeternam salutem esse consecuturum, qui prius a morte fuerit occupatus, quam ad baptismum adduci potuerit; quod longe secus habere iudicamus. Salus enim illis solum adimitur, qui sacrum hunc baptismi fontem contemnunt, aut superbia quadam ab eo, vel contumacia resiliunt; quae importunitas cum in puerorum aetatem non cadat, nihil contra salutem illorum auctoritate Scripturarum decerni potest, immo contra cum illos communis promissio pueros in se compraehendat, optima nobis spes de illorum salute concipienda est.>]

19. *28*. De transusbstantiatione in eucharistia **et**
29. De impanatione, ut vocant, corporis Christi.[43]

Obrepsit etiam in eucharistia periculosissimus error eorum qui docent, contionantur et contendunt, virtute certorum verborum quae minister ad symbola huius sacramenti insusurrat, panem [13v] converti vel (ut ipsi loquuntur) transubstantiari in Christi corpus, et itidem vinum in sanguinem;. *q*/**Quod**[44] sane dogma quoniam Sacris Litteris adversatur, a natura sacramenti discrepat et verum

---

[42]A marginal note in an unknown hand in the MS reads: 'Deinde b', indicating that s. 18 was meant to follow here.
[43]Article 29 of 1553 (28 of 1571).
[44]Cranmer began a new sentence here.

of sins and to adopting integrity of life. If these things are rightly considered, the calumny of those who want to leave the nature of the sacraments worthless and bare will necessarily be silenced.[42]

[<18. Of baptism.

Finally their cruel ungodliness extends to baptism, which they do not want to be administered to infants, though for no reason whatsoever. For the children of Christians do not belong any less to God and the church than the children of the Hebrews once did, and since circumcision was given to them in infancy so also baptism ought to be imparted to our children, since they are participants in the same divine promise and covenant, and have been accepted by Christ with the greatest human kindness.

Likewise there are many errors which are piled up by others in baptism, which some are so impressed by that they think the Holy Spirit emerges from the mere external element itself, as well as [*all*] the force, [**the name**] and power by which we are re-created, and that grace and the other gifts which come from it swim in the very fonts of baptism. In sum, they want our entire regeneration to be owed to that sacred well, which flows into our senses. But the salvation of souls, the indwelling of the Spirit, and the blessing of adoption by which God recognizes us as his children, come from the divine mercy flowing to us through Christ, as well as from the promise which appears in the Holy Scriptures. For the scrupulous superstition of those who combine the grace of God and the Holy Spirit with the elements of the sacraments so closely as to affirm plainly that no child of Christian parents shall receive eternal salvation if he has been seized by death before he has been able to be brought to baptism, must be regarded as ungodly, because we judge it to be quite wrong. For salvation is denied only to those who despise this sacred font of baptism, or who turn away from it because of a certain pride or contumacy, but since this misfortune does not occur at the age of children, nothing can be determined against their salvation by the authority of the Scriptures, but rather the opposite, for since the common promise includes those children in it, the best hope for their salvation ought to be conceived by us.>]

19. *28.* Of transubstantiation in the eucharist **and**
29. Of the impanation, as they call it, of the body of Christ.[43]

There has also appeared in the eucharist the most dangerous error of those who teach, preach and argue that by virtue of certain words which the minister applies to the symbols of this sacrament, the bread is changed or (as they themselves say) is transubstantiated into the body of Christ, and likewise the wine into blood, which[44] doctrine is clearly opposed to Holy Writ, diverges from the nature of a

Christi corpus ita depravat ut vel divinam in illud inducat naturam omnibus locis diffusam, vel ex eo spectrum aut machinam quandam com[9b]miniscatur., *T*/totum[45] hoc papisticae faecis somnium auferri volumus, et naturam veram panis et vini in eucharistia remanentem plane agnosci, quomodo Spiritus Sanctus apertis verbis attestatur. Itaque *non* **nec** in altum tolli sacramentum hoc, nec circumferri [**per agros**] patimur, nec conservari [**in crastinum**], nec adorari; denique null*u*/am relinquimus maiorem eucharistiae venerationem quam baptismi et Verbi Dei. Symbola vero **panis et vini** nisi pium et institutum a Scripturis usum commun*icat**ionis retinent, *eandem omnino* **non maiorem** aestimationem habere volumus quam panis et vinum habent, quae quotidie inter nos in usu habentur. In eodem luto haerent, qui panis et vini substantiam in eucharistia ponunt, sed vi consecrationis *ut aiunt* per ministrum appositae corpus et sanguinem Christi verum et naturalem adiungi putant, et cum symbolorum [14r] naturis permisceri, et subter eas subiici, usque adeo ut sive pii sint sive impii, qui ad Domini mensam se admovent, verum et naturale Christi corpus, et expressum eius sanguinem, una cum pane et vino sumant.[46] Verum symbola sacramentorum quoniam *ita comparata sunt ut rerum significationem afferant et earum repraesentationem quandam habebant, res autem ipsas* **ipsae neque sint neque**[47] *suis* /*in*/ *membris et substantiis non contineant aut exprimant* **res quas significant, non intra se clausas realiter et substantialiter (ut *ita dicamus) contineant* loquuntur) contineant;** deinde cum Sacris Scripturis determinatum sit Christum suam in coelum humanam naturam invexisse, nec cum illa sit in terras ante tempus extremi iudicii decensurus. Praeterea cum haec commentitia naturalis corporis Christi praesentia*m* nullum habeat maius momentum ad aedificationem nostrae religionis quam haec Christi praesentia quae fide p[er/rae]cipitur, **imo multas secum afferat quaestiones inexplicabiles, ac assertiones falsas et portentosas**; absurdam hanc doctrinam qua Christi corpus et sanguis naturaliter et substantialiter (ut illi loquuntur) /ad eucharistiam adrepunt, et in eam includuntur/, prorsus aboleri volumus,. *p*/Peregrinum[48] enim est, et alienum a Sacris Litter[10a]is; deinde contrarium humanae naturae veritati, quam Christus assumpsit, et a conditione sacramentorum longe dissidens; postremo communis quaedam [14v] sentina superstitionum multarum in ecclesiam Dei comport[ta/-]rum.

---

[45]Cranmer removed new sentence here.
[46]The Lutheran doctrine commonly known as 'consubstantiation'.
[47]Added and deleted by Cranmer before he deleted the entire passage.
[48]Cranmer began a new sentence here.

sacrament, and so corrupts the true body of Christ that either it introduces into it a divine nature which extends to every place, or else reduces it to a mere form or device of some kind. We[45] want this entire fantasy of papistical rubbish taken away, and it to be plainly acknowledged that the true nature of bread and wine remain in the eucharist, as the Holy Spirit bears witness in clear words. Therefore we do not allow the sacrament to be elevated, nor carried about [**through the fields**], nor reserved [**for later use**], nor adored; finally, we reject any greater veneration for the eucharist than for baptism and the Word of God. For we want the symbols **of bread and wine**, except when they retain the godly use for communion which was instituted by the Scriptures, to receive *exactly the same* **no greater** consideration *as* **than** bread and wine have, which are in daily use among us. In the same mire stick those who posit the substance of bread and wine in the eucharist, but who think that by the power of consecration, *as they say*, added by the minister, the true and natural body and blood of Christ are added, and that they are mixed with the natures of the symbols and placed under them, to the effect that those who approach the Lord's table, whether they are godly or ungodly, consume the true and natural body of Christ and his very blood along with the bread and wine.[46] But the symbols of the sacraments *are so designed that they carry the meaning of the things and bear some resemblance to them, but* **they themselves are not, and they do not** contain *or express the things themselves in their parts and substances* **the things which they signify, really and substantially (***so to speak* **as they say) within themselves**; and also because it is determined from the Holy Scriptures that Christ took his human nature into heaven, and that he will not descend to earth with it before the time of the last judgment. Moreover, since this fabricated presence of the natural body of Christ has no more significance for the upbuilding of our religion than the presence of Christ which is perceived by faith, **and moreover brings with it many unanswerable questions, as well as false and revolting assertions**, we desire that from henceforth this absurd teaching, by which the body and blood of Christ creep naturally and substantially (as they say) /into the eucharist and are included in it/, shall be abolished. For it is foreign, and alien to Holy Writ, and moreover it is contrary to the truth of human nature which Christ assumed, and totally at variance with the nature of the sacraments; finally, it is some sort of common cesspool of the many superstitions which have been brought into the church of God.

20. 13.[49] De abusu eucharistiae in missis.[50]

*Notetur etiam illorum amentia qui sacramentum eucharistiae non solum in mensa Domini volunt adhiberi, et inter nonnullos communicari, sed illud etiam separatim ad missa*m/s *contra Scripturarum institutum sevocant.* [>In quibus sacrificium Deo Patri credunt oblatum esse, nimirum corpus et sanguinem Domini nostri Iesu Christi vere, quomodoque illi dicunt*ur* realiter, ad veniam peccatorum impetrandam, et salutem tam mortuorum quam vivorum procurandam; **quibus etiam regnum tam licentiosum dant ut illis aliquando minui, nonnunquam omnino tolli purgatorii tormenta statuant.** Qua in re sacrificium illud unicum (quod Christus Dei Filius in cruce Deo Patri repraesentavit et plenissime exhibuit) largiter imminuunt, et sacerdotium quod unius Christi proprium est, ad miserabilem hominum conditionem devolvunt*ur*.<][51]

20. 21. 31. De matrimonio *sublato religiosorum et ministrorum ecclesiae.*[52]

Iam inde a primis ecclesiae temporibus magna fuit haereticorum turba, quae matrimonium aversabatur ut foedam rem et inquinatam, et vel funditus [15r] e coetu fidelium auferebant, vel si semel imbecillitati nostrae p[er/**rae**]mitteretur tamen illud nullo modo repetendum esse putabant;. *q*/**Q**uorum[53] sententia quoniam a regula pietatis, quae Sacris in Litteris lucet, vehementer abhorrebat, ecclesiae censura veteri iam olim explosa est. Sed diabolus pro hac impietate aliam subiecit, nimirum ut omnes qui solitariam vitam profiterentur, aut ad ecclesiae administrationem aggregarentur, matrimonii contrahendi facultatem in omne tempus amitterent. Quod eorum iniquum institutum, quoniam pugnat cum Sacris *Litteris* Scriptis, aboleri penitus, et pro nullo volumus haberi.

21. 22. 32. De Romana ecclesia **et**
33. De potestate Romani pontificis.[54]

Etiam illorum insania legum vinculis est constringenda, qui Romanam ecclesiam in huiusmodi /petra/ fundatam esse existimant, ut nec erraverit, nec errare possit; cum et multi possint eius errores ex superiore maiorum memoria repeti, et etiam

---

[49]An error for 30.
[50]A marginal note in the MS reads: 'Quorundam enim est nimis, etc. fo. 9', referring to s. 9 above.
[51]Moved to section 10 above as indicated by Cranmer in a note which reads: 'Verum Sacrae Scripturae, etc. fo. 9'.
[52]Article 31 of 1553 (32 of 1571).
[53]Cranmer began a new sentence here.
[54]Article 35 of 1553 (37 of 1571).

20. 13.[49] *Of the abuse of the eucharist in masses.*[50]

Likewise the insanity is to be noted of those who not only want the sacrament of the eucharist to be administered at the Lord's table and to be shared by many, but who take it away into private masses, against the command of the Scriptures [>in which they believe that a sacrifice has been offered to God the Father, even the body and blood of our Lord Jesus Christ truly, or as they put it, really, to obtain the forgiveness of sins and procure the salvation of both the dead and the living, **to which they grant** such [licentious *broad*] **power that they maintain that their torments in purgatory are sometimes lessened and occasionally taken away altogether.** In which matter they greatly reduce that one unique sacrifice (which Christ the Son of God offered and fully presented to God the Father on the cross), and bring the priesthood, which is the property of Christ alone, down to the miserable level of men.<]

20. *21. 31.* Of matrimony *removed from religious and ministers of the church.*[52]

Even from the very first times of the church there was a great crowd of heretics which opposed matrimony as a wicked and unjust thing, and either they removed it completely from the fellowship of believers, or they thought that if it were permitted once on account of our weakness, nevertheless it should in no way be repeated. Their[53] opinion, since it is absolutely repugnant to the rule of godliness which shines in Holy Writ, was already long ago exploded by the ancient censure of the church. But the devil substituted another form of ungodliness for this one, to wit that all who profess the solitary life or who are employed in the administration of the church, must abandon any possibility of contracting marriage for all time. Which wicked institution of theirs, since it is repugnant to Holy Writ, we desire that it shall be completely abolished and regarded as null and void.

21. *22. 32.* Of the Roman church **and**
33. Of the power of the Roman pontiff.[54]

Also the insanity of those who think that the Roman church was founded on a /rock/ of such a kind that it has neither erred nor can err, must be restrained by limits imposed by law, since many of its errors can be repeated by the longer

ex hac nostra proferri, partim in his quibus vita nostra debet informari, partim etiam [15v] in his quibus fides debet institui. Quapropter illorum etiam intolerabilis est error, qui totius Christiani orbis universam ecclesiam solius episcopi Romani principatum contineri volunt. Nos enim eam quae cerni potest ecclesiam sic definimus, ut om[10b]nium coetus sit fidelium hominum in quo Sacra Scriptura sincere docetur et sacramenta (saltem his eorum partibus quae necessariae sunt) iuxta Christi praescriptum administrantur.

22. 23. 34. De praedestinatione.[55]

Ad extremum in ecclesia multi feris et dissolutis moribus vivunt, qui cum re ipsa curiosi sint, differti luxu, et a Christi Spiritu prorsus alieni, semper praedestinationem et reiectionem, vel (ut usitate loquuntur), reprobationem in sermone iactant, ut cum aeterno consilio Deus vel de salute vel de interitu aliquid certi constituerit, inde latebram suis maleficiis et sceleribus et omnis generis perversitati quaerant. Et cum pastores dissipatam illorum et flagitiosam vitam coarguunt, in voluntatem Dei criminum suorum culpam conferunt, et hac defensione [16r] profligatas admonitorum repraehensiones existimant; ac ita tandem, duce diabolo, vel in desperation[*is*/**em** *puteum* **praesentem**] abiiciuntur praecipites, vel ad solutam quandam et mollem vitae securitatem, si[n/v]e **aut paenitentia aut scelerum conscientia** dilabuntur. Quae duo mala disparem naturam, sed finem /videntur/ eundem habere. Nos vero Sacris Scripturis eruditi, talem in hac re doctrinam ponimus, quod diligens{*et*} accurata cogitatio de praedestinatione nostra et electione suscepta (de quibus Dei voluntate determinatum fuit antequam mundi fundamenta iacerentur). Haec itaque diligens et seria, quam diximus, his de rebus cogitatio, piorum hominum animos Spiritu Christi afflatos, et carnis et membrorum subiectionem p[*er*/**rae**]s{*enti*}[*sc*]entes, et ad caelestia sursum tendentes, dulcissima quadam et iucundissima consolatione permulcet, quoniam fidem nostram de perpetua salute per Christum ad nos perventura confirm[a/e]t, vehementissimas caritatis in Deum [11a] flammas accendit, mirabiliter ad gratias agendas exsuscitat, ad bona nos opera propinquissime adducit, et a peccatis longissime abducit, *et a peccatis longissime* quoniam a Deo sumus electi et filii eius instituti; quae [16v] singularis et eximia conditio summam a nobis salubritatem morum et excellentissimam virtutis perfectionem requirit. Denique nobis arrogantiam minuit ne viribus nostris geri credamus, quae gratuita Dei beneficientia et infinita bonitate indulgentur. Praeterea neminem ex hoc loco purgationem censemus vitiorum suorum afferre posse; quia Deus nihil ulla in re iniuste constituit, nec ad peccata voluntates nostras unquam invitas truditur. Quapropter omnes nobis admonendi sunt, /ut in/ actionibus suscipiendis ad decreta praedestinationis se non referant, sed universam vitae suae rationem ad Dei leges accommodent; *et* cum **et** promissiones **bonis** *tum* **et** minas **malis** in Sacris Scripturis **generaliter** *sibi*

---

[55]Article 17 of 1553 and 1571.

memory of our elders, and may even be recalled by our memory, partly in those things by which our life ought to be guided and partly also in those things by which our faith ought to be determined. For this reason the error of those who want the universal church of the whole Christian world to be governed by the bishop of Rome alone is intolerable. For we define the visible church like this: it is an assembly of faithful people in which Holy Scripture is sincerely taught and the sacraments (at least in those parts of them which are essential) are administered according to the command of Christ.

22. *23. 34.* Of predestination.[55]

On the fringe of the church there are many who live in a wild and dissolute way, who when they get interested in the subject, being dissipated by excess and completely cut off from the Spirit of Christ, always toss predestination and rejection, or (as they usually call it), reprobation, into their speech, arguing that since God by his eternal counsel has already determined something, both concerning salvation and concerning destruction, they have some excuse for their wrongdoings and crimes and all manner of evil. And when pastors upbraid their dissipated and disgraceful life, they blame God's will for their crimes and by that defence consider that the reprimands of admonitions are wasted, and so also, under the devil's leadership, they are either tossed headlong into [*the well of* **actual**] despair or drawn into some dissolute and soft security of life, **without either repentance or any consciousness of wrongdoing.** Which two evils /appear to/ have a different nature, but the same end result. For we who are taught by the Holy Scriptures, lay down such teaching on this matter that a diligent [[*and*]] careful understanding of our predestination and election may be obtained, (about which it was decided by the will of God before the foundations of the world were laid). Therefore this diligent and serious understanding, as we have said, concerning these things will reward the minds of godly people · ho are full of the Spirit of Christ, who [*feel* **foresee**] the subjection of their flesh and members, and who look upwards to heavenly things with the sweetest and most joyful consolation, since it confirms our faith in the eternal salvation which will come to us through Christ, lights the strongest flames of love towards God, stirs us most remarkably to give thanks, and takes us far away from sin, *and far away from sin* since we have been chosen by God and declared to be his children, which singular and exalted condition demands the highest propriety in behaviour and the most excellent perfection of virtue from us. Furthermore, it reduces our arrogance, lest we believe that we are ruled by our own strength, which is blessed by the free beneficence and infinite goodness of God. Moreover we consider that on this basis no one can achieve the cleansing of his own sins, since God has not established anything unjustly in any matter, nor does he lead our wills into sins against our desires. Wherefore everyone must be warned by us /that in/ undertaking actions they should not rely on the decrees of predestination, but adapt their entire way of life to the laws of God, and contemplate that **both**

propositas contemplentur,. *d*/Debemus enim ad Dei cultum viis illis ingredi et in illa Dei voluntate commorari, *in s*... quam in Sacris Scripturis patefactam esse videmus.

23. Epilogus.

Posset magna colluvies aliarum haeresum accumulari, sed hoc tempore [*solum*] illas nominare. [**solum**] *V*/voluimus,[56] quae potissimum hisce nostris temporibus per ecclesiam diffunduntur; fideles omnes in nomine [17r] Dei et Domini nostri Iesu Christi obtestantes, ut ab his opinionibus pestilentissimis se longissime abducant; et ab illis etiam vehementer contendimus qui rem publicam et ecclesiam administrant, ut istas haereses ex regno nostro penitus evellendas et radicitus extirpandas (quantum in se est) curent.

---

[56]Cranmer joined two sentences into one at this point.

promises *as well as* **to the good and** threats **to the bad** are **generally** set forth *to him* in the Holy Scriptures. For we must go into the worship of God in those ways and dwell in that will of God, *in...* which we see made plain in the Holy Scriptures.

23. Conclusion.

It may be that a great heap of other heresies will pile up, but at this time we desire[56] to name only those which are most powerfully spread throughout the church in these our times, warning all who believe in the name of God and of our Lord Jesus Christ that they should stay as far away as possible from these most pestilential opinions, and we also strongly demand from those who govern the state and church that they try (as far as they can) totally to destroy and uproot these heresies out of our kingdom.

[17r; 11b]   **3. DE IUDICIIS CONTRA HAERESES**[1]

1. *Iudicia haeresum quibus modis procedant et quae sunt in illis specialia.* **Sub quibus iudicibus cognoscatur de haeresi.**[2]

Iudicium de haeresibus informatur quattuor rationibus, inquisitione, vel accusatione, vel evangelica denuntiatione, vel exceptione. *Iudicum peculiaria vero sunt quaedam, quae solum in hoc haeresum iudicio valent, ex quibus unum est quod* Is qui vel accusatione, vel inquisitione, vel evangelica denuntiatione reus fit, quod aliquam haeresim, aut affirmaverit aut defenderit, aut praedica[r/v]it aut docuerit, coram episcopo **suo*** vel archiepiscopo causam dicet. [<Qui vero loci privilegium habent, et exempti dicuntur, apud illos vel episcopos vel archiepiscopos causam dicent intra quorum dioeceses illorum exempti loci constiterint.>][3] Appellatio[4] tamen reo conceditur, ab episcopo ad archiepiscopum, et ab archiepiscopo nostram ad regalem personam,. e/*Et*[5] *ad nos si res deducta fuerit, tres episcopos adhiberi volumus in scientia Sacrarum Litterarum instructissimos, et ad hos assumi duos iuris civilis doctores usu praestantes et doctrina legum, ut ab illis tota causa ratione et ordine pertractari possit.*[>Qui vero **episcopi non sunt et*** loci privilegium habent, et exempti dicuntur, apud illos vel episcopos vel archiepiscopos causam dicent intra quorum dioeceses illorum exempti loci constiterint.<]

[17v] 2. *Inquisitio in haeresis crimen, qualis sit.* **Modus procedendi contra haereticos.**[6]

Primum autem crimen haeresis quoties per inquisitionem *in...* intentatur, **sive** fama *sive* plene contra reum comprobata fuerit, sive reus in eo nullam exceptionem opposuerit, quantumcunque postea negaverit illos ad se articulos pertinere, tamen nisi fideiussores idoneos exhibeat, quod iuri stare velit, tantisper in carcere potest ab episcopo detineri, donec lis ad finem pervenerit. *Si vero de*

---

[1]This chapter was originally part of the preceding one, but was separated out by Cranmer.
[2]Cf. X, 5.1.16 (Fr, II, 737-8), originally a decretal of Pope Innocent III, 11 February 1203; L, 5.5.4, originally c. 10 of the council of Oxford, 1407.
[3]This sentence is found here in F, having been displaced from the end of the paragraph.
[4]A marginal note, possibly in Foxe's hand reads: 'Ordo codicis corrigendus' ('The order of the codex must be corrected').
[5]Cranmer began a new sentence here.
[6]Cf. X, 5.7.13 (Fr, II, 787-9), originally c. 3 of Lateran IV, 1215 (*C.O.D.*, 233-5). See also H.C., 1.2.

3. OF JUDGMENTS AGAINST HERESIES[1]

1. *How judgments of heretics shall proceed and what is peculiar to them.* **By which judges cases of heresy shall be heard.**[2]

Judgment concerning heresies is decided by four means, inquest, accusation, evangelical denunciation and exception. *But certain things are peculiar to judges, which are valid only in this judgment of heresies, of which one is that* He who is inculpated by accusation, inquest or evangelical denunciation, because he has affirmed, defended, preached or taught some heresy, shall plead his cause before **his*** bishop or archbishop. [<And those who have a local privilege and are considered exempt, shall plead their cause before those bishops or archbishops in whose dioceses those exempt places are situated.>][3] Nevertheless[4] the accused is allowed to appeal from the bishop to the archbishop and from the archbishop to our royal person. *And*[5] *if the matter is brought to us, it is our will that three bishops, most learned in the knowledge of Holy Writ, shall be called, and that two doctors of civil law, of exceptional experience and legal learning, shall be added to them, so that the entire cause may be examined by them properly and in order.* [>And those **who are not bishops, and*** who have a local privilege and are considered exempt, shall plead their cause before those bishops or archbishops in whose dioceses those exempt places are situated.<]

2. *What an inquest into the crime of heresy is like.* **The mode of procedure against heretics.**[6]

First of all, every time a crime of heresy is *ex...* examined by inquest, or rumour against the accused has been fully proved, or the accused has deposited no exception to it, however often he may subsequently deny that those articles pertain to him, unless he can produce suitable guarantors that he will stand trial, he may be kept in prison by the bishop until the issue is resolved. *But if he*

errore confiteatur, et dicat se ab eo paratum esse decedere, dimmitendus erit;
hac tamen adhibita cautione, ut si quos vel sermone vel doctrina offenderit, aut
corruperit, illis ordinarii arbitratu satisfaciat, ne contagio serpat erroris, et
foras ad multitu[12a]*dinem emanet.**[7] Praeterea qui propter crimen haeresis in
iudicium a legitimo iudice vocatus fuerit, si negligat et animi contumacia non
adfuerit in tempore, primum in poenam excommunicationis incurrat. Deinde
quamprimum investigari potuerit ab ordinario, et praehendi, coniiciatur in
carcerem, donec locupletes interposuerit fideiussores, quod iuri stare velit.

3. Crimen haeresis quod per inquisitionem aut evangelicam denutiationem
procedit, quomodo tractetur.

Cum vero crimen haeresis per inquisitionem aut [18r] evangelicam
denuntiationem procedit, summatim tractatur, si[n/v]e solemni rerum ad iudicia
pertinentium apparatu,.

3. De haereticis resipiscentibus.[8]

c/Cumque[9] omnia fuerint in utramque partem in iudicia disputata, sive reus fuerit
convictus, sive crimen ipse confiteatur, primum admonendus est ut ab errore
desistat; quod si facturum se spoponderit, iuramento se ad id astringet. Deinde
paenitentiae fructus **iudicum arbitratu***[10] edet et ita demum dimittetur; hoc
tamen proviso, fratrum ut offensioni (si quae fuerit) quantum in se est, medeatur,
et **ne contagio serpat erroris*** quibus in locis errorem prius disseminavit, in
eisdem publice fateatur se in haeresi versatum esse. Quod si suam ad haeresim
pertinaciter adhaeserit, amandetur aliquandiu ad homines scientia praeditos, qui
illum in viam revocare possint. Et si illorum persuasu[-/**m**] sententia decedat,
iuramento interposito, quod haresim velit relinquere, liberari potest, illa semper
repetita conditione quam ante posuimus, nimirum ut paenitentiae certa signa det,
ac contraria doctrina fratres in illis locis erudiat, in quibus eos prius haeresi
contaminaverat.

---

[7]Foxe wrote in the margin of the MS: 'Haec *vero* in *codice* exemplari Cantuariensis stant.'
('*But* these words remain in Canterbury's *codex* copy.')
[8]X, 5.7.9 (Fr, II, 780-2), originally a decree of Pope Lucius III (1181-5); X, 5.34.10 (Fr,
II, 872-4), a decretal of Pope Innocent III, dated 7 May 1199; L, 5.5.2, c. 4 of the council
of Oxford, 1407. Cf. H.C., 1.9.
[9]Cranmer started both a new sentence and a new canon here.
[10]Both this and the next addition are in different ink (though in Cranmer's hand) and were
probably made later.

confesses his error and says that he is prepared to abandon it, he shall be set free; yet subject to this caution, that if he should offend or corrupt others either in preaching or in teaching, he shall render them satisfaction at the ordinary's discretion, lest the contagion of the error spread and seep out to the multitude.[7] Moreover, if whoever has been called into court on a charge of heresy ignores the summons and in the contumacy of his mind, does not present himself in time, he shall first of all incur the pain of excommunication. Then, as soon as he can be tracked down by the ordinary and arrested, he shall be thrown into prison until he has produced a good number of guarantors that he will stand trial.

3. How a crime of heresy which proceeds by inquest or evangelical denunciation shall be handled.

And when a crime of heresy proceeds by inquest or evangelical denunciation, it shall be handled summarily, without the solemn apparatus of things pertaining to judgments.

3. Of repentant heretics.[8]

And[9] when everything on both sides has been argued out in court, and the accused has either been convicted or confesses his crime, he shall first of all be warned to desist from his error, and if he promises to do so, he shall bind himself by oath to do it. After that he shall eat the fruits of penitence **at the discretion of the judges*[10] and then shall be released, but with the proviso that he shall make amends for the offence caused to his brethren (if there was any) as far as he can, and **lest the contagion of error spread,*** he shall state publicly in those places where he previously disseminated the error, that he had been involved in heresy. But if he persists in clinging to his heresy, let him be sent for a while to men of exceptional knowledge, who may be able to call him back to the way. And if he declares that he has been persuaded by their opinion and swears an oath that he will abandon his heresy, he may be set free, always subject to the same condition which we placed above, to wit, that he shall give clear signs of penitence and edify, with the opposite teaching, the brethren in those places in which he had previously contaminated them with heresy.

4. De contumacibus haereticis.[11]

Qui vero nec admonitionem nec doctrinam [18v] ulla ratione admittunt, sed in haeresi prorsus indur[a]uerunt, primum haeretici pronuntientur a iudice, deinde legitim[o/a] ferian[12b]tur excommunicationis supplicio. Quae sententia cum *rite* lata fuerit, si infra spatium sexdecim dierum ab haeresi recesserint, primum exhibeant publice manifesta paenitentiae i[n/u]dicia. Deinde solemniter iurent in illa se nunquam haeresi rursus versaturos. Tertio contraria doctrina publice satisfaciant, ac his omnibus impletis absolvantur, sed illis seria prius et vehemens adhibeatur exhortatio*ne semper*, ut post illud tempus cum a praesenti errore, tum etiam ab **omnibus** aliis haeresibus se longissime disiungant. Cum vero sic penitus insederit error, et tam alte radices egerit, ut ne sententia quidem excommunicationis ad veritatem reus inflecti possit, tum, consumptis omnibus aliis remediis, ad extremum ad civiles magistratus ablegetur puniendus *exilio vel perpetuo carcere*, **vel ut in perpetuum pellatur exilium vel ad aeternas carceris deprimatur tenebras, aut alioqui pro magistratus prudenti consideratione plectendus, ut maxime illius conversioni expedire videbitur.***[12]

5. De his qui abiurant haeresim.[13]

Qui vero iuramentuo se obligaverit ad repudiandam haeresim, primum profiteri debet se ab hac haeresi separatim abhorrere, de qua praesens tractatio sit; deinde contrariam opinionem publice [19r] affirmabit, et aperte testificabitur se tota ea in re hoc sequi, et firme tenere, quod sancta et universa Dei ecclesia Sacrarum Scripturarum auctoritate sequitur, et tenet, nec in haeresim a qua iam destiterit, unquam rursus ullo modo relapsurum.[14]

6. Haeresis quomodo probari debeat.[15]

Et quoniam crimen haeresis magnam atrocitatem et summam contumeliam habet, sola fama plene convinci non potest, nec aliis eius generis semiplenis (ut lex vocat) et curtis probationibus, sed tamen haec ipsa tantam vim habent, ut reo necessitatem afferant se purgandi; quae sane purgatio, si rite non possit ab eo impleri, condemnari [13a] reum in eo ipso stat[im/ui] oportet.

---

[11]See previous canon for references. Cf. Also H.C., 1.3-4.

[12]Added in Peter Martyr's hand, but not in F or 1640. For the punishment, see H.C., 1.5, which follows 25 Henry VIII, c. 14, s. 6, 1533-4 (*S.R.*, III, 454-5).

[13]X, 5.34.10 (Fr, II, 872-4), originally a decretal of Pope Innocent III, dated 7 May 1199; L, 5.5.2, c. 4 of the council of Oxford, 1407. See H.C., 1.9.

[14]MS inserts 'rediturum' over this word, in John Foxe's hand.

[15]25 Henry VIII, c. 14, 1533-4 (*S.R.*, III, 454-5).

4. Of contumacious heretics.[11]

But those who will in no way accept admonition or teaching, but who persist in their heresy, shall first of all be pronounced heretics by the judge, and then punished by a lawful sentence of excommunication. Once this sentence has been pronounced, if within the space of sixteen days they abandon the heresy, they shall first of all publicly display manifest signs of penitence. Then they shall swear that they will never again get involved in that heresy. Thirdly, they shall render satisfaction by teaching the opposite in public, and when they have done all this they shall be absolved, but first of all, a serious and stern exhortation shall be given to them, that after that time they shall distance themselves as far as possible, not only from their present error, but also from **all** other heresies. But when the error has penetrated so far and has put down such deep roots that the accused cannot be turned to the truth even by a sentence of excommunication, then, when all other remedies have been exhausted, he shall be turned over to the civil magistrates to be punished *by exile or perpetual imprisonment,* **either to be forced into perpetual exile or to be bound in the eternal shadows of prison, or to be treated in some other way, at the wise discretion of the magistrate, as shall seem most expedient for his conversion.***[12]

5. Of those who abjure heresy.[13]

And anyone who swears on oath to abandon heresy must first state that he has independently turned away from the heresy which is currently being examined, and then he shall publicly affirm the opposite opinion and openly testify that in this whole matter he follows and holds firmly what the holy and universal church of God follows and holds, by the authority of the Holy Scriptures, and that he will never again in any way fall into the heresy which he has just abandoned.[14]

6. How heresy ought to be proved.[15]

And since the crime of heresy leads to great wickedness and enormous abuse, it cannot be fully proved by rumour alone, nor by other half-complete (as the law says) and inadequate proofs of that kind, yet nevertheless these things are important enough to make it necessary for the accused to purge himself, and if this purgation cannot be duly fulfilled by the accused, he must stand convicted of the offence.

7. Iudicum iniquitas quomodo punienda.[16]

Quemadmodum haereses ex regno nostro prorsus (quantum fieri potest) excludendae sunt, [*ita*] summopere cavendum est ne quisquam in periculum tam horribilis et invidiosi criminis sine iusta [19v] causa vocetur. Itaque si iudex, sive quod oderit quempiam, sive pecuniam ut eliciat, aut ut illi molestiam exhibeat, inique litem hanc haeresis intenderit, et in eo iudicis culpa legitimis probationibus constiterit, arbitrio superioris iudicis supplicium de eo sumetur.

8. Quomodo ferenda sententia sit, et quomodo interrogandi testes.[17]

Cum haeresis crimen cognoscetur, iudices [*in ferenda* **inferenda**] sententia theologorum et iureconsultorum aliquot utentur consilio, qui prius omnia causae acta diligenter perscrutati fuerint. Et testes qui adhibebuntur, ab ipsis iudicibus interrogari par est, nisi forte morbus, aut aliqua iusta causa, iudices impediveri[n]t. Qui si ipsi forte impediuntur, duos substituant pro se viros honestos, quibus hoc testimoniorum interrogandorum munus tuto committi possit.

9. Cum lis in haeresis causa pendet, et reus fugerit, quid sit faciendum.[18]

Si lis in haeresis controversia pende[*a*]t, et interim reus in alium locum dilabatur, ubi prior iudex in iure dicendo pergere nequ[*i*/**ea**]t, [20r] postulabit iudex aut a vicecomite aut praefecto oppidi (quem maiorem vocant) illius loci in quo reus versatur, ut sibi reum et proprio foro restituendum curet; vicecomes autem, sive maior, cum iudicis sententiam intel[13b]lexerit, in litteris iudicis perscriptam et eius signo communitam, statim providebit ut reus appraehendatur, eumque ad proprium iudicem relegabit. Quod si vicecomes aut maior facere neglexerit, in eo ipso quod neglexerit protinus excommunicatus, et ab ecclesia separatus esse *videbitur* **iudicabitur.**

---

[16]25 Henry VIII, c. 14, 1533-4 (*S.R.*, III, 454-5).
[17]Cf. VI, 5.2.11 (Fr, II, 1073-4), a decretal of Pope Clement IV (1265-8), taken over as H.C., 1.11; 32 Henry VIII, c. 15, 1541 (*S. R.*, III, 764); 34-5 Henry VIII, c. 1, 1542 (*S. R.*, III, 894-7).
[18]L, 5.5.4, c. 10 of the council of Oxford, 1407; 23 Henry VIII, c. 9, 1532 (*S.R.*, III, 377-8).

7. How the unfairness of judges is to be punished.[16]

In so far as heresies must be totally excluded (as far as possible) from our kingdom, [*so*] care must above all be taken to ensure than no one is brought into danger of so horrible and unenviable a crime without just cause. Therefore if a judge, either because he hates someone or in order to obtain money, or in order to molest him, handles the suit of heresy unfairly, and the judge's guilt in the matter can be demonstrated by lawful proofs, he shall be punished at the discretion of a superior judge.

8. How the sentence shall be pronounced, and how witnesses shall be examined.[17]

When a crime of heresy is being heard, judges, in pronouncing sentence, shall take the advice of a number of theologians and legal consultants, who have first diligently examined all the proceedings of the cause. And the witnesses who are produced may also be cross-examined by these judges, unless perchance illness or some other just cause shall hinder the judges. And if by chance they themselves are hindered, they shall substitute two honest men, to whom this duty of examining the testimonies may safely be entrusted, in their place.

9. What must be done if the accused escapes while a suit in a cause of heresy is pending.[18]

If a suit in a dispute of heresy is pending, and meanwhile the accused has gone away to another place where the former judge cannot follow him for a trial, the judge shall request either the deputy sheriff or the town prefect (whom they call the mayor) of the place where the accused is dwelling to restore the accused to him and to his own court, and the deputy sheriff or mayor, when he has learned of the judge's sentence, written down in a letter from the judge and bearing his seal, shall immediately see to it that the accused is arrested and sent back to his own judge. And if the deputy sheriff or mayor shall neglect to do this, he shall automatically be excommunicated for that reason, and shall *appear* **be judged** to have been put out of the church.

10. De his qui confessi aut convicti sint quid statuendum sit.[19]

Qui de crimine fuerit haeresis confessus, aut qui sic convictus fuerit ut sententia iudicis contra illum processerit et pronuntiata fuerit, si nec appellaverit, nec intra tempus appellationi concessum resipuerit, et arbitratu sui iudicis pro crimine satisfecerit **nulla illi valebit indulgentia, quin***[20] ex illo tempore sit hac ipsa contumacia factus infamis; nec ad officia publica gerenda, nec ad consilia *percipienda*, nec ad testimonium dicendum ullo [20v] tempore assumatur; i*m*mo nec testamentum illi condere fas erit; praeterea quodcunque negotium illi cum aliis intercesserit, ipse quidem omnibus, illi vero nullus cogatur in iudicio respondere. Crimen enim haeresis publicum esse statuimus; quoniam Dei religio*ne* communis inter omnes cum violatur, in eo publice videtur omnibus iniuria fieri.

11. De ministris ecclesiae resipiscentibus.[21]

Si contingat ecclesiae ministros haeresis esse re*u*/os, et si in eadem convicti sententiam passi fuerint, et post deponant errorem, et resipiscant, tamen communi iure suam ad priorem administrationem ecclesiae non redibunt; quoniam ecclesiae ministros integra fama esse oportet, non solum apud domesticos et suos, verum etiam externos. Quod[22] licet iure communi sic procedere debeat, tamen si huiusmodi tempora inciderint, ut ecclesia bonis ministris admodum denuda[14a]ta sit, aut quietis et concordiae causa id requirat, ecclesiastico iudici id permittimus, ut quos vere suorum errorum paenituerit, suos ad gradus et officia redire [21r] sinat, ut ita necessitatibus ecclesiarum succurri possit, neque pax impediatur; in quo tamen hoc tener[i/e] volumus, ut ad ampliorem in ecclesia locum quam prius habuerint, nunquam ascendant, nisi summa necessitas urserit, cui non possit ulla alia ratione occurri.

---

[19]Cf. 2 Henry V, s. 1, c. 7, 1414 (*S.R.*, II, 181-4).
[20]Added by Cranmer in different ink (probably later).
[21]This stands in contrast to C. 1, q. 1, c. 112 (Fr, I, 402), which was much more generous.
[22]A vertical line in the left margin in the MS singles this sentence out.

10. What is to be done with those who have confessed or been convicted.[19]

If whoever has confessed to the crime of heresy, or who has been so convicted that the sentence of the judge against him has gone forward and been pronounced, has not appealed or repented within the time allotted for the appeal and rendered satisfaction for his crime at the discretion of his judge, **no indulgence shall be allowed to him, but***[20] from that time he shall be blacklisted for his contumacy, and shall never be permitted to hold public office, to *offer* counsel or to give testimony, nor shall it be lawful for him to make a testament. Moreover, in all his dealings with others, he shall be obliged to answer in court to them, but not they to him. For we ordain that the crime of heresy is a public one, since whenever the religion of God which is common to all is violated, harm is seen to be done publicly to all as a result.

11. Of repentant ministers of the church.[21]

If it happens that ministers of the church are guilty of heresy, and if after being convicted they have undergone sentence, and later they abandon their error and repent, still as a general rule they shall not return to their former position in the church, since ministers of the church must be of blameless reputation, not only among their servants and family, but also among those outside. This is how one ought to proceed as a general rule, but if the times are such that the church does not have enough good ministers, or if it is necessary for the sake of peace and harmony, we permit an ecclesiastical judge to allow those who have truly repented of their errors to return to their positions and offices, so that in this way the needs of the churches may be met and peace may not be hindered. Yet we want to keep to this, that they shall never rise to a higher position in the church than the one they previously held, unless the greatest necessity requires it and no other solution is possible.

[22r; 14a]   **4. [DE] BLASPHEMIA *QUIBUS***

1. Quibus in rebus versetur **blasphemia.**[1]

Ex omni peccatorum genere nullum es[*t*/**se**] horribilius nec in quo Dominus Deus noster vehementius indignatur, aut maiore afficitur contumelia, nec in quod acerbum ultionis telum citius intorquet, quam illud blasphemiae scelus, quando vel superbissimo contemptus proposito Deum aversantes, vel [*ef*]fervescente furoris impetu contra illum elati, convitium vel in illum, vel in illa quae ad eius divin[*issim*]am maiestatem pertinent, evomimus. Et haec est inter blasphemiam et haeresim differentia, quod blaspehmia contemptu contumelias in Deum proiicit, et iracundia, sed haeresis errore falsas opiniones suscipit, et inscient[*ia*/**er**].

2. Quomodo punienda sit blasphemia.[2]

Sit igitur hoc a nobis constitutum, ut haec execrabilis blasphemiarum impietas, quam primum de ea rite constiterit, ab episcopis nulla ratione tolleretur, sed eodem supplicio [14b] confixa sit quo pertinax haereticorum insania plectitur. [22v] Nec immerito; cum ira Dei contra hunc blaspehmiae furorem sic priscis temporibus exarsit, ut ad opprimendum et obruendum huius criminis reum, populorum et integrae multitudinis concursus esse voluerit, ut sic publica lapidatione facta, cont/e/r[r]ere*te*tur. Et ipse Deus invectas a se publicas saepe calamitates attestatur, ut in illis blasphemiae flagitium ulcisceretur.

---

[1]L, 1.11.1, c. 9 of the council of Lambeth, 1281.
[2]Lv. xxiv. 11-16.

4. [OF] BLASPHEMY *IN WHICH*

1. In which matters **blasphemy** is involved.[1]

Of all the sins which exist, none is more horrible and there is none at which our Lord God is more greatly angered, or which is burdened with greater reproach, or into which the sharp weapon of revenge more quickly plunges, than the crime of blasphemy, when either we turn against God in an attitude of supreme contempt, or we are incited against him by the burning power of anger, and spew out abuse either against him or against the things which pertain to his most divine majesty. And the difference between heresy and blasphemy is this, that blasphemy hurls invectives against God out of contempt and anger, whereas heresy adopts false opinions in error, and without knowledge.

2. How blasphemy is to be punished.[2]

Therefore let it be decreed by us that as soon as this detestable ungodliness of blasphemy has been duly demonstrated, it shall in no way be tolerated by the bishops, but be punished with the same punishment as that which the persistent madness of the heretics receives. Nor is this unjust, since in early times the wrath of God burned so strongly against this madness of blasphemy, that in order to repress and destroy a man accused of this crime, it was God's will for there to be a gathering of the people and of the whole multitude, that it should be stamped out by public stoning. And God himself bears witness by the public disasters which are often brought by him, that he is avenging the crime of blasphemy against them.

[76r; 14b]   **5. DE SACRAMENTIS**[1]

1. Quid sit sacramentum.[2]

Sacramentum (quomodo nos illud in hoc loco capimus) signum est institutum a
Deo quod videri potest, quo gratia Christi promissis et meritis ad nos perfecta,
condonatioque peccatorum ipsis {*pro*/**re**}missorum [*verbis*] expressa
consignatur; quod duplicem in animis nostris vim habet. Primum etiam horum
externorum sumptio [*signorum*], et attributarum proprie illis virtutum, nobis
recuperatae salutis nostrae pretium in memoriam revocat, et id ut aperte
profiteamur eff[i/e]cit, deinde fidem acuit et exsuscitat, et illi robur addit.
Praeterea caritate[*m inter*] nos mutua[*m*] conserit, et in mentibus nostris Dei
timorem diffundit. Postremo vitam ad sinceram et integram exstimulat. Ex hoc
genere circum*sit*/**cis**io priscis temporibus erat. Nunc baptismus et eucharistia
successerunt.

2. Quid in sacramento quaerendum sit.[3]

Ad sacramenti perfectionem tria concurrere debent. Primum evidens est et
illustris nota, quae manifeste cerni [15a] possit. Secundum est Dei promissum,
quod externo signo nobis repraesentatur [76v] et plane confirmatur. Tertium est
Dei praeceptum, quo necessitas nobis imponitur, ista partim faciendi, partim
comm[*em*]orandi; quae tria cum auctoritate Scripturarum in baptismo solum
occurrant, et eucharistia, nos haec duo sola pro veris et propriis Novi Testamenti
sacramentis ponimus.

3. Quid sit baptismus.[4]

Baptismus est sacramentum, quo secunda generatio nostra nobis externa
consignatur [*aquae*] conspersione, veniaque peccatorum indulgetur, et Spiritus

---

[1]A marginal note in Foxe's hand reads: 'Hic titulus "De sacramentis" in codice Matthaei
Cantuariensis quintus est et sequitur proximo post titulum "De blasphemia"'. ('The title
"On sacraments" is fifth in the codex of Matthew Parker and follows immediately after
the title "On blasphemy"').
[2]Cf. C. 1, q. 1, c. 54 (Fr, I, 379).
[3]Article 26 of 1553 (25 of 1571).
[4]Article 28 of 1553 (27 of 1571).

5. OF SACRAMENTS[1]

1. What a sacrament is.[2]

A sacrament (as we understand it in this context) is a sign instituted by God which may be seen, by which the grace of Christ conveyed to us by promises and merits and the forgiveness of sins {*promised* **remitted**}, expressed to them [*in words*], is sealed, which has a double power in our souls. For first of all, the taking of these external [*signs*], and of the virtues properly attributed to them, recalls to our memory the price of the salvation which has been bought for us, and enables us to profess it openly, and secondly it sharpens and revives faith, giving added strength to it. Furthermore, it strengthens [**us in**] mutual love [*between us*], and pours out the fear of God in our minds. Finally it encourages us to live a sincere and honest life. In former times circumcision was this kind of thing. Now baptism and the eucharist have taken its place.

2. What must be looked for in a sacrament.[3]

Three things must come together for a sacrament to be perfect. First there must be an obvious and appropriate sign, which can be clearly discerned. Second, there is the promise of God which is represented to us and fully confirmed by the external sign. Third, there is the command of God, by which the necessity is placed on us, both to do these things and to commemorate them. Since these three things occur with the authority of the Scriptures only in baptism and the eucharist, we accept only these two as true and proper sacraments of the New Testament.

3. What baptism is.[4]

Baptism is a sacrament by which our second birth is sealed to us by the external pouring [*of water*], forgiveness of sins is received, and the power of the Holy

Sancti virtus infunditur, quemadmodum [*divini promissi*] verbis compraehensum est in baptismo propositis, ut erectior in nobis et perfectior esset fides. Dum autem in aqua demergimur et rursus ex illis emergimus, Christi mors [*nobis*] primum et sepultura commenda[*n*]tur, deinde suscitatio quidem illius et red*d*itus ad vitam; ut isti[**u**]s mortis et vitae monumentis recordemur, et palam testificemur peccatum in nobis [*mersum*] mortuum et sepultum iacere, sed novum [77r] et salutarem Dei Spiritum reviviscere in nobis et reflorescere, tinctoque foras externis aquis corpore, nostras intus animas, abstersis peccatorum sordibus, puras et perpurgatas ad aeternas et caelestes oras se attollere.

4. Quid sit eucharistia, quos fructus habeat.[5]

Eucharistia sacramentum est in quo cibum ex pane *a*sumunt*ur*, et potum ex vino, qui convivae sedent in sacra Domini mensa; cuius panis inter illos et vini communicatione obsignatur gratia Spiritus Sancti, veniaque peccatorum, ad quam ex eo perveniunt, quod fide compraehendunt et percipiunt Christi sacrosanctum corpus respectu[**m**] nostrae salutis ad [15b] crucem [*suf*]fixum, et cruorem pro tollendis fusum nostris peccatis, ut Dei promissa palam ipsa loquuntur. Deinde etiam his illustribus signis, quae coram cerni poss[**u**/**i**]nt, instru*a*/**u**ntur et ad confitendum adducuntur, quod Christus illos enutriat et in illis remaneat, et ipsi vicissim in Christo coll*ec*/[*oc*]ati[6] s*u**/i*nt.[7] Praeterea discunt summam debere esse suam cum ceteris fidelibus [77v] viris omnium officiorum coniunctionem; quoniam omnes membra sunt ad unum et idem Christi corpus agglutinata. Cum autem ad haec omnia nec transubstantiatione*m* opus sit, nec illa quam fingere solebant reali praesentia [*corporis*] Christi, sed [**quidem**] potius haec curiosa hominum inventa sint. Primum contra naturam humanam a Filio Dei nostra causa sumptam, deinde cum Scripturis Divinis pugnent, et praeterea cum universa sacramentorum ratione confligunt, ista tamquam frivola [*quaedam*] somnia merito desecanda curavimus, et oblivione obruenda, praesertim cum magnum ex illis et perniciosum agmen superstitionum in ecclesia Dei [*co*/**i**]mpe/**o**rtatum fuerit.

5. Qui s[*i*/**u**]nt admittendi ad mensam Domini.[8]

Neminem ad mensam Domini volumus admitti, donec fidem in ecclesia professus fuerit.

---

[5] Article 29 of 1553 (28 of 1571).
[6] 1640 has 'collocati'.
[7] 1640 has 'sint'.
[8] L, 1.6.5, c. 4 of the council of Lambeth, 1281.

Spirit is infused, as is contained in the words [*of the divine promise*] pronounced in baptism, so that faith may be strengthened and perfected in us. And when we go down into the waters and emerge from them again, first of all, Christ's death and burial are recalled [*to us*], second his resurrection and return to life, so that we should be reminded of the great events of his death and life, and openly testify that sin in us lies [*covered*], dead and buried, but that the new and lifegiving Spirit of God lives and flourishes in us, and that when our body is dipped on the outside with external water, on the inside our souls rise pure and cleansed, with the stains of sins removed, to the eternal and heavenly shores.

4. What the eucharist is, and what fruits it contains.[5]

The eucharist is a sacrament in which those who sit as guests at the Lord's table consume food of bread and drink of wine. By the sharing of this bread and wine among them the grace of the Holy Spirit is sealed, and the forgiveness of sins, to which they come as a result, if by faith they understand and accept that the most holy body of Christ was crucified for our salvation, and that his blood was shed for taking away our sins, as the promises of God openly state. For then they are taught by these transparent signs, which may be clearly discerned, and are led to believe that Christ feeds them and dwells in them, and that they in turn are[7] united[6] with Christ. Furthermore, they teach that there must be the closest co-operation with other faithful men, since they are all members of, and joined to, the same body of Christ. Moreover, for these things there is no need of transubstantiation, nor of anything which used to be imagined by the real presence of [*the body of*] Christ, but these things are [**just**] the curious inventions of men; they are repugnant both to the human nature which was assumed by the Son of God for our sake, and also to the divine Scriptures, and moreover, they go against the general principle of sacraments; we have seen to it that such [*certain*] frivolous dreams shall rightly be rejected and consigned to oblivion, particularly since a large and dangerous number of superstitions has been introduced into the church of God because of them.

5. Who should be admitted to the Lord's table.[8]

We do not want anyone to be admitted to the Lord's table until he has professed his faith in church.

6. Impositionem manuum esse retinendam.[9]

[78r] In praeficiendis ecclesiarum ministris (quales sunt diaconi, presbyteri et episcopi) ceremoniam manuum imponendarum retineri placet; quoniam illius in Sacris Scripturis mentio [*f*/s]it, et perpetuum habu[er]it usum in ecclesia.

7. Nuptias solemniter celebrandas esse.[10]

Nuptiarum solemnes ritus in oculis omnis ecclesiae summa cum gravitate et fide collocari statuimus, qui[16a]bus si quicquam absit eorum quae nos [*in i*/**nu**]llis sanci[*vi*]mus, pro nullis statim haberi placet.

8. Quo tempore confirmatio esse debe{*a*}t.[11]

Episcopis nostris [*negotium*] [damus/**divinis**] {**ius**} illos confirmandi qui catechismum didicerint, quod in his temporibus nostris praecipue fieri debet, in quibus infantes baptizati suam ipsi fidem ac voluntatem adhuc profiteri non possunt. Itaque confirmationis eorum tempus hanc ad rem aptissimum erit.

9. Pastores visitare debent afflictos.[12]

[78v] Pastores ecclesiarum debiles, afflictos et aegros diligenter visitent et precibus illos ac solationibus, quantum possunt, in difficillimis illorum et periculosissimis temporibus sustentent.

10. Quomodo sit in his procedendum.[13]

Horum formulas universorum officiorum inclusimus in unum librum qui de ceremoniis proprias/e tractat ecclesiarum nostrarum, ex eo volumus rerum administrationem singular[*u*/e]m depromi.

---

[9]D, 23 c. 14 (Fr, I, 84).
[10]C. 30, q. 5, c. 3 (Fr, I, 1105); *ibid.*, c. 6 (Fr, I, 1106); C. 35, q. 5, c. 2 (Fr, I, 1271-4).
[11]L, 1.6.2, c. 8 of the canons of an unknown English diocese, *c.*1222-5 (PC, 141); 2-3 Edward VI, c. 1 (*S.R.*, IV, 37-9). See 1603/60 for later practice similar to this.
[12]L, 1.11.3, c. 15 of the council of Oxford, 1222.
[13]Cf. the act of uniformity, 5-6 Edward VI, c. 1 (*S.R.*, IV, 130-1). The book of common prayer mentioned in that act came into use on 1 November 1552. It was withdrawn by Mary I, with effect from 20 December 1553, but continued to be used clandestinely until it was replaced by a similar text in 1559.

6. The laying on of hands is to be retained.[9]

In ordaining the ministers of the church (such as deacons, presbyters and bishops), the ceremony of the laying on of hands is to be retained, since mention is made of it in the Holy Scriptures and it has always been done in the church.

7. Weddings are to be solemnized.[10]

We ordain that solemnizations of weddings are to be held with the greatest seriousness and faith in front of the whole church, and if any of the things we have sanctioned is missing from them, they shall immediately be declared null and void.

8. At what time confirmation ought to take place.[11]

To our [**divine**] bishops we give [*the task*] {**the right**} to confirm those who have learned the catechism, which must be done particularly in these our times, in which infants who are baptized cannot as yet express their faith and assent. Therefore the time of their confirmation shall be the one most appropriate for that.

9. Pastors must visit the afflicted.[12]

Pastors of churches shall diligently visit the weak, afflicted and sick, and sustain them as far as they can by their prayers and consolations, in their most difficult and dangerous moments.

10. The procedure to be adopted.[13]

We have combined the forms of all these services in one book, which deals with the ceremonies belonging to our churches, and it is our will that every administration of them shall be taken from that book.

[80r; 16a] 6. DE IDOLOLATRIA ET ALIIS HUIUSMODI CRIMINIBUS[1]

1. Quae vitia vitanda sint in ecclesia.[2]

Devitentur prorsus et exterminentur idolorum cultus, magia, divinatio, sortilegium et superstitiones, quibus se criminibus si quisquam contaminaverit, arbitratu iudicum ecclesia[16b]sticorum poenas det, quas si repudiaverit, eiiciatur excommunicationis fulmine ex ecclesia, a quibus ut facilius nos abstineamus, singula separatim per se collocata definiemus.

2. Quid idolorum cultus sit.[3]

Idolo[lat/**ta**]ria, quomodo vulgo loquimur, cultus quid[*a*/e]m est in quo non Creator sed creatura vel hominis aliquod inventu[*m*], adoratur.

3. Quid magia sit.[4]

Magia pactum est vel foedus cum Diabolo percussum et eius ministris, carminibus, precibus, characteribus, vel similibus impietatis instrumentis conflatum, quod vel ad futurorum casuum investigationem refertur, vel ad certarum rerum quas expectimus conqu[*isi*/**aes**]tionem.

[80v] 4. Quid divinatio sit.[5]

Divinatio rerum est secretarum praenuntiatio, mali cuiusdam [*et*] impii spiritus instinctu proveniens et ex auguriis coagmentatur, auspiciis et om[*i*]nibus et reliqua huiusmodi prava levitate, quam in repraehensionem illorum etiam incidit curiosum ingenium, qui specie figurarum astrologiae praeceptis

---

[1] A marginal note in the MS, probably in Foxe's handwriting, reads: 'Titulus sextus in codice Matthaei Cantuariensis habetur.' ('This is chapter six in Matthew Parker's codex'). Something similar to this title can be found in 1636/4.8.
[2] See H.C., 7.1.
[3] Cf. C. 26, q. 5, c. 3 (Fr, I, 1027-8).
[4] C. 26, q. 5, c. 12 (Fr, I, 1030-1); *ibid.*, c. 14 (Fr, I, 1032-6).
[5] D, 37, c. 4 (Fr, I, 136). See H.C., 7.1; also 1566/2.7.

6. OF IDOLATRY AND OTHER LIKE CRIMES[1]

1. What evils are to be avoided in the church.[2]

From henceforth the worship of idols, magic, divination, fortune telling and superstitions are to be avoided and wiped out, and if anyone contaminates himself with such crimes, he shall pay a penalty at the discretion of the ecclesiastical judges. If he refuses to do so, he shall be thrown out of the church by the thunderbolt of excommunication. In order for us to be able to stay away from these things more easily, we shall define each of them separately by itself.

2. What the worship of idols is.[3]

Idolatry, as we commonly call it, is a form of worship in which not the Creator, but a creature or some figment of man's imagination, is worshipped.

3. What magic is.[4]

Magic is a pact or alliance forged with the devil and his servants, which is conflated with songs, prayers, signs and other similar tools of ungodliness, which deal either with the investigation of future events or with the obtaining of certain things which we want.

4. What divination is.[5]

Divination is the announcing of secret things, coming from the intuition of some evil and ungodly spirit, which is supported by auguries, auspices, omens and other such wicked inanity, to which condemnation is added the perverse genius of those who claim to know ways and events, by the form of figures delineated

deli[*ne*/**m**]at[a/**o**]rum, ut videri volunt, rerum, vel furto, vel alia ratione quacunque summotarum, deinde etiam actionum in omni vita susceptarum, vias et eventus se scire profitentur.

5. Quid sortilegium sit.[6]

Sortilegium intelligitur cum per sortes cuiuscunque generis abditae res patefactae sunt, vel futurus praesentium factorum aliquis finis p[*rae*/**er**]significatur.

6. Quid superstitio sit.[7]

Superstitio cultus est ad Deum relatus immenso quodam proficiscens humano studio, vel animi certa pro[17a]pensione, quam vulgo bonam intentionem vocant, et ortum semper habet ex hominis ingenio separatim sine Scripturarum divinarum auctoritate.

[81r] 7. Pastoris in his criminibus officium.[8]

Pastores diligenter populum commonefaciant ut ab his flagitiis tanquam gravissimis quibusdam Christianae fidei pestibus, se longissime abduca*n**t, nec ullo respectu quarumcunque rerum (sive lucrum exempli causa sit, sive voluptas, sive sit honor aut sanitas, aut rerum abstrusarum intelligentia, sive quisquam alius in animis obstrepat aut tumultuetur pravus affectus) *n*unquam huiusmodi impulsu vitio**s**orum motuum diaboli vinculis *nos* **se** teneri patiantur, et [*a*] suavissima Christiana[*e religionis*] libertate des[*c*]is[*c*/**t**]ere.

8. Qui propter haec crimina puniendi sint.[9]

Poenas autem gravissimas non solum illis denuntiamus qui curiosis utuntur et pestiferis artibus, verum etiam illis qui tam sceleratos artifices de rebus suis interrogant, vel illorum ullam operam quacumque ratione suas ad causas accommodant.

---

[6] C. 26, q. 1, c. 1 (Fr, I, 1020), from Isidore, *Etymologiae*, 8.9. See H.C., 7.1.
[7] C. 26, q. 2, c. 6 (Fr, I, 1021-2), from Augustine, *De doct. Chr., II, 19-21. See* H.C., 7.2.
[8] C. 26, q. 7, c. 15 (Fr, I, 1045), attributed to Augustine; c. 42 of the third council of Tours, 813. See H.C., 7.5.
[9] C. 26, q. 5, c. 1 (Fr, I, 1027), c. 12 of a council of Rome, 721. See H.C., 7.3.

by the precepts of astrology, as they want it to seem, by things which are moved either in secret or by some other cause, and finally even by actions encountered in everyday life.

5. What fortune telling is.[6]

Fortune telling is to be understood when hidden things are revealed by drawing lots of any kind, or when some future result of present actions is predicted.

6. What superstition is.[7]

Superstition is worship offered to God which comes from great human effort, or from a certain disposition of mind, which is popularly called 'good intention', and which always has its source in the mind of man independently, without the authority of the divine Scriptures.

7. The duty of the pastor in confronting these crimes.[8]

Pastors must diligently warn their people to distance themselves as much as they can from these crimes, which are some of the most serious plagues to infect the Christian faith, so that they may never allow themselves to be bound by the chains of the devil, either by any respect for these things (whether for example, it is money, or lust, or honour and heath, or the understanding of complex things, or any other evil thought which resounds in their minds or upsets them), or by the impulse of such depraved thoughts, and so depart from the sweetest liberty of the Christian [*religion*].

8. Who should be punished for these crimes.[9]

We decree the most severe punishments not only for those who make use of curious and pestiferous arts, but also for those who inquire of such wicked artificers about their affairs, or who adapt their activity to their own purposes in any way whatsoever.

9. Damnum his artibus datum esse compensandum.[10]

[81v] Si quisquam sceleratis istorum artibus damnum ullum in frumento, fructibus, aedificiis, pecoribus aut quibuscunque bonis suis acceperit, id universum plenissime cogantur restituere.[11]

---

[10]*Dig.*, 44.7.1, originally, Gaius, *Aurea*, 2; *ibid.*, 44.7.4, originally Gaius, *Aurea*, 3.
[11]A marginal note by Foxe reads: 'Proximus titulus in codice Mattahei Cantuariensis sequitur "De contionatoribus", ordine sepimus. Deinde "De matrimonio"'. ('In Matthew Parker's codex the next chapter is "On preachers", the seventh in order. After that, "On matrimony"').

9. Loss on account of these arts must be compensated.[10]

If anyone has suffered any loss because of the wicked arts of these people, either in corn, fruit, buildings, cattle or any of his goods, they shall be obliged to compensate it fully.[11]

[32r; 17b]   **7. DE CONTIONATORIBUS**[1]

1. Contionandi munus quale sit et quomodo suscipi debeat.[2]

Quoniam contionandi munus populo Dei maxime necessarium est, ecclesia nunquam [*illo*] destitui debet. Illud tamen diligentissime providendum est ne quisquam ad officium tam praeclarum assumatur, nisi pietatem ad illum locum et convenientem doctrinam secum adferat. Quod ut melius sciri possit, praesulum auctoritatem ad contionatores in ecclesiis disponend[*o*/i]s intercedere volumus. Nec ulli permittimus ut hoc contionandi munus suscipiat, aut in eo se ipse collocet, nisi legitima potestate eorum quorum interest, fuerit ad illud advocatus. In quo tantam episcoporum diligentiam esse volumus, ut temere non omnes adsciscant quicunque [s/**d**]e Spiritu Dei iactant afflatos, sed illorum vitam et *con*/**eru**ditionem considerent et [*ap*/**per**]pendant, ut ex eo cognosci possit an illorum spiritus a Deo proficiscantur.

2. *De* contionatoribus errores esse cavendos et errorum libros.[3]

Quibus vero contionandi potestas conceditur, [32v] hi vehementer advigilare debent, ne vel errores disseminent in ecclesia, vel inutiles quaestiones, hominum inventa et commenta, voces novas, aut ulla denique superstitionum fermenta; nominatim autem nec Anabaptistarum libellos auctoritate publica toto damnatos in nostro regno, nec aliorum quorumcunque quod sectarios vocant, vel iam explosa volumina, vel quae posthac explodentur, aut ullo modo doceant, [18a] aut tradant, aut illorum nomina proferant, [ad **aut**] [ali/**ante**]quam illius doctrinae partem confirmandam, de qua publice contiona[*n*]tur.

3. Contionatorum mores et doctrinae quales esse debeant.[4]

In contionatoribus vitae magistris, huiusmodi placabilitas et modestia debet inesse, nunquam ut acerbe contendant [**nec**] inter se, nec aliter in alterum maledicta intorqueat, quod si forte quispiam ex illis sit qui doctrinam impiam in

---

[1] Much of this was taken over and included in 1571/6.
[2] 2 Henry IV, c. 15, 1400-1 (*S.R.*, II, 125-8); L, 5.5.1, cc. 1-2 of the council of Oxford, 1407. See H.C., 2.1.
[3] L, 5.4.2, c. 6 of the council of Oxford, 1407. See H.C., 2.2; 1566/2.1.
[4] 1566/2.5.

7. OF PREACHERS[1]

1. What the task of preaching is and how it must be undertaken.[2]

Since the task of preaching is most necessary for God's people, the church ought never to be deprived [*of it*]. But the utmost care must be taken to ensure that no one is admitted to such an important office unless he brings godliness and the right doctrine to it with him. And so that this may be better controlled, it is our will that the authority of the bishops shall be exercised with respect to the preachers [**to be placed**] in the churches [*to be supplied*]. Nor do we allow anyone to take up this task of preaching, or to place himself in it, unless he has been called to it by the lawful power of those responsible for it. In this matter we want the diligence of the bishops to be such that they will not accept all those who claim [that they are **to be**] full of the Spirit of God, but that they will consider and weigh their lives and [*circumstances* **learning**], so that on that basis it may be known whether their spirits come from God or not.

2. *Of* errors and books of errors to be avoided by preachers.[3]

And those to whom the power of preaching is granted must be on the alert not to spread errors in the church, or pointless debates, or the inventions and thoughts of men, or novelties, or finally any seeds of superstition. In particular they shall in no way teach, or handle or mention the names of the books of the Anabaptists, which have been totally condemned by public authority in our kingdom, nor of any others whom they call sectaries, whether the volumes have already been published or shall be published after this, [for the purpose of **before**] supporting part of the doctrine about which they are publicly preaching.

3. What the behaviour and teaching of preachers should be like.[4]

In preachers, who are the teachers of life, there should indwell such pleasantness and modesty that they never argue bitterly [**either**] among themselves, nor hurl invectives at each other. But if by chance there should be one of them who has spread ungodly doctrine in his preaching, he must be warned to acknowledge his

contione per*m*/vulgaverit, admoneri debet, ut publice suum errorem agnoscat, quod si recusaverit facere, iudex illum afficiat haeretici poena, nisi de sententia decesserit, et hoc etiam accuretur, ut ubi perniciosam hanc doctrinam consevit, ibi sanus et pius aliquis contionator eius haeresim convincat, ne populus erroris venenum hauriens [33r] a vera desciscat et communi fide. Contionatores acriter vitiorum improbitatem obiurgent, sed in eo sic illis oratio progrediatur, nullius ut hominis occulta maleficia separatim et proprie demonstrent. Nec quenquam nominatim reum coram multitudine citent, nisi tam importunus quispiam fuerit, ut ecclesiasticas admonitiones antegressas contempserit. Evidens etiam et apertus sit contionatorum sermo, non obscurus nec perplexus; nec verba sponte sic involvant et implicent, ut aeque possint in utramque partem distorqueri.

4. Ad quos proprie contionandi munus pertineat.[5]

Archiepiscopi in hoc contionandi munere principatum habere debent. Succedant episcopi, decani et quicunque sunt in dignitatibus (ut vocant) constituti. Nec hi solum in hac occupatione sanctissima debent esse, sed pastoribus [18b] etiam et parochis eadem potestas in suis gregibus concedi debet, nisi iustae causae subsint, ob quas episcopi sui silentium illis indixerint.

[33v] [5. *In cathedralibus collegiis quis sit ordo contionum.*[6]

Valde nobis convenire videtur ad omnes sacros coetus, quantum fieri potest, ut contio possit haberi. Itaque mandamus ut in omnibus ecclesiis cathedralibus singulis diebus dominicis vel episcopus ipse vel decanus vel aliquis ex numero praebendariorum contionem habeant. Itidem in singulis diebus festis aut aliquis illorum ad populum contionetur, aut homilia saltem recitetur.

6. *In academiis ordo quis sit.*[7]

In academiis contio sit singulis dominicis et festis diebus in templo quod vocant Universitatis, nisi quo die legitima contio et solemnis in aliquo collegio separatim explicatur. Et peragentur hae contiones partim a theologiae baccalaureis, partim doctoribus eiusdem, partim a collegiorum praefectis, qui

---

[5] 1538/9 (*D.E.R.*, 181); 1547/10 (*D.E.R.*, 251).
[6] In the MS there is a note in Cranmer's hand which reads: 'Ponatur hoc in titulo "De divinis officiis", vel "De ecclesiis cathedralibus"'. ('Put this in the title "On the divine offices" [R, 19] or "On cathedral churches" [R, 20.7]'). However, it is not found in either of those titles.
[7] A marginal note in Cranmer's hand reads: 'Ponatur in titulo "De academiis".' ('Put in the title "On universities" [R, 24]'). However, it is not found there.

error publicly, and if he refuses to do so, a judge may punish him with the penalty of a heretic, unless he gives up his opinion and puts matters right, so that where he has previously sown this pernicious doctrine, there some sound and godly preacher may expose his heresy, lest the people imbibe the poison of error and depart from the true and common faith. Preachers shall sharply denounce the wrongness of vices, but in this matter their delivery shall proceed in such a way so as not to reveal the hidden sins of any particular person. Nor shall they accuse anyone by name in front of the congregation, unless someone is so bothersome that he has shown contempt for earlier ecclesiastical warnings. Furthermore, the language of preachers must be clear and open, not obscure and confused, nor should they so twist and turn their words that they can be equally well distorted one way or the other.

4. To whom the task of preaching properly belongs.[5]

In this task of preaching the archbishops must take precedence. Then follow the bishops, deans and those who have been appointed to dignities (as they are called). Nor must they be the only ones engaged in this most holy occupation, but the same power must be granted to pastors and incumbents among their flocks, unless there are valid reasons why their bishops have ordered them to keep silent.

[5. *What the order of preaching is to be in cathedral chapters.*[6]

Really it seems to us to be right for a sermon to be had at every sacred assembly, as often as this is possible. Therefore we command that in all cathedral churches on every Sunday, either the bishop himself or the dean or one of the prebendaries shall preach. Likewise on particular saints' days either one of them shall preach to the people or at least a homily shall be read.

6. *What the order shall be in the universities.*[7]

In the universities there shall be a sermon every Sunday and holy day in what they call the university church, unless on any of those days there happens to be a lawful and serious sermon in one particular college. And these sermons shall be preached partly by bachelors of theology, partly by doctors of the same subject, and partly by the heads of the colleges, as long as the heads are duly

quidem praefecti rite fuerint ad contionandum advocati. Quoniam autem Oxonii cathedralis est ecclesia, singuli in ea collocati canonici quattuor intra tempus unius anni contiones ad populum habebunt. Nec in academiis hanc libertatem damus baccalaureis theologiae, vel doctoribus eiusdem, canonicis aut praefectis collegiorum, [34r] *ut cum illorum erunt contionandi tempora vicarios substituant, qui muneribus illis satisfaciant, nisi morbus illos oppresserit, vel absentia manifeste necessaria sevocet et sevocaverit.*

7. In oppidis et pagis quis sit ordo.[8]

Per oppida quoque contiones *et pagos* **contiones** *peragantur et in illis usurpentur; aut illis interdum deficientibus clara sit homiliarum et distincta lectio, quam, si tempus contione non fuerit occupatum, in omnibus regni nostri ecclesiis singulis dominicis et festis diebus sine ulla exceptione locorum habere volumus; hoc etiam adiicientes amplius ut singulis annis in quibuslibet parochiis, cum minimum erit, quattuor contiones peragantur.*]

5. 8. De convocandis per episcopum contionatoribus.[9]

Et ut contionum sit uberior fructus et contionatorum maior consensus, episcopus omnes contionatores quibus speciale privilegium, hoc est, praecipuam et peculiarem potestatem indulsit, lat*am*/e per universam dioecesim suam contionandi, certis temporibus ad se singulis annis congreget, cum illis de contionibus communicet, ac ex illis p[*er*/**rae**]discat quae vitia, quibus in locis [34v] maxime frequententur, et quibus remediis possit illis facillime occurri, ut communi quadam conspiratione contionatorum improbitas coerceatur, et pietas dilatetur.

6. 9. De his qui interesse debent contionibus.[10]

Quoniam praecipuus sabbatorum cultus in p[*er*/**rae**]cipienda Sacrarum Scripturarum scientia consistit, [*nos*] illos ecclesiasticis [*poenis*] feriri volumus, qui contionibus interesse nolunt, aut negligunt, nisi morbus illos impediat vel necessarium iter, vel alia pietatis exercitia, vel aliqua huiusmodi negotia quae

---

[8]There is a note in the margin in Cranmer's hand which reads: 'Ponatur in titulo "De divinis officiis".' ('Put in the title "On the divine offices" [R, 19]'). It does not appear there, but cf. R, 19.12. Unknown to the compilers of R, there were Anglo-Saxon canons dealing with this subject, e.g. c. 14 of Cloveshoo, 747 (HS, 367); c. 61 of Aelfric, *c.*, 993-5 (WBB, 208).

[9]Cf. 1571/1.3.

[10]5-6 Edward VI, c. 1 (*S. R.*, IV, 130-1).

called to the preaching ministry. And since at Oxford there is a cathedral church, the individual canons appointed to it shall preach sermons to the people four times in the space of one year. Nor do we grant the liberty to bachelors of theology, or to doctors of the same, to canons or to heads of colleges in the universities, that when the times for them to preach come round, they should provide substitutes to perform their tasks, unless illness has reduced them or a manifestly necessary absence has called or will call them away.

7. What the order shall be in towns and villages.[8]

Sermons shall also be preached in towns and villages and be given priority in them; or in their absence there shall be a clear and distinct reading of homilies, which, if the time is not filled with a sermon, it is our will shall take place every Sunday and holy day in all the individual churches of our kingdom without any exception; adding to this more explicitly that every year, in every parish, a minimum of at least four sermons shall be preached.]

5. *8.* Of the assembling of preachers by the bishop.[9]

And so that the fruit of preaching may be richer and the agreement between preachers greater, the bishop shall gather around himself every year at particular times all the preachers to whom he has granted the special privilege, that is, the great and peculiar power to preach throughout the entire diocese, when he shall instruct them about preaching and learn from them what ills are most frequently met with and in what places, and by what remedies they might most easily be dealt with, so that wrongdoing may be corrected by the common desire of the preachers, and godliness spread.

6. *9.* Of those who ought to be present at sermons.[10]

Since the main Sunday worship consists in receiving the knowledge of the Holy Scriptures, [*we*] desire that those who do not want to attend sermons, or who fail to do so, shall be punished by ecclesiastical [*punishments*], unless illness hinders them or an essential journey, or other works of godliness, or some other such

omnino necesse est statim obiri. Et hoc in loco primae partes nobilium et principum virorum esse debent, ut suo pulcherrimo et *orn*/**honor**atissimo exemplo studia plebeiorum et inferiorum invitent, deinde praecipimus ut propter maiorem huius rei disciplinam sanciendam, magistratus, iustitiarii, praefecti civitatum, et reliqui quocunque iurisdictionis nomine censeantur, contionibus intersint, nisi magna illos et omnino non praetermittenda causa detineat.

[19a] 7. *10.* Quid de his statuendum sit qui in contione obstrepunt.[11]

[35r] Si qui tanta importunitate sint, ut contionatore adhuc ex pulpito loquente, vel interfari vel obstrepere velint, vel ad illum aliquo modo **allatrare**, ab ecclesia segregentur, et commun**ion**is sint expertes, donec palam crimen agnoverint et resipuerint. Itidem quicunque vel otiose obambulando vel intempestive garriendo, vel ex coetu sacro sic emigrando, contionis ut contemptus in eo vel contionatoris depraehendi possit, vel quacunque alia ratione populum ad contionem attentum scientes et volentes averterint aut interturbaverint, meritas huiusmodi sceleratae levitatis poenas dabunt, et ecclesiae in eo satisfacient, quod eam su[*o*/**b**] pravissimo exemplo offenderint.

[11]H.C., 10.13. 1 Richard II, c. 15, 1377 (*S.R.*, II, 5).

business which absolutely must be undertaken. And in this matter pride of place belongs to the nobles and leading men, so that by their most attractive and esteemed example they may encourage the zeal of the people and lower orders, and we further ordain that for ensuring the better discipline of this matter, magistrates, justices, mayors of cities, and all others who are recognized as having any kind of jurisdiction, should also attend sermons, unless a great and absolutely unavoidable cause prevents them.

7. *10.* What should be done about those who shout during sermons.[11]

If there are those who are so troublesome as to want to interrupt or shout while the preacher is still speaking in the pulpit, or **rail** at him in some way, they shall be removed from the church and cut off from communion until they have openly acknowledged their crime and repented. Likewise anyone who can be found either walking aimlessly about or chatting at the wrong time or going out of the sacred assembly in such a way as to show contempt for the sermon or for the preacher, or who in any other way diverts or distracts the attention of the people who are trying to pay attention to the sermon, shall pay the penalties deserved by such wicked folly, and shall render satisfaction in this matter to the church, because they have offended it by their most wicked example.

[37r; 19a] **8. DE MATRIMONIO**

1. Matrimonium quid sit.[1]

Matrimonium est legitimus contractus, mutuam et perpetuam viri cum femina coniunctionem Dei iussu inducens et perficiens, in quo tradit uterque alteri potestatem sui corporis, vel ad prolem suscipiendam, vel ad scru/**or**tationem evitandam, vel ad vitam mutuis officiis gubernandam. N[ec/**am**] [n]ullis promissis aut contractibus matrimonium posthac procedere volumus, quotcunque verbis et quibuscunque concurrentibus, nisi fuerit hac formula [*celebratum*], quam hic subiiciendam esse curavimus.

[19b] 2. Matrimonium *quando* **quomodo** contrahatur.[2]

Principio, qui minister est ecclesiae, tribus dominicis aut saltem tribus festis diebus, publice futuras nuptias in ecclesia populo denuntiet. Deinde sponsus et sponsa se palam in ecclesia collocabunt et coram ea[**s**] ceremonias et ritus *adh*/**ob**ibunt, quae nostrae de rebus divinis sanctiones in hoc genere postulant; huic autem formulae tantam auctoritatem damus ut quicquid praeter eam dictum [37v] gestumve fuerit, quacunque ratione matrimonium in eo [*non*] possit existere, sed omnia huiusmodi praeparationes sint, aut pr[*o*/**ae**]lusiones quaedam ad matrimonium, non autem ipsum matrimonium in illis inest. *At*/**Ita**que liberae solutaeque s[*u*/**i**]nt utraeque personae, nec altera potest ab altera matrimonii ius ullum postulare, donec adhibito legitimo ceremoniarum apparatu mutuam fidem coram ecclesia certis verbis dederint et acceperint.

3. Corruptores mulierum quomodo puniendi.[3]

Nec tamen illorum foeda libido gravi poena carere debet, qui simplicitatem puellarum et mulierum innocentiam circumveniunt, et illarum castitatem promissis et blanditiis obside[**ri**]nt, donec turpissime corporibus earum tandem

---

[1] X, 4.1.9 (Fr, II, 663-4), originally a decretal of Pope Alexander III (1159-81); X, 4.1.25 (Fr, II, 670), originally a decretal of Pope Innocent III, 1206.
[2] X, 4.3.3 (Fr, II, 679-80), originally c. 51 of Lateran IV, 1215 (*C.O.D.*, 258). See also H.C., 22.1.
[3] X, 5.16.1 (Fr, II, 805-6), quoted from Ex. xxii. 16ff; X, 5.16.2 (Fr, II, 806), originally a letter of Pope Gregory I (590-604), *Reg.*, 3.43.

8. OF MATRIMONY

1. What matrimony is.[1]

Matrimony is a legal contract, which by the command of God creates and effects a mutual and perpetual union of a man with a woman, in which each of them surrenders power over his or her body to the other, in order to beget children, to avoid prostitution and to govern life by serving one another. Nor is it our will for matrimony any longer to take place by promises or contracts, however many words they may have or whatever accompaniments there may be, unless it is celebrated according to the form which we have appended here.

2. *When* **How** matrimony shall be contracted.[2]

First, the minister of the church, whoever he is, shall make a public announcement of the wedding in front of the people in church, on three Lord's days or at least on three holy days beforehand. Then the bridegroom and the bride will stand openly in front of the church, and take part publicly in those rites and ceremonies which our regulations concerning divine matters require in this instance. Moreover, we give so much authority to this form that if anything is said or done which is in any way contrary to it, [*no*] marriage shall have taken place. For all these things are preparations or rehearsals for marriage, but marriage itself is not contained in them. Therefore both persons are free and at liberty, and one cannot demand any right of marriage from the other until by the lawful form of ceremonies they have pledged and received each other's troth in the presence of the church, using the prescribed words.

3. How seducers of women are to be punished.[3]

But the wicked lust of those who take advantage of the simplicity of girls and innocence of women, and besiege their chastity with promises and enticements until finally they most shamelessly violate their bodies, ought not to escape

illudant. Nam cum pudicitiae thesaurum illis detrah[*a*/**u**]nt, omnibus reliquis opibus et copiis pretiosiorem, in graviore[*m*/**s**] illos *illos* aequum est poenam incidere, quam fures, quorum in rebus externis peccat improbitas. [*Ex*] ecclesi[*is*/**ae**] igitur illos excommunicationis telo praecipimus exturbari. Nec ullum ad eas reditum illis esse, nisi velint illas uxores [38r] ducere, quibus abutebantur prius ut scortis; verum hoc si forte fieri non potest, iudices illorum bona agnoscent, et ex eorum diligenti consideratione tertiam partem ad mulieres sevo[20a]cabunt, quae libidine sunt illorum inquinatae. Quod si bona partitionem hanc non ferant, tamen ad prolem suis impensis sustentandam damnabuntur. Et praeterea tantas sibi poenas impositas habebunt, quantas iudex ecclesiasticus ad ecclesiae tollendam offensionem satis esse putabit, si divulgatum crimen eorum fuerit.

4. Matrimonium sine consensu parentum non valere.[4]

Quoniam Sacrae Scripturae, pietati, iustitiaeque conveniens est ut matrimonia d[*e*/**a**]m[*a*/**ne**]ntur et pro nullis habeantur, quae vel liberi vel orphani, nec scientibus nec consentientibus aut parentibus aut tutoribus contrahunt. Praecipimus, ut nec liberi nec orphani *sumant* uxores **ducant aut** [**nub**/inib/{ine}]**ant**, nisi auctoritas illorum intercesserit in quorum potestate sunt; quod si *sumpserint* **fecerint**, tales nuptias omnino non valere sancimus et ad nihilum recidere. [38v] Quod si parentes vel tutores in providendis nuptiarum [*honestis*] conditionibus nimium cessaverint, aut /in/ illis proponendis nimium duri et acerbi extiterint, ad magistratum ecclesiasticum confugiatur, a quo partes eorum in huiusmodi difficultatibus agi volumus, et eius aequitate totam causam transigi.

5. *Oet..* Aetas, *et* tempus **et locus** matrimonii[**s**] quae sint.[5]

Sequitur, ut certam aetatem ponamus in qua nuptiae concludi possint, et tempora designemus ad quae revocari debeant. Igitur femina cum ad duodecimum annum /plene/ pervenerit, virum sponsum, vir cum ad annum decimum quartum ascenderit, feminam sponsam accipere potest. Nec annos hi[*s*/**c**] inferiores ullo modo nuptiarum participes esse sinimus, tempora vero nulla s[*i*/**u**]nt excepta ad celebrandas nuptias, modo sint huiusmodi, ceremonia[*s*/**e**] ut admitt[*a*/**u**]nt in hac [20b] lege nostra compraehensa[*s*/**e**]. In loco vel (ut vocant) paroechia semper hoc servari placet, ut is sumatur ad nuptias in quo vel sponsa vel sponsus inhabitat. Et si quis minister illos in alio loco matrimonio coniunxerit, [*in*] poena[*m*/**s**] excommunicationis incurret.

---

[4]New here but taken up by 1584/3.2; 1603/100. Cf. M. Bucer, *De regno Christi*, II, 18.
[5]Cf. X, 4.2.1-14 (Fr, II, 672-9); VI, 4.2.1 (Fr, II, 1066-7). Cf. also H.C., 22.17.

severe punishment. For if they deprive them of the treasure of their chastity, which is more precious than all other riches and goods, it is fair that they should receive a greater punishment than thieves, whose wickedness transgresses in external things. Therefore we decree that they shall be driven out of the church with the weapon of excommunication, nor may they go back to these women unless they wish to marry those whom they formerly abused as harlots. But if perchance this cannot be done, the judges shall make an inventory of their goods, and after careful examination, shall confiscate a third of them for the women who have been contaminated by their lust. But if their goods cannot be divided up in this way, they will be forced to pay child support at their own expense. Moreover, they will have as many penalties imposed upon them as the ecclesiastical judge considers necessary to remove the offence to the church, if their crime has become known to the people.

4. Matrimony is not valid without the consent of the parents.[4]

Since it is in accord with Holy Scripture, godliness and justice, that marriages be condemned and considered void when children or orphans contract them without the knowledge and consent of either their parents or their guardians, we enjoin that neither children nor orphans shall marry wives or husbands without the authority of those in whose power they are. If they have done so, we decree that such a wedding is not valid and becomes null and void. But if parents and guardians have failed to provide [*honourable*] conditions for marriage, or if they have been too harsh and strict in setting them out, appeal may be made to the ecclesiastical magistrate, by whom we wish the parties to be guided in their difficulties, and the entire case shall be decided by his judgment.

5. What the age, time **and place** of matrimony should be.[5]

It follows that we must set a fixed age at which marriages may take place and that we must indicate the times to which they ought to be restricted. Thus, when a woman has completed her twelfth year, she may accept betrothal to a man, and when a man reaches his fourteenth year he may accept betrothal to a woman. In no circumstances do we allow parties to a marriage to be any younger than this. But no times have been excluded for the celebration of marriage, as long as they conform to the ceremonies contained in this law of ours. As regards the place or parish (as it is called), the rule is that the wedding shall take place in the one in which either the bride or the bridegroom resides. And if any minister shall join them in marriage in any other place, he will incur the punishment of excommunication.

[39r] 6. De prohibendis nuptiis.[6]

Cum in ecclesia*m* sponsus et sponsa convenerint ut matrimonio coniungantur, si se quispiam interposuerit eo tempore, causamque afferat, aut afferre posse dicat, cur in matrimonio esse non possint, et hanc rem intra mensem proxime consecuturum se probaturum esse spondeat, et nisi ita faciat satisfacturum se plene pro omni apparatu qui fuerat in celebratione nuptiarum futurus, et ad id non solum se, sed etiam pro se fideiussores locupletes obligaverit, tum demum audiatur et matrimonium totum mensem differatur. Haec tamen dilatio quoniam aliquando dolum malum habere potest et fraudem, ut interim novis nuptiis locus esse possit, ad tollendam astutiam omnem, hoc ista lege praecavetur, ut pendente controversia prioris matrimonii, totum mensem exitum illius expectent, nec ad ullas interim novas nuptias divertant. Quam constitutionem nostram si levitate sua violaverint, no[*vum*/**men**] omne huiusmodi matrimoni[*um*/**i**] damnamus et tollimus, et persona quae rea fuerit huius defectionis, excommunicationis poenam sustinebit, donec personae satisfecerit a qua descivit.

[39v] 7. Qu*i*/**ae** *morbi* matrimonium impediant.[7]

Quorum natura perenni aliqua clade sic extenuata est, ut prorsus Veneris participes esse non possint et [*hoc*] coniugem lateat, quamquam consensus mutuus extiterit et omni reli[21a]qua ceremonia matrimonium fuerit progressum, tamen verum in huiusmodi coniunctione matrimonium subesse non potest; destituitur enim altera persona beneficio suscipiendae prolis et etiam usu coniugii care[*n*]t. Verum si nota sit utrique perversitas haec corporis, et tamen mutuus perduret de matrimonio consensus, nuptiae procedant, quoniam volentibus nulla iniuria potest fieri.[8] Par est ratio corporum maleficis artibus excantatorum et enervatorum in quibus quoniam fructus nuptiarum tollitur, ipsas quoque nuptias detrahi necesse est. Praeterea matrimonium dissolvetur si uni personae de altera non constiterit, vel quae fuerit, vel qua conditione *viri* fuerit, conditionem autem hoc in loco capimus vel pro libertatis statu vel servitutis.

---

[6]X, 4.3.3 (Fr, II, 679-80), originally c. 51 of Lateran IV, 1215 (*C.O.D.*, 258); H.C., 22.14.
[7]X, 4.15.2 (Fr, II, 705), originally a decretal of Pope Alexander III (1159-81); X, 4.15.3 (Fr, II, 705), also a decretal of Pope Alexander III.
[8]X, 4.15.4 (Fr, II, 705), originally a decretal of Pope Lucius III (1181-5).

6. Of prohibiting a marriage.[6]

If someone comes forward, when the bridegroom and the bride have come together in the church in order to be joined together in matrimony, and declares a reason, or says that he can declare one, as to why they cannot be joined together in matrimony, he must promise to make good this claim within the following month, and if he does not do so, he must promise that he will pay full compensation for all the preparation made for the celebration of the marriage, and he shall commit not only himself, but also sufficient guarantors on his behalf, after which he shall be heard, and the marriage shall be postponed for a whole month. But since this postponement can sometimes be a bad deception and a fraud, so that in the meantime another marriage might take place, in order to avoid all clever deception, it shall be provided by this law, that as long as the controversy over the former marriage is still pending, they will await the outcome for a whole month, and not go off to contract any other marriage in the meantime. If they break this decree of ours by their wantonness, we condemn and revoke every new marriage so performed, and the person accused of this transgression shall suffer the penalty of excommunication, until he has given satisfaction to the person to whom he has been unfaithful.

7. What *illnesses* are impediments to matrimony.[7]

Those whose nature has been weakened by some permanent injury, so that they cannot engage in sexual relations at all, and who have concealed [*this*] from their spouse, even though there was mutual consent and the marriage took place with all the rest of the ceremony, still a true marriage cannot exist in a union of this kind, for the other party is deprived both of the blessing of bearing children, and of the rights of marriage. But if this bodily defect is known to both parties, and despite that mutual consent to the marriage continues, the wedding may proceed, because no injury can be done to those who are willing.[8] The same principle applies to people whose bodies are enchanted and weakened by evil arts. Since the benefits of marriage are taken away from them, the marriage itself must be cancelled. Moreover, a marriage will be dissolved if one party has not been told the identity of the other party, or what his social standing is. By 'social standing' in this context we mean whether he is a free man or in bondage.

[40r] 8. Quae difficultates non impediant matrimonium.[9]

Mutis et surdis qui mente consistunt matrimonium permittimus, quoniam signis inter se voluntatem et consensum testificari possunt; furiosi vero, nisi quaedam habeant furoris intervalla, quibus res suas ratione moderari possint, omnino [*sunt*] a nuptiis summovendi. Cum his qui non sunt Christiana fide, Christianis matrimonium non instituetur. Nam cum liberos Christianos in fide Christiana par sit enutriri, magnus est metus ne id, nisi utroque Christiano parente, ita esse non possit. Sed si contingat, ut eorum qui iam sunt coniuges diversa religio*ne* fuerit, non temere distrahentur huiusmodi persona*s/e*, sed iuxta Pauli doctrinam respectu Christianae caritatis tam diu cohaerebunt, quam diu persona quae aliena religione **est** una vivere ac cohabitare sustinebit.[10]

9. In absentia coniugis quid sequendum sit.[11]

Si forte coniugum alteruter abfuerit diu a domo, nec de vita quicquam illius vel morte [40v] *certo congnosci* ***possit***,[12] *relicta persona iudices ecclesiasticos adeat, et exposita causa biennium ab illis vel triennium accipiet, in quo personam absentem expectet. In quo tempore diligenter interim perquisit*us/***a*** *si tamen non comparuerit, nec de vita quicquam eius compertum sit, si relicta persona novas nuptias petat, iudex eas concedet. Post quas si prior maritus redierit, uxorem tamen non recuperabit, nisi tantas ostendat fuisse suas difficultates, ut nec ipse celerius redire, nec quicquam de statu suo renuntiare potuerit.*

9. *10.* Omnibus permittendum esse matrimonium.[13]

Quoniam matrimoni[*or*]um legitimus et pius usus est, et turpitudinem multorum flagitiorum exclud*a/*it, illa quo[21b]ties opus *fu*erit, modo rite fiant, repeti posse volumus. Nec ullas personas, cuiuscunque sint conditionis, ordinis aut aetatis,

---

[9]X, 4.1.23 (Fr, II, 669-70), originally a decretal of Pope Innocent III, 15 July 1198; X, 4.1.24 (Fr, II, 670), originally a decretal of Pope Innocent III, 28 Dec. 1204; H.C., 22.10-11.

[10]A marginal note in Foxe's hand reads: 'De his vero quid statuendum sit, qui se segregant a coniugibus, alibi requirendum est, ubi "De adulteriis et divortiis" egimus.' ('But what has been legislated concerning those who separate themselves from their spouses must be sought where we have dealt with "Adultery and divorce"').

[11]A marginal note in Cranmer's hand reads: 'Habetur in titulo "De adulteriis et divortiis".' ('Found in the chapter "On adulteries and divorces"'). Its substance is given in 11.9, but the wording is different. On the content, see X, 4.1.19 (Fr, II, 668), originally a decretal of Pope Clement III (1187-91); H.C., 22.4.

[12]Added by Cranmer.

[13]Marriage of the clergy act, 2-3 Edward VI, c. 21, 1549 (*S.R.*, IV, 67).

8. Difficulties which do not hinder matrimony.[9]

We allow matrimony to the deaf and dumb who are sound of mind, since they can signify their desire and agreement to each other; but the insane are to be prevented from marrying unless they have particular intervals of sanity in which they can manage their affairs rationally. With those who are not of the Christian faith, marriage to Christians is not to be allowed. For since it is right for Christian children to be brought up in the Christian faith there is great fear that that cannot happen unless each parent is a Christian. But if it happens that those who are already husband and wife are of different religions, these persons are not to be carelessly separated, but following the doctrine of Paul with respect to Christian charity, they are to keep together as long as the person who is of a different religion continues to live and cohabit with the other one.[10]

9. What must be done in the absence of a spouse.[11]

If by chance either spouse is absent for a long time from the home, and nothing **can**[12] *be discovered for certain about his life or death, the deserted person shall go to the ecclesiastical judges, and after explaining the case, he or she will be granted a two or three year period by them in which to wait for the missing person. If that person, diligently sought for during this time, is still not found, nor anything about his life is discovered, the judge shall allow a new marriage if the person deserted wants one. If after that the former husband returns, he will not recover his wife unless he shows that there were such great difficulties that he could not return more quickly or send back word of his condition.*

9. 10. Matrimony is to be allowed for everyone.[13]

Since matrimony is a lawful and devout custom, and prevents the evil of many shameful things, it is our will for it to be repeated as many times as necessary, as long as it is done properly. We do not bar anyone from marriage on grounds

a nuptiis abarcemus. Tamen Christianis feminis quae grandes sunt, et aetate multum provectae, consilium damus et illas etiam magnopere cohortamur, ne se [41r] velint cum adolescentibus matrimonio coniungere, [*tum quia* **tumque**] liberos ex illis habere non poss[i/**u**]nt, [*tum quia* **tumque**] in illa levitate magna sit et multiplex perversitas.

10. *11*. Polygamiam esse vitandam.[14]

Polygamiam autem profligari legibus nostris volumus, et in eisdem nuptiis solum ponimus unum atque adeo unicum par; sic enim matrimonium fuit a Deo primo fundatum. Itaque si quis plures uxores acceperit, omnes posteriores am[a/e]ndet et solum retineat quam sumpsit primam, (si maritum velit illum agnoscere); ceteris vero, quibus abeundum est, singulis dotem dispertiat, et ecclesiae praeterea satisfaciat, affectus illa poena quam iudex tanto sceleri convenire existimabit. Tum mulierum etiam nequitia supplicio castigabitur, si scientes ad eundem se virum contulera/int, et si illarum in eo maleficio culpa [*u*/i]lla depraehendi possit.

11. *12*. Propter contentiones et rixas non tolli matrimonium.[15]

Conclus*io* iam [*et perfecto*] matrimonio, si tales rixae, contentiones, iniuriae, concertationes, [41v] acerbitates, contumeliae, luxus, pravitates multiplicis generis tam vehementer exaestuant, ut in eisdem aedibus coniuges commorari nolint, nec cetera matrimonii iura sibi mutuo praestare, poenis implicentur ecclesiasticis et in easdem aedes compellantur, et etiam revocentur ad [*honesta et*] pia inter se communicanda matrimonii officia, modo nulli tales casus inciderint, propter quos ipso iure divortium petere liceat.

[22a] 12. *13*. Matrimonia vi et metu contracta non valent.[16]

Summatim hoc ad omnia matrimonia pertinere volumus, ut si vis et metus illa coegerint, modo tanta fuerint ut in viros constantes iuxta iuris civilis doctrinam cadere poterunt, omnino tales violentes nuptiae distrahantur et pro nullis

---

[14]This may have been intended as an anti-Anabaptist canon, since some of them advocated polygamy. But cf. D, 26 c. 3 (Fr, I, 96-7); C. 24, q. 3, c. 19 (Fr, I, 996); H.C., 22.18 and notes.

[15]X, 2.13.13 (Fr, II, 286-8), originally a decretal of Pope Innocent III (1198-1216); H.C., 23.2.

[16]X, 4.1.19 (Fr, II, 665-6), originally a decretal of Pope Alexander III (1159-81); X, 4.1.30 (Fr, II, 672), originally a decretal of Pope Gregory IX (1227-41), published on or before 5 September 1234; H.C., 22.8.

of social standing, rank, or age; but we advise those Christian women who are aged and very much advanced in years, and also strongly encourage them not to want to marry young men, both because they cannot have children from them, and because there may be great and many different kinds of perversity in such wantonness.

10. *11*. Polygamy is to be avoided.[14]

Furthermore, it is our will that polygamy shall be forbidden by our laws, and we think that in a marriage there should be only one single couple, for this is how marriage was established by God in the first place. Therefore if anyone has taken more than one wife, he must send away all the latter ones and keep only the one whom he first took in hand (if she wishes to acknowledge him as her husband). But he shall grant a dowry to each of the others who will be turned out, and he shall also make amends to the church, in line with whatever punishment the judge shall consider suitable for such an enormity. The wrongdoing of the women shall also be penalized by punishment if they knowingly offered themselves to the same man, and if any guilt on their part can be discerned in this misdeed.

11. *12*. Marriage is not to be dissolved because of disputes and quarrels.[15]

Once a marriage has taken place [*and been consummated*], if quarrels, disputes, insults, controversies, bitterness, abuses, debaucheries and depravities of different kinds boil up to the point that the married couple do not wish to live together in the same house, and the other duties of marriage are not being performed for each other, they shall be subject to ecclesiastical penalties and forced to live in the same house, and they shall also be called back to the [*honourable and*] godly duties of marriage which they are meant to share with one another, as long as nothing has occurred which would constitute lawful grounds for divorce.

12. *13*. Marriages are not valid if contracted by force and fear.[16]

It is our will that this shall apply generally to all marriages, so that if force and fear compel a marriage, as long as they were so extreme that they could have overwhelmed men of firm character, such a forced wedding is by all means to be

habeantur. Quamquam difficillime quidem et vix hae difficultates ad matrimonium irrumpere possunt, si legitimos omnes ritus habeat et tota perpolitum sit illa forma quam ante posuimus tamen vis et metus, si *il...* ulla ratione irruerint, matrimonium ex illis expressum prorsus dissolvi placet.

[42r] 13. *14.* Ut matres propriis uberibus infantes alant.[17]

Inveteravit in uxorum moribus nimium mollis et delicata consuetudo, suam ut prolem a propriis uberibus ablegent, et ad alias nutrices amandent, quae res cum plerumque nullis probabilibus causis nitatur, sed tenera quadam suorum corporum indulgentia fi[a]t, ut sibi ipsae parcant, et honestos et naturales educationis labores subterfugiant, et cum haec inhumana matrum et degener igna[v/n]ia multorum causam malorum afferat, ad officium contionatorum nostrorum arbitramur pertinere, matres ut cohortentur ne prolem in lucem editam inhumaniter destituant, et beneficium illis uberum suorum negent, quibus paulo ante beneficium imp[e/a]rtiverunt suorum uterorum et viscerum.

---

[17]This curious canon has no antecedents, but reflects a sixteenth-century controversy about breastfeeding. The reformers generally believed that a mother should breastfeed her child herself, since this was her God-given duty as a mother, and they regarded the habit of employing wet-nurses as a form of female vanity. See V. A. Fildes, *Breasts, bottles and babies. A history of infant feeding* (Edinburgh, 1986), pp. 98-133, 152-63; *eadem, Wet nursing. A history from antiquity to the present* (Oxford, 1988), pp. 79-100; M. Salmon, 'The cultural significance of breastfeeding and infant care in early modern England and America', *Journal of Social History*, XXVIII (1994), 247-69. For the most recent treatment of the subject, see D. Cressy, *Birth, marriage and death. Ritual, religion and the life-cycle in Tudor and Stuart England* (Oxford, 1997), pp. 87-94.

dissolved and considered null, in accordance with the doctrine of the civil law. Although these problems can afflict a marriage only with great difficulty, if it possesses all the lawful ceremonies and takes place according to the form which we mentioned above, nevertheless, if force and fear enter in for any reason, it is permissible for a marriage performed because of them to be utterly dissolved.

13. *14*. Mothers should breast-feed their babies themselves.[17]

There is an excessively soft and delicate habit which has become ingrained in the behaviour of wives, which causes them to remove their babies from their own breasts and sent them away to wet-nurses. Since for the most part this practice stems from no obvious causes, but occurs because of a kind of lax indulgence towards their own bodies, which lets them spare themselves and avoid the honest and natural burdens of child-rearing, and since this inhuman and degenerate irresponsibility on the part of mothers brings with it the origin of many evils, we believe that it is part of the duty of our preachers to encourage mothers not to desert the children whom they brought into the light in an inhuman way, nor to deny the benefit of their breasts to those on whom they have so recently conferred the benefit of their womb and bowels.

[44r; 22b]9. DE GRADIBUS IN MATRIMONIO PROHIBITIS[1]

1. Inter personas non legitimas non debere matrimonium esse.[2]

Quoniam matrimonium est legitima viri cum femina coniunctio, magna cautio adhiberi debet ne tales personae contra ius et fas ad nuptias accedant, et earum vinculo colligentur, quales divinae leges ad huiusmodi [*convictus* **coniunctionis**] societatem admitti nolunt. Nam id si conti[n]geret, regnum nostrum et ecclesias in illo depositas incestus contaminaret, deinde personas ipsas nefari{i/a}s congressibus turpificatas, necesse esset in Dei summum odium incurrere.

2. Consanguinitas et affinitas quid sint.[3]

Multiplices consanguinitatis et affinitatis gradus sunt in quibus matrimonium consistere non potest. Primum autem ut ipsa capita cognoscantur, consanguinitas in illis intelligatur qui maioribus eisdem procreati sunt, quibus nos generati sumus, vel propagatione carnis et sanguinis [*a nobis*] descenderunt. Affinitas vero per coniunctionem maris et feminae ingreditur. Haec autem duo capita consanguinitatis et affinitatis sic comparata sunt, [44v] ut primum divinae leges, deinde civiles [*certa/os*] in utroque genere gradus annotarint, in quos matrimonium intrare nullo modo debet.

3. Divinum ius in matrimonio prohibendo quale sit.[4]

Deus i[n/**d**] his gradibus certum ius posuit Levitici XVIII[5] et XX[6] capite; quo iure nos *ad* et omnem nostram po*te*steritatem tener[i/**e**] necesse est. Nec enim /haec/ illorum capitum praecepta [23a] veteris Israelitarum rei publicae propria fuerunt, (ut quidam somniant), sed idem auctoritatis pondus habent, quod religio nostra decalogo tribuit, ut nulla possit humana potestas quicquam in illis ullo modo [*secus*] constituere. Itaque pontifex Romanus illam impie sibi facultatem arrogat, et conscientias suas graviter consauciant, quicunque vel a pontifice Romano, vel

---

[1] 1566/4.8; 1571/10.5.
[2] *Clem.*, 4.1.1 (Fr, II, 1177-8); H.C., 22.30.
[3] H.C., 22.28-9.
[4] 32 Henry VIII, c. 38, 1540 (*S.R.*, III, 792).
[5] Lv. xviii. 6-23.
[6] Lv. xx. 10-21.

9. OF DEGREES PROHIBITED IN MATRIMONY[1]

1. No matrimony is to be allowed between persons who are not legally eligible.[2]

Since matrimony is a legal union between a man and a woman, great caution ought to be applied lest persons whom the divine laws do not want to be admitted to the fellowship of a union of this kind enter into marriage against legal right and divine law, and are united in its bonds. For if this should happen, incest would contaminate our kingdom and the churches located in it, and these same persons, corrupted by their heinous union, would then of necessity incur the greatest hatred of God.

2. What consanguinity and relationship by marriage are.[3]

There are many grades of consanguinity and affinity in which marriage cannot take place. But first, in order that these terms may be understood, consanguinity is used to refer to those who were begotten by the same parents by whom we were begotten, or who are descended [*from us*] through procreation of body and blood. Affinity however, derives from the marriage of male and female. Moreover, these two terms, consanguinity and affinity, have been compared in such a way that first divine laws, and then civil ones, have noted [*certain*] grades in each category in which marriage should not be entered into in any way.

3. What kind of divine law prohibits marriage.[4]

God has established a fixed law of these grades in Leviticus 18[5] and 20;[6] we and all our posterity must be bound by this law. For the precepts of those chapters were not peculiar to the commonwealth of the ancient Israelites (as some imagine), but have the same weight of authority as our religion bestows on the ten commandments, so that no human power can decree anything which is in any way [*contrary*] to them. Therefore the Roman pope appropriates this power to himself irreligiously, and those who seek dispensations (as they are called) in this matter, either from the Roman pope or from any other person, hurt their own

a quocunque alio, tales in hac causa dispensationes (ut vocant) conquirunt. Hoc tamen in illis Levitici capitibus diligenter animadvertendum est, minime ibi omnes non legitimas personas nominatim explicari. Nam Spiritus Sanctus illas ibi personas [*solas*] evidenter et expresse posuit, ex quibus [45r] similia spatia reliquorum graduum et differentiae inter se facile possint coniectari et inveniri. Quemadmodum, exempli causa, cum filio non datur uxor mater, consequens est ut ne filia quidem patri{s} coniunx dari po[*ssi*/**tes**]t. Et si patrui non licet uxorem in matrimonio habere, nec cum avunculi profecto coniuge nobis nuptiae concedi possunt.

4. Regulae observandae in iure Levitico.

Ut ergo pellantur omnes errores, reliquae nobis enumerandae sunt et intexendae personae, quae paribus graduum finibus *terminantur, illas sumentes* **coniunctae sunt cum illis personis,** quarum Sacrae Scripturae mentionem [*ap*/**c**]ertam faciunt,. *i*/**In**[7] quo duas regulas magnopere volumus attendi; quarum una est ut qui loci viris attribuuntur, e*a*/**o**sdem *quae* sciamus feminis assignari, paribus semper proportionum et propinquitatum gradibus. Secunda regula est ut vir et uxor unam et eandem inter se carnem habere existimentur, et ita quo quisqu*am*/**e** gradu consanguinitatis quemqu*am*/**e*** contingit, eodem [45v] [*e*]ius uxorem continget affinitatis gradu, quod etiam in contrariam partem eadem ratione valet. Et istis finibus si nos tenebimus, plures non i*u*/**ndi**/**u**cemus *intelligimus* **illegitimas** personas quam Sacrae Scripturae consti[23b]tuunt, et illos gradus integros et inviolatos conservabimus de quibus nobis Deus praecepit.

5. Enumeratio personarum in Levitico prohibitarum.

In Levitico dispositae personae citantur his nominibus, mater, noverca, soror, filia filii, filia filiae, amita, matertera, uxor patrui, nurus, uxor fratris, filia uxoris, filia filii uxoris, filia filiae uxoris, soror uxoris. Personae vero quas praetermittit Leviticus hae sunt: socrus, avia, et quae supra ea[*m*] sunt directa via, quoniam omnes huiusmodi matrum loco nobis esse videntur. Et ex altera parte filia proneptis, et quaecunque infra sunt et ex illis procreantur, a quibus quoniam filiarum similitudinem habe[**a**]nt, nos abstinere debemus. Adiiciuntur fratris filia, sororis filia et quae recta linea descendendo ex eis procreantur, uxor filii fratris, uxor filii sororis, filia fratris uxoris, [46r] filia sororis uxoris, **uxor avunculi,*** [*soror patris uxoris*], soror matris uxoris, filius leviri, filius gloris, maritus sororis patris, maritus sororis matris, maritus filiae fratris, filius privigni, filius privignae.

---

[7]Cranmer began a new sentence here.

consciences greatly. But in these chapters of Leviticus it must be carefully noted that by no means all persons who are not legitimate are there specified by name. For the Holy Spirit there obviously and clearly designated [*only*] those persons from whom similar distances of intervening grades, and differences between them can be inferred and discovered. For example, since a mother is not given to a son as a wife, it follows that a daughter cannot be given to her father. And if it is not lawful to take a paternal uncle's wife in marriage, then neither may a marriage be contracted with a maternal uncle's widow.

4. Rules to be observed in the Levitical law.

Therefore, in order that all mistakes may be avoided, we must enumerate and mention the remaining persons who are *bound* **united** by equal limits of relationship *taking for granted* **with** those people of whom Holy Scripture makes specific mention. In[7] this matter it is our will that two rules above all be observed. One of these is that whatever places have been assigned to men, we understand that the same have been allotted to women, since the degrees of proportions and relationships are always equal. The second rule is that a man and his wife are considered to have one and the same flesh between them, and so wherever a man is related to someone else by a degree of consanguinity, his wife will also be related by the same degree of affinity, because by the same reckoning it is also valid on the other side. If we keep to these limits, we shall not *judge* **make** more persons **illegitimate** than the Holy Scriptures do, and we shall maintain the relationships which God commanded us about, pure and inviolate.

5. An enumeration of persons prohibited in Leviticus.

In Leviticus the persons regulated are specified by these names: mother, step-mother, sister, son's daughter, daughter's daughter, father's sister, mother's sister, wife of father's brother, daughter-in-law, wife of brother, daughter of wife, daughter of wife's son, daughter of wife's daughter, sister of wife. But persons whom Leviticus omits are these: mother-in-law, grandmother and those who are above her in the direct line, since all of these seem to us to be included in 'mothers'. And in the other direction, we ought to keep away from the daughter of a great-granddaughter and those who are below and are begotten from them, since they are like a daughter. To be added are a brother's daughter, a sister's daughter, and those who are begotten of them in a direct line of descent, the wife of a brother's son, the wife of a sister's son, the daughter of a wife's brother, the daughter of a wife's sister, **the wife of a maternal uncle,*** [*the sister of a wife's father*], the sister of a wife's mother, the son of a husband's brother, the son of a husband's sister, the husband of a father's sister, the husband of a mother's sister, the husband of a brother's daughter, the son of a stepson, the son of a stepdaughter.

6. Quae consideranda sint in superiore catalogo.

Et hi superioris legis antegressi gradus duplicem considerationem habent. Primum enim non solum in legitimis matrimoniis talem habent dispositionem qualem iam posuimus, sed e*a*/**un**dem in *omni* corporum *naturali* **illegitima** coniunctione locum habent,. *f*/**F**ilius[8] enim quo iure matrem non potest uxorem sumere, eodem nec patris concubinam habere potest, et pater quomodo filii non debet uxorem contractare, sic ab illa se removere debet, qua filius est abusus. Qua ratione mater nec cum filiae marito iungi debet, nec etiam cum illo congredi [24a] qu[*i*/**ae**] fili[*a*/**u**]m oppresserit. *Et eadem similium causa multarum personarum est.* Secunda cautio est, non solum istas [46v] maritis adhuc superstiti*on*ibus disiungi personas quas diximus, sed etiam illis mortuis idem perpetuo valere. Quemadmodum enim horribile flagitium est in vita patris, fratris, *aut paterni* **patrui, aut** avunculi, audere illorum uxores violare, sic post mortem illorum, *idem crimen* **matrimonium cum illis contrahere,** parem turpitudinem habet.

7. Cognatio spiritualis non impedit nuptias.[9]

Spiritualis illa quae vulgo dicitur necessitudo, cum nec inducta sit Sacris Scripturis, nec ullis fulciatur solidis et firmis rationibus, matrimonii cursum prorsus impedire non debet.

---

[8]Cranmer began a new sentence here.
[9]Cf. X, 4.11.5 (Fr, II, 694-5), originally a decretal of Pope Clement III (1187-91). This is a contradiction (so intended) of that canon.

6. What must be considered in the preceding list.

The above-mentioned degrees of the former law are important for two reasons. In the first place, not only do they play the part in legal marriage which we have already outlined, but they play the same part in *every natural* **the unlawful** union of bodies. For[8] a son cannot legally take his mother as a wife, and so he cannot have his father's concubine either; and just as a father ought not to touch his son's wife in any way, he ought to stay away from any woman whom his son has abused as well. For this reason, a mother ought not to be united in marriage with her daughter's husband, nor with any man who has wronged her daughter. The second point is that those whom we have mentioned are not only to be kept apart while their husbands are still living, but even after they are dead. For just as it is terribly disgraceful in life to dare to dishonour the wives of a father, a brother, a paternal uncle or a maternal uncle, *the same crime* **contracting marriage with them** is equally reprehensible.

7. Spiritual affinity does not hinder marriage.[9]

Since spiritual affinity, as it is commonly called, is not mentioned in the Holy Scriptures and is not supported by any sound or stable principles, it ought not to hinder the course of matrimony in any way.

[48r; 24a]   **10. DE ADULTERIIS ET DIVORTIIS**[1]

1. Adulteria severe punienda esse.

Turpitudo tam horribilis adulteriorum est, ut aperte decalogi praecepto confossa sit,[2] et etiam veteribus divinis legibus per Mosen latis publica populi lapidatione obruta et consepulta esset;[3] denique iure civili etiam capite plecteretur.[4] Rem igitur Deo tam odiosam et a sanctissimis maioribus nostris singulari cruciatu c[*on*/**ruci**]fixam, ecclesiastici iudices nostri non debent sine gravissima poena dimittere.

[24b] 2. Ministri de adulterio convicti quomodo puniendi sunt.[5]

Ordiamur ab ecclesiarum ministris, quorum vitae praecipua quaedam integritas esse deb[**er**]et. Itaque si quis ex illis adulterii, scortationis, aut incestus convictus fuerit, si propriam habuerit uxorem, omnes eius opes et bona devolventur ad eam et ad liberos, si qui sint ex ea, vel ex aliquo priore matrimonio legitime nati. Si vero nec suam uxorem nec liberos habeat, omnes eius facultates, arbitratu iudicis, vel inter pauperes dispertientur, vel in alia pietatis officia [48v] conferentur. Deinde si quod illi beneficium fuerit, postquam adulterii vel incestus vel scortationis convictus fuerit, ex eo tempore protinus illud amittat, nec illi potestas [*sit*] ullum aliud accipiendi. Praeterea vel in perpetuum ablegetur exilium, vel ad aeternas carceris tenebras depri*v*/**matur**.

---

[1] 1597/6.2.

[2] The seventh. Ex. xx. 14; Dt. v. 18.

[3] The Mosaic law does not state the penalty for adultery, either in Ex. xx. 14 (the seventh commandment) or in Lv. xx. 10. That it was by stoning is inferred from other passages of Scripture, *e.g.* Ek. xvi. 38, 40; Jn. viii. 5).

[4] *Dig.*, 48.5.

[5] Cf. X, 3.2.3 (Fr, II, 454), originally a decretal of Pope Alexander III (1159-81); X, 3.2.10 (Fr, II, 457), originally a decretal of Pope Grepory IX (1227-41), published before 5 September 1234; cf. H.C., 4.4-5. This is stricter.

10. OF ADULTERY AND DIVORCE[1]

1. Adultery must be severely punished.

So awful is the wickedness of adultery that it is specifically attacked by one of the ten commandments,[2] and under the ancient divine laws promulgated by Moses, it was also punished by the culprit's being stoned to death by the people and buried under the stones,[3] and furthermore, it was also punishable by death according to the civil law.[4] It therefore follows that a crime so hateful to God and visited by our godly forefathers with a punishment specially designed for it, must not be passed over by our ecclesiastical judges without the most severe punishment.

2. How ministers convicted of adultery shall be punished.[5]

Let us begin with the ministers of the church, whose lives ought to be particularly blameless. If one of them is convicted of adultery, fornication or incest, all his goods and property shall pass to his wife, if he has one of his own, and to the children, whether they were born of her or are the lawful fruit of a previous marriage. But if he has neither wife nor children of his own all his property shall be divided among the poor or devoted to other works of godliness, at the judge's discretion. Furthermore, if he holds a benefice, he shall lose it from the time he is convicted of adultery, incest or fornication, and shall be ineligible to obtain any other. Moreover, he shall either be condemned to perpetual banishment or else consigned to the darkness of the dungeon for life.

3. Laicus quomodo puniendus.[6]

Laicus *crimen* adulterii damnatus uxori suae dotem restituito; deinde bonorum universorum dimidiam partem eidem uxori concedito. Praeterea, vel in perpetuum exilium ito, vel aeternae carceris custodiae mancipator.

4. Uxores sive ministrorum sive laicorum quomodo puniendae.[7]

Uxores ex contraria parte, tam laicorum quam ministrorum, si crimen adulterii contra illas probatum fuerit, et iudex adversus illo/as pronuntiaverit, dotibus carebunt, et omnibus emolumentis quae vel [ex] ullo regni nostri *in re* **iure** vel *m...* consuetudine vel pacto vel promisso poterant ex bonis maritorum ad illas descendere, tum etiam vel in sempiternum exilium eiicientur, vel perpetuae carceris custodiae mandabuntur.

[25a] 5. Integra persona transit ad novas nuptias *legitime*.[8]

[49r] Cum alter coniunx adulterii damnatus est, alteri licebit innocenti novum ad matrimonium (si v[e/o]l[i/e]t) progredi. Nec enim usque adeo debet integra persona crimine alieno premi, coelibatus ut invite possit obtrudi. Quapropter *adultera non habebitur* integra persona **non habebitur adultera**, si novo se matrimonio devinxerit, quoniam ipse causam adulterii Christus ac/excepit.

6. Reconciliationem esse optandam.[9]

Quoniam in matrimonio summa coniunctio rerum omnium est, et tantus amor quantus potest maximus cogitari, vehementer optamus ut integra persona damnatae veniam indulgeat, et illam ad se rursus assumat, si credibilis melioris vitae spes ostendatur; quam animi mansuetudinem licet nullae possint externae leges praecipere, tamen Christiana caritas saepe nos ad eam adducere potest. Quod si damnata persona non possit ad superiorem conditionem admitti, nullum *ex* illi novum matrimonium conced[e/i]tur.

---

[6]On the dowry question, cf. X, 4.20.2 (Fr, II, 725), originally a decretal of Pope Urban III (1185-7). The penalties of exile and of life imprisonment are new and of unprecedented strictness.

[7]Cf. X, 4.19.3 (Fr, II, 720-1), originally a decretal of Pope Alexander III (1159-81); H.C., 23.5.

[8]1597/6.3.

[9]C. 32, q. 1, cc. 7-8 (Fr, I, 1117).

3. How a layman shall be punished.[6]

The layman convicted of *the crime of* adultery shall restore his wife's dowry to her, and in addition shall give her half of all his goods. Moreover, he shall either be condemned to perpetual banishment or committed to prison for life.

4. How wives, either of ministers or of laymen, are to be punished.[7]

On the other hand, if the crime of adultery is proved against wives, either of ministers or of laymen, and the judge gives his decision against them, they shall be deprived of their dowries and of all benefits which might accrue to them from the property of their husbands, either under any law of our realm, or by custom, contract, or covenant; and shall also either be condemned to perpetual banishment or imprisoned for life.

5. The innocent party may *lawfully* contract a fresh marriage.[8]

When one of the spouses has been convicted of adultery the other, being innocent, shall be allowed to proceed to a new marriage (if he or she wishes to do so). For the innocent party ought not to suffer for another's crime to the point that celibacy is forced on him or her unwillingly. Therefore the innocent party is not to be considered guilty of adultery if he binds himself in a new marriage, since Christ himself *ac*/ex cepted adultery as a reason.

6. Reconciliation is preferable.[9]

Since in matrimony there is the closest union of all things and the highest degree of love that can be imagined, we strongly prefer that the innocent party should forgive the guilty one and take him or her back again if there seems to be any real hope of a better life; and although no external laws can teach this forgiving attitude, nevertheless Christian charity can often lead us to it. But if the guilty party cannot be persuaded to adopt a higher way of life, no new marriage is permitted to him.

7. Nemo coniugem arbitratu suo potest relinquere.[10]

Magna res est et ingentem affert totius [49v] familiae perturbationem, cum uxor a viro distrahitur. Quapropter adulterii respectu, nemo suam a se coniugem auctoritate propria removeat et aliam adsciscat, nisi iudex ecclesiasticus totam causam rite prius cognoverit et definiverit. Quod si facere quispiam ausus fuerit, ius omne agendi adversus coniugem amittat. Iudex autem, quoties alterum coniugem adulterii condemnat, alteri sincerae personae libertatem denuntiare debet ad novum matrimonium transeundi; cum [25b] hac tamen exceptione, certum ut tempus assignet in quo superiorem ad coniugem (si velit) redire possit; quod si tempore iam absumpto recuset facere, tum ad aliud matrimonium descendere potest. Et hoc tempus quod iudex indulgebit, omnino volumus anni spatio vel sex mensibus definiri.

8. Divortium propter desertum matrimonium.[11]

Cum alter ex coniugibus aufugerit, seque abalienarit ab altero, si persona absens possit inveniri, consiliis, hortationibus u/et poenis cogatur ut ad coniugem se rursus adiungat, et una cum illo convenienter vivat. Quam ad rem si nulla ratione potest adduci, contumax in eo persona debet accipi, legumque divinarum et humanarum contemptrix; et propterea perpetuae carceris custodiae dedatur, et deserta persona *debet* [50r] novarum potestatem nuptiarum ab ecclesiastico iudice sum{e/**a**}t. Cum autem con[i/**t**]u[n/**ma**]x non possit absens investigari nec erui, ne[**c**] locus ullus in hoc crimine levitati vel temeritati relinquatur, primum absentem personam nominatim requiri volumus illa iuris *nostri* formula, quam viis et modis appellant; quo tempore si se non ostenderit aut eius aliquis vicarius qui causam eius velit agere, iudex illi biennium vel triennium indulgebit, in quo persona possit absens se repraesentare. Quo tempore consumpto, si se ipse non sistat et iustas afferat absentiae tam diuturnae causas, destituta persona nuptiarum vinculis liberabitur, et novum sibi coniugem (si velit) [*as*]sum[e/**a**]t. Desertrix autem persona, si iudicio iam peracto novisque consecutis nuptiis, sero post biennii vel triennii spatium expletum sui potestatem fecerit, in aeternas carceris tenebras *ob...* detrudatur, et secundum matrimonium plenissimo iure valeat.

[26a] 9. Divortium propter nimis longam coniugis absentiam.[12]

Quando non aufugerit coniunx, sed militiam aut mercaturam **aut** aliquam habet huiusmodi legitimam et honestam peregrinationis suae causam, et abfuerit diu

---

[10]X, 4.19.3 (Fr, II, 720-1), originally a decretal of Pope Alexander III (1159-81); H.C., 23.1.
[11]Cf. X, 4.1.9 (Fr, II, 668), originally a decretal of Pope Clement III (1187-91).
[12]Cf. X, 4.1.9 (Fr, II, 668), originally a decretal of Pope Clement III.

7. No one may abandon a spouse of his or her own free will.[10]

It is a serious matter, and causes great disturbance in the family, when a wife is separated from her husband. Therefore, with respect to adultery, no one may put away his wife on his own authority and take another unless an ecclesiastical judge shall first duly examine the whole case and give his decision. If anyone dares to do this, he shall lose all right of action against his wife. Whenever the judge convicts either spouse of adultery, he must inform the other, innocent party, that he or she is free to proceed to a new marriage, but with this reservation, that he shall set a certain period during which the injured party may return to the former marriage partner (if he or she so wishes), and if he or she refuses to do so, he or she may then contract another marriage once the set period has expired. And it is our will that this period which the judge shall allow shall be no more than the space of a year or six months.

8. Divorce on the ground of desertion.[11]

When either of the spouses deserts or withdraws from the other, if the absent party can be found, he or she is to be compelled by advice, exhortations and penalties to return to his or her marriage partner, and live harmoniously together. If there is no way that he or she can be persuaded to do this, he or she shall be considered contumacious in the matter and a despiser of divine and human laws, and for that reason shall suffer perpetual imprisonment; and the deserted party *must* may claim from the ecclesiastical judge the right to contract a new marriage. But when the absent [*spouse* **contumacious person**] cannot be found or located, then it is our will that the absent person shall first be summoned to appear by name, according to the form of *our* legal procedure known as 'ways and means', so that there may be no room left in this crime for wanton and careless behaviour, at which time, if he or she does not come and no representative appears who wishes to act on his or her behalf, then the judge shall allow a delay of two or three years during which the absent party may come forward. On the expiration of this period, if he or she does not appear in person and produce just causes for so long an absence, the deserted person shall be set free from the bonds of matrimony and allowed to marry again (if he or she so wishes). But if, after the proceedings have ended and a new marriage has taken place, the deserting party should come forward when it is too late, after the expiration of the two or three years, he or she is to be thrown into the darkness of prison for life, and the second marriage shall be entirely legal.

9. Divorce on the ground of the unduly protracted absence of the husband.[12]

When one spouse has not deserted, but has military service or business **or** some similarly legitimate and honourable reason for travelling abroad, and has been

domo, nec illius vel de vita vel [*morte*] quicquam certo sciatur, largientur alteri coniugi iudices [50v] (si quidem hoc ab illis requirat) biennii vel triennii spatium, in quo mariti reditum expectet. Quo tempore toto si non revertatur, nec de vita possit illius aliquid esse explorati, cum diligentissime de ea fuerit interim perquisitum, alteri coniugi novas concedi nuptias aequum est; cum hac tamen conditione, prior ut maritus si tandem se repraesentet, uxor illum rursus **ad** se recipiat, si quidem ostendere possit culpa sua factum non esse, quod foras tam diu peregrinatus sit. Tantam enim et tam longi temporis absentiam nisi plen[*e*/**a**] magnaque cum ratione possit excusare, custodiam in perpetuam carceris dimittatur, nullum ad uxorem reditum habeat, et illa secundis in nuptiis rite permaneat.

10. Inimicitiae capitales divortium inducunt.[13]

Inter coniuges si capitales intercedant inimicitiae, tamqu*am*/**e** vehementer exarserint, ut alter alterum aut insidiis aut venenis appetat, aut aliqua vel aperta vi vel occulta peste vitam velit eripere, quamprimum tam horribile crimen probatum fuerit rite in iudicio, divortio volumus huiusmodi personas distrahi. Maiorem enim coniugi facit iniuriam persona, quae salutem et vitam oppugnat, quam ea quae ex consuetudine se coniugis eximit, aut corporis sui potestatem [51r] alteri facit. Nec inter illos ullum consortium esse potest, inter quos capitale periculum cogitari coepit et metui. Cum [26b] igitur una [*non*] poss[*i*/**u**]nt esse, iuxta Pauli doctrinam [*matrimonium*] dissolvi par est.[14]

11. Malae tractationis crimen tandem divortium inducit.[15]

Si vir in uxorem saeviat et acerbitatem in ea nimia{**m**} factorum et verborum expromat, quam diu spes ulla placabilitatis est, cum illo iudex ecclesiasticus agat, nimiam ferociam *a*/**o**biurgans; et si non potest monitis et hortationibus profici, pignoribus oblatis, aut fideiussoribus acceptis, *c*/**e**um cavere compellat de nulla vehement[*e*/**i**] coniugi inferenda iniuria, /et de illa tractanda/ quomodo matrimonii intima coniunctio postulat. Quod si ne pignioribus quidem aut fideiussoribus coerceri potest maritus, nec asperitatem velit isto modo deponere, tum capitalem illum coniugis inimicum esse existimandum est, et illius vitam infestare. Quapropter divortii remedio periclitanti succurrendum erit, non minus quam si vita manifeste fuisset oppugnata. Nec tamen praeterea iuris dempta est[*o*], potestas coercendi uxores quibus modis opus fuerit, si rebelles, contumaces, petulantes, acerbae sint et improbae; modo rationis et aequitatis

---

[13]X, 2.13.13 (Fr, II, 286-8), originally a decretal of Pope Innocent III (1198-1216).
[14]Paul never addressed this question. Presumably the reference is to I Co. vii. 15, where he allowed remarriage in the case of desertion by an unbelieving partner.
[15]X, 2.13.13 (Fr, II, 286-8), originally a decretal of Pope Innocent III.

away from home a long time and it is not known for certain whether he is alive [*or dead*], the judges shall grant to the other spouse, (if she asks them to), a space of two or three years during which she is to await her husband's return. If he does not come back during the whole of this time, and if it is impossible to find out whether he is alive, even when the most thorough inquiry has been made in the meantime, it is fair for the wife to be allowed to contract a new marriage, but on this condition, that if her first husband should return, the wife is to take him back to her, as long as he can prove that it was not his fault that he stayed abroad so long. For unless he can give a full and sufficient reason for so serious and long an absence, he shall be imprisoned for life and have no right to reclaim his wife, and she shall duly continue in her second marriage.

10. Deadly hostility is a ground for divorce.[13]

If deadly hostility should arise between husband and wife, and become so inflamed that one attacks the other, either by treacherous means or by poison, and wants to take the other's life in some way, either by open violence or by hidden malice, it is our will that as soon as so horrible a crime is proved in court, such persons shall be separated by divorce. For a person who attacks health and life does greater injury to his marriage partner than one who separates himself from the other's company, or commits adultery with someone else. For there cannot be any sort of fellowship between those who have begun to plot or to fear mortal harm. Therefore, since they can[*not*] live together, it is right for [*the marriage*] to be dissolved, according to the teaching of Paul.[14]

11. The crime of ill-treatment is also a ground for divorce.[15]

If a man is cruel to his wife and displays excessive harshness of word and deed towards her, as long as there is any hope of improvement, the ecclesiastical judge is to reason with him, rebuking his excessive violence, and if he cannot prevail by admonitions and exhortations, he is to compel him not to inflict any violent injury on his wife, and to treat her as the intimate union of marriage requires, by making him pledge bail, or by taking guarantees. But if the husband cannot be coerced either by bail or by guarantees, and if he refuses to abandon his cruelty by these means, then he must be considered his wife's mortal enemy and a threat to her life. Therefore, in her peril recourse must be had to the remedy of divorce, no less than if her life had been openly attacked. But on the other side, the power given by the law to coerce wives in whatever ways are necessary, if they are rebellious, obstinate, petulant, scolds and of evil behaviour, is not abrogated, as long as the husband does not exceed the limits of moderation and fairness. Both

fines mariti non egrediantur. Et cum in hoc, tum in his superioribus delictis hoc [51v] teneri placet, ut solutae personae novas (si velint) nuptiarum conditiones legant, convictae vero priorum criminum vel exiliis perpetuis, vel aeterna carceris custodia plectantur.

12. Parvae contentiones, nisi perpetuae sint, divortium non inducunt.[16]

Si minores quaedam contentiones aut offensiones obrepserint in matrimonio, Pauli sententia moderatrix earum esse debet,[17] ut aut uxor marito se reconciliet, quod omnibus poenarum *et hortationum* ordinariis et extraordinariis *hortationum* viis [27a] procurari debet, aut absque novo coniugio maneat; id quod et viro pariter faciendum statuimus.

13. Perpetuus morbus non tollit matrimonium.[18]

Si forte coniugum alteruter perpetuum aliquem morbum contraxerit, cuius nulla levatio po[ssi/**tes**]t inveniri, tamen matrimonium in omnibus huiusmodi difficultatibus perdurabit. Quoniam hoc unum esse debet praecipuum et eximium matrimonii commodum, ut mu[tu/**lt**]a mala mutuis coniugum officiis sedari lenirique possint.

14. Durante lite quomodo rea persona sustentabitur.[19]

Quoniam saepe magnam controversiam habent et longissimi sunt temporis lites adulteriorum, veneficiorum, [52r] capitalium insidiarum, et malae tractationis, vir uxorem *aut uxor contra virum* interim honestis et convenientibus impensis sustentet, habita ratione dignitatis et conditionis in qua est.

---

[16]Cf. *Nov.* 117.4; R, 8.11.
[17]I Co. vii. 11.
[18]X, 4.8.1 (Fr, II, 690-1) and X, 4.8.2 (Fr, II, 691), both originally decretals of Pope Alexander III (1159-81).
[19]Cf. 1237/23; H.C., 23.3.

in this and in the above-mentioned offences, it is our will that parties set free in this way may contract a new marriage (if they wish), while those convicted of the said crimes shall be punished either by perpetual exile or by imprisonment for life.

12. Minor disagreements, unless they are permanent, are no ground for divorce.[16]

If minor disagreements or grounds for offence creep into a marriage, the words of Paul should act as a check upon them,[17] namely, that either the wife should be reconciled to her husband, a result which ought to be sought after by all ordinary and extraordinary methods of penalties and exhortations, or she is to remain single, a penalty which we decree shall be equally binding on the man.

13. Incurable disease does not annul a marriage.[18]

If by chance either of the parties has contracted an incurable disease for which no remedy can be found, the marriage will nevertheless continue in spite of all difficulties of this kind. For this ought to be the one principal and distinguishing advantage of matrimony, that [*mutual* **many**] troubles may be soothed and alleviated by the mutual support of the spouses.

14. How the accused party is to be maintained during the lawsuit.[19]

Since cases involving charges of adultery, poisoning, mortal treachery and ill-treatment frequently entail serious controversy and are of very great length, a man is to maintain his wife for the duration on an honourable and sufficient allowance, account being taken of her rank and social standing.

15. Poena falsae accusationis.[20]

Multorum libidines huiusmodi pruritum habent, ut nova subinde matrimonia consectentur, et ad varias uxores devolare concupiscant. Quapropter falsas innocentibus calumnias struent adulteriorum, et aliorum huius generis criminum, nisi sceleribus illorum suppliciorum acerbitate fuerit occursum. Itaque si vir uxorem adulterii vel veneficii ream fecerit, et post causa cadat, dimidia bonorum pars ad uxorem sevocetur. Nec in illis vendendi, distrahendi, legandi, permutandi, donandi, vel alienandi quacunque ratione ius ullum habeat, nisi uxor in id consentiat. Et uxor ex altera parte, si maritum adulterii, [**vel**] veneficii, capitalis iniuriae, vel malae tractationis postulaverit, et li[27b]tem amittat, dote primum careat; deinde orbetur omni emolumento, quod iure per maritum debuit ad illam pervenire, /nisi maritus illi sponte voluerit aliquid aspergere/. Postremo matrimonium inter illos ita ut erat integrum conservetur.

16. Poena falsae accusationis in externa persona.

[52v] Si non coniunx coniugem, sed alterum ex his externa quaedam persona reum faciat, et in iudicio succubuerit, ecclesiasticus iudex illum arbitratu suo magna tamen et acri poena feriat, et etiam coniugi satisfaciat cui damnum dedit. Denique calumniatores huiusmodi nec ad ecclesiam redeant, nec admittantur ad sacro*sanct*amenta, nisi famam eius personae, quam calumnia et mendacio dedecoraverunt, plene restitue*u*/int quantum poss[*u*/i]nt, et paenitentia*e* scelere digna perfuncti fuerint. Et has in hoc genere poenas omnibus sive laicis sive clericis communes esse volumus.

16. Mariti poena suadentis uxori adulterium.[21]

Si maritus uxori suasor aut auctor ulla ratione fuerit adulterii committendi, damnabitur *quidem* illa quidem adulterii, sed et maritus lenocinii reus pronuntiabitur, et matrimonii con*di*/**iunc**tione neuter liberabitur. **Quod et de uxore similiter intelligi volumus.**

---

[20]*Cod. Iust.* 9.46.7, originally a rescript of the emperors Valentinian I and Valens, 26 November 366; *ibid.*, 9.46.8, originally a rescript of the emperors Gratian, Valentinian II and Theodosius I, 8 May 385; *ibid.*, 9.46.9, originally a rescript of the same emperors, 18 May 382; *ibid.*, 9.46.10, originally a rescript of the emperors Honorius and Theodosius II, 6 August 423.

[21]*Dig.*, 48.5.2, originally Ulpian, *Disputationes*, 8; ibid., 48.5.30(29), originally Ulpian, *De adulteriis*, 4; C. 32, q. 1, c. 10 (Fr, I, 1117-18).

15. The penalty for false accusation.[20]

The sensual desires of many men have an urge to pursue a succession of new marriages and they long to go off with different wives. Therefore they will devise false accusations of adultery and of other crimes of that kind against the innocent, unless the punishment for their offences is made severe enough to deter them. Therefore, if a man accuses his wife of adultery or poisoning and the case subsequently fails, then half his property shall be assigned to the wife. Nor shall he in any circumstances have any right to sell, divide, bequeathe, exchange, give, or alienate that property unless his wife consents to it. On the other hand, if the wife shall prosecute the husband for adultery [or] poisoning, mortal injury or ill-treatment, and lose her case, first of all, she shall forfeit her dowry, then she is to be deprived of all emoluments which would have accrued to her by right from her husband, /unless the husband is of his own accord willing to make some provision for her./ Finally, the marriage between them is to be maintained intact, as it was before.

16. The penalty for a third party who makes a false accusation.

If it is not the husband or wife who accuses the other, but some third party accuses one of them, and his case breaks down, the ecclesiastical judge shall inflict some heavy and exemplary punishment on him at his own discretion, and furthermore that party shall pay compensation to the one he wronged. Moreover, such slanderers may neither return to the church, nor be admitted to the sacraments, unless they have to the best of their ability restored the reputation of that person whom they have discredited by calumny and falsehood, and have done penance in proportion to the crime. And we decree that the penalties mentioned here shall be common to all, whether laymen or clergymen.

16. The penalty of the husband who incites his wife to adultery.[21]

If the husband has in any way been the inciter or instigator of his wife's adultery, she shall indeed be convicted of adultery, but the husband shall also be declared guilty of procuring, and neither shall be released from the *state* **bonds** of matrimony. **And it is our will that this shall apply equally to the wife.**

17. Quae poena sit cum per adulterium est in utroque coniuge.[22]

Si persona quae fuerit adulterii convicta, crimen in altero coniuge possit idem ostendere, et ostenderit, priusquam coniunx ad novas nuptias diverterit, utriusque coniugis culpa par in pares incidet poenas, et prius inter illos firmum manebit matrimonium.

[53r; 28a] 18. Receptatorum et fautorum adulterii quae poena sit.[23]

Ne illi quidem iudic[-/i]um ecclesiasticorum diligentiam subterfugere debent qui receptatores sunt adulter[i]orum, aut illorum flagitia, ope, opera, vel consilio quacunque ratione procurant. Quo in genere sunt, exempli causa, qui domum adulteris scientes expediunt, vel locum qualemcunque, qui sermonum, litterarum aut [mun/**num**]erum cuiuscunque generis sint internuntii. Quapropter omnem [*hominum*] huiusmodi faecem quae coenum adulterii quacunque parte commovet, ecclesiasticis poenis et arbitrariis etiam iudicis constringendum esse decernimus.

19. Separatio a mensa et thoro tollitur.[24]

Mensae societas et thori solebat in certis criminibus adimi coniugibus; salvo tamen inter illos reliquo matrimonii iure. Quae constitutio cum a Sacris Litteris aliena sit, et maximam perversitatem habeat, et malorum sentinam in matrimonium comportaverit, illud auctoritate nostra totum aboleri placet.

20. Incestus et scortationes laicorum quomodo puniuntur.[25]

[53v] Incestus [*omnis*], nominatim autem *h*is qui primum ad gradum ascendit, afficietur poena sempitern[*i*/**a**] carceris. Deinde scortationes et vagae licentiosaeque libidines omnis generis magna suppliciorum acerbitate compraehenda[*n*]tur, ut tandem aliquando radicitus ex regno nostro extirpentur. Ecclesiastici igitur iudices diligenter evigilent, ut quascunque personas et cuiuscunque sexus flagitiosis et impuris libidinum congressibus implicatas in excommunicationem eiiciant, nisi [28b] mature moniti resipuerint. Et licet se ipsi correxerint, tamen publice cogantur ecclesiae satisfacere. Praeterea decem libras

---

[22]X, 4.19.5 (Fr, II, 721-2), originally a decretal of Pope Alexander III (1159-81); X, 5.16.7 (Fr, II, 807), originally a decretal of Pope Innocent III, 13 June 1208; 1597/6.3.
[23]*Dig.*, 48.5.9(8), originally Papinian, *De adulteriis*, 2; *ibid.*, 48.5.10(9), originally Ulpian, *De adulteriis*, 4.
[24]See 1597/6.3 for the regulations governing these which were finally adopted in 1603/106-7.
[25]C. 23, q. 5, c. 45 (Fr, I, 944); L, 5.16.12, c. 7 of the council of Lambeth, 1281.

17. What the penalty shall be when both parties are equally guilty of adultery.[22]

If the person who has been convicted of adultery is able to prove the same crime against the other marriage partner, and does so before that party has proceeded to a new marriage, the equal guilt of each party shall incur equal punishment, and the former marriage between them shall remain valid.

18. What the penalty shall be for harbourers and abettors of adultery.[23]

Of course, those who are harbourers of adulter[ers/y], or who in any way promote their wickedness by their help, action or advice must not escape the vigilance of the ecclesiastical judges. Examples of this kind of person are those who knowingly lend their houses to adulterers, or a place of whatever description, and who are intermediaries of messages, letters or [*presents* a **number**] of any sort. Therefore we decree that all such dregs [*of humanity*] who encourage the filth of adultery in any way, must be restrained by ecclesiastical penalties and also at the discretion of the judge.

19. Separation 'from bed and board' shall be abolished.[24]

It used to be that in the case of certain crimes married people were deprived of the right to share bed and board, though in all other respects their marriage remained intact. But since this practice is contrary to Holy Writ, leads to the greatest perversity and has introduced a lot of evils into matrimony, it is our will that the whole thing shall be abolished by our authority.

20. How incest and fornication among the laity shall be punished.[25]

[*All*] incest, especially that which touches the first degree of relationship, shall be punished with the penalty of life imprisonment. Furthermore, fornication and unbridled lusts of every kind are to be checked with great severity of punishment, so that they may eventually be uprooted from our kingdom. Therefore, the ecclesiastical judges must take vigilant care to excommunicate whatever persons of whichever sex have been involved in sensual associations of an impure or dissolute character, unless after being warning they repent in time. And even though they have amended their ways, they are nevertheless to be compelled to

in pauperum cistam ecclesiae suae propriam imponant, vel si minores illorum facultates sunt, tantum *sit* **imponant** quantum de bonis illorum commode detrahi potest.

21. Filius non legitimus quomodo sit alendus.[26]

Filius ex adulterio susceptus, aut ex simplici scoratatione, quemadmodum appellant, patris impensis alatur, si quidem is inveniri poterit. Qui si non poterit erui, mater suum ipsa foetum propriis impensis sustentet.

---

[26]*Dig.*, 25.3.1, originally Ulpian, *Ad edictum*, 34.

make public satisfaction to the church. Moreover, they must put ten pounds in the poor box of their own church, or if their means are insufficient, they must put in it as much of their goods as can conveniently be spared.

21. How an illegitimate child shall be maintained.[26]

A child born of adultery or of mere fornication, to use the common term, is to be maintained at the father's expense, if he can be found. If he cannot be located, the mother shall provide for her child at her own expense.

[58r; 28b] 11. DE ADMITTENDIS AD ECCLESIASTICA BENEFICIA

1.[1]

Quemadmodum reipublicae status ruit, cum a stupidis et flagitiosis et ardentibus ambitione viris temperatur, sic ecclesia Dei nostris hisce temporibus gravissime laborat, quoniam illorum curae committitur, qui tam praeclarum ad munus obeundum omnino sunt inepti; qua in re multum et longe longeque plurimum ab illis beati Pauli formulis recessum est, de quibus ad Titum[2] et Timotheum[3] praescripsit. Quapropter huic tam insigni nostrarum ecclesiarum cladi maturum aliquod remedium a nobis inveniendum est.

2. Diligenter in ministros inquirendum [*esse*].[4]

Omnes quibus aliqua ratione sacerdotium obvenit, diligentissime ritu et praescripto legum nostrarum explo[29a]rentur et pernoscantur, ne temere cuiquam episcopus manum imponat, et alienorum criminum particeps sit. Nec admittatur ullus ad ecclesiam administrandam, nisi prius rite fuerit examinatus.

[58v] 3. Patronorum officium.[5]

Praeterea, patronis beneficiorum ecclesiasticorum praecipimus, ut omnibus seclusis vel necessitudinum vel quorumcunque respectuum affectibus, illorum rationem habeant qui munus hoc sacrum, ad quod adhibendi sunt, possint et velint omnibus partibus implere. Nec enim sacerdotia delata sunt ad patronos, ut illa circumciderent, aut de illis depraedarentur, sed ut [*in*] illorum praesidio et fide **tuto** conquiescerent.

---

[1]D, 38 c. 1 (Fr, I, 140-1), originally c. 24 of the fourth council of Toledo, 633.
[2]Tt. i. 5-9.
[3]I Ti. iii. 1-13.
[4]D, 24 c. 2 (Fr, I, 87); X, 1.12.1 (Fr, II, 124-5), originally a decretal of Pope Innocent III, 15 March 1206; X, 1.14.4 (Fr, II, 126-7), originally a decretal of Pope Alexander III (1159-81). Cf. H.C., 20.10; 1566/4.1.
[5]1571/10.

11. OF THOSE TO BE ADMITTED TO ECCLESIASTICAL BENEFICES

1.[1]

Just as the condition of the state is ruined when it is governed by men who are stupid, demanding and burning with ambition, so in these times the church of God is struggling, since it is committed to the care of those who are totally incompetent to assume so important a task, in which respect it has fallen very far short indeed of those rules of the blessed Paul, which he prescribed to Timothy[2] and Titus.[3] Therefore we must find an appropriate remedy for so serious a plague on our churches.

2. Ministers [*are*] to be carefully examined.[4]

Everyone who obtains a living in any way whatsoever shall be most carefully tested and examined according to the form and procedure of our laws, lest a bishop lay his hand suddenly on someone and so become a partner in the crimes of others. Nor shall anyone be allowed to run a church, unless he has been duly examined beforehand.

3. The duty of patrons.[5]

Furthermore, we order patrons of ecclesiastical benefices to put aside any feeling that they are beholden to particular interests and constraints, and to ensure that those who are to be appointed to this sacred task can and will fulfill it in every respect. For livings are not entrusted to patrons so that they may reduce them or make a profit from them, but so that they may rest in their **safe** keeping and trust.

4. Patronorum deliquentium poena.[6]

Vehementer patronorum interest, ne turpiter et avare sibi quacunque conventione praecaveant in beneficiorum collationibus, de retinendis aedificiis, subducendis decimis, aut ullo se contaminent *huiusmodi* flagitioso quaestu *qualis a nobis in illo capite sublatus est, quod 'De sacerdotiis' inscriptum est 'integre conferendis'*.[7] Quorum si quicquam in hoc genere fuerit contra leges nostras quacunque ratione conventum, patronus collocationis ius illius temporis amittet. Deinde, qui iure fuerat collocationis usurus, quoniam ad iniquam transactionem suam voluntatem accommodavit, et sacerdotio carebit, quod illi designabitur, et ab illis omnibus, quae consequi poterat, excludetur.

[59r] 5. Sacerdotia vacua non esse oportere, **neque antequam vac{a}verint conferri**.[8]

Sacerdotia diu vacua iacere non debent. Itaque nisi spatio sex mensium postquam vacua facta sunt, patroni novos il[29b]lis ministros designaverint, ipso beneficio designationis illo quidem tempore carebunt; et tamen in collocandis sacerdotiis nimium properari nolumus, nec patimur ut patroni certam illorum spem cuiquam ulla scriptorum, aut pignorum, aut pactorum cautione faciant, priusquam vacua sint. Nam huiusmodi conventiones magnam secum vim incommodorum afferunt. Itaque qui talem ullam sacerdotiorum minime vacuorum spem faciunt, ius collocationis illius temporis amittent, et qui /ad/ nondum vacua sic adspiraverunt, ne ad vacua quidem post assumentur, et etiam ab omnibus aliis submovebuntur.

6. Ius designationis *quibus tribuantur* **a patrono ad quos devolvatur**.[9]

Quoties patronus designationis ius amittit, illud in episcopum transire placet, qui spatio sex mensium si neglexerint in vacuum sacerdotium idoneum aliquem imponere, ius in archiepiscopum transferetur; [59v] qui sex mensibus (a quo tempore certior factus est) illo iure si non utatur, nos illud ipsi nobis sumemus. Et si nobis etiam, ex quo id novimus, sex menses effluxerint sacerdotium vacuum non collocantibus, ad patronum rursus ius suum devolvetur, et sic in eodem semper orbe circumferatur, illis quas nominavimus personis mutuo sibi succedentibus, donec tandem aliquis eorum praescripto tempore ius collocationis exequatur.

---

[6] 1571/10.
[7] R, 18. This may be an older version of the title heading.
[8] X, 3.8.2 (Fr, II, 488), originally c. 8 of Lateran III, 1179 (*C.O.D.*, 215); X, 3.38.12 (Fr, II, 613), originally a decretal of Pope Alexander III (1159-81); H.C., 17.1.
[9] X, 3.38.22 (Fr, II, 616), originally a decretal of Pope Alexander III.

4. The penalty for delinquent patrons.[6]

It is most decidedly in the interest of patrons to ensure that when they are conferring benefices they do not behave meanly or in a miserly fashion for any reason whatsoever, by holding on to buildings, deducting tithes or contaminating themselves with any other *such* demand for money, *of the kind which was listed by us in the title headed 'Of conferring priestly offices intact'.*[7] And if anything of this kind shall in any way be agreed against our laws, the patron shall forfeit the right of conferment for that turn. Furthermore, the one who was to benefit from the right of conferment shall forfeit the living which has been granted to him and shall also be excluded from anything else which could have resulted from it, because he has acquiesced in an unjust transaction.

5. Livings ought not to be vacant, **nor conferred before they become vacant.**[8]

Livings must not lie vacant for a long time. Therefore, if the patrons have not assigned ministers to them within the space of six months after they have become vacant, they shall forfeit the appointment to the benefice for that turn. Nevertheless, we not want there to be too much speed in making appointments to livings, nor do we allow patrons to give anyone assurance of obtaining them by any guarantee, written, pledged or agreed, before they become vacant. For habits of that kind bring a great burden of inconveniences with them. Therefore, those who make such a promise of livings not yet vacant shall lose the right of appointment for that turn, and those who thus aspire /to/ livings not yet vacant, shall not be appointed to them later on, when they become vacant, and shall also be debarred from all others.

6. *To* **On** whom the **patron's** right of appointment shall *be given* **devolve**.[9]

Every time a patron forfeits the right of appointment, it shall go to the bishop, and if he has failed to appoint some suitable person to the vacant living within the space of six months, the right shall be transferred to the archbishop, and if he has not exercised that right within six months (from the time he is notified), we shall take it upon ourselves. And if we have also not appointed to the vacant living within the space of six months from the time we learned of it, the right shall return to the patron, and so it shall continue to go round in a circle, with the persons whom we have named following one another in succession, until finally one of them exercises the right of appointment within the time prescribed.

7. Cognitores adhibendos esse.[10]

Quoniam explorandam esse diximus et excutiendam illorum doctrinam et probitatem, qui sacerdotiorum participes erunt, primum episcopus ipse certos cognitores eligat. Deinde quoniam haec cura peculiaris archidiaconorum esse debet, illos in iure suo *v*/**n**olumus interpellare, sed univer[30a]sum hoc cognitionis negotium illis informandum et pertractandum relinquimus; hoc interim proviso, collegas ut vocent ad se, quos episcopus cognitores designaverit, quorum perspecta fu[*er*]it gravis morum integritas, et [60r] in quibus Sacrarum Scripturarum scientia cum usu coniuncta sit, et peritia gubernandarum ecclesiarum. Et etiam episcopum in primis optabile est ipsum (si fieri potest) in hoc cognitionis negotio versari. Munus enim hoc unum est ex omnibus summum, et maximum in quo status ecclesiarum praecipue fundatus est. Quare si minutioribus in plerisque causis ecclesiarum episcoporum praesentia flagitatur, eam in hoc sane principali [mun/**num**]ere desiderari minime convenit.

8. Iuramentum cognitioni praeponendum esse.[11]

Nolumus ad cognitionem descendi, donec iuramentum a petitore fuerit requisitum, ut vere sincereque respondeat ad omnia, quae fuerint ab illo quaesita, modo praesentem ad cognitionem pertineant. Deinde in omnes vitae partes diligenter inquiretur, et in doctrinam penitus intrabitur, ne forte vel inscitia, vel scientia perversa laboret, aut corrupta.

9. In doctrina quid quaerendum sit.[12]

Quantum autem ad doctrinam illorum [60v] spectat, qui sunt ad ecclesiarum moderationem admovendi, his potissimum viis cognitionem procedere volumus, ut eorum sententiae de fide catholica pervestigentur, et sacrosancto Trinitatis mysterio, quantum quidem in illis necessario credendum [*est*]; proximo loco de Sacrarum Scripturarum libro/is, quos canonicos appellant, qualemque credant et quantam Sacrarum Scripturarum auctoritatem. Succedant controversiae [*praesertim*] recentiores nostrorum temporum. In summa catechismum membratim et per partes explicent, in quo praecipua religio[30b]nis capita breviter decursa sunt.[13]

---

[10]D, 23 c. 5 (Fr, I, 81); D, 23 c. 6 (Fr, I, 81); 1237/20; 1566/4.5; 1571/1.6; 1603/39.
[11]D, 23 c. 5 (Fr, I, 81); L, 1.5.1, gloss on *canonice examinatus*.
[12]D, 23 c. 5 (Fr, I, 81); 1566/4.2.
[13]This catechism was composed by Archbishop Cranmer in 1548 as part of the confirmation rite in the 1549 B.C.P.

7. Examiners are to be appointed.[10]

Since we have said that the doctrine and trustworthiness of those who obtain livings must be tried and tested, the bishop himself shall first choose certain examiners. Moreover, since this responsibility ought to belong especially to archdeacons, we do **not** want to interfere with their right, but leave the entire business of examination to be undertaken and carried out by them, subject only to the proviso that they summon colleagues whom the bishop shall appoint as examiners, whose moral integrity has been certified, and in whom knowledge of the Holy Scriptures is coupled with experience and skill in running churches. Moreover it is desirable for the bishop to participate in this business of examination in person (if he can). For this task is the most important and greatest one of them all, as it is mostly on this that the condition of the churches is based. Therefore, if the presence of the bishops is required in many smaller matters pertaining to the churches, it is at the very least appropriate for it to be required in this truly important task as well.

8. An oath is to be taken before the examination.[11]

We do not want the examination to be undertaken until an oath has been demanded from the one seeking admission, to the effect that he will respond truthfully and sincerely to all the things which shall be asked of him, as long as they relate to the present examination. Moreover, careful inquiry shall be made into every aspect of his life, and particularly into his learning, in case he happens to be suffering either from ignorance or from a knowledge which is perverse or corrupt.

9. What is to be asked about learning.[12]

As far as the learning of those who are to be appointed to the running of churches is concerned, it is our will that the examination shall proceed as far as possible along these lines: that their opinions concerning the catholic faith shall be tested, as well as concerning the most holy mystery of the Trinity, which must absolutely be believed by them; next, concerning the books of the Holy Scriptures which they call canonical, what and how great they believe the authority of the Holy Scriptures is. There shall then follow [*in particular*] the more recent controversies of our own times. In conclusion, they shall explain the catechism bit by bit and part by part, in which the main points of religion are briefly set out.[13]

10. Cognoscendum esse an haeretici sint.[14]

Quoniam autem plane sciri debet an ulla sint infecti falsa doctrina, quaerendum ex illis erit quid de materiis universis sentiant, quas in caput 'De haereticis'[15] coniiciendas [*esse*] curavimus. Et ad has interrogationes qui non convenienter et recte responderint, cognitorum iudicio, vel qui Sacrarum Scripturarum scientiae sunt expertes, repudientur. Si vero fuerint haec in illis *bene* bene constituta, tum demum ad reliqua pergendum erit.

[61r] 11. Cognitores quid primum requirent.[16]

Et primum quidem cognitores ex illo sciscitentur, an ad illa beati Pauli praecepta se velit accommodare (quae s[u/i]nt ad Timotheum his verbis: 'Tu vero vigila, in omnibus labora, opus fac evangelistae, ministerium tuum imple'),[17] *suam* ut ecclesiam **suam ad quam apponetur** *huiusmodi*, quantum vires ferent, assiduitate semper administret *ad quam apponetur*, et deinde suum illi plane et aperte declaretur officium, quod in sacerdotio debet exercere.

12. Unicum esse oportere sacerdotium unius ministri.[18]

Quoniam multis sacerdotiis in unum ministrum concurrentibus, singulis m[i/u]nus recte perfecteque satisfieri necesse est, et minus viris doctis (qui adhuc egent neque illis prospectum est) consuli potest, percontentur a candidato cognitores an ullum habeat praesens sacerdotium; et si confiteatur habere se, secundum non impetret quod ab illis petit; alioqui prius sacerdotium volumus vacuum fieri, ac si [31a] possessor eius obiisset, eritque patroni ius et officium loco eius alium quempiam designandi.

[61v] 13. Privilegia pluralitatum, ut vocant, tollenda.[19]

Privilegia quorum auctoritate multa sacerdotia poss[u/i]nt in unum ministrum confluere, posthac nemini volumus indulgeri. Attamen his qui *a nobis* hactenus impetrarunt ut plura sibi permitt[ere/a]ntur administranda sacerdotia, nostram hanc legem fraudi esse nolumus, quominus acquisitis privilegiis libere fruantur.

---

[14]L, 5.5.1, originally cc. 1-2 of the council of Oxford, 1407.
[15]R, 2.
[16]1237/20.
[17]II Ti. iv. 5.
[18]X, 1.14.4 (Fr, II, 126-7), originally a decretal of Pope Alexander III (1159-81); X, 3.5.13 (Fr, II, 468), also originally a decretal of Pope Alexander III; H.C., 19.4; 1571/1.7.
[19]Cf. X, 1.14.4 (Fr, II, 126-7), originally a decretal of Pope Alexander III; 1571/8.

10. They are to be examined to find out whether they are heretics.[14]

And since it must be clearly known if they are infected with false doctrine, they shall be asked what they think about all the matters which we have caused to be included in the chapter 'Of heretics'.[15] And those who do not answer properly and correctly to these questions, or who are deficient in the knowledge of the Holy Scriptures, shall be rejected by the judgment of the examiners. But if these things are well grounded in them, then they may proceed further to the remaining matters.

11. What the examiners shall ask first of all.[16]

And first of all, the examiners shall ask him whether he is willing to conform himself to those precepts of the blessed Paul (which were given to Timothy in these words: 'But you be vigilant, labour in all things, do the work of an evangelist, fulfill your ministry'),[17] that he may always carefully administer the *said* church to which he shall be appointed, as far as his strength allows, and after that the duty which he must perform in the living shall be clearly and openly declared to him.

12. Each minister ought to have only one living.[18]

Since, when there are many livings held by one minister, it is [*necessarily the case that each individual one will be cared for less* **necessary for the task of each to be done**] correctly and perfectly, and there will be fewer livings available for learned men (who are still without them and have little prospect of obtaining any), the examiners shall find out from the candidate whether he already has a living, and if he admits that he has, he shall not obtain the second one which he is asking them for. Furthermore, it is our will that the living shall first be vacant, and if its possessor has died, it will be the right and duty of the patron to appoint someone else in his place.

13. The privileges of pluralism, as it is called, are to be removed.[19]

From now on, we do not want anyone to enjoy the privileges by virtue of which many livings can accrue to a single minister. But we do not want this law to deprive those who have hitherto obtained permission *from us* to administer many livings, but rather that they should freely enjoy their acquired privileges.

14. Absentiae quae possint esse causae.[20]

Quicunque vel annis fuerit gravis, vel morborum incursione multum extenuatus, ut suo munere fungi non valeat, vel si quamcunque iustam aliam habeat temporariae cuiusdam absentiae causam episcopo [a/o]pprobandam, propter quam illum aliquandiu sacerdotio necesse sit abesse, tamen hoc interim [*illi*] p[*ro*/**er**]spiciendum erit, ut probum et laudabilem vicarium suo in loco colloce*n*t. Et diligenter episcopi vigilent, ne cuiuscunque rei respectu dolose quisquam aut astute diutius quam necessitas urget a sacerdotio suo sinatur abesse.

[62r] 15. Quo tempore sit *habitandum* /**ad**/ **eundum** *ad* sacerdoti*a*/**um**.[21]

Quoniam hoc a nobis prius constitutum est ut unusquisque suo in sacerdotio permaneat, nisi temporaria quaedam privilegia nonnullos aliquando liberaveri[n/-]t *(ut ante legitime)*, hoc etiam adiunctum sit, ut cum peracta cognitione quisquam per ordinarii litteras ad sacerdotium adhibetur, duorum mensium spatio continu[*e*/**o**] subsequentium in sacerdotium commeet, nisi morbus aut vehemens necessitas, cui parendum sit, illum distineat; quod si secus fecerit, et sacerdotium praesens illi pe[31b]ribit, et etiam ab aliis omnibus submovebu*n*/itur.

16. Officium praebendariorum *quale sit*.[22]

Immunitatem quandam omnium munerum habere solebant qui beneficiis prius ecclesiasticis fruebantur, curarum (ut *vocant* ipsi interpretati et etiam locuti sunt) expertibus. Nos autem p[*er*/**rae**]didicimus ecclesiarum utilitatibus omnes inservire debere, quicunque vivunt ecclesiae *vectigalibus* **proventibus**. Igitur tum canonicis tum praebendariis, qui certa sibi non habent in ecclesiis dispertita munera, negotium hoc damus, ut ecclesias docendo, contionando, *de** **a*** morbis vel rebus adversis depressos solando, [62v] reliquaque pietatis officia communicando sublevent, vel aliis quibuscunque viis legitimis et rectis quas episcopus et decanus ecclesiae praescripserint.

---

[20]X, 3.6.3 (Fr, II, 482), originally a decretal of Pope Lucius III (1181-5); 1237/10; 1268/10; 9 Edward II, c. 8, 1315 (*S.R.*, I, 172); 21 Henry VIII, c. 13, ss. 28-9, 1529 (*S.R.*, 292-6).

[21]L, 3.6.1, originally c. 9 of the council of Oxford, 1222.

[22]A marginal note in Cranmer's hand reads: 'Ista duo capita melius differentur ad titulum "De praebendariis".' ('These two sections would be better moved to the chapter "On prebendaries"'). On the subject, see 1571/2.3; 1603/44.

14. What the reasons for absence may be.[20]

Anyone who is so advanced in years, or so greatly weakened by the onset of diseases that he is unable to exercise his function, or if he has some other just cause for a particular temporary absence, which has been approved by the bishop, on account of which he must be away from the benefice for a time, must nevertheless ensure that he appoints an honest and praiseworthy vicar to take his place for the duration. And the bishops shall diligently see to it that no one shall contrive to be absent from his living for longer than need requires, by fraud or deceit for any reason whatsoever.

15. At what time the living is to be *resided in* **taken up**.[21]

Since it has already been decided by us that each parson shall reside on his living, except that certain temporary privileges may occasionally dispense some of them from this (*as lawfully above*), let this also be added, that when someone is admitted to a living by letters from the ordinary upon completion of the examination, he should take up residence within the living in the space of two months immediately following, unless illness or urgent necessity, to which he must defer, prevents him. If he does not do so, he shall lose his present living and also be debarred from all others.

16. *What* the duty of prebendaries *is*.[22]

There used to be some who had a certain immunity from all duties because they enjoyed ecclesiastical benefices which (as they themselves *call* have explained and also declared) are free of responsibilities. But we have taught that all who live off the *revenues* **fruits** of the church must serve the needs of the churches. Therefore we give this task to the canons or prebendaries, who do not have particular duties assigned to them in churches, that they should assist the churches by teaching, preaching, comforting those who are laid low by illnesses or misfortunes, and by fulfilling the other duties of godliness, or by whatever other lawful and right ways which the bishop and dean of the church have prescribed.

17. Quinquennii absentiam praebendariis indulgeri.[23]

Hoc autem illis indulgemus, qui vel ad praebendas, vel ad canonicatus, vel ad beneficia certorum munerum expertia sunt ads[*ci*/**er**]ti, quinquennium ut doctrinarum studiis in academiis impendant, hoc adiecto, singulis ut annis litteras scribant cum ad episcopum tum ad integram societatem, quam capitulum vocant, in quibus fideliter rationem vitae reddant et morum et progressionis in doctrina. Cum autem absumptum est quinquennium, in sua beneficia vel ecclesiastica munera rursus introire cogantur.

18. De natalibus ministrorum.[24]

Postquam de vita plene cognitum est, de religione, de scientia, de voluntate sacerdotium administrandi, et in eo remanendi, tandem etiam ad natales et ortus illorum descendatur. Et quamquam stupris parentum et adulteriis filii /non/ premuntur, quantum quidem ad immortalitatem vitae caelestis [*et*] futurae pertinet, tamen Deus quoniam immenso quo[32a]dam [63r] et grandi stuprorum et adulteriorum et flagitiosarum libidinum odio liberos vitio procreatos vehementer interdum affligit, et successores eorum obterit, et propter eandem patrum *importunitatem* **impuritatem** filios in Veteri Testamento *sacrarum* ab ecclesia*rum*/**e** administratione depulit;[25] nos divinae severitatis exemplum secuti, tales vitio generatos filios a contrectatione munerum ecclesiasticorum abarcemus, nisi forte singulares quidam existant eximiis donis instructi, quae sic in illis luceant, ut priores natalium sordes obscurentur, aut virtutum praestantia compensentur, aut nisi summa sit in ecclesia ministrorum paucitas.

19. Patronorum nothos ab ecclesiarum cura removendos esse.[26]

Quorundam tanta est patronorum impudentia, suos ut liberos ex adulteriis et stupris susceptos in illas ecclesias intrudant, quarum ad illos ius designationis pertinet, qui cum paternarum libidinum intempestivi testes sint, potius quam ecclesiarum apti ministri, peccandique quandam auctoritatem affera*n*t tam ingens illorum habita ratio, *prorsus illos ab huiusmodi muneribus ecclesiasticis depelli*

---

[23]X, 5.5.5 (Fr, II, 770-1), originally a decretal of Pope Honorius III, 25 November 1219.
[24]X, 1.17.1 (Fr, II, 135), originally c. 8 of the council of Poitiers, 1087; X, 1.17.14 (Fr, II, 139-40), originally a decretal of Pope Clement III (1187-91); X, 1.17.18 (Fr, II, 141), originally a decretal of Pope Gregory IX (1227-41), published on or before 5 September 1234.
[25]This presumably refers to Hophni and Phineas, the sons of Eli who were deprived and slain because of their father's unfaithfulness. Cf. I Sa. ii. 27-36.
[26]Cf. X, 1.17.15 (Fr, II, 140), originally a decretal of Pope Innocent III, 8 January 1207; X, 1.17.16 (Fr, II, 140), c. 31 of Lateran IV, 1215 (*C.O.D.*, 249); 1947/55.5.

17. Prebendaries shall be granted a five-year leave of absence.[23]

But this we grant to those who have been appointed to prebends, canonries or benefices without specific duties - a five-year period which they may spend in the universities in the pursuit of learning, with this proviso added, that in each of those years they shall write a letter both to the bishop and to that whole fellowship which they call the chapter, in which they shall faithfully render account of their life, behaviour and progress in learning. And when the five-year period is up, they shall be obliged to go back again to their benefices or ecclesiastical duties.

18. Of the family background of ministers.[24]

After full inquiry has been made concerning their life, religion, knowledge and desire to administer the living and reside on it, then let it extend also to their family background and origin. And although they are /not/ discriminated against because of the fornication and adultery of their parents, in matters which pertain to the immortality of the heavenly [*and*] future life, yet since God, out of his great and immense hatred of fornication, adultery and shameful lusts, sometimes grievously afflicts children who have been procreated in sin and hurts their offspring, and because of this same *misbehaviour* **impurity** of the fathers, he deposed sons in the Old Testament from the administration of the *sacred* churches,[25] following the example of the divine severity, we debar such sons, born in sin, from receiving ecclesiastical appointments, unless perchance there are some who have exceptional gifts, which shine in them to such an extent as to blot out the earlier shame of their birth, or who make up for it by their outstanding virtues, or unless there is a serious shortage of ministers in the church.

19. The illegitimate children of patrons are to be removed from the cure of churches.[26]

The impudence of some patrons is such that they appoint children conceived in fornication and adultery to those churches where the right of appointment belongs to them. Because these children are untimely evidences of their parents' lusts rather than suitable ministers of the churches, and because this widespread custom of theirs lends a certain respectability to sin, it is our will that from henceforth *they shall be deprived of such ecclesiastical duties*

volumus **huiusmodi omnes beneficiorum collocationes prorsus irritas esse volumus, et patron[*um*/os] pro eo tempore collocationis iure privari**.

[63v] 20. Vitiis quibusvis corporum ministros non arceri a sacerdotiis.[27]

Offensiones corporum, quae prius homines a susceptione munerum ecclesiasticorum secludebant, tantum posthac momentum non habebunt, ut illis, cuiuscunque generis fuerint, vir doctus et probus ab administrando sacerdotio summoveatur. Ill[*a*/o]rum tamen diligens erit habenda consideratio, qu[*ae*/i] gerendi muneris ecclesiastici facultatem vel [32b] omnino perimunt, [vel **ut**] plane corrumpunt, ut caecitas lectionis officium tollit, ad quod Paulus Timotheum incitat;[28] rursus in ministro si lingua sic titubaverit, vel adhaeserit, vel quacunque calamitate tantopere vitiata fuerit, ut in contione [**a suis**] non po[*ss*/**ter**]it [*a suis*] intelligi, fructum in illo maximum sui muneris interire necesse est. Praeterea si vultu minister sic d[*is*/e]torqueatur, [*aut*] spiritum adeo tetrum habeat et aspernabilem, ut homines ab illius consuetudine colloquioque resiliant, et ita nec publicum nec privatum, vel consilium vel solationem, aliorum necessitatibus impartire possit, desiderari paene omnia in illo videmus, quae suum ad officium pertinent. Igitur has grandes et immanes corporum clades qui sic inustas [64r] habent, ut sacrarum in illis rerum libera non possit administratio procedere, minime ad dignitatem sacerdotiorum gubernandorum perveniant; sed minutiores offensiunculae, licet inspersae sint, illos a sacerdotiis non distinebunt, nec earum deformitatem pecunia redimere debent.

21. Aetas ministrorum.[29]

Sequitur aetas, quae non est in ecclesiae ministris negligenda, quoniam annorum maturitas auctoritatem affert, et adolescentiae temeritas occupationi sanctissimorum munerum et severitati vix convenire potest. Igitur in episcopis, **decanis ecclesiarum cathedralium, et archidiaconis,**[30] quorum maxima perfectio morum esse debet, tricesimum annum expectari volumus, in parochi{*i*}s, ut vocant, vicesimum quintum, in praebendariis eundem, siquidem cura sit illis ulla certorum hominum commissa, quos et contionandi laborem, et sacramentorum communicandorum oportet subire, quoties vel episcopi vel praesides haec illorum curae [*munera*] committunt. Itaque volumus illos respectu

---

[27]D, 49 c. 1 (Fr, I, 175-7); D, 55 cc. 4-13 (Fr, I, 216-19); X, 3.6.2 (Fr, II, 482), originally a decretal of Pope Eugenius III (1145-53); H.C., 18.14.
[28]I Ti. iv. 13.
[29]D, 78, c. 1 (Fr, I, 275); D, 78 c. 4 (Fr, I, 275-6); D, 78 c. 5 (Fr, I, 276); H.C., 18.2.
[30]Added to the MS by Peter Martyr.

all such conferments to benefices shall be void, and that the patron[s] shall be deprived of the right of conferment for that turn.

20. Ministers with particular bodily defects are not to be excluded from livings.[27]

Bodily defects which previously barred men from taking on ecclesiastical duties shall henceforth not have such great importance that a learned and honest man may be debarred from holding a living because of them, whatever they may be. Nevertheless, careful consideration will have to be given to those defects which make it completely impossible to fulfil a particular ecclesiastical duty, [or/**because**] they clearly vitiate it, as for example, blindness excludes the duty of reading, which Paul encourages Timothy to do.[28] Again, if a minister's tongue falters or sticks, or has been so damaged by some misfortune that he cannot be understood by his people when preaching, it is clear that the most important fruit of his task will be lost. Moreover, if the minister's appearance is so distorted, [*or*] if he has such a nasty and repulsive spirit that people refuse to speak or relate to him, and for that reason he cannot give either public or private counsel and consolation to others in need, we see that he is lacking in almost everything which belongs to his office. Therefore, those who have such great and enormous bodily defects, which are so ingrained in them that the administration of sacred things cannot proceed unhindered, shall not be promoted to the dignity of holding livings. But smaller defects, even if they are widespread, shall not bar them from livings, nor shall they have to make any financial recompense for their deformity.

21. The age of ministers.[29]

There follows age, which is not to be overlooked in the ministers of the church, since maturity of years carries authority with it, and the rashness of youth can hardly be appropriate for performing the most sacred tasks and for seriousness. Therefore it is our will that for bishops, **deans of cathedral churches and archdeacons,**[30] who ought to be of the most perfect character, the age of thirty shall be required, for parish priests, as they call them, twenty-five, and the same for prebendaries, if there is any cure of particular people which has been committed to them, and they ought to undertake the labour of preaching and of administering the sacraments as often as their bishops or superiors commit these [*tasks*] to their care. Therefore it is our will that they shall be sent to the

studiorum ad academias ablegari; doctrinam enim et omnem reliquam facultatem [33a] illos secum oportet adferre, priusquam ingrediantur ad ecclesiastica munera.

[64v] 22. Aetas liberorum praebendariorum.[31]

In liberioribus illis et solutioribus praebendis quae certos greges non curant, iuvenes collocari possunt qui vicesimum **primum**[32] annum impleverunt, si cetera cognitores in illis animadverterint recte comparata. Quibus hoc etiam indulgeri potest, ut **si di/a/coni fuerint**,[33] addiscendarum causa Sacrarum Scripturarum ad academias aliquandiu diversentur; sed ille secessus omnino debet quinquennii spatio definiri, **quo exacto nisi presbyterii gradu ini*ic*/tientur, et praebenda iam adepta privabuntur, et ad restituendos fructus superioribus annis ex ea perceptos censuris ecclesiasticis adigentur.**

23. Cognitorum qualis diligentia requiratur.[34]

Cognitores ipsi magna vigilantia summaque debent assiduitate et integritate suum [*munus*] implere. Quod si quisquam eorum praevaricatus fuerit, et vel quaestu vel gratia de iure formularum decesserit, in hac universa cognitione praestitutarum, non solum *eadem* **ea de** re Christo summo iudici respondebit, verum etiam episcopi, cum requisitus fuerit, cogetur iudicium censuramque subire.

[65r] 24. Forma iuramenti ministrorum.[35]

Extremo loco cum finis erit totius cognitionis, si persona videbitur ad suscipiendum sacerdotium apta, iuramento tenebitur ad illa quae sequuntur praestanda. Principio, se permansurum in recepta fide veraque religione, toto vitae spatio, piorumque semper institutorum retinentissimum fore; [33b] monarchiam et tyrannidem Romani pontificis non agniturum; regem Angliae culturum, et veneraturum Ecclesiae Anglicanae summum caput in terris post Christum. Deinde reverentiam, fidem, et submissionem suo exhibiturum

---

[31] Cf. D, 28 c. 5 (Fr, I, 101-2); D, 77 c. 4 (Fr, I, 273).

[32] Added to the MS by Peter Martyr.

[33] Added to the MS by Peter Martyr.

[34] Cf. X, 1.23.7 (Fr, II, 151-2), originally a decretal of Pope Innocent III (1198-1216); X, 1.23.9 (Fr, II, 152), originally a decretal of Pope Innocent III, 23 September 1198.

[35] L, 2.6.3, attributed to Archbishop Richard Winchelsey, 1305. For the protestant aspects of this canon, see 1536/1 (*D.E.R.*, 175-6); 1547/1 (*D.E.R.*, 248); the eleven articles of 1559 (*D.E.R.*, 349-51). The actual form of the oath was not officially determined until Archbishop Whitgift's articles of 19 October 1583, (6), subsequently incorporated into 1603/36.

universities in order to study, for it is necessary that they should bring learning and every other ability with them, before they enter into ecclesiastical duties.

22. The age of free prebendaries.[31]

In cases of freer and more exempt prebends, which do not involve the care of particular congregations, young men who have attained the age of twenty-**one**[32] years may be appointed, if the examiners have noted that they have properly met the other requirements. It may also be granted to them that **if they are deacons**,[33] they may spend some time in the universities for the purpose of learning the Holy Scriptures, but this leave of absence must in all cases be limited to a five-year period. **After that time, if they are not ordained as presbyters, they shall be deprived of the prebend which they have obtained and also be compelled by ecclesiastical censures to repay the revenues which they received from it in previous years.**

23. What diligence is required of examiners.[34]

The examiners themselves must fulfill their [*task*] with great vigilance and with the highest dedication and integrity. If any of them is dishonest, and departs from the regulations laid down for all these kinds of examination, either because he has been bribed or of his own free will, not only will he be answerable to Christ the supreme judge for this, but he shall also be obliged to undergo the judgment and censure of the bishop when he is required to do so.

24. The form of the ministers' oath.[35]

Finally, when the whole examination has come to an end, if the person appears to be suitable to take on a living, he shall be bound by oath to fulfill the following. First, that he will remain in the received faith and true religion for the whole space of his life, and that he shall always adhere closely to godly practices, that he will not recognize the monarchy and tyranny of the Roman pontiff, and that he shall respect and venerate the king of England as the supreme head on earth, after Christ, of the English Church. Next, he shall show reverence, loyalty

episcopo, quo[*a*]d omnia honesta et sancta illius mandata; nihil de iure diminuturum ecclesiae sibi commissae; praeterea nec antea dedisse quicquam, nec postea daturum, aut de dando pactum intercessisse, vel intercessurum, vel ipso auctore, vel alio quocunque procuratore aut vicario, respectu praesentis sacerdotii quod iam sumit; et si quisquam illum celans hoc in genere quicquam molitus est, se quamprimum norit episcopo renuntiaturum, et eius arbitrio cessurum parto sacerdotio; tum autem non gravaturum se ecclesiam suam novis aut auctioribus pensionibus; postremo, si forte sacris ordinibus adhuc imbutus non sit, spatio sex mensium continue subsequentium, diaconum, et deinde spatio succedentis anni presbyterum esse futurum, **vel quamprimum vicesimum quintum annum perfecerit, si forte ante illud ad praebendam liberiorem (ut supra diximus) admissus fuerit.**

[65v] **25. De eis qui temere in beneficia irrumpunt ecclesiastica.**[36]

Et ne quis praeceps in dignitatem aut beneficium irruat ecclesiasticum, volumus ut quicunque absque ordinarii auctoritate, et litteris illius [*sub scripto* subscripta] authentic[*o*/is], beneficium aliquod ecclesiasticum occupaverit, non tantum excid[*e*/i/{a}]t a beneficio quod iniuste invasit, absque spe ulla illius recuperandi, verum etiam nullum aliud imposterum consequi poterit, et ut eius contumacia requirit, excommunicabitur, et a ministerio ecclesiastico suspendetur.[37]

---

[36]Cf. X, 1.7.3 (Fr, II, 98-9), originally a decretal of Pope Innocent III, 21 August 1198.
[37]Here Foxe wrote in the MS: 'Desiderantur hoc loco sex articuli; videlicet "De renuntiatione vel defectione beneficiorum", 2. "De permutatione beneficiorum ecclesiasticorum", 3. "De purgatione", 4. "De dilapidationibus", 5. "De alienatione et elocatione beneficiorum", 6. "De electione", etc. In quibus titulis continentur capitula 39. Haec reperies in codice Matthaei Cantuariensis, folio 58. Adduntur haec in libro impresso.' ('In this place are wanting six chapters, namely, "Of renouncing or resigning benefices", 2. "Of transferring ecclesiastical benefices", 3. "Of purgation", 4. "Of dilapidations", 5. "Of alienating and letting benefices", 6. "Of election", etc. In these chapters are contained 39 headings. You will find them in Matthew Parker's codex, folio 58. They are added in the printed book'). He goes on to add in a second note: '"De dilapidationibus", "alienatione", "elocatione" vide in fine huius codicis.' ('"Of dilapidations", "alienating", "letting", see at the end of this codex').

and obedience to his bishop, in all things honest and holy which are commanded by him; that he will take nothing away as of right from the church committed to him; moreover, that he has not previously given anything, nor shall afterwards give anything, nor has entered into an agreement about giving anything, nor shall enter into one, either in person or through some other proxy or substitute, with respect to the present living which he is now taking up; and if anyone has tried to do anything of the kind by deceiving him, as soon as he finds it out, he shall report it to the bishop, and at his discretion shall surrender the acquired living; and that he shall not burden his church with new and increased pensions; finally, if by chance he has not yet been ordained into holy orders, that within the space of six months immediately following he shall become a deacon, and then within the space of the following year a priest, **or as soon as he has attained his twenty-fifth year, if by chance he has already been admitted to a freer prebend (as we have said above).**

25. Of those who rush in and grab ecclesiastical benefices.[36]

And in order that no one shall rush in and seize an ecclesiastical dignity or benefice, it is our will that anyone who has taken over any ecclesiastical benefice without the authority of the ordinary and his authentic letters [*in his authentic hand*], shall not only have to leave the benefice which he has unlawfully acquired, with no hope of recovering it, but shall also be made ineligible to receive any further benefice, and as his contumacy requires, he shall be excommunicated and suspended from the ministry of the church.[37]

[34a] 12. DE RENUNTIATIONE VEL DESERTIONE BENEFICIORUM

1.[1]

Huiusmodi causae possunt incidere, sacerdotiis ut vel cedi sponte possit, et ut vulgo loquuntur, illis renuntiari, vel eorum etiam ut permutatio fiat; sed hoc quoties usu veniet, omnem dolum et avaritiam et simoniam, non solum crimen sed etiam suspicionem, quantum fieri potest abesse praecipimus.

2. In renuntiatione et permutatione consensus ordinarii necessarius est, et sine illo paciscens, simoniacus est.[2]

Nunquam vel cedi placet beneficiis ecclesiasticis cuiuscunque generis fuerint, vel permutatione moveri propter ullam lucri vel emolumenti spem obiectam; nec ullum in huiusmodi negotiis factum valeat, donec ordinarius illius ecclesiae proprius totam rem consideraverit, et eam auctoritate sua confirmaverit. Quod si quis temere provectus ordinarii consensum in hac causa non adhibuerit, aut de lucro pactus fuerit, in eo ipso simoniae reus erit, nec ullum dimissi beneficii emolumentum unquam percipiet.

3. Resignationis negotium non potest incohari sine auctoritate ordinarii.[3]

Et quoniam vehementer placet omnes non solum causas, sed occasiones maleficiorum amputari, nullam dimittendorum aut aliis permittendorum beneficiorum mentionem fieri patimur, ex qua pactum possit cum quoqu {*am*/e} consequi, donec ordinarius hoc potestate sua liberum fecerit. Nec ordinarius ex altera parte rem hanc procedere sinat, nisi ipse qui [34b] beneficio cessurus est, iuramentum interponat, nec lucrum in hac re, nec ullam simoniacae perversitatis particulam intercessisse vel intercessurum.

---

[1]X, 1.9.5 (Fr, II, 104), originally a decretal of Pope Clement III (1187-91).
[2]X, 1.9.1 (Fr, II, 102-3); X, 1.9.4 (Fr, II, 104), both originally decretals of Pope Alexander III (1159-81); cf. H.C., 16.1-2.
[3]X, 1.9.4 (Fr, II, 104), originally a decretal of Pope Alexander III.

12. OF THE RESIGNATION OR ABANDONMENT OF BENEFICES

1.[1]

Causes may arise making it possible for livings to be given up voluntarily, and renounced, as it is popularly known, or for them to be exchanged, but whenever this occurs, we decree that all trickery, greed and simony - not only the crime itself but also any suspicion of it - shall be as far as possible excluded.

2. In a resignation and exchange the agreement of the ordinary is necessary, and anyone who makes a transaction without it, is a simoniac.[2]

No ecclesiastical benefices of any kind whatsoever may be surrendered or exchanged for any promise made of money or payment, nor shall anything done in transactions of this kind be valid until the ordinary proper to that church has considered the whole matter and confirmed it by his authority. But if someone dares to act in this case without obtaining the agreement of the ordinary, or has made some financial arrangement, he shall stand accused of simony on that account, and shall not receive any emolument whatever from the abandoned benefice.

3. The process of resignation may not be started without the authorization of the ordinary.[3]

And since it is highly desirable that not only all causes but also all occasions of wrongdoing shall be cut off, we do not allow any mention to be made of benefices which are about to be given up or transferred to others, on the basis of which information a financial arrangement may be made with someone, until the ordinary has freed it by his power. Nor shall the ordinary for his part try to advance the matter unless the one who intends to surrender the benefice swears an oath that in this matter no money nor any element of simoniacal perversity has intervened, or shall intervene.

4. Non licet sententiam cessionis mutare.[4]

Si quis semel beneficio cesserit, et post consilium mutans ad illud reditum habere voluerit, frustra sit haec illius secunda et sera voluntas, nisi forte talis aliqua subsit causa, superiorem ut ordinarius cessionem retexendam, et pro nulla putet habendam.

5. Cedi non posse beneficiis ecclesiasticis per procuratores.[5]

Et ut omnia prorsus in hoc negotio sincera sint, procuratores excludimus, nec eos ullo modo patimur ad sacerdotiorum dimissionem admitti. Quod si aliquando contra constitutionem hanc nostram obrepserint vel irruperint, frustra sit illorum cessio, vel (ut vulgo loquuntur) resignatio.

---

[4]1268/33 (PC, 780); X, 1.9.2-3 (Fr, II, 103), both originally decretals of Pope Alexander III (1159-81); cf. H.C., 16.3.
[5]An alteration of *Clem.*, 1.4.1 (Fr, II, 1138); H.C., 16.6.

4. The sentence of surrender may not be changed.[4]

If someone has once surrendered a benefice and later changes his mind and wants to have it back, this second and tardy desire of his shall be null and void, unless perchance there is some other reason for the ordinary to revoke the earlier cession and regard it as invalid.

5. Benefices may not be surrendered by proctors.[5]

And so that from henceforth everything done in this matter may be above board, we exclude proctors, nor do we allow them in any way to be allowed to surrender livings. But if occasionally they ignore this our constitution or break it, any cession or resignation (as it is popularly known) of theirs shall be void.

[34b] 13. DE PERMUTATIONE BENEFICIORUM ECCLESIASTICORUM

1. Quomodo permutatio procedat.[1]

Ecclesiastica beneficia, quocunque nomine censeantur, sine patronorum et ordinariorum auctoritate permutari non licebit. Verum quando locorum et ecclesiarum ratio postulabit, ut qui uno loco minus utiles esse videntur, [35a] alibi se valeant utilius exercere, potest episcopus unum ministrum in alterius locum imponere, si voluntas id ministrorum ferat, et uterque locus in ditione sit episcopi quam dioecesim vocant.

2. Quomodo beneficia diversarum dioecesum permutari possint.[2]

Si quando vero contingat ecclesiastica beneficia quaecunque diversis in dioecesibus poni, de quibus commutandis coeptum est, ad exitum causa non perveniat, donec utriusque ditionis, vel dioecesis ordinarius auctoritatem suam coniunxerit. Qu{i}a in re ut permutationum impensae minuantur, et etiam in toto sit negotio minus molestiae, cuius in ditione minus beneficium inest, ecclesiasticum is suum ius in alterum ordinarium transferat, qui suam ad propriam alterius delegatam, et quasi fidei commissam, potestatem infundens, sua sententia totam permutationis causam concludet.

3. Quae beneficia possunt in omne tempus permutari.[3]

Ecclesiastica beneficia quae sic comparata sunt ut ecclesiae vel collegia ius in illis proprietatis habeant, ordinariorum interposita rite sententia, permutatione possunt in omne tempus ab una societate in aliam transferri.

---

[1]X, 1.19.5 (Fr, II, 522-3), originally a decretal of Pope Urban III (1185-7); H.C., 21.1.
[2]Cf. 1268/29 (PC, 774-7).
[3]Panormitanus on X, 2.1.2.

13. OF THE EXCHANGE OF ECCLESIASTICAL BENEFICES

1. How an exchange shall proceed.[1]

Ecclesiastical benefices, whatever they are called, may not be exchanged without the authorization of the patrons and bishops. But when the right ordering of places and churches strongly suggests that those who appear to be less useful in one place will turn out to function more usefully elsewhere, the bishop may appoint one minister in another's place, if the will of the ministers is agreeable and each place is in the district of the bishop, which is called the diocese.

2. How benefices of different dioceses may be exchanged.[2]

But when it happens that negotiations have begun for an exchange of ecclesiastical benefices which are located in different dioceses, the matter shall not be concluded until the ordinary of each district or diocese has given his authorization. In which matter, in order to keep the expenses of the exchange down and also to minimize the amount of bother involved in the whole business, the ordinary in whose district the lesser benefice is situated shall transfer his ecclesiastical right to the other one, who shall unite his own power with that of the former, which has been delegated and practically entrusted to him, and shall bring the whole matter of exchange to a conclusion by his own decision.

3. Which benefices may be exchanged at any time.[3]

Ecclesiastical benefices which are so established that churches or colleges have property rights over them may be transferred by exchange from one corporation to another at any time, subject to the agreement of the ordinaries.

4. Permutatio, si bona fide non fiat, nulla est.[4]

Quoniam iniquum est homines in eo circumveniri quod illis pro beneficio ius indulget, praesertim cum sanctum est causae genus, et ad ecclesiam pertinet, instituimus ut quoties beneficiis ecclesiasticis cessum est, si veros ad domi[35b]nos et permutationum auctores non perveniant, sed ad alios astute detorquentur, omnis huiusmodi fraus quae non directis fidei, sed fraudis obliquis viis incedit, prorsus tollatur, et ad nihilum recidat, talesque permutationes omnibus modis pro nullis habeantur.

[4]*Clem.*, 3.5.1 (Fr, II, 1161); H.C., 21.3.

4. If an exchange has not been made in good faith, it is void.[4]

Since it is unjust for men to bypass something which the law has ordained for their benefit, especially when the type of cause is holy and pertains to the church, we decree that whenever ecclesiastical benefices are surrendered, if they do not come to their true owners and the authors of the exchanges, but are cleverly diverted to others, all such fraud, which walks not in the straight ways of faith but in the crooked ways of deceit, shall from henceforth be removed and retreat into nothing, and such exchanges shall in all cases be regarded as void.

[35b]   **14. DE PURGATIONE**

1. Cur legitima purgatio sit instituta.[1]

Quoniam omnes leges et instituta debent ad haec duo capita referri, virtus ut venerationem et remunerationem habeat, vitium ut contumelia notetur et supplicio, quemadmodum his legibus nostris procuratum est, nimirum malorum ut improbitas poenarum acerbitate devinciretur, ita nunc tempus est ad secundum ut descendamus, scilicet ut defensionem et praesidium innocentiae comparemus et integritati. Tolerabilius enim est reum praeteriri, quam bonum circumveniri, nec diligentius scelera peccatorum quam calliditates detractorum, ex re publica debent excludi. Primum enim hoc in causa purgationis sit, ut si quis in suspicionem ecclesiastici criminis venerit, et apud bonos et laudabiles viros publice infamis esse coeperit, licet plane non possit de crimine constare, tamen arbitratu iudicis infamata persona suam defensionem instruat.

2. Quando purgationi locus est.[2]

Defensio, quam vulgo purgationem dicunt, habet proprie duo tempora, quorum alterum est cum adversus aliquis infamis rumor publice dimanavit de aliqua persona, praesertim ad honestos et bene moratos homines, alterum est [36a] quando reus aliquis in iudicio factus est, et tamen legitimis probationibus convinci non potest, sed magnis interim et verisimilibus praeiudiciis urgetur.

3. Quando purgatio non indicitur.[3]

Manifesto crimine nullus est defensioni locus, nec rursus ad purgationem reus tradi debet, cum infamia probabilius causis non nititur, sed mendacio et calumnia; sed tamen reus ipse si suae confisus innocentiae cupiat publicos honestatis suae testes in iudicium deducere, aequum est hoc illi concedi.

---

[1]L, 5.14.1, originally c. 12 of the council of Oxford, 1222; H.C., 12.1. See also Panormitanus, on X. 5.34.
[2]X, 5.34.1 (Fr, II, 869-70), c. 68 of the council of Tribur, 895; X, 5.34.13 (Fr, II, 875), originally a decretal of Pope Innocent III, 5 January 1199.
[3]X, 5.34.15 (Fr, II, 875-7), originally a decretal of Pope Innocent III, 10 January 1208.

14. OF PURGATION

1. Why lawful purgation was instituted.[1]

Since all laws and statutes must be in accordance with these two principles, *viz.* that virtue should receive respect and reward and that vice should be branded with shame and punishment, in so far as it has been secured by our laws that the wrongness of so many evils should be overcome by the severity of the penalties, so now it is time to go on to the second aspect, which is that we should give equal consideration to the defence and protection of innocence. For it is more tolerable for the accused to escape than for a good man to be trapped, nor should the crimes of sinners be more diligently excluded from the state than the false insinuations of accusers. For the first reason for allowing purgation is this, that if someone has come under suspicion of having committed an ecclesiastical crime, and has begun to be publicly denounced among good and praiseworthy men, although no criminal activity can be proved, then the defamed person may draw up his own defence, at the judge's discretion.

2. When there is ground for purgation.[2]

The defence, which is popularly known as purgation, may appropriately take place in two circumstances, of which one is when some hostile, defamatory rumour has been circulating publicly about some person, especially among honourable and morally upright people, and the other is when someone has been accused but cannot be convicted by lawful proofs, although he labours under great and plausible suspicions.

3. When purgation is not required.[3]

In the case of manifest crime there is no ground for defence, nor should the accused be handed over for purgation, since it is not evil rumour which appears to be the main problem, but rather wrongdoing and calumny. Nevertheless, if the accused himself protests his innocence and wants to bring public witnesses of his honesty into court, it is fair for this to be granted to him.

4. Damnatis in civili iudicio non est opus ecclesiastica purgatione.[4]

Magnam indignitatem nobis habere videtur, ut ecclesiasticae personae, cum a civilibus nostris legibus capitalis criminis pronuntiantur, rursus ad ecclesiastici fori iudicium relegentur et purg{a/e}ntur. Nam acies in eo nostrae videtur auctoritatis praescindi, et retundi. Etenim cum omnibus regni nostri ordinibus praeficiamur et imperitemus, quare nostra iudicia ab ecclesiasticis rescinduntur? Quisquis alterius retexit iudicium, illum oportet maiore esse superiorique loco. Non igitur nostra possunt iudicia foro ecclesiastico tolli, nisi nostra quoque auctoritas intelligatur ecclesiasticis iudicibus subiacere. Proinde ne talis posthac instituatur purgatio mandamus, cum non solum in eo antehac regali nostrae potestati largiter detrahebatur, verum etiam a iustitia recedebatur, quoniam nulla potest ibi purgationis defensio superesse, certum ubi crimen antegressum est.

5. Quando praemonendus sit reus ante purgationem.[5]

Si quis adversa fama fuerit, et quotidie de illo minime belli rumores increbrescant, sed tamen admodum suspi[36b]ciosi, et is tum suae famae negligens fuerit, episcopus terrorem ecclesiasticarum poenarum obiiciens, omnibus denuntiet, qui quicquam scire videntur, ut id proferant. Et si nullus hac ratione potest accusator elici, personam infamatam ipse primum separatim ad officium adhortetur; si non ita perficietur, duos aut tres testes adhibeat, quibus si non potest flecti, publice cum illo agat; ad extremum si nec ita potest ad officium duci, illum vel a munere ecclesiastico submoveat, vel abarceat ab ecclesiae ingressu, donec legitimam suam infamiam perpurgaverit, ne ulla communis in eo sit offensio ecclesiae. Si vero peccatum erit atrocius, nimirum periurii vel adulterii, commissumque iam ante peccatum dicatur, et magna fuerit in eo ecclesiae offensio, tum protinus praecisa monitorum mora, iudex illum ad defensionem vel purgationem adigere potest. Monitorum enim locum in solutiore vita, mollioreque quam convenit habitu et consuetudine, ceterisque rebus suspiciosis potius quam malis esse placet. Purgationem vero iudex praescribere potest, licet solemnes legum ritus non antegrediantur, vel certi temporis ad accusandum praeparandi, vel suspiciosae personae criminibus inquirendi.

---

[4] Cf. X, 2.1.4 (Fr, II, 240), originally a decretal of Pope Alexander III (1159-81); 1268/6-7 (PC, 754-6); L, 5.14.3, an undated statute of Archbishop John Peckham (1279-92).
[5] X, 5.34.2 (Fr, II, 870), c. 8 of the council of Agde, 506.

4. There is no ground for ecclesiastical purgation in the case of those who have been condemned by a civil court.[4]

It looks like a great insult to us that ecclesiastical persons, when they have been condemned of a capital crime by our civil laws, are sent back to the judgment of the ecclesiastical court and purged. For by doing this it appears that the sword of our authority is withdrawn and blunted. For when we have deliberated and reached a decision according to all the laws of our kingdom, why are our judgments cancelled by the ecclesiastical courts? Someone who has overturned the judgment of another must be greater than he and in a higher position. Therefore our judgments cannot be cancelled by an ecclesiastical court without giving the impression that our authority is also subject to ecclesiastical judges. Hence we order that no such purgation shall be held in the future, since not only was our royal power largely annulled by this procedure in the past, but also it was unjust, since no defence of purgation can overturn a clearly established crime.

5. When the accused should be forewarned before purgation.[5]

If someone has been defamed and nasty rumours about him multiply daily, yet despite that they are somewhat suspect, and the person concerned has failed to protect his reputation, the bishop, using the threat of ecclesiastical penalties, shall order everyone who appears to know something about the matter to state what he knows. And if no accuser can be identified in this way, he shall first privately exhort the defamed person to do his duty. If that does not work, he shall call on two or three witnesses, and if the accused cannot be swayed by them, he shall deal with him publicly. Finally, if all that fails to make him do his duty, he shall either remove him from his ecclesiastical post or bar him from entering the church until he has lawfully purged his infamy, so that there may be no general offence against the church on account of this. But if there is a worse sin, such as that of perjury or adultery, and it is said to have already been committed before this one, and the church has been greatly offended because of it, then after a fixed period of warning, the judge may compel him to make a defence or purgation. For there is a place for warnings in the case of behaviour which is less serious and more excusable than is the usual habit or custom, and when other things are suspect rather than evil. But the judge may prescribe purgation, as long as the solemn procedures of the laws, granting a certain time for preparing an accusation or inquiring into the crimes of the suspect person, have not already been set in motion.

6. Purgationem legitimam aliquando publica denuntiatio praecedit.[6]

Cum defensio vel purgatio personae adversa fama laborantis instituitur, iudex vel propriam eius ecclesiam, vel aliquam aliam illi maxime familiarem deligat, in qua maxima populi frequentia divinorum officiorum tempore coram omnibus proponatur, ut si quis institutae defensionis ordinem, aut cursum impedire velit, aut ullo modo se in hoc negotio interponere, loco, die et tempore constitutis se ostendat, et ibi quicquid ulla ratione velit in hac causa purgationis afferre, coram iudice rite et {*progressu iuris ex*}[37a]promat. Et licet iudex praemittendam existimet huiusmodi proclamationem, tamen is qui adversa est fama si remedium hoc valde flagitaverit, et suis impensis id procurare velit, illi concedi placet.

7. Quando suspenduntur nondum purgati.[7]

Relegatio ab ecclesia, quam suspensionem vocant, nunquam statim ante purgationem distringenda est, nisi sit immane facinus quod in suspicione est, aut ipse reus cui se defendendo supina fuerit et dissoluta negligentia.

8. Ratio purgationis.[8]

Haec formula purgationis esto. Defensor se crimen non admisisse iurato; defensoris liberatores, vel ut vulgo dicunt compurgatores, credere se verum eius iuramentum fuisse iuramento et ipsi affirmanto.

9. Quales esse debent purgatores.[9]

Purgatores omnes (ut usitatum vocabulum sumamus) optimae sint existimationis et perspectae virtutis, ne periurii cadat in illos ulla suspicio. Et qui pro aliena innocentia, praesertim suspecta, iuramento spondebunt, debent talem cum illo habuisse consuetudinem et usum, ut illius vitam et conversationem norint, praesertim a tempore quo crimen commisisse dicitur.

---

[6]X, 5.34.10 (Fr, II, 872-4), originally a decretal of Pope Innocent III, 7 May 1199; H.C., 12.8.
[7]X, 5.34.2 (Fr, II, 870), c. 8 of the council of Agde, 506.
[8]X, 5.34.5 (Fr, II, 870-1), originally a decretal of Pope Innocent III (1198-1216); H.C., 12.2.
[9]X, 5.34.7 (Fr, II, 871), originally a decretal of Pope Alexander III (1159-81); H.C., 12.3.

6. A public denunciation sometimes precedes lawful purgation.[6]

When the defence or purgation of a person suffering from a hostile reputation is instituted, the judge shall appoint that person's church, or another one which is very familiar to him, in which, at the time of divine service, when the greatest number of people is present, the matter shall be laid before them all, so that if anyone wishes to hinder the order or course of the instituted defence, or in any way intervene in the matter, he shall appear at the set place, day and time, and there present whatever he wishes to allege in this cause of purgation before the judge, duly and according to law. And even if the judge thinks that the said presentation should be accepted, nevertheless the victim of the hostile reputation shall be granted the right of reply if he demands it and is prepared to pay for it out of his own pocket.

7. When those who have not yet been purged are suspended.[7]

Relegation from the church, which is called suspension, is never to be carried out immediately before purgation, unless there is some enormous crime which is under suspicion, or the accused himself is too weak and spineless to bother defending himself.

8. The procedure for purgation.[8]

The formula for purgation shall be this. The defendant shall swear that he has not committed the crime, and those who have come to set him free, who are popularly known as compurgators, shall also affirm on oath that they believe that his oath is true.

9. The qualifications of purgators.[9]

All purgators (to use the common word) must be of the highest reputation and of transparent virtue, lest any suspicion of perjury fall on them. And those who swear an oath on behalf of someone else's innocence, especially when doubt has been cast on it, must have had such dealings with, and experience of, that person, that they know his life and behaviour, especially from the time at which the crime is said to have been committed.

10. Numerus purgantium.[10]

Numerus purgatorum iudicis arbitratu constituetur, hoc tamen retento, quod celebrior persona pluribus, obscurior paucioribus utetur integritatis suae testibus. Et episcopus aliquos episcopos et presbyter presbyteros et similiter omnis defensor ex suo ordine pro se [37b] testem adferat.

11. Nemo debet cogi ad alium purgandum.[11]

Quamquam homines in certis causis ad testimonium dicendum inviti possunt trahi, tamen neminem volumus ad purgandum aliquem nolentem trudi.

12. Quando possit ab indicta purgatione appellari.[12]

Cum episcopus plures congregari iubet purgantes liberatores, quam aequitas aut defensoris conditio fert, potest appellatione iudicis acerbitatem declinare.

13. Quomodo purgandi sint infames.[13]

Qui superiorum criminum convicti iure fuerint infames effecti, quoniam ad iurandum adhiberi non possunt, iuramento non liberabuntur, sed illa ratione quae iudici videbitur optima.

14. Rite purgatus per iudicem famae bonae restituatur.[14]

Cum is qui reus sit criminis factus legitime se liberaverit, iudex debet illum integrum et innocentem publice pronuntiare, communem ut hominum improborum et licentiosam dicacitatem auctoritate solemnis sententiae refutet. Itaque cum persona quae rea fuit iudicio pl{a/e}ne satisfecerit, diploma iudex conficiat muneris sui signo conclusum, in quo satisfactio reae personae continebitur. Et cum reus hoc postulaverit, iudex primo quoque commodo tempore tradendum curet.

---

[10]Cf. X, 5.34.10 (Fr, II, 872-4), originally a decretal of Pope Innocent III, 7 May 1199; H.C., 12.4.
[11]Panormitanus on X, 2.21.8.
[12]Panormitanus on X, 5.34.7.
[13]Cf. L, 5.14.3, an undatable canon of Archbishop John Peckham (1279-92); H.C., 12.6.
[14]Cf. L, 5.5.1, originally cc. 1-2 of the council of Oxford, 1407; H.C., 12.5.

10. The number of purgators.[10]

The number of purgators shall be determined at the discretion of the judge, but on the understanding that a better-known person will require more, and a lesser-known person fewer, witnesses of his integrity. And a bishop shall present on his behalf some bishops, a presbyter presbyters, and likewise any defender a witness who belongs to his own order.

11. No one must be forced to purge another person.[11]

Although there are certain causes in which people may be forced to give testimony against their will, nevertheless, we do not want anyone to be obliged to purge someone else unwillingly.

12. When it is possible to appeal against an indicted purgation.[12]

When a bishop orders more purgators to assemble than fairness or the social standing of the defendant warrants, the latter may reject the judge's severity by appealing.

13. How those defamed are to be purged.[13]

Since those who have been convicted of earlier crimes have effectively been defamed by law, they cannot be brought to swear and shall not be set free on oath, but rather in a way which shall seem best to the judge.

14. Someone duly purged shall be restored to good repute by the judge.[14]

When someone who has been accused of a crime has freed himself by lawful means, the judge must publicly pronounce him to be honest and innocent, so as to counter the common and licentious gossip of dishonest men with the authority of a solemn sentence. Therefore, when the person who has been accused has {*clearly* **fully**} satisfied the court, the judge shall prepare a document, sealed with the seal of his office, in which the satisfaction made by the accused person shall be recorded. And when the accused asks for it, the judge shall ensure that it is given to him at the first convenient opportunity.

[38a] 15. Occasiones criminum prohibendae sunt.[15]

Quoniam ad maxima scelera gradibus quibusdam ascenditur, iudex hos ipsos gradus incidat, et causas amputet, quibus flagitia proficisci solent. Nominatim qui suspectus est adulterii, iudex dom{o/**us**} omni{**s**} usu interdicat, qu{*ae*/**o**} possit cum huiusmodi femina intercedere; quod iudicis mandatum si neglectum fuerit, poenam a se prius institutam sine ullo favore contemptori infligat.

16. Poena se non rite purgandis.[16]

Si defensor purgationem omnibus partibus implere non possit, convictus existimetur eius criminis cuius ante quaestio fuit.

17. Poenarum varietas.[17]

Cum reus accusatione convincitur, illum gravis poena subsequatur, sed inquisitione si reus est evictus, nonnihil illi debet parci; et magis etiam adhuc impensiusque indulgeatur cum plene se non potuit purgare. Quamquam enim in his omnibus culpa depraehenditur, tamen ut peccatorum, ita poenarum gradus constitui debent.

18. Quantum efficiat purgatio.[18]

Qui purgationem incohatam et curtam adducit, si causa sit haeresis, non statim illum ad civiles magistratus oportet abripi, quoniam huiusmodi destitutio, praesumptio aut praeiudicium potius quam iudicium est, et non directam veritatem, sed obliquam habet probabilitatem.

[38b] 19. Defensor quando sit beneficio privandus.[19]

Si quis ex ecclesiastica secta, cum adversa fama laboret, se purgare debet, ecclesiastico beneficio non excludatur, donec defensionem instituerit. In ea vero si defecerit, tum demum illi beneficium eripi potest, si peccati magnitudo tantam poenam requirat.

---

[15]D, 81 cc. 20-33 (Fr, I, 286-9). Cf. D, 32 c. 16 (Fr, I, 121), 1268/42 (PC, 786), 1268/52 (PC, 789-91); R, 11.18.
[16]X, 5.34.10 (Fr, II, 872-4), originally a decretal of Pope Innocent III, 7 May 1199.
[17]Panormitanus on X, 5.34.10.
[18]Panormitanus on X, 5.34.10.
[19]X, 5.34.10 (Fr, II, 872-4), originally a decretal of Pope Innocent III, 7 May 1199.

15. Opportunities for crimes are to be prevented.[15]

Since major crimes are the end result of taking one small step at a time, the judge shall anticipate those steps and remove the causes which normally lead to greater wrongdoing. In particular, the judge shall ban anyone suspected of adultery from any house where he might have intercourse with such a woman, and if the decree of the judge is ignored, he shall inflict the penalty which he would have imposed on the man showing contempt, without any favour.

16. The penalty for those who do not duly purge themselves.[16]

If a defendant cannot fulfill all the requirements for his purgation, he shall be regarded as convicted of the crime in question.

17. The variety of penalties.[17]

When the accused is convicted by accusation, a severe penalty shall follow, but if the accused is convicted by inquest, the punishment shall be mitigated, and if he has been unable to purge himself completely, he shall be shown greater and even more generous indulgence. For although guilt may be found in all these things, nevertheless there are different levels of penalty, just as there are of sins.

18. How much purgation can achieve.[18]

Whoever makes an incomplete and inadequate purgation, if the cause is one of heresy, he shall not be turned over immediately to the civil magistrates, since a failure of this kind is more in the nature of a presumption or prejudice than of a judgment, and reveals not the straightforward truth but only an indirect probability.

19. When a defendant must be deprived of his benefice.[19]

When someone of the ecclesiastical order suffers from defamation and has to purge himself, he shall not be put out of his ecclesiastical benefice until he has instituted his defence. But if he fails in that, his benefice may then be taken away from him if the magnitude of the sin requires so great a penalty.

20. Iudex purgantibus se potest aliquando subvenire.[20]

Cum pauper, obscura vel ignota persona non potest satis copiose defensionem instruere, iudex et hominis et causae conditione perspecta, potest illum sublevare. Nam aut pauciores viros aut feminas iudex, si velit admitt{i/e}t, aut etiam solo rei iuramento contentus esse poterit.

21. Superstitiosas purgationes non valere.[21]

Quoniam quantum licet veritatem consectamur, illa prisca defensionis remedia non admittimus, quae ratione et probabilitate non nituntur, sed in omnes partes aeque propendent, et insontes plerumque condemnant, ac sontes absolvunt; qualia sunt singularia certamina, flammae, ferrum candens,[22] vel effervescens aqua. Nam isto modo primum Dei tentabatur omnipotentia, deinde non certitudinis haec aut veritatis indicia sed casus erant, et fortunae ludibria. Omnis igitur huiusmodi pellatur anilis et superstitiosa defensio; quam si quis posthac attulerit, arbitratu iudicis ab illo poena sumetur. Et tamen legitimam idem defensionis formulam post adhibere cogetur.

---

[20]Panormitanus on X, 5.34.10.
[21]X, 5.35.3 (Fr, II, 878), originally a decretal of Pope Honorius III (1216-27).
[22]F has 'cadens' and S has 'cardens', but 'candens' must be the correct reading.

20. A judge may sometimes come to the aid of those making purgation.[20]

When a poor, obscure or unknown person is not able to afford the expense of setting up his defence, the judge, after considering the state of the man and the cause, may come to his aid. For a judge may pardon poorer men and women if he so desires, or may also be content to accept no more than the oath of the accused.

21. Superstitious purgations are invalid.

Since we are looking for the truth as far as possible, we do not allow those primitive forms of defence which do not reflect reason or honesty, but which may go either way and more often than not, condemn the innocent and absolve the guilty. Among these are single combat, fire, burning[22] iron and boiling water. For first, God's omnipotence is tested in this way, and second, these things are not signs of certainty or truth but are accidents and hostages to fortune. Therefore, all mindless and superstitious defences of this kind are to be rejected, and if someone introduces one of them in future, he shall be penalized for doing so at the discretion of the judge. And moreover, he shall still be obliged to undergo the lawful form of defence afterwards.

[270r; 39a]   **15. DE DILAPIDATIONIBUS**

1. In propriis ecclesiis proprietarii debent vicario domum providere.[1]

Ecclesia quae certum aliquem habet ac haereditarium possessorem, si nec aedes habeat in quibus se vicarius collocare possit, nec convenientem aream in qua domus ante posita fuerit, si haereditarius possessor vel aedibus aliis, vel praediis quibuscunque fuerit instructus ad ius ecclesiae pertinentibus, vel ipsas aedes vel solum, in quo domus aedificari possit, episcopus ad vicarium auctoritate sua sevocet, providens in hoc, ut vicarius omni ex parte satis apte commodeque [270v] habit[e/**abi**]t. Et haec quidem habitatio vicarii procedat impensis haereditarii possessoris ecclesiae, ut intra triennium postquam ab episcopo admonitus fuerit perfecte extruatur. In quo si possessorem episcopus repugnare viderit, et durae tractationis causam esse crediderit, vel ecclesiae fructus ab illo d[i/**e**]stineri curet, vel poenis illum ecclesiasticis devinciat. Quod si forte nec proprius episcopus satis ipse vigilaverit, primarius episcopus, (quem metropolitanum [*dicunt* **vocant**]), hanc causam, cum ad se perferetur, cognoscet ac diiudicabit.

2. Quomodo ruinosae domus s[i/**u**]nt reficiendae.[2]

Quibus autem in paroechiis domus pastoribus [271r] aut eorum vicariis praeparatae aliquando fuerint, sed priorum ministrorum vel negligentia vel nuditate aut plane ruerint ad terram, aut diuturnitate temporis [*collabi incipiant, nec quicquam in priorum fortunis* **non**] sit reliquum quo refici possint, episcopus septimam annui portionem emolumenti apud sequestros faciet seponi, donec aut domus [39b] nova omnibus ministri necessitatibus apta denuo construatur, aut ruinosae aedes sartetectae fiant.

---

[1]C. 22 of Winchester I, 1224 (PC, 129); c. 25 of Winchester II, *c.* 1247 (PC, 407); c. 9 of Salisbury III, *c.* 1228-56 (PC, 513). Cf. 1237/10 (PC, 249), 1237/13 (PC, 251); 1268/10 (PC, 759-61).
[2]1268/17 (PC, 766-7); H.C., 30.1. The sequestration of one seventh of the annual income was considerably less than the one fifth enjoined by earlier royal injunctions, cf. 1536/10 (*D.E.R.*, 178) and 1547/16 (*D.E.R.*, 252) and later repeated in 1559/13 (*D.E.R.*, 338).

15. OF DILAPIDATIONS

1. In their own churches, proprietors must provide a house for the vicar.[1]

If a church which has a private and hereditary owner does not have a house in which the vicar may dwell, nor a convenient plot of land on which a house was previously located, and if the hereditary owner has been provided either with another house, or with lands which belong to the jurisdiction of the church, the bishop shall on his own authority set aside either that house or the land on which a house may be built, for the vicar's use, thereby providing that the vicar will have an adequate, suitable and comfortable place to live. And the vicar's dwelling shall be paid for by the hereditary owner of the church, so that within three years after he has been advised by the bishop, it may be fully built. If the bishop sees that the owner is reluctant to do this, and believes that he is the cause of difficulties, he shall either ensure that the fruits of the church are taken away from him, or he shall compel him to do so by ecclesiastical penalties. And if perchance the local bishop is not sufficiently vigilant in this matter, the superior bishop (who is called the metropolitan), shall hear and determine the cause when it is brought to him.

2. How ruined houses are to be repaired.[2]

And in those parishes in which houses were at one time built for the rectors or their vicars, but which because of the negligence or the poverty of previous ministers have either fallen down completely or after a great length of time [*are beginning to collapse, and*] there is nothing left [*from the estates of earlier incumbents*] with which they might be repaired, the bishop shall have the seventh part of the annual income set aside by sequestration, until either a new house suitable for all the needs of the minister is built from scratch, or the ruined building is restored.

3. Qui silvas ecclesiarum vastant quomodo corrigendi s[*i*/**u**]nt.[3]

Si quis arbores, arbusta, lucos, nemora, silvas, saltus, fruticeta, vel huiusmodi quascunque lignorum opportunitates ullius ad se beneficii ecclesiastici iure pertinentes, [271v] licentiosius quam necessitas tulerit sine consensu proprii [*ditionis*] illius [**ditionis**] episcopi vendiderit, succiderit, amputarit, asportarit, aut quocunque modo corruperit et vastarit, pretium is universum, et aestimationem omnium huiusmodi lignorum distractorum et eversorum in cistam pauperum attributam plene conferet. Praeterea tantum in hac re successori satisfaciet, quantum episcopus aequum esse putabit; et prorsus talis erit huius causae ratio qualis prius aedificiorum reficiendorum a nobis posita est.

4. De illis qui morientes aedificia relinquunt ruinosa aut eversa.[4]

Itidem qui praesens est ecclesiae praefectus cum migrat e vita, si superiorem templi partem quam cancellam [272r] vocant, aut alias quascunque domos ad ecclesiae ius spectantes, ruinosas aut vitiosas reliquerit, aut prorsus eversas, successori licebit vel haeredes vel bonorum administratores quocunque nomine censeantur, propter damna [*talium*] ruinarum et vitiorum iure *convincere* convenire. Spatium tamen possessionis erit considerandum, quod si totum annum non impleverit, nihil postulabitur; quantum autem anno fuerit amplius, ad id aequitas iudicis ecclesiastici satisfaciendi rationem accommodabit. Denique si quicquam in talium aedificiorum impensas quacunque ratione collatum fuerit, et id nunquam in eo mi[40a]nister collocarit, haeredes vel administratores annumerent successori, ut is in tam bona causa*m* superioris fidem liberare possit.

[272v] 5. Ruinae aedificiorum ad ecclesias cathedrales, collegia, et xenodochia pertinentium, quomodo resarciendae sunt.[5]

Eadem quoque sit lex de reaedificandis et reparandis domibus quae assignantur illis ecclesiarum beneficiariis, quos vulgo decanos, praebendarios, magistros collegiorum aut hospitalium vocant, sive in urbibus sive ruri sitae fuerint. Illos tamen ad aedificia ruri sita, vel denuo extruenda vel reficienda astringi nolumus, quae citra viginti recentissimos annos inhabitata non fuerint.

---

[3]This was not explicitly stated in earlier legislation, but it follows naturally from it. See L, 3.16.3, c. 5 of Archbishop John Stratford's council, 1342; X, 3.13.6 (Fr, II, 513-14), originally a decretal of Pope Symmachus I at a Roman council in 501 and 503; X, 3.13.11 (Fr, II, 515-16), originally a decretal of Pope Innocent III, 29 March 1206; X, 3.13.12 (Fr, II, 516), c. 44 of Lateran IV, 1215 (*C.O.D.*, 254).
[4]L, 3.27.1, c. 68 of Richard Poore's canons for Salisbury, *c.* 1217-19; H.C., 30.2.
[5]*Ibid.*

3. How those who lay waste the woods of the church are to be corrected.[3]

If anyone shall sell, cut down, remove, disperse or in any way destroy or lay waste, to an extent greater than what need requires, the trees, bushes, groves, copses, forests, woods, orchards or such kinds of trees of any ecclesiastical benefice belonging to him by law, without the consent of his local bishop, he shall pay the full price and the estimated value of all such trees removed and destroyed into the poor box. Moreover, he shall pay his successor such compensation for this as his bishop shall think fair, and after that the matter shall be handled in the same way as we have provided above for the repair of buildings.

4. Of those who die leaving ruined or dilapidated buildings.[4]

Likewise, when the present incumbent of a church departs this life, if he leaves the upper part of the sanctuary, which is called the chancel, or any other buildings subject to the jurisdiction of the church, ruined, damaged, or even destroyed, it shall be lawful for his successor to *convict* call either the heirs or the executors of his goods, whatever they may be called, to pay compensation for [*such*] ruins and damages. Nevertheless, the length of ownership must be taken into consideration, so that if it was less than a full year, nothing may be claimed, but to the extent that it was longer than a year, the ecclesiastical judge shall apportion a satisfactory sum according to what he considers fair. Finally, if anything has been collected in any way for the expenses of such buildings, and the minister has never assigned any of it to that purpose, the heirs or administrators shall pay the sum over to the successor, so that he may fulfill the obligation of his predecessor in so good a cause.

5. How the ruins of buildings belonging to cathedral churches, colleges and hospices are to be repaired.[5]

There shall also be the same law for the rebuilding and repairing of houses which are assigned to those beneficed clergy who are commonly called deans, prebendaries, masters of colleges or boarding schools, whether they are situated in towns or in the country. But with respect to buildings situated in the country, we do not want those which have not been inhabited within the past twenty years to be rebuilt or repaired.

[273v; 40a] 16. DE ALIENATIONE ET ELOCATIONE BONORUM ECCLESIASTICORUM

1. Nihil alienari posse ab ecclesia sine consensu ordinarii et patroni.[1]

Qui gubernandis ecclesiis admoniti sunt, nec domos, nec agros, nec ullas ecclesiarum possessiones aut fructus vendent, permutabunt, donabunt, aut quocunque genere contractus vel conventionis in omne tempus abalienabunt, nisi suum patronus et episcopus consensum interposuerint.

2. Elocatio quemadmodum fieri debeat.[2]

Omnis emolumentorum ecclesiasticorum locatio consistat intra decem annos, vel ultra decennium non excur[40b]rat, nec successorum tempus occupet. [274r] Nam experientia saepissime tales locationes coarguit, quod successorum in illis ius aperte violatur ab his qui priores in illo munere versati sunt, nisi forte necessaria fuit vel utilis locandi causa propter aedium ruinas aut agrorum sterilitatem, et conductores se obligaverint ad domos reficiendas et agros excolendos, et interim integrum ecclesiae pendant annuum vectigal quod superioribus temporibus repraesentari solebat. Sed nec ista quidem ullo modo procedant, nisi patronus in illis et episcopus consenserint.

3. Quattuor alienationis causae.[3]

Nolumus ad alienationem bonorum ecclesiasticorum descendi, nisi subiect[is/a ex quattuor causa/is sit aliqua **causa**] [274v] quae necessitatem alienationis afferat. Prima tum intelligetur, cum ecclesia sic obruitur aere alieno, legitimis ut vectigalibus annuis se ipsa[m] sustentare non possit; deinde, si grandis et evidens utilitas invitabit, statum [*enim* **annuum**] ecclesiarum meliorem fieri facile patimur. Pietatis etiam accedit tertia causa liberandorum e[x/t] servitute Christianorum populorum cum in potestatem hostium nostrae religionis inciderint.[4] Quarta ponatur [*et*] alienationis et ultima ratio, cum aliquid desecatur

---

[1]*Nov.* 7, 67.4, 120; *Liber constitutionum novellarum* 7, 116.
[2]Cf. X, 3.13.7 (Fr, II, 514), originally a decretal of Pope Alexander III (1159-81); 28 Henry VIII, c. 11, 1536 (*S.R.*, III, 666-7).
[3]*Nov.*, 7.2, 6.
[4]*Nov.*, 120.9.

16. OF ALIENATING OR LETTING CHURCH PROPERTY

1. Nothing may be alienated from the church without the consent of the bishop and patron.[1]

Those who have been *warned* appointed to run churches shall not sell, exchange, give or alienate either the houses, the fields or any possessions or fruits of the churches by any form of contract or agreement at any time, unless the patron and the bishop have given their consent.

2. How letting should take place.[2]

Any let of ecclesiastical revenues shall be for a period not longer than ten years, and shall not extend beyond a decade nor into the time of successors. For very often experience shows that such lets are a bad idea, because through them the right of successors is openly violated by those who previously held that office, unless by chance there was a necessary or advantageous reason for letting, *e.g.* because of the ruins of the buildings or the infertility of the fields, and the renters have committed themselves to repair the houses and cultivate the fields, and meanwhile they are paying the full annual assessment to the church which was regularly offered in earlier times. But they shall not proceed even with this in any way, unless the patron and the bishop agree to it.

3. Four reasons for alienation.[3]

We do not want anyone to resort to the alienation of church property except for one [**cause** *of the four causes*] which makes alienation necessary. The first of these shall be understood as occurring when a church is so ruined by debt that it cannot sustain itself on its lawful annual income. The second is if a great and obvious advantage shall suggest it, [*for*] we allow that the [**annual**] state of the church shall be easily improved thereby. The third cause is that of the godliness of freeing Christian people from slavery when they have fallen into the power of the enemies of our religion. The fourth and final reason for alienation occurs

huiusmodi in quo premebatur ecclesia potius quam adiuvabatur. Neque tamen ex his ipsis causis alienationem ecclesiae bonorum sequi placet, nisi sententiam episcopus suam et patronus ad [e/**caus**]am accommodaverint.

[275r] 4. Poena contra leges alienantium.[5]

Quoties autem permutatio, locatio, vel alienatio bonorum ecclesiae secus instituitur quam his legibus nostris constitutum est, primum ipsas conventiones universas ad nihilum recidere volumus, deinde clericos ipsos hu[41a]iusmodi conventionum ulla ratione participes sacerdotiis [*suis*] excludi placet.

---

[5]L, 3.8.1, c. 36 of the council of Oxford, 1222.

when by it something is cut off which was harming the church rather than helping it. Nevertheless, even in these cases alienation of the goods of the church shall not take place unless the bishop and patron express a favourable opinion of [*it* **the cause**].

4. The punishment of those who alienate illegally.[4]

And whenever an exchange, let or alienation of the goods of the church takes place in a way which is contrary to these our laws, it is our will first that all those agreements shall be rendered null and void, and also that those clergy who in any way took part in those agreements shall be deprived of [*their*] livings.

[276v; 41a]   **17. DE ELECTIONE**

1.[1]

Electionum vel in principibus ecclesiis quas cathedrales vocant, vel in collegiis
et scholasticorum coetibus institutorum prorsus eadem formula sit, quae
domesticis singulorum collegiorum institutis sancita est, nisi forte quicquam [*in*]
illis reperiatur, quod reformatae in hoc regno nostro religioni, aut his nostris
constitutionibus ecclesiasticis repugnet.

---

[1]X, 1.6.3 (Fr, II, 49), originally a decretal of Pope Gregory III (731-41).

17. OF AN ELECTION

1.[1]

From henceforth there shall be the same pattern of elections, whether in main churches which are called cathedrals, or in colleges and societies of academic scholars, as has been authorized in the internal statutes of the individual colleges, unless by chance there is something found in them which is repugnant to the reformed religion in this our kingdom, or to these our ecclesiastical constitutions.

[68r; 41a] 18. DE BENEFICIIS ECCLESIASTICIS SINE DIMINUTIONE CONFERENDIS

1. *Puniendos esse mercatores* **Nullae debent esse mercaturae** ecclesiasticorum munerum.[1]

Frustra legum est omnis praestantia, nisi flagitiosa quorundam et immanis avaritia, (iuris salubritatem ad sua commoda detorquentium), ce*ter*tis poenarum vinculis cohibeatur. Etenim cum hoc a maioribus nostris praeclare constitutum fuerit, *ut* ut ecclesiarum ministris uberes, et illorum conditioni convenientes fructus suppeditarentur, ex illis locis, ad quorum moderationem appositi fuer[*u*/i]nt, recentioribus hisce temporibus multorum tanta cupiditas patronorum invenitur, opes un[41b]dique colligendi, beneficiis ut ex suis cum illa collocant, aliquam vel ad se vel ad suos particulam sevocent.

2. Quotuplex sit mercatura munerum ecclesiasticorum.[2]

Quidam fructus beneficiorum ipsi colligunt universos, et eorum omnia emolumenta vel sibi vel suis ex pacto reservant{*ur*}, **ecclesiae** ministris pensiones certas quasdam aspergentes, et illas *etiam* multo minores quam ratio beneficiorum postulat; alii, paulo mitius agentes, solam huiusmodi terram sibi pacto seponunt, quae censeri potest et vulgo gleba dicitur; nonnulli [68v] domos accipiunt et aedificia quae solebant ministris concedi; reliqui paene omnes a misellis ministris vel annuam pensionem comportant, vel quas ipsa ratione [*terrarum*] debent decimas educunt, vel aliquam cert[*e*/is] beneficiis illorum plagam vel apertam vel occultam iniiciunt, usque adeo propemodum, ut nulli sint qui beneficia integra et illibata cum universo iure commodorum omnium gratis in ministros ecclesiarum conferant.

---

[1]X, 3.38.23 (Fr, II, 616-17), originally a decretal of Pope Lucius III (1181-5).
[2]Whole title lined out in the MS, but Cranmer wrote 'stet' in the margin. X, 3.12.1 (Fr, II, 509-12), originally a decretal of Pope Innocent III, 23 September 1198. Cf. also c. 15 of Lateran III, 1179 (*C.O.D.*, 219).

18. OF CONFERRING ECCLESIASTICAL BENEFICES WITHOUT LOSS

1. *Traders* **There must be no trade** in ecclesiastical offices *are to be punished.*[1]

Every statement of the laws is in vain, unless the scandalous and excessive greed of some people (who twist the good intentions of the law to suit themselves), is restrained by *other* **certain** bonds of penalties. For since it was most clearly determined by our ancestors that revenues and fruits sufficient to maintain their status should be supplied to the ministers of churches from those places to whose government they have been appointed, in these more recent times such great greed on the part of many patrons has appeared that they amass wealth from wherever they can, so that when they appoint to benefices they reserve a part of the revenue either for themselves or for their dependants.

2. The many forms which trade in ecclesiastical offices takes.[2]

Some people collect the fruits of their benefices themselves and reserve all their revenues either for themselves or by covenant for their dependants, setting aside certain fixed stipends for the ministers **of the church**, which *moreover* are much smaller than the size of the benefices would suggest. Others, somewhat more generous, reserve for themselves by covenant only that land which can be valued and is commonly called glebe. Some take over houses and buildings which were normally granted to ministers, while almost all the others either collect an annual pension from their unfortunate ministers, or else deduct the tithes which they owe according to the ratable value [*of the lands*], or add some [*particular*] catch, either open or secret, to their [**particular**] benefices, to such an extent that there are none who confer benefices whole and unencumbered, with complete right to free enjoyment of all their privileges, on the ministers of the churches.

3. Pacta in muneribus sacris interposita non valere.[3]

Superiorum igitur difficultatum ut aliqua possit esse levatio, volumus et iubemus ut sive beneficia, sive quaecunque sint ali*qu*ae dignitates ecclesiasticae, gratis condonentur, nec quicquam in illis sit ulla ratione praecisum; et quicquid [*u*/i]llo modo pactum aut conventum fuerit inter patronos ipsos, et illos quorum futura beneficia vel dignitates sunt, sive sit inter illos solos actum, sive per alios irrepserit, utrinque suam ad id operam interponentes, omnia huiusmodi pacta et conventa vel ab ipsis vel ab aliis, illorum respectu, quacunque ratione vel iam instituta, vel quae posthac instituentur, prae[42a]sentis auctoritate legis tolli praecipimus et ad nihilum recidere.

[69r] 4. Inquisitio pactorum qualis esse debeat.[4]

Placet etiam quoties aliquis ordinari {*o*/**us**} se repraesentat, ut priusquam ab illo fuerit ad ullam dignitatem ecclesiasticam admissus, in illum ordinarius inquirat, et quant[u/**a**]m potest odoretur et pervestiget, an ulla fuerint pacta vel conventa huiusmodi qualia prius posita sunt, et in illo volumus ab ordinario requiri iuramentum eius, qui admitti postulat et non eius solum, sed quorumcunque aliorum quos aliquid in hoc negotio credit intelligere, ne[*c*] solis iuramentis ordinarius sed aliis omnibus viis rectis et legitimis veritatem hac in re persequatur.

5. Ordinarius ex probabilibus coniecturis purgationem iudicet.[5]

Cum ordinarius ad plenam et perfectam probationem [*iniu*/**mini**strorum] pactorum pervenire non potest, et tamen ex negotii progressu vel ipse per se probabiliter sus*ci*picatur illa subesse, vel id ex credibilibus aliorum sermonibus coniectat, personam se offerentem non admittat, donec canonum praescriptis se rite perpurgaverit.

---

[3]Whole title lined out in the MS, but Cranmer wrote 'stet' in the margin. X, 1.35.4 (Fr, II, 204-5), originally a decretal of Pope Alexander III (1159-81); X, 1.35.6 (Fr, II, 205), originally a decretal of Pope Alexander III.
[4]L, 2.6.1, c. 23 of the council of Oxford, 1222; 1268/33 (PC, 780); 1547/31 (*D.E.R.*, 256).
[5]X, 5.34.5 (Fr, II, 870-1), originally a decretal of Pope Innocent I (401-17); X, 5.34.12 (Fr, II, 874), originally a decretal of Pope Innocent III, 7 July 1206.

3. Covenants linked to sacred offices are invalid.[3]

Therefore, in order that there may be some alleviation of the above-mentioned difficulties, we desire and command that benefices and any other ecclesiastical dignities, whatever they may be, shall be granted free of charge, nor shall any condition be in any way attached to it, and we decree that whatever may have been agreed or decided between the patrons themselves and those whose future benefices and dignities they are, whether this has been done only between them or whether it has crept in through third parties who have contributed their labour to it, all covenants and agreements of this kind which have in any way whatsoever been made or which shall afterwards be made by them or by others concerning the benefices, shall be annulled by the authority of the present law and made void.

4. What the investigation of pacts should consist of.[4]

It is also fitting, every time some{*one* **ordinary**} presents himself {*to the ordinary*}, that before the ordinary appoints him to any ecclesiastical dignity, he shall inquire of him, and check out as far as possible and thoroughly investigate whether there have been any covenants or agreements of the kind which have been mentioned above, and we desire that in this matter an oath should be required by the ordinary from the one who seeks to be appointed, and not only from him, but from any others whom he believes have some knowledge of the business, nor should the ordinary pursue the truth in this matter by oaths alone, but by all other right and lawful means.

5. The ordinary shall assign purgation on the basis of informed guesswork.[5]

When the ordinary cannot arrive at a full and perfect proof that there have been [*unjust*] covenants [**between the ministers**], but in the course of the business he has either *picked up* **suspected** that there probably were, or has heard it from the credible reports of others, he shall not appoint the person offering himself until the latter has duly purged himself according to the precepts of the canons.

6. Poena paciscentium qualis sit.[6]

Ordinarius si certo cognoverit ulla ratione quod [69v] quisquam vel beneficium vel quamcunque dignitatem ecclesiasticam iniquis pollicitiationibus redemerit, primum evocabit ad se tam patronum aut patroni vicarium, quam ipsum qui vel beneficio vel dignitate sit *affectus* **donatus** ecclesiastica. Deinde, cum illorum mercaturam manifestis argumentis coarguerit et convicerit, personam *affectam* **donatam** beneficio vel [42b] dignitate statim de loco [*d*]eiiciat ad quem deviis et perversis itineribus obrepserat, quoniam cum simoniae labem in se conceperit, in sacris rebus pretium interponens, non solum praesente conditione per scelus occupata carere debet, sed etiam nullius ex tempore illo beneficii vel dignitatis vel muneris ecclesiastici particeps erit.

[6]X, 5.3.11 (Fr, II, 752), originally a decretal of Pope Alexander III.

6. What the penalty shall be for those who make covenants.[6]

If the ordinary somehow knows for certain that someone has purchased a benefice or particular ecclesiastical dignity by unlawful promises, he shall first summon both the patron or the patron's deputy, as well as the man who has been *appointed to* **granted** the benefice or ecclesiastical dignity. Then when he has exposed and condemned their trading by clear arguments, he shall immediately deprive the person *appointed to* **granted** the benefice or dignity of the post into which he has crawled by devious and dishonest means, since because he has conceived the sin of simony in his mind and put a price on sacred things, he ought not only to forfeit the current position which he has acquired by deceit, but also from henceforth to be made ineligible for any benefice, dignity or ecclesiastical office.

[70r; 42b]   **19. DE DIVINIS OFFICIIS**[1]

1. De temporibus divinorum officiorum in cathedralibus ecclesiis et collegiis celebrandorum.[2]

In principialibus ecclesiis quas cathedrales vocant, et *de temporibus divinorum officiorum in cathedralibus ecclesiis et collegiis celebratorum et* in collegiis, divina volumus officia quotidie peragi, quemadmodum ratio dierum postulabit, vel profestorum vel festorum. Quapropter antemeridiano quopiam convenienti tempore preces quas appellant matutinas recitari placet, appositis etiam illis quae pro communionis officio praescripta sunt. Et intercurrat in singulis diebus Mercurii et Veneris illa solemnis supplicatio, quae litania nominata est. Similiter tempore pomeridiano vespertinae preces adhibeantur.

2. Qui divinis officiis interesse debean*tur*.[3]

Omnes quos canonicos vocant et clericos, qui quidem ecclesiarum impensis sustentantur, ad statas preces conveniant, tam matutini quam pomeridiani temporis, et illis in die*bus* intersint, nisi iustam absentiae possin*et* excusationem [43a] afferre. Ceteri vero si non comparuerint, arbitratu decanorum, **vel illis absentibus suorum vicariorum**, certa pecuniae summa plectantur, [70v] sed tamen diebus profestis illorum sane studiis parcimus, qui doctrinae causa se collocaverunt in academiarum collegiis, quos tamen et ipsos in omnibus feriis universos in sacris officiis adesse praecipimus, nisi ob contionandi munus abfuerint.

---

[1] In the MS the original title was: 'De divinorum officiorum *celebratione* **celebratae**.' The alteration was made by Cranmer, but (surprisingly) it is ungrammatical and was replaced at some subsequent stage.
[2] A marginal note in the MS in Foxe's hand reads: 'Animadversio adhibenda' (either 'a penalty to be added' or 'further attention to be given'). The second meaning would tie in with remarks made by Foxe towards the end of his preface, about R, 19.16. Cf. D, 12 c. 14 (Fr, I, 31), c. 1 of the council of Braga, 561. Cf. X, 3.41.1 (Fr, II, 635), c. 9 of the council of Agde, 506.
[3] D, 91 cc. 1-2 (Fr, I, 316); D, 92 c. 9 (Fr, I, 319). Cf. X, 3.4.7 (Fr, II, 461), originally a decretal of Pope Alexander III (1159-81); X, 3.5.32 (Fr, II, 479), originally a decretal of Pope Honorius III (1216-27).

19. OF THE SERVICES OF THE CHURCH[1]

1. Of the times of celebration of divine services in cathedral churches and colleges.[2]

In main churches which are called cathedrals, and *at the times of celebration of divine services in cathedral churches and colleges, and* in colleges, it is our will that divine services shall be held daily, as the calendar of feast days and their eves shall require. Thus it is fitting that in the morning what are called 'morning prayers' shall be said at some convenient time, along with those which are appointed for the office of communion. And every Wednesday and Friday that solemn supplication which is called the litany shall be added. Likewise in the afternoon the evening prayers shall be said.

2. Who ought to be present at the divine services.[3]

All those who are called canons and clergy, who are maintained at the expense of the churches, shall come together for the stated prayers, both in the morning and in the evening, and shall be present *on those days* **at them daily**, unless they can offer a legitimate excuse for being absent. But if they do not appear they shall be fined a certain sum of money at the discretion of the deans, **or in their absence of their deputies**, but on the eves of feasts we are happy to excuse those who have gone to dwell in the colleges of the universities in order to learn on the ground of their studies. But we order them all to be present at the sacred services on normal weekdays, unless they are away because of a preaching engagement.

3. De sacra communione administranda in dominicis et festis diebus.[4]

Diebus dominicis et festis ecclesiarum quas cathedrales vocant, hunc in divinis officiis *esse* ordinem esse iubemus, ut absolutis precibus matutinis, et decursa supplicatione quam appellant litaniam, communio succedat; in qua facilius ut procedi possit, in nomine Dei cohortamur, et per eius gloriam vehementer obtestamur, *ut* primum episcopus ipse si fieri potest ut adsit,[5] deinde decanus et archidiaconus, cum ipsis canonicis et reliquis omnibus clericis, qui participes sunt bonorum illius ecclesiae, pariter ad communionem cum ministro [*ut*] se congregent, tum ut exemplo suo ceteros ad idem officium invitent, tum ut [**in**] hac nota sciri possi*n*t, quod ipsi viva veraque sint Christi et ecclesiae membra.

[71r] 4. De sacra**rum** *communione* **contionum** tempore.[6]

Contiones autem in his ecclesiis antemeridian[a/i]s sane omnes tollimus, ne quisquam illarum occasione legitime desit suae ecclesiae; pomeridiana/**i** vero temporis hora secunda contionibus usque ad *quartam* **tertiam** serviat, et statim ad vespertinas preces descendatur.

5. De sacrarum lectionum pronuntiatione, et psalmorum cantu.[7]

In divinis capitibus recitandis, et psalmis conci*o*nendis, ministri et clerici diligenter hoc cogitare debent, non so[43b]lum a se Deum laudari oportere, sed alios etiam hortatu et exemplo et observatione illorum ad eundem cultum adducendos esse. Quapropter partite voces et distin/c/te pronuntient, et cantus sit illorum clarus et aptus, ut ad auditorum omnia sensum et intelligentiam p[*er*/**ro**]veniant. Itaque vibratam illam et operosam musicam, quae figurata dicitur, auferri placet, quae sic in multitudinis auribus tumultuatur, ut saepe linguam non possit ipsam loquent[*iu*/**e**]m intelligere. Tum auditores etiam ipsi sint in opere simul cum clericis et ministris cert*i*/**as** divinorum officiorum particulas canentes, in quibus Psalmi primum erunt, annumerab*un*/**itur** fidei symbolum, et 'Gloria in excelsis', decem solemnia [*Dei*] praecepta, [71v] ceteraque huiusmodi praecipua religionis capita, quae maximum in communi fide nostra pondus habent; his enim piis divini cultus exercitationibus et invitamentis populus se ips[*e*/**um**] eriget, ac sensum quendam habebit orandi; quorum si nullae nisi auscultandi partes sint, ita friget et iacet mens, ut nullam de rebus divinis vehementem et seriam cogitationem suscipere possit.

---

[4]L, 3.23.4, c. 1 of the council of Lambeth, 1281; 1566/3.3.
[5]Cf. X, 3.41.12 (Fr, II, 643), originally a decretal of Pope Honorius III (1216-27).
[6]Cf. 1547/32 (*D.E.R.*, 256).
[7]D, 12 c. 13 (Fr, I, 30-1), c. 3 of the eleventh council of Toledo, 675; cf. 1547/21-2 (*D.E.R.*, 253).

3. Of the administration of holy communion on Sundays and feast days.[4]

On Sundays and feasts of those churches which are called cathedrals, we command this order to be used in the divine services, that when morning prayers are over and the supplication known as the litany has been recited, communion shall follow. In order for this to proceed more easily, we encourage in the name of God, and for his glory we strongly urge, *either* that first the bishop himself, if it is possible for him to be present,[5] and then the dean and the archdeacon, with the canons and all the remaining clergy who partake of the goods of that church, [*that they*] shall gather together along with the minister for communion, both so that by their example they may encourage others to attend the same service, and that [*by* **in**] this sign *they* **it** may be known that they themselves are living and true members of Christ and the church.

4. Of the time of holy *communion* **sermons**.[6]

And in these churches we abolish practically all morning sermons, so that no one need be lawfully absent from his own church because of them, but there shall be sermons in the afternoon from the second to the *fourth* **third** hour, followed immediately by evening prayers.

5. Of the reading of the sacred lessons and the singing of the psalms.[7]

In reciting the divine chapters and *preaching* **chanting** the psalms, the ministers and clergy must diligently consider this, that not only ought God to be praised by them, but also that by their encouragement and example and practice others ought to be attracted to attend the same worship. For this reason their voices shall enunciate clearly and distinctly, and their chanting shall be clear and appropriate, so that everything may reach the mind and intellect of the hearers. Therefore it is fitting for that complex and elaborate music which is called multipart harmony shall be discontinued, because it makes such a noise in the ears of the congregation that it is often impossible to understand what the tongue is saying. For the hearers are themselves also involved, along with the clergy and ministers, in chanting certain parts of the divine services, of which the Psalms are first, to which may be added the creed, the Gloria, the ten solemn commandments [*of God*] and other such central texts of religion which have the greatest importance for our common faith, for by these godly exercises and encouragements of divine worship, the people [*themselves*] will stir themselves and develop a feeling for prayer. But if they have no part to play other than to listen, their minds will seize up and die, with the result that they will be unable to develop any strong and serious understanding of divine things.

6. Ordo servandus in parochiis urbanis.

Eadem parochiarum in urbibus constitutarum erit omnis ratio, festis et dominicis diebus, quae prius collegiis et cathedralibus ecclesiis (ut vocant) attributa fuit, nisi quod contionandi partes antemeridiano tempore, si fieri potest, obibuntur, aut homilia saltem contionis locum [*obtinebit* **occupabit**], deinde coena Domini sumetur. Temporibus autem pomeridianis contio solis in cathedralibus ecclesiis instituetur, aut huiusmodi convenientibus locis, ad quam ab omnibus undique concurri volumus. Itaque mane parochiarum ministri suum populum commonefaciant ut ad id se praepa[44a]rent. Sed in frequentissimis et celeberrimis urbibus, (ubi magnus est parochiarum numerus et immensum inter eas intervallum, et spissae [72r] populorum catervae), pomeridianis *ibi* contionibus propter parochiarum situs et hominum abundantiam locum concedimus.

7. De coena Domini sumenda.[8]

Hoc erit omnium ecclesiarum commune, quod **nisi gravis aliqua causa [*aliud*] postulet**, coena[**m**] Domini solum in dominicis diebus et ad aliquam Domini propriam memoriam spectantibus sumetur; et nec eo quidem tempore procedi scinimus, donec legitimus numerus se obtulerit illorum qui Domini coenae participes erunt,. q/*Quoniam*[9] *illi* **Qui vero communionem** *sus*/**accepturi** sunt, pridie debent in praesentia ministri se collocare, tempus ut sumere possit ad excutiendas illorum conscientias, et cum illis ut agat, si quid ab illis improbe vel [*suspiciose* **superstitiose**] gestum fuerit, in quo ecclesiae communis aliqua fuerit offensio; deinde fidem etiam illorum exploret, ut vel inscitiam illorum corrigat, vel contumaciam terreat, vel dubitationem confirmet. Nam ad sacrosanctam Domini *coenam* mensam nemo debet assumi, cuius fides omnibus partibus perfecta non sit. Itaque si quis ex illis, qui se ad Domini mensam praepare/ant, in aliqua religionis parte vacillet, aut conscientia sauciat[*us*/**a**] sit, [72v] liberum aditum ad ministrum habeat, et ab illo consolationem et levationem aegritudinis capiat, et si plene se ministro probaverit, [*crimine*], si opus fuerit, solvatur.[10]

8. Deficiente coena Domini quid faciendum [*sit*].[11]

Si mensae Domini legitim[**u/i**]s convivarum numerus defuerit, nullam potius quam solitariam esse [*placet* **volumus**]; sed minister ingratam et impiam populi negligentiam acriter ob[44b]iurgabit, quod ab usu saluberrimi pretiosissimique

---

[8]Picked up in 1603/113.
[9]Cranmer began a new sentence here.
[10]X, 5.38.12 (Fr, II, 887-8), originally c. 21 of Lateran IV, 1215 (*C.O.D.*, 245).
[11]D, 1 *de cons.*, c. 61 (Fr, I, 1311); D, 2 *de cons.*, c. 20 (Fr, I, 1320).

6. The order to be kept in urban parishes.

The exact same pattern as was assigned above to colleges and cathedral churches (as they are called) on Sundays and feast days, shall be followed in urban parishes, except that the preaching slots will be filled in the morning, if possible, or at least a homily will [*obtain* **take**] the place of a sermon, after which the Lord's supper will be eaten. And in the afternoons preaching will take place only in cathedral churches, or in similarly convenient places, which we desire everyone from everywhere to attend. Therefore in the morning the parish ministers will exhort their people to prepare themselves for that. But in the largest and most important cities, (where there is a large number of parishes and a great distance between them, and large crowds of people), [*there*] we make room for afternoon sermons on account of the locations of the parishes and the large number of people.

7. Of eating the Lord's supper.[8]

This will be common to all the churches, that **unless some serious cause demands** [*otherwise*], the Lord's supper shall be eaten only on Sundays and on those days connected to some particular memorial of the Lord, and we do not intend that it shall proceed even at that time unless a lawful number of those who will partake of the Lord's supper shall present themselves. *Since* **And**[9] those who intend to *partake* **receive communion** must gather together the day before in the presence of the minister, so that he may spend time in examining their consciences and deal with them if they have done something dishonest or [*suspicious* **superstitious**], as a result of which the church as a whole has been offended; then too, that he might test their faith in order to correct their ignorance, frighten their insolence and confirm their doubting. For no one ought to be received at the most holy *supper* table of the Lord whose faith is not perfect in all respects. Therefore, if one of those who are preparing themselves for the Lord's table is weak in any aspect of religion, or has been wounded in his conscience, he shall have free access to the minister and receive consolation and alleviation of his sickness from him, and if he has fully proved himself to the minister, he shall be absolved [*from his crime*] if need be.[10]

8. What [*is*] to be done when there is no Lord's supper.[11]

If the lawful number of guests at the Lord's table is lacking, it is [*better* **our will**] that there be no service at all rather than one for a single communicant, but the minister shall sharply condemn the ungrateful and ungodly negligence of the people, because they have removed themselves from partaking in the most

sacramenti se removeant, nec ullo modo convenire solus ut in convivio, propter multos instituto, sedeat, sed has a Domino singulares animorum delicias ad Christianam quandam omnium communitatem piorum relictas fuisse docebit, quod si divinissimum hoc mentis pabulum immani scelere contemnant, vel horribili ingratitudine deserant, suam nullam, sed illorum maximam et flagitiosam esse improbitatem, a se quidem omnia suppeditata esse, caelestis ut iste cibus expediretur, angique se vehementer quod illorum barbarus et profanus vel stupor vel fastus epulas tam pias et necessarias distulerit, et se ab illis maximopere contendere, proximum [*ut* **ne**] diem dominicum [*n*]ullo modo praetermittendum existiment. Praeterea pauperum illis causam diligenter commendet, ut illorum necessitates sublevent.

[73r] 9. Pomeridiano tempore quid faciendum sit.[12]

Pomeridiani temporis horam primam minister explicando catechismo tribuat, et in ea re vel integram horam ponat, vel aliquid eo amplius, si videbitur, modo contioni non sit impedimento, quam in ecclesia cathedrali populus expectabit; omnino enim ill[a/**u**]m praeteriri non placet aut destitui. Catechismum pertractet vel ipse parochus, vel eius vicarius et magnam in eo diligentiam adhibeat; summam enim utilitatem et praestantem usum habet in ecclesia Dei frequens inculcatio catechismi, quem non solum a pueris edisci, sed etiam ab adolescentibus attendi volumus, ut in summa religionis erudiantur, et puerorum piam assiduitatem sua praesentia cohonesten*tur*. Catechismo concluso, statim succedat baptismus, si qui fuerint ad id praeparati pueri.

[45a] 10. Precibus vespertinis ratio collationum et disciplina succedunt.

Confectis precibus vespertinis, ad quas ab omnibus post contionem in propriis ecclesiis attendendas concursus erit, principalis minister, quem parochum vocant, et diaconus, si forte praesentes fuerint, vel absentibus illis, ministri vicarius et seniores, cum populo rationem [73v] pecuniarum ineant ad pios usus sepositarum, quomodo possi[*n*]t rectissime collocari; et ad idem tempus disciplina reservetur. Quorum enim publica fuit aliqua perversitas, quae communem in ecclesia[*e*] offensionem incurrerit, ad peccatorum [*a*/**co**]gnitionem revocentur, et eorum poenas publice dent, ut ecclesia illorum salutari correctione conformetur. Deinde minister cum senioribus nonnullis secedens consilium capiet, quomodo ceteri, quorum pravi mores esse dicuntur, et flagitiosa vita depraehenditur, primum fraterna quadam caritate iuxta Christi praescriptum in evangelio conveniantur a sobriis et frugi viris; quorum monitis si se ipsi

---

[12]Cf. 1559/44 (*D.E.R.*, 344); 1571/4.8; 1603/59.

salutary and precious sacrament, nor is it at all right that he should sit alone at a banquet which was instituted for many, but he shall teach that these singular delights of the mind have been left by the Lord to a Christian community of all the godly, and if they despise this most divine food for the mind by some great wrongdoing, or desert it out of horrible ingratitude, he has done nothing wrong, but they are guilty of a very great and disgraceful sin. For everything has been supplied by him in order to make this heavenly food available, and it pains him deeply that their barbarous and profane indifference and contempt has postponed so godly and necessary a feast, and he shall entreat them as much as he can, so that they will not think that they can miss the following Sunday for any reason. In addition, he shall [**diligently**] commend the cause of the poor to them, so that they may relieve their necessities.

9. What is to be done in the afternoon.[12]

The minister shall devote the first hour of the afternoon to explaining the catechism, and for this purpose he shall set aside a full hour or more, if necessary, as long as it is does not get in the way of the sermon in the cathedral church, which the people shall look forward to; for that must not be missed or cancelled in any way. Either the incumbent himself or his vicar shall go through the catechism and shall devote great diligence to this, for the frequent instilling of the catechism is of the greatest benefit and extraordinary usefulness in the church of God. It is our will that it shall not only be learned by children but also heard by young adults, so that they may be taught the main points of religion and by their presence do honour to the godly dedication of the children. When the catechism is finished baptism shall follow immediately, if there are children ready for it.

10. The counting of the collections and discipline follow after the evening prayers.

When the evening prayers are over, which everyone will go to attend in their own churches after the sermon, the chief minister, who is called the incumbent, and the deacon, if they happen to be present, or in their absence, the minister's vicar and the elders, with the people, shall go into an account of the money left for godly uses, as to how it may best be allocated, and discipline shall be exercised at the same time. For those who have done something wrong, which has offended the whole church, shall be called to acknowledge their sins and make public penance for them, so that the church may be edified by their salutary punishment. Then the minister shall meet privately with some of the elders to take advice as to how others, who are accused of depraved morals and whose evil life has been noted, may first of all be challenged in the Gospel by sober and virtuous men, acting in brotherly love according to the commandment of Christ, and if, after

correxerint, Deo gratia diligenter est habenda; quod si perrexerint in scelere, poenarum ea sunt acerbitate compraehendendi, quam [*in*] evangelio videmus illorum contumaciae praeparatam esse.

11. Excommunicatio quomodo sit exercenda.[13]

Cum autem excommunicationis fulmen [vibr/**urb**]andum erit, primum episcopus adeatur, et eius intelligatur sententia; [74r] qui si consenserit, et auctoritatem suam apposuerit, excommunicationis formula coram universa peragatur ecclesia, disciplinam ut in eo veterem, quantum fieri potest, [*rursus*] introducamus.

12. Ecclesiarum rusticanarum ritus.

In ecclesiis rusticanis festorum dierum matutinis temporibus homiliam in communionem intexi volumus. Po[45b]meridiano tempore descendetur ad catechismum, ad quem ab illis etiam qui grandiores sunt attendi placet, et explicationem catechismi relegamus ad vicarium. Principalis autem minister, quem parochum dicimus, post conclusum catechismum statim ad populum contionabitur, et illa finita, preces vespertinae succed[e/**a**]nt, et ad extremum adiicientur disciplinae et procurationes num*er*/**morum** publice collectorum.

13. *De* **In** sacellis sacra non sunt tractanda.[14]

V/Nolumus in sacellis, nisi singularis quaedam necessitas [74v] urserit, administrari sacramenta, nec reliquam in illis adhiberi sacrorum officiorum rationem; quoniam ita futurum esset, ut proprias homines ecclesias destitueren*tur*, et in solitudine reliquerent. Convenientissimum autem est fidei nostrae communitati, singulas oves ad proprios pastores [*suos*] sevocari, separatimque ab illis omnia pietatis et divini cultus adiumenta requiri.

14. In privatis domibus communio non celebrabitur.[15]

Communionis officium in domibus separatim non instituetur. Nam saepe fit ut in angulis privatarum aedium errores et pestilentes opiniones insusurrentur, et ita saepe numero contingit, ut sacrosancta [*Domini* **Dei**] coena, quae singularis est

---

[13]1571/4.3.
[14]*Nov.*, 57.
[15]*Nov.*, 58; D, 1 *de cons.*, c. 33 (Fr, I, 1302); *ibid.*, c. 34 (Fr, I, 1302); 1571/4.6.

their warnings, they put themselves right, God is diligently to be thanked, but if they continue in sin, they are to be treated with that severity which we see has been designed [*in* **by**] the Gospel for their contumacy.

11. How excommunication is to be exercised.[13]

And when the thunder of excommunication is to be [sounded **published**], the bishop shall first appear and be informed of the sentence, and if he consents and authorizes it, the formula of excommunication shall be read out in front of the entire church, so that by this means we may reintroduce the ancient discipline into the church as much as possible.

12. Services in country churches.

In country churches it is our will that a homily shall accompany the communion on feast days in the mornings. In the afternoon they shall proceed to catechism, which even those who are older shall attend, and we leave the explanation of the catechism to the vicar. And after catechism is over the chief minister, whom we call the incumbent, shall immediately preach to the people, and when the sermon is over, evening prayers will follow, after which shall be added the disciplinary procedures and the distribution of the money which has been publicly collected.

13. Sacred services are not to be held *from* **in** chapels.[14]

Unless some extreme urgency demands it, we do **not** want the sacraments to be administered in chapels, nor the other forms of sacred services to be held there, because then the result would be that people would desert their own churches and remain by themselves. For it is most desirable for the community of our faith that individual sheep shall be gathered to [*their*] own pastors, and that all the requisites of godliness and divine worship shall be sought from them individually.

14. Communion shall not be celebrated in private houses.[15]

The office of communion shall not be held in private houses. For it often happens that in the corners of private houses errors and pestilential opinions are whispered, and thus it very often transpires that when the most holy supper of [*the Lord* **God**], which is in itself a unique witness and sign of love, communion

per se amoris, coniunctionis, et caritatis testis et nota, cum in secessus privatarum aedium distrahatur, non solum omnem propriam amittat et insitam vim, sed etiam hominum immani scelere degeneret in litis occasionem et discordiae.

[75r; 46a] 15. Quid in aegrotis et familiis nobilium teneri debeat.[16]

Aegrotantibus tamen et vehementer debilitatis, coenam Domini flagitantibus, negari nolumus. Principibus etiam et honoratis personis, quorum affluens [*est*] in aedibus et copiosa multitudo, quibusque non licet ipsis occupatione publica distr[*i*/a]ctis in communibus ecclesiis versari, coenam dominicam dom*um*/i percipere licebit, et omnem ibi reliquam sacrorum officiorum rationem cum domestico ministro pertractare. Proviso quod hoc privilegium nullam communis ecclesiae pastoris utilitatem impediat.

16. Quae communiter in omnibus ecclesiis observanda sunt.[17]

Diligens autem imprimis cautio semper adhibeatur in ecclesiarum omni genere, tum etiam in nobilium hominum familiis, denique locis [*in*] universis in quibus sacra peraguntur officia, ne quicquam contra praescripta procedat, et formulas illius libri nostra communi lingua scripti, quem proprium et perfectum omnis divini cultus iudicem et magistrum esse iussimus. Qua in re quicunque peccaveri[n/-]t, ecclesiasticorum iudicum arbitratu poenas culpae magnitudin[i/e] pares sustinebunt*ur*. Si *quae** [75v] vero alia incurrent vacua tempora, praeter haec quae nos posuimus, divini cultus, visitatione et consolatione debilium, aegrotarum, et afflictarum personarum cuiuscunque generis, et reliquis huiusmodi caritatis muneribus ea consumantur. Ad haec accedat institutio domesticorum, disciplinae labor et opera lectionis; et omnino talis in summa festorum temporum partitio sit, ut universa meditatione tractationeque rerum sacrarum et divinarum abeant.

---

[16]Cf. L, 3.23.5, c. 18 of Archbishop John Stratford's council, 1342.
[17]Act of uniformity, 5-6 Edward VI, c. 1, 1552 (*S.R.*, IV, 130-1).

and charity, is taken away into the seclusion of private houses, it not only loses all its own innate force, but also, by the great sin of people, degenerates into an occasion for dispute and argument.

15. What ought to be allowed among the sick and in noble families.[16]

But we do not want those who are sick or seriously handicapped to be denied the Lord's supper if they desire it. Nobles also and public figures, who have a large number of people in their houses and who are [*prevented* **distracted**] by their public business from attending church with everyone else, may be allowed to receive the Lord's supper at home, and there go through all the remaining pattern of sacred offices with their domestic chaplain. Provided that this privilege shall not hinder the usefulness of the church's common pastor.

16. What must be generally observed by all churches.[17]

First of all, diligent care must always be taken in every type of church, as well as in the families of noble persons and in every place in which the sacred services are conducted, that no one shall conduct worship in a way which is contrary to the patterns and forms of that book of ours which is written in the common tongue, which we have ordered to be the proper and perfect judge and master of all divine worship. Anyone who sins in this matter shall undergo punishments at the discretion of the ecclesiastical judges which are commensurate with the seriousness of the crime. And if there are any other times available for divine worship, apart from those which we have mentioned, they shall be taken up with visiting and comforting weak, sick and afflicted persons of whatever kind, and in other such works of charity. In these may be included the education of domestic servants, the work of discipline and the labour of reading, and to sum up generally, feast times shall be so ordered that they may be spent in general meditation and the consideration of sacred and divine things.

[90r; 46b] 20. DE ECCLESIA ET MINISTRIS EIUS, ILLORUMQUE OFFICIIS[1]

[91r] 1. De aedituis.[2]

Aedituus parochia[*no*]rum alatur stipendio. Huius erit pueritiam omnem parochiae suae sibi oblatam in alphabeto et catechismo vulgari lingua [*scripto*] informare, ut pueri cognoscere incipiant et quid sit credendum, ac quomodo orandum, ac bene beateque vivendum. Qui autem id facere recusaverit, et per duos menses officium hoc suum neglexerit, per episcopum aut loci illius ordinarium semel atque iterum admonitus, amoveatur. Porro si parochiani consuetum stipendium vel subtractum vel imminutum detineant, censura ecclesiastica ad id praestandum per episcopum aut loci illius ordinarium cogantur. Sin autem stipendii summa videbitur episcopo nimium exigua, eius erit pro arbitratu suo, amplitudinis parochiae ratione habita, ex parochianorum sumptibus facere auctiorem. *Ad* **Et** huius etiam munus est[*o*], templa purgata conservare, Biblia Sacra, et paraphrasin,[3] ac reliquos libros ecclesiae, nec vel lacerentur vel corrumpantur diligenter curare; campanas, quibus populus vel ad contiones vel ad preces publicas evocantur, vel quando pro agente animam orandum est, vel gravis alioqui ratio aut necessitas humanorum casuum urget, apto tempore pulsare; vestes et pocula, et alia quaevis [*ecclesiae*] ornamenta sacris usibus assignata, ut pura et nitida sint prospicere; et si quid sit vel vetustate confectum, vel casu detritum, vel necessitate aliqua immutandum, gardianos eius rei in tempore admonere; aquam ad baptismum adhibere; panem et vinum ad sacrosanctam coenam Domini celebrandam praeparare; ac pastori tam in con[47a]iugi{*i*/o} [*ritu*] celebrando, quam in cura et visitationis et funeris, et reliquis sacris functionibus omnibus, continenter ministrare et studiose inservire. Quibus in officiis tuendis si parum *studiosus* **diligens** depraehendatur, parochi et gardianorum erit, [91v] eum ad munus suum aut revocare, aut alium *post unam atque alteram admonitionem* **cum semel atque iterum admonitus fuerit**, in eius locum substituere. *Ad* **Et** ad eosdem, parochum inquam et gardianos pertinebit, cum munus huiusmodi vacaverit, idoneum ad *ipsum eligere* **illud assumere**. Qua [*in*] electione si [*consentire non poterunt, episcopi* **consenserint,** *ipsorum*] iudicio res definiatur.

---

[1]Unless otherwise noted, all changes in this chapter are in Dr Walter Haddon's hand.
[2]D, 25 c. 1 (Fr, I, 89-91); X, 1.25.1 (Fr, II, 155), originally a decretal of Pope Leo III (795-816); X, 1.26.1 (Fr, II, 155), attributed to a council of Toeldo, but of unknown origin.
[3]Erasmus' paraphrase of the Gospels. Cf. 1547/7 (*D.E.R.*, 250).

20. OF THE CHURCH AND ITS MINISTERS, AND THEIR OFFICES[1]

1. Of parish clerks.[2]

The parish clerk shall be paid by the parish[*ioners*]. It will be his duty to instruct all the youth of the parish entrusted to him in the alphabet and in the catechism [*written*] in the popular tongue, so that the children may begin to understand what to believe, how to pray and how to live well and blessedly. And whoever refuses to do this and neglects this his duty for two months shall be removed, after having been warned once and again by the bishop or by the local ordinary. Furthermore, if the parishioners withhold the usual stipend, or reduce or diminish it, they shall be compelled by the bishop or the local ordinary, using ecclesiastical censure, to pay it. And if the amount of the stipend shall seem to the bishop to be too small, it will be in his power to augment it at his discretion out of the revenues of the parishioners, bearing in mind the size of the parish. *In addition to this task, he shall* **And it shall be his task to** keep the church buildings clean, and diligently ensure that the Holy Bible, the paraphrase[3] and the other church books are not torn or defaced, to ring the bells at the appropriate time, by which the people are summoned either to sermons or to common prayer, or when a departing soul is to be prayed for, or some serious reason or case of human need requires, to inspect the vestments and silver and any other ornaments [*of the church*] which are designated for holy use to see that they are pure and clean, and if there is something which has been worn out with age, accidentally ruined or is in need of alteration for some necessary reason, to alert the wardens to it in time; to bring water for baptism; to prepare the bread and wine for celebrating the most holy supper of the Lord; and faithfully to assist and dutifully serve the pastor, both in celebrating [*the rite of*] marriage, and in the duty of visiting and conducting funerals, and in all other sacred functions. If someone is found to be insufficiently *dutiful* **diligent** in performing these duties, it will be the responsibility of the incumbent and wardens either to call him back to his task, or to substitute another in his place *after one and another warning* **when he has been warned once and again**. And it will be the responsibility of the incumbent and wardens to *elect* **appoint** a suitable person to the said office when it is vacant. In which election, if [*they have been unable to agree* **they agree**] the matter shall be decided by **their** *the bishop's* judgment.

2. De oeconomis sive gardianis ecclesiarum et sacellorum.[4]

Res omnes in templo necessarias oeconomi parochianorum sumptibus parabunt, [*et easdem*] sic aedituo tradent, ut *sit securitas* **omnino provisum sit** ne quid detrimenti ecclesiae bonis adferatur. Populum Dei sic in ordinem redigent, ut cum aut precationes publicae aut contiones Verbi Domini, aut lectiones sacrae in ecclesia fiant, utque dum aut iniunctiones nostrae, sive episcopi, aut statuta aut mandata quaecunque recitentur, aut sacramenta Domini ministrentur, prorsus nullus audiatur in coetu obambulantium, altius legentium, precantium vel loquentium, aut quoquo modo aliter *perturbantium strepitus* **obstrepentium tumultus**. Quod si quispiam contionatori in ecclesia obstrepere, aut presbytero ministranti obsistere, aut ordinem quemcunque a nobis in ecclesia institutum *perturbare non vereatur* **impedire ausit**, gardianorum erit eum ab ecclesia extrudere, *quoad per episcopum reversurum restituat non reversurum* **nec illi re**{d}**ditus ad ecclesiam nisi per episcopum concedetur**. Episcopi vero debent censura quavis ecclesiastica, **tamquam freno iniecto**, praefractos eiusmodi *ad mentem cogere meliorem* **maiorem ad morum gravitatem et modestiam contorquere**, et gardianos, nisi id fecerint, ecclesiastica/**is** [92r] *censura punire* **poenis devincere**. Gardiani a parochianorum maiori parte eligentur, ac singulis annis circa festum natalis Domini rationem pastori ac parochianis acceptorum et expensorum reddent. [47b] Et qu*i*[oni]am *habent in manibus* **penes se detinent** ecclesiae suppell*ectilia*/**icitatem**, quaeque ipsi ab aliis qui ante se fuerunt in eo munere acceperunt, integra et illibata successoribus consign*ent*/**ata relinquant**. *Ac si ecclesiae ratione reddita oberati sint* **Et confectis rationibus si quicquam apud illos aeris ecclesiastici resideat**, per censuras ecclesiasticas id omne citra festum Paschae proxime futurum cogantur *satisfactionem dare* **restituere**. Gardianorum officium per parochianos impositum *recusare* **qui recusaverit**, primo quoque tempore decem solidos, secundo viginti, tertio quadraginta, ad ecclesiae operas persolvet. Ad visitationem ordinariam quamcunque vocati si non accesserint et officium suum praestiterint, *pro* arbitratu visitatoris punientur.

3. De diaconis.[5]

Diaconus erit patronus pauperum, ut languidos confirmet, soletur vinctos, inopes iuvet; eritque pater orphanis, patronus viduis, et solatium afflictis et miseris, quantum in illo est, omnibus. Nomina etiam *indigentium* **pauperum** parocho diligenter deferet, ut eius suasu ecclesia tota permota necessitatibus illorum prospiciat, ne mendicantes *susque deque latius vagentur fratres* **late fratres obambulent**, [92v] eodem et caelesti Patre nati et pretio redempti. Pastoribus suis a quibus adsciti fuerint in sacris precationibus et *ministeriis* **officiis** perpetuo

---

[4]X, 1.27.1 (Fr, II, 155) and X, 1.27.2 (Fr, II, 156), both of unknown origin; 1571/5; 1603/18.
[5]D, 25 c. 1 (Fr, I, 89-91); 1571/1.4.

2. Of stewards or wardens of churches and chapels.[4]

The churchwardens shall prepare everything needed in the church at the expense of the parishioners, and shall deliver them to the parish clerk, so that it may be *certain* **fully provided** that no harm will be done to the goods of the church. They shall so discipline the people of God that when public prayers or sermons on the Word of God, or sacred lessons are held in the church, as also when injunctions, either from us or from the bishop, or any statutes or orders, are read, or the sacraments of the Lord are administered, no *shouting* **noise** shall then be heard in the congregation of people wandering about, reading out loud, praying or talking, or *disturbing* **interrupting** things in any other way whatsoever. But if someone *is not ashamed* **has dared** to interrupt a preacher in the church, or block a presbyter from ministering, or *disturb* **hinder** any order whatsoever, instituted by us in the church, it will be the wardens' responsibility to expel him from the church, *to which he shall not return until he has been reconciled* **and there shall be no return to the church for him unless it has been allowed** by the bishop. For the bishops must, by using ecclesiastical censure **as a kind of brake imposed**, *compel* delinquents of that kind *to adopt a better attitude* **to develop more serious behaviour and greater modesty**, and they shall *punish* **compel** the wardens, if they have not done this, by ecclesiastical *censure* **penalties**. The wardens shall be elected by the majority of the parishioners, and every year about the time of Christmas they shall render an account of their revenues and expenditures to the pastor and the parishioners. And *those who have in their hands* **since they keep in their possession** the furnishings of the church, **they** shall *consign* **hand** them **on** to their successors wholly and completely, as they themselves received them from those who were in that office before them. And if, *after having rendered account to the church, they are in profit* **once the accounts have been made, there is some church money still remaining with them**, they shall be compelled by ecclesiastical censures to *make satisfaction for* **return** it all before the following feast of Easter. Whoever refuses to take on the office of churchwarden, imposed by the parishioners, shall pay ten shillings to the works of the church on the first occasion, twenty on the second and forty on the third. If they are called to attend a visitation of the ordinary and do not appear or fulfill their duty, they shall be punished at the visitor's discretion.

3. Of deacons.[5]

A deacon shall be the patron of the poor, to strengthen the weak, comfort the downtrodden and help the needy, and he shall be a father to orphans, a patron to widows, and a comfort to all who are afflicted and distressed, in so far as he is able. He shall also diligently report the names of the *indigent* **poor** to the parish priest, so that at the latter's urging the entire church may be stirred up to provide for their needs, so that brethren born of the same heavenly Father and redeemed

adsint. Lectiones ex Verbo [*divino* **Domini**] quotidianas populo recitabunt, et si quando necessitas incumbat, contionabuntur, et sacramenta (modo si episcopi aut ordinarii permissione faciant) administrabunt. His officiis nisi diligenter eos invigilasse per presbyteros ecclesiae *testatum* **demonstratum** sit, episcopi illos ad altiorem gradum *promovere ne audeant* **non promoveant**.

4. De presbyteris.[6]

In presbytero mores eluceant a Domino Paulo descripti [*prima*] ad Timotheum trito[7] et ad Titum primo.[8] Gregem Dei sibi commissum verbo vitae subinde nutriant, et ad *infucatam* **sinceram** tum Deo [48a] tum [*magistratibus* **magistratui ac**] in *sublimiori loco* **dignitate** positis oboedientiam assidue [*al*/**e**]liciant, et ad benevolentiam mutuam Christianos omnes sedulo invitent. Non sint compotores, non aleatores, non aucupes, non venatores, non sycophantae, non otiosi aut supini; sed sacrarum litterarum studiis et praedicationi Verbi et {o}rationibus pro ecclesia ad Dominum diligenter incumbant. [*Nullus aut rasuram aut tonsuram papisticam in vertice gerat.*] Nullus expers coniugii mulierem sexaginta annis natu minorem in aedibus sinat diversari, nisi sit eius mater, aut amita, aut matertera, aut soror. Presbyter quivis Biblia Sacra habeat propria, non [93r] Anglice modo, verum etiam Latine.[9] Vestis sit decens et gravis, quae ministrum deceat, non militem, iui/xta arbitrium episcopi.[10]

5. De archipresbyteris sive decanis ruralibus.[11]

Decanatus quilibet archipresbyterum *ruralem* **rusticanum** habeat, *per episcopum aut loci ordinarium nominandum* **vel ab episcopo vel ecclesiae ordinario praeficiendum**. Munus autem eius erit annuum. Hic tamquam in specula presbyteris, diaconis, gardianis et aedituis, ut singuli quae ad eorum munus attinent praestent, perpetuo invigilabit. De idololatris et haereticis, de simoniacis, de lenonibus et meretricibus, de adulteris et fornicatoribus, de his qui duas uxores simul habent, [*aut quae* **atque**] maritos duos, de magis et veneficis, de calumniatoribus et blasphemis, de sodomiticis et ebriosis, de ultimarum *voluptat...* voluntatum corruptelis et periuriis, de iniunctionum aut nostrarum aut

---

[6]D, 25 c. 1 (Fr, I, 89-91).
[7]I Ti. iii. 1-13.
[8]Tt. i. 5-9.
[9]1547/20 (*D.E.R.*, 253).
[10]D, 32 c. 16 (Fr, I, 121), c. 3 of Nicaea I, 325 (*C.O.D.*, 7).
[11]D, 25 c. 1 (Fr, I, 89-91); X, 1.24.1 (Fr, II, 153), attributed to a council of Toledo but of unknown origin; X, 1.24.2 (Fr, II, 154); X, 1.24.3 (Fr, II, 154); X, 1.24.4 (Fr, II, 154-5), all decretals of Pope Leo III (795-816).

at a price shall not *wander up and down* **travel far and wide** begging. They shall constantly be in attendance on the pastors, by whom they have been employed, at the holy prayers and *services* **offices**. They shall read daily lessons from the *divine* Word **of God** to the people, and whenever necessary, they shall preach and administer the sacraments (as long as they do so with the permission of the bishop or the ordinary). The bishops shall not *presume to* promote them to higher rank unless the presbyters of the church have *testified* **demonstrated** that they have fulfilled these functions diligently.

4. Of presbyters.[6]

In a presbyter, there shall shine those qualities described by the Lord Paul in [*first*] Timothy iii.[7] and in Titus i.[8] They shall regularly feed the flock of God committed to them with the word of life, and they shall constantly nurture all Christians in an *unfeigned* **sincere** obedience both to God, and to the magistrate*s*, [**and to those**] placed in a *higher position* **dignity**, and earnestly encourage them to love one another. They shall not be drunkards, gamblers, fowlers, hunters, hypocrites, sluggards or weaklings, but they shall devote themselves to the study of sacred letters, to the preaching of the Word and to prayers to the Lord for the church. [*None of them shall shave his head or wear a tonsure in the Roman fashion.*] No single man shall allow a woman of less than sixty years of age to dwell in his house unless she is his mother, his father's sister, his mother's sister, or his own sister. Every presbyter shall have his own Holy Bible, not only in English but also in Latin.[9] His attire shall be decent and sober, as befits a minister, not a soldier, as the bishop shall appoint.[10]

5. Of archpresbyters or rural deans.[11]

Every deanery shall have a *rural* **rustic** archpresbyter, to be *named* **appointed** by the bishop or the local ordinary. His term of office shall be for one year. He shall constantly inspect, as in a mirror, the presbyters, deacons, wardens and parish clerks, to see that each of them fulfills the duties which belong to his office. He shall *make inquiry* **inquire** about idolaters and heretics, about simoniacs, about pimps and whores, about adulterers and fornicators, about those who have two wives at the same time [*or who have* **and**] two husbands, about magicians and sorcerers, about slanderers and blasphemers, about homosexuals and drunkards, about falsifiers of last wills and perjurers, and about violators of

episcopi violatoribus, *quaestionem faciat* **inquirat**. Et vocandi ad se, [*et*] examinand*um*/**i** horum scelerum suspectos auctoritatem habeat. Omnem accusationis *originem* **ortum**, sive per famam publicam, sive deferentium testimonio probatum, vel suspectum, episcopo aut eius loci ordinario infra decem dies in scriptis prodet. Qui autem venire ad eum recusaverit, per apparitorem vocatus tamquam con[48b]tumax [*episcopi puniatur arbitr*io/*atu*] {**censebitur**}. Episcopi voluntatem omnibus eius dec[a/o]natus ecclesiis sibi per litteras significatam, quanta poterit [93v] celeritate subinde exponi curabit; alioqui subibit supplicium contemptus. Officii sui sexto quolibet mense episcopum aut loci ordinarium certiorem faciet, quot in eius decanatu {**m**} contiones eo temporis spatio **fuerint habitae**.

6. De archidiaconis.[12]

Archidiaconus sit proximus post episcopum <u>et eius vicarium minister Domini</u>, salvo *nihilominus* **tamen** iure decani quod ad cathedralem ecclesiam **spectat**. Ac propterea sit presbyter et in perpetuis excubiis, ut qui in functionibus sunt inferioribus, diligenter suum officium faciant. Sint itaque oculi episcopi. In archidiaconatu[**m**] resideant, contionentur, pascant, visitent. Quae si non praestiterint, nisi *rationabilem* **iustam** episcopo reddiderint causam, ab eo censuris et poenis ecclesiasticis *cogantur* **ad huiusmodi trudantur officia**. Annis autem singulis bis, aut ad minimum semel, archidiaconatum suum perlustrabit; archipresbyteros et inferiores reliquos ministros omnes non solum suorum admonebit officiorum, sed rationem etiam ab eis repetet, et de templorum ac aedificiorum ruinis, et de *thaus...* thesauri pauperum distributione, et de bonorum ecclesiae vel accessione vel decessione. Quod autem sive in his rebus, sive in illis quae ad archipresbyteri explorationem **referuntur**, peccatum erit, per censuras ecclesiasticas *puniet* **corrigetur**. Ipse, si se recte non gerat, ab episcopo *corrigendus* **castigandus** pro meritorum ratione est. Archidiaconus etiam ante viginti dies post visitationem eius absolutam, [94r] omnes populi querelas, omnes *transgressiones* **offensiones**, omnes inferiorum ministrorum errores, omnem denique actionum suarum seriem episcopo deferet, ut per eum tamquam per oculi organum, quid recte, quid secus, per universam dioecesin geratur, episcopus videat. Et inter ce[49a]tera illius erit episcopo diligenter significare, quaenam in dioecesi parochiae sint, ubi miseris, egenis et aegrotis non subveniatur, prout in

---

[12]D, 25 c. 1 (Fr, I, 89-91); D, 93 c. 6 (Fr, I, 321-2); X, 1.23.1 (Fr, II, 149-50), of unknown origin; X, 1.23.6 (Fr, II, 151), originally a decretal of Pope Alexander III (1159-81); X, 1.23.7 (Fr, II, 151-2), originally a decretal of Pope Innocent III (1198-1216); 1571/3; 1634/25.

either our or the bishop's injunctions. And they shall have the authority to summon those suspected of these crimes to themselves and to examine them. Within ten days they shall inform the bishop or the local ordinary in writing of every *origin* **source** of accusation, whether it has come by public rumour or has been proved or alleged on the testimony of those who have reported it. And whoever shall refuse to come to him when summoned by the apparitor, shall be {**pronounced**} [*punished at the bishop's discretion as*] contumacious. They shall ensure that the will of the bishop, conveyed to him by letters, shall regularly be expounded in all the churches of the deanery as quickly as possible; otherwise he shall suffer the pain of contempt. Every six months he shall make an official report to the bishop or local ordinary as to how many sermons have been preached in his deanery during that time.

6. Of archdeacons.[12]

An archdeacon shall be next after the bishop <u>and his deputy as a minister of the Lord</u>, *nevertheless* **but** saving the right of the dean **with respect** to the cathedral church. In addition he shall be a presbyter and in permanent residence, to make sure that those who are in lower positions do their work diligently. For they are the eyes of the bishop. They shall reside in the archdeaconry, preach, pastor and visit. If they do not do so, they shall be *compelled* **obliged** by the bishop, using ecclesiastical censures and penalties **to perform these duties**, unless they can give him some *reasonable* **just** excuse. And twice a year, or at least once, he shall inspect his archdeaconry, not only reminding the archpresbyters and all the other inferior ministers of their duties, but also demanding from them an account, of the dilapidation of churches and buildings, of the distribution of the funds in the poor box, and of any increase or decrease in church property. And if there is any fault either in these things or in those which **pertain to** the archpresbyter's investigation, it shall be *punished* **corrected** by ecclesiastical censures. If he does not act properly himself, he shall be *corrected* **castigated** by the bishop according to the merits of the case. Also an archdeacon shall report all quarrels of the people, all *transgressions* **offences**, all the mistakes of the inferior ministers, and finally the entire range of their actions to the bishop within twenty days after the completion of his visitation, so that the bishop may see through him, as through the organ of the eye, what is being done correctly, and what wrongly, throughout the entire diocese. And among other things, it will be his responsibility to notify the bishop diligently, which parishes in the diocese there are where no help is being given to the distressed, the poor and the sick, in the

parliamenti constitutionibus nuper decretum est;[13] *quo* **ut** ad officium sedulo ac diligentius faciendum, cum ordinarii tum contionatorum monitionibus acrius incitari possint.

7.[14] De ecclesiis cathedralibus.[15]

Ecclesia cathedralis sit sedes episcopi. Fundatorum statuta iam abhinc antea recepta retinebunt[*ur*] pura et integra, [*quamdiu* **quemadmodum**] Verbo Dei non adversantur, et nostris constitutionibus de religione vel editis vel edendis non repugnant. Hic episcopum visitare, morum vitia emendare, flagitiosos punire, et aperte reluctantes *deprivare* **de loco deiicere**, fas esto.

8. De decanis.[16]

Decani quoque, cum in clero amplam dignitatem et locum honor*ific*/**atum** in ecclesia sortiantur, presbyteri sunto, viri graves, docti et magna prudentia insignes; cathedrales ecclesias iuxta illarum constitutiones regant; [94v] collegio tum canonicorum tum aliorum clericorum ecclesiae maioris praesint, neque disciplinam labi sinant; provideantque summa diligentia ut in sua ecclesia sacri ritus ordine ac iusta ratione peragantur, utque omnia [*cum*] ordine ac *decenti* **convenienti** gravitate ad *aedificationem* **fratrum utilitatem** fiant; ut[*que*] archidiaconi *extra* **foras**, sic illi domi, hoc est in ecclesia cathedrali et eius canonicis et clericis, episcopo sint adiumento, quasi duo eius membra utilissima et necessaria. Quare neque decani abesse debent a sua ecclesia, sine maxima et urgentissima causa per *suum* **proprium** episcopum approbanda.

9. De praebendariis.[17]

Praebendariorum erit non modo sacris ecclesiae cathedralis interesse, ac ea **vicissim** iuxta *vires et* constitutiones collegii pera[49b]gere, sed etiam efficere ut in suo collegio per doctum virum et peritum theologum Sacrarum Litterarum interpretatio *habeatur* **suscipiatur**, atque id *minimum* ter in hebdomada **frequentetur**. Hoc vero munus [*aut*] ipsi per se obeant, aut si quem ad id conduxerint, viginti libras annuatim suppeditent, sive ex communibus collegii

---

[13]5-6 Edward VI, c. 2, 1551-2 (*S.R.*, IV, 131-2). Cf. also 3-4 Edward VI, c. 16, 1549-50 (*S.R.*, IV, 115-17).
[14]In the MS the numbering restarts here.
[15]X, 1.33.16 (Fr, II, 202), originally a decretal of Pope Gregory IX (1227-41), published on or before 5 September 1234.
[16]D, 60 cc. 1-2 (Fr, I, 226); D, 60 c. 3 (Fr, II, 226-7); 1571/2.
[17]1571/2.3; 1603/44.

way that was recently decreed in the statutes of parliament,[13] so that they may be more urgently encouraged by the admonitions of both the ordinary and the preachers to do this duty more earnestly and diligently.

7.[14] Of cathedral churches.[15]

The cathedral church shall be the seat of the bishop. [**They shall retain**] the founders' statutes which have long since been accepted [*shall be retained*] whole and entire, [*as long as* **in so far as**] they are not contrary to the Word of God and are not repugnant to our statutes concerning religion which have been or which shall be published. Here it shall be lawful for the bishop to visit, to correct bad behaviour, to punish the wicked and to *deprive* **remove from their posts** all those who openly resist.

8. Of deans.[16]

Deans also, since they enjoy considerable dignity among the clergy and an honoured place in the church, shall be presbyters, serious men, learned and known for their great wisdom; they shall govern the cathedral churches according to their statutes; they shall preside over the college both of canons and of the other clergy of the greater church, and shall they not allow discipline to slip; they shall provide with the greatest diligence that the sacred rites are conducted in an orderly and proper way in their church, so that everything may be done for **the** *edification* **benefit of the brethren** [*with* **in**] order and with *decent* **appropriate** seriousness [*and*] so that what the archdeacons are *without* **outside**, they may also be at home, that is, assistants to the canons and clergy in the cathedral church, as well as to the bishop, the two together being his most useful and necessary members. Therefore the deacons also must not be absent from their church without the greatest and most urgent cause, which must be approved by their **own** bishop.

9. Of prebendaries.[17]

It shall be the duty of prebendaries not only to be present at the services in the cathedral church, and to conduct them **in turn** according to the *powers and* statutes of the college, but also to ensure that the exposition of Holy Writ is *had* **undertaken** in their college by a learned man and skilled theologian, and this **shall be repeated** *at least* three times a week. Moreover, they shall [*either*] undertake this task themselves, or if they appoint someone else to do it, they shall pay him twenty pounds a year, either from the common funds of the college or

proventibus, sive ex fructibus singularum praebendarum; aut si commodius hoc videatur, certam quandam praebendam huic muneri addictam perpetuo habeant. Decanus item et praebendarii contionem habeant in ecclesia cathedrali singulis dominicis diebus, *ha*/**nec** ab ea neque a theologica lectione licebit **cuiquam** ecclesiae cathedralis clerico *modo praesens adsit* (**si domi fuerit**) abesse *sub poena*. **Si vero absit**, stipendii unius [*mensis*] **mulcta feriatur**, nisi *a* decano, vel si absit, *ab* eius vicario, causa**m** *eius* absentiae **suae** *probata fuerit* **probaverit**.[18]

[95r] 10. De episcoporum gradu ac dignitate in ecclesia.[19]

Episcopi, quoniam inter ceteros ecclesiae ministros locum principem tenent, ideo sana doctrina, gravi auctoritate, atque provido con[c/s]ilio debent inferiores ordines cleri, universumque populum Dei regere ac pascere, non sane ut dominentur eorum fidei, sed ut seipsos vere servos servorum Dei exhibeant; sciantque *regimen* **auctoritatem** et iurisdictionem ecclesiasticam non alia de causa sibi praecipue creditam esse, nisi ut suo ministerio et *sedula opera* **assiduitate** homines quam plurimi Christo *lucri fiant* **iungantur**, quique iam Christi sunt, in eo crescant et **ex**aedificentur, atque si nonnulli deficiant, *et* **ad** pastorem Christum Dominum reducantur, et per salutarem paenitentiam instaurentur.

11. De oboedientia episcopis exhibenda.[20]

Omnes in ecclesia cum pacem sectari debeant, et *unitatis pro viribus esse studiosi, idcirco episcopo* **ad concordiam quantum licet incumbere,** *primum* **episcopo** [*etc.*] qui ecclesiae [50a] praeficitur, non solum decanus, archidiaconus, archipresbyter, et reliqui ministri parebunt, sed omnia etiam Christi membra eius curae commissa *illi sic auscultabunt* **sic ad eius se voluntatem accommodabunt**, ut et in his quae iuxta Verbum Dei praecipiunt, et in illis etiam quae mandabunt ad Christianam disciplinam, et ad nostras ecclesiasticas leges pertinentia *oboediant et obsequantur studiosissime*, **paratissime morem gerant.**

---

[18]A marginal note in Cranmer's hand reads: 'Hoc loco recte adderentur capita 16 et 17 ex titulo "De admittendis ad ecclesiastica beneficia".' ('In this place there ought rightly to be added headings 16 and 17 of the chapter "On those to be admitted to ecclesiastical benefices"').

[19]Cf. D, 23 c. 2 (Fr, I, 79-80); D, 61 c. 6 (Fr, I, 229); X, 1.31.16 (Fr, II, 192-3), originally a decretal of Pope Honorius III (1216-27).

[20]D, 93 cc. 8-10 (Fr, I, 322); X, 1.32.2 (Fr, II, 195-6), attributed to Pope Gregory I (590-604); X, 1.33.4 (Fr, II, 196), originally a decretal of Pope Clement III (1187-91).

from the income of individual prebends, or if it appears to be more convenient, they shall reserve one particular prebend in perpetuity for this purpose. Likewise the dean and the prebendaries shall preach in the cathedral church every single Sunday, and it shall not be lawful for any cleric to be absent from the theological lecture *as long as he is present* (**if he is at home**), *under penalty*. **And if he is absent, he shall be fined** one [*month's*] stipend, unless **he has proved** the reason for his absence *has been approved by* **to** the dean, or in his absence, *by* **to** his deputy.[18]

10. Of the rank and dignity of bishops in the church.[19]

Bishops, because they hold the chief place among the other ministers of the church, must therefore govern and pastor the lower orders of the clergy, as well as the whole people of God, with sound doctrine, sober authority and wise counsel, not indeed in order to lord it over their faith, but that they might prove themselves to be true servants of the servants of God. And they shall know that *the government* **authority** and ecclesiastical jurisdiction has been specially entrusted to them for no other reason than that by their ministry and *hard work* **dedication** as many people as possible may be *made rich in* **joined to** Christ, and that those who are already Christ's may grow in him and be built up, and that, if some fail in this, they shall be led back to their pastor, who is Christ the Lord, and restored by salutary penance.

11. Of the obedience to be shown to bishops.[20]

Since everyone in the church must dwell in peace, and be *concerned as much as they can be with unity, therefore* the bishop's ***primary*** responsibility shall be **to foster harmony**, and not only the dean, archdeacon, archpresbyter and other ministers shall heed him, but also all other members of Christ committed to his cure shall so *listen to him* **conform themselves to his will**, that they shall *obey and carefully follow* **most readily obey**, both in those matters which they teach according to the Word of God and also in those which they shall ordain for the sake of Christian discipline, and those which pertain to our ecclesiastical laws.

12. De variis et multiplicibus episcopi muneribus.[21]

Verbi Dei sanam doctrinam cum primis tum per seipsum, [95v] tum per alios, episcopus tradat in sua ecclesia, quanta diligentia et sedulitate fieri potest; sacros ordines opportuno tempore conferat; sed nemini vel mercede conductus vel temere manus imponat. Idoneos ministros ad ecclesiastica beneficia instituat; indignos vero, ubi graves causae ac *mala eorum merita* **morum perversitas** id requisiverint, submoveat, et ab ecclesiae administratione deiiciat; ecclesiae testimonia et querelas de suis pastoribus audiat; rixas inter ministros et ecclesias subortas componat; vitia et *corruptelas* **contaminatos mores** censuris ecclesiasticis corrigat; *iniunctiones* **edicta** ad meliorem vivendi formam praescribat; eos qui pertinaciter et obstinate reluctantur excommunicet; paenitentes vero in gratiam recipiat; dioecesim totam, tam in locis exemptis quam non [*exemptis*], *singulo* **tertio** quoque *triennio* **anno** visitet *ob emergentes casus*, et consuetas procurationes accipiat; ut vero aliis temporibus, quoties visum fuerit, visitet *ob emergentes casus* **propter novos casus qui incidere possint**, ei liberum esto, modo suis impensis id faciat, et nova onera stipendiorum aut procurationum ab ecclesiis non exigat; statis temporibus [*anni* **annuatim**] synodos habeat; illi quoque sit curae ut *iam apprime catechizatos adolescentes aut si opus fuerit, provectioris aetatis* **paratos et** in **catechismo instructos** certo anni tempore confirmet; testamenta quoque approbet. Et demum omnia et singula episcopis curae sunto, quae [50b] ad eos ex Dei praescripto spectant, et nostrae leges ecclesiasticae illorum cognitioni et iudiciis commiserunt.

13. De familia episcopi.[22]

Quemadmodum necessarium est ut episcopus sit gravibus et sanctis moribus ornatus, ita quoque familiam [96r] eius gravem, modestam et sanctam esse oportet, et *quoad ministeria* **quantum officia** domestica patiuntur, Verbi Dei studiosam, *utque possit* **quoniam potest** ecclesiae Dei ad varias opportunitates esse utilis, nam ex illius domo, tamquam ex *equo Troiano* **quodam thesauro**, sunt *educendi* **depromendi** viri qui *ministeriis* **muneribus** ecclesiasticis praeficiantur. Et certe apud episcopum (si fuerit is qu[*em*/**i**] decet esse) dogmata fidei probe ac solide cognoscere poterunt, et ecclesiae regendae illius exemplo *experientiam sibi non mediocrem comparare* **magnam scientiam colligere**. Caveat autem ne otiosos, vanos, impudicos, aut aleatores nutriat. Alioquin si domui suae praeesse non novit, quomodo ecclesiam Dei curabit? Et sacellanos habeat **circa se** contionatores, qui non tantum *Verbum Dei praedicent supplendo parochorum quando opus erit defectum seu negligentiam* **Sacram Scripturam disseminent, rusticanorum negligentiam et cessationem explentes**, sed qui etiam ad illud munus obeundum alios ex familia, *pro cuiusque illorum captu*

---

[21]X, 1.31.16 (Fr, II, 192-3), originally a decretal of Pope Honorius III; 1571/1.1; 1603/60.
[22]D, 54 c. 23 (Fr, I, 214); C. 2, q. 7, cc. 59-60 (Fr, I, 502).

12. Of the many and various tasks of a bishop.[21]

A bishop shall pass on the sound doctrine of the Word of God, first of all in person, and also through others, in his church, with as much diligence and dedication as he can; he shall confer holy orders at an appropriate time, but he shall not lay hands on anyone suddenly or because he has been bribed. He shall institute suitable ministers to ecclesiastical benefices, and he shall remove the unworthy wherever serious causes and *their wicked deserts* **bad behaviour** require it, and put them out of the administration of the church; he shall listen to the testimonies of the church and complaints concerning his pastors; he shall settle quarrels which have arisen between ministers and their churches; he shall correct vices and *corruptions* **corrupt behaviour** by ecclesiastical censures; he shall prescribe *injunctions* **edicts** for the improvement of morals; he shall excommunicate persistent and deliberate gainsayers; he shall also receive penitents back into grace; he shall also visit his entire diocese, in places both exempt and not [*exempt*], every *three* **third** year*s to deal with cases which have arisen*, and shall receive the usual procurations; and he shall also be free to visit at other times, as often as seems right to him, *to deal with cases which have arisen* **on account of new cases which might occur**, but he shall do so at his own expense and shall not demand fresh levies of stipends or procurations from the churches; he shall hold synods at stated times [*of the* **every**] year; it shall also be his responsibility to confirm those *young people, and if need be, those of a more advanced age, who have been fully catechized* **who have been instructed in the catechism** at a particular time of the year; he shall also prove testaments. And lastly, everything which concerns bishops by the commandment of God shall be their responsibility, and our ecclesiastical laws have been committed to their hearing and judgments.

13. Of the bishop's household.[22]

As it is necessary for a bishop to be adorned with sober and holy morals, so also it is essential for his household to be sober, modest and holy, and studious of the Word of God to the extent that domestic *services* **duties** allow, in order to be as useful to the church of God as possible in different ways, for men who can take charge of ecclesiastical *ministries* **posts** can be *drawn* **obtained** from his house, as from *the Trojan horse* **some treasure store**. For surely they will be able to learn the doctrines of the faith soundly and solidly in the bishop's company (if he is the man he ought to be), and by his example in governing the church, acquire *no small experience* **great knowledge**. However, the bishop must be careful not to sponsor the lazy, the useless, the unchaste or gamblers. For if he cannot control his own house, how shall he care for the church of God? And he shall have preaching chaplains **around him**, who shall not only *preach the Word of God by making up for the defects and negligence of parish priests when need be* **spread Holy Scripture by making up for the negligence and laziness of**

quantum ingenio quisque contendere potest, instituant. Haec sane una est ratio inter alias subveniendi tantae inopiae bonorum atque fidelium ecclesiae ministrorum. Sic *se habuit* **instituta fuit** Augustini domus, et ceterorum patrum qui populo Christi sancte praefuerunt. Sint ad haec uxores episcoporum nequaquam leves, otiosae, *vanae*, aut *sumptuose ornatae* **voluptatibus implicitae, ne[c] pretiose nimis exornentur**. Nam his rebus pii homines mirum in modum offenduntur, et impii evangelicae doctrinae *petulanter* **insolenter** insultant. Et quod est *dictum de* **positum in** uxoribus, ad filios etiam et ad filias [*eorum*] attinet. Quae*quemodo expressivimus* **vero compraehendimus** isto **praesente** decreto de uxore, liberis et familia episcopi, *explicare* **pertinere** volumus *iusta proportione* **eadem aequabiliter** ad decanos, archidiaconos, canonicos, parochos et ceteros [51a] ecclesiae ministros. Et in summa *caveant* **vetent** omnem superbiam, fastum, luxum et *vanitatem* **ineptias omnis generis**, quibus eorum praedicatio et auctoritas *elevetur* **minui possit**.

[96v] 14. De collegiis episcoporum curae in academia commissis.[23]

Ad haec nonnulli episcopi habent aliqua collegia scholasticorum *protectioni* **defensioni** atque tutelae suae commissa. Ideo necessarium est ut ea quam diligentissime curent; nam ibi quoque ecclesia habet suorum ministrorum alterum seminarium. Videant igitur *sedule* **diligenter** ut praefecti *sanae doctrinae quoad religionem sint studiosi* **salubr[i/e]s in Sacra Scriptura, et sincerae doctrinae retinentes sint**, eamque inter socios collegii sui *promoveant* **dilatent**, hostes maxime pertinaces reprimendo et coercendo. Nam si hoc faciant, et *e diverso* **ex altera parte** studiosos evangelicae pietatis tueantur, *promoveant* **sublevent** et iuvent, brevi spatio temporis collegia *re*/**per**purgabuntur. Non sinat episcopus in huiusmodi collegiis lectionem theologicam, (si qua ibi sit), intermitti. Neque ad illam patiatur admitti praelectorem, qui aut alienam doctrinam profiteatur, aut sit [*m*/n]utantis et *dubiae* **incertae** sententiae. Exploret an iustus numerus theologorum in collegio servetur. Inspiciat interdum qui eorum proficiant, qui sint ignavi, ut sciat quos et quot ministros possit habere *ad manus* **paratos**, cum necessitas ecclesiae postularit.

15. De residentia episcoporum.[24]

Nec etiam ullo modo episcopi a suis dioecesibus aut *curis* **ecclesiis** debent abesse, nisi causa ecclesiastica eos abducat, vel maxima rei publicae necessitas. Et ubi in cathedrali ecclesia *residerint* **consederint**, parum convenit ut dominicis

---

[23]L, 5.5.4, c. 10 of the council of Oxford, 1407. Cf. 1529/15 (AC, 55), not enacted at the time; also R, 23.3.
[24]1268/21 (PC, 769-70). This was also a reform of the council of Trent, sixth session, 13 January 1547 (*C.O.D.*, 681-2).

country parsons, but who will also prepare others in the household to undertake the same task, *according to the ability of each one of them* **in so far as each one is able to do so**. Indeed, this is one way among others of supplying the great lack of good and faithful ministers of the church. This was the way in which Augustine's house *operated* **was set up**, and that of other fathers who presided over the people of God in a holy manner. In addition, the wives of bishops must not be frivolous, lazy, *vain* or *sumptuously dressed*, **caught up in desires or too richly clothed**. For godly people are deeply offended by these things, and the ungodly *petulantly* **insolently** insult evangelical doctrine as a result. And what is *said concerning* **laid down for** wives, applies also to [*their*] sons and daughters. **And** it is our will that what we have *expressed* **established** by this **present** decree concerning the wife, children and family of a bishop, shall **also** *extend* **apply** *in just measure* **equally** to deans, archdeacons, canons, parish priests and other ministers of the church. And in sum, they shall *beware of* **exclude** all pride, ostentation, luxury and *vanity* **foolishness of all kinds**, by which their preaching and authority *is taken away* **may be lessened**.

14. Of colleges in the university committed to the care of bishops.[23]

In addition, some bishops have certain colleges of scholars committed to their *protection* **defence** and care. Therefore they must look after them as diligently as possible, for there also the church has another seedbed for its ministers. Therefore they shall *earnestly* **diligently** see to it that heads of houses *are studious of sound doctrine with respect to religion* **strong in Holy Scripture and retentive of sincere doctrine**, and they shall *promote* **spread** it among the fellows of their college, reprimanding and compelling those who are its most persistent enemies. For if they do this, and if on the other hand they look after, *promote* **advance** and assist those who are devoted to evangelical godliness, they shall **completely** reform their colleges in a short space of time. The bishop shall not allow the reading of theology in these colleges (where it exists) to be suspended. Nor shall he allow a lecturer to be admitted to teach theology who either professes some strange doctrine or is of a [*shifting* **empty**] and *doubtful* **uncertain** mind. He shall find out whether the full number of theologians is maintained in the college. Moreover, he shall also investigate to see which of them is doing well, and which are ignorant, so that he may know which and how many ministers he will have *to hand* **ready**, when the need of the church shall require.

15. Of the residence of bishops.[24]

Also, bishops should in no circumstances ever be absent from their dioceses or *cures* **churches**, unless some ecclesiastical cause or very great public need takes them away. And when they are *resident* **present** in the cathedral church, it is

diebus in suis sacellis *agitent* **officia** sacra **tractent**, vel ipsis intersint. Potius eant ad cathedralem ecclesiam; ibi vel ipsi contionentur, aut contionantem audiant, et sacramenta in communione [51b] vel ipsi ministrent [97r] vel cum aliis percipiant. Sic enim coram eis res gravius gerentur, et conventum sacrum praesentia sua ornabunt.

16. De coadiutoribus dandis.[25]

Quemadmodum episcopi ministris inferioribus, cum iam vel **propt**er morbum *incurabilem* **desperatum** vel *per senium ministrare non amplius possunt, dare coadiutores debent* **propter senectutem, ecclesiam [***ad***]ministrare diutius non possint, adiutores apponere debent**, sic etiam illis ob easdem causas *ab archiepiscopo** dabuntur, modo noster consensus interveniat. Et sicut ipsi possunt in sua dioecesi ministros *indignos* **pravos**, gravibus causis id *exigentibus* **postulantibus**, *privare beneficio ecclesiastico* **loco movere**, ita ipsi sciant se, si *prava docuerint* **corruptam doctrinam tradiderint**, ac pertinaciter defenderint, aut *cum scandalo ac turpiter vixerint* **ecclesiam flagitiosis et dissolutis moribus offenderint**, neque moniti resipuerint, auctoritate nostra deponendos fore, **et ab ecclesia submovendos.**

[97v] 17. De archiepiscopis.[26]

Omnia quae de episcopis constituta sunt ad se pertinere archiepiscopi quoque **ipsi** *noverint* **agnoscant**; et praeter illa mun*eri*/**us** eorum est in sua provincia episcopos *ordinare* **collocare**, cum a nobis electi fuerint. Utque totius provinciae suae statum melius intelligat archiepiscopus, semel provinciam suam universam, si possit, ambi{*e*/**bi**}t et visitabit. Et quoties contigerit aliquas vacare sedes episcopales, episcoporum *vices* **locos** non modo in visitatione, sed etiam in beneficiorum coll[**oc**]atione et omnibus aliis functionibus ecclesiasticis implebit. Quin et ubi episcopi sunt, si eos animadvertat in suis muneribus curandis, et praesertim in corrigendis vitiis, *remissos* **tardiores** et negligentiores esse quam in gregis Domin*ici* **praefectis** ferri possit, primum illos paterne monebit; quod si **monitione** non profuerit, illi ius esto *eorum supplere negligentiam* **alios in illorum loco collocare**. Appellantium etiam [52a] ad se querelas causasque audiet et iudicabit. Episcopi suae provinciae, si qua de re *interesse* **inter se**

---

[25]C. 7, q. 1, c. 16 (Fr, I, 573-4), originally c. 2 of the seventh council of Toledo, 646; C. 7, q. 1, c. 17 (Fr, I, 574-5), originally a letter of Pope Zacharias (741-52), written in 748; C. 7, q. 1, c. 18 (Fr, I, 575-6), originally a letter of Pope Pelagius (555-60); VI, 3.5.1 (Fr, II, 1034), originally a decretal of Pope Boniface VIII (1294-1303).

[26]D, 64 c. 1 (Fr, I, 247-8), originally c. 4 of Nicaea I, 325 (*C.O.D.*, 7); D, 64 c. 5 (Fr, I, 248), attributed to Pope Anicetus (157-68); D, 64 c. 8 (Fr, I, 249), originally c. 6 of Nicaea I, 325 (*C.O.D.*, 8-9); 1237/22 (PC, 255); L, 3.15.2, gloss on *metropolitanum*.

hardly right for them to *say* **conduct** the sacred **offices** on Sundays in their chapels, or to worship there. Instead they shall go to the cathedral church where they shall either preach themselves, or hear a preacher, and either administer the sacraments in communion themselves, or take part along with others. For services will be conducted more seriously when they attend, and their presence will grace the sacred assembly.

16. Of supplying coadjutors.[25]

As bishops must *give* **appoint** coadjutors for lower ministers when they are no longer able to serve **a church** either because of some *incurable* **hopeless** illness or because of old age, so also they shall be supplied to the bishops *by the archbishop**, as long as we agree to it. And just as they can *deprive unworthy* **remove wicked** ministers *of their ecclesiastical benefice* **from their post** in their dioceses, so let them also know that if they *teach wicked things* **pass on corrupt doctrine**, and stubbornly defend it, or if they have *lived scandalously and in an evil way* **offended the church by their disgraceful and dissolute morals**, and after being warned have not repented, they shall be deposed by our authority **and removed from the church**.

17. Of archbishops.[26]

Archbishops shall also *know* **recognize** that everything ordained concerning bishops applies to them too, and in addition to those things it shall also be their responsibility to *ordain* **install** bishops in their province, after they have been chosen by us. And if possible, the archbishop shall at some point travel across and visit his whole province in order to have a better understanding of the state of his entire province. And whenever it happens that some episcopal sees are vacant, he shall take the *turns* **places** of the bishops, not only in visitation but also in *collating* **appointing** to benefices and in all other ecclesiastical functions. But where there are bishops, if he notices that they are *remiss* **too slow** in fulfilling their duties and especially in correcting vices, and more negligent than can be tolerated in **heads of** the Lord's flock, he shall first warn them in a fatherly way, and if that **warning** does not work, it shall be lawful for him to *make up for their negligence* **appoint others in their stead**. He shall also hear and judge the quarrels and causes of those who appeal to him. If bishops of his province dispute with or sue each other about something, the archbishop shall be

contenderint aut litigarint, iudex et finitor inter eos esto archiepiscopus. Ad haec audiet et iudicabit accusationes contra episcopos suae provinciae. Ac denique si ullae contentiones aut lites inter [**episcopum et** *ipsos* archiepiscop*os*/**um**] ortae fuerint, nostro iudicio cognoscentur et definientur. Archiepiscopi quoque munus esto synodos provinciales nostro iussu convocare.

18. De synodis.[27]

Si contigerit in ecclesia gravem aliquando *emergere* **exoriri** causam, quae sine multorum con[*c*/**s**]ilio episcoporum haud facile possit finiri, tum archiepiscopus, ad cuius provinciam ea causa pertinet, suos episcopos ad provinciale con[*c*/**s**]ilium [98r] evocabit. Nec eorum quisquam *detiritabit* **recusabit** venire, modo *per* valetudine*m* **adversa** non impediatur; quod si morbo gravatus fuerit, alium *suo loco* **pro se** mittat, qui et suum excuset absentiam, et de his quae tractabuntur pro se respondeat et definiat. Verum con[*c*/**s**]ilia haec provincialia sine nostra voluntate ac iussu nunquam convocentur.

19. De synodo cuiuslibet episcopi in sua dioecesi.[28]

Quilibet episcopus in sua dioecesi habeat synodum, in qua cum suis presbyteris, parochis, vicariis et clericis de his agat rebus quae pro tempore vel constituenda sunt vel emendanda. *Non enim synodus lene medicamen est, ad supplendam* **Etenim aptissima profecto medicina synodus est ad castigandam** negligentiam, et tollendos errores, qui subinde in ecclesiis per diabolum et malos homines disseminantur; fietque ut per huiusmodi synodos coniunctio et caritas inter episcopum et clerum augeatur et servetur. Nam ille suos clericos prop{**r**}ius cognoscet et alloquetur; atque illi vicissim coram eum audient, et *de quibus necessarium duxerint* **quando rei na**[52b]**tura postulabit**, interrogabunt.

20. De tempore et loco synodi episcopalis.[29]

Singulo quoque anno synodus ab episcopo indic{*a*/**e**}tur, curetque diem condictam omnibus pastoribus qui sunt in agro per decanos *rurales* **ruri sparsos** indicari, sua vero in civitate per contionatorem ecclesiae cathedralis et schedas *prae* foribus affixas, diem huiusmodi *publicari* **pervulgari** mandabit, *atque id saltem antea per mensem* **toto mense, priusquam synodum instituat.** Liberum vero et sit quemcunque diem voluerit **ad id** accipere post dominicam secundam quadragesimae. Et nihilominus pr[*o*/**ae**]videat ut parochi et vicarii tam mature

---

[27]D, 18 c. 1 (Fr, I, 53).
[28]D, 18 c. 2 (Fr, I, 54).
[29]D, 18 c. 3 (Fr, I, 54).

the judge and final arbiter between them. In addition, he shall hear and judge accusations made against bishops of his province. And finally, if any disputes or lawsuits arise between the archbishop[*s themselves* **and a bishop**], they shall be heard and decided by our judgment. It shall also be the archbishop's responsibility to convene provincial synods at our command.

18. Of synods.[27]

If it happens that some serious cause *emerges* **arises** in the church at some point, which cannot be easily resolved without the [*council* **counsel**] of many bishops, then the archbishop to whose province that cause belongs shall convene his bishops in a provincial council. Nor shall any of them *hesitate* **refuse** to come, unless they are hindered by **poor** health. But if the illness has become serious, he shall send someone else *in his place* **for him**, who will both explain his absence and respond and decide on his behalf concerning the matters which are discussed. But these provincial councils shall never be convened apart from our will and command.

19. Of the synod of any bishop in his diocese.[28]

Every bishop shall have a synod in his diocese, in which he, along with his presbyters, parish priests, vicars and clergy shall deal with those matters which need to be established or altered at the time. For a synod is *no weak* **the most perfect** medicine for *supplying* **castigating** negligence and removing errors, which are regularly sown in the churches by the devil and by evil people, and it may be by such synods that the links and the love between the bishop and his clergy may be increased and preserved. For the bishop will then know and address his clergy in a more familiar way, and they in turn will hear him directly and be able to question him *about what they think is necessary* **when the nature of the matter demands it**.

20. Of the time and place of the bishop's synod.[29]

A synod shall be convened by the bishop every year, and he shall ensure that the appointed day is made known to all the pastors who are **scattered** in rural deaneries in the countryside. Moreover, in his own city he shall order the said day to be *published* **announced** by the preacher of the cathedral church and by notices posted on the *outer* doors, *and this at least* one **full** month before he opens the synod. But he shall be free to choose whatever day he wishes **for it**, after the second Sunday in Lent. Nevertheless, he shall see to it that parish priests

possint redire, ut die dominic[o/a] palmarum a *suis plebibus* **suo populo** non absint.[30] Locum vero in [*sua*] dioecesi deliget sibi episcopus *vel* [98v] *capitulum vel* quem omnibus *accessuris*, **qui accessuri sunt**, iudicaverit esse *quam* commodissimum. A *synodo* synodo vero nulli ex clericis abesse licebit, nisi cuius excusationem episcopus ipse approbaverit. Et ipse cum primis praesens adesto episcopus, et (quemadmodum par est) synodo praesit; *quem si gravissima causa fortassis abesse coegerit, eius loco synodo praesit archidiaconus.**[31]

21. De forma habend*i*/**ae** synodi.[32]

Ad locum quem episcopus assignaverit die condicta clerus adsit, et mane hora septima ad templum conveniat, primumque in medio *eius* **templo** preces, quae l[i/e]taniae vocantur, solemni ritu decantabuntur. Deinde *archidiaconus, vel*** episcopus ipse, si adsit, contionabitur, idque lingua materna, nisi aliter causa legitima suaserit. Contione vero absoluta, communio celebrabitur; qua peracta, episcopus ad locum aliquem interiorem cum toto clero migrabit, exclusis omnibus laicis, his exceptis quos ipse manere iusserit, omni[53a]busque ordine considentibus, maxima cum gravitate summaque pace de his agetur, quae *magis* **maxime** necessaria visa fuerint.

22. De rebus in synodo episcopali tractandis.[33]

Si qua *impuritas* **corruptio verae** doctrinae obrepserit, coarguatur. In Scripturis quae cum animarum *scandalo* **offensione** perperam exponuntur, iuxta fidei orthodoxae *analogiam* **convenientiam** explicentur; et quae fortassis non intellecta conscientias perturbant, fideliter excutiantur et declarentur. Ceremoniae impiae et superstitiosae, si quae *obrepserunt, abrogentur* **illapsae sint, auferantur.** Ecclesiasticae querelae atque controversiae audiantur, et quantum *pro tempore fieri potuit* **tempus fer**[*a*/e]*t,* definiantur. Et inquiratur quam diligentissime an *quoad* ritu*m*/**s** omnium sacrorum **officiorum**, iuxta formam a nostris legibus praescriptam, in ecclesiis *agatur* **instituantur**. [99r] Et in summa quaecunque ad *aedificationem* **utilitatem** populi Dei visa fuerint pertinere, integra fide ac singulari diligentia tractentur. Ibi de quaestionibus *quoad* res/**rum** controversa*s*/**rum** interrogabuntur singuli presbyteri. Episcopus vero doctiorum sententias patient[*i*/**er**] *aure audiet* **colliget**, neque dicentes, quoad finem fecerint, ab ullo assidentium sinat temere interturbari; nam (ut inquit apostolus) Deus non est confusionis **Deus**, sed pacis.

---

[30]Palm Sunday falls four weeks after the second Sunday in Lent.
[31]A vertical line in the margin may indicate that this deletion was meant to be ignored.
[32]1571/5.
[33]D, 18 c. 5 (Fr, I, 55).

and vicars will be able to return home in good time to be with their people on Palm Sunday.[30] Moreover, the bishop shall designate a meeting place in the diocese, *either the chapterhouse or one* which he judges is most convenient for all those who will attend. Moreover, it shall not be lawful for any of the clergy to be absent from the synod, unless the bishop has approved his excuse. And above all, the bishop shall be present himself and (as is fitting) shall preside over the synod, *but if some very serious cause compels him to be absent, the archdeacon shall preside in his stead.**[31]

21. Of the procedure for the synod.[32]

On the appointed day the clergy shall appear at the place which the bishop has assigned and shall gather in the church at seven o'clock in the morning. First shall come those prayers, which are called the litany, and they shall be solemnly chanted in the midst **of the church**. Then the *archdeacon, or** the bishop himself if he is present, shall preach, and this in his mother tongue, unless some lawful cause persuades him otherwise. Then when the sermon is finished, communion will be celebrated, and when that is over, the bishop shall retire with the clergy to some back room, where the laity shall be completely excluded, apart from those whom he has expressly ordered to remain. And when everyone is seated by order, the business concerning those things which appear to need *more* **most** attention shall be done with the greatest seriousness and in complete peace.

22. Of the matters to be discussed in a bishop's synod.[33]

If some *impurity* **corruption** of **true** doctrine has crept in, it must be condemned. Things in the Scriptures which are being expounded wrongly, to the *scandal* **offence** of souls, shall be explained according to the *analogy* **pattern** of orthodox faith, and things which perhaps have not been understood which disturb consciences shall be faithfully interpreted and clarified. If any ungodly and superstitious ceremonies have *crept* **slipped** in, they shall be *abolished* **removed**. Ecclesiastical quarrels and controversies shall be heard and settled as far as *can be done in the* time **allows**. And it shall be most diligently inquired as to whether the rites of all the sacred **offices** are *done* **conducted** according to the form prescribed by our laws. And in sum, whatever seems to relate to the *edification* **benefit** of the people of God shall be discussed with complete confidence and singular diligence. There individual presbyters shall be asked about questions *pertaining to* **of** controversial matters. Moreover, the bishop shall *listen* **gather** *with a patient ear* **patiently** to the opinions of the more learned, and shall not allow any of the speakers to be rudely interrupted by any of those present until they have finished, for (as the apostle says), God is not **a God** of confusion, but of peace.

23. De synodo concludenda.[34]

Non permittat episcopus ad multos dies *extrahi* **p[ro/er]ferri** synodum, sed illi quam *citius* **primum** fieri po*ter*/**ssit**, finem imponat; quia neque pastoribus neque gregibus conducit ut a se *invicem diutius absint* **diu utri[n]que disiungantur**. Sententiam itaque feret de litibus et querelis, quae illo brevi spatio temporis definiri poterunt. Alias, quae cognitione longiori opus habent, aut alio tempore ad suum tribunal iudicabit, aut per archidiaconum cum Septembri mense ad visitandum dioecesim proficisce[53b]tur, quid decreverit, significabit. De quaestionibus [*vero*] quo/**ae** ad doctrinam et ceremonias **spectant**, canones partim tunc *publicabit* **publice proponet**, partim archidiacono visitaturo *publicandos* **publice proponendos** committet. Decreta vero illius et sententias vel in synodo per ipsum vel per archidiaconum in visitatione *publicatas* **divulgatas**, inferiores ministri ut validas et firmas retinebunt. Quod si quid in eis vel iniustum vel absurdum contineri arbitrati fuerint, id ad *archiepiscopum** **nos***[35] deferant, cuius erit, ab episcopo constitutum, decretum aut sententiam vel confirmare vel emendare, *quo* **ita** tamen *ad* **ut qua parte** illa non correxeri*t**/**mus***[36] *archiepiscopus,** vigorem suum et robur *habebunt* **retineant**. Episcopus itaque in synodo suis promulgatis decretis atque sententiis, ad curam et sollicitudinem commissi gregis clerum adhortabitur, et cum pace et Spiritu Domini eorum quemque ad sua**s ecclesias** reverti iubebit.

---

[34]D, 18 c. 17 (Fr, I, 58).
[35]The emendation 'nos' was added in an unknown hand.
[36]The emendation 'correximus' was made in the same unknown hand as 'nos' above.

23. Of concluding a synod.[34]

The bishop shall not allow a synod to be *extended* **prolonged** for many days, but shall put an end to it as *quickly* **soon** as possible, because it is not to the benefit of the pastors or their flocks that they should be *away* **separated** from one another for *too* long. Therefore he shall pronounce sentence in lawsuits and quarrels which they can decide in that short space of time. Otherwise, those things which need further consideration, he shall either judge at another time in his tribunal, or he shall indicate to the archdeacon when he sets out on his visitation in the month of September, what he has decided. [*But*] **as regards** questions which are matters of doctrine and ceremonies, he shall *publish* **publicly declare** some of the canons and the rest he shall entrust to the archdeacon for *publication* **public declaration** on his next visit. Moreover, the lower ministers shall accept his decrees and sentences, *published* **declared** either by himself in the synod or by the archdeacon on his visitation, as valid and firm. But if there is something in them which they have decided is either unjust or absurd, they shall refer the matter to the *archbishop** **us,***[35] whose duty it will be either to confirm or to modify the bishop's statute, decree or sentence, yet **in such a way that** they shall *have* **retain** their force and strength to the extent that **we have***[36] *the archbishop has** not corrected them. Therefore, by his decrees and sentences promulgated in the synod, the bishop shall order his clergy to care and take concern for the flock entrusted to them, and he shall command them to return every one to their own **churches**, in peace and with the Spirit of the Lord.

[100r; 53b]   **21. DE ECCLESIARUM GARDIANIS**

1.[1]

Gardianorum munera haec sunto, nempe ecclesiarum bona, iura, debita et legata petere et administrare: adulteros, scortatores, incestuosos, [*usuarios*], oblocutores, divinatores, haereticos, simoniacos, periuros et alios gravi infamia notatos in parochia morantes vel delinquentes, ac in ecclesia vel coemeterio rixantes sive pugnantes., N/**n**ecnon[2] eos qui divinis precibus, cultui sacro, vel divinis mysteriis, diebus domini*bu*/**c**is et festivis, (nullis propediti legitimis impedimentis), interesse [*de more*] noluerint, loci ordinario denuntiare; alios vero inter divina in ecclesia tumultuantes, et confabulatione vel strepitu sacra mysteria perturbantes, duabus vicibus ut sileant [54a] adhortari. Quod si eorum, [100v] vel unius eorum hortatibus non *ac*quieverint, infra mensem id loci ordinario, vel per seipsos, vel per litteras, aut a rectore aut a vicario **subscriptas**, significari curabunt. Quae crimina si{*c*} per gardianos delata et legitimis modis probata, poenis ordinariorum iudicio infligendis puniri volumus absque dilatione.

Praeterea, ad gardianos spectabit cancellae, mansionum et domorum ad rectorem, vicarium, praebendarium, collegii vel hospitalis magistrum spectantium ruinas et ceterarum rerum dilapidation*ibus*/**e** defectus, et curatorum seu ministrorum negligentias et errores loci ordinario significare. Necnon ecclesiae parochialis navem, turrim, campanas, libros et alia [101r] ecclesiae ornamenta, ac Sacrae Scripturae sententias parietibus inscribendas, de pecuniis ecclesiae quoties opus fuerit reparare, vel ut fiant procurare; nec non coemeterium clausura decenti cingere. Et si ecclesiae pecuniae ad praemissa perficienda sufficere non valeant, licebit eis, cum consensu quattuor graviorum parochianorum, per eos ad hoc deligendorum, collectam singulis parochianis (modo seipsos ante alios ad iustam portionem solvendam obligent), pro ratione facultatum imponere. Quod si parochiani collectam huiusmodi ad diem per eos constitutum solvere distulerint, seu contumaciter recusaverint, et per gardianos loci ordinario d[*e*/**i**]lati fuerint, ad solvendam collectam huiusmodi cum expensis moderatis per censuras ecclesiasticas erunt per [101v] ordinarium compellendi.

Pecunia in pauperum cista piorum largitione reposita, ad festa Nativitatis Domini et Pentecostes, ac aliis temporibus, si necessitas postula[**veri**]t, per gardianos praedictos, de consilio rectoris, vicarii, vel parochi, et aliorum quattuor

---

[1]C. 12 of Exeter II, 1287 (PC, 1005-8); cf. H.C., 34.1; 1603/85, 89.
[2]This was formerly the beginning of a new sentence.

21. OF CHURCHWARDENS

1.[1]

The tasks of wardens shall be these: namely, to seek and administer the property, rights, dues and legacies of the churches; to report to the local ordinary adulterers, harlots, incestuous persons, [*usurers*], slanderers, diviners, heretics, simoniacs, perjurers and others of notoriously bad reputation who dwell or loiter in the parish, and those who brawl or fight in the churchyard, as[2] well as those who are [*habitually*] unwilling to attend divine prayers, the sacred service, or the divine mysteries, on Sundays and holy days, (being hindered by no lawful impediments); also to give others who make a noise in church during divine service and disturb the sacred mysteries with their talking and shouting two warnings, that they should be silent. But if they, or one of them, shall refuse to obey these warnings the wardens shall ensure that the matter is reported within a month to the local ordinary, either by themselves or by letters **signed** by the rector or the vicar. It is our will that such crimes, {*so* if} reported by the wardens and proved by lawful means, we desire to be punished without delay by penalties to be imposed at the judgment of the ordinaries.

Furthermore, it will be the wardens' responsibility to report to the local ordinary any ruins of the chancel, dwellings, and houses which belong to the rector, vicar, prebendary or master of a college or hospital, as well as any defects arising from the dilapidations, and the omissions and errors of the curates or ministers. They shall also repair the nave of the parish church and the tower, and ensure that the bells, books and other ornaments of the church are provided, and that the verses of Holy Scripture which are meant to be inscribed on the walls actually are. They shall also enclose the churchyard with a decent fence. And if the monies of the church are not enough to cover the above, it shall be lawful for them, with the agreement of four of the more senior parishioners, to be chosen by them for this purpose, to impose a collection on individual parishioners rated according to their ability to pay (provided that they first commit themselves to pay a just portion). But if the parishioners defer payment of this collection, or contumaciously refuse to pay it on the day determined by the wardens, and they are reported by the wardens to the local ordinary, they shall be compelled by the ordinary, using ecclesiastical censures, to pay the said collection along with reasonable expenses.

Money placed in the poor box by the generosity of the godly shall be faithfully distributed among the poor of the parish and assigned to other godly uses, in so far as need demands, at Christmas and Pentecost, and at other times,

ex primoribus parochiae per eos ad h[o/**ae**]c vocandorum, inter pauperes parochiae aut in alios pios usus, prout necessitas po[54b]stulat, fideliter distribuatur.

Gardiani ad ordinariorum visitationes, synodos et capitula vocati, ut suarum administrationum ration*u*/em reddant, (si necesse fuerit), et peccata in parochiis [**in**] quibus degunt commissa referant, per se ipsos compar{*a*/**e**}re non detrectent.

[102r] Si vero gardiani in denuntiandis vel reparandis praemissis, vel in aliquibus aliis faciendis quae ad ipsorum officium spectabunt, negligentes extiterint, et loci ordinario per facti evidentiam, famam publicam, vel alicuius fide digni relationem constiterit, aliquid in parochia corrigendum esse aut reformandum, id (mulctatis ante omnia gardianis negligentibus poena pecuniaria, arbitr[*io*/**atu**] suo pauperum cistae parochiae illius persolvend*um*/**a**) *ordinarius*** **episcopus***[3] ipse ratione sui officii, licet a nullo instigetur, si voluerit, corrigere et reformare poterit.

In capellis vero ultra unum milliare ab ecclesia parochiali distantibus, eodem modo et forma [102v] gardianos eligi et creari volumus atque fit in parochiis, paremque per omnia potestatem exercere valeant, et poenis similibus subiacebunt. Capellas vero ab ecclesiis parochialibus ultra unum milliare non distantes (nisi incolae per inundationem aquarum ecclesiam parochialem multoties adire non valeant) penitus sublatas esse volumus, et ad [**ecclesiarum**] parochialium [*ecclesiarum*] usum omnia ill[*a*/**o**]rum bona converti.

---

[3]Added in the same unknown hand as 'nos' and 'correximus' in the previous chapter.

if need demands, by the aforesaid wardens, on the advice of the rector, the vicar, or the parish priest, and of four other leading members of the parish appointed by them for this purpose.

Wardens summoned to the visitations of the ordinaries, synods and chapters, in order to give an account of their administrations, (if need be), and to report the sins which have been committed in the parishes in which they dwell, shall not fail to appear in person.

And if the wardens turn out to be negligent in reporting or in repairing the above, or in doing anything else which belongs to their office, and the local ordinary is informed that something in the parish must be corrected or reformed by evidence of the fact, public rumour or the report of some trustworthy person, the *ordinary** **bishop***[3] shall be able to correct and reform it himself, by reason of his office, even if the matter has not been instigated by anybody, if he so wishes (having first of all fined the negligent wardens with a financial penalty, to be paid at his discretion to the poor box of that parish).

And in chapels which are more than one mile distant from the parish church, it is our will that wardens shall be elected and created according to the same manner and form, and that they shall be able to exercise the same power in all things as they would in parishes, and that they should be subject to the same penalties. But it is our will that chapels which are less than one mile distant from the parish churches shall be completely subject to them (unless the inhabitants are often unable to get to the parish church because of flooding), and that all their goods shall be turned over to the use of the parish churches.

[104r; 54b]   **22. DE PAROCHIARUM LIMITATIONE**[1]

1.[2]

Si *inter controversiam* in foro ecclesiastico *vertendam* de finibus parochiarum sit contentio, ea per iudicem ecclesiasticum, testibus et aliis probationibus legitimis, terminabitur. Et quo magis parochiarum limites omnibus semper innotescant, decernimus ut singulis annis minister ecclesiae, cum gardianis et aliis quattuor viris per gardianos nominandis, in hebdomada Penteco[55a]stis totam parochiam circumeant, limitesque et terminos pervideant, observentque praesentes antiquos singularum parochiarum fines, **in libroque conscribi faciant quem in ecclesiae cista tuto reponent.** Et si minister vel alius ex praedictis huic nostro decreto contumax et inoboediens unquam reperiatur, simulatque de eiusmodi inoboedientia visitatori aut alii iudici cuicunque idoneo constiterit, in decem libr[a/i]s mulctabitur communi ecclesiae scrinio persolvend[a/i]is.

Ecclesia[s/e] quae per fructuum exilitatem idoneum ministrum sustentare nequeant, per locorum episcopos de consensu patronorum (salvis nobis decimis *ad ipsius aestimationem* per ecclesiam cui fuerit adiuncta annuatim solvendis) vicinori**bus** *alicui* ecclesi*ae*/**is** uniri et annecti permittimus. Quod si patronus ecclesiae annectendae praedictae unioni consentire noluerit, tantum de suo patrimonio impartiat ecclesiae indigenti, quantum ad sufficientem sustentationem idonei rectoris, vel vicarii sufficere videatur; et ad id per loci ordinarium compellatur.

[105r] Latas insuper et spatiosas parochias, [*cum earum maior pars vel saltem* **in quibus**] magna parochianorum pars ultra quattuor milliaria ab ecclesia parochiali distare dinoscitur, dividi et separari per locorum ordinarios volumus, et inter diversos rectores vel vicarios distribui, ut magis expedire visum fuerit, salvis semper nobis ecclesiae decimis prius taxatis, ac patroni ecclesiae iure conservato.

---

[1]This was originally a subsection of the preceding chapter.
[2]X, 2.19.13 (Fr, II, 314), originally a decretal of Pope Honorius III (1216-27); X, 3.29.4 (Fr, II, 555), originally a decretal of Pope Urban III (1185-7); H.C., 32.1.

22. OF PARISH BOUNDARIES[1]

1.[2]

If there is a dispute about parish boundaries *which forms part of a controversy to be heard* in an ecclesiastical court, it shall be decided by an ecclesiastical judge, using witnesses and other lawful proofs. And in order that the parish boundaries shall become ever more familiar to everyone, we decree that every year the minister of the church, with the wardens and four other men to be named by the wardens, shall go about the entire parish in the week of Pentecost, and inspect the boundaries and markers, and observe the present ancient limits of individual parishes, **and have them written in a book which they shall deposit safely in the church chest.** And if the minister or another of the aforesaid persons shall ever be found to be contumacious and disobedient to this our decree, as soon as the visitor or any other suitable ecclesiastical judge finds out about it, he shall be fined ten pounds to be paid to the common fund of the church.

We allow churches which cannot sustain a suitable minister because of the smallness of their fruits to be united and annexed by the local bishops to *some* neighbouring churches, with the consent of the patrons (saving to us the tithes which by his estimation should be paid every year through the church to which it has been joined). But if the patron of the aforesaid church to be annexed does not want to agree to the union, then he shall contribute from his own resources to the impoverished church as much as is needed to sustain a suitable rector, or an amount sufficient for a vicar, and he shall be compelled to do this by the local ordinary.

Moreover, it is our will that broad and large parishes, [*where the majority or at least* **in which**] a large percentage of the parishioners is known to live more than four miles away from the parish church, shall be divided and separated by the local ordinaries, and distributed among different rectors and vicars, as appears to be most expedient, saving always to us the tithes already assessed, and retaining the patron's right to the church.

[106r; 55a]   **23. DE SCHOLIS ET LUDIMAGISTRIS**[1]

1. De scholis habendis in ecclesiis cathedralibus.[2]

Ut Verbi Dei cognitio retineatur in ecclesia, quod absque linguarum peritia vix fieri potest, ut *barbaries non sinatur* **inscitia** inter nostros homines, et praesertim ministros ecclesiae *obrepere* **non regnet**, *utque* doctrina **deinde** quae donum Spiritus Sancti est **ut** quam latissime propagetur, et denique ut feliciora ingenia **litterarum** institutione *litteraria irrogentur et foveantur* **nutriantur et crescant**, volumus ut quaeli[55b]bet ecclesia cathedralis per universum nostrum regnum scholam habeat, *quo* **ut** pueri qui *iam* prima **iam** elementa **praeceptorum labore per**didicerunt *sub tutela et cura ludimagistri* in *sp...* scholis publicis deinceps erudiantur. Atque decano et capitulo erit curae, ut vel ex communibus ecclesiae redditibus, vel ex propriis fructibus praebendarum, singulo quoque anno viginti librae numerentur ludimagistro; aut si hoc fieri non possit, certa aliqua praebenda ad hoc destinetur, ut integri eius fructus scholae praeceptori cedant. Qui **licet** a suis discipulis *nil exiget pro mercede* **nullam mercedem capiat**, non tamen prohibebitur a do/itioribus accipere si quid obtulerint; a pauperioribus [*vero*] *nil prorsus accipiat* **nihil omnino sumet**, cum maxime ad eorum inopiam *re*/**sub**levandam in ecclesiis hoc institutum servari decrev[*er*]imus.

2. A quo scholae praeceptor sit [**d**]{*e*/**i**}l[*e*/**i**]gendus.[3]

Examinatio et admissio ludimagistri ad episcopum pertineat, quamvis in aliquibus ecclesiis fortassis aliter fuerit hactenus constitutum. In eo vero probando haec imprimis observ[*a*/**e**]nt[*o*/**u**]r. Sit in evangelica doctrina sincerus, moribus integris, *conversatione* **vita** gravis, grammatices et human[*io*/**a**]rum litterarum peritus, atque valetudine tam firmus ut docendi labores ferre valeat. Quae si deesse viderit episcopus, [106v] aut si prius quidem ad tempus affuerint, postea vitiata esse et corrupta **intellex**{*er*}**it**, oblatum sibi ad munus docendi non admittet, aut iam admissum *re*/**sub**movebit.

---

[1]This was originally a subsection of chapter 21. All additions to the MS are in an unknown hand.
[2]X, 5.5.1 (Fr, II, 768-9), originally c. 18 of Lateran III, 1179 (*C.O.D.*, 220); X, 5.5.4 (Fr, II, 770), originally c. 11 of Lateran IV, 1215 (*C.O.D.*, 240).
[3]Cf. D, 37 c. 12 (Fr, I, 139); X, 3.1.3 (Fr, II, 449), of uncertain origin; X, 5.5.4 (Fr, II, 770), originally c. 11 of Lateran IV, 1215 (*C.O.D.*, 240); Robert Winchelsey, *Reg.*, fo. 50a (1310); William Courtenay, *Reg.*, fo. 10b (1382); 1571/9.

23. OF SCHOOLS AND SCHOOLMASTERS[1]

1. Of having schools in cathedral churches.[2]

In order for a knowledge of the Word of God to be retained in the church, which is hardly possible without expertise in languages, and in order that *barbarity* **ignorance** shall not be allowed to *creep in* **reign** among our people, and especially the ministers of the church, and so that learning, which is the gift of the Holy Spirit, should be spread as widely as possible, and finally so that sounder minds may be *planted and fostered* **nurtured and grow** by an education **in letters**, it is our will that every cathedral church throughout the whole of our kingdom shall have a school, so that boys who have already *learned* **mastered** the first elements **through the effort of tutors** *under the guidance and care of a schoolmaster* may be further educated in public schools. And it shall be the responsibility of the dean and chapter to pay a schoolmaster twenty pounds a year, either out of the common revenues of the church or out of income belonging to the prebends, or if this cannot be done, that one particular prebend shall be set aside for this purpose so that its entire income may go to the master of the school. Even if the schoolmaster does not *ask* **receive** anything from his pupils by way of remuneration, nevertheless he shall not be prevented from accepting something from the wealthier ones, if they offer it to him, [*but*] he shall not *accept* **take** anything at all from the poorer ones, because we have decreed that the establishment of schools in the churches is designed above all to compensate for their poverty.

2. By whom the master of a school is to be chosen.[3]

The examination and admission of a schoolmaster is the bishop's responsibility, even if in some churches the matter has been decided differently up to now. And in testing him, these are the things which are to be looked for above all. He is to be sincere in his profession of evangelical doctrine, of sound morals, sober in his *behaviour* **lifestyle**, an expert in grammar and the humanities, and strong enough in health to be able to withstand the strains of teaching. If the bishop sees that these qualities are lacking, or if he realizes that although they were once there for a time, they have since become ruined and corrupted, he shall not appoint the candidate to the post of teaching, or if he has already been appointed, he shall remove him.

3. De visitatione scholae.[4]

Bis unoquoque anno loci ordinarius puerorum progressus in studiis explorabit, atque tunc ingenia quae videbuntur ad litteras nimis inepta excludet; libros parum idoneos doceri non sinet, sed utiliores praescribet; praeceptorem vero igna[56a]viae aut *remissae diligentiae* **nimiae cessationis** suspectum coram decano, vel eo absente, vicedecano et duobus praebendariis arguet. Quod si bis **frustra** fecerit *absque fructu*, tertio delinquentem loco movebit.

4. Quae in arbitrio sunt ludimagistri quoad scholam regendam.

Rationem docendi servabit praeceptor, quam ad *captum* **ingenium** et *utilitatem* **indolem** puerorum iudicabit esse commodissimam; tot lectiones habebit quot esse utiles existimaverit; pro conditione ac *profectu* **progressione** scholasticorum distinguet classes, *quoetiam ad horas, cum docendi tum examinandi, exercendi stilum et repetendi ea faciet quae institutioni ac eruditioni iuvenum putaverit magis convenire.* **Reliqua vero docendi, interrogandi, repetendi, stylum exercendi, tempora sic disp[e/a]rtiet, quemadmodum ratio videbitur illorum eruditionis et ingenii postulare.**

5. Quae institutio grammatices retinenda sit.[5]

Mandamus etiam ut in singulis scholis non alia ratio grammatices in usum assumatur, quam quae iam olim a nobis proposita fuit et approbata.

[107r] 6. De catechismo ante omnia tractando.[6]

Statim post primorum *cognitionem* **perceptionem** rudimentorum, singuli discipuli catechismum Latinum discant, neque ad sedes prius transferantur sublimiores, quam ad catechismi quaestiones respondere valeant.

---

[4]Cf. R, 20.14.
[5]1547/34 (*D.E.R.*, 257); 1571/9.2.
[6]The catechism of Archbishop Cranmer, 1548, included in the confirmation rite of the B.C.P., 1549. By the time this text was re-presented to parliament in 1571, there was another catechism, prepared by Alexander Nowell, dean of St Paul's, and submitted to the convocation of Canterbury, which approved it on 3 March 1563.

3. Of the visitation of a school.[4]

Twice in every year the local ordinary shall examine the progress of the boys in their studies, and at that time he shall expel those minds which appear to be less gifted for letters. He shall not allow unsuitable books to be taught, but shall prescribe more helpful ones, and he shall report any teacher suspected of ignorance or of *lack of diligence* **excessive laziness** to the dean, or in his absence, to the vicedean and two prebendaries. But if he has done this twice **in vain** *without result*, on the third occasion he shall remove the delinquent from his post.

4. Matters regarding the governance of a school which are left to the schoolmaster's discretion.

The master shall use the teaching method which he considers most appropriate to the *understanding* **minds** and *benefit* **character** of the boys; he shall give as many lessons as he shall think fit; he shall stream classes according to the condition and *advance* **progress** of the scholars, *and as far as the hours for teaching and examining, for penmanship and for recitation are concerned, he shall do whatever he thinks is most appropriate for the education and learning of the youth.* **And he shall so divide up the times remaining for teaching, questioning, reciting, and penmanship, as the needs of their education and minds shall seem to demand.**

5. What textbook of grammar is to be retained.[5]

Also, we order that in individual schools there shall be no method of grammar brought into use, other than the one which has already been put forward and approved by us.

6. Of studying the catechism above all else.[6]

All the pupils, immediately after *knowing* **picking up** the basic elements, shall learn the Latin catechism, and they shall not be promoted to higher classes until they are able to answer the questions of the catechism.

7. Quid in schola sit agendum in primo ingressu matutino, et postremo egressu vespertino.

Quamprimum hypodidascalus aut ludimagister ingreditur mane **in** scholam, recitabunt omnes discipuli simul clara voce lingua vernacula duodecim *articulos* **capita** fidei, orationem Dominicam et decem praecepta legis, et ad finem [56b] cuiusque praecepti dicent 'Domine miserere', et haec nostris suggere cordibus, atque hoc itidem sub noctem facient priusquam scholam egrediantur.

8. De cura in discipulos diebus festis.[7]

Dominicis autem et festis diebus conveniant pueri mane ad scholam, atque inde a ludimagistro ad templum deducantur, [*atque* **ac**] illic sub eius custodia maneant, quoad sacra fuerint absoluta; idemque pomeridiano tempore fiet, quando vel ad catechismum, vel ad vespertinas preces eundum erit; sic enim cavebitur ne pueri temere a sacris absint, neve in templo strepant aut discurrant dum sacra peraguntur.

[107v] 9. De aetate puerorum admittendorum in scholam.

Cum pueri sunt in scholam recipiendi, non sint minores octo annis, neque natu maiores quattuordecim.

10. De conditionibus admittendorum discipulorum.[8]

Nullus puer in scholam recipiatur, qui non possit Anglice apprime legere, atque catechismum Anglice editum memoriter recitare, atque suum nomen propria manu scribere. Puer item qui non habet Novum Testamentum Anglicum ne admittatur. Nam ludimagister curare debet, ut dominicis diebus in eo se pueri ad annum exerceant. Quod idem fiet post annum in Novo Testamento Latine conscript*um*/**o**. Cetera vero de ludimagistris et puerorum institutione a statutis ecclesiae cathedralis petantur, si qua ibi sint, modo his nostris legibus non repugnent.

---

[7]Cf. 1571/9.4.
[8]Cf. 1536/5 (*D.E.R.*, 177); 1538/5 (*D.E.R.*, 180).

7. What should be done in school at the beginning of the day in the morning and at the end of it in the evening.

As soon as the deputy teacher or schoolmaster enters the school in the morning, all the pupils shall recite in a clear voice and in the vernacular tongue the twelve *articles* **points** of faith, the Lord's prayer and the ten commandments of the law, and at the end of each the tutors shall say 'Lord have mercy', and implant these things in our hearts, and they shall do exactly the same thing at night, before leaving the school.

8. Of caring for pupils on feast days.[7]

And on Sundays and feast days, the boys shall gather at the school in the morning and from there they shall be taken by the schoolmaster to the church, and there they shall remain in his custody until the services are finished; and the same thing shall be done in the afternoon, when they ought to go either to catechism or to the evening prayers, for care must be taken to ensure that the boys are not wilfully absent from the services, and that they do not shout or run about in the church while the services are being conducted.

9. Of the age of boys to be admitted to the school.

When the boys are to be admitted to the school, they shall not be less than eight nor more than fourteen years of age.

10. Of the conditions for admitting pupils.[8]

No boy shall be admitted to the school who cannot read English fluently, and recite by memory the English edition of the catechism, and write his name in his own hand. Likewise, a boy who does not have a New Testament in English shall not be admitted. For the schoolmaster must ensure that the boys shall study it every Sunday for a year. After a year they shall do the same with the New Testament in Latin. Other matters pertaining to schoolmasters and the education of boys shall be found in the statutes of the cathedral church, if there are any, as long as they are not repugnant to these our laws.

[108r; 57a] 24. DE ACADEMIIS ET PRIMUM DE PRAEFECTIS COLLEGIORUM[1]

1.[2]

Curent fundatores ut praefecti **posthac** *sint presbyteri**, *quoad* **veramque** religionem *sinceri* **colant**, *quique* et sanam doctrinam omnibus modis *promoveant* **amplificent**, *et unoquoque anno singuli praefectorum in ecclesia* universitatis ***academiae propria*** *aliquando contionentur.**

2. De iusto scholasticorum numero in collegiis retinendo.[3]

Scholasticorum praescriptus numerus a statutis non imminuatur; qui tamen, si quando vel annonae nimia difficultate, vel alia quapiam necessitate maxima retineri non poterit, attamen in theologica facultate omnino plenus et integer servetur.

3. Scholasticorum negligentia coerceatur.[4]

Qui theologiae aut aliis generibus doctrinarum sunt addicti, si lectiones ad suam facultatem pertinentes tum publicas, tum sui collegii privatas neglexerint, parte sui annui stipendii ad arbitrium praefecti collegii mulctentur, nisi valetudine adversa impediantur.

4. De theologis admittendis ad gradus.[5]

Quando scholastici theologi vel baccalaurei vel doctores creabuntur, de *articulis* **capitibus** in religione controversis diligenter *examinentur* **interrogentur**, neque

---

[1]MS additions are in the same unknown hand as those in the preceding chapters.
[2]L, 5.5.4, c. 10 of the council of Oxford, 1407.
[3]Adapted from 1268/49 (PC, 788).
[4]Cf. 28 Henry VIII, c. 13, s. 2, 1536 (*S.R.*, III, 668-9).
[5]L, 5.5.4, c. 10 of the council of Oxford, 1407; statute of Archbishop Henry Chichele, 6 November 1417 (W, III, 381-2); ibid., 16 July 1421 (W, III, 401-2).

24. OF UNIVERSITIES, PARTICULARLY OF THE HEADS OF COLLEGES[1]

1.[2]

The founders shall ensure that **from now on** the heads *shall be presbyters,* sound in matters of* **and that they practise the true** religion, and that they shall *promote* **advance** sound doctrine in every way, *and every year each of the heads shall preach at some point in the university church.*

2. Of maintaining the proper number of scholars in the colleges.[3]

The number of scholars prescribed by the statutes shall not be decreased, but even if at some point the full quota cannot be maintained, either because of some problem with the funding or because of some other very great necessity, the full and complete number shall be kept up in the theological faculty.

3. The negligence of scholars shall be punished.[4]

If those who are devoted to theology or to other kinds of learning fail to attend the lectures relating to their subject, whether public or private within their college, they shall be fined a part of their annual stipend at the discretion of the head of the college, unless they have been kept away by poor health.

4. Of admitting theologians to degrees.[5]

When theological students are to be made bachelors or doctors they shall be diligently *examined* **questioned** on disputed *articles* **points** in religion, and they

ad hos gradus admittantur, nisi *quoad* legitimam veramque intelligentiam in *articulis illic* **capitibus** propositis *consenserint et subscripserint* [57b] **et sermone et subscriptione velint agnoscere.**

[108v] 5. Ut in academiis non commorentur qui habent sacerdotia.[6]

In academiis et collegiis non *ferantur* **remaneant**, qui sacerdotia sunt adsecuti quibus animarum cura coniuncta est, cum *praesentes* **illorum** ad pascendum gregem sibi commissum **praesentia** requira*n*tur. Quia tamen primitiae ab eis solvendae sunt, *pro* primo/**i** anno/**i respectu**, cum fuerint socii collegiorum, inde tantum emolumenti accipiant, quantum eis daretur ad *annuam substantiam sustentationem* **anni totius impensas sustentandas**, si in collegiis adessent. Qui vero praebendas nacti fuerint absque cura animarum, si primitias cogantur solvere, primo anno impensis collegii sui vivere poterunt, *quo elapso ministro, tum ad suas ecclesias ire* **deinde suis ecclesiis inservire** coge/antur, nisi fortasse ab episcopo et capitulo suo *facultatem habuerint* **potestatem impetraverint** commorandi ad aliquod tempus in academia, ut in *titulis* **capitibus** 'De admittendis ad ecclesiastica beneficia',[7] et 'De praebendariis'[8] antea cautum est; quo tempore suis ipsorum vivent impensis, neque a collegiis *victum* **impensas** accipient, cum illis aliunde prospectum sit.

6. De adiuvandis scholasticis pauperibus.[9]

Providendum est etiam ut ex legatis ad pias causas, et ex eleemosynis extraordinariis aliquid subinde scholasticis pauperibus *erogetur* **distribuatur**, his praesertim qui operam suam ecclesiastico ministerio addixerunt, et praeter sui collegii stipendium nihil habent, quod est saepe numero admodum tenue, quoniam si rationibus his non foveantur et *illis addantur anni* **excitentur illorum studia,** *alio* facile *studia sua conferent* **suas voluntates ad alia detorquebunt,** et ecclesia ministris *idoneis carebit* **aptis destituetur.**

[6]21 Henry VIII, c. 13, ss. 15, 17, 1529 (*S.R.*, III, 292-6); amended by 28 Henry VIII, c. 13, 1536 (*S.R.*, III, 668-9); cf. H.C., 35.4.
[7]R, 11.
[8]R, 20.9.
[9]Cf. 1536/9 (*D.E.R.*, 178); 1547/15 (*D.E.R.*, 252).

shall not be admitted to those degrees unless they have *assented and subscribed to* **been willing to acknowledge both orally and in writing** the lawful and true interpretation of the *articles* **points** *there* set forth.

5. That those who have livings shall not reside in the universities.[6]

Those who have obtained livings to which a cure of souls is attached shall not *be tolerated* **remain** in the universities and colleges, since *they are* **their presence is** required *to be present* in order to pastor the flock entrusted to them. Nevertheless, because the first fruits must be paid by them, *for* **in respect of** the first year, they shall receive from the colleges of which they have been fellows the same salary as would have been given to them *for their yearly maintenance* **to meet their expenses for a full year**, if they had been in the colleges. And those who have found prebends without a cure of souls, if they are compelled to pay the first fruits, may live for the first year at the expense of their college, *but when that duty is fulfilled,* they shall be compelled to *go to* **minister in** their churches, unless by chance they have *received permission* **acquired power** from the bishop and his chapter to reside for some time in the university, as has already been specified in the *titles* **chapters** 'Of admitting to ecclesiastical benefices'[7] and 'Of prebendaries'.[8] During that time they shall live at their own expense, nor shall they receive *board* **expenses** from the colleges, since they have been provided for elsewhere.

6. Of assisting poor scholars.[9]

It shall also be provided that something shall regularly be *reserved* **distributed** to poor scholars from legacies given to godly causes, and from special alms, especially to those who have devoted their labours to the church's ministry and who have nothing besides their college stipend, because that is often so small that if they were not favoured in these ways and *years given to them* **their desire to study aroused**, they might easily *take their studies elsewhere* **turn their wishes aside to other things**, and the church would *lack* **be deprived of** *suitable* **fit** ministers.

[144r; 58a]   **25. DE DECIMIS**[1]

1. Decimas esse solvendas.[2]

Quoniam Dominus noster Iesus Christus hanc ipse legem sancivit, ut qui doctrinam inter homines evangelii con[*s*/**f**]erunt, ex docendi lab/**o**/re praesidia vitae metant,[3] et eiusdem Domini nostri testificatione, digni sunt mercede quicunque sunt in opere,[4] porro divinum ius scriptum bovi trituranti cum os [*al*/**ob**]ligari non sinat,[5] nobis exemplum divinae clementiae repetendum est, et valide videndum ne vel nimia nostrorum hominum avaritia vel negligentia fiat, *vel* **ut** ecclesiarum nostrarum ministris iusti et convenientes fructus ex sanctissimorum occupatione munerum non suppeditentur.

2. Decimae praediales quomodo solvi debent.[6]

Igitur auctoritate nostra constitutum sit, ut omnes singulique subditi nostri, locis et temporibus designatis et legitimis, decimas omnium rerum ex praediis provenientium ministris seponant, sive foenum si[**n**]t, sive fruges qualescunque quorumcunque locorum, sive crocum, sive cannabis, sive linum, sive [144v] sint olera, vel arborum fructus, vel aliae cuiuscunque generis ex fundis utilitates exortae; semper enim quamcunque rationem aut conditionem hae commoditates habeant, decimas [*earum*] univers[*a*/**o**]rum integre et explete rebus ex ipsis exemptas, eadem specie qua prius ex fundis colligebantur, ministris repraesentari placet, exceptis robustis et proceris arboribus quae vicesimum ad annum excrever[*u*/**i**]nt, et aedificiis aut melioribus reservatae propositis, ad focum non praeparantur.

Ex molendinorum fructibus, ex caespitibus[**, carbonibus**] effossis, ex lapidicinis, et aliis omnibus huius generis oppor[58b]tunitatibus decimae sevocentur ad ministros. Similiter ex pascuis, vel ceteris quibuscunque terris, decimae ministris eximantur, in quas equi, iuvenci, boves et effeta quaecunque

---

[1]A marginal note in Cranmer's hand reads: 'This is finished by us, but must be overseen again by Dr Haddon.'
[2]27 Henry VIII, c. 20, 1536 (*S. R.*, III, 551-2).
[3]Cf. Mk. vi. 8-11; Lk. ix. 3-5.
[4]Lk. x. 7.
[5]I Co. ix. 9; I Ti. v. 18, from Dt. xxv. 4.
[6]X, 3.30.21 (Fr, II, 563), originally a decretal of Pope Clement III (1187-91); X, 3.30.22 (Fr, II, 563) and X, 3.30.23 (Fr, II, 563-4), both originally decretals of Pope Celestine III (1191-8).

25. OF TITHES[1]

1. Tithes are to be paid.[2]

Since our Lord Jesus Christ himself ordained this law, that those who [*sow* **preach**] the doctrine of the Gospel among men shall reap their livelihood from their work of teaching,[3] and by the witness of our same Lord, all those who labour are deserving of reward,[4] and further the written divine law does not allow an ox to thresh with his mouth muzzled,[5] we must imitate the example of divine mercy, and valiantly see to it that neither the excessive greed of our people, nor their negligence, shall result in a situation in which the just and appropriate rewards from employment in the most holy duties are not paid to the ministers of our churches.

2. How predial tithes shall be paid.[6]

Therefore let it be decreed by our authority that all and singular our subjects shall, at designated and lawful places and times, set aside tithes of all produce from the fields for the ministers, whether [*it is* **they are**] hay or any kind of fruits of whatever places, or saffron or hemp or flax, or whether they are oils or the fruits of trees or other profits of whatever kind which have come from farms; for whatever quantity or quality these commodities may have, a full and complete tithe of [*them*] all shall always be put aside from the things themselves, in the same form that they were in when they were first collected from the farms, and presented to the ministers, except for strong and tall trees which are more than twenty years old and which are being kept in reserve for buildings or better uses, and which are not intended for the fireplace.

Tithes shall be set aside for the ministers out of the fruits of mills, [**coal**]mines which have been dug, quarries and of all other instances of this kind. Likewise, tithes shall be paid to the ministers from the pastures, or from any other lands onto which horses, donkeys, oxen and any other breeding animals are

animalia sunt [*im*]missa. Decimae deriventur etiam ex fecundorum animalium quibuscunque foetibus aut fructibus, et in hoc numero sunt, exempli causa, vaccae, sues, oves, equae, cygni, gallinae, anseres, columbae, cuniculi, damae, pisces, apes, et alia paris conditionis animalia. Fructus ex eisdem animalibus, butyrum, caseus, lac consideratum sua natura, cum nec in butyrum nec caseum infunditur, lana, [*m/v*]el, cera, quibus quidem ex fructibus universis, non minus quam ex ipsis foetibus, decimas plene et particulatim, nullo nec dolo nec astutia, [145r] volumus ad ministrorum utilitatem secerni.[7]

Denique totum ius decimarum ex omnibus et [**ex**] singulis praediorum commodis et opportunitatibus percipiendarum ad rationem et formam in parliamento praescriptam, quo**d** anno secundo et tertio regni nostri celebratum est, determinari volumus, et eisdem modis et poenis procedere, quae definita sunt in nominati parliamenti tertio decimo capite.[8] Quod parliamenti decretum et eius singula verba ac sententiae praesentem ad concludendam decimarum causam auctoritatem firmam et prorsus inviolatam habebunt, non minus quam si fuissent huc infusa; nisi forte sit in illis aliquid huiusmodi, quod cum praesentibus his legibus nostris manifeste pugnet. Verum illa parliamenti decreta quoniam omnes decimarum repraesentandarum formulas in se non compraehendunt, et multae dubitationes in hanc quotidie causam decimarum incidunt, de quibus in parliamento nihil determinatum fuit, ad minuendas quaestiones ista curavimus intexi, quae sunt ordine consecutura.

[59a] 3. Animalium decima annua quomodo iuxta numeri rationem solvatur.[9]

Si cuiquam obvenerint tantum sex vituli, vel pauciores sex, pro singulis vitulis duos denarios respectu decimae ministro pendat; si septem erunt, [145v] unum ministro segregabit, et minister vicissim sex denarios, aequalitatis constituendae causa, personae refundet a qua vitulum acc[*i/e*]pit. Eodem modo cum octo vituli fuerint, unus eximetur ministro; sed ille rursus cum quattuor denariis exuberantem decimam compensabit. Si vero novem vituli reperiantur, vitulum accipiens duos tantum denarios minister exhibebit. Quod si decimarum malit plenum beneficium minister exspectare, nec suo iure velit uti, donec legitimus decem vitulorum numerus expletus sit, commodum dilationis, (ut multis in rebus iure civili constitutum est), aliqua ex parte feret, hoc est, cum tempus legitimi numeri venerit, uno aut duobus exceptis, ex reliquis sumet decem vitulis quem voluerit. Et eandem illos rationem sequi volumus in pullis equinis et consimilibus. De agnis vero, cygnis et aliis animalibus quibuscunque quorum similis est aestimatio, pro singulo quoque denarius ultro citroque dabitur, cum pauciora quam decem fuerint. In ceteris autem minutioribus animalculis, quae tam exile momentum habent, ut illorum decimae certa ratione non possint iniri,

---

[7]Based on L, 3.16.5,7. See H.C., 24.1.
[8]2-3 Edward VI, c. 13, 1548 (*S.R.*, IV, 55-8).
[9]Based on L, 3.16.5,7. See H.C., 24.1.

put. Tithes shall also be taken from any offspring or fruits of fecund animals, including for example, cows, sows, ewes, mares, swans, hens, geese, doves, rabbits, deer, fish, bees, and other animals of like kind. The fruits of these same animals, butter, cheese, milk considered in its natural state, when it has not been turned into butter or cheese, wool, [*honey,* **and**] wax - it is our will that tithes shall be set aside, fully and particularly, of these as of all fruits, no less than of the offspring themselves, for the use of the ministers, without trickery or deceit.

Finally, it is our will that the whole law of tithes which are to be levied from all and singular profits and revenues of the fields shall be determined according to the pattern and form prescribed in the parliament which was held in the second and third year of our reign, and to have the same procedures and penalties which have been defined in the thirteenth chapter of the said parliament.[8] Which decree of parliament and its very words and sentences shall have direct, firm and absolutely inviolable authority for deciding matters of tithe, no less than if they had been included in this document, unless by chance there happens to be something in them which is clearly repugnant to these present laws of ours. For since those decrees of parliament do not cover all the forms in which tithes can be paid, and many doubts occur daily in this matter of tithes, concerning which nothing has been decided by parliament, we have had the following matters added, so that conflicts may be reduced.

3. How the annual tithe of animals is to be paid according to the calculation of their number.[9]

If someone has only six calves, or fewer than six, he shall pay the minister two pence for each of the calves in respect of tithe; if there are seven, he shall set aside one for the minister and the minister in turn shall refund six pence, in order to restore the balance, to the person from whom he has received the calf. In the same way when there are eight calves, one shall be paid to the minister, but he in turn shall compensate the excess tithe with four pence. And if nine calves are found, the minister who takes a calf shall pay out another two pence. But if the minister prefers to await the full benefit of the tithes, and does not want to exercise his right until the lawful number of ten calves has been reached, he shall nevertheless receive some interest for the delay (as has been decided by the civil law in many cases), that is, that when the time has come that the lawful number has been reached, he shall take the calf of his choice, with one or two exceptions, from the remaining ten. And it is our will that they shall follow the same procedure with respect to foals and the like. And concerning lambs, swans and whatever other animals are reckoned in a similar way, a penny shall be given back and forth for each one, when there are fewer than ten of them. With regard to smaller animals which have such a short lifespan that they cannot be tithed in

consuetudin[i/e] locorum stari debet. Qui tales animantes alienaverit, priusquam ab illis decimae percip[ere/ia]ntur, decimam pretii partem ministro concedat. Cum autem [146r] possessor vel ad usum illa familiae suae peremerit vel amiserit casu, tantum pro decimis minister feret, quantum loci consuetudo postulabit.

4. Divisio decimarum qualis sit.[10]

Si forte contingat ut equi, boves et illius generis animalia, quae ius decimarum superioribus nostris legibus effi[59b]ciunt, ab unius parochiae pascuis in alia d[e/i]migrent, aequabilem decimarum partitionem inter illorum locorum ministros esse volumus, in quibus animalia se pabulo sustentaverunt, inita temporum in utriusque pascuis consumptorum iusta ratione. Sed in hoc partitionis iure nolumus ex ovibus quicquam pro decima exigi a pastore, nisi triginta dies in illius parochia restiterint. Quod si fines ac limites parochiarum, in quibus oberrant animalia, incerti sunt, et liquere non possit, quem ad locum ius decimarum infundi debeat, aut tempore colligendarum decimarum non constet alteri parochiae iuste satisfactum fuisse, in qua prius fuerint, illius loci ministro decimas adiudicari placet, in quo depraehensa sunt animalia legitimo decimarum tempore. Cum autem communia duabus aut pluribus parochiis pascua sunt, in quibus sparsim animalia degunt, aut si terrae vastae sint et publicum usum habentes, [146v] quas nostro sermone dicimus 'waste grounds', in quibus nullum sit proprietatis ius ullius certae parochiae; aut quando *est* talis est vicinarum parochiarum inter se pascuorum communicatio, mutuis ut vicibus in illis pascuorum ius obambulet, certis anni temporibus humano quodam et commodo suae propinquitatis respectu, tum segregetur ad illum locum decimarum ius in quo possessor animalium inhabitat.

5. Decima rerum alienatorum quomodo recuperetur.[11]

Multi decimarum vitandarum et eludendarum causa, vitulos, agnos, oves, et ceter[a/o]rum rerum fructus, inter liberos, cognatos et necessarios spargunt, priusquam legitimum tempus decimarum advenerit. Quorum astutia quoniam ecclesiarum nostrarum ministros iniquum est circumveniri, libertatem illis damus in huiusmodi decimarum iniu[60a]sta div[ul/i]sione vel a divisoribus ipsis decimas integras iure repetendi, vel ab his qui fructus ab illis acceperunt.

---

[10]Based on L, 3.16.6. See H.C., 24.2.
[11]Elaboration of provisions in L, 3.16.5-7; H.C., 24.1-2.

any definite way, the local custom shall prevail. Anyone who sells such animals before tithes on them have been received shall pay one tenth of the price to the minister. But when an owner has either killed the animals for the use of his household or has lost them by accident, the minister shall receive in tithes however much local custom demands.

4. How tithes shall be divided.[10]

If by chance it happens that horses, oxen and animals of that kind, which incur the right of tithes by our foregoing laws, migrate from the pastures of one parish to another, it is our will that there shall be an equal division of the tithes between the ministers of those places in which the animals have fed themselves, in proportion to the time spent in the pastures of each parish. But in this right of division, we do not want anything to be demanded by a pastor in tithe on sheep unless they have remained thirty days in his parish. But if the boundaries and limits of the parishes in which the animals graze are uncertain and it cannot be resolved to which place the right of tithes ought to belong, or at the time of collecting the tithes it is not agreed that the other parish, in which they had previously been, has received just compensation, the tithes shall be assigned to the minister of the place in which the animals were found at the lawful time of tithing. And when there are pastures common to two or three parishes, in which scattered animals graze, or if the lands are vast and open to public use, which we call 'waste grounds' in our language, in which no particular parish has any proprietorial right, or when the pastures of neighbouring parishes are so closely connected that the right of pasture is shared out between them at certain times of the year by mutual arrangement, governed by what suits the convenience of the neighbourhood, then the right of tithes shall be reserved to that place in which the owner of the animals dwells.

5. How the tithe on things which have alienated shall be recovered.[11]

In order to avoid and escape paying tithes, many people disburse calves, lambs, sheep and the produce of other things among their children, relatives and dependants before the lawful time of tithing comes round. Since it is unfair for the ministers of our churches to be cheated by such deceit, we give them the freedom to claim full tithes by right in such an unjust division of tithes, either from the dividers themselves or from those who have received the income from them.

6. De iure vicariorum.

Vicarius quoniam habitat in parochia et in illius curam sedulo incumbit, decimas, oblationes, pensiones, iura, fructus ecclesiasticos omnis generis...[12]

[147r] 6. De commodis quae proveniunt a sacris ritibus.[13]

Omnes oblationes, fructus et utilitates quae solent ex ritibus matrimoniorum, *gratiarum actionis mulierum a partu,* **levatarum puerperarum,** funerum, et bonis defunctorum, et aliis quibuscunque religiosis officiis, ad ministros Ecclesiae [*congregari, et libello rituum Ecclesiae*] Anglicanae [**venire**], non adversant[*ur*/**e**] consuetudine locorum, et praescript[*o*/**a**] constitution[*um*/**e**] a nobis prius ad has res accommodata[*rum*], maxima fide volumus ad ministros affundi; quique deliquerint in hoc genere satisfactionis, illorum ab ordinario plectatur avaritia, donec officium plene praestiterint.

7. De iure vicariorum.[14]

Vicarius, quoniam habitat in parochia, et in illius curam sedulo incumbit, decimas, oblationes, pensiones, iura, fructus ecclesiasticos omnis generis, quae vel a primo illius muneris fundamento, vel ex pacto, consuetudine, vel temporis beneficio, quod praescriptionem vocant, iure vendicari potest, accipiat. Et illi praeterea generatim omnia largimur, quae spatio decem annuorum ante nostrarum divulgationem istarum legum sine contentione percepit et controversia. Nec vel pastor, nec quisquam alius, illum ab [*e*/**ill**]orum possessione depellet. Deinde terras exaret, si quas ad arandum aptas habet, nec decimas ex illis ullas repraesentabit, sive pastori ipsi, sive cuicunque alteri.

[147v] 8. Quando minister ecclesiae ex proventibus ecclesiae ali non potest.[15]

Pastor cum exilitate fructuum necessitates suas commode sustentare non potest, sive contingat·illorum scelera[60b]ta cupiditate, qui decimas illi subtrahunt aut praecidunt, sive quod tam minutae sunt decimae et fructus, ut etiamsi iuste persolverentur, minime illum possent alere, suam in huiusmodi pastorum difficultatibus pietatem episcopus *au*/et auctoritatem interponat, ut illis et illorum familiis possit convenienter prospici. Quod expediri sic poterit, si vel episcopus

---

[12]Removed to 7 below.
[13]1268/16 (PC, 766); H.C., 24.9. Cf. H.C., 25.12-13.
[14]X, 3.5.30 (Fr, II, 478-9), originally c. 32 of Lateran IV, 1215 (*C.O.D.*, 249-50); 1237/12 (PC, 250-1); cf. H.C., 20.23.
[15]Cf. 37 Henry VIII, c. 21, 1545 (*S.R.*, III, 1013-14).

6. Of the right of vicars.

A vicar, since he dwells in the parish and earnestly devotes himself to its care...
tithes, offerings, pensions, rights, ecclesiastical fruits of every kind...[12]

6. Of income which comes from the sacred rites.[13]

It is our will that all offerings, fruits and benefits which [*are*] customarily
[*gathered by* **come** to] ministers of the Church [**of England**] from the rites of
matrimony, *thanksgiving of women after childbirth*, **delivery of children**,
funerals and the goods of the deceased, and any other religious duties, [*and*]
which do not go against [*the Church of England's book of common prayer*], the
custom of the place or the *prescription of the* **prescribed** statute*s* previously
drawn up by us for these matters, shall be paid with complete honesty to the
ministers, and that the greed of those who are delinquent in making
compensation of this kind shall be punished by the ordinary, until they have
fulfilled their duty completely.

7. Of the right of vicars.[14]

A vicar, since he dwells in the parish and earnestly devotes himself to its care,
shall receive tithes, offerings, pensions, rights, ecclesiastical fruits of every kind,
which he may rightfully claim either on the basic principle of his office, or by
agreement, custom, or benefit of time, which is called prescription. Moreover,
we grant to him in general everything which he has received without dispute or
controversy for the space of ten years before the publication of these our laws.
Neither shall the pastor nor anyone else dispossess him. Finally, he shall till the
lands, if he has lands suitable for tilling, and shall not pay any tithes for them,
either to the pastor himself or to anyone else.

8. When a minister of a church cannot be supported from the revenues of the
church.[15]

When a pastor is unable to meet his needs adequately because of the smallness
of the income, whether this happens because, as a result of the wicked greed of
people who subtract from his tithes or cut them short, or because the tithes and
fruits are so small that even if they are paid properly, they are not enough to
maintain him, the bishop shall bring his godliness *or* **and** authority to bear on the
difficulties of such pastors, so that they and their households may be provided
with a decent living. This may be accomplished if the bishop imposes on all

omnibus necessitatem imponat pastoribus in causa decimarum et aliorum fructuum iuste satisfaciendi; quod si adhuc satis non fuerit, hominibus parochiae suadeat pro viribus, ut e facultatibus quae suppetunt praeter decimas *sponte* tantum sponte attribuant, quantum necessarium esse videbitur. Atque his viis si non proficitur, tertia reperiatur minutorum aliquot sacerdotiorum, quae sunt in propinquis locis, in unum corpus et unam ecclesiam coniungendi, quo pastor rem suam familiarem bene alere et nutrire possit. Sin vero ministri qui eg[e/**ueri**]nt, vicarii fuerint, tum episcopus illos adhortetur, qui *quocunque titulo* **quacunque causa** fructus ecclesiarum possident, *ut ratione quae visa fuerit commodior* **viam ut aliquam reperiant,** inopem vicari*o*/**um** ac eius familia*e*/**m** quantum satis erit *contribuant adimia* **sublevandi.**

[148r][16] 9. De decimis colligendis in aliena parochia.[17]

Si quis [*in*] aliena parochia certum locum ad decimas colligendas, aut certam decimarum portionem sibi praescriptione legitima vendica[*ri*]t, ei praecipimus, ne [*i*/**u**]llo praetextu alium quempiam locum ad colligendas decimas, neve alias decimas in illa parochia, usurpare audeat.

10. Parochiae solvendas decimas, non sacello.[18]

Si forte sacellum aliquod in parochia situm fuerit, oblationes, decimae, ceterique fructus ecclesiastici non deriva[61a]buntur in sacellum, sed in parochiam confluent. Si tamen quicquam secus rite convenerit, aequum est ut fides pactorum servetur.

11. De locis qui sunt a decimis liberi.[19]

Pro agris, fundis et [*solo* **loco**] quocunque, sive haereditario iure, sive quavis alia iusta ratione possideatur, decimas persolvere nemo cogatur, si loca huiusmodi per leges, constitutiones huius *f*... regni, legitima privilegia seu praescriptionem, et iusta pacta a decimis libera et· immunia fuerint, modo ea de re fides ecclesiastico iudici evidenter fiat.

---

[16]A blank folio 150 is erroneously inserted immediately before this.
[17]Cf., X, 3.30.29 (Fr, II, 566), originally a decretal of Pope Innocent III, 17 May 1210; H.C., 24.7.
[18]1268/16 (PC, 766); H.C., 24.9.
[19]X, 5.33.6-7 (Fr, II, 851), both originally decretals of Pope Alexander III (1159-81); X, 5.33.22 (Fr, II, 865-6), originally a decretal of Pope Innocent III, 3 October 1213; X, 5.33.31, 33 (Fr, II, 869), both originally decretals of Pope Gregory IX (1227-41), published on or before 5 September 1234.

pastors the need for a full settlement in the case of tithes and other fruits, but if that is still not enough, he may try to persuade the people of the parish, in so far as he is able, that they should voluntarily contribute something beyond their tithes out of their own resources, to the extent that that seems to be necessary. And if these measures do not succeed, a third possibility would be to join together a number of small livings, which are next to one another, into one unit and one church, where a pastor can feed and nourish his own household well. But if the ministers who are in need are vicars, then the bishop shall order those who own the income of the church *by* **for** whatever *title* **reason**, that they should *contribute* **find some way of raising** adequate funds *in a manner which seems to be easier*, for the needy vicar and his household.

9.[16] Of collecting tithes in another parish.[17]

If anyone claims a particular place for collecting tithes in another parish, or claims a certain percentage of the tithes for himself by lawful prescription, we command that he shall not presume to seize any other place for collecting tithes, nor other tithes in that parish, under any pretext.

10. Tithes are to be paid to the parish, not to a chapel.[18]

If there happens to be a chapel situated in the parish, the offerings, tithes and other ecclesiastical fruits shall not be diverted to the chapel but shall flow into the parish. But if something contrary to this has been duly established, it is right for the terms of the agreement to be maintained.

11. Of places which are free of tithes.[19]

For fields, farms and any [*soil* **place**] whatever which may be owned either by hereditary right or by some other lawful means, no one shall be compelled to pay tithes if the said places are free and immune from tithes by the laws, the statutes of this realm, lawful privileges or a prescription and just agreements, as long as proof of this matter has been given to an ecclesiastical judge.

[148v] 12. Consuetudo compensationis tenenda.[20]

Quibus [*in*] locis consuetudo fuit ut pro decimis aliae res subministrarentur, eandem posthac teneri placet, si aequalis pro decimis compensatio fiat.

13. Decimae praediales et personales quibus solvendae.[21]

Decimae praediorum, hoc est, quae ratione praediorum aut fundorum debentur, in illas parochias immigrabunt, in quarum finibus praedia vel fundi constiterint. Decimae vero personarum, hoc est, quae personarum ratione sumi debent, et oblationes omnes, in illas parochias commeabunt, in quibus personae decimas conferentes inhabitant, et rerum divinarum et sacramentorum participes fiunt; nisi vel privilegio, vel longi temporis consuetudine secus observatum fuerit. Cum autem de praediorum finibus ambigitur, qua[*m*/**e**] ad parochiam proprie spectent, episcopus ad illam ecclesiam fructus convertat decimarum, ad quam aequitate credit e[*o*/**a**]s et iure pertinere.

[61b] 14. Solvendas esse decimas personales iuxta consuetudinem urbis Lond[*i*/**o**]n[*ensis*].[22]

Magnam indignitatem habet a tenuibus et laboriosis agricolis decimas annuas ecclesiarum ministris [149r] suppeditari, mercatores autem opibus affluentes, et viros scientiarum et artificiorum copiis abundantes, nihil ferme ad ministrorum necessitates conferre, praesertim cum illis ministrorum officio non minus opus sit, quam colonis. Quapropter, ut ex pari labore **par** *per*consequatur merces, constituimus ut mercatores, pannorum confectores, et artifices reliqui cuiuscunque generis, ac omnes qui scientia vel peritia qual[*i*/**e**]cunque lucrum percipiunt, hoc modo decimas persolvant; pro domibus *nempe* **nimirum**[23] atque terris quibus utuntur, et *de* ill*is*/**arum ratione**[24] decimas praediales non solvunt, quolibet anno dabunt annuae pensionis decima*ru*m partem.

---

[20]X, 1.36.2 (Fr, II, 206), originally a decretal of Pope Alexander III (1159-81).
[21]X, 3.30.18 (Fr, II, 562), originally a decretal of Pope Alexander III; X, 3.30.20 (Fr, II, 562-3), originally a decretal of Pope Lucius III (1181-5).
[22]37 Henry VIII, c. 12, 1545 (*S.R.*, III, 998-9), followed by the decree of Archbishop Thomas Cranmer and others, dated 24 February 1546 (*S.R.*, III, 999-1000); H.C., 25.
[23]In Haddon's hand.
[24]In Haddon's hand.

12. The custom of compensation is to be retained.[20]

In those places where there has been a custom that other things may be given instead of tithes, it shall continue to be maintained, <u>if there is adequate compensation for the tithes</u>.

13. To whom predial and personal tithes shall be paid.[21]

Tithes on the estates, that is, which are owed by reason of estates or farms, shall go to those parishes within which the estates or farms are located. But tithes on persons, that is, which must be paid in respect of persons, and all offerings shall go to those parishes in which the persons paying the tithes reside and take part in divine services and the sacraments. And when there is some doubt about the boundaries of the estates, [*to*] which [*parish they*] properly belong [**to the parish**], the bishop shall hand over the tithe revenue to that church to which he believes they belong in fairness and by right.

14. Personal tithes are to be paid according to the custom of the city of London.[22]

It is extremely unfair that yearly tithes are paid to the ministers of the church by poor and hardworking farmers, when merchants wallowing in riches, and men of letters and manufactures abounding in wealth, contribute nothing in particular to the needs of ministers, particularly when they have just as much need of them as the farmers have. Therefore, in order that there should be equal pay for equal work, we decree that merchants, cloth makers, and other manufacturers of whatever kind, and all who earn money by some knowledge and skill, shall pay tithes in this way - to wit,[23] for their homes and the lands which they use, and *for* **in respect of**[24] which they do not pay predial tithes, shall pay a tenth part of their income every year.

15. Proprietarii quomodo decimas solvent.[25]

Quod si mercator, aut artifex, aut qualiscunque negotiator, aut scientia vel peritia se sustentans, proprietatis ius vel in aedibus habet, in quibus inhabitat, vel in terris circumfusis, quibus ad mercaturam, artificium vel peritiam utitur, hanc cum illis rationem iniri volumus, ut ex una parte minister, et ex altera /parte/ possessor, singuli singulos arbitros sumant, et arbitri sumpti definiant quanti domus et terrae sint, et quo pretio locari possunt, et illius pretii decimam a possessore minister accipiet. Et inter duos arbitros si forte convenire non possit, ordinarius illius ecclesiae proprius tertium assignet virum gravem, et huiusmodi controversiarum callentem, et quod illi videbitur, id in hoc negotio teneri placet.

[149v] 16. Decimas utriusque generis solvendas esse.[26]

Mercatores autem, artifices, et reliquae personae quas diximus, cum decimas personales *contribuerunt* **contulerint**[27] ea for[62a]ma, quam ante posuimus, illas tamen prioris generis, quas praediales vocant, adiicient. Nam si domini sint agrorum, ovium, vaccarum, aut aliorum huiusmodi commodorum, quae superioribus nostris legibus decimarum ius efficiunt, pro illorum respectu ministris plene volumus satisfieri.

17. Causa decimarum inter ipsos ministros non progredietur.[28]

Quoniam ecclesiarum ministri summa debent /inter se/ caritate coniungi, pacatamque vitam et tranquillam degere, magnum habet dedecus, ut propter decimarum fructus turpissimis altercationibus et immanibus etiam impensis inter se conflictentur. Ut igitur huiusmodi morum labes et perniciosa discordiarum exempla tollantur et extermina/entur, /hanc decimarum causam nullo modo patimur/ inter ministros ipsos consistere, nec unus illorum ab altero decimas ullorum respectu ecclesiasticorum fructuum excipia[n]t.

---

[25]L, 3.16.5, of uncertain origin (PC, 794).
[26]2-3 Edward VI, c. 13, 1548 (*S.R.*, IV, 55-8).
[27]Added by the same unknown hand which made most of the corrections in chapters 22-3 above.
[28]For the spiritual principle behind this, see D, 90 c. 1 (Fr, I, 313). On the particular matter in question, see 13 Edward I, c. 4, 1285 (*S.R.*, I, 101-2), abolishing the writ of *Indicavit*, by which such litigation was originally conducted.

15. How proprietors shall pay their tithes.[25]

But if a merchant or manufacturer or some kind of trader, or someone who supports himself by knowledge or a skill, has the right of ownership either to the house in which he resides, or to the surrounding lands, which he uses for his commerce, manufacturing or skill, we desire that this pattern shall be adopted with them, that on the one hand the minister, and on the other /hand/ the owner shall each appoint arbitrators, and that the appointed arbitrators shall determine how much the house and the lands are worth, and for what amount they can be let, and the minister shall receive a tenth of that amount from the owner. And if by chance the two arbitrators cannot agree, the ordinary proper to that church shall appoint a third responsible man, and one experienced in such disputes, and what seems right to him will be accepted in this matter.

16. Tithes of either kind must be paid.[26]

However, merchants, manufacturers and the other people whom we have mentioned, when they have *contributed* **paid**[27] personal tithes in the form which we have indicated above, shall nevertheless also pay those of the first kind, which are called predial. For if they are lords of fields, sheep, cows or other such assets, which by our above laws are subject to the right of tithe, we wish full satisfaction with respect to them to be given to the ministers.

17. A tithe case between ministers shall not go forward.[28]

Since the ministers of the churches must be united in the highest love for one another, and lead a peaceful and tranquil life, it is a great scandal for them to argue over tithe revenues among themselves with the most bitter altercations and even at huge expense. Therefore, in order to remove and extinguish such moral lapses and wicked examples of discord, we forbid this kind of thing to develop into a tithe case between ministers, nor may any one of them receive tithes from another with respect to any ecclesiastical revenues.

[18. Consuetudo non solvendi decimas invalida sit.[29]

Cum decimae omni humano iure sine aliqua diminutione solvendae sint, et Salvatoris nostri Christi pastoribus ubique terrarum debeantur; et cum pluribus in locis propter non solutas decimas animarum curam habentibus adeo exigua portio,[30] ut ex eo nequeant congrue sustentari, relinquatur, itaque fiat ut pauci inveniantur pastores, qui ullam [*vel* et] modicam habent peritiam Sacrarum Litterarum; cumque inter cetera quae ad salutem populi Christiani spectant, pabulum Verbi Dei maxime noscatur esse necessarium, osque bovis ligari non debeat triturantis, sed qui altari servit de altari vivere debeat;[31] statuimus ut consuetudine qualibet non obstante, integrae cuiuscunque rei decimae solvantur, omnemque contrariam consuetudinem irritam esse decernimus.][32]

---

[29]Cf. X, 1.4.1 (Fr, II, 36), originally a rescript of Pope Gregory I (590-604), *Reg.*, 1.66. This canon was moved here from R, 46.5.

[30]In MS Harleian 426 Foxe copied this as 'exiguo pretio', and F has 'exiguum pretium' ('a small sum'). Probably the missing Parker MS had 'ptio', with a ligature under the 'p', and Foxe simply misread it.

[31]I Co. ix. 9; I Ti. v. 18, from Dt. xxv. 4. See also Nm. xviii. 8-24.

[32]A marginal note in the MS, in Foxe's hand, reads: 'Hoc caput in codice Matthaei Cantuariensis refertum hic omissum fuerat.' ('This heading, found in the codex of Matthew Parker, was left out here'). Foxe proceeded to include it in the MS.

[18. The custom of not paying tithes shall be invalid.[29]

Since tithes are to be paid without any reduction according to all human law, and are owed everywhere on earth to the pastors of our Saviour Jesus Christ, and since in many places, because of unpaid tithes, so tiny a portion[30] is left to those who have the cure of souls that they are unable to support themselves adequately on it, and thus it comes about that there are few pastors who may be found who have even limited expertise in Holy Writ, and since, among other things which pertain to the salvation of the people of God, the food of the Word of God is recognized to be most necessary, and the mouth of the threshing ox should not be muzzled, but who serves the altar ought to live off the altar,[31] we decree that, any custom notwithstanding, full tithes shall be paid on everything, and we decree that any custom to the contrary shall be void.][32]

[151r; 62b]   [*25. 19 DE PENSIONIBUS*][1]

19. De pensionibus.[2]

Quoniam pensiones, quae ad illos deferuntur, qui aliis suis cedunt sacerdoti*a*/**is**,[3] solent ignaviam illorum et avaritiam nutrire, qui laboris expertes lucri participes esse volunt, huiusmodi fucos aliorum sudores depascere non feremus. Itaque nullum cuiquam c*a*/**en**sum huiusmodi annuum relinquimus, nisi cuius vel propter morbum, vel propter senectutem habenda sit ratio. Quae cum occurrunt impedimenta, proprius illorum locorum episcopus adeatur, is tant[*a*/**u**]m constituet pensionem, quantam aequam esse putabit, quam summa fide successor persolvet. Sed aetas et valetudo quamdiu ferent, omnino nullum a sacerdotio ministrum discedere patimur, alioqui nullum ex relicto sacerdotio fructum cuiuscunque generis iure vendicabit.

Vicarii, quoniam in laboribus parochiae assidue versantur, et tenues proventus ad se alendos et familiam plerumque habent, par est ut *ab* omni genere pensionum solvendarum eximantur. Statuimus itaque ut nullus pastor, patronus, aut quivis alius ab eis posthac nomine pensionis annuae quicquam omnino exigat*ur*.

---

[1]In the MS this is a separate chapter.
[2]26 Henry VIII, c. 3, 1534 (*S. R.*, III, 493-9); H.C., 28.1-2. Pensions from former monastic lands were covered by 34-5 Henry VIII, c. 19, 1542-3 (*S. R.*, III, 918-19).
[3]This alteration was made in Haddon's hand.

[*25.19 OF PENSIONS*][1]

19. Of pensions.[2]

Since pensions which are paid to those who surrender their livings to others, usually feed the ignorance and greed of those who want to get rich without having to work for it, we shall not allow such parasites to live off the sweat of others. Therefore, we leave no yearly stipend of this kind to anyone, unless there is a reason for it either because of illness or because of old age. When these impediments occur, the bishop belonging to those places shall be called, and he shall fix a pension in the amount which he thinks is fair, which his successor will pay with the greatest faithfulness. But as long as age and health hold up, we do not allow any minister to leave his living, nor shall he claim any income of any kind by right from a living which he has left.

Since vicars are deeply involved in the work of a parish, and usually have slender resources on which to feed themselves and their household, it is fair that they should be exempt from having to pay any sort of pension. Therefore, we decree that from now on no pastor, patron or anyone else shall in any way demand anything at all from them in the name of an annual pension.

[151v; 62b]   **26. DE VISITATIONIBUS**[1]

1. Cur ecclesiae visitandae sint.[2]

Archiepiscopi, episcopi, archidiaconi, denique reliqui quorum interest, et qui ius ecclesiasticum dicere possunt, ecclesias suas visitent et considerent, et solemnes ac [u/**vi**]sitatos in illis coetus in tempore celebrent, ut populus illorum curae commissus salubriter [63a] a pastoribus et ordine gubernetur, et ut assiduis *et* ac piis ministrorum officiis ecclesiarum ipsarum status recte conservetur.

2. Quae sint in visitationibus quaerenda.[3]

Haec autem in statis huiusmodi congressibus potissimum quaerantur: An Sacrae Scripturae diligenter et sincere pertractentur; an apta sit et recta sacramentorum administratio; deinde disciplina qualis ecclesiarum sit, et quantum habeat roboris; ac[4] postremo, formulae publicarum supplicationum an recte [**et**] tempestive[*que*] conserventur; et an cetera rite peragantur universa, quibus ecclesiarum procuratio continetur.

3. Forma visitationis.[5]

Iam ut ista facilius procedant, universa multitudo, quemadmodum usitate fieri solet, maximeque videbitur convenire, in unum aliquem locum congregetur, et [152r] interpositis syndicorum, et aliorum iuramentis solemnium testium, crimina diligentissime pervestigentur personarum omnis generis, quae ad ius pertinent ecclesiasticum; et cum plene fuerint intellecta, iustas legibus poenas dent, et acerbum ab illis supplicium capiatur.

---

[1]The changes in the MS of this chapter are in Dr Haddon's hand.
[2]Visitations by archbishops and bishops are mentioned in 1237/22 (PC, 255); visitations by archdeacons in 1237/20 (PC, 254).
[3]VI, 3.20.3 (Fr, II, 1057-8), a decretal of Pope Boniface VIII (1294-1303). Cf. H.C., 29.2.
[4]The MS leaves a space here (about a third of a line) which may have been intended for additional material.
[5]C. 35, q. 6, c. 7 (Fr, I, 1279).

26. OF VISITATIONS[1]

1. Why churches must be visited.[2]

Archbishops, bishops, archdeacons and finally everyone else whose concern it is, and who can pronounce on ecclesiastical law, shall visit their churches and deliberate, and celebrate the solemn and [customary **visited**] assemblies in them at the proper time, so that the people committed to their charge may be properly governed by pastors and order, and that the state of those churches may be maintained by the constant and godly services of the ministers.

2. What shall be inquired of in visitations.[3]

And these are the main things which must be inquired of in assemblies of this kind: Whether the Holy Scriptures are expounded diligently and sincerely, whether the administration of the sacraments is appropriate and right; what the discipline of the churches is like and how much effect it has; and[4] lastly, whether the forms of the public prayers are maintained in the right way and at the right times, and whether everything else by which the welfare of the churches is maintained is being properly conducted.

3. The form of visitation.[5]

Now in order for these things to proceed more easily, the whole congregation shall come together in one single place, as is customarily done and seems to be most convenient, and when the oaths of the churchwardens and other important witnesses have been taken, the crimes of persons of every kind, which pertain to the ecclesiastical law, shall be most diligently investigated, and when the crimes have been fully examined, the persons concerned shall pay the just penalties according to the laws and receive severe punishment.

4. Quae sint et a quibus praestanda.[6]

Deinde providendum erit, ut qui beneficiis ecclesiasticis utuntur, omnes domos ad se pertinentes emendent et reconcinnent, hoc excepto, quod superiorum in ecclesiis locorum, quae cancella vocantur, instaurationem et refectionem non ad vicario[re]s devolvi, sed ad rectores ipsos perpetuo referri volumus. Reliquae vero templorum partes his qui in parochia habitant tuendae corrigendaeque relinquentur *et illorum etiam erit ut aedituum suis communibus expensis sustentent, illum quidem quem ecclesiae pastor ad hoc munus aptum existimabit.* Prae[63b]terea, coemeteriis undique communiendis, vasis et instrumentis omnibus ecclesiasticis perpurgandis, et suo in loco collocandis, invigilabunt. *Syndici vero, quos gardianos vocant, ecclesiasticorum bonorum sibi creditorum quotannis rationem reddent, et communis thesauri reliquum integrum et illibatum illis tradent, quorum est proxima successio.*

[152v] 5. Punienda in syndicis negligentia.[7]

Videndum etiam erit an in rebus fidei suae commissis iuste sint et diligenter versati. Quique non paruerint, aut officio functi [**non**] fuerint in omnibus illis causis, quas ante posuimus, in excommunicationis poenam incidant, aut ordinarii puniantur arbitratu.

6. Solvendam visitatoribus iustam mercedem.[8]

Quoniam autem labor praemio carere non debet, archiepiscopus si provinciam, vel episcopus dioecesim, vel archidiaconus proprias sui muneris ecclesias, aut alii suas, quocunque praefectorum ecclesiasticorum nomine censeantur, visitent et perlustrent, et coetus ibi solemnes et usitatos habeant, reliquosque visitationis legitimos ritus adhibeant; omnibus fruantur emolumentis, quae pertinent ad commun[iu/e]m huiusmodi negotiorum administrationem. Nec in hoc genere quicquam minuatur illorum, quae vel consensu, vel consuetudine, vel quacunque legitima ratione, solebant ad illos deferri. Et ut hac in re facilior sit progressio, si qui negligant, aut nolint huiusmodi mercedem expedire qualem visitationis munus postulat, potestas erit his qui visitandi labores obeunt, beneficiorum

---

[6]1268/17 (PC, 766-7); X 3.48.1 (Fr, II, 652), originally c. 25 of the sixth council of Arles, 813; X, 3.48.4 (Fr, II, 653), originally a decretal of Pope Alexander III (1159-81); H.C., 30.1.
[7]L, 2.6.2, c. 14 of the synod of Archbishop Boniface, 1261.
[8]X, 3.39.23 (Fr, II, 632), c. 33 of Lateran IV, 1215 (*C.O.D.*, 250); also VI, 3.20.3 (Fr, II, 1057-8), a decretal of Pope Boniface VIII (1294-1303). See H.C., 29.1,4.

4. What must be presented and by whom.[6]

Furthermore it shall be provided that those who enjoy ecclesiastical benefices shall repair and refashion all the houses belonging to them, with the exception that the restoration and repair of the upper parts of the churches, which are called chancels, shall not fall on the vicars, but it is our will that they shall always be turned over to the rectors. And the remaining parts shall be left to those who reside in the parishes to be maintained and put right, *and it shall also be their responsibility to support a parish clerk, the man whom the pastor of the church shall think fit for that task, out of their common funds.* Moreover, they shall see to it that cemeteries are everywhere maintained, that the vessels and all church implements are fully cleaned and stored in their proper place. *And the syndics, who are called wardens, shall every year give an account of the ecclesiastical goods entrusted to them, and hand over whatever is left in the common fund fully and completely to those who are their immediate successors.*

5. The negligence of wardens is to be punished.[7]

Inspection shall also be made as to whether they have acted rightly and been diligently involved in the things of faith which have been committed to them. Those who have not complied or [**not**] fulfilled their duty in all these cases which we have set out above shall incur the penalty of excommunication or be punished at the discretion of the ordinary.

6. A fair wage is to be paid to the visitors.[8]

And since work must not go without reward, the archbishop (if it is the province), or the bishop (in the diocese), or the archdeacon (in the churches of his jurisdiction) or others, by whatever title given to ecclesiastical officers they may be known, shall visit and survey their own churches, and there hold the solemn and customary assemblies, and perform the other lawful rites of visitation; they shall enjoy all the emoluments which pertain to the [**common**] administration of [*common*] business of this kind. Nor shall any of the things of this kind which are customarily paid to them either by agreement, or custom or any lawful means, be cut back. And so that there may be easier expedition in this matter, if some people neglect or refuse to pay a wage of this kind such as the task of visitation demands, those who devote their labours to visiting shall have

fructus segregare, reliquamque omnem impedire utilitatem, [153r] imo vero poenas etiam alias ecclesiasticas expromere, donec [*plene*] sibi fuerit ab illis satisfactum.

[64a] 7. Privilegia locorum exemptorum moderanda.[9]

Quoniam libertates et immunitates ecclesiastica*e*/s[10] licentiosam videmus saepe numero afferre peccandi securitatem, volumus ut episcopis liceat in omnia collegia, societates et coetus, quae quidem in dioecesibus illorum constiterint, quantumcunque privilegiis praemuniantur, inspectare, poenasque peccatis illorum assignare, non solum communibus visitationum, sed omnibus aliis temporibus, cum magnitudo criminum postulabit; et eandem archiepiscopus in sua provincia potestatem habebit.

8. Poena peccatorum in collegiis et huiusmodi coetibus unde proficisci debeat.[11]

Cuicunque tamen hoc **peculiare ius tribuitur, quod** praerogativum *est* **vocatur**, ut in aliquo collegio, vel **certo** cuiuscunque generis coetu*i speciatim* **separatim** iuris dicendi potestatem habeat, et in *crimina animadvertendi* **coercendis maleficiis** sit fas ei iure suo uti; ita tamen ut disciplinam vel archiepiscopi vel episcopi non impediat. Quapropter hanc rem ita moderamur, ut si primum ille de suorum criminibus [*coeperit iudicare* i{*n*/u}**dicaverit**], eius sit omnis illorum castigatio, nisi reus ill[*u*/a]m appellatione vitaverit. Si vero peccata prius [153v] ad *e...* episcopum vel archiepiscopum perferantur, et illi coeperint causam cognoscere, illorum iudicio stare/i placet. Et hanc sane cautionem in solis criminum controversiis diiudicandis ita teneri placet, ut *quoad* cetera immunitatis iura et consuetudines inviolata et salva *re*maneant.

---

[9]This goes against the old canon law, cf. *e.g. Clem.*, 5.7.2 (Fr, II, 1187), originally published by Pope Clement V following the council of Vienne (1311-12). Also Panormitanus on X, 2.1.5.

[10]In addition to the change, the word 'ecclesiasticas' was written in the margin by Dr Haddon.

[11]X, 5.33.3 (Fr, II, 849-50), originally c. 9 of Lateran III, 1179 (*C.O.D.*, 215-17).

the power to set aside the income of the benefices and block all further use of them, and may also employ other ecclesiastical penalties until they have been [*fully*] satisfied by them.

7. The privileges of exempt places are to be controlled.[9]

Since we see that ecclesiastical[10] liberties and immunities often provide a licentious safety to sin, it is our will that it shall be lawful for bishops to inspect all colleges, societies and associations which exist in their dioceses, however many privileges they may enjoy, and assign penalties for their transgressions, not only at the common times of visitation but at all other times, whenever the magnitude of the crimes demands it, and the archbishop shall have the same power in his province.

8. Where the penalty for transgressions in colleges and similar associations ought to come from.[11]

Nevertheless *someone has the* **this particular right which is called a** prerogative **is granted to someone** in order that he may have the power in a college or particular association of whatever kind, to pronounce the law *specially* **separately** for it, and it shall be lawful for him to make use of that right to *punish crimes* **coerce wrongdoers**, yet not in such a way as to hinder the discipline of the archbishop or bishop. Therefore, we regulate this matter so that if he has first [*begun to judge* **judged**] the crimes of his own people, their entire punishment shall be his responsibility, unless the accused has avoided it by an appeal. But if the transgressions have previously been referred to the bishop or archbishop, and they have begun to hear the case, their judgment shall stand. And this restriction shall be maintained only in deciding criminal disputes, so that other rights and customs of immunity shall remain safe and inviolate.

[277r; 64b]   **27. DE TESTAMENTIS**

1. Quid sit testamentum.[1]

Testamentum est nostrae voluntatis et perfectae mentis definita sententia de rerum nostrarum post mortem collocatione, quod nominat et instituit certum haeredem, qui nunc executor vulgo dicitur. Testamenta vero quisquis vel universa retexit, vel ullam illorum partem quacunque ratione sciens violat, anathemate percutiatur, et ex communitate Christianae societatis exturbetur.

2. De testibus {*adhi*/**ha**}bendis.[2]

Testamentum legitimis testibus communitum sit, et hi nominatim ponantur [*quantum quidem commode fieri potest*], ipse minister, et ecclesiae [**syndici**],[3] quos gardianos appellant [*ut maior testamentorum auctoritas es... existat; qui cum forte sumi non possunt*], aut duo vel tres as[*ci*]s[*c*/**ist**]antur viri spectatae probitatis et exploratae fidei, aut denique testamentum ipsum manu testatoris, [*vel* **et**] duorum vel trium testium, [*consignetur*].

3. De testamento nuncupativo.[4]

Si quis ex vita subito migraverit, trium probatae fidei testium consensus accipietur, licet testamentum scriptis mandatum non sit. Et in utroque testamenti genere, tam scripto quam sermone testatoris excepto, quod nuncupativum vocant, satis erit si testamenti sui testator haeredem nominaverit.

---

[1]*Dig.*, 28.1.1, originally Modestinus, *Pandectae*, 2; ibid., 48.10.2, originally Paulus, *Ad Sabinum*, 3; *Inst.*, 2.20.34.

[2]X, 3.26.10 (Fr, II, 541), originally a latter of Pope Alexander III (1159-81) to the canonist Hostiensis. Cf. H.C., 31.2.

[3]This word is not in the MS, though there is a blank space which was evidently intended for it.

[4]Cf. X, 3.26.13 (Fr, II, 542), originally a decretal of Pope Innocent III, 1202.

27. OF TESTAMENTS

1. What a testament is.[1]

A testament is the definite expression of our will and determined intention concerning the distribution of our goods after death, which names and appoints a particular heir, who is nowadays popularly called the executor. And anyone who alters the entire testament, or knowingly violates any part of it for any reason whatsoever, shall be punished by excommunication and put out of the community of Christian fellowship.

2. Of {*providing* **having**} witnesses.[2]

A testament shall be backed by lawful witnesses, and the following in particular shall be included [*as far as may conveniently be done*]: the minister himself, the [**syndics**][3] of the church, who are called wardens [*so that the testament may enjoy greater authority, and if for some reason these people cannot be employed*], either two or three men of known integrity and proved faith shall be added, and finally the testament itself [*shall be signed*] by the hand of the testator [*or* **and**] two or three witnesses.

3. Of a nuncupative testament.[4]

If someone departs this life suddenly, the common testimony of three witnesses of proved trustworthiness shall be accepted if no testament has been committed to writing. And in either kind of testament, whether written or taken from the speech of the testator, which is called 'nuncupative', it will be enough if the testator of the testament has named an heir.

[277v] 4. Quod testamentum valere debeat.[5]

Semper hoc teneri placet, ut omnis auctoritas ad postremum testamentum accommodetur, et quaecunque sunt antegressa pro nullis habeantur, nisi certarum in illis positarum rerum testator aperte iusserit in postremo testamento [65a] rationem haberi. Quod si contigerit, illae solum res consist[a/e]nt, de quibus separatim testator cavit.

5. De codicillis.[6]

Quoniam saepe contingit ut, perfecto conclusoque testamento, multa testatori veniant in mentem, de quibus in testamento non praecaverit, et quae vehementer ad illud apponi velit, propterea concedimus ut ista posteriora non minus habeant roboris, quam ea quae sunt in testamento collocata; si litteris illa custodiri providerit, aut a praesentibus duobus aut tribus probatae fidei testibus petat, ut illa velint attestari.

6. Quo tempore liceat contra testamentum agere.[7]

Si quis contra testamentum in iudicio quicquam afferre velit, vel id interponat cum tempus est comprobandi testamenti, vel anni spatio tempus hoc consequentis. Si vero longius expecta[ri]t, excludatur causa, nisi forte vel aetatis excusationem, vel longinquae peregrinationis, ut de testamento nihil audierit, adferre et probare possit [*vel ignorationis rei gestae pro se alleget*]. [278r] Has autem excusationes ita volumus definiri, primum quibus aetas est impedimento, tum demum illos audiri placet, cum grandes erunt et ad agendum maturi. Primum autem aetatis legitimae sum[a/e]nt annum: quem si praetermiserint, agendi ius universum amittant. Qui vero mare transmiser{u/i}nt, his post reversionem sex menses indulgemus: cuius beneficio temporis si non uta[n]tur, illis etiam actio nulla relinquetur. [*Ignoratio quidem facti, quoniam aliquando si fraude caret, veniam meretur, mensem sibi tributum habebit, in quo nisi ius suum actor prosequatur, omnino post in iudicio non consistat.*]

---

[5]Cf. *Dig.*, 28.3.2, originally Ulpian, *ad Sabinum*, 2; ibid., 28.1.2, originally Ulpian, *Disputationes*, 4; *Cod. Iust.*, 6.23.28, originally a rescript of the Emperor Justinian I, 27 March 530.
[6]*Dig.*, 29.7.2, originally Julian, *Digesta*, 37; *Inst.*, 2.25.
[7]X, 2.28.5 (Fr, II, 411), originally a decretal of Pope Alexander III (1159-81). Cf. C. 2, q. 6, c. 41 (Fr, I, 481-3); C. 3, q. 3, c. 4 (Fr, I, 510-11), which is a quote from *Cod. Iust.*, 3.11.1, originally a rescript of the emperors Diocletian and Maximian, 18 March 293.

4. What value a testament ought to have.[5]

It must always be maintained that all authority shall be given to the last testament, and that any which have gone before shall be regarded as void, unless the testator has openly stated in the last testament that some of the provisions contained in them are still valid. If this is the case, only those things of which the testator has made particular mention shall stand.

5. Of codicils.[6]

Since it often happens that after a testament is completed and closed, many things come to the testator's mind which he has not given directions about in the testament, and which he strongly desires to attach to it, we therefore allow that these afterthoughts shall have no less force than the matters which are contained in the testament, if he has provided for them to be written down and asks two or three witnesses of proved trustworthiness to observe this and bear witness to them.

6. At what time it shall be lawful to contest a testament.[7]

If someone wishes to object to a testament in a court of law, he shall either deposit his objection at the time when the testament is proved or within a year following that. If he delays any longer, his case shall be rejected, unless he can offer the excuse of age or prove that he was on a long journey and so had heard nothing about the testament [*or claims that he was ignorant of what had happened*]. However, we want these excuses to be defined as follows: first, with respect to those for whom age is an impediment, they shall be heard as soon as they are older and have attained their legal majority. And they shall bring their objection in the first year of their lawful age of majority, but if they let it go by, they shall lose any right to act. As for those who have gone overseas, we grant them six months after their return, and if they do not make use of this time allowance, there shall likewise be no recourse left to them. [*Ignorance of the fact, which sometimes is genuine, deserves to be excused, and such a person shall have one month allotted to him, in which if he has not acted on his right, he shall not subsequently appear in court.*]

7. Quibus liceat vel non liceat testamentum facere.[8]

Omnes, cuiuscunque sexus vel conditionis sint, potestatem habebunt testamentorum instituendorum, nisi fuerit in his aliquid, quod praesentibus his legibus nostris ad[65b]versetur. Illos autem principio summovemus, qui sui iuris non sunt, sed in aliena potestate detinentur, quales sunt nominatim uxor, servus, liberi minores annis quattuordecim[is].[9] Deinde furiosos non admittimus, nec mente captos, nisi forte sanitatis huiusmodi tempora quaedam intercurrant, in quibus ratione res suas moderari possunt. Arceantur praeterea qui nec fari ipsi possunt, nec aliorum sermones intelligere, nec cogitationes suas litteris mandare, nisi nutibus et signis utantur tam evidentibus et perspicuis, [ut/-] idonei testes afferri possint illorum [278v] certae voluntatis et indubitatae sententiae. Porro nec haereticis testamentorum libertatem concedimus, nec his qui mortis vel exilii perpetui, vel sempiternorum vinculorum sententiam acceperunt.[10] Careant etiam hoc beneficio qui concubinas ante extrema non dimiserint tempora. Feminarumque ex altera parte similis sit poena, quoties similis est causa. Quas ad personas annumerentur, qui duas uxores eodem tempore compraehenderint, vel feminae duos maritos sumentes, nisi legitimum in priore persona divortium antegressum posterioris ius conditionis firmum effecerit. Ab[le]legentur etiam quicunque famosorum damnati sunt scriptorum quomodocunque compositorum, qui meretriciam vel lenoniam exercita[ri]nt, nisi publicas publicorum criminum poenas subierint. Ad extremum et foeneratores, aut (ut crassissime vulg[ar]i modo loquamur) usurarii, nisi forte vel usuras refuderint, vel de refundendis plene caverint, aut propter illas aliqua ratione alia integre satisfecerint.[11] His igitur omnibus positis personis nec testament[um/i] componendi, nec haeredem instituendi ius erit. Et generatim hoc intelligendum erit, test[at]orum illam esse conditionem excutiendam et sequendam, quae iam morientium, non quae longe ante testantium fuerit.

[66a] 8. Quomodo qui communi iure testamentum condere non possunt, tamen ad pias causas legata relinqu[a/u]nt.[12]

Ad extremum vitae tempus qui concubinam asservant, vel duas retinent uxores, itidem mulieres quarum similis pravitas est, ad pias causas [279r] bona sua possunt accommodare. Similiter qui meretriciam vel lenoniam publice

---

[8]*Inst.*, 2.12; *Dig.*, 28.1.5, originally Ulpian, *Ad Sabinum*, 6.
[9]By 34-5 Henry VIII, c. 5, s. 7, 1542-3 (*S.R.*, III, 901-4), the minimum age was twenty-one.
[10]Cf. X, 5.7.10 (Fr, II, 782-3), originally a decretal of Pope Innocent III, 25 March 1199.
[11]Cf. X, 5.19.9 (Fr, II, 813-14), originally a decretal of Pope Alexander III (1159-81).
[12]Cf. X, 3.26.11 (Fr, II, 541), originally a decretal of Pope Alexander III.

7. Who has, and who does not have the right to make a testament.[8]

Everyone, of whatever sex or status they may be, shall have the power to make a testament, unless there is something about them which is contrary to these our present laws. First of all, we exclude those who cannot act in their own right, but are subject to someone else's authority, such as for example a wife, a servant and children under fourteen years of age.[9] Next, we do not accept the insane or the mentally handicapped, unless by chance there are intervals when they are lucid, when they are able to control their affairs rationally. Moreover, those who are unable to speak for themselves and who cannot hear the speech of others, or commit their thoughts to writing, shall be excluded, unless they use gestures and signs which are so obvious and clear that suitable evidence can be gained from them of their definite will and undoubted intention. Furthermore, we do not grant the liberty of making testaments to heretics, nor to those who have received a sentence of death, perpetual exile, or life imprisonment.[10] Also those who do not send their concubines away before their final days shall not enjoy this privilege either. On the other side, women shall be placed under similar restrictions, to the extent that their case is similar. To these persons shall be added those who have kept two wives at the same time, or women who have taken two husbands, unless a lawful divorce has first taken place which gives the second situation a firm legal standing. Also excluded are those who have been condemned for spreading defamatory documents, however they may have been composed, and who have engaged in prostitution or pimping, unless they have undergone public penalties for their public crimes. Finally, money lenders, or (as we say in the crudest vulgar way) usurers, unless perchance they have refunded the usury or were fully intending to do so, or have made full reparation for it in some other way.[11] Therefore for all these persons mentioned there shall be no right either to make a testament or to appoint an heir. And it shall be generally understood that the will of the testator is to be executed and followed as it was at the time of his death, and not as it may have been long before that.

8. How those who cannot make a testament in common law may nevertheless leave legacies to pious causes.[12]

Those who, at the end of their lives, keep a concubine or have two wives, and likewise women whose depravity is similar, can leave their goods to pious causes. Similarly, those who have publicly engaged in prostitution or pimping,

exercuerint, aut foeneratores fuerint, nec ad bonam frugem unquam se revocaverint, tamen si piis officiis extrema voluntate sua quicquam impendant, honestas has, etiam in malis personis, cogitationes valere placet.

9. Quae sunt [**piae**] causae [*piae*].[13]

Ad pias autem causas hae adnumerantur; cum aliquid ad vinctorum levationem, ad pauperum recreationem, [*ad*] orphanorum, viduarum et afflictarum omnis generis personarum sustentationem confertur, nominatim et maxime cum ad puellarum tenuium nuptias, ad scholasticorum in academiis degentium nuditatem propellendam, ad publicarum viarum refectionem quippiam testamento designatur. Cum autem quicquam superstitiose potius quam pie legatum fuerit, episcopus auctoritatem suam interponat, ut legatum [*in*] pias [**in**] causas distribuatur.

10. Qualis distributio bonorum esse debeat, vel ex testamento, vel ab intestato.[14]

Bonorum vel testamento collocandorum, vel sine testamento relictorum, huiusmodi partitio sit. Qui coniugem et liber[o/i]s habet, tertiam bonorum partem ad uxorem segreget, liber[i/o]s deinde suam tertiam assignet, et adhuc tertiam quae superest portionem arbitratu suo collocet. Quod si decesserit sine testamento, suas aequales tertias habebunt [66b] uxor primum, deinde liberi, reliquam vero solam administratores tertiam partem [*ipsi*] dispartient. Quod si proles testatori [279v] defuerit, apud uxorem dimidia bonorum pars resideat, et quod erit reliqui, quomodo voluerit, de eo constituat. Et si moriens testamento destitutus fuerit, hoc idem reliquum in administratorum potestate solum erit, uxoris salva semper et illibata sorte. Si vero testator sobolem ex uxore susceperit, et uxor, illa superstite, sit mortua, tum ad h[o/**an**]c ipsam sobolem dimidium placet omnium bonorum revocari, residuum autem ad voluntatem referatur testatoris; quem si forte mors sine testamento depraehenderit, iure sobolis inviolato, quod relinquetur ad auctoritatem devolvatur administratorum. Fortunarum autem talis ratio debet *iniri* iniri, semper ut aes alienum, et omnes funeris impensae deducantur. Liberorum vero ius, quoniam propter variam eorum multitudinem incertum esse potest, aequalitatis perpetua regula definiatur, ut quotcunque sint, suam quisque propriam habeat pro facultatum ratione particulam, nisi forte pater in testamento nominatim aliquid secus posuerit. Et cum tenuior erit parentum conditio licebit filiis in tertia bonorum parte, cuius integrum ius habent, tantum parentes sublevare quantum illis videbitur. Quae res ut facilius possit progredi, reliquas portiones, quas uxoribus et liberis reservavimus, si locus eorum vacuus fuerit, ad parentes collocupletandos infundi

---

[13]L, 3.13.6, gloss on *pias causas*.
[14]21 Henry VIII, c. 5, s. 2, 1529 (*S.R.*, III, 285-8). Cf. H.C., 31.11.

or who have been money lenders and have not brought themselves back to good works, if in their last will they donate something to godly purposes, such honourable intentions, even in wicked persons, shall nevertheless be valid.

9. What pious causes are.[13]

The following may be regarded as pious causes: when someone gives towards the release of captives, to the rehabilitation of the poor, [to] the support of orphans, widows and distressed persons of all kinds, especially and above all when something is designated in a testament for the marriage of poor brides, for the clothing of scholars in the universities and for the repair of the public highways. But when something is left for superstitious rather than for godly reasons, the bishop shall intervene by his authority and ensure that the legacy is distributed to pious causes.

10. How a person's goods shall be distributed, whether he has made a testament or not.[14]

The division of the goods which have either been allocated by testament or which have been left without a testament, shall be as follows. Whoever has a spouse and children shall set aside one third of his goods for his wife, and then he shall assign one third to the children, and after that he may allocate the remaining third at his discretion. But if he should die without a testament, the goods shall be divided equally into thirds and the wife shall have hers first, then the children, and then the administrators [*themselves*] shall share out the remaining third. But if the testator has no children, half of his goods shall remain with his wife and he may do as he wishes with the remainder. And if the deceased has no testament, this remainder shall be in the hands of the administrators, leaving always the wife's portion untouched. And if the testator has offspring by his wife, and his wife is dead but the offspring is still alive, then half of all his goods shall be reserved for that offspring, and the remainder shall be disbursed according to the will of the testator; and if by chance death has struck him down without a testament, the right of the offspring shall be inviolate and what remains shall fall to the authority of the administrators. Such a reckoning should be made of fortunes, but always deducting any debts and all expenses of the funeral. And the right of the children, which may be uncertain on account of the variable number of them, shall be defined by the constant rule of equality, so that for as many as there are, each one shall have his proportionate amount, unless perchance their father has expressly put something different in his will. And since the testator's parents' standard of living will be reduced, they shall have every right as parents to take as much of the third part belonging to the children as they shall think fit. In order for this matter to be more easily expedited, the remaining portions which we have reserved for the wives and children may be added to the parents' portion if there is no wife and no child to claim it. Finally,

posse placet. Denique si testator[i/e]s, vel cum testamento vel sine testamento morientis, filium etiam mors oppresserit, et is filius liberos habeat, quantum ex avi bonis ad filium erat descensurum, [*tantum*] ad nepotes proveniat, ut latissime legum nostrarum humanitas [*ad omnes*] dimanare possit.

[280r; 67a] 11. Qui filii portione legitima carere possint.[15]

Nullus filius in testamento patris praetermitti debet, nisi quem prius vel ante conclusum testamentum, vel in ipso testamenti condendi tempore disertis verbis pater exhaeredaverit. Abdicatio tamen ipsa non valebit, nisi iustam aliquam habuerit causam appositam: quas, ut plane cognoscerentur, hic ordine subi[i/e]ci[e]mus.

Itaque primum et gravissimum est, si filius patri manum iniecerit;

deinde si gra*t*/v**i** aliqua et insigni iniuria volens et sciens violaverit;

si criminis in foro coarguerit non reipublicae causa, sed vel malitia vel odio intestino;

si cum incantatoribus illi*s* vel maleficis usus fuerit;

si patris [**aut matris**] saluti tetenderit insidias;

si cum [*patris coniuge* **noverca**] vel patris concubina incestum commiserit;

si calumnia famam patris oppugnaverit, aut eius facultates obtriverit;

si pro patre*nte* requirente vel fideiussor esse, vel vadimonium obire negaverit;

si patri sit impedimento ne vel testamentum instituat, vel quacunque ratione corrigat.

Filia vero testamenti beneficio careat, si meretriciis institutis vixerit, vel corpus pervulgaverit, cum interim pater honestam nuptiarum conditionem obtulerit. Nam pater si vicesimum quintum annum in filia neglexerit, et matrimonium non praeparaverit, negligentia patris culpa filiam exsolvet, aut saltem quam ipse tam grandem suo vitio virginem apud se detinuerit, [280v] eam nec familia nec testamento po[*si*/**tes**]t excludere.

Plect[*a*/**e**]tur etiam exhaereditationis poena filiorum ingratitudo, qui patres vel furiosos vel mente captos non (quantum res illorum ferent) sustentaverint, vel si captivos aliquam non reperirint liberandi viam; si prolabantur in haeresim et in ea permanserint; si lenoniis vel meretriciis artibus usi fuerint.

---

[15]*Nov.*, 115,3. The 'lawful portion' or *legitim*, was provided for in the *Lex Falcidia* of 40 BC, and was subsequently modified by Justinian. It seems to have faded out in medieval England, or at least to have become variable according to local custom, though this may be evidence of its continuing vitality as late as 1552. See R. H. Helmholz, '*Legitim* in English legal history', *University of Illinois Law Review*, MCMLXXXIV (1984), 659-74, reprinted in *idem, Canon law and the law of England* (London, 1987), pp. 247-62.

if death has taken away the son of the testator also, whether he has a testament of his own or not, and that son has children, as much of the grandfather's goods as would have gone to the son, [*so much*] shall go to the grandchildren, so that the humanity of our laws may extend as widely as possible [*to everyone*].

11. Which sons may lose their lawful portion.[15]

No son must be overlooked in his father's testament, unless the father has explicitly disinherited him beforehand, either before composing the testament or at the time of writing it. Nevertheless, this exclusion shall be invalid unless it has some just cause attached, which we list here, so that they may be fully known.

The first and most important is if a son has laid hands on his father,

then if he has willingly and knowingly harmed him by some *uncalled for* **serious** and significant wound,

if he has convicted him into a criminal court, not for the sake of the state but out of malice or hatred,

if he has made use of enchanters or sorcerers,

if he has conspired against the safety of his father [**or mother**],

if he has committed incest with his [*father's wife* **stepmother**] or his father's concubine,

if he has defamed his father with calumny or wasted his resources,

if he has refused to be a guarantor for his *parent* **father** when asked, or to provide bail for him,

if he has prevented his father either from making a testament or from amending it in any way.

And his daughter shall lose the benefit of the testament if she has lived in prostitution or flaunted her body when her father had offered her a decent dowry for marriage. But if a father has failed to notice that his daughter has reached the age of twenty-five and has not arranged her marriage, the father's negligence shall absolve the daughter of guilt, or at least if he has kept such an old maid through his own fault, he may not exclude her either from his household or from his testament.

Also, the ingratitude of the children shall be punished with the penalty of disinheritance, if they have not looked after their fathers (as far as they are able) when they are either insane or mentally handicapped, or who have not found some way of liberating them if they have been taken captive, if they have fallen into heresy and remained in it, and if they have resorted to the arts of the pimp or prostitute.

[67b] 12. Parentes etiam pauperes, cur a filiis in testamento praeteriri possint.[16]

Parentes, ex altera parte, si turpiter liberos destituant, aut execrabili quodam et immani odio a se proiiciant, vel in magnum vitae periculum eiiciant, ab illis in testamento praeteriri possunt:

si venenis aut artibus quibuscunque magicis salutis damnum filiis inferre moliantur, aut uxor[*um*/**is**] pudicitiam expugnent;

itidem si filiis testamentorum libertatem instituendorum interceperint;

si furiosos illos non curaverint; si convicti fuerint haeresis, et ab ea nolint removeri;

causis omnibus his filii possunt ad pa*r*rentes in testamento praetereundos uti, proviso semper in his duobus capitibus quod nomine patris etiam mater intelligatur.

13. Cur uxores praeterire liceat in testamento.[17]

Semper etiam uxorum in testamentis mariti rationem habere debent, nisi *si* iusta possit offensionis causa proferri, quam nec ipsam admitti volumus, nisi firmis argumentis nitatur. Nec enim illis per calumniam ius suum eripi debet; [281r][18] quam et in filiorum et in tenuium parentum causis aequitatem teneri volumus, ne ulla iniuria ius suum amittant. Uxores autem mariti propter haec [*testamentis*] excludere possunt:

si vi in illos incurrerint;

si quicquam ad eorum perniciem machinatae sint;

si maleficis aut magicis artibus se contaminaverint;

si prudens et sciens uxor famam aut fortunas mariti calumnia vel accusatione falsa perverterit;

si viro fuerit impedimento ne testamentum vel perficeret vel emendaret, aut quacunque ratione commutaret;

vel illum si furiosum, delirum, aut implicatum gravi morbo non foverit;

si salutem eius prodiderit ulla [*alia*] nisi reipublicae causa;

si captivum vel pecunia vel aliqua ratione non recuperaverit, quantum [68a] quidem in se fuerit;

si arripiat haeresim nec ab ea dimoveri velit;

si filiam vel [*aliam*] quamcunque domesticam quorumcunque libidini patefecerit aut obiecerit;

denique si digressa fuerit a viro, nec ad illum revocari possit.

---

[16]*Nov.*, 115,4.

[17]Widows were brought under the *Lex Falcidia* by *Nov.* 53,6. This was then adapted from *ibid.*, 115,3, in order to cover them.

[18]Folios 281-8 are not actually numbered as such in the MS. In December 1875 they were numbered 260-7 respectively.

12. Why parents, even if they are poor, may be passed over by their children in a testament.[16]

Parents, on the other hand, if they have wickedly deserted their children, or out of some execrable and incomprehensible hatred have rejected them, or have thrust them into great danger of life, may be passed over by the children in their testament:

if they have attempted to bring harm to their children's health by poisons or any kind of magic arts, or impugned the chastity of their [*wives* **wife**],

likewise if they have interfered with the freedom of their children to make testaments,

if they have not cared for them if they are insane, if they have been convicted of heresy and have refused to renounce it,

for all these reasons children may pass over their *fathers* **parents** in their testament, provided always that in these two chapters the word 'father' shall include the mother as well.

13. Why wives may be passed over in a testament.[17]

Husbands must always take account of their wives in their testaments, except *if* a just cause of offence be produced, which we do not want to be accepted unless it is supported by firm arguments. For their right must not be taken away from them by calumny,[18] which fairness we also want to be respected in cases of children and poor parents, so that they do not lose their right by any adverse action against them. However, husbands may exclude their wives [*from their testaments*] for these reasons:

if they attack their husbands by force,

if they have schemed up something to their husbands' detriment,

if they have contaminated themselves by sorcery or magic arts,

if cunningly and knowingly a wife has injured the reputation or fortunes of her husband by calumny or false accusation,

if she has prevented her husband from completing or amending his testament, or altering it for any reason, or if she has not cared for him when insane, delirious or weighed down with serious illness,

if she has betrayed his interests for any [*other*] reason than that of the state,

if she has not rescued him with money or in some other way when he was captured, in so far as she was able,

if she has adopted a heresy and been unwilling to be turned away from it,

if she has exposed or subjected a daughter or any [*other*] domestic servant to the lusts of any others,

finally if she has deserted her husband and cannot be brought back to him.

14. Qui nec haeredes institui, nec legatorum participes esse possunt.[19]

Nec haeredes instituentur, nec ullo beneficio utentur testamentorum, qui pertinaces sunt haeretici, nec qui mortis sententiam acceperunt, aut exilii perpetui vel aeterni carceris, nec qui concubinatu se polluunt, nec duas qui coniuges uno tempore contra omne ius et fas conservant; nec feminae quarum in crimine pari par est culpa. Adnumerabuntur huc qui procuratorum ullo modo vel sparsorum [281v] damnati sunt scriptorum infamium, quae lex civilis famosa vocat, qui lenoniis vel meretriciis institutis palam [*vi*/**ut**]unt[**ur**]. Pellentur etiam foeneratores ab omnibus testamentorum emolumentis. Tempus autem *illud** minime **illud*** spectetur, in quo testamentum est institutum, vel in quo testator est ipse mortuus, sed in illo tempore personarum mores excuti placet, in quo vel *ab illis* haereditas **ab illis** est adeunda, vel legata ei[**u**]s incipiunt deberi.

15. De iniqua vel impossibili conditione legati.[20]

Si quis rem certam in testamento cuiquam leget, conditionem [*vel*] iniquam vel impiam apponens, legatarius rem amittet, nisi fidem suam interposuerit se conditionem repudiaturum. Ad quod si nolit adduci, legata res episcopi arbitratu in pium aliquod institutum impendatur. Si vero talis fuerit conditio quae non possit praestari, frustra debet addita videri, quapropter huiusmodi conditiones nec haeredum iura nec legatariorum impedient, praesertim hoc si ostenderint, se [68b] quidem, quantum in ipsis positum esset, elaboravisse conditiones ut procederent, nec illorum diligentiae quicquam abfuisse.

16. Quando haeredes bona testatoris capere possunt.[21]

Haeredibus ad bona mortuorum aditus non erit, nisi commentarium ut quendam eorum conficiant, quem indicem vocant, et tantum ut sumant quantum funeris impensis satis erit, donec testamenta [282r] vel episcopo, vel eius ditionis proprio iudici, quem ordinarium saepissime communi nomine dicimus, plene probata fuerint; et donec ab haeredibus apud ordinarium syngrapha obligatoria praecautum fuerit, se toto in hoc negotio commissorum sibi bonorum integre et sincere progressuros, et rationem illi red{*d*}ituros suae fidei cum eam ordinarius poposcerit, et ipsum ordinarium omni ratione salvum et quietum semper praestituros. Nam episcoporum est proprium [*ius*] testamenta confirma[*ndi*/**re**],

---

[19]*Dig.*, 28.1.5, originally Ulpian, *Ad Sabinum*, 6; L, 3.13.5, c. 7 of Archbishop John Stratford's council of 1342.
[20]*Dig.*, 28.7.1, originally Ulpian, *Ad Sabinum*, 5; ibid., 28.7.6, originally Ulpian, *Ad Sabinum*, 9; ibid., 28.7.8, originally Ulpian, *Ad edictum*, 50; ibid., 28.7.9, originally Paulus, *Ad edictum*, 45; ibid., 28.7.14, originally Marcian, *Institutiones*, 4.
[21]The statute of Archbishop Henry Chichele on wills, 1 July 1416 (W, III, 377-8).

14. Who cannot be appointed heirs nor share in legacies.[19]

Those who are persistent heretics shall neither be appointed as heirs nor share in any benefit from testaments, neither shall those who have received a sentence of death, or of perpetual exile or life imprisonment, nor those who have polluted themselves in concubinage, nor those who, against all law and right, have kept two wives at the same time, nor women whose guilt is equal in a like crime. To their number shall be added those who have been condemned for any kind of procuring or for spreading defamatory writings, which the law calls infamous, who openly make use of pimps or prostitutes. Money lenders shall also be refused any funds from testaments. Moreover, the morals of the individuals concerned will be examined not at the time at which the testament was made, or at which the testator himself died, but at the time at which they are either due to receive an inheritance or [*a* **their**] legacy is due [*to them*].

15. Of an unfair or impossible condition in a legacy.[20]

If a person leaves a particular item to someone in a testament, adding a condition to it which is [*either*] unfair or ungodly, the legatee shall forfeit the item in question, unless he has sworn his faith that he will repudiate the condition. If he cannot be persuaded to do this, the legacy will be paid to some godly institution, at the bishop's discretion. And if the condition is such that it cannot be fulfilled, it must be regarded as having been added in vain, with the result that such conditions shall not block the rights of either the heirs or the legatees, particularly if they demonstrate that they have tried their best to fulfill the conditions, and that there has been nothing lacking in their diligence.

16. When the heirs may take possession of the goods of the testator.[21]

The heirs shall not have access to the goods of the deceased, except in order to prepare a commentary on them, which is called an inventory, and also to withdraw a sum sufficient to pay the funeral expenses, until the testaments have been fully proved either by the bishop, or by the judge belonging to his jurisdiction, whom we most often call by the common name of ordinary, and until the heirs have indicated to the ordinary, by compulsory bond, that they will proceed in all this business of the goods entrusted to them with integrity and sincerity, that they will give account of their trust when the ordinary shall request it and that they will in every way keep the ordinary himself immune and untroubled. For it is the proper [*right*] of bishops to confirm testaments [*and to*

[*potestatemque concedendi suorum scriptorum auctoritate*], bonorum administrationem etiam designare, si testamenta mortuorum non extiterint. Itaque [*v*/**n**]olumus hoc illorum ius loco movere, nisi singulare privilegium intercurrerit, aut aliquo consensu legitimo secus constitutum fuerit, vel aliqua consuetudo recta, vel spatium temporis iure definitum (quam praescriptionem vocant) hanc auctoritatem ad alios aut [*ad*] homines aut locos deducat.

17. De mercede iudicis et ministrorum.[22]

Cum bona testatorum summam quinque librarum non transcendunt, nihil vel iudici vel eius administris pro confirmatione testamentorum rependetur: scriba tantum sex denarios percipiet, quod iudicis sententiam et testamenti exemplar in acta retulerit. Iudex autem huiusmodi testamentum, quando firmum et solidum esse statuit, ap[69a]posito signo gratis muniet: [282v] membranae ver*o**/**ae***, cerae, scripturaeque sumptus ad illos aequum est devolvi, ad quos ex eisdem utilitas perveniet. Si vero testatorum facultates ultra quinque libras ascendant, et tamen intra quadraginta libras subsistent, ad iudicem et ministros quadraginta denarii seponentur, ex quibus duodecim eximentur scribae, reliquum iudici remanebit et suis administris. Cum autem res testatoris pretium quadraginta librarum superant, ad iudicem et ministros quinque solidi corrivabuntur, de quo dimidium ad scribam perveniet: at in eo si non acquiesc[*a*/**e**]t, hanc conditionem sumet, ut pro decimo quoque testamenti versu denarium percipiat, proviso quod singuli versus decem pollicum latitudinem [*longitudine*] exaequent.

18. Quod haeredes et administratores rationem reddent bonorum.[23]

Nulli privilegio tantum tribui volumus, ut [*vel*] haeredes bonorum (quos executores vocant) vel administratores a reddenda legatorum ratione abducat, quam in omnibus, qui vel cum testamento vel sine testamento moriuntur, constare placet. Quapropter qui talibus privilegiis praemuniti sunt, eorum nisi beneficium deponant et repudient, nolumus illos ullum in tractandorum bonorum negotio ius habere, nec ad eorum administrationem quacunque ratione adhiberi.

---

[22]L, 3.13.7, c. 23 of Archbishop John Stratford's council of 1342; 21 Henry VIII, c. 5, ss. 2-3, 1529 (*S.R.*, III, 285-8).
[23]*Clem.*, 3.6.1 (Fr, II, 1161), published by Pope Clement V (1305-14) after the council of Vienne (1311-12).

give effect to them by the authority of his letters], and also to allocate the administration of the goods, if the deceased have left no testaments. Therefore we [**do not**] desire this right of theirs to be transferred elsewhere unless it comes up against some particular privilege or is seen to be contrary to some lawful agreement, or some proper custom or space of time defined by law (which is called a prescription) transfers this authority to others, either [*to*] people or places.

17. Of the fee for the judge and his servants.[22]

When the goods of the testators do not exceed the sum of five pounds, nothing shall be paid either to the judge or to his staff for the confirmation of the testaments; only the scribe shall receive six pence for putting the judge's sentence and a copy of the testament into the records. Moreover, the judge shall validate such a testament, when he has stated that it is firm and solid, by affixing his seal free of charge, *and** it is fair that the costs of the **true*** parchment, wax, and writing shall fall upon those who derive the benefit from them. But if the estate of the testators goes above five pounds, yet does not reach the sum of forty pounds, forty pence shall be set aside for the judge and his servants, out of which twelve shall be paid to the scribe and the rest shall remain with the judge and his staff. But when the value of the testator's goods surpasses forty pounds, five shillings shall be turned over to the judge and his ministers, of which half shall go to the scribe, and if he is not satisfied with this, he shall accept this arrangement, that for every tenth line of the testament he shall receive a penny, provided that each line equals the width of ten inches [*in length*].

18. That heirs and administrators must give account of the goods.[23]

We do not want any privilege to be given which would exempt [*either*] the heirs of the goods (who are called executors) or the administrators from having to give an account of the legacies, for such an account must be given in all cases, whether the deceased has left a testament or not. Therefore, we do not want those who have such privileges to have any right in the business of dealing with goods unless they give up and renounce the use of the privileges, nor shall they be employed in any way in administering the goods.

[283r] 19. De sigillo defuncti.[24]

Quoniam multa solent astute fieri quando signum hominis mortui interceptum est, iubemus ut quamprimum aliquis excesserit e[x] vita, signum eius qualecunque sit quod ad scripta solebat affigere, quandam in arculam vel crumenam seponatur, ubi tuto conservari possit, et praeterea trium signis honestarum personarum illa crumena vel arcula obfirme[69b]tur, ut ita signum testatoris salvum ad iudicem primo quoqu[e/**am**] tempore deducatur. Cum vero [**vel**] haeredes vel executores signum ad iudicem deportaverint, ille statim imaginem et formam signi pervertat et deleat, materiam vero illis restituat, nec ullo modo sibi reservet.

20. De bonorum indicibus conficiendis.[25]

Haeredes vel administratores duos evocabunt ad se, qui vel aliquid testatori debebant, vel nonnihil ex eius testamento percipient, [*vel* **aut**] hi si *non* [*negaverint*] vel [**omnino**] non affirmerint [**negaverintve**], duos existimationis honestae, qui defuncto necessarii fuerint, vel omnibus his absentibus, duos cuiuscunque conditionis, modo probos et integros; et hi rationes omnium rerum scriptis mandandas curent plene et perfecte: quorum scriptorum, vel ut vulgo dicunt inventariorum, sibi reservent unum exemplar, alterum iudicis fidei committ[a/**e**]nt, qui cum iuramentum ab illis de scriptorum [283v] fide et sinceritate poposcerit et acceperit, ipsa scripta prompte sumet, comprobabit, et in tuto loco conservabit, nam et testamentorum et i{*n*/**u**}dic[**i**]um vel inventariorum (ut vocant) exemplaria diligenter a iudice vel a iudicis administris custodiri praecipimus, ut hi quorum intererit, quoties illa requisiverint, praesto esse possint. Cum autem haec scripta postulabuntur, statim illa placet et alacriter exhiberi, et merces his rebus transcribendis illa sit, quam ante posuimus; aut, ita si scriba /sibi/ voluerit satisfieri, numerum secutus versuum pro decimo quoqu[*e*/**am**] singulos denarios excipiat, et illa versibus longitudo constet, quam ante praescripsimus. Quod si vel iudicis vel administr[*at*]orum avaritia plus ad se derivaverit quam nos assignavimus, et merces primum omnis ipsa detrahatur, deinde iactura ferientur decem librarum, de [70a] quibus dimidium in cistam pauperum secedet, reliquum ad eum perveniet, cuius negotium fuit, si reos facere velit et causam iure p[*ro*/**er**]sequi.

[24]21 Henry VIII, c. 5, s. 5, 1529 (*S.R.*, III, 285-8).
[25]L, 3.13.5, c. 7 of Archbishop John Stratford's council of 1342. Cf. H.C., 31.11, where it is mentioned in passing.

19. Of the seal of the deceased.[24]

Since many things are often done by deceit when the seal of a dead man has been intercepted, we order that as soon as someone departs this life, his seal, of whatever kind it may be, which he used to affix to documents shall be put away in some box or purse where it may be kept safely, and furthermore that that purse or box shall be fastened with the seals of three honest persons, so that the seal of the testator may be taken safe and sound to the judge at the first available opportunity. And when [**either**] the heirs or the administrators take the seal to the judge, he shall immediately deface and destroy the image and shape of the seal, and return the object to them, nor shall he ever keep it for himself.

20. Of drawing up inventories of the goods.[25]

The heirs or administrators shall summon two people to them, who either owe something to the testator or who will receive something from his testament, or if they neither [*deny* **affirm**] nor [*affirm* **deny**], to men of honourable reputation, who were dependants of the deceased, or if all of these are absent, two men of any sort, as long as they are honest and true, and they shall ensure that accounts of all the goods are recorded fully and completely in writing, of which documents, or inventories, as they are commonly called, they shall keep one copy for themselves and entrust another to the judge who, after he has asked for and received an oath from them regarding the trustworthiness and reliability of the documents, shall quickly take up the documents, prove them and keep them in a safe place, for we order the copies of the testaments and indexes or inventories (as they are called) to be kept diligently by the judge or by the judge's staff, so that those who have an interest in them may have access to them as often as they need them. And when these documents shall be demanded, they shall be immediately and readily provided, and the fee for transcribing these things shall be the same as the one we have laid down above, or if the scribe wants to satisfy himself, he shall receive a penny for every ten lines, and the length of the lines shall be what we have prescribed above. But if the greed of either the judge or the administrators diverts more to them than we have assigned, first of all, their entire fee shall be seized, and then they shall be fined ten pounds, of which half shall go to the poor box and the rest to the person whose business it was, if he wants to accuse them and pursue the case at law.

21. Haeredes vel administratores sol[*a*/**u**]m indic[**i**]um fidem sequi debere.[26]

Aequum non est ut vel haeredes vel bonorum administratores plus exhibere cogantur, quam in illis scriptis [*reperiri potest* **reperitur**], quos indices dicimus, si tamen ipsis indicibus plene fides constiterit.

[284r] 22. Dubitatio cum [*oc*/**in**]currit de testamento vel haeredibus, quid sequendum sit.[27]

Cum nec de testamenti pondere, nec de personis qui bonorum ad moderationem adhibendi sint, in ecclesiastico foro iure possit constare, iudex, ut interim de facultatibus [**nihil**] intercidat, illas fidorum sequestrorum custodiae committet, [**donec aliquid in his rebus certi possit intelligi**]. Haeres autem si tempus ad cogitandum sumpserit, nec statim credat negotium tam implicatum debere suscipi, litteras ordinarius illi curet confici, quarum auctoritate dissipatas testatoris facultates [*intelligere* **recolligere**] possit; modo scriptis legitime cautum sit, ut haeres sex mensium spatio proxime consecuturorum, rationem omnium rerum reddat ullo iure testatoris a se conquisitarum, nec secus ad opes testatoris contrectandas intret, nisi perfecto bonorum omnium incorrupto veroque indice, eo modo quo paulo ante est praescriptum. Hanc etiam rationem administratores sequentur, qui sine testamentis ad hominum facultates admoventur.

[70b] 23. Poena recusantium haeredum quae sit.[28]

Qui nominatim in testamento constituuntur haeredes, cum ordinarius illos admonuerit et certum *p*... tempus posuerit in quo debent testamenti tractationem suscipere, vel ordinarii monita licet non intercesserint, nec is quicquam in hac re cum illis egerit, si totos sex menses effluere sinant [284v] mortem testatoris excipientes, et ad testamenti pertractationem se non adiungant, nec causam afferant iustam qua cog[*u*/**a**]ntur ab illo abesse, statim ordinarius illos a testamento discludat, nec quicquam ex eo patiatur ad illos emolumenti pervenire. Restituant autem et reponant plene et integre si quicquam prius [*de* **in**] testamento delibaverint: et mortui propinquis hoc negotium a iudice committatur.

---

[26]21 Henry VIII, c. 5, s. 2, 1529 (*S.R.*, III, 285-8); H.C., 31.11.
[27]The statute of Archbishop Henry Chichele on wills, 1 July 1416 (W, III, 377-8); H.C., 31.15.
[28]X, 3.26.3 (Fr, II, 539), originally a letter of Pope Gregory I (590-604), *Reg.*, 4.8; H.C., 31.12.

21. Heirs and administrators must seek [*only*] the truth of the inventories [**alone**].[26]

It is not fair that either the heirs or the administrators should be compelled to report more than what [*can be* **is**] found in those documents, which we call inventories, as long as the inventories themselves are fully trustworthy.

22. What is to be done when there is some doubt about the testament or the heirs.[27]

When neither the validity of the testament nor the persons who have been appointed to administer the goods can be lawfully verified in an ecclesiastical court, the judge shall for the time being entrust the property to the care of reliable sequestrators, so that [**none of**] the property shall disappear, [**until something definite can be ascertained about these matters**]. But if the heir has taken time to think it over and does not believe that so complicated a business should be undertaken straightaway, the ordinary shall see to it that letters are sent to him, by the authority of which he can [*claim* **recoup**] the disbursed property of the testator, as long as it is lawfully stated in the documents that the heir shall give an account of all the goods received by him by any right of the testator, within six months immediately following, nor shall he otherwise claim possession of the goods of the testator as long as a perfect, true and complete inventory of all the goods has not been made in the manner just described above. Also, the administrators who are assigned to the property of people without testaments shall also follow the same procedure.

23. What the penalty shall be for those who refuse to act as heirs.[28]

When the ordinary has notified those who have been named as heirs in a testament and appointed a fixed time in which they must undertake the execution of the testament, or even if the ordinary has given no notification and has had nothing to do with them in this matter, if they allow six months to go by after the testator's death and do not devote themselves to the execution of the testament, nor offer any just cause by which they are compelled to stay away from it, the ordinary shall immediately exclude them from the testament nor shall he allow anything from it to come to them as reward. Moreover if they have already taken something [*from* **in**] the testament, they shall restore and replace it fully and completely, and the business shall be entrusted by the judge to relatives of the deceased.

24. De distributione bonorum inter haeredes vel administratores.[29]

Cum plures haeredes vel administratores fuerint, aequas sibi bonorum particulas sument, ut alter ab altero cum iniuriose tractabitur, singulis ad suum ius recuperandum via esse possit. Ordinarius igitur hoc vehementer providebit, ut haec inter illos bonorum aequalitas semper conservetur, nisi forte secus ipsi inter se pacti fuerint, aut propter viduam et filiorum causam [*aliud*] consilium ordinarius capiendum esse putet.

25. Quae legantur piis causis, quando solvenda sunt.[30]

Quamprimum aes alienum fuerit dissolutum, statim hoc in pias causas collocetur, quod illis testator impendit, in qua re si illi quorum interest ultra sex menses a testamenti approbatione tardaverint, episcopus [*e*/**au**]t ordinarius [71a] ecclesiasticarum auctoritate censurarum [285r] universam non solum sortem, sed accessiones etiam quascunque comportari curet, et ad testatoris voluntatem accommodari, nisi tempus solvendorum legatorum in testamento diserte sit expressum.

26. Moriens legatarius quando legatum transmittit ad haeredem.[31]

Postquam res legata deberi coepit, si legatarius e vita prius excedat quam haereditas adita fuerit, in legati ius haeres legatarii succed[*a*/**e**]t. Sed res legata tradi non potest, donec testamentum per iudicem confirmetur.

27. Quando legatum ab haerede non solvitur.[32]

Haeres necessitate solvendae rei legatae non tenetur, cum ea donatione legatario primum obveniens aut ulla lucrosa causa, post in eiusdem legatarii possessione collocetur; nec enim bis in eodem beneficio quisquam adiuvari debet: sed quam rem *ante* legatarius ante pretio comparaver[*a*/**i**]t, eam si dempto pretio testator donaverit, eius benevolentiam emptio non impedit, quoniam in ea non lucrum sed onus inesse videtur.

---

[29]L, 3.13.5, gloss on *propriis suis bonis*; 1268/15, gloss on *libertatem*; H.C., 31.14.
[30]Cf. The statute of Archbishop Henry Chichele on wills, 1 July 1416 (W, III, 377-8), which allowed a year's grace for this.
[31]25 Edward III, s. 5, c. 5, 1351 (*S.R.*, II, 319-24); H.C., 31.21.
[32]L, 3.13.5, gloss on *titulo emptionis*.

24. Of the distribution of goods among their heirs and administrators.[29]

When there are many heirs or administrators, they shall take an equal share of the goods, so that if one is cheated by another there may be some way for particular individuals to recover their rights. Therefore the ordinary shall strongly insist that this equality of goods shall always be maintained among them, unless by chance they have made some other arrangement among themselves, or the ordinary thinks that [*other*] advice must be taken because of the widow and the cause of the children.

25. When things which have been left to pious causes shall be paid.[30]

As soon as all debts have been cleared, the money which the testator gave to pious causes shall be allocated to them, but if the interested parties delay in doing this for more than six months beyond the probation of the testament, the bishop [*and* **or**] the ordinary shall see to it that not only the whole amount, but also whatever additions may have accrued to it, and which conform to the will of the testator, shall be delivered under the authority of ecclesiastical censures, unless the time for paying the legacies is explicitly stated in the testament.

26. When a dying legatee may transfer his legacy to an heir.[31]

If a legatee should depart this life after the time that the legacy is owed but before the inheritance has come to him, the legatee's heir shall succeed to the right of the legacy. But the legacy may not be handed over until the testament has been confirmed by the judge.

27. When a legacy is not paid by the heir.[32]

The heir will not be bound of necessity to pay the legacy when it has already come into the legatee's possession by gift or by some other profitable means, and then is later allocated to the possession of the same legatee, for no one ought to be helped twice over by the same benefit, but if the legatee has already purchased the thing, if the testator has given it to him for a reduced price, the purchase shall not impede his benevolence, since it appears that there is more of a burden than a profit in it.

28. Quando legata non valent.[33]

Legata valere non possunt nec praestari debent, cum legatarius a testatoris proposito receda/it; aut si conditio non extiterit ad quam legatum referebatur; aut ipsa si legata quocunque casu vel fortuita calamitate [**prius**] effluant et colliquescant, quam haereditas adeatur; aut si legata fuerint quae aedificiis sunt coniuncta, nisi vel corruant vel diruantur aedificia.

[285v; 71b] 29. Quando legata minui poss[i/**u**]nt.[34]

[*Quando* **Cum**] haereditas sic extenuata fuerit, ut omnia legata plene si repraesentarentur, vel uxori vel liberis suum non possit ius integrum relinqui, tantum ex ea volumus decerpi, quantum ad explendam uxoris et liberorum sortem satis erit.

30. Quid a legatariis promittendum sit.[35]

Cuicunque quicquam expresse legatum est, id illi non tradatur, nisi legitime praecaverit se restituturum quod accep[**er**]it, si c[*u*/**e**]rta fuerit haereditas, et onera sustentare non possit.

31. De fidei commissis.[36]

Quoties vel haereditas vel legata in testamento cuiuscunque personae fidei committuntur, hoc est, illi sic ad tempus mandantur, ut eadem post voluntate testatoris alio transferantur, fidei commissarii nec ad haereditates ullo modo, nec ad legata [**admitti**] debent [*admitti*], donec vel fideiuss[*or*/**ion**]ibus idoneis vel etiam pignoribus caverint, se salvas haereditates et inviolata legata prorsus eisdem conditionibus esse repraesentaturos, quas testator in suprema voluntate sua legitime vel significavit vel expressit.

---

[33]Cf. X, 3.26.5 (Fr, II, 540), originally a decretal of Pope Gregory IX (1227-41), published on or before 5 September 1234.
[34]*Dig.*, 35.2.1, originally Paulus *Ad legem Falcidiam*, 1.
[35]*Dig.*, 35.3.1, originally Ulpian, *Ad edictum*, 79.
[36]*Inst.*, 2.23-4; *Dig.*, 36.1.1, originally Ulpian, *Fideicommissa*, 3. Cf. VI, 3.11.1 (Fr, II, 1044-5), originally a decretal of Pope Boniface VIII (1294-1303).

28. When legacies are not valid.[33]

Legacies are not valid, nor shall they be fulfilled, when a legatee rejects the testator's conditions, or if there is no condition which applies to the legacy, or if the legacy itself disappears and evaporates by some accident or chance mishap [**before**] the inheritance comes, of if the legacy was tied to buildings and the buildings are either falling down or are in ruins.

29. When legacies may be reduced.[34]

When an inheritance has been so reduced that if all the legacies were to be fully paid, nothing would be left either to the wife or to the children, it is our will that enough to pay the wife and children their portion shall be withheld from it.

30. What must be promised by the legatees.[35]

A legacy shall not be handed over to anyone to whom it has been expressly left until he lawfully swears that he will give back what he has received if the inheritance is [*small* **limited**] and cannot bear the burden.

31. Of things held in trust.[36]

Whenever either an inheritance or a legacy in anyone's testament is given to some person in trust, that is, is committed to him for the time being in such a way that afterwards, according to the will of the testator, it shall be transferred to someone else, the trustees must not be granted any access either to the inheritance or to the legacy until they have given assurances either by suitable sureties or even by bonds that they will pay out what the testator has lawfully either signified or expressed in his last will.

32. Quomodo sit utendum mortui bonis.[37]

Haeredes ex bonis testatoris nihil ad se vel pretio sevoce[n]t, vel inter se mutua donatione spargant, [*vel* **aut**] alio respectu cuiuscunque generis invadant, et quasi proprium assumant, nisi quod vel in testamento fuerit illis aperte attributum, vel pro quo iustum pretium numeraverint co[72a]ram idoneis testibus, qua formula bonorum etiam administratores uti placet.

[286r] 33. Sine consensu nihil esse alienandum.[38]

Distrahi nihil aut alienari patimur ex facultatibus testatoris, cuiuscunque generis res aut possessio sit, nec scriptis quicquam acceptum ferri, vel, ut vulgo loquuntur, acquietantiam ullam dari vel ab haeredibus vel a bonorum administratoribus, nisi communis sit omnium in eo consensus, qui iuramento se prius obligaverint. Et qui secus fecerint, illos excommunicationis poena coerceri volumus.

34. Testamentum annuo spatio [**impleri**] debet [*impleri*].[39]

Haeredes vel administratores, cum ad testamentorum collocationem semel admoti sunt, intra spatium proximi *sequentis anni* succedentis anni, vel, ut planius loquamur, intra duodecim menses ex [*eo*] tempore quo testamentorum administrationem susceperunt, omnes rerum legatarum particulas emetientur, et quantum testatoris voluntas ac haereditatis ratio ferent, totum hoc negotium illis commissum plenissime conficient, quod si definito tempore munus hoc suum non concludant, cum ordinarius illorum diligentiam excitarit, si illi poscenti iustam non ostenderint causam suae cessationis, ecclesiasticis suppliciis compraehendantur, et etiam omnibus careant *fructibus* fructibus, qui fuer[u/a]nt ad illos ex testamentis perventuri.

35. Quando separatim haeredes in testamento versari possint.[40]

Si complures fuerint haredes vel administratores eodem iure constituti, contingatque quempiam ex illis vel morte [72b] tolli, vel necessaria [**nostra**]

---

[37]The statute of Archbishop Henry Chichele on wills, 1 July 1416 (W, III, 377); H.C., 31.19.
[38]21 Henry VIII, c. 4 (*S.R.*, III, 285).
[39]X, 3.26.3 (Fr, II, 539), originally a letter of Pope Gregory I (590-604), *Reg.*, 4.8; X, 3.26.6 (Fr, II, 540), attributed to a council of Mainz, but its origin is uncertain.
[40]VI, 3.11.2 (Fr, II, 1045), originally a decretal of Pope Boniface VIII (1294-1303); H.C., 31.8.

32. How the goods of the deceased are to be used.[37]

The heirs shall neither set aside anything from the goods of the testator for themselves, by paying for it, nor shall they hand things out to one another by mutual donation, or seize, as if to appropriate, anything else of this kind for any reason, unless it has either been openly allotted to them in the testament or for which they have paid a just price in the presence of reliable witnesses, and administrators of goods shall follow the same procedure also.

33. Nothing may be alienated without consent.[38]

We do not permit that any of the testator's property, of whatever nature the thing or possession may be, may be removed or alienated, nor shall anything be accepted in writing, or as is commonly said, no receipt shall be given either by the heirs or by the administrators of the goods, unless there is common consent from all parties in the matter, who shall first bind themselves to this by oath. And it is our will that those who do otherwise shall be punished with the penalty of excommunication.

34. The testament must be executed within the space of a year.[39]

Heirs and administrators, when once they have been appointed to the execution of testaments, shall pay out all the particulars of the legacies, and in so far as the will of the testator and the means of the inheritance allow, they shall completely fulfil all this business committed to them within the space of a year immediately *following* succeeding, or, as we might say more clearly, within twelve months from the time at which they undertook the administration of the testaments, but if they do not conclude their task within the appointed time, and when the ordinary stirs up their diligence, if they do not show him on request a just cause for their delay, they shall be compelled by ecclesiastical punishments and shall also forfeit all the fruits which would have come to them from the testaments.

35. When heirs can act separately in a testament.[40]

If there are several heirs or administrators empowered with the same right, and it happens that one of them is either taken away by death, or is away for some

causa peregrinari, vel sic impediri, ut intra sex menses aut nolit aut [286v] non possit operam cum aliis suam communicare, reliquis licebit totum pertractare testamentum, et omnes res ad exitum perducere, nec enim tutum aut aequum est testatorum voluntatem ex uno religatam diu suspendi, et res eius incertas relinqui.

36. De successoribus haeredum et administratorum.[41]

Cum solitaria mulier (quam [**viduam**] appellamus [*viduam*]) vel haeres vel bonorum administratrix instituta sit, et eadem post virum sumpserit, vir, sive mortua sive superstite coniuge, per iudicem qui administrationem vel executionem illam commisit, trudetur ad omnem testatoris implendam voluntatem. Et hoc adeo in omnibus legitimis haeredum [*et administratorum*] successoribus teneri volumus, [u/e]t quaecunque priores onera testamentorum agnoscebant, eadem intelligant posteriores ad se pertinere, quantum quidem hoc angustia bonorum et haereditatum fieri sinet ad se quacunque ratione perlatorum.

37. Haeredes diversarum dioecesium quomodo iure convenientur.[42]

Cum plures haeredes ad unum testamentum confluxerint, licet in oris diversis et dioecesibus, ut vocant, dissiti sint, tamen ad illum iudicem revocabuntur, qui testamentum confirmavit, et eius auctoritate suscipient omnia munera, quaecunque ad [**haeredum**] fidem [*haeredum*] et officium pertinent, quod etiam de bonorum administratoribus intelligi volumus.

[287r] 38. Quomodo ratio sit ab haeredibus reddenda.[43]

Ordinarii vel alii quicunque iudices, quibus confirmare licet ac consignare testamenta, quibus[*que*] bonorum sine testa[73a]mento relictorum commissa est auctoritas administrationis [*in*/**re**]stituendae, post annum ab haeredibus et administratoribus sui muneris gesti rationem flagitare possunt et debent. In quo si vide[*tur*/**nt**] integre illos et incorrupte versatos esse, prorsus illos in omne tempus dimittant. Hoc tamen excipimus, ut si forte quicquam ex mortui fortunis non fuerit, ut oportet, distributum quod adhuc coll{**oc**}atum non sit, vel ad eos deferatur, qui in eo ius habent, vel haeredes aut administratores arbitratu iudicis id ad sanctum aliquod propositum accommodent.

[41]1268/15, gloss on *libertatem*; L, 3.13.5, gloss on *propriarum uxorum*. See H.C., 31.20 and accompanying note.
[42]L, 3.13.5, gloss on *laicis*; 1268/15, gloss on *fidem*; H.C., 31.13.
[43]Cf. 13 Edward I, c. 1, s. 23, 1285 (*S.R.*, 83); 4 Henry IV, c. 8, 1402 (*S.R.*, II, 195-6); the statute of Archbishop Henry Chichele on wills, 1 July 1416 (W, III, 377).

necessary reason [**in our service**], or is so hindered that within six months he is unwilling or unable to undertake his task along with the others, it shall be permissible for the others to execute the entire testament, and carry out all matters towards its conclusion, for it is neither safe not fair for the will of the testator to be held up for long simply because of one person, and for the testator's affairs to be left undecided.

36. Of the successors of heirs and administrators.[41]

When a solitary woman (whom we call a widow) has been appointed either an heir or an administrator of the goods, and has then remarried, that husband shall be permitted by the judge who has assigned that administration or execution, to fulfil all the will of the testator, whether his wife is dead or alive. And it is our will that this shall be maintained in all the lawful successors of heirs [*and administrators*], so that whatever the former recognized as the duties of the testaments, the latter shall understand the same as applying to them, in so far as the extent of the goods and inheritance which have been transmitted to them in whatever way allows.

37. How heirs from different dioceses shall be brought together by law.[42]

When many heirs come together in one testament, and they happen to be scattered, as they say, on different shores and in different dioceses, they shall nevertheless be summoned to the same judge who confirmed the testament, and by his authority they shall undertake all the tasks which pertain to the trust and duty of heirs, and it is our will that the same shall be understood of administrators of goods.

38. How an account is to be given by the heirs.[43]

The ordinaries, and any other judges who are permitted to confirm and countersign testaments, [*and*] to whom the authority to establish the administration of goods which have been left without a testament has been entrusted, can and must demand from the heirs and administrators an account of their transactions after a year. If it appears that they have acted honestly and without corruption in this matter, he shall then dismiss them for all time. Nevertheless, we make this exception, that if by chance something from the fortune of the deceased has not been distributed as it should have been, what has not yet been allocated shall either be referred to those who have the right in this matter, or the heirs and administrators shall apply it to some holy purpose, at the discretion of the judge.

39. Poena eorum qui testamenta violant.[44]

Testamentarii qui falsa testamenta subiecerint aut ob[*sign*/**lig**]averint, vel testamentum per se verum ulla ratione perverterint, vel addendo, vel demendo, vel mutando, vel interline[**a**]ndo, vel quocunque genere fraudis aut depravationis utendo, si tam atrocis flagitii manifeste convincantur, pellantur tanquam falsarii omnibus in iure concessis muneribus, et omni careant emolumento corruptorum testamentorum.

40. Qui s[*i*/**u**]nt sine testamento.[45]

Testamentum non dicuntur relinquere, primum qui scriptis non mandant, nisi subitanea irruat mors; deinde qui nominatim haeredem aliquem non ponunt; vel si negant haeredes qui relinquuntur et suscipere [287v] nolunt, aut huiusmodi sint ut suscipere non possint. Et sine testamento iudicandi sunt esse, cum testamentum tam male comparatum est, ut a iudice legitimo confirmari non possit.

[73b] 41. Testamentum vitiosum impleri debet.[46]

Quando testamentum pro nullo capitur et facultates distribuendae sunt ab administrat{*or*/**ion**}ibus, hoc a iudice debet summe provideri, tantam ut testatoris habeat voluntatis rationem, quant{*a*/**o**} omnino maxima esse potest. Quanquam enim legitimum non fuerit testamentum, tamen legum civilium humanitatem libenter sequimur, ut in propriis bonis ultimas hominum voluntates et iudicia nunquam ad se reditura (quantum fieri potest) firma et inviolata conservemus.

42. Quibus administratio bonorum committenda sit, et quid mercedis habere debeant.[47]

Quoties aliquis sine testamento moritur, ad bonorum eius administrationem uxor primo loco sumatur, secundo qui cognatione fuerint propinquissima, vel, si iudex [*ita*] censebit, una potest illos in hoc munere cum uxore coniungere. Hoc tamen perpetuo stet, ut quibuscunque fuerit munus administrationis attributum, fideiussores afferant prius, aut etiam pignora deponant, quibus plene possit et

---

[44]*Dig.*, 48.10.2, originally Paulus, *Ad Sabinum*, 3; H.C., 5.4.
[45]21 Henry VIII, c. 4 (*S.R.*, III, 285); *ibid.*, c. 5 (*S.R.*, III, 285-8); H.C., 31.5.
[46]Same sources as previous.
[47]L, 3.13.4, c. 5 of the council of 1329; L, 3.13.7, c. 23 of Archbishop John Stratford's council of 1342; 31 Edward III, c. 11, 1357 (*S.R.*, I, 351); 21 Henry VIII, c. 5, s. 4, 1529 (*S.R.*, III, 285-8).

39. The penalty for those who violate testaments.[44]

Testamentaries who have submitted or signed false testaments, or who have in any way corrupted a testament by themselves, either by adding or deleting or altering or inserting something, or by using any other kind of fraud or deception, if they have been clearly convicted of so atrocious a crime, those falsifiers shall be deprived of all the offices assigned to them in law, and shall forfeit any reward from such corrupt testaments.

40. Those who are intestate.[45]

The following are said not to have left a testament: first, those who do not commit it to writing before sudden death intervenes; then, those who have not named an heir; or if the heirs who are left refuse and do not wish to undertake the execution, or are such that they are unable to undertake it. Also to be judged intestate are those whose testament is so badly composed that it cannot be confirmed by a lawful judge.

41. A defective testament must be fulfilled.[46]

When a testament is nullified and the property is to be distributed by administrators, the judge must above all ensure that the administration should follow the pattern of the testator's will as far as possible. For although the testament is not legitimate, nevertheless we willingly follow the humanity of the civil laws, and preserve the last wills of people concerning their own goods and decisions, which they would never withdraw, firm and inviolate (as much as possible).

42. To whom the administration of goods is to be entrusted, and what fee they should receive.[47]

Every time someone dies without a testament, the wife shall be appointed to the administration of his goods in the first instance, and secondly those who were the closest acquaintances, or if the judge [*so*] thinks, he may unite them in this task with the wife. Nevertheless, it shall always be the case that whoever the task of administration has been committed to shall first offer guarantees or even deposit bonds, by which it may be fully and lawfully affirmed that they will proceed in

legitime praecaveri, quod in hoc negotio sincere sint et sine ulla fraude processuri, quod ordinarii omnibus partibus incolumitatem praestabunt, postremo quod rerum gestarum rationem red{*d*}e[*n*]t quandocunque iudex eam legitime poposcerit. Quod si forte nonnunquam evenerit, ut propter aequalem cognationis [288r] propinquitatem multorum ad facultates administrandas concursus sit, quoniam in illorum pari causa par videtur ius requiri, tum iudex tanquam honorarius arbiter litem determinet, suoque arbitratu munus hoc administrationis aut uni illorum aut pluribus collocet. Cum autem in pari multorum [74a] cognatione aliquis unus existit qui beneficium administrationis petit, vel in dispari cognatione si multi cupiunt ad hoc negotium assumi, iudex uxorem mortui potest et vel illum singularem virum, si velit, in hoc munere copulare, vel ex ceteris quoslibet designare suo arbitratu, modo merces in hac re nulla interveniat. Nec iudici ex administratorum designatione lucri quicquam [*esse*] debet [**esse**], nisi bona supra quinque libras {ascenderint; scriba [*tamen*] etiam in his fortunis, quae ad quinque libras}[48] non perveniunt, sex denarios accipiet. Quod si facultates quinque librarum aestimationem vincant, et tamen quadraginta libris angustiores sint, ad iudicem et eius administros triginta denarii confluent.

43. Quae desunt huic capiti unde petenda s[*i*/**u**]nt.[49]

Quoniam acervi dubitationum et controversiarum in hoc testamentorum caput comportari solent, dum infinita virorum avaritia mortuorum voluntatem circumvenire molitur, omnibus partibus illorum perversitati placet occurri. Quapropter quarum rerum in his constitutionibus medicina vel levatio non potest inveniri, de illis ad iuris Caesarei auctoritatem [288v] confugiendum erit; cum hac tamen exceptione, nihil ut inde sumatur huiusmodi, quod vel cum decretis hisce nostris ecclesiasticis pugnet, vel a municipali iure regni nostri dissideat.

[48]This line is omitted in S.
[49]Cf. 25 Henry VIII, c. 19, s. 5, 1534 (*S.R.*, III, 460-1). See also H.C., 31.22.

this business sincerely and without any fraud. Then the ordinary shall promise safety to all parties, and finally they shall give an account of their transactions whenever the judge shall lawfully ask for it. But if, as sometimes happens, there is competition among many for the right to administer the goods, on account of equidistant relationships, since it appears that they all have equal entitlement in the matter, the judge, as the honest broker, shall decide the case, and at his discretion shall assign the task of administration to one or to several of them. And when there is one in particular among the many equal relatives who desires the benefit of administration, or if there are many in different relationships who desire to undertake this business, the judge can couple the wife of the deceased and either that one man, if he wishes, in this task, or at his discretion designate whomever he wishes out of the others, as long as no fee enters into the matter. Nor shall the judge receive any reward for assigning the administration, unless the goods {exceed} five pounds, {but the scribe, [*even*] in those fortunes which} do not reach {five pounds},[48] shall receive six pence. But if the property is worth more than five pounds, and yet is less than forty pounds in value, thirty pence shall go to the judge and his staff.

43. Where matters which are not contained in this chapter are to be looked for.[49]

Since a lot of doubts and controversies are usually connected with this chapter on testaments, and because the boundless greed of men tries to circumvent the will of the deceased, their perversity may appear on all sides. Therefore whenever medicine or remedy for these things cannot be found in these statutes, recourse must be had concerning them to the authority of the law of Caesar, but with this exception, that nothing shall be taken from that law which is either repugnant to these our ecclesiastical decrees or which differs from the common law of our realm.

[74b]   **28. DE POENIS ECCLESIASTICIS**

1. Poena culpae par esse debet.[1]

Quoniam poena culpae par esse debet, ecclesiastici iudices diligentissimam cautionem adhibeant, ut in criminibus plectendis locum, personam, tempus et ceteras omnes flagitiorum circumstantias considerent, et aequitatis regula supplicii magnitudinem definiant.

2. Idem crimen non debet bis puniri.[2]

Aequum non est ut in idem crimen bis animadvertatur. Itaque qui semel peccati poenam his legibus nostris dedit, non debet ab ullo iudice ecclesiastico, quocunque nomine appelletur, rursus ad supplicium vocari, nisi forte rursus ad eandem peccandi licentiam devolvatur; tum enim nova culpa novam poenam requirit.

3. Clerici quomodo puniendi.[3]

Qui sunt ex ordine ecclesiastico, quos vulgo clericos dicunt, si de suis ipsi criminibus confiteantur, aut in illis legitime convincantur, illorum proprii iudices cum personarum omnes et causarum circumstantias perquisiverint, vel temporariis vel perpetuis vinculis illos arbitratu suo mandare posse concedimus.

4. Aetati nulli parcendum esse.[4]

Impunitas delicti propter aetatem non detur, si quis ea sit aetate, in quam crimen quod intenditur cadere potest.

---

[1]X, 5.38.3 (Fr, II, 884-5), a decretal of Pope Alexander III (1159-81); X, 5.38.8 (Fr, II, 886), a decretal of Pope Innocent III, 19 April 1201; cf. H.C., 13.1.
[2]L, 5.16.12, gloss on *canonicas sanctiones*; cf. H.C., 13.2.
[3]VI, 5.9.3 (Fr, II, 1091), a decretal of Pope Boniface VIII (1294-1303); cf. H.C., 13.3.
[4]*Cod. Iust.*, 9.47.7, originally an undated rescript of Emperor Alexander Severus (222-35) to Isidore; cf. H.C., 13.5.

28. OF ECCLESIASTICAL PENALTIES

1. The penalty must be equal to the crime.[1]

Since the penalty must be equal to the crime, the ecclesiastical judges shall use the utmost caution, so that when punishing crimes, they shall take into consideration the place, the person, the time and all other circumstances of the misdemeanours, and determine the seriousness of the punishment by the rule of equity.

2. The same crime must not be punished twice.[2]

It is not fair that the same crime should be punished twice. Therefore, those who have paid the penalty for their sin once, according to these our laws, must not be called back for punishment by any ecclesiastical judge, by whatever name he may be called, unless perchance he has fallen into the same licence of sinning, for then fresh guilt demands a fresh penalty.

3. How clergy are to be punished.[3]

If those who are of the ecclesiastical order, who are commonly called clergy, themselves confess their crimes, or if they are lawfully convicted of them, we grant their own judges the power to consign them to temporary or life imprisonment, at their discretion, after they have examined all the circumstances of persons and causes.

4. No age is to be exempt.[4]

Immunity from prosecution is not to be granted on account of age, if a person is of an age at which the crime in question can be committed.

[75a] 5. Poena debet auctorem sequi.[5]

Poena semper auctorem sequatur, et in illo terminetur, ut non ulterius progrediatur metus quam inveniatur delictum.

6. Iudices in veneratione esse debere.[6]

Quicunque iudicum dignitatem sermone, facto, vel actione violat, aut quicunque de illorum aestimatione decerpit, ipsorum iudicum arbitratu contumaciae poenas et impudentiae dent{**ae**}.

7. Gravidis feminis parcendum ad tempus.[7]

Gravidarum mulierum uteris parci volumus, qui donec subsidant, nec grave supplicium ab illis sumatur, nec ad tribunal ita pertrahantur, ut ullum ex eo foetui periculum creari possit.

8. Ubi legitima deest, ibi sit arbitraria poena.[8]

Si quorum huiusmodi peccata fuerint, ut his legibus nostris certae poenae non constituantur, arbitratu iudicis supplicium ab illis sumatur.

9. Poena minui potius quam augeri debet.[9]

Interpretatio legum poenas minuere debet potius quam augere, benignissimam ut etiam in hac re iuris civilis regulam sequamur, quae dubiis in causis clementiorem sententiam eligit.

---

[5]*Cod. Iust.*, 9.47.22, originally a rescript of the emperoros Arcadius and Honorius to Eutychianus, 25 July 399; cf. H.C., 13.6.
[6]X, 5.37.11 (Fr, II, 882-3), a decretal of Pope Innocent III, 5 January 1211; cf. H.C., 13.9.
[7]*Dig.*, 48.19.3, originally Ulpian., *Ad Sabinum*, 14; cf. H.C., 13.11.
[8]Cf. *Dig.*, 48.19.41, originally Papinian, *Definitiones*, 2; cf. H.C., 13.17.
[9]VI, 5.13.49 (Fr, II, 1123), a rule of Pope Boniface VIII (1294-1303) taken from *Dig.*, 48.19.42, originally Hermogenianus, *Epitomae*, 1; cf. H.C., 13.15.

5. A penalty must follow its author.[5]

A penalty must always follow its author, and end with him, so that fear may not extend any farther than wrongdoing is found.

6. Judges must be respected.[6]

Anyone who violates the dignity of judges in word, deed or action, or whoever detracts from their reputation, shall pay the penalties of contumacy and impudence, at the discretion of the judges themselves.

7. Pregnant women are to be spared during their term.[7]

It is our will that the wombs of pregnant women shall be spared, so that no severe punishment shall be exacted from them until they give birth nor shall they be brought to trial in a way which might create some danger for the foetus.

8. Where there is no fixed penalty, an arbitrary one shall be imposed.[8]

If the wrongdoings of some are such that there are no fixed penalties established by these our laws, punishment shall be exacted from them at the discretion of the judge.

9. A penalty ought to be mitigated rather than increased.[9]

Interpretation of the laws ought to mitigate punishments rather than increase them, so that in this matter also we shall follow the most benign rule of the civil law, which prefers a lighter sentence in doubtful cases.

[75b] 10. Institutio carceris qualis sit.[10]

Quoniam homines ad peccandum facile solent accedere, carcerem unum aut alterum, vel plures etiam, si res poposcerit, in propria ditione, quam dioecesim vocant, episcopus habeat; ut eo dimittantur, qui se vitiis in his legibus positis obstrinxerint, vel contumeliose aut irreverentes contra iudicem pro tribunali sedentem se gesserint.

11. Pecuniaria poena quomodo admitti possit.[11]

Paenitentias ecclesiasticas nolumus in poenas mutari pecuniarias, nisi aliqua gravis intercesserit et necessaria causa. Quoties autem ita fiat, omnes rei nummos, quibus crimen eius plectitur, in communem thesaurum, quem cistam pauperum vocant, comportari placet, et eos ibi deponi ubi habitat, aut {*ubi* **si**} crimen commissum est. Idque testatius ut esse possit, aedituis vel syndicis praesentibus geratur, et tempus sumatur celebrationis divinorum officiorum, et pecunias ibi manibus ips{*i*/**e**} suis collocet qui peccavit, et dies quidem sit festus, ut plures reus testes facti sui colligat. Et is sit dies quem iudex illi praescripserit, vel ordinarius reo certas constituat pias causas, in quibus pecunia omnis expromi possit. Si quis autem culpam eandem geminaverit, nullum illi praesidium in pecunia relinquimus.

---

[10]L, 5.15.5, c. 29 (25) of the council of Lambeth, 1261 (PC, 684).
[11]C. 44 of Winchester II, *c.* 1247 (PC, 409); c. 58 of Wells, *c.* 1258 (PC, 616), c. 96 of Winchester III, *c.* 1262-5 (PC, 721).

10. What kind of prisons there shall be.[10]

Since people often fall into wrongdoing quite easily, the bishop shall have a prison or two, or even several, if the situation demands it, in his own jurisdistion, which is called the diocese, that those who have engaged in the crimes mentioned in these our laws, or who have behaved obnoxiously or irreverently towards the judge seated in the court, may be sent there.

11. How a monetary penalty may be allowed.[11]

We do not want ecclesiastical penances to be commuted into monetary penalties, unless some grave and necessary cause requires it. And every time that is done, all the coins of the accused, with which he pays for his crime, shall be put in the common chest which is called the poor box, and they are to be deposited where he resides, or {*where* **if**} the crime was committed. And for this to be more clearly witnessed, it shall be done in the presence of the parish clerks or wardens, and at the time of the celebration of the divine services, and the person who has offended shall put the money in there with his own hands, and it shall be on a feast day, so that the accused may assemble many to witness to his act. And this shall be a day which the judge has prescribed to him, and the ordinary shall assign certain pious causes to the accused, to which all his money shall be paid. But if someone repeats the same crime, we allow him no monetary commutation.

[76a]   **29. DE SUSPENSIONE**

1. Suspensionis varietas.[1]

Principio genus ipsum suspensionis ad utrumque ordinem pertinebit, ecclesiasticum et popularem, vel (ut res notior communibus vocabulis esse possit) ad ecclesiasticos et laicos, et huius poenae moderationis varietas erit, ut aliquando rei prorsus in ecclesiam non introeant, nisi forte velint ad comminationem subauscultare, nonnunquam ut ab usu sacramentorum abarceantur, et interdum ab administratione sacramentorum excludantur. Cum igitur varia sunt suspensionis genera, iudex nominatim et expresse dicet, cum hac poena ream personam afficit, quam ex his potissimum velit intelligi. Nunquam tamen a familiari hominum commercio arcet suspensio.[2]

2. Quae causae sunt suspensionis.[3]

Quidam suis vitiis in poenam suspensionis incurrunt, cum ad bonam frugem se ipsi revocant, aut impositas sibi criminum poenas suscipiunt. Hi donec omnem exple{**ve**}rint integre iudicis voluntatem et ecclesiae satisfecerint, si peccati magnitudo satisfactionem requirit, in hoc supplicio detinentur. Aliquando pertinacia vel negligentia reorum hanc a rebus sacris relegationem pati cogitur, cum iudex in minore delicto fulmen excommunicationis vibrandi non portat, et saepe contingit, ut licet crimina non possunt ipsa depraehendi, tamen suspiciones, praesertim atrocium peccatorum, si modo longo tempore inveteraverint, et infamiam attulerint, ab ecclesiis amandandae sunt, quoniam magna sequeretur bonorum perturbatio, si cum huiusmodi perso[76b]nis infamibus sacramenta communicarent.

3. Quomodo terminatur suspensio.[4]

Cum homines ad tempus a sacris ablegantur, vel ut crassissime loquamur, cum talis est ratio suspensionis, ut certum tempus habeant reditus ad ecclesiam,

---

[1]L, 1.2.1, gloss on *suspensionis*.
[2]This is the lesser excommunication. See Panormitanus on X, 5.39.
[3]C. 2, q. 5, c. 13 (Fr, I, 459), originally c. 13 of the council of Ilerda, 546; C. 2, q. 5, c. 18 (Fr, I, 461).
[4]VI, 5.11.24 (Fr, II, 1106-7), originally a decretal of Pope Boniface VIII (1294-1303).

29. OF SUSPENSION

1. The different types of suspension.[1]

First of all, the same kind of suspension shall apply to either order, the ecclesiastical and the popular, or (as the matter may be better known under the common words), to the clergy and the laity, and there shall be different ways in which this penalty shall be applied, so that sometimes those accused shall not enter into the church any more, unless perchance they wish to attend the commination, sometimes they shall be banned from participation in the sacraments, and occasionally they shall be prevented from administering the sacraments. Therefore, since the kinds of suspension vary, when the judge imposes this penalty on the accused person he shall say spcifically and expressly which of these he prefers to be understood. Nevertheless, suspension shall never bar anyone from familiar association with other people.[2]

2. What the causes of suspension are.[3]

Those who incur the penalty of suspension through their own wrongdoing, shall either call themselves back to good works or receive the penalties of their crimes which have been imposed on them. If the magnitude of their sin demands satisfaction, these people shall be kept in this punishment until they have fulfilled completely the will of the judge and satisfied the church. Sometimes the stubbornness or negligence of the accused must be punished by this relegation from sacred things, since the judge does not carry the vibrating thunderbolt of excommunication for a minor offence, and it often happens that even if actual crimes cannot be proved, nevertheless suspicions, especially of atrocious crimes, must be punished by the church if they have lasted a long time and attracted bad publicity, since good people will be deeply upset if the sacraments are administered to such infamous people.

3. How suspension is brought to an end.[4]

When people are suspended from the sacraments for a period of time, or as we say in the most vulgar manner, when the suspension is of such a kind that those affected have a set time when they can return to the church, as soon as that time

quamprimum advenerit, absque ulla relaxatione vel absolutione reus liber erit. Sed tempus si non fuerit constitutum, sed institutum aliquid quod reus suscipere debeat, nullo modo reum mitti placet, donec ordinarius ex eo perfecte intellexerit omnia rite et ordine a se gesta esse, quae illi mandata sunt. Quam rem si iudici plene probaverit, tum demum culpa illum evolvi patimur. Cuius autem in quaestionem bona fama vocatur, is tantisper haereat in iudicio, donec legitime suspensiones amolitus sit, quibus oppugnatur.

4. Suspensus totum annum excommunicetur.[5]

Si quis a sacris relegatus adeo iudicis sententiam contemnat, ut relegatus annum integrum maneat, pellatur coetu Christianorum, et in horribile supplicium excommunicationis detrudatur, et sacerdotio, si quod habuerit, excludatur.

5. Quomodo puniri debent qui iudicis sententiam violant.[6]

Si quando minister ecclesiae vel loco motus ab episcopo, vel in formulam suspensionis prolapsus fuerit, et quicquam eorum audeat facere quae sunt illi negata, nec se mature corrigat, cum episcopus illum officii admonet, et excommunicationis poena plectetur et desecrationis acerbitate vel degradationis, ut vulgo loquuntur, ut omnibus exua[77a]tur ornamentis status ecclesiastici. Si vero minister non fuerit, sed ex ordine laico, excommunicatione ferietur.

6. Poena illorum qui suspensis aut excommunicatis contra leges favent.[7]

Quicunque publicas preces, sacramenta, aut ceremonias ecclesiasticas vel ipsi administrant, vel aliis administrandi auctores fuerint, coram his qui poena vel suspensionis vel excommunicationis correpti sunt, aut illos in ecclesia quicunque retentant, cum a ministris legitime admonentur, nisi a ministro repraehensi temeritate destiterint, excommunicationis et ipsi supplicio repraehendantur.

---

[5]Cf. X, 1.14.8 (Fr, II, 128), originally a decretal of Pope Celestine III (1191-8).
[6]VI, 5.11.20 (Fr, II, 1104-5), originally a decretal of Pope Boniface VIII (1294-1303).
[7]X, 5.39.15 (Fr, II, 894-5), originally a decretal of Pope Clement III (1187-91); X, 5.39.29 (Fr, II, 900-1), originally a decretal of Pope Innocent III, 16 May 1199.

arrives, the accused shall be free from any need for a pardon or absolution. But if no time limit is set, but some penance is assigned which the guilty person has to undergo, under no circumstances shall he be dispensed until the ordinary has been fully informed that he has completely fulfilled everything which was demanded of him, correctly and in the right way. If the judge has certified that he has done so, then once that is done we allow him to be released from guilt. And the person whose good reputation is called into question shall remain under judgment until he has lawfully served the suspensions laid against him.

4. Anyone suspended for a full year shall be excommunicated.[5]

If someone who has been barred from the sacraments so despises the judge's sentence that he remains barred for a full year, he shall be expelled from the fellowship of Christians and relegated to the horrible punishment of excommunication, and he shall be put out of his living if he has one.

5. How those who violate the judge's sentence must be punished.[6]

When the minister of a church is either removed by the bishop or has fallen under a form of suspension, if he presumes to do one of the things which are forbidden to him, and does not correct himself immediately when the bishop reminds him of his duty, he shall suffer both the penalty of excommunication and the harshness of desecration, or degradation, as it is commonly known, and shall be divested of all the marks of his ecclesiastical status. And if he is not a minister, but from the lay order, he shall be punished by excommunication.

6. The penalty for those who illegally support those who have been suspended or excommunicated.[7]

Anyone who administers the public prayers, sacraments or ecclesiastical ceremonies either themselves, or by appointing others to do so, in the presence of those who have been bound by the penalty of suspension or excommunication, or whoever retains them in the church, after they have been lawfully warned by the ministers, shall also be bound by the punishment of excommunication if they do not desist from their boldness after being reprimanded by a minister.

7. Poena suspensorum et excommunicatorum si pertinaciter {e} templ{um/o} exire recusent.[8]

Qui vero ab ecclesia religati, vel quibus ecclesia prorsus est interdictum, aut, ut usitate loquamur, qui suspensi vel excommunicati sunt, si (quando supplicii ratio postulet) se ab ecclesia non abalienant, isto modo contra illorum pertinaciam procedi iubemus. Si sunt ex ordine ecclesiastico et beneficia habeant ulla ecclesiastica, illorum emolumentis ad tempus denudentur ordinarii arbitratu. Si fructus ad illos ex ecclesia nullus redeat, omnes actiones ecclesiasticorum munerum erunt eis interdictae; et licet prioribus vinculis liberentur suspensionis vel excommunicationis, tamen integrum annum in hac munerum ecclesiasticorum intermissione permaneant. Qui vero sunt ordine laico si talis pertinaciae rei fuerint, arbitratu iudicis gravissime puniantur.

[77b] 8. Quomodo ferenda suspensionis et excommunicationis sententia.[9]

Cui (qui plus est) excommunicare licet, illi (quod minus est) suspendere licebit, sed nullus harum poenarum sententiam publice recitabit, nisi litteris compraehensam et iudicis legitimo signo munitam.

9. In morte sacramenta sunt concedenda.[10]

Qui criminum ecclesiasticorum rei sunt, licet ab ecclesiae sacramentis removeantur, tamen ex hac vita si forte migraturi sint, et verae paenitentiae signa dederint, Christianae caritatis est sacramentorum illis usum exhibere. Qui vero mortis sententiam acceperunt, si in carcere detenti coenae Domini participes esse non possunt, diligenter ab aliquo pio viro instrui debent Christum sacramentis alligatum non esse, sed ab illo sacramentorum auctoritatem et vim proficisci. Quapropter ad illum si mentem sursum erigant, et in illius mortem stabili ac immota fide dirigant, Christi carnem manducaverunt, et eius sanguinem combiberunt. Qua in re ut melius confirmari possint, aliquem pium et doctum ecclesiae ministrum ad eos adhiberi mandamus, qui unum vel duos dies ad illorum fidem confirmandam et exaedificandam sumat, priusquam ad mortem trudantur, ut alacrioribus animis ex hac vita decedant, et patientiam ac solatium ex Sacris Scripturis colligentes, scelerum desperatione sublata, fidenter ac certa spe ad Deum misericordiae patrem et Christum nostrae salutis auctorem pergant.

---

[8]L, 1.2.1, gloss on *suspensionis*.
[9]C. 11, q. 3, c. 106 (Fr, I, 674); VI, 5.11.1 (Fr, II, 1093-4), originally a decretal of Pope Innocent IV (1243-54).
[10]Cf. C. 26, q. 6, c. 13 (Fr, I, 1040); X, 5.38.11 (Fr, II, 887), originally a decretal of Pope Innocent III (1198-1216); VI, 5.11.22 (Fr, II, 1105), originally a decretal of Pope Bonifcace VIII (1294-1303).

7. The penalty for those who have been suspended or excommunicated if they stubbornly refuse to leave the church building.[8]

Those who have been barred from the church, or to whom the church is from henceforth forbidden, or as we usually say, those who have been suspended or excommunicated, if (when the nature of their punishment demands) they do not absent themselves from the church, we order that their stubbornness shall be dealt with in this way. If they are of the ecclesiastical order and have any ecclesiastical benefices, they shall be temporarily deprived of their emoluments at the discretion of the ordinary. If no income comes to them from the church, the exercise of all ecclesiastical offices shall be barred to them, and even after they have been freed from the bonds of suspension or excommunication, they shall still remain in this forfeiture of their ecclesiastical offices for a full year. And if members of the lay order have been accused of such stubbornness, they shall be most severely punished at the discretion of the ordinary.

8. How the sentence of suspension and excommunication is to be imposed.[9]

Anyone who may be excommunicated (which is more serious) may also be suspended (which is less serious), but no one shall publicly announce the sentence of these penalties unless he has a written confirmation of it, bearing the judge's lawful seal.

9. The sacraments shall be granted to a dying man.[10]

Those who are accused of ecclesiastical crimes, although they have been barred from the sacraments of the church, nevertheless, if they are about to depart this life and have shown signs of true repentance, it is the custom of Christian charity to offer them the sacraments. And those who have received a sentence of death, if they cannot partake of the Lord's supper while being held in prison, they must be diligently instructed by some godly man that Christ is not bound by the sacraments, but that the power and authority of the sacraments proceed from him. Therefore, if they lift up their minds to him, and concentrate on his death with a fixed and unmoved faith, they have eaten the flesh of Christ and have drunk his blood. And so that they may be better confirmed in this belief, this godly man shall spend one or two days confirming and building up their faith before they are handed over to death, in order that they may depart this life with more alert minds, and by deriving patience and comfort from the Holy Scriptures, and leaving the despair of their crimes behind, they may with faith and a certain hope approach God the Father of mercy and Christ the author of our salvation.

[78a] 30. DE FRUCTUUM DEDUCTIONE VEL SEQUESTRATIONE, UT VULGO DICITUR, PROPTER VARIAS CAUSAS

1. Ratio sequestrationis qualis esse debeat.[1]

Quicunque benefciis ecclesiasticis fruuntur, superiorem templi partem, quam cancellam vocant, sart{*e*/**am**}tectam conservare debent, et ceterorum etiam aedificiorum convenientem rationem habere, quae suam ad ecclesiam pertinent. Praeterea quaecunque impensae ad illorum curam referuntur ecclesiae respectu, illas debent omnes facultatibus suis facere et sustentare, sive ius ita scriptum postulet, sive legitima loci consuetudo. Quod si recusent facere, deducantur ecclesiae fructus, et ab illis tantisper detineantur, donec integre suum officium et explete praestiterint: et cumulentur aliis etiam ecclesiasticis poenis, si iudicibus id illos promereri videbitur. Quo in loco nullum ut illis profugium relinquatur, fructus ecclesiarum erui volumus, sive proprietarius eos, sive colonus, sive quis illos alius aut perceperit aut percepturus sit. Cum autem haec fructuum erit deductio (quam vulgo sequestrationem vocant) illi quorum fidei fructus committuntur, vel illorum legitimi vicarii, possunt eos distrahere, et pecuniam ita collocare quomodo necessaria postulat ecclesiae ratio. Et hoc etiam provideant fructuum distractores, ut omnia interim ecclesiae divina suppeditentur officia. Tandem vero cum omnibus legitimis impensis abunde satisfactum est, fructus ad priorem dominum revolvantur. Colonus autem, vel conductor, de vectigali annuo tantum ad se derivabit, quantum potest cum omni deductorum fructuum damno compensa[78b]ri, quantumcunque scriptis locat{*o*/**u**}r de mercede integra sibi praecaverit.

2. Sequestratio locum habet in litigioso beneficio.[2]

Si ius incertum sit ecclesiastici beneficii, nec adhuc, cum vacuum sit, constare possit ad quem beneficium pervenire debeat, quamdiu controversum est, fructus de beneficio deduci per iudicem ecclesiasticum debent, et quamprimum causa legibus determinata fuerit, statim ad legitimum dominum pariter cum omnibus emolumentis beneficium commeet, exceptis impensis quibus ecclesiae necessitatibus interim subservitum est. Si quis autem ex litigatoribus beneficium

---

[1]X, 2.16.3 (Fr, II, 305); X, 3.4.16 (Fr, II, 464), both originally decretals of Pope Gregory IX (1227-41), published on or before 5 September 1234; H.C., 33.1, 3.
[2]*Clem.*, 2.6.1 (Fr, II, 1146), originally a decretal of Pope Clement V (1305-14), published after the council of Vienne (1311-12); H.C., 33.2.

30. OF THE DEDUCTION OF FRUITS OR SEQUESTRATION, AS IT IS COMMONLY CALLED, FOR DIFFERENT REASONS

1. What the procedure of sequestration ought to be.[1]

Those who enjoy ecclesiastical benefices must maintain the upper part of the church, which is called the chancel, roofed, and must also keep a reliable account of the other buildings which belong to their church. Moreover, they must do this and maintain them all with their resources, whatever expenses are allocated for their upkeep in respect of the church, whether a written law or the lawful custom of the place demands it. But if they refuse to do so, the income of the church shall be deducted and shall be held back from them until they have fulfilled their duty wholly and completely, and they shall also be covered with other ecclesiastical penalties if it seems to the judges that they deserve them. In which case, so that there may be no escape left for them, it is our will that the income of the church shall be taken away, whether it is the proprietary, or the farmer or someone else who receives or shall receive them. And since this shall be the deduction of the income (which is commonly called sequestration), those to whose trust the income is committed, or their lawful deputies, may remove it, and use the money in whatever way the needs of the church dictate. And those who sequester the income shall also provide that in the meantime all the divine offices of the church shall be funded. And when everything has been satisfactorily arranged by all lawful expenditures, the income shall be restored to its former owner. And the farmer or the middleman shall set aside for his own use as much as he can be compensated with, given all the loss of the deducted income, and he shall give notice in writing of what percentage of the total sum he has reserved for himself.

2. Sequestration is appropriate in a contested benefice.[2]

If the right to an ecclesiastical benefice is uncertain, and it has not been possible thus far, while it is vacant, to determine to whom the benefice ought to go, as long as the matter is under litigation, the income from the benefice ought to be sequestered by the ecclesiastical judge, and as soon as the case has been decided by the laws, the benefice shall go immediately to its lawful owner along with all its emoluments, except for the expenses which have been used for the needs of the church, in the meantime. And if one of the litigants has occupied and taken

praeoccupaverit et possederit, et post sententia iudicis contra illum possessorem proferatur, ille vero sententiae plagam appellationis remedio declinaverit, huiusmodi beneficii fructus quantumcunque possessi iure videntur deduci posse, etiam appellatione adhuc pendente, et minime terminata. Quanquam enim legum auctoritas civilium multa possessoribus indulget, tamen ea contra iudicis sententiam in causa ancipiti valere non placet.

3. De sequestratione mulierum in causa nuptiarum.[3]

Cum de matrimonio lis incidit, et mulier loci vel incolarum difficultatibus oppressa, metu vel mercede vel aliqua prava causa videtur nonnihil subticere aut occulere, potest ecclesiastici iudicis auctoritate novas in aedes aut aliud in oppidum transmoveri, donec de toto negotio conclusum sit.

[79a] 4. Poena delinquentium contra sequestrationem.[4]

Si quisquam sequestratione rite facta se interponat, aut contra legum in hac re constitutionem quocunque modo tumultuetur, ecclesiasticis poenis eius importunitatem constringi oportet.

5. De sequestratione fructuum post mortem possessoris.[5]

Quoties vacuum fuerit beneficium ecclesiasticum, iudex legitimus efficiet ut omnes vacui beneficii fructus deducantur, et ad tempus in tuto loco seponantur: quos universos plene et integre reddet is, in cuius custodia conquieverunt, et quantum illis aberit, tantum et amplius etiam duabus partibus restituet: quae simul omnia novum ad dominum statim, nulla nisi necessaria interposita mora, comportabuntur. Illas tamen impensas iudex aestimet, quibus legitima praesidia cuiuscunque generis ecclesiae subministrata sunt, sive ius illa constituit, sive legitima consuetudo recepit.

[3]Cf. X, 2.19.14 (Fr, II, 314-15); H.C., 33.4.
[4]L, 2.4.1, c. 15 of Archbishop John Stratford's council of 1342; H.C., 33.6.
[5]28 Henry VIII, c. 11 (*S.R.*, III, 666-7); 1268/15 (PC, 765-6).

possession of the benefice, and afterwards the sentence of the judge is given against that possessor, and he has gone on to contest the sentence, using the remedy of appeal, the income of the said benefice may be legally sequestered in so far as it appears to have been possessed, even if the appeal is still pending and not yet terminated. For although the authority of the civil laws grants much to possessors, yet it cannot prevail against the sentence of the judge in an unresolved case.

3. Of the sequestration of women in a cause of matrimony.[3]

When a matrimonial suit occurs, and the woman is oppressed by difficulties created by the place or its inhabitants, and she appears to be hiding or concealing something out of fear, or because she has been bribed, or for some other wicked reason, she may be transferred to a new house or to another town by the authority of the ecclesiastical judge, until the whole matter has been concluded.

4. The penalty for those who disregard the sequestration.[4]

If someone tries to block a sequestration which has been duly made, or creates some kind of disturbance against the established order of the laws in this matter, his misbehaviour ought to be punished by ecclesiastical penalties.

5. Of sequestration of the income after the owner's death.[5]

Whenever an ecclesiastical benefice falls vacant, a lawful judge shall ensure that all the income of the vacant benefice shall be sequestered and set aside in a safe place temporarily. And the person in whose custody it is placed shall give it all back fully and completely, and whatever is missing from it he shall restore twice over, all of which shall be transferred to the new owner immediately, with no more delay intervening than is necessary. Nevertheless the judge shall calculate the expenses to which the lawful upkeep of any kind of church is subject, whether the law has established it or a lawful custom has accepted it.

[79a]   **31. DE DEPRIVATIONE**

1. Deprivatio flagitiis atrocibus convenit.[1]

Deiectio de dignitate, vel, ut vulgo loquuntur, deprivatio, quoniam singularem quandam inter poenas ecclesiasticis legibus constitutas acerbitatem habet, maximis et teterrimis vitiis est reservanda. Quapropter ista securis in homicidis, adulteris, et huiusmodi consceleratis personis [79b] defigatur, cum manifestis i{*u*/**n**}dici{**i**}s depraehensa fuerit illorum immanitas.

2. Deprivatio qualis sit in episcopo.[2]

Cum episcopus in amittendi status sui periculum venit, archiepiscopum et duos episcopos alios arbitratu nostro sumi volumus, moribus et doctrina praestantes viros, qui iudicium hoc exercebunt; et hi totam rem diligenter inspectam et consideratam prudentia et pietate sua definiant.

3. Deprivatio qualis sit in dignitate vel beneficio.[3]

Quando cuiquam vel diripi dignitas, vel eripi beneficium ecclesiasticum formula deprivationis debet, principio proprius illum episcopus ad se rite evocet; deinde ad reliquum onme negotium pertractandum episcopus adsit, et duos ad se doctos et integros presbyteros asciscat, quorum auctoritate et decreto stari placet.

4. Nunquam iudex deprivationis sententiam pronuntiet, nisi re apertissima.[4]

Sententia deprivationis, quoniam cruenta est, et totum hominem conficit, tam horribile telum nec in venerandum episcopi statum intorqueatur, nec in sanctum ordinem quarumcunque personarum ecclesiasticarum mittatur, nisi reus vel trium

---

[1]23 Henry VIII, c. 1, 1531 (*S.R.*, III, 362-3); ibid., c. 11 (*S.R.*, III, 379).
[2]C. 6, q. 4, c. 1 (Fr, I, 563). Formerly, only the pope could deprive a bishop. See Panormitanus on X, 2.1.1.
[3]X, 1.31.16 (Fr, II, 192-3), originally a decretal of Pope Honorius III (1216-27); X, 2.22.15-16 (Fr, II, 353), both originally decretals of Pope Gregory IX (1227-41), published on or before 5 September 1234; 1268/5 (PC, 752-4).
[4]Panormitanus on X, 2.1.10.

31. OF DEPRIVATION

1. Deprivation is appropriate in cases of heinous crimes.[1]

Since removal from a dignity, or as it is commonly called, deprivation, has an exceptional harshness among the penalties established by the ecclesiastical laws, it is to be reserved for the greatest and most terrible crimes. Therefore this axe is to be applied to homicides, adulterers and such criminal persons, when their wickedness has been revealed by manifest {*judgments* **indications**}.

2. How a bishop shall be deprived.[2]

When a bishop is in danger of losing his status, we desire that the archbishop and two other bishops, men who are outstanding in morals and doctrine, shall be appointed by our authority to execute this judgment, and they shall decide the entire matter after diligently looking into it and considering it with their wisdom and godliness.

3. How deprivation shall be handled in a dignity or benefice.[3]

When someone is to be deprived of a dignity or an ecclesiastical benefice, the procedure of deprivation must be as follows. First, his bishop shall duly summon the man to him, and then the bishop shall be present for the handling of the rest of the business, and he shall call on two learned and honest presbyters, whose authority and decree shall be final.

4. The judge shall never pronounce a sentence of deprivation unless the matter is extremely clear.[4]

Since a sentence of deprivation is devastating and involves every aspect of a man's life, it is such a horrible weapon that it shall neither detract from the honour due to the status of a bishop nor be used against the sacred order of any ecclesiastical persons whatsoever, unless the accused has been convicted by the

vocibus idoneorum et locupletum testium convincatur, vel se ipse iudicet, vel re tam evidenti et perspicua coarguatur, ut nullam onmino dubitationem habere possit.

voices of three reliable and trustworthy witnesses, or unless he condemns himself, or unless the matter is so evident and clear that no doubt about it is possible.

[80a]   **32. DE EXCOMMUNICATIONE**

1. Quid sit excommunicatio.[1]

Excommunicatio (melius est enim parum Latine quam parum apte loqui) potestas est et auctoritas ad ecclesiam a Deo profecta, quae facinorosas personas, vel de religione nostra corrupte sentientes, et ad suam improbitatem adhaerescentes, a perceptione sacramentorum, et etiam Christianorum fratrum usu, tantisper summovet, donec sensus sanos recollegerint, et salutarium cogitationum apta signa dederint, et poenas etiam ecclesiasticas adierint, quibus ferocia carnis comprimitur, ut spiritus salvus fiat.

2. Quibus excommunicatio committitur.[2]

Ecclesia claves accepit a Christo, quibus ligandi potestas et solvendi continetur. Quoniam autem ad haec recte debet et ordine procedi, quemadmodum administratio sacramentorum, et ex Sacris Scripturis contionandi munus, certis viris deferuntur, ita potestas excommunicationis in ministris et gubernatoribus ecclesiarum consedit, ut illi Sacrarum Scripturarum sententia et regula disciplinam in sacrosancta Domini coena sanciant, et diiudicent quae personae mensa pellendae divina, quae sint ad eam assumendae; nominatim vero moderatores et ecclesiarum duces sunt archiepiscopi, episcopi, archidiaconi, decani, denique quicunque sunt ab ecclesia ad hoc munus adhibiti.

3. Quibus in causis excommunicatio debet adhiberi.[3]

Non debet excommunicatio minutis in delictis versari, sed ad horribilium criminum atrocitatem admo[80b]venda est, in quibus ecclesia gravissimam infamiam sustinet, vel quod illis evertatur religio, vel quod boni mores pervertuntur. Illius autem generis sunt de quibus Paulus dicit, qui talia faciunt in

---

[1]This is the greater excommunication. See Panormitanus on X, 5.39. X, 5.39.59 (Fr, II, 912), originally a decretal of Pope Gregory IX (1227-41), published on or before 5 September 1234.
[2]L, 1.3.1, gloss on *censura ecclesiastica*. Cf. L, 5.17.5, c. 13 of the council of Lambeth, 1261. Also 1571/4.3.
[3]L, 5.17.6, c. 11 of the council of Reading, 1279. Cf. C. 6, q. 3, c. 5 (Fr, I, 563).

32. OF EXCOMMUNICATION

1. What excommunication is.[1]

Excommunication (for it is better to express it in poor Latin than to express it poorly) is the power and authority conveyed to the church by God, which bars wicked persons, or those who have a corrupt understanding of our religion and persist in their error, from the reception of the sacraments, and also from the society of Christians, until they recover their senses and give appropriate signs of their salutary opinions, and also submit to ecclesiastical penalties, by which the lust of the flesh is repressed in order that the spirit might be saved.

2. To whom excommunication is entrusted.[2]

The church has received from Christ the keys in which the power to bind and to loose is contained. And since these things must be approached rightly and in order, just as the administration of the sacraments and the task of preaching from the Holy Scriptures is reserved for certain men, so the power to excommunicate resides in the ministers and governors of the churches, that by the teaching and rule of the Holy Scriptures they may impose discipline in the most sacred supper of the Lord, and determine which persons ought to be excluded from the divine table and which are to be admitted to it; and the following are the moderators and leaders of the churches: the archbishops, bishops, archdeacons, deans, and finally whoever have been appointed to this office by the church.

3. The cases in which excommunication must be applied.[3]

Excommunication must not be used for minor offences, but is to be reserved for the wickedness of horrible crimes, by which the church endures the most grievous disrepute, either because religion is overturned by them or because good morals are perverted. Of this type are those of which Paul says that those who do

regnum Dei non introibunt,[4] vel regni Dei non erunt haeredes,[5] vel quod propter haec venit ira Dei in filios incredulos.[6] Haec immania facinora telo debent excommunicationis confringi, ut qui sunt illorum rei, in hoc supplicium incurrant, nisi mature bonam ad frugem se revocaverint, et cum arguuntur, se ab huiusmodi sceleribus quamprimum alienant, ac etiam plene velint omne damnum luere, quod ecclesia in illorum peccatis passa est. Etenim excommunicationis acerbitas nunquam expromi debet, nisi cum homines in sceleribus obduruerunt: quod duobus modis evenit, vel cum a salubribus se monitis avertunt, et vocati se non ostendunt, vel si praesto sint et iudicum decretis stare nolint.

4. Excommunicanda persona debet ante sententiam admoneri.[7]

Nullus iudex excommunicatione quemquam percutiet, nisi semel atque iterum, et etiam tertio, si res id requirit, illum praemonuerit, ut se ipse, si fieri potest, tempestive corrigat. Tum etiam reo certum tempus ad deliberationem relinquatur, in quo secum ipse constituat, utrum sanis consiliis obsecuturus sit. Sed qui rite fuerit evocatus, si tempore suo non adfuerit, huius pertinacia statim in excommunicationem incidat.

5. Universitas aut collegium non potest excommunicari.[8]

Integri coetus, quos universitates vel collegia vocant, excommunicationis poena compraehendi non debent. Cum enim ibi varietas magna sit personarum cuiusque generis, [81a] aliquorum innocentia violaretur: nostra vero clementia potius malis parcit quam bonos plectit. Itaque soli poenis plectentur, quicunque in huiusmodi coetu soli peccaverunt.

6. Excommunicatio prudenter et deliberate debet institui.[9]

Quoniam ex poenis omnibus ecclesiasticis acerbissisimam ponimus excommunicationem, acutissimum eius mucronem sine magna maturaque deliberatione distringi nolumus. Ut autem in hac re vitiosissimos superiorum temporum ritus emendare possimus, primum in nulla permittimus una persona potestatem excommunicationis collocari. Totius autem ecclesiae consensus

---

[4]I Co. vi. 9-10; Ga. v. 21. The New Testament has 'inherit' rather than 'enter'.
[5]Ep. v. 5.
[6]Ep v. 6. The original text has 'disobedient' instead of 'unbelieving'.
[7]VI, 5.11.5 (Fr, II, 1095), originally a decretal of Pope Innocent IV (1243-54); VI, 5.11.9 (Fr, II, 1101-2), originally a decretal of Pope Gregory X (1271-6); H.C., 14.12.
[8]VI, 5.11.5 (Fr, II, 1095), originally a decretal of Pope Innocent IV; H.C., 14.12.
[9]Cf. C. 24, q. 2, c. 2 (Fr, I, 984-5) for the idea that it is the *church* which excommunicates. See also 1571/4.3.

them will not enter into the kingdom of God,[4] or be heirs of God's kingdom,[5] or because it is for these things that the wrath of God comes on his unbelieving children.[6] These enormous evils must be restrained by the weapon of excommunication, so that those who are accused of them shall incur this punishment unless they call themselves back to good works in time, and when they are reprimanded, immediately distance themselves from crimes of this kind, and also are willing to make up any damage which the church has suffered because of their sins. Moreover the harshness of excommunication must never be employed, except when people persist in their crimes, which happens in two ways - either when they turn away from healthy warnings and do not appear when summoned, or if they are present but are unwilling to obey the decrees of the judges.

4. A person who is to be excommunicated must be warned before the sentence is given.[7]

No judge shall sentence anyone to excommunication unless he has forewarned him once, twice, and even a third time if the matter requires it, so that the person concerned may correct himself in time, if that is possible. For then a certain time is left to the accused to reconsider, during which he can make up his mind whether he will follow wise counsels. But if someone has been duly summoned and does not appear at the right time, his stubbornness shall lead to immediate excommunication.

5. A university or college may not be excommunicated.[8]

Entire societies, which are called universities or colleges, may not be bound by a penalty of excommunication. For as there is a great variety of persons of all kinds there, the innocence of some would be violated, and our clemency prefers to spare the wicked rather than punish the good. Therefore only those in such a society who have sinned shall be punished.

6. Excommunication must be applied prudently and with careful consideration.[9]

Since we regard excommunication as the harshest of all ecclesiastical penalties, we do not want its very sharp edge to be used without great and careful consideration. And in order that we might remedy the most disgraceful practices of earlier times, first of all we do not allow the power of excommunication to be concentrated in one single person. For although the agreement of the whole

quanquam imprimis esset optabilis, tamen quoniam difficillime colligi potest et conquiri, sic excommunicatio procedat, ut archiepiscopus vel episcopus vel alius quicunque legitimus iudex ecclesiasticus unum ad se publicae pacis nostrae custodem, quem vulgo iustitiarium vocant, aggreget, ac proprium illius ecclesiae ministrum in qua reus inhabitat, vel aliquem cui minister suas vices committat: deinde sumantur etiam duo vel tres, arbitratu iudicis, docti beneque morati presbyteri, quorum in praesentia, cum res ipsa diligentissime tractata gravissimeque ponderata fuerit, tandem ad decernendam excommunicationem d{*i*/e}scendatur.

7. De excommunicatione scriptis mandata.[10]

Sententia non valeat excommunicationis, nisi scriptis mandata fuerit: cuius exemplum incorrupte sincereque transcriptum iudex reo tradat, quo id tempore postulaverit, atque adeo intra sex dies sine ulla exceptione scriptum hoc reo requirenti concedatur.

[81b] 8. Poena iudicis non legitime excommunicantis.[11]

Quicunque iudex vel reum non praemonuerit, vel ceteras cautiones non adhibuerit, quas nos in hanc causam contulimus, primum in ecclesiam toto mensis spatio non introeat, nisi sacrae communionis percipiendae causa; deinde iudex superior, a quo petenti reo succurretur, priorem contra leges progressam excommunicationem universam retexet, excommunicationis auctorem ad solvendas omnes impensas iniustae litis damnabit, et etiam alias poenas arbitratu suo cumulabit, ut metu iudices conterreantur, ne tam magnam in calamitatem homines sine gravissimis causis detrudant. Cum autem iudex intellexerit, quod caecus et praeceps in illo iudicio ferebatur, et propterea sententiam vel temere latam ipse per se tollere, priusquam ad superiorem iudicem reus digressus fuerit, nec tamen is assentiri velit, qui procuravit excommunicationem, nisi reus illi satisfaciat, et ad hoc auxilium superioris iudicis imploret, iudex inferior hanc eius duram et acerbam appellationem negligens, sui potius commodi memorem quam communis inter Christianos caritatis, sententiam suam dissolvat, in qua manifestum animadvertit priorem suum errorem. Nam si addubitaverit, pignoribus a reo datis, quod sententiae et decreto superioris iudicis, quem appellavit, obediet, ita tandem iudex indictam a se prius excommunicationem rescindat et aboleat. Quae cum omnia rite fecerit, omni se legum nostrarum poena liberabit.

---

[10]VI, 5.11.1 (Fr, II, 1093-4), supposedly from Lyon I, 1245, but not recorded in the acts of the council.
[11]X, 5.39.48 (Fr, II, 909-10), c. 47 of Lateran IV, 1215 (*C.O.D.*, 255-6).

church would in principle be preferable, nevertheless, because it can be difficult to gather and obtain, excommunication shall proceed as follows: the archbishop or bishop or some other lawful ecclesiastical judge shall associate himself with a guardian of our public peace, who is called a justice, and the particular minister of that church in which they accused resides, or someone to whom the minister delegates his powers, and in addition two or three learned and respectable presbyters shall be appointed, at the discretion of the judge, in whose presence proceedings leading to excommunication may be initiated after the matter has been thoroughly investigated and most deeply pondered.

7. Of ordering excommunication in writing.[10]

A sentence of excommunication shall not be valid unless the order has been put in writing, a copy of which, transcribed without corruption or error, the judge shall hand over to the accused whenever he asks for it, and in any case this document shall be granted to the accused on demand within six days, without any exception.

8. The penalty for a judge who excommunicates unlawfully.[11]

Any judge who either has not forewarned the accused or taken the other precautions which we have decreed in this matter, shall first of all not enter the church for the space of a full month, except for the purpose of receiving holy communion. Then a superior judge, to whom the accused has appealed for help, shall completely rescind the former excommunication enacted against the laws, and shall order the author of the excommunication to pay all the expenses of the unjust suit, and shall also add other penalties at his discretion, so that judges may be terrified by fear, and not push people into such great disasters without the most serious reasons. And if a judge realizes that he was led blindly and precipitously into that judgment, and furthermore has himself lifted the rashly pronounced sentence before the accused has appealed to a superior judge, but the person who obtained the excommunication is not willing to agree to this unless the accused gives him satisfaction, and begs the superior judge for help in obtaining this, the inferior judge, disregarding this hard and cruel appeal, which reflects his own selfish interests rather than any mutual love among Christians, shall annul his sentence, in which he recognizes his earlier manifest error. For if he has doubts, and bonds have been given by the accused, promising to obey the sentence and decree of the superior judge to whom he has appealed, then the judge shall rescind and abolish the excommunication which he had previously imposed. And when he has duly done all these things, he shall be immune from any penalty contained in our laws.

9. Excommunicatorum denuntiatio.[12]

Cum legitimus iudex excommunicationis sententiam pronuntiaverit, statim id significet ecclesiae, in qua reus [82a] inhabitat, ut omnes ab illo tanquam a putri et proiecto membro se abstineant. Nec una tantum rei propria ecclesia rei gestae certior sit, sed disseminetur et emanet ad vicinos ministros et ecclesias, ut maiore sentiat ille pudore se undique exclusum et destitutum. Minister autem ecclesiae propriae, cum {h/e}is qui legitime sunt ad hoc negotium adhibiti, consequente dominico die, formula qua illi praescriptum est, Evangelio recitato, protinus excommunicationem, quibus verbis praescriptum est, apte et publice coram ecclesia expediat et legat, et populum condocefaciat excommunicationis fulmine perstrictam personam ex ecclesia quasi cadaver eiici debere, nec coenae Domini participem, nec divinorum officiorum, nec Christianae societatis, sed a sinu communis Christianorum matris ecclesiae revulsam, et abruptam a corpore Christi, coelo simul et terra esse exturbatam, diabolo et eius consceleratis ministris mancipatam, et sempiternis flammarum cruciatibus addictam, nisi mature suam salutem Satanicis ex vinculis expediat, vitam suam salubribus institutis ad probitatem revocet, maximum ex superioribus peccatis dolorem capiat, et, quantum in se est, omne damnum illius flagitiis ecclesiae datum nova innocentia et integritate compenset. Donec igitur Deo reconciliatus et ecclesiae fuerit, ea formula, quam post subiiciemus, pro Christiano fratre non accipiatur, sed tanquam extorris et naufragus et advena ignoti orbis obambulet, expers coenae Domini et sacramentorum et divinorum quorumcunque officiorum. Idem in aliis fiet ecclesiis, ad quas mandatum iudicis perveniet.

10. Excommunicatorum poena.[13]

Cum excommunicato non resipiscente nec in Domini mensa scienter communicandum est, nec in ullis cum illo divinis officiis versandum. Atque ista quidem poena nul[82b]lam exceptionem habeat. Deinde ne cibum quidem aut potum una cum illo capere, vel osculari, vel salutare, vel ad aedes tuas invitare fas erit. In quo tamen debet indulgeri; nam reus licet in aedes alienas commeare non debet, tamen propria eius domus solitaria non relinquetur, nec a pactis civilibus excludetur, et usitatis negotiis, quibus necessariae res humanae vitae suppeditantur: et si quis illum admonendi causa visitaverit et ad probitatem reflectendi, non debet in officio tam pio impediri. Nec illos ad ecclesiastica beneficia sumi fas est, quos ad mensam vel ad colloquium adhibere nefas existimatur. Et beneficiorum auctores illius temporis ius amittant. Quod si reus ipse, priusquam legitime liberatus fuerit, ad sacramenta vel communicanda vel

---

[12]L, 5.17.6, c. 11 of the council of Reading, 1279; L, 3.28.5, gloss on *excommunicati*.
[13]HC 14.2 and note.

9. The denunciation of excommunicates.[12]

When a competent judge has pronounced a sentence of excommunication, he shall signify it immediately to the church in which the accused dwells, so that everyone may avoid him as they would avoid a gangrenous and rejected member. Nor shall only the particular church of the accused be informed, but it shall be circulated and distributed to the neighbouring ministers and churches, so that he may feel even greater shame at being excluded and deprived. And the minister of his own church, with the documents which lawfully related to this business, shall proceed on the following Sunday, according to the form which is prescribed in his case, after the reading of the Gospel, to declare and read the excommunication, in the words prescribed, clearly and publicly in the presence of the church, and by reading the sentence of excommunication he shall inform the people that the person so restricted ought to be thrown out of the church as if he were a corpse, and not partake of the Lord's supper, or attend the divine services, or associate with Christians, but should be thrown out of the bosom of the church, the common mother of Christians, and amputated from the body of Christ and shunned by heaven and earth alike, bound over to the devil and his equally wicked servants, and consigned to the eternal tortures of the flames unless he effects his salvation from the bonds of Satan in time and calls his life back to honesty by salutary practices, and develops the greatest grief for his previous sins, and as far as he is able, repays any damage caused to the church by those crimes with a new innocence and integrity. Therefore, until he has been reconciled to God and the church by that form which we have appended to this title, he shall not be accepted as a Christian brother, but shall wander the earth as an outcast, a shipwrecked man and a stranger, cut off from the Lord's supper and the sacraments and all other divine services. The same thing shall be done in the other churches to which the judge's order comes.

10. The penalty of excommunication.[13]

As long as an excommunicate is not repentant he is not knowingly to be admitted to communion at the Lord's table, nor are any divine services to be conducted with him present. And moreover this penalty shall have no exception. Also, it shall not be lawful to eat or drink together with him, or to embrace or greet him, or to invite him to your house. Nevertheless, there must be certain relaxations to this, for although an accused person ought not to enter someone else's house, nevertheless his own house shall not be left empty, nor shall he be excluded from civil contracts, and the usual business by which things necessary to human life are supplied, and if someone should visit him in order to admonish him and to turn him back to righteousness, he must not be hindered in so godly a work. Nor is it right for people whom it is thought wrong to invite to dinner or engage in conversation with to be appointed to ecclesiastical benefices. And the patrons of benefices shall lose their right of presentation for that turn. But if the accused man himself shall presume to force his way into the sacraments either to receive

administranda irrumpere audeat, si ex ordine ecclesiastico clericus fuerit, beneficio careat et officio deiiciatur: si ex promiscuo populo, et, ut vulgo dicitur, laicus, arbitratu legitimi iudicis gravissime puniatur.

11. Poena communicantium cum excommunicatis.[14]

Quicunque cum excommunicatis non resipiscentibus in ullis actionibus se commiscet, nisi quas excipiebamus, poenam cum illis communem habebit, si semel admonitus ab illis non deflexerit.

12. Quamdiu vitandi sunt excommunicati.[15]

Qui excommunicatione fuerint ab ecclesia dimoti, tam diu ad societatem Christianorum fratrum non admittentur, quamdiu ecclesiae quantum possunt non satisfecerint, et beneficiorum liberationes a legitimo iudice impetraverint, aut ad minimum fidem iudici obstrinxerint suam, legitimis se illius mandatis obtemperaturos.

[83a] 13. Quid obstinatis debeat excommunicatis fieri.[16]

Cum in excommunicationis acerbissima solitudine quadraginta dies reus iacuerit, et nullam levationis honestam et piam rationem exquisiverit, ordinarius qui prius excommunicationi praefuit, litteras nostro munitas ecclesiarum causarum proprio signo nostrum ad forum aequitatis transmittat, quod vulgo cancellariam vocant, in quibus more regni nostri pertinacia reae personae perscrib{a/e}tur. Nos autem, quamprimum litteras nostras, ut in huiusmodi causis fieri solet, ad ministros legitimos, nimirum vicecomites et ballivos, ut vocant, perferri volumus, qui spatio quindecim dierum si reos non eruerint, compraehenderint, et in carcerem condiderint, sed illis vel avare propter lucrum, vel iniuste propter gratiam pepercerint, et ius longius indulserint, quam huius ratio decreti nostri fert, si fuerint apud legitimum iudicem in hac re convicti, triplum expensarum omnium in excommunicationis universo negotio collocatarum exsolvent, et in illum ecclesiae thesaurum, quem vulgo cistam pauperum vocant, illud deponent, quem ordinarius hoc beneficio dignissimum esse iudicaverit. Quod si per alios quindecim dies eorundem ministrorum nostrorum culpa cessatum fuerit, illud triplum, quod solvere debent, conduplicabunt. Deinde si praehensos reos et in

---

[14]X, 5.39.55 (Fr, II, 912), originally a decretal of Pope Gregory IX (1227-41), published on or before 5 September 1234. See also H.C., 14.1 and note.
[15]X, 5.39.15 (Fr, II, 894-5), originally a decretal of Pope Clement III (1187-91); X, 5.39.51 (Fr, II, 910), originally a decretal of Pope Honorius III (1216-27); H.C., 14.7.
[16]H.C., 14.20 and note.

them or to administer them, before he has been lawfully set free, he shall forfeit his benefice and be deposed from his office if he is of the clerical order. If he is from the general populace, and, as is commonly said, a layman, he shall be most severely punished at the discretion of a lawful judge.

11. The penalty for those who have dealings with excommunicates.[14]

Anyone who involves himself in any dealings with unrepentant excommunicates, apart from those which we have named as exceptions shall share the same penalty, if he does not turn away from them after having been warned.

12. How long excommunicates are to be shunned.[15]

Those who have been put out of the church by excommunication shall not be admitted to the society of Christian brethren for as long as they have not given as much satisfaction to the church as they shall seek the return of their benefices from a lawful judge, or at least make their pledge to the judge that they all conform to his lawful orders.

13. What should be done with obstinate excommunicates.[16]

When an accused person has lain for forty days in the very harsh loneliness of excommunication, and has given no honest and godly reason why this should be lifted, the ordinary who earlier presided over the excommunication shall send letters bearing the proper seal of ecclesiastical causes to our court of equity, which is popularly called the chancery, to which the stubbornness of an accused person is referred according to the custom of our kingdom. And it is our will that our letters shall be delivered as quickly as possible, as is customary in such cases, to lawful ministers, to wit, to the sheriffs and bailiffs, as they are called, who, if they have not located the accused within the space of fifteen days, arrested him and put him in prison, or if they have spared him either because of greed for money or from a wrong sense of compassion, and have delayed implementing the law for longer than the terms of this our decree will bear, if they have been convicted in this matter before a lawful judge, they shall pay three times the expenses allocated in the entire business of excommunication and shall put it into that chest in the church which is popularly called the poor box, which the ordinary has decided is the most worthy recipient of this benefit. But if this guilt on the part of our ministers continues for a further fifteen days, the triple amount which they had to pay shall be doubled. Furthermore, if the sheriffs or guards

carcere inclusos, nulla interveniente nostrarum litterarum auctoritate, vicecomites aut custodes liberaverint, aut elabi permiserint, antequam episcopo excommunicati se submiserint, et superioribus impensis plectentur, et decem addent alias libras arbitratu iudicis in cistam pauperum infundendas. Si vero negent aut differant has ita pecunias ponere, quomodo nos hoc decreto nostro iussimus, custodes pu[83b]blicae nostrae pacis invocati statim opem ferant, nisi nostrae velint auctoritatis contemptores haberi: quibus si ita visum fuerit, in bona licebit et possessiones eorum intrare, et illa seponere et segregare, donec plene sit ab illis omni ratione satisfactum.

14. Excommunicatus non liberatur nisi resipuerit.[17]

Cum ratio Sacris in Scripturis proposita, consuetudoque sanctorum patrum, ab auctoritate Scripturarum repetita, non permittat excommunicatos liberari poenarum suarum vinculis, donec violatam ecclesiae pacem et integritatem, quantum in se est, emendarint, et priori statui restituerint,[18] (nec enim aequum est illos in ecclesiae corpus inseri, donec peccata formulis ecclesiasticis eluerint, nec salus ab ecclesia unquam ostenditur, nisi prius ad probitatem se ipse reus revocaverit,) haec igitur cum ita sint, iudex cum plane cognorit reum in ecclesiae disciplina mansuete et clementer acquieturum, et si quem privatim offenderit, illi plene satisfacturum; tum demum ad ministrum proprium curet reum remitti, ministrumque certiorem faciat quomodo reus in loco suo rursus collocari possit, postquam ecclesiae se rite submiserit, ad extremum omni cum officio perfunctus sit, in ecclesiam reus inducatur, et ibi rite a legitimo ministro dimittatur, et ad veram Christianae caritatis omnem societatem adhibeatur, nisi forte simulatio sit aliqua rei in hoc negotio depraehensa, planeque de eo constet, quod non sincere sed fu{c/g}ate se gerat. Minister autem imprimis curet, ut ad legitimum iudicem totam rem perscribat quomodo tractata sit, et reus iam liber ipse novae nuntius suae fortunae, se quamprimum ad iudicem conferat: vel sic ministrumque certiorem faciat de ritu et forma paenitentiae, et de tem[84a]pore quo reus astrictus sit ecclesiam, quam malo exemplo offenderit, emendare. Minister vero et syndici, aut praestantes aliquot parochiae viri, imprimis curent, ut ad legitimum iudicem bona fide et mature rescribant, an reus mandatam a iudice poenam submisse et plene luerit, et externo corporis habitu animi vere paenitentis signa declaraverit, an sic se gesserit, ut aut contumaciae aut simulationis notas aliquas palam ostenderit. Iudex vero cum reum omni officio praescripto perfunctum esse cognoverit, illum a vinculis excommunicationis liberabit, curabitque ut ministri omnes qui excommunicatum declararunt, iam rursus liberatum et ecclesiae

---

[17]Cf. X, 5.38.5 (Fr, II, 885), originally a decretal of Pope Alexander III (1159-81). See also Panormitanus on X, 5.39.13.

[18]Cf. *e.g.* I Co. v. 1-5; II Co. vii. 8-12; I Ti. 1. 20. The Scriptural basis for this procedure is rather unclear.

have set the accused free, after they have been arrested and imprisoned, without any authority by letters from us to do so, or have allowed them to escape before the excommunicates have submitted to the bishop, they shall both be punished with higher fines and they shall pay a further ten pounds to be deposited into the poor box at the judge's discretion. But if they refuse or delay the deposit of this money, as we have ordered in this our decree, the guardians of our public peace shall be summoned to do their duty straightaway, unless they wish to be held in contempt of our authority, and if it seems right to them, they may seize their goods and possessions and take them away and imprison them until they receive full satisfaction from them on all counts.

14. An excommunicate shall not be set free unless he repents.[17]

As the procedure found in the Holy Scriptures, and the custom of the holy fathers, which is based on the authority of the Scriptures, does not permit excommunicates to be set free from their bonds until they have mended the violated peace and integrity of the church, as far as they can, and have restored them to their earlier state,[18] (and neither is it fair for them to be readmitted to the body of the church until they have washed their sins away by the ecclesiastical forms, nor is salvation ever held out by the church until the accused person himself returns to righteousness), therefore, since this is the case, when the judge has plainly recognized that the accused person will acquiesce humbly and peacefully in the church's discipline, and give full satisfaction to anyone he may have offended, then following that he shall ensure that the accused is handed over to his own minister, and shall inform the minister as to how the accused person may be reinstated in his post. After he has duly submitted to the church and after he has performed all his duty, the accused shall be led into the church and there he shall be duly absolved by a lawful minister and be re-admitted to the full fellowship of true Christian love, unless perchance some insincerity on the accused person's part is discovered in this business, and it turns out that he has not acted honestly but deceitfully about it. Then the minister shall first of all ensure that he reports the whole matter in detail to a competent judge, and the accused, already freed, shall himself announce his new fortune to the judge as soon as possible. The accused shall also inform the minister of the form and manner of his penance, and of the time at which he was compelled to make amends to the church which he had offended by his bad example. And the minister and churchwardens, or some leading men of the parish, shall first of all ensure that they report in good faith and as soon as possible to a competent judge, whether the accused has fully and submissively wiped out the penalty ordered by the judge, and by the outward clothing of his body has declared the signs of a truly penitent mind, or whether he has behaved in such a way as to show certain signs of contumacy or pretence openly. And when the judge recognizes that the accused has fulfilled all the obligations prescribed, he shall release him from the bonds of excommunication and see to it that all the ministers who announced the excommunication shall also declare to the people

reconciliatum esse populo divulgent. Haec vero semper ita procedant, nisi mortis periculum in excommunicatione reum depraehenderit; tum enim illum statim dimitti placet, si promissis pignoribus caverit se integre satisfacturum omni ratione, si fuerit saluti restitutus. Cum autem convaluerit, si mutaverit sententiam, et nolit ecclesiae disciplinam subire, rursus illius in excommunicationem perfidia relabatur.

15. Cum appellatur ab excommunicante quid fiat.[19]

Pronuntiata semel excommunicationis sententia, non potest {*a*} quoquam nisi ab ipso illo auctore rescindi, vel eius legitimo vicario; nisi reus appellationis usus remedio causam superiorem ad iudicem transmoverit. Tum autem si reus vel iniuria se dicat excommunicatum, vel iniuste ab ecclesia, quam omnibus officiis legitime conquisierit, auctor excommunicationis accersetur, et nisi is quindecim dierum spatio postquam ad causam dicendam evocatus fuerit, aperte possit ostendere, quod recte et iuste contra reum processum fuerit, eius prior sententia tanquam iniqua reiicietur, et ad ni[84b]hilum recidet. Verum auctor excommunicationis si superiori iudici suam sententiam probaverit, rursus in eius potestate reus erit, pignoribus tamen ab illo interim providebitur, ut impensae praestentur, et ut omnibus qui violati fuerunt aut affecti iniuria, satisfaciat, sed dum haeret in iudicio haec excommunicationis causa, reus auctoritate superioris iudicis excommunicationis supplicio potest eximi. Sed si post reus litem amiserit, et in iudicio succubuerit, vel ipse sibi diffisus deseruerit appellationem, tum aut spatio viginti dierum posteriorem damnationem vel relictam appellationem consequentium, omnia faciat perfecte et abundanter, quae superiori sententia peragere iussus est, aut si recusarit, rursus in luto prioris excommunicationis haereat.

16. De reis qui mortis sententiam acceperunt.[20]

Cum civilis magistratus aliquis flagitiosos homines adhuc non excommunicatos praeoccuparit, in carcerem abduxerit, hi si post sententiam mortis acceperint, et nos illis postea pepercerimus, nolumus tum indulgentia nostra ecclesiae disciplinam impediri. Iudex igitur ecclesiasticus illos satisfactionis et reliquorum officiorum commonefaciat: quae si non omnia rite perficiant, excommunicationis virga tantisper flagellentur, donec salubriores cogitationes susceperint.

---

[19]VI, 5.11.7 (Fr, II, 1096-1101), originally a decretal of Pope Innocent IV (1243-54).
[20]Cf. *Clem.*, 5.9.1 (Fr, II, 1190), originally published by Pope Clement V (1305-14) after the council of Vienne (1311-12). H.C., 13.16.

that he has been set free again and reconciled to the church. And these things shall always proceed in this manner unless danger of death has overtaken the accused during the time of his excommunication, for then he may be released immediately, if he has indicated by bonds posted that he will give full satisfaction in every way if he should be restored to health. But if when he recovers he changes his mind and does not want to undergo the discipline of the church, he shall fall back into excommunication by reason of his perfidy.

15. What is to be done when an excommunicate appeals.[19]

When once the sentence of excommunication has been pronounced, it cannot be rescinded by anyone except by him who was its author, or by his lawful deputy, unless the accused has transferred the case to a higher judge by making use of the facility of appeal. And then, if the accused claims that he has been excommunicated by malice, or that he has been put out of the church unjustly, when in fact he has performed all his duties lawfully, the author of the excommunication shall be summoned and unless he can clearly demonstrate that he proceeded rightly and justly against the accused within the space of fifteen days from the time when he was summoned to present his case, his former sentence shall be rejected as unfair and shall be annulled. But if the author of the excommunication has vindicated his sentence before the higher judge, the accused shall once again be in his power, but in the meantime it shall be provided, by bonds posted by him, that the expenses will be paid and that he will give satisfaction to all those who have been injured or damaged by the harm he has done, but as long as this case of excommunication is pending in judgment, the accused shall be exempt from the punishment of excommunication, by the authority of the higher judge. But if, after the accused has lost his suit and has succumbed to judgment, or else has lost his self-confidence and abandoned the appeal, then he shall either fulfil, perfectly and adequately, all the things which he has been ordered to do by the sentence of the higher judge, within the space of twenty days immediately following the second condemnation or the abandonment of the appeal, or if he refuses, he shall remain still in the trap of the earlier excommunication.

16. Of accused who have received a death sentence.[20]

When some civil magistrate has arrested wicked people who have not yet been excommunicated and imprisoned them, if they subsequently receive a death sentence and we then pardon them, we do not then want the discipline of the church to be hindered by our clemency. Therefore, the ecclesiastical judge shall advise them of the satisfaction they must give and of their other duties, and if they do not duly complete them all, they shall be beaten with the rod of excommunication until they acquire sounder opinions.

[83r; 84b]   **33. FORMULA RECONCILIATIONIS
EXCOMMUNICATORUM**[1]

Primum omni[*um*] eo tempore quod ab ordinario constitutum fuerit, reus ad
ecclesiam accedens coram foribus subsistet, illo prorsus omni corporis habitu
quem legitimus iudex assignavit. Pastor autem ex altera parte occurret, ac illum
in ecclesia[*e*] frequenti coetu sic affabitur:

'Visne, frater [85a] N. in Christo carissime, peccatum coram Deo
tuum **et in huius ecclesiae conspectu confiteri detestarique** [*tuum
tandem*], ut animum intelligamus a pravitate, qua prius tenebaris,
abalienatum esse, teque ut rursus ad ecclesiae nostrae societatem
aggregemus, a qua prius singulari perversitate tua revulsus eras.'

Et subiiciat reus:

'Valde volo, meque quamprimum ad superiorem meam
conditionem, unde turpiter et miserabiliter excidi, Dei beneficio et
vestro revocari vehementer postul*atum*/**o**.'

Tum pastor eum in templum introducat, et ad omnem circumfusam
multitudinem hanc orationem habeat:

'Viri fratres, adduximus ante oculos vestros, et in vestra praesentia
collocavimus, quemadmodum muneris nostri ratio fert, reum hunc,
fratrem nostrum, qui suos ut plane nobis probet emendatos sensus et
correctam morum labem, peccati sui deformitatem, qua Dominum
communem nostrum Deum, et sacrosanctam hanc eius ecclesiam
offendit, publice coram vobis paratus est *co*/**agnoscere**. Quae res licet
pudorem [83v] illi nonnullum allatura sit, tamen Dei gloriam et
ecclesiae nostrae statum vehementer amplificabit. Ad hoc igitur praebet
se, vobiscum ut rursus coram Deo coniungatur, et fraternam recens

---

[1]In the MS there is a marginal note in Foxe's hand which reads: 'Ante formulam hanc
praevenit alius titulus de excommunicatione in aliis exemplaribus; in quo titulo
continentur 16 capitula quae hic desiderantur.' ('Before this formula in the other copies
there comes another chapter on excommunication, in which chapter are contained 16
headings which are missing here'). See C. 11, q. 3, c. 108 (Fr, I, 674). This title is referred
to in the *General notes of matters to be moved by the clergy*, 1563, 3.46 (*A.C.*, 736). See
also 1571/11.

33. A FORM FOR RECONCILING EXCOMMUNICATES[1]

First [*of all*], at whatever time may be fixed by the bishop, the accused shall come to the church and stand at the doors, fully dressed in the clothing which a competent judge has determined. Then the pastor shall approach from the other side and when a congregation is present, shall address him like this:

'Dearest brother in Christ N., do you desire **in the sight of this church to confess and [also] condemn** your sin in the presence of God, that we may know that your mind is delivered from that depravity in which you were formerly held, and that we may join you once more to the fellowship of our church, from which you were formerly alienated by your own perversity?'

And the accused shall reply:

'Indeed I desire and I ask earnestly that above all things I may be called back by God's kindness and yours to my former state, from which I wickedly and pitifully fell.'

Then the pastor shall lead him into the church and with the whole congregation standing around shall deliver this address:

'Men and brethren, in accordance with our duty, we have brought before your eyes and have gathered in your presence this accused man, our brother, who is ready to acknowledge publicly before you the deformity of his sin, by which he offended our common Lord God and this his most holy church, so that he may prove to us openly that his mind has been changed and that his moral failure has been corrected. Which matter, although it has brought much shame on him, shall nevertheless greatly increase the glory of God and the standing of our church. Therefore it is for this reason that he presents himself, that he may once more be united with you before God, and again enjoy that brotherly intercourse which was recently interrupted. In which matter

intermissam ut iterum necessitudinem colat. In quo meae partes sunt, ut ex Sacris apud vos Scripturis repetam primum quid separatim ac proprie de praesentis rei crimine statui debeat, deinde quae communis omnibus nobis de communi fragilitate nostra cogitatio suscipienda sit. Principio Sacrarum Scripturarum auctoritas duo nos de peccato docet: alterum est quod omnes sine ulla exceptione peccatorum in carcerem detrudimur: alterum quod ad hunc finem vincula nostra referuntur, non ut semper in illis iaceremus, sed ut ex illis immensa[**m**] et infinita[**m**] Dei Patris misericordia[**m**] propter Christum explicaremu[*r*/**s**]. Quibus rebus facile possumus intelligere quid [85b] ipsi de nostris, deinde de aliorum criminibus cogitare possimus, et quis in illis [**nostri**] sensus [*noster*] esse debeat. Communitas enim illa peccandi quae prius ad omnes pertinere dicebatur, in eo nos erudit, naturam sane nostram universam ipsam per se semper ad omne flagitiorum genus ferri. Quapropter, offensiones aliorum [*admirabiles* **miserabiles**] nobis videri [*non*] debent, nec fratres decet in officiis vel claudicantes vel ruentes aut atrociter accusare aut superbe despicere: sed hoc potius Christianae coniunctionis est, ut non minor nobis in fratrum ruinis, quantumcunque magnis et capitalibus, dolor acci[*p*/**d**]eret[*ur*], quam si nos ipsi concidissemus. Imo [84r] vero fratrum in nostrorum occasu, nostram ipsi debilitationem et praecipitationem contemplemur, et de illa flebiliter communi voce coram Deo Patre nostro conqueramur. Nam illud si vere nobiscum [*ipsi*] cogit[*e*/**a**]mus, quod omnium hominum natura peccati dedecus concipit, in eo [*nimis* **minus**] acerbe nunquam alios insectabimur in quo nos teneri [*posse*] videmus; imo potius mansuete et submisse [*Deo*] gratias agemus, quod in tam grande crimen ipsi non sumus prolapsi, nostraeque constantiam innocentiae vehementissimis [*a Deo* **adeo**] et ardentissimis votis flagitemus. Et quoniam quidem omnes peccatorum mancipia su[*mus*/**nt**] illis in miserabilem servitutem dedita, *nos*/**n** *solum illa nos inter nos agnoscamus, sed toleremus etiam et patienter feramus* **illa non**/s **s invicem** *a*/resi**piscentibus et supplicibus condonemus**. Nam si secus faceremus, ipsi contra nos testimonium diceremus, in eo frat[*ru*/**erna**]m improbitatem accusantes, in quo nostra pravitas similiter delinquit. Cum autem in caeno peccatorum omnes ita volutemur, ut nulla nostrorum operum perfectione vel excellentia possimus ex illo extrahi, sed ex sola Dei Patris propter Christum et gratuita misericordia nobis levatio sit, ut eius ex eo nomen in summa celebritate versetur, et sempiterna gloria, maturus nobis ad pietatem et officium reditus esse debeat, et tempestivus ad singularem Dei misericordiam respe[86a]ctus, qui nos in carissimo filio et haerede Christo tam arcte complexus est, ut omnem peccatorum nostrorum poenam in illum derivaverit, et acerbissimis eius tormentis condonaverit, si nos in sceleribus nostris ipsi coarg[u/u]amus, nec flagitiorum nostrorum excusationem quaerentes, culpam [84v] in Deum et divinarum legum acerbitatem deflectamus, sed potius ad illos

it is my part that I should read to you out of the Holy Scriptures; first of all, what ought to be decided separately and particularly concerning the crime of the accused here present; then, what common understanding we all ought to acquire concerning our common frailty. First of all, the authority of the Holy Scriptures teaches us two things about sin: the first is that we have all, without exception, been bound in the prison of sins, and the second is that our chains are borne for this purpose, not that we should lie in them for ever, but that we should [*be delivered from* **expound by**] them [*by*] the immense and infinite mercy of God the Father for Christ's sake. By these things we can easily understand what we ourselves may think about our crimes, as well as about those of others, and what our attitude[**s**] toward them should be. For that shared inheritance of sinning which was earlier on said to apply to everyone, teaches us that our common nature is always led by itself to all manner of sins. Therefore, the offences of others ought [*not*] to seem [*admirable* **pitiful**] to us, nor is it seemly either bitterly to accuse or proudly to despise brethren who are limping or failing in their duties, but the Christian attitude is rather this, that we should be no less grieved by the ruin of brethren, however great and important it may be, than if we ourselves had fallen. But in the fall of our brethren let us contemplate our own weakness and vulnerability, and approach God our Father tearfully with one voice. For if we [*ourselves*] are honest enough to admit that the nature of all people conceives the disgrace of sin, we shall never condemn others [*too* **less**] harshly for what we see that we [*may be* **are**] bound by; rather we shall gently and humbly give thanks [*to God*] that we have not fallen into such a great crime, and we shall [**furthermore**] ask [*God*], with the most earnest and ardent prayers, for the power to remain innocent. And moreover since [*we are*] all [**are**] slaves of sins, given over in miserable servitude to them, not only should we recognize them among ourselves, but we should *also tolerate them and patiently endure them* **forgive them by mutual repentance and prayers.** For if we do otherwise we bear witness against ourselves, accusing our brethren of wrongdoing which our depravity has also committed. But since we are all wallowing in the mire of sins and cannot be hauled out of it by any perfection or excellence in our own works, our only release is in the sole and free mercy of God the Father for Christ's sake, which is why his name is held in the highest esteem and eternal honour. Our return to godliness and duty ought to be speedy, and our regard for the singular mercy of God timely, for he has embraced us so closely in Christ, his most dear son and heir, that he has laid on him the penalty for all our sins, and forgiven us by his most bitter torments. If we come to terms with our crimes and do not seek the forgiveness of our sins, we project the guilt and the harshness of the divine laws onto God, but we should rather take refuge in those treasuries of mercy, which God the Father has

clementiae thesauros confugiamus, quos Deus Pater in Filio Iesu Christo condidit, et ad ill[*u*/**a**]m perpetuo sol[*u*/**a**]m adhaerescentes, salutarem eius et propitium favorem uno consensu animorum firme et sincere postulemus. Neque vero lautus est in his rebus aut delicatus Dominus et Pater noster Deus ut ad misericordiam eliciendam aut emendicandum favorem pompa nobis et apparatu verborum opus sit, animum enim exp[*e*/**a**]ndit, verba non numerat, [*et*] si nos intimis mentium fibris veram et s[*eri*/**aev**]am conquestionem deprompserimus, ac optima fide contra nequitiam nostram ipsi constiterimus, et cum ea dimicaverimus, et ad eius gratiam recolligendam certa spe vota fecerimus, praesto statim est Deus, etiam antequam invocetur, ad amplexus se nostros offert, et voces antevertit priusquam illas ulla ratione moliri possimus. Imo vero salubrem hanc et necessariam peccatorum agnitionem animis nostris infundit, et hac disciplina condocefactos ipse suis humeris imponit, et ad beatissimum ovile suum devehit, et, magis exultat in unica persona tandem ad sanitatem revocata, quae vera peccatorum agnitione et morum emendatione se recuperaverit, quam in nonaginta novem iustis et perfectis viris, quos prius regni sui participes habuit. Haec igitur cum ita sint, fratres carissimi, et collocatus hoc tempore sit in conspectu [85r] vestro reus frater, qui peccati sui turpitudinem coram vobis agnoscere, poenamque illius a Domino Deo communi Patre nostro deprecari velit, vestra in praesentia, quam veluti sanctissi[86b]mam Dei veneratur et revereretur ecclesiam, et suppliciter petat, ut hac submissa sui deiectione viam ad coetum vestrum invenire possit, et ad superiorem suum inter vos ordinis fraterni locum pervenire, Christian[*i*/**ae**] vos ex vestra parte mansuetudinis recordari debetis, et vestra delicta cum huius praesentis rei fratris nostri peccatis coniungere, perpetuamque quandam et similem nostrarum [*offensionum* **affectionum**] consuetudinem esse statuere, sed et arrogantiam nostram et spiritus frangat, et contumaciam minuat huius abiectio nostri fratris et sui despicientia, qui se quemadmodum ipse quodammodo deserit, et fugit pudore vitiorum confusus et perculsus, eadem vestra sit coram Deo scelerum memoria vestrorum et verecundia. Deinde cum ad huius rei publicam et apertam criminum confessionem attende[*ritis*/**entes**], et illam optima fide propositam existimaveritis, exemplo Domini Dei Patris illum in humeros vestros iniiciatis, fractaque et quassata gravissimis peccatorum ruinis eius membra clementi fraternae caritatis lenitate sustentetis; sic enim misericordiae mutuis officiis peccatorum nostrorum onera sublevantes, legem illam Christi novam et auream [*san*/**fa**]ciendae caritatis inter nos [*auctorem*] *ple*... praeclare conservabimus, et proficiscantur ad Deum Patrem cum huius rei precibus vestrae preces, p{*er*/**rae**}g{**n**}ant cum eius lacrimis etiam vestri [85v] fletus, et ita demum certam divini favoris fiduciam anim[*is*/**o**] suscipie[*nte*/**ti**]s, quod propter Christum immensam nobis et infinitam misericordiam impartire velit, omnes una cum hoc reo fratre

established in his Son Jesus Christ, and cling constantly to [*him* **it**], and firmly and sincerely demand his salutary and propitious favour with singleminded purpose. For our Lord and Father God is not so strict and particular in these matters as to demand ceremony and fancy words from us in order to obtain his mercy or receive his favour, for he examines the mind and does not count the words, [*and*] if in the deepest fibres of our mind we have shown true and [*serious* **bitter**] contrition, and with the best faith have turned against our wrongdoing, and have broken with it, and if we have prayed with a sure hope to receive his grace, God is right there even before we ask, he offers himself for our embrace, and he hears our voices before we can prepare them in any way. But rather he pours this healthful and necessary admission of sins into our minds, and places those who have been taught by this discipline on his shoulders, and leads them to his blessed sheepfold, and he rejoices more in one person who has been brought back to health, who has restored himself by a true acknowledgment of sins and change of behaviour, than in ninety-nine just and perfect men, whom he already had as partakers of his kingdom. Therefore, since these things are so, most dear brethren, and at this time this accused brother is placed before your eyes, who desires to acknowledge the wickedness of his sin before you, and in your presence to pray that his penalty may be remitted by the Lord God, our common Father, since he venerates and reveres the most holy church of God, and humbly begs that by humbling himself like this he may find his way into your fellowship and reach a higher degree of brotherly rank among you, you for your part ought to remember [**Christian**] mercy [*as Christians*], and unite your transgressions with the sins of this our accused brother here present, and acknowledge that this is an innate habit which is like our own [*offences* **feelings**], but our brother's humility and self-deprecation ought to break our arrogance and spirits, and lessen our stubbornness. For as he is in some sense abandoning himself and fleeing in confusion and defeat from the shame of his sins, so likewise ought to be the memory of your crimes and sense of shame at them before God. Then when you have heard the accused's public and open confession of his crimes, and concluded that it was made in the best of faith, following the example of our Lord God and Father, you shall put him on your shoulders and support his members which have been broken and crushed by the most grievous ruins of his sins by the kind lenience of brotherly love, for by thus showing mercy to one another we shall remove the burdens of our sins and maintain that new and golden law of Christ, [*the author*] of [*sanctioning* **making**] love among us, and your prayers will reach God along with the prayers of this accused, your cries {*will **also** reach him* **are pregnant**} with his tears, and so you will receive sure confidence of divine favour in your mind. Because God desires to impart immense and infinite mercy to us for Christ's sake, let

nostro veniam peccatorum expectemus, et id ipsi, reum ad nos fratrem pie et officiose suscipientes, nostris quomodo possumus studiis contestemur. Quae maiore ut in luce versentur, et facilius cerni possint, reum hunc carissimum fratrem, interposita mei muneris ratione, membrum assumamus et agnoscamus communis in Christo nostri cor[87a]poris; et **ut*** intimus *ut** noster affectus *ut* in hoc corporis nostri recuperato membro testatior sit, publicis illum et precibus et gratulationibus et ad extremum etiam osculis consignemus. Tu vero, mi frater, primum et ante omnia in te ipse d[e/i]scende, ac tuum ipsius animum, testem et iudicem adhibens Deum, omnibus partibus perscrutare; [*cogita te* **cogitato**] coram Deo consistere, non coram hominibus solum apparere, nec in hoc saeculo tantum haec cum hominibus te tractare puta, sed in caelo praecipue [*cum* **coram**] Domino [*Deo*] Patre nostro. Quapropter diligentissime tibi circumspicienda sunt omnia, ne religione mei muneris ad illudendum Deo et Spiritu[*i*] Sancto turpiter abutare. Certe quidem, mi frater, utcunque nos tumultuamur miseri, Deus [*non irridetur* **nos erudiet**]. Itaque vehementer et iterum atque iterum provide, ne quicquam in hoc negotio sanctissimo veteratorie vel dissimulanter feceris. Nos extern[e/**i**] testes sumus [*tuae*] [86r] submissionis [**tuae**], quam contemplati sumus; sed Deus in secretos et penitus abstrusos mentis tuae secessus intrat, et ulciscetur gravissime, si quicquam in te perfid/**ia**/e depraehenderit. Quapropter amplifica, mi frater, quantum in te est, Dei gloriam; quod uberrime facies, si tuorum vitiorum sordes vehementer et serio detestatus fueris, et prorsus eorum omnem memoriam [*ex*/**ab**]horr[*ueri*/**ea**]s. Is enim maximus est divinae gloriae splendor, ut nos ipsi aversantes et abiicientes, Dei favorem p[*ropt*]er Christi Filii sanctissimum nomen imploremus. Et hoc unum est excellens divinae bonitatis lumen, ut spretis omnibus /aliis/ et conculcatis, sola Dei Patris et gratuita misericordia conservemur; quam tibi salutem, et nobis etiam omnibus, largiatur Deus Pater, cui cum Filio sit et Spiritui Sancto sempiternus honos. Amen.'

Hanc orationem cum pastor explicuerit, reus in oculis et auribus ecclesiae circumfusae verba, quae sequuntur, *plane* clare distincteque pronuntiabit.

'Aeterne Deus, omnium rerum auctor et parens, [87b] tu caelum et terram et quaecunque collucentia sunt in illis ornamenta iam inde ab initio tui nominis ad gloriam et usum vitae nostrae praeparavisti, tui nos ut honoris et laudis maximam semper rationem haberemus, et ad sanctissimam voluntatem tuam omnes actiones nostras dirigeremus. Verum ego teterrimus inter omnes et aerumnosissimus peccator, ab hoc tuo tam sancto salubrique consilio resiliens, tuam divinissimam maiestatem immani perversitate mea gravissime violavi, summoque meo damno et periculo purissimam illam innocentiae vestem, qua me [86v]

us all wait alongside our accused brother for the forgiveness of sins, and let us also bear witness to it as far as possible by our own efforts, in taking this accused brother back in a godly and dutiful manner. So that these things may be done in fuller light and be more easily perceived, by the office given to me, let us admit this accused, a most dear brother, and let us recognize him as a member of our common body in Christ, and so that our deep affection for this member of our body who has been recovered may be more evident, let us affirm him by public prayers, greetings and embraces also. And you, my brother, look into yourself first and above all, and examine your mind in every way, calling on God as witness and judge; [*think that you* **let it think that it**] stand[**s**] before God, and not just that it appears before men, and do not imagine that you have to deal only with men in this world, and not primarily [*with* **before**] the Lord [*God*] our Father in heaven. Therefore you must diligently investigate all things, to ensure that you do not wickedly abuse the dignity of my office in order to deceive God and the Holy Spirit. For it is certain, my brother, that however we poor men are tossed about, God will [*not be mocked* **instruct us**]. Therefore watch out again and again, lest you do something in this most holy business by craft or deceit. We are the external witnesses of your submission, which we have observed, but God enters into the secret and totally hidden recesses of your mind, and is most deeply offended if he finds any trace of perfidy in you. Therefore my brother, increase God's glory as much as in you lies, which you shall do most abundantly if you have truly and earnestly hated the wickedness of your sins and utterly abhor all memory of them. For it is the greatest splendour of the divine glory that we may turn and repent, and beg for God's favour for the sake of the most holy name of Christ the Son. And this is the most outstanding light of divine goodness, that when all other things have been cast out and despised, we shall be preserved solely by the free mercy of God the Father, which salvation God the Father shall bestow on you and on us all, to whom with the Son and the Holy Spirit be eternal honour. Amen.'

When the pastor has concluded this address, the accused, in the sight and hearing of the church surrounding, shall *plainly,* clearly and distinctly say the words which follow:

'Eternal God, author and parent of all things, you have prepared the heaven and the earth and all the shining ornaments in them from the beginning for the glory of your name and the benefit of our life, so that we may always have the greatest reason to honour and praise you, and direct all our actions to your most holy will. But I, the most terrible and despicable sinner of them all, have turned away from this, your most holy and healthful counsel, and have most grievously offended your most divine majesty by my enormous perversity, and by falling into sin,

baptismi sacramento per Christum Servatorem nostrum cooperueras, labe scelerum infeci et pollui, deinde ad extremum a me perdite prorsus abieci, meque ab ecclesia, cui per baptism[*i*/**um** *vim*] infundebar, perfidiose disiunxi. Quo factum est, ut in miserabilem peccatorum servitutem detrusus fuerim, et a tua maiestate nihil praeter horribilem poenam et sempiternum exitium expectare possim. Sed tamen ingenti promissorum tuorum fiducia, quibus favorem et veniam omnibus denuntias, quantumcunque scelestis et flagitiosis, qui Christi merita certa fide prensantes, et ad illa[**m**] semper incubantes, acrem et magnum ex suis criminibus dolorem accipiunt, et in illorum recordatione gemunt et lugent, peccatum coram te meum, mi Pater, et coram his fratribus meis, in hac ecclesia praesenti tua collocatis, libenter profiteor, agnosco, detestor, et execror. Quapropter parce mihi, Domine Deus, miserere meae prorsus miserabilis et afflictae conditionis; tuam appello misericordiam infinitam, immensam. Teterrimus peccator, appello tuam [*omni*] cogitatione[**m**] superiorem misericordiam, [*Deus*] O Deus Pater, propter Filium tuum et Servatorem meum Iesum Christum, qui pro communibus omnium peccatis incredibili quodam humani generis amore ad atrocem et infamem crucis mortem trusus est, mise[88a]rere mei, mei inquam abiectissimi et luctuosissimi et facinorocissimi peccatoris miserere *mei*. Tu[*i*]que posthac tantum robur mihi Spiritus infunde, tuum [87r] ut semper nomen perpetua beneficiorum tuorum memoria colam, et clementiae tuae laudem, actionum et officiorum constanti integritate, privatim et publice, testificar[*i*/**e**] dilatareque possim.'

Cum haec recitarit, erectus astet, [*ac*] in altiorem aliquem locum translatus, ex quo facile videri possit et audiri, clare dicat ea quae sequuntur et aperte.

'Fateor, O viri fratres, fateor me gravissimis sceleribus meis *et** Deum meum imprimis, deinde vos etiam omnes, incredibiliter offendisse, meque adeo fateor omnibus modis indignissimum ut ad ecclesiam vestram rursus assumar, ac ad membra pretiosissimi corporis Christi adnumerer; quoniam sanctissima caelestis mei Patris mandata flagitiosissime scelestissimeqne proieci et conculcavi, et Christi Servatoris mei sacrosanctum sanguinem, quo sum ex faucibus inferni ereptus, quantum in me fuit, immani flagitio profanavi, vobisque fratres, peccandi licentiam et impietatis exemplum subministravi.'

Deinde suum intexat [*proprium*] peccatum cuius reus est factus, et eo exposito, sic instituto sermone pergat.

have infected and polluted to my own very great hurt and danger, that most pure vesture of innocence with which you had clothed me in the sacrament of baptism through Christ our Saviour, until at last in my lost condition I utterly rejected it, and wickedly separated myself from the church, to which I was joined by [*the power of*] baptism. Thus it happened that I was cast into the pitiful slavery of sins, and could expect nothing from your majesty other than a horrible penalty and everlasting death. But yet by great confidence in your promises, in which you proclaim favour and forgiveness to all, however sinful and wicked they may be, who trust with sure faith in the merits of Christ, and relying always on [*them* it], develop a sharp and great sorrow from their sins, and groan and mourn at the remembrance of them, I freely confess, acknowledge, repudiate and denounce my sin before you, my Father, and before these my brethren, gathered in this church here present. Therefore spare me, Lord God, have mercy on my utterly miserable and afflicted condition, I call upon your infinite and immense mercy. A terrible sinner, I call upon your [**mind as**] superior mercy [*with all my mind, God*] O Father God, for the sake of your Son and my Saviour Jesus Christ, who for the sins common to all, out of unbelievable love for the human race, was handed over to the wicked and shameful death of the cross, have mercy on me, I say, have mercy on me, a most abject, sorrowful and wicked sinner. And finally pour into me such great power of your Spirit that I may always worship your name in perpetual memory of your blessings, and that I may bear witness and proclaim the grace of your kindness, both privately and publicly, by the continual righteousness of my deeds and behaviour.'

After he has read this, he shall stand up, [*and*] being taken to some higher place, where he may be easily seen and heard, he shall say clearly and distinctly the words which follow:

'I confess, O men and brethren, I confess that I have unbelievably offended my God first of all, as well as all of you, by my most grievous sins, and I further confess that I am in every way most unworthy to be readmitted to your church, and counted among the members of the most precious body of Christ, since I have most wickedly and sinfully rejected and broken the most holy commandments of my heavenly Father, and by my enormous transgression have profaned as much as I could the most holy blood of Christ my Saviour, by which I have been rescued from the jaws of hell, and I have given you, brethren, licence to sin and an example of ungodliness.'

Then he shall reveal the [*particular*] sin of which he has been accused, and when that has been expounded, shall continue with the following speech:

'In hac igitur mea tam inquinata vivendi ratione, mihi ipse sum gravis, et maleficii mei labes *est ea quidem** omnibus modis **est*** mihi intolerabilis; atque adeo vos omnes per Deum immortalem obtestor, ne meo corruptissimo quisquam exemplo maleficium ad hoc praesens meum aut [*ullum*] huiusmodi aliud adducatur. Imo terreri potius miseria vos mea [88b] decet, [87v] ne simili vos dedecore contaminetis. Deinde suppliciter a vobis peto, per immensam Domini nostri Iesu Christi caritatem, per eius acerbissimam mortis in cruce perpessionem, qua totum genus humanum a diaboli vinculis liberavit, ut praesens hoc crimen meum condonetis, in quo praeclarissimam ecclesiae vestrae societatem turpiter inquinavi. Deinde vos etiam magnopere rogo, me rursus ut ad coetum vestrum, quantacunque perversitate fuerim, clementer aggregetis.'

Tum pastor circumfusam ecclesiam sic interroget.

'Vultis, viri fratres, huic reo resipiscenti, suam condonare culpam, qua coetum hunc vestrum offendit, et eius causam communibus vestris precibus Deo Patri commendare, suam ut illi misericordiam impartiat, et quod nos hic in terris facimus, ille velit idem in caelo confirmare?'

Respondeat populus, 'Volumus.'
Rursus pastor sic interroget.

'Vultisne reum hunc in vestrum coetum recipere, carissimorumque posthac in numero fratrum habere?'

Respondeat populus, 'Volumus.'
Tum pastor reum in genua inclinatum sic alloquatur.

'Carissime frater, quoniam in conspectu totius *totius* ecclesiae professus es maximum et summum te tuo ex flagitio dolorem cepisse, et intimis propter illud [88r] sensibus commotum fuisse; praeterea cum ecclesiasticae disciplinae [*poenam*] tranquille et submisse subieris; deinde cum a Deo criminis veniam depoposceris, et [*e/*t]**andem a fratribus demisse et suppliciter requisiveris**, vehementer ab illis contendens, ne tuo [89a] exemplo ad delinquendum abutantur, sed potius fruantur ad recte vivendum; denique cum illorum tibi caritas veniam concesserit, et ad suam societatem rursus apposuerit.'

(Hic pastor, rei cap[*ut/***ite**] contract[*ans/***o**], ita pergat:)

'Therefore, I have become a burden to myself in this my deeply wicked way of life, the fault of my wrongdoing is [*itself*] in every way intolerable to me, and furthermore I beseech you all by the immortal God, that no one may be led by my most corrupt example into this my present wrongdoing or [*anything*] else like it. But rather it is fitting that you should be frightened by my misery, so that you may not be tainted with a similar disgrace. Next I humbly beg you, by the immense love of [*the* **our**] Lord Jesus Christ, by his most bitter suffering of death on the cross, by which he delivered the entire human race from the chains of the devil, that you may pardon this my present crime, in which I have wickedly offended the most noble fellowship of your church. Finally I also most earnestly ask you to take me back into your fellowship, however wicked I may have been.'

Then the pastor shall ask the church gathered around as follows:

'Men and brethren, do you wish to pardon the guilt of this repentant sinner, by which he has offended this your fellowship, and commend his cause to God the Father by your common prayers, so that God may impart his mercy to him, and be willing to confirm in heaven what we are doing here on earth?'

The people shall respond: 'We do.'
The pastor shall again ask as follows:

'Do you wish to receive this accused into your fellowship, and henceforth regard him as one of your very dear brethren?'

The people shall respond: 'We do.'
Then the pastor shall address the accused, kneeling on his knees, as follows:

'Most dear brother, since you have confessed in front of the whole church that you have reaped the greatest and deepest sorrow from your sin, and have been troubled on account of it in your inner mind, and furthermore since you have quietly and submissively undergone [*the penalty of*] ecclesiastical discipline; and since you have asked forgiveness of your crime from God, and have humbly and suppliantly asked the same of your brethren, earnestly urging them not to use your example in order to sin themselves, but rather to learn from it how to live rightly, and since their love has granted you forgiveness and taken you back into their fellowship,'

(Here the pastor, touching the head of the accused, shall continue as follows:)

> 'Ego [**te**] coram hac ecclesia, cuius mihi administratio commissa est, te tuorum poena delictorum et excommunicationis exsolvo vinculis, per auctoritatem Dei, potestat[*is*/**em**] Iesu Christi, et Spiritus Sancti, consentientibus huius ecclesiae praesentibus membris, et etiam ordinario suffragante; tibique rursus pristinum in ecclesia tuum locum et plenum ius restituo.'

His rebus conclusis, pastor reum complectatur et osculo sancto fratrem agnoscat, eumque manibus attollat, et medio templo prope mensam deducat communioni praeparatam, accinens interim, 'Te Deum' vel 'Gloria in excelsis' vel ut maxime convenire videbitur; et chorus in alternis versibus perpetuo succedat. Ad finem pastor addat, 'Sit nomen Domini laude affectum.' Respondeat populus, 'Ex hoc tempore usque ad omnem *perpetuitatem* **aeternitatem**.' Sequatur his verbis oratio.

> 'Agimus tibi gratias, clementissime Pater, quod hunc fratrem nostrum a lata via, quae sempiternum ad exitium descendit, mature tua singulari misericordia revocaveris, [88v] et salutarem resipiscendi spiritum illi suppeditaveris, qui dux ad vitam aeternam est, ut ex pestiferis diaboli paludibus emergens, in dulcissima Iesu Christi Servatoris nostri pascua commigra[*re*/**vi**]t, ac proprium se rec[*i*/**e**]per[*e*/**i**]t ad gregem, a quo periculosissime iam ante peregrinabatur. Itaque tuum in perpetuo sit honore nomen, tua semper laus perpetua commemo[89b]ratione nostra dilatetur, tua nobis gloria continuis [*sermonum* **officiorum** nostrorum *officiis* **sermonibus**] usurpetur, et frequentetur, cum in omni reliqua infinita bonitate tua, tum in hoc particulatim fratre nostro, quem nostra communi laetitia et exultatione reduxisti in viam, ut ex eius *parte* **per te** recuperata salute maximum gaudium caperemus, qui sua prius calamitosissima ruina summum nobis dolorem afferebat. Quapropter [*a te*] quaesumus, ut haec ad te pro fratre [**nostro**] fusa vota perveniant, et in illis ipse pondus et firmitatem [*in*]esse velis, ut ille nobiscum, et nos una cum illo, timore, fide, spe, dilectione, reliquorum compraehensione tuorum mandatorum ad tuam voluntatem vitam omnem nostram conformemus, et in perpetua veneratione tui nominis semper acquieseamus. Animadverte, Deus Pater, animadverte, nobisque Spiritum tuum tuis famulis largire, propter Iesum Christum, qui tecum vivit et regnat in unitate [*Sancti*]Spiritus [**Sancti**] Deus.'

Cum pastor extremam hanc orationem terminaverit, ad reum iam plane reconciliatum se convertat, et cum illo vehementer agat, ne rursus ad peccandi licentiam recidat, ostendens quam periculosae sint secundae ruinae, quibus, auctoritate Scripturarum, extrema necesse est prioribus [89r] esse deteriora; deque e[*o*/**a**] re[*i*] publicam requirat professionem, quod firme secum ipse

'Before this church, the government of which has been entrusted to me, I absolve you of the penalty of your transgressions and release you from the bonds of excommunication, by the authority of God, the power of Jesus Christ and the Holy Spirit, with the agreement of all the members of this church here present and also with the assent of the bishop, and I restore you to your former place and full rights in the church.'

When these things are concluded, the pastor shall embrace the accused and acknowledge him as his brother with a holy kiss, and he shall take him by the hands and lead him to the middle of the church next to the table prepared for communion, all the while chanting the 'Te Deum' or the 'Gloria in excelsis' or whatever seems most appropriate, and the choir shall each time respond in alternate verses. At the end the pastor shall add: 'May the name of the Lord be covered in praise.' The people shall respond: 'From this time forth, and to all *perpetuity* **eternity**.' An address shall follow in these words:

'We give you thanks, most merciful Father, that by your singular mercy you have called this our brother back in time, from the broad way which goes down to everlasting death, and have supplied him, being penitent, with a healthful spirit, to guide him to eternal life, so that coming out of the pestiferous swamps of the devil, he may go over into the sweetest pastures of our Saviour Jesus Christ and be received into his own flock, from which he had previously wandered in a most perilous way. Therefore, may your name be for ever honoured, may your praise be always proclaimed by our perpetual commemoration, may your glory be upheld and kept in remembrance by the continual [*service of our*] words [**of our services**], as in all the rest of your infinite goodness, so especially in this our brother, whom you have brought back to the way, to our common joy and exultation, so that we might obtain the greatest joy through the salvation recovered, [**by you,** *from him*] who previously had brought the greatest grief to us by his most calamitous ruin. Therefore we ask [*of you*] that these prayers, poured out to you for this [**our**] brother may reach you, and that according to your will there may be such weight and firmness in them that he with us, and we together with him, may conform our entire life to your will in the fear, faith, hope, love and understanding of your other commandments, and that we may always rest in the perpetual veneration of your name. Hear, Father God, hear and bestow your Spirit on us your servants, for the sake of Jesus Christ, who lives and reigns with you in the unity of the Holy Spirit, God.'

When the pastor has finished this final address, he shall turn to the accused, now fully reconciled, and shall earnestly admonish him not to fall back into the licence of sin, showing how dangerous are second lapses, since by the authority of the Scriptures the latter must be worse that the first, and he shall require a

constituerit, quemadmodum a Deo se postulat et sperat adiuvari, diligentissimam et summam adhibere cautionem, ne Dei posthac in iram incurrat, et a sanctissimis eius mandatis tam longe peregrinetur, ut rursus publico fidelium coetu sit illi merito carendum. Deinde et Deum ipse rogabit, et ad id communes ecclesiae preces postulabit, ut suum Deus hoc institutum constabiliat, et in Christo [**Iesu**] corroboret.

Quoties aliquis excommunicatione*m* propter peccatorum magnitudinem eiectus ex ecclesia, {*propri[or]um*} auctoritate iudicum ad hoc adhibita, rursus in suum coe[90a]tum hac, quae ante[**pro**]gressa est, formula receptus fuerit, {*et*} crimine solutus, curet ut ad certum tempus sibi praescriptum, ordinarius suae reconciliationis certior fiat, et illam syngrapha [*publico signo consignata compraehensam mittat, in qua syngrapha*] subscribat primum ipse pastor, vel eius vicarius, et aliquot ex gravissimis et integerrimis in ecclesia viris, qui rei gestae interfuerint, partim ut ipsa reconciliatio testatior esse possit, [**partim ut ordinarius, cum actum fuerit, intelligat**], et in eo quod pie Christianeque factum est, communem cum aliis laetitiam percipiat.[2]

---

[2]A note in Foxe's hand reads: 'Sequitur proxime titulus "De iudiciis" in aliis codicibus.' ('In the other codices there follows immediately the chapter "On judgments"').

public profession concerning this matter [*from the accused*] that he has firmly decided in himself that he will demand and expect God's help in applying the most diligent and greatest caution so as not to incur the wrath of God from now on or go so far away from his most holy commandments that he will deservedly forfeit the public company of faithful people once more. Then he shall ask God himself, and request the common prayers of the church that God will confirm this intention and strengthen it in Christ [**Jesus**].

Whenever someone is thrown out of the church by excommunication, on account of the magnitude of his sins, he shall be reconciled to its fellowship by this form aforegoing, which has been appointed for this purpose by the authority of the {*proper*} judges, {*and*} being released from his crime, he shall ensure that the ordinary is informed of his reconciliation within a certain time prescribed to him, and first, [*he shall send it, with the original copy signed with his public seal, on which original copy*] the pastor himself, or his deputy, and a number of the most serious and honest men in the church, who took part in the proceedings, will sign [**it on the original copy**], partly so that the reconciliation may be better attested, [**and partly so that the ordinary may know that it has occurred**], and that the accused may share with others in the common joy that the matter has been handled in a godly and Christian manner.[2]

[182r; 90a] 34. DE IUDICIIS, ET UBI QUIS AGERE VEL CONVENIRI DEBEAT

1. Quid iudicium.[1]

Iudicium est actus legitimus rite ac ordine pervestigandi et decidendi, quae in controversia[*m*] apud iudicem producuntur.

2. *Quid sit iudicium ordinarium* De iudiciis ordinariis.[2]

Ordinaria iudicia sunt, in quibus ea omnia requiruntur, quae in legitima causarum cognitione observari debent.

3. *Quid requiratur ad sententiae pronuntiationem in iudiciis ordinariis.* <Ordine enim iuris non servato, processus redditur nullus, si iudicium fuerit ordinarium.>[3]

In iudiciis ordinariis civilibus, ad pronuntiandam [*sententiam* **summam**] sufficiat plena cognitio causae. Verum in criminalibus propter periculum acerrima indagatio adhibeatur, neque in illis pronuntietur, nisi cognitio causae habeatur ple[90b]nissima, et probationes fuerint ipsa luce clariores.

[182v] 4. De iudiciis extraordinariis.[4]

In extraordinariis iudiciis procedendi ordo non observatur quo ad omnia. D[*i*/e]s[*t*/c]rib[*u*]untur autem [*in*] iudicia summaria, de plano et sine strepitu, et sine forma et figura iudicii.

---

[1]This and the following headings in this chapter are in Cranmer's hand. The numbers are supplied for this edition. Cf. Panormitanus on X, 2.1.
[2]*Ibid.*
[3]Moved by Cranmer from 36.6 below. Cf. Panormitanus, *ibid.*
[4]*Ibid.*

34. OF JUDGMENTS, AND WHEN SOMEONE OUGHT TO TAKE ACTION OR AGREE TO THEM

1. What a judgment is.[1]

A judgment is the lawful act of investigating and deciding the matters of controversy which are brought before a judge duly and in an orderly way.

2. *What an ordinary judgment is* Of ordinary judgments.[2]

Ordinary judgments are those in which everything which ought to be observed in the lawful hearing of causes is required.

3. *What is required for pronouncing sentence in ordinary judgments.* <For if the order of the law is not followed, the hearing is made null, if it was an ordinary judgment.>[3]

In ordinary civil judgments, a full hearing of the cause shall suffice for pronouncing [*sentence* the summary]. But in criminal ones, because of the danger involved, the most careful investigation shall be employed, and no pronouncement shall be made until the fullest hearing of the cause has been had, and the proofs have been clarified in the light of them.

4. Of extraordinary judgments.[4]

In extraordinary judgments the order of procedure is not followed in all respects. And [treated as] summary judgments are [*divided into*] those which are made informally and without fuss, and those which lack the form and shape of a judgment.

5. De iudiciis summariis.[5]

In summariis iudiciis lites absque exacta probatione possunt definiri, ut si actio sit ad exhibendum, et quo ad omnes [*ill*/ali]as quaestiones quae circa indagationem principalis causae emergunt, modo tales fuerint, ut earum definitio non pariat *praeiudicium* praeiudicium litigantibus, quominus ius suum alio iudicio prosequi poss[i/**u**]nt. Illa quoque summaria sunt iudicia, in quibus probationes adversus absentem admittuntur.

6. *Iudicium* Processus de plano et sine strepitu iudicii.[6]

Quandoque de plano, vel (ut dicitur) sine strepitu procedi potest, quando [*scilicet*] a iudice extra locum ordinarium, dum pro tribunali non sedet, et feriis [183r] *ob necessitatem hominis inventis* non observatis iudicium agitatur, recipiendo libellum actionis, aut litteras appellationum, et quicquid est eorum, quae parti adversae non pariunt praeiudicium. Quanquam et integras causas nonnunquam de plano cognosci posse volumus, ut cum levia delicta sunt punienda; in quo tamen iudicii genere ceteras observationes iuridic{*i*}alis processus non volumus prorsus omitti.

[91a] 7. Processus absque forma et figura iudicii.[7]

Processus absque forma et figura iudicii tunc sit, quando ea tantum, quae sunt iuris naturalis, in processu conservantur, [*u*/e]t citatio, legitima[*tio*/**rum**] personarum, qua [*scilicet*] mandatum exhibeant, qui postulare quippiam nomine alterius velint, petitio, defensio, et alia huiusmodi. Ea vero, quae solius iuris [183v] civilis et positivi sunt, re[*sec*/**cit**]antur, ut libellus, fieri[8] ob necessitatem hominum constitutae, litis contestatio et similia.[9]

---

[5]*Speculum*, 1.1, *De officio omnium iudicum*, 8.16.
[6]*Ibid.*, 8.3, 8. *Clem.*, 2.1.2 (Fr, II, 1143), originally a decretal of Pope Clement V (1305-14), published after the council of Vienne (1311-12).
[7]*Ibid.* Cf. H.C., 35.1.
[8]This is the reading of both the MS and the printed versions, but it must be an error for 'feriae' ('holidays'). F tries to make sense of it by repunctuating as follows: 'ut libellus fieri ob necessitatem hominum, constitutae litis contestatio, et similia.' ('that a libel be made because of people's need, the contesting of the established suit, and similar things.')
[9]F (followed by S) makes sense of this be punctuating as follows: '...ut libellus fieri ob necessitatum hominum, constitutate litis contestatio et similia.' This would then translate as: '...that a libel should be made for the needs of men, the contestation of the suit once it has been put together, and other similar things.'

5. **Of summary judgments.**[5]

In summary judgments, suits may be concluded without a full probation, for example, if an action has yet to be presented and the [**other**] questions arising in connexion with the investigation of the main cause are only such that deciding them would not prejudice the litigants in such a way that they would be less able to pursue their rights in another judgment. Summary judgments are also those in which proofs against an absent party are accepted.

6. The process of **a judgment which is made informally and without fuss.**[6]

Whenever it is possible to proceed informally, or (as is said) without fuss, when [*that is*] the judgment is carried out by the judge away from the ordinary place, when he is not sitting on the bench, and the ceremonies *invented for the needs of men* are not observed, by receiving the libel of the action, or the letter of appeal, or anything like that which does not prejudice the opposite party. However, it is also our will that whole causes shall sometimes be heard informally, as when trivial crimes are to be punished, although in that kind of judgment we do not want the other observances of the judicial process to be completely omitted.

7. **A process without the form or shape of a judgment.**[7]

A process without the form or shape of a judgment may occur when only those things which are matters of natural law are retained in the process, like [*citation, the legitimation of* **citation of lawful**] persons, by which [*that is*] those who wish to demand something in the name of another shall show their warrant for doing so, such as a petition, a defence or something similar. But those things which are matters only of civil and positive law, shall be cut out, like the libel, holidays[8] established for the needs of men, the joinder of issue and things like that.[9]

8. Quando procedere licet summarie, et de plano, et sine strepitu ac forma iudicii.[10]

Iudex *inferior mox regia maiestate* in cognitione causae nequaquam pro suo arbitrio summatim de plano et absque figura et forma iudicii procedat, sed tantum cum id ei nominatim a legibus nostris permittitur *vel a nobis in delegatione causae mandatum fuerit.* **In causis beneficialibus, matrimonialibus, etc. ut folio sequente.**[11] **In causis, etc.**[12] [<In causis beneficialibus, matrimonialibus, testamentariis, nec non decimarum et usurar[**iar**]um, ac eas quoquo modo tangentibus, simpliciter, ac de plano, el sine strepitu et figura iudicii processus fiat. In aliis autem civilibus iudiciis et criminalibus non notoriis, ordinem iudiciorum observari volumus, nisi ex consensu partium aliud statuatur, vel ex commissione nostra reg[*ia*/**ali**] rescribatur.>]

---

[10]*Speculum,* 1.1, *De officio omnium iudicum,* 8.1-20.
[11]Added by Cranmer, who wanted the latter part of 35.3 moved here.
[12]Added to MS by Foxe.

8. When it is permissible to proceed summarily, and informally, and without fuss or form of judgment.[10]

A judge *who is lower in rank that his royal majesty* shall in no case proceed with the hearing of a cause summarily, informally and without the form or shape of judgment, at his own discretion, but only when it is explicitly permitted to him by our laws *or has been ordered by us in the delegation of a cause. **In benefice causes, matrimonial causes, etc., see the next page**[11]. **In causes, etc.**[12] [<In benefice, matrimonial, and testamentary causes, as well as those concerning tithes and usury, and those which in some way touch on them, the process shall be conducted simply and informally, without fuss or shape of judgment. But in other civil judgments and in criminal ones which are not notorious, it is our will that the order of judgments shall be observed, unless something else is decided by the agreement of the parties, or has been prescribed by our royal commission.>]

[183v; 91a]   **35. DE CRIMINIBUS**[1]

1.[2]

Criminalia iudicia tunc agi dicantur, quando in iudicio ipso de crimine agitur, [*ut* **vel**] animadversione iuridic{i}a puniantur; quod interdum fiat per accusatores, quandoque per denuntiatores, qui ad iudicem de eo referant. Nonnunquam iudex ex of[91b]ficio suo inquirat, non existente accusatore aut [184r] denunitatore; aliquando vero per exceptiones inter litigantes obiectas. An vero in his criminalibus iudex ordinarie vel extraordinarie procedere debeat, partim ex legibus, partim ex verbis commissionis factae sibi a nobis, intellig[*e*/**a**]t.

2. De criminibus notoriis.[3]

Quando crimen est notorium, non requiritur observatio iudiciarii ordinis, sed [*ex*] evidentia[4] (cum iam constet a quo crim[en/**ine**] sit commissum), satis esto citari obnoxium ad audiendam sententiam, ut, si quas habeat, probabiles afferat causas, propter quas ad hanc vel ad illam poenam condemnari non debeat.

    Et si crimen sit notorium, null[*i*/**a**] tamen legitima sui defensio neganda est,[5] cum de crimine const[*a*/**e**]t notori[*e*/**o**], seu citatus veniat, seu non veniat, contra [184v] eum summarie procedatur.

3. De crimine non notorio.[6]

De crimine si qua dubitatio fuerit, cum eam probationibus tolli sit necessarium, et quidem luce clarioribus, iudiciarium ordinem severissime servari volumus. Etenim error in his non potest esse nisi nocentissimus.

    Statuimus ut [>in causis beneficialibus, matrimonialibus testamentariis, nec non decimarum et usurarum, ac eas quoquo modo tangentibus, simpliciter, ac de

---

[1]In the MS this is part of the preceding chapter.
[2]Hostiensis, *Summa aurea*, c. *De iudiciis*; Speculum, 3.1, *De criminibus et eorum cognitionibus*, preface.
[3]X, 5.1.9 (Fr, II, 734), originally Augustine (354-430), on Gn. iv.
[4]F (followed by S) ends the sentence here and begins the next one with 'Cum', but without the brackets.
[5]In the MS the sentence ends here.
[6]Cf. L, 5.15.7, gloss on *delicto notorio*, for an explanation of this.

35. OF CRIMES[1]

1.[2]

Criminal judgments are said to take place when the judgment itself is concerned with a crime, [*so that* or] the matters in question are to be punished by a juridical penalty. This sometimes occurs through accusers, and sometimes through denouncers who refer the matter to a judge. Sometimes the judge shall inquire on his own authority, when there is no accuser or denouncer, and sometimes by exceptions put forward by each of the litigants. But whether the judge should proceed ordinarily or extraordinarily in these criminal cases, he shall decide partly by the laws and partly by the words of the commission given to him by us.

2. Of notorious crimes.[3]

When a crime is notorious, the observance of the juridical order is not required, but [*from*] the evidence[4] (since it is already clear by whom the crime was committed), shall suffice for the accused to be summoned to hear his sentence, in order that he may present convincing reasons, if he has any, as to why he should not be condemned to this or to that penalty.

But even if a crime is notorious, no lawful defence of it is to be refused.[5] When it is agreed that a crime is notorious, the person cited shall be proceeded against summarily, whether he appears in court or not.

3. Of a crime which is not notorious.[6]

If there is some doubt about the crime, since it is necessary for that doubt to be removed by proofs, and also clarified by the light, it is our will that the juridical order shall be most strictly observed. For a mistake in these matters can only be most harmful.

We decree that [>in benefice, matrimonial, and testamentary causes, as well as those concerning tithes and usury, and those which in some way touch on

plano, vel sine strepitu et figura iudicii processus fiat. In aliis autem civilibus iudiciis et criminalibus non notoriis, ordinem iudiciorum observari volumus, nisi ex consensu partium aliud statuatur, vel ex commissione nostra regia rescribatur.<][7]

4. De criminali accusatione.[8]

Ad accusandum criminaliter nemo admittatur, [185r] nisi [*se*] prius astrinxerit ad [*subeundam* **scribendum**] poenam, cui accusatus victus subiici debuer[*i*/a]t, si succumbat in iudicio, et nisi fideiussores dederit, quibus de lite prosequenda caveat. *Si de fuga dubitetur, tam accusator quam accusatus sub custodia detineri possunt donec de crimine constet.*

Qui perpetratis delictis vel aufugiunt vel latitant, ne in iudicium trahantur, cum per edicta de more vocati fuerint, si non compareant, eorum bona sequestrentur. Quod ubi factum fuerit, rursus edictis et citationibus evocentur; et si neque ita comparuerint, et bona eorum et *confiscabuntur, et illi cum appraehendi potuerint, absque dilatione capientur.*

[185v] 5. *Aetas iudicis.*[9]

Iudicem minorem octodecim annis esse non permittimus, etiamsi ex consensu litigantium postuletur.[10]

---

[7]Moved from here to 34.8 on Cranmer's instructions, though the change was not actually made in the MS copy. Cranmer wrote in the margin: 'ponatur folio praecedente' ('let it be placed on the preceding folio'.)

[8]*Dig.*, 2.13.1, originally Ulpian, *Ad edictum*, 4.

[9]Cf. *Dig.*, 5.1.12.2, originally Paulus, *Ad edictum*, 17.

[10]A marginal note in Cranmer's hand reads: 'Ponatur folio praecedente' ("Let it be put in the preceding folio'). This would have included it at the end of 34.8, but in fact it was added to 36.3, on the following folio.

them, the process shall be conducted simply and informally, without fuss or shape of judgment. But in other civil judgments and in criminal ones which are not notorious, it is our will that the order of judgments shall be observed, unless something else is decided by the agreement of the parties, or has been prescribed by our royal commission.<][7]

4. Of a criminal accusation.[8]

No one shall be allowed to make a criminal accusation unless he has first promised to [*undergo* **subscribe to**] the penalty to which the party accused and convicted would have to be subjected, if his case collapses in court, and unless he gives guarantees, that he will pursues the issue.

If there is some fear that one of the parties might run away, both the accuser and the accused may be held in custody until the crime is decided.

Those who, after committing crimes, either run away or hide so that they may not be brought to judgment when they have been summoned by edicts, as the custom is, shall have their goods sequestered if they do not appear. And when that has been done, they shall again be summoned by edicts and citations, and if they still do not appear, their goods shall be confiscated and when they can be arrested, they shall be imprisoned without delay.

5. *The age of a judge.*[9]

We do not allow a judge to be less than eighteen years of age, even if that is requested by the agreement of the litigants.[10]

[185v; 92a]   **36. DE IUDICIIS**[1]

1. Iudex non suus ex consensu fit suus.[2]

Iurisdictio cuiuslibet iudicis non sui, qui tribunali praeest, vel aliam iurisdictionem habet, ex partium litigantium consensu prorogari possit, at privatorum consensus iudicem eum non facit, qui nulli praeest iurisdictioni, nec quod [e]is statuit, rei iudicatae continet auctoritatem.

Non solum expresse sed etiam tacite prorogatio fieri possit. Nam si litigatores iudicem non suum scienter ad[*iv*/**mis**]erint, iurisdictionem illius prorogare intelliguntur.

Si quis in aliquem iudicem coram ipso et cum [186r] suo adversario consentit, [*quoad* **quod ob**] certam aliquam causam, non potest in ea illum declinare.

Non videtur in iudicem consensisse, qui edi sibi genus apud eundem iudicem desiderat actionis.

2. *Post iudicis obitum successor procedat.*[3]

>Mortuo iudice succedens in eius locum potest procedere iuxta formam retroactam, prout ille potuit, in cuius locum successit.<[4]

2. **De iudici[*bu*/i]s delegatis.**[5]

Cum iudex ordinarius unum ex pluribus delegatis iudicare vetat, ceteris id committere videtur.[6]

---

[1]In the MS, this chapter is not distinguished from the preceding one.
[2]*Dig.*, 5.1.1, originally Ulpian, *Ad edictum*, 2; ibid., 5.1.2, originally Ulpian, *Ad edictum*, 3; *Cod. Iust.*, 3.13.1, originally a rescript of the emperors Severus and Antoninus, 11 January 214; *ibid.*, 3.13.3, originally a rescript of the emperors Diocletian and Maximian, 27 December 293.
[3]*Dig.*, 5.1.60, originally Paulus, *Ad Sabinum*, 14.
[4]Moved by Cranmer to the heading of c. 5 below.
[5]Cf. Hostiensis, *Summa aurea*, c. *De recusatione iudicis delegati*.
[6]In the MS this is crossed out, but the same word is written in Foxe's hand at the end of the preceding line. It seems that he wanted to avoid confusion which might have resulted from the subsequent division of the canon into two. As it stood originally, a careless reader might have thought that 'videtur' was the first word of the next canon.

36. OF JUDGMENTS[1]

1. A judge who is not one's own becomes one's own by agreement.[2]

The jurisdiction of any judge, other than one's own, who presides over the court or who has another jurisdiction, may be extended by the agreement of the litigants, but the agreement of private parties does not make a judge out of someone who presides over no jurisdiction, nor does what he decrees [**for them**] carry the authority of something which has been judged.

Extension may be secured not only expressly but silently as well. For if the litigators knowingly accept a judge who is not their own, they are understood to be extending his jurisdiction.

If someone accepts a certain judge, in his presence and in that of his opponent, in respect of some particular cause, he cannot reject him in it.

Someone who wants a kind of action to be published for him by a judge is not seen to have given his consent to that same judge.

2. *After the death of a judge his successor shall proceed.*[3]

>When a judge dies his successor in the post may proceed retroactively according to the form, exactly as the one to whose post he has succeeded could have done.<[4]

2. **Of delegated [*judges* judgments].**[5]

When an ordinary judge forbids one of many delegates to judge, he is understood to be extending this prohibition to the others.[6]

3.[7] **Qui iudices [*esse*] nequeunt** [esse].[8]

Non *autem* omnes **homines indiscriminatim** iudices [*dari* **esse**] possunt,.
q/Quidam[9] enim natura impediuntur, ut surdus, mutus, et perpetuo furiosus, *et
impubes* quia iudicio carent. Quidam lege impediuntur, ut infames, quidam
moribus, [186v] ut feminae et servi, non quia iudicium non habent, sed quia
receptum est, ut civilibus non fungantur officiis. **Quidam [*aetate*], ut impubes,
et minor octodecim annis, tales enim iudices esse non permittimus, etiam si
ex consensu litigantium postulentur.**

[92b] 4. **De recusatione iudicis.**[10]

Iudex etiam ordinarius potest recusari ex omni causa [*per*] qua[*m*] verisimiliter
in favorem alterius partis inclinare praesumitur. Sed qui recusat, causas debet
exponere ac verisimiles ostendere.

    Si alter ex litigatoribus iudicem solum haeredem, vel ex parte [*aut*]
executorem fecerit, alius iudex necessario sumendus est, quia iniquum est
aliquem suae rei iudicem fieri.

    Observandum est ne is iudex detur, quem altera pars nominatim petit; id
enim iniqui exempli esse iudicamus, nisi hoc specialiter a nobis ob dignitatem
iudicis petiti permittatur.

[187r] 5. **Succedens iudex supplere potest quod praecedens non praestiterat.
<Mortuo iudice, succedens in eius locum potest procedere iuxta formam
retroactam, prout ille potuit, in cuius locum successit.>**[11]

Si iudex, cui certa tempora praestita erant, decesserit, et alius in eius locum datus
fuerit, tanta ex integro in persona eius praestita intelligemus, quamvis delegans
nominatim hoc in sequenti datione non expresserit, quanta prior iudex, *ante
obitum fecerat* qui decessit, *habuerat* **praestiterat**: ita tamen, ut legitima
tempora non excedant.

    Qui iudex est in iudicio possessorio, idem esse debet in petitorio, ne causae
continentia dividatur.[12]

---

[7]This heading was originally part of section 2 and was separated out by Cranmer.
[8]*Dig.*, 5.1.12.2, originally Paulus, *Ad edictum*, 17.
[9]Cranmer divided the sentence here.
[10]Hostiensis, *Summa aurea*, c. *De recusatione iudicis delegati*; Speculum, 1.1, *De
recusatione*, 4.1; Panormitanus on X, 2.1.18.
[11]Moved here by Cranmer from c. 2a above. *Dig.*, 5.1.60, originally Paulus, *Ad Sabinum*,
14.
[12]*Dig.*, 5.1.62, originally Ulpian, *Ad edictum*, 39.

3.[7] **Who cannot be judges.**[8]

However, not all people can be [*appointed*] judges indiscriminately. For[9] some are impeded by nature, like the deaf, the dumb and the permanently insane, *and infants*, because they lack judgment. Some are impeded by law, like those of ill repute, some by custom, like women and servants, not because they lack judgment but because it is generally agreed that they do not hold public office. **Some [*by age*], like infants, and those under the age of eighteen, For we do not allow such people to be judges even if they are requested by the agreement of the litigants.**

4. **Of the rejection of a judge.**[10]

A judge, even an ordinary one, may be rejected for any reason which makes it likely that he will be inclined to favour the other party. But the one who rejects him must explain the reasons and show that they are well-founded.

If one of the litigators has made a judge sole or part heir, [*or*] executor, another judge must necessarily be appointed, because it is unfair for someone to be made the judge of his own case.

Care is to be taken that a man whom one of the parties specifically asks for is not appointed judge, for we consider that to be an example of unfairness, unless this has been specially allowed by us because of the dignity of the judge requested.

5. **The succeeding judge may complete what the preceding one has not fulfilled. <When a judge dies his successor in the post may proceed retroactively according to the form, exactly as the one to whose post he has succeeded could have done.>**[11]

If a judge appointed for a fixed term should die, and another is appointed in his place, we understand that fully as much time shall be allotted to his person as the former judge who died had **fixed *before he died***, even if the delegator has not specifically expressed this in the second appointment, yet so as not to exceed the lawful term limit.

The one who was judge in the judgment of possession ought to be the same again in the judgment of petition, so that the general flow of the proceedings is not interrupted.[12]

6. Tres iudicii partes.[13]

Tres partes habet iudicium, principium usque ad litis contestationem, medium usque ad conclusionem in causa, et finem per sententiam.

>*Ordine iuris non servata, processus redditur nullus* [187v] *si iudicium fuerit ordinarium.*<[14]

7. De citatione.[15]

Per citationem incohatur iudicium, et iurisdictio perpetuatur.

Eum qui in ius vocandus est, non tribus edi[93a]ctis, sed uno peremptorio pro omnibus (ut circuitus evitetur) vocari placuit.

8. Quando partes procuratores mittere possunt.[16]

Iuris esse ambiguum non videtur, iudicem ordinarium sive delegatum iubere non posse alterutram partium coram se personaliter comparere, nisi causa fuerit correctionis, vel nisi pro veritate dicenda, vel pro iuramento calumniae faciendo, aut alia iuris necessitas partes coram eo exigeret personaliter praesentari.

[188r] Principales personae non [*per*] procuratores, aut advocatos, super facto in iudicio proposito, sed p[*er*/**ro**] se ips[*a*/**i**]s respondere debent, si iudex eas interrogandas vel examinandas fore duxerit.

9. Citatus comparere debet coram iudice etiam non suo.[17]

Si quis ex aliena iurisdictione ad iudicem vocetur, debet venire; iudicis enim est existimare an sua sit iurisdictio, vocati autem est non contemnere auctoritatem iudicis. Nam et privilegiati in ea sunt causa, ut in ius vocati veniant privilegia sua allega[**n**]tur[*i*].

---

[13]Hostiensis, *Summa aurea*, c. *De iudiciis.*
[14]Moved by Cranmer to 34.3 above.
[15]Speculum, 1.1, *De officio omnium iudicum*, 6.7.
[16]*Dig.*, 3.3.33.2, originally Ulpian, *Ad edictum*, 9; X, 2.1.14 (Fr, II, 245), originally a decretal of Pope Innocent III, 19 December 1203; VI, 2.1.1 (Fr, II, 995), originally a decretal of Pope Innocent IV (1243-54).
[17]This contradicts X, 1.3.28 (Fr, II, 31), c. 37 of Lateran IV, 1215 (*C.O.D.*, 251-2).

6. The three parts of judgment.[13]

A judgment has three parts: the beginning, up to the joinder of issue; the middle, up to the conclusion of the cause; and the end, through to the sentence.

>*For if the order of the law is not followed, the hearing is made null, if it was an ordinary judgment.*<[14]

7. Of citation.[15]

A judgment begins by citation and the jurisdiction is maintained throughout.

The man who is to be summoned may be called not by three edicts, but by one peremptory one which will do for them all (to avoid going around in a circle).

8. When the parties may send proctors.[16]

There seems to be no doubt in the law that neither the ordinary judge nor his delegate can order either of the parties to appear before him in person, unless it is a cause of correction or unless it is to take the oath for telling the truth or the oath against calumny, or some other necessity demands that the parties appear personally before him.

The main persons must not respond through proctors or advocates, concerning the matter put forward for judgment, but must answer for themselves, if the judge has called them forward to be questioned and examined.

9. The person cited must appear before the judge even if he is not his own.[17]

If someone is called before a judge from another jurisdiction he must come, for it is the judge's responsibility to determine whether it is his jurisdiction and it is not up to the person summoned to despise the judge's authority. For even the privileged are in the position that they must come to court when summoned in order to defend their privileges.

10. Mutatio *sui* loci post citationem non sufficit ad declinationem fori.[18]

Si quis, posteaquam in ius vocatus est, alterius fori esse coeperit, exceptio illius fori non obstabit, *quasi* **quod** ab alio sit iam praeventus.

[188v] 11. **Citatis tutus sit ad iudicem accessus et recessus.**[19]

Ad iudicium ecclesiasticum vocatus per *officialem seu* iudicem saecularem, cuiuscunque sit privilegii, eundo, stando, vel re[93b]deundo non molestetur, vel realiter capiatur, sub poena decem librarum applicandarum cistae pauperum.

12. *Quae reo solvendae sunt impensae* De solvendis impensis.[20]

Si reus vocatus ad iudicium comparuerit, et actor *absens fuerit* **nihil obiecerit**, reus exhibita copia citationis, et fide facta super diem compar[i/a]tionis, una cum expensis dimittatur.

Eum quem temere adversarium suum in iudicium vocasse constiterit, viatica litisque sumptus adversario suo reddere oportebit.

<Victum victori iudex condemnabit in expensis, nisi iusta causa ei qui succumbit subveniat.

Expensas litis iudicis est post sententiam in executione taxare, et deinde iuramentum super veritate earundem parti vincenti deferre.>[21]

[189r] 13. *Actio sequetur forum rei* De foro iudiciali.[22]

Iuris ordo est, ut actor rei, et non reus actoris forum sequatur. (**Rei quattuor rationibus forum sortiuntur, in titulo 'De officio** [*et*/in] **iurisdictione omnium iudicum',**[23] **et ibi** [*expungitur* exponantur].) *Nam ubi domicilium habet reus, ibi eum convenire oportet vel ubi crimen commisit* **Cum reus potest conveniri in pluribus locis, tunc est in arbitrio actoris positum, ubi velit eum convenire.**

---

[18]Cf. *Cod. Iust.*, 8.35(36).13, originally a rescript of the emperors Honorius and Theodosius II, 28 August 415.

[19]X, 1.29.35 (Fr, II, 179-80), originally a decretal of Pope Innocent III (1198-1216). Cf. VI, 1.14.13 (Fr, II, 981-2), originally a decretal of Pope Boniface VIII (1924-1303).

[20]X, 5.37.4 (Fr, II, 881), c. 9 of the council of Tours, 1163.

[21]Moved here by Cranmer from 36.20a below.

[22]*Cod. Iust.*, 3.13.2, originally a rescript of the emperors Diocletian and Maximian, 10 October 293.

[23]This was originally 37.15a but was later moved to 36.14 (the next section) without any change being made to this sentence.

10. **Change of residence after citation is not sufficient reason for refusing the court's jurisdiction.**[18]

If someone goes to live in another court's jurisdiction after he has been summoned to court, the immunity of that jurisdiction shall not stand in the way, *as if* **since** he had already been called by the other one.

11. **There shall be safe conduct to and fro for those who have been cited before a judge.**[19]

Someone who has been summoned before an ecclesiastical court shall not be molested by a*n official or* secular judge, whatever privilege the latter may have, on his way there, or when he is standing before the court, or on his way back home, nor shall his property be seized, under pain of ten pounds to be paid into the poor box.

12. *What expenses are to be paid to the accused* **Of the payment of expenses.**[20]

If the accused appears in court when summoned and the plaintiff *is absent* **does not object**, the accused shall be dismissed with his expenses after he has shown a copy of his citation and given his pledge that he will appear on the day appointed.

Anyone who has decided to call an opponent into court for no good reason shall be obliged to reimburse him the costs of his journey and of the suit.

<The judge shall impose the winner's expenses on the loser, unless for some good reason he comes to the latter's aid.

It is the judge's responsibility to set the expenses of the suit after the sentence is in execution, and then to administer the oath concerning truth of these things to the winning party.>[21]

13. *The action goes to the court of the accused* **Of the judicial forum.**[22]

The rule of the law is that the plaintiff shall go to the court of the accused, and not the accused to the court of the plaintiff. (**The accused are allocated a court in four ways, in the title 'Of the office [***and***/in] jurisdiction of all judges',**[23] **and it is there [***expunged* explained].**) *For where the accused has his domicile, there he must be summoned, or where he committed the crime* **When the accused can be summoned in many places, then it is left to the discretion of the plaintiff, where he wishes to summon him.**

[<Clericus in foro civili si quempiam convenerit, in eodem potest ab adversario suo reconveniri, ac ibidem iudicabitur, non tamen quoad criminalia. Ubi coeptum est semel [*iudicium*], ibi et finem accipere debet.>][24]

[<14. Quattuor modis potest reus forum sortiri.[25]

Rei *quinque* **quattuor** rationibus forum sortiuntur; aut propter domicilium (a iudice quippe loci ubi quis habitat est iudicandus); aut ob delictum commissum (ibi enim quis iudicatur, ubi peccatum admisit et depraehensus fu[er]it); a[u/-]t [94a] ob locum ubi sita res fuerit de qua contenditur. (Nam si de beneficio ecclesiastico, aut de *agris vel domibus* **decimis agrorum aut domuum**, litigetur, iudex loci earum rerum est adeundus). Aut propter locum contractus: siquidem ubi quis contraxit, plerumque de contractu est litigandum.>][26]

15. Ordinarius iudex non potest mutare locum consuetum.[27]

Ordinarius iudex in loco maiorum ius reddere, et in eodem sententiam proferre debet, nisi de consensu partium alius locus deputetur.

16. *Sufficit actore in libello simpliciter narrare factum.* De libello.[28]

Actionem in libello actor non tenetur exprimere, *f...* sed factum ipsum et rei veritatem pure et simpliciter, ut ex eo ius agendi colligatur, narrare sufficit.

Iudex quandocunque de ineptitudine libelli ei constiterit, reum absolvere debet: ita tamen quod si [189v] actor aptum et congruentem libellum porrexerit, reus nihilominus respondere teneatur.

---

[24]This whole sentence was moved here from 17a below, on the instructions of Archbishop Cranmer who wrote: 'Clericus tantum in foro civili etc., ut folio sequente' in this place in the MS.

[25]Ibid.

[26]Moved here from 37.15a on Cranmer's instructions, but not found in the MS.

[27]Cf. *Dig.*, 5.1.59, originally Ulpian, *Ad Sabinum*, 51.

[28]X, 2.1.6 (Fr, II, 241), originally a decretal of Pope Alexander III (1159-81); X, 2.1.15 (Fr, II, 245), originally a decretal of Pope Innocent III, 24 March 1207.

[<If a cleric has summoned someone to appear in a civil judgment, he can also be summoned to appear in the same judgment by his adversary, and there be judged, but not in criminal cases. Once a hearing has begun in a particular place, it must also be brought to an end there.>][24]

[<14. An accused person may be allocated a court in four ways.[25]

Accused people may be allocated a court in *five* **four** ways, either because of his domicile (the place where a person resides is to be determined by the judge), or on account of the crime committed (for a man shall be judged in the place where he committed the crime and was arrested), or according to the place where the thing which is being contested is situated. (For if the litigation concerns an ecclesiastical benefice, or **tithes on** fields or houses, the judge of the place where those things are is to be called). Or according to the place of the contract, if someone has signed a contract somewhere and most of the litigation is about the contract.>][26]

15. **An ordinary judge cannot change the customary place.**[27]

An ordinary judge must render the law in the customary place, and pronounce sentence there also, unless another place is substituted with the agreement of the parties.

16. *It is enough for the plaintiff to narrate the fact simply in the libel* **Of the libel.**[28]

A plaintiff is not obliged to express his action in the libel, but it is enough if he recites the fact itself and the pure and simple truth of the matter, so that his right to act may be determined on this basis.

Whenever a judge has decided that a libel is foolish, he must absolve the accused, but in such a way that if the plaintiff presents a suitable and relevant libel, the accused shall nevertheless be obliged to respond.

17. Iudicium quando solvitur.[29]

Iudicium solvitur vetante eo qui iudicare iusserat, vel etiam eo qui maius imperium in eadem iurisdictione habet, vel etiam si ipse iudex eiusdem imperii esse coeperit, cuius est qui iudicare iussit.

Si unus ex litigatoribus habens procuratorem post litem contestatam decesserit, iudicium non solvitur. Nam iudex contra procuratorem tanquam dominum litis, usque [*ad*] sententiam inclusive procedere poterit: executio tamen contra executorem, seu bonorum administratorem de mortui, et non contra procuratorem fiet.

[190r] *17a. De foro iudiciali.*

Ubi ac*ceptum est semel iudicium, ibi et finem accipere debet.* [>Clericus in foro civili si quempiam convenerit, in eodem potest ab adversario suo reconveniri, ac ibidem iudicabitur, non tamen quoad criminalia, ubi coeptum est semel iudicium, ibi et finem accipere debet.<][30]

17b. De iudicio possessorio.[31]

Possessorium priusquam petitorium in iudiciis discutiatur.

Si de vi et possessione quaeratur, prius cognoscendum de vi quam de possessione rei decernimus.

18. De causis incidentibus.[32]

Quoties in causa et lite pendente coram iudice, aliqua causa incidens seu emergens concurrit, nihil prohibet quin [94b] apud eundem iudicem huiusmodi causa terminetur, licet principaliter super eandem cognoscere non possit.

[190v] Iudicium valet super emergenti, etiam super quo iudex non pronuntiat, sed ultra processit.

---

[29]*Dig.*, 5.1.58, originally Paulus, *Ad Sabinum*, 13; *ibid.*, 3.3.15, originally Ulpian, *Ad edictum*, 8.

[30]A marginal note in Cranmer's hand reads: 'Supra folio praecedente' ('Above, on the preceding folio'). It was eventually moved to 36.13 above.

[31]*Dig.*, 5.5.2, originally Caius, *Ad edictum provinciale*, 6; *ibid.*, 43.24.11.12, originally Ulpian, *Ad edictum*, 71; X, 2.12.2 (Fr, II, 276), originally a decretal of Pope Celestine III (1191-8); X, 2.12.3 (Fr, II, 276-7), originally a decretal of Pope Innocent III, 7 February 1200; X, 2.13.10 (Fr, II, 284), originally a decretal of Pope Lucius III (1181-5).

[32]*Speculum*, 1.1, *De officio omnium iudicum*, 8.5.

17. When a judgment is dissolved.[29]

A judgment is dissolved when either the person who ordered it or someone who has greater authority in the same jurisdiction forbids it to continue, and also if the judge himself is promoted to the same authority as the person who originally ordered the judgment to take place.

If one of the litigators has a proctor and should die after the issue is joined, the judgment is not dissolved. For the judge may proceed against the proctor as if he were the principal of the suit, up to and including the sentence, but the execution of it will be made against the executor or the administrator of the goods of the deceased, and not against the proctor.

17a. Of a judicial forum.

Once a hearing has begun in a particular place, it must also be brought to an end there. [>If a cleric has summoned someone to appear in a civil judgment, he can also be summoned to appear in the same judgment by his adversary, and there be judged, but not in criminal cases. Once **a hearing*** has begun in a particular place, it must also be brought to an end there.<][30]

17b. Of possessory judgment.[31]

Possessory judgments shall be deliberated before petitory ones.

If it is a question of power as well as possession, we order that the question of power must be heard before that of possession.

18. Of incidental causes.[32]

Whenever in a cause or suit pending before a judge, some other cause occurs or emerges alongside it, there is nothing to prevent that cause from being determined by the same judge, although he cannot hear it as if it were the main cause.

The judgment in an emergent cause is valid, even if the judge does not pronounce on it as such, but goes on beyond it.

18a. **Iudex dolo malo offendens damna partium persolvet.**[33]

Non quicquid iudicis potestati permittitur, id subiicitur iuris necessitati. Iudex si quid adversus legis praecepta in iudicando dolo malo praetermiserit, legem offendit, et damna partium (quae inde forte sequentur), persolvet.

19. Infra annum causae omnes terminentur.[34]

Cum nonnunquam lites plus iusto per superfluas allegationes et dilationes protelentur, ideo *tam* causas *spirituales quam* ecclesiasticas **omnes**, post litem contestatam, infra annum terminar[i/e] volumus; alias peribit instantia.

Si iudex negligens causam infra annum sua culpa non finierit, poena viginti librarum, fisco nostro solvenda, ultra [191r] interesse partium, punietur: et partes nihilominus, (nisi inter se concordarint), pergant coepta processus forma litem prosequi.

Si causa infra statuta tempora propter unius litigantium negligentiam non terminetur, tum iudex partem negligentem in expensis et damnis adversario restituendis, ac in poena decem librarum fisco nostro solvenda, condemnabit, et partes nisi inter se concordarint, coepta forma processus litem prosequent*em*/**ur**.

20. De officio iudicis.[35]

Iudici in causa **instantionata**, cuius instantia elapsa fuerit, testes et instrumenta recipere ex suo officio, ut tollatur omnis suspicio, non permittitur.

Iudices oportet imprimis rei qualitatem plena [191v] inquisitione discutere, et tunc utramque partem interrogare saepius, numquid novi addi desiderent: ac deinde tam [**in**] allegationibus facti, quam iuris pensatis, suam sententiam definitivam in scriptis proferre.

De qua re cognoverit iudex, de ea quoque pronuntiare per superiorem cogendus est.

---

[33]*Dig.*, 5.1.15, originally Ulpian, *Ad edictum*, 21.
[34]Cf. X, 1.29.4 (Fr, II, 158), originally a decretal of Pope Alexander III (1159-81), for the principle.
[35]*Inst.*, 4.17. Basically this is a summary of principles which can be found scattered throughout the canon law and the commentators.

18a. A judge who offends by malicious fraud shall pay the parties' damages.[33]

A judge is not allowed to do whatever he likes, but is subject to the demands of the law. If a judge does something in his judging by malicious fraud, against the precepts of the law, he offends against the law, and shall pay the damages of the parties (which may result from that).

19. All causes shall be terminated within a year.[34]

Since suits are sometimes prolonged beyond what is right by superfluous allegations and delays, therefore it is our will that **all** ecclesiastical causes, *both spiritual and ecclesiastical*, shall be brought to an end within a year after the issue is joined; otherwise an instance cause will die.

If a negligent judge has not brought a cause to an end within a year and the fault is his, he shall be punished with a penalty of twenty pounds payable to our treasury, as well as the expenses of the parties, but nevertheless the parties (unless they come to an agreement among themselves), may continue to pursue the issue according to the form of process already begun.

If a cause has not been brought to an end within the stated time because of the negligence of one of the litigants, then the judge shall condemn the negligent party to reimburse his opponent's expenses and damages, and to pay ten pounds to our treasury, and unless the parties have reached an agreement among themselves, they may pursue the issue according to the form of process already begun.

20. Of the office of a judge.[35]

In **an instance** cause, <u>whose time limit has expired</u>, in order for all suspicion to be removed, a judge is not allowed to accept witnesses and instruments *ex officio*.

First of all judges ought to deliberate the merits of the case by a full inquest, and then question both parties quite often, in case they wish to add anything new, and then he shall set out his final sentence in writing, both in allegations of fact and in considerations of law.

A judge is to be compelled by his superior to pronounce sentence in any case which he has heard.

20a. *Victus victori solvet impensas.*[36]

>*Victum victori iudex condemnabit in expensis, nisi iusta causa ei qui succumbit subveniat.*

Expensas litis iudicis est post sententiam in executione taxare, et deinde iuramentum super veritate earundem parti vincenti deferre.<[37]

Iudex post conclusionem in causa non potest ex suo officio [95a] aliquid facere, nisi super prius [192r] actitatis, si fuerint obscura.

21. Poena iudicis scienter ferent[i/e]s sententiam iniustam.[38]

Iudex *si litem suam faciat* parti ad interesse tenetur. *Iudex tunc litem suam facere intelligitur, cum dolo malo in fraudem legis sententiam dixerit; dolo malo hoc facere videtur* si evidenter arguatur eius sententia vel gratia, vel inimicitia, vel etiam sordibus lata: tunc volumus, ut veram aestimationem litis praestare cogatur.

22. Absens contumaciter non est audiendus si appellet.[39]

Sciendum est ex peremptorio absentem condemnatum, si appellet, non esse audiendum, si modo p*ro*/**er** contumaciam defuerit; sin minus, audietur.

23. De nondum adultis.[40]

Cum qui[**s**] ad aetatem adultam pervenerit, et a tutoribus liberat[u/**ore**]s sui iuris esse coeperit, per se aut [192v] per procuratorem iudicium suscipere posse certi iuris est. At infra id tempus, p[*er*/**ro**] se agere aut defendere non poterit, sed per tutores eius lites (cum inciderint) agitabuntur.[41]

---

[36]X, 5.37.4 (Fr, II, 881), c. 9 of the council of Tours, 1163.
[37]Transferred to 36.12 above.
[38]*Dig.*, 5.1.15, originally Ulpian, *Ad edictum*, 21.
[39]*Cod. Iust.*, 7.65.1, originally a rescript of the Emperor Antoninus, 7 July 214.
[40]VI, 2.1.3 (Fr, II, 996), originally a decretal of Pope Boniface VIII (1294-1303).
[41]A note in Foxe's hand reads: '"De officiis et iurisdictione omnium iudicum" require in folio 232'. ('"On offices and the jurisdiction of all judges" see on folio 232').

20a. *The loser shall pay expenses to the winner.*[36]

>The judge shall impose the winner's expenses on the loser, unless for some good reason he comes to the latter's aid.

It is the judge's responsibility to set the expenses of the suit once the sentence is in execution, and then to administer the oath concerning truth of these things to the winning party.<[37]

After the conclusion of the cause, the judge cannot do anything *ex officio*, except to clarify matters already dealt with, if they were obscure.

21. The penalty for a judge who knowingly imposes an unjust sentence.[38]

A judge is bound to the interest of the party, *if he makes a suit his own. A judge is understood to be making a suit his own when by malicious fraud he pronounces a sentence which is against the law; he appears to have done this by malicious fraud*, if it is openly proved that his sentence was imposed either because of favouritism, or hatred, or even greed, in which case we want him to be compelled to pay the true cost of the suit.

22. A person who is contumaciously absent is not to be heard if he appeals.[39]

It is to be understood that if an absentee has been condemned peremptorily and then appeals, he is not to be heard, as long as his absence was due to his contumacy. If not, he shall be heard.

23. Of those who are not yet adults.[40]

When someone reaches adult age and has been released from his guardians, he has a definite right to undertake a judgment either by himself or through a proctor. But until that time he cannot act or defend himself, and his suits (if there are any) shall be conducted by his guardians.[41]

[232r; 95a]   37. DE OFFICIO ET IURISDICTIONE OMNIUM
IUDICUM[1]

1. Iurisdictio ordinaria et delegata.[2]

Inter iurisdictionem ordinariam et delegatam hoc interest, quod ordinaria vel lege, vel privilegio, compositione aut consuetudine, delegata *quidem* **vero** ab homine datur et conceditur.

[95b] 2. Iurisdictio regis.[3]

Rex tam in archiepiscopos, episcopos, clericos, et alios ministros, quam in laicos infra sua regna et dominia plenissimam iurisdictionem, tam civilem quam ecclesiasticam, habet et exercere potest, cum omnis iurisdictio et ecclesiastica et saecularis ab eo tanquam ex uno et eodem fonte d[e/i]riva[n]tur.

3. Iurisdictio archiepiscopi, episcoporum, archidiaconorum et *etc.* aliorum.[4]

Archiepiscopi, episcopi infra suas dioeceses, et [232v] *capitulum*, *archiepiscopus*, **capitulum**, sede vacante, iurisdictionem ordinariam ex lege; archidiaconi vero ac ceteri ecclesiarum praelati solum ex privilegio, compositione, aut consuetudine praescripta acquirunt et habent.

 Iurisdictionem ordinariam ex privilegio, compositione, vel consuetudine praescripta ante has leges nostras ecclesiasticas per quemcunque ecclesiae praelatum acquisitam, in suo robore (ubi his [233r] legibus nostris non adversatur) permansuram fore iudicamus.

 Iurisdictionem ex privilegio, compositione, vel consuetudine praescripta, per archiepiscopos, antehac infra suas provincias usitatam (si his legibus nostris non repugnet) non solum consistere, sed etiam per eosdem in futurum exercere posse placuit.

---

[1]The headings in this chapter are all in Cranmer's hand. Numbers have been supplied for this edition.
[2]*Speculum*, 1.1, *De iurisdictione omnium iudicum*, preface.
[3]26 Henry VIII, c. 1, 1534 (*S.R.*, III, 492).
[4]VI, 1.16.5 (Fr, II, 988), originally a decretal of Pope Boniface VIII (1294-1303).

37. OF THE OFFICE AND JURISDICTION OF ALL JUDGES[1]

1. **Ordinary and delegated jurisdiction.**[2]

The difference between ordinary and delegated jurisdiction is that ordinary jurisdiction is appointed and granted by law, privilege, composition, or custom, *whereas* **but** delegated jurisdiction is appointed and granted by another person.

2. **The jurisdiction of the king.**[3]

The king has and can exercise the most complete jurisdiction, both civil and ecclesiastical, within his kingdoms and dominions as much over archbishops, bishops, clergy and other ministers, as over lay people, since all jurisdiction, both ecclesiastical and secular, is derived from him as from one and the same source.

3. **The jurisdiction of an archbishop, bishops, archdeacons and *etc.* others.**[4]

Archbishops, bishops within their dioceses, and when a see is vacant, the ***archbishop*** chapter acquire and have ordinary jurisdiction by law, but archdeacons and other prelates of the churches have it only by privilege, composition, or prescribed custom.

We order that ordinary jurisdiction acquired by privilege, composition or prescribed custom by any prelate of the church, before these our ecclesiastical laws were passed, shall continue and remain in force (where it does not conflict with these our laws).

Jurisdiction by privilege, composition or prescribed custom previously exercised by the archbishops within their provinces shall not only continue, but shall also be exercised by them in future (if it is not repugnant to these our laws).

4. Iudicis officium.[5]

Congruit bono et gravi iudici ex officio suo curare, ut pacata et quieta **et ad pietatem dedita** iurisdictio sit, quam regit; quod non difficile obtinebit, si sollicite *agat ut* **de** malis hominibus *iurisdictio careat, eosque* conquirat, et prout quisque deliquerit, in eum animadvertat, atque fama vel i[n/**u**]diciis potest iudex descendere ad inquisitionem.

[96a] 5. Iurisdictio delegata.[6]

Cui iurisdictio data est, ea quoque concessa esse videtur, sine quibus iurisdictio explicari non potuit; et ideo potest delegatus partes citare, et contumaces severitate ecclesiastica [233v] coercere, etiamsi litterae commissionis id non contineant.

6. Iurisdictio episcoporum et praelatorum.[7]

Habeant episcopi in suis dioecesibus, et alii ecclesiarum praelati in suis iurisdictionibus, liberam potestatem de adulteriis et sceleribus, quae ad suum forum pertinent, inquire*re*/**ndi**, ulcisce*re*/**ndi**, et iudica*re*/**ndi**, absque impedimento alicuius. Et cum opus fuerit, iudicium convocent saeculare.

7. De loco iudicii.[8]

Placuit, ut episcopus in quolibet loco suae dioeceseos, et archidiaconus, et alii praelati iurisdictionem habentes in locis solitis per se vel per alium sedere pro tribunali, causas ecclesiasticas audire, delinquentium excessus corrigere, et cetera, [234r] quae ad [*suum*] officium spectant, libere exercere poss[i/**u**]nt. Nemo tamen pro tribunali, in quo[**rum**]cunque loco, sedere de consensu ordinarii loci prohibeatur.

8. Archiepiscopi privilegium.[9]

Archiepiscopus potest eligi in iudicem a subditis suffraganeorum, licet suffraganei ig/n/orent.

---

[5]*Speculum*, 1.1, *De iurisdictione omnium iudicum*, 2.1.
[6]Cf. X, 1.29.11 (Fr, II, 161), originally a decretal of Pope Alexander III (1159-81).
[7]VI, 1.16.7 (Fr, II, 988), originally a decretal of Pope Boniface VIII (1294-1303).
[8]L, 2.2.4, c. 25 of Archbishop John Stratford's council of 1342.
[9]Hostiensis on X, 1.31.11.

4. The office of a judge.[5]

It is fitting for a good and sober judge to ensure by reason of his office that the jurisdiction which he governs shall be peaceful and quiet, **and dedicated to godliness,** which he will achieve without difficulty, if he carefully *acts so that his jurisdiction is empty of* **subdues** human evils, *and subdues them,* and that each time anyone sins he punishes him, and the judge may initiate an inquest on the basis of rumour or [evidence **judgments**].

5. Delegated jurisdiction.[6]

To the person to whom a jurisdiction is delegated, those things without which the jurisdiction cannot be exercised will also be assumed to be granted, and therefore a delegated judge may cite parties and compel the contumacious by ecclesiastical punishment, even if the letters of his commission do not include this.

6. The jurisdiction of bishops and prelates.[7]

In matters of adultery and crimes, bishops in their dioceses and other prelates of the churches in their jurisdictions shall have every power of inquest, punishment and judgment which belongs to their court, without any impediment. And when necessary, they may call upon secular judgment.

7. Of the place of judgment.[8]

A bishop may sit on the bench, hear ecclesiastical causes, correct the excesses of delinquents, and freely exercise everything else which pertains to [*his* **the**] office, in any place in his diocese, in person or through some other judge, as may also the archdeacon and other prelates who have jurisdiction in the usual places. Nevertheless, no one shall be prevented from sitting on the bench in any place whatsoever, if he has the local ordinary's consent.

8. The archbishop's privilege.[9]

An archbishop may be chosen as judge by the subjects of his suffragans, even if the suffragans are unaware of it.

9. Poena in contumaces.[10]

Iudices ecclesiastici in contumaces et non oboedientes poenas ecclesiasticas proferant, atque eccleslasticae iurisdictionis contemptores huiusmodi poenis coerceant.

[96b] ## 10. Cancellarius.[11]

Vicarius episcopi iudex est ordinarius, neque iurisdictionem habet subdelegatam. Vicarii iurisdictio, eo mortuo qui eum fecit vicarium, desinit.[12]

[234v] ## 11. Aetas iudicis.[13]

Iudex non deputetur minor viginti quinque annis.

12. Quando impune non paretur iudici.[14]

Extra territor[i/-]um ius dicenti impune non paretur. Idem est {*et*/**ac**} si supra iurisdictionem suam velit ius dicere.

13. *Qui delegare iudices possunt.* De delegatione iurisdictionis.[15]

More maiorum ita comp[*er*/**ara**]tum est, ut is demum iurisdictionem mandare possit, qui eam suo iure, non alieno beneficio, habet.

Cui aliqua causa est delegata, illam alteri /sub/delegare non potest, nisi a nostra regia maiestate causa fuerit ei commissa. Nam tunc non solum delegare potest, sed etiam alios cogere ad causam acceptandam, quam ipsis delegaverit; si tamen industria personae eius in commissione causae [235r] depraehendatur elect[*a*/**or**], ipsam totam delegare non poterit. **Delegatus tamen nostrae maiestatis subdelegato suo non potest dare facultatem subdelegandi.**

---

[10]X, 2.1.1 (Fr, II, 239), possibly from an African council.

[11]VI, 1.4.2 (Fr, II, 944), originally a decretal of Pope Boniface VIII (1294-1303).

[12]VI, 1.14.15 (Fr, I, 982-3), originally a decretal of Pope Boniface VIII.

[13]This was the age of majority in Roman law, *Dig.*, 4.4.1, originally Ulpian, *Ad edictum*, 11. But cf. X, 1.29.41 (Fr, II, 182), originally a decretal of Pope Gregory IX (1227-41), published on or before 5 September 1234, where the age was twenty, and *Dig.*, 42.1.57, originally Ulpian, *Disputationes*, 2, where eighteen was allowed.

[14]*Dig.*, 2.1.20, originally Paulus, *Ad edictum*, 1.

[15]VI, 1.14.12 (Fr, II, 980-1); VI, 1.14.15 (Fr, II, 982-3), both originally decretals of Pope Boniface VIII. Here the king has taken the place of the pope.

9. The penalty for the contumacious.[10]

Ecclesiastical judges shall impose ecclesiastical penalties on the contumacious and disobedient, and they shall coerce the despisers of ecclesiastical jurisdiction by similar penalties.

10. A chancellor.[11]

The bishop's deputy is an ordinary judge and does not have delegated jurisdiction.

    The jurisdiction of a deputy ceases on the death of the one who appointed him his deputy.[12]

11. The age of a judge.[13]

No one under twenty-five years of age shall be appointed a judge.

12. When a judge may not act with impunity.[14]

The one who pronounces the law is not allowed to act with impunity outside his territory. This applies even if he wants to pronounce the law concerning his own jurisdiction.

13. *Who may delegate judges.* Of the delegation of jurisdiction.[15]

It has been established by ancestral custom that the only person who can delegate jurisdiction is the one who has it by right, not by some other benefit.

    If a cause has been delegated to someone, that person cannot subdelegate it to another unless the cause has been entrusted to him by our royal majesty. For then not only can he delegate, but he can also compel others to take the cause which he has delegated to them, but even if the energy of the person to whom the cause has been entrusted is found to be exceptional, he still may not delegate the whole thing to him. **[*Only* Nevertheless] someone delegated by our majesty cannot give the power of delegation to his subdelegate.**

Delegatus etiam maiestatis nostrae non potest subdelegare, adiiciendo hanc clausulam, appellatione remota, licet ipse cum ea fuerit delegatus.[16]

Solvi mandatum non dubitatur, si is, [*qui*] mandaverit iurisdictionem, decesserit, antequam res ab eo, cui mandata est, geri coeperit.

Potest iudex ordinarius suam iurisdictionem mandare, et aut omnem mandat, aut speciem unam. Nam et is, cui mandata iurisdictio est, fungitur vice eius, qui [97a] mandavit, non sua.

Delegatus regius vices *regiae maiestatis* **nostras** gerit; unde in causa illa superior est et maior illis, quorum causam suscepit terminandam. Ideo si quis litigantium rebellis [*au*/e]t contumax fuerit, *servi* **secundum** qualitatem facti poterit a iudice delegato per censuras ecclesiasticas coerceri.

[235v] Delegatus *regiae maiestatis* potestatem habet non solum in partes principales, sed etiam in alios, qui suam iurisdictionem impediant, ac eos districtione ecclesiastica coercer[*e*/i] poterit.

Delegatio facta dignitati, non expresso nomine personae, ad successorem transit, nisi fortasse in commissione fiat mentio anteactae vitae, doctrinae, aut acuminis, et similium, quae personam, non dignitatem, describunt. Sin vero fiat per nomen proprium, morte delegati expirat.[17]

Delegatio causae illis quoque personis fieri potest, quae fuer[*i*/u]nt inferiores partibus litigantibus.

[236r] Si duobus causa committitur, etiamsi non in[s/f]eritur, ut unus sine altero procedat, *procedat* in ea, nihilominus unus ex ipsis sive suo coniudici, sive alii, vices suas committere potest.

Si causa tribus committitur, cum clausula, quod si omnes interesse nequiverint, duo eam nihilominus exequantur, priusquam de impotentia tertii appareat, duo nihil in causa agere valeant: sed si aliquis ex ipsis, cum possit, noluerit interesse, tunc duo in causa procedant, licet tertius sit arguendus, pro eo quod mandata/**um** superioris subterfugiat aut contemnat, idem quoque per omnia dicimus observandum, in causa quae committitur duobus, eo [*a*/o]pposito, ut si ambo interesse nequiverint, alter nihilominus exequatur.[18]

[236v] Iurisdictio pluribus delegata sine conditione, si non omnes interesse possint, qui vale[a]nt adesse, procedant; uno eorum mortuo expirat.

Si plures iudices delegati fuerint, omnes oportet actis interesse, nisi expressum [*fuerit* **sit**] in commissione, aliquo vel aliqui[97b]bus eorum non valentibus adesse, reliquos debere in causa procedere: quo tamen casu, collega sive collegae debent a reliquis requiri, an poss[i/u]nt an velint adesse.[19]

---

[16]Moved by Cranmer from the following section.

[17]X, 1.29.14 (Fr, II, 162), originally a decretal of Pope Alexander III (1159-81).

[18]X, 1.29.21 (Fr, II, 164-6), originally a decretal fo Pope Celestine III (1191-8).

[19]X, 1.29.22 (Fr, II, 166), originally a decretal of Pope Innocent III, 1 November 1198.

Also, a person delegated by our majesty cannot subdelegate by adding this clause: 'without appeal', even if it was part of the delegation as given to him.[16]

There is no doubt that a delegate's mandate is dissolved if the person who mandated the jurisdiction should die before the matter mandated by him has begun to be handled by him.

An ordinary judge can mandate his jurisdiction, and he may mandate the whole of it or only a part. For the person to whom the jurisdiction is mandated acts on behalf of the person who mandated him, not on his own behalf.

A royal delegate acts on **our** behalf *of the king's majesty*, for which reason he is in that cause superior to, and greater than, those whose cause he has undertaken to determine. Therefore, if any of the litigants has been rebellious or contumacious, he may be coerced by the delegated judge by ecclesiastical censures in accordance with the seriousness of the matter.

A delegate *of the king's majesty* has power not only over the principal parties but also over others who may impede his jurisdiction, and he may coerce them by ecclesiastical punishment.

A delegation made to a dignity passes to a successor when the name of the individual is not specified, unless it happens that in the commission mention is made of some preceding life, doctrine or ability, and such things, which describe the individual and not the dignity. But if it is made by proper name, it shall expire on the death of the delegate.[17]

The delegation of a cause may also be made to persons who were inferior to the litigating parties.

If a cause is entrusted to two delegates, even if it is not inserted that one may proceed with it without the other, nevertheless, one of them may entrust his powers either to his co-judge or to someone else.

If the cause is entrusted to three delegates, with a clause which states that if they cannot all be present, nevertheless two of them may undertake it, the two must not do anything in the cause before the inability of the third becomes clear, but if one of them does not wish to be present, even though he is able to be, then the two shall proceed in the cause, although the third may be charged on the ground that he has undermined or despised the orders of his superior. And we say that the same must be observed in all things, in a cause which is entrusted to two, with this added, that if both are unable to be present, the one who can be shall nevertheless proceed.[18]

If a jurisdiction is delegated to several people without any condition, but not all of them can be present, those who can shall proceed; but if one of them dies the jurisdiction shall expire.

If several judges have been delegated, all of them ought to be present for the hearings unless it is explicitly stated in the commission that if one or more of them is unable to be there, the others should proceed in the cause. But in that case, a colleague or colleagues must be requested by the others, if they can and are willing to come.[19]

Licet delegatus ordinarii inferioris a principe subdelegare non possit, tamen unam speciem, sive aliquam partem eiusdem causae committere licitum existat.[20]

[237r] Delegatum ordinarii inferioris a principe ad universitatem causarum subdelegare posse non dubitatur, cum ordinarius et delegatus ad universitatem causarum in iure propemodum assimulantur.

Delegatus, si sit de iurisdictione delegantis, onus commissionis in se suscipere tenetur sub poena contemptus.[21]

14. Iurisdictio delegati re integra morte mandantis expirat.[22]

Si quis se asserat /esse/ delegatum principis, vel cum mandatis secretis missum, sciant omnes ei, (cuiuscunque sit dignitatis), non esse credendum, nisi id scriptis probaverit.

[237v] Si delegatus pronuntiaverit se iurisdictionem non habere, ipsam etiam de consensu partium non reassumat.[23]

Subdelegatus, postquam coepit causam cognoscere, non potest per delegantem removeri. Vicarius autem episcopi removeri potest, quandocunque voluerit episcopus, quia non est eius delegatus.[24]

Delegatus iure regiae maiestatis subdelegato suo non potest dare facultatem subdelegandi.

Delegatus etiam regiae maiestatis iure non potest subdelegare adiiciendo hanc clausulam, appellatione remota; licet ipse cum ea fuerit delegatus.[25]

Subdelegatus inferioris a principe aliquem [238r] articulum causae potest subdelegare, et actum (ut appellant) **non**[26] iurisdiction[*al*]em, quemadmodum est citatio, et similia.

Causa potest alicui delegari hoc mandato, ne ad eius decisionem procedatur, nisi adhibito consilio vel delegantis, vel nominati alicuius prudentis viri; quod si fiat, necessarium erit, subdelegatum priusquam sententiam ferat, consilium audire iuxta mandatum: non tamen cogetur iuxta illud ferre sententiam. Poss[*e*/**i**]t enim fieri, ut esset iniustum, et contrarium ordini iuris; et sententia[**m**] tum secundum conscientiam [98a] tum secundum iura ferenda est.

Illi, cui commissum fuerit excommunicare, vel absolvere [238v] aliquos, vel pro delictis paenitentias iniungere, liceat hoc demandare; quia non sibi

---

[20]X, 1.29.27 (Fr, II, 171-2), originally a decretal of Pope Innocent III, 27 March 1204.
[21]X, 1.29.28 (Fr, II, 172-3), originally a decretal of Pope Innocent III, 19 December 1203.
[22]A marginal note in Foxe's hand explains that this is the title of the next section. It reads simply: 'Titulus.'
[23]Rubric to X, 1.29.30 (Fr, II, 175), a decretal of Pope Innocent III (1198-1216); X, 1.29.31 (Fr, II, 175), originally a decretal of Pope Innocent III, 23 August 1208.
[24]X, 1.29.37 (Fr, II, 181), originally a decretal of Pope Honorius III (1216-27).
[25]Moved by Cranmer to the preceding section.
[26]Added by Foxe.

Although the delegate of an ordinary who is lower than the king cannot subdelegate, nevertheless he may lawfully entrust one aspect or one part of the cause to someone else.[20]

There shall be no doubt that anyone delegated to the whole range of causes by an ordinary lower than the king shall be able to subdelegate, since the ordinary and a plenary delegate are practically one and the same.

If a delegate is from the jurisdiction of the one delegating, he is obliged to undertake the burden of the commission, under pain of contempt.[21]

14. The jurisdiction of a delegate expires on the death of the one delegating, if the case has not yet begun.[22]

If someone claims /to be/ a delegate of the king, or to have been sent with secret orders, let all know that he is not to be believed (whatever his dignity), unless he proves it in writing.

If a delegate has decreed that he does not have jurisdiction, he shall not take it up again, even with the agreement of the parties.[23]

A subdelegate, once he has begun to hear the cause, cannot be removed by the one delegating him. But a bishop's deputy may be removed whenever the bishop wishes to do so, because he is not his delegate.[24]

A delegate in right of subdelegation by the king's majesty cannot grant the power of subdelegating.

Also, a delegate in right of the king's majesty cannot subdelegate by adding the clause: 'without appeal', even if it was part of the delegation as given to him.[25]

A subdelegate of someone lower than the king can subdelegate some section of the cause, as well as a **non**[26] jurisdictional act, such as citation and similar things.

A cause may be delegated to someone with this order, that he shall not proceed to decide it unless he seeks the advice of the person delegating or of some prudent man who has been named, but if that happens, it shall be necessary for the subdelegate, before he pronounces the sentence, to take advice according to his mandate, but he shall not be compelled to pronounce sentence according to that advice. For it may happen that it is unjust and contrary to the order of law, and a sentence is to be pronounced both according to conscience and according to the laws.

Anyone empowered to excommunicate, or absolve people, or enjoin penances for sins, may also delegate the same, because it is not a jurisdiction but

iurisdictio, sed certum ministerium potius committitur: et tamen excommunicare potest impedientes eum exercere suum ministerium iniunctum, ne illusoria et sine exitu esset talis commissio.

A delegato ad delegantem appellari debere non ambigitur.

Est receptum ut si [*quis*] maior vel aequalis subiiciat se iurisdictioni alterius, possit **et pro** eo et adversus eum ius dici.[27]

Omnis reus apud proprium iudicem debet conveniri.

[239r] 15. **Audiat iudex tantum ea quae suae sunt iurisdictionis.**[28]

Primum debet iudex, quando a[**u**]dit{*ur*}, id explorare, an iurisdictio earum rerum, personarum, aut criminum, quae in iudicio proponuntur, ad se pertineat: cumque illi constiterit ea suae iurisdictionis esse, iudicandi munus aggrediatur. Sin vero animadvert[*er*]it ad suam iurisdictionem non pertinere, causam remittat ad proprium iudicem, reum ab observatione sui tribunalis absolvat, et actorem in expensis, si quae intercesserint, condemnabit.

[>15a. **Quattuor modis potest reus forum sortiri.**

Rei *quinque* **quattuor** rationibus forum sortiuntur; aut propter domicilium (a iudice quippe loci ubi quis habitat est iudicandus); aut ob delictum commissum (ibi enim quis iudicatur, ubi peccatum admisit et depraehensus fu[**er**]it); aut ob locum ubi sita res fuerit de qua contenditur (nam si de beneficio ecclesiastico, aut de *agris vel domibus* **decimis agrorum aut domuum**, [239v] litigetur, iudex loci earum rerum est adeundus); aut propter locum contractus: (siquidem ubi quis contraxit, plerumque de contractu est litigandum).<][29] *Demum sortiuntur quandoque forum propter originem, ibi videtur ut quis iudicetur unde est oriundus; quae causa movit Pilatum ut Christum remitteret ad Herodem, nempe audito quod est Galilaeus.*[30]

Actor sequatur forum rei.

Quando reus conveniri potest in pluribus locis, tunc est in arbitrio rei **actoris** *positum, ubi velit eum convenire.*

---

[27]*Dig.*, 2.1.4, originally Ulpian, *Ad edictum*, 39.
[28]X, 1.29.38 (Fr, II, 181), originally a decretal of Pope Gregory IX (1227-41), published on or before 5 September 1234; VI, 1.16.5 (Fr, II, 988), originally a decretal of Pope Boniface VIII (1294-1303).
[29]A marginal note in Foxe's hand reads: 'De foro competenti', which is the title of the next section. A note in Cranmer's hand reads: 'Ponatur hoc in titulo "De iudiciis, etc."'. ('Put this in the chapter "On judgments, etc."'). This seems to be an error for 'De foro iudiciali' (36.14) which is where the text was subsequently moved.
[30]Lk. xxiii. 6.

only a particular function which is entrusted to him, but he may excommunicate any who hinder him from exercising his appointed ministry, so that this commission may not appear to be illusory and without effect.

There is no doubt that an appeal may be made from a delegate to the one who delegated him.

It is accepted that if someone greater or equal submits himself to the jurisdiction of another, the law may be pronounced **either for** him or against him.[27]

Every accused person must be summoned before his own judge.

15. A judge shall hear only those cases which belong to his jurisdiction.[28]

First of all, when a case is heard, a judge must examine it to see whether the jurisdiction over these things, persons or crimes presented for judgment belongs to him, and if he confirms that they are within his jurisdiction, the task of judging shall proceed. But if he notices that the cause does not belong to his jurisdiction, he shall refer it to the proper judge, shall release the accused from having to obey his court and shall order the plaintiff to pay expenses, if there have been any.

[>15a. An accused person may be allocated a court in four ways.

An accused person may be allocated a court in *five* **four** ways, either because of his domicile (the place where a person resides is to be determined by the judge), or on account of the crime committed (for a man shall be judged in the place where he committed the crime and was arrested), or according to the place where the thing which is being contested is situated. (For if the litigation concerns an ecclesiastical benefice, or **tithes on** fields or houses, the judge of the place where those things are is to be called). Or according to the place of the contract, if someone has signed a contract somewhere and most of the litigation is about the contract.<][29] *Finally whenever possible, they shall allocate a court according to the person's origin, so that he may be judged in the place where he comes from. This was the factor which caused Pilate to send Christ to Herod, for it was heard that he was a Galilean.*[30]

The plaintiff shall go to the court of the accused.

When an accused person can be summoned in several places, then it shall be left to the discretion of the accused ***plaintiff in the case*** *where he wishes to* summon him.

16. De foro competenti.[31]

Clerici litigaturi suum episcopum seu eius vicarium adeant, et absque illius consensu et voluntate in nullum alium iudicem consentiant.

[240r]*Cum ordinarius delegavit aut rex suum munus delegatum oportet adire.* De criminibus mere ecclesiasticis nemo quenquam nisi apud iudicem ecclesiasticum conveniat.

17. Causae ecclesiasticae.[32]

Hae sunt vero causae subsequentes iurisdictionis ecclesiasticae, beneficiales, matrimoniales et divortii, causae testamentariae, et bonorum administrationis defunctorum, subtractionis legatorum, mortuariorum, decimarum, obla[98b]tionum et aliorum iurium ecclesiasticorum, necnon et usurarum, et haeresium, incestus, adulterii, fornicationis, sacrilegii, periurii, blasphemiae, fidei laesionis, defamationis, et convitii, iniectionis manuum violentarum in clericum, perturbationis divinorum, [240v] morum correctionis et reformationis, computus ecclesiarum et oeconomorum, causaeque debiti ecclesiis earumque ministris, reparationis et dilapidationis ecclesiae, coemeterii, ac aliorum aedificiorum ecclesiasticorum. In his namque causis cum suis incidentibus, emergentibus, dependentibus, et connexis quibuscunque, atque in omnibus aliis causis, quod ad correctionem peccati spectat, iudex ecclesiasticus, et nullus alius, se intromittat, cognoscat, [e/**au**]t iudicet.

Causa vero iurispatronatus et annuae pensionis ecclesiasticae ita coniuncta et connexa est spiritualibus causis, quod non nisi ecclesiastico iudicio valeat definiri.

[241r] 18. De recusatione iudicis.[33]

Ordinarius iudex quando ut suspectus recusatus fuerit, expeditum et consultum id est, ut sine mora causam alicui deleget, in quem partes, tanquam in non suspectum, consentiant. Quod si iusta aliqua ratione motus facere nolit, causas suspicionis a recusante coram se iubeat assignari, de quibus an iustae sint cognoscent et pronuntiabunt arbitri, vel a litigantibus, vel a iudice et reo (si nullus fuerit actor) electi; et ne res diutius p[ro/**er**]trahatur, terminus arbitris est praefigendus, quo de caus[is/**a**] suspicionis constituant, an iustae vel iniustae

---

[31]X, 2.2.1 (Fr, II, 248), originally c. 9 of the council of Chalcedon, 451 (*C.O.D.*, 91); X, 2.2.2 (Fr, II, 248-9), originally c. 6 of the council of Paris, 615.
[32]9 Edward II, c. 1, 1316 (*S.R.*, I, 171-4).
[33]X, 1.29.39 (Fr, II, 181-2), originally a decretal of Pope Gregory IX (1227-41), published on or before 5 September 1234; X, 2.2.4 (Fr, II, 249), originally a decretal of Pope Gregory I (590-604), *Reg.*, 11.77.

16. Of the competent court.[31]

Clergy who want to litigate shall go to their own bishop or his deputy, and they shall agree on no other judge without his consent and will.

When the ordinary or the king has delegated his office, it is necessary to go to the delegate. Concerning crimes which are purely ecclesiastical, no one shall summon anybody except to an ecclesiastical judge.

17. Ecclesiastical causes.[32]

The following causes belong to the ecclesiastical jurisdiction: benefices, matrimony and divorce, testaments, the administration of the goods of the deceased, the deduction of legacies, mortuaries, tithes, offerings and other ecclesiastical rights, as well as usury, heresies, incest, adultery, fornication, sacrilege, perjury, blasphemy, breach of faith, defamation and slander, laying violent hands on a clergyman, disturbance of divine services, correction and reform of behaviour, the accounts of churches and churchwardens, and causes involving debt owed to churches or their ministers, repair and dilapidation of a church, cemetery and other ecclesiastical buildings. Furthermore in causes which accidentally emerge during any of these, or are dependent on any of them, or linked with any of them, and in all other causes which have to do with the correction of sin, the ecclesiastical judge and none other shall get involved, hear it and pass judgment.

And a cause of patronage and the annual church pension is so related and connected to spiritual causes that it is not valid unless it is decided by an ecclesiastical judgment.

18. Of the rejection of a judge.[33]

When an ordinary judge is rejected as suspect, it is fitting and proper for him to delegate the cause without delay to someone else, whom the parties can agree on as not being suspect. But if there is some good reason why he does not want to do this, he shall order the reasons for suspicion to be presented before him by the person rejecting, and arbitrators chosen by the litigants, or by the judge and the accused (if there is no plaintiff), shall find out whether they are justified and decide on them. And so that the matter is not drawn out, a time limit is to be given to the arbitrators, within which they must decide whether the cause[*s*]

videantur; qui si non concordarint, una pars unum, et altera alterum del[*i*/e]g{*a*/e}t, qui intra certum terminum pronuntient. [241v] At si non consenserint, ad se tertium advocent, et quod duo decreverint, id esto iudicatum. Et si definitum fuerit suspicionis causas non esse iustas, tum ordinarius munere suo fungatur. Sin vero pronuntientur iustae, ordinarius aut litigantes transmittat ad superiorem iudicem, vel det illis delegatum, in quem tanquam in non suspectum consentiant. Cum vero iudex ordinarius fuerit vicarius episcopi, [99a] aut inferior episcopo, tum episcopus ipse de causis suspicionis iudicabit, neque arbitros adhibere opus erit, nisi episcopus forte extra dioecesim fuerit, aut in loco mult[*um*/o] distanti agat; nam tunc arbitri, prout dictum est, eligentur.

19. Causae recusationis.[34]

Causae, quibus iudex recusari potest, permultae sunt: [242r] ut si recusans *causam* cum iudice, tanquam cum privato, causam habeat: si iudex cum recusantis dignitate causam habeat: si iudex noluit recusantem admittere ad osculum pacis, vel ea exhibere illi officia, quae his praestare mos est, qui sunt paris aut consimilis gradus: si iudex minatus fuerit parti, se velle illi nocere, si praebeatur occasio: si noluerit eum salutare, ut antea consueverat: si iudex cum inimicis recusantis frequenter versatur: si mortem aut gravia damna conatus est inferre: si accusavit eum criminaliter: si iudex sit dominus partis adversae: si sit eius vasallus: si sit eius suffraganeus: si consanguineus: si fuit advocatus partis **adversae** in eadem causa: si iudex habet cum alio consimilem causam. Potest denique iudex [242v] *denique* recusari, si partis sit socius, aut [**si**] *concanonicus* concanonicus, aut si simul habitet, aut si partis fuerit doctor, aut discipulus; *au*/et si quae aliae inveniuntur causae harum similes.

20. A iudice iuste recusato potest appellari.[35]

Iudex suspectus, qui recusatus fuerit iuste, ac secundum formam nostrarum legum, si recusationem non admiserit, ab eo appelletur.
    Extra suam dioecesim iudicii causa nullus trahatur invitus.

---

[34]X, 2.1.18 (Fr, II, 246), originally a decretal of Pope Innocent III, *c*.1206-7.
[35]Cf. *Cod. Iust.*, 7.62.30, originally a rescript of the emperors Arcadius and Honorius, 7 June 399. See also Panormitanus on X, 2.1.12.

appear[s] to be justified or not. If they do not agree, one party shall appoint one of the arbitrators and the other party the other, and the two of them shall decide within a fixed period. But if they do not agree, they shall call a third person to join them, and what two of them decide shall stand as the judgment. And if it is decided that the causes of suspicion are not justified, then the ordinary shall exercise his duty. But if it is decided that they are justified, the ordinary shall either transfer the litigants to a higher judge, or shall appoint a delegate for them, whom they agree is not suspect. And when the ordinary judge is the bishop's deputy, or inferior to the bishop, then the bishop himself shall assess the causes of suspicion, and there will be no need to appoint arbiters unless the bishop happens to be out of the diocese, or working in some very distant place, for then arbitrators shall be elected as has been said above.

19. **Reasons for rejection.**[34]

The reasons for which a judge may be rejected are many: if the person rejecting him is laying a suit against the judge as a private person, if the judge has a suit against the dignity of the rejecting party, if the judge does not want to admit the rejecting party to the kiss of peace, or perform those services for him which it is customary to offer to those who are of equal or similar rank, if the judge has threatened the party, saying that he wanted to do him harm if the opportunity should present itself, if he has been unwilling to greet him as he was formerly used to doing, if the judge spends a lot of time with enemies of the rejecting party, if he has tried to inflict death or serious damages, if he has made a criminal accusation against him, if the judge is the master of the other party, or if he is his servant, if he is his suffragan or blood relative, if he has ever been the **other** party's advocate in the same cause, if the judge has a similar cause against someone else. Finally, the judge can be rejected if he is a colleague of the party, or a fellow canon, or if they live together, or if he has been the party's teacher or pupil, *or* **and** if any other reasons similar to these are discovered.

20. **It is possible to appeal from a judge who has been justifiably rejected.**[35]

A suspect judge who has been justifiably rejected, and if he has not accepted this rejection according to the form of our laws, may be appealed from.

Nobody shall be taken out of his diocese against his will for the sake of judgment.

21. Episcopus non delegat causam extra dioecesim.[36]

Ordinarius non deleg{*e*/**a**}t causas ad se pertinentes ad locum extra dioecesim, nisi fortasse partes tum temporis ibi commorentur.

[99b] 22. Episcopos negligentes archiepiscopus corripiet.[37]

Si episcopus fuerit negligens in administranda iustitia, pertinet ad eius archiepiscopum ipsum compellere ad ius dicendum, illique terminum praescribet, quem si non [243r] observaveri[**n**]t absque legitimo impedimento, non modo censuris ecclesiasticis puniet, verum et in aestimationem iustam litis damnabit.

Iudex negligens modo fuerit interpellatus, litem facit suam, et in aestimationem iustam litis condemnabitur.

Si quis iudex laicus clericis aut ecclesiasticis personis iustitiam administrare deneget, tertio de hoc requisitus iurisdictionem suam amittat.

Iudex ecclesiasticus inhibere potest iudici laico, ne in illa causa procedat, quae ab ea pendet, quam ipse actu cognoscit.

23. De delegatione ad tempus.[38]

Instantia elapsa, iudex in causa nihil ulterius aget. Quae prius tamen acta fuer[*i*/**u**]nt non per*h*ibunt, [243v] sed ad litem p[*er*/**ro**]sequendam sub altero iudice inservient: si qua tamen post [*elapsam*] instantiam fiant, pro cassis et irritis habebuntur.

De causis quae infra certum tempus decidendae committuntur, statutum est, quod nisi dies praefixus de communi consensu partium prorogetur, [*eo*] transact[*o*/**um**] mandatum expirat.

24. Iudex non habenti advocatum providere potest.[39]

Quoniam litigando pars compelli non potest ad respondendum, nisi advocatum habeat, ad officium iudicis [**non**] pertinebit advocatum illi parti providere, quae advocatum habere non potest, et si videatur, suum domesticum dare poterit.

---

[36]Cf. VI, 1.16.5 (Fr, II, 988), originally a decretal of Pope Boniface VIII (1294-1303); VI, 2.2.1 (Fr, II, 996-7), originally a decretal of Pope Innocent IV (1243-54).

[37]X, 1.10. 3 (Fr, II, 116), originally a decretal of Pope Innocent III (1198-1216); X, 1.31.13 (Fr, II, 191), originally c. 7 of Lateran IV, 1215 (*C.O.D.*, 237).

[38]X, 1.29.4 (Fr, II, 158), originally a decretal of Pope Alexander III (1159-81); X, 1.29.24 (Fr, II, 169-70), originally a decretal of Pope Innocent III.

[39]X, 1.32.1 (Fr, II, 194-5), originally a decretal of Pope Honorius III (1216-27).

21. A bishop shall not delegate a cause outside the diocese.[36]

The ordinary shall not delegate causes belonging to him to a place outside the diocese, unless it happens that the parties are dwelling there temporarily.

22. The archbishop shall discipline negligent bishops.[37]

If a bishop has been negligent in administering justice, it is the duty of his archbishop to compel him to pronounce the law and to prescribe a time limit for him, and if he does not observe it without lawful impediment, not only shall the archbishop punish him with ecclesiastical censures but he shall also force him to pay a reasonable sum for the expenses of the suit.

A negligent judge who has been accused creates his own suit, and he shall be obliged to pay a reasonable sum for the expenses of the suit.

If some lay judge refuses to administer justice to clergy or to ecclesiastical persons, he shall lose his jurisdiction after having been asked for the third time.

An ecclesiastical judge may inhibit a lay judge from proceeding in a cause which depends on one which he is in the process of hearing.

23. Of temporary delegation.[38]

If the commission has expired, the judge shall do no more in the cause. But what has already been done will not be lost, but will carry over to the prosecution of the suit under another judge, yet if it happens after the commission [*expires*], it shall be regarded as null and void.

As for causes which are set to be decided within a fixed time, it is determined that unless the set day is postponed by the common agreement of the parties, the mandate shall expire when the date has passed.

24. The judge may provide an advocate to someone who does not have one.[39]

Since a party, when litigating, cannot be compelled to answer if he does not have an advocate, it shall [**not**] be the judge's duty to provide an advocate for that party which cannot have an advocate, and if it shall seem right, he may give him a member of his own staff.

Potest etiam cogere quem voluerit alium advocatum ad patrocinandum indigenti pro congrua mercede, quam potest ei solvere; et si omnino solvere non possit, ad gratis patrocinandum.

[244r] 25. **Iudex fugientem repetere potest a iudice loci ad quem fug[*eri*/ia]t.**[40]

Quando grave delictum commissum fuerit, iudex eius loci /potest petere a iudice loci/ quo reus fugi[a]t, ut illum ad se [*re*]mittat.

[100a] 26. **Iudices mutuo opem ferre debent.**[41]

Sententia lata a iudice loci, ubi delinquitur, vel ubi domicilium habetur a reo, executioni mandetur (si oportuerit) a iudice, in cuius *dioecesi* ditione rei sita sunt bona, modo a iudice, qui sententiam tulit, id requiratur: quandoquidem iudex unius dioeceseos non potest exequi in alia dioecesi.

27. **Iudex aliis excommunicatum absolvendi ius committere potest.**[42]

Iud[*ex*/ici], qui absolvere ab excommunicatione potest, aliis huiusmodi absolutionem committere liceat.

27a. *Iudex...*

Qui iurisdictioni praeest neque sibi ius dicere debet, neque uxori vel liberis suis vel ceteris quos sicut *secum habet.*
[244v] *Licet princeps sit solutus legibus, tamen illius delegatus leges in suo processu sequi et observare debeat, et si eius commissio aliquid de plenitudine potestatis sapuerit, huiusmodi commissio tamquam per obreptionem concessa non valebit.*

---

[40]Cf. C. 21, q. 5, c. 4 (Fr, I, 860), originally c. 4 of the fourth council of Arles, 524; Speculum, 1.4, *De teste*, 3.16.
[41]X, 1.31.8 (Fr, II, 189), originally a decretal of Pope Innocent III, 1 June 1198.
[42]X, 1.31.20 (Fr, II, 194), originally a decretal of Pope Gregory IX (1227-41), published on or before 5 September 1234.

He may also compel any other advocate he may wish to take on the case of a poor person for any fee which he can afford to pay him, and if he cannot pay anything, to take the case free of charge.

25. The judge can seek the extradition of a fugitive from the place to which he has fled.[40]

When a serious crime has been committed, the judge of that place can ask the judge of the place to which the accused has fled to turn him over to him.

26. Judges must support each other.[41]

A sentence passed by the judge of the place where the offence was committed, or where the accused is resident, shall be ordered for execution (if necessary) by the judge in whose *diocese* jurisdiction the goods of the accused are situated, provided that this is requested by the judge who has passed the sentence, for the judge of one diocese can never pass sentence in another diocese.

27. A judge can entrust the right to absolve an excommunicate to others.[42]

A judge who is able to absolve from excommunication may entrust the said absolution to others.

27a. *A judge...*

Whoever is in charge of a jurisdiction must not pass judgment on himself, or on his wife or children, or on anyone else in his household.

Although the king is above the law, his delegate must nevertheless follow and observe the laws in his process, and if his commission indicates that he has absolute power, the said commission will be invalid, as it has been granted by deceit.

28. Poena arbitraria.[43]

Ubi certa poena in iure non reperitur, iudex ordinarius sive delegatus arbitrariam imponere potest.

29. Iudex appellationis non probabit testamentum, neque bonorum administrationem concedet.[44]

Si quaestio super viribus testamenti, sive super administratione bonorum defuncti concedenda coram iudice ordinario fuerit, et in causa illa appellatio ad superiorem interposita extiterit, iudex ille superior super *iudice* iustitiae causa pronuntiare habe{n}t; et is ordinarius, ad quem pertinet, debet testamentum probare, seu administrationem concedere, [245r] ac alia requisita et [ea] necessaria in ea parte facere, in quibus iudex appellationis nullo modo sine expresso consensu ordinarii se intromittat.

30. De prorogatione iurisdictionis iudicis delegati.[45]

Per procuratorem non habentem mandatum iurisdictio delegati de re ad rem prorogari non potest, cum procura[100b]tor ad illa solummodo intelligatur constitutus, quae in commissionis litteris inveniuntur expressa, nisi dominus hoc scit et patitur.

31. Excommunicatus ab uno ab alio absolvi non potest.[46]

Excommunicatus a suo iudice ab aliis est vitandus, nec iudex alter eum absolvere possit, nisi sit superior, qui per viam appellationis vel querelae aditus fuerit.
    Si a regia maiestate super aliqua causa ecclesiastica rescriptum ad lites impetratur, et aliud postea in [245v] *eadem causa, non facta mentione prioris rescripti, emanaverit, iudices supersedere debent in utriusque executione, donec principis voluntatem plenius exinde cognoscant.*[47]

---

[43]Speculum, 1.1, *De iurisdictione omnium iudicum*, preface.
[44]The outcome of a dispute in the upper house of the convocation of Canterbury concerning the archbishop's prerogative, 1512 (W, III, 653-7).
[45]X, 1.29.32 (Fr, II, 175-7), originally a decretal of Pope Innocent III, 1209.
[46]X, 1.31.8 (Fr, II, 189), originally a decretal of Pope Innocent III, 1 June 1198.
[47]A note in Foxe's hand at the end of this chapter reads: '"De litis contestatione" require folium 162.' ('"On contesting a suit", see folio 162').

28. Arbitrary penalty.[43]

When there is no fixed penalty in law, an ordinary judge or his delegate may impose one arbitrarily.

29. An appeal judge shall not prove a testament, nor shall he grant administration of goods.[44]

If a question concerning the validity of a testament or of granting the administration of the goods of a deceased person comes before an ordinary judge, and in that cause an appeal is lodged with a higher judge, that higher judge has to pronounce on the *judge* cause of justice, and the ordinary to whom it belongs must prove the testament or grant the administration, and do the other things which are demanded and necessary in that respect, in which matters the appeal judge shall in no way interfere without the express consent of the ordinary.

30. On the extension of the jurisdiction of the judge delegate.[45]

The jurisdiction of a delegate cannot be extended from one matter to another by a proctor who does not have a mandate to do so unless his superior knows and approves, since the proctor is understood to be appointed only for those things which are specifically indicated in his letters of commission.

31. A person excommunicated by one judge cannot be absolved by another.[46]

A person who has been excommunicated by his own judge is to be avoided by others, and no other judge can absolve him, unless it is a higher judge who has come in on the case by way of appeal or quarrel.

If a rescript for suits concerning some ecclesiastical cause has been obtained from the king's majesty, and afterwards another appears in relation to the same cause, making no mention of the earlier rescript, the judges must refrain from executing either of them until they learn the king's will in the matter more fully.[47]

[162r; 100b]   **38. DE LITIS CONTESTATIONE**[1]

1. Litis contestatio quid sit.[2]

Litis contestatio est fundamentum iudicii; ex ea enim vere demum lis existit, et in ea versatur, oriturque ex congruo responso rei, seu ad libellum, seu ad petitiones, vel in scriptis datas, vel in scripta iussu iudicis redactas: neque respicit litis contestatio incidentia, vel emergentia, sed principale caput controversiae. Et quando in forma et figura iudicis/i procedendum est, si ommissa fuerit, inanibus laboribus et sumptibus vexantur litigantes.

2. De confessione.[3]

Cum libello iam oblato reus confitetur, ex illius confessione lis est contestata, si quidem iudex ea habita potest ad sententiam ferendam progredi: sin vero confessio praecedat oblationem libelli, ex ea non fit litis contestatio, neque sententia fertur, sed tantum iudex reo praecipere debet, ut intra certum tempus, quod debuerit, persolvat. Si quis ad libellum vel ad petitiones respondeat, praemittendo protestationem, qua se affirmat per illas responsiones in animo non habere, ut litem [162v] contestetur, lis non erit contestata.[4]

[101a] 3. **Contestatio litis non requirit praesent/i/am actoris.**[5]

Contestatio litis etiam absente actore fieri potest, modo libellus datus [*sit*], aut petitiones in scripta redactae, quas iudex reo proponere possit ad respondendum in iudicio. Nam si sequatur responsum, quo vel affirme[n]tur vel nege[n]tur petita, sive protestatione alieni animi a lite contestanda, lis (quamvis actor absit) erit contestata.

In responsione, quae requiritur ad litis contestationem, minime refert, sive per verba credulitatis, sive per verba veritatis respondeatur a reo.

---

[1]The headings in this chapter were added by Cranmer.
[2]X, 2.5.1 (Fr, II, 257-8), originally a decretal of Pope Gregory IX (1227-41), published on or before 5 September 1234.
[3]*Dig.*, 42.2.1, originally Paulus, *Ad edictum*, 56.
[4]Speculum, 2.2, *De litis contestatione*, 2.14.
[5]*Ibid.*, 5.5.

38. OF THE JOINDER OF ISSUE[1]

1. What the joinder of issue is.[2]

The joinder of issue is the basis of all judgment, for in the final analysis it is because of that that the suit exists and in that that it consists, and it emerges out of the corresponding response of the accused, either to the libel, or to the questions, which are either given in writing or written up on the judge's orders; nor does the joinder of issue depend on accidents or chance occurrences, but on the main point of controversy. And since the form and shape of the judgment makes this procedure necessary, the litigants are burdened with useless labours and expenses if it is overlooked.

2. Of confession.[3]

When the accused confesses after the libel has been submitted, and the suit is joined on the basis of his confession, the judge can proceed to pass sentence, once those things are obtained, but if the confession precedes the submission of the libel, then there shall not be any joinder of the issue, nor shall sentence be passed, but the judge must only inform the accused that he must pay what he owes within a certain time. If someone responds to the deposition or to the petitions by putting forward a protest in which he claims that when he made those responses he did not intend that the issue should be joined, the issue shall not be joined.[4]

3. The joinder of issue does not require the presence of the plaintiff.[5]

The issue may be joined even if the plaintiff is absent, as long as the libel [*is*] submitted, or the questions are written up, which the judge may present to the accused so that he may respond in the judgment. For if there follows a response in which the matters questioned are either affirmed or denied, or there is a protestation of an intention which is hostile to the joinder of the issue, the issue will be joined (even though the plaintiff is absent).

In the response, which is required for the issue to be joined, it does not matter whether the accused answers with a statement of what he believes to be true or with a statement of what he knows to be true.

4. Quare [s/f]it litis contestatio.[6]

Litis contestatio in causis idcirco *requirit* exigitur, ut inde liquere possit, quaenam sit inter [163r] litigantes de principali negotio controversia, quod nisi planis et perspicuis verbis cum petatur, tum respondeatur, fieri non poterit. Ideo a iudice omnes ambiguitates et obscuritates hinc removeri volumus.

5. Reus in litis contestatione certum dabit responsum.[7]

Si reus ad petitiones responderit, se illas neque fateri, neque negare, quoniam perinde est, ac si nihil respondisset, ad certum *quid respondendum* **aliquod responsum** urgeri debet.

6. Reus ad singulas petitiones seorsim respondebit.[8]

Cum in libello multa petuntur, non est permittendum ut una responsione reus omnia simul in universum neget. Sic enim facile iudicium eluderetur, nec de lite inter actorem [163v] et reum constaret, neque iudex posset litem iusta sententia dirimere. Nam saepe contingit, ut ex multis petitioni[101b]bus aliquae verae sint, aliquae falsae, ad quas cum una eademque responsione satisfieri non possit, volumus ut reus de singulis seorsim respondeat.

7. Contumax contra se ipsum praeiudicium facit.[9]

Per contumaciam non comparentis **minime** fit litis *t...* contestatio. Verum contumax habebitur, vel pro confitente, vel pro negante, prout magis in eius praeiudicium vergit.

8. Exceptiones dilatoriae litis contestationem impediunt.[10]

Dilatoriae exceptiones litem prorsus non contestantur; imo si probatae fuerint (saltem ad tempus) vetant ne lis contestetur, quia [164r] circa principale negotium controversiae non versantur, de quo proprie fieri debet litis contestatio.

---

[6]*Ibid.*, 5.7.
[7]Speculum, 2.2, *De positionibus*, 9.9.
[8]Speculum, 2.2, *De litis contestatione*, 2.1.
[9]*Dig.*, 42.1.53, originally Hermogenianus, *Iuris epitomae*, 1.
[10]Speculum, 2.1, *De exceptionibus et replicationibus*, 1.5; cf. *ibid.*, 2.2, *De litis contestatione*, 5.1.

4. **Why an issue is joined.**[6]

The joinder of issue in causes is *required* obligatory in order to make it possible to resolve by means of it whatever controversy there may be between the litigants concerning the main business, which cannot happen unless plain and transparent answers are given to the questions asked. Therefore we want all ambiguities and obscurities to be removed by the judge.

5. **In the joinder of issue the accused shall give a definite answer.**[7]

If the accused answers the questions by saying that he can neither confirm nor deny them, that is exactly as if he has not answered at all, and he must be forced to give a clear answer.

6. **The accused shall answer the individual questions one at a time.**[8]

When many things are asked in a libel, the accused is not allowed to deny them all at once by a single answer. For that way judgment can easily be avoided, nor will the issue between the plaintiff and the accused be resolved, nor will the judge be able to conclude the suit with a just sentence. For it often happens that some of the many questions are right and others are wrong, so since it is impossible to answer them properly by one and the same response, it is our will that the accused shall reply to each one of them in turn.

7. **A contumacious person creates a prejudice against himself.**[9]

An issue shall **not** be joined if someone fails to appear through contumacy. But a contumacious person will be considered either to have confessed or to have denied the matter, whichever does him more harm.

8. **Dilatory exceptions impede the joinder of issue.**[10]

Dilatory exceptions do not allow the issue to be joined; rather if they have been proved (at least in time) they prevent the issue from being joined, because they do not concern the main business of the controversy, which is what the joinder of issue ought to be about.

9. Similiter exceptiones peremptoriae.[11]

Quaedam exceptiones peremptoriae litem, n*on*/e contestetur, impediunt, ut exceptio transactionis, rei iudicatae, et litis finitae. Quare iudex de exceptionibus dilatoriis, et his peremptoriis, (quae litis contestationem impediunt), ab initio causae cognoscere et pronuntiare debet. Aliae autem exceptiones praeter enumeratas, litis contestationem (si obiiciantur) non prohibent.

10. Testes ante litis contestationem non admittuntur ad probandum causam principalem, sed ad probandum exceptiones dilatorias et peremptorias.[12]

Testes ante litis contestationem possunt [164v] admitti, non sane quoad principale totius causae caput, sed ad probandas vel improbandas exceptiones dilatorias, et *illas* perempto[102a]rias, quae litis contestationem impediunt.

11. Test*ibu*/es ad perpetuam rei memoriam ante litis contestationem admitti possunt.[13]

Quamvis communi regula testes ante litis contestationem recipi non debeant, attamen si de morte illorum timeatur, aut absentia diutina, sive periculum *sit* fuerit (quando negotium perplexum est, et i[nv/**mm**]ol[u/**a**]tum), ne rerum gestarum et ordinis obliviscantur, ad testandum recipien*dum*/**tur** senes valetudinarii, et quorum vel diuturna absentia, vel oblivio suspecta est, et[*iam*] cum lis non adhuc [165r] fuerit contestata, praemissa nihilominus partis citatione; quae si haberi praesens non possit, actorem oportebit suum convenire adversarium tempore, quod iudex illi assignabit, computando a die quo primum conveniri poterit, vel illi saltem (cum possibile fuerit) huiusmodi testium admissionem renuntiare; quod si facere *nex*... neglexerit, recepta testimonia non valebunt.

12. In quibus causis testes admittantur de principali causa, ante litis contestationem.[14]

Poterunt etiam de principali capite negotii admitti testes, absque litis contestatione, cum agitur de electione praelatorum, de postulationibus, provisionibus, dignitatibus, *personatis, officiis,* [165v] personatibus, officiis,

---

[11]VI, 2.3.2 (Fr, II, 998), originally a decretal of Pope Boniface VIII (1294-1303); Speculum, 2.2, *De litis contestatione*, 2.24.

[12]Speculum, 1.4, *De teste*, 2.3.

[13]X, 2.6.5 (Fr, II, 263-5), originally a decretal of Pope Innocent III, 1209.

[14]Speculum, 1.4, *De teste*, 2.1-7.

9. Likewise with peremptory exceptions.[11]

Certain peremptory exceptions prevent the issue from being joined, like the exception of transaction, of the matter judged, and of the suit ended. Therefore the judge must hear and pronounce upon dilatory exceptions and these peremptory ones (which hinder the joinder of issue), at the beginning of the cause. But exceptions other than the ones listed do not prevent the joinder of issue (if they are objected).

10. Witnesses are not admitted to prove the main cause before the joinder of issue, but to prove dilatory and peremptory exceptions.[12]

Witnesses may be admitted before the joinder of issue, not indeed with respect to the main point of the whole cause, but in order to prove or disprove dilatory exceptions, and *those* peremptory ones, which hinder the joinder of issue.

11. Witnesses can be admitted before the joinder of issue in order for there to be a perpetual record of the matter.[13]

Although by the general rule witnesses ought not to be admitted before the joinder of issue, nevertheless, if it is feared that they might die, or be absent for a long time, or when there is danger (when the business is complicated and involved), the elderly and infirm, and those whose long absence or forgetfulness is suspected, will be admitted to testify, even if the issue has not yet been joined, in order for the events and their order not to be forgotten, although only after the party has been cited. If the party is unable to be present, the plaintiff will have to summon his adversary at a time which the judge shall assign to him, reckoning from the day on which he will first be able to appear, or else he must (if possible) reject the admission of such witnesses, and if he neglects to do this, the testimonies received will not be valid.

12. In which causes witnesses may be admitted concerning the main cause, before the issue is joined.[14]

Witnesses may also be admitted concerning the main point of the business, without joinder of issue, when it is a matter of the election of prelates, of postulations, provisions, dignities, *parsonages, offices*, parsonages, offices,

canonicatibus, praebendis, seu quibusvis beneficiis ecclesiasticis, decimis, usuris, et notoriis, quibus addimus [etiam] matrimoniales causas. In his enim simpliciter de plano, absque forma et figura iudicii, procedi permittimus. *Nec etiam requiritur litis contestatio, quando testes examinantur ad perpetuam memoriam;* quando *quod interdum fit, cum quis timet aliquod sibi creandum periculum aut praeiudicium, nisi quod contigit, dum potest fieri, confirmetur per testes.*

In criminalibus actionibus, quando crimen [*non*] est notorium, testes recipiendi non sunt, nisi lis [166r] fuerit contestata, cum is, cuius agitur causa, in eis gravissime periclitatur.

[102b] 13. **Quando non requiritur litis contestatio.**[15]

Non requiritur contestatio litis, ubi non agitur contra certam personam, sed tantum iudici concluditur; quamvis aliorum utcunque utilitas et praeiudicium attingatur. Item ubi causa mere spiritualis fuerit, quae absque alicuius incommodo tractetur, in sententiis interlocutoriis, et sententi*ae*/**is** censurae, nec non quaestionibus emergentibus, in omnibus notoriis et summariis processibus, atque cum ius agendi ad publicum commodum dirigitur.

In inquisitione criminum si eam quispiam [166v] impetravit, et eius prosecutor fuerit, litis contestatio adhibeatur: sed si iudex ex officio suo sponte moveatur, litis contestatione minime opus erit.

Ubi litis contestatio non requiritur, volumus ut *ps* **primus** actus, qui post litem contestatam fieri solet (ut est receptio testium et id genus alia) exceptiones dilatorias, quas ipsa litis contestatio excludere solebat, penitus excludat, vimque et effectum ipsius litis contestationis etiam in ceteris omnino habeat.

[167r] 14. Vel de litis contestatione sic scribatur.[16]

Quandoquidem in causis ad forum nostrum ecclesiasticum pertinentibus quibuscunque, nullus libellus, sed petitio duntaxat simplex in actis redacta, requiratur, statuimus, quod nec litis contestatio in praefatis causis quovismodo exigatur, sed absque ea ad finem usque causarum omnino procedatur. Volumus autem, quod primus actus, qui post litem contestatam fieri solet, (ut testium receptio et id genus alia), exceptiones dilatorias, (quas ipsa litis contestatio excludere solebat), penitus excludat, vimque et effectum ipsius litis contestationis etiam in ceteris omni[*no*/**bus**] habeat [**et obtineat**].[17]

---

[15]Speculum, 1.1, *De officio omnium iudicum*, 2.15.

[16]Speculum, 2.2, *De litis contestatione*, 5.1-4. In MS Harleian 426 this heading appears to be the beginning of a separate title.

[17]A note in Foxe's hand at the top of [167v] reads: '"De iuramento et periuriis" require in folio 24.' ('For "On oaths and perjury" see folio 24').

canonries, prebends or any ecclesiastical benefices, tithes, usury and well-known matters, to which we add matrimonial causes **also**. For in these we allow proceedings to be held simply and informally, without the form and shape of judgment. *Nor is the contesting of a suit required when witnesses are examined in order to make a permanent record,* since *because it sometimes happens that someone is afraid that a danger or prejudice to him might be created unless the relevant evidence is confirmed by witnesses while that is still possible.*

In criminal actions, when the crime is [*not*] notorious, witnesses are not to be admitted unless the issue has been joined and the person whose cause it is is in desperate need of them.

13. **When the joinder of issue is not required.**[15]

The joinder of issue is not required when it is not directed against a particular person, but involves only the judge, even if the interests and prejudice of others are sometimes affected. Likewise when the cause is purely spiritual and may be handled without inconvenience to anyone; in interlocutory sentences and sentences of censure, as well as questions which emerge in passing; in all notorious and summary processes, and when the right to act is directed towards the public good.

In the investigation of crimes, if anyone requests a joinder of issue and has been its prosecutor, it shall be done, but if the judge acts spontaneously on the basis of his office, there will be no need to join the issue.

When a joining of the issue is not required, it is our will that the **first** act which is normally done after the issue has been joined (like the admission of witnesses and other things of that kind) should completely exclude those dilatory exceptions which the joinder of issue itself would normally exclude, and that this shall have the complete force and effect of the joinder of issue itself, in other matters as well.

14. Or this shall be written concerning the joinder of issue.[16]

In any causes pertaining to our ecclesiastical court, whenever no libel is required, but only a simple petition recorded in the proceedings, we ordain that neither shall a joinder of issue be required in any way in the aforesaid causes, but that the causes shall proceed to their end without that. Moreover, we desire that the first act which is normally done after the issue has been joined (like the admission of witnesses and other things of that kind) should completely exclude dilatory exceptions which the joinder of issue itself would normally exclude, and that this shall have [**and obtain**] the [*complete*] force and effect of the joinder of issue itself, in other matters as well.[17]

[24r; 103a]   **39. DE IURAMENTIS ET PERIURIIS**

1. De differentia iuramentorum.[1]

Quemadmodum iuramenta, quae ad Dei gloriam el ad fratrum utilitatem aliquid afferunt, Christianis concessa sunt (modo suscipiantur in iudicio, iustitia, et veritate) sic illa iurandi levitas ex animis et sermonibus nostris exterminari debet, quae familiaribus quotidianis in colloquiis nostris volitat. Posterioribus enim istis Dei reverentia minuitur, et in periuria facile incurritur. Quare qui perversa iurandi consuetudine contaminati sunt, et moniti[s] ab ea absterreri non possunt, illos (quoniam Dei nominis contemptores sunt et divinarum rerum) iusto supplicio coerceri oportet.

2. De poena temerarii iuramenti.[2]

Qui temere iurantem audierit aut sine iusta causa quamcunque personam, statim eam admoneat, ut duodecim denarios proximo die dominico conferat in communem thesaurum, quem cistam pauperum vocant, et in illius loci cista pecuniam deponat, in quo iurandi *crimine* crimen est admissum. Et hoc si facere persona rea neglexerit, nomen eius [24v] ab illo, qui audierit, ad ordinarium deferatur, [*et*] is ad se personam evocabit, et illi culpae poenam publice implendam praescribet; nec tamen a mulcta duodecim denariorum liberabitur.

3. **Forma** publicae poenae *forma et legitimi iuramenti.*[3]

Publica poena temere iurantis haec erit, ut nudo capite astet ante suggestum, et altiore loco quam sunt ceteri, tantisper donec homilia die dominico recitatur, et illa termi[103b]nata, statim in eodem loco confiteatur, se temeritatis suae vehementer paenitere, qua sine causa iurando Dei sacrosancto nomine sit abusus.

---

[1]C. 22, q. 1, c. 3 (Fr, I, 862), originally Augustine (354-430), *Ep.* 154; C. 22, q. 1, c. 13 (Fr, I, 864), originally Isidore of Seville, *Sententiae*, 2.31; cf. *Dig.*, 12.2.33, originally Ulpian, *Ad Sabinum*, 28; Article 38 of 1553 (39 of 1571).
[2]Cf. C. 22, q. 2, c. 3 (Fr, I, 867), originally Augustine, *De verbis Apostoli*, sermon 38. The penalty was new and did not become law until 21 James I, c. 20, 1623 (*S.R.*, IV, 1229-30).
[3]The alteration is in Foxe's hand. Cf. C. 22, q. 1, c. 10 (Fr, I, 863), attributed to Pope Pius I (*c.*140-55).

39. OF OATHS AND PERJURY

1. Of the different oaths.[1]

Since oaths which contribute something to the glory of God and the well-being of the brethren have been permitted to Christians (as long as they are taken in judgment, justice and truth) so any levity of swearing, which flies about in our everyday conversations with friends, must be completely cut out of our minds and speech. For reverence for God is diminished by these latter kinds, and easily falls into perjury. Therefore, if those who are contaminated by the perverse habit of swearing cannot abstain from it after having been warned to do so, they must be coerced by just punishment (since they are despisers of God's name and of divine things).

2. Of the penalty for swearing rashly.[2]

Whoever hears any person swearing rashly, or without good reason, shall immediately admonish him to pay twelve pence on the following Sunday to the common fund which is called the poor box, and to place the money in the box of that place in which the crime of swearing has been committed. And if the accused person neglects to do this, his name shall be referred to the ordinary by the person who heard him swear, [*and*] he shall summon the person and prescribe a penalty for his fault which shall be paid publicly, nor shall he be dispensed from the fine of twelve pence.

3. The form of the public penalty *and of a lawful oath.*[3]

The public penalty for someone who swears rashly shall be this, that he shall stand with his head bared in front of the pulpit, and in a place higher than where everyone else is, during the reciting of the homily on Sunday, and when that is finished he shall immediately confess, in the same place, that he earnestly repents of the rashness by which he abused the most holy name of God by swearing without cause.

4.[4] Forma legitimi iuramenti.[5]

Legitimum autem iuramentum eis verbis, et nullis aliis, suscipi volumus: 'Ita me Deus *adiuvet* per Dominum nostrum Iesum Christum adiuvet.'

5. *4*. Periurium quid sit.[6]

Ut facilius a scelere periuriorum abesse possimus, primum explicanda nobis erit eius natura, deinde patefaciendum quam gravis in eo sit Dei offensio. Periurium autem est mendacium iuramento confirmatum, vel iuramenti liciti violatio.

[25r] Periurus autem *his* habetur, qui sciens et proposito fallendi iuramento quemquam dolose circumvenit, aut qui volens iuramentum licitum violat, aut qui iurans verba tam perplexe involvit, ut iuramenti sensus non percipiatur; contra quam fraudem hanc regulam semper tenere volumus, ut id iurasse credatur, quod is, ad quem iuramentum referebatur, communi loquentium more *in eo* intelligit.

6. *5*. De iudicibus iuramentum postulantibus.[7]

Gravissimum est periurii crimen; primum enim contra Dei praeceptum est; deinde Deus in eo rei falsae testis adhibetur. Postremo iuramentum, quo veritas, res humanae societati maxime necessaria, confirmari debet, ad suffulcienda mendacia detorquetur. Cum igitur tam vehementer in periuriis peccetur, iudic{e/**i**}s in postulandis iuramentis non s[*i*/**u**]nt faciles, praesertim cum ex iuramentis periuria consecutura non obscure coniiciunt.

[104a] 7. *6*. De peierantium poena.[8]

Clerici, qui scientes et volentes iuramenta de rebus licitis et honestis interposuerint, si fidem post fefellerint quam servare poterant, aut si iuramento confirmaverint quae, cum iurarent, [25v] ipsi falsa esse sciebant, primum ordinis gradu *ap*pellantur in quo sunt; deinde beneficiis, ut vocant, excludantur, et non solum praesentibus careant, sed etiam ab his omnibus, quae forte consequi poterant, perpetuo submoveantur. Laicus qui fuerit in crimine periurii convictus, si facultates iudici videbuntur hoc ferre posse, decem libras in cistam conferet pauperum eius loci, in quo periurium est admissum, et publica confessione coram

---

[4]Originally part of the preceding section.
[5]Cf. C. 35, q. 6, c. 6 (Fr, I, 1279); C. 35, q. 6, c. 7 (Fr, I, 1279-80).
[6]C. 22, q. 5, c. 10 (Fr, I, 886), attributed to John Chrysostom (d. 407); cf. H.C., 6.2.
[7]Cf. *Dig.*, 12.2.4, originally Ulpian, *Ad edictum*, 36.
[8]*Novellae of the Emperor Leo VI*, 7.6 (888); X, 2.24.10 (Fr, II, 362), originally a decretal of Pope Alexander III (1159-81); H.C., 6.9.

4.[4] **The form of a lawful oath.**[5]

It is our will that a lawful oath shall be taken in these words and no others: 'May God so help me through our Lord Jesus Christ.'

5. *4.* What perjury is.[6]

In order that we may more easily distance ourselves from the crime of perjury, its nature must first be explained to us, and then it must be shown how serious is the offence given to God by it. For perjury is a lie confirmed by oath, or a violation of a lawful oath.

A perjurer is defined as someone who knowingly and cleverly cheats someone with an oath designed to deceive, or who willingly violates a lawful oath, or who twists his words when swearing in such a complicated way that the meaning of the oath is not clear. Against this deceit we want this rule to be always maintained, that what the person to whom the oath is sworn understands *by it* according to the normal custom of speech, is what will be believed as having been sworn.

6. *5.* Of judges demanding an oath.[7]

The crime of perjury is extremely serious, first of all because it is against the commandment of God, and secondly because God is called by it to witness to something which is false. Finally it is because an oath, by which the truth, a thing most necessary for human society, [**ought to be confirmed**], is twisted into supporting lies. Therefore, since someone who commits perjury sins as seriously as this, judges shall not be easygoing in demanding oaths, especially when perjury is such an obviously possible consequence of oathtaking.

7. *6.* Of the penalty of perjurers.[8]

If clergy who knowingly and willingly swear oaths concerning things which are lawful and honest, afterwards betray the commitment which they could have kept, or if they confirm on oath what they knew was false at the time they swore, they shall first be expelled from the rank of the order in which they are, and then they shall be excluded from their benefices, as they are called, and they shall not only forfeit their present ones, but they shall also be for ever debarred from any others which they might perhaps have obtained. If a layman has been convicted of the crime of perjury and the judge thinks that his resources can bear it, he shall pay ten pounds into the poor box of that place in which the perjury was committed, and shall testify that he abhors his fault by public confession before

ecclesia suam sibi culpam displicere contestabitur. Si vero rei convicti non sint tantae opes, ut mulcta possit ad decem libras pervenire, tum in ecclesiae conspectu publice crimen suum agnoscat, et ante suggestum astet capite et pedibus nudis toto tempore, quo vel homilia periurium tractans recitatur, vel contio peragitur; atque haec universa patiatur isto modo tribus diebus dominicis continue succedentibus, et in cistam pauperum conferet, quantum eius facultates iudicabuntur ferre posse. Iudici tamen ecclesiastico potestas erit, ut pro circumstantiarum ratione sua sapientia vel demat de praescripta poena, vel ad eam addat. Interim hoc ipsis iudicibus nostris vehementer imperamus, ut in hoc horribili crimine periurii, cuius nullum modum aut finem homines inveniunt, non conniveant. Nam si [26r] quicquam eorum neglexerint, quae a nobis in hoc genere proposita sunt, iam antea denuntiamus, illis hanc illorum flagitiosam socordiam in summum *suc*/**in**cursurum[9] nostrum odium. Quin et hoc aequissime videtur a nobis adiiciendum esse, ut quicunque causam periurio scientes dederint, eisdem poenis compraehendantur, quibus periurii convictos ante subiec[**er**]imus. Hoc autem summatim ad omnes [104b] pertineat, in quibus crimen periurii convincitur, ut infames sint, nec ad testimonium dicendum admittantur, nec unquam post tempus periurii iuramentum illis deferatur, nisi forte oneris iuramentum sit, in quo suam ipsi causam deteriorem faciant. Denique quicunque *fratri* **periurio alteri** damnum dederit, cogatur illi plene pro damno satisfacere.

8. *7.* De legitimis iuramentis non detrectandis.[10]

Nec tamen eis periurii poenis homines ab omni genere iuramentorum abalienari volumus. Itaque si quis auctoritate[**m**] legitima iurare, vel iuramento interposito respondere iussus sit, iudici hoc rite postulanti non negabit; et si forte negare voluerit, in eo contumax censebitur, et excommunicationis poenam sustinebit, si maior sit quattuordecim annis et mente integra.

[26v] 9. *8.* De fide laesa *in causis ecclesiasticis.*[11]

Firmissimum est vinculum humanae societatis fides; quapropter in ea custodienda legibus homines constringi debent. Itaque si pa[c/**r**]ta vel promissa non consistant nec impleantur, in quae vel a iuratis vel non iuratis consensum est vel serio tantum affirmantibus, illos qui fidem /huiusmodi/ suam fefellerint, primum arbitrariis poenis a iudicibus ecclesiasticis affici volumus; deinde cogantur, ut illis personis plene satisfaciant, quae sunt illorum perfidia deceptae.

[9]This change is in Haddon's hand.
[10]*Dig.*, 12.2.38, originally Paulus, *Ad edictum*, 33.
[11]Cf. X, 2.24.27 (Fr, II, 371), originally a decretal of Pope Innocent III (1198-1216); H.C., 6.1.

the church. But if the wealth of the man accused and convicted is not so great that the fine can reach ten pounds, then he shall acknowledge his crime publicly in the sight of the church, and he shall stand in front of the pulpit with bare head and feet for the whole time that either the homily dealing with perjury is read or a sermon is preached, and he shall do all this in the same way for three successive Sundays, and put as much into the poor box as his resources are thought to be able to bear. Nevertheless, the ecclesiastical judge shall have the power to lessen or increase the prescribed penalty using his own wisdom, according to the nature of the circumstances. Meanwhile we strongly order these same judges of ours that they shall not connive at this horrible crime of perjury, to which people know no bounds or limits. For if any of them neglect what has been set out by us in this respect, we already declare to them in advance that this disgraceful carelessness of theirs shall *attract* **incur**[9] our greatest displeasure. Moreover it also seems fair that this should be added by us, that whoever knowingly gives cause for perjury shall be included in the same penalties which we have already imposed on those convicted of perjury. Furthermore, to sum up, this shall apply to everyone who is convicted of the crime of perjury: they shall be blacklisted and not admitted to give testimony, nor shall any oath ever be offered to them after the time of their perjury, unless perchance the burden of the oath is such that they would make their own case worse by swearing it. Finally, anyone who has done harm to *a brother* **another by perjury** shall be compelled to pay him full compensation for the damage done.

8. 7. Of not declining lawful oaths.[10]

Nevertheless, we do not want people to be put off taking any kind of oath because of these penalties for perjury. Therefore, if someone swears by lawful authority, or has been ordered to answer on oath, he shall not say no to a judge who asks him in the right way, and if by chance he wants to refuse, he shall be regarded as contumacious and shall suffer the penalty of excommunication if he is more than fourteen years old and of sound mind.

9. 8. Of breach of faith *in ecclesiastical causes.*[11]

Faith is the strongest bond of human society, for which reason people must be obliged by the laws to keep it. Therefore, if contracts or promises which have been agreed either on oath or without oaths, but with at least a serious affirmation, do not hold and are not fulfilled, it is our will that those who have thus betrayed their faith shall first of all be punished by the ecclesiastical judges with arbitrary penalties, and then compelled to pay full compensation to those people who have been deceived by their perfidy.

10. *9.* Exceptiones in periurii*s* /et/ fidei laesae culpis /quae sint/.[12]

Verum superiores hae leges duas exceptiones habere debent. Altera est, illos non debere periuros videri, nec fidei laesores, qui cum omnia summa fecerint, ut iuramentum et fi[105a]dem servarent, tamen aliqua sunt huiusmodi ratione impediti, quam vitare non poterant. Istis enim satis erit iudicibus probare suam voluntatem et operam; secundo loco, nec illi sunt fidei laesores aut periuri*i* censendi, quibus exciderunt subito nec cogitantibus nec opinantibus promissa rerum iniquarum, inhonestarum, aut quae fieri non poss[*i*/**u**]nt, [27r] vel si primum recta fuerint, et progressu temporis in hanc absurditatem degeneraverint. Hoc tamen posito et retento, quod volens et sciens qui rem inhonestam, iniustam, aut quae fieri non possit, iuraverit aut promiserit, illum quidem hoc crimine non teneri, si iurata non praestet; sed tamen ecclesiastico iudici iustas temeritatis suae poenas daturum esse.

11. *10.* Generalia iuramenta et promissa qualia esse debe[*a*]nt.[13]

Qui summatim iurat vel promittit statuta vel consuetudines ecclesiarum, capitulorum, universitat[*u*/**e**]m, vel huiusmodi quorumcunque locorum vel societatum se conservaturum esse, non potest talis iuramenti vel promissi auctoritate compelli, res ut iniquas suscipiat, aut eas quae fieri non possunt. Nec enim iurantis vel promittentis anim[*u*/**i**]s ullum honestum ad talem perversitatem respectum habere potest. Quapropter in conclusionibus talium iuramentorum et promissorum hoc attexi placet: 'Haec omnibus partibus servabo, quibus cum sacra Scriptura cum legibus civilibus et ecclesiasticis huius regni consentient, et quantum vires meae patientur.'[14]

---

[12]X, 2.24.18 (Fr, II, 365-6), originally a decretal of Pope Innocent III, 5 April 1199; X, 2.24.23 (Fr, II, 368), originally a decretal of Pope Innocent III, 3 February 1204; H.C., 6.3, 7, 9.
[13]X, 2.24.21 (Fr, II, 367), originally a decretal of Pope Innocent III, 14 November 1198; VI, 2.11.1 (Fr, II, 1003-4), originally a decretal of Pope Nicholas III (1277-81).
[14]A note at the top of [27v] in Foxe's hand reads: '"De iuramento calumniae" require folium 168.' ('"On the oath of calumny" see folio 168').

10. *9.* What the exceptions are in faults of perjury and breach of faith.[12]

But these foregoing laws must allow two exceptions. The first is that those who have done everything in their power to keep their oath and faith, but who have been prevented from doing so for some reason which they could not avoid, shall not be regarded as perjurers or breakers of faith. In their cases it will be enough for the judge to prove their good will and their efforts. In the second place, those who have rashly given oaths without thinking or realizing that the promises were of things which are unfair, dishonest or impossible to do, or else were right at first but in the course of time degenerated into this absurdity, are not to be counted as perjurers or breakers of faith. But it shall be established and maintained that whoever has knowingly and willingly sworn or promised something which is dishonest, unjust or which cannot be done, shall not be guilty of this crime if he has not sworn on oath, but he shall nevertheless pay the just penalties of his rashness to the ecclesiastical judge.

11. *10.* What general oaths and promises ought to be like.[13]

In sum, whoever swears or promises that he will abide by the statutes or customs of churches, chapters, universities or of any such places or societies whatsoever, cannot be compelled, on the basis of such oath or promise, to undertake unfair things, or things which cannot be done. For the intention of the one swearing or promising cannot have any connexion with such perversity. Therefore at the end of such oaths and promises the following shall be added: 'I shall abide by these things in all parts which agree with Holy Scripture, with the civil and ecclesiastical laws of this kingdom and as far as my strength allows.'[14]

[168r; 105b]   **40. DE IURAMENTO CALUMNIAE**[1]

1. Tam actor quam reus initio litis praestet iuramentum calumniae.[2]

Quoniam calumniantes odimus, et summo studio et cura aversamur, libidinem [*ill*/e]orum, qui facile ac temere ad litigandum proceder{e/i}nt, reprimere summopere cupientes, necessarium duximus et praesentem legem ponere, per quam sancimus, quod non aliter neque actor neque reus in quibusvis causis ecclesiasticis (nam et in his frequenter calumniari solet) ad litis certamina admittatur, quam si in ipso litis exordio iusiurandum calumniae subeat uterque.

2. Iudex, cum primum ad munus admittitur, praestet iuramentum de calumnia.[3]

Iudex, licet de calumnia in singulis causis non iuret, tamen hoc iuramenti genus quoad omnes causas in universum a se tractandas [168v] ab initio, cum suscipit iudicandi munus, praestare debet.

3. Forma iuramenti calumniae.[4]

Tam actor quam reus, cum de calumnia iurant, haec praecipue *trac*/estentur: se putare iustam habere causam, nolle in universa actione (quae subsecutura est) quicquam calumniari, nilque largitos esse, aut largituros, aut per se aut per alios, vel ad iudicem vel ad alios corrumpendos, per quos iudicium administratur, nolle tergiversari, aut dolos in probationibus nectere, neque dilationes vel in fraudem adversarii, vel ad protrahendam litem petere, et denique se fideliter esse responsuros his omnibus, quae in iudicio (modo ad causam pertineant) ab ipsis requirentur.

---

[1]The headings in this chapter were added by Cranmer.
[2]Gaius, *Institutes*, IV, 176; Speculum, 2.2, *De litis contestatione*, 2.28.
[3]Cf. Speculum, 2.2, *De iuramento calumniae*, 3.1. Was this provision intended to be a relaxation of the demand that a judge take the oath every time?
[4]Speculum, 2.2, *De iuramento calumniae*, 4.7.

40. OF THE OATH AGAINST CALUMNY[1]

1. At the beginning of a suit both the plaintiff and the accused shall swear an oath against calumny.[2]

Since we hate slanderers and oppose them with the greatest effort and care, and want above all to repress the desire of those who easily and rashly proceed to litigation, we have felt it necessary to pass the present law, by which we ordain that neither the plaintiff nor the accused shall be admitted to the deliberations of a suit in ecclesiastical causes (for even in these there is often a lot of slandering) unless each of them takes the oath against calumny at the beginning of the suit itself.

2. When a judge is first admitted to his office, he shall swear an oath against calumny.[3]

Although a judge does not have to swear an oath against calumny in individual causes, he must nevertheless swear this kind of oath with respect to all the causes which he shall ever handle, at the beginning of his term of office as a judge.

3. The form of swearing an oath.[4]

Both the plaintiff and the accused, when they swear the oath against calumny, shall *cover* **include** the following in particular: that they think that they have a just cause; that they do not want to slander anyone during the entire course of the action (which is about to follow); that they have paid nothing and will pay nothing either by themselves or through others, either to the judge or to others by whom judgment is administered, in order to bribe them; that they do not want to evade the issues or devise tricks in the proofs, or introduce delays either to cheat the other party or to drag out the proceedings; and finally that they will faithfully answer all the questions which may be put to them in the judgment (provided that they are pertinent to the cause).

[169r; 106a] 4. **Iuramentum malitiae.**[5]

Licet iuramentum calumniae semel exigatur quoad totam causam post litis contestationem, attamen iuramentum malitiae in omnibus litis partibus exigi potest, cum iudici visum fuerit, neque manifestum periurium timetur.

5. Discrimen inter iuramentum malitiae et iuramentum calumniae.[6]

Iuramentum malitiae a iuramento calumniae hoc differt, quod hoc iuramentum (non ut illud) ad totam litem refertur, sed ad illud tantum quod tunc malitiose agi praesumitur, debetque is, a quo exigitur, iurare se non esse conscium sibi ullius malitiae aut fraudis, qua studea*tur*, in eo quod proponit aut agit, adversarium circumvenire. Potestque hoc iuramenti genus et ante [169v] litis contestationem et postea exigi, non solum a dominis litis, sed etiam ab eorum procuratoribus et substitutis, ut dictum est, quoties praesumptio est malitiose agi.

6. Iuramentum aut per dominum litis fiat, aut per procuratorem.[7]

Dominus causae de calumnia iurare debet, quando facile haberi potest; alioqui iuramentum sufficiet procuratoris, modo speciale mandatum habeat ad iurandum in ea causa de calumnia. Attamen si a domino fuit ante discessum universalis constitutus procurator negotiorum eius, non erit opus speciali mandato.

Si domini litis de calumnia iurarunt, et deinde suos procuratores instituer[*u*/i]nt ad litem [170r] prosequendam, procuratores etiam de calumma iurare debebunt, sed ad hoc speciali mandato non opus erit.

[106b] 7. Iurans debet non levem habere causae notitiam.[8]

Oeconomum seu procuratorem aut syndicum, qui ad iurandum de calumnia est admittendus, iustam et non levem causae notitiam habere oportet.

---

[5]*Ibid.*, 1.6.
[6]*Ibid.*, 1.9.
[7]X, 2.7.3 (Fr, II, 266), originally a decretal of Pope Eugenius I (655-7); VI, 2.4.2-3 (Fr, II, 998), both originally decretals of Pope Boniface VIII (1294-1303).
[8]Speculum, 2.2, *De iuramento calumniae*, 3.1-2.

4. The oath against malice.[5]

Although the oath against calumny is only required once with respect to the entire cause after the issue has been joined, nevertheless an oath against malice may be required at any point during the suit, if it seems good to the judge and there is no fear of manifest perjury.

5. The difference between an oath against malice and the oath against calumny.[6]

An oath against malice differs from the oath against calumny in that (unlike the other) it does not apply to the entire suit, but only to that which is presumed to be done maliciously at the time, and the person from whom it is demanded must swear that he is not aware of any malice or fraud in what he is proposing or doing, by which he is trying to cheat the other party. This kind of oath may also be demanded both before and after the joinder of issue, not only from the principal of the suit, but also from his proctors and substitutes, as they are called, whenever there is a presumption of malicious behaviour.

6. The oath shall be taken either by the principal of the suit or by his proctor.[7]

The principal of the cause must take the oath against calumny if he is readily available; otherwise the oath of the proctor will suffice, provided that he has a special mandate to swear against calumny in that cause. But if it has already been decided by the principal that the proctor of his affairs may act on his behalf in any circumstances, there will be no need of a special mandate.

If the principals of the suit swear and then later appoint proctors to pursue the suit, the proctors must also swear the oath against calumny, but for this there shall be no need of a special mandate.

7. The person swearing must not have a light attitude towards the cause.[8]

The agent, proctor or warden who is to be admitted to take the oath against calumny, must have a right and not a frivolous attitude towards the cause.

8. Mortuo/a *actore* altera parte, successor idem praestabit iuramentum.[9]

Quando is qui litem instituer[a/i]t mortuus fuerit, haeres aut successor eius, qui litem est prosecuturus, iuramentum calumniae praestare debet, licet qui mortuus est iuraverit.

9. In appellatione iurandum.[10]

In appellationis quoque causa de calumnia iurandum est, quamvis ab initio institut*um*/ae litis [170v] iuratum fuerit.

10. Recusans iuramentum calumniae causa cad[e/a]t.[11]

Is a quo iuramentum calumniae seu malitiae requiritur, si recuset ipsum praestare, causa cadet, sive re*ctor*/us fuerit sive actor.

11. Iuramentum calumniae non est omittendum.[12]

Sed quia veremur, ne forsitan partes collusione quadam utentes remittant sibi invicem huiusmodi sacramentum, et vel [*hoc*] pacto sanctionem nostram deludant, praecipimus (quandoquidem non pro commodo privatorum tantummodo, verumetiam pro communi utilitate praesentem legem posuimus) quod iudices minime patiantur iusiurandum istud, nedum expresse, sed ne tacite quidem remitti, sed illud (ut p*er*/raemittitur) omnino [171r] exigant, et nullo modo praeter[107a]mittant. Est enim hoc iuramentum calumniae inter legitimas observationes iudiciorum numeratu*r*/m,. *q*/Quod[13] si iudex neglexerit, praesertim a parte monitus, sententia eius iure cassabitur.[14]

---

[9]*Ibid.*, 2.7.
[10]VI, 2.4.2 (Fr, II, 998), originally a decretal of Pope Boniface VIII (1294-1303).
[11]X, 2.7.7 (Fr, II, 268), originally a decretal of Pope Gregory IX (1227-41), published on or before 5 September 1234.
[12]Speculum, 2.2, *De iuramento calumniae*, 5.3-6.
[13]Cranmer divided the sentence here.
[14]A note at the top of [171v] in Foxe'hand reads: '"De probationibus" require folium 154.' ('"On trials" see folio 154').

8. If *the plaintiff* either party should die, his successor shall swear the same oath.[9]

When the person who has brought the suit dies, his heir or successor, who is to continue the suit, must swear the oath against calumny, even if the dead person had already sworn it.

9. What must be sworn in an appeal.[10]

In a cause of appeal an oath against calumny must also be sworn, even if it has already been sworn at the beginning of the suit.

10. Anyone who refuses to swear the oath against calumny shall drop out of the cause.[11]

If anyone from whom the oath against calumny is required refuses to swear it, he shall drop out of the cause, whether he is the *rector* **accused** or the plaintiff.

11. The oath against calumny must not be omitted.[12]

But because we are afraid that perhaps the parties will collude to allow each other to omit this oath, and by [*this*] agreement escape our punishment, we command (in that we have passed the present law not only for the benefit of private individuals but also for the common good), that judges shall not allow this oath to be omitted under any circumstances, either expressly or tacitly, but that they shall always demand it of everyone. For this oath against calumny is counted among the lawful observances in judgments. But[13] if the judge neglects it his sentence shall be nullified by law, especially if he has been reminded by one of the parties.[14]

[154r; 107a]   **41. DE PROBATIONIBUS**[1]

1. Probatio quid sit.[2]

Probatio est rei dubiae per legitima documenta ostensio.

2. Reo confi{*t*/d}ente, non est opus probatione.[3]

Quid [*igitur*] est opus causam in examen trahere, quam reus sua confessione certam facit et indubitatam? Proinde non est quaerenda probatio, cum reus id /quod/ contra eum principaliter propositum est, fatetur.

Probationis facultas amplianda potius, quam restringenda est, ut veritas in omnibus causis eluce{*sc*}at.

3. Species probationis.[4]

Sive igitur per testes, instrumenta, praesumptiones, i[*n*/**u**]dicia *e*/**aut** famam, probationes offerantur, prudens iudex, (cui multum quoad hoc tribuendum esse iudicamus), **facile existimabit, (pensatis rerum et personarum circumstantiis), quatenus cuique credendum sit.** [154v]

Neque enim ad unam probationis speciem iudex sese alligare debet, sed ex iusta animi sui sententia*m* aestimabit, quid aut credat, aut parum probatum sibi videatur, cum intelligat multa saepe coniunctim evincere, seorsim vero accepta nequaquam fidem facere.

---

[1]The headings in this chapter were added by Cranmer.
[2]Hostiensis, *Summa aurea*, c. *De probationibus*; X, 5.40.10 (Fr, II, 914), originally Isidore of Seville, *Etymologiae*, 18.15.
[3]X, 2.18.2 (Fr, II, 305-6), originally a decretal of Pope Innocent III, 1200.
[4]*Dig.*, 22.5.3, originally Callistratus, *Cognitiones*, 4.

41. OF TRIALS[1]

1. What a trial is.[2]

A trial is the demonstration of a doubtful matter by lawful documents.

2. If the accused confesses, there is no need for a trial.[3]

What [*therefore*] is the need to bring a cause to trial if the accused makes the matter clear and undoubted by his confession? Therefore no trial is to be sought when the accused admits to the main point charged against him.

The right to a trial is to be extended rather than restricted, so that the truth may be elucidated in all causes.

3. Kinds of trials.[4]

Therefore whether trials are held by witnesses, instruments, presumptions, [*indications* judgments] *or* and report, a wise judge (who has an important part to play in this, we think), **will easily figure out, (after weighing the circumstances of the matters and persons), how much of what each one says is to be believed.**

For a judge must not limit himself to one type of proof, but by using the right intuition of his mind, he shall figure out what to believe and what appears to be unproved, since he understands that often many things are convincing when taken together, but the same things are unpersuasive when taken one at a time.

[107b] 4. **Probatio non est admittenda, nisi reo praesente, aut per contumaciam absente.**[5]

Quanquam vi/ero iudici, et non parti, fides facienda sit, [n/v]olumus tamen aliquod probationis genus adversus *q*... aliquem admitti vel exhiberi, nisi ips[e/o] aut praesens fuerit, aut per contumaciam absens.

5. **Probatio facienda est in iudicio [*et*] coram iudice.**[6]

Probatio recipienda est coram iudice, et in iudicio, non extra iudicium, neque coram notario aut tabellione.

6. **Actori non reo interest probare.**[7]

Actore non probante, reus (etiam si nihil praestiterit), *absolvendus est, nisi tantae adversus* [155r] absolvendus est, nisi tantae adversus ipsum praesumptiones insurgant, ut in eum probationes transferr[e/i] poss[u/i]nt. Alioqui enim non convenit, ut actore palam profitente, se probare non posse quod asseveravit, re{r}um necessitate monstrandi contrarium astringat; cum per rerum naturam factum negantis nulla probatio sit. In negativis tamen, coarctatis loco et tempor[i/e], veterem modum probandi observari volumus.

7. **Contrariae probationes.**[8]

Si ab una et eadem parte contrariae probationes aliquando producantur, invicem sibi ipsis et merito derogare debent. At si a diversis partibus contraria fortassis allegantur, et proponentibus huiusmodi probationes adhibitae fuerint, fortiori probation[i/e] adhaerendum erit. Sed si de ea non constet, favend*ae*/**um** est reo, nisi [155v] favor reipublicae, salus animarum, aut natura causae aliud suaserit.

[108a] 8. **In communibus iudiciis tam reo quam actori incumbit probatio.**[9]

In communibus iudiciis, tam actor quam reus probationibus onerantur, isque vincet, qui meliores et efficaciores probationes attulerit. Sed si omnia huiusmodi aequalia s[u/i]int, pro possessore iudicabitur, nisi favor causae aliud suaserit.

---

[5]Hostiensis, *Summa aurea*, c. *De probationibus*.
[6]Speculum, 2.2, *De probationibus*, 1.14.
[7]*Dig.*, 22.3.2, originally Paulus, *Ad edictum*, 69.
[8]Speculum, 2.2, *De probationibus*, 1.23; 2.4.
[9]X, 2.19.3 (Fr, II, 307), originally a decretal of Pope Lucius III (1181-5).

4. A trial is not to be started unless the accused is present, or else absent because of his contumacy.[5]

But although trust must be placed in the judge and not in a party, even so we do [*not*] want any sort of trial to be initiated or conducted against anyone, unless he is either present or else absent by contumacy.

5. A trial is to be held in a courtroom [*and*] before a judge.[6]

A trial is to be held before a judge and in a courtroom, not outside a courtroom nor before a notary or recorder.

6. The plaintiff must appear at the trial more than the accused.[7]

If the plaintiff does not appear at the trial, the accused (even if he does not appear), *shall be absolved unless there are so many* shall be absolved unless there are so many presumptions which rise against him that the burden of proof may be transferred to him. For otherwise, if the plaintiff has made an open accusation and then cannot prove what he has asserted, it is not right that he should force the accused to demonstrate the opposite, since in the nature of things it is impossible to prove a negative. But in negative cases, which are restricted in place and time, we want the old method of proving them to be observed.

7. Contrary proofs.[8]

If contrary proofs are ever produced by one and the same party, they must cancel each other out, and rightly so. But if by chance contrary proofs are alleged by different parties, and such proofs are presented to the proposers, the stronger proof must be adhered to. But if that cannot be agreed on, the accused is to be favoured unless the interest of the state, the salvation of souls, or the nature of the case suggests otherwise.

8. In common judgments the burden of proof lies with the accused as well as with the plaintiff.[9]

In common judgments the plaintiff and the accused share the burden of proof, and the one who produces better and more effective proofs shall win. But if all other things are equal, judgment shall be given for the possessor, unless the weight of the case suggests otherwise.

9. Post publicationem non licet contrarias probationes afferre.[10]

Si de impedimento aliquo, (etiam in causa matrimoniali), probationes aliquae publicatae sunt, non licebit alteri parti contrarias probationes aliquando inferre vel producere.

10. In omni actu iudiciali adesse oportet aut notarium aut duos testes.[11]

In recipiendis probationibus, atque in omnibus aliis actibus iudicialibus iudex debet publicum notarium [156r] aut duos, loco illius, hon[*o*/e]stos viros adhibere, per quos cuncta quae aguntur fideliter scribi mandamus; ut si quae postea super actitatis oriatur controversia, ea penitus per ipsa originalia publica et communia tollatur.

11. Affirmanti incumbit probatio, non neganti.[12]

Ut creditor, qui pecuniam petit, numerat[a/u]m probare cogitur, ita rursus debitor, qui solutam affirmat, eius rei probationem praestare debet. Ei enim incumbit probatio, qui affirmat, non qui negat.

12. Aliena a causa nihil probant.[13]

Probationes vero, vel necessario vel praesum/p/tive, inferre [108b] debent id de quo agitur. Quae vero aliena sunt a causa seu controversia nihil probant.

13. Accusatores in iudicium deferre non debent rem quae probari [*non*] possit.[14]

Sciant cuncti accusatores, eam se rem deferre in publicam no[ti]tionem debere, quae munita /sit/ idoneis **testibus**, [156v] vel instructa apertissimis documentis, vel i[*n*/u]diciis ad probationem indubitatis, et luce clarioribus expedita.

---

[10]X, 2.19.6 (Fr, II, 308), originally a decretal of Pope Clement III (1187-91).
[11]X, 2.19.11 (Fr, II, 313-14), originally c. 38 of Lateran IV, 1215 (*C.O.D.*, 252).
[12]*Speculum*, 2.2, *De probationibus*, 1.9.
[13]*Ibid.*, 2.1.
[14]*Cod. Iust.*, 4.19.25, originally a rescript of the emperors Gratian, Valentinian II and Theodosius I, 18 May 382.

9. After publication no contrary proofs may be alleged.[10]

If proofs have been published concerning some impediment (even in a matrimonial cause), the other party may not allege or produce contrary proofs at any time.

10. In every judicial act either a notary or two witnesses must be present.[11]

In receiving proofs and in all other judicial acts, the judge must have a public notary or two honest men in his place, by whom we order that every transaction shall be accurately recorded, so that if some controversy should later arise concerning what was done, it may be resolved immediately by these public and common original documents.

11. Proof lies with the one who affirms, not with the one who denies.[12]

As a creditor who asks for money is obliged to check the amount, so also the debtor who claims that it is paid must provide proof of the matter. For proof lies with him who affirms, not with him who denies.

12. Matters extraneous to the cause prove nothing.[13]

Proofs, both necessary and presumptive, must support the matter which is being discussed. But those which are extraneous to the cause or controversy prove nothing.

13. Accusers must not refer a matter to judgment which can[*not*] be proved.[14]

Let all accusers know that any matter which they bring to public attention must be backed up with suitable **witnesses**, presented in the clearest documents and supported by undoubted [*indications* **judgments**] which are clearer than light.

14. Testes synodales.[15]

Testibus tamen synodalibus, ac aliis probationibus ex magnis [*ac* et] vehementioribus suspicionibus exortis, ant[*i*/e]quam vim veteremque auctoritatem reservamus.

15. Officium iniunctum quisque probare tenetur se implevisse.[16]

Quotie/s/cunque aliquis ex officio sibi iniuncto aliquid facere tenetur, ipse semper probare debet, quod officium suum huiusmodi ac onus iniunctum fideliter adimplevit, vel per eum non stetit, quominus adimplevit.

16. Monumenta publica.[17]

Census et monumenta publica potiora testibus esse censemus.

17. Reus potest probandi onus in se suscipere.[18]

Potest *enim* reus onus probandi in se assumere, et docere de iure suo, licet ad hoc nullo iure astringatur.

[157r] 18. Reus exceptiones suas probare debet.[19]

Qui dolo aliquid factum esse dicit, seu excipit, ipse de dolo [109a] docere debet. In exceptionibus quoque omnibus reus actoris partes *partes* sustinebit, ipsamque exceptionem (ut actor suam intentionem) implere cog[*i*/e]tur.
    Qui mutatam voluntatem dicit, probare hoc necesse habet.

---

[15]Cf. X, 2.21.7 (Fr, II, 343), originally a decretal of Pope Celestine III (1191-8); VI, 5.10.1 (Fr, II, 1093), originally a decretal of Pope Innocent IV (1243-54), who referred to them as *quaestores* ('questmen'). The *testes synodales* were the ancestors of the modern sidesmen (i.e. 'synodsmen').
[16]C. 22, q. 4, cc. 1-23 (Fr, I, 875-82); X, 2.24.3 (Fr, II, 360), a decretal of Pope Gregory III (731-41); VI, 2.11.1 (Fr, II, 1003-4), a decretal of Pope Nicholas III (1277-80). See H.C., 6.3.
[17]*Dig.*, 22.3.10, originally Marcellus, *Digesta*, 3.
[18]Speculum, 2.2, *De probationibus*, 1.12.
[19]*Dig.*, 44.1.1, originally Ulpian, *Ad edictum*, 4; Cf. VI, 2.12.1 (Fr, II, 1004-5), originally a decretal of Pope Innocent IV; Speculum, 2.1, *De exceptionibus et replicationibus*, 4.2.

14. Synodical witnesses.[15]

But synodical witnesses and other proofs which are based on great and quite persuasive suspicions shall retain their ancient force and old authority.

15. Each person is obliged to prove that he has fulfilled his appointed office.[16]

Whenever someone is obliged to do something by virtue of the office to which he has been appointed, he must always prove that he has faithfully fulfilled that office and appointed task, or that if he has not fulfilled it, it was not his fault.

16. Public records.[17]

We consider that registers and public records are of more force than witnesses.

17. An accused person may take the burden of proof on himself.[18]

For an accused person may take the burden of proof on himself, and explain his rights, even if he is not bound by any law to do so.

18. An accused person must prove his exceptions.[19]

Anyone who says or objects that something was done by trickery, must himself explain the trickery. Also, in all exceptions the accused shall take upon himself the part of the plaintiff and shall be compelled to prove the exception (as a plaintiff would have to prove his case).

Whoever says that he has changed his mind must prove this.

19. Ad probandum ea quae nihil causam iuvant, nemo admittatur.[20]

Ad probationem illius rei nemo admitti debet, quae etiam probata nihil relevaret, ne ex/t partes inanibus expensis onerentur, et lites plus iusto differeru/antur.

20. Quando confessio omnibus probationibus sit praeferenda.[21]

Probationes *equidem* omnes confessioni partis [157v] merito cedere debent. Sive igitur contra instrumenta, testes, aut sententiam, in favorem suum introductam sive latam, aliquid confitetur, locum semper obtinebit, contrariis probationibus {*non*} obsistentibus, nisi animae periculum in causa [*u*/**ver**]tatur, aut leges confessioni huiusmodi resistant, et nisi confessio pro causa confitentis faciat.

21. Probationes valent, etiam nullo designato termino ad probandum.[22]

Probationes *enim* non censentur reprobatae, licet sine assignatione alicuius termini, aut nulla ad probandum concessa dilatione, factae reperiantur.

22. Probationes inductae ad unum effectum valent ad alium.[23]

Probationes inductas ad unum effectum facere fidem ad alium effectum inter easdem personas [158r] aequum esse *dubitamus* iudicamus.

[109b] 23. Alleganti statuti ignorantiam non facile creditur.[24]

Alleganti constitutionis aut statuti ignorantiam non est credendum, nisi probationem suae ignorantiae adducat, aut praesumptiones verisimiles; quibus iudex (consideratis rei et personae circumstantiis) possit in plenam probationem alleganti ignorationem iuramentum differre.

---

[20]Speculum, 1.4, *De teste*, 3.1.
[21]*Dig.*, 42.2.1, originally Paulus, *Ad edictum*, 56; ibid., 42.2.3, originally Paulus, *Ad Plautinum*, 9.
[22]Speculum, 2.1, *De dilationibus*, 4.8.
[23]X, 2.20.11 (Fr, II, 319), originally a decretal of Pope Alexander III (1159-81).
[24]D, 37 c. 16 (Fr, I, 140), originally Augustine, *Quaestiones*, 67. Cf. Speculum, 2.2, *De iuramenti delatione*, preface.

19. **No one shall be allowed to try matters which do not help the cause in any way.**[20]

No one must be allowed to try a matter which reveals nothing even if it is proved, and merely burdens the parties with pointless expenses and prolongs the suits more than is right.

20. **When confession is to be preferred to all proofs.**[21]

Proofs, *moreover*, must all give way before the confession of a party, and rightly so. Therefore if he confesses anything contrary to the documents, witnesses or sentence produced or delivered in his favour, he shall always carry the day, proofs to the contrary {*not*} withstanding, unless the danger of a soul is involved in the cause or the laws reject a confession of this kind, and unless the confession works on behalf of the cause of the one confessing.

21. **Proofs are valid, even when there is no fixed time limit for proving has been set.**[22]

For proofs are not regarded as invalid even if they have been made without any time limit having been set or any delay allowed for proving.

22. **Proofs brought for one purpose are valid for another.**[33]

We *doubt* judge that it is fair for proofs brought for one purpose to be valid for another purpose if the same persons are involved.

23. **Someone who pleads ignorance of a statute is not to be readily believed.**[24]

Someone who pleads ignorance of a constitution or statute is not to be believed unless he offers proof or plausible presumptions of his ignorance, by which the judge (having considered the matter and the person), may delay the oath of the person alleging ignorance until he receives full proof.

24. **Probatio per iuramentum.**[25]

Quando aliquid ad conscientiam solam pertinet, per iuramentum admittitur probatio.

25. **Aliquando negativa probanda est.**[26]

Ab ea parte quae dicit adversarium suum ab aliquo iure prohibitum esse speciali lege vel constitutione, id probari oportet. Idem respondendum est, si quis neget [158v] aliquid recte factum, *ipse p...* ips[*u*/a]m praestare debere probationem.

26. **Antiquitatis probatio.**[27]

In finibus ac rebus antiquis *ap*probandis, fama ac testes de auditu, librique antiqui sine suspicione aliqua confecti, custoditi, et reperti, possunt iudicem ad credulitatem adducere, ut recte *et* pro sic probante sententiam ferat, nisi **adversae** partis fortiores probationes aliud requirant.

27.[28] **Acta iudicii fideliter custodienda.**[29]

Acta iudicii plenam inducunt probationem. Volumus igitur eadem omnia et singula fideliter descripta ac more solito clausa transmitti ad iudices appellationis, illud requirentes seu exigentes, ut ex illis colligant, an per inferiorem iudicem recte iudicatum existat.

---

[25]Hostiensis, *Summa aurea*, c. *De assertorio iuramento*, 4; cf. X, 2.20.27 (Fr, II, 324), originally a decretal of Pope Celestine III (1191-8).
[26]Speculum, 2.2, *De probationibus*, 1.1-7.
[27]X, 2.19.9 (Fr, II, 311-12), originally a decretal of Pope Innocent III (1198-1216); X, 2.19.13 (Fr, II, 314), originally a decretal of Pope Honorius III (1216-27).
[28]This was originally part of 26, but was separated from it by Cranmer.
[29]X, 2.19.15 (Fr, II, 315), originally a decretal of Pope Gregory IX (1227-41), published on or before 5 September 1234.

24. **Proof by oath.**[25]

When something is only a matter of conscience, proof by oath may be allowed.

25. **Sometimes negative statements must be proved.**[26]

A party who says that his adversary is prohibited from enjoying some right by a special law or constitution, must prove it. Likewise, if someone denies that something has been done properly, the answer must be that he himself has to present proof of that.

26. **Proof from antiquity.**[27]

In proving ancient boundaries and things, rumour and oral witnesses, and ancient books which have been made, kept and discovered without any suspicion, may persuade the judge to believe them, so that he may pass sentence rightly *and* in favour of the man proving his case, unless stronger proofs from the **other** party demand otherwise.

27.[28] **The acts of the judgment are to be faithfully kept.**[29]

The acts of the judgment constitute full proof. Therefore we desire that each and every one of them shall be accurately copied and sealed in the usual manner and transmitted to the appeal judges when they request or demand them, so that from them they may gather whether a lower judge has decided rightly.

[159r; 110a]   **42. DE POSSESSIONE**

1.[1]

Possessori non incumbit onus probandi res possessas ad se pertinere, cum, actore in probatione deficiente, dominium apud possessorem manere debeat.

In possessionis iure is superior et victor existimabitur, qui de antiquiore possessione fidem facere possit, maxime si illa aliquo titulo iustificata sit; nisi altera pars meliores et efficaciores probationes introduxerit, possessionem suam iustificantes.[2]

Possessiones quas ad te pertinere dicis, more iudiciorum persequere; non enim possessori incumbit onus probandi eas ad se pertinere, cum te in probatione cessante dominium apud eum remanebit.[3]

Res alienas possidens, licet iustam causam tenendi fortassis non habeat, non nisi intentionem suam implenti restituere cogitur.

Si fraude [*tamen*] vel violentia possessionem rei alienae aliquis nactus fuerit, illa possessio non solum [159v] illi non proderit, sed eum fortiori probatione aggravat, si ipse rem ipsam vel suam vel sibi debitam postea affirmet.[4]

---

[1]*Cod. Iust.*, 4.19.1, originally a rescript of Emperor Septimius Severus, 30 June 196.
[2]X, 2.19.9 (Fr, II, 311-12), originally a decretal of Pope Innocent III (1198-1216).
[3]*Cod. Iust.*, 4.19.2, originally a rescript of Emperor Antoninus, 17 November 215.
[4]X, 2.13.11 (Fr, II, 284-5), originally a decretal of Pope Celestine III (1191-8); X, 2.13.18 (Fr, II, 290), originally c. 39 of Lateran IV, 1215 (*C.O.D.*, 252-3). A note at the end of the chapter in Foxe's hand reads: '"De fide instrumentorum" require in folio 194.' ('"On the reliability of documents" see folio 194').

42. OF POSSESSION

1.[1]

The burden of proving that his possessions belong to him does not lie with the possessor, since if the plaintiff cannot prove his case, control ought to remain with the possessor.

In the right of possession, the one who can give proof that he had more ancient possession shall be considered the superior and the winner, especially if his claim is backed by some title, unless the other party produces better and more effective proofs which justify his possession.[2]

Pursue the possessions which you say belong to you by means of judgments, for the burden of proving that they belong to the possessor does not lie with him, since if you give up the trial, control will remain with him.[3]

Someone who possesses things which do not belong to him is not forced to restore them, even if by chance he has no just cause for holding them, except to the one who proves his case.

[*Nevertheless*] if someone has gained possession of someone else's goods by fraud or violence, that possession shall not only be of no benefit to him, but shall subject him to a greater burden of proof, if he later states that the thing in question is either his or is owed to him.[4]

[194r; 110a] 43. DE FIDE [*INSTRUMENTORUM*][1]

1. [De fide instrumentorum.][2]

In persequendis litibus eandem vim obtineant fides instrumentorum et depositiones testium.[3]

2. Instrument*orum*/a *partitio* publica.[4]

Instrumentorum alia sunt publica, alia privata. Publica, quae a notario nostra auctoritate creato cum [*testium*] *subscriptione* subscriptione [**testium**] fiunt. Quae autem nostri, alicuiusve archiepiscopi, episcopi, archidiaconi eiusve commissarii, seu of[110b]ficialis, aut alterius cuiuscunque, publicum gerentis officium, sigilli appensione muniuntur, authentica recte nuncupentur.

3. **Instrumenta privata.**[5]

Scripta privata dicimus, quae a privatis personis conficiuntur, nec aliquo publico seu authentico **sigillo** coadiuvantur; quae nisi ex archivo [194v] publico causam in se complectentia proferantur, vel ali[*ter*/i] probata fuerint, fidem facere nolumus.

4. **Privata scripta non valent, nisi trium testium subscriptione firmentur.**[6]

Privata scripta, quibus inter aliquas personas contrahitur, tum in iudicio valida sunto, et robur habento, si trium testium subscriptione firmentur, ne manus ambiguitate atque characterum collatione cum utriusque partis periculo sit laborandum, neve perfide negandi quae acta sunt, detur occasio.

---

[1]The section headings in this chapter were added by Archbishop Cranmer.
[2]This heading was originally the chapter title.
[3]*Dig.*, 22.4.1, originally Paulus, *Sententiae*, 1; *Cod. Iust.*, 4.21.15, originally a rescript of the Emperor Constantine I, 21 July 317.
[4]Hostiensis, *Summa aurea*, c. *De fide instrumentorum*; Panormitanus on X, 2.22.
[5]X, 2.22.2 (Fr, II, 344), originally a decretal of Pope Alexander III (1159-81); X, 2.22.6 (Fr, II, 346-9), originally a decretal of Pope Innocent III, 16 April 1199.
[6]*Cod. Iust.*, 4.21.20, originally a rescript of Emperor Justinian I, 19 March 530.

43. OF [*THE*] CREDENCE [*GIVEN TO DOCUMENTS*][1]

1. [Of the credence given to documents.][2]

In pursuing suits the credence of documents and the depositions of witnesses are of equal force.[3]

2. *Types of* public **documents.**[4]

Some documents are public and others private. Public ones are those which have been made by a notary appointed by our authority and carry the signature of witnesses. Those which are backed by the impress of the our seal, or of the seal of any archbishop, bishop, archdeacon or his commissary or official, or of anyone else holding public office, shall rightly be regarded as authentic.

3. **Private documents.**[5]

We call private documents those which are composed by private persons and which are not supported by any public or authentic **seal**, but we do not want them to have credence unless they are brought out of a public archive, as containing the entire cause in themselves, or have otherwise been proved.

4. **Private documents are invalid, unless they are signed with the signature of three witnesses.**[6]

Private documents, by which an agreement is made between certain persons, shall be valid in judgment and have force if they are signed with the signature of three witnesses, so that no harm may be done to either party by the ambiguity of the handwriting and a comparison of the letters, nor any opportunity be given for perfidiously denying what has been done.

5. Libri mercatorum.[7]

Exemplo perniciosum est, ut ei scripturae credatur, qua unusquisque annotatione
propria debitorem sibi aliquem constituit, unde neminem ex suis subnotationibus
debiti probationem praebere posse oportet, mercatorum tamen et aliorum artem
aliquam approbatam exercentium, libris et [195r] rationibus, cum aliis
adminiculis, plenam fidem adhiberi volumus.

6. Modus conficiendi instrumenta.[8]

In conficiendo instrumento hanc seriem observari volumus, ut scriba cum primis
a Dei nomine auspic{i}etur, annum Domini subdat, regis nomen, *et regni eius*
nomen **titulum et *annum* regni annum**, posthac mensem et diem eius, et nomen
loci ubi contractus initur. Deinde narrentur quae sunt exponenda, testes [111a]
adscribantur, aut subscribant. Notarii quoque obsignatio cum subscriptione ac
proprio signo in fine adiiciatur. **Scriptura [*t*/c]um alieno sigillo m[*uni*/inu]ta**
non minorem facit fidem quam si proprio esset obsignata, si hoc ipsum et
causa in eadem exprimatur.

7. Scripturarum comparatio.[9]

Scripturae legitimo modo comparatae semiplenam faciant probationem.

8. Instrumenta ipsa in iudicio exhibenda sunt.[10]

Instrumento publico causam suam probaturus [195v] ipsum exhibeat in iudicio.
Exemplaria nempe nihil faci[*e*/**a**]nt, nisi congrui iudicis auctoritate descripta
fuerint.

Instrumento semel in iudici[*um*/**o**] producto, viso, ac p[*er*/**rae**]lecto, sufficiat
verum ipsius exemplum, fideliter cum originali auctoritate iudicis collatum, actis
iudicii esse insertum.

---

[7]Cf. *Cod. Iust.*, 4.21.17, originally a rescript of Emperor Justinian I, 1 June 528. See
Panormitanus on X, 2.22.2.
[8]Speculum, 2.2, *De instrumentorum editione*, 2.4-9.
[9]Speculum, 2.2, *De probationibus*, 3.28.
[10]X, 2.22.1 (Fr, I, 344), originally a letter of Pope Gregory I (590-604), *Reg.*, 3.3.

5. Books of merchants.[7]

For example, it is pernicious for credence to be given to a document in which somebody has made another person his debtor by his own handwriting, and so no one must be allowed to offer proof of debt on the basis of his own notes, but we want full credence to be given to the books and accounts, along with other papers of merchants and others who engage in some approved trade.

6. How documents are to be composed.[8]

In composing a document we want the following order to be observed: first the scribe shall invoke the name of God, then add the year of the Lord, the name of the king and the *name* **title and year** of his reign, after that the month and the day, and the place where the contract was entered into. Then the matters to be explained shall be listed, and witnesses shall be mentioned or else they shall sign. The attestation of the notary shall also be added at the end with his signature and particular seal. **A document bearing the seal of someone else shall have no less credence than if it had been signed with the right one, if this fact and the reason for it are explained in the document.**

7. The preparation of documents.[9]

Documents prepared in a lawful way shall constitute partial proof.

8. The documents themselves must be produced in the judgment.[10]

Someone who intends to prove his cause by a public document shall produce the same in the judgment. Copies will obviously prove nothing unless they have been written by the authority of the relevant judge.

Once a document has been produced, verified and read in the judgment, it shall suffice for a true copy of the same, faithfully compared with the original on the judge's authority, to be inserted in the proceedings of the judgment.

9. Instrumenta quando exhibenda sunt.[11]

Unusquisque instrumenta usque ad *condictionem* **conclusionem** in causa, vel in causis, in quibus non concluditur, usque ad secundam termini ad audiendam sententiam assignationem exhibendi facultatem habeat. Et non po[te]st, nisi iudici, qui de causa cognoscit, ex iusta causa aliter visum fuerit.

[196r] 10. Contraria scripta.[12]

Sibi imputet, qui contrarias inter se scripturas in iudicio protulerit, fidem sibi invicem derogantes; cum in ipsius fuerit potestate quam maluerit non proferre.

11. Instrumenta publica valent mortuis testibus.[13]

Scripta publica propter mortem testium in eisdem descri[111b]ptorum deficere nulla ratio permittit.

12. De exustis /aut amissis/ instrumentis.[14]

Sicut iniquum est, instrumentis vi ignis consumptis, debitores renuere solutionem, ita non statim casum conquerentibus facile credendum est. Intelligere itaque debetis, non existentibus instrumentis, aliis argumentis probare *debet* debere fidem petitionibus adesse *cum instrumentis non intervenientibus*.

Apud eos, qui rem gestam ignoraverunt, amissorum instrumentorum habita testatio [196v] nihil ad probationem veritatis prodesse potest.[15]

---

[11]X, 2.22.9 (Fr, II, 350), originally a decretal of Pope Innocent III, 17 March 1207.

[12]*Cod. Iust.*, 4.21.14, originally a rescript of the Emperor Constantine I, 4 May 333; X, 2.22.13 (Fr, II, 352), originally a decretal of Pope Gregory IX (1227-41), published on or before 5 September 1234.

[13]Speculum, 2.2, *De instrumentorum editione*, 10.3.

[14]*Cod. Iust.*, 4.21.5, originally a rescript of Emperor Gordian III, 30 May 240; *Dig.*, 22.4.4, originally Gaius, *Formula hypothecaria*, 1; ibid., 22.4.5, originally Callistratus, *Quaestiones*, 2.

[15]*Cod. Iust.*, 4.21.13, originally a rescript of the emperors Diocletian and Maximian, 17 December 287.

9. When documents are to be produced.[11]

Anyone shall have leave to produce documents up to the *sentencing* **conclusion** of a cause, or in causes which have not been concluded, up to the second appointment of a time limit for hearing the sentence. And [*not afterwards* **he cannot**], unless the judge hearing the cause decides for some just cause to do otherwise.

10. Conflicting documents.[12]

Anyone who produces mutually conflicting documents in a judgment, which cancel each other out, shall bear the blame, since it was in his power to decide which of them he would rather not have produced.

11. Public documents are valid even after the death of the witnesses.[13]

There is no reason at all why public documents should be invalidated because of the death of the witnesses mentioned in them.

12. Of burnt /or lost/ documents.[14]

Just as it is unfair for debtors to renege on payment if the documents have been consumed by the force of fire, so also those who claim that there has been an accident are not to be readily believed. You must therefore understand that if there are no extant documents, you must prove whether credence can be given to the petitions by other arguments, **when there are no documents to support them**.

Among those who were ignorant of the transaction, testimony taken from lost documents can do nothing to help prove the truth.[15]

13. De instrumentis *rasis* suspectis.[16]

Instrumentum, si in loco minus suspecto sit abrasum, per hoc non censetur vitiosum, nec corruit ex fractura sigilli.

Si loco suspecto instrumentum vel rasuram vel lit*a*/**u**ram habeat, aut aliud aliquod nota**bi**le vitium, corruptum quidem est, et improbatur; verum non in universum, sed solummodo quoad illud caput, ubi vitium est depraehensum. Quo vero ad alia capita po[*te*]st fidem facere: secus tamen statuimus,[17] cum aliqua sua parte instrumentum falsum convincitur; quoniam tunc totum suspectum redditur, et ut falsum improbari potest.

Si sculptura sigilli eius dignitati vel officio, qui imposuisse dicitur, minus conveniat, instrumentum [197r] redditur suspectum.

13a. Scriptura alieno sigillo signata. [18]

Scriptura alieno sigillo munita non minorem facit fidem, quam si proprio esset obsignata, si hoc ipsum et causa in eadem exprimatur.

Cum cartam scriptura multo vetust*at*/**ior**em, vel dissimilitudinem in cera videas, instrumentum non immerito suspectum habeas.

Instrumenti fides, in quo una littera vel syllaba alterius loco apponitur, vel deest, si de sensu liquere possit, per hoc non vacillat.

Propter falsum Latinum ex unius litterae vel syllabae appositione loco alterius, aut litterarum transposi[197v]tione, vel similibus resultans, instrumentum corruere nolumus.

[112a] 14. Instrumenti improbatio.[19]

Si aliquod instrumentum quasi falsum [*confutare* **improbare**] in iudicio quis voluerit, primum iuramento se obstringat, quo se nil calumniandi causa esse d[*i*/**u**]cturum testetur; alioqui non audiatur.

Ad aliquod instrumentum improbandum quattuor aut quinque testes ad minimum exig[*u*/**a**]ntur, qui sint probatae fidei, et iudici omnino videantur idonei.

---

[16]X, 2.22.3 (Fr, II, 345), originally a decretal of Pope Alexander III (1159-81); X, 5.20.9 (Fr, II, 821-2), originally a decretal of Pope Innocent III, 19 November 1198.

[17]F altered the punctuation in order to make sense of the text. There, it reads: 'ad alia capita, post fidem facere secus tamen stauimus, cum...' ('to other chapters, but we decree that for them to be trusted afterwards is wrong, since...')

[18]X, 2.22.11 (Fr, II, 352), originally a decretal of Pope Honorius III, 17 November 1216.

[19]Hostiensis, *Summa aurea*, c. *De iuramento in litem dando*. This type of oath could be used for almost anything; cf. Gaius, *Institutes*, IV, 172, 176.

13. Of *erased* suspect documents.[16]

If a document is erased in a place which is not really suspect, it shall not be considered invalid on that account, nor does it lose its authority by the breaking of the seal.

If the document has an erasure or blot, or some other noticeable fault, in a suspect place, it is corrupt and invalid; however, not entirely, but only with respect to that chapter where the fault is discovered. As far as the other chapters are concerned, credence may be given to them, although we decree otherwise[17] when a document is proved to be false in some other part of it, since then the whole thing is rendered suspect and may be invalidated on the ground that it is false.

If the impress of the seal does not correspond to that of the dignity or official who is supposed to have affixed it, the document is rendered suspect.

13a. A document signed with someone else's seal.[18]

A document bearing the seal of someone else shall have no less credence than if it had been signed with the right one, if this fact and the reason for it are explained in the document.

When you notice that the parchment is much older than the document, or that there is some variation in the wax, you shall rightly hold the document suspect.

The credence of a document in which one letter or syllable is written in by someone else, or is missing, is not lessened for that reason, if it is possible to determine the meaning.

We do not want a document to lose its authority on account of bad Latin resulting from the addition of one letter or syllable by someone else, by the transposition of letters, or things like that.

14. The invalidation of a document.[19]

If someone wants to [*reject* **invalidate**] a particular document in the judgment, as being false, he must first bind himself with an oath by which he testifies that he will say nothing in order to slander anyone. Otherwise he shall not be heard.

In order to invalidate a document, at least four or five witnesses of proved trustworthiness, who appear to the judge to be entirely suitable, are required.

Cum instrumentis non intervenientibus venditio facta rata maneat, consequenter amissis quae intercesserant, non tolli substantiam veritatis placuit.[20]

[198r] *Statum tuum,* tu *natali professione perdita non esse mutilatum, si eundem aliter probare poteris, certi iuris est.*[21]

Si adversarius tuus apud acta praesidis, cum fides instrumenti quod proferebat in dubium revocaretur, non usurum se testatus est, vereri non debes ne ex ea scriptura, quam non esse veram ex professione eius constiterit, negotium denuo repetatur.[22]

15. De instrumentorum custodia.[23]

Si de tabulis testamenti vel aliis instrumentis communibus deponendis agatur, et dubitetur apud quem ea deponi oporteat, semper seniorem iuniori, et amplioris honoris inferiori, et marem feminae praeferemus.

[198v] 16. Instrumentum a diversis tabellionibus factum.[24]

Instrumentum ab aliquo tabellione inceptum, necdum vel propter subitaneam fortasse mortem, vel propter diuturnum impedimentum perfectum, auctoritate ordinarii, et eis requirentibus, quorum interest, potest a quovis alio tabellione perfici, perpetuam ut habeat fidem.

17. Descriptio vetusti instrumenti.[25]

Si instrumentum propter vetustatem vel aliam iustam causam describi petatur, congruo iudici offeratur; qui si diligenter inspectum in nulla sui parte vitiatum repererit, per publicam personam praecipiat describi, eandem auctoritatem per hoc cum originali habiturum.

---

[20]*Cod. Iust.*, 4.21.10, originally a rescript of the emperors Diocletian and Maximian, 25 October 287.

[21]*Cod. Iust.*, 4.21.6, originally a rescript of the emperors Diocletian and Maximian, 20 January 286.

[22]*Cod. Iust.*, 4.21.3, originally a rescript of the emperor Alexander Severus, 3 December 223.

[23]*Dig.*, 22.4.6, originally Ulpian, *Ad edictum*, 50.

[24]X, 2.22.15 (Fr, II, 353), originally a decretal of Pope Gregory IX (1227-41), published on or before 5 September 1234.

[25]X, 2.22.16 (Fr, II, 353), originally a decretal of Pope Gregory IX, published on or before 5 September 1234.

Since a sale which has been made without supporting documents remains valid, it follows that the substance of the truth is not removed even if the documents which supported it have been lost.[20]

Your status is not impaired because evidence of your birth has been lost; if you can prove it in some other way, your rights are assured.[21]

If your opponent has testified in the records of the presiding judge, when the credibility of the document which he has produced is called into question, that he would not make use of it, you must not be afraid that the business will be repeated all over again on the basis of that document, which he himself has admitted is not reliable.[22]

15. Of storing documents.[23]

If it is a question of depositing the sheets of a testament or other common documents, and there is some doubt as to with whom they ought to be deposited, we always give preference to an older over a younger, to one of higher honour over one of lower, and to a male over a female.

16. A document made by different recorders.[24]

A document begun by one recorder and not yet completed, either because of his death, which may have been sudden, or because of some long hindrance, may be completed by some other recorder acting on the authority of the ordinary at the request of the interested parties, so that it may have permanent credence.

17. The recopying of an old document.[25]

If a document needs to be recopied because it is old, or for some other good reason, it shall be presented to the relevant judge, who, if after carefully inspecting it, finds no defect in any part of it, shall order it to be copied by a public person, so that in this way it shall have the same authority as the original.

18. Antiquitatis probatio.[26]

In factis antiquis, et quae hominis excedunt memoriam, libros antiquos, et id genus alias privatas scripturas [199r] in [112b] archivo publico, [*seu*] alias fideliter custoditas plenam fidem facere statuimus.

19. Scripturis authenticis detrahitur fides, si unus ex testibus contradixerit.[27]

Sigillis authenticis, ac instrumentis quibus ipsa appenduntur seu adhibentur, consuetam fidem volumus adhiber[*i*/e], donec per probationes contrarias reprobentur; meritoque fides illius instrumenti vacillabit, cui vel unus testis in eodem descriptus contradixerit.

20. Adversarius non est cogendus in medium proferre quod contra se faciat.[28]

Actori deliberandum est antequam agat, quibus probationibus uti voluerit, frustra expectaturus, ut adversarius suus cogatur aliquid, quod contra se faciat, in medium proferre. Civilium tamen legum dispositioni, quoad instrumentorum editionem, per hanc legem nolumus derogari.

20a. *De chirographo cancellato.*[29]

Si chirographum cancellatum fuerit, licet p...

---

[26]Panormitanus on X, 2.22.2.
[27]Speculum, 2.2, *De instrumentorum editione*, 8.11.
[28]X, 2.19.1 (Fr, II, 306), originally a letter of Pope Gregory I (590-604), *Reg.*, 9.122.
[29]*Dig.*, 22.3.24, originally Modestinus, *Reg.*, 4. The full quotation reads: 'Si chirographum cancellatum fuerit, praesumptione debitor liberatus esse videtur, in eam tamen quantitatem, quam manifestis probationibus creditor sibi adhuc deberi ostenderit, recte debitor convenitur.' ('If the handwriting has been crossed out, the debtor is deemed by presumption to be excused, but the debtor is rightly obliged to pay the sum that the creditor can demonstrate by manifest proofs is still owed to him.').

18. Proof by reason of age.[26]

We decree that in questions concerning ancient facts, which extend beyond a person's memory, old books and other private documents of the same type, which have been faithfully kept in the public archive [*or*] elsewhere, shall have full credence.

19. The credence of authentic documents is diminished if one of the witnesses contradicts it.[27]

It is our will that the usual credence shall be accorded to authentic seals, and to the documents to which they are appended or affixed, until they are disproved by contrary proofs, but the credence of the document will rightly be weakened if one of the witnesses mentioned in it should contradict it.

20. The opposing party cannot be compelled to produce something which goes against him.[28]

A plaintiff must decide before he acts, what proofs he wants to use, for he cannot expect that his opponent can be compelled to produce something which goes against his interests. [*Only* Nevertheless] we do not want, by this law, to detract from the provision of the civil laws with respect to the publication of documents.

20a. *Of cancelled handwriting.*[29]

If the handwriting has been cancelled, although...

21. De rationibus defuncti.[30]

Rationes defuncti, quae in bonis eius inveniuntur, ad probationem sibi debitae quantitatis solae sufficere non possunt, nec etiam si in ultima voluntate defunctus certam pecuniae quantitatem aut etiam res certas sibi de[b/l]eri significavit.[31]

---

[30]*Cod. Iust.*, 4.19.6, originally a rescript of the Emperor Philip, 15 March 245.
[31]At the top of [199v] a note in Foxe's hand reads: "'De crimine falsi" require in folio 112'. ("'On the crime of forgery" see folio 112').

21. Of the accounts of the deceased.[30]

The accounts of the deceased which are found among his goods cannot by themselves suffice to prove the amount of debt owed to him, not even if in his last will, the deceased indicated a particular amount of money or even that he was owed certain things.[31]

[112r; 112b]   **44. DE CRIMINE FALSI**

1. Crimen fals[*i*/**um**] quid sit, et quando committatur.[1]

Crimen falsi veritatis est immutatio, quae dolo malo [*f*/**s**]it, et cum iactura fratris coniungitur, et cum [113a] in verbis tum in scriptis committitur, denique in omnibus quae in iudicio et usu publico rata et firma esse debent. Principio in hoc crimen incidunt qui falsa testimonia dicunt; deinde etiam qui mercede adducuntur, vel ut testimonium non ferant, vel ut ferant.

2. Quibus in rebus hoc crimen versetur.[2]

In eodem crimine sunt, qui testamenta, supremas hominum voluntates, codicillos, acta, instrumenta, syngraphas, vel alia[*s*] eius generis quascunque probationes, (ex quibus in iudiciis fides fieri possit), [*immut*/**nunti**]averint, vel ulla ratione perverterint, vel ad opprimendam, [*aut* **vel**] occulenda[*m veritatem*] ista celaverint, diffregerint, combusserint, aut sponte *sub* submoverint, aut quorumcunque [112v] scriptorum huius generis signa corruperint, seu ipsa scripta deleverint, seu quocunque modo interleverint. Nec solum auctores ipsi sunt rei, verum etiam et illi tenentur, qui scripta vel adulterata vel ullo modo depr[*a*/**i**]vata descripserint, obsignaverint, recitaverint, et /**in**/duxerint, allegaverint ad iudicium, vel qui talia scripta fieri pro[*cur*/**nunti**]averint aut consenserint ut fierent, modo scientes haec egerint et dolo malo. Tenentur etiam, qui citationes, inhibitiones, decreta, edicta, acta, vel scripta sive civilis fori, sive ecclesiastici, malitia violaverint quocunque modo, vel eorum obsignationes et signa seu corruperint, seu pro veris falsa subiecerint.

Hoc falsi crimen etiam in illis haeret, qui nomina ponunt in scriptis absentium, quasi praesentes fuissent, vel ipsa nomina distorquent, pervertunt, aut immutant dolo malo. Itidem, qui falsas litteras vel edicta falsa in nomine iudicum, tam civilium quam ecclesiasticorum, mittunt aut divulgant. Ad illos etiam crimen falsi pertinet, qui signis,⸳ quomodocunque detractis aut dimotis, alienas litteras patefaciunt, licet sint forte privatorum hominum, et eas vel ipsi legunt, vel adversario eius, a quo sunt scriptae, legendas ullo [113b] modo curant

---

[1]Panormitanus on X, 5.20.
[2]*Dig.*, 48.10.1, originally Marcian, *Institutes*, 14; *ibid.*, 48.10.25, originally Ulpian, *Ad edictum*, 7; *Cod. Iust.*, 9.25.1, originally a rescript of the emperors Diocletian and Maximian, 18 December 293; *ibid.*, 9.22.8, originally a rescript of the emperors Valerian and Gallienus, 29 June 259; H.C., 5.1.

44. OF THE CRIME OF FORGERY

1. What the crime of forgery is, and when it is committed.[1]

The crime of forgery is an alteration of the truth which is done with malicious intent, both when the deception of a brother is involved, and whether it is committed orally or in writing, as well as in all things which ought to be firm and certain in a judgment and in public affairs. First, those who give false testimony fall into this crime, as also do those who are bribed either to give testimony, or not to give it.

2. In what matters this crime occurs.[2]

Guilty of the same crime are those who [*alter* **announce**], or who for any reason pervert testaments, people's last wills, codicils, acts, documents, bonds or other proofs of that kind whatsoever, (on the basis of which credence may be had in a judgment), who hide, tear, burn or remove them of their own volition, either in order to suppress or to distort [*the truth*], or who corrupt the seals of any documents of this kind whatsoever, or who delete the writing or in any way insert extra material. Nor shall only the authors themselves be accused, but those who have copied, signed, read, produced and alleged writings which have been adulterated or in any way [*corrupted* **diminished**] in judgment, shall also be arrested, along with those who have [*had* **ordered**] such writings to be made or who have agreed that they should be made, provided that they did so knowingly and with malicious intent. Also those who from malice have in any way violated citations, inhibitions, decrees, edicts, acts or writings, either of the civil court or of the ecclesiastical, or who have corrupted their signatures or seals, or who have substituted falsehood for truth.

This crime of forgery also applies to those who put the names of absent parties in documents, as if they were present, or who twist, corrupt or alter the names with malicious intent. Likewise those who send or publish false letters or false edicts in the name of judges, both civil and ecclesiastical. The crime of falsehood also applies to those who open other people's letters by somehow breaking or removing the seals, even if they belong to private people, and either read them themselves or permit or somehow see to it that they are read by the

aut permittant; illo semper [113r] proviso, quod scientes et dolo malo faciant. Huius etiam criminis rei sunt, qui apud se deposita quaecunque instrumenta cum illis, qui contrarii/as [**etiam**] partes tuentur, communicant*ur*, nisi iudicis assensu fecerint, aut illius, qui instrumenta deposuit, et cui subserviunt. Eadem est illorum causa, et par culpa, qui testamentum clausum aut quomodocunque involutum explicant et evolvunt, si fraus suberat, et si nullum in patefaciendo ius habebant, ut id iuste possent facere; quod eodem modo valet in his, qui codices rationarios, praesertim mercatorum, quacunque ratione corrumpunt, vel folia ex illis aliqua*m* eximunt. Participes sunt huius criminis ipsi etiam notarii et scribae, cum testes scriptorum adhibent rerum omnium, quae tractantur, ignaros; si scientes hoc et dolo malo fecerint. Similiter peccant, qui supplicando aut petendo quippiam a principibus me[*nti*/**tu**]untur, seu veritatem ad rem praesentem necessariam tacent.[3]

Omnis igitur ad principes talis obrep{*s*/**t**}io iustissimum habere videtur hoc supplicium, ut *in* illis omnibus careant, ad quae non veritate sed mendacio et simulatione pervenerint. Deinde involvuntur omnes in hoc *crimine* crimen, qui litteras, instrumenta, syngraphas et huius generis alia quaecunque [113v] scripta, cum illa sciant vitiata vel depr[a/i]vata esse, tamen eadem apud se detinent, et illa nec rumpunt, nec exurunt, nec ullo modo abolent; immo ne notam quidem apponunt ullam, qua secerni possint. Nam damnum ex illis ad posteros saepe descendit. Denique illos etiam aequum est huc adnumerari, quorum tam insatiabilis et hians cupiditas est, ut eandem rem solidam et integram diversis pactis distrahant, et diversis hominibus divendant.

[114a] 2. *3.* Huius criminis rei et suspecti quomodo conveniuntur.[4]

Hos igitur ac eorum similes, contra quos falsi crimen obiici potest, iudex istis quattuor rationibus conveniet, **per** inquisitionem nimirum, aut accusationem, vel exceptionem, vel denuntiationem. Qui vero falsi non obscure suspectus fuerit, eum iudex appraehendi curabit, et appraehensum non liberabit, donec illi de veritate plane constit[**u**]erit.

---

[3] *Dig.*, 48.10.29, originally Modestinus, *De enucleatis casibus*, 1; cf. X, 5.20.1 (Fr, II, 816-17), attributed to Augustine (354-430).
[4] X, 5.1.16 (Fr, II, 737-8), originally a decretal of Pope Innocent III, 11 February 1203; X, 5.1.24 (Fr, II, 745-7), originally c. 8 of Lateran IV, 1215 (*C.O.D.*, 237-9). Cf. Speculum, 3.1, *De criminibus et eorum cognitionibus*, preface.

other party, against whom they were written, provided always that they do so knowingly and with malicious intent. Also accused of this crime are those who *share* **transmit** whatever documents are deposited with them *with* **to** those *which* who **are protecting** the opposite parties *are keeping* [**also**], unless they do so with the agreement of the judge or of the person who deposited the documents, and whose interests they serve. Similar is the case, and equal the guilt, of those who open and unravel a testament which has been somehow closed and wrapped up, if some fraud was intended and if they had no right to open it, in which case they could have done it justly. The same obtains for those who for any reason corrupt account books, especially those of merchants, or who remove pages from them. Also sharing in this crime are the notaries and scribes themselves, if they call on people to witness documents when they know nothing of the matters being transacted in them, and have done this knowingly and with malicious intent. Those who lie when asking or begging for something from the authorities, or fail to reveal truth which is necessary and relevant to the matter, are also guilty of this crime.[3]

Therefore every such deception against the authorities shall be seen to have this most just punishment, that they shall forfeit everything which they have acquired not by truth but by lying and pretence. Then all those who keep letters, documents, bonds and any other writings of this kind in their possession, even though they know that they are corrupt and have been tampered with, and do not tear them up, burn them or in some way destroy them, and do not even put some mark on them by which they may be detected, are also involved in this crime. For out of these things harm often comes to descendants later on. Finally, it is fair to add to the list those whose greed is so insatiable that they divide up one solid and complete thing and sell it to different people.

2. *3.* How those who are accused and suspected of this crime are summoned.[4]

Therefore, a judge may summon these and those like them, against whom the crime of forgery may be alleged, in these four ways, **by** inquest obviously, or accusation, or exception or denunciation. But the judge may see to it that anyone who is openly suspected of forgery is arrested, and once arrested he shall not release him until he tells the truth plainly.

3. *4.* Convictorum poenae.[5]

Qui vero *cum* accusati fuerint et legitime convicti, si conquiri possint et inveniri, poenas ecclesiasticas subibunt iudicum arbitrio rite pronuntiatas. [114r] Deinde fructibus carebunt et emolumentis, quae fuerant ex scripturis corruptis, aut ulla ratione perversis, ad se perventura, et illis etiam quae iam pervenerint. Praeterea cogentur, quantum facultates sinent, illis omnibus plene satisfacere, quorum conditio illorum fraude ulla in re deterior facta est. Infames etiam erunt, officiis et beneficiis, si quae sunt, removebuntur et pellentur, et nec officiorum nec beneficiorum unquam capaces erunt, ex eo tempore, quo in hoc genere criminis convicti damnatique sunt. Et si ministri fuerint, munere quo funguntur in ecclesia eos excludi oportet.

4. *5.* De scriptis corruptis quid statuendum sit.[6]

Quoniam diximus falsariis quid faciendum sit, consequens est ut videamus quid de scriptis ipsis statuendum sit; quae quoniam corrupta depravataque sunt, nullius illa momenti [*volumus*] aut ponderis esse [**volumus**], nec in iudicium introduci. Quin et illud praecautum sit, ut sententia si fuerit a iudicibus aliqua vel falsorum testium, vel scripturarum vio[114b]latarum auctoritate perlata, revocetur eadem et ret[*e*/**a**]xatur, *o...* et omnino pro nulla sit, et alia [114v] nova pronuntietur, quae conveniens sit regulae veritatis et iustitiae.

5. *6.* Fraus et dolus malus spectantur in crimine falsi.[7]

Interdum evenire potest, ut aliquis non dolo malo, nec sciens, sed ignorans, et ipse deceptus ab alio, falsum instrumentum pro vero sumat, et eo utatur. Quod si accidat, et is qui scripto sit usus, innocentiam in hac re suam iudici probare possit, illum omnino volumus hoc crimine liberari, quod nunquam consistere potest, nisi fraus et dolus malus ibi concurrerint.

6. *7.* Scribae vitium negligentia inductum quomodo puniatur.[8]

Accidit etiam, ut cum ex arch*i*etypo, vel (ut vulgo nominant) originali*a*, describitur aliquod instrumentum, scriba negligens et non satis animadvertens

---

[5]Cf. X, 1.3.43 (Fr, II, 35), originally a decretal of Pope Gregory IX (1227-41), published on or before 5 September 1234; X, 5.20.7 (Fr, II, 820-1), originally a decretal of Pope Innocent III (1198-1216).
[6]X, 1.3.11 (Fr, II, 20), originally a decretal of Pope Lucius III (1181-5).
[7]H.C., 5.7.
[8]X, 1.3.20 (Fr, II, 25), originally a decretal of Pope Innocent III, 17 November 1208.

MS Petyt 538/38, fos. 231r-246r (Inner Temple)

[231r] 3. *4*. The punishments of persons convicted.[5]

And those that shall be accused and lawfully convicted, if they can be sought out and found, shall suffer ecclesiastical pains, rightfully to be uttered by the discretion of the judges. Moreover, they shall lose their profits and gains that they /might have/ had by false writings or otherwise by any wrong means to come unto them or the which they have had heretofore. Besides that they shall be forced so far as they are able to satisfy and to make full amends unto all them whose state or condition through their deceit in anything hath been the worse. They shall also be disfamed persons, and shall lose their offices and benefices whatsoever, and be put out of them, neither shall they, from the time that they have been convicted and condemned for any such kind of crime, be apt to receive any office or benefice ever hereafter. /And if they be ministers, they shall lose that office in the church, the which they have./

4. *5*. What order is to be taken with false writings.[6]

Because we have said what is to be done with forgers of writings, now it remaineth that we see what order is to be taken with the writings self, the which because they are false and forged, we will not that they be of any value or moment, nor yet to be brought in to judgment, but this we will be forewarned, that if any judgment or sentence /hath/ been given by the judges, either through false witnesses or forged writings, we will the same be revoked, altered and altogether taken for no sentence, and another sentence be given, the which is agreeable to the rule of truth and justice.

5. *6*. Fraud and evil deceit are seen in the offence of forging.[7]

It may chance sometimes that a man may not by evil deceit, nor yet writing, but ignorantly, and deceived himself by some other, take a false writing for a true, and use the same, the which thing if it be chance, and he that hath used the writing can prove his innocency to the judge in this behalf, we will that such a man be altogether void of this offence, the which evil or wickedness can never be, but when fraud and evil deceits be meet together.

6. *7*. How should a clerk's or writer's offence committed by negligence be punished.[8]

It happeneth often that when any writing is taken or copied out of the original, a careless writer, or one that taketh no heed, doth err [231v] and putteth in

erret, ac aliquid secus ponat, qu[*am*/**od**] in originali collocatum est. Quod si nulla fraude factum esse, nec dolo malo, scriba defenderit et obtinuerit, falsi quidem non damnabitur, sed tamen negligentiae poenam dabit quam iudex assignaverit. Etenim illum oporte[*ba*]t in eo vigilare, ut suam scripturam ad primum exemplum [115r] diligenter accommodaret. Scriptum autem ipsum, in quo sic aberratum est, null[a/**u**]m omnino fidem habere potest.

7. *8.* Sigilla universitatum et societatum sine consensu praefecti et maioris partis universitatis non valent.[9]

Sigilla capitulorum, ecclesiarum, universitatum, hospitalium, et ali*o*/**arum** id genus societatum, non apponentur ad ullum diploma vel scriptum quodcunque, nisi praesens sit, aut [115a] consentiat, qui in societate praefectus est ceteris, et nisi cum praefecto conspiret *etiam* etiam maior pars canonicorum, vel sociorum, vel collegarum, vel eius cuiuscunque universitatis, penes quam eo tempore rerum gerendarum auctoritas est. Qua in re qui secus fecerint, aut fieri procuraverint, acerbe iudicum ecclesiasticorum arbitratu puniantur, et instrumenta vel diplomata vel scripta cuiuscunque generis secus obsignata quam praecepimus, ut falsa removeri volumus, et pro nullis haberi. Et si forte per illa quicquam damni fuerit cuiusquam rebus illatum, pro illo plene satisfiet ab his, qui vel ipsi consigna/r/unt, vel effecerunt vel consenserunt ut consignarentur scripta secus, quam a nobis prius est constitutum.[10]

---

[9]H.C., 5.3.
[10]A note in Foxe's hand on [115v] reads: '"De testibus eorumque dictis" require in folio 119'. ('"On witnesses and their statements" see folio 119').

something otherwise than is in the original. That if the writer can avow the same to be done, without fraud, or 'male engine', and that it so fall out, he shall not be condemned of forging, and yet he shall be punished for his negligence in such sort as the judge shall think good. For it is his part to be in that behalf very careful, that his writing do agree with the original, /and the writing itself that hath so erred, cannot have any authority or credit at all./

7. *8.* A seal of any university, society or college, without the consent of the head and the greater part of the university is of no force.[9]

Let no seals of chapter, churches, universities, hospitals and all other fellowships of like sort be put to any evidence or writing whatsoever, except he be present or be assenting unto it, that is the head over others, and except the *whole company* greater part of the canons, fellows, collegioners or any other company whatsoever, who at that time have authority to deal therein, be agreeing thereunto. Wherein if anyone do otherwise, or procure to be done otherwise, let them be sharply punished by the discretion and will of the ecclesiastical judges, and farther we will that all letters patents, evidence or writings whatsoever, otherwise sealed than we have commanded, be rejected as false and be of no value. That if any harm do happen to any man by any such writings, he shall be well satisfied of them that either have sealed any such writings themselves, or have compassed or presented that any such writings should be sealed otherwise, than before hath been by us approved.

[119r; 115a]   **45. DE TESTIBUS, EORUMQUE DICTIS**[1]

1. Quando testes examinandi sunt ante litem contestatam.[2]

Considerandum est, an probatio per testes fienda sit in causa principali, an in causa accessoria et emergenti. Si in causa incidenti et accessoria, (cuiusmodi sunt, quae oriuntur ex oppositis exceptionibus dilatoriis, et declinatoriis iudicii, atque etiam peremptoriis quibusdam, ut est exceptio transactionis rei iudicatae, litis finitio per iusiurandum), non est opus ut expectetur litis contestatio, quia tales controversiae obstant, quominus fieri iudicium de principali quaestione possit, nisi de illis prius constet id, quod constare non potest, si non [a/o]fferantur probationes. Necesse est itaque testes [119v] ad probandas tales exceptiones ante litis contestationem in principali causa factam admitti. In causa vero principali regulariter non admittitur testium probatio, [115b] nisi lis contestata sit; quia ante litis contestationem constitui non potest, quae sit inter litigantes principalis controversia. Ineptus itaque esset iudex, qui admitteret eius rei probationem fieri, de cuius controversia nondum ei satis constaret. Nonnunquam tamen et principalis negotii testes recipiuntur ante litis contestationem; sed hoc fit certis solum ex causis, et ex beneficio quodam iuris; ut si quis diuturnam absentiam aut mortem [*eorum*] metuat [**eorum**], quibus compertum sit negotium, quod in controversiam venire possit, [120r] curare potest, ut ad aeternam memoriam publico instrumento eorum testimonia describantur; vel si lis iam [m/n]ota sit, ut a iudice examinentur, lite nondum contestata. Ubicunque autem id fuerit factum, necesse est ut depositiones testium consignentur, et quamprimum fieri possit, denuntientur illis, quos metuat quis sibi futuros adversarios ea in re; nec publicentur, donec elapsus sit annus post receptionem talium testium, aut lis sit contestata, ne fraudi sit illis ignorasse ea de re receptos esse testes.

2. Dilatio ad producendum testes.[3]

Ea pars cui incumbit probatio, potest petere sibi dari dilationem a iudice ad producendum [120v] testes; quam ei dare iudex tenetur, adhibita competenti moderatione temporis, secundum spatia quibus distat testium habitatio a iudicis

---

[1]A marginal note on [118r] in Cranmer's hand reads: 'For Mr. Morres'.
[2]Speculum, 1.4, *De teste*, 2.1-7.
[3]*Ibid.*, 3.7.

45. OF WITNESSES AND THEIR SAYINGS[1]

1. When are witnesses to be examined before the contestation of the controversy, or issue joining.[2]

It is to be considered whether the proof by witnesses ought to be made in the principal cause, or in the accessory or happening cause that falleth out upon the matter. If it be to be done in the incident or accessory cause (as those causes are that rise /of/ exceptions, restrictings and declinings of judgment, and also of [232r] certain peremptory exceptions, as exceptions of transaction, of a thing judged, the ending of controversy by an oath), it is not needful that in these cases the joining of issue be looked for, because such controversies are a let that judgment cannot be given of the principal cause, except the others be known before, the which cannot appear except the proofs be offered. It is necessary therefore that the witnesses be admitted to prove such exceptions before the issue contested in the principal cause. But the proof of witnesses commonly is not admitted in the principal cause, except the issue be contested. For before the joining of issue, it *is* cannot be determined what is the chief controversy betwixt the parties that do contend. Foolish therefore were that judge who would admitted proof to be made of that thing whereof he did not yet know the controversy. And yet sometimes witnesses are received even of the principal cause, before issue joining, but this is done for certain causes only, and for an especial benefit of the laws. As for example, if a man do fear the long absence or death of them unto whom the matter is well known, that is like to come in law, he may provide that for an eternal memory, their testimony may be written in a public instrument, or if the matter be commenced, he may make suit to have the witnesses examined of the judge, although the issue be not yet contested. But wheresoever this thing shall be done, it is necessary that the deposition of witnesses be consigned, and as soon as may be, showed unto them, whom a man feareth will be his adversaries, and not published, till a year be past after the receipt of such witnesses, or that issue be contested, lest it be a hurt to them to be ignorant that witnesses were taken upon that matter.

2. Respiting to bring forth witnesses.[3]

That party who must prove may ask time of the judges to bring forth witnesses, the which the judge is bound to give [232v] unto him, allowing reasonable time, according as the witnesses do dwell from the judge's house. And whilst the time

domicilio. Et dum durat tempus datae dilationis, potest producens vel una vel terna vice ad iudicem nomina eorum, quos producturus est testes, referre; quarta vice hoc ei [*non*] conceditur, nisi iuret de calumnia.

3. Articuli probationis.[4]

Relatis ad iudicem nominibus testium, simul exibenda sunt capita dicendi testimonii.

[116a] 4. Testium citatio.[5]

Producens vero testes curet eos a iudice citari, et eis certum constitui tempus deponendi [121r] suum testimonium. Suspecti enim habentur testes, qui [*ultro*] se [**ultro**] obtrudunt iudici ad perhibendum testimonium. Ad fidem tamen rei gestae etiam non rogati testes sufficiunt.

5. Adversae partis citatio.[6]

Non solum autem testes, sed et pars, contra quam illi producuntur, vocanda est ad audiendum et videndum testes produci, generali clausula citationum adiecta, quod sive venturus sit, sive non, tamen iudicem processurum in causa, quantum de iure possit. Estque simul ei facienda copia articulorum, quos ille, qui testes produxit, iudici exhibuit; ut si ei libeat, interponere possit suas interrogationes.

[121v] 6. Interrogationes.[7]

Interrogari autem potest et de personae fide, et de negotii circumstantiis. Ad personae fidem spectant explorandam studia, mores, voluntates, fortunae, **aetas, cognatio, totiusque vitae** conditio. Ad negotii vero circumstantias pertinent quomodo in eius rei notitiam testis pervenerit, an ips[*e*/**i**] negotio interfuerit, an ab aliis acceperit, et quare factum, quodque sit, quo tempore, quo loco, qua spe, quo consilio.

---

[4]*Ibid.*, 3.4.
[5]*Ibid.*, 3.6. *Dig.*, 22.5.11, originally Pomponius, *Ad Sabinum*, 33.
[6]X, 2.20.2 (Fr, II, 315-16), originally a letter of Pope Gregory I (590-604), *Reg.*, 13.45.
[7]*Dig.*, 22.5.2, originally Modestinus, *Regulae*, 8; ibid., 22.5.3, originally Callistratus, *De cognitionibus*, 4.

of this respiting doth continue, he that bringeth to the judge once or thrice the names of those folk whom he will produce for witnesses, may refuse them the first time. That much is granted unto him, except he do swear 'De calumnia', the which is that he doth not seek maliciously any man's vexation.

3. Articles of probation.[4]

When the names of the witnesses are relayed unto the judge, the chief points of the testimony that they would give ought also to be exhibited.

4. The calling of the witnesses.[5]

He that doth bring forth the witnesses ought to provide that they be cited and called by the judge, and that they may have a time appointed unto them, to give their testimony. For those witnesses are to be suspected that voluntarily offer themselves to the judge, because they would bear witness. And yet to /make/ prove /of/ a thing done, witnesses not desired are thought sufficient.

5. Citation of the contrary party.[6]

Neither yet only be the witnesses to be called, but also the contrary party, against whom the said witnesses are produced, is to be called to hear and see the witnesses produced, with *those* this general clause of citation added, that whether the party do come or do not come, yet the judge will proceed in the cause so far forth as by law he may. And the party also must have a copy of the articles, the which were exhibited /to the judge/ by him, that produced the witnesses, that if he list, he may put forth /his/ interrogatories.

[233r] 6. Interrogatories.[7]

Interrogatories may be made both of the faith and trust of the man, and also of the circumstances of the matter.

And for the trial of a man's honesty these things are to be considered - his bringing up, his manner of life, his disposition, his state, **his age, his kindred or stock,** and his **whole** condition **of his life**. Touching the circumstances, these things are to be weighed, how the witnesses came to the knowledge of that thing, whether they were there present at the business or that they heard it of others, and wherefore everything was done, by what counsel, way or means.

7. Dilatio ad interrogationes concipiendas.[8]

Ad has autem interrogationes concipiendas itidem potest peti dilatio a parte, contra quam testes producuntur. *Nec*non autem debet *et* iudex interrogationum copiam facere parti *m*... [122r] producenti testes, ne eos ex his ad respondendum instituat.

[116b] 8. Protestatio in exhibitione interrogationum.[9]

Potest quoque pars in exhibitione interrogationum protestari, quod eatenus velit admittere testes productos, ut sibi salvum maneat ius reprobandi eorum personas et dicta per alios testes. Nisi enim quis ante publicationem testimoniorum de reprobatione testium protestatus fuerit, postea non auditur, nisi iuret se nulla malitia nec dolo ad protrahendam litem, ad faciendum talem reprobationem induci, et nunc primum se id reperisse, quod testibus obiecturus sit.

9. Iuramentum testium.[10]

Requiritur autem, ut testes iuramentum [122v] praestent, antequam quicquam depona[*nt*/**tur**]; quia testi non iurato, (quantumvis religiosus ille fuerit), non creditur in alterius praeiudicium. Iurabunt autem totam dicturos veritatem, quam norunt, de re super qua iurant, nec ullam admixturos falsitatem; quod pro utraque parte dicent veritatem, quam sciunt ad negotium pertinere, etiam non interrogati; et quod nec pretio, nec amore aut odio, nec timore aut commodo quocunque dicent testimonium. Nihilominus partibus invicem re[*mitt*/**nu**]entibus ut non iurent testes, creditur etiam non iuratis. Iuramentum testium extendere volumus ad omnem causam, et etiam interrogatoria qua*nt*/**ecu***m*/**n**que legitimae rei, nisi specialiter super [123r] uno articulo producantur.

10. Diebus feriatis non iuretur.[11]

Testes diebus feriatis iuramentum ne praestent, cum de processu iuris sit, et actus iudicialis.
    Examinari vero testes iurati quocunque tempore possunt, quia examinatio testium non est iudicialis actus, sed seorsim et secreto loco fit, [117a] ut

[8]Cf. Hostiensis, *Summa aurea*, c. *De dilationibus*.
[9]Speculum, 1.4, *De teste*, 10.1-5.
[10]*Ibid.*, 4.1. Cf., X, 2.20.39 (Fr, II, 332), originally a decretal of Pope Innocent III, 22 March 1208; X, 2.20.51 (Fr, II, 339), originally a decretal of Pope Honorius III, 1 March 1225.
[11]X, 2.9.1 (Fr, II, 270), originally c. 37 of the council of Mainz, 813.

7. Respiting for the interrogatories to be conceived.[8]

A time also may be desired to conceive these interrogatories by the party against whom the witnesses are produced. Neither ought the judge give any copy of the interrogatories to him that produced the witnesses, lest he should thereby instruct his witnesses /how/ to make answer.

8. A protestation upon the establishing of the interrogatories.[9]

The party may, when he doth exhibit his interrogatories, protest that he will so far forth admit the witnesses produced as that he may by law object against their persons and sayings, by other witnesses. For except a man do protest to reprove witnesses, before publication of them, he shall not afterwards be heard, except he do swear unto the judge that he doth not bring any such reproving against the witnesses for any malice or fraud, to prolong the matter, and that he did now and not before find out the matter that he hath to object against the witnesses.

9. The oath of the witnesses.[10]

It is further required that the witnesses take a proposed oath before they do depose anything, because a witness that is not sworn [233v] although he be a religious man, is not believed to the prejudice of another man. They shall swear to tell the whole truth that they know in the *nigh* things whereof they do swear, and that they will not impart any falsehood, but that they will say the truth for both parties, that they know belongeth to the matter, although they were not asked, and that neither for greed, nor love nor hatred nor fear, nor yet for any worldly profit, they will bear witness. And yet notwithstanding, although the parties upon both sides do refuse to swear, [...] they are believed, although they do not swear. We will that the oath of the witnesses be extended unto the whole cause, and that all interrogatories whatsoever of a lawful matter be produced, but specially upon one article.

10. No oath to be taken upon the holy days.[11]

Let no witnesses take an oath upon the holy days forasmuch as an oath taking is part of the process of the law and a judicial act.

And sworn witnesses may be examined at any time, because the examination of witnesses is no judicial act, but is done severally and in a secret place, that

liberiores sint testes ad dicendum testimonium. Nam testimonium habetur pro nullo, quod palam omnibus dictum est.

11. Del[e/i]gatio examinationis.[12]

Potest autem iudex vel ipse testes examinare, vel id munus alteri committere; verum is, [c/q]ui commiserit testium examinationem, non potest porro alii delegare, quia eius industria videtur esse electa.

[123v] 12. Reiectio testium quando fienda.[13]

Testes admitti volumus ad dicendum testimonium, etiam si contra eorum personas obiectum sit; nisi obiecta sit eis excommunicatio, aut [o/a]pponens afferat promptam suae oppositionis probationem.

13. Testes per iudicem cogendi sunt, si venire recusant.[14]

Si qui testes requisiti venire recusaverint, hi iudicis auctoritate compellendi sunt, cum non minus fere delinquat is, qui veritatem supprimere conatur, quam qui false/o deposuerit.

14. Qui in testimonium venire cogi non possunt.[15]

Testes non temere evocandi sunt per longum [124r] iter, multoque minus milites a suis signis vocandi sunt, perhibendi testimonii causa, *ceterum quoad hoc consuetudinem cuiusque provinciae regni nostri quoad testes evocandos observari praecipimus.*

---

[12]*Speculum*, 1.4, *De teste*, 7.1.
[13]*Ibid.*, 1.31-2.
[14]X, 2.21.1 (Fr, II, 341), originally a decretal of Pope Alexander III (1159-81).
[15]*Dig.*, 22.5.3.6, originally Callistratus, *De cognitionibus*, 4; *ibid.*, 22.5.19, originally Ulpian, *De officio proconsulis*, 8.

witnesses may be more free to give their testimony. For that testimony is /had for/ no testimony, that is spoken openly before all men.

11. Appointing of examination.[12]

The judge himself may either examine witnesses or else he may commit that office to another. But he unto whom the examination of the witnesses is committed cannot appoint the same unto others, because his diligence and travail seemeth to be chosen.

12. When are witnesses to be rejected.[13]

We will that witnesses be admitted to give evidence, although there be matter laid against their persons, except excommunication be laid against them, or he that doth lay in matter doth bring ready proof thereof.

[234r] 13. Witnesses are to be forced by the judge to come, if they do refuse to come.[14]

If any witnesses be required to come and do refuse, they are to be compelled by the authority of the judge to appear, because he doth no less offend, that seeketh to suppress or to hide the truth, than he doth that deposeth a falsehood or untruth.

14. Who cannot be compelled to bear witness.[15]

Witnesses are not rashly to be called a great way off, and much less are soldiers to be called from their ensigns to bear witness. *But with regard to this, we order that the custom of each province of our kingdom be observed in the matter of calling forth witnesses.*

15. Ad nobiles et debiles eundum est p*er*/**ro** illorum examinatione*m*.[16]

Si testes in maiori aliqua dignitate constituti [*sunt* **fuerint**], aut aliquo naturali inevitabili*qu*/ve *vi* impedimento detenti, ut ad [117b] iudicium congrue [*ac* **et**] commode venire non possunt, tunc iudex aut ad eosdem descendat, aut examinationem illorum bono viro committat.

16. Officium testium.[17]

Officium testis in hoc maxime versatur, ut de rebus sibi bene notis veritatem expr*om*/**n**at. [124v] Prohibemus igitur, ne qui testes cuiuscunque status, conditionis, seu nominis existant, iudicandi officium in se assumant, neque de criminibus aliquibus aliquid statuant, nec etiam inquirant, nisi ad mandatum illius iudicis, qui *per has leges nostras* cognitionem ipsius causae, (in qua aliquid agere conantur), habere dinoscatur, sub poena contemptus.

17. Qui a testimonio repellendi sunt.[18]

Repelli volumus a testimonio omnes de crimine aliquo famoso condemnatos, inimicos capitales, domesticos, quibus imperari potest ratione patriae vel dominicae potestatis, parentes etiam, et eos qui loco parentum sunt, impuberes, ac [125r] mente captos, palam quaestum facientes, proxenetas et causarum sollicitatores in illis causis, quas sollicitasse noscuntur (nisi utraque pars consentiat). Nec non eos, qui in re sua testimonium dicere conantur: a testimonio penitus arceantur.

De criminibus autem suspecti, mercenarii (alias probi, et honesti) amici, mulieres, consanguinei, cum quibus matrimonium de iure divino *non* **non**[19] prohibetur, qui ante [*in*] alteram partem testimonium dixerint, ad testimonium admitti possunt. Sed bonus iudex ex fide, dignitate, moribus, gravitate constantiaque illorum, ac rei, de qua controvertitur, mole, facile existimare poterit, quid aut credat, aut [125v] parum per ipsos probatum opinari debeat.

---

[16]Cf. X, 2.20.8 (Fr, II, 318), originally a decretal of Pope Eugenius III (1145-53).
[17]Cf. Hostiensis, *Summa aurea*, c. *De testibus*, 5; Baldus, *De teste* in Speculum, 1.4, *idem*.
[18]*Dig.*, 22.5.4, originally Paulus, *Ad legem Iuliam et Papiam*, 2; *ibid.*, 22.5.5, originally Gaius, *Ad legem Iuliam et Papiam*, 4; *ibid.*, 22.5.6, originally Licinius Rufinus, *Regulae*, 2; *ibid.*, 22.5.7, originally Modestinus, *Regulae*, 3; *ibid.*, 22.5.8, originally Scaevola, *Regulae*, 4.
[19]Added in an unknown hand after having been deleted.

15. Noblemen and sick folk must be gone unto, when they are to be examined.[16]

If the witnesses be in any high estate of degree, or by any natural /sickness/ or incurable let detained, that they cannot well appear in judgment, then the judge must come unto them, or else must commit the examination of them to some honest man.

16. The duty of witnesses.[17]

It is the /chief/ duty of witnesses to speak the truth of those things that they do best know. We do therefore forbid witnesses of what condition, estate or degree soever they are, that they take not upon them to be judges, neither determine upon any offences, nor yet inquire upon them, except by the commandment of that judge who is known to have understanding *by these our laws* of that cause wherein they seek to deal, under pain of contempt or disobedience.

17. Who are to be removed from giving witness.[18]

We will that all those shall be removed from giving witness that are condemned of any heinous offence, such as are deadly enemies to the party, of household to the party, over whom the party hath power to command by reason of his fatherly or lordly power, parents and those that are instead of parents, young folk under years, mad folk, open gain getters, attorneys or solicitors of <*meet*> such causes, wherein they are known to have travailed, except both the parties be agreed thereunto. And those also that would bear witness in their own cause, all such must altogether be removed from giving witness.

/And yet/ such as are suspected of crimes, hirelings /or men that take wages/ (otherwise being honest and good men), friends, women, kinsfolk to whom marriage is not[19] forbidden by the law of God, that have given witness before upon the other side, may be admitted to bear witness. But a good judge may easily discern by the uprightness, dignity, behaviour, [234v] gravity and constancy of them, and by consideration of the weight of the matter whereof the testimony riseth, what he may /either/ believe or ought to think that is not sufficiently proved by them.

[118a] 18. Quorundam testimonia repellenda sunt.[20]

Qui falso vel varia testimonia dixerint, vel utrique parti causam prod*ux*/**id**erint, quique ob testimonium dicendum, vel non dicendum, pecuniam [*acce*/**reci**]pisse iudicati fuerint, non solum fide omni carebunt, sed etiam a iudicibus condigne punientur, et parti laesae satisfaci[*e*/**a**]nt.

19. Qui a testimonio repellendi sunt.[21]

Particeps criminis minorque viginti annis in criminalibus causis testimonium reddere non debent; nec is etiam qui ante in simili causa testimonium in eum dixisse probabitur. Procuratores, advocati, [126r] ceterique negoti[*orum*/**a**] alicuius gerentes ad testimonium pro dominis suis non admitt[*u*/**a**]ntur.

At si adversa pars eorum testimoniis uti voluerit, veritatem, quam noverint, (post depositum officium) dicere cogentur.

20. Testes de universitate.[22]

Singuli de universitate aliqua possunt esse testes in causa ipsius universitatis, si non principaliter de iure ipsius testis agatur, aut de singulari suo et non universitatis commodo agatur.

21. Testes domestici quando adhiberi possunt.[23]

Usu compertum est, nonnullos (sive taedio prioris [126v] coniugii affectos, sive spe secundi magis prosperi matrimonii d*o*/**u**ctos), crimen adulterii coniugibus suis impingere. Sit igitur iudex in hac parte prudens, nec facile sibi imponi permittat, nec quibuscunque credat, qui *susp*... suspicione aliqua laborent, quive dictorum suorum probabilem aliquam et concludentem rationem non attulerint. Sed quando de natura istius actus [118b] non solent testes adhiberi, domesticis (alias honestis et fide dignis) credi potest, nisi partis accusatae bona fama et inculpata vita conversatioque honesta praeponderet.

---

[20]*Dig.*, 22.5.16, originally Paulus, *Sententiae*, 5.
[21]*Dig.*, 22.5.20, originally Venuleius, *De iudiciis publicis*, 2.
[22]Speculum, 1.4, *De teste*, 1.22; cf. X, 1.38.7 (Fr, II, 215-16), originally a decretal of Pope Innocent III (1198-1216).
[23]Speculum, 1.4, *De teste*, 1.19, 39; Panormitanus on X, 1.40.7.

18. <*When are*> /certain/ testimonies /to be/ refused.[20]

They that have falsely testified or varied in their witness greatly, or uttered the matter to both the parties, or those that have taken money, either to bear witness or not to bear witness, they shall not /only/ lose their credit for ever, but also they shall worthily be punished of the judges, and shall make recompense to the party offended.

19. Who are to be rejected from giving witness.[21]

Partakers of the crime and he that is younger than twenty years cannot bear witness in criminal causes. Neither he that in a like cause hath borne witness, by proof, against the same man. Proctors, advocates and all others that deal in the affairs of other men cannot bear witness for their lords. That if the contrary party will use their testimonies, they shall be enforced to say the truth that they know (when they are out of office).

20. Witnesses of a corporation or university.[22]

Every/one/ of any body <*b...*> politic may be witness in a cause of the same body, if dealing be not principally of the right of a witness, or of his private commodity, and not of the universal profit of the body politic.

21. When may domestical witnesses be brought in.[23]

It falleth out by daily experience that many men, either weary of their former marriage or else for hope of a second, better marriage, do lay adultery to their wives. Let the judge therefore be wise in this behalf, neither let him suffer himself to be easily deceived, neither let him believe everybody that may anything be suspected or the which be not held to give a probable and concluding reason of their sayings. But when witnesses are not to be had of the nature of this act, domestical persons, being otherwise honest, and to be lettered, are to be trusted, except the good fame and undefiled life of the contrary party and her honest conversation be of more weight and validity than their reports or sayings are.

[127r] 22. Qui semel approbat personam testis semper videtur approbare, nisi nova emerserit exceptio.[24]

Qui approbat personam testis in uno actu, approbat eam in omni alio, nisi nova infirmandi causa supervenerit. Ideo contra personam testis, quem quis semel produx[er]it, non potest [o/a]pponere, nisi causa de novo emerserit; contra eius tamen dicta licebit opponere.

23. In aliena causa plures testes ex eadem familia adhiberi possunt.[25]

Ni[hi]l obstat, quominus plures etiam testes ex eadem familia alieno negotio semper possunt adhiberi.

24. Teste/is alicuius scripti propter crimen postea commissum aut patefactum reiici non debent.[26]

Si quis ex testibus testamenti quidem, aut alterius [127v] cuiusquam instrumenti, confectionis tempore (in quo ipse testis describitur) liber aut ab omni crimine alienus communi hominum aestimatione et opinione habebatur, testimonium ipsius ex crimine aliquo latenti, seu ex delicto aliquo postea detecto, patefacto, seu commisso, infici non debet, nec quicquam fidei illius detrahendum est, nisi testator per tres menses a crimine *homini* **huiusmodi** patefacto supervixerit, nec alium loco illius submittendum curaverit.

[119a] 25. Qui paenitentiam egerunt, ad testimonii fidem restitui possunt.[27]

Ceterum cum nos semper pro pietate nostra in subditos nostros magis cupiamus eos semper [128r] lucrari, quam in desperationem adigere, si quis criminosus crimini suo penitus renuntiaverit, ac condignam paenitentiam ecclesiae iudicio pro eodem peregerit, ac ad frugaliorem vitam redierit, testimonii tunc dicendi facultatem illi restituendam duximus.

---

[24]Speculum, 1.3, *De teste*, 1.26-7, 41.
[25]*Dig.*, 22.5.17, originally Ulpian, *Regulae*, 1.
[26]Speculum, 1.4, *De teste*, 1.27.
[27]*Ibid.*, 1.86.

[235r] 22. He that doth once allow the person of a witness doth always seem to allow him, except some new exception do arise.[24]

He that doth allow the person of a witness in one act doth allow the same in all other acts, except some new cause of information do happen. Therefore none can object to the person of the witness whom he hath once allowed, except a new cause do rise thereupon, and yet it is lawful to object against his sayings.

23. Many witnesses of one family may be brought to depose in another man's cause.[25]

There is no let but that many witnesses of one family may be brought to depose in another man's cause.

24. A witness of some writing ought /not/ to be rejected for any fault that he doeth afterwards, being brought to light.[26]

If any witness, at the time of a will making, or of any other kind of writing wherein the witness's *is* name is written, being then free from all kind of crime, by the common opinion of men, the same man's testimony ought not to be discredited for any hidden offence or crime, afterwards detected and known to be bared, neither ought any credit to be taken from him, except the said estator do overlive three months after **such** an offence known *to the man*, and <*neither*> seeketh /not/ to appoint some other person in his place.

25. Those that have done penance may be restored to grave witnesses.[27]

But forasmuch as we do ever desire for the love and zeal that we have to our subjects, rather to win them than that they should fall into desperation, if any open offender do renounce utterly his offence and do worthy penance for the same, according to the judgment of the church, and becometh a man of better life, we thought good to give /power/ unto him to bear witness.

26. Quibus testibus fides sit habenda.[28]

Testibus iuratis et non testimoniis convenit fidem adhibere: illis tamen testibus credendum est, qui concludenter aut praesumptive rem, de qua agitur, approbant.

27. Super eisdem aut contrariis articulis non licet saepius testes producere.[29]

Quicunque semel, aut plur[*i*]es testes aliquos produxerit, ac testificata tractaverit, aut [128v] quoquo modo eadem didicerit, non habebit ipse licentiam vel eosdem vel alios super eisdem vel directo contrariis articulis producendi.

28. Quando testes repeti possunt.[30]

Testes plene examinandi sunt, nec a suis negotiis saepe avocandi. Si tamen aut dolo iudicis aut negligentia debito modo examinati non sunt, id parti recte libellanti, seu articulos proponenti, nocere non debet, quin eidem testes repeti possunt. Ceterum si partis culpa aut negligentia defectus aliquis in testium dictis depraehendatur, illi nusquam succurretur, nec ipsi testes postea repetiti sive ex officio, sive ad [129r] eius instantiam aliquid sibi prodesse poterunt.

[119b] 29. Poena testium pe{**r**}iurantium.[31]

Si quis posthac adeo officii sui immemor fuerit, ut aliqua [*caeca*] affectione ductus falsa aut mult*a**/**um*** varia reddidisse depraehendatur testimonia, is extraordinarie pro arbitrio iudicis, quem in hac parte offenderit, punietur. *Volentes* **Volumusque** omnes ministros nostros in executione poenarum huiusmodi falsis testibus inflictarum, sive infligendarum, ad requisitionem dictorum iudicum promptos ac paratos semper *futuros* esse, sub poena contemptus.

---

[28]*Dig.*, 22.5.2, originally Modestinus, *Regulae*, 8; *ibid.*, 22.5.3, originally Callistratus, *Cognitiones*, 4.
[29]*Dig.*, 22.5.23, originally Venuleius, *De iudiciis publicis*, 1.
[30]Speculum, 1.4, *De teste*, 8.5.
[31]Panormitanus on X, 5.20.1.

26. What witnesses are to be trusted.[28]

Faith ought to be given to sworn witnesses and not to the testimonies or sayings of men. And those witnesses are to be believed the which do prove the matter, the which they take in hand, either concludently or else by good likelihoods and presumptions.

27. Witnesses ought not often to be produced upon the same, or contrary articles.[29]

Whosoever hath once produced diverse witnesses and handled their testimonies, or by any means hath /learned or/ rehearsed again the same, it shall be lawful for him to produce of new, either the same witnesses or others [235v] upon the same articles or else upon another that are directly contrary.

28. When may witnesses be repeated.[30]

Witnesses ought to be fully examined, neither should they be often called from their business. That if they be not examined as they ought to be, either by the deceit or the negligence of the judge, the same ought not to hurt the party that hath duly put in his deposition, or proponed his articles, but that the said witnesses may be repeated. But if any default be found in the sayings of the witnesses, by any default or negligence of the party, he shall never be holpen, neither the witnesses, being afterwards repeated, either by office or at the instance of the party, shall do him any good at all.

29. The punishment of perjured witnesses.[31]

If any /man/ hereafter be so forgetful of his duty that he be found for affection's sake to have uttered any untruth, or to have varied in his depositions, the same man shall be punished extraordinarily by the discretion of the judge, whom in this behalf he hath offended. And we will that all our officers shall be ready to do execution upon such false witnesses when they are required by the learned judges and doctors to do this same, upon pain of contempt and disobedience.

30. Quando testis rationem sui dicti reddere teneatur.[32]

Testis in acti[*bu*]s omnibus sensu corporeo [129v] percepti[*bi*]libus debet reddere rationem dicti sui per illum sensum ita demum si fuerit interrogatus. At in rebus sensibus huiusmodi non subiectis, debet rationem reddere non interrogatus.

31. De testibus extraiudicialibus.[33]

Dictum testis iudiciale non tollitur per dictum suum extraiudiciale contrarium; sed nisi aliquam iustam rationem, quod tam varia aut repugnantia protulerit testimonia, reddere idem testis poterit, multum fidei illius detrahetur.

32. Testibus expensae sunt solvendae.[34]

Quotiescunque testes a suis negotiis pro [130r] ferendo testimonio avocantur, id fieri volumus expensis partis eos producentis, qui expensas illorum tempore a[*rr*/**cc**]epti itineris, donec iterum ad habitationes suas reversi fuerint, sustinebit.

33. Reprobatorii testes non sunt per alios reprobandi.[35]

Reprobatorii reprobatoriorum testium admittendi non sunt, ne si producendi quartos contra tertios et sic deinceps [120a] licentia tribueretur, negotium longius quam par est protelari contingeret.

34. Dicta testium interpretanda sunt secundum loquendi consuetudinem.[36]

Testium dicta non cavillanda, sed potius benigne interpretanda sunt, maxime vero secundum communem usum ac ipsius testis loquendi consuetudinem.

---

[32]Speculum, 1.4, *De teste*, 1.60.
[33]Cf. *ibid.*, 12.1.
[34]Speculum, 2.3, *De expensis*, 6.21.
[35]X, 2.20.49 (Fr, II, 338), originally a decretal of Pope Honorius III (1216-27); X, 2.20.15 (Fr, II, 320), originally a decretal of Pope Alexander III (1159-81).
[36]Speculum, 2.2, *De probationibus*, 3.27.

30. When shall the witness be forced to give a reckoning of his saying.[32]

The witness ought to give a reason of his saying in all acts that are to be comprehended by the bodily sense, with the self same sense, so that he be asked thereupon. But in other matters that are not subject to the bodily senses he must give a reason, although he be not asked.

31. Of witnesses extrajudicial.[33]

A judicial saying of a witness is not taken away by a contrary saying extrajudicial. And yet except the same witness can give some good reply, why he doth so vary and speaketh contrary, he shall <*lose*> /diminish/ greatly his credit.

32. Witnesses must have their charges borne.[34]

Whensoever witnesses are called from their own business to bear witness for others, we will that the same be done at the charge of the party that doth produce them, who shall have their charges from the time of their journey that they take until they return home again to their own houses.

[236r] 33. Reprobatory witnesses are not to be reproved by others.[35]

Witnesses reprobatory, that would reprove them that have reproved other, are not to be admitted, lest that if you bring the fourth reprover against the third, and so licence might be given to proceed further, affairs would be longer prolonged or deferred than meet or reason it were.

34. The saying of witnesses must be expounded according to the common use of speaking.[36]

We ought not to cavil upon the saying of witnesses, but they ought rather *gently* favourably to be expounded according to the common use and the plain custom of speaking of the witnesses.

[130v] 35. Quando dictum unius testis **suppletur** per dictum alterius.[37]

Dictum quoque unius testis suppletur per dictum alterius testis plenius deponentis; interpretationemque a pleniori illo dicto *iuxta veteres leges* merito recipiet, si modo constet, quod de uno et eodem facto deponere conentur.

35a. Praferendi sunt testes qui absolvunt, his qui condemnant.

Cum ad absolvendum potius quam ad condemnandum promptiora sunt iura nostra, volumus, quod si testes aliqui faciant pro bona fama seu innocentia alicuius, ac rursus alii pro mala fama seu noxa, quod praeferantur hi, qui pro innocentia fecerint, modo alias ipsi testes inter se aequales fuerint.[38]

[131r] 36. Testis inconstantia.[39]

Testes, qui adversus fidem testationis suae vacillant, audiendi non sunt.

37. Pars intentionem suam obscuram interpretari potest.[40]

Si testes clare de re aliqua testificantur, quae obscure fortassis a parte proponebatur, potest tamen pars suam intentionem interpretari, ut dicta testium illi prosint.

38. Testes pro utraque parte deponere debent, si requira[n]tur.[41]

Testes pro utraque parte deponere debent, si requirantur vel a iudice, vel a parte non producente, licet a parte principaliter producente expensas recipiunt.

39. Examinatio testium.[42]

Notarii opera, et non industria in examinatione [131v]testium videtur electa. Ideo ad mandatum iudicis debent scribere dicta testium, etiam extensive, prout

---

[37]Speculum, 1.4, *De teste*, 12.2, 4.
[38]This was crossed out here, probably after it was realized that it was already included as no. 46 below.
[39]*Dig.*, 22.5.2, originally Modestinus, *Regulae*, 8.
[40]Cf. Speculum, 1.4, *De teste*, 5.9; *ibid.*, 2.2 *De positionibus*, 4.5-6; Albericus de Rosate, *De testibus*, 3.36 (*Tractatus universi iuris*, V, 187).
[41]Speculum, 1.4, *De teste*, 1.69-70, 4.1.
[42]*Ibid.*, 7.11.

35. When **is** the saying of one witness **supplied by** the saying of another witness.[37]

The saying of one witness is supplied by the more full deposing of another witness and shall receive understanding of that more full saying so that it be known that they have endeavoured themselves to depose of one and the same fact.

35a. Those witnesses are to be preferred that do absolve before those that do condemn.

Forasmuch as our laws are more ready to absolve and favour than to condemn and cast away, we will that if any witnesses do testify for one's good name or innocency and others do depose against the same, those shall be preferred that do testify for the innocency, so that the same witnesses be otherwise equal among themselves.[38]

36. The inconstancy of a witness.[39]

Those witnesses that do waver against the truth of their depositions are not to be heard.

37. The party may expound his meaning when it is obscure and dark.[40]

If the witnesses do clearly depose of some matter, the which perhaps were obscurely proponed by the party, the party may yet expound his meaning, that the saying of the witnesses may do him good.

38. Witnesses ought to depose for both parties if they be required thereunto.[41]

Witnesses ought to depose for both parties if they be required either of the judge or of the party that doth not produce them, although they may require their charges of the party principal that doth produce them.

39. Examination of witnesses.[42]

The travail of the registrar and not the industry doth seem to be required in examination of witnesses. Therefore he ought to write upon the commandment

unusquisque locutus fuerit, [120b] cum in verbis omissis plus aliquando efficaciae reperitur, quam in eis, quae a notariis quibusdam describuntur.

40. Testes singulares.[43]

Testes singulares nihil probant; adeo ut veteres non permittebant iuramentum, etiam in defectu probationis, tales testes producenti deferre, nisi huiusmodi singularitas tendat ad unum et eundem finem: quod et no{s/n} approbamus.

41. Variatio testium.[44]

Si qui tamen testes deponant de aliqua [132r] summa debita, aliqui de maiori, aliqui rursus de minori, ac in una aliqua summa numerus sufficiens concordat, potest illis iudex fidem adhibere, si nihil aliud est, quod illorum fidei detrahat.

42. Testimonia de scire et credere.[45]

Licet testes saepe adeo rudes sunt et ignorari, ut nihil distinguant inter verba veritatis assertiva (ut scio), ac illa quae nihil necessario ponunt (ut credo, videtur, et recordatur), tamen nolumus fidem huiusmodi testibus adhiberi, si ipsi de natura horum verborum a iudicibus nostris admoniti (quod semper fieri volumus), congrua non reddiderint testimonia. In casibus tamen illis, [132v] in quibus veteres leges fidem huiusmodi testimoniis adhiberi voluerunt, idem observandum [esse] duximus.

43. De testibus examinatis coram arbitris.[46]

Testibus examinatis coram arbitris non tenetur quis stare coram iudice, si vivunt, sed potest petere eos iterum examinari, si velit; sed si sunt mortui, non requiritur ulterior examinatio, sed standum erit eis, sicut si coram iudice fuissent recepti, salvo tamen iure obiiciendi contra personas et dicta.

[43] *Ibid.*, 11.7.
[44] Hostiensis, *Summa aurea*, c. *De testibus*.
[45] Speculum, 1.4, *De teste*, 7.15; Baldus, *De teste*, in Speculum, 1.4, *idem*.
[46] Cf. X, 1.43.6 (Fr, II, 234), originally a decretal of Pope Innocent III, 20 March 1207.

of the judge, the sayings of the witnesses, [236v] very largely as every one hath spoken, for as much as there is oftentimes more sense found in words omitted than in all those things that the registrar hath written.

40. Singular witnesses.[43]

Singular witnesses do not prove anything at all so that in old time they would not /suffer to/ minister any oath when any such witnesses were brought upon want of proof, except the same singularity or one /sole/ witness /do tend/ to one and the same end, the which we also do allow.

41. The varying of witnesses.[44]

If any witnesses do depose of any sum of debt, some of more and some of less and in some one sum, a sufficient number do agree, the judge may give credit unto them if there be nothing else to hinder their credit.

42. Testimonies of knowledge and believing.[45]

Although witnesses be oftentimes so rude and ignorant that they cannot /know/ the difference betwixt words expressly affirming the truth (as for example: 'I do know') and betwixt those words that do not necessarily allege /or affirm anything/ as for example: 'I do believe', 'It seemeth unto me' or 'He remembereth' yet we will not that any trust shall be given unto such witnesses, if they being <*warning*> /warned/ by our judges of such words (the which always we will that it be done), they do not aptly give their report /and judgment/. And yet in those cases where the old laws will that faith be given to such witnesses, we have thought good the same should be observed also.

43. Of witnesses to be examined before arbitrators.[46]

When witnesses are examined before arbitrators, none are forced to appear before a judge if they be living, but the party may require to have them examined again, if he will, that if they be dead, there is no further examination required, but their testimonies must be stand unto, as if they were received before a judge, saving the right of law to object against their persons and their sayings.

[121a] 44. Quomodo iudex de multis testibus iudicabit.[47]

Si testes omnes eiusdem honestatis et existimationis sunt, et negotii qualitas ac iudicis etiam motus cum *his* [*h*/e]is concurrat, sequenda sunt omnia testimonia. [133r] Si vero ex his quidam illorum aliud dixerint, licet impari numero, credendum est quod naturae negotii convenit, et quod inimicitiae aut[*em*] gratiae suspicione careat, confirmabitque iudex motum animi sui ex argumentis et testimoniis, quae et rei aptiora et vero proximiora esse compererit; neque enim ad multitudinem respici oportet, sed ad sinceram testimoniorum fidem, et testimonia quibus potius lux veritatis assis[*t*/c]it.

45. Variatio testium quando non noceat.[48]

Si testes in circumstantiis non necessariis (ad quas simplices homines non solent magnopere respicere) varii aliquando inveni[*a*/u]ntur, in rei tamen, de qua agitur, substantia conveniant, plena fides illis adhibe*re*/**nda** [133v] est. Neque enim omnis ve/**arietas** reprobata est, sed ea tantum, quae contrarietatem quandam et incompassibilitatem in se contineat, nihilque nocet narrandi diversita*tem*/**s**, cum eadem dicuntur.

46. Praferendi sunt testes qui absolvunt, his qui condemnant.[49]

Cum ad absolvendum potius quam ad condemnandum promptiora sunt iura nostra, volumus, quod si testes aliqui faciant pro bona fama seu innocentia alicuius, ac rursus alii pro mala fama seu noxa, quod praeferantur hi, qui pro innocentia fecerint, modo alias ipsi testes inter se aequales fuerint.

[121b] 47. De numero testium.[50]

Quanquam quibusdam legibus amplissim[*u*/i]s numerus testium definitus sit, tamen hanc licentiam ad sufficientem numerum coarctamus, ut iudices *tantum* **tamen** [134r] moderentur, et [*e*/c]um solum numerum, quem necessarium esse putaverint, evocari patiantur, ne effrenata potestate ad vexandos homines superflua testium multitudo protrahatur. At ubi numerus testium non requiritur, duo testes probabunt.

---

[47]*Dig.*, 22.5.21.3, originally Arcadius, *De testibus*, 1.
[48]Hostiensis, *Summa aurea*, c. *De testibus*.
[49]X, 2.19.3 (Fr, II, 307), originally a decretal of Pope Lucius III (1181-5).
[50]Cf. X, 2.20.37 (Fr, II, 330-1), originally a decretal of Pope Innocent III, 22 June 1206; *Dig.*, 22.5.12, originally Ulpian, *Ad edictum*, 37.

[237r] 44. <*When*> how a judge shall judge of many witnesses.[47]

If all the witnesses be of like honesty and estimation, and the quality of the matter and the judge's mind also do concur together, all those testimonies are to be followed. That if some of those witnesses have said otherwise, although in number unequal, <*the judge*> /we/ must believe that which agreeth to the nature of the business, and that which wanteth suspicion of hatred or favour, and the judge shall confirm the motion of his mind, by arguments and testimonies, that he shall perceive are most apt and nighest to the matter, neither ought he have an eye to the multitude, but to the faithful reports of the witnesses and their testimonies, wherein the light of truth doth rather consist.

45. When doeth not the varying of witnesses any harm at all.[48]

If witnesses be found to vary in circumstances not necessary unto the which simple folk have no great respect, and yet do agree in the substance of the matter intreated, they ought wholly to be trusted. Neither all varying is to be reproved, but that only the which hath contrariety in itself, neither doth the variety of saying hurt anything /at all/, when one thing in substance <*st...*> is said.

46. Those witnesses are to be preferred that do absolve before those that do condemn.[49]

Forasmuch as our laws are <*most*> more ready to absolve and favour than to condemn and cast away, we will that if any witnesses do testify for one's good name or innocency and others do depose against the same, those shall be preferred that do testify for the innocency, so that the same witnesses be otherwise equal among themselves.

47. Of the number of witnesses.[50]

Although by some laws, a marvellous great number of witnesses are to be appointed, yet we have arraigned their licence to a sufficient number that the judges may moderate them, and that they cause such a number only to be called *that* /as/ they think necessary, lest a superfluous multitude of witnesses of inordinate power be brought forth to vex men. But in those cases where a number of witnesses are not required, those witnesses shall suffice to prove.

48. Iudex testibus iubere potest silentium, et mutare articulorum ordinem in examinatione.[51]

Iudicis *equidem* est cuncta rimari, [*ac* **et**] v[*eri*/**arie**]tatem plena inquisitione discutere. Ideo ei permittimus ut [*in*]iungat testibus iuramenti religione, ne dicta sua contestibus aut aliis quibusvis propalent, ac ut testes (non observato ordine articulorum) super omnibus examinare possit, prout ei videbitur {*expedire*}.

49. In animae periculo iuramentum exigi potest.[52]

Si acta nihil probaverint, iudex iuramentum exigere [134v] potest a parte principali, ubicunque animae periculum vertitur.

50. Testimoniorum copia partibus non *sunt* **est** neganda.[53]

Iudex post testium publicationem testimoniorum copiam faciat partibus petentibus, ipso retinente originale. Et iudicis est illis constituere terminum, intra quem publicata testimonia evertant, aut t[*u*/**en**]eantur,[54] cum hac interminati[122a]one, quod si istud facere neglexerint, deinceps non sit admissurus ut id facia[*n*]t.

51. Testimoniorum publicatio.[55]

Examinatis testibus, ea pars cui maxime interest testimonia esse nota, petere potest a iudice, ut ea publicentur. Id vero ut rite fiat, necesse est partes citari ad audiendum testimonia publicari. Ita vero fiet publicatio, si aut ipse iudex aut publicus notarius praesentibus partibus palam testimonia recit[*e*/**a**]t, *e*/**au**t coram exhibeat cartam, in qua ea d[*e*/**i**]scripta sunt, et clara voce testetur in ea contineri [135r] depositiones testium productorum fideliter annotatas, quas sua exhibitione publi*t*/**c**atas velit. Postea iudex partibus constituet terminum, intra quem accepturi s[*i*/**u**]nt exempla testimoniorum, et alium terminum, intra quem disputaturi sint, si velint.

---

[51]Speculum, 1.4, *De teste*, 4.2.
[52]X, 5.34.5 (Fr, II, 870-1), originally a decretal of Pope Innocent I (401-17).
[53]Speculum, 2.2, *De instrumentorum editione*, 5.12; 6.10.
[54]Here the translator read 'timeantur' and took it as an introduction to what follows. But both the MS and the Foxe edition read 'or they may be retained', 'tueantur' being virtually synonymous with 'teneantur' in this context.
[55]Speculum, 1.4, *De teste*, 8.1.

[237v] 48. The judge may command the witnesses to keep silence and may alter the order of the articles in the examination.[51]

It belongeth to the judge to search all things and to discuss the full [*truth* >**variety**<] by inquisition. Therefore we do suffer him that he do enjoin the witnesses upon their oaths, that they do not utter their sayings to their fellow witnesses or to any other, and that the witnesses, without any order keeping of the articles, may be examined upon all points as it shall seem good unto the judge.

49. An oath may /be/ taken upon peril of the soul.[52]

If the acts do not prove anything the judge may take an oath of the parties principal, wheresoever peril of the soul lieth.

50. The copy of testimonies *are* **is** not to <*the*> be denied to the parties.[53]

Let the judge give copies to the parties that do ask, after publication of witnesses, keeping to himself the original witnesses. It belongeth also to the judge to appoint unto them a term, within the which they may overthrow the witnesses published, or to fear the parties[54] with this threatening, that if they refuse so to do, they shall not afterwards be admitted to do it.

51. Publication of witnesses.[55]

When the witnesses are examined, that party whom it behoveth most that the testimonies and sayings of the witnesses be known, may ask of the judge that they may be published. And to the end it may be well done, it is needful that the parties be called to hear the witnesses published. And thus shall publication be, if either the judge himself or the public notary do openly rehearse the sayings of the witnesses, the parties being present and before them, doth exhibit the paper where they are written and doth openly declare that in the same paper are contained the depositions of the witnesses, faithfully <*producted*> written, the which he would exhibit to be published. Afterwards the judge shall appoint a term within the which they shall take copies of the witnesses and any other term, wherein they shall dispute of the matter if they list.

52. Testium productio post testimoniorum publicationem.[56]

Quamvis partibus non regulariter permittatur, ut post testimoniorum publicationem denuo alios testes producant, iudex tamen ratione sui officii, non solum [**potest**] post testimoniorum [*publicationem* **receptionem**], sed et postquam in causa conclusum est, testes examinatos potest denuo interrogare de re, quam sua depositione non satis declarasse videtur, si eius notitia necessaria aut utilis appareat ad causae cognitionem. Et si iudex ex s[*e*/**cr**]ip[*s*/**t**]o hoc non faciat, possunt partes petere a iudice, ut id fiat.

53. Quando admittitur probatio post testium publicationem.[57]

Rursus si post testium publicationem quisquam probare [135v] aliquid voluerit, quod in prioribus suis articulis, quo[122b]ad necessitatem facti et probationis, inesse dinoscatur, id ei nullatenus permittatur. Sed si quid inopinatum, et de quo quis facile cogitare non poterat, a{*b*} [*ad*/**di**]versa parte probatum fuerit, quod causae alterius magnopere noceat, non incongruum esse putamus id a parte laesa (si potest) reprobatum iri, publicatione testium non obstante.

In causis etiam matrimonialibus favore animarum olim constitutum erat, ut testium publicatio aliorum testium productioni non obstaret; quod nos moderantes ita temperamus, ut publicatio in his causis non noceat. Si testes illi post publicationem producendi omni exceptione maiores fuerint, ac tales qui omni careant suspicione, ac quibus merito credendum est; alioqui iudex eos vel non admittat, vel fidem, quam voluerit, illis adhibere poterit.

[136r] 54. Neque testes neque dicta testium refelli possunt post primam assignationem ad audiendum [**sententiam**].[58]

Si quid in dictis testium a veritate alienum depraehenditur, aut persona illius reprobari aliquando possit, id usque ad primam assignationem ad audiendum *futurum* **sententiam** proponi permittimus, sive quis protestatus fuerit contra eos, sive non est protestatus.

[56]*Ibid.*, 8.2.
[57]*Ibid.*, 8.3.
[58]X, 2.20.31 (Fr, II, 326), originally a decretal of Pope Innocent III (1198-1216).

52. Production of witnesses after publication of their sayings.[56]

Although it is not commonly granted unto the parties that after publication of witnesses they should produce other witnesses, yet the judge [**may**] by virtue of his office, not only after [*publication* >**reception**<] of witnesses [238r] but also after the cause is concluded, examine the witnesses again upon interrogatories in that matter, the which seems by their depositions not to be fully declared, if the knowledge of that matter seem necessary or profitable to the better understanding of the cause, and if the judge do not put this in writing, the parties may desire the judge that it may be so.

53. When is probation admitted after publication of witnesses.[57]

Again, if any man after publication of witnesses will prove anything that in his former articles is thought to be of the necessity of the fact and proof, the same must not be granted unto him at all. But if anything that was not thought upon before, or that was likely a man could not think of, be proved by the contrary party, that may greatly hurt the other's cause, we think it not amiss that the same be <*p...*> reproved of the party harmed, notwithstanding any publication of witnesses.

And in causes of matrimony, it hath been heretofore ordained in favour of men's souls, that the publication of witnesses should not hinder the producting of other witnesses, the which matter we, moderating, do thus temper, that publication in such causes shall not do any hurt if those witnesses that are to be producted after publication be <*with*> above all exception and such as are without all suspicion, and whom a man may well believe. Otherwise the judge ought not admit them, or else may give credit unto them as he shall think good.

54. Neither the witnesses nor yet their sayings can be rejected after the first assignation to hear [**sentence**].[58]

If anything be found untrue in the saying of the witnesses or that his person may be reproached, we are contented that the same shall be proponed unto the first assignation to hear *his future* **sentence**, if anyone do protest against them or do not protest.

55. Officium iudicis in examinandis testibus.[59]

Pertinet autem peculiariter ad officium iudicis, diligenter testes examinare de singulis negotii circumstantiis, ut quod per partes vel earum advocatos omissum forte sit in articulis et interrogatoriis c{*onci*/**u**}piendis, illud ipse suppleat.[60]

---

[59]*Dig.*, 22.5.22, originally Venuleius, *De officio praeconsulis*, 2.
[60]A note on [136v] reads: '"De consuetudine", require in folio 160'. ('"On custom", see folio 160').

55. The duty of the judge in examining of witnesses.[59]

It belongeth to the judge to examine diligently the witnesses of every circumstance of the matter, that such things which are either omitted by the parties or their counsels, the same may the [238v] judge supply either in the articles or else in {*conceiving of* **desiring**} the interrogations.[60]

[160r; 123a]   **46. DE CONSUETUDINE**

1. Consuetudo quid sit.[1]

Consuetudo est ius quoddam moribus institutum, quod pro lege suscipitur, cum deficit lex, seu ius quoddam moribus seu usibus populi totius vel maioris partis ratione initiatum, continuatum, et constitutum, legis habens auctoritatem,. *e*/**Ex**[2] non scripto enim ius venit quod usus approbavit. Nam diuturni mores consensu utentium comprobati legem *im*mitantur.

2. Consuetudo non valet contra rationem aut legem.[3]

Quamvis consuetudinis ususque longaevi non sit vilis auctoritas, verumtamen non est usque adeo valitura, ut aut rationem vincat aut legem, [160v] seu iuri positivo praeiudicium generare debeat.

3. Consuetudo non valet contra ius divinum aut naturale.[4]

Cum peccata tanto sint graviora, quanto diutius infelicem animam detinent alligatam, nemo sanae mentis intelligit iuri divino aut **naturali** (cuius transgressio periculum salutis inducit) quacunque consuetudine (quae dicenda est verius in hac parte corruptela) poss[*e*/**it**] aliquatenus derogari,. *q*/**Quaelibet**[5] enim consuetudo, quantumvis vetusta, quantumvis vulgata, veritati omnino est postponenda, et usus, qui veritati est contrarius, est abolendus.

---

[1] D, 1 c. 5 (Fr, I, 2).
[2] Cranmer began a new sentence here.
[3] D, 8 cc. 7-8 (Fr, I, 15); D, 11 c. 4 (Fr, I, 23-4); X, 1.4.11 (Fr, II, 41), originally a decretal of Pope Gregory IX (1227-41), published on or before 5 September 1234.
[4] D, 8 c. 6 (Fr, I, 14-15); D, 9 c. 1 (Fr, I, 16); X, 1.4.11 (Fr, II, 41), originally a decretal of Pope Gregory IX, published on or before 5 September 1234.
[5] Cranmer began a new sentence here.

46. OF CUSTOM

1. What is custom.[1]

Custom is a certain right brought in by usage and manners of men, the which is taken for a law when the law doth fail, or else it is a certain right begun, continued and constituted by usage of the whole people or by indulgence of the most part, having authority of a law. For[2] without writing the law came and was confirmed by use, for continual usages, allowed by consent of the /users/ *users, have* do follow the nature of a law.

2. Custom is of no value, made against reason and law.[3]

Although the authority of custom and long use is of no small force, yet it is not of such force that either it may overcome reason or law, or bring any prejudice to a positive statute or law.

3. Custom is not good against the law of God and the law of nature.[4]

Forasmuch as sins are the more grievous the longer they do detain and keep bound the unhappy soul, no man of understanding thinketh that the law of God or the law **of nature**, the transgression whereof bringeth damnation of soul, may be in any part defaced or undone by any custom whatsoever, the which ought rather to be called a corruption, for[5] every custom, although it be never so old, although it be never so common, ought altogether give place unto the truth, and that use or custom, the which is contrary unto the truth, ought to be abolished.

4. Statuta et consuetudines ecclesiae cathedralis non sunt mutandae,[6] sine episcopi et capituli consensu.[7]

Propterea quod **Quia** novitates saepe numero pariunt [161r] discordiam, non immerito statuendum videtur, ne quis episcopus absque consensu capituli statuta aut consuetudines ecclesiae cathedralis antiquas [123b] immutare, aut novas facere possit; itidem nec capitulum sine episcopo. Quod si aliter facta fuerint, decernantur irrita, nisi statuta et consuetudines huiusmodi **priores**[8] verbo Dei aut ecclesiae aedificationi repugnent.

[*5. Consuetudo non solvendi decimas invalida sit.*

*Cum decimae omni humano iure sine aliqua diminutione solvendae sunt, et Salvatoris nostri Christi pastoribus ubique terrarum debeantur, et cum pluribus in locis propter non solutas decimas animarum curam habentibus adeo exigua portio, ut ex ea nequeant congrue sustentari, relinquantur, ita**que** fiat, ut pauci inveniantur pastores qui ullam [161v] vel modicam habeant peritiam sacrarum litterarum, cumque inter cetera, quae ad salutem populi Christiani spectant, pabulum Verbi Dei maxime noscatur esse necessarium, usque bovis ligari non debeat triturantis, sed qui altari servit de altare vivere debeat, statuimus ut (consuetudine qualibet non obstante) integre cuiusque rei decimae solvantur, omnemque contrariam consuetudinem irritam esse decernimus.*][9]

---

[6]The comma was added by Cranmer.
[7]X, 1.4.9 (Fr, II, 41), originally a decretal of Pope Honorius III, 2 March 1221.
[8]Added to the MS by Peter Martyr.
[9]In the MS this passage is marked with a marginal note in Peter Martyr Vermigli's hand which reads: 'In titulo "De decimis" est prospectum.' ('Covered in the chapter "On tithes"'). See 25.18. A note at the end of the chapter, in Foxe's hand, reads: '"De praescriptionibus" require in folio 208.' ('"On prescriptions", see folio 208').

4. The statutes and customs of cathedral churches ought not to be altered[6] without consent of the bishop and the chapter.[7]

Because innovations do oftentimes bring discord, it ought upon good cause to be established that no bishop, without consent of the chapter, *do* may alter or make new, any ancient statutes or old customs of the cathedral church, neither the chapter ought to do anything without the bishop, that if things be otherwise done, let the same be void, except such **former**[8] statutes and customs be against the Word of God or edifying of the church.

[*5. The custom of not paying tithes is not valid.*

Since tithes are to be paid without any reduction according to all human law, and are owed everywhere on earth to the pastors of our Saviour Jesus Christ, and since in many places, because of unpaid tithes, so small a sum is left to those who have the cure of souls that they are unable to support themselves adequately on it, and thus it comes about that there are few pastors who may be found who have even limited expertise in sacred letters, and since, among other things which pertain to the salvation of the people of God, the food of the Word of God is recognized to be most necessary, and the mouth of the threshing ox should not be muzzled, but who serves the altar ought to live off the altar, we decree that, any custom notwithstanding, full tithes shall be paid on everything, and we decree that any custom to the contrary shall be void.][9]

[208r; 123b]   **47. DE PRAESCRIPTIONIBUS**

1. Praescriptio quid sit.[1]

Praescriptio est ius quoddam ex tempore congruens, auctoritate legum vim capiens, poenam negligentibus inferens, et finem litibus imponens, quod non in totum a naturali iure recedit, nec per omnia ei servit,. *q*/**Q**uemadmodum[2] enim natura aequum est neminem debere locupletari cum alterius iactura, ita naturali rationi congruum est et negligentibus poenam inferri et finem litibus imponi.

2. Praescriptio decimarum in aliena parochia.[3]

Si una ecclesia decimas in alterius parochia quadraginta annos possederit, volumus de iure [208v] meliorem conditionem fieri possidentis: quia quadragenalis praescriptio omnem prorsus actionem exclud{*i*/**a**}t.

3. Malae fidei possessor praescribere non potest.[4]

Nulla antiqua dierum possessio iuvat aliquem malae fidei p[oss/**rof**]essorem, <u>nisi resipuerit, postquam s[*e*/**i**] aliena noverit possidere</u>,[5] cum bonae fidei p[oss/**rof**]essor dici non po[*ssi*/**tes**]t. Derogandum enim erit omni constitutioni atque consuetudini, quae absque mortali peccato non potest observari. Oportet igitur eum, qui praescribit, ut in nulla temporis parte rei ha[124a]beat conscientiam alienae, sitque in bona fide constitutus, sine qua nulla valet praescriptio ecclesiastica.

---

[1]Panormitanus on X, 2.26.
[2]Cranmer began a new sentence here.
[3]X, 2.26.6 (Fr, II, 383), originally a decretal of Pope Alexander III (1159-81).
[4]X, 2.26.5 (Fr, II, 383), originally a decretal of Pope Alexander III.
[5]A marginal note by Peter Martyr reads: 'Ista non faciunt ad legem' ('These things have nothing to do with the law').

[239r]   **47. OF PRESCRIPTIONS**

1. What is prescription.[1]

Prescription is a certain right through time, meet and taking taking [*sic*] force by authority of laws, punishing the negligent and ending controversies, the which thing doth not *much* /wholly/ dissent from the law of nature, neither in all things doth it agree with nature. For[2] as it is natural that none ought to be made rich with another's harm, so it is agreeing with natural reason that negligent men should be punished and controversies should have an end.

2. Prescription of tenths in another parish.[3]

If one church hath had tenths in another parish by the space of forty years, we will that in law his condition be the better that is in possession, because that forty years prescription excludeth all manner of action.

3. A possessor upon an evil *grounds or* /known/ conscience, cannot prescribe.[4]

No old or long continuance of possessing doth help any man that is [owner >**claimant**<] by wrong and evil conscience, except he do repent and be sorry, when he knoweth that he doth possess another's right[5] and therefore cannot /be/ said to be owner in good conscience. Yea and all customs are to be broken that cannot be kept without deadly sin. Therefore it is meet that he who doth prescribe should not have his conscience troubled with the possession of any other man's goods, but he ought to be in posse upon good faith and conscience, without the which no prescription of the church is anything worth.

[209r] 4. Interruptio tollit praescriptionem.[6]

Si de praescriptione et interruptione mota fuerit quaestio *si* **cum**[7] receptis testibus seu probationibus (quae recipi debent ab utraque parte) probata fuerit interruptio, praescriptio non tenebit.

5. Contra visitantes nemo praescribere potest.[8]

Quia secundum apostolum, qui spiritualia seminat, non est magnum si metat carnalia, (cum nemo suis stipendiis militare cogatur), *statuendum est* **statuimus**,[9] ne subditus contra superiorem visitationem,[10] aut procurationem ratione visitationis debitam, in seipso praescribere possit. Allegantes igitur se non meminisse procurationem solvisse aut petitam [209v] fuisse, audiendos non fore decernimus; sed negantes poena condigna afficiendos., *N*/**nec**[11] non ad condignam satisfactionem compellendos, quacunque praescriptione temporis non obstante, statuimus.

6. Praescriptio ecclesiarum vel decimarum in aliena dioecesi.[12]

Episcopum qui ecclesias et decimas in aliena dioecesi se legitime praescripsisse proponit, oportet huiusmodi praescriptionis titulum allegare, et (cum ius commune contra ipsum faciat) probare,. *n*/**Nam**[13] licet ei, qui rem praescribit ecclesiasticam, si sibi non est contrarium ius commune, vel contra eum praesumptio non habetur, sufficiat [210r] bona fides. Ubi tamen est ei ius commune contrarium, vel habetur praesumptio contra ipsum, bona fides non sufficit, sed est necessarius titulus, qui possessori causam tribuat praescribendi, nisi tan[124b]ti temporis allegetur praescriptio, *co...* cuius contrarii/**a** memoria non existit.

---

[6]X, 2.26.8 (Fr, II, 384), originally a decretal of Pope Alexander III (1159-81).
[7]This alteration seems to have been made by Peter Martyr.
[8]X, 2.26.11 (Fr, II, 385), originally a decretal of Pope Innocent III, 23 February 1199; X, 2.26.16 (Fr, II, 388-9), originally a decretal of Pope Innocent III, 28 November 1202.
[9]Altered by Cranmer.
[10]A marginal note by Peter Martyr reads: 'Puto de visitationibus hoc idem propemodum haberi.' ('I think that this is more or less what one should expect from visitations').
[11]Punctuation changed in MS, but not be Cranmer.
[12]Panormitanus on X, 2.26.6.
[13]Cranmer began a new sentence here.

4. Interruption or claiming of right breaketh prescription.[6]

If there be a question *if* **upon**[7] prescription and claim of right, by *<and>* witnesses *<with>* /and/ proofs, the which ought to be brought in upon both parties, and that the interruption or claim be proved, the prescription shall not be of any force.

5. No man ought to prescribe against visitors.[8]

Because according to the apostle, he that doth sow spiritual things, it is no great matter if he do reap carnal things, for that no man is bound to go on war upon his own wages, we do ordain[9] that no subject do prescribe in himself against [239v] any superior visitation,[10] or procuration due by reason of any visitation. And we do further decree that they are not to be heard if they do allege that they remember not that ever they paid any proxy money, or that any such money was asked of them, but we will that such as do deny any such duty be duly punished and[11] be compelled to make full satisfaction to the parties' injuried, any prescription of time whatsoever to the contrary notwithstanding.

6. Prescription of churches and tenths in another diocese.[12]

It behoveth a bishop that *<he>* doth lay that he hath lawfully prescribed churches and tenths in another diocese to allege the title of such his prescription, and to prove it when the common law is against him. For[13] he that /doth/ prescribe anything of the church, if the common law be not against him, neither /yet/ any *<prescription>* presumption, may lawfully enjoy the same, and his good conscience may suffice to prove possession. But where the common law is against him, or else presumption may be gathered, his good conscience cannot suffice /in this case/ to prescribe. But there ought to be a necessary title that giveth cause unto the possessor to prescribe, and the prescription ought to be alleged of so long time as the contrary memory of man cannot be had.

7. Praescriptio vel interrumpi potest vel cessare vel impediri.[14]

Praescriptio aliquando cessat, aliquando interrumpitur, sed non idem aestimandum quando cessat, et quando [*inter*]rumpitur. Cessare praescriptio dicitur, quando propter aliquod privilegium personae cuius res est, aut conditionem ipsius rei, non habet locum praescriptio. [210v] Similis huic cessationi videri potest impeditio, quando praescriptio quasi intersistit, ut cum propter publicum aliquem motum iudicia exercere, et ius suum requirere non licet, ut in tempore belli, **vel quando in loco ius non redditur,** et **defectu iudicis *ut*** [vel] **rei[p],**[15] **atque tempore pestis.**[16] In quo/**ibus** cas*u*/**ibus**[17] et similibus praescriptio non prorsus intermoritur, sed vi quadam impedita interquiescit, **et praesertim cum actoris protestatio intercedit.**[18]

Interrumpi vero naturaliter praescript{*i*}o dicitur, cum coepta retrahitur, ne progredi possit. Id vero fit, cum possessio nobis non vi legitima, (quam vocant compulsiva[*m*]), sed violenta eripitur. Et ratio est, quia sine possessione praescriptio non procedit. Est autem in naturali [211r] interruptione hoc regulare, quod ea prodest omnibus, qui habent ius in re.

Rumpitur etiam praescriptio, quando is, cuius res est, illam *in* contestata lite in iudicio repetit, quamvis litem non perficiat; item per alluvionem maris, aut fluminis, per solutionem pensionis aut partis debiti, per secundam cautionem a debitore factam. Impeditur ad haec praescriptio ne currat, quando is, cuius res est, illam non potest repetere; ut sunt impuberes, quique adhuc sub aliena potestate continentur, et furiosi, quibus etiam adnumeres excommunicatos; nam dum ita sunt, non audiuntur sua repetentes. Praescriptioni coniunctae cum bona fide ne[125a]mo per suum pactum potest renuntiare; cum praescriptio sit propter bonum publicum inventa, ne scilicet dominia rerum sint incerta, et ius publicum pacto privatorum non remittatur.

Ad praescribendum in rebus [*in*]corporalibus, ut est servitus praedii, iurisdictio, et consimilia, non requiritur possessio, sed scientia et patientia adversarii.

Interrumpitur quoque praescriptio, ne currat protestatione coram iudice, vel si eius copia non fiat coram notario et testibus; quo protestationis genere principes inter se utuntur ad impediendam praescriptionem, cum sese non possunt convenire sub iudice, qui sit utrique parti communis.

Quiete dicitur quis possidere, quando non vocatur in iudicio, sincere autem, quando cum bona fide. Bona autem fides in dubio praesumitur, /et

---

[14]A digest of Panormitanus on X, 2.26.8-10.
[15]*Sic*. Possibly short for 'reipublicae'.
[16]Added by Peter Martyr.
[17]Alteration made by Peter Martyr.
[18]Added by Peter Martyr.

7. Prescription may either be interrupted, or cease, or hindered.[14]

Prescription doth sometimes cease and sometimes it is interrupted. But we must not think all one, when prescription ceaseth and when it is [*interrupted* >**broken**<]. The prescription is then said to cease when it hath no place, because of some privilege of the person that hath the thing, or else for condition or property in the thing itself. Hindering or letting is like unto this <*prescription*> ceasing, when the prescription doth stay after a sort, as when upon occasion of some common tumult or commotion, law cannot take place and none can have /or may ask/ their own, as in time of battle, **or when law is not exercised in a place** [>**either**<] **for want of the judge** /[or] **matter/,**[15] <*then*> **or in time of plague.**[16]

[240r] In which cases[17] and such like, prescription doth not wholly die, but doth rest for a time, being hindered by some force, **and especially when the protestation of the actor is inserted.**[18]

A prescription is said to be naturally interrupted, when that it being begun, is holden back that it cannot go forward. And that is when possession is taken from us not by lawful force, (the which is called compulsive force), but by violence and strong hand. And the reason is that no prescription can be had without possession. This is a general rule in all natural interruptions, that the same doth profit them that have any right therein.

Prescription is broken when /he/ unto whom the goods do appertain doth require the same in judgment, winning issue thereupon, although he do not prosecute the same. Likewise, by gathering upon the sea or flood or river, by paying of pension or the debt of the party, by a second caution made from the debtor. Prescription is also hindered that it cannot continue when he unto whom the goods do belong cannot ask his own, as those cannot do that are under years, although they are under another man's ward, and those /also/ that are mad, and likewise excommunicate persons. For so long as they are so they cannot be heard to ask their own by prescription issued with good conscience. No man can forsake or renounce by his private pact or consent, for that prescription was intended for a public benefit, that the dominions and lordship of things should not be uncertain, and the public right remitted by the part of private persons.

Possession is not necessary to be required for prescribing in things incorporal, as fealty and homage are, jurisdiction, royalties and such others, but the knowledge and patience of the adversary may suffice.

Prescription is also interrupted that it may not continue, by protestation making before a judge, or if acceptation not be had to him, before a notary and witnesses, the which kind of protestation princes do use among themselves to hinder prescription when they cannot meet together before a judge that were indifferent to them both.

A man is then said to possess quietly when he is not sued in law, and then he is said to possess truly and sincerely when he enjoineth things with a good faith and conscience. A good conscience is presumed to be when the

quando non habetur notitia rei alienae/.[19] Mala vero probatur variis modis; primo per confessionem propriam possidentis; secundo per famam quae erat in vicinia; tertio per denuntiationem factam tempore contracus; denique per incidentes coniecturas, et si contra ius fuit acquisita, et non observata iuris solemnitate. Praescriptio contra bona ecclesiae vel pia legata non currit minor quadragenaria, post quam elapsam potest ecclesia in integrum restitui: si tamen restitutio intra quadr{i}ennium petita fuerit; nam post hoc tempus non audietur. Mala fides praescriptionem impedit, priusquam terminus eius elabatur. Ac cum perfecta fuerit praescriptio, bonam habens fidem coniunctam, si postea res praescripta noscatur fuisse aliena, minime cogitur, qui praescripsit, eam restituere. Nam quando novit alterius eam fuisse, iam non alienam, sed suam coeperat possidere; nam leges et iura ei addixerunt. [211v] Qui alieno nomine possidet, non praescribit.

Usucapionis trium annorum spatium assignatur; praescriptionis autem, quoad prae[125b]sentes decem, quoad absentes viginti; longior est triginta, longissima vero quadraginta annorum; utque usucapio ad res mobiles pertinet, ita praescriptio ad immobiles.[20]

---

[19]Added in the margin by Peter Martyr.

[20]A marginal note reads: 'Peter Martyr's hand'. A note at the end of the chapter, in Foxe's hand, reads: '"De violenta percussione clericorum" require in folio 116.' ('"On violence done to clerics" see folio 116').

matter is /in/ doubt and no certain knowledge had of another's right.[19] [240v] An evil right or faith is said to be diverse ways. First, by the proper confession of him that is in possession, again by the fame and common report of the country; thirdly, by denunciation made at the time of the bargain, and moreover by incident conjectures, and if the same were gotten against law, and the solemnity of law not observed. There is no prescription against the goods of the church or godly legacies within less time than forty years, after the which time expired, the church may be restored to the whole again, so that yet restitution be required within some years, for after that time all asking is in vain. Evil conscience in prescription hindereth the <*posses...*> continuance before the time be expired. But when the prescription is fully ended, that was begun in good faith and conscience, if after prescription, the same is known to be another's, he shall <*b...*> not be sued that hath prescribed, to make restitution back. For when he knew afterwards that it belonged to another man, he began then to possess not another man's right, but his own right, for the laws and all right have adjudged the same unto him. He that doth possess in another man's name doth not prescribe.

The space of three years is assigned for taking of anything by use. The space for prescription amongst those that are present is reckoned ten years, and amongst those that are absent, it is reckoned twenty years, and a longer prescription is thirty years, and the longest of all is forty years, /and as/ the usage taking (called 'usucapio') doth belong property to things <*to things*> moveable; so doth prescription appertain to things immoveable.[20]

[116r; 125b] 48. DE VIOLENTA PERCUSSIONE CLERICORUM

1. Vis contra clericum quibus poenis afficiatur.[1]

Quicunque manus violentas in clericum sciens iniecerit, nisi voluerit arbitratu iudicum ecclesiasticorum ei satisfacere, paenitentiamque subire tam atroci scelere dignam, in excommunicationem ruet. A qua nullo modo patimur illum sublevari, donec paenitentia plene sit perfunctus, ordinarii sui arbitratu *indicta vel* indicenda.

2. Quae sunt exceptiones in hac causa.[2]

Quoniam omnis honesta ratio relinqui debet expediendae salutis, si quis se legitime defendens, aut iustitiae serviens, ad vim contra clericum progressus sit *et contra superioris legis verba quicunque commiserit*, si coram ordinario suo patefecerit vim his causis profectam esse, quas posuimus, omnino illum liberari volumus, et sine poena dimitti.

Esto quoque par clericorum poena, si violentas manus in laicos homines iniecerint.[3]

---

[1] 9 Edward II, c. 3, 1315 (*S.R.*, I, 171). Cf. C. 17, q. 4, c. 29 (Fr, I, 822-3), originally c. 15 of Lateran II, 1139 (*C.O.D.*, 200); X, 5.39.4 (Fr, II, 890), originally a decretal of Pope Alexander III (1159-81).
[2] Panormitanus on X, 5.39.3. Cf. 28 Henry VIII, c. 1, 1536 (*S.R.*, III, 651-2).
[3] Panormitanus on X, 5.39.23. A note at the end reads: '"De praesumptionibus" require in folio 138.' ('"On presumptions" see folio 138').

48. OF VIOLENT STRIKING OF CLERKS

1. How violence used against a clerk shall be punished.[1]

Whosoever doth willingly lay violent hands upon a clerk, except he will make him amends by the discretion of the ecclesiastical judges, and do condign penance for such a wicked deed, he shall be excommunicated, neither shall he be absolved from the same *<unti...>* in any wise till he have done full penance, according to the will and pleasure of the ordinary.

[241r] 2. What exceptions are there in this cause.[2]

Because all honest means ought to be left for men to save themselves and to withstand wrong, if any man do deal with a clerk in his own defence, to do justice and to withstand violence, *and if anyone has committed a crime against the words of the above law,* if he do prove the same before the ordinary, that he withstand violence in his own defence, or before hath been declared, we will that the same man be clearly acquitted and dismissed without any punishment at all.

The like punishment the clerks shall have if they lay violent hands upon any laymen.[3]

[138r; 125b]   **49. DE PRAESUMPTIONIBUS**[1]

1. Praesumptio quid sit.[2]

Praesumptio est alicuius rei ex variis circumstantiis collecta coniectura.

2. Praesumptio temeraria et probabilis.[3]

Temeraria praesumptio ex mera suspicione proficiscitur, et nulli vestigio rei gestae incumbit. Probabilis vero rei *gestae* ve[126a]stigiis inhaeret, licet per seipsam non toll[a/i]t dubitationem, sed tantum credulitatem inducat.

Probabilis praesumptio, vel un[i]us testis assertione aut aliqua semiplena probatione adiuta, plenam fidem facit. Temeraria vero prorsus est reiicienda.

3. Praesumptio violenta.[4]

Violenta praesumptio est, quae i[n/u]diciis adeo [138v] apertis innititur, ut id, quod esse contenditur, inde quodammodo necessario sequi videatur.

Iudex non ad unam speciem probationis animum suum coarctabit; et ideo in causis, quae de sui natura directe probari nequeunt, praesumptionibus ad ferendam sententiam adduci poterit.

Ex violenta praesumptione iudicem posse ferre sententiam exemplo regis Salomonis docemur, qui causam inter duas mulieres audiens, atque [ex] naturali unius amore alteriusque odio erga infantem veram matrem discernens, eundem mulieri, quae divisionem abhorrebat, adiudicavit (*III Regum capite trito*). Curet attamen iudex, ut violenta praesumptio, qua motus [139r] est ad ferendam sententiam, scripta extet in actis, quo appareat sententiae latae fundamentum.[5]

---

[1]All chapter headings are in Cranmer's hand.
[2]Speculum, 2.2, *De praesumptionibus*, preface.
[3]*Ibid.*, 2.1-2.
[4]*Ibid.*, 2.3.
[5]X, 2.23.2 (Fr, II, 353), originally I Ki. iii. 24.

49. OF PRESUMPTIONS[1]

1. >What a presumption is.<[2]

A presumption is a conjecture of some one thing, gathered upon diverse circumstances.

2. Presumptions rash and probable.[3]

A rash presumption doth rise upon mere suspicion, and doth not lean upon any part of the thing done. A probable presumption doth lie hid within the matter *done*, although of itself it doth not take away all doubt, but only doth bring with it a likelihood or credulity that the thing should so be.

A probable presumption being holpen by the affirmation of any one witness, or with any halfful proof, doth make faith and persuadeth. But a rash presumption is wholly to be rejected.

3. A violent or vehement presumption.[4]

A violent presumption is that doth lean upon so evident [*tokens* >**judgments**<] and marks that the same thing, the which is affirmed to be seemeth necessarily to follow thereupon.

The judge shall trim his mind and straighten it to one kind of proof. And therefore in those causes that of their own nature cannot be proved directly, he may /be/ brought unto the same by presumptions to give sentence.

We are thaught by the example of King Solomon that a judge may give sentence upon /a/ violent presumption, who hearing a cause betwixt two women and discerning betwixt the natural love of the one and the hatred of the other /against the child/, who was the mother, adjudged the same child to the woman that was loth, or rather abhorred, to have her child parted or cut in two *(I Kings iii.)*. Let the judge yet provide that when [241v] he seeth a presumption whereby he is moved to give sentence, that same be put in writing and committed to the acts whereby the foundation of the sentence given may appear.[5]

4. Probatio carnalis copulae per praesumptiones.[6]

Violenta praesumptione probari carnalem commistionem nullus dubitet, veluti si masculus et femina, solus cum sola, nudus cum nuda, in eodem lecto iacentes depraehensi fuerint.

In probanda commixtione maris et feminae, sufficiat probatio actuum propinquorum ad eam, dum tamen testium accedat credulitas.

Uxor cui maritus non abs re denuntiabit, ne cum eo, quem suspectum habuerit, colloqueretur, secretove consortio uteretur, si mariti denuntiationem spernat, adultera censeatur.

[139v] 5. Quis sit habendus pro patre.[7]

Eius filius esse praesumitur, in cuius domo, et cuius ex uxore quis nascitur, licet uxor forsitan tempore conceptionis [126b] cum alio concubuerit, nisi mariti diuturna absentia, adversave valetudo, aut alia iusta causa, aliud suadeat.

6. Praesumptio mali animi.[8]

Is, qui contra legum interdicta, quicquam molitur, malam fidem semper habere praesum[*i*/a]tur.

Depraehensi in delicto semper praesumitur malus animus. Itaque qui cum nocuisset alicui, ioco se id fecisse dicit, tanquam obnoxius tenetur, nisi suam probet innocentiam.

7. Praesumptio boni animi.[9]

Per exteriora, quae intus sunt praesum[*un*/a]tur. Quemcunque igitur studere virtutibus, praesertim simplicitati et modestiae, videris, huius bonum et rectum [*esse*] animum intelligas.

[140r] Ex transacta cuiuslibet vita di{g}noscere possumus quid de subsequenti eius conversatione praesumamus: quia praeteritorum consideratio nos instruit de futuris.

---

[6]X, 2.23.11 (Fr, II, 355); X, 2.23.12 (Fr, II, 355-6), both originally decretals of Pope Alexander III (1159-81); X, 2.23.13 (Fr, II, 356), originally a decretal of Pope Clement III (1187-91).
[7]X, 4.17.8 (Fr, II, 712-13), originally a decretal of Pope Alexander III.
[8]*Speculum*, 2.2, *De praesumptionibus*, 2.9-10.
[9]*Ibid*.

4. A proof of carnal knowledge by presumption.[6]

No man doubteth but that carnal knowledge may be proved by violent presumption, as for example, if a man and woman *<found>* /be found alone/, both naked and /lying/ in one bed, *<be found>* together and so be taken with the manner.

The *<profits>* proofs of damage, most nigh unto the act, are sufficient to show carnal knowledge, so that witnesses do suppose the same to be true.

Let a wife be thought an adulterous woman *<if>* /that contemneth/ her husband's /commandment, who not/ *<upon not>* without cause will warn her, that she do not talk with him, or secretly be in his company, whom he suspecteth with her.

5. Who is to be counted a father.[7]

The child is to be thought his son, in whose house and of whose wife he is born, although the wife perhaps at the time of conception hath lain with another, except the long absence of her husband or his great sickness or some other cause do persuade the contrary.

6. A presumption of an evil mind.[8]

He that purposeth anything against the prohibition of the laws, let him always be presumed to /have/ an evil mind.

His mind is ever thought to be evil that is taken with any offense. Therefore, he that sayeth, when he hath hurt another, that he *<it>* did it out in sport, let /him/ be counted an offender, except he prove his innocency.

7. A presumption of a good mind.[9]

The inward things are presumed from outward shows; whomsoever therefore you shall see give himself to virtue, and namely to plainness and modesty, you may /well think/ that the same man's mind is good and right.

We may judge by a man's forelife past what we may presume of his conversation and behaviour hereafter. Because the consideration of things past doth give us good instructions for things to come.

8. Qui ad obiecta crimina tacet, suspectus est.[10]

Si quis ad crimina, quae sibi fuerint obiecta, vel proposita in iudicio ad respondendum, taceat, praesumptionem haud levem praebet [*probabilem*] defensionem se non habere.

9. Qui subterfugia quaerit, malam causam habere praesumitur.[11]

Quisquis dilationibus iudicium subterfugere conatur, is malam causam semper fovere praesumatur.

10. Quando ignorantia non est praesumenda.[12]

Ea quae publice aguntur, et quae quis indagare debet, nemo ignorare censetur.
[127a] Latere non potest vicinos, quod ad nos in longinquo [140v] pervenit; vicinis enim cum res praesuma{n}tur notiores esse, quam remotis, illis cum primis creditur.

11. De fama.[13]

Communis et pervulgata fama de aliquo gravem inducit praesumptionem.

12. Praesumptio continentiae.[14]

Non praesumitur incontinens in senili aetate, qui in iuventute continuit; atque id maxime si divinarum litterarum studiis incumbit, et eo genere doctrinae apprime fuerit ornatus.

13. Praesumptio ex habitu.[15]

Talis quisque praesumitur in quali habitu reperitur.

---

[10]X, 2.23.5 (Fr, II, 354), originally a sermon of Pope Gregory I (590-604), *Hom.* 18.
[11]X, 2.23.4 (Fr, II, 354), originally a rescript of Pope Boniface I, 13 June 419.
[12]X, 2.23.8 (Fr, II, 354), originally a letter of Pope Gregory I, *Reg.*, 12.29.
[13]Speculum, 2.2, *De probationibus*, 1.30; *ibid.*, *De praesumptionibus*, 2.2.
[14]X, 2.23.15 (Fr, II, 358), originally a decretal of Pope Innocent III, 7 July 1206.
[15]VI, 5.11.12 (Fr, II, 1102-3), originally a decretal of Pope Boniface VIII (1294-1303); 1268/5.

[242r] 8. **He that holdeth his peace when he is charged with a fault is to be suspected.**[10]

If any man do hold his peace and maketh no purgation unto faults that are laid unto his charge, it is no /small/ presumption that he is not well able to defend himself.

9. **He that seeketh starting holes is presumed to have an evil cause.**[11]

Whosoever seeketh by delays to avoid judgment, it is to be presumed that he cherisheth a wrong cause.

10. **When ignorance is not to be presumed.**[12]

Those things that are commonly done, and the which men ought to search out and know, no man is thought to be ignorant of them.

That can/not/ be ignorant to those that are at hand, that cometh to our knowledge afar off. Neighbours therefore are <*chiefly*> thought to know and understand things better than those that are further off, are first of all and chiefly to be believed.

11. **Of fame.**[13]

A common and open fame of any man bringeth great presumption with it.

12. **Presumption of continence.**[14]

He is not presumed to have incontinence in his old years that in his youth lived chaste, and especially if he gave himself to the study of divinity and were well imbued with that kind of learning.

13. **Presumption by apparel.**[15]

Everyone is thought to be such a one as the garments are which he doth wear.

14. Praesumitur neminem velle p[er/ro]dere sua.[16]

Praesumitur neminem esse qui sua bona velit e/**aut** prodigere aut perdere.

15. Praesumitur non mutari voluntatem, nisi probetur.[17]

Quilibet praesumitur manere in eadem voluntate, qua semel fuisse constat. Proinde qui mutatam [141r] asserit voluntatem, probare debet.

16. Iud/*ex*/icis sententia praesumitur bona.[18]

Propter religion*is*/**em** iudicantis semper pro eius sententia est praesumendum, nisi per appellationem fuerit suspensa.

[127b] 17. Praesumitur pro scripto.[19]

Praesumitur pro script[*o*/**ura**], nisi aliud actum aliud[*q*]ue scriptum esse probetur.

18. Praesumptio iuris et de iure.[20]

Praesumptio non est tanti momenti, quin contraria probatione elidatur; nisi sit praesumptio iuris, et de iure, quam sola eius *conf...* confessione, de cuius commodo agitur, tolli posse putamus.

19. Pares praesumptiones se mutuo conficiunt.[21]

Duae praesumptiones paris potentiae invicem se collidunt, et maior minorem vincit, prorsusque enervat.

---

[16]Speculum, 2.2, *De praesumptionibus*, 2.11 (additions).
[17]A. Alciatus, *De praesumptionibus*, in *Tractatus universi iuris* (18 vols., Lyon, 1549), V, 131a.
[18]Baldus, *De sententia*, in Speculum, 2.3, *idem*.
[19]Baldus, *De praesumptionibus*, in Speculum, 2.2, *idem*.
[20]Speculum, 2.2, *De praesumptionibus*, 2.7.
[21]Baldus, *De praesumptionibus*, in Speculum, 2.2, *idem*.

14. It is a presumption that no man will lose his own.[16]

It is a presumption that no man will waste away, or wilfully lose his own goods.

15. It is presumed that the will is not changed, except it be proved.[17]

Everybody is presumed to keep the same will that he once made. Therefore he that will say that will is changed, must prove it [242v] prove it (*sic*).

16. The sentence of a judge is presumed to be good.[18]

For the reverence of him that judgeth, men must presume that the sentence, the which he gave, is good, except the same by an appeal be suspended.

17. Presumption in the behalf of a writing.[19]

Presumption is with the <*s...*> writing, except some other thing is proved to be done or written.

18. Presumption of law and by law.[20]

A presumption is not of such force but it may be overthrown by a contrary proof, except it be prescription of law and by law, the which we think may be taken away by his only confession, <*of his*> /upon whose/ profit, all the contention and matter of law is.

19. Like presumptions do overthrow one another.[21]

Those presumptions of like power do overthrow the one the other, and the greater overthroweth the less, and doth utterly make it to be of no force.

20. Praesumptio infirmitatis tollitur per actum.[22]

Praesumptione[m] infirmitatis tolli per exercitium actus non compassibilis cum infirmitate, [141v] manifesti iuris est.

21. Iudex ex circumstantiis iudicabit.[23]

Si probationes rei et actoris tantum praesumptive concludant, iudicis est ex diligenti circumstantiarum consideratione iudicare. Ut cum vir se sponsam suam cognovisse affirmat, illa vero illud negat, matronaeque aliquae, (quae corpus inspiciebant), cum illa consentiant, iudex considerata opportunitate cognoscendi, mora, et diutina conversatione, et aetate utriusque, et matronarum fide et peritia, quid sequendum sit, [*facile*] iudicabit.[24]

---

[22]Cf. A. Alciatus, *De praesumptionibus*, in *Tractatus universi iuris*, V, 131b-132a.
[23]X, 2.19.4 (Fr, II, 307), originally a decretal of Pope Gregory VIII (1118-21).
[24]A note at the end in Foxe's hand reads: '"De defamationibus" require folium 268.' ('"On defamations" see folio 268').

20. **A presumption of infirmity is taken away by *<any>* /an/ act done.**[22]

It is plain law that the presumption of weakness is taken away by exercise of an act that is /not/ compatible with the sickness.

21. **A judge shall judge by circumstances.**[23]

If the proofs of the defendant and the acts do only conclude presumptorily, it is the duty of a judge, having diligent consideration of the circumstances, to judge thereupon, as for example, when a man saith that he had carnal knowledge with his spouse, and she denieth the same, and certain women, the which had view of her body, *<do>* be of the same mind /with her/, the judge, having consideration upon the opportunity for the one to know the other, their abode and long conversation, the age of them both, the honesty and skill of the matrons will [*easily*] judge what is to be thought and said in their behalf.[24]

[268r; 127b]   **50. DE DEFAMATIONIBUS**

1. Obtrectatores legibus esse puniendos.[1]

Quoniam omnes Christiani mutua caritate veros se debent Christi discipulos esse
ostendere, coercenda quorundam improborum malevolentia est, qui fratres odii/o
tam capitali prosequuntur, ut illos falsi criminibus ca[128a]lumniose velint
opprimere. Quo fit ut legum frena illorum licentiae sentiamus iniicienda, quorum
mentes Christiana caritas, (quae prorsus illis abest), mollire non potest; et quos
ipsum per se non movet officium, illos iuris acerbitate de[*vinc*/**nunt**]iemus.

2. Obtrectatores quando et quomodo puniantur.[2]

Primum igitur hoc constitutum sit, ut quicunque [*prudens et sciens* **malitiosa
voluntate ac**] dolo malo famam cuiusquam crimine conficto ac ementito
violaverint, aut ullo modo /ut/ violaretur effecerint, aut sermone contumelioso
contra quenquam utuntur, aut libellum famosum vel ipsi componunt aut scribunt,
/vel/ ab aliis compositum aut scriptum, /cum invenerint, [*aut*] non continuo
rumpunt/, aut ignibus cremant, sed divulgant aut in lucem proferunt, aut
proferendum curant, primum quidem ab eo cui haec facta est iniuria (si modo
velit iniuriam prosequi) deducantur ad ecclesiae pastorem et seniores, qui talium
obtrectatorum importunitatem [268v] [*acri*] vehementique sermone
perterrefaciant. In quorum auctoritate si acquiescere velint, et hominis
existimationem quam ante calumniis oppuguaverant, recolligere parati sint,
(quantum in se est), et recuperare, in eo ipso causa terminetur; nec ille, qui
calumniis fuerit appetitus, ullam suis obtrectatoribus exhibebit aliam molestiam,
nec illos ad iudices ordinarios trahet. Nam praecipua semper ratio salutis
animarum esse debet, et sumptus non necessarii, quantum licet, sunt amputandi.
Verum huiusmodi calumniatores et obtrectatores si nolunt salutaribus pastorum
et seniorum praeceptis inflecti, tum demum ad ipsos iudices ecclesiasticos
illorum nomina deferantur, apud quos (cum manifestis probationibus de
calumniis illorum et obtrectationibus plene constiterit) damnentur sententia
iudicum ad illas pecuniarum summas in cistas pauperum infundendas, quae
suarum ecclesiarum propriae sunt, [128b] quas illorum opes commode
videbuntur ferre posse; et etiam excommunicationis poena plectantur,

---

[1]13 Edward I, c. 4, 1285 (*S.R.*, I, 101-2); 9 Edward II, s. 1, c. 4, 1316 (*S.R.*, I, 171); cf. 37
Henry VIII, c. 10 (*S.R.*, III, 997); L, 5.17.6, c. 11 of the council of Reading, 1279.
[2]H.C., 9.1; *Cod. Iust.*, 9.36.1.

[243r] **50. OF DEFAMATIONS**

1. Backbiters and slanderers are to be punished by the law.[1]

Because all Christians ought to show themselves with love and charity one to another that they are the true disciples of Christ, the naughtiness of certain evil persons is to be corrected, that do so deadly hate their brethren that they will go about to undo them for ever with false slanders maliciously devised. Therefore, to the end their licentiousness may be bridled, who*se*/m Christian charity (the which they do wholly want), cannot mollify or temper, and whom duty /of itself/ doth not stir, we will [>*have them bridled* **denounce them**<] by the sharpness of the law.

2. Slanderers, when and how they should be punished.[2]

First of all let this be ordained, that whosoever [>*wittingly and willingly*<] doth take away a man's good name, by [>**malicious will and**<] false and feigned slander, or procure by any manner, that any man be slandered, or use any contumelious words against any man, or make or write any slanderous book or bill, or when they /find/ any such book or bill written do not either tear it or burn it, but publish the same to others or cast it abroad, or procure it to be brought abroad; the same man shall first be brought by him that is thus injuried, if he will prosecute this <*pro...*> wrong, to the pastor and elders of the church, that they may rebuke with all vehement speech the naughtiness of such slanderers, unto whose authority if they will yield and be quiet, and be ready to speak well of him again, /and make him amends as they may/ whom before they have slandered, then we will that the matter go no farther. Neither shall he that is slandered trouble any such backbiters any more, nor yet bring them to any ordinary judge. For the chief care ought to be for the soul's health, and unnecessary charges ought to be cut off, as much as may be. But if such slanderers and backbiters will not amend by the wholesome warnings of the pastor and elders, they let them be sent unto the ecclesiastical judges, before whom, when there shall be evidently <*ev...*> convicted upon such slander, let them be condemned by sentence of the judge in such sums of money as their ability may show, and the same to be put into the poor man's box, and they farther to be excommunicated,

a qua nullo modo volumus illos liberari, donec arbitratu iudicis ecclesiastici satisfactum est illi, cui iniuria facta est, et etiam ea perfuncti sint paenitentia, quae tanto crimini convenire videbitur.

3. Qui probant crimen obiectum, non puniantur.[3]

Quoniam reipublicae vehementer interest, ut crimina suppliciis coerceantur, et [*ut*] sua cuique iusta defensio reservetur, constituimus, ut si quis aliquem [269r] reum fecerit accusatione, denuntiatione, vel exceptione, vel alia quacunque ratione legitima et solemni, iudicique criminis obiecti fidem fecerit, illum (quoniam non calumniam, sed veritatem secutus sit) omni[**um**] legis istius poena liberari debere. Si vero qui accusaverit fuerit causa deiectus, poenis legis teneatur, nisi possit ostendere, quod non proposito male dicendi, nec calumniandi voluntate, sed aliqua iusta ratione fuerit ad hoc institutum adductus.[4]

---

[3]*Ibid.*
[4]A note at the end of the chapter in Foxe's hand reads: '"De dilationibus" require in folio 172.' ('"On delays" see folio 172').

[243v] from the which they shall not be absolved until /by the discretion of the judge/ they have satisfied the party whom they have injured and done such penitence as were meet for such an offence.

3. Let not them be punished that have proved the fault wherewith they have charged another.[3]

Because it is for the common weal behove, that offenses should be punished and that every man may have his just defence, we do ordain that if any man do /do/ [*sic*] prove another guilty by any accusation, <*the same*> /denunciation or exception, or by any other lawful means and persuaded the judge therein the same/ man shall be void of [>*all*<] penalty [>**of all**<], because he hath not slandered the man, but has said the truth. That if the accuser be found faulty by law, let him be punished by law, except he can show that he was induced hereunto, not upon purpose to slander, or upon will to take a man's good name away, but upon some other just cause he was brought to say as he did.[4]

[172r; 128b]   **51. DE DILATIONIBUS**[1]

1. Dilatio quid sit.[2]

Dilatio est agendi facultas infra tempus vel a legibus, [*vel a iudice*], vel ex conventione partium praescriptum.

2. Dilationum species.[3]

Dilationum alia est legalis, quae a legibus *est* definitur; ad appellandum enim, et petendum restitutionem /*realiter*/ in integrum, et similia, tempus a legibus praescribitur.

Iudicialis, quae datur arbitrio iudicis,.

c/Conventionalis,[4] quae terminum [129a] habet ex conventione partium.

Ex dilationibus iudicialibus citatoria datur *citatoria datur* a iudice, ad comparendum.

Deliberatoria[5] oblato libello datur ad deliberandum de his, quae [172v] petuntur, vel de cedendo, vel de lite sus[*cip*/**pic**]ienda.

Recusatoria terminum concedit ad proponendas [*omnes*] exceptiones [**omnes**], et ad declinandum seu differendum iudicium.

Probatoria datur ad probandum et allegandum in causa.

Definitoria datur ad negotium definiendum.

Iudicatoria datur condemnatis ad patiendum vel solvendum iudicata.

Appellatoria *quae* datur ad appellandum.

3. Dilationes, quantum fieri potest, amputandae sunt.[6]

Materias dilationum ubique amputare volumus, et hac ratione iudicibus *c*... non concedimus dandae dilationis, quoties voluerint, facultatem, sed quatenus rerum urgentissima ratio *flagitaverit*, et necessitas desideratae instructionis **exegerit**. Idcirco non nisi [173r] iusta de causa petenti, bonaque fide imploranti dilatio

---

[1] All headings in this chapter are in Cranmer's hand.
[2] Speculum. 2.1, *De dilationibus*, preface.
[3] *Ibid.*
[4] Cranmer began a new sentence here.
[5] The translation here is wrong. 'Dilation' should read: 'deliberatory appointment'.
[6] *Ibid.*, 4.1.

51. OF RESPITINGS OR DILATIONS[1]

1. What is a dilation?[2]

A dilation is a leave to plead within time either prescribed by law, [>*or by the judge*<], or by the agreement of the parties.

2. The kinds of appointments <*of*> or dilations.[3]

Of appointments to plead some are by law, such as law doth ordain; for to appoint and to ask to be restored to the whole, and suchlike, a time is appointed by law.

A judicial appointment is that which is given by discretion of the judge.

A conventional[4] is that, the which is given by agreement of the parties.

Among the judicial appointments, the citation is given by the judge for the party to appear.

A dilation[5] is given when the libel is offered, to deliberate [244r] upon those things that are asked, either to yield or to proceed in the cause.

A recusatory appointment doth grant a term to propound all exceptions and to eschew or defer the judgment.

A probatory appointment is given to prove and to gather matter in the cause.

A definatory appointment is to end the matter.

A judicatory time is granted unto the parties condemned to suffer or to pay things judged.

Appellatory time is *what is* given to appeal.

3. All dilations or <*dis..*> appointing of time ought to be cut off as much as may be.[6]

We will that the matter of all dilations be cut off. And for this cause we will /not/ give leave to the judge to grant time, so often as he will, but when urgent cause *demands it* and great necessity for informations to be given **do so require**. Therefore dilation or <*t...*> respiting of time ought not to be granted but when it

concedi debet. Proinde si mo*de*randae solutionis gratia a debitore falsi crimen obiicitur, nihilominus salva executione criminis, debitorem ad solutionem compelli volumus,. *quodque* **Et**[7] idem in consimilibus faciendum existimamus.

4. Certa dilationum spatia.[8]

Quamvis iure antiquo receptum sit, ut quaelibet citatio spatium decem dierum concedat, et dentur ad deliberandum viginti dies pro testibus et instrumen*d*/**t**is producen*t*/**d**is, quando fuerint in provincia, tres menses; quando in locis provinciae contiguis, sex, quando in transmarinis regionibus, novem, actori vero contumaci triginta dies; istas nihilominus dilationes [173v] iudicum arbitrio (ratione habita personarum, locorum et causarum) magis minusve contrahi volumus, prorogari vero nullo modo,. *c*/**C**umque[9] iudex e[129b]as multum contraxerit, causas exprimat, quae in actis inserantur ut appellandi materia praecidatur. Appellatoria tamen dilatio iudicis arbitrio non mutabitur: semper enim erit quindecim die*s*/**rum**, qui/*s* neque contrahentur, neque ampliabuntur.[10]

5. Dilationes quae ad causae cognitionem pertinent, iudice sedente, et parte adversa praesente, fiant.[11]

Dilationes citatoriae atque deliberatoriae, licet a iudice non sedente, sed ambulante in loco iudicii, concedi possint, attamen quae causae cognitionem requirunt, a iudice sedente dari volumus, et dum adversaria pars adest; ut si reclamet, et de dilatio[174r]nibus huiusmodi quaestio emergat, sententia iudicis lis dirimatur.

6. Si iudex tempore probation[*i*/um] praescripto ius non dicat, pars ad tempus amissum restituetur.[12]

Si tamen non stat per partem, quominus facere possit suas probationes in dilatione ei data, sed stat per iudicem, quia non reddit ius in illo die, tunc non est danda nova dilatio; sed volumus partem eandem restitui ad tempus amissum.

---

[7]Cranmer began a new sentence here.
[8]*Cod. Iust.*, 3.11.1, originally a rescript of the emperors Diocletian and Maximian, 18 March 293.
[9]Cranmer began a new sentence here.
[10]Speculum, 2.3, *De appellationibus*, 5.7, where the delay is ten days.
[11]Speculum, 2.1, *De dilationibus*, 2.1.
[12]*Ibid.*, 3.9.

is asked upon just cause and in good faith. And therefore if a debtor do object the crime of forging or falsehood because he would be prohibited for payment of the money that he is condemned to pay, yet we will that the debtor be compelled to pay the money, saving the examination of the crime. *Which* **And**[7] the same we think ought to be done in like things.

4. Certain terms or spaces of dilations or appointments.[8]

Although by the old /law/ it hath been received that every citation should have ten days respite and twenty days for deliberation, for witnesses and writings when the parties are within the province three months, when they are /in places/ nigh the province, six months, when they are beyond the seas, nine months, and to the acts thirty days together. Yet we will that these appointments shall be shortened by the discretion of the judges, respect had to the persons, places and causes, but in no wise that any longer days be given. And[9] when the judge shall much shorten those appointments, let him give a reason wherefore, and the same to be inserted in the acts, that all matter of appeal may be taken away. [244v] But the appealing dilation shall not be altered by the discretion of the judge, for it shall always be <*twelve*> fifteen days, the which shall neither be shorter nor yet longer.[10]

5. Let dilations be made such as belong to the cause, when the judge and the contrary party is present.[11]

All citatory and deliberatory dilations or appointments may be granted by the judge, not sitting but walking in the place of judgment. But those things that do appertain to the knowledge of the cause, we will that the same be given by the judge sitting, and when the contrary party is present, that if he do reclaim, and question do rise upon such appointments of time, the same may be decided by the sentence of the judge.

6. If the judge do not utter his law at the time of process appointed, the party shall be restored to his lost time.[12]

If the party be not behind to bring in his process that were by appointment ordained for him to bring in, but there the judge is a let, because he doth not <*sit in*> give judgment that day, then is there not a new dilation to be given, but we will that the party shall be restored to his lost time.

7. Terminus dilationis utrique parti communis sit.[13]

Ubicunque a iudice data erit dilatio, statuimus, ut idem terminus sit communis utrique parti; ita ut utraque possit in illo probare. Sed si is, cui data est dilatio, re integra renuntiaverit dilationi, adversarium ratione *hu*/eiusdem dilationis posse probare [*n*/**v**]olumus.

[174v; 130a] 8. Dilatio *ad* certum tempus praescribere[14] habet.[15]

Volumus dilationem a iudice partibus datam, certam esse, vel per numerationem dierum, vel ad certum tempus.

9. Data dilatione cessat iudicis officium *ad tempus praescriptum*, dum durat dilatio.[16]

Data dilatione iudicis **officium** conquiescere decernimus, donec petiti temporis defluxerint curricula, feriis illi tempori non excludendis, sed connumerandis.

10. *Si q..* Qui p[*er*/ro]diderit acta, ad aliam probationem non admittetur.[17]

Si quis probaverit intentionem suam per testes, vel per aliud simile, et postea p[*er*/**ro**]diderit acta, etiam si casum possit probare, nullam esse ei amplius dandam dilationem volumus.

11. Libellus, si in citatione inseratur, excludit dilationem ad deliberandum.[18]

Cum in citando exemplum libelli reo transmittitur, vocaturque ad respondendum, deliberatoriae dilationes ei non dabuntur, modo citatio [175r] aequum et decentem contineat terminum; alioqui dilationes ad deliberandum habebit *atque hoc non solum in civili iudicio, sed in criminali quoque observari volumus.*

---

[13]*Ibid.*, 4.14.
[14]It appears that Cranmer went back and added the prefix later.
[15]*Ibid.*, 1.3.
[16]*Cod. Iust.*, 3.11.3, originally a rescript of the Emperor Constantine I, 7 February 318.
[17]Speculum, 2.2, *De probationibus*, 2.5.
[18]*Novellae*, 53.3.1, where there is a delay of twenty days.

7. The term of appointment is common unto both parties.[13]

Wheresoever any appointment shall be given by the judge<*ment*>, we do ordain that the same term be common unto both the parties, so that both of them may prove at the same time, but if he unto whom the time is appointed will then renounce his time, the matter then standing whole, we will [*>not<*] that his adversary shall bring in his process at the selfsame time.

8. An appointment ought to have a certain time prescribed.[14-15]

We will that the appointment granted by the judge unto the parties be certain, either by number of days or else at a certain prefixed time.

[245r] 9. When an appointment is given, the judge's office doth cease *for the prescribed time* during the time of that appointment.[16]

When a time is appointed, we do decree that the judge's **office** shall cease until that time be run out, and the holy days in the same account not to be excluded but to be reckoned.

10. He that hath [*>lost* betrayed<] his acts shall not be admitted to any other probation.[17]

If any shall prove his intent by witnesses or by any other like thing, and afterwards do [*>lose* **betray**<] the acts, although he can prove the loss, we will notwithstanding that he have not any further or other time appointed unto him.

11. If a libel be inserted in a citation, it doth exclude appointment for deliberation.[18]

When upon a citation, the example of a libel is transmitted to the defendant and is called to answer, the defendant shall not have respite or any other time appointed for deliberation, so that the citation do contain an indifferent and meet term to answer, otherwise he shall /have/ his time appointed to deliberate, *and we wish this to be observed not only in civil judgment but in criminal judgment also.*

12. In causae initio non dabitur actori tempus ad deliberandum.[19]

Deliberatoriae dilationes ab initio causae actori non conced[*e*/**u**]ntur, (existimatur enim venire instructus); attamen si reus excipiat, vel illum reconveniat, dilationem aliquam ad deliberandum iure habebit.

[130b] 13. **Mutatio libelli non semper requirit novam dilationem ad respondendum.**[20]

Si libellus mutatur in eo, quod non alterat primam petitionem, quominus de ea certus esse possit reus, non erunt novae dilationes deliberatoriae concedendae. Nam cum plene quis [175v] potuit instrui per primum libellum, licet aliquid addatur, quod non mutat naturam negotii, novae non erunt impartiendae dilationes.

14. **Prorogatio dilationis.**[21]

Plures dilationes, quam leges nostrae permittunt, nolumus alicui dari: tamen decernimus eas posse prorogari ex causa, et illae non erunt novae dilationes, sed priores prorogatae. Prorogatio enim debet fieri antequam primum tempus dilationis sit finitum; tempore autem toto finito, nolumus tunc posse habere locum prorogationem, sed erit nova dilatio.

15. **Secunda dilatio ex causa dari potest.**[22]

Secundam dilationem ex causa dandam esse statuimus, et hoc solummodo respectu temporis, in quo impeditus fuit aliquis, et respectu eius [176r] rei, in qua fuit impeditus. Et ideo si aliquis impeditus fuerit producere unum testem, et procuravit, quantum potuit, in prima dilatione eundem producere, *certe* dabitur [*dilatio*] nova [**dilatio**] ad producendum illum testem, et non alios, quos non procuravit in prima dilatione producendos.

---

[19]Speculum, 2.1, *De dilationibus*, 1.18-19.
[20]Speculum, 4.1, *De libellorum conceptione*, 7.9.
[21]Speculum, 2.1, *De dilationibus*, 2.4.
[22]*Ibid.*, 2.5.

12. At the beginning of the cause, the actor shall not have time to deliberate.[19]

Time*s* for deliberation shall not be granted to the actor at the beginning of the cause, (for it is thought that he cometh instructed). And yet if the defendant do except, or reconvent him, he shall have by the law some time to deliberate.

13. The alteration of the libel doth not always require new time to answer.[20]

If the libel be altered in that, that it doth not alter the first petition, but that the defendant may be certain of it, there are no*ne* new appointments to be given, for when a man may be fully informed by the first libel (although something be added, the which doth not alter the nature of the business) new appointments of time are not to be granted.

14. A prorogation of an appointment.[21]

We will /not/ that any man have any more delays of time than the laws do grant, and yet we do decree that the same may be prorogued upon cause. And they shall not be called new appointments, but former appointments prorogued, for a prorogation ought to be made before the first time of the appointment [244v] be expired. But when the whole time is ended, we will not that then afterwards it shall be called a prorogation, but a new appointment.

15. A second appointment may be granted upon cause.[22]

We do ordain that a second delay or appointment may be granted upon cause, and that only upon respect of time when one hath been hindered and upon respect of the matter whereby he was hindered. And therefore if any man were hindered to bring forth one witness, and yet he did his best to bring forth the same in the first appointment of time, he shall *certainly* have a new appointment of time granted unto him, to bring forth the same witness and none other, because he did not make means in the first appointment to bring them forth.

16. Dilatio [*potest*] quando [potest] revocari.[23]

Dilatio, quae de partium consensu data est, altera parte invita non debet sine causa revocari; sed quando iudex ex [131a] officio suo dilationem praefixit, si causa tollatur, quae illum movit, {*ea*/**cu**}m potest revocare.

17. Dilatio data reo ad iurandum intelligenda est dari actori ad probandum.[24]

Decernimus dilationem datam reo [176v] ad iurandum etiam intelligi debere datam actori ad probandum per testes vel instrumenta.

18. Dilatio quando reus opponit exceptiones.[25]

Utrique parti dilationem dari debere de iuribus suis decernimus, quando reus opponit exceptiones.

19. Dilatio ad consulendum.[26]

Potest a principio dilatio peti ad illos consulendos, quorum consilium arduitas causae requirit, et quos aliqua ex parte negotium tangit, ut ab eis, is qui citatus est, informetur.

Si pendente causa, super quopiam emergente positiones *obs*/**ff**erantur , dandae sunt induciae procuratori, ut dominum suum consulere possit, si tale sit emergens, ut probabiliter nihil ab initio **de hoc** [177r] scire potuerit dominus constituens. Nam si ab initio praevideri potuisset, et a causa principali perspicuam dependentiam haberet, tempus ei, ut dominum suum consulat, non dabitur. Est enim quod dominus sibi imputet, quare ab initio, (ut debuit), procuratorem suum plene non instruxerit.

20. Citatio peremptoria.[27]

Citationi peremptoriae nimis brevis terminus non affigatur, nisi maxima necessitas id suggerat. Alioqui parti sic vocatae licebit appellare.

---

[23]*Ibid.*, 4.13.
[24]*Ibid.*, 4.6.
[25]Speculum, 2.1, *De exceptionibus et replicationibus*, 3.4.
[26]X, 2.8.2 (Fr, II, 269), originally a decretal of Pope Celestine III (1191-8).
[27]X, 2.8.1 (Fr, II, 268-9), originally a decretal of Pope Alexander III (1159-81).

16. When may an appointment be called back.[23]

An appointment of time granted by consent of the parties cannot be revoked without cause, against the good will of one of the parties. But when the judge hath appointed by office a certain prefixed time, if the cause be taken, no one that moved him to appoint that time, he may revoke the same appointment of time.

17. When an appointment of time is given unto the defendant to swear, the same time is understanded to be given unto the agent to prove.[24]

We do decree that when an appointment of time is granted unto the defendant to swear, it ought to be understanded that the same time is given to the agent to prove his matter by witnesses and by writings.

18. Appointment of time when the defendant putteth exceptions.[25]

We do decree that both the parties should have their appointments of time granted <*up...*> unto them, when the defendant doth put in his exceptions.

[245r] 19. An appointment of time to ask counsel.[26]

An appointment or respiting of time may be asked from the beginning to ask counsel of those whose counsel the greatness of the cause doth require, or whom the matter concerneth by any means, that he who is cited may be informed of them.

If positions are offered upon some emergent cause that riseth upon the matter, in the time that <*t...*> the cause yet hangeth, respiting of time should be granted unto the proctor, that he may ask counsel of his lord, if any such thing hath fallen out that by all likelihood his lord that appointed him to be proctor, could not from the beginning know anything **of it**. For if from the beginning it might have been foreseen and that it had plain and evident dependency upon the principal cause, there shall no time be given unto him to ask counsel of his lord. For the lord may blame himself, because he did not fully instruct his proctor from the beginning as he ought to have done.

[End of the MS]

20. Peremptory citation.[27]

An extremely short time limit shall not be set for a peremptory citation unless the greatest necessity demands this. Otherwise a party so summoned may appeal.

[131b] 21. **Propter iniustas dilationes licet appellare.**[28]

Si iudex absque causa et iniuste dilationes vel contrahat vel ampliet, ab eo licet appellare.

22. **Citatio terna.**[29]

Citatoriae dilationes aut sunto tres, aut [177v] una esto peremptorie inscripta, sed quae spatium temporis id concedat, quod tribus aequari et congruere possit.

Praeter citatoriam primam et secundam dilationem aliae sunto peremptoriae, licet fortasse non sic inscribantur.[30]

23. **Absens reipublicae causa a iudicio excusabitur.**[31]

Absens reipublicae causa tantisper a terminis in iudicio sibi praefixis excusatur, quamdiu *impedimentum* **causa** absentiae durat.

Qui fuerit spoliatus atque suis bonis vi deiectus, ut respondeat adversariis suis in iudicio compelli non potest, nisi prius restituatur. Deinde restitutus in integrum ad comparendum [178r] *quattuor aut sex mensium dilationem habebit.*

24. **De remoto ab administratione.**[32]

De [*di*]lapidatione suspectus, et ob id ab administratione remotus, quamvis nondum sit restitutus, in iudicio respondere cogitur, neque restituetur, nisi causa cognita absolvatur.

25. **Quando idem terminus duobus actis praescribi potest.**[33]

Licebit eundem terminum duobus actibus praefigere, quando simul et in idem tempus possunt concurrere, ut ad producendum testes probatorios, et ad producendum reprobatorios, *et si actus ordine successivo sint explicandi eundem terminum* nihil enim vetat iudicem testes admittere simul, super principali, et reprobatorios. At si actus ordine successivo sint explicandi, eundem terminum

---

[28]Speculum, 2.3, *De appellationibus*, 2.5-6.
[29]Speculum, 2.1, *De citatione*, 3.3.
[30]In F and subsequent printed editions, this sentence is read as part of the heading of the next canon.
[31]*Dig.*, 49.11.2, originally Marcian, *De appellationibus*, 2.
[32]C. 3, q. 2, c. 8 (Fr, I, 508-9), see Gratian's comment in pt. 2.
[33]Speculum, 2.2, *De probationibus*, 1.2.

21. It is permissible to appeal because of unjust delays.[28]

If a judge either establishes or extends delays without cause and unjustly, it is permissible to appeal from that.

22. Threefold citation.[29]

Citation delays shall either be three or one, written peremptorily, but which allows the space of time which would equal and be appropriate for three.

Beyond the first and second citations, the others shall be peremptory, even if they are not written as such.[30]

23. Someone absent on state business shall be excused from judgment.[31]

Someone absent on state business shall be excused from the time limits imposed on him in judgment, as long as the *hindrance* **cause** of absence lasts.

Anyone who has been robbed and deprived of his goods by force shall not be compelled to answer his adversaries in judgment unless he gets them back first. After getting them all back he shall have a delay of four or six months in which to appear.

24. Of someone removed from administration.[32]

Someone suspected of dilapidation and removed from his administration for that reason, is obliged to answer in judgment even though he has not yet been restored, and he shall not be restored unless he is absolved in the cause being heard.

25. When the same time limit can be prescribed for two actions.[33]

It will be permissible to appoint the same time period for two actions, when they may run together and at the same time, for the purpose of producing both supporting witnesses and hostile witnesses, *and if the actions must be heard in succession, a common time period....* for nothing prevents a judge from admitting witnesses in the principal cause, including hostile ones, at the same time. But if the actions must be heard in succession they will not be able to share one

communem habere non poterunt. [178v] Iudici licet dilationem dando, vel adhuc pendente, quae iam data est, terminum ad alium actum successive explicandum statuere, tam eidem quam alteri parti; quo[132a]niam sic dilationi iam concessae nullum fit praeiudicium: ut si decem dies ad instrumenta producenda, et quinque ad testes assignentur; non enim [**hi**] se mutuo [*hi*] actus impediunt. At si unus actus pendet ab altero, id facere non convenit. Male quippe darentur decem dies ad positiones producendas, et decem ad intentionem probandam; quia positiones fortasse tam erunt clarae, ut probatione non egeant, vel [*erunt*] adeo [**erunt**] ineptae, ut omnino sint repudiandae.

26. Iudex uni parti parcere non potest in alterius partis praeiudicium.[34]

Tametsi iudex propitius nonnihil potest reo [179r] contumaci parcere (unum scilicet aut alterum diem illum, post terminum peremptorium, expectando) id tamen in praeiudicium partis ne faciat, neque ita ut impensas non iubeat recompensari.

27. Diebus feriatis iudicia non fiant.[35]

Feriis institutis ad honorem Dei, ut sunt omnes festi dies, a litibus et iudiciis abstineri volumus; neque testes his temporibus dicent testimonia atque processus tunc facti, et sententia lata non valebit.

    Repentinae feriae, quae iussu nostrae regiae maiestatis indicuntur vel ob res feliciter gestas, vel propter inaugurationem regni, vel publicas supplicationes, feriis institutis ad honorem Dei sunto pares et eiusdem rationis, ut**que** illis contendere non licet in [179v] iudicio, (etiam volentibus partibus), ita in istis non concedatur.

28. Quae in feriis liceant.[36]

Repentinis feriis nec non institutis ad honorem Dei **In feriis**, quae ad pacem et concordiam pertinent, fieri permittimus, ut iuramenta, [*p*/**f**]acta, transactiones. Licebit etiam his diebus miserabilium personarum causas agere. *Quaestiones quoque ac tormenta latronibus propter has ferias non remittentur.*

---

[34]Speculum, 2.1, *De dilationibus*, 4.14.
[35]X, 2.9.1 (Fr, II, 270), originally c. 37 of the council of Mainz, 813.
[36]Speculum, 2.1, *De feriis*, 2.1.

common time period. It is permissible for a judge, when granting a delay, or while one which has already been granted is still pending, to give either of the parties a time period for the other action which must be heard subsequently, since there is no prejudice to a delay already granted - for example, if ten days are allowed for producing documents and five are appointed for witnesses, for these actions do not hinder one another. But if one action depends on another, it is not appropriate to do that. Indeed it would be bad to grant ten days for producing statements and ten for proving a case, since the statements may perhaps be so clear that they do not need any proof, or else so silly that they must be totally rejected.

26. A judge cannot pardon one party in prejudice to another party.[34]

Even if the judge is disposed to pardon someone accused of contumacy (for example, by waiting an extra day or two for him after the end of the peremptory time limit), nevertheless he shall not do this in prejudice to any party, nor in such a way that he will not order expenses to be paid.

27. Judgments are not to be held on holidays.[35]

On holidays instituted for the honour of God, as all feast days are, we want no suits or judgments to be held, nor shall witnesses give testimonies at those times, and processes held then and any sentence passed shall not be valid.

Other holidays, which are appointed at the command of our king's majesty, either because of happy occurrences, or because of the beginning of the reign, or for public prayers, are equal to holidays instituted for the honour of God and of the same nature, so just as it is not permissible to debate in judgment on the former days, (even if the parties want to), so it is not allowed on the latter days either.

28. What is permitted on holidays.[36]

On remaining holidays not instituted for the honour of God **On holidays**, we allow things which pertain to peace and concord to be done, like oaths, [*contracts* **acts**], transactions. It shall also be permissible to hear the causes of poor people on those days. *Also, thieves are not spared interrogations and tortures because of these holidays.*

[132b] 29. **Citationes non fiant diebus feriatis.**[37]

Citationes quae fiant die feriato non valent; et cum nominatim diem feriatum praefigunt ad comparendum, sunt temerariae. Proinde citet iudex ad certum diem, et adiiciat, quod si dies is fuerit feriatus, proximo venias.

[180r] 30. **De messe et vindemia.**[38]

His feriis quae ad hominum utilitatem sunt institutae, (ut messis et vindemiarum), partes pro suo arbitrio renuntiare poss[u/i]nt,. *q*/**Q**uod[39] si faciant, et processus iudicialis et sententia lata valebit. Testes tamen compelli non possunt, ut his diebus testificentur, si nolint.

Feriis hominum causa institutis, non solum partes renuntiare queunt, sed certis de causis cogi possunt, ut ad iudicium veniant; ut si res tempore sit peritura, nec patiatur moram. Ad haec, sententia, quae ante has ferias lata fuit, per eas mandari potest executioni, **et gravia in Deum scelera cognosci possunt et puniri.**

31. **De certis feriis.**[40]

Toto quadragesimae tempore, septem diebus [180v] post resurrectionis festum, et septem diebus ante natalem Domini, quiescant iudicia.[41]

[37]Speculum, 2.1, *De citatione*, 1.13-14.
[38]*Dig.*, 2.12.1, originally Ulpian, *De omnibus tribunalibus*, 4; X, 2.9.5 (Fr, II, 272-3), originally a decretal of Pope Gregory IX (1227-41), published on or before 5 September 1234.
[39]Cranmer began a new sentence here.
[40]Speculum, 2.1, *De feriis*, 1.2; *Cod. Iust.*, 3.12.5(6), originally a rescript of the emperors Gratian, Valentinian II and Theodosius I, 27 March 380; ibid., originally a rescript of the emperors Valentinian II, Theodosius I and Arcadius, 7 August 389.
[41]A note at the bottom of the page in Foxe's hand reads: '"De exceptionibus" require in folio 202.' ('"On exceptions" see folio 202').

29. **Citations are not to be made on holidays.**[37]

Citations which are made on a holiday are not valid, and when they specify a holiday for appearing in court, they are out of order. Therefore the judge shall summon for a certain day, and shall add that if that day happens to be a holiday, you shall come the day after.

30. **Of harvest and vintage.**[38]

On those holidays which are instituted for the benefit of people, (like harvest and vintage), the parties may refuse to appear at their own discretion. But[39] if they come, both the judicial process and the sentence passed shall be valid. Nevertheless, witnesses cannot be compelled to testify on those days if they do not want to.

On holidays instituted for the sake of people, although the parties can in principle refuse to appear, in certain cases they can be compelled to come to judgment, for example, if the matter is on the point of being lost and cannot allow any delay. In such cases, a sentence which has been passed before these holidays may be ordered for execution during them, **and serious crimes against God can be heard and punished.**

31. **Of certain holidays.**[40]

There will be no judgments held during the whole time of lent, the seven days following the feast of the resurrection and the seven days before the birth of the Lord.[41]

[202r; 132b]   **52. DE EXCEPTIONIBUS**[1]

1. **Exceptio quid sit.**[2]

Exceptio est defensio, qua conventus in iudicio conatur agentem a se depellere, atque ab actione vel eius effectu excludere.

[133a] 2. **Exceptiones peremptoriae et dilatoriae.**[3]

Peremptoriae exceptiones, si probentur susceptas actiones seu lites penitus tollunt: dilatoriae vero illas tantum differunt. Et inter dilatorias aliquae appellantur declinatoriae, sumunturque ab observatione iudiciorum a ratione personarum, loci, et temporis, ac rescripti, et iudicium conantur declinare.

3. **Exceptiones reales et personales.**[4]

Reacles exceptiones ita rebus, de quibus agitur, cohaerent, ut ad omnes illos devolvantur, ad quos res extenduntur, de quibus agitur. Exceptio enim [202v] quae convenit reo, convenit etiam eius fideiussori. Personales autem sic certe alicui personae sunt propriae, ut ad alios non transeant.

4. **Exceptiones peremptoriae semper possunt obiici.**[5]

Exceptiones peremptoriae sunt perpetuae. Nam semper obstant agentibus, neque illis praescribitur, quominus in omni parte iudicii actori obiici valeant.

---

[1]In this chapter, the first four headings are in Cranmer's hand and the rest are in Peter Martyr's.
[2]*Dig.*, 44.1.2, originally Ulpian, *Ad edictum*, 74.
[3]Hostiensis, *Summa aurea*, c. *De exceptionibus*.
[4]*Dig.*, 44.1.7, originally Paulus, *Ad Plautium*, 3.
[5]*Dig.*, 44.1.3, originally Gaius, *Ad edictum provinciale*, 1.

52. OF EXCEPTIONS[1]

1. What an exception is.[2]

An exception is a defence, by which someone summoned to judgment tries to fend off the plaintiff and prevent him from launching his action and succeeding in it.

2. Peremptory and dilatory exceptions.[3]

If peremptory exceptions are proved they totally annul actions or suits which have been undertaken, but dilatory exceptions only postpone them. And some dilatory ones are known as declinatory, being taken from the observation of judgments made on the basis of the persons, the place, the time and the rescript, and they try to avoid judgment.

3. Real and personal exceptions.[4]

Real exceptions are tied to the matters under litigation in such a way that they apply to all those to whom the matters under litigation extend. For an exception which is appropriate for the accused is also appropriate for his guarantor. But personal exceptions are so definitely particular to a certain person that they do not extend to others.

4. Peremptory exceptions may be presented at any time.[5]

Peremptory exceptions are permanent. For they block the plaintiffs for ever, nor are they restricted in such a way that they may not validly be objected against the plaintiff at any point in the judgment.

5. Quae exceptiones sint temporariae.[6]

Dilatoriae atque declinatoriae exceptiones temporariae sunt. Nam illis qui utuntur, causar*rum*/i solent tempus (aut solutioni condictum, aut intra quod leges agere prohibent), nondum elapsum esse, vel conditionem appositam nondum extare, vel iudicem non esse competentem, et alia id genus. Exceptiones huiusmodi actorem in perpetuum non vetant [203r] quin agat, sed ob mutationem rerum et temporum facile potest contingere, ut amplius locum non habeant. Sunt etiam ea de causa temporariae, quoniam si quis eis non utatur tempore [133b] a iure praescripto, illis deinceps uti non poterit.

6. Declinatoriae exceptiones quando sint opponendae, et quando probandae.[7]

Omnes exceptiones declinatorias (cum processum iudicii impediant, non autem causam perimant) ante litis contestationem, vel primum causae actum, si lis non sit contestanda, proponi volumus; et si quis ante litem contestatam vel primum actum eas proponere omiserit, illis postea non utatur: quoniam eas praetereundo actis videtur consensisse. Atque huiusmodi exceptiones cum obiectae [203v] fuerint, probari a reo volumus, priusquam vel ad litis contestationem vel ad primum causae actum veniatur.

7. Exceptiones dilatoriae quando proponendae et probandae.[8]

Dilatoriae vero exceptiones (quibus non processus iudicii sed actoris intentio impeditur) cum ad negotium et rem, quae agitur, pertineant, et ipsae proponantur ante litis contestationem; sed eas probare nullus reus cogatur, antequam ipse actor suam intentionem probare coeperit. Attamen etiam si post litis contestationem proponantur, non erunt repellendae a iudicio.

8. Declinatoria exceptio contra iudicem ante omnes alias proponenda.[9]

Exceptio declinatoria, quae contra iudicem est *est*, non solum ante litis contestationem debet proponi, sed ante omnes alias, sive dilatorias, [204r] sive declinatorias. Nam si de aliis incipiat reus respondere in iudicio, iudicem videbitur ut suum approbare.

---

[6]*Ibid.*
[7]Hostiensis, *Summa aurea*, c. *De exceptionibus.*
[8]*Ibid.*
[9]*Ibid.*

5. Which exceptions are temporary.[6]

Dilatory and declinatory exceptions are temporary. For those who make use of them usually do so because the time (either that specified for payment, or that within which the laws forbid them to act), has not yet expired, or the affixed condition has not yet been met, or the judge is not competent, and other things like that. Exceptions of this kind do not permanently prevent the plaintiff from acting, but because of the change of circumstances and times it may easily happen that they have no further relevance. For this reason also they are temporary, since if someone does not make use of them within the time prescribed by the law, he may not make any further use of them.

6. When declinatory exceptions must be put forward and when they must be proved.[7]

It is our will that all declinatory exceptions (since they hinder the process of judgment but do not invalidate the cause) shall be set out before the joinder of issue, or before the first act in the cause, if the issue is not to be joined, and if anyone neglects to set them out before the issue is joined or before the first act, he shall have no further recourse to them, since by overlooking them he is regarded as having agreed to the proceedings. And when exceptions of this kind have been raised, it is our will that they shall be proved by the accused before coming to the joinder of issue or the first act in the cause.

7. When dilatory exceptions must be set out and proved.[8]

Moreover, dilatory exceptions (by which it is not the process of judgment but the plaintiff's case which is held up), when they pertain to the business and matter under discussion, shall also be set out before the issue is joined, but no accused person shall be compelled to prove them before the plaintiff himself has begun to prove his case. But even if they are set out after the joinder of issue, they shall not be rejected by the court.

8. A declinatory exception against a judge is to be put forward before any others.[9]

A declinatory exception which is against a judge must not only be set out before the joinder of issue, but also before any others, whether they are dilatory or declinatory. For if the accused starts to answer the others in court, it will look as if he approves of his judge.

[134a] 9. **Terminum esse proponendum /a iudice/ ante litis contestationem ad omnes dilatorias exceptiones proponendas.**[10]

Ne dilatoriis exceptionibus lites malitiose protrahantur, iudici mandamus, ut ante litis contestationem certum aliquem terminum praescribat, *co*/intra quem si reus omnes dilatorias non opponat, deinceps de eis non audiatur, nisi fortassis aliqua ex tempore oriatur inter agendum, aut si prius fuit, reo non er[*a*/i]t cognita, aut si fuit cognita, tunc non habuit, ex quo illam probaret, quod postea illi occurrit. Qua de re priusquam audiatur, iuramento malitiae interponat.

[204v] 10. **Tempus proponendarum exceptionum peremptoriarum.**[11]

Peremptoriae exceptiones, quae iudicium impediunt et causam perimunt, ut exceptio rei iudicatae, transactionis et litis finitae, possunt et ante et post litis contestationem opponi. Quae vero solum causam et negotium perimunt, ut est exceptio pacti de non petendo et similia, recte opponuntur lite demum contestata.

11. **Quae exceptiones per totam causam obiici poss[*i*/u]nt.**[12]

Exceptiones excommunicationis et falsi procuratoris per totam causam obiici possunt.

12. **Exceptio excommunicationis intra octo dies est** [post] **probanda.**[13]

Ut vero lites plus iusto non protelentur, praecipimus, ut is qui excommunicationem obiicit, speciem illius et nomen excommunicatoris exprimat, sciturus eam rem se deferre debere in [134b] publicam notionem, quam intra [205r] octo dierum spatium (die in quo proponitur minime computato) probare valeat apertissimis documentis. Quod si non probaverit iudex, in causa procedere non omittat, reum in expensis, quas actor ob hoc, diebus illis se fecisse docuerit, (praehabita taxatione) condemnans.

---

[10]*Ibid.*
[11]*Ibid.*
[12]Speculum, 2.1, *De exceptionibus et replicationibus*, 2.16, 3.15.
[13]Speculum, 2.1, *De dilationibus*, 1.15.

9. A time limit for setting out all dilatory exceptions must be put forward by the judge, before the joinder of issue.[10]

In order that suits may not be maliciously prolonged, we order the judge to fix some definite time limit, before the joinder of issue, and if the accused has not set out all the dilatory exceptions *by* **within** that time, he shall not be heard again on the subject, unless perchance something crops up in the proceedings, or if it was there previously, it was not known to the accused, or if it was known, he did not then have the means to prove it which he subsequently obtained. Before the matter is heard, he shall swear an oath against malice.

10. The time for setting out peremptory exceptions.[11]

Peremptory exceptions which block the judgment and invalidate the cause, like an exception of judgment rendered, transaction and suit completed, can be raised both before and after the joinder of issue. But those which invalidate the cause and business, like the exception of agreement not to sue and suchlike, are rightfully presented only once the issue has been joined.

11. Which exceptions may be raised at any point during the cause.[12]

Exceptions of excommunication and of false proctor may be raised at any point during the cause.

12. An exception of excommunication must be proved within eight days [afterwards].[13]

Moreover, in order that suits should not be unduly prolonged, we order that someone who objects on the ground of excommunication shall explain what kind it is and give the name of the excommunicator, and shall understand that the matter must be published in a public announcement, which must be proved by the most evident documents within the space of eight days, (not counting the day on which it is put forward). And if the judge does not prove it he shall not fail to proceed with the cause, ordering the accused to pay the expenses which the plaintiff claims (by prior estimate) to have incurred on that account.

13. De [*mixtis*] exceptionibus [mixtis].[14]

Exceptiones mixtae, quae sic dicuntur, ut partim dilatoriae sunt et partim peremptoriae, si post litis contestationem proponantur, vim dilatoriarum non habebunt, sed tantum peremptoriae censebuntur.

14. Dilatoria iudicii processum impediens omissa in prima instantia in appellatione non poterit obiici.[15]

Exceptio dilatoria, quae iudicii processum impedit, in causa principali non opposita, in appellatione obiici non poterit.

[205v] 15. Peremptoriae omissae in prima instantia possunt in appellatione obiici.[16]

Si peremptoriae exceptiones in instantia omissae fuerint, et quidem non ex malitia, neque ad vexandum adversarium, in appellatione produci poterunt; non autem declinatoriae aut dilatoriae illae exceptiones, quae iudicii processum elidunt, sed illas tantum licebit obiicere, quae negotium ipsum et rei summam spectant, modo prius ex malitia non fuerint omissae.

16. Quid sit replicatio, et quando sit probanda.[17]

Ad reorum exceptiones actores replicationes adhibere solent, quae nihil aliud sunt, quam allegationes actorum, [135a] per quas exceptio solvitur; neque actor cogi debet ad suam replicationem probandam, nisi prius reus probaverit exceptionem.

17. An iudex de replicationibus pronuntiare debeat.[18]

Ut iudex de replicationibus pronuntiet non est [206r] necessarium: quia vires earum satis intelligi poterunt, cum iudex de ipsis exceptionibus constituerit, an admittendae [*sint*] vel repudiandae [**sint**].

---

[14]Speculum, 2.1, *De exceptionibus et replicationibus*, 1.8.
[15]*Ibid.*, 2.5.
[16]*Cod. Iust.*, 8.35(36).8, originally a rescript of the emperors Diocletian and Maximian, 17 November 293.
[17]*Dig.*, 44.1.2, originally Ulpian, *Ad edictum*, 74.
[18]Speculum, 2.1, *De exceptionibus et replicationibus*, 5.4.

13. Of mixed exceptions.[14]

If mixed exceptions, which are so called because they are partly dilatory and partly peremptory, are set out after the joinder of issue, they shall not have delaying power, but shall be considered to be exclusively peremptory.

14. A dilatory exception blocking the process of judgment, which was omitted in the first instance, cannot be raised at the appeal.[15]

A dilatory exception which blocks the process of judgment, which was not presented in the principal cause, cannot be raised at the appeal.

15. Peremptory exceptions omitted in the first instance can be raised at the appeal.[16]

If peremptory exceptions were omitted in the hearing, and that was not done out of malice or with a desire to annoy the opponent, they may be produced at the appeal; however, not those declinatory or dilatory exceptions which extend the process of judgment, but only those which relate to the business itself and the essence of the matter may be raised, as long as they were not omitted out of malice at an earlier stage.

16. What a reply is and when it must be proved.[17]

Plaintiffs normally attach replies to the exceptions raised by the accused, which are nothing other than allegations on their part by which the exception is refuted, nor must a plaintiff be compelled to prove his reply before the accused has first proved his exception.

17. Whether a judge ought to pronounce on replies.[18]

It is not necessary for a judge to pronounce on replies, since their validity will be sufficiently evident once the judge has decided whether to admit or reject the exceptions themselves.

18. Quantum possit replicatio paris criminis.[19]

Replicatio paris criminis repellit excipientem. Nam exceptio alicuius criminis ab illo non debet opponi, qui eodem laborare convincitur.

19. Neque excipiens neque replicans omnia fatetur, quae dicit excipiendo vel replicando.[20]

Excipiens non est censendus fateri omnia, quae in eius exceptione includuntur; quemadmodum et actor non omnia iudicabitur fateri, quae in replicatione continentur.

20. De exceptione contra testes, cuius[ce]modi sit, et quamdiu valeat.[21]

Exceptio contra testes, cum non sit dilatoria, indirecte et oblique est peremptoria. Nam ea spectat [206v] ut probationem tollat, qua sublata ius actoris eliditur. Ea vero duplex est: nam vel contra personas testium excipitur, cum criminosi dicuntur, vel aliqua alia ratione non idonei, vel contra testium dicta, ut cum falsi arguuntur. Exceptio igitur contra personas testium usque ad sententiam potest obiici et pro[135b]bari. Postea vero non audietur, nisi ad appellationem ventum fuerit. Ibi enim poterit obiici. Si vero excipiatur testes falsum dixisse, usque ad viginti annos locum habet exceptio, ne dum in appellatione; quod tamen accipi volumus, cum in agendo non fuit proposita. [207r] Nam si tunc obiecta est, et non probata, minime valebit eius vis ad annos viginti, sed tantum in appellatione repeti poterit.

21. De exceptione /contra testes/,[22] et replicatione testium.[23]

Testis contra quem excipitur de crimine, si contra excipientem de eodem crimine replicet, ob id non admittetur ad testimonium. Quia non relatione criminis reus purgatur, sed si se innocentem ostenderit.[24]

---

[19]*Dig.*, 44.1.2, originally Ulpian, *Ad edictum*, 74.
[20]X, 2.25.6 (Fr, II, 377-8), originally a decretal of Pope Innocent III, 5 August 1206.
[21]Hostiensis, *Summa aurea*, c. *De testibus*.
[22]Added by Peter Martyr.
[23]*Ibid.*
[24]A note at the bottom of the page reads: '"De sententia et re iudicata" require in folio 246.' ('"On sentence and case decided" see folio 246').

18. **How much a reply of equal crime is worth.**[19]

A reply of equal crime defeats the one making the exception. For an exception of some crime must not be presented by someone who has been convicted of doing the same thing himself.

19. **Neither the person making the exception nor the respondent confesses everything which he says in his exception or reply.**[20]

A person making an exception is not regarded as confessing everything which is contained in the exception, just as the plaintiff also is not judged to be confessing everything which is contained in his reply.

20. **Of an exception against witnesses: what kind of thing it is and how long it is valid.**[21]

An exception against witnesses, since it is not dilatory, is indirectly and obliquely peremptory. For its intention is to remove proof, and once that is taken away, the right of the plaintiff is destroyed. Moreover it is of two kinds: either the exception is against the persons of the witnesses, e.g. if they are said to be criminals, or unsuitable for some other reason, or it is against the statements of the witnesses, as when they are condemned as false. Therefore an exception against individuals can be raised and proved right up to the sentence. But after that it shall not be heard unless the matter comes to appeal, where it may be raised. But if it is excepted that the witnesses have told a lie, the exception may be brought for up to twenty years, and not just in an appeal; and it is our will that it shall be accepted, even if it was not brought up during the proceedings. For if it was raised at that point and not proved, its validity will not extend to twenty years, and it may only be repeated at an appeal.

21. **Of an exception /against witnesses/,[22] and the reply of the witnesses.**[23]

If a witness against whom an exception has been made because of a crime replies by accusing the person making the exception of the same crime, he shall not be allowed to testify for that reason. For the accused is not purged by repeating the crime, but by proving that he is innocent.[24]

[246r; 135b]   **53. DE SENTENTIA ET RE IUDICATA**[1]

1. Iudex quando allegata et probata sequi potest contra conscientiam.[2]

Utile est quod a doctis et sapientibus praecipitur, ne quis in iudicando sequatur aliquam suam cogitationem, quam secum domo attulerit in iudicium, sed secundum allegata et probata pronuntiet. Sed haec regula locum habere debet, quando iudex levibus quibusdam argumentis ductus existime/at aliter se rem habere quam probatum sit. Nam isto casu potius sequi debet allegata et probata, quam suam opinionem et conscientiam ex quadam imaginatione conceptam. Si vero iudex habet conscientiam [246v] rei indubitatam, tunc nullo modo debet aliquid statuere contra eam, propter allegata et probata. Sed et in hoc ca[u]su *debet* rursum distingui debet. Nam si iudex habeat conscientiam contra reum, et tamen in actis reus proba[136a]tur innocens, tum propter suam conscientiam, qua scit eum [**in**]nocentem, condemnare eum non debet, sed illum, secundum id quod probatum est, absolvere. Quia etiam{*si*} hoc faciat, non tamen po[*ssi*/**tes**]t dici eum contra conscientiam fecisse, cum reum non ut innocentem, sed ab instantia*m* iudicii tantum absolvat. Si vero iudex habeat conscientiam pro reo contra [247r] allegata et probata, tum non debet contra indubitatam conscientiam in causa decernere. Quia iudici credendum *sit* est, qui allegat conscientiam in praeiudicium alterius, si eam probare posc/sit.[3]

Quoniam iudex non potest supplere omissa in facto, operae pretium est iudicare, quonam modo possit conscientiam suam pro reo contra allegata et probata adducere, ut non impingat in constitutiones, quibus prohibetur aliquid supplere in facto. In tali igitur casu iudex per consultationem superiori iudici declaret suam conscientiam.

Petat igitur a parte urgente ac precibus instet, ut det[*ur*] sibi spatium consulendi superiorem iudicem. Cui suam cum exposuit conscientiam, potestatem facit, ut s[e/i] tanquam veritatis testem audiat, ac deinceps iuxta allegata et probata sententiam pronuntiet; neque ut iudex factum supplet, sed ut minister iustiti*t*/ae cavet [*in*/ne] eius culpa innocentia proximi oneretur.

---

[1]Unless otherwise indicated, the additions and alterations in MS of this chapter are in Peter Martyr's hand.

[2]*Speculum*, 2.3, *De sententia*, 5.1.

[3]A marginal note by Peter Martyr reads: 'Videtur redundare.' ('This seems to be redundant').

53. OF THE SENTENCE AND JUDGMENT RENDERED[1]

1. When a judge can follow charges and proofs against his conscience.[2]

What is decreed by the learned and wise is helpful, that no one should follow any thought of his own which he has brought with him from home to the judgment, but he should decide according to the charges and proofs. But this rule must obtain when a judge is led by certain frivolous arguments to think that he understands the case differently from what has been proved. For in that case he must follow the charges and proofs rather than his opinion and conscience which is formed by something in his imagination. But if the judge has an undoubted conscience concerning the matter, then he must in no way determine anything against it, on account of the charges and proofs. But even in that case, a distinction must be made. For if a judge has a conscience against the accused, and yet in the trial the accused is proved to be innocent, then he must not condemn him on the basis of his conscience, by which he knows that he is [*guilty* **innocent**], but absolve him according to what has been proved. For even {*if*} he does so, it cannot be said that he has done it against his conscience, because he has absolved the accused not as an innocent man, but only on the basis of the process of judgment. But if the judge has a conscience in favour of the accused, in spite of what is charged and proved, then he must not decide against his undoubted conscience. For a judge is to be believed if he alleges conscience in support of another person, if he can prove it.[3]

Since a judge cannot supply elements missing from the trial, he must determine how he can bring his conscience to bear in favour of the accused, in spite of the charges and proofs, in such a way that he does not impinge on those constitutions by which it is forbidden to add anything to the trial. Therefore in such a case he should declare his conscience to a superior judge by consulting with him.

Therefore he shall ask the plaintiff and plead with him that he might [*be*] allow[*ed*] time to consult a higher judge. When he has unburdened his conscience to that judge, he makes it possible to hear himself as a witness to the truth, and then he can pronounce sentence according to the charges and proofs, and not add something to the trial as a judge, but as a servant of justice make sure that the innocence of a neighbour is not harmed by his guilt.

[247v] 2. Iudex primum certam exquirere debet facti notitiam.[4]

Iudex in hoc potissimum incumbat, ut ante omnia certus sit de facto, et praecipue d... in criminalibus quosvis audiat, innocentiam cuiusvis probaturos, donec in plenam causae cognitionem veniat. Nam in iudiciis ordinariis iudices iubentur plena inquisitione rei qualitatem discutere. In criminalibus vero iudiciis tam clara requiritur facti notitia, ut noti permittatur iuramenti dilatio in de fa/ectu apertarum probationum, sicut in causis civilibus.

[136b] 3. Deinde exquirat quod in facto ius sit.[5]

Post certam facti *notitiam* cognitionem proximum [248r] est ut sententia, qua declaraturus est ius, *acc...* facto probata/o sit conveniens, et iuri atque consuetudini, quibus quaeque regio aut civitas in ea specie facti utitur. Si vero neque ex lege neque ex consuetudine manifesta iudici constare possit, quid in casu proposito pro iure habendum sit, procedendum illi est de similibus ad similia iura, donec, argumento aliquo ex usitato iure ducto, constituere possit, quid eum sequi in pronuntiando oporteat.

4. Si ambigat, favendum est reo.[6]

Si vero neque id quidem consequi sua investigatione aut [*ex*] peritorum consultatione possit, [248v] tum in dubio iuris potius pro reo quam pro actore pronuntiandum est, **nisi actor foveat causam favorabiliorem**.

5. Quid sit sententia.[7]

Hactenus traditum est quae sunt iudici consideranda, antequam ad ferendam sententiam progrediatur. Statuendum nunc est de ipsa sententia, ut intelligi possit quae pronuntiatio iudicis mereatur dici sententia.[8] *Proprie igitur loquendo,* ea

---

[4]Panormitanus on X, 2.27.1.

[5]Speculum, 2.3, *De sententia*, 5.3; Baldus, *De disputationibus et allegationibus*, in Speculum, 2.2, *idem.*

[6]X, 2.27.26 (Fr, II, 409), originally a decretal of Pope Gregory IX (1227-41), published on or before 5 September 1234.

[7]Speculum, 2.3, *De sententia*, preface; *Cod. Iust.*, 7.45.3, originally a rescript of the Emperor Alexander Severus, 1 October 223; *ibid.*, 7.45.9, originally a rescript of the emperors Diocletian and Maximian, 5 April 293.

[8]A marginal note by Peter Martyr reads: 'Redundat.' ('Redundant').

2. First of all the judge must demand definite confirmation of the fact.[4]

A judge's first responsibility is that above all else, he must be certain of the fact, and particularly in criminal cases, if he hears of people who can prove the innocence of someone, before he comes to the full hearing of the cause. For in ordinary judgments judges are required to assess the nature of the case in a full inquest. Moreover, in criminal cases, so clear must the confirmation of the fact be that deferral of the standard oath is allowed *in fact* **for want** of clear proofs, as it is in civil cases.

3. Then he shall ask what the law is regarding the fact.[5]

After receiving definite *confirmation* knowledge of the fact, the next thing is that the sentence, by which he will declare the law once the fact has been proved, shall be appropriate to the law and custom which each region or city uses in that type of case. But if the judge cannot decide what should be regarded as right in the case before him, either by the law or by any clear custom, he must proceed to compare it to other similar laws, until by some argument drawn from the law as it is actually used he may be able to decide what principles he must follow when pronouncing sentence.

4. If there is any doubt, the accused is to be favoured.[6]

But if he cannot reach a decision based on his own investigation or [*by*] consulting the experts, and if the law is in doubt, he must pronounce in favour of the accused rather than in favour of the plaintiff, **unless the plaintiff has presented a better case.**

5. What a sentence is.[7]

Thus far have been listed those things which the judge must consider before he proceeds to pass sentence. Now the rules for the sentence itself must be set out, so that one may know what pronouncement of the judge deserves to be called a sentence.[8] *Therefore properly speaking*, only that pronouncement of the judge

solum pronuntiatio iudicis meretur dici sententia, qua finis imponitur controversiae legitima disceptatione in iudicium *de*ductae. [*Restat nunc ut modus indicetur, quo sententia rite feratur*.]⁹

6. Quomodo sententia recte feratur.¹⁰

Statuimus igitur, ut in observatione solemnita*tis*¹¹ [249r] circa ferendas sententias, partes ad sententiam audiendam citentur. Alioqui (cum maximi praeiudicii sit sententia) eam partibus non citatis pro nulla haberi volumus. Deinde statuimus, ut praesentibus partibus, vel altera contumaciter absente, sententia a iudice pro tribunali vel alio loco hone[137a]sto [*et* **vel**] publico sedente promulgetur; quodque sententia concepta ex breviculo, in quo est descripta, per iudicem aut tabellarium recitetur, iudice clare attestante, se iuxta recitata ex scripto de causa pronuntiare; **nisi talis sit casus, de quo verbo tenuis absque breviculo liceat pronuntiare.**

Si lis debeat **per**¹² sententiam dirimi inter [249v] contendentes, necesse est eius orationem non esse exegeticam,¹³ sed definitivam et decisoriam. Porro non sufficit sententiam esse absolutoriam, vel condemnatoriam, nisi in ea etiam diserte res exprimantur, ad quas praestandas aut ferendas reum condemnet, aut a quibus eum liberet. Est enim iudici omnino conandum, ut quam fieri possit, sententiam ferat certam, **et praecipue secundum libelli petitionem dirigenda est certitudo sententiae.**¹⁴

Vitandum quoque est *iudici*¹⁵ ratione*m* certitudinis, quae in causarum decisione requiritur, ne sententia sub conditione feratur.

Operae pretium non est ut causa, quae iudicem [250r] movet ut sententiam ferat, in sententia exprimatur. Verum si propter ineptitudinem libelli lata sit sententia, tunc necesse est ut causa ineptitudinis sententiae inseratur, qua reus ab instantia iudicii absolvatur.¹⁶

Sed tamen est necessarium in causa [*appellationis* approbationis], ut iudex, ad quem appellatum est, semper inserat causam in sententia. Nam iudicare eum oportet, quare latam sententiam ab inferiori iudice vel approbet vel improbet.

---

⁹A marginal note by Peter Martyr reads: 'Redundat.' ('Redundant').
¹⁰X, 1.38.2 (Fr, II, 212), originally a decretal of Pope Alexander III (1159-81); VI, 2.14.5 (Fr, II, 1014), originally a decretal of Pope Boniface VIII (1294-1303).
¹¹'Solemnitatis' was restored in the 1640 edition.
¹²This was added by Cranmer.
¹³F has 'exegentiam' and a marginal note which reads: 'Alias exegeticam'. This may reflect an error in the Parker MS.
¹⁴Speculum, 2.3, *De sententia*, 5.7.
¹⁵On top of this word Peter Martyr wrote: 'Abdundat' ('Redundant').
¹⁶*Ibid.*, 5.14.

deserves to be called a sentence, by which an end is put to a controversy which has been brought to judgment by lawful process. [*There remains now to indicate the way in which the sentence ought to be passed.*][9]

6. The right way to pass sentence.[10]

Therefore we decree that in the observation *of*[11] solemnity surrounding the passing of sentences, the parties shall be summoned to hear the sentence. Otherwise (since the sentence is of the greatest importance) it is our will that it shall be nullified if the parties have not been summoned. Next, we decree that the sentence is to be read by the judge, sitting on the bench or in another honourable place, in the presence of the parties, or of one of them if the other is absent because of his contumacy, and that the prepared sentence shall be read by the judge or recorder from the brief in which it has been copied, and the judge shall clearly state that he is pronouncing on the cause according to what has been read from the brief, **unless the case is such that it is permissible to pronounce orally, without a brief.**

If the suit between the contending parties is to be ended **by**[12] the sentence, it is essential that its recitation not be tentative,[13] but definitive and decisive. Moreover, it is not enough for a sentence to be absolutory or condemnatory, unless the things which the judge orders the accused to perform or to suffer, or the things from which he is releasing him, are clearly expressed in it. For the judge must always try as far as he can to pass a definite sentence, **and the definiteness of the sentence is to be expounded above all according to the petition of the libel.**[14]

Also to be avoided *by the judge* is a long explanation of the reasoning, which is required in deciding causes, so that the sentence will not appear to have been passed subject to some condition.

There is no need for the reason which persuades *the judge*[15] to pass sentence to be expressed in the sentence. But if the sentence has been passed because of the inadequacy of the libel, then the reason for this inadequacy must be included, by which the accused is dispensed from the consequences of the judgment.[16]

But nevertheless in a cause of [*appeal* approbation], the judge to whom the appeal is made must always include the reason in the sentence. For he must decide whether he approves or disapproves of the sentence passed by the lower judge.

7. Sententiarum species.[17]

Forma sententiarum generali absoluta, tandem ad sententiarum species est descendendum, *et primum de interlocutoria est decernendum, quia ad eam et* et primum de interlocutoria est decernendum, quia ad eam ordine procedendi in causis prius pervenitur.[18]

8. De sententia interlocutoria.[19]

Sententiam igitur interlocutoriam eam [250v] esse decernimus, [137b] qua aditus ad principalis causae *causae* cognitionem paratur. Id vero duobus fit modis: aut enim iudex simpliciter aliquid imperat litigantibus ut faciant, aut remoras exceptionum, (quas utrinque attulerunt), sua pronuntiatione aufert, ut absque obstaculis ad decisionem principalis causae venire possit. Unde eam sic definiri volumus. Interlocutoria sententia est, quae inter principium et finem causae fertur, super eis quae incidunt vel emergunt citra principalis causae cognitionem. Talis igitur sententiae non sit tanta vis, quanta in definitiva. Nam ea lata semper potest revocari per iudicem, nisi per eam iusserit [251r] partem alteri aliquid restituere vel dare. Tunc enim iudex eam revocare non potest, quia definition/**vae** speciem habet; ut cum propter [**aliquam**] contumaciam, aliqua pars alteri condemnatur in expensis solvendis, **aut si iusserit expoliatum restitui in possessionem, priusquam procedatur in petitorio.** Idem censendum est de omnibus exceptionibus peremptoriis. Nisi enim lata de eis sententia firma haberetur, [*sed* **at**] iudici liceret, quoties illi visum esset, eam revocare, tum incerta admodum esset progressio ad principalis causae decisionem.

9. De sententia definitiva.[20]

Impensius vero in sententia definitiva (qua de principali causa pronuntiatur) operam navari decernimus. Nam si quid ex illis, **quae** ci*r*ca [*solemnitatem*] [251v] actus, aut quae in ipsa forma orationis observanda esse iudicavimus, omissum sit, tanquam illegitimam eam reiiciendam esse volumus.

---

[17]*Ibid.*, 1.2.
[18]A marginal note by Peter Martyr reads: 'Redundat.' ('Redundant').
[19]*Ibid.*, 2.1.
[20]*Ibid.*, 2.3.

7. Types of sentences.[17]

Having covered the general form of sentences, it is time to go on to specific types of sentence, *and first of all to define an interlocutory sentence, because to it* and first of all to define an interlocutory sentence, because by the order of procedure in causes it comes up first.[18]

8. Of an interlocutory sentence.[19]

Therefore we define an interlocutory sentence as one by which the way is cleared for the hearing of the main cause. And this may be done in two ways: either the judge simply orders the litigants to do something, or by his pronouncement he lifts the delays imposed by the exceptions (which both sides have brought), so that he can get to the decision of the main cause without obstacles. Whence we want it to be defined like this. An interlocutory sentence is one which is passed between the beginning and the end of a cause, concerning matters occurring or arising within the hearing of the main cause. Therefore, the force of such a sentence will not be as great as that of a final sentence. For once it is passed it can always be revoked by the judge, unless in it he has ordered one party to restore or to give something to the other. For then the judge cannot revoke it, since it has the appearance of something definitive, as when on account of [**some**] contumacy one party is ordered to pay expenses to the other, **or if he orders the dispossessed party to be restored to possession, before proceeding with the case.** The same thing is to be done with all peremptory exceptions. For unless the sentence passed concerning them is considered to be firm, the judge might revoke it whenever he wishes, and progress towards a decision of the main cause would remain uncertain.

9. Of the final sentence.[20]

We declare that greater care shall be taken with a final sentence (in which the main cause is decided). For if one of the things surrounding [*the solemnity of*] the act, or which we have ordered to be observed in the form of pronouncement itself, is omitted, then it is our will that the sentence shall be rejected as unlawful.

10. Sententia definitiva retractari non potest nisi contra ius divinum feratur.[21]

Porro si nihil talium in sententia definitiva desideretur, ut tanquam illegitimo modo **lata**, pro nulla haberi possit, [138a] nec ab ea intra spatium, quo appella[*tio*/**ri**] permissa est, appellatum sit, tunc eam in rem iudicatam transire volumus, hoc est, talem consequ*atur*/**i** auctoritatem, ut contravenire nemo possit: nec iudici quidem liceat eam revocare, mutare, aut aliquam eius partem tollere, vel emendare, sive bene sive male [252r] *iudex* suo officio in ea [**parte**] *re*ferenda functus sit. Sed in hac regula magnopere observandum, quod sententia contra ius litigantium male lata transeat in rem iudicatam, modo ab ea appellatum non sit. Sed secus esse statuimus, si sententia contra ius divinum aut naturale lata sit. Nam sententia manifestam iniquitatem continens est ipso iure nulla, nec debet quis iure cogi ut ei stet, etiamsi ab ea appellare sit prohibitus.[22] Proinde sententia, quae sine peccato mortali serv*atur*/**ri** non potest, recte a iudice revocatur, et a litigantibus tanquam nulla negligitur; [252v] quia transire in rem iudicatam non potest propter offensionem conscientiae, **licite etiam iudex mutabit sententiam, si viderit eam obesse reipublicae.**

11. Iudici quando liceat sententiam mutare, addere, et minuere.[23]

Vitium grammaticum si quod est in verbis sententiae, illud per iudicem tolli liceat. Porro iudex sententiam definitivam latam non solum mutare, sed et supplere in pronuntiando de accessionibus et immunitionibus actionum, si tamen eadem die, qua ferat sententiam, id ab eo fiat, et antequam pronuntietur in actis, id petitum sit. Nefas enim videtur, peracto semel iudicio, iterum permittere, ut ex sopita lite nova lis de *accessionibus* **actionibus** [253r] et immunitionibus actionum moveatur.

[138b] 12. De impugnatione sententiae.[24]

Porro nobis nunc pergendum est, ut de impugnatione sententiae interlocutoriae et definitivae decernamus.[25] Cum *enim* proclive admodum sit falsam sententiam ferre, operae pretium est modos quosdam tenere, quibus occurri *illis* **ei** possit, ne nobis fraudi sit *eorum* **illius** ratihabitio, aut nostra in *illis* **ea** admittend*is*/**a** supinitas. Ceterum antequam quis conetur sententiam impugnare, videre debet, an secundum allegata et probata, et ut exig[*u*/**a**]nt iura et consuetudo atque legitima forma, cum observatione solemnitatum lata sit. Nam si tale quid circa

---

[21]X, 2.27.1 (Fr, II, 393), originally a letter of Pope Gregory I (590-604), *Reg.*, 2.40.
[22]X, 2.27.9 (Fr, II, 395), originally a decretal of Pope Alexander III (1159-81).
[23]Speculum, 2.3, *De sententia*, 5.10-12.
[24]Speculum, 2.3, *De executione sententiae*, 8.1-10; *ibid.*, 2.3, *De appellationibus*, 1.11.
[25]A marginal note by Peter Martyr reads: 'Redundat.' ('Redundant').

10. A final sentence cannot be retracted unless it is passed against the divine law.[21]

Moreover if there is nothing missing from the final sentence so that it might be nullified as **having been passed** in an unlawful way, and there has been no appeal within the time [*in*] which [*an appeal*] is allowed [**to the appellant**], then it is our will for the matter to advance to the status of a judgment rendered, that is, for it to take on such authority that no one may go against it, nor may even the judge revoke, alter or remove any part of it, or add to it, whether *the judge* **he** has performed his function well or badly in that [**respect**]. But particular care must be taken in observing the rule that a sentence which has been wrongly passed, against the right of the litigants, shall become law as long as it has not been appealed. But that shall not be the case if the sentence has been passed against divine or natural law. For a sentence which contains manifest injustice is automatically void, and no one shall be compelled by law to obey it, even if he is forbidden to appeal it.[22] Likewise, a sentence which cannot be kept without mortal sin is rightly revoked by a judge, and ignored by the litigants as being null and void, because it cannot become law on account of the offence it gives to conscience, **and the judge may also alter the sentence if he sees that it is in the interest of the state to do so.**

11. When a judge may change, increase or lessen a sentence.[23]

If there is some grammatical error in the wording of a sentence, the judge may remove it. Moreover, he may not only alter the sentence but also add to it by pronouncing on additions and deletions of actions, but only if this is done by him on the same day that the sentence was passed, and if he is asked to do it before it is recorded. For once the judgment is completed, it shall be regarded as wrong to allow a new suit to be created out of the old one, concerning *additions* **actions** and [*deletions* **preventions**] of actions.

12. Of impugning a sentence.[24]

Moreover we must now go on to establish rules for impugning an interlocutory or a final sentence.[25] *For* since it is relatively easy to pass a false sentence, it is necessary to have certain ways by which *they* **it** may be remedied, lest *their* **its** ratification appear to be fraud on our part, or else weakness in permitting *them* **it**. But before someone tries to impugn a sentence, he must see whether it was passed according to the charges and proofs, and as the laws and custom demand, and in a lawful form, with observance of the solemnities. For if there is

eam [253v] non observatum esse appareat, non est opus eam impugnare, quia ipso iure illam pro null[*a*/**o**] haberi volumus, quae manifestum iuris errorem continet, adeo ut nec in rem iudicatam transeat, etiamsi ab ea appellatum non sit, aut provocatio ab ea facta deserta sit.

Igitur contra quem talis sententia lata est, defendere se nullitatis exceptione potest, si ex ea conveniatur; et talis exceptio competit illi perpetuo, hoc est, quadraginta annis, quibus omnis actio et obligatio tollitur.

In casibus, quibus iudex sententiam suam revocare potest, sententiae eius emendationem [254r] simpliciter petitam esse sufficiat: quia in talibus casibus, aut evidens est **causa**[26] eius revocandae, aut solemnitas processus iudicari[*i*] non requiritur. Sed si ratione nullitatis petatur mutari aut corrigi sententia, necesse est errorem aut fraudem iudicis legitimis documentis declarari, ut causa, (propter quam contenditur [*esse nulla*]), fiat manifesta.

Ut **Et probandum erit** si quid eorum, quae ad cognitionem legitimam necessario requiruntur, a iudice **neglectum fuerit**, ut si [*o*/**a**]missa sit citatio partium, aut non oblatus libellus, aut lis non contestata, aut de calumnia non [254v] iuratum, aut sententia **non sit** lata secundum legitimam formam, quae supra [139a] est descripta, tunc ea debet dici nulla: quia ea iudiciorum recte constituendorum causa observari iubentur, ut iudex ri/**ec**te et ordine pervenire in causae notitiam possit.

Quoties vero exigit casus, ut de nullitate sententiae pronuntietur, non apud alium iudicem superiorem, (sicut in appellationibus), sed apud eundem, qui de causa principali iudicavit, causa agenda est. Sed hoc [**tunc**] solum fit, quando coram ordinario causa agitata est, non cum apud del[e/**i**]gatum iudicem. Nam eius iurisdictio extinguitur, cum ab eo male iudicatum est **quoad sententiam definitivam;** *non* et **non interlocutoriam revocare potest, neque propter illam officio suo est** [*de*] **functus. Verum si definitiva sententia male iudicavit,** [255r] *et* potest ab eo ad delegantem appellari, ac peti, ut aut ipse causam cognoscat, aut alter*um* eam cognoscendam demandet.

13. Subsidium impugnationis sententiae.[27]

Reliquum est ut de subsidio impugnandae sententiae aliquid decernamus, quod huc videtur referendum, nempe querela falsi. Nam et illud subsidium generaliter omnibus competit, qui falsorum instrumentorum aut testium auctoritate et subornatione, se iudicio succubuisse ostendere possunt. Si in pervestigatione causae cognitum de crimine falsi non sit, et apparet iudicem specie talium probationum [255v] deceptum esse, tunc propter odium eius crimini*e*/**s** non

---

[26]This may have been added by Archbishop Cranmer.
[27]Speculum, 2.3, *De sententia*, 9.8.

something like this about it which does not seem to have been observed, there is no need to impugn it, because it is our will that what contains a manifest error of law shall be automatically nullified, and moreover shall not become law, even if there has been no appeal from it, or a referral made from it has been abandoned.

Therefore the person against whom such a sentence has been passed can defend himself by the exception of nullity, if it arises from it, and that exception invalidates it for ever, that is, for forty years, during which all action and obligation is removed.

In cases in which the judge can revoke his sentence, it shall suffice for the amendment to the sentence simply to be asked for, since in such cases, either **the reason for**[26] revoking it is evident or the solemnity of a process is not required for reaching a decision. But if the way of nullity is used to make a change or correction of the sentence, the error or deceit of the judge must be declared by lawful documents, so that the reason (for which it is argued [*that it is void*]), may be made clear.

So that **And it shall be proved** if something which is absolutely essential for a lawful hearing **has been overlooked** by the judge, for example, if the citation of the parties has been omitted, or the libel has not been presented, or the issue has not been joined, or the oath against calumny has not been taken, or the sentence **has not been** passed according to the lawful form, which is described above, then it must be said to be void, because these things are ordered to be observed for the correct formulation of judgments, so that the judge may come to an understanding of the cause *duly* **rightly** and in an orderly manner.

But whenever the situation demands that a pronouncement of the nullity of a sentence must be made, the matter is to be handled not by some other higher judge (as in appeals), but by the same one who decided the main cause. But this is only done [**then**], when the cause has been heard before an ordinary judge, not when it has been heard before a delegated one. For the jurisdiction of the latter is extinguished when he has decided wrongly **with respect to the final sentence, nor can he revoke an interlocutory sentence, nor is [*he to be dismissed* his duty finished] because of it. But if he has decided wrongly in the final sentence,** it is possible to appeal from him to the one who delegated him, and to request either that the superior hear the cause himself or that he appoint someone else to hear it.

13. Appendix to the impugning of a sentence.[27]

It remains for us to make a rule for an appendix to the impugning of a sentence, which it seems ought to be mentioned here, namely a quarrel of falsehood. This appendix generally applies to anyone who can show that he has been subjected to judgment on the authority and at the instigation of false documents or witnesses. If nothing has been heard about the crime of forgery during the investigation of a cause, and it appears that the judge has been deceived by a form of such proofs, then, because of our revulsion against that crime, not only

solum iubemus sententiam rescindi, antequam ab ea appellatum sit, sed volumus, ut postquam ea transierit in rem iudicatam, laesus per eam in integrum restituatur, ut denuo experire/i iudicium possit. Ac si quid secundum eam solutum sit, liceat ei illud repetere.

14. De re iudicata.[28]

Decisio litis est res iudicans, sed illud quod in ea decisione [139b] statuitur [f/s]it res iudicata, si ea rite et legitime facta sit, ita ut tanquam nulla impugnari [*non*][29] possit, nec ab ea appellatum sit.

[256r] 15. Quando res inter quosdam iudicata praeiudicat aliis.[30]

Et cum tanta sit vis rei iudicatae, obiter considerandum venit, an illis solum ea praeiudicet, inter quos iudicatum est, an illis etiam, quos controversia de qua iudicatum est, (vel ratione communis rei, vel contractus) contingat. Videndum igitur quam late ius sententiae se extendat, ad nocendum aliis, vel eos iuvandos.[31] Est *autem* generalis regula, quod res inter quosdam gesta non nocet aliis. Et habet haec regula locum, sive in iudicio sive extra iudicium aliquid actum sit. In re autem in iudicio acta [256v] hoc addendum est regulae: quod ne tum quidem nobis praeiudicent acta *illorum* aliorum, si nostro nomine quid fecerint, si id si[n/v]e nostro mandato aut ratihabit[at]ione factum sit. Licet autem haec regula *admodum* sit generalis,[32] attamen si quid fiat, (me sciente et non prohibente), ab eo, qui commune ius in ea re, de qua actum est, mecum habeat, cum potuerim eum prohibere, tum sententia contra eum lata mihi praeiudicium parit,. s/Secus[33] est si eius molitionem nescierim, neque potestatem eum prohibendi habuerim.

[257r] Suntque casus, in quibus sententia simpliciter omnibus praeiudicat, quorum interest non esse ita iudicatum, si ea in rem iudicatam transiit: ut si querela inofficiosi testamenti resciscum sit testamentum, ea, quae ex eius dispositione nomine legatorum debita fuissent, si contra illud non fuisset iudicatum, peti non possunt, imo etiam soluta repetuntur.

Cum ubi maius est periculum, ibi cautius [*sit* **est**] agendum, aeternique tribu/n/al iudicis illum reum non habere certum sit, quem iniuste iudex

---

[28]*Ibid.*, 6.11.

[29]Marked for deletion in the MS, but not actually deleted.

[30]*Cod. Iust.*, 7.60.1, originally a rescript of the emperors Diocletian and Maximian, 28 March 293; *ibid.*, 7.60.2, originally a rescript of the same emperors, 13 April 293; X, 2.27.25 (Fr, II, 409), originally a decretal of Pope Gregory IX (1227-41), published on or before 5 September 1234.

[31]A marginal note by Peter Martyr, referring to the entire section up to this point, reads: 'Redundat.' ('Redundant').

[32]A marginal note by Peter Martyr reads: 'Redundat.' ('Redundant').

[33]Cranmer began a new sentence here.

do we order that the sentence shall be withdrawn before it is appealed, but we also wish that after the case has been terminated, the person damaged by it shall be compensated in full, so that the judgment may begin afresh. And if something has been paid because of it, it must be refunded to him.

14. Of a judgment rendered.[28]

The decision of the suit is the judgment being given, but what is decreed in that decision, if it has been done duly and lawfully, so that it may neither [*not*][29] be impugned nor appealed, is the judgment rendered.

15. When a judgment rendered between two people prejudices third parties.[30]

And since the force of a judgment rendered is so great, it must also be considered whether it affects only those for whom it has been rendered, or whether it also affects those whom the controversy which has been judged touches (either by way of common interest or contract). Therefore it must be seen how far the application of the sentence extends, whether it hurts third parties or helps them.[31] *Moreover* there is a general rule, that a thing done between two people should not harm third parties. And this rule has its place, whether something is done in judgment or outside of it. For in a matter which is done in judgment, this is to be added to the rule: that *their* acts of others are not prejudicial to us, even if they have done something in our name, if it was done [*without* **either by**] our mandate or agreement. But although this rule is *fairly* general,[32] nevertheless, if something is done (with my knowledge and without my forbidding it), by someone who has a common right with me in the matter which has been acted on, when I could have prevented it, then the sentence passed against him creates a prejudice against me; but this is not the case[33] if I was unaware of his intention and had no power to forbid him.

There are also cases in which a sentence is simply prejudicial to everyone if it passes into law, because it is not in their interest for it to be so judged - for example, if a testament has been withdrawn by a quarrel of improper testament, the things which by its provision were owed in the name of legacies cannot be claimed, if there has been no decision against it, and even things which have already been paid out must be returned.

Since where the danger is greater, the matter must be handled more cautiously, and the tribunal of the eternal judge will not hold him guilty, whom

condemnat, maximopere cavendum est ecclesiasticis [257v] iudicibus *ceterisque omnibus*, atque prudenter attendendum, ut in causarum quibuscunque processibus nihil vendicet odium vel [140a] favor usurpet, sed timor exulet, praemium aut expectatio praemii iustitiam non evertat; sed stateram in manibus gestent accept[at]ionem personarum non habentes, lances [*aequo*] **pro**[34] libramine appendentes, ut in omnibus, quae in causis agenda fuerint (praesertim in concipiendis sententiis et ferendis) prae oculis habeant solum Deum, illius imitantes exemplum, qui querelas populi (tabernaculum ingressus) ad Dominum referebat, ut secundum [258r] eius imperium iudicaret.[35] Quisquis enim iudex ordinarius sive etiam delegatus, famae suae prodigus, et proprii persecutor honoris, contra conscientiam et contra iustitiam in gravamen alterius partis quicquam per gratiam vel per sordes in iudicio fecerit, per annum ab executione officii noverit se remotum, ad aestimationem litis, parti, quam laeserit, nihilominus condemnandus.[36]

---

[34]The MS has been altered by an unknown hand. 'Pro' was written in above 'aequo' which was underlined, but not deleted.

[35]This was the office of the high priest in ancient Israel, cf. Lv. xvi. 23-4. In the Christian covenant, Jesus fulfills this rôle, cf. He. v. 1-4.

[36]VI, 2.14.1 (Fr, II, 1007), originally a decretal of Pope Innocent IV (1243-54). At the end of this chapter there is a note in Foxe's hand which reads: 'Quattuor modis potest reus forum sortiri. Rei quattuor rationibus forum sortiuntur, aut propter domicilium, etc., vide folium' ('There are four ways in which the accused can get a hearing. The accused may get a hearing for four reasons, either because of residence, etc.; see folio...'). The reference is to 36.14. On [258v] a note in the same hand reads: '"De appellationibus" require in fol. 213.' ('"On appeals" see folio 213').

a judge unjustly condemns, ecclesiastical judges *and all others* must take special care, and pay close attention, so that in any trials of causes neither hatred shall claim nything, nor favouritism take over, but fear shall be banished, and bribery or the expectation of a bribe shall not overthrow justice, but let those who have no respect of persons hold the scale in their hands, adding yardsticks [**for** *equal*][34] measure, so that in all things which are done in the causes (especially in framing and passing sentences), they should have only God before their eyes, imitating his example, who (on going into the temple) referred the quarrels of the people to the Lord,[35] so that he might decide according to his authority. For what ordinary judge, or even a delegate, would be so heedless of his reputation and such a persecutor of his own honour as to do something in judgment against conscience and against justice, to the hurt of the other party, either by kindness or out of meanness, when he knows that he will be debarred from the execution of his office for a year, and furthermore be ordered to pay the costs of the suit to the party which he has harmed?[36]

[213r; 140a]   **54. DE APPELLATIONIBUS**[1]

1. [*Quid*] **Appellatio** [quid] **sit.**[2]

Appellatio (ut a definitione incipiamus) est a minore ad maiorem provocatio, et per eam legitime interpositam et pronuntiatam et iurisdictio iudicis quoad illam causam suspenditur, et ipsius cognitio et examen ad superiorem transfertur. Distinguitur autem in iudicialem et extraiudicialem.

2. **De appellatione iudiciali.**[3]

Appellatio iudicialis est, cum in iudicio provocatur ad superiorem iudicem a definitiva, ab interlocutoria, vel a gravaminibus, quae in agendo causam quandoque partibus infliguntur: cumque appellatur a definitiva sententia sufficit dixisse: 'Ab iniqua hac sententia appello', sed quando ab interlocutoria [213v] vel gravamine aliquo provocatur, causa omnino assignanda est, quae vera sit iusta et expressa. [140b] Et si proprie loqui velimus, appellatio non est, nisi in iudicio; quae vero fit extra iudicium, provocatio dici poterit.

3. **De appellatione extraiudiciali.**[4]

Extraiudicialis appellatio est a praesenti seu verisimiliter futuro gravamine ad superiorem provocatio, antequam ad iudicium veniatur; in qua probabilis et verisimilis ratio debet assignari, quae si reddita fuerit, causam ad superiorem iudicem transfert. Et appellatione huiusmodi pendente, nil in appellantis praeiudicium tentari potest a iudice, a quo est appellatum.

---

[1]A marginal note by Cranmer reads: 'For Mr Morres'. The section headings in this chapter, and all other additions or alterations to the MS (unless otherwise noted) are all by Peter Martyr.

[2]Hostiensis, *Summa aurea*, c. *De appellationibus*; Panormitanus on X, 2.28.

[3]Hostiensis on X, 2.28; *Clem.*, 2.12.5 (Fr, II, 1154-5), originally published by Pope Clement V (1305-14) after the council of Vienne (1311-12); H.C., 36.2.

[4]Panormitanus on X, 2.28.

54. OF APPEALS[1]

1. What an appeal is.[2]

An appeal (to begin with the definition) is a referral from a lesser to a greater, and through it, once it has been lawfully lodged and pronounced, the jurisdiction of the judge with respect to that cause is suspended, and his hearing and examination of it is transferred to a superior. Moreover, there are two different types of appeal: judicial and extrajudicial.

2. Of a judicial appeal.[3]

An appeal is judicial when it is referred in the judgment to a higher judge, either from a final sentence, or an interlocutory sentence, or grievances which were inflicted on the parties at some point during the trial, and when the appeal is from the final sentence it is enough to have said: 'I appeal against this unjust sentence', but when it is referred from an interlocutory sentence or from some grievance, a reason must always be given which is true, just and specific. And if we wish to speak properly, there is no appeal except in the judgment, and what is done outside the judgment could be called a referral.

3. Of an extrajudicial appeal.[4]

An extrajudicial appeal is the referral of a present or foreseeably future grievance to a superior, before it comes to judgment, in which a probable and likely reason must be indicated. If that has been given, the cause is transferred to a higher judge. And nothing can be attempted by the judge from whom it has been appealed in prejudice to the appellant, while an appeal of this kind is pending.

[214r] 4. **Appellare licet etiam in [*actis* causis], extraiudicialibus.**[5]

In actis extraiudicialibus appellare licet, ut ab electionibus, postulationibus, provisionibus, et ceteris huiusmodi. Sed interponere oportet appellationem infra dies decem a notitia, qua quis gravari se intellexit. Nam elapsis decem diebus, per viam appellationis non amplius audietur: sed per alia remedia iuris petere poterit, ut [*in*] integrum restituatur et revocetur gravamen.

5. **Quae sit vis appellationis extraiudicialis.**[6]

Appellatio extraiudicialis, si interponatur ex probabilibus et verisimilibus causis, adeo devolvit causam ad superiorem, ut actus gestus contra eam sit nullus. Unde si quis appellaverit, ne [*in*] possessione molestetur, cum se molestandum verisimiliter suspicetur, [214v] si ea spoliatur, restituitur ante omnia in statum, in quo erat tempore appellationis emissae.

In extraiudiciali appellatione si appellans et eius adversarius diversos habeant iudices, licebit appellanti ad e[141a]um [*pro*/**re**]vocare, qui sibi ordine competit, et valida erit eius appellatio.

6. **In iudicio non licet appellare a futuro gravamine.**[7]

In iudicio non potest appellari a gravamine futuro etiam sub conditione; ut si, ne gravaveris, appelles; sed debet prius expectare/i gravamen et postea appellare. Ut enim a futuro gravamine appelletur, solum extra iudicium conceditur.

7. **Si appellatio scripta porrigatur iudici, satis est, nec requiritur ut coram eo legatur.**[8]

Appellatio in scriptis iudici porrecta non potest, [215r] quod coram eo la/ecta non fuerit, legitime impugnari.

---

[5]VI, 2.15.8 (Fr, II, 1017-18), originally a decretal of Pope Boniface VIII (1294-1303).
[6]Panormitanus on X, 2.28; X, 2.28.17 (Fr, II, 415); X, 2.28.7 (Fr, II, 412),both originally decretals of Pope Alexander III (1159-81); X, 2.28.51 (Fr, II, 429-31), originally a decretal of Pope Innocent III, 21 November 1205.
[7]*Cod. Iust.*, 7.65.7, originally a rescript of the emperors Gratian, Valentinian II, Theodosius I and Arcadius, 15 February 385.
[8]VI, 2.15.9 (Fr, II, 1018), originally a decretal of Pope Boniface VIII.

4. **Right of appeal even in extrajudicial [*acts* causes].**[5]

There is a right to appeal in extrajudicial acts, for example, from elections, requests, provisions and other things like that. But the appeal must be lodged within ten days from the notice by which someone learns that he has been grieved. For once the ten days have expired he shall no longer be heard by way of appeal, but he may seek full restitution by using other legal remedies and also to have his grievance revoked.

5. **What the force of an extrajudicial appeal is.**[6]

If an extrajudicial appeal is lodged on probable and likely grounds, it refers the cause to a superior in such a way that any act done against it is void. Whence if someone has appealed not to be disturbed in possession when he suspects that he is probably going to be troubled, and if he is then deprived of it, he shall first of all be restored to the position in which he was when the appeal was lodged.

   If the appellant and his opponent have different judges in an extrajudicial appeal, the appellant may refer it to the one who corresponds to himself in rank, and his appeal will be valid.

6. **There is no right of judicial appeal against a future grievance.**[7]

In a judgment there can be no appeal against a future grievance, even on condition, as if you were appealing in order not to be grieved, but one must wait for the grievance to occur first and then appeal it. For the only way to appeal from a future grievance is by the extrajudicial procedure.

7. **If the appeal is handed to the judge in writing, that is enough, and it does not have to be read out in front of him.**[8]

An appeal handed to the judge in writing cannot lawfully be impugned on the ground that it has not been *delivered* **read** in front of him.

8. Quid agendum sit, si iustus metus impediat ab appellando.[9]

Si iustus metus vel iudicis vel adversarii vel municipalis legis, quae prohibeat ab aliquibus causis appellari, fortasse impediat quenquam ab appellando, excusabitur; et esse volumus ac si appellaverit, modo coram iudice protestetur, a quo gravatur de metu, si audeat, et fieri possit, vel eius copiam habeat. Quod si non est ausus, et copiam illius non habuit, si fieri possit, coram iudice, ad quem decernit appellare, suam interponat appellationem. Quod si non succedat, satis ei tunc esto, coram uno aut pluribus viris bonis, not[a/o]rio adhibito ac testibus, de hoc metu protestari, appellare, [215v] et causas, propter quas appellant, exprimere; atque ab eo vel ab [ill/e]is apostolos obtinere, coram quibus appellat. Curandum tamen est, ut iudici appellatio huiusmodi quoquo modo intimetur intra decem dies a gravamine vel a sententia. Alioqui si ad [141b] ulteriora in causa procederet, quae ageret non essent invalida. Adversarii vero praesentia, dum sic appellatur, non est necessaria. Sufficit enim e/ut ei fiat intimatio. Cum vero neque iustus metus obstat, et iudicis copia potest haberi, semper coram eo tam iudicialis **quam extraiudicialis** appellatio fieri debet, atque in scriptis porrigi, nisi a definitiva sententia statim, ut di[c/s]tum est, [*viva* **unica**] voce sit appellatum.[10]

9. Quibus casibus appellare non licet, aut frustra appellatur.[11]

Neque a correctione neque ab execut[or/**ion**]i/e licet [216r] appellare, nisi modus excedatur, atque tunc causa, et ea quidem vera exprimenda est. In not[o/a]riis etiam prohibemus appellationem.[12] A poena quoque iuris non licet appellare: sed a sententia iudicis appellatur, qua pronuntiavit litigantem in poenam iuris incidisse. In omnibus, in quibus iura prohibent appellationem, iudex non cogitur ei deferre, cum interponitur, nisi causa diserte exprimatur; atque isto casu appellando a definitiva sententia causam exprimere necessarium est, cum alias non requiratur. Ad haec in his, quae dilationem temporis non admittunt, appellatio non recipiatur.[13] Si appellatio [216v] est manifeste frivola, iudex eam admittendo non recte agit.[14] Tertio appellare ab eodem articulo vel ab eadem sententia non licet.[15] Ab arbitrio appellare etiam non licet, neque in enormi et

[9]X, 2.28.73 (Fr, II, 443), originally a decretal of Pope Gregory IX (1227-41), published on or before 5 September 1234.
[10]*Dig.*, 49.1.2, originally Macer, *De appellationibus*, 1.
[11]*Dig.*, 49.1.4, originally Macer, *De appellationibus*, 1; X, 2.28.3 (Fr, II, 410); X, 2.28.29 (Fr, II, 419-20), both originally decretals of Pope Alexander III (1159-81).
[12]X, 2.28.13 (Fr, II, 413-14); X, 2.28.14 (Fr, II, 414), both originally decretals of Pope Alexander III; X, 2.28.61 (Fr, II, 437-8), originally c. 48 of Lateran IV, 1215 (*C.O.D.*, 256-7).
[13]*Dig.*, 49.5.7, originally Paulus, *De appellationibus*, 1.
[14]Cf. X, 2.28.19 (Fr, II, 415-16), originally a decretal of Pope Alexander III.
[15]X, 2.28.65 (Fr, II, 440), originally a decretal of Pope Honorius III (1216-27).

8. **What must be done if justified fear prevents someone from appealing.**[9]

If justified fear of a judge, of an opponent or of the common law, which may forbid appeal in certain cases, should happen to prevent someone from appealing, he shall be excused, and it is our will that it shall be as if he had appealed, as long as he makes his fear clear to the judge by whom he was wronged, if he dares to do so and it can be done, and the judge is available. But if he has not dared, or has not been able to get hold of the judge, let him lodge his appeal, if he can, before the judge to whom he decides to appeal. But if he does not succeed in this, then it shall suffice if he states his fear and appeals in the presence of one or several good men, accompanied by a [*notary* **prominent person**] and witnesses, and expresses the reasons why he is appealing, and obtains letters of appeal from the person or persons before whom he is appealing. Nevertheless, care is to be taken that an appeal of this kind shall somehow be communicated to the judge within ten days of the grievance or the sentence. Otherwise if the judge should proceed to further matters in the cause, what he does will not be invalid. Moreover, the opponent's presence is not required when the matter is appealed in this way. For it is enough for him to be informed *also*. But when there is no justified fear in the way, and a judge is available, both a judicial **and an extrajudicial** appeal ought always to be made before him, and be presented in writing, unless, as has been said, there is an immediate [*oral* **unanimous**] appeal from the final sentence.[10]

9. **Cases in which it is not permissible, or is pointless to appeal.**[11]

It is not permissible to appeal from a correction or an execut[*or*/**ion**], unless the norms have been exceeded, and then the reason, and it must indeed be the true one, shall be expressed.[12] We also forbid an appeal [*in notorious cases* **against notaries**]. It is also not permissible to appeal against a legal penalty, but the sentence of a judge by which he has decreed that the litigant has incurred a legal penalty may be appealed. In all matters in which the laws forbid an appeal, the judge is not compelled to defer to it when it is lodged, unless the reason for it is clearly stated; and for this to happen it is necessary, when appealing from the final sentence, to express the reason, which is not required otherwise. In addition, an appeal shall not be accepted in those causes which do not allow a delay of time.[13] If the appeal is manifestly frivolous, a judge does not act rightly by allowing it.[14] To appeal a third time from the same article or the same sentence is not permitted.[15] It is also not permitted to appeal from a discretionary

gravi scelere. Qui appellat post decem dies non audiatur per viam appellationis, quamvis conqueri possit, et alia ratione agere, ut in integrum *non* restituatur. In civilibus unus pro alio non appellat, nisi eius intersit.[16] Cum quis in iudicio confessus fuerit, non admittitur eius appellatio, modo per seipsum non per procuratorem sit confessus, neque confessio per tormenta aut eorum metum sit extorta: imo etiam id requiritur, ut de eo, quod est confessus in [217r] iudicio, sit con[142a]victus. Et appellationi f[*a*/**o**]venti aliquam iniustitiam vel iniquitatem nunquam est deferendum: neque recipietur appellatio, quando a nostra regia maiestate causa subdelegata est sub conditione ut inde non appelletur.

10. Quando ante sententiam definitivam liceat appellare in causis ecclesiasticis.[17]

In causis ecclesiasticis ante sententiam definitivam appellare sive querelare prohibemus, nisi a sententia censurarum aut correctionis, ubi modus excedatur, aut ubicunque damnum aut gravamen illatum per appellationem a definitiva non est reparabile. In quibus casibus appellare et etiam querelare ante sententiam definitivam licebit.

11. Quo ordine appellandum sit [*ad superiores iudices*].[18]

Ab archidiaconis, decanis, et his, qui sunt in[*f*/t]ra [217v] pontific*a*ciam dignitatem, et iurisdictionem ecclesiasticam habent, ad episcopum liceat appellare, ab episcopo ad archiepiscopum, ab archiepiscopo vero ad nostram maiestatem. Quo cum fuerit causa devoluta, eam vel concilio provinciali definir[*i*/e] volumus, si gravis sit causa, *alioqui a duobus tribusve* **vel a tribus quattuorve** episcopis, a nobis ad id constituendis. Quibus rationibus cum res fuerit definita et iudicata, per appellationem amplius cognosci non poterit. Observari tamen praeter haec volumus, ut si causa fuerit subdelegata, semper ad subdelegantem appelletur, a quo si rursus [*appellandum*] fuerit [**appellandum**], ordo iam descriptus conservetur.

12. Quomodo a pluribus iudicibus appelletur.[19]

Si plures iudices fuerint, lata ab eis sententia, vel gravamine aliquo inflicto, cum omnes simul haberi [142b] non possint, coram maiori parte illorum

---

[16]*Dig.*, 49.9.1, originally Ulpian, *Liber de appellationibus*, 4.
[17]An extension of the previous canon. See also H.C., 36.4.
[18]VI, 2.15.3 (Fr, II, 1015-16), originally a decretal of Pope Innocent IV (1243-54).
[19]*Clem.*, 2.12.1 (Fr, II, 1153-4), originally published by Pope Clement V (1305-14) after the council of Vienne (1311-12); cf. H.C., 36.1.

judgment, nor in an enormous and serious crime. Whoever appeals after ten days shall not be heard by way of appeal, although he may still complain and pursue another course in order *not* to be restored in full. In civil cases one person shall not appeal on behalf of another, unless he is also involved.[16] When someone has confessed in a judgment his appeal shall not be allowed, as long as he has confessed in person and not through a proctor, and that his confession has not been extorted by tortures or fear of them; moreover, it shall also be required that he stand convicted of what he has confessed in court. An appeal must never be allowed to anyone who [*favours* **encourages**] some injustice or iniquity, nor shall an appeal be accepted when a cause has been subdelegated by our kingly majesty on the condition that there shall be no appeal from it.

10. **When there is a right of appeal before the final sentence in ecclesiastical causes.**[17]

In ecclesiastical causes we forbid appeals or suits before the final sentence, unless it is from a sentence of censures or correction where the rules have been broken, or wherever the harm or grievance incurred cannot be put right by an appeal from the final sentence. In such cases it will be permissible to appeal and even to sue before the final sentence.

11. **The order of appeal [*to higher judges*].**[18]

Appeal may be made to the bishop from archdeacons, deans and those below the episcopal dignity who have ecclesiastical jurisdiction, from the bishop to the archbishop, and from the archbishop to our majesty. And when the cause has been referred, we want it to be decided either by a provincial council, if it is serious, or else by *two* **three** or *three* **four** bishops, to be appointed by us for that purpose. When the matter has been decided and judged by these means, it cannot be heard by further appeal. Nevertheless, in addition to these things, we want it to be observed that if the cause has been subdelegated, an appeal can always be made to the one who subdelegated it, and if it is to be appealed any further, the order already described shall be kept.

12. **How to appeal from several judges.**[19]

If there were many judges and a sentence was passed or some grievance was inflicted by them, it shall be permissible to appeal before a majority of them

appellare licebit, et apostoli peti seorsim ab eis poter[u/i]nt. Sed tamen appellatio ipsa, delatio ad certum iudicem, et praefixus terminus adversario, si non adfuerit, sunt intimanda.

12a. *In causa communi plurium unius appellatio reliquos etiam iuvat.*[20]

Si plures qui communi iure iuventur idem [218r] *negotium et eandem defensionis causam habent, cum una sententia condemnati fuerint, unius eorum appellatio et eius victoria ceterorum iuri et causae suffragatur.*

13. **Qui per appellationem in una causa liberatur a suo iudice, in aliis tamen ei debet respondere.**[21]

Pendens appellatio non est sufficiens et idonea causa, ut iudex, a quo appellatum est, in aliis causis repudietur. Unde cum quis duas diversasque causas habet sub eodem iudice, licet quoad unam earum appellaverit, de altera tamen cogetur iudici respondere a quo appellavit.

14. **Non obstat prior appellatio deserta, quando propter novum gravamen rursus appellari possit ab eodem iudice.**[22]

Qui appellavit, et appellationem deseruit, rediitque ad iudicem, a quo appellavit, si rursus ab eo gravetur, denuo poterit appellare.

[218v] 15. **In causa communi plurium unius appellatio alios etiam iuvat.**[23]

Si ex pluribus una sententia condemnatis, qui communi interesse iure iu[v/b]entur, idemque habeant negotium et eandem causam defensionis, unus appellaverit, eius victoria proderit aliis. Et si fortasse is unus qui appellavit, ceteris tacentibus et scientibus, appellationem deseruerit, quivis alius ex illis eam prosequi poterit.

---

[20]X, 2.28.72 (Fr, II, 443), originally a decretal of Pope Gregory IX (1227-41), published on or before 5 September 1234; *Dig.*, 49.1.10, originally Ulpian, *Disputationes*, 8; H.C., 36.9.

[21]*Dig.*, 49.12.1, originally Ulpian, *De appellationibus*, 4; X, 2.28.6 (Fr, II, 411); X, 2.28.22 (Fr, II, 416-17); X, 2.28.24 (Fr, II, 417), all originally decretals of Pope Alexander III (1159-81).

[22]Panormitanus on X, 2.28.39.

[23]*Dig.*, 49.1.10, originally Ulpian, *Disputationes*, 8; X, 2.28.72 (Fr, II, 443), originally a decretal of Pope Gregory IX, published on or before 5 September 1234; H.C., 36.9.

if they are not all available at the same time and letters of appeal can be requested from each of them individually. But if the opponent was not present the appeal itself, the referral to a particular judge and the fixed time limit must be communicated to him.

12a. *In a cause which is common to several people, an appeal from one of them will also help the others*[20].

If several people who are supported by the same law have the same business and the same cause of defence, the appeal of one of them and his victory will support the right and cause of the others, since they have been condemned by the same sentence.

13. **Someone who has been released by his judge on appeal in one cause must nevertheless answer to him in others.**[21]

A pending appeal is not a sufficient or suitable reason for the judge from whom the appeal has been made, to be rejected in other causes. Therefore when someone has two different causes under the same judge, even if he has appealed one of them, he shall nevertheless be compelled to answer the judge from whom he has appealed, as far as the other one is concerned.

14. **An earlier, abandoned appeal does not stand in the way when a new grievance gives rise to another appeal from the same judge.**[22]

Someone who has appealed and abandoned the appeal, and returns to the judge from who he appealed, may appeal again if he is grieved by him a second time.

15. **In a cause which is common to several people, an appeal from one of them will also help the others.**[23]

If out of several people who have been condemned by the same sentence, who are [*supported* **ordered**] by an interest in the same law, have the same business and the same cause of defence, the appeal of one of them and his victory will benefit the others. And if by chance the one who appealed, while the others remained silent but knew of it, should abandon the appeal, any one of the others may take it up.

16. An iuramentum interpositum prohibeat appellationem.[24]

Si quis iuraverit se staturum iudicatis et definitis in ali[143a]quo iudicio, quoniam iuramenta semper ad causas honestas contrahenda sunt et verisimiliter cogitatas, ideo si eveniat, ut sententia vel mandatum iudicis et honestatis et iu*d*/stitiae limites excedat, licite qui iuravit inde potest appellare, cum iuramentum his [219r] casibus non urgeat. Verum si hoc non accidat, sua ipsius promissione astringitur ut non appellet.

17. Ob suspectum locum licet appellare.[25]

Locus iudicii exercendi, ad quem iudex citaverit, debet esse to/utus domino et omnibus his qui pro eo interveniunt, ut ad locum possint ire secure. Alias proposita exceptione de loco suspecto libere [*possit* licet] appellare.

18. Tam in maioribus quam in minoribus causis licet appellare.[26]

Et in maioribus et in minoribus causis appellandi facultas non denegetur. Nec enim iud*icem*/ex iniuriam sibi fieri debet existimare, eo quod litigator appellat. Quia quantitas causae non fe/acit, quare sit appellandum, sed iniquum gravamen.

[219v] 19. Qualis causa reddenda sit in appellationibus.[27]

Cum sit extra iudicium **appellatio**, causa potest assignare/i, quae sit generalis et incerta respectu personarum seu gravaminis, cum fiat saepissime de futuro, quod minime potest determinate sciri. Sed in appellatione iudiciali, quando reddenda est causa, illam et certam et specialem esse oportet, cum semper ferme sit vel de praesenti vel de praeterito gravamime.

Praeterea in iudicio causa appellandi debet esse [143b] vera. Sed extra iudicium satis est quod causa sit verisimilis et probabilis, ut puta: 'Verisimiliter timui gravari in possessione [*alicuius* **alterius**] rei, licet adhuc non sum gravatus, tamen extra iudicium possum appellare.'

---

[24]Cf. X, 2.28.20 (Fr, II, 416), originally a decretal of Pope Alexander III (1159-81).
[25]X, 2.28.47 (Fr, II, 428), originally a decretal of Pope Innocent III, 22 April 1202.
[26]X, 2.28.11 (Fr, II, 413), originally a decretal of Pope Alexander III.
[27]X, 2.28.18 (Fr, II, 415), originally a decretal of Pope Alexander III.

16. **Whether an oath taken can prevent an appeal.**[24]

If someone has sworn that he will abide by the judgments and decisions of some court, since oaths are always to be sworn in honest cases which are reasonably well argued, and it happens that the sentence or order of the judge goes beyond the bounds of honesty and justice, the person who swore may legitimately appeal, since in those cases his oath is not binding. But if that is not the case, he is bound by his promise not to appeal.

17. **Right of appeal on account of a suspect place.**[25]

The place where a judgment is held, to which a judge has issued his summons, must be *whole* **safe** for the principal and for all those who intervene on his behalf, so that they may go to the place in safety. Otherwise, it is [*possible* **permissible**] to appeal freely, by putting forward an exception on the ground of suspect place.

18. **Right of appeal in both major and minor causes.**[26]

The right of appeal shall not be denied either in major or in minor causes. For a judge must not think that any harm is done to him because a litigator appeals. For it is not the size of the cause, but an unfair grievance which *gave* **gives** ground for appeal.

19. **What kind of reason ought to be given for an appeal.**[27]

When **an appeal** is extrajudicial, a reason may be given which is general and unspecific with respect to persons or a grievance, as most often happens with respect to the future, which cannot be known exactly. But in a judicial appeal, when a reason must be given, it must be definite and specific, since it is almost always about a present or a past grievance.

Moreover, in a judicial appeal the reason for it must be true. But in an extrajudicial one it is enough for the reason to be probable and likely, for example: 'I was genuinely afraid of being molested in possession of some [other] thing, even though I have not yet been molested, nevertheless I can appeal extrajudicially.'

[220r] 20. **Cum appellatur a definitiva, licet aliter agere quam in aliis appellationibus permittatur.**[28]

In appellatione a definitiva sententia cum non sit necessarium causam exprimere, appellans, cum unam causam exposuerit in agendo, aliam poterit prosequi, et post eam, aliam, quoad ei suppetent. Sed in aliis appellationibus, cum debeat causa[*m*] exprimi, non poterit citra expressam alia tractari in prosecutione.

21. **Coram quo iudice appellationis causa sit proponenda, et coram quo iustificanda.**[29]

Causa appellationis cum est exprimenda, coram iudice, a quo appellatum est, proponetur, nisi metus obest, et si copia eius haberi potest; sed coram iudice, ad quem appellatum, iustificabitur.

22. **Si exceptiones legitimae cum probationibus offerantur iudici, si re[*ie*]ctae fuerint, et licit[a]e appellatur, et iustificatur appellatio.**[30]

Exceptiones legitimae et earum probationes, quando iudici oblatae fuerint, si ab eo non admittantur, [220v] iusta causa praebetur appellandi; quin et appellatio coram iudice, ad quem provocatum est propter hoc iustificabitur, licet veritas exceptionis non probetur.[31]

Insuper ordinamus non **Non tamen volumus** sufficere appellanti, si dicat se materiam sive exceptionem legitimam et veram proposuisse et appellasse, nisi doceat propter exceptionem non admissam appellasse.

[144a] [<23. **Iustificata appellatione, non est probata [*ob id* obiter] exceptio.**[32]

Constituimus praeterea, ut talis oblatio probationis iustificet solum appellationem, quoad devolutionem causae, non autem ut exceptio habeatur pro probata in praeiudicium partis adversae.>][33]

---

[28]Cf. *Clem.*, 2.12.5 (Fr, II, 1154-5), originally published by Pope Clement V (1305-14) after the council of Vienne (1311-12).
[29]X, 1.3.29 (Fr, II, 31), originally a decretal of Pope Honorius III (1216-27).
[30]X, 2.28.63 (Fr, II, 439-40), originally a decretal of Pope Honorius III.
[31]In the MS, John Foxe wrote this word again at the beginning of the next paragraph, to indicate that the two should be joined up.
[32]*Ibid.*
[33]A marginal note in Peter Martyr's hand reads: 'Inseratur hic hoc quod inferius est ad hoc signum *'. ('Insert here what comes below under the sign *'). This heading originally came between 25 and 26 below.

20. When a final sentence is appealed, it may be done differently from what is allowed in other appeals.[28]

Although it is not necessary to state the reason for an appeal from a final sentence, the appellant, when he has given one reason in the judgment, may add another, and yet another, as they occur to him. But in other appeals, when the reason must be stated, he cannot deal with other matters under the heading of the one stated in the prosecution.

21. Before which judge a reason for appeal is to be put forward, and before which one it must be justified.[29]

When a reason for appealing must be stated, it shall be put forward before the judge from whom the appeal has been made, unless fear stands in the way, and if his presence can be had, but it shall be justified before the judge to whom the appeal has been made.

22. If lawful exceptions have been offered to the judge and have been rejected, this may be lawfully appealed and the appeal is justified.[30]

When lawful exceptions and their proofs have been offered to a judge and have not been accepted by him, a just cause for appeal is provided; furthermore, the appeal shall be justified on this account before the judge to whom it has been referred, even if the truth of the exception has not been proved.[31]

In addition we decree that it is not **Nevertheless we do not want it to be** enough for an appellant merely to say that he has put forward and appealed a true and lawful matter or exception, without adding that he has appealed because the exception has not been accepted.

[<23. The justification of an appeal does not mean that the exception has been proved.[32]

Moreover we decree that such an offer of proof merely justifies the appeal with respect to the referral of the cause, and not that the exception must be regarded as proved, in prejudice to the other party.>][33]

24. Ob quas alias iniurias et cavillationes iudicis, licet ab eo appellare.[34]

Praeterea si iudex procedat ad ulteriora, exceptione vel materia neglecta, licet expresse eam non repulerit, potest ab eo appellari. Ad haec si iudex non procedat ad ulteriora, sed supersedeat vexando excipientem vel materiam proponentem, [221r] quem saepe citat ad audiendum deliberationem suam, vel ad idem saepe assignavit terminum, tunc volumus, quod si iudex bis humiliter requisitus non pronuntiat, possit ab hoc gravamine appellari.

25. Quomodo in diversis appellationibus processus iustificetur.[35]

Et licet processus primi iudicis iustificari vel impugnari non possit, quando appellatur ab interlocutoria, nisi ex actis coram eo in appellatione, tamen **in appellatione**[36] a definitiva sententia, potest iudex ad quem, ex novis actis coram eo habitis, suum processum iustificare, et contrarium primae sententiae pronuntiare. Quia non allegatum vel [*non*] probatum in causa principali, potest allegari et probari in causa appellationis.

[>*25a. Iustificata appellatione, non est probata [*ob id* obiter] exceptio.[37]

Constituimus praeterea, ut talis oblatio probationis iustificet solum appellationem, quoad devolutionem causae, non autem *vel* **ut** exceptio habeatur pro probata in praeiudicium partis adversae.<][38]

26. Ad quid inventae s[*i*/u]nt appellationes.[39]

Appellationes non ad deprimendam cuiusquam iustitiam sunt inventae, sed ut gravamen impositum reparetur, et ad [144b] corrigendam iniquitatem et imperitiam iudicis, et nonnunquam ad ipsius afflicti succurrendum inscitiae. Nam in appellatione persaepe locum habet, quod iactatur: 'Non probatum probabo, et quod non est oppositum opponam.' Etenim quae in prima instantia sunt omissa, frequenter in secunda locum habent.

---

[34]X, 2.28.48 (Fr, II, 428), originally a decretal of Pope Innocent III, 14 May 1204; X, 2.28.49 (Fr, II, 429), also a decretal of Pope Innocent III (1198-1216); X, 2.28.50 (Fr, II, 429), also a decretal of Pope Innocent III, 10 February 1205.

[35]Hostiensis, *Summa aurea*, c. *De appellationibus*, 23; cf. H.C., 36.5.

[36]Added by Peter Martyr.

[37]See R, 54.23.

[38]Moved at Peter Martyr's suggestion to 23 above, but not actually changed in the MS.

[39]*Dig.*, 49.1.1, originally Ulpian, *De appellationibus*, 1.

24. For what other injuries and hesitations of a judge there is a right of appeal from him.[34]

Moreover, it is possible to appeal from the judge if he goes on to further matters, passing over the exception or matter without specifically rejecting it. Also, if a judge does not go on to further matters, but proceeds to trouble the person making the exception or putting the matter forward, by frequently citing him to hear his own deliberation or by often cutting the matter short, then it is our will that if the judge does not pronounce after having been twice respectfully requested to do so, this grievance may be appealed.

25. How a procedure may be justified in different appeals.[35]

And although the procedure of the first judge may not be justified or impugned when an appeal is lodged from the interlocutory sentence, unless it comes from the records before him in the appeal, nevertheless **in an appeal**[36] from a final sentence, the judge to whom the appeal is made may justify his procedure on the basis of new proceedings held before him, and quash the first sentence. For what has not been charged or [*not*] proved in the main cause may be charged and proved in the appeal cause.

[>*25a. The justification of an appeal does not mean that the exception is proved.[37]

Moreover we decree that such an offer of proof merely justifies the appeal with respect to the referral of the cause, and not **that** the exception must be regarded as proved, in prejudice to the other party.<][38]

26. What appeals have been devised for.[39]

Appeals have been devised not for depriving someone of justice, but so that a grievance imposed might be put right, and for correcting the unfairness and inexperience of a judge, and sometimes for coming to the rescue of the ignorance of the person affected. For very often in an appeal there is room for the boast: 'I shall prove the unproved, and I shall oppose what has not been opposed.' Furthermore, things which have been overlooked in the first instance often find a place in the second.

27. In causa appellationis aliquae exceptiones repeti possunt, quae in prima instantia locum non habuerunt.[40]

Cum peremptoria exceptio in instantia non [222r] fuit admissa, interposita appellatione a definitiva sententia in causa appellationis, denuo poterit obiici et probari. Idemque licebit, si eadem exceptio peremptoria in priori instantia vel negligentia vel oblivione omissa fuerit. Verum exceptiones illae quae in pr/i/ori instantia necessario erant opponendae ante litis contestationem, in causa appellationis obiici non poterunt.

28. Lapsus termini quandoque non obest.[41]

Lapsus termini ad appellandum vel appellationem finiendum non praeiudicabit appellanti, quominus ex causa legitima audiatur, saltem per beneficium restitutionis in integrum; et fiet restitutio usque ad tantum tempus quantum fuit tempus impedimenti. Quia si impedimentum non fuisset, habuisset [222v] effectum suum appellatio. Volumus tamen ut suam diligentiam ostendat infra tempus impedimenti, quia aliter constare non poss[e/i]t impedimentum causam praestitisse; neque sufficit probare impedimentum fuisse, nisi doceatur id impedimentum fuisse causam non agendi, quod probatur probando tunc temporis diligentiam.

[145a] 29. Terminus ad appellandum est decem dierum.[42]

Appellationes et nullitatum querelas infra decem dies utiles a tempore notitiae latae sententiae aut gravaminis, a quo per constitutiones nostras appellare sive querelare licet, coram iudice, a quo provocatur, fieri volumus.

30. De terminis ad prosequendam et ad finiendam causam appellationis.[43]

Cum quis appellaverit, vel de nullitate conquestus fuerit, nisi infra duos menses a [223r] tempore appellationis sive querelae interpositae eandem prosecutus fuerit, et iudicem a quo de prosecutione huiusmodi per citationem vel inhibitionem superioris certiorem fecerit, ac infra sex menses, a fine ipsorum

---

[40]Cf. *Clem.*, 2.12.7 (Fr, II, 1156), originally published by Pope Clement V (1305-14) after the council of Vienne (1311-12), where the provision is different.
[41]X, 2.28.8 (Fr, II, 412), originally a decretal of Pope Alexander III (1159-81).
[42]Cf. H.C., 36.1.
[43]X, 2.28.4 (Fr, II, 410-11); X, 2.28.5 (Fr, II, 411), both originally decretals of Pope Alexander III (1159-81); *Clem.*, 2.12.3 (Fr, II, 1154), originally published by Pope Clement V after the council of Vienne (1311-12); H.C., 36.6.

27. In an appeal cause some exceptions which were unsuccessful in the first instance can be repeated.[40]

When a peremptory exception has not been allowed in a hearing, it may be presented in an appeal cause once the appeal has been lodged from the final sentence, and proved again. This may be done if the same peremptory exception was overlooked in the first instance by negligence or forgetfulness. But those exceptions which of necessity should have been presented in the former instance before the joinder of issue, cannot be presented in an appeal case.

28. When the expiry of a time limit is not an impediment.[41]

The expiry of a time limit for appealing or for finishing an appeal shall not prejudice the appellant from being heard for a lawful reason, at least for the purpose of restitution in full, and restitution shall be made up to the same length of time as the period of impediment. For if there had been no impediment, his appeal would have gone through. Nevertheless, it is our will that he shall show his diligence during the period of impediment, because otherwise he cannot prove that the impediment has brought about the cause, nor is it enough to prove that there was an impediment, if it is not shown that the impediment was the cause of not acting, which is proved by proving his diligence during that time.

29. The time limit for appeal is ten days.[42]

It is our will that appeals and suits of nullity shall be lodged with the judge from whom the referral has been made within ten working days from the time of the notice of the sentence passed or of the grievance, from which our constitutions allow one to appeal or sue.

30. Of time limits for pursuing and finishing an appeal case.[43]

When someone has appealed or sued for nullity, unless he has pursued it within two months from the time the appeal or suit for nullity was lodged, and has informed the judge from whom he is appealing of the said prosecution by a citation or inhibition from a superior, and obtained an end to this appeal or suit within six months, counting from the end of the previous two months (barring

duorum mensium numerandos, ipsam appellationem sive querelam (legitimo impedimento cessante, quod a iudice, a quo appellatum est, approbandum erit) fie/**niri** obtinuerit, sententiae contra eum prius latae stare compelletur: et debebit eius appellatio deserta censeri. Terminum vero ad prosequendam litem datum a lege concedimus cum a iudice tum ab appellante posse imminui, non autem prorogari.

31. Lata sententia definitiva non est ante decem dies mandanda executioni.[44]

Illis decem diebus a lata sententia, quibus appellare licet, iudicatum non mandetur executioni; quod [223v] non modo in civilibus, verum et in criminalibus observari decernimus. Volumus etiam ut in ipsis criminalibus, etiam invito condemnato, quivis alius pro eo possit appellare.

32. Quomodo labatur terminus in extraiudiciali appellatione.[45]

In appellatione extraiudiciali, propter gravamen aut fu[145b]turum aut iam inflictum interposita, terminus vel a iure datus vel a iudice vel appellante praefixus ad litem prosequendam, non a die appellationis fluere incipiet, sed a die qua oppressus cognovit se gravatum; qui nihilominus terminus si fuerit elapsus, non obstabit quin oppressus a superiori iudice audiatur, non quidem appellationis via sed querelae: cum in appellatione appellans, qui semel eam deseruerit, quoad ipsam non amplius audiri debeat.

[224r] 33. Terminus finiendae causae appellationis a iudice, a quo appellatur, non potest mutari.[46]

Iudex a quo est appellatum, licet valeat praefigere terminum appellationis prosequendae, non tamen illius finiendae alium terminum potest constituere ab eo, quod ius concedit.

---

[44]Speculum, 2.3, *De appellationibus*, 5.10; Panormitanus on X, 2.27. Cf. X, 2.24.19 (Fr, II, 366), originally a decretal of Pope Innocent III, 1200.

[45]Cf. X, 2.28.12 (Fr, II, 413), originally a decretal of Pope Alexander III (1159-81).

[46]X, 2.28.33 (Fr, II, 420-1), originally a decretal of Pope Alexander III; X, 2.28.50 (Fr, II, 429), originally a decretal of Pope Innocent III, 10 February 1205.

lawful impediment, which must be approved by the judge from whom the case is appealed), he shall be compelled to abide by the sentence previously passed against him, and his appeal will have to be considered abandoned. But we allow the time limit given by the law for pursuing the suit to be shortened either by the judge or by the appellant, but not to be prolonged.

31. Once the final sentence has been passed, it shall not be put into effect until ten days have elapsed.[44]

For the ten days after the passing of a sentence, during which an appeal is allowed, the judgment shall not be put into effect, and we decree that this shall be observed not only in civil matters but in criminal ones also. For even in criminal cases it is our will that even if the condemned person does not want to do so, someone else may appeal on his behalf.

32. How the time limit may expire in an extrajudicial appeal.[45]

In an extrajudicial appeal lodged on account of a grievance which is either future or has already been inflicted, the time limit established by law or by the judge, or fixed by the appellant for pursuing the suit, shall not be counted from the day of the appeal but from the day on which the accused found out that he had been grieved. But if that time limit has already expired, there shall be no bar to the accused's being heard by a higher judge, not indeed by appeal but by suit. But once an appellant has abandoned his appeal it shall not be heard again.

33. The time limit for finishing an appeal cause cannot be altered by the judge from whom it has been appealed.[46]

Although the judge from whom an appeal is made can fix the time limit for pursuing the appeal, he cannot set a time limit for finishing it which is different from the one which the law allows.

34. Si compromissum interponatur, non labitur terminus.[47]

Si appellatione interposita partes consenserint in compromissum terminus/m ad prosequendam appellationem, currere nolumus, nisi iudex, animadvertens ex nimia dilatione imminere periculum, in causa iuberet progredi.

35. De generibus apostolorum.[48]

Apostoli non omnes sunt eiusdem generis. Aliqui sunt dimissorii, atque **tunc** *tru*dantur, cum iudex appellationi defert: sunt et refutatorii, qui dantur cum appellatio non est a[*d*]missa: tertio [224v] loco dicuntur alii reverentiales, hique dantur quando non merito causae, sed propter honorem iudicis, ad quem appellatum est, defertur appellationi. Postremo apostoli, si quandoque in appellatione dantur extraiudiciali, vel conventionales vel testimoniales dici consueverunt.

[146a] 36. Quando sit opus apostolis et quando non.[49]

In appellatione iudiciali semper onus est apostolis, non item in appellatione extraiudiciali.

37. Quando petendi apostoli, et quis terminus eorum *eorum* petendorum concedatur.[50]

Quando iudex appellatione interposita praefixit diem ad dandos apostolos, appellans tunc ad eos petendos debet compara/ere; quod si non faciat, sententia contra illum lata poterit executioni mandari. Et cum spatium termini praefixi [225r] ad apostolos dandos amplum fuerit, appellantem satis erit aliquando comparere, et loco et tempore congruo apostolos instanter petere. At si iudex aperte dixerit, se nolle dare, vel si praefixo termino aut ex malitia aut [*ex*] negligentia non dederit, poterunt litigantes appellationem sine illis prosequi. Et si iudex, qui non dederit, procedere attentet in causa, omnia quae fecerit erunt

---

[47]X, 2.28.47 (Fr, II, 435-7), originally a decretal of Pope Innocent III, 9 July 1209; *Clem.*, 2.12.4 (Fr, II, 1154), originally published by Pope Clement V (1305-14) after the council of Vienne (1311-12).
[48]Hostiensis, *Summa aurea*, c. *De appellationibus*. Cf. *Dig.*, 49.6.1, originally Marcian, *De appellationibus*, 2.
[49]Speculum, 2.3, *De appellationibus*, 3.11.
[50]VI, 2.15.6 (Fr, II, 1017), originally a decretal of Pope Innocent IV (1243-54); *Clem.*, 2.12.2 (Fr, II, 1154), originally published by Pope Clement V, after the council of Vienne (1311-12).

34. If a compromise is reached, the time limit does not expire.[47]

If the parties agree to compromise on a time limit for pursuing an appeal once it has been lodged, we do not want this to stand unless the judge, realizing that danger is imminent if there is too long a delay, has ordered the case to proceed.

35. Of the types of letters of appeal.[48]

Not all letters of appeal are of the same type. Some are dimissory, and are **then** introduced when the judge defers to an appeal. There are also refutatory ones, which are given when the appeal is not allowed. In the third place, others are called reverential, and these are given when a matter is referred to appeal not because of the merit of the case but because of the honour of the judge to whom the appeal is made. Lastly when letters of appeal are given in an extrajudicial appeal, they are usually called either conventional or testimonial.

36. When letters of appeal are needed and when not.[49]

Letters of appeal are always needed in a judicial appeal, but it is not the same in an extrajudicial one.

37. When letters of appeal are to be sought, and what time limit is allowed for seeking them.[50]

If the judge, once an appeal has been lodged, sets a day for giving letters of appeal, the appellant must appear at that time in order to ask for them. If he does not do so, the sentence passed against him may be put into effect. And if the space of time allotted for giving letters of appeal is adequate, it will be enough for the appellant to appear at some point and ask for the letters of appeal on the spot, at a convenient time and place. But if the judge has openly stated that he does not want to give them, or if out of malice or negligence, he has not given them within the set time, the litigants may pursue the appeal without them. And if the judge who has not given them tries to proceed with the cause, everything

invalida;[51] et a iudice, ad quem appellatum est, arbitraria poena plectetur. Tempus autem quoad apostolos dandos longissimum, et quod proferri non possit, triginta dies esse volumus, intra quod spatium, si appellans eos instanter loco et tempore congruo non p*ot*/**eti**erit, appellationi renuntiasse censebitur.

[225v] 38. **Quid in apostolis contineri debeat.**[52]

In apostolis appellationis causa exponetur; et an admissa sit appellatio, vel non admissa declarabitur. Et a quocunque dentur apostoli, illis apponendum est eius sigillum, a quo dantur. Cumque iudex apostolos dederit, appellanti quoque terminum prosequendae appellationis constituet. [146b] Verum ex apostolis datis vel praefixo termino non intelligetur iudex appellationi interpositae detulisse. Nam apostoli facile potest fieri ut sint refutatorii; et constituitur terminus ad malitiam litigantium compescendam, ne superfluis moris lites extrahant.

39. **Appellanti non est fraudi, si post *appellationem* gravamen [*aliquid agat* alligat] ad tribunal iudicis, *a quo appellavit* nec ob id impeditur, [*quin* quando] intra decem dies ab eo appellari possit.**[53]

Quando aliquis [**est**] in iudicio [*est*] gravatus, licet post gravamen ad iudicem venerit, qui eum gravavit, et aliquid ad eius tribunal egerit, propter huiusmodi acta [226r] non eripitur ei facultas, quin infra decem dies ab inflicto gravamine appellare possit, praesertim cum ea, **quae** post gravamen egit, non sponte, sed vi iudicis adactus egerit.

40. **Appellans si quid cum protestatione agat coram iudice a quo appellavit, n[*on*/e] propterea deserit appellationem.**[54]

Quando aliquis appellavit, licet ad iudicem, a quo appellatum est, post appellationem interpositam venerit, et aliquid ad eius tribunal egerit, modo protestetur, se non ob id velle appellationem de[*sere*/**fer**]re, non iudicabitur illi [**non**] renuntiasse.

[51]VI, 2.15.4 (Fr, II, 1016), originally a decretal of Pope Innocent IV.
[52]VI, 2.15.1 (Fr, II, 1014-15), supposedly promulgated at Lyon I, 1245; Speculum, 2.3, *De appellationibus*, 3.10.
[53]Cf. *Dig.*, 49.12.1, originally Ulpian, *De appellationibus*, 4.
[54]X, 2.28.54 (Fr, II, 432-3), originally a decretal of Pope Innocent III, 12 December 1207; H.C., 36.8.

which he does will be invalid,[51] and he shall be punished with a discretionary penalty by the judge to whom the appeal has been made. However it is our will that the longest time during which letters of appeal may be given shall be thirty days, which may not be extended, during which period, if the appellant [*cannot* **does not ask for**] them on the spot, at a convenient time and place, he shall be regarded as having abandoned the appeal.

38. What ought to be contained in letters of appeal.[52]

In letters of appeal the reason for the appeal shall be set out, and it shall be declared whether the appeal has been allowed or not. And the seal of whoever gives these letters of appeal shall be affixed to them. And when a judge gives letters of appeal, he shall also set a time limit for the appellant to pursue the appeal. But it shall not be understood, merely on the basis of letters of appeal given or a time limit set, that the judge defers to the appeal lodged. For it is easy for letters of appeal to be drawn up in such a way that they are refutatory, and a time limit is set in order to contain the malice of the litigants, lest they drag suits out by superfluous delays.

39. It is not wrong for an appellant, if after the *appeal* grievance he [*does something at* brings something to] the tribunal of the judge *from whom he has appealed,* and he is not prevented from doing so, [*as long as* if] he can appeal within ten days.[53]

If someone is grieved in a judgment and after the grievance has occurred he comes to the judge who has grieved him and does something in his tribunal, the right to appeal from the inflicted grievance within ten days shall not be taken away from him on account of these proceedings, especially if the things **which** he did after the grievance, he did not do of his own free will, but because he was compelled by the power of the judge.

40. An appellant, if he does something under protest before the judge from whom he has appealed, does not thereby abandon the appeal.[54]

When someone has appealed, even if he comes to the judge from whom he has appealed, after lodging the appeal, and does something in his tribunal, he shall not be judged to have [**not**] abandoned the appeal as long as he protests that he does not on that account want to [*abandon* **defer**] it.

41. Post appellationem debet iudex a tota causa supersedere, nisi gravamen inflictum revocet.[55]

Quamvis appellatio interdum certum aliquem causae articulum spectet, nihilominus ea interposita, iudex a quo appellatum est, a tota ipsa causa supersedebit. Non enim quispiam cogi debet, ut illi iudici respondeat in ea causa, in qua [147a] se [226v] [*se*] gravatum ab eo sentit; neque amplius ad illum comparere adigitur, ut respondeat, neque ut de gravamine doceat, nisi fortasse citetur ad audiendam gravaminis illati revocationem. Quam revocationem si iudex fecerit, sive comparente eo, qui appellavit, sive non comparente, et ad solvendas expensas, si quas appellans fecerit, sese obtulerit, et adeundus est, et sub eo agendum. Nam causam, a qua fuit appellatum, potest reassumere, et ad ulteriora procedere. Quod tamen tunc solum habet locum, quando appellationi minime detulit. Nam si eam fortasse receperit, neque gravamen revocare, neque causam potest resumere. Etenim iurisdictio eius, quoad illam causam, prorsus transfusa est in iudicem superiorem. [227r] Poterit nihilominus postea de illa cognoscere, si iudex, ad quem est appellatum, illam ad eum remiserit. Itaque deferendo appellationi causam illam iudex omnino a se abdicat, nisi de[*s*/f]eratur appellatio, et terminus praefixus elapsus fuerit, intra quem appellans debuit prosequi appellationem. Isto siquidem casu lis denuo ad illum redit.

42. Quae attentantur post appellationem sunt irrita.[56]

Quae attentantur contra et post appellationem, sive iudicialem sive extraiudicialem, sunt ipso iure nulla. Potest attamen iudex, a quo appellatum est, omnia ea facere pendente appellatione, quae ad eius faciliorem exitum tendant.

43. Quae innovata post appellationem a iudice appellationis revocari debeant, et quae non.[57]

Innovata post appellationem a definitiva, aut inter sententiam et appellationem, ante omnia [227v] per appellationis iudicem revocari debent. Innovata vero post appellationem [147b] ab interlocutoria seu gravamine, donec appellationis causam veram esse constiterit, revocari non debent, nisi post inhibitionem (ne procederet in causa) a superiore factam, inferior iudex processit. Nam irritum est et invalidum, quicquid agitur post inhibitionem.

---

[55]X, 2.28.60 (Fr, II, 437), originally c. 36 of Lateran IV, 1215 (*C.O.D.*, 251); VI, 2.15.10 (Fr, II, 1018), originally a decretal of Pope Boniface VIII (1294-1303).
[56]VI, 2.15.7 (Fr, II, 1017), originally a decretal of Pope Boniface VIII.
[57]*Ibid.*

41. After an appeal the judge ought to withdraw from the entire cause, unless he revokes the grievance inflicted.[55]

Although an appeal refers only to one particular aspect of the cause, nevertheless, once it has been lodged, the judge from whom it has been appealed shall withdraw from the entire cause. For no one must be compelled to answer to that judge in a cause in which he feels that he has been grieved by him, nor shall he be expected to appear before him any more in order to answer or to explain the grievance, unless perchance he is summoned to hear the revocation of the grievance inflicted. If the judge makes such a revocation, whether the person who has appealed appears or not, and offers to pay expenses, if the appellant has incurred any, he shall then come and the trial will take place in his court. For he may once again take up the cause from which the appeal was made, and proceed to further matters. But this may only take place when he has not deferred to the appeal at all. For if perchance he has accepted the appeal, he can neither revoke the grievance nor resume the cause. Moreover, his jurisdiction with respect to that cause is henceforth transferred to a higher judge. Nevertheless, he may be able to hear it later on, if the judge to whom it has been appealed remits it to him. Therefore, by deferring to the appeal, a judge withdraws completely from the cause, unless the appeal is [*abandoned* **deferred**], and the set time limit, within which the appellant ought to have pursued the cause, has expired. In that case the suit goes back to him again.

42. Whatever is attempted after an appeal is invalid.[56]

Whatever is attempted against and after an appeal, whether it is judicial or extrajudicial, is automatically void. Nevertheless the judge from whom a cause has been appealed can do anything which helps towards an easier resolution of it, while the appeal is still pending.

43. Which innovations made after the appeal ought to be revoked by the judge, and which not.[57]

Innovations made after an appeal from the final sentence, or made between the sentence and the appeal, must first of all be revoked by the appeal judge. But innovations made after an interlocutory sentence or a grievance, must not be revoked until the true reason for the appeal has been established, unless the lower judge proceeds after an inhibition (that he should not proceed in the cause) has been issued by a higher judge. For anything which is done after an inhibition is null and void.

44. Quatenus iudex, a quo appellatur, de appellationis iustitia po[*si*/tes]t cognoscere.[58]

Iudex, a quo appellatur, de appellationis iustitia potest cognoscere, quo sese instruat, an illi sit deferendum: non autem in praeiudicium appellationis. Nam h[*o*/ae]c ad iudicem pertinet, ad quem est appellatum.

45. Quando iudex appellationis causam debeat ad inferiorem iudicem remittere.[59]

Inferior iudex quando appellationi **a definitiva** minime [228r] detulit, debet superior, vanitate seu malitia cognita illius, appellationis causam ad illum remittere, ac eodem die appellantem iniuste condemnare quoad expensas. Cum vero iudex inferior appellationi detul[er]it, in potestate superioris erit causam ad eum remittere vel apud se retinere, quod accipiendum est, si prosecutio coram superior{*i*/e} fiat.[60]

Item *volumus* cum superior appellationem ab interlocutoria sive gravamine frivolam esse [**causam**] cognoverit, causam ipsam remittat. Si vero ipsam appellationem ex veris et iustis causis fuisse interpositam cognoverit, causam principalem in suam accipiet potestatem. Nec ulterius eam ad [228v] inferiorem iudicem remittat.

46. Iudex ad quem appellatum est non prohibeat inferiorem, nisi prius ei constet legitime appellatum esse.[61]

Prohibemus ne iudex, ad quem appellari seu querelari contigerit, iudici, a quo appellatum est, prius inhibeat, quam appellatum sive querelatum legitime sibi fuisse constiterit. [148a] Nisi a definitiva statim, iudic*io*/e pro tribunali sedente, viva voce apud acta fuerit appellatum sive querelatum: quo casu sufficiet iudici, ad quem appellatum est, de hoc per appellantis aut procuratoris eiusdem habentis mandatum, iuramento constare.

---

[58]L, 2.7.2, gloss on *pallietur*.
[59]VI, 2.15.5 (Fr, II, 1016-17), originally a decretal of Pope Clement IV (1265-8).
[60]In the MS, John Foxe wrote 'item, etc.' after this word, to show that the next paragraph should be joined up with this one.
[61]X, 2.28.38 (Fr, II, 422-3), originally a decretal of Pope Clement III (1187-91); VI, 2.15.7 (Fr, II, 1017), originally a decretal of Pope Boniface VIII (1294-1303); H.C., 36.3 (slightly abridged). Cf. *Dig.*, 49.1.1, originally Macer, *De appellationibus*, 1.

44. To what extent the judge from whom the appeal is made may conduct a hearing about the justice of the appeal.[58]

The judge from whom the appeal is made can conduct a hearing about the justice of the appeal, on the basis of which he shall decide whether he ought to defer to it, but not, however, to the prejudice of the appeal. For this belongs to the judge to whom the case has been appealed.

45. When the appeal judge must remit the cause to the lower judge.[59]

When a lower judge has not deferred to an appeal **from the final sentence**, his superior, recognizing his vanity or malice, must remit the appeal case to him, and at the same time he shall order the person who is appealing unjustly to pay expenses. But when the lower judge defers to the appeal, the higher one shall have the power to remit the case to him or keep it himself, because it must be accepted if a prosecution is to take place before the higher judge.[60]

Likewise *we wish that* when the higher judge knows that the appeal from an interlocutory sentence or from a grievance is [a] frivolous [**case**], he shall remit the case. But if he knows that the appeal itself has been lodged for true and just reasons, he shall take the main cause into his power. Nor shall he later remit it to the lower judge.

46. The judge to whom appeal is made shall not inhibit the lower judge until he ascertains that the appeal is lawful.[61]

We forbid the judge to whom a case must be appealed or sued to inhibit the judge from whom it has been appealed before he ascertains that the appeal or suit to him is lawful, unless it has been appealed or sued immediately, orally during the proceedings, while the judge was seated on the bench, in which case it will be enough for the judge to whom the case has been appealed to confirm this by an oath from the appellant or a proctor who has his mandate.

47. Sententiae excommunicationis et suspensionis non revocandae a iudice appellationis, nisi vocatis partibus.[62]

Non solum statuimus, ut si negetur per appellationem negotium devolutum, non inhibeat iudex appellationis iudicem a quo, in causa procedere; nisi de [*de*]volutione constiterit. **Verum** sententias quoque suspensionis sive [229r] excommunicationis in appellantem ab eo, a quo appellatum proponitur, pro[m/v]ulgatas, nullatenus (nisi vocatis partibus et de appellatione constiterit) **volumus** iudices appellationes revoc*ent*/**are** aut denunti*ent*/**are** esse nullas.

48. Puniendus quomodo sit iudex, qui iustae appellationi non detulerit.[63]

Si iudex legitimae appellationi non detulerit, est puniendus; et si criminalis fuerit causa, deponetur. Sin vero civilis, a superiori arbitraria poena mulctabitur.

49. Non est necessaria citatio partium in causa appellationis.[64]

In cognoscendo de appellatione primum omnium esse *esse* videretur, ut partes citarentur ad iustificandam et impugnandam appellationem. Sed hoc necessario non requiritur, cum tempus praefixum habent ad prosequendam appellationem.

Quando iudex, *ad quem* a quo appellandum [229v] est, puniendus fuerit a iudice, ad quem fuit provocatum, debet citari: quin et si volet, assidere iudici superiori poterit, dum causam a se iudicatam retractat, ne quid in eius praeiudicium fiat.

[148b] 50. Iudex a quo appellatum est non punietur a superiori, nisi citatus, et illi assidebit in causa retractanda, si visum fuerit.[65]

Quando iudex, ad quem appellatum est, definit contra sententiam inferioris iudicis propter novas rationes coram ipso allatas, quae in priori iudicio non

---

[62]VI, 2.15.3 (Fr, II, 1015-16), originally a decretal of Pope Innocent IV (1243-54).
[63]X, 2.28.31 (Fr, II, 420), originally a decretal of Pope Alexander III (1159-81); *Cod. Iust.*, 7.62.19, originally a rescript of the Emperor Constantine I, 1 September 331; *ibid.*, 7.62.21, originally a rescript of the emperors Constantius II and Constans, 25 July 355; *ibid.*, 7.62.24, originally a rescript of the emperors Valentinian I and Valens, 4 February 364.
[64]VI, 2.6.2 (Fr, II, 1000), originally a decretal of Pope Boniface VIII (1294-1303). But such a citation was lawful, cf. 23 Henry VIII, c. 9, s. 3, 1531 (*S. R.*, III, 377-8).
[65]Cf. Hostiensis, *Summa aurea*, c. *De re iudicata*, 5; Speculum, 2.3, *De appellationibus*, 10.1.

47. Sentences of excommunication and suspension must not be revoked by the appeal judge, unless the parties are summoned.[62]

We **not only** decree that if the business referred to appeal is rejected, the appeal judge shall not inhibit the judge from whom the appeal has been made from proceeding in the cause, unless the referral has been agreed to; **but** also **we do not in any way want** judges **to** *shall not* revoke appeals or declare that sentences of suspension or excommunication which have been promulgated against the appellant by the judge from whom the appeal has been made are invalid (unless the parties have been called and the appeal has been agreed to).

48. How a judge who has not deferred to a just appeal is to be punished.[63]

If a judge does not defer to a lawful appeal, he shall be punished, and if the case was a criminal one, he shall be deposed. But if it was a civil one, he shall be fined a discretionary penalty by his superior.

49. A citation of the parties is not necessary in an appeal cause.[64]

In hearing an appeal cause it must first of all be made certain that the parties are summoned to justify or to impugn the appeal. But this is not required of necessity, since they have a set time in which to pursue an appeal.

When the judge *to* from whom the appeal has been made, is to be punished by the judge to whom it has been made, he must be summoned, and if he wishes, he may sit with the higher judge while he reviews the case judged by him, so that nothing may be done in prejudice to him.

50. The judge from whom the appeal has been made shall not be punished by a higher judge unless he has been summoned, and if he wishes, he shall sit with him as the case is reviewed.[65]

When the judge to whom the appeal has been made decides against the sentence of the lower judge, on account of new factors brought to his attention which had

fuerunt agitatae, non simpliciter dicet in sententia inferiorem iudicem male iudicasse, sed cum adiectione ob defectum probationum, quae tum non fuerunt adductae.

51. Iudex ad quem appellatur, pro arbitrio non potest appellationem [*vel reiicere* requirere] vel admittere.[66]

Non est in facultate iudicis, ad quem appellatum fuerit, vel [*sus*/re]cipere vel renuere appellationem, quin si iusta [*sit* fuerit], eam recipere cogitur. Iudicandi quippe munus publicum est, neque [*illi*] ab e {*o*/a} renuntiari potest, qui iudicandi munus occupat.

[230r] 52. Partes quandoque possunt renuntiare appellationi.[67]

Partes de mutuo consensu valent interpositae appellationi renuntiare, et ad iudicem, a*d* quo appellatum est, reverti: neque ad hoc faciendum sufficit unius partis voluntas, et etiam fieri non potest, si iudex appellationi detulit. Quia tunc eam eandem causam non amplius iudicare valebit, nisi vel iudex, ad quem appellatum est, illam ad se remiserit, vel terminus praefixus eius prosequendae fuerit elapsus.

53. Suspectus appellans aut fide iubeat aut custodiatur.[68]

Si appellans fuerit suspectus de fuga, vel det fideiussores de [149a] prosequenda appellatione, vel custodiatur.

54. Inferior iudex exequetur a se sententiam latam, si confirmetur a superiori.[69]

Si lata sententia confirmetur per iudicem, ad quem appellatum fuit, executioni mandabitur a iudice, a quo [*appellatum*] est [appellatum].

---

[66]*Cod. Iust.*, 7.62.6, originally a rescript of the emperors Diocletian and Maximian (no date - between 285-305).
[67]*Cod. Iust.*, 7.62.28, originally a rescript of the emperors Arcadius and Honorius, 23 July 396; ibid., 7.63.5.6, originally a rescript of the Emperor Justinian I, 17 November 529.
[68]Cf. *Cod. Iust.*, 7.62.12, originally a rescript of the Emperor Constantine I, 17 April 314.
[69]VI, 2.15.3.10 (Fr, II, 1015-16), originally a decretal of Pope Innocent IV (1243-54). Cf. Speculum, 2.3, *De appellationibus*, 4.13; 10.4; Hostiensis, *Summa aurea*, c. *De re iudicata*, 7.

not been mentioned in the earlier judgment, he shall not simply say in his sentence that the lower judge had decided wrongly, but shall add that it was because of a lack of proofs, which were not produced at that time.

51. The judge to whom the appeal has been made cannot [*either reject require*] or allow the appeal at his own discretion.[66]

The judge to whom the appeal has been made cannot choose whether to accept or to reject the appeal; rather, if it is just, he is obliged to accept it. For the office of judging is a public one, and cannot be refused by the person who occupies it.

52. When the parties can abandon an appeal.[67]

By mutual consent, the parties may abandon an appeal they have lodged and go back to the judge from whom they appealed, but the will of one of the parties is not enough to do this, nor may it be done if the judge has deferred to the appeal. For then it is no longer valid for him to judge that same cause unless either the judge to whom it had been appealed has remitted it to him, or the time set for pursuing it has expired.

53. A suspect appellant shall either post guarantees or be imprisoned.[68]

If it is suspected that an appellant might flee, he shall either give guarantees that he will pursue the appeal, or else be imprisoned.

54. A lower judge shall carry out a sentence passed by him, if it is confirmed by a higher judge.[69]

If a sentence passed is confirmed by the judge to whom the appeal was made, it shall be put into effect by the judge from whom it was appealed.

55. In appellatione a definitiva gravamen quodcunque per interlocutoriam illatum, a iudice appellationis revocari potest.[70]

Cum a sententia definitiva appellatum vel [230v] de nullitate querelatum fuerit, gravamen quodcunque, quod per interlocutoriam illatum fuit, licite per appellationis iudicem emendari possit.

56. Appellans cum deserit appellationem, condemnatur adversario prosequenti in expensis.[71]

Cum quis appellationem interpositam deserit, et adversarius eam prosequitur, desertor ei condemnabitur in expensis.

57. Qui non sui adversarii appellationi defert, sciat suae quoque non deferendum.[72]

Si quis appellationi interpositae a suo *ordinario* **adversario** non detulerit, nec suae, si postea in eadem causa interponatur, cogi poterit adversarius ut deferat.

58. Post appellationem non est denuntianda excommunicatio.[73]

Si appellatio fuerit interposita, priusquam excommunicatio [149b] sit denuntiata, denuntiationem eius impedit.

59. Excommunicatio post appellationem lata[*m*] est invalida.[74]

Et sicut non tenet excommunicatio lata post appellationem iudicialem, ita neque [*post*] appellationem extraiudicialem. Timen*ti*/s ergo iniuste excommunicari appellat extra iudicium, et suspendit iurisdictionem iudicis. Sed post gravamen inflictum necesse est appellare.

---

[70]VI, 2.15.12 (Fr, II, 1018), originally a decretal of Pope Boniface VIII (1294-1303); H.C., 36.5.
[71]X, 2.28.26 (Fr, II, 418-19), originally c. 6 of Lateran III, 1179 (*C.O.D.*, 214); X, 2.28.64 (Fr, II, 440), originally a decretal of Pope Honorius III (1216-27).
[72]X, 2.28.23 (Fr, II, 417), originally a decretal of Pope Alexander III (1159-81).
[73]Speculum, 2.3, *De appellationibus*, 5.7; cf. H.C., 36.7.
[74]X, 2.28.55 (Fr, II, 433-5), originally a decretal of Pope Innocent III, 5 January 1207.

55. In an appeal from the final sentence, any grievance arising from an interlocutory sentence may be revoked by the appeal judge.[70]

When an appeal or suit for nullity is lodged from the final sentence, any grievance which had arisen from an interlocutory sentence may rightfully be cancelled by the appeal judge.

56. When an appellant abandons his appeal, he shall be ordered to pay his opponent's expenses if the latter pursues it.[71]

When someone deserts an appeal he has lodged, and his opponent pursues it, the deserter shall be ordered to pay his expenses.

57. Whoever does not defer to his opponent's appeal shall know that his own appeal will not be deferred to either.[72]

If someone has not deferred to an appeal lodged by his *ordinary* **opponent**, neither shall his opponent be obliged to defer to his appeal, if later on he lodges one in the same cause.

58. Excommunication is not to be pronounced once an appeal has been lodged.[73]

If an appeal has been lodged before an excommunication has been pronounced, that appeal bars the pronouncement.

59. An excommunication [passed] after an appeal [*has been passed*] is invalid.[74]

And just as an excommunication does not hold if passed after a judicial appeal, so also it does not hold [*after*] an extrajudicial appeal either. Therefore someone who is afraid of being excommunicated unjustly can appeal extrajudicially and suspend the judge's jurisdiction. But after a grievance has been inflicted, an appeal is necessary.

[231r] 60. **Revocatio causae ab episcopo facta vel a superiori iudice quanti sit momenti.**[75]

Episcopus causas ad se revocare potest, quae coram suo vicario aguntur, et revocatio alicuius causae per superiorem facta magis iurisdictionem suspendit inferioris iudicis, quam appellatio.

61. **Post appellationem legitimam a sequestro appellans libere fructus percipit.**[76]

Si a sequestro fuerit appellatum, et appellatio legitime prosecuta fuerit, ea pendente, possessores bonorum sequestratorum, et alii eorum nomine libere et impune utantur eisdem.[77]

---

[75]X, 2.28.56 (Fr, II, 435), originally a decretal of Pope Innocent III, 23 September 1198.
[76]Panormitanus on X, 2.17.1.
[77]A note on [231v] in Foxe's hand reads: "'De regulis iuris" require in folio 260.' ('"On the rules of law" see folio 260').

60. What force the revocation of a case made by a bishop or by a higher judge has.[75]

A bishop may revoke cases which are being heard before his deputy to himself, and the revocation of any cause made by a higher judge suspends the jurisdiction of the lower judge more effectively than an appeal.

61. After a lawful appeal against sequestration, the appellant shall freely receive the income.[76]

If a sequestration has been appealed, and the appeal has been lawfully pursued, the possessors of the sequestered goods and others in their name shall freely and without penalty enjoy the use of them while the appeal is pending.[77]

[260r; 150a]   **55. DE REGULIS IURIS**[1]

1.[2] Quod non est licitum in lege, necessitas facit licitum.

2.[3] Quae propter necessitatem introducta sunt, non debent in argumentum trahi.

3.[4] Semel malus semper praesumitur esse malus.

4.[5] Quod omnes tangit, debet ab omnibus approbari.

5.[6] Refertur ad universos, quod publice fit per maiorem partem.

6.[7] Cum tempus in testamento adiicitur, credendum est pro haerede adiectum, nisi alia mens fuerit testantis.

[260v] 7.[8] Quae in testamento ita scripta sunt ut intelligi non possint, perinde sunt, ac si scripta non essent.

8.[9] In poenalibus causis benignius interpretandum est.

9.[10] Fere in omnibus poenalibus iudiciis et aetati et imprudentiae succurritur.

10.[11] Imperitia culpae adnumeratur.

11.[12] Generi per speciem derogatur.

12.[13] Semper generalibus specialia insunt.

13.[14] In toto pars continetur.

14.[15] Accessorium naturam sequi congruit principalis.

[261r] 15.[16] Cum principalis causa non consistit, nec ea quae sequuntur locum habent.

---

[1]This title is inspired by X, 5.41 (Fr, II, 927-8) and especially by VI, 5.13 (Fr, II, 1122-4), which was composed by Pope Boniface VIII (1294-1303) and appended to the *Liber sextus* when it was promulgated on 3 March 1298. Marginal references in Cranmer's hand in the MS give the sources. As these do not relate to modern editions, they have been omitted and current references have been supplied instead.

[2]X, 5.41.4 (Fr, II, 927).

[3]VI, 5.13.78 (Fr, II, 1124).

[4]VI, 5.13.8 (Fr, II, 1122).

[5]VI, 5.13.29 (Fr, II, 1122).

[6]*Dig.*, 50.17.160 (120), originally Ulpian, *Ad edictum*, 76.

[7]*Dig.*, 50.17.17, originally from Ulpian, *Ad Sabinum*, 23.

[8]*Dig.*, 50.17.73, originally Quintus Mucius Scaevola, *Definitiones*, 1.

[9]VI, 5.13.49 (Fr, II, 1123); *Dig.*, 50.17.155 (197), originally Paulus, *Ad edictum*, 65.

[10]*Dig.*, 50.17.108, originally Paulus, *Ad edictum*, 4.

[11]*Dig.*, 50.17.132 (174), originally Gaius, *Ad edictum provinciale*, 7.

[12]VI, 5.13.34 (Fr, II, 1123); *Dig.* 50.17.80, originally Papinian, *Quaestionum*, 1.

[13]VI, 5.13.35 (Fr, II, 1123); *Dig.* 50.17.189, originally Gaius, *Ad edictum provinciale*, 24.

[14]VI, 5.13.80 (Fr, II, 1124); *Dig.*, 50.17.113, originally Gaius, *Ad edictum provinicale*, 3.

[15]VI, 5.13.42 (Fr, II, 1123).

[16]VI, 5.13.39 (Fr, II, 1123).

55. OF THE RULES OF LAW[1]

1.[2] Necessity makes permissible what is not permissible in law.

2.[3] Things which have been introduced because of necessity must not be drawn into dispute.

3.[4] Someone who is once evil is presumed to be always evil.

4.[5] What affects everyone must be approved by everyone.

5.[6] What is done publicly by a majority applies to all.

6.[7] When a time limit is included to a testament, it is to be believed that it was included for the heir, unless the testator intended otherwise.

7.[8] Things in a testament which are so written that they cannot be understood, are exactly as if they had not been written.

8.[9] In penal cases the most favourable interpretation is to be made.

9.[10] In almost all penal judgments there is mitigation on grounds of age and ignorance.

10.[11] Inexperience is counted as a fault.

11.[12] The general may be deduced from the particular.

12.[13] The particular always inheres in the general.

13.[14] The part is contained in the whole.

14.[15] It is fitting for the secondary to be compatible with the principal.

15.[16] When the main cause is not valid, those which follow have no standing.

16.[17] Non debet, cui quod plus est licet, quod minus est non licere.

17.[18] Non potest dolo carere, qui imperio magistratus non obtemperat.

18.[19] Haereditas est successio in universum ius, quod defunctus habuit tempore mortis.

19.[20] Qui*bus* rebus mobilibus praeficiuntur per defuncti testamentum, haeredes testamentarii sive executores appellamus.

20.[21] Haeredis appellatione omnes significari successores credendum est.

[261v; 150b] 21.[22] Nulla mora ibi intelligitur ubi nulla petitio est.

22.[23] Qui dolo desiit possidere, pro possessore damnatur.

23.[24] Quicquid calore iracundiae vel fit [*vel*/{**a**}**ut**] dicitur, non prius ratum est, quam si perseverantia apparuerit iudicium animi fuisse.

24.[25] Quoties idem sermo duas sententias exprimit, ea potissimum accipiatur, quae rei gerendae aptior est.

25.[26] In dubiis benigniora sunt praeferenda.

26.[27] In obscuris quod minimum est sequendum.

[262r] 27.[28] Secundum naturam est, commoda cuiusque rei eum sequi, quem sequuntur {*in*}commoda.

28.[29] Vani t[*im*/**emp**]oris non iusta excusatio est.

29.[30] Ratihabit{*at*}io retrahitur, et mandato aequiparatur.

30.[31] Ratum quis habere non potest, quod ipsius nomine gestum non est.

31.[32] Cum sint partium iura obscura, reo favendum est potius quam actori.

32.[33] Ignorantia facti non iuris excusat.

33.[34] Odia restringi, favores convenit ampliari.

---

[17]VI, 5.13.53 (Fr, II, 1123); *Dig.*, 50.17.21, originally Ulpian, *Ad Sabinum*, 27.

[18]VI, 5.13.24 (Fr, II, 1122); *Dig.* 50.17.199 (159), originally Javolenus, *Epistulae*, 6.

[19]VI, 5.13.46 (Fr, II, 1123); *Dig.*, 50.16.24, originally Gaius, *Ad edictum provinciale*, 6; ibid., 50.17.62, originally Julian, *Digesta*, 6.

[20]According to Cranmer's marginal note, this was based on *Dig.*, 50.16.70, originally Paulus, *Ad edictum*, 73, but it is greatly altered. This source makes no mention of *bona mobilia*, nor does the word 'executores' appear with this meaning anywhere in the *Corpus iuris civilis*.

[21]*Dig.*, 50.16.170, originally Ulpian, *Ad Sabinum*, 33.

[22]*Dig.*, 50.17.88, originally Scaevola, *Quaestiones*, 5; cf. VI, 5.13.25 (Fr, II, 1122).

[23]VI, 5.13.36 (Fr, II, 1123), *Dig.*, 50.17.181 (173), originally Paulus, *Ad edictum*, 22.

[24]*Dig.*, 50.17.48, originally Paulus, *Ad edictum*, 35.

[25]*Dig.*, 50.17.67, originally Julian, *Digesta*, 87.

[26]*Dig.*, 50.17.56, originally Gaius, *De legatis ad edictum urbicum*, 3.

[27]VI, 5.13.30 (Fr, II, 1122); *Dig.*, 50.17.9, originally Ulpian, *Ad Sabinum*, 15.

[28]*Dig.*, 50.17.10, originally Paulus, *Ad Sabinum*, 3.

[29]*Dig.*, 50.17.184 (144), originally Celsus, *Digesta*, 7.

[30]VI: 5.13.10 (Fr, II, 1122); cf. *Dig.*, 50.17.252 (194), originally Ulpian, *Ad edictum*, 69.

[31]VI, 5.13.9 (Fr, II, 1122).

[32]VI, 5.13.11 (Fr, II, 1122).

[33]VI, 5.13.13 (Fr, II, 1122).

[34]VI, 5.13.15 (Fr, II, 1122).

16.[17] It is not right that the one who may do what is greater may not do what is less.

17.[18] The person who does not obey the magistrate's authority cannot be innocent.

18.[19] Inheritance is succession into the full rights which the deceased had at the time of his death.

19.[20] Those who are put in charge of moveable goods by the testament of the deceased, we call testamentary heirs or executors.

20.[21] It is to be believed that all successors are intended by the name 'heir'.

21.[22] No delay shall be assumed where there is no request for one.

22.[23] One who has fraudulently ceased to be the possessor is condemned as the possessor.

23.[24] Something done or said in the heat of anger shall not be confirmed until it appears from perseverance to be the judgment of someone's mind.

24.[25] Whenever the same words have two meanings, the one which is more appropriate to the matter in question is to be preferred.

25.[26] In doubtful cases the more favourable choices are to be preferred.

26.[27] In obscure cases, the least damaging option is to be followed.

27.[28] It is according to nature that the advantages of something should follow him whom the {*dis*}advantages follow.

28.[29] Empty [*fear* **time**] is not a valid excuse.

29.[30] Ratification is withdrawn and is made equivalent to the mandate.

30.[31] No one can ratify something which has not been done in his name.

31.[32] When the rights of the parties are unclear, the accused is to be favoured over the plaintiff.

32.[33] Ignorance of the fact, but not of the law, is an excuse.

33.[34] It is fitting for hatred to be restrained and for favours to be extended.

34.[35] Decet concessum a principe beneficium esse mansurum.

[262v] 35.[36] Indultum a iure beneficium non est alicui auferendum.

36.[37] Nullus pluribus uti defensionibus prohibetur.

37.[38] Quod semel placuit, amplius displicere non potest.

38.[39] Non debet aliquis alterius odio praegravari.

39.[40] Sine culpa *non*, nisi subsit causa, non est aliquis puniendus.

40.[41] Scienti et conscienti non fit iniuria neque dolus.

41.[42] Utile per inutile non debet vitiari.

42.[43] Ex eo non debet quis fructus consequi, quod visus est impugnare.

[263r] 43.[44] Cum quid prohibetur, prohibentur omnia quae sequuntur ex eo.

44.[45] Pluralis locutio duorum numero est contenta.

[151a] 45.[46] Imputari non debet ei, per quem non stat, si non facit quod per eum fuerat faciendum.

46.[47] Qui tacet, consentire videtur.

47.[48] Qui tacet, non fatetur, sed nec utique negare videtur.

48.[49] Praesumitur ignorantia, ubi scientia non probetur.

[263v] 49.[50] Non praestat impedimentum, quod de iure non sortitur effectum.

50.[51] Qui prior est tempore, potior est iure.

51.[52] Quod ob gratiam alicuius conceditur, non est in eius dispendium retorquendum.

52.[53] Nullus ex consilio (dummodo fraudulentum non sit) obligatur.

53.[54] Exceptionem obiiciens non videtur de intentione adversarii confiteri.

54.[55] Quod suo nomine non licet, nec alieno licebit.

55.[56] Potest quis per alium, quod potest facere per seipsum.

---

[35]VI, 5.13.16 (Fr, II, 1122).
[36]VI, 5.13.17 (Fr, II, 1122).
[37]VI, 5.13.20 (Fr, II, 1122).
[38]VI, 5.13.21 (Fr, II, 1122).
[39]VI, 5.13.22 (Fr, II, 1122).
[40]VI, 5.13.23 (Fr, II, 1122).
[41]VI, 5.13.27 (Fr, II, 1122).
[42]VI, 5.13.37 (Fr, II, 1123).
[43]VI, 5.13.38 (Fr, II, 1123).
[44]VI, 5.13.39 (Fr, II, 1123).
[45]VI, 5.13.40 (Fr, II, 1123).
[46]VI, 5.13.41 (Fr, II, 1123).
[47]VI, 5.13.43 (Fr, II, 1123).
[48]VI, 5.13.44 (Fr, II, 1123); *Dig.*, 50.17.142 (184), originally Paulus, *Ad edictum*, 16.
[49]VI, 5.13.47 (Fr, II, 1123).
[50]VI, 5.13.52 (Fr, II, 1123).
[51]VI, 5.13.54 (Fr, II, 1123).
[52]VI, 5.13.61 (Fr, II, 1123).
[53]VI, 5.13.62 (Fr, II, 1124).
[54]VI, 5.13.63 (Fr, II, 1124).
[55]VI, 5.13.67 (Fr, II, 1124).
[56]VI, 5.13.68 (Fr, II, 1124).

34.[35] It is proper for a benefit granted by the king to remain.

35.[36] A benefit allowed by right is not to be taken away from anyone.

36.[37] No one is prohibited from making use of several defences.

37.[38] What once pleased, cannot later displease.

38.[39] No one must be burdened by the hatred of another.

39.[40] No one is to be punished without guilt, *not* unless there is some underlying reason.

40.[41] No harm or malice is done to someone who knows about and is conscious of it.

41.[42] What is useful must not be ruined by what is useless.

42.[43] No one should reap the rewards of what he has been seen to impugn.

43.[44] When something is forbidden, everything which follows from it is also forbidden.

44.[45] A plural expression may refer to only two in number.

45.[46] If someone does not do what was supposed to have been done by him, what he does not abide by ought not to be attributed to him.

46.[47] Whoever keeps silent is regarded as consenting.

47.[48] Whoever keeps silent does not confess, but neither does it appear that he denies.

48.[49] Ignorance is presumed where knowledge is not proved.

49.[50] What has no effect in law does not constitute an impediment.

50.[51] Whoever is earlier in time is stronger in law.

51.[52] What is allowed by someone's grace is not to be twisted to his disadvantage.

52.[53] No one is responsible for giving advice (as long as it is not fraudulent).

53.[54] Someone raising an exception is not regarded as accepting his opponent's claim.

54.[55] What is not permissible in one's own name is not permissible in someone else's name either.

55.[56] Someone may do through another what he may do by himself.

[264r] 56.[57] Quod alicui gratiose conceditur, non debet ab aliis in exemplum trahi.

57.[58] Delictum personae in detrimentum ecclesiae non debet redundare.

58.[59] In generali concessione non veniunt ea, quae quis non esset verisimiliter in spem[60] concessurus.

59.[61] Bona fides non patitur, ut bis idem exigatur.

60.[62] Cum quid una via prohibetur alicui, ad id alia non debet admitti.

61.[63] Infamibus non patent portae dignitatis.

62.[64] Is committit in legem, qui legis verba complectens contra legis nititur voluntatem.

[264v] 63.[65] Non quicquid iudicis potestat[i/e] permittitur, iuris necessitati subiicitur.

64.[66] De qua re cognov[er]it iudex, de ea quoque pronuntiare cogendus est.

65.[67] Nullus existimandus est dixisse, quod non mente prius agitaverit.

[151b] 66.[68] Pronuntiatio sermonis in sexu masculino ad utrumque sexum plerumque porrigitur.

67.[69] Quae esui, potui, cultuique corporis, quaeque ad vivendum huiusmodi necessaria sunt, vestimenta quoque et stramenta, et cetera, quibus vivendi curandive corporis nostri gratia utimur, victus verbo continentur.

[265r] 68.[70] Parent[i/e]s appellatione pater avus proavus et omnes superiores continentur; sed et mater avia et proavia.

69.[71] Liberorum appellatione nepotes et pronepotes ceterique qui ex his descendunt, continentur.

70.[72] Filii appellatione sicuti filia ita et nepos compraehenditur.

71.[73] Intestatus est, non tantum qui testamentum non facit, sed etiam is, cuius ex testamento haereditas [a/e]dita non est.

---

[57]VI, 5.13.74 (Fr, II, 1124).
[58]VI, 5.13.76 (Fr, II, 1124).
[59]VI; 5.12.81 (Fr, II, 1124).
[60]This is the reading of both the MS and the printed texts, but it is an error for 'specie' or 'speciem', as the original source attests.
[61]VI, 5.13.83 (Fr, II, 1124).
[62]VI, 5.13.84 (Fr, II, 1124).
[63]VI, 5.13.87 (Fr, II, 1124).
[64]VI, 5.13.88 (Fr, II, 1124).
[65]*Dig.*, 5.1.40, originally Papinian, *Quaestiones*, 4.
[66]*Dig.*, 5.1.74, originally Julian, *Digesta*, 5.
[67]*Dig.*, 33.10.7, originally Celsus, *Digesta*, 19.
[68]*Dig.*, 50.16.195, originally Ulpian, *Ad edictum*, 46.
[69]*Dig.*, 50.16.43-4, originally Ulpian, *Ad edictum*, 58 and Gaius, *Ad edictum provinciale*, 22 respectively.
[70]*Dig.*, 50.16.51, originally Gaius, *Ad edictum provinciale*, 23.
[71]*Dig.*, 50.16.220, originally Callistratus, *Quaestiones*, 2.
[72]*Dig.*, 50.16.201, originally Julian, *Digesta*, 81.
[73]*Dig.*, 50.16.64, originally Paulus, *Ad edictum*, 67.

56.[57] What is granted to someone by grace must not serve as a precedent for others.

57.[58] The crime of an individual must not redound to the detriment of the church.

58.[59] Those things which someone would probably not grant in particular[60] do not come by way of a general concession.

59.[61] Good faith does not allow the same thing to be demanded twice.

60.[62] When something is forbidden to somebody one way, he must not be allowed to have it in another way.

61.[63] The gates of dignity are not open to those of bad repute.

62.[64] The person who tries to go against the intention of the law by complicating the words of the law, commits a crime against the law.

63.[65] Not everything is allowed [*to* **by**] a judge's power; it is subject to the necessity of the law.

64.[66] A judge is obliged to pronounce on the same case which he has heard.

65.[67] No one must be thought to have said what has not previously crossed his mind.

66.[68] The use of the masculine gender often applies to both sexes.

67.[69] In the term 'sustenance' are included those things which are necessary for eating, drinking, clothing of the body, and whatever of that kind is needed for living, clothes also and coverings, and other things which we freely make use of for the survival and care of our body.

68.[70] In the term 'parent' are included the father, grandfather, great-grandfather and all ancestors, as well as the mother, grandmother and great-grandmother.

69.[71] In the term 'children' are included grandchildren, great-grandchildren and others who descend from them.

70.[72] In the term 'son' both a daughter and a grandson are included.

71.[73] It is not only someone who does not make a will who is intestate, but also someone whose inheritance is not mentioned in the testament.

[265v] 72.[74] Impensae necessariae sunt, quae si non faciant, res aut peritura est aut deterior fiet; utiles, quae rem meliorem faciunt; voluptuariae, quae speciem dumtaxat ornant.

73.[75] Usura pecuniae in fructu non est, quia non ex ipso corpore, sed ex alia causa est, id est, ex nova obligatione.

74.[76] Qui mortui quique abortivi ante septimum mensem aut octavum **nascuntur**, neque nati neque procreati videntur.

75.[77] Ea mulier creditur filium habere cum moriretur, qu[ae/i] exciso ventre eded/re possit; tamen falsum est eam peperisse, cui mortuae filius exsectus est.

[266r] 76.[78] Hominis appellatione tam feminam quam masculum contineri non dubitatur.

77.[79] Pueri appellatione etiam puella significatur.

78.[80] Solutionis verbo satisfactionem quoque omnem accipiendam placet, quam creditor acceptare voluerit.

79.[81] Qui in utero est, pro iam nato habetur, cum de ipsius commodo quaeritur.

80.[82] Duobus negativis verbis quasi permittit lex magis quam prohibet.

[266v; 152a] 81.[83] Silva caedua est, quae in hoc habetur ut cr{a}edatur, et quae succisa rursus ex stirpibus aut radicibus renascitur.

82.[84] Authentica sigilla declaramus nostra, archiepiscoporum, episcoporum, decanorum, ecclesiarum cathedralium et earundem ecclesiarum capitulorum, archidiaconorum, et eorum officialium. Quae penes ipsos aut ipsorum legitimos deputatos, et nullo modo apud suos registrarios seu actorum scribas, custodiri volumus.

---

[74]*Dig.*, 50.16.79, originally Paulus, *Ad Plautium*, 6.
[75]*Dig.*, 50.16.121, originally Pomponius, *Ad Quintum Mucium*, 6.
[76]*Dig.*, 50.16.129, originally Paulus, *Ad legem Iuliam et Papiam*, 1.
[77]*Dig.*, 50.16.141, originally Ulpian, *Ad legem Iuliam et Papiam*, 8.
[78]*Dig.*, 50.16.152, originally Gaius, *Ad legem Iuliam et Papiam*, 10.
[79]*Dig.*, 50.16.163, originally Paulus, *Ad Sabinum*, 2.
[80]*Dig.*, 50.16.176, originally Ulpian, *Ad Sabinum*, 45.
[81]Adapted from *Dig.*, 50.16.131, originally Paulus, *Ad senatusconsultum Tertullianum*, 1.
[82]*Dig.*, 50.16.237, originally Gaius, *Ad legem duodecim tabularum*, 5.
[83]*Dig.*, 50.16.30, originally Gaius, *Ad edictum provinciale*, 7; also L, 5.18.1, originally c.6 of the constitutions of Archbishop John Stratford, 1342.
[84]1237/28 (PC, 257-8).

72.[74] Necessary expenses are those which, if they were not made, would cause the matter would either to collapse or to deteriorate; useful expenses are those which make a thing better; voluptuary expenses are those which only decorate the appearance.

73.[75] Interest on money is not part of the income because it does not come from the capital sum itself, but from another source, that is, from a new obligation.

74.[76] Those who are **born** dead or who have been aborted before the seventh or eighth month are not regarded as having been born or procreated.

75.[77] A dying woman is regarded as having a child if she can give birth to him when her womb is cut open, but it is wrong to say that she has given birth if the child is taken out of her after she has died.

76.[78] In the term 'man' it is not to be doubted that both the masculine and the feminine are included.

77.[79] By the term 'boy' a girl is also meant.

78.[80] By the word 'payment' all satisfaction is to be understood which the creditor is willing to accept.

79.[81] One who is in the womb is regarded as already born, when it is a question of his interest.

80.[82] By a double negative the law permits something rather than prevents it.

81.[83] A timber wood is one which has trees which can be felled, and which when felled will grow back again from the stems or roots.

82.[84] We declare the following seals to be authentic: ours, those of the archbishops, bishops, deans, cathedral churches and the chapters of those churches, archdeacons, and their officials. These we wish to be kept by them or by their lawful deputies, and under no circumstances by their registrars or recorders.

APPENDIXES

1. THE FOLIO PAGES IN MS HARLEIAN 426 (British Library)

MS Harleian 426 contains a number of folio pages which are blank, or almost so, and others which have indexes or other jottings made at different times. There are also two different systems of numbering them, of which the first is original and the second was added by a curator of the British Museum in December 1875. For the main text of this edition, the original numbers have been used, but the following tables make it possible to correlate the two systems and detect which folios are blank (or nearly so). When something has been written on an otherwise blank folio page, that is indicated next to the number in the list of blank folios, except when the notes are too extensive, in which cases they are given in separate tables at the end. The running heads were put there by Archbishop Cranmer; additions in John Foxe's hand are indicated as such.

A. Correlation of the folio numbers

Original	1875	Original	1875
-	1	142-3	-
-	2	144-7	129-32
-	3	150	-
1-4	4-7	148-9	133-4
5	-	151-80	135-64
6-27	8-29	181	-
32-54	30-52	182-92	165-75
58-65	53-60	193	-
68-78	61-71	194-9	176-81
79	-	200-1	-
80-102	72-94	202-58	182-238
103	-	259	-
104-8	95-9	260-6	239-45
109-11	-	267	-
112-36	100-24	268-9	246-7
137	-	269-80	248-59
138-41	125-8	-	260-7

B. Blank folios

Original	1875	
-	1	Cranmer's list of titles (see below)
-	2r	John Foxe's list of titles (see below)
-	2v	-
-	3r	De summa Trinitate et fide catholica (title page)
-	3v	-
5	-	-
21v	23v	-
23r	25r	A partial list of titles and headings in John Foxe's hand (see below)
23v	25v	-
27v	29v	Foxe: De iuramento calumniae, require fol. 168.
28-31	-	Moved to 112-15.
35v	33v	De contionatoribus (running head)
36r	34r	De matrimonio (title page)
36v	34v	-
42v	40v	De matrimonio (running head)
43	41	De matrimonio (running head)
47	45	De gradibus in matrimonio prohibitis (running head)
54	52	De adulteriis et divortio (running head)
55	-	Missing from the MS.
56-7	-	Moved to 116-17.
66-7	-	Moved to 268-9.
79	-	-
82r	74r	Formula reconciliationis excommunicatorum (title page)
82v	74v	-
89v	81v	-
90r officiis	82r	De ecclesia et ministris eius illorumque (title page)
90v	82v	-
99v	91v	-
103	-	-
105v	96v	-
109-11	-	-
115v	103v	De crimine falsi (running head) Foxe: De testibus eorumque dictis require in fo. 119.
116v	104v	De violenta percussione clericorum (running head)

117	105	De violenta percussione clericorum (running head)
118r	106r	De testibus (title page). For Mr Morres.
118v	106v	-
136v	124v	-
137	-	-
142-3	-	-
150	-	- (Misplaced between 147 and 148).
167v fol.	151v	Foxe: De iuramento et periuriis, require in 24.
171v	155v	Foxe: De probationibus, require fol. 154.
181	-	-
193	-	-
199v	181v	Foxe: De crimine falsi, require in fol. 112.
200-1	-	-
207v	187v	-
212r	192r	De appellationibus (title page). For Mr Morres.
212v	192v	-
231v	211v	Foxe: De regulis iuris, require in fol. 260.
258v	238v	Foxe: De appellationibus, require in fol. 263.
259	-	-
267	-	-
269v	247v	-
269 (2)r	248r	De dilapidationibus. De alienatione et elocatione bonorum ecclesiasticorum. De electione. (title page)
269 (2)v	248v	-
273r	252r	-
275v	254v	-
276v	255v	-

C. List of titles in Archbishop Cranmer's hand

The titles in italics were crossed out by Cranmer when he rearranged them.

De summa Trinitate et fide Catholica	fo. 1r-4v
De haeresibus	fo. 6r-17r
De iudiciis contra haereses	fo. 17r-21r
De blasphemia	fo. 22r-22v
De iuramentis et periuriis	fo. 24r-27r
De crimine falsi	*fo. 28r-31r*
De contionatoribus	fo. 32r-35r
De matrimonio	fo. 37r-42r
De gradibus in matrimonio prohibitis	fo. 44r-46v
De adulteriis et divortiis	fo. 48r-53v
De violenta percussione clericorum	*fo. 56r*
De admittendis ad ecclesiastica beneficia	fo. 58r-65v
De defamationibus	fo. 66r-67r[1]
De beneficiis ecclesiasticis sine diminutione conferendis	fo. 68r-69v
De divinorum officiorum celebratione	fo. 70r-75v
De sacramentis	fo. 76r-78v
De idolatria et aliis huiusmodi criminibus	fo. 80r-81r
Formula reconciliationis excommunicatorum	fo. 83r-89r
De ecclesia et ministris eius	fo. 91r-99r
De ecclesiarum gardianis	fo. 100r-102v
De parochiarum limitatione	fo. 104r-105r
De scholis in ecclesiis cathedralibus	fo. 106r-107v
De academiis	fo. 108r-108v
De crimine falsi	fo. 112r-115r
De violenta percussione clericorum	fo. 116r
De testibus	fo. 119r-136v
De praesumptionibus	fo. 138r-141v
De decimis[2]	fo. 144r-149v
De pensionibus (et visitationibus)	fo. 151r-153v
De probationibus	fo. 154r-158v
De possessione	fo. 159r-159v
De consuetudine	fo. 160r-161v
De litis contestatione	fo. 162r-167r
De iuramento calumniae	fo. 168r-171r
De dilationibus	fo. 172r-180v
De iudiciis	fo. 182r-192v
De fide instrumentorum	fo. 194r-199v

[1]Moved in the MS but not crossed out.
[2]In the MS, fo. 1v begins here.

Added later in another hand:

Added by John Foxe:

Haec capita hic desiderantur:

[3]"Cap[ut] alt[erum]' is crossed out next to this in the MS.

D. List of titles in John Foxe's hand

Ordo titulorum in codice Domini Matthaei Cantuariensis
[Order of the titles in the manuscript of Archbishop Matthew Parker]

1.	De summa Trinitate
2.	De haeresibus
3.	De iudiciis contra haereses
4.	De blasphemia
5.	De sacramentis
6.	De idololatria et aliis huiusmodi
7.	De contionatoribus
8.	De matrimonio
9.	De gradibus in matrimonio prohibitis
10.	De adulteriis et divortiis
11.	De admittendis in ecclesiastica beneficia
12.*	De renuntiatione vel desertione beneficiorum
13.*	De permutatione beneficiorum
14.*	De purgatione
15.*	De dilapidationibus
16.*	De alienatione vel elocatione beneficiorum
17.*	De electione
18.	De beneficiis sine diminutione conferendis
19.	De temporibus divinorum officiorum in cathedralibus etc.
20.	De ecclesia et ministris eius illorumque officiis
21.	De ecclesiae gardianis
22.	De parochiarum limitatione
23.	De scholis habendis in ecclesiis cathedralibus
24.	De academiis
25.	De decimis
26.	De pensionibus
27.	De visitationibus
28.	De testamentis
29.	De poenis ecclesiasticis
30.	De suspensione
31.	De fructuum deductione vel sequestratione
32.	De deprivatione
33.	De excommunicatione
34.	Formula reconciliationis excommunicatorum
35.	De iudiciis
36.	De officio et iurisdictione omnium iudicum
37.	De litis contestatione
38.	De iuramentis et periuriis
39.	De iuramento calumniae
40.	De probationibus

41.   De fide instrumentorum
42.   De crimine falsi
43.   De testibus eorumque dictis
44.   De consuetudine
45.   De praescriptionibus
46.   De violenta percussione clericorum
47.   De praesumptionibus
48.   De defamationibus
49.   De dilationibus
50.   De exceptionibus
51.   De sententia et re iudicata
52.   De appellationibus
53.   De regulis iuris

*A line linking these is accompanied by the notation: 'Vide fol. 65b' ('See folio 65v').

This list correlates with the present edition as follows:

1-25 are the same in both.
26 is now 25.19.
27-34 correspond to 26-33.
35 is now divided into 34-6.
36-40 correspond to 37-41.
The last section of 40 is now chapter 42.
41-53 correspond to 43-55.

E. The list on folio 23r of the MS (in John Foxe's hand)

The words in italics were susbequently crossed out.

De sacramentis	fo. 76
De baptismo	fo. eod.
De eucharistia	fo. 77
De admittendis ad ecclesiastica beneficia	fo. eod.
De impositione manuum	fo. 78
De nuptiis celebrandis, etc.	ibid.
De tempore confirmationis	eod.
De pastorum visitatione	eod.
Quomodo in his procedendum	eod.
De idolatria et aliis huiusmodi criminbus	fo. 80
Quae vitanda	
De idolorum cultu	eod.
De magia	eod.
De divinatione	eod.
De sortilegio	eod.
De superstitione	eod.
De pastoris officio in his criminibus	fo. 81
Qui propter haec crimina puniendi	eod.
De damno compensando	eod.
De contionatoribus a capite 1 ad caput 6	

In exemplari Cantuariensis haec inseruntur capita, quae in hoc codice desiderantur.

Contionandi munus quale sit et quomodo suscipi debeat	*fo. 32*
Contionatoribus errores esse vitandos **cavendos**[4] *et*	
errorum libros	*fo. eod.*
Contionatorum et mores et doctrina quales esse debeant	*fo. eod.*
Ad quos contionandi munus proprie pertineat	*fo. 33*
De consecrandis per episcopum contionatoribus	*fo. 34*
De his qui interesse debent contionatoribus	*fo. eod.*
Quid de his statuendum qui contionibus obstrepunt	*fo. 35*

De matrimonio	fo. 37-47
De adulteriis et divortiis	fo. 48-58

---

[4] 'Vitandos' was crossed out and replaced by 'cavendos' which was then crossed out along with the rest of the title.

De admittendis ad ecclesiastica beneficia   fo. 58

Repeated at top right hand of page:

De sacramentis   fo. 76
    De baptismo   fo. eod.
    De eucharistia   fo. 77

2. TITLES OF THE *DECRETALS*

The following is a list of the titles of all the chapters in the *Decretals* of Pope Gregory IX, together with their correspondences in the other parts of the *Corpus iuris canonici*, which are the *Liber sextus* (VI), the *Clementinae* (C), the *Extravagantes Iohannis XXII* (EJ) and the *Extravagantes communes* (EC), as well as in the *Provinciale* of William Lyndwood, the Henrician canons of 1535 and the *Reformatio legum ecclesiasticarum* in its final 1571 form. (*N.B.* The correspondence of titles is not always exact, and does not necessarily mean that the content is identical - or even very similar.)

Book I

Title (in X)	X	VI	C	EJ	EC	L	HC	R
De summa Trinitate et fide Catholica	1	1	1			1	1	1
De constitutionibus	2	2				2		
De rescriptis	3	3	2					
De consuetudine	4	4			1	3		46
De postulatione praelatorum	5	5			2			
De electione	6	6	3	1	3		15	17
De translatione episcopi	7							
De auctoritate et usu palliae	8				4			
De renuntiatione	9	7	4				16	12
De supplenda negligentia praelatorum	10	8	5				17	
De temporibus ordinationum et qualitate ordinandorum	11	9				4	18	
De scrutinio in ordine faciendo	12					5		
De ordinatis ab episcopo qui renuntiavit episcopatui	13							
De aetate et qualitate et ordine praeficiendorum	14	10	6					
De sacra unctione	15					6		
De sacramentis non iterandis	16					7		5
De filiis presbyterorum ordinandis vel non	17	11				8		
De servis non ordinandis et eorum manumissione	18							
De obligatis ad ratiocinia ordinandis vel non	19							

Title (in X)	X	VI	C	EJ	EC	L	HC	R
De corpore vitiatis ordinandis vel non	20							
De bigamis non ordinandis	21	12						
De clericis peregrinis	22					9		
De officio archidiaconi	23					10		20
De officio archipresbyteri	24					11		20
De officio primicerii	25							20
De officio sacristae	26							20
De officio custodis	27				5		34	21
De officio vicarii	28	13	7			12		
De officio et potestate iudicis delegati	29	14	8		6			37
De officio legati	30	15						
De officio iudicis ordinarii	31	16	9		7	13		37
De officio iudicis	32							37
De maioritate et oboedientia	33	17		2	8	14		
De treuga et pace	34				9	15		
De pactis	35	18						
De transactionibus	36					16		
De postulando	37					17		
De procuratoribus	38	19	10			18		29
De syndico	39							
De his quae vi metusve causa fiunt	40	20						
De in integrum restitutione	41	21	11					
De alienatione iudicii mutandi causa facta	42							
De arbitris	43	22						

Book II

Title	X	VI	C	EJ	EC	L	HC	R
De iudiciis	1	1	1		1	1		34 -6
De foro competenti	2	2	2			2		
De libelli oblatione	3							
De mutuis petitionibus	4							
De litis contestatione	5	3						38
Ut lite non contestata non procedatur ad testium receptionem vel ad sententiam definitivam	6							
De iuramento calumniae	7	4						40
De dilationibus	8				2			51
De feriis	9					3		
De ordine cognitionum	10							
De plus petitionibus	11							
De causa possessionis et proprietatis	12		3					42

Title (in X)	X	VI	C	EJ	EC	L	HC	R
De restitutione spoliatorum	13	5						
De dolo et contumacia	14	6	4		3			
De eo qui mittitur in possessionem causa rei servandae	15	7						
Ut lite pendente nihil innovetur	16	8	5					
De sequestratione possessionum et fructuum	17		6				4 33	30
De confessis	18	9						
De probationibus	19		7					41
De testibus et attestationibus	20	10	8					45
De testibus cogendis vel non	21							
De fide instrumentorum	22							43
De praesumptionibus	23					5		49
De iureiurando	24	11	9			6		39
De exceptionibus	25	12	10					52
De praescriptionibus	26	13						47
De sententia et re iudicata	27	14	11					53
De appellationibus, recusationibus et relationibus	28	15	12			7	36	54
De clericis peregrinantibus	29							
De confirmatione utili vel inutili	30							

Book III

	X	VI	C	EJ	EC	L	HC	R
De vita et honestate clericorum	1	1	1		1	1		
De cohabitatione clericorum et mulierum	2					2		
De clericis coniugatis	3	2				3		
De clericis non residentibus in ecclesia vel praebenda	4	3				4	19	
De praebendis et dignitatibus	5	4	2	3	2	5		
De clerico aegrotante vel debilitato	6	5						
De institutionibus	7	6				6	20	11
De concessione praebendae et ecclesiae non vacantis	8	7	3	4		7		
Ne sede vacante aliquid innovetur	9	8		5	3			
De his quae fiunt a praelato sine consensu capituli	10							
De his quae fiunt a maiore parte capituli	11							
Ut ecclesiastica beneficia sine diminutione conferantur	12							18
De rebus ecclesiae alienandis vel non	13	9	4		4	8		
De precariis	14							

Title (in X)	X	VI	C	EJ	EC	L	HC	R
De commodato	15							
De deposito	16							
De emptione et venditione		17				5		
De locato et conducto	18					9		16
De rerum permutatione	19	10	5				21	13
De feudis	20							
De pignoribus et aliis cautionibus	21					10		
De fideiussoribus	22							
De solutionibus	23							
De donationibus	24					11		
De peculio clericorum	25					12		
De testamentis et ultimis voluntatibus	26	11	6			13	31	27
De successionibus ab intestato	27							
De sepulturis	28	12	7		6	14		
De parochis et alienis parochianis	29					15	32	22
De decimis, primitiis et oblationibus	30	13	8		7	16	24	25
De regularibus et transeuntibus ad religionem	31	14	9		8	17		
De conversione coniugatorum	32							
De conversione infidelium	33							
De voto et voti redemptione	34	15		6		18		
De statu monachorum et canonicorum regularium	35	16	10			19		
De religiosis domibus, ut episcopo sint subiectae	36	17	11	7	9	20		
De capellis monachorum et aliorum religiosorum	37	18						
De iure patronatus	38	19	12			21		
De censibus, exactionibus et procurationibus	39	20	13		10	22	28	25
De consecratione ecclesiae et altaris	40	21						
De celebratione missarum et sacramento eucharistiae et divinis officiis	41		14		11	23		19
De baptismo et eius effectu	42		15			24		
De presbytero non baptizato	43							
De custodia eucharistiae, chrismatis et aliorum sacramentorum	44					25		
De reliquiis et veneratione sanctorum	45	22	16		12	26		
De observatione ieiuniorum	46							
De purificatione post partum	47							
De ecclesiis aedificandis vel reparandis	48					27	30	15
De immunitate ecclesiarum, coemeterii et rerum ad eas pertinentium	49	23	17		13	28		

Title (in X)	X	VI	C	EJ	EC	L	HC	R
Ne clerici vel monachi saecularibus negotiis se immisceant	50	24				29		

Book IV

Title (in X)	X	VI	C	EJ	EC	L	HC	R
De sponsalibus et matrimoniis	1	1				1	22	8
De desponsatione impuberum	2	2				2		
De clandestina desponsatione	3					3		
De sponsa duorum	4							
De conditionibus appositis in desponsatione vel in aliis contractibus	5							
Qui clerici vel voventes matrimonium contrahere possunt	6							
De eo qui duxit in matrimonium quam polluit per adulterium	7							
De coniugio leprosorum	8							
De coniugio servorum	9							
De natis ex libero ventre	10							
De cognatione spirituali	11	3					9	
De cognatione legali	12						9	
De eo qui cognovit consanguineam uxoris suae vel sponsae	13						9	
De consanguinitate et affinitate	14		1				9	
De frigidis et maleficiatis et impotentia coeundi	15							
De matrimonio contracto contra interdictum ecclesiae	16							
Qui filii sint legitimi	17							
Qui matrimonium accusare possunt vel contra illud testari	18							
De divortiis	19						23	10
De donationibus inter virum et uxorem, et de dote post divortium restituenda	20							
De secundis nuptiis		21						

Book V

Title (in X)	X	VI	C	EJ	EC	L	HC	R
De accusationibus, inquisitionibus et denuntiationibus	1	1				1	11	
De calumniatoribus		2					9	50

Title (in X)	X	VI	C	EJ	EC	L	HC	R
De simonia, et ne aliquid pro spiritualibus exigatur vel promittatur	3				1	2	3	
Ne praelati vices suas vel ecclesias sub annuo censu concedant	4					3		
De magistris, et ne aliquid exigatur pro licentia docendi	5		1			4		23 -4
De Iudaeis, Sarracenis et eorum servis	6		2	8	2			
De haereticis	7	2	3		3	5		2- 3
De schismaticis et ordinatis ab eis	8	3			4			
De apostatis et reiterantibus baptisma	9					6		
De his qui filios occiderunt	10					7		
De infantibus et languidis expositis	11							
De homicidio voluntario vel casuali	12	4	4			8		
De torneamentis	13			9				
De clericis pugnantibus in duello		14						
De sagitariis	15							
De adulteriis et stupro	16						4	10
De raptoribus, incendiariis et violatoribus ecclesiarum	17							
De furtis	18				5	9		
De usuris	19	5	5					
De crimine falsi	20			10	6		5	44
De sortilegiis	21						7	6
De collusione detegenda	22							
De delictis puerorum	23							
De clerico venatore	24					10		
De clerico percussore	25							
De maledicis	26						8	4
De clerico excommunicato, deposito vel interdicto ministrante	27							
De clerico non ordinato ministrante	28							
De clerico per saltum promoto	29							
De eo qui furtive ordinem suscepit	30					11		
De excessibus praelatorum et subditorum	31	6	6			12		10
De novi operis nuntiatione	32							
De privilegiis et excessibus privilegiatorum	33	7	7	11	7	13		
De purgatione canonica	34					14	12	14
De purgatione vulgari	35						12	14
De iniuriis et damno dato	36	8						
De poenis	37	9	8	12	8	15	13	28

Title (in X)	X	VI	C	EJ	EC	L	HC	R
De paenitentiis et remissionibus	38	10	9		9	16		
De sententia excommunicationis	39	11	10	13	10	17	14	32, 48
De verborum significatione	40	12	11	14		18		
De regulis iuris	41	13						55

3. THE *REFORMATIO* AND THE *DECRETALS*

The following tables list the titles which were taken up and used by the *Reformatio*, giving them first in the order of the *Dceretals* (X) and then in that of the *Reformatio*, both in the 1571 printed edition (given first) and in the 1552 MS. The form of the titles is that found in the *Reformatio*.

X	1571/1552	
1.1	1	De summa Trinitate et fide Catholica
1.4	46/29	De consuetudine
1.6	17/44	De electionibus
1.9	12	De renuntiatione
1.16	5/13	De sacramentis
1.23-6	20/16	De ecclesia et ministris eius
1.27	21/17	De gardianis
1.29, 31-2	37/38	De iudicibus
2.1	34-6/33	De iudiciis
2.5	38/30	De contestatione litis
2.7	40/31	De iuramento calumniae
2.8	51/32	De dilationibus
2.12 ?	42/28	De possessionibus
2.17	30	De sequestratione
2.19	41/27	De probationibus
2.20	45/23	De testibus
2.22	43/34	De fide instrumentorum
2.23	49/24	De praesumptionibus
2.24	39/5	De iuramentis
2.25	52/35	De exceptionibus
2.26	47/36	De praescriptionibus
2.27	53/39	De sententia et re iudicata
2.28	54/37	De appellationibus
3.7	11/10	De admittendis ad ecclesiastica beneficia
3.12	18/11	De beneficiis sine diminutione conferendis
3.18	16/43	De alienatione bonorum ecclesiasticorum
3.19	13	De permutatione beneficiorum

765

X	1571/1552	
3.26	27/45	De testamentis
3.29	22/18	De paroechiarum limitatione
3.30	25/25	De decimis
3.39	25.19/26	De visitationibus
3.41	19/12	De divinis officiis
3.48	15/42	De dilapidationibus
4.1	8/7	De matrimonio
4.11-14	9/8	De consanguinitate et affinitate
4.19	10/9	De divortio
5.2	50/41	De defamationibus
5.5	23/19	De scholis
	24/20	De collegiis
5.7	2, 3	De haereticis
5.16	10/9	De adulteriis
5.20	44/21	De crimine falsi
5.21	6/14	De idololatria
5.26	4	De blasphemia
5.34-5	14	De purgatione
5.37	28	De poenis ecclesiasticis
5.39	32	De excommunicatione
	48/22	De violenta percussione clericorum
5.41	55/40	De regulis iuris

1571 (Foxe)	X	1552 (MS)	X
1	1	1	1
2	5.7	2	5.7
3	5.7	3	5.7
4	5.26	4	5.26
5	1.16	5	2.24
6	5.21	6	
7		7	4.1
8	4.1	8	4.11-14
9	4.11-14	9	4.19; 5.16
10	4.19; 5.16	10	3.7
11	3.7	11	3.12
12	1.9	12	3.41
13	3.19	13	1.16
14	5.35-6	14	5.21
15	3.48	15	(5.39)
16	3.18	16	1.23-6
17	1.6	17	1.27
18	3.12	18	3.29
19	3.41	19	5.5
20	1.23-6	20	5.5
21	1.27	21	5.20
22	3.29	22	5.2
23	5.5	23	2.20
24	5.5	24	2.23
25	3.30	25	3.30
26	3.39	26	3.39
27	3.26	27	2.19
28	5.37	28	2.12 ?
29	(5.39)	29	1.4
30	2.17	30	2.5
31	(5.39)	31	2.7; 5.2
32	5.39	32	2.8
33	(5.39)	33	2.1
34	2.1	34	2.22
35	2.1	35	2.25
36	2.1	36	2.26
37	1.29, 31-2	37	2.28
38	2.5	38	1.29, 31-2
39	2.24	39	2.27
40	2.7; 5.2	40	5.41
41	2.19	41	5.2
42	2.12 ?	42	3.48
43	2.22	43	3.18
44	5.20	44	1.6

1571 (Foxe)	X	1552 (MS)	X
45	2.20	45	3.26
46	1.4		
47	2.26		
48	(5.39)		
49	2.23		
50	5.2		
51	2.8		
52	2.25		
53	2.27		
54	2.28		
55	5.41		

4. FROM THE HENRICIAN CANONS TO THE *REFORMATIO*

The following tables list the Henrician canons of 1535 in order and show how they were taken up by the compilers of the *Reformatio* at the different editorial stages which we can recover from the MS evidence. The latter are as follows:

A. The original scribal order (in so far as this can be recovered).
B¹. Archbishop Cranmer's first reordering (1552).
B²⁻³. Archbishop Cranmer's second reordering, plus additions (1552).
C. The order of Archbishop Matthew Parker's MS (probably 1553).

The Roman numerals in A stand for different scribal hands. The numbering of C (which is the order also followed by Foxe's printed version) has been modified to correspond to the present edition.

1535	A	B¹	B²⁻³	C
1	I, 1	1	1	1
2	I, 6	7	6	7
3				
4	I, 9	10	9	10
5	I, 5	6	21	44
6	I, 4	5	5	39
7				
8	I, 3	4	4	4
9	I, 12	13	41	50
10				
11				
12				14
13				28
14				32
15			III, 21 (44)	17
16				12
17				
18				
19				
20	I, 11	12	10	11
21				13

1535	A	B¹	B²⁻³	C
22	I, 7	8	7	8
23	I, 9	10	9	10
24	I, 18	26	25	25
25				
26				
27				
28				
29				
30			III, 19 (42)	15
31			IV, 1 (45)	27
32	III, 2	21	18	22
33				30
34	III, 1	20	17	21
35	III, 8	31	30	38
36	III, 15	38	37	54

There is slightly more correspondence if the 1535 titles are arranged in groups as follows:

1535	B¹	B²⁻³
Group 1 (1-10)	(1, 2, 6)	(1, 2, 7)
Group 2 (11-14)	-	6
Group 3 (15-21)	2-3	3
Group 4 (22-31)	2, 6	2, 5
Group 5 (32-4)	4	4
Group 6 (35-6)	6	7

Within the *Reformatio* itself, the evolution of the order of the titles can be charted as follows:

A	B^1	B^2	C
I, 1	1	1	1
I, 2	2-3	2-3	2-3
I, 3	4	4	4
I, 4	5	5	39
I, 5	6	21	44
I, 6	7	6	7
I, 7	8	7	8
I, 8	9	8	9
I, 9	10	9	10
I, 10	11	22	48
I, 11	12	10	11
I, 12	13	41	50
I, 13	14	11	18
I, 14	18	15	33
I, 15	19	16	20
I, 16	22	19	23
I, 17	23	20	24
I, 18	26	25	25
I, 19	27	26	25.19-26
II, 1	15	12	19
II, 2	16	13	5
II, 3	17	14	6
III, 1	20	17	21
III, 2	21	18	22
III, 3	24	23	45
III, 4	25	24	49
III, 5	28	27	41
III, 6	29	28	42
III, 7	30	29	46
III, 8	31	30	38
III, 9	32	31	40
III, 10	33	32	51
III, 11	34	33	34-6
III, 12	35	34	43
III, 13	36	35	52
III, 14	37	36	47
III, 15	38	37	54

A	B¹	B²	C
III, 16	39	38	37
III, 17	40	39	53
III, 18	41	40	55

		[B³]	
		III, 19 (42)	15
		III, 20 (43)	16
		III, 21 (44)	17
		IV, 1 (45)	27
			12
			13
			14
			28
			29
			30
			31
			32

5. THE *REFORMATIO* IN BISHOP EDMUND GIBSON'S *CODEX*

Bishop Edmund Gibson's *Codex iuris Ecclesiae Anglicanae* first appeared in 1713 and soon established itself as a standard work on the subject of ecclesiastical law. His comments on the *Reformatio* thus acquired a semi-canonical status of their own, which lasted at least until Edward Cardwell produced a complete edition of the work in 1850. All Gibson's comments and quotations are reproduced below, for ease of reference, with the chapter and page of the *Codex* preceding the title and chapter of the *Reformatio* (R). The extracts are given in the order in which they appear in the *Codex*, with a reverse index appended at the end.

Preface (ix): For method's sake, the constituent parts of this work shall be first divided into several heads, and then each head shall be spoken to briefly, and as far only as is necessary by way of preface: viz. 1. Statutes, 2. Constitutions, 3. Canons, 4, Rubrics, 5. Articles, 6. Abridgment, 7. Commentary, 8. Rules of Common and Canon Law, 9. Appendix, 10. Index.

    (xiv, under 'Commentary'): The citations of ancient and modern councils and synods which have been held at home and abroad (as they are annexed here by way of commentary to our present laws) are designed to show, on one hand, that though many of the laws are modern, the constitution is ancient; and on the other hand to facilitate the improvement of this constitution by suggesting such useful rules of order and discipline as have been established abroad or attempted at home. With which last view it is that may of the passages out of the body of ecclesiastical laws entitled *Reformatio legum etc.* are grafted into this commentary as candidates for a place in our constitution in case the convocation shall think them deserving, or at least as not unworthy the consideration of that learned and venerable assembly.

I, 4 (10-11). R, 48.1-2. Agreeably to this (i.e. X, 5.39.2) the *Reformatio legum* has fixed it: 1. *Quicunque manus violentas in clericum sciens iniecerit, nisi voluerit arbitratu iudicum ecclesiasticorum ei satisfacere, paenitentiamque subire tam atroci scelere dignam, in excommunicationem ruet. A qua nullo modo patimur illum sublevari, donec paenitentia plene sit perfunctus, ordinarii sui arbitratu indicenda.* To all which rules the practice of the Church of England hath been conformable, both before and since the reformation, as appears by the forms of absolution which we frequently meet with in our ecclesiastical records.

I must not omit what the same *Reformatio legum* adds: 2... *Esto quoque par clericorum poena, si violentas manus in laicos homines iniecerint.*

II, 3 (63). R, 37.2. King Edward VI, in whose reign the *Reformatio legum* thus expresses the notion they had of the royal supremacy: *Rex tam in archiepiscopos, episcopos, clericos, et alios ministros, quam in laicos infra sua regna et dominia plenissimam iurisdictionem, tam civilem quam ecclesiasticam, habet et exercere potest, cum omnis iurisdictio et ecclesiastica et saecularis ab eo tanquam ex uno et eodem fonte derivantur.*

V, 3 (158). R, 20.16. And the *Reformatio legum* urges that, by parity of reason, coadjutors ought to be assigned to bishops: *Quemadmodum episcopi ministris inferioribus, cum iam vel propter morbum incurabilem desperatum vel...propter senectutem, ecclesiam ministrare diutius non possint, adiutores apponere debent; sic etiam illis ob easdem causas ab archiepiscopo dabuntur, modo noster consensus interveniat.*

XVII, 3 (410). R, 3.1. The rule laid down in the *Reformatio legum* is thus: *Is qui vel accusatione, vel inquisitione, vel evangelica denuntiatione reus fit, quod aliquam haeresim, aut affirmaverit aut defenderit, aut praedicaverit aut docuerit, coram episcopo vel archiepiscopo causam dicet. Qui vero loci privilegium habent, et exempti dicuntur, apud illos vel episcopos vel archiepiscopos causam dicent intra quorum dioeceses illorum exempti loci constiterint. Appellatio tamen reo conceditur, ab episcopo ad archiepiscopum, et ab archiepiscopo nostram ad regalem personam.*

XIX, I (453). R, 19.9. In the *Reformatio legum* there is an excellent rule upon this head: *Pomeridiani temporis horam primam minister explicando catechismo tribuat ... aliquid eo amplius, si videbitur .... Catechismum pertractet vel ipse parochus, vel eius vicarius et magnam in eo diligentiam adhibeat; summam enim utilitatem et praestantem usum habet in ecclesia Dei frequens inculcatio catechismi, quem non solum a pueris edisci, sed etiam ab adolescentibus attendi volumus, ut in summa religionis erudiantur, et puerorum piam assiduitatem sua praesentia cohonestent.*

XIX, 2 (454). R, 20.12. The *Reformatio legum* seems to direct annual confirmations: *... statis temporibus annuatim synodos habeat; illi quoque sit curae ut ... in catechismo instructos certo anni tempore confirmet ...*

XXII, 1 (499). R, 9.6. There are two rules in the *Reformatio legum* which conduce much to the true understanding of the Levitical decrees: ... *non solum in legitimis matrimoniis talem habent dispositionem qualem iam posuimus, sed eundem in corporum illegitima coniunctione locum habent. Filius enim quo iure matrem non potest uxorem sumere, eodem nec patris concubinam habere potest, et pater quomodo filii non debet uxorem contrectare, sic ab illa se removere debet, qua filius est abusus. Qua ratione mater nec cum filiae marito iungi debet, nec etiam cum illo congredi quae filiam oppresserit.*

     ... *non solum istas maritis adhuc superstitibus disiungi personas quas diximus, sed etiam illis mortuis idem perpetuo valere. Quemadmodum enim horribile flagitium est in vita patris, fratris, patrui, aut avunculi, audere illorum uxores violare, sic post mortem illorum matrimonium cum illis contrahere parem turpitudinem habet.*

     To the first of these rules may be referred the case of Haynes and Jephcot (*Modern Reports* V, p. 168), in which a prohibition was prayed to the spiritual court on a suit there against a man for marrying his sister's bastard daughter, as not within the Levitical law. But it was urged against the prohibition that in this case, legitimacy or illegitimacy made no difference, and that if a bastard be not within the rule *ad proximum sanguinis non accedat*, then a mother may marry her bastard son. The court inclined not to grant a prohibition, but the cause was adjourned and it appears not what became of it.

XXII, 3 (507). R, 8.4. To this prohibition, the *Reformatio legum* adds: *Quod si fecerint, tales nuptias omnino non valere sancimus, et ad nihilum recidere.* And I have observed that a remedy of this mischief hath more than once been attempted in parliament, particular bills to that effect having been brought in *anno* 32 Henry VIII [1540], and lately, in the year 1689. And inasmuch as parents may sometimes deal hardly with their children in this matter, the *Reformatio legum* goes on thus: *Quod si parentes vel tutores in providendis nuptiarum conditionibus nimium cessaverint, aut in illis proponendis nimium duri et acerbi extiterint, ad magistratum ecclesiasticum confugiatur, a quo partes eorum in huiusmodi difficultatibus agi volumus, et eius aequitate totam causam transigi.*

XXII, 17 (535). R, 10.19. This form of divorce (separation from bed and board) was to have been wholly taken away by the *Reformatio legum*, in these words: *Mensae societas et thori solebat in certis criminibus adimi coniugibus; salvo tamen inter illos reliquo matrimonii iure. Quae constitutio cum a sacris litteris aliena sit, et maximam perversitatem habeat, et malorum sentinam in matrimonium comportaverit, illud auctoritate nostra totum aboleri placet.*

XXII, 17 (536). R, 10. 5, 17. But because our Saviour, in another place, prohibiting divorces and new marriages thereupon, specially excepts the case of

fornication [Mt 19:9], therefore the *Reformatio legum* expressly allows the injured party the liberty of marrying again [10.5]: *Cum alter coniunx adulterii damnatus est, alteri licebit innocenti novum ad matrimonium (si volet) progredi. Nec enim usque adeo debet integra persona crimine alieno premi, coelibatus ut invite possit obtrudi. Quapropter integra persona non habebitur adultera, si novo se matrimonio devinxerit, quoniam ipse causam adulterii Christus excepit.* Upon which principle several acts of parliament for the divorce of particular persons in the case of adultery [5-6 Edward VI, c. 10; 13 William III, c. 3] have expressly allowed a liberty to the innocent persons of marrying again. But the same *Reformatio legum* makes a special exception to that liberty, where both parties are guilty [10.17]: *Si persona quae fuerit adulterii convicta, crimen in altero coniuge possit idem ostendere, et ostenderit, priusquam coniunx ad novas nuptias diverterit, utriusque coniugis culpa par in pares incidet poenas, et prius inter illos firmum manebit matrimonium.*

XXX,1 (688). R, 16.1. The ancient rule of alienations is thus set down in the book entitled *Reformatio legum*: *Qui gubernandis ecclesiis admoti sunt, nec domos, nec agros, nec ullas ecclesiarum possesiones aut fructus vendent, permutabunt, donabunt, aut quocunque genere contractus vel conventionis in omne tempus abalienabunt, nisi suum patronus et episcopus consensus interposuerint.*

XXX, 8 (726). R, 25.2. After divers acts of Parilament for the framing and compiling of a body of ecclesiastical laws, it was at length finished in the reign of Edward VI but never ratified and confirmed. In it we are referred, for the law of tithes, to the statute made upon that head in the second and third year of Edward VI, with some few variations. [Comment on 27 Henry VIII, c. 20 s. 4, referring to 2-3 Edward VI, c. 13.]

XXXII, 3 (791). R, 15.3. The rule in the *Reformatio legum* is as follows: *Si quis arbores, arbusta, lucos, nemora, silvas, saltus, fruticeta, vel huiusmodi quascunque lignorum opportunitates ullius ad se beneficii ecclesiastici iure pertinentes, licentiosius quam necessitas tulerit sine consensu proprii illius ditionis episcopi vendiderit, succiderit, amputarit, asportarit, aut quocunque modo corruperit et vastarit, pretium is universum, et aestimationem omnium huiusmodi lignorum distractorum et eversorum in cistam pauperum attributam plene conferet. Praeterea tantum in hac re successori satisfaciet, quantum episcopus aequum esse putabit.*

XXXIV, 4 (840-1). R, 11.5. The rule in the *Reformatio legum* is as follows: *[non] patimur ut patroni certam [beneficiorum] spem cuiquam ulla scriptorum, aut pignorum, aut pactorum cautione faciant, priusquam vacua sint. Nam*

huiusmodi conventiones magnam secum vim incommodorum afferunt. Itaque qui talem ullam sacerdotiorum minime vacuorum spem faciunt, ius collocationis illius temporis amittent, et qui ad nondum vacua sic adspiraverunt, ne ad vacua quidem post assumentur, et etiam ab omnibus aliis submovebuntur.

XXXIV, 4 (845). R, 11.24. In the chapter of the *Reformatio legum* which is entitled 'Forma iuramenti ministrorum', the oath [against simony] is: *[Se] nec antea dedisse quicquam, nec postea daturum, aut de dando pactum intercessisse, vel intercessurum, vel ipso auctore, vel alio quocunque procuratore aut vicario, respectu praesentis sacerdotii quod iam sumit; et si quisquam illum celans hoc in genere quicquam molitus est, se quamprimum norit episcopo renuntiaturum, et eius arbitrio cessurum parto sacerdotio.*

XXXIV, 5 (850). R, 11.7. The *Reformatio legum*, speaking of the 'cognitores' or examiners to be appointed by the bishop, in order to the instituting of a clerk, adds: *Et etiam episcopum in primis optabile est ipsum (si fieri potest) in hoc cognitionis negotio versari. Munus enim hoc unum est ex omnibus summum, et maximum in quo status ecclesiarum praecipue fundatus est. Quare si minutioribus in plerisque causis ecclesiarum episcoporum praesentia flagitatur, eam in hoc sane principali munere desiderari minime convenit.*

XXXIV, 11 (869). R, 12.5. Resignation must be made in person, and not by proxy. There is in the register of writs, one entitled 'Littera procuratoria ad resignandum' by which the person constituted proctor was enabled to do all things necessary to be done, in order to an exchange (and of these things, resignation was one), and Lyndwood [2.5.1, gloss on *renuntians*] supposes that any resignation may be made 'per procuratorem', but the doctrine of the *Reformatio legum* is: ... *ut omnia prorsus in hoc negotio sincera sint, procuratores excludimus, nec eos ullo modo patimur ad sacerdotium dimissionem admitti.*

XLI, 6 (989). On 25 Henry VIII c. 16 s. 4 'established and declared': Pursuant to the powers given by this act, not only the thirty-two persons were appointed for reformation of the canon law, but they had drawn the whole into form, so as nothing was wanting but the confirmation of the king, as appears by the letter or act of confirmation which was ready prepared and which is now prefixed to the book entitled *Reformatio legum, etc.* [A reference to the Henrician canons of 1535.]

XLI, 6 (990-1). 3-4 Edward VI, c. 11, followed by the letter of Edward VI authorizing the choosing of a committee of thirty-two, followed by an extract from the preface of R as follows: *Nec longum erat quin regis voluntati satisfactum sit. Res enim, tanquam pensum, in varias distributa operas felicitate non minori quam celeritate confecta est, hoc observato ordine; ut duo hi et triginta (quos diximus) in quattuor classes aequa proportione ita dividerentur, ut in singulis octonariis duo episcopi, duo item theologi, rursusque duo iuris utriusque similiter et communis iuris consulti totidem continerentur. Inter quos sic denique conventum est, ut quod in singulis classibus conclusum et definitum esset, id per reliquas classes considerandum atque inspiciendum transmitteretur. Quamquam vero ex hoc ipso omni numero octo potissimum selecta fuerunt capita, quibus prima operis praeformatio quasique materiae praeparatio commitebatur, quorum nomina regis in Edovardi epistula compraehensa videre liceat.*

[...] Summae negotii praefuit Thomas Cranmerus, archiepiscopus Cantuariensis. Orationis lumen et splendorem addidit Gualterus Haddonus, vir disertus, et in hac ipsa iuris facultate non imperitus. Quin nec satis scio an Iohannis Checi, viri singularis, eidem negotio adiutrix adfuerit manus. Quo factum est, ut cultiori stylo concinnatae sint istae leges, quam pro communi ceterarum legum more.

[...] Nec dubium quin parliamentari etiam auctoritate eaedem sanctiones istae constabilitae atque in publicum usum consecratae fuissent, si vita regi paulo longior suppetisset.

This design of a body of ecclesiastical laws, having been defeated by the death of King Edward VI, rested until the year 1562 when it was proposed in convocation to move Her Majesty, that 'certain learned men, bishops and others, might be appointed to set down ecclesiastical orders and rules in all ecclesiastical matters, for the good government of the Church of England, as should by them be thought most meet; and the same in this present session of parliament, whatsoever they shall order or set down within one year next, to be effectual and for law confirmed by act of parliament, at or in this session'.

Afterwards, by the endeavours of Archbishop Parker, it was set afoot in the parliament of the 13 Elizabeth, and by a leading member recommended to the consideration of the House of Commons, but after that we hear no more of it.

Preparatory to the gaining a parliamentary establishment at that time, care was taken to have the whole work published as we now see it, by John Foxe; the conclusion of whose preface plainly intimates the main design of the publication: *...optandum, quod per praematuram mortem regis illius negatum est ecclesiae felicitati, per feliciora tempora serenissimae reginae nostrae Elizabethae suppleatur, accedente publica huius nunc parlamenti auctoritate, simulque faventibus doctorum hominum suffragiis. Quos ut nostram hanc in edendo audaciam boni consulant, impense rogamus.*

XLII, 8 (1011-12). R, 20.5. In the *Reformatio legum* the rule (regarding rural deans) is: *Decanatus quilibet archipresbyterum rusticanum habeat, vel ab episcopo vel ecclesiae ordinario praeficiendum.*

[Later in the same section.]... in the *Reformatio legum*, the rule is: *Munus... erit annuum.*

[Later in the same section.] The like description of this office is also found in the *Reformatio legum* (comparing it with X, 1.24.4): *Hic tamquam in specula presbyteris, diaconis, gardianis et aedituis, ut singuli quae ad eorum munus attinent praestent, perpetuo invigilabit.* And after an enumeration of divers crimes,it follows: *...vocandi ad se, et examinandi horum scelerum suspectos auctoritatem habeat. Omnem accusationis ortum, sive per famam publicam, sive deferentium testimonio probatum, vel suspectum, episcopo aut eius loci ordinario infra decem dies in scriptis prodet.*

XLV, 5 (1078). R, 32.16. In this place, it may not be improper to subjoin the rule of the *Reformatio legum* concerning the right of the church to proceed in a spiritual way against criminals, after sentence in the temporal courts and pardon: *Cum civilis magistratus aliquis flagitiosos homines adhuc non excommunicatos praeoccuparit, in carcerem abduxerit, hi si post sententiam mortis acceperint, et nos illis postea pepercerimus, nolumus tum indulgentia nostra ecclesiae disciplinam impediri. Iudex igitur ecclesiasticus illos satisfactionis et reliquorum officiorum commonefaciat: quae si non omnia rite perficiant, excommunicationis virga tantisper flagellentur, donec salubriores cogitationes susceperint.*

XLV, 6 (1080). R, 54.26. The end and design of appeals is thus set forth in the *Reformatio legum: Appellationes non ad deprimendam cuiusquam iustitiam sunt inventae, sed ut gravamen impositum reparetur, et ad corrigendam iniquitatem et imperitiam iudicis, et nonnunquam ad ipsius afflicti succurrendum inscitiae. [...] Etenim quae in prima instantia sunt omissa, frequenter in secunda locum habent.*

XLVI, 1 (1088). R, 14.8. This was the rule of the ancient canon law (X, 5.34.5) which, after the oath of the person, speaking of the compurgators, says: 'Deinde compurgatores super Sancta Dei Evangelia iurabunt, quod ipsi credunt eum verum iurasse'. And from thence it is thus described in the *Reformatio legum: Haec formula purgationis esto. Defensor se crimen non admisisse iurato; defensoris liberatores, vel ut vulgo dicunt compurgatores, credere se verum eius iuramentum fuisse iuramento et ipsi affirmanto.*

XLVI, 3 (1092). R, 28.11. That there be no commutation [of penance] at all, but for very weighty reasons and in cases very particular. So saith the *Reformatio legum: Paenitentias ecclesiasticas nolumus in poenas mutari pecuniarias, nisi aliqua gravis intercesserit et necessaria causa.*

[Later in the same section.] That the money be applied to pious or charitable uses, to the poor of the parish, saith the *Reformatio legum*, with this addition, that the offender himself put the money in the poor's chest, in time of divine service, and in presence of the churchwardens. [Gibson does not quote the text, which follows immediately after the preceding and reads: *Quoties autem ita fiat, omnes rei nummos, quibus crimen eius plectitur, in communem thesaurum, quem cistam pauperum vocant, comportari placet, et eos ibi deponi si habitat, aut ubi crimen commissum est. Idque testatius ut esse possit, aedituis vel syndicis praesentibus geratur, et tempus sumatur celebrationis divinorum officiorum, et pecunias ibi manibus ipse suis collocet qui peccavit, et dies quidem sit festus, ut plures reus testes facti sui colligat.*]

[Later in the same section.] That the favour of commutation shall not be granted a second time to the same person for the same fault, as it is in the *Reformatio legum: Si quis autem culpam eandem geminaverit, nullum illi praesidium in pecunia relinquimus.*

XLVI, 3 (1093). R, 29.5. And lastly, both [types of suspension], if unduly performed, are attended with further penalties; that of the clergy with irregularity, if they act in the meantime, and that of the laity (as I conceive) with excommunication, if they either presume to join in communion during their suspension or do not in due time perform those things, the performance whereof such suspension was designed to enforce. [Gibson refers his readers to the following passage without actually quoting it: *Si quando minister ecclesiae vel loco motus ab episcopo, vel in formulam suspensionis prolapsus fuerit, et quicquam eorum audeat facere quae sunt illi negata, nec se mature corrigat, cum episcopus illum officii admonet, et excommunicationis poena plectetur et desecrationis acerbitate vel degradationis, ut vulgo loquuntur, ut omnibus exuatur ornamentis status ecclesiastici. Si vero minister non fuerit, sed ex ordine laico, excommunicatione ferietur.*]

XLVI, 4 (1095). R, 32.3-4. That [excommunication] be used by way of punishment only for great and heinous crimes. So is the rule in the *Reformatio legum* (32.3): *Non debet excommunicatio minutis in delictis versari, sed ad horribilium criminum atrocitatem admovenda est, in quibus ecclesia gravissimam infamiam sustinet, vel quod illis evertatur religio, vel quod boni mores pervertuntur.* Which matter was intended to be the subject of an act of parliament in the reign of King James I, upon a message from the king to that purpose, as appears by the journal of the House of Lords.

[Later in the same section.] [Excommunication is not to] be pronounced rashly and precipitately. Against which the foregoing constitutions provided so

far as to forbid the doing of it without previous monition or notice to the party. But the *Reformatio legum* goes further and enjoins time to be also given to the party for mature deliberation, though he appears and is obstinate (32.4): *Nullus iudex excommunicatione quemquam percutiet, nisi semel atque iterum, et etiam tertio, si res id requirit, illum praemonuerit, ut se ipse, si fieri potest, tempestive corrigat. Tum etiam reo certum tempus ad deliberationem relinquatur, in quo secum ipse constituat, utrum sanis consiliis obsecuturus sit.* But in case he did not appear, then the rule was: ... *huius pertinacia statim in excommunicationem incidat.*

XLVI, 4 (1096). R, 34.10. [Commenting on 3 James I, c. 5 s. 11, according to which a person excommunicated may not sue.] Upon this head, the *Reformatio legum* says: *Nec [excommunicatos] ad ecclesiastica beneficia sumi fas est, quos ad mensam vel ad colloquium adhibere nefas existimatur.* Which, as well as the disability to sue and be an advocate, is agreeable to the rule of the canon law.

XLVI, 9 (1116). R, 31.3. Although by the *Reformatio legum* the proper bishop might deprive without any other bishop, and with assistance only of two presbyters, yet was the process throughout to be not before officers only, as it is here, but before, but before the bishop himself: *Quando cuiquam vel diripi dignitas, vel eripi beneficium ecelesiasticum formula deprivationis debet, principio proprius illum episcopus ad se rite evocet; deinde ad reliquum onme negotium pertractandum episcopus adsit, et duos ad se doctos et integros presbyteros asciscat, quorum auctoritate et decreto stari placet.*

Passages of the *Reformatio* quoted or alluded to by Gibson's *Codex*

R	Gibson (chapter)	Gibson (page)
Preface	XLI, 6	989-91
3.1	XVII, 3	410
8.4	XXII, 3	507
9.6	XXII, 1	499
10.5	XXII, 17	536
10.17	XXII, 17	536
10.19	XXII, 17	535
11.5	XXXIV, 4	840-1
11.7	XXXIV, 5	850
11.24	XXXIV, 4	845
12.5	XXXIV, 11	869
14.8	XLVI, 1	1088
15.3	XXXII, 3	791

R	Gibson (chapter)	Gibson (page)
16.1	XXX, 1	688
19.9	XIX, 1	453
20.5	XLII, 8	1011-12
20.12	XIX, 2	454
20.16	V, 3	158
25.2	XXX, 8	726
28.11	XLVI, 3	1092
29.5	XLVI, 3	1093
31.3	XLVI, 9	1116
32.3-4	XLVI, 4	1095
32.16	XLV, 5	1078
34.10	XLVI, 4	1096
37.2	II, 3	63
48.1-2	I, 4	10-11
54.26	XLV, 6	1080

INDEXES OF SOURCES AND REFERENCES

1. TO HOLY SCRIPTURE

In these indexes, references in *italics* are to the Henrician canons of 1535; other references are to the *Reformatio legum ecclesiasticarum*.

Old Testament

Ex. xx. 14	10.1
Ex. xxii. 16	*4.3*; 8.3
Lv. xvi. 23-4	53.15
Lv. xviii. 6-23	9.3
Lv. xx. 10	10.1
Lv. xx. 10-21	9.3
Lv. xxiv. 11-16	4.2
Nm. xviii. 8-24	25.18
Dt. v. 18	10.1
Dt. xxv. 4	25.1, 18
I Sa. ii. 27-36	11.18
I Ki. ii. 24	49.3
Ek. xvi. 38	10.1
Ek. xvi. 40	10.1
Am. viii. 11	Intro. n. 495

Apocrypha

Wi. vi. 2, 4, 10-11	*Preface*

New Testament

Mt. xii. 31	2.9
Mt. xix. 9	Intro.n. 526

2. TO CANONS OF ECUMENICAL COUNCILS

	C. O. D.	H. C./R
Chalcedon (451)		
6	90	*18.4*
9	91	37.16
25-6	98-9	*34.1*
Lateran II (1139)		
15	200	48.1
Lateran III (1179)		
3	212	*15.12*
5	214	*18.7*
6	214	*36.7*; 54.56
8	215	*20.7*; 11.5
9	215-17	26.8
15	219	18.2
18	220	23.1
23	222-3	*26.1*
25	223	*20.17*
Lateran IV (1215)		
1	230-1	1.2-3
2	231-2	1.2
3	233-5	Intro.n. 554; *1.3, 7, 10*; 3.2
6	236-7	*4.6*
7	237	*10.14*; 29.4; 37.22
8	237-9	*11.14, 17*; 44.2

	C. O. D.	*H. C.*/R
10	239-40	*29.3*
11	240	23.1-2
15	242-3	*10.1*
21	245	*10.10*; 19.7
23	246	*15.1*
24	246-7	*15.1, 21*
26	247-8	*17.2*
31	249	11.19
32	249-50	*20.23*
33	250	*29.1, 3*; 26.6
35	251	*36.4*
36	251	54.41
37	251-2	36.9
38	252	41.10
39	252-3	42.1
44	254	15.3
47	255-6	*14.8, 10*; 32.8
48	256-7	54.9
49	257	*14.11*
50	257-8	Intro. n. 583
51	258	*22.1, 14*; 8.2, 6
55	260	*24.4*

Lateran V (1512-17)

11	636	*18.8*

Lyon I (1245)

5	285	*15.6*
19	291	*14.8-9*
20	291-2	*14.5*
21	292	*14.3*

	C. O. D.	*H. C.*/R
Lyon II (1274)		
10	321	*18.9*
13	321-2	*18.2*
15	322	*18.2*
Nicaea I (325)		
3	7	20.4
4	7	20.17
6	8-9	20.17
Trent (1545-63)		
4.1	663-4	1.6, 8
4.2	664-5	1.13
6	681-2	20.15

3. TO THE *CORPUS IURIS CANONICI*

Decretum Gratiani	Friedberg (Vol. I)	H. C./R
D. 60 c. 2	226	20.8
D. 60 c. 3	226-7	20.8
D. 61 c. 6	229	20.10
D. 64 c. 1	247-8	20.17
D. 64 c. 5	248	20.17
D. 64 c. 8	249	20.17
D. 70 c. 1	256-7	*18.4*
D. 70 c. 2	257	*18.4*
D. 71 c. 2	258	*18.4*
D. 72 c. 2	259-60	*18.4*
D. 75 c. 2	265-6	*34.1*
D. 77 c. 4	273	11.22
D. 77 c. 5	273	Intro. n. 590; *18.2*
D. 77 c. 6	273-4	Intro. n. 590; *18.2*
D. 77 c. 7	274	Intro. n. 590; *18.2*
D. 78 c. 1	275	11.21
D. 78 c. 4	275-6	11.21
D. 78 c. 5	276	11.21
D. 81 cc. 20-33	286-9	14.15
D. 90 c. 1	313	25.17
D. 91 c. 1	316	19.2
D. 91 c. 2	316	19.2
D. 92 c. 9	319	19.2
D. 93 c. 6	321-2	20.6
D. 93 c. 8	322	20.11
D. 93 c. 9	322	20.11
D. 93 c. 10	322	20.11
C. 1 q. 1 c. 54	379	5.1
C. 1 q. 1 c. 112	402	3.11
C. 1 q. 2 c. 4	409	*3.2*
C. 2 q. 3 cc. 1-6	450-1	*11.3*
C. 2 q. 3 c. 8	453-4	*11.2*
C. 2 q. 5 c. 13	459	29.2
C. 2 q. 5 c. 18	461	29.2
C. 2 q. 6 c. 41	481-3	27.6
C. 2 q. 7 c. 59	502	20.13
C. 2 q. 7 c. 60	502	20.13
C. 3 q. 2 c. 8	508-9	51.24
C. 3 q. 3 c. 4	510-11	27.6
C. 3 q. 11 c. 2	535	*11.4*
C. 3 q. 11 c. 3	535	*11.5*
C. 6 q. 3 c. 5	563	32.3

Decretum Gratiani	**Friedberg (Vol. I)**	*H. C./R*
C. 26 q. 6 c. 13	1040	29.9
C. 26 q. 7 c. 15	1045	*7.5*; 6.7
C. 30 q. 5 cc. 1-5	1104-6	*22.6*
C. 30 q. 5 c. 3	1105	*22.13*; 5.7
C. 32 q. 1 c. 7	1117	10.6
C. 32 q. 1 c. 8	1117	10.6
C. 32 q. 1 c. 10	1117-18	10.16
C. 32 q. 7 c. 3	1140-1	*23.10*
C. 32 q. 7 c. 5	1141	*23.10*
C. 33 q. 3		
DP, 1, c. 14	1161	*13.13*
C. 34 qq. 1-2 c. 1	1256-7	*22.18*
C. 35 qq. 2-3, c.18	1268	*22.28*
C. 35 q. 5 c. 2	1271-4	5.7
C. 35 q. 6 c. 6	1279	39.4
C. 35 q. 6 c. 7	1279-80	26.3; 39.4
C. 36 q. 1 c. 2	1288-9	*4.2*
D. 1 *de cons.*, c. 33	1302	19.14
D. 1 *de cons.*, c. 34	1302	19.14
D. 1 *de cons.*, c. 61	1311	19.8
D. 2 *de cons.*, c. 20	1320	19.8
D. 3 *de cons.*, c. 23	1417-18	*1.1*
D. 5 *de cons.*, c. 39	1423	1.2
D. 5 *de cons.*, c. 40	1424	1.2

Liber extra	**Friedberg (Vol. II)**	*H. C./R*
1.1.1	5-6	1.2-3
1.1.2	6-7	1.2
1.3.11	20	44.4
1.3.20	25	44.6
1.3.28	31	36.9
1.3.29	31	54.21
1.3.43	35	44.3
1.4.1	36	25.18
1.4.9	41	46.4
1.4.11	41	46.2-3
1.6.1	48	*19.6*
1.6.2	48-9	*15.17*
1.6.3	49-50	*15.18*; 17.1
1.6.9	52-3	*15.12*
1.6.11	53	Intro. n. 73; *15.11*

Liber extra	Friedberg (Vol. II)	*H. C./R*
1.6.22	64-6	*15.16*
1.6.27	71	*15.3*
1.6.30	74-6	*15.23*
1.6.32	77-9	*15.24*
1.6.33	79	*15.25*
1.6.36	82-3	*15.2*
1.6.39	84	*15.9*
1.6.41	88	*15.1*
1.6.42	88-9	*15.1*
1.6.44	89-90	*17.2*
1.6.45	90	*15.27*
1.6.47	90-1	*15.13*
1.6.49	91	*15.3*
1.6.54	93-4	*15.10*
1.7.3	98-9	Intro. n. 596; 11.25
1.9.1	102-3	*16.1*; 12.2
1.9.2	103	*16.3*; 12.4
1.9.3	103	*16.3*; 12.4
1.9.4	104	*16.2*; 12.2-3
1.9.5	104	12.1
1.9.10	107-12	*10.14*
1.9.13	113-14	*16.4*
1.10.3	116	*17.1*; 37.22
1.10.4	116-17	*17.1*
1.10.5	117-18	*17.1*
1.11.3	118	*18.1*
1.11.13	121-2	*18.7*
1.11.15	122-3	*18.3*
1.12.1	124-5	*20.10*; 11.2
1.13.2	125	*18.10*
1.14.3	126	*20.11*
1.14.4	126-7	*18.12*; 11.2, 12-13
1.14.8	128	29.4
1.17.1	135	11.18
1.17.14	139-40	11.18
1.17.15	140	11.19
1.17.16	140	11.19
1.17.18	141	11.18
1.18.2	141-2	*18.13*
1.20.1-7	144-6	*18.14*
1.22.1-4	148-9	*18.15*
1.23.1	149-50	20.6
1.23.6	151	*29.3*; 20.6

Liber extra	Friedberg (Vol. II)	H. C./R
1.23.7	151-2	11.23; 20.6
1.23.9	152	11.23
1.24.1	153	20.5
1.24.2	154	20.5
1.24.3	154	20.5
1.24.4	154-5	20.5
1.25.1	155	Intro. n. 611; 20.1
1.26.1	155	Intro. n. 612; 20.1
1.27.1	155	Intro. n. 618; 20.2
1.27.2	156	20.2
1.29.4	158	36.19; 37.23
1.29.11	161	37.5
1.29.14	162	37.13
1.29.21	164-6	37.13
1.29.22	166	37.13
1.29.24	169-70	37.23
1.29.27	171-2	37.13
1.29.28	172-3	37.13
1.29.30	175	37.14
1.29.31	175	37.14
1.29.32	175-7	37.30
1.29.35	179-80	36.11
1.29.37	181	37.14
1.29.38	181	37.15
1.29.39	181-2	37.18
1.29.41	182	37.11
1.31.8	189	*36.7*; 37.26, 31
1.31.13	191	*10.14*; 37.22
1.31.15	192	*29.3*
1.31.16	192-3	20.10, 12; 31.3
1.31.20	194	37.27
1.32.1	194-5	37.24
1.32.2	195-6	20.11
1.33.4	196	20.11
1.33.16	202	20.7
1.35.4	204-5	18.3
1.35.6	205	18.3
1.36.2	206	25.12
1.38.2	212	53.6
1.38.6	214-15	*14.4*
1.38.7	215-16	45.20
1.40.7	222	45.21
1.43.6	234	45.43

Liber extra	**Friedberg (Vol. II)**	*H. C./R*
2.1.1	239	31.2; 37.9
2.1.2	239	13.3
2.1.4	240	14.4
2.1.5	240	26.7
2.1.6	241	36.16
2.1.10	242	31.4
2.1.12	242	37.20
2.1.14	245	36.8
2.1.15	245	36.16
2.1.18	246	36.4; 37.19
2.2.1	248	37.16
2.2.2	248-9	37.16
2.2.4	249	37.18
2.3.1	255-6	*35.1*
2.5.1	257-8	38.1
2.6.5	263-5	38.11
2.7.3	266	40.6
2.7.7	268	40.10
2.8.1	268-9	51.20
2.8.2	269	51.19
2.9.1	270	45.10; 51.27
2.9.5	272-3	51.30
2.12.2	276	36.17b
2.12.3	276-7	36.17b
2.13.10	284	36.17b
2.13.11	284-5	42.1
2.13.13	286-8	*23.2*; 8.11; 10.10-11
2.13.18	290	42.1
2.16.3	301	*33.3*; 30.1
2.17.1	302-4	54.61
2.18.2	305-6	41.2
2.19.1	306	43.20
2.19.3	307	41.8; 45.46
2.19.4	307	49.21
2.19.6	308	41.9
2.19.9	311-12	41.26; 42.1
2.19.11	313-14	41.10
2.19.13	314	*32.1*; 22.1; 41.26
2.19.14	314-15	*33.4*; 30.3
2.19.15	315	41.27
2.20.2	315-16	45.5
2.20.8	318	45.15
2.20.11	319	41.22

Liber extra	Friedberg (Vol. II)	H. C./R
2.20.15	320	45.33
2.20.27	324	41.24
2.20.31	326	45.54
2.20.37	330-1	45.47
2.20.39	332	45.9
2.20.49	338	45.33
2.20.51	339	45.9
2.21.1	341	45.13
2.21.7	343	41.14
2.21.8	343	14.11
2.22.1	344	43.8
2.22.2	344	43.3, 5, 18
2.22.3	345	43.13
2.22.6	346-9	43.3
2.22.9	350	43.9
2.22.11	352	43.13a
2.22.13	352	43.10
2.22.15	353	31.3; 43.16
2.22.16	353	31.3; 43.17
2.23.2	353	49.3
2.23.4	354	49.9
2.23.5	354	49.8
2.23.8	354	49.10
2.23.11	355	49.4
2.23.12	355-6	49.4
2.23.13	356	49.4
2.23.15	358	49.12
2.24.3	360	*6.3*; 41.15
2.24.10	362	*6.9*; 39.7
2.24.12	363	*6.8*
2.24.18	365-6	39.10
2.24.19	366	54.31
2.24.21	367	39.11
2.24.23	368	39.10
2.24.25	368-9	*23.8*
2.24.27	371	*6.1*
2.24.35	373	*6.10*
2.24.37	371	39.9
2.25.6	377-8	*5.2*; 52.19
2.26.5	383	47.3
2.26.6	383	47.2, 5
2.26.8	384	47.4
2.26.9	384	47.7
2.26.10	384	47.7

Liber extra	Friedberg (Vol. II)	*H. C./R*
2.26.11	385	47.5
2.26.16	388-9	47.5
2.27.1	393	53.2, 10
2.27.2	393	*35.1*
2.27.9	395	53.11
2.27.25	409	53.15
2.27.26	409	53.4
2.28.3	410	54.9
2.28.4	410-11	*36.1, 6*; 54.30
2.28.5	411	*36.1*; 27.6; 54.30
2.28.6	411	54.13
2.28.7	412	54.5
2.28.8	412	54.28
2.28.11	413	54.18
2.28.12	413	*36.4*; 54.32
2.28.13	413-14	54.9
2.28.14	414	54.9
2.28.16	414-15	*36.7*
2.28.17	415	54.5
2.28.18	415	54.19
2.28.19	415-16	54.9
2.28.20	416	54.16
2.28.22	416-17	54.13
2.28.23	417	54.57
2.28.24	417	54.13
2.28.26	418-19	*36.7*; 54.56
2.28.29	419-20	54.9
2.28.31	420	54.48
2.28.33	420-1	*36.1*; 54.33
2.28.38	422-3	*36.3*; 54.46
2.28.39	423	54.14
2.28.40	423	*36.7*
2.28.47	428	*36.1*; 54.17, 34
2.28.48	428	54.24
2.28.49	429	54.24
2.28.50	429	54.24, 33
2.28.51	429-31	54.5
2.28.54	432-3	*36.8*; 54.40
2.28.55	433-5	*36.7*; 54.59
2.28.56	435	54.60
2.28.59	437	*36.4*
2.28.60	437	54.41
2.28.61	437-8	54.9
2.28.63	439-40	54.22-3

Liber extra	**Friedberg (Vol. II)**	**H. C./R**
2.28.64	440	54.56
2.28.65	440	54.9
2.28.72	443	*36.9*; 54.12a, 15
2.28.73	443	54.8
3.1.3	449	23.2
3.1.9	450-1	*10.1*
3.1.14	452-3	*10.1*
3.2.3	454	*4.4*; 10.2
3.2.10	457	*4.5*; 10.2
3.4.7	461	19.2
3.4.11	462-3	*19.1*
3.4.16	464	*33.1*; 30.1
3.5.13	468	11.12
3.5.30	478-9	*20.23*; 25.7
3.5.32	479	19.2
3.6.2	482	11.20
3.6.3	482	*19.6*; 11.14
3.6.4	482	*18.14*
3.6.5	482	*19.7*
3.7.3	483-4	*20.1*
3.7.6	485-6	*20.5*
3.7.7	487	*20.2*
3.8.1	488	*20.8*
3.8.2	488	*20.7*; 11.5
3.8.3	488	*20.8*
3.8.15	499-500	*20.9*
3.9.1	500-1	*20.13*
3.10.6	503-4	*20.15*
3.10.9	505	*20.16*
3.11.1	506	*20.17*
3.11.4	509	*20.18*
3.12.1	509-12	*20.19*; 18.2
3.13.6	513-14	15.3
3.13.7	514	16.2
3.13.11	515-16	15.3
3.13.12	516	15.3
3.19.5	522-3	*21.1*
3.19.9	524-5	*21.2*
3.26.3	539	*31.6, 12*; 27.23; 27.34
3.26.5	540	27.33
3.26.6	540	*31.6*; 27.34
3.26.10	541	*31.2*; 27.2

Liber extra	Friedberg (Vol. II)	*H. C./R*
3.26.11	541	27.8
3.26.13	542	27.3
3.26.17	545	*31.4*
3.28.5	550	*13.7*
3.28.12	553	*10.12*
3.29.4	555	*32.1*; 22.1
3.30.3	556-7	*24.6*
3.30.4	557	*24.5*
3.30.13	560-1	*24.3*
3.30.18	562	25.13
3.30.20	562-3	25.13
3.30.21	563	25.2
3.30.22	563	25.2
3.30.23	563-4	25.2
3.30.29	566	*24.7*; 25.9
3.30.34	568-9	*24.4*
3.38.12	613	11.5
3.38.16	616	11.6
3.38.23	616-17	18.1
3.39.11	624	*28.6*
3.39.15	626	*28.5*
3.39.23	632	*29.1, 3*; 26.6
3.41.1	635	19.1
3.41.12	643	19.3
3.48.1	652	26.4
3.48.2	652	*26.1*
3.48.4	653	26.4
4.1.9	663-4	*23.11*; 8.1, 8-9
4.1.11	664-5	*22.7*
4.1.15	666-7	*22.5*
4.1.19	668	*22.4*; 8.(9), 12
4.1.21	668-9	*22.8*
4.1.22	669	*22.19*
4.1.23	669-70	*22.10*; 8.8
4.1.24	670	*22.11*; 8.8
4.1.25	670	8.1
4.1.30	672	*22.9*; 8.12
4.1.31	672	*22.19*
4.2.1-14	672-9	*22.12*; 8.5
4.3.3	679-80	*22.1, 14*; 8.2, 6
4.4.4	681	*22.20*
4.5.6	683-4	*22.21*
4.5.7	684	*22.23*

Liber extra	**Friedberg (Vol. II)**	*H. C./R*
4.8.1	690-1	10.13
4.8.2	691	10.13
4.8.3	691	*22.24*
4.9.4	692-3	*22.25*
4.11.15	694-5	9.7
4.13.2	696-7	*22.26*
4.13.3	697	*22.27*
4.13.5	697-8	*22.27*
4.14.8	702-3	Intro. n. 583
4.15.2	705	8.7
4.15.3	705	*22.31*; 8.7
4.15.4	705	*22.32*; 8.7
4.17.5	711	*22.34*
4.17.8	712-13	49.5
4.17.12	713-14	*22.33*
4.18.1	717-18	*22.35*
4.18.3	718-19	*22.36*
4.18.5	719	*22.37*
4.18.6	719-20	*22.38*
4.19.3	720-1	*23.1, 4*; 10.4, 7
4.19.4	721	*23.5*
4.19.5	721-2	10.17
4.20.2	725	10.3
4.21.2	730	*22.4, 18; 23.9*
5.1.1	733	*11.6*
5.1.4	733	*11.7*
5.1.5	734	*11.8*
5.1.6	734	*11.9*
5.1.7	734	*11.10*
5.1.9	734	*11.11*; 35.2
5.1.11	735	*11.12; 23.3*
5.1.15	737	*11.13*
5.1.16	737-8	*11.14*; 3.1; 44.2
5.1.17	738-9	*11.15*
5.1.19	740-1	*11.16*
5.1.20	741	Intro. n. 77; *11.18*
5.1.23	744-5	*11.19*
5.1.24	745-7	*11.14, 17*; 44.2
5.1.25	747	*4.6*
5.1.26	747	*11.22*
5.1.27	748	*11.20*
5.3.1	749	*3.1, 2*
5.3.4	750	*3.1*

Liber extra	**Friedberg (Vol. II)**	*H. C./R*
5.3.10	751	*3.3*
5.3.11	752	18.6
5.3.18	754-5	*3.2*
5.3.19	755-6	*3.5*
5.3.30	759-60	*3.5*
5.3.45	767	*3.1*
5.5.1	768-9	23.1
5.5.4	770	23.1-2
5.5.5	770-1	11.17
5.7.3	778	2.11
5.7.7	779	2.5
5.7.9	780-2	*1.8*; 3.3-4
5.7.10	782-3	27.7
5.7.13	787-9	Intro. n. 554; *1.3, 7, 10*; 3.2
5.9.5	791-2	*10.2*
5.9.6	792	*10.3*
5.10.3	793	*10.4*
5.12.5	794	*10.5*
5.16.1	805-6	*4.3*; 8.3
5.16.2	806	8.3
5.16.3	806	*23.6*
5.16.7	807	*23.7*; 10.17
5.19.9	813-14	27.7
5.20.1	816-17	44.1
5.20.7	820-1	44.3
5.20.9	821-2	43.13
5.21.1	822	*7.1*
5.24.1	825	*12.6*
5.26.2	826-7	*8.1*
5.27.2	827	*14.14*
5.27.3	827	*14.15*
5.27.7	830-1	*14.17*
5.27.9	832	*14.16*
5.28.1	833	*10.6*
5.31.8	837	*10.8*
5.31.9	837	*10.9*
5.33.3	849-50	26.8
5.33.5	850-1	*10.11*
5.33.6	851	25.11
5.33.7	851	25.11
5.33.22	865-6	25.11
5.33.31	869	25.11
5.33.33	869	25.11

Liber extra	**Friedberg (Vol. II)**	*H. C./R*
5.34.1	869-70	14.2
5.34.2	870	14.5, 7
5.34.5	870-1	*12.2*; 14. 8; 18.5; 45.49
5.34.7	871	*12.3*; 14.9, 12
5.34.10	872-4	*1.9*; *12.4, 8*; 3.3-5; 14.6, 10, 16-20
5.34.12	874	18.5
5.34.13	875	14.2
5.34.15	875-7	14.3
5.35.1	877-8	*12.7*
5.35.2	878	*12.7*
5.35.3	878	*12.7*; 14.21
5.36.9	880	Intro. n. 680
5.37.1	880	*13.8*
5.37.3	880-1	*10.11*
5.37.4	881	36.12, 20a
5.37.11	882-3	*13.9*; 28.6
5.38.3	884-5	*13.1*; 28.1
5.38.5	885	32.14
5.38.8	886	*13.1*; 28.1
5.38.11	887	29.9
5.38.12	887-8	*10.10*; 19.7
5.39.3	890	48.2
5.39.4	890	48.1
5.39.13	893	32.14
5.39.15	894-5	*14.1*; 29.6; 32.12
5.39.17	895	*14.4*
5.39.18	895-6	*14.1*
5.39.23	897	48.2
5.39.29	900-1	29.6
5.39.31	901-2	*14.2*
5.39.40	906-7	*14.5*
5.39.48	909-10	*14.8, 10*; 32.8
5.39.51	910	*14.7*; 32.12
5.39.55	912	*14.3*; 32.11
5.39.57	912	*14.22*
5.39.59	912	32.1
5.40.10	914	41.1
5.40.24	921	*14.6*
5.41.4	927	55.1

Liber sextus	Friedberg (Vol. II)	*H. C./R*
1.3.1	938	*19.3*
1.4.2	944	37.10
1.6.1	945-6	*15.22*
1.6.2	946	*15.6*
1.6.5	949-50	*15.19*
1.6.6	950	*15.7*
1.6.8	950-1	*15.5*
1.6.11	952	*18.9*
1.6.14	953-4	*15.4; 18.2*
1.6.15	954	*18.2*
1.6.22	961	*15.28*
1.6.26	962	*15.8*
1.6.27	962	*15.14*
1.6.37	966	*15.26*
1.6.46	970	*15.21*
1.9.3	975-6	*18.5*
1.10.1	976	*18.12*
1.14.12	980-1	37.13
1.14.13	981-2	36.11
1.14.15	982-3	37.10, 13
1.16.5	988	37.2, 15, 21
1.16.7	988	37.6
2.1.1	995	36.8
2.1.2	995	*11.29*
2.1.3	996	*11.29*; 36.23
2.2.1	996-7	37.21
2.3.2	998	*35.2*; 38.9
2.4.2	998	40.6, 9
2.4.3	998	40.6
2.6.2	1000	54.49
2.11.1	1003-4	*6.3, 10*; 39.11; 41.15
2.12.1	1004-5	41.18
2.14.1	1007	53.15
2.14.5	1014	53.6
2.15.1	1014-15	54.38
2.15.3	1015-16	54.11, 47, 54
2.15.4	1016	54.37
2.15.5	1016-17	54.45
2.15.6	1017	54.37
2.15.7	1017	*36.3*; 54.42-3, 46
2.15.8	1017-18	54.4
2.15.9	1018	54.7

Liber sextus	Friedberg (Vol. II)	*H. C./R*
2.15.10	1018	54.42
2.15.12	1018	54.55
3.1.1	1019	*10.1*
3.5.1	1034	*19.8*; 20.20.16
3.8.1	1041-2	*20.14*
3.11.1	1044-5	27.31
3.11.2	1045	*31.7-8*; 27.35
3.13.2	1048-50	*24.5*
3.20.3	1057-8	*29.1-2*; 26.2, 6
3.21.1	1059	*3.4*
4.1.1	1065-6	*22.22*
4.2.1	1066-7	8.5
5.2.4	1070-1	*1.4*
5.2.11	1073-4	*1.11*; 3.8
5.2.20	1078	*1.10*
5.9.1	1090	*13.10*
5.9.3	1091	*13.3*; 28.3
5.10.1	1093	41.14
5.10.3	1093	*14.3*
5.11.1	1093-4	*14.8-9, 19*; 29.8; 32.7
5.11.5	1095	*14.12*; 32.4-5
5.11.7	1096-1101	*3.7; 14.5*; 32.15
5.11.7a	1096-1100	*14.5*
5.11.8	1101	*14.13*
5.11.9	1101-2	32.4
5.11.12	1102-3	49.13
5.11.20	1104-5	29.5
5.11.22	1105	*14.18*; 29.9
5.11.24	1106-7	29.3
5.13.8	1122	55.3
5.13.9	1122	55.30
5.13.10	1122	55.29
5.13.11	1122	55.31
5.13.13	1122	55.32
5.13.15	1122	55.33
5.13.16	1122	55.34
5.13.17	1122	55.35
5.13.20	1122	55.36
5.13.21	1122	55.37
5.13.22	1122	55.38

Liber sextus	Friedberg (Vol. II)	*H. C./R*
5.13.23	1122	55.39
5.13.24	1122	55.17
5.13.25	1122	55.21
5.13.27	1122	55.40
5.13.29	1122	55.4
5.13.30	1122	55.26
5.13.34	1123	55.11
5.13.35	1123	55.12
5.13.36	1123	55.22
5.13.37	1123	55.41
5.13.38	1123	55.42
5.13.39	1123	55.15, 43
5.13.40	1123	55.44
5.13.41	1123	55.45
5.13.42	1123	55.14
5.13.43	1123	55.46
5.13.44	1123	55.47
5.13.46	1123	55.18
5.13.47	1123	55.48
5.13.49	1123	*13.15*; 28.9; 55.8
5.13.52	1123	55.49
5.13.53	1123	55.16
5.13.54	1123	55.50
5.13.58	1123	*6.7*
5.13.61	1123	55.51
5.13.62	1124	55.52
5.13.63	1124	55.53
5.13.67	1124	55.54
5.13.68	1124	55.55
5.13.74	1124	55.56
5.13.76	1124	55.57
5.13.78	1124	55.2
5.13.80	1124	55.13
5.13.81	1124	55.58
5.13.83	1124	55.59
5.13.84	1124	55.60
5.13.87	1124	55.61
5.13.88	1124	55.62

Clementinae	**Friedberg (Vol. II)**	***H. C./R***
1.3.1	1135	*15.20*
1.3.8	1138	*15.15*
1.4.1	1138	*16.6*; 12.5
1.9.1	1140-1	*10.14*
2.1.2	1143	*35.1*; 34.6
2.6.1	1146	*33.2*; 30.2
2.12.1	1153-4	54.12
2.12.2	1154	54.37
2.12.3	1154	54.30
2.12.4	1154	54.34
2.12.5	1154-5	54.20
2.12.7	1156	54.27
2.12.15	1154-5	54.2
3.4.2	1160	*20.20*
3.5.1	1161	*21.3*; 13.4
3.6.1	1161	*31.9*; 27.18
4.1.1	1177-8	*22.30*; 9.1
5.3.1	1181-2	*1.12*
5.7.2	1187	26.7
5.9.1	1190	*13.16*; 32.16
5.10.2	1191-2	*14.17*

4. TO THE LEGATINE CONSTITUTIONS OF OTHO (1237) AND OTHOBON (1268)

5. TO WILLIAM LYNDWOOD'S *PROVINCIALE*

Lyndwood	*H. C./R*
1.2.1	29.1, 7
1.3.1	32.2
1.4.3	*18.4*
1.4.4	*18.6*
1.5.1	11.8
1.6.2	5.8
1.6.5	5.5
1.9.1	*10.7*
1.11.1	4.1
1.11.3	5.9
2.2.4	37.7
2.4.1	*33.6*; 30.4
2.5.1	*16.5*
2.6.1	18.4
2.6.2	26.5
2.6.3	11.24
2.7.2	54.44
3.4.4	Intro. n. 79; *19.2*
3.5.2	*19.4*
3.6.1	11.15
3.6.3	*20.6*
3.6.4	*20.6*
3.7.1	*28.2-3*
3.8.1	16.4
3.13.3	*31.7*
3.13.4	*31.17*; 27.42
3.13.5	*31.1, 11, 13-14, 18, 20*; 27.14, 20, 24, 27, 36-7
3.13.6	27.9
3.13.7	27.17, 42
3.15.2	20.17
3.16.3	*24.1*; 15.3

6. TO OTHER ENGLISH CANONS

Provincial statutes	*H. C./R*
Cloveshoo (747)	
14	7.(7)
Lambeth (1261)	
19-22	*31.1*
Diocesan statutes	*H. C./R*
Chichester II (1289)	
23	*22.17*
24	*22.2*
Exeter II (1287)	
7	*22.13, 17*
12	Intro. n. 617; *34.1*; 21.1
London II (*c.* 1245-59)	
43	*22.2*
47	*22.17*
Salisbury I (*c.* 1217-19)	
83	*22.2*

Diocesan statutes	*H. C./R*

Salisbury III (*c.* 1228-56)

9	15.1

Wells (*c.* 1258)

12	*22.17*
58	28.11

Winchester I (1224)

22	15.1

Winchester II (*c.* 1247)

25	15.1
44	28.11

Winchester III (*c.* 1262-5)

28	*22.17*
96	28.11

Worcester II (1229)

21	*25.11*

York I (*c.* 1241-55)

24	*22.17*
25	*22.2*

7. TO OTHER CANONS

H. C./R

Irish canons of 1634 (1635)

25   20.6

Scottish canons of 1636

4.8   6

***Codex iuris canonici* (1917)**

1076   *22.28*

***Codex iuris canonici* (1983)**

1091   *22.28*

8. TO THE *CORPUS IURIS CIVILIS*

Institutes of Gaius	*H. C./R*
4.172	43.14
4.176	40.1; 43.14

Institutiones Iustiniani	*H. C./R*
2.12	*31.3*; 27.7
2.20.34	27.1
2.23	27.31
2.24	27.31
2.25	27.5
4.17	36.20

Digesta	*H. C./R*
2.1.4	37.14
2.1.20	37.12
2.12.1	51.30
2.13.1	35.4
3.3.15	36.17
3.3.33.2	36.8
4.4.1	37.11
5.1.1	36.1
5.1.12.2	35.5; 36.3
5.1.15	36.18a, 21
5.1.40	55.63
5.1.58	36.17
5.1.59	36.15
5.1.60	36.2, 5
5.1.62	36.5
5.1.74	55.64
5.5.2	36.17b
12.2.4	39.6
12.2.33	39.1
12.2.38	39.8
22.3.2	41.6

9. TO THE STATUTES OF THE REALM

	Vol. III	*H. C./R*
34-5/1 (1543)	894-7	3.8
34-5/5 (1543)	901-4	27.7
34-5/19 (1543)	918-19	25.19
35/16 (1544)	976	Intro. n. 82, 92
37/9 (1545)	996-7	Intro. n. 650
37/10 (1545)	997	50.1
37/12 (1545)	998-9	*25.1*; 25.14
37/21 (1545)	1013-14	25.8

	Vol. IV	*H. C./R*

Edward VI (28 January 1546 - 6 July 1553)

1/1 (1547)	2-3	*1.1*
1/12 (1547)	18-22	Intro. n. 565, 601
2-3/1 (1548-9)	37-9	5.8
2-3/13 (1548-9)	55-8	Intro. n. 624; 25.2, 16
2-3/21 (1548-9)	67	Intro. n. 228, 581; 8.9
3-4/11 (1549-50)	111-12	Intro. n. 122
3-4/16 (1549-50)	115-17	20.6
5-6/1 (1551-2)	130-1	Intro. n. 174, 574, 601; 5.10; 7.6; 19.17
5-6/2 (1551-2)	131-2	20.6

Mary I (19 July 1553 - 24 July 1554)

1/2 (1553)	202	Intro. n. 240

Philip and Mary I (25 July 1554 - 17 November 1558)

1-2/6 (1554)	244	Intro. n. 554

Elizabeth I (17 November 1558 - 24 March 1603)

1/1 (1559)	350-5	Intro. n. 556
1/2 (1559)	355-8	Intro. n. 601
5/16 (1563)	446-7	Intro. n. 566

George III (25 October 1760 - 29 January 1820)

53/127   (12 July 1813)   Intro. n. 604, 637

George IV (29 January 1820 - 26 June 1830)

7-8/28   (21 June 1827)   Intro. n. 679

William IV (26 June 1830 - 20 June 1837)

6-7/71 (13 August 1836)   Intro. n. 626

Victoria (20 June 1837 - 22 January 1901)

1-2/106 (14 August 1838)   Intro. n. 595
3-4/115 (11 August 1840)   Intro. n. 593
18-19/41 (26 June 1855)   Intro. n. 681
37-8/85 (7 August 1874)   Intro. n. 8
55-6/32 (27 June 1892)   Intro. n. 607
61-2/48 (12 August 1898)   Intro. n. 600

George V (6 May 1910 - 20 January 1936)

26/43 See under Edward VIII

Edward VIII (20 January 1936 - 11 December 1936)

1/43   (31 July 1936)   Intro. n. 626

George VI (11 December 1936 - 6 February 1952)

1-2/45   (13 July 1938)   Intro. n. 628

Elizabeth II (6 February 1952 -)

1963/measure no. 1 (31 July 1963)   Intro. n. 649
1966/2   (24 February 1966)   Intro. n. 622

10. TO THE ROYAL INJUNCTIONS

11. TO THE ARTICLES OF RELIGION

1553 (42)	1571 (39)	R
1	1	1.2
2	2	1.3
3	3	1.3
4	4	1.3-4
5	6	1.6-9
6	7	2.4
7	8	1.7
8	9	Intro. n. 550; 2.7
13	14	2.8
14	15	2.8-9
15	16	2.9
17	17	2.22
22	21	1.14
23	22	2.10
26	25	Intro. n. 236; 2.17; 5.2
28	27	2.18; 5.3
29	28	2.19; 5.4
-	29	Intro. n. 553
31	35	2.20
35	37	2.21
38	39	39.1
39	-	2.12
40	-	2.12
41	-	Intro. n. 550

12. TO THE HENRICIAN CANONS OF 1535

H.C.	R
1.2	3.2
1.3	3.4
1.4	3.4
1.5	3.4
1.9	3.3-5
2.1	7.1
2.2	7.3
4.4	10.2
4.5	10.2
5.1	44.1
5.3	44.7
5.4	27.39
5.7	44.5
6.1	39.9
6.2	39.5
6.3	39.10; 41.15
6.7	39.10
6.9	39.7, 10
7.1	6.1, 4-5
7.2	6.6
7.3	6.8
7.5	6.7
9.1	50.2-3
10.3	7.7
12.1	14.1
12.2	14.8
12.3	14.9
12.4	14.10
12.5	14.14
12.6	14.13
12.8	14.6
13.1	28.1
13.2	28.2
13.3	28.3
13.5	28.4
13.6	28.5; 32.16

13. TO THE MEDIEVAL CANONISTS

Albericus de Rosate   *H. C./R*

De testibus 3.36   45.37

Alciatus

De praesumptionibus   49.15, 20

Baldus

De disputationibus et allegationibus	53.3
De praesumptionibus	49.17, 19
De sententia	49.16, 18
De teste	45.16, 42

Hostiensis

Summa aurea

De appellationibus	54.1, 25, 35
De assertorio iuramento	41.24
De dilationibus	45.7
De exceptionibus	52.2, 6-10
De fide instrumentorum	43.2
De iudiciis	35.1; 36.6
De iuramento in litem dando	43.14
De probationibus	41.1, 4
De recusatione iudicis delegati	36.2, 4
De re iudicata	54.50, 54
De testibus	45.16, 41, 45; 52.20-1

X, 1.31.11	37.8
X, 2.28	54.2

Panormitanus	*H. C./R*
X, 1.40.7	45.21
X, 2.1	34.1-4
X, 2.1.1	31.2
X, 2.1.2	13.3
X, 2.1.5	26.7
X, 2.1.10	31.4
X, 2.1.12	37.20
X, 2.1.18	36.4
X, 2.17.1	54.61
X, 2.21.8	14.11
X, 2.22	43.2
X, 2.22.2	43.5, 18
X, 2.26	47.1
X, 2.26.6	47.6
X, 2.26.8	47.7
X, 2.26.9	47.7
X, 2.26.10	47.7
X, 2.27	54.31
X, 2.27.1	53.2
X, 2.28	54.1, 3, 5
X, 2.28.39	54.14
X, 5.20	44.1
X, 5.20.1	45.29
X, 5.34	14.1
X, 5.34.7	14.12
X, 5.34.10	14.17-18, 20
X, 5.39	29.1; 32.1
X, 5.39.3	48.2
X, 5.39.13	32.14
X, 5.39.23	48.2

Speculum	*H. C./R*

1.1. *De iurisdictione omnium iudicum*

Preface	37.1, 28
2.1	37.4

1.1. *De officio omnium iudicum*

2.15	38.13
6.7	36.7
8.1-20	34.8

SUBJECT INDEX

In the following subject index, references in *italics* are to the Henrician canons and those in normal type are to the *Reformatio legum ecclesiasticarum*.

Absolution

Accusation(s)

Adultery See also **Divorce**

Archbishops

Archdeacons

Astrology

- permitted   *7.7*

Baptism   See also **Sacraments**

- definition of   5.3
- necessity of   2.18
- rejection of infant, by Anabaptists   *1.1*; 2.18
- unlawful administration of   *10.7*

Benefices   See also **Dilapidation**; **Patrons**; **Pluralism**; **Sequestration**

- absence of incumbent   11.14-15
- appointment of perpetual vicar(s)   *20.23*; 25.7
- accusations against clergy on admission to   *11.19*
- admission to   *3.6*; 11.1-2
- age for receiving (minimum)   *18.12*
- appropriated to monasteries   *20.16, 20, 22-3*
- collation of   *3.6; 20.19*
- deprivation of   See **Deprivation**
- diminution of, forbidden   *20.19*; 18.1-6
- division of, forbidden   *19.5*
- examination before admission to   11.2, 7-11, 23
- exchange of   *21.1-3*; 13.1-4
- held by students   *35.4*; 11.17; 20.9; 24.5
- induction to   *20.5*
- institution to   *20.1-23*
- intrusion into   *13.4; 20.12*; 11.25
- letters of admission to   *20.6*
- must not be conferred on excommunicates   *14.17*
- not to be granted unless vacant   *20.7-8, 21-2*
- oath required for admission to   11.24
- presentation to   *17.1*; 11.5
- residence in   *19.1-3*
- resignation of   *3.5; 16.1-6; 21.3; 28.2*; 12.1-5; 13.4
- revenue of   18.1-2
- purchase of   18.3-6
- sequestration of   *33.2-3*; 30.1-2, 5
- union of   *10.8; 20.20, 22*; 22.1
- vacancy of   *20.7-8, 13*; 11.5

Colleges and universities

Defamation

Delay(s)

Denunciation, evangelical

Documents

- accounts kept by merchants	43.5
- composition of	43.6-7
- copies of	43.17; 44.6
- credence given to	43.1
- defamatory	*9.1*; 50.2-3
- destroyed	43.12
- false	*5.1-2, 6-7*; 44.1, 5
- lost	43.12
- made by more than one person	43.16
- mutually conflicting	43.10
- private	43.3-4
- required for excommunication	*14.8*
- storing of	43.15
- to be produced in judgments	43.8
- types of	43.2
- unlawful alteration of	*5.6*
- validity of	43.4, 11, 13-14, 18-19

Drugs, use of

- to induce impotence	*10.5*

Elections

- annulment of	*15.2, 5-9*
- bribery in	*15.17*
- confirmation of	*15.10-12, 18-19, 21*
- expenses of, to be reimbursed	*15.27*
- form of	*15.1*; 17.1
- in colleges and exempt places	*15.28*
- in general	*15.1-28*; 17.1
- institution following	*15.7*
- irregularities in	*15.22*
- majority rule to prevail	*20.17*
- minimum age for	*15.3-4*
- minority rights in	*15.2*
- objections to	*15.5, 22*
- payment of expenses	*15.27*
- procedure to be followed in cathedrals	*15.1*
- refusal by person elected	*15.8*
- validity of	*15.6*

Scripture, Holy

Seals

Sentence

Suspension

Synods

Testaments

BIBLIOGRAPHY

Letters in bold after an entry indicate the way references to the work are abbreviated in the notes.

Primary sources: the Henrician canons and the *Reformatio legum ecclesiasticarum*

Manuscripts

Additional 48040 (British Library, London). Formerly Yelverton 45. Fos. 14-103 contain the only extant version of the Henrician canons of 1535.

Harleian 426 (British Library, London). This is a draft of the *Reformatio legum ecclesiasticarum* which may be dated to mid-October 1552.

Petyt 538/38 (Inner Temple, London). Fos. 231r-46r contain a sixteenth-century translation of R, 44.3-51.19. There is no author or date.

Printed texts

Reformatio legum ecclesiasticarum, ed. J. Foxe, London, 1571. This is the complete text, based on a manuscript which is now lost. R.S.T.C. 6006. [**F**]

Reformatio legum ecclesiasticarum, printed by Thomas Harper and Richard Hodgkinson, London, 1640. A reprint of the former, with corrections. R.S.T.C. 6007-8. [**S**]

Reformatio legum ecclesiasticarum, printed by the Stationers' Company, London, 1641. A re-issue of the 1640 edition, with some changes in punctuation and wording. The former are generally improvements, but not the latter. R.S.T.C. (Wing) 6828.

Cardwell, E., *The reformation of the ecclesiastical law as attempted in the reigns of King Henry VIII, King Edward VI, and Queen Elizabeth*, Oxford, 1850. A critical edition of F, with an appendix containing most of the variants found in MS Harleian 426. (Facsimile reprint, Farnborough, 1968).

Spalding, J. C., *The reformation of the ecclesiastical laws of England, 1552*, Sixteenth Century Essays and Studies, 19, Kirksville, Mo, 1992. A translation of MS Harleian 426.

Primary sources: medieval canonists and civil lawyers

N. B.: The following 'sources' were not necessarily used by the compilers of the *Reformatio*, but they can be shown to provide precedents which the compilers certainly drew on.

Albericus de Rosate, died 1351. His treatise *De testibus* was published in the *Tractatus universi iuris*, 18 vols., Lyon, 1549 (V, 187).

Andreas Alciatus (Andrea Alciati), born 1492; died 1550. His collected works were published as *Opera omnia*, 4 vols., Venice, 1546-9. The treatise *De praesumptionibus* was also published in the *Tractatus universi iuris*, 18 vols., Lyon, 1549 (V, 131b-132a).

Baldus de Ubaldis, born about 1327; died 1400. He wrote a number of additions to the *Speculum iudiciale* of William Durand which are included in the printed edition of the latter, Lyon, 1547.

Durand, William ('The Speculator'), born 1231; died 1296. He completed his *Speculum iudiciale* about 1271 and revised it about 1287. It was printed at Lyon, 1547 (facsimile reprint, Assen, 1975).

Hostiensis (Henricus de Segusio), born *c.* 1190-1200; died 1271. His two major works are the *Summa Aurea*, completed in 1250-1 and a *Lectura* on the *Liber extra*, completed in 1271. The *Summa aurea* was printed at Lyon, 1587 (facsimile reprint, 1963), and the *Lectura* was printed at Venice, 1581 (facsimile reprint, 1965).

Panormitanus (Nicholas de Tudeschis), born 1386; died 1445. His major work is a *Lectura* on the *Liber extra*. It was printed in nine volumes at Venice, 1475, in six volumes at Lyon, 1524 and in ten volumes at Venice, 1617.

Speculum. See Durand, William.

Other primary sources

Acts of the privy council of England, ed. J. R. Dasent, 32 vols., London, 1890-1907. Vol. III (1891), covers the period 1550-2.

The Anglican canons, 1529-1947, ed. G. L. Bray (Church of England Record Society , VI), Woodbridge, 1998. [**A.C.**]

Bucer, Martin, *De regno Christi*, ed. F. Wendel, Paris, 1955. Translated (except for the titles on divorce) by W. Pauck, *Melanchthon and Bucer*, Philadelphia, 1969. The titles on divorce were translated by John Milton and published on 15 July 1644. A critical edition of the text can be found in *Complete prose works of John Milton*, 8 vols., New Haven, 1953-82, II, 416-79.

Calendar of letters, despatches and state papers relating to the negotiations between England and Spain, preserved in the archives at Vienna, Simancas, Besançon and Brussels, 13 vols., London, 1862-1954.

Calendar of the patent rolls preserved in the Public Record Office: Edward VI, 4 vols., London, 1926.

Calendar of state papers, domestic series, of the reigns of Edward VI, Mary, Elizabeth and James I, ed. R. Lemon and M. A. E. Green, 12 vols., London, 1856-72.

Cardwell, E., *Synodalia. A collection of articles of religion, canons and proceedings of convocations in the province of Canterbury, from the year 1547 to the year 1717*, 2 vols., Oxford, 1842.

Church of England: a booke of certaine canons, London, 1571; repr. Amsterdam, 1971.

Cobbett, W., *The parliamentary history of England from the Norman conquest in 1066 to the year 1803*, 36 vols., London, 1806-20.

Codex iuris ecclesiastici Anglicani, ed. E. Gibson, 2 vols., London, 1713.

Collection of statutes for the universities and colleges of Cambridge, London, 1811.

A collection of the laws and canons of the Church of England from its first foundation to the conquest, and from the conquest to the reign of King Henry VIII, ed. J. Johnson, 2 vols., London, 1720; new edn., ed. John Baron, Oxford, 1850-1.

Concilia Magnae Britanniae et Hiberniae a synodo Verulamiensi AD 446 ad Londiniensem AD 1717, ed. D. Wilkins, 4 vols., London, 1737. [**W**]

Conciliorum oecumenicorum decreta, see *Decrees of the ecumenical councils*

Corpus iuris canonici, ed. E.L. Richter and E. Friedberg, 2 vols., Leipzig, 1879-81. [**Fr**]

Corpus iuris civilis, ed. T. Mommsen and P. Kruger, 3 vols., Berlin, 1954.

Councils and ecclesiastical documents relating to Great Britain and Ireland, ed. A. W. Haddan and W. Stubbs, 3 vols., Oxford, 1869-73. [**HS**]

Councils and synods, with other documents relating to the English Church, 2 vols., Vol. I, ed. D. Whitelock, M. Brett, C.N.L. Brooke, Oxford, 1981. [**WBB**] Vol. II ed. F. M. Powicke and C. R. Cheney, Oxford, 1964. [**PC**]

Cranmer, T., *A defence of the true and catholick doctrine of the sacrament*, London, 1550.

Decrees of the ecumenical councils. Conciliorum oecumenicorum decreta, ed. Norman P. Tanner, 2 vols., London and Washington, 1990. [**C.O.D.**]

Documentary annals of the Church of England, ed. E. Cardwell, 2 vols., Oxford, 1839.

Documents of the English reformation, ed. G.L. Bray, Cambridge, 1994. [**D.E.R.**]

England in the reign of King Henry the eighth. A dialogue between Cardinal Pole and Thomas Lupsed, by Thomas Starkey, ed. J. M. Cowper, Early English Texts Society, Extra series, XII, 2, London, 1871.

Foxe, J., *Acts and monuments of these latter and perillous days, touching matters of the church*, London, 1563.

Gaius, *Institutes*, ed. and translated by W. M. Gordon and O. F. Robinson, London, 1988.

Gleanings of a few scattered ears, during the period of the reformation in England, ed. G. C. Gorham, London, 1857.

The journals of the house of commons, London, 1547-. Vol. I covers the period 1547-1625.

The journals of the house of lords, London, 1509-. Vol. I covers the period 1509-77.

Literary remains of King Edward VI, ed. J. G. Nichols, London, 1857.

Letters and papers, foreign and domestic, of the reign of Henry VIII, 1509-47, ed. J. S. Brewer, J. Gairdner and R. H. Brodie, 21 vols., London, 1862-1910. *Addenda* to Vol. 1, London, 1929-32.

Lyndwood, W., *Constitutiones provinciales, seu Provinciale,* Oxford, 1679. [**L**]

*Lyndwood's **Provinciale**,*trans. J. V. Bullard and H. C. Bell, London, 1929.

MacLure, M., *Register of sermons preached at Paul's cross 1534-1642,* revised edition, Ottawa, 1989.

Original letters relative to the English reformation, written during the reigns of King Henry VIII, King Edward VI, and Queen Mary, chiefly from the archives of Zürich, ed. H. Robinson, 2 vols., Cambridge, 1846-7 (Parker Society, 52-3).

Penry, J., *A treatise wherein is manifestlie proved, that reformation and those that favor the same, are unjustly charged to be enemies, unto hir majestie,* Edinburgh, 1590 (R.S.T.C., 19612).

Proceedings in the parliaments of Elizabeth I, ed. T. E. Hartley, 3 vols., Leicester, 1981-95.

Puritan manifestoes, ed. W. H. Frere and C. E. Douglas, London, 1907.

Sacrorum conciliorum nova et amplissima collectio, ed. J. D. Mansi, cont. I. B. Martin, L. Petit, 53 vols., Florence, Venice, Paris, Leipzig, 1759-1927.

Statutes of the realm, 12 vols., London, 1810-26. [**S.R.**]

Synodalia. A collection of articles of religion, canons and proceedings of convocations in the province of Canterbury, from the year 1547 to the year 1717, ed. E. Cardwell, 2 vols., Oxford, 1842.

Tudor royal proclamations, ed. P. L. Hughes and J. F. Larkin, 3 vols., New Haven, 1964-9.

Wright, T., ed., *Letters relating to the suppression of monasteries,* London, 1843.

Secondary works

Ackroyd, P., *The life of Thomas More*, London, 1998.

Ayliffe, J., *Parergon iuris canonici anglicani, or a commentary, by way of supplement to the canons and constitutions of the Church of England*, London, 1726.

Baker, J. H., *Monuments of endlesse labours*, London, 1998.

Beckwith, R. T., *The Old Testament canon of the New Testament church*, London, 1985.

Bellomo, M., *The common legal past of Europe, 1000-1800*, Washington, DC, 1995.

Berlioz, J., *L'atelier du médiéviste 1: identifier sources et citations*, Mechelen, 1994.

Bernard, E., *Catalogi librorum manuscriptorum Angliae et Hiberniae in unum collecti*, Oxford, 1697.

Bindoff, S. T., *The house of commons, 1509-58*, 3 vols., London, 1982.

Borkowski, A., *Textbook on Roman law*, 2nd edn., London, 1997.

Borrie, M. A. F., *The British Library catalogue of additions to the manuscripts. The Yelverton manuscripts*, 2 vols., London, 1994.

Bourguignon, H. J., *Sir William Scott, Lord Stowell. Judge of the high court of admiralty*, Cambridge, 1987.

Bray, G. L., 'The strange afterlife of the *Reformatio legum ecclesiasticarum*', *English canon law. Essays in honour of Bishop Eric Kemp*, ed. N. Doe, M. Hill and R. Ombres, Cardiff, 1998.

Briden, T. and Hanson, B., *Moore's introduction to English canon law*, 3rd edn., London, 1992.

Brundage, J. A., *Law, sex and Christian society in medieval Europe*, Chicago, 1987.

Brundage, J. A., *Medieval canon law*, London, 1995.

Burn, R., *Ecclesiastical law*, 2nd edn., 4. vols., London, 1767.

Burnet, G., *The history of the reformation of the Church of England*, 2 vols., London, 1850.

The canon law of the Church of England, being the report of the archbishops' commission on canon law, together with proposals for a revised body of canons, London, 1947.

The canons of the Church of England. Canons ecclesiastical promulged by the convocations of Canterbury and York in 1964 and 1969 and by the general synod of the Church of England from 1970 London, 1969. 5th edn. with supplements, London, 1996.

Carlson, E. J., *Marriage and the English reformation*, Oxford, 1994.

Chapman, C. R., *Ecclesiastical courts, officials and records. Sin, sex and probate*, 2nd edn., Dursley, 1997.

Cheney, C. R., *A handbook of dates for students of British history*, 3rd edn., Cambridge, 1997.

Churchill, I. J., *Canterbury administration. The administrative machinery of the archbishops of Canterbury, illustrated from original records*, 2 vols., London, 1933.

Clarke, F., *Praxis Francisci Clarke, tam ius dicentibus quam aliis omnibus qui in foro ecclesiastico versantur apprime utilis*, ed. T. Bladen, Dublin, 1666.

Consett, H., *The practice of the spiritual or ecclesiastical courts*, London, 1685.

Coote, H. C., *The practice of the ecclesiastical courts with forms and tables of costs*, London, 1847.

Cressy, D., *Birth, marriage and death. Ritual, religion and the life-cycle in Tudor and Stuart England*, Oxford, 1997.

Cross, C., *The royal supremacy in the Elizabethan church*, London, 1969.

Davies, C. and Facey, J., 'A reformation dilemma. John Foxe and the problem of discipline', *Journal of Ecclesiastical History*, XXXIV (1988), 37-65.

Dibdin, Sir Lewis and Chadwyck-Healey, C. E. H., *English church law and divorce*, London, 1912.

Dickens, A. G., *Thomas Cromwell and the English reformation*, London, 1959.

Didier, N., 'Henri de Suse en Angleterre (1236?-1244)', *Studi in onore di Vincenzo Arangio-Ruiz nel XLV anno del suo insegnamento*, 4 vols., Napoli, 1953.

Doe, N., *Canon law in the Anglican communion*, Oxford, 1998.

Doe, N., *The legal framework of the Church of England*, Oxford, 1996.

Drew, C., *Early parochial organisation in England. The origins of the office of churchwarden*, York, 1954.

Duffy, E., *The stripping of the altars. Traditional religion in England, 1400-1580*, New Haven and London, 1992.

Duncan, G. I. O., *The high court of delegates*, Cambridge, 1971.

The ecclesiastical courts. Principles of reconstruction, being the report of the commission on ecclesiastical courts set up by the archbishops of Canterbury and York in 1951 at the request of the convocations, London, 1954.

Ecclesiastical Law Journal, Vol. I- (1987-).

Elton, G. R., *The parliament of England, 1559-1581*, Cambridge, 1986.

Elton, G. R., *Reform and renewal: Thomas Cromwell and the common weal*, Cambridge, 1973.

Elton, G. R., *Studies in Tudor and Stuart politics and government*, 4 vols., Cambridge, 1974-92.

Emden, A. B., *A biographical register of the university of Oxford to A. D. 1500*, 3 vols., Oxford, 1957-9.

Emden, A. B., *A biographical register of the university of Oxford, A. D. 1501 to 1540*, Oxford, 1974.

Epstein, W., 'Issues of principle and expediency in the controversy over prohibitions to ecclesiastical courts in England', *Journal of legal history*, I (1980), 211-61.

Ferme, B. E., 'The *Provinciale* of William Lyndwood. The sources, contents and influence', D.Phil. dissertation, University of Oxford, 1987.

Fildes, V. A., *Breasts, bottles and babies. A history of breast feeding*, Edinburgh, 1986.

Fildes, V. A., *Wet nursing. A history from antiquity to the present*, Oxford, 1988.

First report of the commissioners appointed by her majesty to enquire into the law of divorce, and more particularly into the mode of obtaining divorces a vinculo matrimonii, London, 1853.

Foster, J., *Alumni Oxonienses*, 4 vols., Oxford, 1891.

Freeman, T. S., 'Thomas Norton, John Foxe and the parliament of 1571', *Parliamentary History*, XVI (1997), 131-47.

Friedberg, E. See *Corpus iuris canonici*.

Gaudemet, J., *Les sources du droit canonique VIIIe-XXe siècle*, Paris, 1993.

Gaudemet, J., *Les sources du droit de l'église en occident du IIe au VIIe siècle*, Paris, 1985.

General report made to his majesty by the commissioners appointed to enquire into the practice of the ecclesiastical courts in England and Wales, London, 1832.

Godolphin, J., *The orphan's legacy, or a testamentary abridgement*, London, 1674.

Godolphin, J., *Repertorium canonicum, or an abridgement of the ecclesiastical laws of this realm, etc.*, 3rd edn., London, 1687.

Graves, M. A. R., 'The management of the Elizabethan house of commons. The council's men of business', *Parliamentary History*, II (1983), 11-38.

Graves, M. A. R., *Thomas Norton, the parliament man*, Oxford, 1994.

Hair, P., *Before the bawdy court*, New York, 1972.

Hale, W. H., *A series of precedents and proceedings in criminal causes, extending from the year 1475 to 1640, extracted from the act-books of the ecclesiastical courts in the diocese of London, illustrative of the discipline of the Church of England*, London, 1847.

Hall, B., 'John a Lasco, the humanist turned protestant, 1499-1560', in *idem*, *Humanists and protestants*, Edinburgh, 1990.

Halsbury's laws of England, 2nd edn., 28 vols., London, 1931-42, XI and 4th edn., 56 vols., London, 1975-, XIV.

Halsbury's statutes of England, 4th edn., London, 1986-95, XIV and continuation.

Hasler, P. W., *The house of commons, 1558-1603*, 3 vols., London, 1981.

Haugaard, W., *Elizabeth and the English reformation*, Cambridge, 1968.

Head, R. E., *Royal supremacy and the trials of bishops, 1558-1725*, London, 1962.

Helmholz, R. H., '*Legitim* in English legal history', *University of Illinois Law Review*, MCMLXXXIV (1984), 659-74, reprinted in idem, *Canon law and the law of England* (London, 1987), pp. 247-62.

Helmholz, R. H., *Roman canon law in reformation England*, Cambridge, 1990.

Helmholz, R. H., *The spirit of classical canon law*, Athens, Ga., 1996.

Hill, M., *Ecclesiastical law*, London, 1995.

Holdsworth, W. S., *A history of English law*, 7th edn., 16 vols., London, 1956.

Houlbrooke, Ralph, *Church courts and the people during the English reformation, 1520-1570*, Oxford, 1979.

Ingram, Martin, *Church courts, sex and marriage in England 1570-1640*, Cambridge, 1987.

Jones, N. L., 'An Elizabethan bill for the reformation of the ecclesiastical law', *Parliamentary History*, IV (1985), 171-87.

Joyce, J. W., *England's sacred synods. A constitutional history of the convocations of the clergy, from the earliest records of Christianity in Britain to the date of the promulgation of the present book of common prayer*, London, 1855.

Keble, J., *Sequel to the argument against unduly repealing the laws which treat the nuptial bond as indissoluble*, Oxford, 1857.

Kelly, J. N. D., *The Athanasian creed*, London, 1964.

Kelly, J. N. D., *Early Christian creeds*, 3rd edn., London, 1972.

Kelly, M., 'The submission of the clergy', *Transactions of the Royal Historical Society*, 5th series, XV (1965), 97-119.

Kemp, E. W., *An introduction to canon law in the Church of England*, London, 1957.

Leeder, L., *Ecclesiastical law handbook*, London, 1997.

Lehmberg, S. H., *The reformation parliament 1529-1536*, Cambridge, 1970.

Levack, B. P., *The civil lawyers in England, 1603-1641. A political study*, Oxford, 1973.

Loades, D., *The reign of Mary Tudor. Politics, government and religion in England, 1553-1558*, 2nd edn., London, 1991.

Logan, F. D., 'Doctors' commons in the early sixteenth century: a society of many talents', *Historical Research*, LXI (1988), 151-65.

Logan, F. D., 'The first royal visitation of the English universities', *English Historical Review*, CVI (1991), 861-88.

Logan, F. D., 'The Henrician canons', *Bulletin of the Institute of Historical Research*, XLVII (1974), 99-103.

Logan, F. D., 'Thomas Cromwell and the vicegerency in spirituals: a revisitation', *English Historical Review*, CIII (1988), 658-67.

MacCaffrey, W. T., *Queen Elizabeth and the making of policy, 1572-1588*, Princeton, NJ, 1981.

MacCulloch, D., *Thomas Cranmer*, New Haven and London, 1996.

McLelland, J. C., *The visible Word of God: an exposition of the sacramental theology of Peter Martyr Vermigli*, Grand Rapids, 1957.

McNair, P., 'Peter Martyr in England', in *Peter Martyr Vermigli and Italian reform*, ed. J. C. McLelland, Waterloo, ON, 1980, pp. 85-105.

Maitland, F. W., *Roman canon law in the Church of England*, London, 1898.

Makower, F., *The constitutional history and constitution of the Church of England*, London, 1895.

Marchant, R. A., *The church under the law 1560-1640*, Cambridge, 1969.

Maurer, W., *Historical commentary on the Augsburg Confession*, Philadelphia, 1986.

Metzger, B., *The canon of the New Testament. Its origin, development and significance*, Oxford, 1987.

Miller, P., *The life of the mind in America from the revolution to the civil war*, New York, 1965.

Moore, E. G. See Briden, T.

Mullinger, J. E., *The university of Cambridge from the earliest times to the royal injunctions of 1535*, Cambridge, 1873.

Neale, J. E., *Elizabeth I and her parliaments*, 2 vols., London, 1953-7.

Null, J. A., 'Thomas Cranmer's doctrine of repentance', PhD. dissertation, University of Cambridge, 1994.

Nys, E., *Pages de l'histoire du droit en Angleterre. Le droit des gens et le collège des docteurs en droit civil*, Brussels, 1910.

Oughton, T., *Ordo iudiciorum, sive methodus procedendi in negotiis et litibus in foro ecclesiastico-civili Britannico et Hibernico*, 2 vols., London, 1728.

Phillimore, R. J., *The ecclesiastical law of the Church of England*, 2nd edn., 2 vols., London, 1895.

Phillimore, R. J., *The practice and courts of civil and ecclesiastical law*, London, 1848.

Purvis, J. S., *An introduction to ecclesiastical records*, London, 1953.

Report of the royal commission on divorce and matrimonial causes, London, 1912.

Ridley, T., *A view of the civile and ecclesiastical law*, 3rd edn., Oxford, 1662.

Rodes, R. E., Jr, *Ecclesiastical administration in medieval England*, Notre Dame, 1977.

Rodes, R. E., Jr, *Law and modernization in the Church of England. Charles II to the welfare state*, London, 1992.

Rodes, R. E., Jr, *Lay authority and reformation in the English Church*, Notre Dame, 1982.

Sachs, L., 'Thomas Cranmer's *Reformatio legum ecclesiasticarum* of 1553 in the context of English church law from the later middle ages to the canons of 1603',

J. C. D. Dissertation, Catholic University of America, Washington, D. C., 1982.

Senior, W., *Doctors' commons and the old court of admiralty. A short history of the civilians in England*, London, 1922.

Simpson, A. W. B., *Biographical dictionary of the common law*, London, 1984.

Slatter, M. D., 'The records of the court of arches', *Journal of Ecclesiastical History*, IV (1953), 139-53.

Spalding, J. C., 'The *Reformatio legum ecclesiasticarum* of 1552 and the furthering of discipline in England', *Church History*, XXXIX (1970), 162-71.

Special report made to his majesty by the commissioners appointed to inquire into the practice and jurisdiction of the ecclesiastical courts in England and Wales, London, 1832.

Squibb, G. F., *Doctors' commons. A history of the college of advocates and doctors of law*, Oxford, 1977.

Strype, J., *Annals of the reformation and establishment of religion*, 7 vols., Oxford, 1824.

Strype, J., *Ecclesiastical memorials*, 6 vols., Oxford, 1822.

Strype, J., *Memorials of Thomas Cranmer*, 3 vols., Oxford, 1840.

Sunderland, E. S. S., *Dibdin and the English establishment*, Bishop Auckland, 1995.

Swanson, R.N., *Church and society in late medieval England*, Oxford, 1989.

Swinburne, H., *A briefe treatise of testaments and last willes, very profitable to be understoode of all the subjects of this realme of England*, London, 1590-1.

Swinburne, H., *Of spousals*, London, 1686.

Tarver, A., *Church court records. An introduction for family and local historians*, Chichester, 1995.

Thomas, K., *Religion and the decline of magic*, London, 1971.

Usher, R.G., *The reconstruction of the Church of England*, 2 vols., New York, 1910.

Van Caenegem, R. C., *The birth of the English common law*, 2nd edn., Cambridge, 1988.

Venn, J. and Venn, J. A, *Alumni Cantabrigienses*, 4 vols., Cambridge, 1922-7.

Watkins, O. D., *Holy matrimony. A treatise on the divine laws of marriage*, London, 1895.

Williams, G., 'Two neglected London Welsh clerics: B. Richard Gwent', *Transactions of the Honourable Society of Cymmrodorion*, 1961, 33-43.

Church of England Record Society

'The object of the Society shall be to advance knowledge of the history of the Church in England, and in particular of the Church of England, from the sixteenth century onwards, by the publication of editions or calendars of primary sources of information.'

Membership of the Church of England Record Society is open to all who are interested in the history of the Church of England. Enquiries should be addressed to the Executive Secretary, Miss Melanie Barber, at the above address.

PUBLICATIONS

1. VISITATION ARTICLES AND INJUNCTIONS OF THE EARLY STUART CHURCH. VOLUME I. Ed. Kenneth Fincham (1994)
2. THE SPECULUM OF ARCHBISHOP THOMAS SECKER: THE DIOCESE OF CANTERBURY 1758–1768. Ed. Jeremy Gregory (1995)
3. THE EARLY LETTERS OF BISHOP RICHARD HURD 1739–1762. Ed. Sarah Brewer (1995)
4. BRETHREN IN ADVERSITY: BISHOP GEORGE BELL, THE CHURCH OF ENGLAND AND THE CRISIS OF GERMAN PROTESTANTISM 1933–1939. Ed. Andrew Chandler (1997)
5. VISITATION ARTICLES AND INJUNCTIONS OF THE EARLY STUART CHURCH. VOLUME II. Ed. Kenneth Fincham (1998)
6. THE ANGLICAN CANONS 1529–1947. Ed. Gerald Bray (1998)
7. FROM CRANMER TO DAVIDSON. A CHURCH OF ENGLAND MISCELLANY. Ed. Stephen Taylor (1999)
8. TUDOR CHURCH REFORM. THE HENRICIAN CANONS OF 1534 AND THE *REFORMATIO LEGUM ECCLESIASTICARUM*. Ed. Gerald Bray (2000)

Forthcoming Publications

LETTERS OF THE MARIAN MARTYRS. Ed. Tom Freeman

PROPHESYINGS, CONFERENCES AND EXERCISES IN THE ELIZABETHAN AND JACOBEAN CHURCH OF ENGLAND. Ed. Patrick Collinson

THE BRITISH DELEGATION AND THE SYNOD OF DORT. Ed. Anthony Milton

THE UNPUBLISHED CORRESPONDENCE OF ARCHBISHOP LAUD. Ed. Kenneth Fincham

THE DIARY OF SAMUEL ROGERS, 1634–1638. Ed. Tom Webster

THE 1669 RETURN OF NONCONFORMIST CONVENTICLES. Ed. David Wykes

THE CORRESPONDENCE OF THEOPHILUS LINDSEY. Ed. G.M. Ditchfield

THE DIARIES OF BISHOP BEILBY PORTEUS. Ed. Andrew Robinson

THE DIARY OF AN OXFORD PARSON: THE REVEREND JOHN HILL, VICE-PRINCIPAL OF ST EDMUND HALL, OXFORD, 1805–1808, 1820–1855. Ed. Grayson Carter

ALL SAINTS SISTERS OF THE POOR. AN ANGLICAN SISTERHOOD IN THE NINETEENTH CENTURY. Ed. Susan Mumm

ANGLO-CATHOLIC COMMUNICANTS' GUILDS AND SOCIETIES IN THE LATE NINETEENTH CENTURY. Ed. Jeremy Morris

Suggestions for publications should be addressed to Dr Stephen Taylor, General Editor, Church of England Record Society, Department of History, University of Reading, Whiteknights, Reading RG6 2AA.